D1573283

ORGANIZATIONAL COMPLIANCE AND ETHICS

ASPEN CASEBOOK SERIES

ORGANIZATIONAL COMPLIANCE AND ETHICS

BABAK BOGHRATY

Lecturer
Boston University School of Law

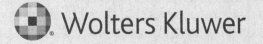 Wolters Kluwer

Published by Wolters Kluwer in New York.

Wolters Kluwer Legal & Regulatory U.S. serves customers worldwide with CCH, Aspen Publishers, and Kluwer Law International products. (www.WKLegaledu.com)

To contact Customer Service, e-mail customer.service@wolterskluwer.com, call 1-800-234-1660, fax 1-800-901-9075, or mail correspondence to:

> Wolters Kluwer
> Attn: Order Department
> PO Box 990
> Frederick, MD 21705

Printed in the United States of America.

1 2 3 4 5 6 7 8 9 0

ISBN 978-1-4548-9345-5

Library of Congress Cataloging-in-Publication Data

Names: Boghraty, Babak, author.
Title: Organizational compliance and ethics / Babak Boghraty, Lecturer,
  Boston University School of Law.
Description: New York : Wolters Kluwer, 2019. | Series: Aspen casebook series
  | Includes bibliographical references and index.
Identifiers: LCCN 2018036569 | ISBN 9781454893455
Subjects: LCSH: Corporation law—United States—Criminal provisions. |
  Commercial crimes—Law and legislation—United States. | Criminal
  liability of juristic persons—United States. | Corporate governance—Law
  and legislation—United States. | International business enterprises—Law
  and legislation—United States—Criminal provisions. | LCGFT: Casebooks
  (Law)
Classification: LCC KF9351 .B64 2019 | DDC 345.73/0268--dc23 LC record available at
https://lccn.loc.gov/2018036569

About Wolters Kluwer Legal & Regulatory U.S.

Wolters Kluwer Legal & Regulatory U.S. delivers expert content and solutions in the areas of law, corporate compliance, health compliance, reimbursement, and legal education. Its practical solutions help customers successfully navigate the demands of a changing environment to drive their daily activities, enhance decision quality and inspire confident outcomes.

Serving customers worldwide, its legal and regulatory portfolio includes products under the Aspen Publishers, CCH Incorporated, Kluwer Law International, ftwilliam.com and MediRegs names. They are regarded as exceptional and trusted resources for general legal and practice-specific knowledge, compliance and risk management, dynamic workflow solutions, and expert commentary.

To Brenda, and to Iranbanu, Lili, and Parvin

Summary of Contents

Contents   xi
Preface   xxi
Acknowledgments   xxiii

PART **I**   **Federal Prosecution of Business Organizations**   1
CHAPTER **1**   Theoretical Underpinnings of Corporate Criminal Liability   5
CHAPTER **2**   Federal Sentencing Guidelines for Organizations ("FSGO")   37
CHAPTER **3**   Prosecutorial Guidelines for Organizations   79
PART **I**   *Test Your Knowledge: Exercising Prosecutorial Discretion*   127

PART **II**   **The Foreign Corrupt Practices Act**   133
CHAPTER **4**   The FCPA Accounting Provisions   145
CHAPTER **5**   The FCPA Anti-Bribery Provisions   255
PART **II**   *Test Your Knowledge: FCPA Violations*   409

PART **III**   **The Effective Compliance Program**   413
CHAPTER **6**   The Ten Hallmarks of an Effective Compliance Program   415
PART **III**   *Test Your Knowledge: Evaluating a Compliance Program*   535

PART **IV**   **The Business Ethics Program**   561
CHAPTER **7**   The Responsible Business Enterprise ("RBE")   565
CHAPTER **8**   Building the Ethics Program   611
CHAPTER **9**   OECD Guidelines for Multinational Enterprises   661
PART **IV**   *Test Your Knowledge: Formulating a Responsible Business*
                Strategy for an Enterprise Operating in a Frontier Market 767

Table of Cases   775
Index   777

Contents

Preface   xxi
Acknowledgments   xxiii

PART **I**

FEDERAL PROSECUTION OF BUSINESS ORGANIZATIONS   1

CHAPTER **1**

Theoretical Underpinnings of Corporate Criminal Liability   5

  I. *Respondeat Superior*   5
     N.Y. Cent. & Hudson River R.R. Co. v. United States   7
     Hypothetical: Scope of Employment   12
 II. The Collective Knowledge Doctrine   13
     United States v. Bank of New England, N.A.   13
     Hypothetical: Collective Knowledge   22
III. The Collective Entity Rule   23
     Braswell v. United States   23
     Hypothetical: Collective Entity Rule   35

CHAPTER **2**

Federal Sentencing Guidelines for Organizations ("FSGO")   37

  I. History of the FSGO   37
    A. The 1991 FSGO   39
    B. The 2004 Revisions to the FSGO   41
    C. *United States v. Booker*   47
 II. Structure of the Current FSGO   52
    A. Section 8B1: Restitution   53
    B. Section 8B2: Effective Compliance and Ethics Programs   53
       1. Subsection (a)   54
       2. Subsection (b)   55
       3. Subsection (c)   62
          Federal Sentencing Guidelines: Sentencing of Organizations   64

III.	Fine Calculation	70
	Hypothetical: Determining a Corporate Sentence Under the Organizational Guidelines	73
IV.	Part 8D: Probation	74

CHAPTER **3**

Prosecutorial Guidelines for Organizations 79

I.	The Thompson Memo and Its Progeny	80
	United States v. Fokker Services B.V.	85
	Hypothetical: Negotiating a Diversion Agreement	95
II.	The Yates Memo	95
III.	The United States Attorneys' Manual ("USAM")	97
	United States Attorneys' Manual	97
IV.	Shepherding Compliance Programs	103
	United States Attorneys' Manual	103
V.	Rewarding Disclosure and Cooperation	105
	United States Attorneys' Manual	106
	Hypothetical: Throwing Your Employees Under the Bus	113
VI.	Monitoring Future Compliance	117
	United States Attorneys' Manual	118

PART **I** *Test Your Knowledge: Exercising Prosecutorial Discretion* 127

PART **II**

THE FOREIGN CORRUPT PRACTICES ACT 133

Legislative Background of the FCPA	134
FCPA's Revival in the New Century	136
Testimony Before the Senate Committee on Foreign Relations on the OECD Convention on Combating the Bribery of Foreign Public Officials in International Business Transactions	138
A Resource Guide to the U.S. Foreign Corrupt Practices Act: Introduction	141

CHAPTER **4**

The FCPA Accounting Provisions 145

I.	Introduction	145
	Recordkeeping and Internal Controls Provisions Section 13(b) of the Exchange Act 15 U.S.C. § 78m	146
II.	What Is Covered Under the Books and Records Provision of the FCPA Accounting Provisions?	147
	Hypothetical: Expense Reports	149
III.	What Is Covered Under the Internal Controls Provision of the FCPA Accounting Provisions?	150
	SEC v. World-Wide Coin Investments, Ltd.	152
	SEC v. Oracle Corp.	167
	A. The COSO Framework	171

1. Defining Internal Control		172
2. Objectives		173
3. Components of Internal Control		174
4. The Seventeen Principles		178
Hypothetical: Initiatives to Prevent Foreign Corruption		179
Hypothetical: Confidential Hotline		180
Volkswagen to Spend Up to $14.7 Billion to Settle Allegations of Cheating Emissions Tests and Deceiving Customers on 2.0 Liter Diesel Vehicles		180
State of New York v. Volkswagen Aktiengesellschaft		182
In the Matter of BHP Billiton Ltd. and BHP Billiton Plc		187
Hypothetical: Automated Data Check		196
United States v. Daimler AG		196
IV. Who Is Covered Under the FCPA Accounting Provisions?		**206**
A. Issuers and Their Subsidiaries		206
Hypothetical: Minority-Held Subsidiaries and the FCPA		206
In the Matter of BellSouth Corp.		207
B. Affiliates		211
Hypothetical: Books and Records of Third Parties		212
V. Interplay Between the FCPA Accounting Provisions and the Sarbanes-Oxley Act of 2002 ("SOX")		**212**
Report of Investigation by the Special Investigative Committee of the Board of Directors of WorldCom, Inc.		213
The Fall of Enron: How Could It Have Happened?		227
A. Section 302: Officer Certification		231
B. Section 404: Reporting on the Adequacy of Internal Controls		232
Commission Guidance Regarding Management's Report on Internal Control over Financial Reporting under Section 13(a) of 15(d) of the Securities Exchange Act of 1934		233
In the Matter of Marc Sherman		245

CHAPTER **5**

The FCPA Anti-Bribery Provisions **255**

I. Introduction		**255**
A Treaty Against Bribes		258
U.S. Targets Overseas Bribery; KBR Exec's Plea Widens Probe		259
II. What Is Covered Under the FCPA Anti-Bribery Provisions?		**263**
A. The Business Purpose Test		266
A Resource Guide to the U.S. Foreign Corrupt Practices Act		266
Hypothetical: Business Purpose Test		267
B. "Anything of Value"		268
Hypothetical: Payment of Medical Expenses		269
In the Matter of JP Morgan Chase & Co.		271
1. Charitable Donations		295
Hypothetical: Charitable Donation		296
2. Gifts, Travel, and Entertainment		297
Gifts, Meals, and Entertainment		298
3. Exceptions and Affirmative Defenses to "Anything of Value"		305

a. Local Law Affirmative Defense 305
b. Reasonable and Bona Fide Expenditures Affirmative Defense 305
Hypothetical: Gifts, Travel, and Entertainment 306
c. Exception for Facilitating or Expediting Payments 308
Facilitation Payments 309
Hypothetical: Facilitating Payments 312
Hypothetical: Facilitating Payments 312
C. Meaning of "Foreign Official" 313
A Resource Guide to the U.S. Foreign Corrupt Practices Act 314
Hypothetical: Hiring Royal Family Member as Consultant 317
United States v. Esquenazi 322
Hypothetical: Government Instrumentality 331
D. Prohibited Intent (Corruptly, Willfully, Knowingly) 332
A Resource Guide to the U.S. Foreign Corrupt Practices Act 333
United States v. Kozeny 337
Hypothetical: Head in the Sand 345
E. Successor Liability 345
A Resource Guide to the U.S. Foreign Corrupt Practices Act 346
FCPA Opinion Procedure Release No. 14-02 349
Hypothetical: Successor Liability Where Acquired Company
Was Not Previously Subject to the FCPA 352
Hypothetical: Successor Liability Where Acquired Company
Was Already Subject to the FCPA 354
II. Who Is Covered Under the FCPA Anti-Bribery Provisions? 356
A. Scope of the Extraterritorial Application of the FCPA 356
A Resource Guide to the U.S. Foreign Corrupt Practices Act 357
B. The Presumption Against Extraterritoriality 359
Morrison v. National Australia Bank Ltd. 360
C. Jurisdictional Scope of the FCPA Anti-Bribery Provisions
in Light of the Presumption Against Extraterritoriality 373
1. Issuers (15 U.S.C. § 78dd-1) 373
15 U.S.C. § 78dd-1 374
*House Report: International Anti-Bribery and Fair
Competition Act of 1998* 374
Hypothetical: Extraterritorial Application of the FCPA 375
2. Domestic Concerns (15 U.S.C. § 78dd-2) 376
*House Report: International Anti-Bribery and Fair Competition
Act of 1998* 377
Hypothetical: Foreign Employee of a Domestic Concern 378
3. Territorial Jurisdiction (15 U.S.C. § 78dd-3) 378
15 U.S.C. § 78dd-3 380
*House Report: International Anti-Bribery and Fair Competition
Act of 1998* 380
D. Responsibility for the Conduct of Others 382
1. Agency 382
*Department of Justice, Office of Public Affairs, FOR IMMEDIATE
RELEASE, Monday, April 22, 2013* 383
Hypothetical: Agency 384

        2. Concert of Action   385
            A Resource Guide to the U.S. Foreign Corrupt Practices Act   386
            Pinkerton v. United States   388
            United States v. Hoskins   391
            United States v. JGC Corp.   400

PART **II**   *Test Your Knowledge: FCPA Violations*   409

PART **III**
THE EFFECTIVE COMPLIANCE PROGRAM   413

CHAPTER **6**
The Ten Hallmarks of an Effective Compliance Program   415

      Overview of Corporate Anti-Corruption Programmes   416
   I. **Commitment from Senior Management and a Clearly
      Articulated Policy Against Corruption**   419
      Hypothetical: Top-Level Commitment   420
      Hypothetical: The Anticorruption Policy Statement   421
  II. **Code of Conduct and Compliance Policies and Procedures** 421
      Hypothetical: Preparing the Code of Conduct   423
 III. **Oversight, Autonomy, and Resources**   424
  IV. **Risk Assessment**   425
      A. Measuring and Mitigating Risk   426
          1. Step One   426
          2. Step Two   426
             Geographic Risk   426
             Sectoral Risk   427
             Transaction Risk   428
             Business Opportunity Risk   428
             Business Partnership Risk   428
          3. Step Three   429
          4. Step Four   430
          5. Step Five   430
      B. Documenting the Results   431
          *OECD Foreign Bribery Report: An Analysis of the Crime
             of Bribery of Foreign Public Officials*   435
          Hypothetical: Assessing and Mitigating a Specific Risk 450
   V. **Training and Continuing Advice**   451
      Hypothetical: Compliance Training Program   454
  VI. **Incentives and Disciplinary Measures**   455
 VII. **Third-Party Due Diligence and Payments**   457
      A. Defining the Scope of the Process   458
      B. Assessing Risk   459
          1. Agency   459
          2. Accounting and Internal Control Practices   459
          3. Geography   460
          4. Industry/Sectoral Risk   460

5. Products		460
6. History of Prior Misconduct		460
7. Identity of the Third Party, Its Owners, and Key Employees		460
8. Nature of the Third Party's Involvement and Compensation		461
9. Risk Ratings		461
C. Conducting Due Diligence		461
1. Obtain Relevant Information from the Third Party		461
2. Verification of Data and Resolution of Red Flags		464
a. Internet and Database Searches		464
b. Boots on the Ground		465
c. Audits		465
D. Approving and Monitoring the Program		465
A Resource Guide to the U.S. Foreign Corrupt Practices Act		466
Case Story: Integrity Due Diligence		467
Hypothetical: Third-Party Vetting		477
Hypothetical: Large-Scale Screening of Third Parties		480
VIII. Confidential Reporting and Internal Investigations		480
A. The Confidential Hotline and Whistleblowers		481
Knowing When to Blow the Whistle		483
Internal Reporting and Whistle-Blowing		485
2015 Annual Report to Congress on the Dodd-Frank Whistleblower Program		490
Hypothetical: Evaluating a Whistleblower Tip		494
B. Internal Investigations		495
1. Should We Investigate?		495
2. Who Should Conduct the Investigation?		495
3. What Should Be the Scope of the Investigation?		496
4. Should the Investigation Be Referred to Outside Counsel?		496
C. Self-Disclosure and Cooperation		498
The Fraud Section's Foreign Corrupt Practices Act Enforcement Plan and Guidance		500
Hypothetical: First Response After Discovery of a Potential Violation		507
IX. Continuous Improvement: Periodic Testing and Review		508
A. Monitoring		509
B. Auditing		510
Hypothetical: Defining the Scope of an Audit		512
X. Pre-Acquisition Due Diligence and Post-Acquisition Integration		512
FCPA Opinion Procedure Release No. 03-01		514
FCPA Opinion Procedure Release No. 08-02		516
FCPA Opinion Procedure Release No. 08-01		521
Hypothetical: Failure to Conduct Pre-Acquisition Due Diligence		533
PART III *Test Your Knowledge: Evaluating a Compliance Program*		535
At Siemens, Bribery Was Just a Line Item		535
U.S. v. Siemens Aktiengesellschaft		542
U.S. Department of Justice Criminal Division Fraud Section Evaluation of Corporate Compliance Programs		554

PART **IV**
THE BUSINESS ETHICS PROGRAM — 561

CHAPTER **7**
The Responsible Business Enterprise ("RBE") — 565

I. Responsible Conduct — 565
Business Ethics: A Manual for Managing a Responsible Business Enterprise in Emerging Market Economies — 566
Hypothetical: Absence of a Sophisticated Legal System — 568
The Bhopal Disaster and Its Aftermath: A Review — 569
In re Union Carbide Corp. Gas Plant Disaster at Bhopal, India, 634 F. Supp. 842 (S.D.N.Y. 1986) — 576
Deepwater: The Gulf Oil Disaster and the Future of Offshore Drilling — 583
U.S. and Five Gulf States Reach Historic Settlement with BP to Resolve Civil Lawsuit Over Deepwater Horizon Oil Spill (Press Release) — 589
II. Responsible Governance — 590
Business Ethics: A Manual for Managing a Responsible Business Enterprise in Emerging Market Economies — 591
Hypothetical: Eduardo's Legacy — 593
Looking Toward the Future: The Business Case for Corporate Governance — 595
III. Responsible Management — 604
Business Ethics: A Manual for Managing a Responsible Business Enterprise in Emerging Market Economies — 605
Hypothetical: #Purpose #Values #Vision — 610

CHAPTER **8**
Building the Ethics Program — 611

I. The Program's Objective — 611
The Coca-Cola Company: Myanmar Investment Due Diligence 2015 Annual Update Report — 614
II. Program Components — 624
  A. The Ethics Code of Conduct — 625
    Business Ethics: A Manual for Managing a Responsible Business Enterprise in Emerging Market Economies — 625
  B. Ethics Program Infrastructure (Autonomy, Oversight, Resources) — 632
    Business Ethics: A Manual for Managing a Responsible Business Enterprise in Emerging Market Economies — 632
    Hypothetical: Fusing the Compliance and Ethics Programs — 639
  C. Ethics Training — 639
    Business Ethics: A Manual for Managing a Responsible Business Enterprise in Emerging Market Economies — 639
    Hypothetical: Ethics Training Program — 647
  D. Incentives and Disciplinary Measures — 647
    Business Ethics: A Manual for Managing a Responsible Business Enterprise in Emerging Market Economies — 648
    Hypothetical: Incentives and Deterrents — 651

E. Reporting and Investigations   651
    Business Ethics: A Manual for Managing a Responsible Business
        Enterprise in Emerging Market Economies   652
F. Continuous Assessment and Monitoring   655
    Business Ethics: A Manual for Managing a Responsible Business
        Enterprise in Emerging Market Economies   655

CHAPTER **9**
OECD Guidelines for Multinational Enterprises   661

I. Introduction   661
    A. RBC Due Diligence   662
    B. Meaningful Stakeholder Engagement   663
        OECD General Policies   664
        Final Report, Kinross Gold Corporation/Association of
            Neighborhoods of Paracatu, Allegation of Non-Compliance
            NCP No. 01/2014   671
II. Disclosure   680
    OECD Disclosure   681
    Hypothetical: Disclosure of Payments to Government   683
    U.S. National Contact Point for the OECD Guidelines for Multinational
        Enterprises, Final Statement, Specific Instance between Greenpeace
        and Herakles Farms and Herakles Capital   684
III. Human Rights   686
    OECD Human Rights   697
    Hypothetical: Suppressing Free Speech in China   700
    Hypothetical: Sale of Surveillance Software to Bahrain   701
    Hypothetical: Sale of Military Equipment to the Kingdom of Saudi Arabia 701
    U.S. National Contact Point for the OECD Guidelines for Multinational
        Enterprises, Final Statement, Specific Instance between European
        Centre for Democracy and Human Rights, Defenders for Medical
        Impartiality, and Arabian Rights Watch Association, and The
        Boeing Company and Lockheed Martin Corporation   702
IV. Employment and Industrial Relations   710
    OECD Employment and Industrial Relations   710
    Hypothetical: Doing Business in the Kurdish Region of Turkey   715
    Hypothetical: Sweatshops   716
    Hypothetical: Collective Bargaining   716
    Hypothetical: Enforcing the Islamic Dress Code   717
    U.S. National Contact Point for the OECD Guidelines for Multinational
        Enterprises, Final Statement, Specific Instance between the International
        Union of Food, Agricultural, Hotel, Restaurant, Catering, Tobacco and
        Allied Workers' Associations and PepsiCo, Inc.   717
V. Environment   724
    OECD Environment   728
    Hypothetical: GM Seeds   732
    Irish National Contact Point, OECD Guidelines for Multinational Enterprises 732
VI. Consumer Interests   742

A. Health and Safety   742
B. Consumer Awareness and Education   743
C. Dispute Resolution   744
D. Consumer Data Protection and Privacy   744
    OECD Consumer Interests   745
    Hypothetical: Defective Handlebars   748
    Statement by the UK National Contact Point on National Grid Transco   749
VII. Science and Technology   751
    OECD Science and Technology   751
    *Communiqué of the Argentine National Contact Point (ANCP) for the OECD
        Guidelines for Multinational Enterprises*   753
VIII. Competition   757
    OECD Competition   757
    *Final Statement of the Korean NCP for the OECD Guidelines for
        Multinational Enterprises, Complaint from Korean Metal Workers'
        Union et al. against Hydis Technologies Co., Ltd., E Ink Holdings,
        Inc. and Yuen Foon Yu, Inc.*   759
IX. Taxation   762
    OECD Taxation   763
    Hypothetical: Transfer Pricing   766

PART **IV**   *Test Your Knowledge: Formulating a Responsible Business
               Strategy for an Enterprise Operating in a Frontier Market*   767

Table of Cases   775
Index   777

PREFACE

Compliance as a distinct field is born out of a paradigm shift in the U.S. criminal justice system—one that leaves the executive branch, instead of Article III courts, primarily in charge of punishing corporate crime. The resultant system gives corporations two options: Institute effective programs to prevent and detect misconduct; or, face draconian sanctions should any employee or agent violate the law. As companies rationally opt to invest in the design and implementation of compliance programs, an entire industry has sprung to meet their urgent needs.

Although management of legal risk should be the province of lawyers, we have not fully seized this new field as our own. Compliance has not been a standard part of law school curricula, and some of the most dynamic and exciting facets of the field—say scouting opportunities in high-risk foreign markets or designing systems that support, rather than hinder, business operations—have been largely left to non-lawyers.

To be sure, compliance involves competencies not traditionally included in a lawyer's skillset—notably, formulation of strategy to deal with what *can* happen in the future rather than with past events. Compliance lawyers must understand an enterprise's long-term business objectives and align them with evolving regulatory trends; in essence help steer the enterprise through a complex and changing global landscape. While legal institutions have been slow to embrace this new role, law students exhibit no such hesitancy. They often walk into my class having never heard of compliance and leave expressing enormous enthusiasm for the content and the prospect of pioneering a new field. This generation of law students is unafraid to break with tradition for the sake of a rewarding career path.

The book is designed to impart a foundational understanding of compliance as a coherent field in law and familiarize students with the basic tools for managing legal risk in various business contexts. It is meant as a platform for a career in compliance; and as such, focuses on theory and practice that are broadly applicable across different industries.

I have used the Foreign Corrupt Practices Act ("FCPA") to showcase a wide range of compliance-related subjects under a single umbrella. The FCPA's breadth and extraterritorial reach make it relevant to all multinational firms, and the statute lends itself to in-depth analysis of legal risk in operations spanning different jurisdictions and cultures.

Going forward, prosecutors and regulators will increasingly focus on whether compliance programs go beyond detecting and preventing violations of law to create values-based cultures. There is an emerging consensus that no compliance program, no matter how elaborate, can be effective in the absence of such an organizational culture. The next frontiers in the development of this field lie in defining the parameters of an organization's ethical obligations and transforming the compliance function from a cost center to a value center. By making culture a focal point throughout the book and dedicating the last three chapters to corporate social responsibility, I hope to signal to this generation of students their critical leadership role in shaping the norms of responsible business conduct in the global economy.

Babak Boghraty, August 2018

ACKNOWLEDGMENTS

This book is in large part the work of a group of dedicated law students and in many ways reflects their vision of a desired profession. I am deeply grateful to my lead editors, Morgan Phillips, Sana Shakir, and Gregg Oberg, for their friendship, insight, and immense substantive input and to Marco Ehrat, Catherine Gregory, Joe Saladino, Arianna Guardiola, Galina Vujovic, Matthew Natoli, Julia Li, Stephanie Cohen, Jacqueline Cangero, Michael Whittington, Ashley Paquin, Hannah Levin, and Alex Forney for their invaluable editorial contribution.

I am grateful to Dean Maureen O'Rourke for encouraging me to pursue my dream of teaching and for her continual support and guidance; Professor Tamar Frankel for being a true friend and mentor; and Professor Fred Tung for his immense help in developing BU Law's compliance curriculum.

I would like to thank my publisher, Wolters Kluwer, especially Joe Terry, as well as Kathy Langone and Sarah Hains of the Froebe Group for their indispensable help and support in developing the book.

A special thanks to my dear colleagues, Felix Ehrat and Jacqueline Arango, for their decades-long friendship and their generosity in sharing their expert perspectives on the issues covered in the book.

My love and gratitude as always to my wife Brenda for being the wind beneath my wings.

We thank copyright holders for permission to reprint excerpts from the following items:

Edward Broughton, The Bhopal Disaster and Its Aftermath: A Review, May 10, 2005. Reprinted with Permission of the Environmental Health Journal.

Susan Côté-Freeman, Overview of Corporate Anti-Corruption Programmes, Business Against Corruption: Case Stories and Examples. Copyright Transparency International, 2006. Reprinted with Permission.

Environment and the OECD Guidelines for Multinational Enterprises: Corporate Tools and Approaches, September 5, 2005. Copyright OECD 2005. Reprinted with permission.

T. Christian Miller, At Siemens, Bribery Was Just a Line Item, ProPublica, December 20, 2008. Reprinted with permission.

T. Christian Miller, U.S. Targets Overseas Bribery; KBR Exec's Plea Widens Probe, ProPublica, September 9, 2008. Reprinted with permission.

OECD Bribery Report: An Analysis of the Crime of Bribery of Foreign Public Officials, 2008. Copyright OECD 2008. Reprinted with Permission.

OECD Guidelines for Multinational Enterprises, 2009. Copyright OECD 2009. Reprinted with permission.

Michael Price, Case Story: Integrity Due Diligence, Business Against Corruption: Case Stories and Examples. Copyright Statoil, 2006. Reprinted with Permission.

Jeremy Simon, Knowing When to Blow the Whistle, Texas Enterprise, University of Texas at Austin, June 10, 2013. Reprinted with Permission.

John D. Sullivan and Anna Nadgrodkiewicz, Looking Toward the Future: The Business Case for Corporate Governance, January 31, 2013. Reprinted with Permission of CIPE Economic Reform Feature Service.

José A. Tabuena & Chris Mondini, Internal Reporting and Whistle-Blowing, Business Against Corruption: Case Stories and Examples. Copyright Deloitte Financial Advisory Services LLP, 2006. Reprinted with Permission.

Alexandra Wrage, Gifts Meals and Entertainment, Business Against Corruption: Case Stories and Examples. Copyright TRACE International, 2006. Reprinted with Permission.

Alexandra Wrage and Kerry Mandernach, Facilitation Payments, Business Against Corruption: Case Stories and Examples. Copyright TRACE International, 2006. Reprinted with Permission.

FEDERAL PROSECUTION OF BUSINESS ORGANIZATIONS

If criminal justice is about personal accountability, how can we justify punishing a fictional entity—like a corporation—that has no persona? This is a long-standing question that Edward Thurlow, Lord Chancellor of England, first posed in the eighteenth century. "Did you ever expect a corporation to have a conscience," he asked, "when it has no soul to damn and no body to kick?"[1]

Two key developments have revived this question and given it special urgency. First, as the global economy has become more integrated, the size and power of multinational enterprises have grown exponentially—as has their ability to do harm. As Professor Sara Sun Beale of Duke Law School explains, "[m]odern corporations not only wield virtually unprecedented power, but they do so in a fashion that often causes serious harm to both individuals and to society as a whole."[2] These massive and complex multinational enterprises control "vast resources [and] have the ability to engage in misconduct that dwarfs that which could be accomplished by individuals."[3]

Recent history is replete with examples of such misconduct. In 1984, Union Carbide's failure to institute proper safety standards in its plant in Bhopal, India, led to the release of tons of deadly gas into the nearby slums, sending thousands to their deaths and permanently maiming tens of thousands more.[4] Criminal conduct by BP in 2010 caused the Deepwater Horizon oil spill—the largest marine oil spill in history—killing eleven people and decimating "one of the most productive ocean ecosystems in the world."[5] Volkswagen's "cheat devices,"

---

1. John C. Coffee, Jr., *"No Soul to Damn: No Body to Kick": An Unscandalized Inquiry into the Problem of Corporate Punishment*, 79 MICH. L. REV 386, 386 (1981) (quoting First Baron Edward Thurlow, who lived from 1731 to 1806).

2. Sara S. Beale, *A Response to the Critics of Corporate Criminal Liability*, 46 AM. CRIM. L. REV. 1481, 1483 (2009).

3. *Id.* at 1484.

4. Edward Broughton, *The Bhopal Disaster and Its Aftermath: A Review*, ENVIRONMENTAL HEALTH (May 10, 2005), https://doi.org/10.1186/1476-069X-4-6.

5. Louis Sahagun, *Toxins Released by Oil Spills Send Fish Hearts into Cardiac Arrest*, L.A. TIMES (Feb. 13, 2014), http://www.latimes.com/science/sciencenow/la-sci-sn-tuna-hearts-oil-spill-toxins-20140213-story.html#ixzz2tbQVLgxI. In November 2012, BP pled guilty to felony counts for the deaths of 11 workers and paid a $4 billion fine. Clifford Krauss and John Schwartz, *BP Will Plead Guilty and Pay Over $4 Billion*, N.Y. TIMES (Nov. 15, 2012), http://www.nytimes.com/2012/11/16/business/global/16iht-bp16.html. Transocean

installed in millions of cars sold around the world between 2009 and 2015, were designed to fool regulators and the public into believing its cars were "green," when in fact they spewed many times more toxins into the air than permitted by law.[6] Siemens, the largest industrial manufacturing firm in Europe, engaged in a systematic effort to corrupt senior government officials in Asia, Africa, Europe, the Middle East, and Latin America, paying almost $1.4 billion in bribes to secure public contracts from the mid-1990s through 2007.[7]

These crimes were not committed by a few rogue employees, but rather undertaken as part of pervasive institutional cultures and business strategies. In this sense, argues Professor Beale, "corporations are not, fundamentally, fictional entities [but] very real and enormously powerful actors whose conduct often causes very significant harm."[8]

Against this background, a second key development has inhibited the government's ability to punish and deter corporate crime: collateral harm to innocent bystanders, including shareholders, employees, and others who took no part in the misconduct. As Preet Bharara, former United States Attorney for the Southern District of New York, notes, corporate defendants "may not be able to survive indictment, much less conviction and sentencing."[9] Bharara points to the "corporate corpses of Arthur Andersen, E.F. Hutton [and] Drexel Burnham

---

pled guilty to a misdemeanor charge as part of its total $1.4 billion fine. Clifford Krauss, *Transocean Chief Admits Crew Shortcomings in Oil Spill*, N.Y. TIMES (Mar. 19, 2013), http://www.nytimes.com/2013/03/20/business/energy-environment/executive-says-crew-should-have-acted-to-prevent-spill.html.

The U.S. Department of Justice filed criminal charges against Kurt Mix, a senior BP engineer, for destroying messages showing BP's knowledge of higher-than-disclosed volumes of oil flow and knowledge that the "Top Kill" operation was likely to fail. John Rudolf, *Kurt Mix, BP Engineer, Faces First Oil Spill Charges (UPDATES)*, HUFFINGTON POST (last updated Dec. 6, 2017). Senior managers Donald Vidrine and Robert Kaluza faced manslaughter and negligence charges in their supervision of safety tests and for their failure to take appropriate action "[i]n the face of glaring red flags." Suzanne Goldenberg and Dominic Rushe, *BP to Pay $4.5bn Penalty Over Deepwater Horizon Disaster*, THE GUARDIAN (Nov. 15, 2012), https://www.theguardian.com/environment/2012/nov/15/bp-deepwater-horizon-gulf-oil-spill. David Rainey, former BP vice president of exploration in the Gulf of Mexico, was charged with "obstruction of Congress and false statements related to the size of the spill." Margaret Cronin Fisk and Allen Johnson, Jr., *Three BP Managers Plead Not Guilty to Gulf Spill Charges*, BLOOMBERG (Nov. 28, 2012). Additionally, Anthony Badalamenti was charged with destruction of evidence related to Halliburton's cement job on the blown-out Macondo well. *Halliburton Manager Gets 1 Year Probation in Gulf Oil Spill*, CBS NEWS (Jan. 21, 2014).

None of the charges resulted in prison time, and no upper level executives were charged. Kurt Mix received 6 months' probation, Donald Vidrine paid a $50,000 fine and received 10 months' probation, and Anthony Badalamenti received one year's probation. David Rainey and Robert Kaluza were acquitted. James Gill, *James Gill: Disaster Prosecution Is, Well, a Disaster*, THE NEW ORLEANS ADVOCATE (Mar. 12, 2016); Loren Steffy, *Blowout*, TEXAS MONTHLY (Oct. 2016); *Halliburton Manager Gets 1 Year Probation in Gulf Oil Spill*, CBS NEWS (Jan. 21, 2014).

6. Coral Davenport & Jack Ewing, *VW Is Said to Cheat on Diesel Emissions; U.S. to Order Big Recall*, N.Y. TIMES (Sept. 18, 2015), https://www.nytimes.com/2015/09/19/business/volkswagen-is-ordered-to-recall-nearly-500000-vehicles-over-emissions-software.html.

7. Eric Lichtblau and Carter Dougherty, *Siemens to Pay $1.34 Billion in Fines*, N.Y. TIMES (Dec. 15, 2008), http://www.nytimes.com/2008/12/16/business/worldbusiness/16siemens.html.

8. Beale, *supra* note 2, at 1482.

9. Preet Bharara, *Corporations Cry Uncle and Their Employees Cry Foul: Rethinking Prosecutorial Pressure on Corporate Defendants*, 44 AM. CRIM. L. REV. 53, 73 (2007).

Lambert," to argue that corporations are "eggshell defendants" for whom prosecution is akin to a death sentence.[10]

Since the early 1990s, the U.S. government has sought to balance these two competing interests—that is, its interest in deterring corporate crime against its interest in avoiding collateral harm by doing what Lord Thurlow thought impossible: getting corporations to develop a conscience. Specifically, the criminal justice system has employed a "carrot-and-stick" system aimed at encouraging corporations to self-police.

> This carrot-and-stick approach aim[s] to convert organizations from passive bystanders who hoped employees would behave well, into active advocates of an ethical culture in the workplace—in short, enlisting companies themselves in the fight against corporate crime. Given the potentially serious consequences of corporate misconduct and the limited ability of after-the-fact prosecutions to undo the damage or deter future law breaking, the [government] hope[s] that corporate self-policing through strong compliance and ethics programs [can] reduce the frequency and severity of misconduct.[11]

The stick wielded by the government is the threat of financially debilitating penalties, penalties large enough in some situations to divest the corporations of all its assets. The carrot, on the other hand, is the offer of substantial leniency: up to a 95 percent reduction in the sentence—if a corporation maintains an effective compliance and ethics program. A compliance and ethics program is an internal policing system designed to ensure that a corporation's employees and agents obey the law and behave ethically. It is meant to be autonomous and independent from business operations and to act as a check on those operations' pursuit of profit. Experience shows that these programs work when properly designed and implemented and that they significantly reduce the incidence of corporate misconduct.[12]

In the ideal world envisioned by the government, every corporation will have an effective compliance and ethics program, obviating the need to ever criminally charge a corporation and risk collateral harm to innocent bystanders. This would also be an optimal allocation of public resources, because corporations are far better positioned than is the government to police their own employees.

Since its inception, this new regime has made great strides toward its objective of encouraging corporate self-policing:

> [N]otably the vigorous efforts by many U.S. companies and other organizations to adopt comprehensive compliance/ethics programs [and] a new profession of compliance/ethics professionals, who now number in the thousands, to develop and implement the new corporate programs. In addition, . . . boards of directors and senior corporate management in many companies have taken on leadership roles in promoting law-compliant and ethical cultures. Numerous books and

---

10. *Id.*
11. Ethics Resource Center, The Federal Sentencing Guidelines for Organizations at Twenty Years 1 (2012) [hereinafter Examination of the FSGO], https://www.theagc.org/docs/f12.10.pdf.
12. *Id.* at 2.

articles have been written and conferences convened to help them know how to do that, and companies have identified best practices to help build compliance into everyday decision-making.[13]

This "revolution," as one commentator calls it,[14] has been possible thanks to an unprecedented exercise of government control over private enterprise, supplanting the role of the board of directors as the corporation's governing body:

> The contemporary compliance function serves a core governance function, yet its origins cannot be traced to a board delegation or other traditional source of governance authority. . . . Compliance is a de facto government mandate imposed upon firms by means of ex ante incentives, ex post enforcement tactics, and formal signaling efforts. . . . [T]he government is not simply making rules that firms must follow, as it does when it passes new laws and regulations . . . . Instead, through compliance, the government . . . [is] imposing specific governance structures . . . designed to change how the firm conducts its business.[15]

Thus, much as a cart driver deals with a reluctant mule, federal prosecutors use the threat of indictment as the stick and the possibility of avoiding indictment as the carrot to compel business organizations—large and small, foreign and domestic—to agree to wide-scale reforms.

---

13. *Id.*
14. Sean J. Griffith, *Corporate Governance in an Era of Compliance*, 57 WM. & MARY L. REV. 2075, 2077 (2016).
15. *Id.* at 2078.

CHAPTER 1

Theoretical Underpinnings of Corporate Criminal Liability

I. *Respondeat Superior*
II. The Collective Knowledge Doctrine
III. The Collective Entity Rule

Three legal doctrines—*respondeat superior*, collective knowledge, and collective entity—impose extraordinarily broad liability on corporations. As a result, "a corporation, though deemed a 'person' for most purposes, does not have the same ability as a natural person"[2] to defend against a criminal enforcement action. This liability scheme underpins the government's power to compel corporations to self-police.

> The history of American constitutional law in no small measure is the history of the impact of the modern corporation upon the American scene.
>
> *Felix Frankfurter*[1]

I. *Respondeat Superior*

Under the common law, corporations were deemed incapable of committing crimes—although their members could be prosecuted for committing crimes in their individual capacities.[3] Industrialization and the increasing importance of corporations led to the gradual erosion of that view; and by the twentieth century, English courts held corporations criminally liable for the conduct of persons who "represent[ed] the directing mind and will of the corporate entity."[4] The doctrine which permits corporate liability under U.K. law is known as

---

1. Felix Frankfurter, *The Commerce Clause Under Marshall, Taney, and Waite* 63 (1937).
2. Preet Bharara, *Corporations Cry Uncle and Their Employees Cry Foul: Rethinking Prosecutorial Pressure on Corporate Defendants*, 44 AM. CRIM. L. REV. 53, 65 (2007).
3. William Blackstone, *Commentaries on the Laws of England*, 464 (1765).
4. HANS DE DOELDER & KLAUS TIEDEMANN, CRIMINAL LIABILITY OF CORPORATIONS 372 (Kluwer Law International 1996).

"identification," the merger of the corporate personality with those of the persons who control it.[5]

In the United States, corporate criminal liability has evolved through the dual state/federal legal systems. Before the Civil War, federal programs and activities were relatively limited and most criminal laws were passed at the state level.[6] The U.S. Constitution recognizes only treason,[7] piracy,[8] and counterfeiting as federal crimes[9]—though it authorizes Congress to make all laws "necessary and proper" to effectuate its delegated powers.[10]

Massive economic growth following the Civil War and consequent expansion of interstate commerce led to a dramatic increase in the number of federal crimes created by Congress. In 1890, Congress passed the Sherman Act,[11] which prohibited monopolies and conspiracies to restrain commerce.[12] In 1903, following the election of President Roosevelt on a platform calling for new laws to regulate corporate conduct, Congress passed the Elkins Act,[13] which held railroad companies criminally liable for any violation committed by an "officer, agent, or other person acting for or employed by any common carrier acting within the scope of his employment."[14]

Holding a corporation responsible for the acts of its agents and employees was permitted under a common law tort doctrine known as *respondeat superior*, which literally means "let the master answer."[15] In the American federal courts it was used primarily to impose civil liability on corporations for damages tortiously caused by their employees.[16] In 1909, the U.S. Supreme Court incorporated this doctrine into criminal law, upholding as constitutional the Elkins Act's imposition of vicarious criminal liability on corporations. The Court's decision in *New York Central Railroad Co. v. United States*[17] serves to this day as the predicate for imposing corporate criminal liability under federal law.

5. Pamela H. Bucy, *Corporate Criminal Responsibility*, Encyclopedia of Crime and Justice (The Gale Group 2002), https://www.encyclopedia.com/law/legal-and-political-magazines/corporate-criminal-responsibility.

6. Sara S. Beale, *The Development and Evolution of the U.S. Law of Corporate Criminal Liability*, Duke Law Scholarship Repository (2014), https://scholarship.law.duke.edu/faculty_scholarship/3205.

7. U.S. Const. art. III, § 3.

8. U.S. Const. art. I, § 8.

9. U.S. Const. art. I, § 8.

10. *See* Beale, *supra* note 6, at 2.

11. Sherman Antitrust Act, ch. 647, 26 Stat. 209 (1890) (codified at 15 U.S.C. §§ 1–7).

12. *Id. See also* Beale, *supra* note 6, at 3.

13. Elkins Act, Pub. L. No. 57-103, ch. 708, 32 Stat. 847 (1903).

14. *Id.* at § 1.

15. *Respondeat superior*, Black's Law Dictionary (10th ed. 2014).

16. Beale, *supra* note 6, at 5.

17. 212 U.S. 481 (1909). Cases following *New York Central* have broadened its scope, holding that criminal liability can attach where the corporation derived no benefit from the alleged misconduct, and even if the offender was a menial employee. *See* Standard Oil Co. of Tex. v. United States, 307 F.2d 120, 127 (5th Cir. 1962); Bharara, *supra* note 2, at 63 (citing United States v. Automated Med. Labs., Inc., 770 F.2d 399, 407 (4th Cir. 1985)).

N.Y. Cent. & Hudson River R.R. Co. v. United States

Supreme Court of the United States, 212 U.S. 481 (1909)

OPINION

Mr. Justice Dᴀʏ delivered the opinion of the court:

. . . .

The second count charges the making and publishing of a through tariff rate upon sugar by certain railroad companies, including the plaintiff in error, fixing the rate at 23 cents per 100 pounds from New York city to Detroit, and charges the railroad company's general traffic manager and assistant traffic manager with entering into an unlawful agreement and arrangement with the shippers, the American Sugar Refining Company of New York and the American Sugar Refining Company of New Jersey, and the consignees of the sugar, . . . whereby it was agreed that, for sugar shipped over the line, the full tariff rate being paid thereon, the railroad company should give a rebate of 5 cents for each 100 pounds. . . .

. . . .

Numerous objections and exceptions were taken at every stage of the trial to the validity of the indictment and the proceedings thereunder. The principal attack in this court is upon the constitutional validity of certain features of the Elkins act. 32 Stat. at L. 847, chap. 708, U. S. Comp. Stat. Supp. 1907, p. 880. That act, among other things, provides:

> "(1) That anything done or omitted to be done by a corporation common carrier subject to the act to regulate commerce, and the acts amendatory thereof, which, if done or omitted to be done by any director or officer thereof, or any receiver, trustee, lessee, agent, or person acting for or employed by such corporation, would constitute a misdemeanor under said acts, or under this act, shall also be held to be a misdemeanor committed by such corporation; and, upon conviction thereof, it shall be subject to like penalties as are prescribed in said acts, or by this act, with reference to such persons, except as such penalties are herein changed.
>
> "In construing and enforcing the provisions of this section, the act, omission, or failure of any officer, agent, or other person acting for or employed by any common carrier, acting within the scope of his employment, shall, in every case, be also deemed to be the act, omission, or failure of such carrier, as well as that of the person."

It is contended that these provisions of the law are unconstitutional because Congress has no authority to impute to a corporation the commission of criminal offenses, or to subject a corporation to a criminal prosecution by reason of the things charged. The argument is that to thus punish the corporation is in reality to punish the innocent stockholders, and to deprive them of their property without opportunity to be heard, consequently without due process of law. And it is further contended that these provisions of the statute deprive the corporation of the presumption of innocence—a presumption which is part of due process in criminal prosecutions. It is urged that, as there is no authority shown by the board of directors or the stockholders for the criminal acts of the agents of the company, in contracting for and giving rebates, they could not be lawfully charged against the corporation. As no action of the board of directors could legally authorize a crime, and as, indeed, the stockholders could not do so, the arguments come to this: that, owing to the nature and character of its organization and the extent of its power and authority, a corporation cannot commit a crime of the nature charged in this case.

Some of the earlier writers on common law held the law to be that a corporation could not commit a crime. It is said to have been held by Lord Chief Justice Holt (Anonymous, 12 Mod. 559) that "a corporation is not indictable, although the particular members of it are." In Blackstone's Commentaries, chapter 18, § 12, we find it stated: "A corporation cannot commit treason, or felony, or other crime in its corporate capacity, though its members may, in their distinct individual capacities." The modern authority, universally, so far as we know, is the other way. In considering the subject, Bishop's New Criminal Law, § 417, devotes a chapter to the capacity of corporations to commit crime, and states the law to be:

> "Since a corporation acts by its officers and agents, their purposes, motives, and intent are just as much those of the corporation as are the things done. If, for example, the invisible, intangible essence or air which we term a corporation can level mountains, fill up valleys, lay down iron tracks, and run railroad cars on them, it can intend to do it, and can act therein as well viciously as virtuously."

Without citing the state cases holding the same view, we may note Telegram Newspaper Co. v. Com. 172 Mass. 294, 44 L.R.A. 159, 70 Am. St. Rep. 280, 52 N. E. 445, in which it was held that a corporation was subject to punishment for criminal contempt; and the court, speaking by Mr. Chief Justice Field, said:

> "We think that a corporation may be liable criminally for certain offenses of which a specific intent may be a necessary element. There is no more difficulty in imputing to a corporation a specific intent in criminal proceedings than in civil. A corporation cannot be arrested and imprisoned in either civil or criminal proceedings, but its property may be taken either as compensation for a private wrong or as punishment for a public wrong."

It is held in England that corporations may be criminally prosecuted for acts of misfeasance as well as nonfeasance. R. v. Great North of England R. Co. 9 Q. B. 315.

It is now well established that, in actions for tort, the corporation may be held responsible for damages for the acts of its agent within the scope of his employment. Lake Shore & M. S. R. Co. v. Prentice, 147 U. S. 101, 109, 111, 37 L. ed. 97, 102, 103, 13 Sup. Ct. Rep. 261.

And this is the rule when the act is done by the agent in the course of his employment, although done wantonly or recklessly or against the express orders of the principal. In such cases the liability is not imputed because the principal actually participates in the malice or fraud, but because the act is done for the benefit of the principal, while the agent is acting within the scope of his employment in the business of the principal, and justice requires that the latter shall be held responsible for damages to the individual who has suffered by such conduct. Lothrop v. Adams, 133 Mass. 471, 43 Am. Rep. 528.

A corporation is held responsible for acts not within the agent's corporate powers strictly construed, but which the agent has assumed to perform for the corporation when employing the corporate powers actually authorized, and in such cases there need be no written authority under seal or vote of the corporation in order to constitute the agency or to authorize the act. Washington Gaslight Co. v. Lansden, 172 U. S. 534, 544, 43 L. ed. 543, 547, 19 Sup. Ct. Rep. 296.

In this case we are to consider the criminal responsibility of a corporation for an act done while an authorized agent of the company is exercising the authority conferred upon him. It was admitted by the defendant at the trial that, at the time mentioned in the indictment, the general freight traffic manager and the assistant freight traffic manager were authorized to establish rates at which freight should be carried over the line of the New York Central & Hudson River Company, and were authorized to unite with other companies in the establishing, filing, and publishing of through rates, including the through rate or rates between New York and Detroit referred to in the indictment. Thus, the subject-matter of making and fixing rates was within the scope of the authority and employment of the agents of the company, whose acts in this connection are sought to be charged upon the company. Thus clothed with authority, the agents were bound to respect the regulation of interstate commerce enacted by Congress, requiring the filing and publication of rates and punishing departures therefrom. Applying the principle governing civil liability, we go only a step farther in holding that the act of the agent, while exercising the authority delegated to him to make rates for transportation, may be controlled, in the interest of public policy, by imputing his act to his employer and imposing penalties upon the corporation for which he is acting in the premises.

It is true that there are some crimes which, in their nature, cannot be committed by corporations. But there is a large class of offenses, of which rebating under the Federal statutes is one, wherein the crime consists in purposely doing the things prohibited by statute. In that class of crimes we see no good reason why corporations may not be held responsible for and charged with the knowledge and purposes of their agents, acting within the authority conferred upon them. 2 Morawetz, Priv. Corp. § 733; Green's Brice, Ultra Vires, 366. If it were not so, many offenses might go unpunished and acts be committed in violation of law where, as in the present case, the statute requires all persons, corporate or private, to refrain from certain practices, forbidden in the interest of public policy.

It is a part of the public history of the times that statutes against rebates could not be effectually enforced so long as individuals only were subject to punishment for violation of the law, when the giving of rebates or concessions inured to the benefit of the corporations of which the individuals were but the instruments. This situation, developed in more than one report of the Interstate Commerce Commission, was no doubt influential in bringing about the enactment of the Elkins law, making corporations criminally liable.

This statute does not embrace things impossible to be done by a corporation; its objects are to prevent favoritism, and to secure equal rights to all in interstate transportation, and one legal rate, to be published and posted and accessible to all alike. New York, N. H. & H. R. Co. v. Interstate Commerce Commission, 200 U. S. 399, 50 L. ed. 524, 26 Sup. Ct. Rep. 272; Armour Packing Co. v. United States, 209 U. S. 56, 52 L. ed. 681, 28 Sup. Ct. Rep. 428.

We see no valid objection in law, and every reason in public policy, why the corporation, which profits by the transaction, and can only act through its agents and officers, shall be held punishable by fine because of the knowledge and intent of its agents to whom it has intrusted authority to act in the subject-matter of making and fixing rates of transportation, and whose knowledge and purposes may well be attributed to the corporation for which the agents act. While the law should have regard to the rights of all, and to those of corporations no less than to those of individuals, it cannot shut its eyes to the fact that the great majority of business transactions in modern times are conducted through these bodies, and particularly that interstate commerce is almost entirely in their hands, and to give them immunity from all punishment because of the old and exploded doctrine that a corporation cannot commit a crime would virtually take away the only means of effectually controlling the subject-matter and correcting the abuses aimed at.

There can be no question of the power of Congress to regulate interstate commerce, to prevent favoritism, and to secure equal rights to all engaged in interstate trade. It would be a distinct step backward to hold that Congress cannot control those who are conducting this interstate commerce by holding them responsible for the intent and purposes of the agents to whom they have delegated the power to act in the premises.

. . . .

We find no error in the proceedings of the Circuit Court, and its judgment is **_affirmed._**

Notes and Questions

The *New York Central* opinion evokes the old adage that bad facts make bad law. The context in which the case was decided—strong public support for the Roosevelt administration's enforcement of federal criminal laws against corporations—explains the court's simpleminded and utilitarian response to the expanding role and power of corporations in interstate commerce.[18] As Professor Beale points out, this approach was influenced by Oliver Wendell Holmes, who was a member of the Court when *New York Central* was decided and is famous for the following quote:

> The life of the law has not been logic; it has been experience. The felt necessities of the time, the prevalent moral and political theories, intuitions of public policy, avowed or unconscious, and even the prejudices which judges share with their

---

18. *See* William S. Laufer, *Corporate Liability, Risk Shifting, and the Paradox of Compliance*, 52 Vand. L. Rev. 1343, 1363–64 (1999).

fellow-men, have had a good deal more to do than syllogism in determining the rules by which men should be governed. The law embodies the story of a nation's development through many centuries, and it cannot be dealt with as if it contained only the axioms and corollaries of a book of mathematics.[19]

Holmes also advocated "prevention . . . [as] the chief and only universal purpose of punishment," and argued that criminal law should abandon its traditional focus on moral culpability.[20] *New York Central*'s emphasis on deterring corporate crime is consistent with Holmes's view. The opinion's reference to "the old and exploded doctrine that a corporation cannot commit a crime"[21] reflects a view of law that "rejects legal formalism and allows criminal as well as civil law to develop to meet the needs of the time."[22]

Although the narrow issue before the court in *New York Central* was the constitutionality of the Elkins Act, the breadth of the opinion "has been understood to be a strong endorsement of corporate criminal liability and the respondeat superior test, which is now applied to other federal offenses in all federal courts."[23] Federal courts have applied the doctrine to impute the intentions and actions of agents directly to the corporation; it is as though the agents were the organization.[24] A multinational enterprise with thousands of employees around the world, "despite its best efforts to prevent wrongdoing in its ranks, can still be held criminally liable for any of its employees' illegal actions."[25] Criminal liability attaches for the misconduct of a low-level employee,[26] "even if the employee acted directly contrary to company policy and instructions"[27] and the corporation derived no benefit from the illegal conduct.[28]

Legal literature has been generally critical of the *New York Central* opinion.[29] The problem with the criminal application of *respondeat superior*, scholars note, is that it overlooks a crucial difference between tort law and criminal law: While tort law functions to distribute the loss from an adverse event, criminal law requires "conscious wrongdoing" on the part of the defendant.[30] As Professor Bucy explains:

---

19. Beale, *supra* note 6, at 8 (quoting OLIVER WENDELL HOLMES, THE COMMON LAW 1 (1881)).

20. *Id.* (quoting OLIVER WENDELL HOLMES, THE COMMON LAW 46, 49–50 (1881)).

21. N.Y. Cent. & Hudson River R.R. Co. v. United States, 212 U.S. 481, 496 (1909).

22. Beale, *supra* note 6, at 7.

23. *Id.* at 8.

24. *Id.* at 5.

25. Paula Desio, *An Overview of the Organizational Guidelines*, UNITED STATES SENTENCING COMMISSION (on file with the USSC), https://www.ussc.gov/sites/default/files/pdf/training/organizational-guidelines/ORGOVERVIEW.pdf.

26. *See, e.g.*, Standard Oil Co. of Tex. v. United States, 307 F.2d 120, 127 (5th Cir. 1962) ("corporation may be criminally bound by the acts of subordinate, even menial, employees").

27. Desio, *supra* note 25.

28. *See, e.g.*, *Standard Oil Co.*, 307 F.2d at 128–29 ("The act is no less the principal's if from such intended conduct either no benefit accrues, a benefit is undiscernible, or, for that matter, the result turns out to be adverse.").

29. Beale, *supra* note 6, at 10.

30. Philip A. Lacovara & David P. Nicoli, *Vicarious Criminal Liability of Organizations: RICO as an Example of a Flawed Principle in Practice*, 64 ST. JOHN'S L. REV. 725, 734 (2012).

The assumption underlying tort liability is that it is more equitable for the employer of the *tort-feasor* to absorb the financial loss caused by its agent's conduct than for the individual victim to do so. Except in rare tort cases, intent is not an issue in holding a corporation liable. . . . Moreover, even though the threat of tort liability may deter conduct, collection of damages, not deterrence of future conduct, is the paramount concern of a tort action. Lastly, in all but unusual cases, tort liability carries no moral or punitive stigma; it is simply a cost of doing business.[31]

By contrast, "[s]ince the element of moral culpability is fundamental to the proper application of the criminal law, generally deterrence is not sufficient to justify criminal prosecution and punishment unless the defendant actually engaged in the misconduct personally or expressly authorized and directed the misconduct."[32]

The Court in *New York Central* acknowledged this problem, but it claimed it could not "shut its eyes" to the importance of corporations to modern commerce and give them "immunity from all punishment."[33] Is this justification valid? Is it true that without corporate criminal liability, the crimes committed by individual employees of corporations would go unpunished? Why would criminal prosecution of culpable employees be inadequate to address those crimes?

Hypothetical: Scope of Employment

Beacon Inc. ("Beacon") is a corporation based in the United States that manufactures and sells pharmaceutical products, with subsidiaries in 35 countries, including Tajikistan. In 2016, a sales agent in Beacon's Tajik subsidiary began demanding that customers pay him an additional 10 percent commission on sales of Beacon products. The commissions were paid directly to the sales agent's bank account without Beacon's knowledge or consent.

One of Beacon's customers contacted the DOJ and reported the extra payments. Subsequently, the DOJ began an enforcement action against Beacon for tax fraud for failing to report the commissions as income.

Can the sales agent's conduct be imputed to Beacon under the doctrine of *respondeat superior*?

31. Bucy, *supra* note 5.
32. Lacovara & Nicoli, *supra* note 30, at 737.
33. N.Y. Cent. & Hudson River R.R. Co. v. United States, 212 U.S. 481, 495–96 (1909).

II. The Collective Knowledge Doctrine

A corollary of the *respondeat superior* doctrine is the collective knowledge doctrine, which holds that in a collective institution, such as a business organization, "knowledge is the sum of the knowledge of all of the employees."[34] This doctrine operates to aggregate the information and states of minds of all the employees, such that the corporation can be held criminally liable even where no single employee intended to commit the crime.[35]

United States v. Bank of New England, N.A.

United States Court of Appeals, First Circuit 821 F.2d 844 (1987)

OPINION

Bownes, Circuit Judge.

The Bank of New England appeals a jury verdict convicting it of thirty-one violations of the Currency Transaction Reporting Act (the Act) 31 U.S.C. §§ 5311–22 (1982). Department of Treasury regulations promulgated under the Act require banks to file Currency Transaction Reports (CTRs) within fifteen days of customer currency transactions exceeding $10,000. 31 C.F.R. § 103.22 (1986). The Act imposes felony liability when a bank willfully fails to file such reports "as part of a pattern of illegal activity involving transactions of more than $100,000 in a twelve-month period. . . ." 31 U.S.C. § 5322(b).

I. THE ISSUES

The Bank was found guilty of having failed to file CTRs on cash withdrawals made by James McDonough. It is undisputed that on thirty-one separate occasions between May 1983 and July 1984, McDonough withdrew from the Prudential Branch of the Bank more than $10,000 in cash by using multiple checks—each one individually under $10,000—presented simultaneously to a single bank teller. The Bank contends that such conduct did not trigger the Act's reporting requirements. It also urges that felony liability should not have been imposed because it did not engage in a pattern of illegal activity. In addition, the Bank avers that, if it did commit a felony violation, it did not commit thirty-one of them. The Bank also argues that the trial judge's instructions on willfulness were fatally flawed, and that, in any event, the evidence did not suffice to show that it willfully failed to file CTRs on McDonough's transactions. Finally, the Bank submits that during her charge to the jury, the trial judge erroneously alluded to evidence of the Bank's conduct after the dates specified in the indictment.

---

34. United States v. Bank of New England, 821 F.2d 844, 855 (1st Cir. 1987); *see also* Bharara, *supra* note 2, at 63.

35. *Bank of New England*, 821 F.2d at 855–56.

The Bank had been named in a federal grand jury indictment which was returned on October 15, 1985. Count One of the indictment alleged that between May 1983 and May 1985, James McDonough, the Bank, and Carol Orlandella and Patricia Murphy—both of whom were former head tellers with the Bank's Prudential Branch—unlawfully conspired to conceal from the IRS thirty-six of McDonough's currency transactions. The trial court directed a verdict of acquittal on this count. Defendants Murphy and Orlandella were found not guilty of charges that they individually aided and abetted the failure to file CTRs on McDonough's transactions.

The bulk of the indictment alleged that the Bank, as principal, and McDonough, as an aider and abettor, willfully failed to file CTRs on thirty-six occasions between May 1983 and July 1984. Five counts were dismissed because, on those occasions, McDonough received cashier's checks from the Bank, rather than currency. McDonough was acquitted of all charges against him. The Bank was found guilty on the thirty-one remaining counts. We affirm.

. . . .

IV. WILLFULNESS OF THE BANK'S CONDUCT

A. The Trial Court's Instruction on Willfulness

Criminal liability under 31 U.S.C. § 5322 only attaches when a financial institution "willfully" violates the CTR filing requirement. A finding of willfulness under the Reporting Act must be supported by "proof of the defendant's knowledge of the reporting requirements and his specific intent to commit the crime." [Citation omitted.] Willfulness can rarely be proven by direct evidence, since it is a state of mind; it is usually established by drawing reasonable inferences from the available facts. [Citation omitted.]

The Bank contends that the trial court's instructions on knowledge and specific intent effectively relieved the government of its responsibility to prove that the Bank acted willfully. The trial judge began her instructions on this element by outlining generally the concepts of knowledge and willfulness:

> Knowingly simply means voluntarily and intentionally. It's designed to exclude a failure that is done by mistake or accident, or for some other innocent reason. Willfully means voluntarily, intentionally, and with a specific intent to disregard, to disobey the law, with a bad purpose to violate the law.

The trial judge properly instructed the jury that it could infer knowledge if a defendant consciously avoided learning about the reporting requirements. The court then focused on the kind of proof that would establish the Bank's knowledge of its filing obligations. The judge instructed that the knowledge of individual employees acting within the scope of their employment is imputed to the Bank. She told the jury that "if any employee knew that multiple checks would require the filing of reports, the bank knew it, provided the employee knew it within the scope of his employment, . . ."

The trial judge then focused on the issue of "collective knowledge":

In addition, however, you have to look at the bank as an institution. As such, its knowledge is the sum of the knowledge of all of the employees. That is, the bank's knowledge is the totality of what all of the employees know within the scope of their employment. So, if Employee A knows one facet of the currency reporting requirement, B knows another facet of it, and C a third facet of it, the bank knows them all. So if you find that an employee within the scope of his employment knew that CTRs had to be filed, even if multiple checks are used, the bank is deemed to know it. The bank is also deemed to know it if each of several employees knew a part of that requirement and the sum of what the separate employees knew amounted to knowledge that such a requirement existed.

After discussing the two modes of establishing knowledge—via either knowledge of one of its individual employees or the aggregate knowledge of all its employees—the trial judge turned to the issue of specific intent:

> There is a similar double business with respect to the concept of willfulness with respect to the bank. In deciding whether the bank acted willfully, again you have to look first at the conduct of all employees and officers, and, second, at what the bank did or did not do as an institution. The bank is deemed to have acted willfully if one of its employees in the scope of his employment acted willfully. So, if you find that an employee willfully failed to do what was necessary to file these reports, then that is deemed to be the act of the bank, and the bank is deemed to have willfully failed to file.
>
> . . . .
>
> Alternatively, the bank as an institution has certain responsibilities; as an organization, it has certain responsibilities. And you will have to determine whether the bank as an organization consciously avoided learning about and observing CTR requirements. The Government to prove the bank guilty on this theory, has to show that its failure to file was the result of some flagrant organizational indifference. In this connection, you should look at the evidence as to the bank's effort, if any, to inform its employees of the law; its effort to check on their compliance; its response to various bits of information that it got in August and September of '84 and February of '85; its policies, and how it carried out its stated policies.
>
> . . . .
>
> If you find that the Government has proven with respect to any transaction either that an employee within the scope of his employment willfully failed to file a required report or that the bank was flagrantly indifferent to its obligations, then you may find that the bank has willfully failed to file the required reports.

The Bank contends that the trial court's instructions regarding knowledge were defective because they eliminated the requirement that it be proven that the Bank violated a known legal duty. It avers that the knowledge instruction invited the jury to convict the Bank for negligently maintaining a poor communications network that prevented the consolidation of the information held by its various employees. The Bank argues that it is error to find that a corporation possesses a particular item of knowledge if one part of the corporation has half the information making up the item, and another part of the entity has the other half.

A collective knowledge instruction is entirely appropriate in the context of corporate criminal liability. [Citations omitted.] The acts of a corporation are, after all, simply the acts of all of its employees operating within the scope of their employment. The law on corporate criminal liability reflects this. [Citations omitted.] Similarly, the knowledge obtained by corporate employees acting within the scope of their employment is imputed to the corporation. [Citation omitted.] Corporations compartmentalize knowledge, subdividing the elements of specific duties and operations into smaller components. The aggregate of those components constitutes the corporation's knowledge of a particular operation. It is irrelevant whether employees administering one component of an operation know the specific activities of employees administering another aspect of the operation:

> [A] corporation cannot plead innocence by asserting that the Information obtained by several employees was not acquired by any one individual who then would have comprehended its full import. Rather the corporation is considered to have acquired the collective knowledge of its employees and is held responsible for their failure to act accordingly.

United States v. T.I.M.E.—D.C., Inc., 381 F. Supp. at 738. Since the Bank had the compartmentalized structure common to all large corporations, the court's collective knowledge instruction was not only proper but necessary.

Nor do we find any defects in the trial court's instructions on specific intent. The court told the jury that the concept of willfulness entails a voluntary, intentional, and bad purpose to disobey the law. Her instructions on this element, when viewed as a whole, directed the jury not to convict for accidental, mistaken or inadvertent acts or omissions. It is urged that the court erroneously charged that willfulness could be found via flagrant indifference by the Bank toward its reporting obligations. With respect to federal regulatory statutes, the Supreme Court has endorsed defining willfulness, in both civil and criminal contexts, as "a disregard for the governing statute and an indifference to its requirements." [Citations omitted.] Accordingly, we find no error in the court's instructions on willfulness.

B. Evidence of Willfulness

The Bank asserts that the evidence did not suffice to show that it had willfully failed to comply with the Act's reporting requirements. We review the evidence in the light most favorable to the government. *United States v. Medina*, 761 F.2d 12, 16 n. 3 (1st Cir.1985); *United States v. Tierney*, 760 F.2d 382, 384 (1st Cir.), *cert. denied*, 474 U.S. 843, 106 S.Ct. 131, 88 L.Ed.2d 108 (1985).

As already discussed, the language of the Treasury regulations itself gave notice that cash withdrawals over $10,000 were reportable, regardless of the number of checks used. Primary responsibility for CTR compliance in the Bank's branch offices was assigned to head tellers and branch managers. Head tellers Orlandella and Murphy, who knew of the nature of McDonough's transactions, also knew of the CTR filing obligations imposed by the Bank. The jury heard testimony from former bank teller Simona Wong, who stated that she knew

McDonough's transactions were reportable, and that the source of her knowledge was head teller Murphy.

Even if some Bank personnel mistakenly regarded McDonough as engaging in multiple transactions, there was convincing evidence that the Bank knew that his withdrawals were reportable. An internal memo sent in May 1983 by project coordinator Jayne Brady to all branch managers and head tellers stated that "'[r]eportable transactions are expanded to include multiple transactions which aggregate more than $10,000 in any *one day*.' This includes deposits or withdrawals by a customer to or from more than one account." (Emphasis in original.) The Prudential Branch Manual instructed that if Bank personnel know that a customer has engaged in multiple transactions totalling $10,000 or more, then such transactions should be regarded as a single transaction. In addition, since 1980, the instructions on the back of CTR forms have directed that reports be filed on multiple transactions which aggregate to over $10,000. Finally, a Bank auditor discussed with Orlandella and Murphy, the Bank's obligation to report a customer's multiple transactions in a single day which amount to more than $10,000. We do not suggest that these evidentiary items in themselves legally bound the Bank to report McDonough's transactions; it is the language of the regulations that impose such a duty. This evidence, however, proved that the Bank had ample knowledge that transactions like McDonough's came within the purview of the Act.

Regarding the Bank's specific intent to violate the reporting obligation, Simona Wong testified that head teller Patricia Murphy knew that McDonough's transactions were reportable, but, on one occasion, deliberately chose not to file a CTR on him because he was "a good customer." In addition, the jury heard testimony that bank employees regarded McDonough's transactions as unusual, speculated that he was a bookie, and suspected that he was structuring his transactions to avoid the Act's reporting requirements. An internal Bank memo, written after an investigation of the McDonough transactions, concluded that a "person managing the branch would have to have known that something strange was going on." Given the suspicions aroused by McDonough's banking practices and the abundance of information indicating that his transactions were reportable, the jury could have concluded that the failure by Bank personnel to, at least, inquire about the reportability of McDonough's transactions constituted flagrant indifference to the obligations imposed by the Act.

We hold that the evidence was sufficient for a finding of willfulness.

. . . .

Affirmed.

Notes and Questions

In his article *Collective Corporate Knowledge and the Federal False Claims Act,* Professor Sam Halabi uses the example of the Ford Pinto to illustrate how the collective knowledge doctrine can suggest culpable intent where none existed.[36] The Ford Pinto became infamous after 27 people died between 1973 and 1980 because of a design error that caused the gas tank to explode on rear impact, engulfing the car and its passengers in flames.

When different bits of information about company processes were pieced together, it appeared as though Ford had consciously compromised on safety to save costs. One piece of information related to the strategy articulated by the CEO—Lee Iacocca—called the "two thousand, two thousand" rule, which set a goal to produce a car that weighed under 2,000 pounds and cost less than $2,000.[37] The effort to meet those criteria led to mistakes that made the gas tank susceptible to rupture.

Another piece of information revealed a separate and unrelated effort by Ford to oppose new safety standards that required installation of special valves in cars and trucks to prevent fuel leakage. In a report commissioned by Ford as part of that opposition effort, a value of $200,000 was attached to each victim of the kind of accident targeted by the regulations.[38] When combined, these two separate facts suggested that Ford had calculated the total human cost of future fuel tank explosions and concluded it would be less than the cost of making the cars safe.[39]

Halabi questions whether the collective knowledge doctrine provides the right methodology for measuring a business organization's "knowledge"—an element of many federal crimes that must be proven in a corporate prosecution.[40] He queries whether, for example, Enron Corporation "knew" that its executives were using fraudulent accounting to mislead investors about the company's true financial profile; or that Walmart knew that its operations in Brazil, China, India, and Mexico were bribing local officials; or that Merck was aware of statistically insignificant findings in drug trials showing an increased risk of heart attacks in patients taking its analgesic Vioxx.[41]

Halabi argues that, in each of these cases, "illicit or tortious conduct was possible through the loss or distortion of information in large, complex business organizations."[42] As information travels through the corporate structure and is disseminated among various individuals with differing responsibilities, "a range of distorting influences may compromise the integrity of that knowledge or otherwise prevent it from playing a role in legal compliance."[43] Halabi further explains:

---

36. Sam F. Halabi, *Collective Corporate Knowledge and the Federal False Claims Act*, 68 BAYLOR L. REV. 265, 272–273 (2016).

37. *Id.* (citing John M. Darley, *How Organizations Socialize Individuals into Evildoing*, in CODES OF CONDUCT: BEHAVIORAL RESEARCH INTO BUSINESS ETHICS 13, 23 (David M. Messick & Ann E. Tenbrunsel eds., 1996)).

38. *Id.*

39. *Id.*

40. *Id.* at 267–68.

41. *Id.* at 273–74.

42. *Id.* at 274.

43. *Id.*

In any organization, information must flow "upward" from employees that are directly connected to products and customers, to mid-level managers, and finally to executives. A key task for any firm becomes devising a system that identifies important data and quickly moves it to the desk of the most appropriate manager or executive. Information arrives at the top of a firm's managerial chain only after having been filtered through multiple layers. "Positive information will move more quickly to the top," but "[n]egative information will travel more slowly, if at all, and will be more subject to skewing."[44]

Halabi argues that notwithstanding a firm's declared commitment to maintaining the quality of information passed through corporate channels, "[t]o the extent that any given employee fears the possibility of being fired or dead-ended in light of a candid portrayal of the situation . . . distortion or concealment becomes a dominant strategy."[45] In the Ford Pinto example, Iacocca's insistence on producing a small, affordable car that could compete with Japanese rivals created barriers to the flow of negative information upward to middle and upper management.[46] These barriers prevented managers from being candid with their superiors about what was and was not possible—distorting information as it passed up the chain.[47]

Courts have over the years expressed doubt about the collective knowledge doctrine as the standard for determining what a corporation knew and intended. In *United States v. Science Applications Int'l Corp.*,[48] the D.C. Circuit held that the collective knowledge doctrine was inapplicable in cases involving the False Claims Act ("FCA"), stating:

> In non-FCA cases, we have expressed a good deal of skepticism about corporate intent theories that rely on aggregating the states of mind of multiple individuals. In *Saba v. Compagnie Nationale Air France*, we held that the plaintiff had failed to establish that the defendant engaged in the "willful misconduct" necessary to impose liability under Article 22 of the Warsaw Convention, we explained that though "negligent acts of employees can be fairly imputed to the corporation[,] [i]ndividual acts of negligence on the part of employees . . . cannot . . . be combined to create a wrongful corporate intent." More recently, in *United States v. Phillip Morris USA Inc.*, we explained that "[l]ike . . . other courts, we are dubious of the legal soundness of the 'collective intent' theory," under which, as we explained, a corporation's specific intent to defraud can be inferred if the company's public statements contradict the accumulated "collective knowledge" of the corporation's employees. In contrast to these two non-FCA cases, Congress defined the FCA's scienter element to require "no proof of specific intent." We nonetheless believe that under the FCA, "collective knowledge" provides an inappropriate basis for proof of scienter because it effectively imposes liability, complete with treble damages and substantial civil penalties, for a type of loose

---

44. *Id.* at 276 (footnotes omitted).
45. *Id.* at 277 (quoting Donald C. Langevoort, *Organized Illusions: A Behavioral Theory of Why Corporations Mislead Stock Market Investors (and Cause Other Social Harms)*, 146 U. Pa. L. Rev. 101 (1997)).
46. *Id.* at 276–78.
47. *Id.*
48. 626 F.3d 1257 (D.C. Cir. 2010).

constructive knowledge that is inconsistent with the Act's language, structure, and purpose.

Congress established the FCA's scienter requirement when it amended the Act in 1986 "to clarify" that even absent evidence of specific intent to defraud, "defendants were subject to liability . . . if they had 'actual knowledge' of the falsity of their claims or acted with 'deliberate ignorance' or 'reckless disregard' of the truth or falsity of their claims." According to the Senate Committee Report to the 1986 amendments, Congress adopted this definition of "knowingly" to capture the "'ostrich-like' conduct which can occur in large corporations" where "corporate officers . . . insulate themselves from knowledge of false claims submitted by lower-level subordinates." That said, Congress clearly had no intention to turn the FCA, a law designed to punish and deter fraud, into a vehicle for either "punish[ing] honest mistakes or incorrect claims submitted through mere negligence" or imposing "a burdensome obligation" on government contractors rather than a "limited duty to inquire." The resulting statutory language demonstrates the care Congress took to balance competing objectives. Although Congress defined "knowingly" to include some forms of constructive knowledge, its definition of that term imposes liability for mistakenly false claims only when the defendant deliberately avoided learning the truth or engaged in aggravated gross negligence.

Lacking such balance and precision, the "collective knowledge" theory allows "a plaintiff to prove scienter by piecing together scraps of 'innocent' knowledge held by various corporate officials, even if those officials never had contact with each other or knew what others were doing in connection with a claim seeking government funds." In other words, even absent proof that corporate officials acted with deliberate ignorance or reckless disregard for the truth by submitting a false claim as the result of, for instance, a communication failure, the factfinder could determine that the corporation knowingly submitted a false claim. In this case, the district court's instruction goes even further, drawing no distinction between the knowledge of corporate officers and that of potentially thousands of ordinary employees, including the knowledge of all employees in the "collective pool" of information imputed to the corporation. The district court's instruction thus allowed the jury to find that SAIC knowingly submitted false claims for payment even if the jury also concluded (1) that no individual at SAIC was simultaneously aware (or was recklessly unaware) of the company's NRC contract and its relationships with other companies involved in the recycling of radioactive materials, and (2) that SAIC, acting on the basis of the knowledge of its individual employees, took reasonable steps to identify potential conflicts.

We know of no circuit that has applied the "collective knowledge" theory to the FCA. Indeed, in a closely analogous case involving claims that were legally false because of undisclosed conflicts of interest, the Fourth Circuit recognized the theory's troubling implications for FCA liability.

Defending the district court's instruction, the government relies primarily on *United States v. Bank of New England*, in which the First Circuit held in a non-FCA case that a collective knowledge instruction was "entirely appropriate." That case is easily distinguishable. First, as we explained in *Saba*, although the First Circuit in *Bank of New England* allowed the jury to infer corporate knowledge of facts through the accumulation of individual knowledge, proof of "the proscribed intent" in that case "depended on the wrongful intent of specific employees." By contrast, the "collective knowledge" instruction in this case gave the jury an alternative basis for finding the requisite scienter. Second, and more important, the First Circuit's justification for the "collective knowledge" theory has no applicability here. There the court concluded that in the context of corporate criminal liability, the trial court's "collective knowledge" instruction "was not only proper but necessary" to prevent corporations from evading liability by "compartmentaliz[ing] knowledge, subdividing the elements of specific duties and operations into smaller components." This "compartmentalization" problem, however, is exactly what Congress had in mind when it defined "knowing" and "knowingly" in the 1986 FCA amendments. Under the FCA, if a plaintiff can prove that a government contractor's structure prevented it from learning facts that made its claims for payment false, then the plaintiff may establish that the company acted in deliberate ignorance or reckless disregard of the truth of its claims. But if the plaintiff in such a scenario fails to prove that the corporation acted with deliberate ignorance or reckless disregard, then no liability may attach under the FCA's plain language.

. . . .

To be sure, the district court did instruct the jury that for the government to satisfy its burden of proof, "more than an honest mistake or mere negligence [on the part of SAIC] must be found." But by providing an alternate route to proof of scienter, the "collective knowledge" instruction undermined the clarity of this separate "no mere negligence instruction" and allowed the jury to impose liability for what is essentially negligence or mistake by another name. Given the essential role that proof of scienter plays under the FCA, and given our lack of confidence that the jury here based its verdict on the proper legal standard, we decline to affirm on the ground that the error was harmless . . . . We shall thus vacate the judgment for the government with respect to its two FCA causes of action.[49]

Although the decision in *Science Applications* is expressly limited to FCA cases, its critical examination of the collective knowledge doctrine casts doubt on the doctrine's continued validity.[50]

Nonetheless, in 2016, the government used the collective knowledge theory to obtain a jury verdict against the Pacific Gas and Electric Company ("PG&E") for willful violations of the Natural Gas Pipeline Safety Act of 1968 and for obstructing the federal investigation into the 2010 fatal pipeline explosion in San Bruno.[51] This was the first time in almost 30 years that the government had successfully prosecuted a corporation under the collective knowledge doctrine.[52]

---

49. *Id.* at 1274–77 (citations omitted).

50. *See* Halabi, *supra* note 36, at 305; *The Decline of the Collective Knowledge Doctrine*, Law360 (May 10, 2011), https://www.foley.com/files/Publication/0f01a39a-609d-49ff-8469-70002bf2f166/Presentation/PublicationAttachment/731f62be-2b76-4550-aeb0-7104300cf6f6/TheDeclineOfTheCollectiveKnowledgeDoctrine.pdf.

51. Press Release, U.S. Attorney's Office, PG&E Found Guilty of Obstruction of an Agency Proceeding and Multiple Violations of the Natural Gas Pipeline Safety Act (Aug. 9, 2016) [hereinafter USAO Press Release], https://www.justice.gov/usao-ndca/pr/pge-found-guilty-obstruction-agency-proceeding-and-multiple-violations-natural-gas.

52. Steven P. Solow & Mark L. Farley, *What Does a Corporation Have to Know to Be Guilty of a Crime? The Conviction of PG&E Based on Corporate Collective Knowledge*, Daily Environment Report (Aug. 22, 2016), https://www.kattenlaw.com/files/162466_PGE_Solow_Farley.pdf.

The district court gave the following instructions to the jury:

> The corporation is . . . considered to have acquired the collective knowledge of its employees. The corporation's "knowledge" is therefore the totality of what its employees know within the scope of their employment.
>   . . . The willfulness of corporate employees acting within the scope of their employment is imputed to the corporation. Accordingly, if a specific employee acted willfully within the scope of his or her employment, then the corporation can be said to have acted willfully.[53]

The jury convicted PG&E of acting knowingly and willfully.[54]

Regardless of whether the collective knowledge doctrine will in the future define how knowledge is measured in a business organization, the challenges inherent in the organizational flow of information will continue to demand solutions. Federal regulations and agency guidance—discussed in Part Two — require business organizations to construct appropriate channels of information to ensure the flow of quality information both internally within the organization and externally with the outside stakeholders such as the investing public and the government. Those efforts should include, for example, training of personnel and providing confidential hotlines to facilitate reporting legal and ethical violations.

Hypothetical: Collective Knowledge

Fairmont, Inc. ("Fairmont") is a U.S. corporation engaged in the manufacture and sale of heavy machinery. In 2016, Fairmont sold certain products to a customer in Germany who in turn exported the goods to Syria—a country on the U.S. sanctions list to which exportation of U.S. products was prohibited. At the time, at least one Fairmont sales manager was aware that the German customer had an ongoing business relationship with the government of Syria, but the manager did not investigate whether the customer intended to resell Fairmont's products. Fairmont's shipping department removed all labels from the shipping containers at the request of the German customer, concealing the origin of the goods. After the shipment, Fairmont's accounting department received payment for the shipment from a bank account in Germany in the name of the government of Syria.

A few months later, the DOJ was alerted to the presence of Fairmont's products in Syria and began an investigation of Fairmont. Following the investigation, the DOJ indicted Fairmont for violating U.S. sanctions laws.

Sanctions regulations against Syria prohibit the export of any goods or services to any country if the exporter knows or has reason to know that the goods are ultimately destined for Syria.

Explain the DOJ's likely theory of liability.

---

53. Order Regarding Jury Instructions on Intent Elements for Regulatory Counts, United States v. Pac. Gas & Elec. Co., No. 14-CR-00175, 2016 BL 240175, at *2, *4 (N.D. Cal. Aug. 9, 2016).
54. USAO Press Release, *supra* note 51.

III. The Collective Entity Rule

A third doctrine—called the collective entity rule—holds that corporations are not entitled to the constitutional right against self-incrimination afforded to individuals under the Fifth Amendment.[55] The logic behind this rule is that the right against self-incrimination is a personal right, and because a collective entity has no persona, it cannot refuse to respond to a subpoena on Fifth Amendment grounds. The Supreme Court reaffirmed this rule in *Braswell v. United States*, where it held that, even where the custodian of records of a corporation was the sole shareholder, the corporation was not entitled to quash a subpoena on Fifth Amendment grounds.[56]

Braswell v. United States

Supreme Court of the United States, 487 U.S. 99 (1988)

OPINION

Chief Justice REHNQUIST delivered the opinion of the Court.

This case presents the question whether the custodian of corporate records may resist a subpoena for such records on the ground that the act of production would incriminate him in violation of the Fifth Amendment. We conclude that he may not.

. . . .

There is no question but that the contents of the subpoenaed business records are not privileged. See *Doe, supra; Fisher v. United States*, 425 U.S. 391, 96 S.Ct. 1569, 48 L.Ed.2d 39 (1976). Similarly, petitioner asserts no self-incrimination claim on behalf of the corporations; it is well established that such artificial entities are not protected by the Fifth Amendment. *Bellis, supra.* Petitioner instead relies solely upon the argument that his act of producing the documents has independent testimonial significance, which would incriminate him individually, and that the Fifth Amendment prohibits Government compulsion of that act. The bases for this argument are extrapolated from the decisions of this Court in *Fisher, supra,* and *Doe, supra.*

In *Fisher,* the Court was presented with the question whether an attorney may resist a subpoena demanding that he produce tax records which had been entrusted to him by his client. The records in question had been prepared by the client's accountants. In analyzing the Fifth Amendment claim forwarded by the attorney, the Court considered whether the client-taxpayer would have had a valid Fifth Amendment claim had he retained the records and the subpoena

---

55. Braswell v. United States, 487 U.S. 99, 104–05 (1988) (discussing the long-recognized rule that, "for purposes of the Fifth Amendment, corporations and other collective entities are treated differently from individuals").

56. *Id.* at 119.

been issued to him. After explaining that the Fifth Amendment prohibits "compelling a person to give 'testimony' that incriminates him," 425 U.S., at 409, 96 S.Ct., at 1580, the Court rejected the argument that the contents of the records were protected. The Court, however, went on to observe:

> "The act of producing evidence in response to a subpoena nevertheless has communicative aspects of its own, wholly aside from the contents of the papers produced. Compliance with the subpoena tacitly concedes the existence of the papers demanded and their possession or control by the taxpayer. It also would indicate the taxpayer's belief that the papers are those described in the subpoena. *Curcio v. United States*, 354 U.S. 118, 125 [77 S.Ct. 1145, 1150, 1 L.Ed.2d 1225] (1957). The elements of compulsion are clearly present, but the more difficult issues are whether the tacit averments of the taxpayer are both 'testimonial' and 'incriminating' for purposes of applying the Fifth Amendment. These questions perhaps do not lend themselves to categorical answers; their resolution may instead depend on the facts and circumstances of particular cases or classes thereof." *Id.*, at 410, 96 S.Ct., at 1581.

The Court concluded that under the "facts and circumstances" there presented, the act of producing the accountants' papers would not "involve testimonial self-incrimination." Id., at 411, 96 S.Ct., at 1581.

Eight years later, in *United States v. Doe, supra*, the Court revisited the question, this time in the context of a claim by a sole proprietor that the compelled production of business records would run afoul of the Fifth Amendment. After rejecting the contention that the contents of the records were themselves protected, the Court proceeded to address whether respondent's act of producing the records would constitute protected testimonial incrimination. The Court concluded that respondent had established a valid Fifth Amendment claim. It deferred to the lower courts, which had found that enforcing the subpoenas at issue would provide the Government valuable information: By producing the records, respondent would admit that the records existed, were in his possession, and were authentic. 465 U.S., at 613, n. 11, 104 S.Ct. 1242, n. 11.

Had petitioner conducted his business as a sole proprietorship, *Doe* would require that he be provided the opportunity to show that his act of production would entail testimonial self-incrimination. But petitioner has operated his business through the corporate form, and we have long recognized that, for purposes of the Fifth Amendment, corporations and other collective entities are treated differently from individuals. This doctrine—known as the collective entity rule—has a lengthy and distinguished pedigree.

The rule was first articulated by the Court in the case of *Hale v. Henkel*, 201 U.S. 43, 26 S.Ct. 370, 50 L.Ed. 652 (1906). Hale, a corporate officer, had been served with a subpoena ordering him to produce corporate records and to testify concerning certain corporate transactions. Although Hale was protected by personal immunity, he sought to resist the demand for the records by interposing a Fifth Amendment privilege on behalf of the corporation. The Court rejected that argument: "[W]e are of the opinion that there is a clear distinction . . . between an individual and a corporation, and . . . the latter has no right to refuse to submit its books and papers for an examination at the suit of the State." *Id.*, at 74, 26 S.Ct., at 379. The Court explained that the corporation "is a creature of the State," *ibid.*, with powers limited by the State. As such, the State may, in the exercise of its right to oversee the corporation, demand the production of corporate records. *Id.*, at 75, 26 S.Ct., at 379.

The ruling in *Hale* represented a limitation on the prior holding in *Boyd v. United States*, 116 U.S. 616, 6 S.Ct. 524, 29 L.Ed. 746 (1886), which involved a court order directing partners to produce an invoice received by the partnership. The partners had produced the invoice, but steadfastly maintained that the court order ran afoul of the Fifth Amendment. This Court agreed. After concluding that the order transgressed the Fourth Amendment, the Court declared: "[A] compulsory production of the *private* books and papers of the owner of goods sought to be forfeited . . . is compelling him to be a witness against himself, within the meaning of the Fifth Amendment to the Constitution. . . ." *Id.*, at 634–635, 6 S.Ct., at 534 (emphasis added). *Hale* carved an exception out of *Boyd* by establishing that corporate books and records are not "private papers" protected by the Fifth Amendment.

Although *Hale* settled that a corporation has no Fifth Amendment privilege, the Court did not address whether a corporate officer could resist a subpoena for corporate records by invoking his personal privilege—Hale had been protected by immunity. In *Wilson v. United States*, 221 U.S. 361, 31 S.Ct. 538, 55 L.Ed. 771 (1911), the Court answered that question in the negative. There, a grand jury investigating Wilson had issued a subpoena to a corporation demanding the production of corporate letterpress copybooks, which Wilson, the corporation's president, possessed. Wilson refused to produce the books, arguing that the Fifth Amendment prohibited compulsory production of personally incriminating books that he held and controlled. The Court rejected this argument, observing first that the records sought were not private or personal, but rather belonged to the corporation. The Court continued:

> "[Wilson] held the corporate books subject to the corporate duty. If the corporation were guilty of misconduct, he could not withhold its books to save it; and if he were implicated in the violations of law, he could not withhold the books to protect himself from the effect of their disclosures. The [State's] reserved power of visitation would seriously be embarrassed, if not wholly defeated in its effective exercise, if guilty officers could refuse inspection of the records and papers of the corporation. No personal privilege to which they are entitled requires such a conclusion. . . . [T]he visitatorial power which exists with respect to the corporation of necessity reaches the corporate books without regard to the conduct of the custodian." *Id.*, at 384–385, 31 S.Ct., at 546.
>
> ". . . When [Wilson] became president of the corporation and as such held and used its books for the transaction of its business committed to his charge, he was at all times subject to its direction, and the books continuously remained under its control. If another took his place his custody would yield. He could assert no personal right to retain the corporate books against any demand of government which the corporation was bound to recognize." *Id.*, at 385, 31 S.Ct., at 546.

In a companion case, *Dreier v. United States*, 221 U.S. 394, 31 S.Ct. 550, 55 L.Ed. 784 (1911), the Court applied the holding in *Wilson* to a Fifth Amendment attack on a subpoena addressed to the corporate custodian. Although the subpoena in *Wilson* had been addressed to the corporation, the Court found the distinction irrelevant: "Dreier was not entitled to refuse the production of the corporate records. By virtue of the fact that they were the documents of the corporation in his custody, and not his private papers, he was under the obligation to produce them when called for by proper process." 221 U.S., at 400, 31 S.Ct., at 550.

The next significant step in the development of the collective entity rule occurred in *United States v. White*, 322 U.S. 694, 64 S.Ct. 1248, 88 L.Ed. 1542 (1944), in which the Court held that a labor union is a collective entity unprotected by the Fifth Amendment. There, a grand jury had issued a subpoena addressed to a union requiring the production of certain union records. White, an assistant supervisor of the union, appeared before the grand jury and declined to produce the documents "'upon the ground that they might tend to incriminate [the union], myself as an officer thereof, or individually.'" *Id.*, at 696, 64 S.Ct., at 1250.

We upheld an order of contempt against White, reasoning first that the Fifth Amendment privilege applies only to natural individuals and protects only private papers. Representatives of a "collective group" act as agents "[a]nd the official records and documents of the organization that are held by them in a representative rather than in a personal capacity cannot be the subject of the personal privilege against self-incrimination, even though production of the papers might tend to incriminate them personally." *Id.*, at 699, 64 S.Ct., at 1251. With this principle in mind, the Court turned to whether a union is a collective group:

> "The test . . . is whether one can fairly say under all the circumstances that a particular type of organization has a character so impersonal in the scope of its membership and activities that it cannot be said to embody or represent the purely private or personal interests of its constituents, but rather to embody their common or group interests only. If so, the privilege cannot be invoked on behalf of the organization or its representatives in their official capacity. Labor unions— national or local, incorporated or unincorporated—clearly meet that test." *Id.*, at 701, 64 S.Ct., at 1252.

In applying the collective entity rule to unincorporated associations such as unions, the Court jettisoned reliance on the visitatorial powers of the State over corporations owing their existence to the State—one of the bases for earlier decisions. *See id.*, at 700–701, 64 S.Ct., at 1252.

The frontiers of the collective entity rule were expanded even further in *Bellis v. United States*, 417 U.S. 85, 94 S.Ct. 2179, 40 L.Ed.2d 678 (1974), in which the Court ruled that a partner in a small partnership could not properly refuse to produce partnership records. Bellis, one of the members of a three-person law firm that had previously been dissolved, was served with a subpoena directing him to produce partnership records he possessed. The District Court held Bellis in contempt when he refused to produce the partnership's financial books and records. We upheld the contempt order. After rehearsing prior precedent involving corporations and unincorporated associations, the Court examined the partnership form and observed that it had many of the incidents found relevant in prior collective entity decisions. The Court suggested that the test articulated in *White, supra,* for determining the applicability of the Fifth Amendment to organizations was "not particularly helpful in the broad range of cases." 417 U.S., at 100, 94 S.Ct., at 2189. The Court rejected the notion that the "formulation in *White* can be reduced to a simple proposition based solely upon the size of the organization. It is well settled that no privilege can be claimed by the custodian of corporate records, regardless of how small the corporation may be." *Ibid.* Beilis held the partnership's financial records in "a representative capacity," *id.,* at 101, 94 S.Ct., at 2189, and therefore, "his personal privilege against compulsory self-incrimination is inapplicable." *Ibid.*

The plain mandate of these decisions is that without regard to whether the subpoena is addressed to the corporation, or as here, to the individual in his capacity as a custodian, see *Dreier, supra; Bellis, supra,* a corporate custodian such as petitioner may not resist a subpoena for corporate records on Fifth Amendment grounds. Petitioner argues, however, that this rule falls in the wake of *Fisher v. United States,* 425 U.S. 391, 96 S.Ct. 1569, 48 L.Ed.2d 39 (1976), and *United States v. Doe,* 465 U.S. 605, 104 S.Ct. 1237, 79 L.Ed.2d 552 (1984). In essence, petitioner's argument is as follows: In response to *Boyd v. United States,* 116 U.S. 616, 6 S.Ct. 524, 29 L.Ed. 746 (1886), with its privacy rationale shielding personal books and records, the Court developed the collective entity rule, which declares simply that corporate records are not private and therefore are not protected by the Fifth Amendment. The collective entity decisions were concerned with the contents of the documents subpoenaed, however, and not with the act of production. In *Fisher* and *Doe,* the Court moved away from the privacy-based collective entity rule, replacing it with a compelled-testimony standard under which the contents of business documents are never privileged but the act of producing the documents may be. Under this new regime, the act of production privilege is available without regard to the entity whose records are being sought. *See In re Grand Jury Matter (Brown),* 768 F.2d 525, 528 (CA3 1985) (en banc) ("[*Fisher* and *Doe*] make the significant factor, for the privilege against self-incrimination, neither the nature of entity which owns the documents, nor the contents of documents, but rather the communicative or noncommunicative nature of the arguably incriminating disclosures sought to be compelled").

To be sure, the holding in *Fisher*—later reaffirmed in *Doe*—embarked upon a new course of Fifth Amendment analysis. *See Fisher,* supra, 425 U.S., at 409, 96 S.Ct., at 1580. We cannot agree, however, that it rendered the collective entity rule obsolete. The agency rationale undergirding the collective entity decisions, in which custodians asserted that production of entity records would incriminate them personally, survives. From *Wilson* forward, the Court has consistently recognized that the custodian of corporate or entity records holds those documents in a representative rather than a personal capacity. Artificial entities such as corporations may act only through their agents, *Bellis, supra,* 417 U.S., at 90, 94 S.Ct., at 2184, and a custodian's assumption of his representative capacity leads to certain obligations, including the duty to produce corporate records on proper demand by the Government. Under those circumstances, the custodian's act of production is not deemed a personal act, but rather an act of the corporation. Any claim of Fifth Amendment privilege asserted by the agent would be tantamount to a claim of privilege by the corporation—which of course possesses no such privilege.

The *Wilson* Court declared: "[B]y virtue of their character and the rules of law applicable to them, the books and papers are held subject to examination by the demanding authority, the custodian has no privilege to refuse production although their contents tend to criminate him. In assuming their custody he has accepted the incident obligation to permit inspection." 221 U.S., at 382, 31 S.Ct., at 545. "Nothing more is demanded than that the appellant should perform the obligations pertaining to his custody and should produce the books which he holds in his official capacity in accordance with the requirements of the subpoena." *Id.*, at 386, 31 S.Ct., at 546.

This theme was echoed in *White*:

> "But individuals, when acting as representatives of a collective group, cannot be said to be exercising their personal rights and duties nor to be entitled to their purely personal privileges. Rather they assume the rights, duties and privileges of the artificial entity or association of which they are agents or officers and they are bound by its obligations. In their official capacity, therefore, they have no privilege against self-incrimination. And the official records and documents of the organization that are held by them in a representative rather than in a personal capacity cannot be the subject of the personal privilege against self-incrimination, even though production of the papers might tend to incriminate them personally." 322 U.S., at 699, 64 S.Ct., at 1251.

In *Dreier*, 221 U.S. 394, 31 S.Ct., at 549 (1911), and *Bellis*, 417 U.S. 85, 94 S.Ct. 2179, 40 L.Ed.2d 678 (1974), the subpoenas were addressed to the custodians and demanded that they produce the records sought. In both cases, the custodian's act of producing the documents would "tacitly admi[t] their existence and their location in the hands of their possessor," *Fisher, supra*, 425 U.S., at 411–412, 96 S.Ct., at 1581. Nevertheless, the Court rejected the Fifth Amendment claims advanced by the custodians. Although the Court did not focus on the testimonial aspect of the act of production, we do not think such a focus would have affected the results reached. "It is well settled that no privilege can be claimed by the custodian of corporate records. . . ." *Bellis, supra*, 417 U.S., at 100, 94 S.Ct., at 2189.

Indeed, the opinion in *Fisher*—upon which petitioner places primary reliance—indicates that the custodian of corporate records may not interpose a Fifth Amendment objection to the compelled production of corporate records, even though the act of production may prove personally incriminating. The *Fisher* Court cited the collective entity decisions with approval and offered those decisions to support the conclusion that the production of the accountant's workpapers would "not . . . involve testimonial self-incrimination." 425 U.S., at 411, 96 S.Ct., at 1581. The Court observed: "This Court has . . . time and again allowed subpoenas against the custodian of corporate documents or those belonging to other collective entities such as unions and partnerships and those of bankrupt businesses over claims that the documents will incriminate the custodian despite the fact that producing the documents tacitly admits their existence and their location in the hands of their possessor." *Id.*, at 411–412, 96 S.Ct., at 1581. The Court later noted that "in *Wilson, Dreier, White, Bellis,* and *In re Harris,* [221 U.S. 274, 31 S.Ct. 557, 55 L.Ed. 73 (1911)], the custodian of corporate, union, or partnership books or those of a bankrupt business was ordered to respond to a subpoena for the business' books even though doing so involved a 'representation that the documents produced are those demanded by the subpoena,' *Curcio v. United States,* 354 U.S., at 125 [77 S.Ct., at 115]." *Id.*, at 413, 96 S.Ct., at 1582 (citations omitted). In a footnote, the Court explained: "In these cases compliance with the subpoena is required even though the books have been kept by the person subpoenaed and his producing them would itself be sufficient authentication to permit their introduction against him." Id., at 413, n. 14, 96 S.Ct., at 1582, n. 14. The Court thus reaffirmed the obligation of a corporate custodian to comply with a subpoena addressed to him.

That point was reiterated by Justice BRENNAN in his concurrence in *Fisher. Id.*, at 429, 96 S.Ct., at 1589 (concurring in judgment). Although Justice BRENNAN disagreed with the majority as to its use of the collective entity cases to support the proposition that the act of production is not testimonial, he nonetheless acknowledged that a custodian may not resist a subpoena on the ground that the act of production would be incriminating. "Nothing in the language of [the collective entity] cases, either expressly or impliedly, indicates that the act of production with respect to the records of business entities is insufficiently testimonial for purposes of the Fifth Amendment. At most, those issues, though considered, were disposed of on the ground, not that production was insufficiently testimonial, but that one in control of the records of an artificial organization undertakes an obligation with respect to those records foreclosing any exercise of his privilege." *Id.*, at 429–430, 96 S.Ct., at 1590; *see also id.*, at 430, n. 9, 96 S.Ct., at 1590 n. 9. Thus, whether one concludes—as did the Court—that a custodian's production of corporate records is deemed not to constitute testimonial self-incrimination, or instead that a custodian waives the right to exercise the privilege, the lesson of *Fisher* is clear: A custodian may not resist a subpoena for corporate records on Fifth Amendment grounds.

Petitioner also attempts to extract support for his contention from *Curcio v. United States,* 354 U.S. 118, 77 S.Ct. 1145, 1 L.Ed.2d 1225 (1957). But rather than bolstering petitioner's argument, we think Curcio substantiates the Government's position. *Curcio* had been served with two subpoenas addressed to him in his capacity as secretary-treasurer of a local union, which was under investigation. One subpoena required that he produce union books, the other that he testify. Curcio appeared before the grand jury, stated that the books were not in his possession, and refused to answer any questions as to their whereabouts. Curcio was held in contempt for refusing to answer the questions propounded. We reversed the contempt citation, rejecting the Government's argument "that the representative duty which required the production of union records in the *White* case requires the giving of oral testimony by the custodian." *Id.*, at 123, 77 S.Ct., at 1149.

Petitioner asserts that our *Curcio* decision stands for the proposition that although the contents of a collective entity's records are unprivileged, a representative of a collective entity cannot be required to provide testimony about those records. It follows, according to petitioner, that because *Fisher* recognizes that the act of production is potentially testimonial, such an act may not be compelled if it would tend to incriminate the representative personally. We find this reading of *Curcio* flawed.

The *Curcio* Court made clear that with respect to a custodian of a collective entity's records, the line drawn was between oral testimony and other forms of incrimination. "A custodian, by assuming the duties of his office, undertakes the obligation to produce the books of which he is custodian in response to a rightful exercise of the State's visitorial powers. But he cannot lawfully be compelled, in the absence of a grant of adequate immunity from prosecution, to condemn himself by his own *oral testimony*." 354 U.S., at 123–24, 77 S.Ct., at 1149 (emphasis added).

In distinguishing those cases in which a corporate officer was required to produce corporate records and merely identify them by oral testimony, the Court showed that it understood the testimonial nature of the act of production: "The custodian's act of producing books or records in response to a subpoena *duces tecum* is itself a representation that the documents produced are those demanded by the subpoena. Requiring the custodian to identify or authenticate the documents for admission in evidence merely makes explicit what is implicit in the production itself." *Id.*, at 125, 77 S.Ct., at 1150. In the face of this recognition, the Court nonetheless noted: "In this case petitioner might have been proceeded against for his failure to produce the records demanded by the subpoena *duces tecum*." *Id.*, at 127, n. 7, 77 S.Ct., at 1151, n. 7. As Justice BRENNAN later observed in his concurrence in *Fisher*: "The Court in *Curcio*, however, apparently did not note any self-incrimination problem [with the testimonial significance of the act of production] because of the undertaking by the custodian with respect to the documents." 425 U.S., at 430, n. 9, 96 S.Ct., at 1590, n. 9.

We note further that recognizing a Fifth Amendment privilege on behalf of the records custodians of collective entities would have a detrimental impact on the Government's efforts to prosecute "white-collar crime," one of the most serious problems confronting law enforcement authorities. "The greater portion of evidence of wrongdoing by an organization or its representatives is usually found in the official records and documents of that organization. Were the cloak of the privilege to be thrown around these impersonal records and documents, effective enforcement of many federal and state laws would be impossible." *White*, 322 U.S., at 700, 64 S.Ct., at 1252. If custodians could assert a privilege, authorities would be stymied not only in their enforcement efforts against those individuals but also in their prosecutions of organizations. In *Bellis*, the Court observed: "In view of the inescapable fact that an artificial entity can only act to produce its records through its individual officers or agents, recognition of the individual's claim of privilege with respect to the financial records of the organization would substantially undermine the unchallenged rule that the organization itself is not entitled to claim any Fifth Amendment privilege, and largely frustrate legitimate governmental regulation of such organizations." 417 U.S., at 90, 94 S.Ct., at 2184.

Petitioner suggests, however, that these concerns can be minimized by the simple expedient of either granting the custodian statutory immunity as to the act of production, 18 U.S.C. §§ 6002, 6003, or addressing the subpoena to the corporation and allowing it to choose an agent to produce the records who can do so without incriminating himself. We think neither proposal satisfactorily addresses these concerns. Taking the last first, it is no doubt true that if a subpoena is addressed to a corporation, the corporation "must find some means by which to comply because no Fifth Amendment defense is available to it." The means most commonly used to comply is the appointment of an alternate custodian. But petitioner insists he cannot be required to aid the appointed custodian in his search for the demanded records, for any statement to the surrogate would itself be testimonial and incriminating. If this is correct, then petitioner's "solution" is a chimera. In situations such as this—where the corporate custodian is likely the only person with knowledge about the demanded documents—the appointment of a surrogate will simply not ensure that the documents sought will ever reach the grand jury room; the appointed custodian will essentially be sent on an unguided search.

This problem is eliminated if the Government grants the subpoenaed custodian statutory immunity for the testimonial aspects of his act of production. But that "solution" also entails a significant drawback. All of the evidence obtained under a grant of immunity to the custodian may of course be used freely against the corporation, but if the Government has any thought of prosecuting the custodian, a grant of act of production immunity can have serious consequences. Testimony obtained pursuant to a grant of statutory use immunity may be used neither directly nor derivatively. 18 U.S.C. § 6002; *Kastigar v. United States*, 406 U.S. 441, 92 S.Ct. 1653, 32 L.Ed.2d 212 (1972). And "[o]ne raising a claim under [the federal immunity] statute need only show that he testified under a grant of immunity in order to shift to the government the heavy burden of proving that all of the evidence it proposes to use was derived from legitimate independent sources." *Id.*, at 461–462, 92 S.Ct., at 1665. Even in cases where the Government does not employ the immunized testimony for any purpose—direct or derivative—against the witness, the Government's inability to meet the "heavy burden" it bears may result in the preclusion of crucial evidence that was obtained legitimately.

Although a corporate custodian is not entitled to resist a subpoena on the ground that his act of production will be personally incriminating, we do think certain consequences flow from the fact that the custodian's act of production is one in his representative rather than personal capacity. Because the custodian acts as a representative, the act is deemed one of the corporation and not the individual. Therefore, the Government concedes, as it must, that it may make no evidentiary use of the "individual act" against the individual. For example, in a criminal prosecution against the custodian, the Government may not introduce into evidence before the jury the fact that the subpoena was served upon and the corporation's documents were delivered by one particular individual, the custodian. The Government has the right, however, to use the corporation's act of production against the custodian. The Government may offer testimony—for example, from the process server who delivered the subpoena and from the individual who received the records—establishing that the corporation produced the records subpoenaed. The jury may draw from the corporation's act of production the conclusion that the records in question are authentic corporate records, which the corporation possessed, and which it produced in response to the subpoena. And if the defendant held a prominent position within the corporation that produced the records, the jury may, just as it would had someone else produced the documents, reasonably infer that he had possession of the documents or knowledge of their contents. Because the jury is not told that the defendant produced the records, any nexus between the defendant and the documents results solely from the corporation's act of production and other evidence in the case.

Consistent with our precedent, the United States Court of Appeals for the Fifth Circuit ruled that petitioner could not resist the subpoena for corporate documents on the ground that the act of production might tend to incriminate him. The judgment is therefore

Affirmed.

Notes and Questions

It is difficult to find a coherent theme in the Supreme Court's treatment of corporate constitutional rights. Corporations enjoy some constitutional rights, including "a First Amendment right to free speech; a Fourth Amendment protection against unreasonable searches and seizures; a Fifth Amendment right to due process and protection against double jeopardy; Sixth Amendment rights to counsel, jury trial, speedy trial, and to confront accusers, and to subpoena witnesses; and Eighth Amendment protection against excessive fines."[57] But corporations also lack other constitutional rights, including the right to vote, Fourteenth Amendment rights, Fifth Amendment rights against self-incrimination, Article IV Privileges and Immunities Clause rights, and Due Process liberty rights.[58]

---

57. CHARLES DOYLE, CONG. RESEARCH SERV., R43293, CORPORATE CRIMINAL LIABILITY: AN OVERVIEW OF FEDERAL LAW 2 (2013); *see also* Brandon L. Garrett, *The Constitutional Standing of Corporations*, 163 U. PA. L. REV. 95, 97 (2014).

58. Garrett, *supra* note 57, at 98.

Professor Brandon Garrett observes that legal scholars have called the Court's rulings on this subject "'ad hoc,' 'right-by-right,' 'arbitrary,' 'sporadic,' inconsistent, and incoherent."[59] Those objections have only intensified after two separate decisions in which the Court held that corporations have both the right to free expression and religious liberty.[60]

In *Citizens United v. Federal Election Commission*,[61] the Court struck down as unconstitutional a law that banned corporations from using "general treasury funds to make independent expenditures for speech [that advocates for] the election or defeat of a candidate."[62] In so doing, the Court reiterated its view "that the First Amendment applies to corporations"[63] and therefore "the Government may not suppress political speech based on the speaker's corporate identity."[64] The Court's reasoning appeared to take for granted that corporations are generally entitled to the same constitutional rights as everyone else:

> Premised on mistrust of governmental power, the First Amendment stands against attempts to disfavor certain subjects or viewpoints or to distinguish among different speakers, which may be a means to control content. The Government may also commit a constitutional wrong when by law it identifies certain preferred speakers. There is no basis for the proposition that, in the political speech context, the Government may impose restrictions on certain disfavored speakers. Both history and logic lead to this conclusion.[65]

Sketching how far this reasoning can extend, Justice Stevens wrote in his dissent: "Under the majority's view, I suppose it may be a First Amendment problem that corporations are not permitted to vote, given that voting is, among other things, a form of speech."[66] Justice Sotomayor remarked during oral argument, "[T]here could be an argument made that that was the Court's error to start with . . . the fact that the Court imbued a creature of State law with human characteristics."[67]

The Court's subsequent decision in *Burwell v. Hobby Lobby Stores*[68] continues the trend in recognizing corporations' humanity. There, the Court held that a for-profit corporation qualified as a "person" under the Religious Freedom Restoration Act of 1993 ("RFRA"), which prohibits the "Government [from] substantially burden[ing] a *person's* exercise of religion."[69] The majority opinion interestingly notes:

> [T]he purpose of extending rights to corporations is to protect the rights of people associated with the corporation, including shareholders, officers, and

---

59. *Id.* at 99 (footnotes omitted).
60. *See id.*
61. 130 S.Ct. 876 (2010).
62. *Id.* at 886.
63. *Id.* at 883.
64. *Id.* at 885.
65. *Id.* at 882–83.
66. *Id.* at 948 (Stevens, J., concurring in part and dissenting in part).
67. Transcript of Oral Argument at 33, Citizens United v. Fed. Election Comm'n, 130 S.Ct. 876 (2010) (No. 08-205).
68. 134 S.Ct. 2751 (2014).
69. *Id.* at 2767, 2769 (citing 42 U.S.C. § 2000bb–1 (2012)).

employees. Protecting the free-exercise rights of closely held corporations thus protects the religious liberty of the humans who own and control them.[70]

The logic of *Citizens United* and *Hobby Lobby*—that corporations are entitled to the same rights as other "persons"—appears to contradict the collective entity rule, reaffirmed in *Braswell*, that "artificial entities are not protected by the Fifth Amendment."[71] Do *Citizens United* and *Hobby Lobby* suggest a trend where, "[a]s with Prometheus, and possibly Dr. Frankenstein, the Supreme Court . . . breathe[s] new life into an inanimate object"?[72] Will this trend ultimately restore corporations' Fifth Amendment rights against self-incrimination?

The *New York Times* recently pondered this possibility and put it this way:

> The Supreme Court was closely divided in the *Braswell, Citizens United* and *Hobby Lobby* decisions, each decided on a 5-4 vote of the justices. The court decided the *Braswell* case in 1988, well before the more recent cases involving corporate constitutional rights articulated the view that organizations are an embodiment of the individuals who choose to associate themselves. There is a sharp contrast in how the court has treated corporations in these areas, relying on the legal fiction of a separate organizational existence to deny the Fifth Amendment protection to corporations while piercing through it to protect First Amendment rights.[73]

If indeed the Supreme Court is moving toward recognizing corporations as full persons under the Constitution, it would be overlooking one important fact: Although corporations act like persons in some ways, they "also possess supernatural powers, particularly perpetual existence."[74]

For now, the collective entity rule remains firmly in place. In combination with her sisters, *respondeat superior* and the collective knowledge doctrines, it holds a corporation criminally liable even where:

- Top management did not participate in and was unaware of the criminal conduct.
- The conduct was committed by a low-level employee.
- The corporation did not benefit from the conduct.
- The conduct violated the company's explicit instructions.
- The company had a robust compliance program in place.
- None of the participants in the criminal conduct had the requisite intent or knowledge to violate the law.
- All employees who participated in the criminal conduct were acquitted of the offense.[75]

---

70. *Id.* at 2755.
71. Braswell v. United States, 487 U.S. 99, 102 (1988).
72. Robert Sprague & Mary E. Wells, *The Supreme Court as Prometheus: Breathing Life into the Corporate Supercitizen*, 49 Am. Bus. L. J., no. 3, 2012, at 4-5, https://ssrn.com/abstract=1973942.
73. Peter J. Henning, *Treating Corporations as People*, N.Y. Times (May 26, 2015), https://www.nytimes.com/2015/05/27/business/dealbook/treating-corporations-as-people.html.
74. Sprague & Wells, *supra* note 72, at 3.
75. *See* Bharara, *supra* note 2, at 64–65 (footnotes omitted).

Hypothetical: Collective Entity Rule

Arlington, Inc. ("Arlington") is a U.S. corporation engaged in the provision of engineering consulting services around the world. In 2015, Arlington entered into a contract with the government of Nigeria to provide engineering advice regarding oil and gas exploration. Prior to entering into the contract, Arlington paid bribes to several Nigerian government officials in violation of U.S. law. Arlington's CEO used his work email to exchange several emails with a friend in the United States wherein he joked about some of the "dirty work" he had to do to make a living and referenced "taking care of government officials in Africa."

After a whistleblower informed the DOJ of the bribery, the DOJ indicted Arlington and issued a subpoena for all corporate records relating to the Nigerian transaction, including emails. Arlington withheld the CEO's email exchange with his friend on Fifth Amendment grounds, arguing that the emails were private in nature and did not fall within the corporation's records. The DOJ filed a motion to compel the production of the emails.

How should the judge rule on the DOJ's motion?

CHAPTER 2

Federal Sentencing Guidelines for Organizations ("FSGO")

I. History of the FSGO
   A. The 1991 FSGO
   B. The 2004 Revisions to the FSGO
   C. *United States v. Booker*
II. Structure of the Current FSGO
   A. Section 8B1: Restitution
   B. Section 8B2: Effective Compliance and Ethics Programs
      1. Subsection (a)
      2. Subsection (b)
      3. Subsection (c)
III. Fine Calculation
IV. Part 8D: Probation

I. History of the FSGO

Notwithstanding the broad liability scheme established by *respondeat superior* and the collective entity and collective knowledge doctrines, corporate prosecutions were rare before the 1980s, and total annual fines against corporations averaged only in the tens of thousands of dollars.[2] Under federal law, corporations faced the same fines as individual offenders regardless of their size, which meant that a conviction for, say, felony mail fraud carried a

> Criminal liability can attach to an organization whenever an employee of the organization commits an act within the apparent scope of his or her employment, even if the employee acted directly contrary to company policy and instructions. An entire organization, despite its best efforts to prevent wrongdoing in its ranks, can still be held criminally liable for any of its employees' illegal actions. Consequently, when the Commission promulgated the organizational guidelines, it attempted to alleviate the harshest aspects of this institutional vulnerability by incorporating into the sentencing structure the preventive and deterrent aspects of systematic compliance programs. The Commission did this by mitigating the potential fine range—in some cases up to 95 percent—if an organization can demonstrate that it had put in place an effective compliance program. This mitigating credit under the guidelines is contingent upon prompt reporting to the authorities and the non-involvement of high level personnel in the actual offense conduct.
>
> *Paula Desio, Deputy General Counsel, U.S. Sentencing Commission*[1]

1. Paula Desio, *An Overview of the Organizational Guidelines*, UNITED STATES SENTENCING COMMISSION (on file with the USSC), https://www.ussc.gov/sites/default/files/pdf/training/organizational-guidelines/ORGOVERVIEW.pdf.
2. *See, e.g.*, Richard S. Gruner, *Beyond Fines: Innovative Corporate Sentences Under Federal Sentencing Guidelines,* 71 WASH. U. L.Q. 261, 262 (1993).

fine of only $1,000.[3] "[F]ines were low enough for large corporations to safely ignore them, giving them an incentive to commit crimes if doing so offered a chance of significant profit."[4]

In 1984, Congress passed the Sentencing Reform Act ("SRA") "with the primary purposes of decreasing unwarranted sentencing disparity, increasing sentencing uniformity and certainty, and for some select offenses, increasing sentence severity in order to more effectively deter and more justly punish convicted offenders."[5] The SRA created a separate statutory framework for sentencing organizations, defined as any "person other than an individual[,]"[6] and authorized courts to fine organizations the greatest of:

1) The fine prescribed by statute;
2) $500,000;
3) Twice the gross gain derived by the defendant from the offense; or
4) Twice the gross loss caused by the offense to anyone other than the defendant.[7]

Hence, the same felony mail fraud that resulted in a $1,000 fine before the SRA would result in a fine of at least $500,000 afterwards, and possibly much larger depending on the type of offense and its impact.[8]

The SRA also created an independent commission inside the judicial branch called the United States Sentencing Commission ("Commission"),[9] and assigned it the responsibility to:

1) provide certainty and fairness by avoiding unwarranted sentencing disparities while maintaining sufficient flexibility for adjustment of sentences by mitigating or aggravating factors;[10]
2) "reflect . . . advancement in knowledge of human behavior as it relates to the criminal justice process";[11] and
3) track the effectiveness of sentencing, penal, and correctional practices.[12]

As Professors Nagel and Swenson observed:

> The [statute] clearly reflect[ed] Congress' decision to take back from individual judges much of the sentencing discretion it previously had delegated to them, and to vest that discretion instead in the Commission, a single administrative body. Congress created the Commission specifically to devote its full attention

---

3. Timothy A. Johnson, *Sentencing Organizations After Booker*, 116 Yale L.J. 632, 641 (2006).

4. *Id.* at 640.

5. Ilene H. Nagel & Winthrop M. Swenson, *The Federal Sentencing Guidelines for Corporations: Their Development, Theoretical Underpinnings, and Some Thoughts About Their Future*, 71 Wash. U. L.Q. 205, 206 (1993).

6. 18 U.S.C. § 18 (2012).

7. 18 U.S.C. § 3571(c)–(d) (2012).

8. *See* Johnson, *supra* note 3, at 642.

9. 28 U.S.C. § 991(a) (2012).

10. 28 U.S.C. § 991(b)(1)(B) (2012).

11. 28 U.S.C. § 991(b)(1)(C) (2012).

12. 28 U.S.C. § 991(b)(2) (2012).

to developing a uniform sentencing policy, based on research and reflection, and to implement that policy through a system of guidelines and policy statements.[13]

A. The 1991 FSGO

The SRA did not explicitly require the Commission to formulate organizational guidelines.[14] After completing proposals relating to sentencing of individual offenders in 1987, and unsure of whether to undertake this task, the Commission conducted a review of corporate sentencing practices in federal courts.[15] The review found that median fines imposed on convicted corporations were substantially lower that the economic loss caused by the offense[16] and that "some courts imposed such sanctions as 'corporate imprisonment' or the compulsory endowment of a faculty chair in ethics[,]" which were "ineffective or inconsistent with the goals of sentencing articulated in the enabling legislation."[17]

Another problem revealed by the study was inconsistency in organizational sentencing among federal judges:

> There [were] many instances where virtually identical crimes and losses result[ed] in different sanctions, both absolutely and in terms of the calculated sanction/loss and fine/loss multiples.
> . . . For example, the sample contained two similar cases of odometer tampering with very different sentencing outcomes. In one case, the total sanction was over three times the loss, as the firm was ordered to pay full restitution and given a fine over twice the loss. In the other case, the firm was fined about 1/3 the loss and no restitution was ordered. A second example of disparity concerns two virtually identical instances of mislabeling beef. In one case, the fine was 2 1/2 times the loss; in the other it was only 4% of the loss. Solvency did not appear to be an issue in any of these cases.[18]

In light of those findings, the Commission concluded that drafting organizational guidelines was within its "broader mandate of establishing sound and effective sentencing policies for the federal courts"[19] and began a three-year effort that included publication of four sets of draft guidelines.[20]

During the Commission's deliberations, a consensus slowly emerged around the idea that the guidelines should "be designed to reduce fines for two primary reasons: to recognize an organization's relative degree of culpability; and to encourage desirable organizational behavior[.]"[21]

---

13. Nagel & Swenson, *supra* note 5, at 207.
14. *Id.* at 213.
15. *Id.* at 207–08.
16. *Id.* at 215.
17. *Id.* at 216–17.
18. *Id.* at 215 (quoting Mark A. Cohen et al., Report on Sentencing of Organizations in the Federal Courts, 1984–1987, *in* U.S. Sentencing Comm'n, Discussion Materials on Organizational Sanctions (1988)).
19. *Id.* at 216.
20. *Id.* at 226.
21. *Id.* at 228 (quoting U.S. Sentencing Comm'n, Supplementary Report on Sentencing Guidelines for Organizations (1991)).

> [T]hese concepts—organizational culpability and what many eventually termed "carrot and stick" incentives to control crime—[were] in fact surrogates for the traditional sentencing principles of just punishment and deterrence. These goals became the cornerstones for the fine provisions of the organizational guidelines.[22]

Discussion of incentives focused primarily on a company's efforts to "'prevent and detect violations of law'—a species of a compliance program."[23] Additionally:

> During the many notice and comment periods on the various draft guidelines, the corporate community strongly argued in favor of compliance programs having a substantial mitigating effect on any potential fine. Corporate counsel asserted, for example, that this factor reveals more about a company's "good citizenship" with respect to lawbreaking than any other effort. Although the Commission largely agreed, it determined that compliance programs should receive credit only if they bear strong indicia of an institutional commitment and due diligence in seeking both to prevent and detect violations of law.[24]

On May 1, 1991, after extensive research, debate, and input from advisory groups, federal agencies, and the general public, the Commission put into effect Chapter 8 of the U.S. Sentencing Guidelines, which applied to organizational offenders.[25] As Diana Murphy, the Commission's chair[26] explained, the organizational guidelines were based on a "novel sentencing approach" that recognized "[a]n organization is not a typical offender."[27] While the guidelines for individual offenders focus on "punishment and incapacitation," organizational guidelines "focus on providing restitution and an appropriate fine range . . . . geared toward deterrence."[28] They "not only encourage corporations to exemplify 'good corporate citizenship,' but also provide a means to 'rehabilitate' corporations . . . . by requiring them, as a term of probation, to institute and maintain effective compliance programs."[29]

An effective compliance program under the original guidelines was defined as meeting seven broad criteria:

1) Compliance standards and procedures must be established to deter crime.
2) High-level personnel must be involved in oversight.
3) Substantial discretionary authority must be carefully delegated.
4) Compliance standards and procedures must be communicated to employees.

---

22. *Id.* at 228 (footnote omitted).
23. *Id.* at 236 (quoting U.S. Sentencing Guidelines Manual §§ 8C2.5(f), 8D1.l(a)(3) (U.S. Sentencing Comm'n 1992)).
24. *Id.* at 236 (footnotes omitted).
25. Diana E. Murphy, *The Federal Sentencing Guidelines for Organizations: A Decade of Promoting Compliance and Ethics*, 87 Iowa L. Rev. 697, 701–02 (2002).
26. From 1999 until 2004. Murphy, Diana E., https://www.fjc.gov/history/judges/murphy-diana-e (last visited Mar. 4, 2018).
27. Murphy, *supra* note 25, at 702.
28. *Id.* at 702–03.
29. *Id.* at 703 (footnotes omitted).

5) Steps must be taken to achieve compliance in establishment of monitoring and auditing systems and of reporting systems with protective safeguards.

6) Standards must be consistently enforced.

7) Any violations require appropriate responses, which may include modification of compliance standards and procedures and other preventive measures.[30]

Leveraging organizations' special vulnerability to criminal prosecution under existing case law, the guidelines gave organizations a simple choice: self-police or risk severe punishment. As Paula Desio, the Commission's General Counsel, noted:

> Criminal liability can attach to an organization whenever an employee of the organization commits an act within the apparent scope of his or her employment, even if the employee acted directly contrary to company policy and instructions. An entire organization, despite its best efforts to prevent wrongdoing in its ranks, can still be held criminally liable for any of its employees' illegal actions. Consequently, when the Commission promulgated the organizational guidelines, it attempted to alleviate the harshest aspects of this institutional vulnerability by incorporating into the sentencing structure the preventive and deterrent aspects of systematic compliance programs. The Commission did this by mitigating the potential fine range—in some cases up to 95 percent—if an organization can demonstrate that it had put in place an effective compliance program. This mitigating credit under the guidelines is contingent upon prompt reporting to the authorities and the non-involvement of high level personnel in the actual offense conduct.[31]

B. The 2004 Revisions to the FSGO

Ten years after the original guidelines went into effect, the Commission empaneled an Ad Hoc Advisory Group ("Advisory Group") to assess their general effectiveness.[32] Shortly after this review began, the U.S. economy was rocked by a series of corporate scandals "involving rampant misconduct at the highest reaches of some of the largest companies in the United States."[33] In 2001, Enron Corporation—then the seventh largest corporation in the United States—declared bankruptcy amid allegations that it had systematically defrauded the investing public.[34] Several Enron executives pled guilty to felony charges and Enron's accounting firm, Arthur Andersen, was convicted of obstructing justice in connection with the DOJ's investigation of Enron.[35]

---

30. *Id.* at 703–4 (citing U.S. Sentencing Guidelines Manual ch. 8 (U.S. Sentencing Comm'n 2001)).

31. Desio, *supra* note 1.

32. U.S. Sentencing Comm'n, Report of the Ad Hoc Advisory Group on the Organizational Sentencing Guidelines 38 (Oct. 7, 2003) [hereinafter Advisory Group Report], https://www.ussc.gov/sites/default/files/pdf/training/organizational-guidelines/advgrprprt/AG_FINAL.pdf.

33. *Id.* at 35.

34. *Id.*

35. *Id.* at 36.

Allegations of misconduct were later leveled against Adelphia Communications, Tyco, WorldCom, Quest, Xerox, Kmart, McKesson HBOC, and HealthSouth.[36] Martha Stewart, the business tycoon declared by New York Magazine as "the definitive American woman of our time,"[37] was convicted of crimes related to insider trading.[38] These events captured the nation's attention and provided new impetus for the government's corporate reform agenda—culminating in the passage of the Sarbanes-Oxley Act of 2002 ("SOX").[39] Among other things, SOX directed the Sentencing Commission to review and amend the organizational guidelines, as appropriate, to ensure that they "are sufficient to deter and punish organizational criminal misconduct."[40]

The Advisory Group undertook an extensive study that "canvassed the practice commentary and scholarly literature, surveyed current representatives of the U.S. Department of Justice regarding prosecutorial decision making, and familiarized itself with the policies of a variety of other governmental agencies and departments."[41] The group "continuously kept abreast of Congress's response to the corporate scandals, most notably in the Sarbanes-Oxley Act of 2002, as well as the relevant output of public and private regulators."[42]

On October 7, 2003, the Advisory Group presented its report to the full Commission.[43] The report concluded that "the organizational sentencing guidelines [had] been successful in inducing many organizations, both directly and indirectly, to focus on compliance and to create programs to prevent and detect violations of law."[44] However, even though the scandals did not necessarily indicate that the original guidelines were deficient, it was still troubling that "much of [the] misconduct was perpetuated by senior management and was only belatedly discovered *despite the existence of auditing and other internal reporting systems.*"[45] The Advisory Group concluded that "changes can and should be made to give organizations greater guidance regarding the factors that are likely to result in *effective* programs to prevent and detect violations of law."[46]

Combining the lessons of the corporate scandals with ten years of experience in applying the guidelines, the Advisory Group proposed amendments to the guidelines that would "give greater guidance regarding the factors that are likely

---

36. *Id.* at 36–37.

37. Barbara Lippert, *Our Martha, Ourselves*, N.Y. MAGAZINE, May 15, 1995, http://nymag.com/news/media/48253/.

38. ADVISORY GROUP REPORT, *supra* note 32, at 37.

39. *Id.*

40. *Id.* (quoting Sarbanes-Oxley Act of 2002, Pub. L. No. 107-204, § 805(a), 116 Stat. 802, 802 (2002)).

41. *Id.* at 1.

42. *Id.* at 2.

43. Ketanji B. Jackson & Kathleen C. Grilli, *"Carrot and Stick" Philosophy: The History of the Organizational Sentencing Guidelines and the Emergence of Effective Compliance and Ethics Programs*, at 1.66 (2014) (on file with the USSC), https://www.ussc.gov/sites/default/files/pdf/training/annual-national-training-seminar/2014/org_article.pdf.

44. ADVISORY GROUP REPORT, *supra* note 32, at 3.

45. *Id.* at 38.

46. *Id.* at 3.

to result in truly effective programs."[47] The amendments added § 8B2.1 (Effective Compliance and Ethics Program), which "identifie[d] for the first time in the body of the sentencing guidelines the purposes of an effective compliance program, set[] forth more clearly the seven minimum steps for such a program, and provide[d] greater guidance for their implementation."[48]

Mary Beth Buchanan, U.S. Attorney for the Western District of Pennsylvania, testified the following before the Commission:

> The proposed amendments will communicate to the corporate community, with greater emphasis and clarity, the federal policy of encouraging self-policing through effective compliance programs and self-reporting if violations of law are detected. Moreover, the continuing policy of ascribing a benefit to having such programs will, we believe, likely lead to better compliance programs and practices and increased information to corporations about monitoring their own conduct and self-reporting any misconduct.[49]

Specifically, the Advisory Group proposed three major departures from the original guidelines' compliance paradigm:

> (1) Extend . . . compliance efforts *beyond mere law compliance* to the development of an organizational culture that encourages a more effective commitment to compliance with the law, including ethics-based standards and procedures;
> (2) Recognize the responsibilities and accountability of organizational leadership for compliance efforts; and
> (3) Explicitly require organizations to focus their compliance efforts by conducting careful risk assessments of probable types and sources of misconduct in company operations and then using the results of these assessments to target compliance efforts and tailor compliance program features.[50]

The first proposed change, which compelled organizations to transcend compliance to create a values-based culture, drew vociferous objections from the legal and business communities.[51] Expressing the general substance of these objections, David T. Buente of Sidley Austin Brown & Wood LLP on behalf of the American Chemistry Council, commented:

> [T]he role of the Organizational Guidelines is to address the specific issue of criminal noncompliance with legal requirements and not to expand into general issues of corporate social responsibility or ethics that are not directly regulated by criminal law.
>   . . . For example, requiring an "integrity and ethics based system," however admirable, is not necessarily related to preventing, detecting or reporting

---

47. *Id.* at 48.

48. *Organizational Sentencing Guidelines: Testimony of the U.S. Dep't. of Justice Before the U.S. Sentencing Comm'n*, at 3 (Mar. 17, 2004) (statement of Mary Beth Buchanan), https://www.ussc.gov/sites/default/files/pdf/amendment-process/public-hearings-and-meetings/20040317-19/Buchanan-DOJ.pdf.

49. *Id.* at 4.

50. *Id.* at 37–38 (emphasis added).

51. *See, e.g.,* Julie R. O'Sullivan, *Some Thoughts on Proposed Revisions to the Organizational Guidelines*, 1 Ohio St. J. Crim. L. 487, 509 (2004).

criminal conduct. . . . Criminal conduct is defined in a discrete set of federal statutes. Individuals and organizations are convicted and sentenced because of specific violations of specific statutory provisions. They are not convicted or sentenced because they may in some manner be unethical or lack integrity—even if that is the case.

. . . [U]nlike the defined realm of criminal offenses, there is no agreed-upon set of ethical criteria against which organizations can be measured. Encouraging organizations to create an "ethics infrastructure" that goes beyond compliance with criminal law is a laudable goal. However, the presence or absence of such an ethical infrastructure should not have consequences in the very serious context of sentencing those convicted of crimes. . . .

The *Organizational Guidelines* are used by courts to sentence those convicted of crimes. . . . However, almost all of the comments submitted to the Commission thus far treat the *Organizational Guidelines* as a guidance manual or educational tool on how to implement effective compliance systems, and do not discuss how these changes would be implemented in the *sentencing* context. . . .

. . . It is a happy development that the *Organizational Guidelines* are being integrated with aspirational ethics programs. It would be wrong, however, for organizations now to be punished more severely for not having taken these "leading," "best practice" steps[.] The threat of increased criminal penalties should not be used to "encourage" organizations to upgrade their compliance assurance systems into "ethics programs."[52]

Unmoved by this criticism, the Advisory Group pointed to mounting evidence that a values-based organizational culture was necessary to the development of an effective compliance program:

For several years, academics and others have advocated organizational culture as being a key contributor towards improving the effectiveness of corporate compliance. For example, in 1994, Professor Lynn Sharp Paine, described the important role organizational culture can play in supporting compliance efforts. The "task of management," she wrote, is to:

Define and give life to an organization's guiding values, to create an environment that supports ethically sound behavior, and to instill a sense of shared accountability among employees. . . . The need to obey the law is viewed as a positive aspect of organizational life, rather than an unwelcome constraint imposed by external authorities.

Testimony presented to the Advisory Group indicates that during the 1990s, as organizations shared best practices, many came to a similar conclusion as Dr. Paine, namely that the effectiveness of compliance programs could be enhanced if, in addition to due diligence in maintaining compliance programs, organizations also took steps to build cultures that encouraged employee commitment to compliance.

---

52. *Id.* at 509–11 (quoting Letter from David T. Buente, Sidley Austin Brown & Wood LLP, on behalf of the American Chemistry Council, to B. Todd Jones, Chair, U.S. Sentencing Commission's Advisory Group on the U.S. Sentencing Guidelines for Organizations regarding the August 21, 2002 Request for Public Comment (Oct. 11, 2002)).

An organizational culture that encourages a commitment to compliance with the law is one in which compliance with the law is the expected behavior. Rather than solely emphasizing conduct restrictions and information gathering activities aimed at preventing and detecting violations of law, [it] includes positive actions which demonstrate that law compliance is a key value within the organization. In general, organizational culture, in this context, has come to be defined as *the shared set of norms and beliefs that guide individual and organizational behavior*. These norms and beliefs are shaped by the leadership of the organization, are often expressed as shared values or guiding principles, and are reinforced by various systems and procedures throughout the organization.[53]

This trend, the Advisory Group argued, increased social expectations of corporate conduct—particularly in the aftermath of the scandals:

This emphasis on ethics and values is . . . reflected in recent legislative and regulatory reforms. Several recent reforms encourage organizations to promote honest and ethical conduct through codes of ethics or business conduct. For example, the Sarbanes-Oxley Act of 2002 encourages companies to adopt "codes of ethics" which include "standards that are reasonably necessary to promote honest and ethical conduct." Recent Securities and Exchange Commission regulations recognize that a "code of ethics" should include "written standards that are reasonably designed to deter wrongdoing and to promote honest and ethical conduct." Furthermore, in this same vein, new listing requirements proposed by the New York Stock Exchange emphasize the importance of a commitment to ethics and culture as a means of improving law compliance. Recently, in separate speeches, Securities and Exchange Commission Chair William Donaldson and Commissioner Cynthia Glassman emphasized the importance of organizational culture in ensuring effective compliance.[54]

The proposed guidelines' second major departure from the original guidelines was in recognizing that "unless the proper tone is set at the top—that is, unless the organizational leadership makes clear that compliance with the law is an organizational priority—no compliance program is likely to succeed."[55] The Advisory Group observed:

[T]he guidelines should better address the role of organizational leadership in ensuring that compliance programs are valued, supported, periodically re-evaluated, and operate for their intended purpose.
. . . [T]he current total silence in the organizational sentencing guidelines relating to the role of the governing authority fails to state what may otherwise be obvious: ultimately the governing authority is responsible for the activities of the organization.[56]

The proposed revisions thus "amplif[ied] the role of the governing authority, [and] provid[ed] direct access between the governing authority (or one of its

---

53. ADVISORY GROUP REPORT, *supra* note 32, at 51–52 (emphasis added) (footnote omitted).
54. *Id.* at 52 (footnotes omitted).
55. O'Sullivan, *supra* note 51, at 507.
56. ADVISORY GROUP REPORT, *supra* note 32, at 3, 58.

committees) and a company's compliance officer, ensuring prompt and unfiltered communications."[57]

Finally, the Advisory Group proposed an explicit requirement that organizations perform "risk assessments," a methodical process of reviewing operations to identify violations that are likely to occur, and *tailoring* the compliance program to mitigate those specific risks.[58] Risk assessment, the Advisory Group proposed, "need[s] to be made at all stages of the development, testing, and implementation of a compliance program to ensure that compliance efforts are properly focused and effective."[59]

On April 8, 2004, the Commission adopted the revisions proposed by the Advisory Group, "elevat[ing] the criteria for an effective compliance program from [a] commentary into a separate guideline, USSG § 8B2.1 (Effective Compliance and Ethics Program), . . . '[i]n order to emphasize the importance of compliance and ethics programs and to provide more prominent guidance on the requirements for an effective program.'"[60] The new guideline introduced added rigor to the criteria for an effective compliance program, "imposing significantly greater responsibilities on the organization's governing authority and executive leadership."[61]

Following the 2004 revisions, the Commission made one more set of major revisions to the organizational guidelines in 2010. The most significant of those revisions was to allow mitigation credit for an effective compliance program despite the involvement of high-level or substantial authority personnel in the offense when four conditions are met:

1) The individual or individuals with operational responsibility for the compliance and ethics program have direct reporting obligations to the governing authority;

2) The compliance and ethics program detected the offense before discovery by outsiders;

3) The organization promptly reported the offense to appropriate governmental authorities; and

4) No individual with operational responsibility for the compliance and ethics program participated in, condoned, or was willfully ignorant of the offense. [62]

---

57. *Id.* at 58.

58. *Id.* at 87–91.

59. *Id.* at 87.

60. Jackson & Grilli, *supra* note 43, at 1.70 (quoting U.S. Sentencing Guidelines app. C, amend. 673 (U.S. Sentencing Comm'n 2004)).

61. *Id.* at 1.71 (quoting U.S. Sentencing Guidelines app. C, amend. 673 (U.S. Sentencing Comm'n 2004)).

62. U.S. Sentencing Comm'n Public Meeting Minutes, at 55 (Apr. 7, 2010) (on file with the USSC), https://www.ussc.gov/sites/default/files/pdf/amendment-process/public-hearings-and-meetings/20100407/20100407_Minutes.pdf.

C. *United States v. Booker*

In 2005, the U.S. Supreme Court decided *United States v. Booker*,[63] which held that mandatory application of federal sentencing guidelines to individual offenders violated their constitutional right to trial by jury under the Sixth Amendment of the U.S. Constitution.[64] *Booker* struck down as unconstitutional 18 U.S.C. § 3553(b)(1)—the provision of the SRA that made all of the sentencing guidelines mandatory—and in so doing rendered all sentencing guidelines non-binding.[65]

Booker held that sentencing courts may, but are not required to, take the guidelines into account in making sentencing decisions.[66] It preserved the Sentencing Commission and its functions, however, leaving that body in place to "writ[e] Guidelines, collect[] information about actual district court sentencing decisions, undertake[] research, and revise[] the Guidelines accordingly."[67]

Two year later, in *Kimbrough v. United States*,[68] the Court stressed that a district court must at least consider the Guidelines range as one of many possible factors to be weighed in sentencing, but may depart from them in his or her discretion.[69] Then in *Gall v. United States*,[70] the Court held that courts of appeal are to accord a high degree of deference to the sentencing decisions of district courts.[71]

After *Booker*, the Sentencing Commission and other actors in the criminal justice system took immediate steps to put into place an advisory guideline system.[72] As the Commission noted in its 2012 report on the impact of *Booker*:

> The Commission continues to promulgate sentencing guidelines that courts must properly consider and guideline ranges that courts must properly determine in all federal criminal cases. Since *Booker*, the Commission has promulgated 96 amendments to the guidelines, . . . carefully consider[ing] data, public comment, and other relevant information. The Commission continues to collect, analyze, and report sentencing data systematically to detect new criminal trends, to determine whether federal crime policies are achieving their goals, and to serve as a clearinghouse for federal sentencing statistics. The Commission resolves conflicting judicial interpretations of the guidelines by studying appeals court decisions on sentencing issues and promulgating guideline amendments to ensure uniform interpretation.[73]

---

63. 543 U.S. 220 (2005).
64. *Id.* at 267.
65. *Id.* at 245.
66. *Id.* at 264.
67. *Id.*
68. 552 U.S. 85 (2007).
69. *Id.* at 108–9.
70. 552 U.S. 38 (2007).
71. *Id.* at 51.
72. U.S. Sentencing Comm'n, Final Report on the Impact of *United States v. Booker* on Federal Sentencing 37 (2006) (on file with the USSC), https://www.ussc.gov/sites/default/files/pdf/news/congressional-testimony-and-reports/submissions/200603-booker/Booker_Report.pdf.
73. U.S. Sentencing Comm'n, Report on the Continuing Impact of *United States v. Booker* on Federal Sentencing 11 (2012) (footnotes omitted), https://www.ussc.gov/research/congressional-reports/2012-report-congress-continuing-impact-united-states-v-booker-federal-sentencing.

Notes and Questions

Although developments in federal law were the main drivers of the idea of corporate self-policing, state law has also played a significant role—most notably, the 1996 decision by the legendary Delaware Chancery Court judge William T. Allen in *In re Caremark International Inc. Derivative Litigation*.[74] When the Advisory Group issued its report in 2003, it made the following observation about the case:

> The court's observations in *Caremark* have raised the prospect, however attenuated, of directors' derivative liability for others' failures to ensure that adequate compliance programs are in place. Consequently, the *Caremark* decision, "gave the movement toward corporate self-policing—known as compliance planning—a kick in the pants."[75]

Caremark involved "claims that the members of Caremark's board of directors (the "Board") breached their fiduciary duty of care to Caremark in connection with alleged violations by Caremark employees of federal and state laws and regulations applicable to health care providers."[76] Because of those alleged violations, the company had been subject to a four-year investigation by the United States Department of Health and Human Services and the DOJ.[77] In 1994, Caremark was indicted with multiple felonies and entered into a plea agreement with the DOJ in which Caremark pleaded guilty to a single felony of mail fraud and agreed to pay civil and criminal fines of approximately $250 million.[78] Following the settlements with the government, a derivative shareholder's suit was filed in the Delaware Chancery Court in 1994, seeking damages on behalf of the company from the individual members of the Caremark board of directors.[79]

Addressing the fairness of a settlement reached between the plaintiffs and the board, Judge Allen held:

> The ultimate issue then is whether the proposed settlement appears to be fair to the corporation and its absent shareholders . . . .
>
> . . . Legally, evaluation of the central claim made entails consideration of the legal standard governing a board of directors' obligation to supervise or monitor corporate performance. For the reasons set forth below I conclude, in light of the discovery record, that there is a very low probability that it would be determined that the directors of Caremark breached any duty to appropriately monitor and supervise the enterprise. Indeed the record tends to show an active consideration by Caremark management and its Board of the Caremark structures and programs . . . .
>
> . . . .
>
> Director liability for a breach of the duty to exercise appropriate attention

---

74. *In re* Caremark Int'l Inc. Derivative Litig., 698 A.2d 959 (Del. Ch. 1996).
75. ADVISORY GROUP REPORT, *supra* note 32, at 32.
76. *In re Caremark Int'l*, 698 A.2d at 960.
77. *Id.*
78. *Id.*
79. *Id.*

may, in theory, arise in two distinct contexts. First, such liability may be said to follow *from a board decision* that results in a loss because that decision was ill advised or "negligent." Second, liability to the corporation for a loss may be said to arise from *an unconsidered failure of the board to act* in circumstances in which due attention would, arguably, have prevented the loss. The first class of cases will typically be subject to review under the director-protective business judgment rule, assuming the decision made was the product of *a process* that was *either* deliberately considered in good faith or was otherwise rational. What should be understood, but may not widely be understood by courts or commentators who are not often required to face such questions, is that compliance with a director's duty of care can never appropriately be judicially determined by reference to *the content of the board decision* that leads to a corporate loss, apart from consideration of the good faith *or* rationality of the process employed. That is, whether a judge or jury considering the matter after the fact, believes a decision substantively wrong, or degrees of wrong extending through "stupid" to "egregious" or "irrational," provides no ground for director liability, so long as the court determines that the process employed was either rational or employed in *a good faith* effort to advance corporate interests. To employ a different rule—one that permitted an "objective" evaluation of the decision—would expose directors to substantive second guessing by ill-equipped judges or juries, which would, in the long-run, be injurious to investor interests. Thus, the business judgment rule is process oriented and informed by a deep respect for all *good faith* board decisions.

Indeed, one wonders on what moral basis might shareholders attack a *good faith* business decision of a director as "unreasonable" or "irrational." Where a director *in fact exercises a good faith effort to be informed and to exercise appropriate judgment*, he or she should be deemed to satisfy fully the duty of attention. If the shareholders thought themselves entitled to some other quality of judgment than such a director produces in the good faith exercise of the powers of office, then the shareholders should have elected other directors. Judge Learned Hand made the point rather better than can I. In speaking of the passive director defendant Mr. Andrews in *Barnes v. Andrews*, Judge Hand said:

> True, he was not very suited by experience for the job he had undertaken, but I cannot hold him on that account. After all it is the same corporation that chose him that now seeks to charge him . . . . Directors are not specialists like lawyers or doctors. . . . They are the general advisors of the business and if they faithfully give such ability as they have to their charge, it would not be lawful to hold them liable. Must a director guarantee that his judgment is good? Can a shareholder call him to account for deficiencies that their votes assured him did not disqualify him for his office? While he may not have been the Cromwell for that Civil War, Andrews did not engage to play any such role.

In this formulation Learned Hand correctly identifies, in my opinion, the core element of any corporate law duty of care inquiry: whether there was good faith effort to be informed and exercise judgment.

. . . The second class of cases in which director liability for inattention is theoretically possible entail circumstances in which a loss eventuates not from a decision but from unconsidered inaction. Most of the decisions that a corporation, acting through its human agents, makes are, of course, not the subject of director attention. Legally, the board itself will be required only to authorize the most significant corporate acts or transactions: mergers, changes in capital structure, fundamental changes in business, appointment and compensation of the CEO, etc. As the facts of this case graphically demonstrate, ordinary business decisions that are made by officers and employees deeper in the interior of the organization can, however, vitally affect the welfare of the corporation and its ability to achieve its various strategic and financial goals. If this case did not prove the point itself, recent business history would. Recall for example the displacement of senior management and much of the board of Salomon, Inc.; the replacement of senior management of Kidder, Peabody following the discovery of large trading losses resulting from phantom trades by a highly compensated trader; or the extensive financial loss and reputational injury suffered by Prudential Insurance as a result its junior officers' misrepresentations in connection with the distribution of limited partnership interests. Financial and organizational disasters such as these raise the question, what is the board's responsibility with respect to the organization and monitoring of the enterprise to assure that the corporation functions within the law to achieve its purposes?

Modernly this question has been given special importance by an increasing tendency, especially under federal law, to employ the criminal law to assure corporate compliance with external legal requirements, including environmental, financial, employee and product safety as well as assorted other health and safety regulations. In 1991, pursuant to the Sentencing Reform Act of 1984, the United States Sentencing Commission adopted Organizational Sentencing Guidelines which impact importantly on the prospective effect these criminal sanctions might have on business corporations. The Guidelines set forth a uniform sentencing structure for organizations to be sentenced for violation of federal criminal statutes and provide for penalties that equal or often massively exceed those previously imposed on corporations. The Guidelines offer powerful incentives for corporations today to have in place compliance programs to detect violations of law, promptly to report violations to appropriate public officials when discovered, and to take prompt, voluntary remedial efforts.

. . . .

[I]n recent years the Delaware Supreme Court has made it clear . . . the seriousness with which the corporation law views the role of the corporate board. Secondly, I note the elementary fact that relevant and timely *information* is an essential predicate for satisfaction of the board's supervisory and monitoring role under Section 141 of the Delaware General Corporation Law. Thirdly, I note the potential impact of the federal organizational sentencing guidelines on any business organization. Any rational person attempting in good faith to meet an organizational governance responsibility would be bound to take into account this development and the enhanced penalties and the opportunities for reduced sanctions that it offers.

. . . .

Thus, I am of the view that a director's obligation includes a duty to attempt in good faith to assure that a corporate information and reporting system, which the board concludes is adequate, exists, and that failure to do so under some circumstances may, in theory at least, render a director liable for losses caused by non-compliance with applicable legal standards. I now turn to an analysis of the claims asserted with this concept of the directors' duty of care, as a duty satisfied in part by assurance of adequate information flows to the board, in mind.

. . . .

In order to show that the Caremark directors breached their duty of care by failing adequately to control Caremark's employees, plaintiffs would have to show either (1) that the directors knew or (2) should have known that violations of law were occurring and, in either event, (3) that the directors took no steps in a good faith effort to prevent or remedy that situation, and (4) that such failure proximately resulted in the losses complained of . . . .

. . . .

Here the record supplies essentially no evidence that the director defendants were guilty of a sustained failure to exercise their oversight function. To the contrary, insofar as I am able to tell on this record, the corporation's information systems appear to have represented a good faith attempt to be informed of relevant facts. If the directors did not know the specifics of the activities that lead to the indictments, they cannot be faulted.

The liability that eventuated in this instance was huge. But the fact that it resulted from a violation of criminal law alone does not create a breach of fiduciary duty by directors. The record at this stage does not support the conclusion that the defendants either lacked good faith in the exercise of their monitoring responsibilities or conscientiously permitted a known violation of law by the corporation to occur. The claims asserted against them must be viewed at this stage as extremely weak.

. . . .

. . . Under the settlement agreement, plaintiffs have been given express assurances that Caremark will have a more centralized, active supervisory system in the future. Specifically, the settlement mandates duties to be performed by the newly named Compliance and Ethics Committee on an ongoing basis and increases the responsibility for monitoring compliance with the law at the lower levels of management. In adopting the resolutions required under the settlement, Caremark has further clarified its policies concerning the prohibition of providing remuneration for referrals. These appear to be positive consequences of the settlement of the claims brought by the plaintiffs, even if they are not highly significant. Nonetheless, given the weakness of the plaintiffs' claims the proposed settlement appears to be an adequate, reasonable, and beneficial outcome for all of the parties. Thus, the proposed settlement will be approved.[80]

In response to *Caremark,* industry groups, lawyers, and compliance providers expanded their offerings to help companies create effective compliance programs. The result was "a substantial increase in the size and scope of corporate

---

80. *Id.* at 961–72 (citations omitted) (footnotes omitted).

compliance activities and ultimately the creation of vast compliance bureaucracies within the organization."[81]

Commentators have long wondered why *Caremark* has had such an outsized impact. It is a largely advisory opinion that creates an extremely narrow path to liability. What is the explanation in your opinion?

II. Structure of the Current FSGO

As originally conceived in 1991, the guidelines comprised three main parts: (1) Remedying Harm, which addressed payment of restitution to victims; (2) Fine Calculation, which set forth the methodology for calculating the fine; and (3) Organizational Probation, which gave the sentencing court continuing jurisdiction to monitor the defendant's post-sentencing conduct.[82] The 2004 revisions added a fourth part titled "Effective Compliance and Ethics Programs," a separate, stand-alone section that set forth the characteristics of an effective compliance program.[83]

The Introductory Commentary to the guidelines articulates four guiding principles corresponding to these four parts:

> First, the court must, whenever practicable, order the organization to remedy any harm caused by the offense. The resources expended to remedy the harm should not be viewed as punishment, but rather as a means of making victims whole for the harm caused.
>
> Second, if the organization operated primarily for a criminal purpose or primarily by criminal means, the fine should be set sufficiently high to divest the organization of all its assets.
>
> Third, the fine range for any other organization should be based on the seriousness of the offense and the culpability of the organization. The seriousness of the offense generally will be reflected by the greatest of the pecuniary gain, the pecuniary loss, or the amount in a guideline offense level fine table. Culpability generally will be determined by six factors that the sentencing court must consider. The four factors that increase the ultimate punishment of an organization are: (i) the involvement in or tolerance of criminal activity; (ii) the prior history of the organization; (iii) the violation of an order; and (iv) the obstruction of justice. The two factors that mitigate the ultimate punishment of an organization are: (i) the existence of an effective compliance and ethics program; and (ii) self-reporting, cooperation, or acceptance of responsibility.
>
> Fourth, probation is an appropriate sentence for an organizational defendant when needed to ensure that another sanction will be fully implemented, or to ensure that steps will be taken within the organization to reduce the likelihood of future criminal conduct.

---

81. Charles M. Elson & Christopher J. Gyves, In Re Caremark: *Good Intentions, Unintended Consequences*, 39 WAKE FOREST L. REV. 691, 701 (2004).

82. U.S. SENTENCING GUIDELINES MANUAL ch. 8 (U.S. SENTENCING COMM'N 1991).

83. U.S. SENTENCING GUIDELINES MANUAL § 8B1.1 (U.S. SENTENCING COMM'N 2004).

These guidelines offer incentives to organizations to reduce and ultimately eliminate criminal conduct by providing a structural foundation from which an organization may self-police its own conduct through an effective compliance and ethics program. The prevention and detection of criminal conduct, as facilitated by an effective compliance and ethics program, will assist an organization in encouraging ethical conduct and in complying fully with all applicable laws.[84]

A. Section 8B1: Restitution

Section 8B1, titled Remedying Harm from Criminal Conduct, aims to ensure that "regardless of the culpability or fault of a corporation in committing an offense, [the corporation] should 'take all appropriate steps to provide compensation to victims and otherwise remedy the harm caused or threatened by [that] offense.'"[85] This principle, which is distinct from the punitive aspects of the guidelines,[86] is referred to as "restitution" and is intended to "make victims whole again."[87]

Section 8B1.1 states:

> (a) In the case of an identifiable victim, the court shall—
> (1) enter a restitution order for the full amount of the victim's loss . . .; or
> (2) impose a term of probation or supervised release with a condition requiring restitution for the full amount of the victim's loss . . . .[88]

The Commentary explains:

> The purposes of a remedial order are to remedy harm that has already occurred and to prevent future harm. A remedial order requiring corrective action by the organization may be necessary to prevent future injury from the instant offense, *e.g.*, a product recall for a food and drug violation or a clean-up order for an environmental violation.[89]

B. Section 8B2: Effective Compliance and Ethics Programs

Section 8B2.1 is divided into three subsections: subsection (a) stresses the importance of preventive due diligence and organizational culture in creating an effective compliance program; subsection (b) lists the seven minimum attributes that should be present in all compliance programs; and subsection (c) requires organizations to perform "risk assessments" as part of constructing and

---

84. U.S. Sentencing Guidelines Manual ch. 8, introductory cmt. (U.S. Sentencing Comm'n 2004).

85. Nagel & Swenson, *supra* note 5, at 232 (quoting U.S. Sentencing Guidelines Manual ch. 8, introductory cmt. (U.S. Sentencing Comm'n 1992)).

86. *See id.* (footnote omitted).

87. *Id.* (footnote omitted).

88. U.S. Sentencing Guidelines Manual § 8B1.1(a) (U.S. Sentencing Comm'n 2016) [hereinafter FSGO].

89. *Id.* § 8B1.2 cmt. background.

operating a generally effective program to prevent and detect violations of law.[90] Each subsection is quoted and discussed in detail below.

1. Subsection (a)

(a) To have an effective compliance and ethics program . . . an organization shall—
> **(1) exercise due diligence to prevent and detect criminal conduct; and**
> **(2) otherwise promote an organizational culture that encourages ethical conduct and a commitment to compliance with the law.**[91]

Neither the guideline nor the commentary elaborates on the specific meaning of the terms "culture" and "ethics" in Subsection (a), but in proposing the language, the Advisory Group noted:

> An organizational culture that encourages a commitment to compliance with the law includes positive actions which demonstrate that law compliance is a key value within the organization. Such a culture is demonstrated by organizational actions which encourage employees to choose lawful behaviors and to expect that their conduct will be evaluated by others within the organization in terms of how well the employees have pursued lawful conduct.[92]

Addressing the legal community's concerns about the difficulty in measuring "culture" and "ethical values," the Advisory Group clarified that organizations can satisfy subsection (a) by simply satisfying the seven steps outlined in subsection (b)(1)-(7):

> [I]t is not the Advisory Group's intention to require organizations to go beyond . . . [building] an effective program to prevent and detect violations of the law. Rather, the Advisory Group anticipates that the dual objectives of reasonable prevention and positive culture will be taken into account by organizations as they shape and implement [their programs].
> . . . By focusing only on aspects of organizational culture affecting affirmative support of an organization's compliance with the law, the proposed guideline is intended to limit the assessments of sentencing courts, prosecutors and other interested parties to evaluations of program elements aimed at building support for compliance with the law. The proposal avoids the need for determinations of whether a particular organization has adopted a good "set of values" or appropriate "ethical standards," subjects which may be very difficult, if not impossible, to evaluate in an objective, consistent manner.[93]

Notably, § 8B2.1, Application Note 1, defines "violations of law" to include "violations of any law, whether criminal or noncriminal (including a regulation), for which the organization is, or would be, liable."[94]

---

90. *See* ADVISORY GROUP REPORT, *supra* note 32, at 50–51.
91. FSGO, *supra* note 88, § 8B2.1(a).
92. *See* ADVISORY GROUP REPORT, *supra* note 32, at 55.
93. *Id.*
94. *Id.* at 54.

2. Subsection (b)

(b) Due diligence and the promotion of an organizational culture that encourages ethical conduct and a commitment to compliance with the law within the meaning of subsection (a) minimally require the following:

(1) Establish standards and procedures to prevent and detect criminal conduct.[95]

According to the Commentary, this provision refers to "standards of conduct and internal controls that are reasonably capable of reducing the likelihood of criminal conduct."[96] Standards of conduct articulate the corporation's expectations of its employees and agents and are usually compiled into a written employee manual or code of conduct. Among other things, the code of conduct addresses the areas where a company's operations may be susceptible to violations; explains the applicable law and sets forth penalties for violations; and provides information regarding how to report a violation. The code of conduct or manual is one part of the company's internal control system: the processes that ensure company expectations of employees are met, usually in the form of approvals, reporting channels, verifications, training, audits, and other similar processes.

(2) The organization's governing authority shall be knowledgeable about the content and operation of the compliance and ethics program and shall exercise reasonable oversight with respect to the implementation and effectiveness of the compliance and ethics program.

(B) High-level personnel of the organization shall ensure that the organization has an effective compliance and ethics program, as described in this guideline. Specific individual(s) within high-level personnel shall be assigned overall responsibility for the compliance and ethics program.

(C) Specific individual(s) within the organization shall be delegated day-to-day operational responsibility for the compliance and ethics program. Individual(s) with operational responsibility shall report periodically to high-level personnel and, as appropriate, to the governing authority, or an appropriate subgroup of the governing authority, on the effectiveness of the compliance and ethics program. To carry out such operational responsibility, such individual(s) shall be given adequate resources, appropriate authority, and direct access to the governing authority or an appropriate subgroup of the governing authority.[97]

This provision imposes two separate obligations on the "governing authority,"[98] which is defined as the board of directors or similar governing body within the organization: (1) to be knowledgeable about the compliance and ethics program; and (2) to exercise reasonable oversight over the program.[99] Being

---

95. *See* FSGO, *supra* note 88, § 8B2.1(b).
96. *Id.* § 8B2.1 cmt. n.1.
97. FSGO, *supra* note 88, § 8B2.1(b)(2).
98. *See id.* § 8B2.1 cmt. n.1.
99. *See id.* § 8B2.1(b)(2)(A).

"knowledgeable" means that the board should acquire three types of information about the program and its function:

1) Practical information about the major risks of unlawful conduct facing their organization;
2) The primary compliance program features aimed at counteracting those risks; and,
3) The types of problems with compliance that the organization and other parties with similar operations have encountered in recent activities.[100]

The guidelines do not dictate the "fact finding procedures or methods that members of a governing authority should use in acquiring this type of information"[101] and leave it to "particular organizations to gather and deliver this sort of information to governing authority members in the ways that best fit the organization's overall operations."[102] Board members typically receive relevant information "through reports from senior organization managers or other experts (in large organizations), or through . . . day-to-day management and oversight of related organizational activities (in small organizations)."[103] The guidelines require that such reporting occur "at least annually, and more frequently when legal changes or shifts in organizational activities raise new compliance risks for the organization."[104]

With respect to the board's obligation to "exercise reasonable oversight" over the program, the Advisory Group notes:

[O]versight of compliance programs . . . is a key part of the duties of top level organizational officials . . . . [E]ffective management requires that governing authorities be *proactive* in seeking information about compliance problems, evaluating that information when received, and monitoring the implementation and effectiveness of responses when compliance problems are detected.[105]

Other than the governing authority, subsection (b)(2) refers to the "organizational leadership" as comprising "high-level personnel of the organization."[106] "[T]hese parties represent the key decision makers within organization management—the range of leaders who set directions for organizational actions and who determine when organizational performance is successful in attaining organizational goals."[107] High-level personnel can include "a director; an executive officer; an individual in charge of a major business or functional unit of the organization, such as sales, administration, or finance; and an individual

100. *See* Advisory Group Report, *supra* note 32, at 61.
101. *Id.* at 60.
102. *Id.*
103. *Id.* (emphasis added).
104. *Id.*
105. *Id.* at 61.
106. *Id.*
107. *Id.*

with a substantial ownership interest."[108] In most companies, high-level personnel are the CEO and the officers that serve directly under her, such as the Chief Financial Officer ("CFO"), Chief Operational Officer ("COO"), Chief Technical Officer ("CTO"), and so on.

Subsection (b)(2)(B) requires high-level personnel to ensure that the company has a compliance and ethics program patterned after the guidelines[109] and that at least one person in a high-level role takes overall responsibility for the program.[110] In practice, this means that the CEO takes charge of building the compliance and ethics program and appoints a Chief Compliance Officer ("CCO") to manage the program. In this way, subsection (b)(2)(B) aims to "ensure that the official charged with implementing [the] program has the formal authority, access to senior management, and the respect needed to manage and oversee the implementation of a program." [111]

Subsection (b)(2)(C) requires that the program have its own dedicated staff with "day-to-day operational responsibility for the . . . program."[113] Those individuals are required to report to the CCO, and, importantly, they are to "be given adequate resources, appropriate authority, and direct access to the governing authority or an appropriate subgroup of the governing authority."[114] As the Advisory Group observed, "[t]he allocation of these sorts of resources is needed to ensure that a company's compliance program is not just a paper program, but rather a substantial management effort with the resources needed to succeed."[115] Thus, when a business executive tries to overrule a compliance officer, or where senior management is apparently involved in or supports the illegal conduct, the CCO is able to bypass senior management and directly report the misconduct to the board.[116]

> The CEO takes charge of building the compliance and ethics program and appoints a Chief Compliance Officer ("CCO") to manage the program. In this way, subsection (b)(2)(B) aims to "ensure that the official charged with implementing [the] program has the formal authority, access to senior management, and the respect needed to manage and oversee the implementation of a program."
>
> *Report of the Advisory Group on the FSGO*[112]

(3) The organization shall use reasonable efforts not to include within the substantial authority personnel of the organization any individual whom the organization knew, or should have known through the exercise of due diligence, has engaged in illegal activities or other conduct inconsistent with an effective compliance and ethics program.[117]

---

108. FSGO, *supra* note 88, § 8A1.2 cmt. n.3(B).
109. *See id.* § 8B2.1(b)(2)(B).
110. *Id.*
111. Advisory Group Report, *supra* note 32, at 62.
112. *Id.*
113. FSGO, *supra* note 88, § 8B2.1(b)(2)(C).
114. *Id.*
115. Advisory Group Report, *supra* note 32, at 62.
116. *See id.* at 62–63.
117. FSGO, *supra* note 88, § 8B2.1(b)(3).

The logic of subsection (b)(3) is clear: "[e]ven absent the incentives of the organizational sentencing guidelines, organizations would . . . want to ensure that those with significant responsibilities are law abiding and likely to act in accordance with company policies."[118] The advisory group explained that organizations should appropriately screen employees—particularly those in positions of substantial authority—balancing "the need for gathering employee information while at the same time avoiding intrusive policies that stifle vital internal communications."[119]

The Commentary lists three factors that organizations must consider when hiring an individual with a history of misconduct:

1) "relatedness of the individual's illegal activities and other misconduct (*i.e.*, other conduct inconsistent with an effective compliance and ethics program) to the specific responsibilities the individual is anticipated to be assigned";[120]
2) "the recency of the individual's illegal activities and other misconduct";[121] and
3) "whether the individual has engaged in other such illegal activities and other such misconduct."[122]

> (4) The organization shall take reasonable steps to communicate . . . its standards and procedures . . . by conducting effective training programs and otherwise disseminating information appropriate to . . . individuals' respective roles and responsibilities.[123]

During the public hearings, one Advisory Group member asked: "Would anyone here regard as effective a compliance program that has no training and simply relied on a fairly detailed employee code of ethical conduct?"[124] In the discussion that ensued, members agreed not only that training was necessary but also that such training should do more than merely "communicate . . . [organizational] standards and procedures."[125] Training should be a tool, the Advisory

---

118. ADVISORY GROUP REPORT, *supra* note 32, at 66.
119. *Id.* at 67. The advisory Board cautioned, however, that:

> In applying the "history of engaging in violations of law" standard, it should be kept in mind that many states have enacted statutes that restrict an employer's ability to request information concerning a job applicant's criminal history, or from considering such information in making employment decisions. While federal anti-discrimination law does not expressly prohibit employers from basing employment decisions on the criminal history of an applicant or employee, as noted above, the consideration of criminal history may give rise to a disparate impact claim if a disappointed candidate can demonstrate that it operates to exclude those groups who are disproportionately the subject of reported criminal conduct. *Id.* (footnotes omitted).

120. *See* FSGO, *supra* note 88, § 8B2.1 cmt. n.4(B).
121. *Id.*
122. *Id.*
123. *Id.* § 8B2.1(b)(4)(A).
124. ADVISORY GROUP REPORT, *supra* note 32, at 68–69.
125. *Id.* at 70.

Board noted, for inspiring, motivating, and teaching employees to do the right thing.[126] Quoting compliance expert Joe Murphy, the Advisory Board observed:

> While there are certainly a large number of transgressions because of ignorance, the truly serious violations that reach the newspapers and incur multi-million dollar fines are typically the result of deliberate wrongdoing. They do not usually happen because a hapless employee lacked knowledge or needed to be told that the company valued ethical behavior. Regrettably, there are genuinely bad actors in corporate America (as in all parts of society), and there are others who may too readily yield to temptation or pressure to break the rules. These people are not necessarily helped or deterred by training that delivers only detailed information. Instead they need training that helps to motivate them and to deter misconduct.[127]

The Advisory Group clarified, however, that training need not be formal or expensive—especially in the case of smaller companies:

> By substituting the phrase "conducting effective training" for "requiring participation in training programs," the Advisory Group sought to ensure that small organizations would not be overly burdened in meeting the training obligations specified in the proposed guideline. For such small entities, effective training could occur during orientation sessions, monthly staff meetings, or even casual conversations between a manager and her subordinates. The larger the organization, the more appropriate it may be to have a more formal training program with appropriate documentation and dedicated resources and tools to measure the training program's impact.[128]

> (5) The organization shall take reasonable steps—
> (A) to ensure that the organization's compliance and ethics program is followed, including monitoring and auditing to detect criminal conduct;
> (B) to evaluate periodically the effectiveness of the organization's compliance and ethics program; and
> (C) to have and publicize a system, which may include mechanisms that allow for anonymity or confidentiality, whereby the organization's employees and agents may report or seek guidance regarding potential or actual criminal conduct without fear of retaliation.[129]

Another lesson of the corporate scandals in the early 2000s was that, once a compliance program is in place in an organization, it must be continually tracked to gauge its effectiveness over time and to ensure that it is, in fact, being followed.[130] This is accomplished through "monitoring" and "auditing" systems:

> The importance of independent compliance monitoring and auditing [was] . . . illustrated by the role of independent auditing practices in revealing and stopping

---

126. *See id.*
127. *Id.* at 70–71 (quoting Joseph E. Murphy, Training "In a Practical Manner," Corporate Compliance (1999)).
128. *Id.* at 71 (footnote omitted).
129. FSGO, *supra* note 88, § 8B2.1(b)(5).
130. *See* Advisory Group Report, *supra* note 32, at 76.

. . . incidents of corporate fraud. For example, internal audits of the company's payment and accounting practices, coupled with the reporting of detected misconduct to the corporation's board, were responsible for detecting and stopping one of the biggest corporate frauds in U.S. history—WorldCom's multi-billion dollar misstatement of corporate expenses. Similar systematic monitoring of compliance in other areas should aid companies in detecting and stopping misconduct in a variety of contexts, provided that it is done by independent evaluators having the ability to invoke board access when compliance problems are found.[131]

The Advisory Board underscored that monitoring and auditing systems must "scrutinize two separate organizational characteristics:

(1) the adherence of organizational activities to applicable laws and compliance program requirements; and
(2) the sufficiency of . . . an organization's compliance program. . . ."[132]

The first task involves verifying that transactions conform to applicable laws and program directives, which may be accomplished either through observation in real time (monitoring) or through periodic review of transaction samples (auditing).[133] The second task encompasses testing the sufficiency of the program itself; that is, ensuring that all the constituent parts of the program are functioning as intended.[134] Again,

[O]rganizations [are] free to choose their own reasonable means for ensuring that their compliance programs are being followed and for periodically evaluating the effectiveness of those programs. Compliance monitoring and auditing systems should be used to detect organizational violations of law. Differently focused monitoring and auditing practices may be used to assess the effectiveness of an organization's compliance program.[135]

Large and small organizations are expected to employ different monitoring and auditing practices:

In small organizations, periodic evaluations of compliance in the course of day-to-day business operating practices will often be adequate monitoring steps so that further auditing or evaluations will not be needed. In larger organizations, however, separate audits of compliance performance will usually be warranted, with such audits being conducted by internal or external parties who are independent of the managers overseeing the performance under scrutiny.[136]

Subsection (b)(5)(C) relates to reporting systems. The Advisory Group considered it "axiomatic that organizations should have internal reporting

---

131. *Id.* at 74.
132. *Id.* at 76.
133. *See id.*
134. *See id.*
135. *Id.*
136. *Id.* at 77.

mechanisms that actually encourage reporting of suspected wrongdoing,"[137] as "[o]rganizations necessarily must depend in large part on information from employees and agents in order to correct potential or actual wrongdoing within the organization."[138] It is important, the Advisory Group noted, "to encourage employees and agents to utilize an organization's internal reporting mechanism to seek guidance even when they are not sure that a violation of law has occurred." [139]

A vexing issue relating to internal reporting was how to address employees' "fear of retaliation, including retaliation by co-workers,"[140] while preserving the corporation's prerogative to disclose information received through the hotline when legally required to do so. [141] "Once documents and testimony are produced in response to . . . litigation demands," the Advisory Group noted, "maintaining confidentiality as to the identity of the individual who reported certain information is no longer a viable possibility." [142]

> Thus, organizations cannot in good faith promise total confidentiality to their employees and agents when asking them to report suspected wrongdoing. . . . This reality, of course, may well serve to chill the reporting individual's willingness to come forward and prevent the organization from learning facts that would have assisted the organization in preventing and detecting wrongdoing at the earliest possible opportunity.[143]

Ultimately, the Advisory Group recognized the limitations faced by organizations in providing assurances of confidentiality, and therefore the provision gave corporations substantial leeway in striking the right balance:

> An organization . . . might legitimately choose not to assure an employee of confidentiality because, inter alia, the organization might be legally obligated to disclose the employee's report of wrongdoing or the organization might want to preserve the option to report voluntarily to law enforcement agencies the information provided by the individual employee or agent. The Advisory Group therefore concluded that the proper balance between fostering an organization's ability to provide a viable assurance of confidentiality to encourage employee and agent reports of wrongdoing and the organization's need for flexibility in disclosing such reports is best left to the judgment of the individual organization.[144]

>> (6) The organization's program to prevent and detect violations of law shall be promoted and enforced consistently through appropriate *incentives* to perform in accordance with such program and *disciplinary measures* for

---

137. *Id.*
138. *Id.*
139. *Id.* at 83.
140. *Id.* at 78.
141. *Id.* at 81–82.
142. *Id.* at 81.
143. *Id.* at 82.
144. *Id.* at 84.

engaging in violations of law and for failing to take reasonable steps to prevent or detect violations of law.[145]

In proposing this requirement, the Commentary states: "[a]dequate discipline of individuals responsible for an offense is a necessary component of enforcement; however, the form of discipline that will be appropriate will be case specific."[146] Neither the guideline nor the Advisory Group defines "incentives," however, which precede disciplinary measures in subsection (b)(6). The subject of incentivizing compliance with the law and ethical conduct has been the subject of much debate and will be discussed in detail in Part Three.

> (7) After a violation of law has been detected, the organization shall take reasonable steps to respond appropriately to the violation of law and to prevent future similar violations of law, including making any necessary modifications to the organization's program to prevent and detect violations of law.[147]

The Commentary explains that Subsection (b)(7) has two aspects. First, it requires an appropriate response to the particular misconduct that has been detected, which means taking several specific steps:

1) Payment of restitution to identifiable victims;
2) Self-reporting to the authorities; and,
3) Cooperation with authorities in the investigation of the crime and prosecution of responsible individuals.[148]

The second aspect of this provision requires taking steps to "prevent further similar criminal conduct, including assessing the compliance and ethics program and making modifications necessary to ensure the program is effective."[149] Each failure must therefore lead to the improvement of the program.

3. Subsection (c)

(c) In implementing subsection (b), the organization shall periodically assess the risk of criminal conduct and shall take appropriate steps to design, implement, or modify each requirement set forth in subsection (b) to reduce the risk of criminal conduct identified through this process.

Although the Advisory Group concluded that "need for risk assessment in designing and operating such a program [was] implicit"[150] in the original guidelines, it proposed to make this requirement explicit to stress that "[a] detailed risk assessment is required to appropriately *tailor* a compliance program to a

---

145. *Id.* at 86 (emphasis added).
146. FSGO, *supra* note 88, § 8B2.1 cmt. n.5.
147. Advisory Group Report, *supra* note 32, at 87.
148. *See* FSGO, *supra* note 88, § 8B2.1 cmt. N.6.
149. *Id.*
150. Advisory Group Report, *supra* note 32, at 87.

company's business circumstances."[151] Tailoring is a term often used to describe the process of building a "risk based" compliance program. It essentially means allocating the company's compliance resources and designing the program's features to fit the specific type of business engaged in by the organization and the offenses most likely to occur as the result.[152] The Advisory Group noted that subsection (c) addresses two separate aspects of risk assessment and "its relationship to broader features of effective programs to prevent and detect violations of law": [153]

> First, risk assessment . . . should be ongoing. The nature of the legal obligations of an organization and the ways that specific organizational activities interact with those obligations . . . change over time. Periodic reviews of compliance risks . . . will be needed to ensure that a company's present efforts to prevent and detect violations of law are matched to the company's current business activities.
>
> Second, . . . the results of risk assessments should influence the design and implementation of a broad range of features of an effective program. . . . For example, risk assessments identifying an organization's legal obligations and the types of practices that may cause an organization not to meet those obligations can provide valuable information for decisions on compliance program standards and procedures. These assessments may be able to specify actions that employees and other organizational agents should take to ensure compliance with legal requirements. Similarly, risk assessments that identify likely means of violating legal standards in an organization's operating context can help the organization develop training programs for preventing and detecting its most probable forms of unlawful conduct. Additionally, risk assessments identifying a company's law violation risks will help company auditors and compliance program evaluators target the frequency and content of program evaluations in order to make the most effective and efficient use of these studies.[154]

Reflecting these two criteria, the Commentary to subsection (c) requires organizations to periodically perform risk assessments and to specifically take into account (1) the likelihood that a certain criminal conduct may occur (its probability), and (2) the "nature and seriousness" of such conduct (its magnitude). [155] As the Commentary explains:

> For example, an organization that, due to the nature of its business, employs sales personnel who have flexibility to set prices shall establish standards and procedures designed to prevent and detect price-fixing. An organization that, due to the nature of its business, employs sales personnel who have flexibility to represent the material characteristics of a product shall establish standards and procedures designed to prevent and detect fraud.[156]

---

151. *Id.* at 45 (emphasis added).
152. *Id.* at 20.
153. *Id.* at 90.
154. *Id.* at 90–91.
155. *See* FSGO, *supra* note 88, § 8B2.1 cmt. n.7(A).
156. *Id.*

The Advisory Group clarified that organizations are free to use the risk assessment framework of their choice, as long as the process involves scrutiny of the organization's "operating circumstances, legal surroundings, and industry history to gain a practical understanding of the types of unlawful practices that may arise in future organizational activities."[157]

Federal Sentencing Guidelines: Sentencing of Organizations

18 U.S.C. app. § 8B (2012)

§ 8B2.1. Effective Compliance and Ethics Program

(a) To have an effective compliance and ethics program . . . an organization shall—

(1) exercise due diligence to prevent and detect criminal conduct; and

(2) otherwise promote an organizational culture that encourages ethical conduct and a commitment to compliance with the law.

Such compliance and ethics program shall be reasonably designed, implemented, and enforced so that the program is generally effective in preventing and detecting criminal conduct. The failure to prevent or detect the instant offense does not necessarily mean that the program is not generally effective in preventing and detecting criminal conduct.

(b) Due diligence and the promotion of an organizational culture that encourages ethical conduct and a commitment to compliance with the law within the meaning of subsection (a) minimally require the following:

(1) The organization shall establish standards and procedures to prevent and detect criminal conduct.

(2) (A) The organization's governing authority shall be knowledgeable about the content and operation of the compliance and ethics program and shall exercise reasonable oversight with respect to the implementation and effectiveness of the compliance and ethics program.

(B) High-level personnel of the organization shall ensure that the organization has an effective compliance and ethics program, as described in this guideline. Specific individual(s) within high-level personnel shall be assigned overall responsibility for the compliance and ethics program.

(C) Specific individual(s) within the organization shall be delegated day-to-day operational responsibility for the compliance and ethics program. Individual(s) with operational responsibility shall report periodically to high-level personnel and, as appropriate, to the governing authority, or an appropriate subgroup of the governing authority, on the effectiveness of the compliance

---

157. ADVISORY GROUP REPORT, *supra* note 32, at 91 (footnote omitted).

and ethics program. To carry out such operational responsibility, such individual(s) shall be given adequate resources, appropriate authority, and direct access to the governing authority or an appropriate subgroup of the governing authority.

(3) The organization shall use reasonable efforts not to include within the substantial authority personnel of the organization any individual whom the organization knew, or should have known through the exercise of due diligence, has engaged in illegal activities or other conduct inconsistent with an effective compliance and ethics program.

(4) (A) The organization shall take reasonable steps to communicate periodically and in a practical manner its standards and procedures, and other aspects of the compliance and ethics program, to the individuals referred to in subparagraph (B) by conducting effective training programs and otherwise disseminating information appropriate to such individuals' respective roles and responsibilities.

   (B) The individuals referred to in subparagraph (A) are the members of the governing authority, high-level personnel, substantial authority personnel, the organization's employees, and, as appropriate, the organization's agents.

(5) The organization shall take reasonable steps—

   (A) to ensure that the organization's compliance and ethics program is followed, including monitoring and auditing to detect criminal conduct;

   (B) to evaluate periodically the effectiveness of the organization's compliance and ethics program; and

   (C) to have and publicize a system, which may include mechanisms that allow for anonymity or confidentiality, whereby the organization's employees and agents may report or seek guidance regarding potential or actual criminal conduct without fear of retaliation.

(6) The organization's compliance and ethics program shall be promoted and enforced consistently throughout the organization through (A) appropriate incentives to perform in accordance with the compliance and ethics program; and (B) appropriate disciplinary measures for engaging in criminal conduct and for failing to take reasonable steps to prevent or detect criminal conduct.

(7) After criminal conduct has been detected, the organization shall take reasonable steps to respond appropriately to the criminal conduct and to prevent further similar criminal conduct, including making any necessary modifications to the organization's compliance and ethics program.

(c) In implementing subsection (b), the organization shall periodically assess the risk of criminal conduct and shall take appropriate steps to design, implement, or modify each requirement set forth in subsection (b) to reduce the risk of criminal conduct identified through this process.

COMMENTARY

Application Notes:

1. **Definitions**—For the purposes of this guideline:

    "Compliance and ethics program" means a program designed to prevent and detect criminal conduct.

    "Governing authority" means the (A) the Board of Directors; or (B) if the organization does not have a Board of Directors, the highest-level governing body of the organization.

    "High-level personnel of the organization" and *"substantial authority personnel"* have the meaning given those terms in the Commentary to § 8A1.2 (Application Instructions—Organizations).

    "Standards and procedures" means standards of conduct and internal controls that are reasonably capable of reducing the likelihood of criminal conduct.

2. **Factors to Consider in Meeting Requirements of this Guideline. —**

    (A) **In General.**—Each of the requirements set forth in this guideline shall be met by an organization; however, in determining what specific actions are necessary to meet those requirements, factors that shall be considered include: (i) applicable industry practice or the standards called for by any applicable governmental regulation; (ii) the size of the organization; and (iii) similar misconduct.

    (B) **Applicable Governmental Regulation and Industry Practice.**—An organization's failure to incorporate and follow applicable industry practice or the standards called for by any applicable governmental regulation weighs against a finding of an effective compliance and ethics program.

    (C) **The Size of the Organization.—**

    (i) **In General.**—The formality and scope of actions that an organization shall take to meet the requirements of this guideline, including the necessary features of the organization's standards and procedures, depend on the size of the organization.

    (ii) **Large Organizations.**—A large organization generally shall devote more formal operations and greater resources in meeting the requirements of this guideline than shall a small organization. As appropriate, a large organization should encourage all organizations (especially those that have, or seek to have, a business relationship with the large organization) to implement effective compliance and ethics programs.

    (iii) **Small Organizations.**—In meeting the requirements of this guideline, small organizations shall demonstrate the same degree of commitment to ethical conduct and compliance with the law as large organizations. However, a small organization may meet the requirements of this guideline with less formality and fewer resources than would be expected of large organizations. In appropriate circumstances, reliance on existing resources and simple systems can demonstrate a degree of commitment that, for a large organization, would only be demonstrated through more formally planned and implemented systems.

Examples of the informality and use of fewer resources with which a small organization may meet the requirements of this guideline include the following: (I) the governing authority's discharge of its responsibility for oversight of the compliance and ethics program by directly managing the organization's compliance and ethics efforts; (II) training employees through informal staff meetings, and monitoring through regular "walk-around" or continuous observation while managing the organization; (III) using available personnel, rather than employing separate staff, to carry out the compliance and ethics program; and (IV) modeling its own compliance and ethics program on existing, well-regarded compliance and ethics programs and best practices of other similar organizations.

(D) **Recurrence of Similar Misconduct.**—Recurrence of similar misconduct creates doubt regarding whether the organization took reasonable steps to meet the requirements of this guideline. For the purposes of this subparagraph, *"similar misconduct"* has the meaning given that term in Commentary to §8A1.2 (Application Instructions-Organizations).

3. **Application of Subsection (b)(2).**—High-level personnel and substantial authority personnel of the organization shall be knowledgeable about the content and operation of the compliance and ethics program, shall perform their assigned duties consistent with the exercise of due diligence, and shall promote an organizational culture that encourages ethical conduct and a commitment to compliance with the law.

If the specific individual(s) assigned overall responsibility for the compliance and ethics program does not have day-to-day operational responsibility for the program, then the individual(s) with day-to-day operational responsibility for the program typically should, no less than annually, give the governing authority or an appropriate subgroup thereof information on the implementation and effectiveness of the compliance and ethics program.

4. **Application of Subsection (b)(3).**—

(A) **Consistency with Other Law.**—Nothing in subsection (b)(3) is intended to require conduct inconsistent with any Federal, State, or local law, including any law governing employment or hiring practices.

(B) **Implementation.**—In implementing subsection (b)(3), the organization shall hire and promote individuals so as to ensure that all individuals within the high-level personnel and substantial authority personnel of the organization will perform their assigned duties in a manner consistent with the exercise of due diligence and the promotion of an organizational culture that encourages ethical conduct and a commit-ment to compliance with the law under subsection (a). With respect to the hiring or promotion of such individuals, an organization shall consider the relatedness of the individual's illegal activities and other misconduct (*i.e.*, other conduct inconsistent with an effective compli-ance and ethic program) to the specific responsibilities the individual is anticipated to be assigned and other factors such as: (i) the recency of the individual's illegal activities and other misconduct; and (ii) whether the individual has engaged in other such illegal activities and other such misconduct.

5. **Application of Subsection (b)(6).**—Adequate discipline of individuals responsible for an offense is a necessary component of enforcement; how-ever, the form of discipline that will be appropriate will be case specific.

6. **Application of Subsection (b)(7).**—Subsection (b)(7) has two aspects. First, the organization should respond appropriately to the criminal conduct. The organization should take responsible steps, as warranted under the cir-cumstances, to remedy the harm resulting from the criminal conduct. These steps may include, where appropriate, providing restitution to identifiable victims, as well as other forms of remediation. Other reasonable steps to respond appropriately to the criminal conduct may include self-reporting and cooperation with authorities.

   Second, the organization should act appropriately to prevent further similar criminal conduct, including assessing the compliance and ethics pro-gram and making modifications necessary to ensure the program is effec-tive. The steps taken should be consistent with subsections (b)(5) and (c) and may include the use of an outside professional advisor to ensure adequate assessment and implementation of any modifications.

7. **Application of Subsection (c).**—To meet the requirements of subsection (c), an organization shall:

   (A) Assess periodically the risk that criminal conduct will occur, including assessing the following:

       (i) The nature and seriousness of such criminal conduct.

       (ii) The likelihood that certain criminal conduct may occur because of the nature of the organization's business. If, because of the nature of an organization's business, there is a substantial risk that certain types of criminal conduct may occur, the organization shall take reasonable steps to prevent or detect that type of criminal conduct. For example, an organization that, due to the nature of its busi-ness, employs sales personnel who have flexibility to set prices shall establish standards and procedures designed to prevent and detect price-fixing. An organization that, due to the nature of its business, employs sales personnel who have flexibility to represent the mate-rial characteristics of a product shall establish standards and proce-dures designed to prevent and detect fraud.

(iii) The prior history of the organization. The prior history of an organization may indicate types of criminal conduct that it shall take actions to prevent and detect.

(B) Prioritize periodically, as appropriate, the actions taken pursuant to any requirement set forth in subsection (b), in order to focus on preventing and detecting the criminal conduct identified under subparagraph (A) of this note as most serious, and most likely, to occur.

(C) Modify, as appropriate, the actions taken pursuant to any requirement set forth in subsection (b) to reduce the risk of criminal conduct identified under subparagraph (A) of this note as most serious, and most likely, to occur.

Background: This section sets forth the requirements for an effective compliance and ethics program. This section responds to the section 805(a)(5) of the Sarbanes-Oxley Act of 2002, Public Law 107-204, which directed the Commission to review and amend, as appropriate, the guidelines and related policy statements to ensure that the guidelines that apply to organizations in this chapter "are sufficient to deter and punish organizational criminal misconduct."

The requirements set forth in this guideline are intended to achieve reasonable prevention and detection of criminal conduct for which the organization would be vicariously liable. The prior diligence of an organization in seeking to prevent and detect criminal conduct has a direct bearing on the appropriate penalties and probation terms for the organization if it is convicted and sentenced for a criminal offense.

Questions

According to the FSGO, "[t]he failure to prevent or detect [an] offense does not necessarily mean that the program is not generally effective in preventing and detecting criminal conduct." [158]

1) Given that an effective compliance program must "prevent and detect" crime, what is the purpose of this statement?
2) Section 8B2.1 refers to both compliance and ethics. Does it require two separate programs or a single program that addresses both compliance and ethics?
3) What are the duties of the board of directors under § 8B2.1?
4) What are the duties of senior management under § 8B2.1?
5) What types of information flow does § 8B2.1 require?
6) What are the limitations to the FSGO's effectiveness in compelling enterprises to self-police?

---

158. FSGO, *supra* note 88, § 8B2.1(a).

III. Fine Calculation

Chapter 8C of the FSGO sets forth the formula for calculating a fine. Convicted organizations are first divided into two groups: "Criminal purpose organizations" and all other organizations. Criminal purpose organizations are those that operate "primarily for a criminal purpose or primarily by criminal means."[159] These criminal enterprises systematically commit legal violations as part of their normal *modus operandi*, and include, for example, companies operating a fraud scam or habitually committing environmental crimes.[160] For that group, the commission determined that the purpose of the sentence should be incapacitation; that is, setting the penalty at a sufficiently high level "to divest the organization of its assets, if possible."[161]

For all remaining organizations, the guidelines provide a formula for calculating the fine amount. Under this formula, the judge first calculates the "base fine" and then adjusts it by the defendant's "culpability score." To calculate the base fine, the judge first refers to the "Offense Level Fine Table" in § 8B2.4(d) to determine the fine applicable to the defendant's offense level.[162] For example, an offense level 8 corresponds to a fine of $15,000, whereas an offense level 37 corresponds to a fine of $100 million. The offense level fine is then compared to (1) the pecuniary gain derived by the defendant from the offense; and (2) the pecuniary loss caused by the offense. The base fine is the greatest of those three amounts.[163]

"Pecuniary loss" is defined as "the greater of actual loss or intended loss."[164] Actual loss is "the reasonably foreseeable pecuniary harm that resulted from the offense."[165] Intended loss, by contrast, is the "'pecuniary harm that was intended to result from the offense' and includes loss that would have been impossible or unlikely."[166] Intended loss "need not be calculated with precision" so long as it is

---

159. Nagel & Swenson, *supra* note 5, at 232 (quoting U.S. Sentencing Guidelines Manual § 8C1.1 (U.S Sentencing Comm'n 1992)).

160. *Id.* at 232–33.

161. *Id.* at 233 (quoting U.S. Sentencing Guidelines Manual § 8C1.1 (U.S Sentencing Comm'n 1992)). *See also* U.S. Sentencing Comm'n, Primer on Fines Under the Organizational Guidelines 2 (2017) [hereinafter Primer on Organizational Fines], https://www.ussc.gov/sites/default/files/pdf/training/primers/2017_Primer_Organizational_Fines.pdf] ("'Net assets' means the assets remaining after payment of all legitimate claims against assets by known innocent bona fide creditors.").

162. The guidelines do not address fines for offenses "involving environmental pollution, food, drugs, agricultural and consumer products, civil/individual rights, administration of justice . . . or national defense." Primer on Organizational Fines, *supra* note 161, at 3. Fines for those offenses are determined pursuant to § 8C2.10 (Determining the Fine for Other Counts). *Id.*

163. *See* FSGO, *supra* note 88, § 8C2.4(a)(1)–(3). If the organizational defendant is unable to pay the fine called for by § 8C2.7(a), a determination of the fine range is unnecessary since, pursuant to § 8C3.3 (Reduction of Fine Based on Inability to Pay), no fine would be imposed. *See also* Primer on Organizational Guidelines, *supra* note 161, at 3 (citing FSGO, *supra* note 88, § 8C2.2(a)).

164. FSGO, *supra* note 88, § 2B1.1 cmt. N.3(A).

165. *Id.* § 2B1.1 cmt. N.3(A)(i).

166. U.S. Sentencing Comm'n, Office of Gen. Counsel, An Overview of Loss in USSG § 2B.1 2 (2009) [hereinafter Loss Overview] (footnote omitted), https://www.ussc.gov/sites/default/files/pdf/training/online-learning-center/supporting-materials/Loss_Overview_2009_April.pdf.

within "the realm of permissible computations."[167] Judges have discretion to use either the actual or intended loss in their calculation of the base fine.[168]

"Pecuniary gain" means the net profits derived by the defendant as a result of the misconduct.[169] As the Commentary explains:

> Gain can result from either additional revenue or cost savings. For example, an offense involving odometer tampering can produce additional revenue. In such a case, the pecuniary gain is the additional revenue received because the automobiles appeared to have less mileage, *i.e.*, the difference between the price received or expected for the automobiles with the apparent mileage and the fair market value of the automobiles with the actual mileage. An offense involving defense procurement fraud related to defective product testing can produce pecuniary gain resulting from cost savings. In such a case, the pecuniary gain is the amount saved because the product was not tested in the required manner.[170]

"Sentencing judges are cautioned against 'abandoning a loss calculation in favor of a gain amount where a reasonable estimate of the victims' loss is feasible' "[171]—since "[s]ubstituting the gain for the loss . . . 'ordinarily underestimates the loss.' "[172] Thus, pecuniary gain can only be used as an alternative measure of loss when the loss cannot reasonably be determined[173] or "when there is no identifiable loss to the victims."[174]

After calculating the base fine, the culpability score is calculated by taking into account several factors enumerated in the guidelines that measure a corporation's "good citizenship"—that is, the company's "crime-controlling" both before and after the offense was committed.[175] Pre-offense conduct is judged by a single measure: the effectiveness of the defendant's compliance program in preventing and detecting violations of law.[176] "Good citizenship" post-offense turns on how a corporation responds to a violation once it has been discovered. If the corporation "in essence ratified the criminal conduct by obstructing justice,"[177] its culpability score will increase, whereas if the corporation "strongly signaled its intolerance of lawbreaking by voluntarily disclosing the offense [and] fully cooperating with enforcement officials in the investigation,"[178] its score will decrease.

> Assume, for example, that a defendant has committed an offense level 20 crime, which corresponds to an offense level fine of $1 million. Assume further that the defendant derived a net profit of $500,000, and that the offense result in a $2 million loss to the victims. The base fine in that case is $2 million, the greater of the three numbers.

---

167. *Id.* at 3.
168. *Id.* at 1.
169. *See* FSGO, *supra* note 88, § 8A1.2 cmt. n.3(H).
170. *Id.*
171. Loss Overview, *supra* note 166, at 6.
172. *Id.* (footnote omitted).
173. *See id.*
174. *Id.*
175. *See* Nagel & Swenson, *supra* note 5, at 236.
176. *Id.*
177. *Id.* At 237 (footnote omitted).
178. *Id.* (footnotes omitted).

In addition to a corporation's pre- and post-offense conduct, the culpability score considers two additional factors: (1) involvement in or tolerance of the offense by the corporation's senior leadership, and (2) the corporation's prior history of misconduct:

> "Involvement in or Tolerance of Criminal Activity". . . gauges the hierarchical level and degree of discretionary authority of the individuals actually involved in the offense. Generally, the more senior the position, and the greater the degree of total discretion possessed by those involved, the higher the culpability score and potential fine. The impetus for using this factor as a measurement of organizational culpability or just punishment emerged from the debate surrounding vicarious liability. Some questioned the basic premise of vicarious liability and argued that the Guidelines should impose no fine unless senior management was directly implicated in the offense. This argument tracked a proposal in the Model Penal Code that criminal liability generally should not attach to the corporation unless a "high managerial official" was involved. The Commission responded to this argument by recognizing that it is simply beyond the Commission's authority to revisit the doctrine of vicarious liability. The Commission acknowledged, however, that some justification may exist for distinguishing between companies at the sentencing phase based on the level and extent of managerial involvement.[179]

A prior history of misconduct "indicate[s] an ambivalent corporate attitude toward violations of the law under certain circumstances [and is] an indicator of higher culpability."[180] This is not necessarily always the case, however; for example, a large organization with many separate divisions and lines of business may experience isolated misconduct in one division or line of business. Therefore, prior misconduct is only considered relevant when it is "similar" to the offense or occurred within the same "separately managed line of business"[181]—indicating a systemic weakness of the compliance program.

The culpability score corresponds to a "minimum multiplier" and a "maximum multiplier," which can be found in the table in § 8C2.6. Those multipliers are applied to the Base Fine amount to produce a fine range.

> For example, assume that the Base Fine for the loss from a criminal episode is determined to be $10 million. Assume further that the culpability score for the organization is nine: the five points with which the calculation begins, plus five points for the organization's size and level of management participation, and minus one point for acceptance of responsibility. Reference to the multiplier chart at § 8C2.6 indicates that a culpability score of nine means that by multiplying the base fine (here, $10 million) by the culpability multipliers that correspond to the culpability score (here, 1.80 and 3.60), the guideline fine range is between $18 million and $36 million.
>
> . . . If in the hypothetical case, the organization had earned three points for an effective compliance program, its culpability score would have been reduced to six, its multipliers to 1.20 and 2.40, and its final fine range to between $12 million and $24 million. If the organization had self-reported, cooperated, and pleaded guilty, even without an effective compliance program, its culpability score would have been five, its multipliers 1.00 and 2.00, and its fine range between $10 million and $20 million.
>
> *Report of the Advisory Group on the FSGO*[182]

---

179. *Id.* at 238 (footnotes omitted).
180. *Id.* at 239 (footnote omitted).
181. FSGO, *supra* note 88, § 8C2.5(c).
182. Advisory Group Report, *supra* note 32, at 20–21.

Judges normally require a great deal of information to make these complex determinations.[183] This information is compiled in a presentence report prepared by a probation officer after an investigation.[184] In addition, the judge may hold hearings to gather additional evidence and order expert studies.[185]

Hypothetical: Determining a Corporate Sentence Under the Organizational Guidelines

Rosepatch, Inc. ("Rosepatch") is a U.S. corporation that provides civil engineering services and employs 30,000 persons around the world. In 2014, Rosepatch entered into a contract with the government of Senegal in connection with the construction of a dam in the vicinity of a natural preserve and several villages. The contract, valued at $100 million over two years, was completed in 2016.

In April 2016, several months after the dam went into operation, a construction flaw led to the build-up of excessive pressure behind the dam, forcing dam operators to release massive amounts of water, submerging the natural preserve, and inflicting significant damage on nearby villages. An independent study estimated the damage to exceed $1 billion, including loss of revenue from tourism.

Shortly after the disaster, Senegalese authorities discovered that the officials in charge of the dam construction project had received bribes from several multinational corporations involved in the project, including Rosepatch, in exchange for awarding government contracts. Rosepatch was indicted in the United States in December 2016 for violating the Foreign Corrupt Practices Act ("FCPA"), among other U.S. laws, and the case proceeded to trial in 2017.

During the trial, counsel for Rosepatch began negotiations with federal prosecutors regarding a possible plea bargain. The prosecution offered a deal whereby Rosepatch pleaded guilty to one count of violating the FCPA and paid a fine of $150 million.

When defense counsel presented this offer to Rosepatch's CEO, the CEO was surprised, noting that the proposed fine was much bigger than any profits Rosepatch made from the deal. She then asked, "What is the maximum sentence Rosepatch could face if we lose at trial?"

Assume that:

a) For each violation, the FCPA provides that corporations are subject to a fine of up to $2 million; and,

b) Rosepatch's culpability score corresponds to a 1.9 minimum multiplier and a 3.8 maximum multiplier.

What is the answer to the CEO's question?

---

183. *See* Johnson, *supra* note 3, at 644.
184. *See* Fed. R. Crim. P. 329(c)–(d).
185. *See* Fed. R. Crim. P. 32(i); *see also* Johnson, *supra* note 3, at 644–45.

IV. Part 8D: Probation

Since organizations cannot be jailed, the only available punishment against them other than fines and dissolution is probation.[187] Before 1991, federal courts only imposed organizational probation as a means of monitoring the collection of fines and restitution and the completion of community service.[188] Section 8D1.1 of the guidelines significantly expanded the conditions for imposing probation, and it allows the court to exercise continuing jurisdiction over the organization to ensure that it institutes appropriate reforms, including the creation of a compliance program or modification of an existing program. Specifically, § 8D mandates probation for the following reasons:

> Proceeding with a somewhat cautious approach, the Commission recognized that the concept of corporate probation is still relatively new. . . . Accordingly, the Commission identified a number of specific, mandatory grounds for probation, as well as a list of recommended probationary conditions; beyond these directives, the Commission left the courts substantial discretion to impose probation in appropriate circumstances.
>
> *Ilene H. Nagel & Winthrop M. Swenson*[186]

(1) if [the] sentence is necessary to secure payment of restitution (§ 8B1.1), enforce a remedial order (§ 8B1.2), or ensure completion of community service (§ 8B1.3);

(2) if the organization is sentenced to pay a monetary penalty (*e.g.,* restitution, fine, or special assessment), the penalty is not paid in full at the time of sentencing, and restrictions are necessary to safeguard the organization's ability to make payments;

(3) if, at the time of sentencing, (A) the organization (i) has 50 or more employees, or (ii) was otherwise required under law to have an effective compliance and ethics program; and (B) the organization does not have such a program;

(4) if the organization within five years prior to sentencing engaged in similar misconduct, as determined by a prior criminal adjudication, and any part of the misconduct underlying the instant offense occurred after that adjudication;

(5) if an individual within high-level personnel of the organization or the unit of the organization within which the instant offense was committed participated in the misconduct underlying the instant offense and that individual within five years prior to sentencing engaged in similar misconduct, as determined by a prior criminal adjudication, and any part of the misconduct underlying the instant offense occurred after that adjudication;

(6) if such sentence is necessary to ensure that changes are made within the organization to reduce the likelihood of future criminal conduct;

(7) if the sentence imposed upon the organization does not include a fine; or

(8) if necessary to accomplish one or more of the purposes of sentencing set forth in 18 U.S.C. § 3553(a)(2).[189]

---

186. Nagel & Swenson, *supra* note 5, at 234.
187. *See* Gary S. Green, *Organizational Probation Under the Federal Sentencing Guidelines*, 62 Fed. Prob. 25 (1998).
188. *Id.*
189. FSGO, *supra* note 88, § 8D1.1.

Data collected by the Commission between 1991 and 1996 showed that most convicted corporations were sentenced to probation as part of the sentence, and "the most prevalent special condition of probation, given in one in five probation sentences, was an order to develop a compliance program."[190] In ensuring that the organization complies with the probationary terms, including the institution of a compliance program, the "court may impose restrictive probation conditions such as appointment of a special master or creation of auditing and monitoring groups."[191]

---

190. Green, *supra* note 187, at 28.
191. Murphy, *supra* note 25, at 708 (footnotes omitted).

Figure 2-1. Quick Facts About Prosecution of Organizational Offenders

▶ THERE WERE 132 CASES INVOLVING AN ORGANIZATIONAL OFFENDER REPORTED TO THE UNITED STATES SENTENCING COMMISSION IN FISCAL YEAR 2016.[1]

▶ THE MOST COMMON OFFENSES COMMITTED BY ORGANIZATIONAL OFFENDERS WERE FRAUD AND ENVIRONMENTAL CRIMES.

Quick Facts

Organizational Offenders[1]

What is an Organizational Offender?

Chapter Eight of the *Guidelines Manual* governs the sentencing of persons other than individuals. This group includes corporations, partnerships, unions, trusts, pension funds, and non-profits.

For some crimes, Chapter Eight provides a formula to calculate the minimum and maximum fine applicable to a defendant after consideration of several factors pertaining to culpability. In other cases, such as those involving environmental crimes, the *Guidelines Manual* instructs the sentencing judge to "determine the appropriate fine by applying the provisions of 18 U.S.C. §§ 3553 and 3572." Chapter Eight also provides guidance for the imposition of a term of probation or other costs (such as forfeiture) against a defendant.

In fiscal year 2016, there were 132 organizations convicted of a federal offense, a decrease of 27.1% from the previous year.

Organizational Offender Characteristics

- In fiscal year 2016, most organizational offenders were established in the United States (81.8%).

- Most of these organizations were owned by private entities: closely-held or private corporations (63.8%), limited liability companies (20.2%), and sole proprietorships (8.5%). Only one (1.1%) was a publicly-traded corporation.

- The majority of the organizational offenders employed fewer than 50 workers (74.3%). Nearly one-tenth of the organizational offenders employed 1,000 employees or more (7.1%).

- Slightly more than one-fifth (22.0%) of the organizations had a history of misconduct, including previous criminal or civil adjudications against the organization or pending charges.

Offense Characteristics

- The most common offenses committed by organizations were environmental (23.5%), fraud (23.5%), and food and drug (12.9%) crimes.

- Of the types of environmental offenses, 64.5% were water related, 19.4% were wildlife related, 12.9% were hazardous material related, and 3.2% were air related.

- Of the types of fraud offenses, 48.4% were mail or wire fraud, 25.8% were false statements, and 25.8% were other types of fraud (including false claims, health care fraud, and other).

- Over half (53.8%) of all organizational cases involved at least one related individual who was separately convicted in addition to the organization.

Number of Organizational Cases

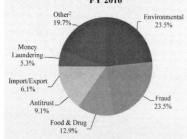

Organizational Cases by Primary Offense FY 2016

Environmental 23.5%
Fraud 23.5%
Food & Drug 12.9%
Antitrust 9.1%
Import/Export 6.1%
Money Laundering 5.3%
Other[2] 19.7%

Types of Fraud Offenses FY 2016

False Statements 25.8%
Mail or Wire 48.4%
False Claims 9.7%
Healthcare 9.7%
Other 6.5%

[1] Only organizations convicted of a federal offense are included in Commission data. The Commission does not collect data on other dispositions, including non-prosecution or deferred prosecution agreements.

[2] The "Other" primary offense category includes: bribery, other, drugs, immigration, racketeering, copyright/trademark infringement, obstruction of justice, tax, firearms, foot stamps, and gambling offenses.

Figure 2-1. *continued*

Quick Facts

Chapter Eight Application

- Over one-third (36.6%) of the 132 organizational offenders were sentenced pursuant to the Chapter Eight fine provisions (found in USSG §§8C2.1-8C2.9). The remaining offenders were sentenced pursuant to §8C2.10.

- Of the 48 organizations sentenced under §§8C2.1-8C2.9:

    - Twenty-one (44.7%) organizations had fewer than ten employees.

    - Two organizations (4.3%) had a prior criminal or administrative violation.

    - No organization had violated a judicial order or condition.

    - One organization (2.1%) obstructed justice.

    - One (2.1%) organization had an effective compliance and ethics program.

    - Twenty-nine (61.7%) of the organizations received an adjustment for cooperating with the investigation and accepting responsibility for the offense.

    - An additional twelve organizations (25.5%) accepted responsibility for the offense but did not cooperate in the investigation.

Punishment

- In fiscal year 2016, 97.7% of all organizational offenders pled guilty.

- Sixty percent (60.6%) of the organizations were sentenced to probation.

- Approximately one-fifth (20.5%) of all organizational offenders were ordered to develop a compliance and ethics program, usually as a condition of probation.

- Of the organizational offenders, 84.1% were sentenced to pay a fine, restitution, or both.

    - A fine was imposed on over three-quarters (78.0%) of these organizations. The median fine amount ordered was $200,000 and the average fine amount was $12,616,605.

    - Slightly more than one-quarter (28.0%) were ordered to pay restitution. The median restitution amount ordered was $174,778 and the average restitution amount was $4,982,025.

- One-quarter (24.2%) of the organizational offenders were ordered to forfeit money. The median forfeiture amount was $737,471 with an average forfeiture amount of $858,548.

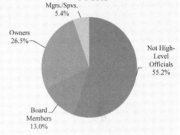
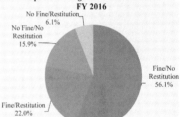
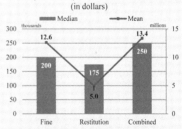

For other Quick Facts publications, visit www.ussc.gov/research/quick-facts.

One Columbus Circle, N.E.
Suite 2-500, South Lobby
Washington, DC 20002-8002
T: (202) 502-4500
F: (202) 502-4699
www.ussc.gov
@theusscgov

SOURCE: United States Sentencing Commission Organizational Datafiles, 2012 through 2016, CORP12-CORP16.

Source: United States Sentencing Commission Organizational Datafiles, 2012 through 2016, CORP12-CORP16.

CHAPTER 3

Prosecutorial Guidelines for Organizations

I. The Thompson Memo and Its Progeny
II. The Yates Memo
III. Current United States Attorneys' Manual
IV. Shepherding Compliance Programs
V. Rewarding Disclosure and Cooperation
VI. Monitoring Future Compliance

Figure 3-1 illustrates the stages of the criminal process, which begins when the government files criminal charges against a defendant in the form of an indictment or information and ends at sentencing when the judge imposes a sentence based on the carrot-and-stick regime of the sentencing guidelines.[1] The central premise of this system is that a corporate defendant can *avoid* harsh punishment if it meets the criteria for mitigation of its sentence.

But the events following the indictment of Arthur Andersen in 2003 took a radically different path: for the venerable accounting firm, punishment came swiftly after indictment in the form of a death sentence—not by the government, but by a far less merciful and just enforcer: the market. To use the Sentencing Commission's own terminology, the mule was beaten to death before it could be offered a carrot.

The demise of Arthur Andersen and other indicted firms shifted the government's focus from sentencing to the earliest stage of the criminal process: the decision to prosecute. Under the principle of Separation of Powers embedded in the U.S. Constitution, "[d]ecisions to initiate charges, or to dismiss charges once brought, 'lie[ ] at the core of the Executive's duty to see to the faithful execution of the laws.'"[2] The executive agency vested with that decision-making power

---

1. An indictment must be filed in cases involving felonies punishable by imprisonment of more than one year, and it must be returned by a grand jury. *See* FED. R. CRIM. P. 7. All other cases may be charged by an information, which is signed by the government's attorney. *See id.* "The indictment or information must be a plain, concise, and definite written statement of the essential facts constituting the offense charged and must be signed by an attorney for the government. . . . For each count, the indictment or information must give the official or customary citation of the statute, rule, regulation, or other provision of law that the defendant is alleged to have violated." FED. R. CRIM. P. 7(c)(1).

2. United States v. Fokker Services B.V., 818 F.3d 733, 741 (D.C. Cir. 2016).

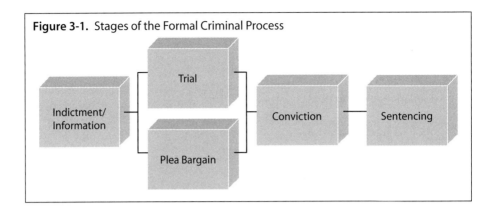

Figure 3-1. Stages of the Formal Criminal Process

is the DOJ. Federal prosecutors employed by the Offices of the United States Attorneys ("USAO"), a division of the DOJ, exercise wide discretion in making charging decisions.

I. The Thompson Memo and Its Progeny

Since 1999, the DOJ has issued broad directives to guide federal prosecutors in exercising their discretion in corporate prosecutions. The first set of such directives was communicated by then-Deputy Attorney General Eric Holder in a memorandum to all Component Heads and United States Attorneys. The "Holder Memo," as it came to be known, was advisory in nature and encouraged federal prosecutors to consider a corporation's cooperation in making charging decisions, including the corporation's willingness to waive attorney-client privilege and produce information that could otherwise be legally withheld.[3]

The Holder Memo gave USAOs two options when confronted with evidence that a corporation had committed a crime: to prosecute or to walk away. Thus, when the DOJ learned in 2002 that Arthur Andersen had shredded millions of documents in connection with the investigation of Enron, it had no choice but to indict—causing the firm's collapse. The resultant losses to Arthur Andersen's innocent shareholders and employees prompted an intense debate within the DOJ regarding whether those two options were sufficient to balance the public interest in deterring corporate crime against the interest in avoiding collateral losses.[4] As then-Attorney General John Ashcroft observed, "[o]ne of the bedrock principles of administering justice in America is to avoid causing serious harm to innocent bystanders . . . [including] the loss of jobs, pensions, and

3. *See* Memorandum from Eric H. Holder, Jr., Deputy Attorney Gen., U.S. Dep't of Justice, Bringing Criminal Charges Against Corporations (June 16, 1999) [hereinafter Holder Memo] (on file with the DOJ).

4. John Ashcroft & John Ratcliffe, *The Recent and Unusual Evolution of an Expanding FCPA*, 26 NOTRE DAME J.L. ETHICS & PUB. POL'Y 25, 31–32 (2012).

investments of innocent parties who were neither aware of, nor played any role in, the criminal conduct."[5] Prosecutors needed a third option—a middle ground between indictment and leaving the crime unpunished—to avoid such collateral harm.[6]

Soon after Arthur Andersen's demise, the DOJ decided to give prosecutors this third option by allowing them to settle with corporations accused of criminal conduct *in lieu* of indictment. Such settlements—referred to as "diversion agreements" because they bypassed the judicial process—had previously been used in cases involving juveniles and drug offenders.[7] In January 2003, Ashcroft's Deputy Attorney General Larry Thompson revised the Holder Memo to invite use of diversion agreements in corporate prosecutions.[8] The revised directives were set forth in a new memo from Thompson to department heads, stating:

> [G]ranting a corporation . . . pretrial diversion may be considered in the course of the government's investigation. In such circumstances, prosecutors should refer to the principles governing non-prosecution agreements generally. . . . These principles permit a non-prosecution agreement in exchange for cooperation when a corporation's "timely cooperation appears to be necessary to the public interest and other means of obtaining the desired cooperation are unavailable or would not be effective."[9]

A pretrial diversion agreement can take two forms: a Deferred Prosecution Agreement ("DPA") or a Non-prosecution Agreement ("NPA"). While DPAs and NPAs are functionally the same, they differ with regard to the filing of criminal charges. "With an NPA, 'formal charges are not filed and the agreement is maintained by the parties rather than being filed with a court.'"[10] By contrast, a DPA is filed in court as part of formal criminal proceedings against a corporation, and the proceedings are then stayed during the probation period.[11]

> DPAs, along with their out-of-court analogues, [NPAs], afford a middle-ground option to the prosecution when, for example, it believes that a criminal conviction may be difficult to obtain or may result in unwanted collateral consequences for a defendant or third parties, but also believes that the defendant should not evade accountability altogether. Both DPAs and NPAs generally include an admitted statement of facts, require adherence to "conditions designed . . . to promote compliance with applicable law and to prevent recidivism," and remain in effect for a period of one to three years. During that period, if the defendant fails to abide by the terms of the agreement, the government can prosecute based

---

5. *Id.* at 31–32.
6. *See id.* at 31.
7. *See id.* (footnote omitted).
8. *See* Memorandum from Larry D. Thompson, Deputy Attorney Gen., U.S. Dep't of Justice, Principles of Federal Prosecution of Business Organizations (Jan. 20, 2003) [hereinafter Thompson Memo] (on file with the DOJ).
9. *Id.* at 6 (citation omitted).
10. United States v. Fokker Services B.V., 818 F.3d 733, 738 (D.C. Cir. 2016).
11. *See, e.g.*, United States v. HSBC, No. 12-CR-763, 2013 WL 3306161 (E.D.N.Y. July 1, 2013).

on the admitted facts. While prosecutors at one time seldom relied on NPAs and DPAs, their use has grown significantly in recent years.[12]

As Lanny Breuer, former Assistant Attorney General and head of the DOJ's Criminal Fraud Division, remarked in his speech at the NYC Bar Association on September 13, 2012:

> A DPA has the same punitive, deterrent, and rehabilitative effect as a guilty plea: when a company enters into a DPA with the government, or an NPA for that matter, it almost always must acknowledge wrongdoing, agree to cooperate with the government's investigation, pay a fine, agree to improve its compliance program, and agree to face prosecution if it fails to satisfy the terms of the agreement. All of these components of DPAs are critical for accountability.[13]

Unlike the Holder Memo that preceded it, the Thompson Memo's directives were mandatory. It required federal prosecutors to consider the following nine factors in deciding whether to charge a corporation, enter into a DPA or NPA, or decline to take any action:

1) Nature and seriousness of the offense;
2) Pervasiveness of misconduct within the corporation;
3) Corporation's history of similar misconduct;
4) Corporation's timely and voluntary disclosure of wrongdoing and its willingness to cooperate in the investigation of its agents, including, if necessary, the waiver of corporate attorney-client and work product privileges;
5) Existence and adequacy of the corporation's compliance program;
6) The corporation's remedial actions, if any;
7) Collateral consequences of a corporate criminal conviction;
8) The adequacy of the prosecution of responsible individuals; and
9) The adequacy of civil and regulatory action.[14]

As with so many other aspects of corporate criminal liability, the Thompson Memo placed policy above legal formalism and altered the relationship between the government and corporations in ways that offended traditional notions of fair play. It effectively gave prosecutors power over the life or death of a corporation—creating a dynamic where, "[o]nly the prosecutor can be merciful, and for his mercy the corporation rationally chooses to cooperate in any way demanded."[15] As such, the Thompson Memo "move[d] the process . . . away from the form the Founders expressly meant it to take—an accusatorial system—and toward something they feared—an inquisitorial system . . . by shifting power

---

12. United States v. Fokker Services B.V., 818 F.3d 733, 738 (D.C. Cir. 2016).
13. Lanny A. Breuer, Assistant Attorney Gen., Speech at the New York City Bar Association, JUSTICE NEWS (Sept. 13, 2012), https://www.justice.gov/opa/speech/assistant-attorney-general-lanny-breuer-speaks-new-york-city-bar-association.
14. *See* Thompson Memo, *supra* note 8, at 3.
15. Preet Bharara, *Corporations Cry Uncle and Their Employees Cry Foul: Rethinking Prosecutorial Pressure on Corporate Defendants*, 44 AM. CRIM. L. REV. 53, 86-87 (2007).

from courts and juries to the Department of Justice and the U.S. Attorneys who work for it."[16]

In a series of decisions that came to be known as the *Stein* cases, Judge Kaplan of the District Court for the Southern District of New York rebuked the Thompson Memo's excessive grant of prosecutorial powers, noting that the government had "let its zeal get in the way of its judgment" and "violated the Constitution it is sworn to defend."[17] The case arose out of a grand jury investigation of the accounting firm KPMG and several of its partners and employees related to fraudulent tax shelters.[18] KPMG eventually entered into a DPA, admitting wrongdoing, paying a $456 million fine, and agreeing to cooperate in the government's investigation and prosecution of its partners and employees.[19]

When the government later indicted the KPMG partners and employees, Judge Kaplan dismissed the indictment against all defendants, ruling that the Thompson Memo had allowed the government to "conduct[] itself in a manner that evidenced a desire to minimize the involvement of defense attorneys,"[20] thereby violating defendants' Sixth Amendment right to counsel. He also held that the government had forced KPMG to give its employees a choice between waiving their Fifth Amendment rights against self-incrimination and getting fired. Judge Kaplan explained:

> Many companies faced with allegations of wrongdoing are under intense pressure to avoid indictment, as an indictment—especially of a financial services firm—threatens to destroy the business regardless of whether the firm ultimately is convicted or acquitted. That is precisely what happened to Arthur Andersen & Co., one of the world's largest accounting firms, which collapsed almost immediately after it was indicted—and the Supreme Court's eventual reversal of its conviction did not undo the damage. So any entity facing such catastrophic consequences must do whatever it can to avoid indictment.
>
> The DOJ and other federal agencies have capitalized on this, in part by altering the manner in which suspected corporate crime has been investigated, prosecuted, and, when proven, punished. The Thompson Memorandum is a part of this change. In cases involving vulnerable companies, the pressure exerted by it and by the prosecutors who apply it inevitably sets in motion precisely what occurred here—the exertion of enormous economic power by the employer upon its employees to sacrifice their constitutional rights.
>
> In this case, the pressure that was exerted on the Moving Defendants was a product of intentional government action. The government brandished a big stick—it threatened to indict KPMG. And it held out a very large carrot. It offered KPMG the hope of avoiding the fate of Arthur Andersen if KPMG could deliver to the USAO employees who would talk, notwithstanding their constitutional right to remain silent, and strip those employees of economic means of defending themselves. In two instances, that pressure resulted in statements that

---

16. Christopher A. Wray & Robert K. Hur, *Corporate Criminal Prosecution in a Post-Enron World: The Thompson Memo in Theory and Practice*, 43 Am. Crim. L. Rev. 1095, 1095 (2006) (footnote omitted).

17. United States v. Stein, 435 F.Supp.2d 330, 336 (S.D.N.Y 2006).

18. *See id.* at 338.

19. *See id.* at 349.

20. *Id.* at 353.

otherwise would not have been made. In seven, the evidence does not warrant that conclusion. The coerced statements and their fruits must be suppressed.

It is no answer for the government to say that these aspects of the Thompson Memorandum are needed to fight corporate crime. Those responsible should be prosecuted and, if convicted, punished. But the end does not justify the means.[21]

Judge Kaplan's decision was affirmed by the Second Circuit,[22] prompting the DOJ to revise its directives several times to address the constitutional issues raised in the *Stein* cases. The most controversial of these issues has revolved around demands by prosecutors that the corporation turn over privileged materials as part of its cooperation with the government. Following *Stein*, two so-called DAG Memos (McCallum and McNulty) attempted to resolve this issue by restricting the right of prosecutors to demand privileged information. But criticism continued.[23]

Finally, in 2008, the Filip Memo authored by then Deputy Attorney General Mark Filip prohibited prosecutors from demanding privileged information as a pre-condition for leniency. The Filip Memo directed prosecutors to focus on whether the corporate defendant had disclosed material facts regarding the underlying conduct and away from the waiver of privilege.[24] It did, however, allow defendants to voluntarily disclose and receive credit for factually relevant information that could otherwise be withheld as privileged.[25]

Notes and Questions

As discussed, after a DPA is negotiated, it is filed in the district court along with the indictment, but the process is stayed pending a defendant's performance of the terms of the DPA. Can a court presiding over such a case deny the parties' request for a stay on the ground that it disapproves of the terms of the DPA—for example, because the punishment meted out to the defendant is either too lenient or too harsh?

The issue came before the District of Columbia Circuit in 2016 in *United States v. Fokker Services B.V.*[26] The district court had disapproved the DPA—not because of prosecutorial overreach, as in the *Stein* cases—but the opposite: The court had deemed it too lenient on the corporate defendant. The appellate court's reversal of the district court's decision further consolidated prosecutorial power by rendering DPAs effectively unreviewable.

---

21. United States v. Stein, 440 F.Supp.2d 315, 338 (S.D.N.Y. 2006).

22. The Second Circuit affirmed Judge Kaplan's ruling on Sixth Amendment grounds and did not reach Judge Kaplan's ruling on the government's violation of defendants' Fifth Amendment rights. *See* United States v. Stein, 541 F.3d 130 (2nd Cir. 2008).

23. *See* Memorandum from Robert D. McCallum, Jr., Deputy Attorney Gen., U.S. Dep't of Justice, Principles of Federal Prosecution of Business Organizations (Oct. 21, 2005) (on file with the DOJ); Memorandum from Paul J. McNulty, Deputy Attorney Gen., U.S. Dep't of Justice, Principles of Federal Prosecution of Business Organizations (Dec. 12, 2006), https://www.justice.gov/sites/default/files/dag/legacy/2007/07/05/mcnulty_memo.pdf.

24. *See* Memorandum from Mark Filip, Deputy Attorney Gen., U.S. Dep't of Justice, Principles of Federal Prosecution of Business Organizations (Aug. 28, 2008), https://www.justice.gov/sites/default/files/dag/legacy/2008/11/03/dag-memo-08282008.pdf.

25. *See id.*

26. *See* United States v. Fokker Services B.V., 818 F.3d 733 (D.C. Cir. 2016).

United States v. Fokker Services B.V.

United States Court of Appeals, District of Columbia 818 F.3d 733 (2016)

OPINION

S<small>RINIVASAN</small>, Circuit Judge:

The Constitution allocates primacy in criminal charging decisions to the Executive Branch. The Executive's charging authority embraces decisions about whether to initiate charges, whom to prosecute, which charges to bring, and whether to dismiss charges once brought. It has long been settled that the Judiciary generally lacks authority to second-guess those Executive determinations, much less to impose its own charging preferences. The courts instead take the prosecution's charging decisions largely as a given, and assume a more active role in administering adjudication of a defendant's guilt and determining the appropriate sentence.

In certain situations, rather than choose between the opposing poles of pursuing a criminal conviction or forgoing any criminal charges altogether, the Executive may conclude that the public interest warrants the intermediate option of a deferred prosecution agreement (DPA). Under a DPA, the government formally initiates prosecution but agrees to dismiss all charges if the defendant abides by negotiated conditions over a prescribed period of time. Adherence to the conditions enables the defendant to demonstrate compliance with the law. If the defendant fails to satisfy the conditions, the government can then pursue the charges based on facts admitted in the agreement.

This case arises from the interplay between the operation of a DPA and the running of time limitations under the Speedy Trial Act. Because a DPA involves the formal initiation of criminal charges, the agreement triggers the Speedy Trial Act's time limits for the commencement of a criminal trial. In order to enable the government to assess the defendant's satisfaction of the DPA's conditions over the time period of the agreement—with an eye towards potential dismissal of the charges—the Speedy Trial Act specifically allows for a court to suspend the running of the time within which to commence a trial for any period during which the government defers prosecution under a DPA.

In this case, appellant Fokker Services voluntarily disclosed its potential violation of federal sanctions and export control laws. After extensive negotiations, the company and the government entered into an 18–month DPA, during which Fokker would continue cooperation with federal authorities and implementation of a substantial compliance program. In accordance with the DPA, the government filed criminal charges against the company, together with a joint motion to suspend the running of time under the Speedy Trial Act pending assessment of the company's adherence to the agreement's conditions. The district court denied the motion because, in the court's view, the prosecution had been too lenient in agreeing to, and structuring, the DPA. Among other objections, the court disagreed with prosecutors' decision to forgo bringing any criminal charges against individual company officers.

. . . .

In vacating the district court order, we have no occasion to disagree (or agree) with that court's concerns about the government's charging decisions in this case. Rather, the fundamental point is that those determinations are for the Executive—not the courts—to make. We therefore grant the government's petition for a writ of mandamus and remand for further proceedings consistent with this opinion.

I.

A.

The Speedy Trial Act establishes time limits for the completion of various stages of a criminal prosecution. *See* 18 U.S.C. §§ 3161–3174. For instance, the Act requires the commencement of trial within seventy days of the filing of an information or indictment by the government. *Id.* § 3161(c)(1). The Act also excludes various pretrial periods from the running of that seventy-day time clock. Of particular relevance, the Act excludes "[a]ny period of delay during which prosecution is deferred by the attorney for the Government pursuant to written agreement with the defendant, with the approval of the court, for the purpose of allowing the defendant to demonstrate his good conduct." *Id.* § 3161(h)(2).

That exemption exists to enable prosecutors to resolve cases through DPAs. DPAs, along with their out-of-court analogues, non-prosecution agreements (NPAs), afford a middle-ground option to the prosecution when, for example, it believes that a criminal conviction may be difficult to obtain or may result in unwanted collateral consequences for a defendant or third parties, but also believes that the defendant should not evade accountability altogether. Both DPAs and NPAs generally include an admitted statement of facts, require adherence to "conditions designed . . . to promote compliance with applicable law and to prevent recidivism," and remain in effect for a period of one to three years. U.S. Attorney's Manual § 9–28.1000 (2015). During that period, if the defendant fails to abide by the terms of the agreement, the government can prosecute based on the admitted facts. While prosecutors at one time seldom relied on NPAs and DPAs, their use has grown significantly in recent years.

DPAs differ from NPAs primarily with regard to the filing of criminal charges. With an NPA, "formal charges are not filed and the agreement is maintained by the parties rather than being filed with a court." Craig S. Morford, *Selection and Use of Monitors in Deferred Prosecution Agreements and Non–Prosecution Agreements with Corporations,* at 1 n. 2 (Mar. 7, 2008). A DPA, by contrast, "is typically predicated upon the filing of a formal charging document by the government." *Id.*

For that reason, a DPA's viability depends on the specific exclusion of time for such agreements set forth in the Speedy Trial Act, 18 U.S.C. § 3161(h)(2). The filing of an information or indictment would ordinarily trigger the Act's seventy-day clock within which trial must commence. *See id.* § 3161(c)(1). But in the case of a DPA, if the defendant were to fulfill the agreement's conditions, the prosecution would move to dismiss all charges with prejudice at the end of the specified time period, ordinarily one to three years. Without the statutory exclusion of time for DPAs provided in § 3161(h)(2), the government would relinquish its ability to prosecute based on the conceded facts if the defendant were to violate the agreement after seventy days. That would largely eliminate the leverage that engenders the defendant's compliance with a DPA's conditions. The statutory exclusion of time for DPAs therefore is essential to the agreements' effective operation.

B.

Fokker Services, a Dutch aerospace services company, provides technical and logistical support to owners of aircraft manufactured by its predecessor company. In 2010, Fokker voluntarily disclosed to the United States Departments of Treasury and Commerce that it had potentially violated federal sanctions and export control laws concerning Iran, Sudan, and Burma. At the time Fokker came forward, no government agency had initiated any investigation focused on the company.

Over the course of the next four years, Fokker cooperated in the wide-ranging investigation conducted by federal authorities. The company facilitated interviews of relevant witnesses, expedited the government's requests to Dutch authorities for documents under the Mutual Legal Assistance Treaty, and initiated its own internal investigation. Fokker's internal investigation revealed that, from 2005 to 2010, the company had participated in 1,147 illicit transactions through which it earned some $21 million in gross revenue. The company instituted remedial measures to improve its sanctions compliance program, adopting a set of procedures to track parts and bolstering its employee training requirements. It also fired its president and demoted or reassigned other employees who had been involved in the violations. The company's compliance efforts have been described by government officials as "a model to be followed by other corporations." Gov't Supp. Mem. in Support of DPA Reached with Fokker Services, B.V., at 15.

In light of Fokker's cooperation, remediation efforts, and other mitigating factors, federal agencies negotiated a global settlement with the company. The settlement included, as an integral component, an 18–month DPA. During the DPA's 18–month period, Fokker was to: continue full cooperation with the government, implement its new compliance policy, and pay fines and penalties totaling $21 million (a sum equaling the gross revenues gained by the company from the illicit transactions). Fokker also accepted responsibility for the acts described in the stipulated factual statement accompanying the DPA.

On June 5, 2014, pursuant to the agreement, the government filed with the district court a one-count information against Fokker, together with the DPA. The information charged Fokker with conspiracy to violate the International Emergency Economic Powers Act. *See* 18 U.S.C. § 371; 50 U.S.C. § 1705. The same day, the government and Fokker filed a joint motion for the exclusion of time under the Speedy Trial Act, in order to "allow [the company] to demonstrate its good conduct and implement certain remedial measures." Joint Consent Motion for Exclusion of Time Under the Speedy Trial Act, at 1.

The district court then held a series of status conferences, during which it repeatedly emphasized its concerns about the absence of any criminal prosecution of individual company officers. Tr. of Status Conference (June 25, 2014), at 4; Tr. of Status Conference (July 9, 2014), at 5. The court requested several additional written submissions from the government. The government was asked to explain why the interests of justice supported the court's approval of the deal embodied by the DPA, and also to address whether Fokker's initial disclosures to the government had in fact been voluntary. *See* Tr. of Status Conference (June 25, 2014), at 3–4; Tr. of Status Conference (July 9, 2014), at 5–6. In response, the government described why the "proposed resolution with Fokker Services is fair and is an appropriate exercise of the government's discretion," Gov't Mem. in Support of DPA Reached with Fokker Services, B.V., at 2, and affirmed the absence of any indication "that Fokker Services was motivated to make its disclosures out of fear about a nonexistent U.S. government investigation," Gov't Status Report, at 15. The district court later expressed that it might still reject the DPA because it was "too good a deal for the defendant." Tr. of Status Conference (Oct. 29, 2014), at 4.

On February 5, 2015, the district court denied the joint motion for the exclusion of time. In explaining the reasons for its decision, the court criticized the government for failing to prosecute any "individuals . . . for their conduct." *United States v. Fokker Services, B.V.*, 79 F.Supp.3d 160, 166 (D.D.C.2015). According to the court, approval of an agreement in which the defendant had been "prosecuted so anemically for engaging in such egregious conduct for such a sustained period of time and for the benefit of one of our country's worst enemies" would "promote disrespect for the law." *Id.* at 167. The court further noted that certain employees had been permitted to remain with the company; that the DPA contained no requirement for an independent monitor; and that the amount of the fine failed to exceed the revenues Fokker gained from the illegal transactions. *Id.* at 166. Based on those considerations, the court rejected the DPA as an "[in]appropriate exercise of prosecutorial discretion." *Id.* at 167.

The district court's order marks the first time any federal court has denied a joint request by the parties to exclude time pursuant to a DPA. Both parties filed a timely notice of appeal. Because both parties seek to overturn the district court's denial of their joint motion to exclude time, we appointed an amicus curiae to present arguments defending the district court's action.

II.

Although we face a threshold question concerning our jurisdiction to review the district court's interlocutory order, our assessment of the jurisdictional issue is substantially informed by our consideration of the merits of the parties' challenge to the district court's action. Consequently, in accordance with our approach in parallel circumstances, *see In re Kellogg Brown & Root, Inc.*, 756 F.3d 754 (D.C.Cir.2014), we first consider whether the district court legally erred in its denial of the joint motion to exclude time pursuant to the DPA. We conclude that it did.

By rejecting the DPA based primarily on concerns about the prosecution's charging choices, the district court exceeded its authority under the Speedy Trial Act. The Act excludes any period of time "during which prosecution is deferred by the attorney for the Government pursuant to written agreement with the defendant, with the approval of the court, for the purpose of allowing the defendant to demonstrate his good conduct." 18 U.S.C. § 3161(h)(2). While the exclusion of time is subject to "the approval of the court," there is no ground for reading that provision to confer free-ranging authority in district courts to scrutinize the prosecution's discretionary charging decisions. Rather, we read the statute against the background of settled constitutional understandings under which authority over criminal charging decisions resides fundamentally with the Executive, without the involvement of—and without oversight power in—the Judiciary. So understood, the statute's "approval of the court" requirement did not empower the district court to disapprove the DPA based on the court's view that the prosecution had been too lenient.

A.

The Executive's primacy in criminal charging decisions is long settled. That authority stems from the Constitution's delegation of "take Care" duties, U.S. Const. art. II, § 3, and the pardon power, *id.* § 2, to the Executive Branch. *See United States v. Armstrong,* 517 U.S. 456, 464, 116 S.Ct. 1480, 134 L.Ed.2d 687 (1996); *In re Aiken Cnty.,* 725 F.3d 255, 262–63 (D.C.Cir.2013). Decisions to initiate charges, or to dismiss charges once brought, "lie[ ] at the core of the Executive's duty to see to the faithful execution of the laws." *Cmty. for Creative Non–Violence v. Pierce,* 786 F.2d 1199, 1201 (D.C.Cir.1986). The Supreme Court thus has repeatedly emphasized that "[w]hether to prosecute and what charge to file or bring before a grand jury are decisions that generally rest in the prosecutor's discretion." *United States v. Batchelder,* 442 U.S. 114, 124, 99 S.Ct. 2198, 60 L.Ed.2d 755 (1979); *see Bordenkircher v. Hayes,* 434 U.S. 357, 364, 98 S.Ct. 663, 54 L.Ed.2d 604 (1978).

Correspondingly, "judicial authority is . . . at its most limited" when reviewing the Executive's exercise of discretion over charging determinations. *Pierce,* 786 F.2d at 1201; *see ICC v. Bhd. of Locomotive Eng'rs,* 482 U.S. 270, 283, 107 S.Ct. 2360, 96 L.Ed.2d 222 (1987). The decision whether to prosecute turns on factors such as "the strength of the case, the prosecution's general deterrence value, the [g]overnment's enforcement priorities, and the case's relationship to the [g]overnment's overall enforcement plan." *Wayte v. United States,* 470 U.S. 598, 607, 105 S.Ct. 1524, 84 L.Ed.2d 547 (1985). The Executive routinely undertakes those assessments and is well equipped to do so. By contrast, the Judiciary, as the Supreme Court has explained, generally is not "competent to undertake" that sort of inquiry. *Id.* Indeed, "[f]ew subjects are less adapted to judicial review than the exercise by the Executive of his discretion in deciding when and whether to institute criminal proceedings, or what precise charge shall be made, or whether to dismiss a proceeding once brought." *Newman v. United States,* 382 F.2d 479, 480 (D.C.Cir.1967). "Judicial supervision in this area" would also "entail[ ] systemic costs." *Wayte,*

470 U.S. at 608, 105 S.Ct. 1524. It could "chill law enforcement," cause delay, and "impair the performance of a core executive constitutional function." *Armstrong,* 517 U.S. at 465, 116 S.Ct. 1480 (quotation omitted). As a result, "the presumption of regularity" applies to "prosecutorial decisions and, in the absence of clear evidence to the contrary, courts presume that [prosecutors] have properly discharged their official duties." *Id.* at 464, 116 S.Ct. 1480 (internal quotation marks, quotation, and alterations omitted).

B.

Those settled principles counsel against interpreting statutes and rules in a manner that would impinge on the Executive's constitutionally rooted primacy over criminal charging decisions. Of particular salience, Rule 48(a) of the Federal Rules of Criminal Procedure requires a prosecutor to obtain "leave of court" before dismissing charges against a criminal defendant. Fed.R.Crim.P. 48(a). That language could conceivably be read to allow for considerable judicial involvement in the determination to dismiss criminal charges. But decisions to dismiss pending criminal charges—no less than decisions to initiate charges and to identify which charges to bring—lie squarely within the ken of prosecutorial discretion. *See e.g., Newman,* 382 F.2d at 480. To that end, the Supreme Court has declined to construe Rule 48(a)'s "leave of court" requirement to confer any substantial role for courts in the determination whether to dismiss charges. Rather, the "principal object of the 'leave of court' requirement" has been understood to be a narrow one—"to protect a defendant against prosecutorial harassment . . . when the [g]overnment moves to dismiss an indictment over the defendant's objection." *Rinaldi v. United States,* 434 U.S. 22, 29 n. 15, 98 S.Ct. 81, 54 L.Ed.2d 207 (1977). A court thus reviews the prosecution's motion under Rule 48(a) primarily to guard against the prospect that dismissal is part of a scheme of "prosecutorial harassment" of the defendant through repeated efforts to bring—and then dismiss—charges. *Id.*

So understood, the "leave of court" authority gives no power to a district court to deny a prosecutor's Rule 48(a) motion to dismiss charges based on a disagreement with the prosecution's exercise of charging authority. For instance, a court cannot deny leave of court because of a view that the defendant should stand trial notwithstanding the prosecution's desire to dismiss the charges, or a view that any remaining charges fail adequately to redress the gravity of the defendant's alleged conduct. *See In re United States,* 345 F.3d 450, 453 (7th Cir.2003). The authority to make such determinations remains with the Executive.

. . . [T]he context of a DPA, like that of Rule 48(a), concerns the prosecution's core prerogative to dismiss criminal charges. While dismissal under a DPA follows from the defendant's adherence to agreed-upon conditions over a specified period, the decision to seek dismissal pursuant to a DPA—as under Rule 48(a)—ultimately stems from a conclusion that additional prosecution or punishment would not serve the public interest. Dismissal in either situation thereby fulfills the Executive's duty under Article II to see that the laws are faithfully executed. *See Pierce,* 786 F.2d at 1201.

. . . As with conventional charging decisions, a DPA's provisions manifest the Executive's consideration of factors such as the strength of the government's evidence, the deterrence value of a prosecution, and the enforcement priorities of an agency, subjects that are ill-suited to substantial judicial oversight. *Id.*

To be sure, the criminal charges filed as part of a DPA remain on the court's docket throughout the time of the agreement (i.e., pending assessment of whether the defendant has satisfied the agreement's conditions, upon which the prosecution seeks dismissal of the charges). . . . For instance, defendants who violate the conditions of their DPA face no court-ordered repercussions. Rather, the prosecution—and the prosecution alone—monitors a defendant's compliance with the agreement's conditions and determines whether the defendant's conduct warrants dismissal of the pending charges. . . .

. . . .

The Senate Committee Report accompanying the Speedy Trial Act reinforces that circumscribed understanding of a district court's "approval" authority under § 3161(h)(2). The report describes the phrase, "with the approval of the court," as designed to "assure[ ] that the court will be involved in the decision to divert and that the procedure will not be used by prosecutors and defense counsel to avoid the speedy trial time limits." S.Rep. No. 93–1021, at 37 (1974). That statement suggests that the judicial-approval requirement was not intended to impinge on the Executive's traditional independence over charging decisions. Rather, the requirement enables courts to assure that a DPA does not exist merely to allow evasion of speedy trial time limits, but instead serves the bona fide purpose of confirming a defendant's good conduct and compliance with law. The Senate Committee Report further describes § 3161(h)(2) as generally intended to "encourage the current trend among United States attorneys" of holding criminal charges in abeyance while defendants participate in rehabilitation programs. *Id.* at 36. Interpreting § 3161(h)(2) to empower courts to scrutinize the prosecution's underlying charging decisions would tend to discourage—not encourage—the prosecution's use of DPAs, contradicting the provision's apparent overarching object.

D.

In defending the notion that § 3161(h)(2)'s "approval of the court" language gives district courts substantial authority to second-guess the prosecution's charging decisions, amicus seeks to analogize a court's review of a DPA under § 3161(h)(2) to a court's review of a proposed plea agreement under Rule 11 of the Federal Rules of Criminal Procedure. That argument fails.

To begin with, even in the context of reviewing a proposed plea agreement under Rule 11, a district court lacks authority to reject a proposed agreement based on mere disagreement with a prosecutor's underlying charging decisions. Rule 11 states that a district court may "accept the agreement, reject it, or defer a decision until the court has reviewed the presentence report." Fed.R.Crim.P. 11(c)(3)(A). Although "district courts must exercise discretion in deciding whether to accept or reject a guilty plea, that discretion is not unfettered." *United States v. Maddox,*

48 F.3d 555, 556 (D.C.Cir.1995). In particular, we have explained, "trial judges are not free to withhold approval of guilty pleas . . . merely because their conception of the public interest differs from that of the prosecuting attorney." *United States v. Ammidown*, 497 F.2d 615, 622 (D.C.Cir.1973).

In addition, a district court's authority to "accept" or "reject" a proposed plea agreement under Rule 11 is rooted in the Judiciary's traditional power over criminal *sentencing,* as the Rule itself indicates in permitting the court to "defer a decision until the court has reviewed the presentence report." Fed.R.Crim.P. 11(c)(3)(A). Plea agreements can take roughly two forms: (i) charge bargains, in which a defendant agrees to plead guilty to certain charges in exchange for the dismissal of other charges; and (ii) sentence bargains, in which the defendant agrees to plead guilty to a particular charge after the parties agree upon a sentence, which the prosecution then recommends to the sentencing court. *See United States v. Robertson,* 45 F.3d 1423, 1437 (10th Cir.1995). In light of the Executive's traditional power over charging decisions and the Judiciary's traditional authority over sentencing decisions, *see Ammidown,* 497 F.2d at 619, some of our sister circuits have concluded that district courts have more limited authority to reject charge bargains than sentence bargains. *See Robertson,* 45 F.3d at 1439; *In re Vasquez–Ramirez,* 443 F.3d 692, 697–98 (9th Cir.2006). Regardless, even in the case of a charge bargain, the court reviews the defendant's admitted conduct and enters a judgment of *conviction,* which in turn carries immediate sentencing implications.

The context of a DPA is markedly different. Unlike a plea agreement—and more like a dismissal under Rule 48(a)—a DPA involves no formal judicial action imposing or adopting its terms. Whereas a district court enters a judgment of conviction and then imposes a sentence in the case of a plea agreement, the court takes no such actions in the case of a DPA. Rather, the entire object of a DPA is to enable the defendant to *avoid* criminal conviction and sentence by demonstrating good conduct and compliance with the law. And a DPA's provisions are agreed to by the parties, not the court, with no occasion for the court to adopt the agreement's terms as its own. The court never exercises its coercive power by entering a judgment of conviction or imposing a sentence. It instead merely approves the prosecution's judgment that further pursuit of criminal charges is unwarranted, as it does when it approves a prosecutor's motion to dismiss charges under Rule 48(a). And as is the case when confronted with a motion to dismiss charges under Rule 48(a), a district court lacks authority to disapprove a DPA under § 3161(h)(2) on the ground that the prosecution has been too lenient in its exercise of charging discretion.

E.

Judged by those principles, the district court in this case erred in denying the parties' motion for exclusion of time under § 3161(h)(2). There is no indication that the parties entered into the DPA to evade speedy trial limits rather than to enable Fokker to demonstrate its good conduct and compliance with law. Rather, the district court denied the exclusion of time based on its view that the prosecution should have brought different charges or sought different remedies. In doing so, the court exceeded its authority under § 3161(h)(2).

From the first status conference concerning the DPA, the district court repeatedly criticized the government for failing to bring charges against individual company officers. *See Fokker Services, B.V.,* 79 F.Supp.3d at 166; Tr. of Status Conference (June 25, 2014), at 4; Tr. of Status Conference (July 9, 2014), at 5. Noting its belief that illegal conduct had been "orchestrated at the highest levels of the company," 79 F.Supp.3d at 166, and unpersuaded by the government's efforts to ground its charging decisions in traditional prosecutorial considerations such as the strength of the evidence and the value of pursuing of different charges, *e.g.,* Gov't Mem. in Support of DPA Reached with Fokker Services, B.V., at 18–19, the district court questioned why no individuals would be held separately accountable. 79 F.Supp.3d at 166. The court also faulted the government for "not requiring Fokker Services to pay as its fine a penny more than the $21 million in revenue it collected from its illegal transactions." *Id.* In addition, the court thought the prosecution should have required an independent monitor as part of the DPA's terms. *See id.* The district court denied the motion for the exclusion of time for those reasons.

Even if the district court's criticisms of the prosecution's exercise of charging authority were entirely meritorious—an issue we have no occasion to address— the court should not have "assume[d] the role of Attorney General," *Microsoft,* 56 F.3d at 1462. Rather, the court should have confined its inquiry to examining whether the DPA served the purpose of allowing Fokker to demonstrate its good conduct, as contemplated by § 3161(h)(2). There is no reason to question the DPA's bona fides in that regard, *see* Deferred Prosecution Agreement, at 4–7; Gov't Supp. Mem. in Support of DPA Reached with Fokker Services, B.V., at 15–16, and the district court made no suggestion otherwise. And insofar as a court has authority to reject a DPA if it contains illegal or unethical provisions, *see United States v. Saena Tech Corp.,* —— F.Supp.3d ——, ——, 2015 WL 6406266, at *17–19 (D.D.C. Oct. 21, 2015); *United States v. HSBC Bank USA, N.A.,* 2013 WL 3306161, at *7 (E.D.N.Y. July 1, 2013), the district court again made no such suggestion here. The court instead denied the exclusion of time under § 3161(h)(2) based on a belief that the prosecution had been unduly lenient in its charging decisions and in the conditions agreed to in the DPA. The court significantly overstepped its authority in doing so.

. . . .

For the foregoing reasons, we vacate the district court's order and remand for further proceedings consistent with this opinion.

Notes and Questions

DPAs have in some ways succeeded in accomplishing what the FSGO could not: inducing multinational enterprises—both U.S. and foreign—to undertake wide-scale reforms aimed at self-policing through compliance and ethics programs.

But, DPAs are entirely based on the premise that the normal criminal process is not available for corporations because they are "eggshell defendants" that would break in the process. Critics of DPAs refer to this premise as the "too big to jail effect" and view it as an excuse to protect large business enterprises.[27] Perhaps in response to this criticism, the DOJ has begun to alter its assumption that corporations are too fragile to be criminally charged.

Since 2014, the DOJ has obtained guilty pleas from several of the world's largest financial institutions—marking the first time since 1989 that large financial institutions have pled guilty to crimes.[28] In May 2014, Credit Suisse pled guilty to conspiracy and aiding and abetting U.S. taxpayers in filing false returns.[29] Then, just a few months later, BNP Paribas—France's largest private bank—pled guilty to crimes involving sanctions violations and agreed to pay almost $9 billion in fines.[30] In May 2015, five more major global banks—Citicorp, JPMorgan Chase & Co., Barclays PLC, The Royal Bank of Scotland plc, and UBS AG—pled guilty to crimes including conspiring to manipulate currency prices and agreed to pay fines in excess of $2.5 billion.[31] Yet, none of those institutions collapsed following their guilty pleas.

For additional information on the current state of federal prosecution of banks, *see* Brandon L. Garrett, *The Rise of Bank Prosecutions*, 126 YALE L. J. F. 33 (2016).

1) Following *Fokker Services*, are there any circumstances under which a court can reject a DPA?
2) As the opinion notes, the Speedy Trial Act gives the court authority to "approve" the DPA. Did the opinion effectively nullify that authority?
3) While criminal proceedings are held in abeyance under the Speedy Trial Act, what is the scope of the court's authority to monitor the defendant's adherence to the terms of the DPA? What is the scope of the prosecutor's authority to monitor such compliance?
4) What is the likely impact of *Fokker Services* on the development of corporate compliance programs?

---

27. *See* Court E. Golumbic & Albert D. Lichy, *The "Too Big to Jail" Effect and the Impact on the Justice Department's Corporate Charging Policy*, 65 Hastings L.J. 1293, 1337–40 (2014) (footnotes omitted).

28. *Id.* at 1337–38 (footnotes omitted).

29. Press Release, U.S. Dep't. of Justice, Credit Suisse Pleads Guilty to Conspiracy to Aid and Assist U.S. Taxpayers in Filing False Returns (May 19, 2014), https://www.justice.gov/opa/pr/credit-suisse-pleads-guilty-conspiracy-aid-and-assist-us-taxpayers-filing-false-returns.

30. Press Release, U.S. Dep't. of Justice, BNP Paribas Pleads Guilty to Conspiring to Violate U.S. Economic Sanctions in Manhattan Federal Court (July 9, 2014), https://www.justice.gov/opa/pr/bnp-paribas-pleads-guilty-conspiring-violate-us-economic-sanctions-manhattan-federal-court.

31. Press Release, U.S. Dep't of Justice, Five Major Banks Agree to Parent-Level Guilty Pleas (May 20, 2015), https://www.justice.gov/opa/pr/five-major-banks-agree-parent-level-guilty-pleas.

Hypothetical: Negotiating a Diversion Agreement

CrimCo is a U.S. company with operations in multiple foreign jurisdictions, and a net worth of approximately $1 billion. CrimCo is under investigation for paying bribes to foreign government officials, which resulted in $50 million in gains for CrimCo. CrimCo's counsel has determined that, should CrimCo resist the charges and go to trial, it will face a maximum penalty of $100 million. CrimCo has begun negotiations with the DOJ to explore a DPA or NPA in lieu of indictment.

1) What is the maximum penalty that CrimCo should consider paying to avoid a criminal prosecution?

CrimCo's attorneys have discovered a novel jurisdictional defense under customary international law and believe it can be asserted in good faith. CrimCo's attorneys are considering raising this jurisdictional defense during their negotiations with the DOJ as a bargaining tool to mitigate CrimCo's penalty.

2) Would raising the jurisdictional defense be a good negotiating strategy?

II. The Yates Memo

DAG Memos issued by the DOJ since the Thompson Memo have reflected the changing policies and priorities of successive administrations, and the DOJ's continuing struggle to find the right approach to the prosecution of business organizations.[32] In 2008, as the U.S. economy faced its worst crisis since the Great Depression, there was significant public pressure to hold large financial institutions and their senior managers accountable for causing the crisis. The DOJ refrained from prosecuting large corporations, fearing the potential wider consequences on the economy—a phenomenon that came to be known as "too big to jail." It was in this context that the district court in *Fokker Services*[33] declined to approve the DPA—echoing public criticism of the leniency exercised by the DOJ in deciding whether to charge corporations.

The 2013 case of HSBC Holding Plc. ("HSBC") stands out as an extreme example. As Matt Taibbi noted in his 2013 *Rolling Stone* magazine article, "Gangster Bankers: Too Big to Jail":

---

32. *See* Robert J. Higdon, Jr. & John S. Davis, Williams Mullen, *The Yates Memo: The Department of Justice Attempts to Refocus Corporate Investigations on Individual Wrongdoers in Both Criminal and Civil Investigations*, http://www.williamsmullen.com/sites/default/files/files/Yates_Long_HigdonDavis_Sept2015%20-%20Higdon%20%26%20Davis%20Alert.pdf.

33. *See* United States v. Fokker Services B.V., 79 F.Supp.3d 160 (D.D.C. 2015).

For at least half a decade, the storied British colonial banking power helped to wash hundreds of millions of dollars for drug mobs, including Mexico's Sinaloa drug cartel, suspected in tens of thousands of murders just in the past 10 years. . . . The bank also moved money for organizations linked to Al Qaeda and Hezbollah, and for Russian gangsters; helped countries like Iran, the Sudan, and North Korea evade sanctions; and, in between helping murderers and terrorists and rogue states, aided countless common tax cheats in hiding their cash.[34]

And yet no criminal charges were brought against the bank or any individual. The bank negotiated a DPA and paid $1.9 billion—"about five weeks' profits"[35]— in fines. Criticism in the media was followed by criticism in Congress. Senator Elizabeth Warren pointed out in a Senate Banking Committee Hearing:

> If you are caught with an ounce of cocaine, the chances are good you are going to go to jail. If it happens repeatedly, you may go to jail for the rest of your life. But evidently, if you launder nearly one billion dollars for drug cartels and violate our international sanctions, your company pays a fine and you go home and sleep in your own bed at night, — every single individual associated with this. I think that is fundamentally wrong.[36]

Former Assistant Attorney General Lanny Breuer responded to this criticism by explaining that, "[h]ad the U.S. authorities decided to press criminal charges, . . . HSBC would almost certainly have lost its banking license in the U.S., the future of the institution would have been under threat and the entire banking system would have been destabilized."[37] Making the same argument, then-Attorney General Eric Holder testified before the Senate Judiciary Committee that some financial institutions can "become[] so large . . . it does become difficult for us to prosecute them when, . . . if you do bring a criminal charge, it will have a negative impact on the national economy, perhaps even the world economy."[38]

Senator Warren renewed her criticism in 2016 after Wells Fargo Bank was caught creating more than a million checking accounts and issuing around 600,000 credit cards to customers without their knowledge. After Wells Fargo was fined only $185 million, Warren appeared on both NBC and CNN, stating "[y]ou cannot have a scandal this size and not have some senior management who are personally responsible[.]"[39] Attorney General Loretta Lynch had recently replaced Eric Holder, and mere days after Warren's public criticisms, the Lynch DOJ issued a new DAG Memo—the Yates Memo, authored by then Deputy Attorney General Sally Yates—that prioritized the prosecution of

---

34. Matt Taibbi, *Gangster Bankers: Too Big to Jail*, Rolling Stone (Feb. 14, 2013), https://www.rollingstone.com/politics/news/gangster-bankers-too-big-to-jail-20130214.

35. *Id.*

36. *Patterns of Abuse: Assessing Bank Secrecy Act Compliance and Enforcement Hearing Before the S. Comm. On Banking, Housing, & Urban Affairs*, 113 Cong. 14 (2013) [hereinafter *Hearing*] (statement of Sen. Elizabeth Warren).

37. Taibbi, *supra* note 34 (quoting Assistant Attorney Gen. Lanny Breuer).

38. *Hearing*, *supra* note 36, at 70 (statement of Attorney Gen. Eric Holder).

39. Shawn Tully, *Elizabeth Warren Blasts Bankers: You're Not Too Big to Jail*, Fortune (Sept. 16, 2016) (quoting Sen. Elizabeth Warren), http://fortune.com/2016/09/16/elizabeth-warren-wells-fargo-lehman-banks-jail.

individuals responsible for committing corporate crimes. Specifically, the Yates Memo set forth several key steps intended to strengthen the DOJ's prosecution of individual corporate wrongdoing, including:

1) Requirement that corporations provide to the DOJ all relevant facts relating to the individuals responsible for the misconduct in order to qualify for any cooperation credit;

2) Focus would be on individual accountability from the inception of the investigation;

3) Absent extraordinary circumstances or approved departmental policy, the DOJ would not release culpable individuals from civil or criminal liability when resolving a matter with a corporation.[40]

III. The United States Attorneys' Manual ("USAM")

In substance, the current version of the *United States Attorneys' Manual* preserves the relationship dynamics between federal prosecutors and corporations set up by the Thompson Memo. It also continues the federal project that began with the FSGO: using a carrot-and-stick approach to compel business organizations to self-police. Below are the USAM provisions that set forth and explain the factors prosecutors should weigh in making their charging decisions. These are referred to by the DOJ as the "Filip Factors," after their author, Deputy Attorney General Mark Filip.

United States Attorneys' Manual

9-28.000 — Principles of Federal Prosecution of Business Organizations

9-28.010—FOUNDATIONAL PRINCIPLES OF CORPORATE PROSECUTION

The prosecution of corporate crime is a high priority for the Department of Justice. By investigating allegations of wrongdoing and bringing charges where appropriate for criminal misconduct, the Department promotes critical public interests. These interests include, among other things: (1) protecting the integrity of our economic and capital markets by enforcing the rule of law; (2) protecting consumers, investors, and business entities against competitors who gain unfair advantage by violating the law; (3) preventing violations of environmental laws;

---

40. *See* Memorandum from Sally Quillian Yates, Deputy Attorney Gen., U.S. Dep't of Justice, Individual Accountability for Corporate Wrongdoing (Sept. 9, 2015), https://www.justice.gov/archives/dag/file/769036/download.

and (4) discouraging business practices that would permit or promote unlawful conduct at the expense of the public interest.

One of the most effective ways to combat corporate misconduct is by holding accountable all individuals who engage in wrongdoing. Such accountability deters future illegal activity, incentivizes changes in corporate behavior, ensures that the proper parties are held responsible for their actions, and promotes the public's confidence in our justice system.

Prosecutors should focus on wrongdoing by individuals from the very beginning of any investigation of corporate misconduct. By focusing on building cases against individual wrongdoers, we accomplish multiple goals. First, we increase our ability to identify the full extent of corporate misconduct. Because a corporation only acts through individuals, investigating the conduct of individuals is the most efficient and effective way to determine the facts and the extent of any corporate misconduct. Second, a focus on individuals increases the likelihood that those with knowledge of the corporate misconduct will be identified and provide information about the individuals involved, at any level of an organization. Third, we maximize the likelihood that the final resolution will include charges against culpable individuals and not just the corporation.

[new November 2015]

9-28.100 — DUTIES OF FEDERAL PROSECUTORS AND DUTIES OF CORPORATE LEADERS

Corporate directors and officers owe a fiduciary duty to a corporation's shareholders (the corporation's true owners) and they owe duties of honest dealing to the investing public and consumers in connection with the corporation's regulatory filings and public statements. A prosecutor's duty to enforce the law requires the investigation and prosecution of criminal wrongdoing if it is discovered. In carrying out this mission with the diligence and resolve necessary to vindicate the important public interests discussed above, prosecutors should be mindful of the common cause we share with responsible corporate leaders who seek to promote trust and confidence. Prosecutors should also be mindful that confidence in the Department is affected both by the results we achieve and by the real and perceived ways in which we achieve them. Thus, the manner in which we do our job as prosecutors—including the professionalism and civility we demonstrate, our willingness to secure the facts in a manner that encourages corporate compliance and self-regulation, and also our appreciation that corporate prosecutions can harm blameless investors, employees, and others—affects public perception of our mission. Federal prosecutors must maintain public confidence in the way in which we exercise our charging discretion. This endeavor requires the thoughtful analysis of all facts and circumstances presented in a given case.

[revised November 2015]

9-28.200 — GENERAL CONSIDERATIONS OF CORPORATE LIABILITY

A. General Principle:

Corporations should not be treated leniently because of their artificial nature nor should they be subject to harsher treatment. Vigorous enforcement of the criminal laws against corporate wrongdoers, where appropriate, results in great benefits for law enforcement and the public, particularly in the area of white collar crime. Indicting corporations for wrongdoing enables the government to be a force for positive change of corporate culture, and a force to prevent, discover, and punish serious crimes.

B. Comment:

In all cases involving corporate [these guidelines apply equally to all types of business organizations, not merely the corporate form] wrongdoing, prosecutors should consider the factors discussed in these guidelines. In doing so, prosecutors should be aware of the public benefits that can flow from indicting a corporation in appropriate cases. For instance, corporations are likely to take immediate remedial steps when one is indicted for criminal misconduct that is pervasive throughout a particular industry, and thus an indictment can provide a unique opportunity for deterrence on a broad scale. In addition, a corporate indictment may result in specific deterrence by changing the culture of the indicted corporation and the behavior of its employees. Finally, certain crimes that carry with them a substantial risk of great public harm—*e.g.*, environmental crimes or sweeping financial frauds—may be committed by a business entity, and there may therefore be a substantial federal interest in indicting a corporation under such circumstances.

In certain instances, it may be appropriate to resolve a corporate criminal case by means other than indictment. Non-prosecution and deferred prosecution agreements, for example, occupy an important middle ground between declining prosecution and obtaining the conviction of a corporation. These agreements are discussed further in USAM 9-28.1100 (Collateral Consequences). . . .

Prosecutors have substantial latitude in determining when, whom, how, and even whether to prosecute for violations of federal criminal law. In exercising that discretion, prosecutors should consider the following statements of principles that summarize the considerations they should weigh and the practices they should follow in discharging their prosecutorial responsibilities. Prosecutors should ensure that the general purposes of the criminal law—appropriate punishment for the defendant, deterrence of further criminal conduct by the defendant, deterrence of criminal conduct by others, protection of the public from dangerous and fraudulent conduct, rehabilitation, and restitution for victims—are adequately met, taking into account the special nature of the corporate "person."

[revised November 2015]

9-28.210 — FOCUS ON INDIVIDUAL WRONGDOERS

A. General Principle:

Prosecution of a corporation is not a substitute for the prosecution of criminally culpable individuals within or without the corporation. Because a corporation can act only through individuals, imposition of individual criminal liability may provide the strongest deterrent against future corporate wrongdoing. Provable individual culpability should be pursued, particularly if it relates to high-level corporate officers, even in the face of an offer of a corporate guilty plea or some other disposition of the charges against the corporation, including a deferred prosecution or non-prosecution agreement, or a civil resolution. In other words, regardless of the ultimate corporate disposition, a separate evaluation must be made with respect to potentially liable individuals.

B. Comment:

It is important early in the corporate investigation to identify the responsible individuals and determine the nature and extent of their misconduct. Prosecutors should not allow delays in the corporate investigation to undermine the Department's ability to pursue potentially culpable individuals. Every effort should be made to resolve a corporate matter within the statutorily allotted time, and tolling agreements should be the rare exception. In situations where it is anticipated that a tolling agreement is unavoidable, all efforts should be made either to prosecute culpable individuals before the limitations period expires or to preserve the ability to charge individuals by tolling the limitations period by agreement or court order.

If an investigation of individual misconduct has not concluded by the time authorization is sought to resolve the case against the corporation, the prosecution authorization memorandum should include a discussion of the potentially liable individuals, a description of the current status of the investigation regarding their conduct and the investigative work that remains to be done, and, when warranted, an investigative plan to bring the matter to resolution prior to the end of any statute of limitations period. If a decision is made at the conclusion of the investigation to pursue charges or some other resolution with the corporation but not to bring criminal or civil charges against the individuals who committed the misconduct, the reasons for that determination must be memorialized and approved by the United States Attorney or Assistant Attorney General whose office handled the investigation, or their designees.

Under the doctrine of *respondeat superior*, a corporation may be held criminally liable for the illegal acts of its directors, officers, employees, and agents. To hold a corporation liable for these actions, the government must establish that the corporate agent's actions (i) were within the scope of his duties and (ii) were intended, at least in part, to benefit the corporation. In all cases involving wrongdoing by corporate agents, prosecutors should not limit their focus solely to individuals or the corporation, but should consider both as potential targets.

Agents may act for mixed reasons—both for self-aggrandizement (direct and indirect) and for the benefit of the corporation, and a corporation may be held liable as long as one motivation of its agent is to benefit the corporation. *See United States v. Potter*, 463 F.3d 9, 25 (1st Cir. 2006) (stating that the test to determine whether an agent is acting within the scope of employment is "whether the agent is performing acts of the kind which he is authorized to perform, and those acts are motivated, at least in part, by an intent to benefit the corporation."). In *United States v. Automated Medical Laboratories, Inc.*, 770 F.2d 399 (4th Cir. 1985), for example, the Fourth Circuit affirmed a corporation's conviction for the actions of a subsidiary's employee despite the corporation's claim that the employee was acting for his own benefit, namely his "ambitious nature and his desire to ascend the corporate ladder." *Id.* at 407. The court stated, "Partucci was clearly acting in part to benefit AML since his advancement within the corporation depended on AML's well-being and its lack of difficulties with the FDA." *Id.; see also United States v. Cincotta*, 689 F.2d 238, 241-42 (1st Cir. 1982) (upholding a corporation's conviction, notwithstanding the substantial personal benefit reaped by its miscreant agents, because the fraudulent scheme required money to pass through the corporation's treasury and the fraudulently obtained goods were resold to the corporation's customers in the corporation's name).

Moreover, the corporation need not even necessarily profit from its agent's actions for it to be held liable. In *Automated Medical Laboratories*, the Fourth Circuit stated:

> [B]enefit is not a "touchstone of criminal corporate liability; benefit at best is an evidential, not an operative, fact." Thus, whether the agent's actions ultimately redounded to the benefit of the corporation is less significant than whether the agent acted with the intent to benefit the corporation. The basic purpose of requiring that an agent have acted with the intent to benefit the corporation, however, is to insulate the corporation from criminal liability for actions of its agents which may be *inimical* to the interests of the corporation or which may have been undertaken solely to advance the interests of that agent or of a party other than the corporation.

770 F.2d at 407 (internal citation omitted) (quoting *Old Monastery Co. v. United States*, 147 F.2d 905, 908 (4th Cir. 1945)).

[new November 2015]

9-28.300 — FACTORS TO BE CONSIDERED [FILIP FACTORS]

A. General Principle:

. . . In conducting an investigation, determining whether to bring charges, and negotiating plea or other agreements, prosecutors should consider the following factors in reaching a decision as to the proper treatment of a corporate target:

1. the nature and seriousness of the offense, including the risk of harm to the public, and applicable policies and priorities, if any, governing the prosecution of corporations for particular categories of crime (*see* USAM 9-28.400);
2. the pervasiveness of wrongdoing within the corporation, including the complicity in, or the condoning of, the wrongdoing by corporate management (*see* USAM 9-28.500);
3. the corporation's history of similar misconduct, including prior criminal, civil, and regulatory enforcement actions against it (*see* USAM 9-28.600);
4. the corporation's willingness to cooperate in the investigation of its agents (*see* USAM 9-28.700);
5. the existence and effectiveness of the corporation's pre-existing compliance program (*see* USAM 9-28.800);
6. the corporation's timely and voluntary disclosure of wrongdoing (*see* USAM 9-28.900);
7. the corporation's remedial actions, including any efforts to implement an effective corporate compliance program or to improve an existing one, to replace responsible management, to discipline or terminate wrongdoers, to pay restitution, and to cooperate with the relevant government agencies (*see* USAM 9-28.1000);
8. collateral consequences, including whether there is disproportionate harm to shareholders, pension holders, employees, and others not proven personally culpable, as well as impact on the public arising from the prosecution (*see* USAM 9-28.1100);
9. the adequacy of remedies such as civil or regulatory enforcement actions (*see* USAM 9-28.1200); and
10. the adequacy of the prosecution of individuals responsible for the corporation's malfeasance (*see* USAM 9-28.1300)

B. Comment:

The factors listed in this section are intended to be illustrative of those that should be evaluated and are not an exhaustive list of potentially relevant considerations. Some of these factors may not apply to specific cases, and in some cases one factor may override all others. For example, the nature and seriousness of the offense may be such as to warrant prosecution regardless of the other factors. In most cases, however, no single factor will be dispositive. In addition, national law enforcement policies in various enforcement areas may require that more or less weight be given to certain of these factors than to others. Of course, prosecutors must exercise their thoughtful and pragmatic judgment in applying and balancing these factors, so as to achieve a fair and just outcome and promote respect for the law.

[revised November 2015]

IV. Shepherding Compliance Programs

Pursuant to USAM § 9-28.800,[41] federal prosecutors have discretion to give mitigating credit to corporations for existing compliance programs or for agreeing to institute one as part of the DPA. Providing no "formulaic requirements," § 9-28.800 allows corporations to design their compliance program to fit their operations.[42]

United States Attorneys' Manual

9-28.000 — Principles of Federal Prosecution of Business Organizations

9-28.800 – CORPORATE COMPLIANCE PROGRAMS

A. General Principle:

Compliance programs are established by corporate management to prevent and detect misconduct and to ensure that corporate activities are conducted in accordance with applicable criminal and civil laws, regulations, and rules. The Department encourages such corporate self-policing, including voluntary disclosures to the government of any problems that a corporation discovers on its own. *See* USAM 9-28.900. However, the existence of a compliance program is not sufficient, in and of itself, to justify not charging a corporation for criminal misconduct undertaken by its officers, directors, employees, or agents. In addition, the nature of some crimes, *e.g.*, antitrust violations, may be such that national law enforcement policies mandate prosecutions of corporations notwithstanding the existence of a compliance program.

B. Comment:

The existence of a corporate compliance program, even one that specifically prohibited the very conduct in question, does not absolve the corporation from criminal liability under the doctrine of *respondeat superior*. *See United States v. Basic Constr. Co.*, 711 F.2d 570, 573 (4th Cir. 1983) ("[A] corporation may be held criminally responsible for antitrust violations committed by its employees if they were acting within the scope of their authority, or apparent authority, and for the benefit of the corporation, even if . . . such acts were against corporate policy or express instructions."). As explained in *United States v. Potter*, 463 F.3d 9 (1st Cir. 2006), a corporation cannot "avoid liability by adopting abstract rules" that forbid its agents from engaging in illegal acts, because "[e]ven a specific directive to an agent or employee or honest efforts to police such rules do not automatically free the company for the wrongful acts of agents." *Id.* at

---

41. U.S. Dep't of Justice, U. S. Attorneys' Manual § 9-28.000, §9-28.800 (2015) [hereinafter USAM], https://www.justice.gov/usam/usam-9-28000-principles-federal-prosecution-business-organizations#9-28.010.
42. *See id.*

25-26. *See also United States v. Hilton Hotels Corp.*, 467 F.2d 1000, 1007 (9th Cir. 1972) (noting that a corporation "could not gain exculpation by issuing general instructions without undertaking to enforce those instructions by means commensurate with the obvious risks"); *United States v. Beusch*, 596 F.2d 871, 878 (9th Cir. 1979) ("[A] corporation may be liable for acts of its employees done contrary to express instructions and policies, but . . . the existence of such instructions and policies may be considered in determining whether the employee in fact acted to benefit the corporation.").

While the Department recognizes that no compliance program can ever prevent all criminal activity by a corporation's employees, the critical factors in evaluating any program are whether the program is adequately designed for maximum effectiveness in preventing and detecting wrongdoing by employees and whether corporate management is enforcing the program or is tacitly encouraging or pressuring employees to engage in misconduct to achieve business objectives. The Department has no formulaic requirements regarding corporate compliance programs. The fundamental questions any prosecutor should ask are: Is the corporation's compliance program well designed? Is the program being applied earnestly and in good faith? Does the corporation's compliance program work? In answering these questions, the prosecutor should consider the comprehensiveness of the compliance program; the extent and pervasiveness of the criminal misconduct; the number and level of the corporate employees involved; the seriousness, duration, and frequency of the misconduct; and any remedial actions taken by the corporation, including, for example, disciplinary action against past violators uncovered by the prior compliance program, and revisions to corporate compliance programs in light of lessons learned. Prosecutors should also consider the promptness of any disclosure of wrongdoing to the government. In evaluating compliance programs, prosecutors may consider whether the corporation has established corporate governance mechanisms that can effectively detect and prevent misconduct. For example, do the corporation's directors exercise independent review over proposed corporate actions rather than unquestioningly ratifying officers' recommendations; are internal audit functions conducted at a level sufficient to ensure their independence and accuracy; and have the directors established an information and reporting system in the organization reasonably designed to provide management and directors with timely and accurate information sufficient to allow them to reach an informed decision regarding the organization's compliance with the law. *See, e.g., In re Caremark Int'l Inc. Derivative Litig.*, 698 A.2d 959, 968-70 (Del. Ch. 1996).

Prosecutors should therefore attempt to determine whether a corporation's compliance program is merely a "paper program" or whether it was designed, implemented, reviewed, and revised, as appropriate, in an effective manner. In addition, prosecutors should determine whether the corporation has provided for a staff sufficient to audit, document, analyze, and utilize the results of the corporation's compliance efforts. Prosecutors also should determine whether the corporation's employees are adequately informed about the compliance program and are convinced of the corporation's commitment to it. This will enable the prosecutor to make an informed decision as to whether the corporation has adopted and implemented a truly effective compliance program that, when consistent with other federal law enforcement policies, may result in a decision to charge only the corporation's employees and agents or to mitigate charges or sanctions against the corporation.

Compliance programs should be designed to detect the particular types of misconduct most likely to occur in a particular corporation's line of business. Many corporations operate in complex regulatory environments outside the normal experience of criminal prosecutors. Accordingly, prosecutors should consult with relevant federal and state agencies with the expertise to evaluate the adequacy of a program's design and implementation. . . .

[revised November 2015]

Notes and Questions

USAM § 9-28.800 states:

Prosecutors should therefore attempt to determine whether a corporation's compliance program is merely a "paper program" or whether it was designed, implemented, reviewed, and revised, as appropriate, in an effective manner.[43]

1) What is the difference between a "paper program" and one that is well designed?
2) Are federal prosecutors qualified to evaluate corporate compliance programs?

V. Rewarding Disclosure and Cooperation

Because a compliance program cannot prevent every violation, the USAM sets forth the steps that corporations are expected to take once a violation is detected internally. Section 9-28.700 encourages corporations to conduct "internal investigations" and to disclose the relevant facts to the government; and, pursuant to the Yates Memo, conditions mitigation credit on the company's cooperation in the prosecution of responsible individuals.

---

43. *Id.* § 9-28.800(B).

United States Attorneys' Manual

9-28.000 — Principles of Federal Prosecution of Business Organizations

9-28.700 — THE VALUE OF COOPERATION

Cooperation is a mitigating factor, by which a corporation—just like any other subject of a criminal investigation—can gain credit in a case that otherwise is appropriate for indictment and prosecution. Of course, the decision not to cooperate by a corporation (or individual) is not itself evidence of misconduct, at least where the lack of cooperation does not involve criminal misconduct or demonstrate consciousness of guilt (*e.g.*, suborning perjury or false statements, or refusing to comply with lawful discovery requests). Thus, failure to cooperate, in and of itself, does not support or require the filing of charges with respect to a corporation any more than with respect to an individual.

A. General Principle:

In order for a company to receive any consideration for cooperation under this section, the company must identify all individuals involved in or responsible for the misconduct at issue, regardless of their position, status or seniority, and provide to the Department all facts relating to that misconduct. If a company seeking cooperation credit declines to learn of such facts or to provide the Department with complete factual information about the individuals involved, its cooperation will not be considered a mitigating factor under this section. Nor, if a company is prosecuted, will the Department support a cooperation-related reduction at sentencing. *See* [FSGO] § 8C2.5(g), cmt. (n. 13) ("A prime test of whether the organization has disclosed all pertinent information" necessary to receive a cooperation-related reduction in its offense level calculation "is whether the information is sufficient . . . to identify . . . the individual(s) responsible for the criminal conduct."). If a company meets the threshold requirement of providing all relevant facts with respect to individuals, it will be eligible for consideration for cooperation credit. To be clear, a company is not required to waive its attorney-client privilege and attorney work product protection in order satisfy this threshold. *See* USAM 9-28.720. The extent of the cooperation credit earned will depend on all the various factors that have traditionally applied in making this assessment (*e.g.*, the timeliness of the cooperation, the diligence, thoroughness and speed of the internal investigation, and the proactive nature of the cooperation).

B. Comment:

In investigating wrongdoing by or within a corporation, a prosecutor may encounter several obstacles resulting from the nature of the corporation itself. It may be difficult to determine which individual took which action on behalf of the corporation. Lines of authority and responsibility may be shared among operating divisions or departments, and records and personnel may be spread throughout the United States or even among several countries. Where the criminal conduct continued over an extended period of time, the culpable or knowledgeable personnel may have been promoted, transferred, or fired, or they may have quit or retired. Accordingly, a corporation's cooperation may be critical in identifying potentially relevant actors and locating relevant evidence, among other things, and in doing so expeditiously.

This dynamic—*i.e.*, the difficulty of determining what happened, where the evidence is, and which individuals took or promoted putatively illegal corporate actions—can have negative consequences for both the government and the corporation that is the subject or target of a government investigation. . . . For example, it may not matter under the law which of several possible executives or leaders in a chain of command approved of or authorized criminal conduct; however, that information if known might bear on the propriety of a particular disposition short of indictment of the corporation. It may not be in the interest of a corporation or the government for a charging decision to be made in the absence of such information, which might occur if, for example, a statute of limitations were relevant and authorization by any one of the officials were enough to justify a charge under the law. Moreover, a protracted government investigation of such an issue could disrupt the corporation's business operations or even depress its stock price.

For these reasons and more, cooperation can be a favorable course for both the government and the corporation. Cooperation benefits the government by allowing prosecutors and federal agents, for example, to avoid protracted delays, which compromise their ability to quickly uncover and address the full extent of widespread corporate crimes. With cooperation by the corporation, the government may be able to reduce tangible losses, limit damage to reputation, and preserve assets for restitution. At the same time, cooperation may benefit the corporation—and ultimately shareholders, employees, and other often blameless victims—by enabling the government to focus its investigative resources in a manner that will not unduly disrupt the corporation's legitimate business operations. In addition, cooperation may benefit the corporation by presenting it with the opportunity to earn credit for its efforts.

The requirement that companies cooperate completely as to individuals does not mean that Department attorneys should wait for the company to deliver the information about individual wrongdoers and then merely accept what companies provide. To the contrary, Department attorneys should be proactively investigating individuals at every step of the process —before, during, and after any corporate cooperation. Department attorneys should vigorously review any information provided by companies and compare it to the results of their own investigation, in order to best ensure that the information provided is indeed complete and does not seek to minimize the behavior or role of any individual or group of individuals.

Department attorneys should strive to obtain from the company as much information as possible about responsible individuals before resolving the corporate case. In addition, the company's continued cooperation with respect to individuals may be necessary post-resolution. If so, the corporate resolution agreement should include a provision that requires the company to provide information about all individuals involved and that is explicit enough so that a failure to provide the information results in specific consequences, such as stipulated penalties and/or a material breach.

[updated November 2017]

9-28.710 — ATTORNEY-CLIENT AND WORK PRODUCT PROTECTIONS

The attorney-client privilege and the attorney work product protection serve an extremely important function in the American legal system. The attorney-client privilege is one of the oldest and most sacrosanct privileges under the law. *See Upjohn v. United States*, 449 U.S. 383, 389 (1981). As the Supreme Court has stated, "[i]ts purpose is to encourage full and frank communication between attorneys and their clients and thereby promote broader public interests in the observance of law and administration of justice." *Id.* The value of promoting a corporation's ability to seek frank and comprehensive legal advice is particularly important in the contemporary global business environment, where corporations often face complex and dynamic legal and regulatory obligations imposed by the federal government and also by states and foreign governments. The work product doctrine serves similarly important goals.

For these reasons, waiving the attorney-client and work product protections has never been a prerequisite under the Department's prosecution guidelines for a corporation to be viewed as cooperative. Nonetheless, a wide range of commentators and members of the American legal community and criminal justice system have asserted that the Department's policies have been used, either wittingly or unwittingly, to coerce business entities into waiving attorney-client privilege and work-product protection. Everyone agrees that a corporation may freely waive its own privileges if it chooses to do so; indeed, such waivers occur routinely when corporations are victimized by their employees or others, conduct an internal investigation, and then disclose the details of the investigation to law enforcement officials in an effort to seek prosecution of the offenders. However, the contention, from a broad array of voices, is that the Department's position on attorney-client privilege and work product protection waivers has promoted an environment in which those protections are being unfairly eroded to the detriment of all.

The Department understands that the attorney-client privilege and attorney work product protection are essential and long-recognized components of the American legal system. What the government seeks and needs to advance its legitimate (indeed, essential) law enforcement mission is not waiver of those protections, but rather the facts known to the corporation about the putative criminal misconduct under review. In addition, while a corporation remains free to convey non-factual or "core" attorney-client communications or work product—if and only if the corporation voluntarily chooses to do so—prosecutors should not ask for such waivers and are directed not to do so. The critical factor is whether the corporation has provided the facts about the events, as explained further herein.

[new August 2008]

9-28.720 — COOPERATION: DISCLOSING THE RELEVANT FACTS

Eligibility for cooperation credit is not predicated upon the waiver of attorney-client privilege or work product protection. Instead, the sort of cooperation that is most valuable to resolving allegations of misconduct by a corporation and its officers, directors, employees, or agents is disclosure of the relevant *facts* concerning such misconduct. In this regard, the analysis parallels that for a non-corporate defendant, where cooperation typically requires disclosure of relevant factual knowledge and not of discussions between an individual and his attorneys.

Thus, when the government investigates potential corporate wrongdoing, it seeks the relevant facts. For example, how and when did the alleged misconduct occur? Who promoted or approved it? Who was responsible for committing it? In this respect, the investigation of a corporation differs little from the investigation of an individual. In both cases, the government needs to know the facts to achieve a just and fair outcome. The party under investigation may choose to cooperate by disclosing the facts, and the government may give credit for the party's disclosures. If a corporation wishes to receive credit for such cooperation, which then can be considered with all other cooperative efforts and circumstances in evaluating how fairly to proceed, then the corporation, like any person, must disclose the relevant facts of which it has knowledge.

a. Disclosing the Relevant Facts—Facts Gathered Through Internal Investigation

Individuals and corporations often obtain knowledge of facts in different ways. An individual knows the facts of his or others' misconduct through his own experience and perceptions. A corporation is an artificial construct that cannot, by definition, have personal knowledge of the facts. Some of those facts may be reflected in documentary or electronic media like emails, transaction or accounting documents, and other records. Often, the corporation gathers facts through an internal investigation. Exactly how and by whom the facts are gathered is for the corporation to decide. Many corporations choose to collect information about potential misconduct through lawyers, a process that may confer attorney-client privilege or attorney work product protection on at least some of the information collected. Other corporations may choose a method of fact-gathering that does not have that effect—for example, having employee or other witness statements collected after interviews by non-attorney personnel. Whichever process the corporation selects, the government's key measure of cooperation must remain the same as it does for an individual: has the party timely disclosed the relevant facts about the putative misconduct? That is the operative question in assigning cooperation credit for the disclosure of information—*not* whether the corporation discloses attorney-client or work product materials. Accordingly, a corporation should receive the same credit for disclosing facts contained in materials that are not protected by the attorney-client privilege or attorney work product as it would for disclosing identical facts contained in materials that are so protected. On this point the Report of the House Judiciary Committee, submitted in connection with the attorney-client privilege bill passed by the House of Representatives (H.R. 3013), comports with the approach required here:

> [A]n . . . attorney of the United States may base cooperation credit on the facts that are disclosed, but is prohibited from basing cooperation credit upon whether or not the materials are protected by attorney-client privilege or attorney work product. As a result, an entity that voluntarily discloses should receive the same amount of cooperation credit for disclosing facts that happen to be contained in materials not protected by attorney-client privilege or attorney work product as it would receive for disclosing identical facts that are contained in materials protected by attorney-client privilege or attorney work product. There should be no differentials in an assessment of cooperation (*i.e.*, neither a credit nor a penalty) based upon whether or not the materials disclosed are protected by attorney-client privilege or attorney work product.

H.R. Rep. No. 110-445 at 4 (2007).

In short, the company may be eligible for cooperation credit regardless of whether it chooses to waive privilege or work product protection in the process, if it provides all relevant facts about the individuals who were involved in the misconduct. But if the corporation does not disclose such facts, it will not be entitled to receive any credit for cooperation.

Two final and related points bear noting about the disclosure of facts, although they should be obvious. First, the government cannot compel, and the corporation has no obligation to make, such disclosures (although the government can obviously compel the disclosure of certain records and witness testimony through subpoenas). Second, a corporation's failure to provide relevant information about individual misconduct alone does not mean the corporation will be indicted. It simply means that the corporation will not be entitled to mitigating credit for that cooperation. Whether the corporation faces charges will turn, as it does in any case, on the sufficiency of the evidence, the likelihood of success at trial, and all of the other factors identified in USAM 9-28.300. If there is insufficient evidence to warrant indictment, after appropriate investigation has been completed, or if the other factors weigh against indictment, then the corporation should not be indicted, irrespective of whether it has earned cooperation credit. The converse is also true: The government may charge even the most cooperative corporation pursuant to these Principles if, in weighing and balancing the factors described herein, the prosecutor determines that a charge is required in the interests of justice. Put differently, even the most sincere and thorough effort to cooperate cannot necessarily absolve a corporation that has, for example, engaged in an egregious, orchestrated, and widespread fraud. Cooperation is a potential mitigating factor, but it alone is not dispositive.

b. Legal Advice and Attorney Work Product

Separate from (and usually preceding) the fact-gathering process in an internal investigation, a corporation, through its officers, employees, directors, or others, may have consulted with corporate counsel regarding or in a manner that concerns the legal implications of the putative misconduct at issue. Communications of this sort, which are both independent of the fact-gathering component of an internal investigation and made for the purpose of seeking or dispensing legal advice, lie at the core of the attorney-client privilege. Such communications can naturally have a salutary effect on corporate behavior—facilitating, for example, a corporation's effort to comply with complex and evolving legal and regulatory regimes. Except as noted in subparagraphs (b)(i) and (b)(ii) below, a corporation need not disclose and prosecutors may not request the disclosure of such communications as a condition for the corporation's eligibility to receive cooperation credit.

Likewise, non-factual or core attorney work product—for example, an attorney's mental impressions or legal theories—lies at the core of the attorney work product doctrine. A corporation need not disclose, and prosecutors may not request, the disclosure of such attorney work product as a condition for the corporation's eligibility to receive cooperation credit.

(i) Advice of Counsel Defense in the Instant Context

Occasionally a corporation or one of its employees may assert an advice-of-counsel defense, based upon communications with in-house or outside counsel that took place prior to or contemporaneously with the underlying conduct at issue. In such situations, the defendant must tender a legitimate factual basis to support the assertion of the advice-of-counsel defense. . . . The Department cannot fairly be asked to discharge its responsibility to the public to investigate alleged corporate crime, or to temper what would otherwise be the appropriate course of prosecutive action, by simply accepting on faith an otherwise unproven assertion that an attorney—perhaps even an unnamed attorney—approved potentially unlawful practices. Accordingly, where an advice-of-counsel defense has been asserted, prosecutors may ask for the disclosure of the communications allegedly supporting it.

(ii) Communications in Furtherance of a Crime or Fraud

Communications between a corporation (through its officers, employees, directors, or agents) and corporate counsel that are made in furtherance of a crime or fraud are, under settled precedent, outside the scope and protection of the attorney-client privilege. *See United States v. Zolin*, 491 U.S. 554, 563 (1989); *United States v. BDO Seidman, LLP*, 492 F.3d 806, 818 (7th Cir. 2007). As a result, the Department may properly request such communications if they in fact exist.

. . . .

[updated November 2017]

9-28.730 — OBSTRUCTING THE INVESTIGATION

Another factor to be weighed by the prosecutor is whether the corporation has engaged in conduct intended to impede the investigation. Examples of such conduct could include: inappropriate directions to employees or their counsel, such as directions not to be truthful or to conceal relevant facts; making representations or submissions that contain misleading assertions or material omissions; and incomplete or delayed production of records.

In evaluating cooperation, however, prosecutors should not take into account whether a corporation is advancing or reimbursing attorneys' fees or providing counsel to employees, officers, or directors under investigation or indictment. Likewise, prosecutors may not request that a corporation refrain from taking such action. This prohibition is not meant to prevent a prosecutor from asking questions about an attorney's representation of a corporation or its employees, officers, or directors, where otherwise appropriate under the law. Neither is it intended to limit the otherwise applicable reach of criminal obstruction of justice statutes such as 18 U.S.C. § 1503. If the payment of attorney fees were used in a manner that would otherwise constitute criminal obstruction of justice—for example, if fees were advanced on the condition that an employee adhere to a version of the facts that the corporation and the employee knew to be false—these Principles would not (and could not) render inapplicable such criminal prohibitions.

Similarly, the mere participation by a corporation in a joint defense agreement does not render the corporation ineligible to receive cooperation credit, and prosecutors may not request that a corporation refrain from entering into such agreements. Of course, the corporation may wish to avoid putting itself in the position of being disabled, by virtue of a particular joint defense or similar agreement, from providing some relevant facts to the government and thereby limiting its ability to seek such cooperation credit. Such might be the case if the corporation gathers facts from employees who have entered into a joint defense agreement with the corporation, and who may later seek to prevent the corporation from disclosing the facts it has acquired. Corporations may wish to address this situation by crafting or participating in joint defense agreements, to the extent they choose to enter them, that provide such flexibility as they deem appropriate.

Finally, it may on occasion be appropriate for the government to consider whether the corporation has shared with others sensitive information about the investigation that the government provided to the corporation. In appropriate situations, as it does with individuals, the government may properly request that, if a corporation wishes to receive credit for cooperation, the information provided by the government to the corporation not be transmitted to others—for example, where the disclosure of such information could lead to flight by individual subjects, destruction of evidence, or dissipation or concealment of assets.
[new September 2008]

9-28.740 — OFFERING COOPERATION: NO ENTITLEMENT TO IMMUNITY

A corporation's offer of cooperation or cooperation itself does not automatically entitle it to immunity from prosecution or a favorable resolution of its case. A corporation should not be able to escape liability merely by offering up its directors, officers, employees, or agents. Thus, a corporation's willingness to cooperate is not determinative; that factor, while relevant, needs to be considered in conjunction with all other factors.

[new August 2008]

9-28.900 — VOLUNTARY DISCLOSURE

In conjunction with regulatory agencies and other executive branch departments, the Department encourages corporations, as part of their compliance programs, to conduct internal investigations and to disclose the relevant facts to the appropriate authorities. . . .

Even in the absence of a formal program, prosecutors may consider a corporation's timely and voluntary disclosure, both as an independent factor and in evaluating the company's overall cooperation and the adequacy of the corporation's compliance program and its management's commitment to the compliance program. *See* USAM 9-28.700 and 9-28.800. However, prosecution may be appropriate notwithstanding a corporation's voluntary disclosure. Such a determination should be based on a consideration of all the factors set forth in these Principles. *See* USAM 9-28.300.

[new November 2015]

Notes and Questions

USAM § 9-28.720 states that "a corporation need not disclose and prosecutors may not request the disclosure of [privileged] communications as a condition for the corporation's eligibility to receive cooperation credit."

Are there any circumstances under which defense counsel should consider voluntarily disclosing such privileged communications?

Hypothetical: Throwing Your Employees Under the Bus

The following excerpt is from the opinion in *United States v. Stein*, 440 F. Supp. 2d 315, 320-24 (S.D.N.Y. 2006), reflecting KPMG's efforts to avoid an indictment by fully cooperating with the DOJ's investigation.

Facts

. . . .

The February 25, 2004 Meeting Between the KPMG and the USAO

. . . Suffice it to say for present purposes that the prosecutors and KPMG attorneys met on February 25, 2004. The KPMG lawyers were well aware of the Thompson Memorandum. . . .

The KPMG lawyers made clear to prosecutors that KPMG believed that an indictment would be fatal to the organization. They said that KPMG intended to cooperate in order to save the firm and that it would not protect individual employees. Later in the meeting, Robert Bennett and Kenneth Bialkin of Skadden, Arps, Slate, Meagher & Flom, the senior lawyers representing KPMG, told the USAO that KPMG's "common practice" had been to pay legal fees for employees in connection with legal matters arising out of their doing their jobs. Although KPMG still was checking on its legal obligations, they said, it would not pay legal fees for employees who declined to cooperate with the government, or who took the Fifth Amendment, as long as it had discretion to take that position. Mr. Bennett made clear also that KPMG would recommend to individual employees "lawyers who understand cooperation is the best way to go in this type of case." He expressed also the view that "it [wa]s in the best interests of KPMG for its people to get attorneys that will cooperate with" the government.

KPMG Gets the Message

Shortly after the February 25, 2004 meeting, Mr. Bennett got back to Justin Weddle, one of the prosecutors, on the legal fee issue. He reported that KPMG did not think it had any binding legal obligation to pay employee legal fees, but that "it would be a big problem" not to do so because the firm was a partnership. He said that KPMG was planning on putting a cap, or limit, on fees and conditioning their payment for any given partner or employee on that individual "cooperating fully with the company and the government." Apparently satisfied with the government's response, KPMG began to implement the policy.

On March 4, 2004, Mr. Pilchen of Skadden spoke to Mr. Townsend, an attorney for defendant Carol Warley. He told Townsend that KPMG wanted to pay Ms. Warley's attorneys' fees but that the government did not want it to do so. In consequence, KPMG was "doing a balancing act" it would "advance something . . . provided that Ms. Warley cooperated . . . with the government." He made clear that no fees would be paid if Ms. Warley invoked her Fifth Amendment privilege.

On March II, 2004, the Skadden team had a conference call with the USAO. Mr. Bennett assured the USAO that KPMG would be "as cooperative as possible" so that the office would not exercise its discretion to indict the firm. Mr. Weddle urged that KPMG tell its people to be "totally open" with the USAO, "even if [that meant admitting] criminal wrongdoing." He commented that this would give him good material for cross-examination.

The Thompson Memorandum and the actions of the USAO had the desired effect. On the same date, Skadden's Mr. Rauh wrote to the USAO, enclosing among other things a form letter that Skadden was sending to counsel for the KPMG Defendants then employed by KPMG who had received subject letters from the government or otherwise appeared to be under suspicion. The form letter stated that KPMG would pay an individual's legal fees and expenses, up to a maximum of $400,000, on the condition that the individual "cooperate with the government and . . . be prompt, complete, and truthful."

The Proffers

The KPMG lawyers met again with the USAO on March 29, 2004. In an effort to demonstrate that KPMG was cooperating, Skadden asked the government to notify it if any current or former KPMG employee refused to meet with prosecutors or otherwise failed to cooperate.

. . . .

As noted, each of the Moving Defendants received the form letter that stated that KPMG would pay an individual's legal fees and expenses, up to a maximum of $400,000, on the condition that the individual "cooperate with the government and . . . be prompt, complete, and truthful." Each subsequently made proffers to the government pursuant to the USAO's standard proffer agreement after receiving the letter or, in one case, after having been told its substance but before receiving it. Six of the nine left KPMG before they made their statements and do not claim that they made their statements under a threat of loss of their employment. There is no evidence that Mr. Gremminger, one of the three who made a proffer while still employed by KPMG, ever was threatened with firing if he did not make a statement. The situations of the other two, Mr. Smith and Ms. Warley, were different.

Mr. Smith initially refused to make a proffer. Ms. Warley, on the other hand, made a proffer on April 21, 2004. This led to a dispute between her Texas counsel and the USAO in which the attorney demanded agreement by the government with a number of conditions as a prerequisite to a further session.

On May 18, 2004, AUSA Weddle informed Skadden that (1) Mr. Smith had refused to meet with the government and (2) although Ms. Warley had met with prosecutors once, she had refused to meet again except on conditions unacceptable to the USAO. Within days, Eugene O'Kelly, then chairman of KPMG, told Mr. Smith that he understood that "there were concerns about whether [Mr. Smith] was cooperating with the investigation" and told Mr. Smith that "he did not want [him] to put [Mr. O'Kelly] in a position where he was forced to take action against" him. Mr. Smith quite reasonably interpreted this comment as meaning that KPMG would fire him if he did not proffer to the government.

On May 28, 2004, promptly after the O'Kelly-Smith conversation, Skadden forwarded copies of Mr. Weddle's letter to counsel for Smith and Warley. The cover letters stated in relevant part:

> Absent an indication within the next ten business days from the government that your client no longer refuses to meet with the government pursuant to its standard proffer agreement, KPMG will cease payment of [the client's legal] fees.

> Finally, please note that KPMG will view continued non-cooperation as a basis for disciplinary action, including expulsion from the Firm.

Shortly after this threat, Mr. Smith–acting against the advice of his attorney and in order to keep his job–changed his position. He entered into the IJSAO's standard proffer agreement on June 16, 2004 and met with prosecutors on that date, June 17, and November 23, 2004.

The record does not fully disclose what transpired next between Ms. Warley and the USAO. In any event, she returned for a second proffer session on October 19, 2004 that lasted less than twenty minutes. Ms. Warley's counsel advised the government that Ms. Warley believed that certain Texas statutes precluded her from voluntarily revealing client information without the clients' permission and asked for a grand jury subpoena, compliance with which would be mandatory. The government obliged, but the USAO then terminated the proffer session despite Ms. Warley's request to continue. A few days later, Ms. Warley appeared before the grand jury but invoked the Fifth Amendment.

On November 10, 2004, Mr. Weddle again wrote to Skadden, informing it that "notwithstanding [Ms. Warley's] counsel's representations that she would cooperate with the investigation, [she] continues to refuse to cooperate." On November 15, 2004, Skadden forwarded the government's letter to Ms. Warley's counsel and advised him that KPMG had ceased payment of her legal fees, effective November 10, 2004. It added:

"In addition, absent an indication from the government within the next ten business days that your client no longer refuses to cooperate with the investigation, KPMG will consider additional actions, including Ms. Warley's separation from the Firm."

In the end, Ms. Warley's counsel disputed the claim that she had not cooperated, but she nevertheless was terminated by KPMG. Subsequent negotiations between Ms. Warley's counsel and the government concerning a further proffer were not successful.

In sum, then, all of the proffers followed KPMG's conditioning of the payment of attorneys' fees on employees' cooperation with the government. In addition, Mr. Smith's proffer and that of Ms. Warley on October 19, 2004 both followed explicit threats of employment termination.

KPMG's Claims That It Successfully Pressured Employees to Talk

KPMG repeatedly claimed that there was a direct causal connection between its actions and the proffers by some of its employees.

In a November 2, 2004 letter to the USAO, which obviously was intended to demonstrate that KPMG should not be indicted because, among other things, it had cooperated with the government, Skadden wrote:

"KPMG has repeatedly directed all current and former personnel to cooperate with the investigation and has conditioned payment of attorney's fees upon prompt, complete, and truthful cooperation with the government's inquiry. Whenever your Office has notified us that; individuals have not rendered prompt, complete, and truthful cooperation, KPMG has promptly and without question encouraged them to cooperate and threatened to cease payment of their attorney fees and (if applicable) to take personnel action, including termination. *In certain instances, KPMG's action has led previously non-cooperating individuals to meet with your Office.* In other instances, KPMG has ceased payment of fees and expenses."

At later meetings, and in a so-called "White Paper" that argued against indictment of the firm, Mr. Bennett "noted that KPMG had 'hinged attorneys' fees on whether people would talk to [the government]'" and "that KPMG had cut off fees for several individuals for non-cooperation and had terminated two partners for noncooperation," including for *"asserting . . . [the] 5th Amendment right not to testify."* A memorandum of a June 13, 2005 meeting with the DOJ discloses that Mr. Bennett argued that "We [KPMG] said we'd pressure–although we didn't use that word–our employees to cooperate" and when employees did not cooperate, "Justin [AUSA Weddle] or Stan [AUSA Okula] would tell us," and the firm then cut off fee payments and/or fired the individual. Indeed, KPMG's final submission to the DOJ argued that it had fully cooperated by, among other things, "pressuring current and former personnel to cooperate fully with the investigation."

1) Under these facts should KPMG receive full cooperation credit?
2) Did KPMG go too far in forcing its employees to incriminate themselves?
3) Did the DOJ act appropriately?

VI. Monitoring Future Compliance

DPAs typically provide for a period of probation during which the corporate defendant institutes compliance and ethics programs and other self-policing measures. During this probation period, the prosecutor may appoint an independent monitor to verify the corporation's adherence to the terms of the DPA.[44]

USAM Criminal Resource Manual § 163 sets forth the criteria for the use of monitors:

> A monitor's primary responsibility is to assess and monitor a corporation's compliance with the terms of the agreement specifically designed to address and reduce the risk of recurrence of the corporation's misconduct, and not to further punitive goals. . . . [I]t may be appropriate to use a monitor where a company does not have an effective internal compliance program, or where it needs to establish necessary internal controls.
>
> . . . .
>
> In negotiating agreements with corporations, prosecutors should be mindful of both: (1) the potential benefits that employing a monitor may have for the

---

44. *See* U. S. Dep't of Justice, U.S. Attorneys' Manual, Criminal Resource Manual § 163 (2008) [hereinafter USAM CRM].

corporation and the public, and (2) the cost of a monitor and its impact on the operations of a corporation.[45]

As this provision recognizes, appointment of a monitor is a costly and intrusive proposition. Holding a broad mandate to "reduce the risk of recurrence of the corporation's misconduct," the monitor and her staff roam the corporation and scrutinize different aspects of operations at will.[46]

United States Attorneys' Manual

Criminal Resource Manual 163. Selection and Use of Monitors in Deferred Prosecution Agreements and Non-Prosecution Agreements with Corporations

March 7, 2008
MEMORANDUM FOR HEADS OF DEPARTMENT COMPONENTS
UNITED STATES ATTORNEYS

FROM: Craig S. Morford
Acting Deputy Attorney General

SUBJECT: Selection and Use of Monitors in Deferred Prosecution Agreements and Non-Prosecution Agreements with Corporations

INTRODUCTION

The Department of Justice's commitment to deterring and preventing corporate crime remains a high priority. The Principles of Federal Prosecution of Business Organizations set forth guidance to federal prosecutors regarding charges against corporations. A careful consideration of those principles and the facts in a given case may result in a decision to negotiate an agreement to resolve a criminal case against a corporation without a formal conviction—either a deferred prosecution agreement or a non-prosecution agreement. As part of some negotiated corporate agreements, there have been provisions pertaining to an independent corporate monitor. The corporation benefits from expertise in the area of corporate compliance from an independent third party. The corporation, its shareholders, employees and the public at large then benefit from reduced recidivism of corporate crime and the protection of the integrity of the marketplace.

The purpose of this memorandum is to present a series of principles for drafting provisions pertaining to the use of monitors in connection with deferred prosecution and non-prosecution agreements (hereafter referred to collectively as "agreements") with corporations. Given the varying facts and circumstances of each case—where different industries, corporate size and structure, and other

45. *Id.*
46. *Id.*

considerations may be at issue—any guidance regarding monitors must be practical and flexible. This guidance is limited to monitors, and does not apply to third parties, whatever their titles, retained to act as receivers, trustees, or perform other functions.

A monitor's primary responsibility is to assess and monitor a corporation's compliance with the terms of the agreement specifically designed to address and reduce the risk of recurrence of the corporation's misconduct, and not to further punitive goals. A monitor should only be used where appropriate given the facts and circumstances of a particular matter. For example, it may be appropriate to use a monitor where a company does not have an effective internal compliance program, or where it needs to establish necessary internal controls. Conversely, in a situation where a company has ceased operations in the area where the criminal misconduct occurred, a monitor may not be necessary.

In negotiating agreements with corporations, prosecutors should be mindful of both: (1) the potential benefits that employing a monitor may have for the corporation and the public, and (2) the cost of a monitor and its impact on the operations of a corporation. Prosecutors shall, at a minimum, notify the appropriate United States Attorney or Department Component Head prior to the execution of an agreement that includes a corporate monitor. The appropriate United States Attorney or Department Component Head shall, in turn, provide a copy of the agreement to the Assistant Attorney General for the Criminal Division at a reasonable time after it has been executed. The Assistant Attorney General for the Criminal Division shall maintain a record of all such agreements.

This memorandum does not address all provisions concerning monitors that have been included or could appropriately be included in agreements. Rather this memorandum sets forth nine basic principles in the areas of selection, scope of duties, and duration.

. . . .

SELECTION

1. Principle: Before beginning the process of selecting a monitor in connection with deferred prosecution agreements and non-prosecution agreements, the corporation and the Government should discuss the necessary qualifications for a monitor based on the facts and circumstances of the case. The monitor must be selected based on the merits. The selection process must, at a minimum, be designed to: (1) select a highly qualified and respected person or entity based on suitability for the assignment and all of the circumstances; (2) avoid potential and actual conflicts of interests, and (3) otherwise instill public confidence by implementing the steps set forth in this Principle.

To avoid a conflict, first, Government attorneys who participate in the process of selecting a monitor shall be mindful of their obligation to comply with the conflict-of-interest guidelines set forth in 18 U.S.C. § 208 and 5 C.F.R. Part 2635. Second, the Government shall create a standing or ad

hoc committee in the Department component or office where the case originated to consider monitor candidates. United States Attorneys and Assistant Attorneys General may not make, accept, or veto the selection of monitor candidates unilaterally. Third, the Office of the Deputy Attorney General must approve the monitor. Fourth, the Government should decline to accept a monitor if he or she has an interest in, or relationship with, the corporation or its employees, officers or directors that would cause a reasonable person to question the monitor's impartiality. Finally, the Government should obtain a commitment from the corporation that it will not employ or be affiliated with the monitor for a period of not less than one year from the date the monitorship is terminated.

Comment: Because a monitor's role may vary based on the facts of each case and the entity involved, there is no one method of selection that should necessarily be used in every instance. For example, the corporation may select a monitor candidate, with the Government reserving the right to veto the proposed choice if the monitor is unacceptable. In other cases, the facts may require the Government to play a greater role in selecting the monitor. Whatever method is used, the Government should determine what selection process is most effective as early in the negotiations as possible, and endeavor to ensure that the process is designed to produce a high-quality and conflict-free monitor and to instill public confidence. If the Government determines that participation in the selection process by any Government personnel creates, or appears to create, a potential or actual conflict in violation of 18 U.S.C. § 208 and 5 C.F.R. Part 2635, the Government must proceed as in other matters where recusal issues arise. In all cases, the Government must submit the proposed monitor to the Office of the Deputy Attorney General for review and approval before the monitorship is established.

Ordinarily, the Government and the corporation should discuss what role the monitor will play and what qualities, expertise, and skills the monitor should have. While attorneys, including but not limited to former Government attorneys, may have certain skills that qualify them to function effectively as a monitor, other individuals, such as accountants, technical or scientific experts, and compliance experts, may have skills that are more appropriate to the tasks contemplated in a given agreement.

Subsequent employment or retention of the monitor by the corporation after the monitorship period concludes may raise concerns about both the appearance of a conflict of interest and the effectiveness of the monitor during the monitorship, particularly with regard to the disclosure of possible new misconduct. Such employment includes both direct and indirect, or subcontracted, relationships.

Each United States Attorney's Office and Department component shall create a standing or ad hoc committee ("Committee") of prosecutors to consider the selection or veto, as appropriate, of monitor candidates. The Committee should, at a minimum, include the office ethics advisor, the Criminal Chief of the United States Attorney's Office or relevant Section Chief of the Department component, and at least one other experienced prosecutor.

Where practicable, the corporation, the Government, or both parties, depending on the selection process being used, should consider a pool of at least three qualified monitor candidates. Where the selection process calls for the corporation to choose the monitor at the outset, the corporation should submit its choice from among the pool of candidates to the Government. Where the selection process calls for the Government to play a greater role in selecting the monitor, the Government should, where practicable, identify at least three acceptable monitors from the pool of candidates, and the corporation shall choose from that list.

SCOPE OF DUTIES

A. INDEPENDENCE

2. <u>Principle</u>: A monitor is an independent third-party, not an employee or agent of the corporation or of the Government.

<u>Comment</u>: A monitor by definition is distinct and independent from the directors, officers, employees, and other representatives of the corporation. The monitor is not the corporation's attorney. Accordingly, the corporation may not seek to obtain or obtain legal advice from the monitor. Conversely, a monitor also is not an agent or employee of the Government.

While a monitor is independent both from the corporation and the Government, there should be open dialogue among the corporation, the Government and the monitor throughout the duration of the agreement.

B. MONITORING COMPLIANCE WITH THE AGREEMENT

3. <u>Principle</u>: A monitor's primary responsibility should be to assess and monitor a corporation's compliance with those terms of the agreement that are specifically designed to address and reduce the risk of recurrence of the corporation's misconduct, including, in most cases, evaluating (and where appropriate proposing) internal controls and corporate ethics and compliance programs.

<u>Comment</u>: At the corporate level, there may be a variety of causes of criminal misconduct, including but not limited to the failure of internal controls or ethics and compliance programs to prevent, detect, and respond to such misconduct. A monitor's primary role is to evaluate whether a corporation has both adopted and effectively implemented ethics and compliance programs to address and reduce the risk of recurrence of the corporation's misconduct. A well-designed ethics and compliance program that is not effectively implemented will fail to lower the risk of recidivism.

A monitor is not responsible to the corporation's shareholders. Therefore, from a corporate governance standpoint, responsibility for designing an ethics and compliance program that will prevent misconduct should remain with the corporation, subject to the monitor's input, evaluation and recommendations.

4. <u>Principle</u>: In carrying out his or her duties, a monitor will often need to understand the full scope of the corporation's misconduct covered by the

agreement, but the monitor's responsibilities should be no broader than necessary to address and reduce the risk of recurrence of the corporation's misconduct.

Comment: The scope of a monitor's duties should be tailored to the facts of each case to address and reduce the risk of recurrence of the corporation's misconduct. Among other things, focusing the monitor's duties on these tasks may serve to calibrate the expense of the monitorship to the failure that gave rise to the misconduct the agreement covers.

Neither the corporation nor the public benefits from employing a monitor whose role is too narrowly defined (and, therefore, prevents the monitor from effectively evaluating the reforms intended by the parties) or too broadly defined (and, therefore, results in the monitor engaging in activities that fail to facilitate the corporation's implementation of the reforms intended by the parties).

The monitor's mandate is not to investigate historical misconduct. Nevertheless, in appropriate circumstances, an understanding of historical misconduct may inform a monitor's evaluation of the effectiveness of the corporation's compliance with the agreement.

C. COMMUNICATIONS AND RECOMMENDATIONS BY THE MONITOR

5. Principle: Communication among the Government, the corporation and the monitor is in the interest of all the parties. Depending on the facts and circumstances, it may be appropriate for the monitor to make periodic written reports to both the Government and the corporation.

Comment: A monitor generally works closely with a corporation and communicates with a corporation on a regular basis in the course of his or her duties. The monitor must also have the discretion to communicate with the Government as he or she deems appropriate. For example, a monitor should be free to discuss with the Government the progress of, as well as issues arising from, the drafting and implementation of an ethics and compliance program. Depending on the facts and circumstances, it may be appropriate for the monitor to make periodic written reports to both the Government and the corporation regarding, among other things: (1) the monitor's activities; (2) whether the corporation is complying with the terms of the agreement; and (3) any changes that are necessary to foster the corporation's compliance with the terms of the agreement.

6. Principle: If the corporation chooses not to adopt recommendations made by the monitor within a reasonable time, either the monitor or the corporation, or both, should report that fact to the Government, along with the corporation's reasons. The Government may consider this conduct when evaluating whether the corporation has fulfilled its obligations under the agreement.

Comment: The corporation and its officers and directors are ultimately responsible for the ethical and legal operations of the corporation. Therefore, the corporation should evaluate whether to adopt recommendations made by the monitor. If the corporation declines to adopt a recommendation by the monitor, the Government should consider both the monitor's recommendation and the corporation's reasons in determining whether the corporation is complying with the agreement. A flexible timetable should be established to ensure that both a monitor's recommendations and the corporation's decision to adopt or reject them are made well before the expiration of the agreement.

D. REPORTING OF PREVIOUSLY UNDISCLOSED OR NEW MISCONDUCT

7. <u>Principle</u>: The agreement should clearly identify any types of previously undisclosed or new misconduct that the monitor will be required to report directly to the Government. The agreement should also provide that as to evidence of other such misconduct, the monitor will have the discretion to report this misconduct to the Government or the corporation or both.

<u>Comment</u>: As a general rule, timely and open communication between and among the corporation, the Government and the monitor regarding allegations of misconduct will facilitate the review of the misconduct and formulation of an appropriate response to it. The agreement may set forth certain types of previously undisclosed or new misconduct that the monitor will be required to report directly to the Government. Additionally, in some instances, the monitor should immediately report other such misconduct directly to the Government and not to the corporation. The presence of any of the following factors militates in favor of reporting such misconduct directly to the Government and not to the corporation, namely, where the misconduct: (1) poses a risk to public health or safety or the environment; (2) involves senior management of the corporation; (3) involves obstruction of justice; (4) involves criminal activity which the Government has the opportunity to investigate proactively and/or covertly; or (5) otherwise poses a substantial risk of harm. On the other hand, in instances where the allegations of such misconduct are not credible or involve actions of individuals outside the scope of the corporation's business, the monitor may decide, in the exercise of his or her discretion, that the allegations need not be reported directly to the Government.

DURATION

8. <u>Principle</u>: The duration of the agreement should be tailored to the problems that have been found to exist and the types of remedial measures needed for the monitor to satisfy his or her mandate.

<u>Comment</u>: The following criteria should be considered when negotiating duration of the agreement (not necessarily in this order): (1) the nature and seriousness of the underlying misconduct; (2) the pervasiveness and duration of misconduct within the corporation, including the complicity or involvement of senior management; (3) the corporation's history of similar misconduct; (4) the nature of the corporate culture; (5) the scale and complexity of any remedial measures contemplated by the agreement, including the size of the entity or business unit at issue; and (6) the stage of design and implementation of remedial measures when the monitorship commences. It is reasonable to forecast that completing an assessment of more extensive and/or complex remedial

measures will require a longer period of time than completing an assessment of less extensive and/or less complex ones. Similarly, it is reasonable to forecast that a monitor who is assigned responsibility to assess a compliance program that has not been designed or implemented may take longer to complete that assignment than one who is assigned responsibility to assess a compliance program that has already been designed and implemented.

9. Principle: In most cases, an agreement should provide for an extension of the monitor provision(s) at the discretion of the Government in the event that the corporation has not successfully satisfied its obligations under the agreement. Conversely, in most cases, an agreement should provide for early termination if the corporation can demonstrate to the Government that there exists a change in circumstances sufficient to eliminate the need for a monitor.

Comment: If the corporation has not satisfied its obligations under the terms of the agreement at the time the monitorship ends, the corresponding risk of recidivism will not have been reduced and an extension of the monitor provision(s) may be appropriate. On the other hand, there are a number of changes in circumstances that could justify early termination of an agreement. For example, if a corporation ceased operations in the area that was the subject of the agreement, a monitor may no longer be necessary. Similarly, if a corporation is purchased by or merges with another entity that has an effective ethics and compliance program, it may be prudent to terminate a monitorship.

Notes and Questions

In a 2014 *New York Times* article on the efficacy of corporate monitors, Steven Davidoff Solomon referred to the appointment of a monitor as a "nice gift" that will earn millions for the monitor but "do little more than that."[47] The article noted: "[o]ne of the main criticisms of these programs is that they perpetuate an 'old boys' network,' rewarding former federal prosecutors with a job that pays millions of dollars."[48] "[M]onitors are . . . picked in a rather murky way," often through an anonymous committee in the U.S. Attorney's office, and their reports are never made public.[49]

The article mentioned several appointments of former Justice Department officials as monitors, including former Attorney General John Ashcroft, former Deputy Attorney General Paul McNulty, and former U.S. Attorney Bart Schwartz.[50] Congress held hearings on this issue in March 2008, which "[s]pecifically . . . explored New Jersey U.S. Attorney Christopher Christie's appointment

---

47. Steven Davidoff Solomon, *In Corporate Monitor, a Well-Paying Job but Unknown Results*, N.Y. Times: Dealbook (Apr. 15, 2014), https://dealbook.nytimes.com/2014/04/15/in-corporate-monitor-a-well-paying-job-but-unknown-results/.
48. *Id.*
49. *Id.*
50. *See id.*

of John Ashcroft, his former Attorney General, to serve as an independent corporate monitor and collect fees potentially between $28 and $52 million."[51]

The DOJ has defended its practice of keeping monitor reports confidential on the grounds that:

> Disclosing that information would harm [companies] because it would expose [companies'] sensitive, commercial information . . . [and] would also harm the DOJ's ability to obtain similar information from other companies in the future and its ability to reduce recidivism of corporations that commit crimes. Companies . . . that have been convicted of crimes often need monitors to review their compliance programs and ensure that those programs are effective. If the information that a monitor gives the DOJ can be obtained through FOIA, companies and their employees are not likely to be candid with monitors. This would harm the DOJ's enforcement efforts because the DOJ would be less likely to receive reliable information from companies under monitorships. Consequently, the DOJ would have inadequate and insufficient information to determine whether companies had improved their compliance programs as required by agreements between the companies and the DOJ.[52]

The Morford Memorandum, issued only days before the March 2008 Congressional hearings, was intended to address criticism of the compliance monitor selection process. Subsequently, several additional memoranda have been issued by the DOJ to further clarify the process:

- The Breuer Memorandum of June 2009 elaborated on the selection process.[53] Specifically, it required that:

  > [T]he selection process . . . (i) instill public confidence in the process and (ii) result in the selection of a highly qualified person or entity, free of any actual or potential conflict of interest or appearance of a potential or actual conflict of interest, and suitable for the assignment at hand.[54]

- The Grindler Memorandum of March 2010 set forth a process for companies to reject a monitor's recommendations as too costly.[55] It provided that:

  > With respect to any Monitor recommendation that the company considers unduly burdensome, impractical, unduly expensive, or otherwise inadvisable, the company need not adopt the recommendation immediately; instead, the company may propose in writing an alternative policy, procedure, or system designed to achieve the same objective or purpose.[56]

---

51. H.R. REP. No. 110-941, at 84 (2009), https://www.congress.gov/110/crpt/hrpt941/CRPT-110hrpt941.pdf.

52. Memorandum for U.S. Dep't of Justice at 2, 100Reporters LLC v. U.S. Dep't of Justice, No. 1:14-cv-01264-RC (D.D.C. Mar 22, 2016).

53. *See* Memorandum from Lanny A. Breuer, Assistant Attorney Gen., U.S. Dep't of Justice, Selection of Monitors in Criminal Division Matters (June 24, 2009) [hereinafter Breuer Memo], https://www.justice.gov/sites/default/files/criminal-fraud/legacy/2012/11/14/response3-supp-appx-3.pdf.

54. *Id.* at 2.

55. *See* USAM CRM, *supra* note 44, § 166.

56. *Id.*

1) Is it appropriate for current U.S. Attorneys to appoint former U.S. Attorneys as monitors, particularly in light of their exorbitant fees?
2) Should reports of monitors be made public?
3) Do former U.S. Attorneys generally possess sufficient knowledge and experience in corporate matters to competently serve as corporate monitors?

TEST YOUR KNOWLEDGE
Exercising Prosecutorial Discretion

In 2010, acting on a tip from a whistleblower employed by HSBC Holdings plc ("HSBC Group"), the DOJ began an investigation of the UK-based bank for:

1) Failing to maintain an adequate anti-money laundering compliance program, and
2) Violating U.S. sanctions by conducting business with Iran and Sudan.

HSBC Group fully cooperated—turning over all relevant documents and data and facilitating witness interviews with its employees. After completing its investigation, the DOJ issued the following press release on December 11, 2012:

> WASHINGTON—. . . [HSBC Group] —a United Kingdom corporation headquartered in London—and HSBC Bank USA N.A. (HSBC Bank USA) (together, HSBC)—a federally chartered banking corporation headquartered in McLean, Va.—violat[ed] the Bank Secrecy Act (BSA), the International Emergency Economic Powers Act (IEEPA) and the Trading with the Enemy Act (TWEA). According to court documents, HSBC Bank USA violated the BSA by failing to maintain an effective anti-money laundering program and to conduct appropriate due diligence on its foreign correspondent account holders. The HSBC Group violated IEEPA and TWEA by illegally conducting transactions on behalf of customers in Cuba, Iran, Libya, Sudan and Burma—all countries that were subject to sanctions enforced by the Office of Foreign Assets Control (OFAC) at the time of the transactions.
>
> . . . .
>
> "HSBC is being held accountable for stunning failures of oversight—and worse—that led the bank to permit narcotics traffickers and others to launder hundreds of millions of dollars through HSBC subsidiaries, and to facilitate hundreds of millions more in transactions with sanctioned countries," said Assistant Attorney General Breuer. "The record of dysfunction that prevailed at HSBC for many years was astonishing. Today, HSBC is paying a heavy price for its conduct, and, under the terms of today's agreement, if the bank fails to comply with the agreement in any way, we reserve the right to fully prosecute it."
>
> . . . .

The AML Investigation

According to court documents, from 2006 to 2010, HSBC Bank USA severely understaffed its AML compliance function and failed to implement an anti-money laundering program capable of adequately monitoring suspicious transactions and activities from HSBC Group Affiliates, particularly HSBC Mexico, one of HSBC Bank USA's largest Mexican customers. This included a failure to monitor billions of dollars in purchases of physical U.S. dollars, or "banknotes," from these affiliates. Despite evidence of serious money laundering risks associated with doing business in Mexico, from at least 2006 to 2009, HSBC Bank USA rated Mexico as "standard" risk, its lowest AML risk category. As a result, HSBC Bank USA failed to monitor over $670 billion in wire transfers and over $9.4 billion in purchases of physical U.S. dollars from HSBC Mexico during this period, when HSBC Mexico's own lax AML controls caused it to be the preferred financial institution for drug cartels and money launderers.

A significant portion of the laundered drug trafficking proceeds were involved in the Black Market Peso Exchange (BMPE), a complex money laundering system that is designed to move the proceeds from the sale of illegal drugs in the United States to drug cartels outside of the United States, often in Colombia. According to court documents, beginning in 2008, an investigation . . . identified multiple HSBC Mexico accounts associated with BMPE activity and revealed that drug traffickers were depositing hundreds of thousands of dollars in bulk U.S. currency each day into HSBC Mexico accounts.

As a result of HSBC Bank USA's AML failures, at least $881 million in drug trafficking proceeds—including proceeds of drug trafficking by the Sinaloa Cartel in Mexico and the Norte del Valle Cartel in Colombia—were laundered through HSBC Bank USA. HSBC Group admitted it did not inform HSBC Bank USA of significant AML deficiencies at HSBC Mexico, despite knowing of these problems and their effect on the potential flow of illicit funds through HSBC Bank USA.

The Sanctions Investigation

According to court documents, from the mid-1990s through September 2006, HSBC Group allowed approximately $660 million in OFAC-prohibited transactions to be processed through U.S. financial institutions, including HSBC Bank USA. HSBC Group followed instructions from sanctioned entities such as Iran, Cuba, Sudan, Libya, and Burma, to omit their names from U.S. dollar payment messages sent to HSBC Bank USA and other financial institutions located in the United States. The bank also removed information identifying the countries from U.S. dollar payment messages; deliberately used less-transparent payment messages, known as cover payments; and worked with at least one sanctioned entity to format payment messages, which prevented the bank's filters from blocking prohibited payments.

Specifically, beginning in the 1990s, HSBC Group affiliates worked with sanctioned entities to insert cautionary notes in payment messages including "care sanctioned country," "do not mention our name in NY," or "do not mention Iran." HSBC Group became aware of this improper practice in 2000. In 2003, HSBC Group's head of compliance acknowledged that amending payment messages "could provide the basis for an action against [HSBC] Group for breach of sanctions." Notwithstanding instructions from HSBC Group Compliance to terminate this practice, HSBC Group affiliates were permitted to engage in the practice for an additional three years through the granting of dispensations to HSBC Group policy.

Court documents show that as early as July 2001, HSBC Bank USA's chief compliance officer confronted HSBC Group's Head of Compliance on the issue of amending payments and was assured that "Group Compliance would not support blatant attempts to avoid sanctions, or actions which would place [HSBC Bank USA] in a potentially compromising position." As early as July 2001, HSBC Bank USA told HSBC Group's head of compliance that it was concerned that the use of cover payments prevented HSBC Bank USA from confirming whether the underlying transactions met OFAC requirements. From 2001 through 2006, HSBC Bank USA repeatedly told senior compliance officers at HSBC Group that it would not be able to properly screen sanctioned entity payments if payments were being sent using the cover method. These protests were ignored.

. . . .

Manhattan District Attorney Cyrus R. Vance Jr., said, "New York is a center of international finance, and those who use our banks as a vehicle for international crime will not be tolerated. My office has entered into Deferred Prosecution Agreements with two different banks in just the past two days, and with six banks over the past four years. Sanctions enforcement is of vital importance to our national security and the integrity of our financial system. The fight against money laundering and terror financing requires global cooperation, and our joint investigations in this and other related cases highlight the importance of coordination in the enforcement of U.S. sanctions. I thank our federal counterparts for their ongoing partnership."

Queens County District Attorney Richard A. Brown said, "No corporate entity should ever think itself too large to escape the consequences of assisting international drug cartels. In particular, banks have a special responsibility to use appropriate due diligence in monitoring the cash transactions flowing through their financial system and identifying the sources of that money in order not to assist in criminal activity. By allowing such illicit transactions to occur, HSBC failed in its global responsibility to us all. Hopefully, as a result of this historical settlement, we have gained the attention of not only HSBC but that of every other major financial institution so that they cannot turn a blind eye to the crime of money laundering."[1]

In addition to fully cooperating with the DOJ's investigation, HSBC immediately undertook the following remedial measures:

a. HSBC Group . . . [installed] a new leadership team, including a new CEO, Chairman, Chief Legal Officer, and Head of Global Standards Assurance.

---

1. Press Release, U.S. Dep't of Justice, HSBC Holdings Plc. and HSBC Bank USA N.A. Admit to Anti-Money Laundering and Sanctions Violations, Forfeit $1.256 Billion in Deferred Prosecution Agreement (Dec. 11, 2002), https://www.justice.gov/opa/pr/hsbc-holdings-plc-and-hsbc-bank-usa-na-admit-anti-money-laundering-and-sanctions-violations.

b. HSBC Group . . . simplified its control structure so that the entire organization [was] aligned around four global businesses, five regional geographies, and ten global functions. This allows HSBC Group to better manage its business and communication, and better understand and address risks worldwide.

c. Since January 2011, HSBC Group [applied] a more consistent global risk appetite and, as a result, has sold 42 businesses and withdrawn from 9 countries.

d. HSBC Group [undertook] to implement single global standards shaped by the highest or most effective anti-money laundering standards available in any location where the HSBC Group operates. This new policy will require that all HSBC Group Affiliates will, at a minimum, adhere to U.S. anti-money laundering standards.

e. HSBC Group . . . elevated the Head of HSBC Group Compliance position to a Group General Manager, which is one of the 50 most senior employees at HSBC globally. HSBC Group has also replaced the individual serving as Head of HSBC Group Compliance.

f. The Head of HSBC Group Compliance [was] given direct oversight over every compliance officer globally, so that both accountability and escalation now flow directly to and from HSBC Group Compliance.

g. Eighteen of the top twenty-one most senior officers at HSBC Group [were replaced] since the beginning of 2011.

h. Material or systemic AML control weaknesses at any affiliate that [were] reported by the Regional and Global Business Compliance heads [and] shared with all other Regional and Global Business Compliance heads facilitating horizontal information sharing.

i. The senior leadership team that attends HSBC Group Management Board meetings is collectively and individually responsible for reviewing all of the information presented at the meeting, as well as all written documentation provided in advance of the meeting, and determining whether it affects their respective entity or region. In addition, if an executive believes that something occurring within his or her area of responsibility affects another business or affiliate within HSBC Group, it is that executive's responsibility to seek out the executives from that business or affiliate and work to address the issue.

j. HSBC Group . . . restructured its senior executive bonus system so that the extent to which the senior executive meets compliance standards and values has a significant impact on the amount of the senior executive's bonus, and failure to meet those compliance standards and values could result in the voiding of the senior executive's entire year-end bonus.

k. HSBC Group . . . commenced a review of all [Know Your Customer ("KYC")] files across the entire Group. The first phase of this remediation will cost an estimated $700 million to complete over five years.

l. HSBC Group . . . defer[red] a portion of the bonus compensation for its most senior officers, namely its Group General Managers and Group Managing Directors, during the pendency of the deferred prosecution agreement, subject to EU and UK legal and regulatory requirements.

m. HSBC Group . . . adopted a set of guidelines to be taken into account when considering whether HSBC Group should do business in countries posing a particularly high corruption/rule of law risk as well as limiting business in those countries that pose a high financial crime risk.

n. Under HSBC Group's new global sanctions policy, HSBC Group will be utilizing key [government] sanctions lists to conduct screening in all jurisdictions, in all currencies.[2]

Assume that you are the Assistant United States Attorney in charge of HSBC's investigation. Based on the foregoing facts,

1) Would you indict, enter into a DPA, or walk away? Why?
2) Is it appropriate to appoint a corporate monitor? If so, what should be the scope of the monitor's responsibilities?
3) Critically evaluate HSBC's remedial measures. Are they sufficient? Do they align with the standards articulated by the FSGO? Are there any additional measures that HSBC should implement?
4) What, if any, additional information would you like to have to complete your analysis?

---

2. Statement of Facts, United States v. HSBC Bank USA, N.A., No. 1:12-cr-00763 (E.D.N.Y., filed on Dec. 11, 2012), https://www.justice.gov/sites/default/files/opa/legacy/2012/12/11/dpa-attachment-a.pdf.

PART ⬤ **II**

THE FOREIGN CORRUPT
PRACTICES ACT

L egal advice has traditionally identified the precise location of the red line between legal and illegal. As Justice Oliver Wendell Holmes, Jr. wrote, "a fair warning should be given to the world, in language that the common world will understand, of what the law intends to do if a certain line is passed. To make the warning fair, so far as possible the line should be clear."[1] In Justice Holmes's world, most legal resources were invested in identifying the red line of the law. This was a sensible investment, because once a business enterprise knew the precise location of the red line, it could freely take advantage of all the market opportunities available to it without crossing that line.

Now imagine a world where interpreting the law is the exclusive province of prosecutors, who can keep the lines fuzzy and move them at will. In such a world, the red line is replaced with a grey zone in which the particular conduct may or may not be deemed illegal by prosecutors, forcing business enterprises to either forgo opportunities or accept the risk of prosecution.

According to former Attorney General Ashcroft, whose deputy Larry Thompson inked the Thompson Memo, the enhanced power and discretion vested in prosecutors by the Thompson Memo has brought about exactly such a shift. Ashcroft points in particular to recent Foreign Corrupt Practices Act ("FCPA") enforcement trends as exemplifying this shift.[2] By resolving the vast majority of FCPA enforcement actions through DPAs or similar pretrial diversions, he argues, prosecutors have kept even the most basic terms of the statute undefined—giving them the option of altering their interpretation to fit the circumstances of each case.[3]

> [T]his unbridled power has allowed prosecutors to become corporate gover-
> nance bullies, forcing corporate defendants to accept the government's interpre-
> tation of the FCPA—no matter how unreasonable or dubious it may appear to be
> ... As a result, ... the FCPA, as an area of law being created outside of the normal
> judicial process with little judicial scrutiny, is providing far too much interpretive

1. McBoyle v. United States, 283 U.S. 25, 27 (1931).
2. John Ashcroft & John Ratcliffe, The Recent and Unusual Evolution of an Expanding FCPA, 26 Notre Dame J.L. Ethics & Pub. Pol'y 25, 33-34 (2012).
3. *Id.*

power to DOJ and SEC prosecutors to set precedents based solely upon unilateral demands on corporate defendants.[4]

Ashcroft is not alone in lodging this criticism.[5] But why was the FCPA "plucked out of relative obscurity"—as the Wall Street Journal suggested in a 2012 article—for special prosecutorial attention?[6] Why did the FCPA suddenly become the Justice Department's number two priority,[7] behind terrorism?[8]

Legislative Background of the FCPA

To understand how the FCPA became such an important prosecutorial tool, we must examine its history. The investigation around the Watergate scandal that toppled President Nixon discovered corporate slush funds being used for illegal political contributions in the U.S. and for bribing foreign government officials. In all, 400 U.S. companies admitted to paying more than $300 million in foreign bribes.[9] The scandal called into question the fundamental idea that business enterprises were capable of acting morally. As the Association of the Bar of the City of New York commented:

> No single issue of corporate behavior has engendered in recent times as much discussion in the United States—both in the private and public arenas—and as much administrative and legislative activity, as payments made abroad by corporations. In part, this interest derives from the important issue of integrity in public life. In part, it derives from the impact of the political and social controversies which eddy about corporate enterprise and the free enterprise system—Are multinational corporations good or bad? Should the center of gravity of corporate governance be under state or federal control? Are the concepts of private management and initiative consistent with notions of corporate ethics?[10]

Senator Frank Church, who conducted the first hearings touching on foreign bribery in 1975, believed that corporate corruption was marring the very idea

---

4. *Id.* (sentences reorganized from original source).

5. *See* SEC v. Vitesse Semiconductor Corp., 771 F. Supp. 2d 304, 309 (S.D.N.Y. 2011) (describing the current state of FCPA enforcement as "a stew of confusion and hypocrisy"); Allen R. Brooks, Comment, *A Corporate Catch-22: How Deferred and Non- Prosecution Agreements Impede the Full Development of the Foreign Corrupt Practices Act*, 7 J.L. Econ. & Pol'y 137, 156 (2010) ("[T]he number of precedents developed under the FCPA remains quite low despite great legal uncertainty surrounding the law, in large part due to the use of DPAs and NPAs.").

6. Joe Palazzolo, *From Watergate to Today, How FCPA Became So Feared*, Wall St. J. (Oct. 2, 2012, 12:01 AM), http://www.wsj.com/articles/SB10000872396390444752504578024791676151154.

7. Lanny Breuer, Assistant Attorney General, Speech before the 24th National Conference on the Foreign Corrupt Practices Act (Nov. 16, 2010), http://www.justice.gov/criminal/pr/speeches/2010/crm-speech-101116.html.

8. Palazzolo, *supra* note 6.

9. *Id.*

10. Mike Koehler, *The Story of the Foreign Corrupt Practices* Act, 73 Ohio St. L.J. 929, 936 (2012) (quoting *Unlawful Corporate Payments Act of 1977: Hearings Before the Subcomm. on Consumer Prot. and Fin. of the H. Comm. on Interstate and Foreign Commerce*, 95th Cong. 63 (1977)).

of free enterprise and undermining America's Cold War foreign policy.[11] "The Communist bloc chortles with glee at the sight of corrupt capitalism,"[12] he said on the Senate floor.

Two proposals emerged out of the hearings, each using a different approach to address the problem of corruption.[14] One proposal criminalized corrupt payments to foreign officials.[15] Opponents of this approach, including the SEC and the State Department, argued that such a law would be impossible to enforce and could be perceived by other countries as an American attempt to impose its moral standards upon the international community.[16]

The other proposal, advanced by the SEC, targeted corporate corruption in general by strengthening existing securities laws.[18] In testimony before Congress, the SEC argued:

> [W]e believe that any legislation in this area should embody a prohibition against the falsification of corporate accounting records. . . [Additionally], we believe that any legislation should require management to establish and maintain its own system of internal accounting controls designed to provide reasonable assurances that corporate transactions are executed in accordance with management's general or specific authorization; and that such transactions . . . are properly reflected on the corporation's books and records . . . .[19]

> Corporate bribery is bad business. In our free market system it is basic that the sale of products should take place on the basis of price, quality, and service. Corporate bribery is fundamentally destructive of this basic tenet. Corporate bribery of foreign officials takes place primarily to assist corporations in gaining business. Thus foreign corporate bribery affects the very stability of overseas business. Foreign corporate bribes also affect our domestic competitive climate when domestic firms engage in such practices as a substitute for healthy competition for foreign business.
>
> *— Senate Report No. 95-114*[13]

> When the Foreign Corrupt Practices Act became law, many critics claimed it to be 'Polly Anna-ish' [sic] legislation, and an example of the United States enforcing its values on the rest of the world. Today, 20 years later, those critics have been silenced. U.S. businesses are recognized worldwide as among the cleanest. In many cases, it also makes U.S. business men and women more innovative, and safer because criminals around the world now know that U.S. businesses must comply with anti-bribery laws.
>
> *—Jesse Helms, Chairman, Committee on Foreign Relations*[17]

Senator William Proxmire, who chaired the hearings after Senator Church, combined both recommendations into a single bill which for the first time: 1) obligated public companies to maintain accurate books and records; 2) obligated public companies to maintain adequate internal controls; and 3) prohibited corrupt payments to foreign officials.[20] This bill, which became the FCPA, was

---

11. Palazzolo, *supra* note 6.

12. *Id.*

13. U.S. Dep't. of Just. & U.S. Sec. and Exch. Comm'n, FCPA: A Resource Guide to the U.S. Foreign Corrupt Practices Act 4 (2012) [hereinafter FCPA Guide] quoting S. Rep. No. 95-114, at 4 (1977).

14. Koehler, *supra* note 10, at 984.

15. *Id.*

16. *Id.*

17. S. Exec. Comm. Rep. No. 105-19, at 47 (1998) (statement of Chairman Helms).

18. Koehler, *supra* note 10, at 986.

19. *Id.* (quoting U.S. Sec. & Exch. Comm'n, Rep. on Questionable and Illegal Corporate Payments and Practices 58 (Comm. Print 1976).

20. *See* Koehler, *supra* note 10, at 987–88.

designed as a two-pronged attack targeting not only corporate corruption, but also its link to state corruption. President Jimmy Carter signed the bill into law in 1977.[21]

FCPA's Revival in the New Century

For three decades, the FCPA was rarely enforced, existing largely as an expression of American idealism; that is, until 2002 when corrupt accounting practices led to the demise of corporate giants, including Enron and WorldCom.[22] The shocking revelations and massive losses in capital markets caused a public outcry that put corporate corruption front and center on Congress's agenda.[23] Congress passed the Sarbanes-Oxley Act of 2002 ("SOX") almost unanimously just months after the failures, giving sharp teeth to the FCPA.[24] SOX holds corporate officers and directors personally liable for their companies' non-compliance with the accounting and internal control provisions of the FCPA, dramatically increasing the consequences of non-compliance.[25]

Another development that contributed to the FCPA's revival was globalization. As planned economies around the world transitioned to free markets and opened to foreign investment, a global consensus formed against the use of private funds to corrupt fledgling public institutions in emerging economies.[26] That consensus allowed the U.S. to lead the charge in 1997 to forge the Organisation for Economic Co-operation and Development Anti-Bribery Convention ("OECD Convention"),[27] which required OECD members to pass legislation patterned after the FCPA—prohibiting foreign corruption and mandating accurate books and records.[28]

> It is the sense of the Congress that the President should pursue the negotiation of an international agreement, among the members of the Organization of Economic Cooperation and Development, to govern persons from those countries concerning acts prohibited with respect to issuers and domestic concerns by the amendments made by this section. Such international agreement should include a process by which problems and conflicts associated with such acts could be resolved.
>
> —*Omnibus Trade and Competitiveness Act of 1998, § 5003(d)*[29]

---

21. *See* Palazzolo, *supra* note 6.
22. Id. at 4–5.
23. *Id.*
24. Sarbanes-Oxley Act of 2002, Pub. L. No. 107-204, 116 Stat. 745 (codified in scattered sections of 11, 15, 18, 28 and 29 U.S.C.).
25. *Id.*
26. FCPA GUIDE, *supra* note 13, at 7–8.
27. *See generally* Convention on Combating Bribery of Foreign Public Officials in International Business Transactions, Dec. 17, 1997, S. TREATY DOC. 105-43, 2802 U.N.T.S. 225 [hereinafter OECD Anti-Bribery Convention].
28. *Id.* at arts. 1, 8; *see also* ORG. FOR ECON. CO-OPERATION AND DEV., CONVENTION ON COMBATTING BRIBERY OF FOREIGN PUBLIC OFFICIALS IN INT'L BUSINESS TRANSACTIONS AND RELATED DOCUMENTS 20-21 (2011) [hereinafter OECD CONVENTION COMMENTARIES, RECOMMENDATIONS, AND GUIDELINES].
29. FCPA GUIDE, *supra* note 13, at n.18 (citation omitted).

This was the first time that advanced economies—the source of nearly all investments in emerging markets—criminalized corrupt payments to foreign officials.[30] The FCPA was amended in 1998 to conform to U.S. treaty obligations under the OECD Convention.[31]

These amendments expanded the FCPA's scope to: (1) include payments made to secure "any improper advantage"; (2) reach certain foreign persons who commit an act in furtherance of a foreign bribe while in the United States; (3) cover public international organizations in the definition of "foreign official"; (4) add an alternative basis for jurisdiction based on nationality; and (5) apply criminal penalties to foreign nationals employed by or acting as agents of U.S. companies.[32]

The United Nations ("UN") followed suit in 2000, with the UN Convention Against Corruption.[33] With this international consensus, the stage was finally set for the FCPA's resurgence.

In November 2012, the DOJ and SEC jointly compiled their interpretations of the FCPA and the requirements of an effective FCPA compliance program into a single guide titled *A Resource Guide to the U.S. Foreign Corrupt Practices Act* ("FCPA Guide").[36] Because of the dearth of case law interpreting the FCPA's provisions, and the increasing prevalence of diversion agreements that bypass the judicial process, the FCPA Guide has emerged not only as the most authoritative guide to the FCPA, but also as a "universal"[37] guide to the type of compliance program that the DOJ and SEC consider "effective" for purposes of deciding whether to indict, enter into a DPA or walk away.

> At the urging of the United States, the OECD adopted in 1994 a Recommendation on Combating Bribery in International Business Transactions. . . . A Revised Recommendation on Combating Bribery in International Business Transactions was approved at a May 1997 meeting of OECD Ministers. . . . Three rounds of negotiations were held in July, October, and November. The Convention was signed in Paris on December 17th, 1997, and was submitted to the Senate on May 4, 1998.
>
> —*Senate Executive Report Number 105-19*[38]

---

30. OECD Convention Commentaries, Recommendations, and Guidelines, *supra* note 28, at 22.

31. FCPA Guide, *supra* note 13, at 4.

32. *Id.*

33. *See generally* United Nations Convention Against Corruption, Oct. 31, 2003, S. Treaty Doc. 109-6, 2349 U.N.T.S. 41.

34. Ashcroft & Ratcliffe, *supra* note 2, at 33–34.

35. *Id.*

36. *See* FCPA Guide, *supra* note 13.

37. Marshall L. Miller, Principal Deputy Assistant Attorney Gen., Criminal Div., Remarks at the Advanced Compliance and Ethics Workshop (Oct. 7, 2014), https://www.justice.gov/opa/speech/remarks-principal-deputy-assistant-attorney-general-criminal-division-marshall-l-miller-0.

38. S. Exec. Rep. No. 105-19, at 2 (1998) (report of the Senate Committee on Foreign Relations regarding the OECD Anti-Bribery Convention).

Testimony Before the Senate Committee on Foreign Relations on the OECD Convention on Combating the Bribery of Foreign Public Officials in International Business Transactions

Fritz F. Heimann, Transparency Int'l U.S. (June 9, 1998)[39]

I am here to urge prompt action by the Senate to ratify the OECD Convention to Combat Bribery of Foreign Public Officials. The Convention would take bribery out of the equation in international business. This would level the playing field between U.S. companies and foreign competitors, resulting in more orders for American companies and more jobs for American workers. The Convention would also contribute to other key U.S. objectives, by helping to overcome the effects of corruption on international development programs and on the stability of struggling democracies in Central and Eastern Europe and elsewhere.

The Convention has the overwhelming support of a broad coalition of major business organizations, including the Business Roundtable, the U.S. Council on International Business, the National Foreign Trade Council, the National Association of Manufacturers, and the Emergency Committee for American Trade.

. . . .

I. WHY CORRUPTION HAS BECOME A CRITICAL INTERNATIONAL ISSUE

During the past five years there has been a remarkable transformation in the willingness of the international community to confront the cancer of corruption. This is a development of which the United States can be justly proud, and for which the U.S. Congress deserves particular credit.

In 1977 the Foreign Corrupt Practices Act passed the Senate 87-0 and the House 349-0. The FCPA was an historic step, the first time any country made it a crime to bribe foreign officials. It was expected that other countries would follow the American example. After all, the same bribery scandals which prompted Congress to act had created major reverberations in Japan, Italy, the Netherlands, Indonesia, and Honduras. This expectation proved wrong. Not a single country acted to curb foreign bribery.

Since the FCPA went into effect, U.S. companies have lost orders amounting to many tens of billions of dollars to foreign competitors who remained free to pay bribes.

The U.S. Department of Commerce estimates that 139 international commercial contracts valued at $64 billion may have involved bribery by foreign firms and that U.S. firms lost 36 of those contracts valued at $11 billion. In many countries, including Germany and France, bribes continued to be treated as tax-deductible business expenses. Foreign governments not merely condoned, but effectively subsidized foreign bribes. Notwithstanding the failure of other countries to act, the U.S. Congress refused to repeal or water down the FCPA and insisted on retaining the moral high ground. In the past five years the tide has finally began to turn.

---

39. *Id.* at 50–54.

There is now widespread recognition that international bribery should no longer be tolerated. This change reflects the following factors:

- The end of the Cold War has resulted in the spread of democratic governments around the world. Political processes have become more open and corruption is harder to cover up. There is more freedom of the press, more independent prosecutors and judges.
- Corruption has been identified as a major obstacle to the transition to democracy and market economies in Central and Eastern Europe. Much of the failure of international development programs to improve the economies of the world's poorest countries is now widely attributed to corruption. The World Bank . . . has made corruption a high-priority issue.
- The Asian crisis has discredited the claim that rapid economic growth can continue notwithstanding endemic corruption. The IMF is making transparency a key element in its assistance programs.
- Massive bribery scandals in highly industrialized countries, including Italy, Japan, Korea, Spain, France and Belgium, have demolished the common excuse for inaction, that corruption is a serious problem only in developing countries. This has clearly created support for the OECD program.
- There is increasing recognition by international business leaders that a global economy requires common rules, and that these rules must be morally defensible. This has resulted in the development by the International Chamber of Commerce of strong Rules of Conduct to Combat Extortion and Bribery.
- Transparency International has grown with extraordinary speed and has helped raise public awareness of the costs of corruption. TI actively promotes the development of systemic reforms such as the OECD Convention.

These factors have produced a tidal change in public perceptions around the world. There now is widespread recognition that action against corruption is required. There are still entrenched groups who oppose reforms. Corruption obviously has powerful beneficiaries: corrupt companies, corrupt officials, and a legion of middlemen. However the prospects for reform have never been better.

II. WHY OECD CONVENTION PROVIDES SOLID FRAMEWORK FOR COMBATING INTERNATIONAL CORRUPTION

The OECD Convention is the most important achievement to date of the international drive for reform. The OECD is the ideal forum for tackling the supply side of international corruption because the industrialized countries that belong to the OECD are the home bases of practically all major international companies.

The Convention is the product of four years of hard work. The U.S. Government deserves great credit for diplomatic skill, forcefulness, and above all perseverance. The Convention provides a solid framework for an effective international system to prohibit bribery of foreign public officials.

. . . .

Sanctions for foreign bribery must be comparable to those for bribery of domestic officials, and must include effective criminal penalties or equivalent civil sanctions.

The Convention also calls for establishing accounting and auditing standards, including prohibition of off-the-books accounts.

. . . .

As noted before, the Convention tackles the supply side of corruption. The demand side—corruption by public officials—must also be addressed. The World Bank and others are working on procurement reforms, increased transparency, and other programs to combat demand-side abuses. The credibility of efforts . . . to promote reforms in the developing world will be greatly strengthened by the OECD effort to end foreign bribery by the industrialized countries.

. . . .

To conclude, the Convention will make foreign bribery a crime in the world's major exporting nations. It will significantly raise the standards for global competition, thereby improving American competitiveness, and strengthening international development, market reforms, and democratization programs. The Convention deserves strong support from your Committee on both practical and moral grounds. . . .

Notes and Questions

1) Does the following statement by Heimann tell the whole story?

Notwithstanding the failure of other countries to act, the U.S. Congress refused to repeal or water down the FCPA and insisted on retaining the moral high ground.[40]

2) What was the Asian crisis, and how did it "discredit[] the claim that rapid economic growth can continue notwithstanding endemic corruption?"[41]

3) Heimann states:

There is increasing recognition by international business leaders that a global economy requires common rules, and that these rules must be morally defensible.[42]

By what standard should moral defensibility be judged?

---

40. *Id.* at 51.
41. *Id.* at 52.
42. *Id.*

A Resource Guide to the U.S. Foreign Corrupt Practices Act: Introduction[43]

THE COSTS OF CORRUPTION

Corruption is a global problem. In the three decades since Congress enacted the FCPA, the extent of corporate bribery has become clearer and its ramifications in a transnational economy starker. Corruption impedes economic growth by diverting public resources from important priorities such as health, education, and infrastructure. It undermines democratic values and public accountability and weakens the rule of law. And it threatens stability and security by facilitating criminal activity within and across borders, such as the illegal trafficking of people, weapons, and drugs. International corruption also undercuts good governance and impedes U.S. efforts to promote freedom and democracy, end poverty, and combat crime and terrorism across the globe.

Corruption is also bad for business. Corruption is anti-competitive, leading to distorted prices and disadvantaging honest businesses that do not pay bribes. It increases the cost of doing business globally and inflates the cost of government contracts in developing countries. Corruption also introduces significant uncertainty into business transactions: Contracts secured through bribery may be legally unenforceable, and paying bribes on one contract often results in corrupt officials making ever-increasing demands. Bribery has destructive effects within a business as well, undermining employee confidence in a company's management and fostering a permissive atmosphere for other kinds of corporate misconduct, such as employee self-dealing, embezzlement, financial fraud, and anti-competitive behavior. Bribery thus raises the risks of doing business, putting a company's bottom line and reputation in jeopardy. Companies that pay bribes to win business ultimately undermine their own long-term interests and the best interests of their investors.

. . . .

NATIONAL LANDSCAPE: INTERAGENCY EFFORTS

DOJ and SEC share enforcement authority for the FCPA's anti-bribery and accounting provisions. They also work with many other federal agencies and law enforcement partners to investigate and prosecute FCPA violations, reduce bribery demands through good governance programs and other measures, and promote a fair playing field for U.S. companies doing business abroad.

DEPARTMENT OF JUSTICE

Department of Justice DOJ has criminal FCPA enforcement authority over "issuers" (i.e., public companies) and their officers, directors, employees, agents, or stockholders acting on the issuer's behalf. DOJ also has both criminal and civil enforcement responsibility for the FCPA's anti-bribery provisions over "domestic

---

43. FCPA GUIDE, *supra* note 13, at 2–8

concerns"—which include (a) U.S. citizens, nationals, and residents and (b) U.S. businesses and their officers, directors, employees, agents, or stockholders acting on the domestic concern's behalf—and certain foreign persons and businesses that act in furtherance of an FCPA violation while in the territory of the United States. Within DOJ, the Fraud Section of the Criminal Division has primary responsibility for all FCPA matters. FCPA matters are handled primarily by the FCPA Unit within the Fraud Section, regularly working jointly with U.S. Attorneys' Offices around the country.

. . . .

SECURITIES AND EXCHANGE COMMISSION

SEC is responsible for civil enforcement of the FCPA over issuers and their officers, directors, employees, agents, or stockholders acting on the issuer's behalf. SEC's Division of Enforcement has responsibility for investigating and prosecuting FCPA violations. In 2010, SEC's Enforcement Division created a specialized FCPA Unit, with attorneys in Washington, D.C. and in regional offices around the country, to focus specifically on FCPA enforcement. The Unit investigates potential FCPA violations; facilitates coordination with DOJ's FCPA program and with other federal and international law enforcement partners; uses its expert knowledge of the law to promote consistent enforcement of the FCPA; analyzes tips, complaints, and referrals regarding allegations of foreign bribery; and conducts public outreach to raise awareness of anti-corruption efforts and good corporate governance programs.

. . . .

INTERNATIONAL LANDSCAPE: GLOBAL ANTI-CORRUPTION EFFORTS

In recent years, there has been a growing international consensus that corruption must be combated, and the United States and other countries are parties to a number of international anti-corruption conventions. Under these conventions, countries that are parties undertake commitments to adopt a range of preventive and criminal law measures to combat corruption. The conventions incorporate review processes that allow the United States to monitor other countries to ensure that they are meeting their international obligations. Likewise, these processes in turn permit other parties to monitor the United States' anti-corruption laws and enforcement to ensure that such enforcement and legal frameworks are consistent with the United States' treaty obligations. U.S. officials regularly address the subject of corruption with our foreign counterparts to raise awareness of the importance of fighting corruption and urge stronger enforcement of anti-corruption laws and policies.

OECD WORKING GROUP ON BRIBERY AND THE ANTI-BRIBERY CONVENTION

The OECD was founded in 1961 to stimulate economic progress and world trade. As noted, the Anti-Bribery Convention requires its parties to criminalize the bribery of foreign public officials in international business transactions. As of November 1, 2012, there were 39 parties to the Anti-Bribery Convention: 34 OECD member countries (including the United States) and five non-OECD member countries (Argentina, Brazil, Bulgaria, the Russian Federation, and South Africa). All of these parties are also members of the OECD Working Group on Bribery (Working Group).

The Working Group is responsible for monitoring the implementation of the Anti-Bribery Convention, the 2009 Recommendation of the Council for Further Combating Bribery of Foreign Public Officials in International Business Transactions, and related instruments. Its members meet quarterly to review and monitor implementation of the Anti-Bribery Convention by member states around the world. Each party undergoes periodic peer review. This peer-review monitoring system is conducted in three phases. The Phase 1 review includes an in-depth assessment of each country's domestic laws implementing the Convention. The Phase 2 review examines the effectiveness of each country's laws and anti-bribery efforts. The final phase is a permanent cycle of peer review (the first cycle of which is referred to as the Phase 3 review) that evaluates a country's enforcement actions and results, as well as the country's efforts to address weaknesses identified during the Phase 2 review. All of the monitoring reports for the parties to the Convention can be found on the OECD website and can be a useful resource about the foreign bribery laws of the OECD Working Group member countries.

The United States was one of the first countries to undergo all three phases of review. The reports and appendices can be found on DOJ's and SEC's websites. In its Phase 3 review of the United States, which was completed in October 2010, the Working Group commended U.S. efforts to fight transnational bribery and highlighted a number of best practices developed by the United States. The report also noted areas where the United States' anti-bribery efforts could be improved, including consolidating publicly available information on the application of the FCPA and enhancing awareness among small- and medium-sized companies about the prevention and detection of foreign bribery. This guide is, in part, a response to these Phase 3 recommendations and is intended to help businesses and individuals better understand the FCPA.

U.N. CONVENTION AGAINST CORRUPTION

The United States is a state party to the United Nations Convention Against Corruption (UNCAC), which was adopted by the U.N. General Assembly on October 31, 2003, and entered into force on December 14, 2005. The United States ratified the UNCAC on October 30, 2006. The UNCAC requires parties to criminalize a wide range of corrupt acts, including domestic and foreign bribery and related offenses such as money laundering and obstruction of justice. The UNCAC also establishes guidelines for the creation of anti-corruption bodies, codes of conduct for public officials, transparent and objective systems of procurement, and enhanced accounting and auditing standards for the private sector. A peer review mechanism assesses the implementation of the UNCAC by parties to the Convention, with a focus in the first round on criminalization and law enforcement as well as international legal cooperation. The United States has been reviewed under the Pilot Review Programme, the report of which is available on DOJ's website. As of November 1, 2012, 163 countries were parties to the UNCAC.

OTHER ANTI-CORRUPTION CONVENTIONS

The Inter-American Convention Against Corruption (IACAC) was the first international anti-corruption convention, adopted in March 1996 in Caracas, Venezuela, by members of the Organization of American States. The IACAC requires parties (of which the United States is one) to criminalize both foreign and domestic bribery. A body known as the Mechanism for Follow-Up on the Implementation of the Inter-American Convention Against Corruption (MESICIC) monitors parties' compliance with the IACAC. As of November 1, 2012, 31 countries were parties to MESICIC.

The Council of Europe established the Group of States Against Corruption (GRECO) in 1999 to monitor countries' compliance with the Council of Europe's anticorruption standards, including the Council of Europe's Criminal Law Convention on Corruption. These standards include prohibitions on the solicitation and receipt of bribes, as well as foreign bribery. As of November 1, 2012, GRECO member states, which need not be members of the Council of Europe, include more than 45 European countries and the United States.

Notes and Questions

1) Why did the United States deem it necessary to bring about an international consensus against corruption?
2) Should the United States impose its moral standards on other countries where bribing government officials might be perceived as acceptable?
3) How did the SEC's proposals combat international corruption?

CHAPTER 4

The FCPA Accounting Provisions

I. Introduction
II. What Is Covered Under the Books and Records Provision of the FCPA
Accounting Provisions?
III. What Is Covered Under the Internal Controls Provision of the FCPA Accounting
Provisions?
 A. The COSO Framework
  1. Defining Internal Control
  2. Objectives
  3. Components of Internal Control
  4. The Seventeen Principles
IV. Who Is Covered Under the FCPA Accounting Provisions?
 A. Issuers and Their Subsidiaries
 B. Affiliates
V. Interplay Between the FCPA Accounting Provisions and the Sarbanes-Oxley Act
of 2002 ("SOX")
 A. Section 302: Officer Certification
 B. Section 404: Reporting on the Adequacy of Internal Controls

I. Introduction

The Foreign Corrupt Practices Act ("FCPA") accounting provisions mandate a foundational structure for a corporate self-policing system.[2] Because a corporation's power to act derives primarily from its financial resources, the first step in preventing misconduct is to institute a system that controls as well as documents the use of corporate assets. This system has two main components:

First, under the "books and records" provision, [corporations] must make and keep books, records, and accounts that . . . accurately and

> Although the accounting provisions were originally enacted as part of the FCPA, they do not apply only to bribery-related violations. Rather, the accounting provisions ensure that all public companies account for all of their assets and liabilities accurately and in reasonable detail, and they form the backbone for most accounting fraud and issuer disclosure cases brought by DOJ and SEC.
>
> —*FCPA Guide*[1]

---

1. U.S. Dep't. of Just. & U.S. Sec. and Exch. Comm'n, FCPA: A Resource Guide to the U.S. Foreign Corrupt Practices Act 4 (2012) [hereinafter FCPA Guide], at 38.
2. *Id.*, at 38–45.

fairly reflect . . . transactions and dispositions of . . . assets. Second, under the "internal controls" provision, [corporations] must devise and maintain a system of internal accounting controls sufficient to assure management's control, authority, and responsibility over the firm's assets. . . . In combination with the internal controls provision, the requirement that [corporations] maintain books and records that accurately and fairly reflect the corporation's transactions "assure[s], among other things, that the assets of the [corporation] are used for proper corporate purpose[s]."[3]

The FCPA accounting provisions apply to public companies whose shares are registered with the SEC, whether U.S.-based or foreign.[4] But the true reach of these provisions is much broader and extends to public companies' global networks of subsidiaries, agents, consultants, distributors, joint-venture partners, and other collaborators.[5]

Recordkeeping and Internal Controls Provisions Section 13(b) of the Exchange Act 15 U.S.C. § 78m

§ 13. Periodical and Other Reports

. . . .

(b) Form of Report; Books, Records, and Internal Accounting; Directives

. . . .

(2) Every issuer which has a class of securities registered pursuant to section 78l of this title and every issuer which is required to file reports pursuant to section 78o(d) of this title shall—

(A) make and keep books, records, and accounts, which, in reasonable detail, accurately and fairly reflect the transactions and dispositions of the assets of the issuer;

(B) devise and maintain a system of internal accounting controls sufficient to provide reasonable assurances that—

(i) transactions are executed in accordance with management's general or specific authorization;

(ii) transactions are recorded as necessary (I) to permit preparation of financial statements in conformity with generally accepted accounting principles or any other criteria applicable to such statements, and (II) to maintain accountability for assets;

(iii) access to assets is permitted only in accordance with management's general or specific authorization; and

(iv) the recorded accountability for assets is compared with the existing assets at reasonable intervals and appropriate action is taken with respect to any differences

. . . .

---

3. *Id.* at 38–39 (citing S. Rep. No. 95-114, at 7 (1977)).

4. *Id.* at 2.

5. *See Foreign Corrupt Practices Act*, U.S. Sec. & Exch. Comm'n (Feb. 2, 2017), https://www.sec.gov/spotlight/fcpa.shtml.

(4) No criminal liability shall be imposed for failing to comply with the requirements of paragraph (2) of this subsection except as provided in paragraph (5) of this subsection.

(5) No person shall knowingly circumvent or knowingly fail to implement a system of internal accounting controls or knowingly falsify any book, record, or account described in paragraph (2).

(6) Where an issuer which has a class of securities registered pursuant to section 78l of this title or an issuer which is required to file reports pursuant to section 78o(d) of this title holds 50 per centum or less of the voting power with respect to a domestic or foreign firm, the provisions of paragraph (2) require only that the issuer proceed in good faith to use its influence, to the extent reasonable under the issuer's circumstances, to cause such domestic or foreign firm to devise and maintain a system of internal accounting controls consistent with paragraph (2). Such circumstances include the relative degree of the issuer's ownership of the domestic or foreign firm and the laws and practices governing the business operations of the country in which such firm is located. An issuer which demonstrates good faith efforts to use such influence shall be conclusively presumed to have complied with the requirements of paragraph (2).

(7) For the purpose of paragraph (2) of this subsection, the terms "reasonable assurances" and "reasonable detail" mean such level of detail and degree of assurance as would satisfy prudent officials in the conduct of their own affairs.

. . . .

II. What Is Covered Under the Books and Records Provision of the FCPA Accounting Provisions?

The books and records provision of the FCPA is codified in § 13(b)(2)(A) of the Securities Exchange Act of 1934 ("Exchange Act") and requires public companies "to make and keep books, records, and accounts, which, in reasonable detail, accurately and fairly reflect the transactions and dispositions of the assets of the [company]."[6] This requirement aims to prevent manipulation of records to mask transactions—including placing a transaction into an erroneous category, mischaracterizing it, or burying it in some other way.[7] For example, bribes have been disguised as:

- Commissions or royalties
- Consulting fees
- Sales and marketing expenses

---

6. 15 U.S.C. § 78m(b)(2)(A) (2012).
7. FCPA GUIDE, *supra* note 1, at 38.

- Travel and entertainment expenses
- Rebates or discounts
- Miscellaneous expenses
- Petty cash withdrawals
- Free goods
- Write-offs[8]

Registering a Bribe: An Accountant's Nightmare

Whether a payment is made directly by a corporation or through an intermediary, an entry must be made to reflect the transaction in the accounts of the local subsidiary or affiliate and also in the consolidated accounts of the mother company. How will a bribe be accounted for? No ready or adequate answer is available; actually the accountant, who has to make an entry in the books, will be faced with a dilemma. Indeed, under the legislation passed during the last decade and under generally accepted accounting practices, it has become impossible to identify a payment as a bribe, as this would be an admission of an offence. It has also become unacceptable to falsely identify the payment (as for instance "promotion expenses"). Falsified accounts lead to false financial reporting, which, if discovered, could destroy the company's reputation.

Wrong accounting, truncated entries, use of false documents, misinformation for the board of directors, the shareholders and the investors' public—all of that contributes to a heavy price to be paid by a company for a single, risky and shady bribing transaction.

— *François Vincke, International Chamber of Commerce Anti-Corruption Commission*[16]

The FCPA does not define what specific books and records fall under this provision, but we know that its scope is very broad.[9]

> Congress' use of the term "records" suggests that virtually any tangible embodiment of information made or kept by an issuer is within the scope of section 13(b)(2)(A) of the FCPA, such as tape recordings, computer print-outs, and similar representations.[10]

Determining whether a record is covered involves a weighing of factors.[11] In general, the more relevant a record is to: 1) the preparation of financial statements; 2) the adequacy of internal controls; or 3) the performance of audits, the more likely the record will be subject to the terms of the provision.[12] Records such as corporate minutes, documents relating to corporate transactions, and authorizations for expenditures fall into the category of records that are relevant to the preparation of financial statements.[13] Records that relate to the design and functioning of internal controls are covered because they impact the accuracy of the financial statements.[14] Finally, the FCPA covers any records that bear on the audit of financial statements.[15]

The books and records provision does not require absolute accuracy. It requires

---

8. *Id.*

9. *See id.* at 38–45.

10. Sec. and Exch. Comm'n v. World-Wide Coin Invs., Ltd., 567 F. Supp. 724, 748–49 (N.D. Ga 1983).

11. *See* FCPA Guide, *supra* note 1, at 39 (quoting H.R. Rep. No. 100-576, at 917 (1988)).

12. *See* Stuart H. Deming, *FCPA Prosecutions: The Critical Role of the Accounting and Recordkeeping Provisions*, Bus. L. Today, Aug. 2, 2010, at 1–2, https://www.americanbar.org/content/dam/aba/publications/blt/2010/08/fcpa-prosecutions-201008.authcheckdam.pdf.

13. *Id.* at 2.

14. Michael S. Schachter, *Defending an FCPA Books and Records Violation*, N.Y. L.J., Jan. 24, 2013, at 2, http://www.willkie.com/~/media/Files/Publications/2013/01/Defending%20an%20FCPA%20Books%20and%20Records%20Violation/Files/DefendinganFCPABooksandRecordsViolationpdf/FileAttachment/Defending_an_FCPA_Books_and_Records_Violation.pdf.

15. *See* Deming, *supra* note 12, at 2.

16. John Bray et al., Business Against Corruption: Case Stories and Examples 44 (2006).

"reasonable detail," defined by statute to mean "detail that would satisfy prudent officials in the conduct of their own affairs."[17] The DOJ and SEC interpret this phrase to mean "that the issuer's records should reflect transactions in conformity with accepted methods of recording economic events."[18]

The FCPA's legislative history provides that the required degree of detail "of necessity contemplates the weighing of a number of relevant factors, including the costs of compliance."[19] This involves a cost-benefit analysis to determine whether additional investment in accuracy is worth the benefit.[20]

For purposes of civil liability, a violation of the books and records provision does not require proof of scienter. As the Ninth Circuit has observed:

> The concept that the books and records provision of the Act embodies a scienter requirement would be inconsistent with the language of section 13(b)(2)(A), which contains no words indicating that Congress intended to impose such a requirement. Furthermore, either inadvertent or intentional errors could cause the misapplication or unauthorized use of corporate assets that Congress seeks to prevent. Also, a scienter requirement is inappropriate because the difficulty of proving intent would render enforcement extremely difficult. As a practical matter, the standard of accuracy in records will vary with the nature of the transaction involved.[21]

Therefore, civil liability can attach as a result of an error in a company's books and records regardless of the motivations of those responsible.[22]

Hypothetical: Expense Reports

US Co., whose shares trade on the New York Stock Exchange ("NYSE"), was exploring business opportunities in Indonesia and sent VP John Smith there to visit potential partners.

During the trip, Smith used cash to pay for his expenses, because his credit card was not working. On his return, Smith submitted an expense report totaling $4,500 and requested reimbursement for that amount. Smith inadvertently miscalculated his expenses, however, and he requested $1,000 more than he spent. He only submitted receipts for $1,500 to US Co.'s accounting department. Nonetheless, US Co.'s accounting department reimbursed the $4,500 claimed in the expense report, because its policy only required receipts for travel expenses exceeding $10,000.

Was there a violation of the FCPA by:

1) US Co.?
2) Smith?

---

17. FCPA GUIDE, *supra* note 1, at 39 (quoting 15 U.S.C. § 78m(b)(7) (2012)) (internal quotations omitted).
18. *Id.*
19. *Id.* (quoting H.R. REP. No. 100-576, at 917 (1988)).
20. *Id.* (stating that "[c]onsistent with the FCPA's approach to prohibiting payments of any value that are made with a corrupt purpose, there is no materiality threshold under the books and records provision.").
21. Sec. & Exch. Comm'n v. World-Wide Coin Invs., Ltd., 567 F. Supp 724, 749 (N.D. Ga. 1983).
22. *Id.*

III. What Is Covered Under the Internal Controls Provision of the FCPA Accounting Provisions?

Section 13(b)(2)(B) of the Exchange Act, commonly called the internal controls provision, requires public companies to devise and maintain a system of internal accounting controls sufficient to provide "reasonable assurances" that:

> (i) transactions are executed in accordance with management's general or specific authorization;
>
> (ii) transactions are recorded as necessary (I) to permit preparation of financial statements in conformity with generally accepted accounting principles or any other criteria applicable to such statements, and (II) to maintain accountability for assets;
>
> (iii) access to assets is permitted only in accordance with management's general or specific authorization; and
>
> (iv) the recorded accountability for assets is compared with the existing assets at reasonable intervals and appropriate action is taken with respect to any differences . . . .[23]

Like the "reasonable detail" requirement in the books and records provision, the FCPA defines "reasonable assurances" as "such . . . degree of assurance as would satisfy prudent officials in the conduct of their own affairs."[24] Once again, this determination involves a cost-benefit analysis, as noted by the Ninth Circuit:

> The concept of "reasonable assurances" contained in section 13(b)(2)(B) recognizes that the costs of internal controls should not exceed the benefits expected to be derived. It does not appear that either the SEC or Congress, which adopted the SEC's recommendations, intended that the statute should require that each affected issuer install a fail-safe accounting control system at all costs. It appears that Congress was fully cognizant of the cost-effective considerations which confront companies as they consider the institution of accounting controls and of the subjective elements which may lead reasonable individuals to arrive at different conclusions. Congress has demanded only that judgment be exercised in applying the standard of reasonableness. The size of the business, diversity of operations, degree of centralization of financial and operating management, amount of contact by top management with day-to-day operations, and numerous other circumstances are factors which management must consider in establishing and maintaining an internal accounting controls system.[25]

There is no fixed set of controls that companies must implement—executive judgment guides this process. Companies have flexibility to develop and maintain a system of controls tailored to their particular needs and circumstances. As the FCPA Guide explains, controls must:

> [T]ake into account the operational realities and risks attendant to the company's business, such as: the nature of its products or services; how the products or

---

23. 15 U.S.C. § 78m(b)(2)(B) (2012).
24. FCPA GUIDE, *supra* note 1, at 40 (quoting 15 U.S.C. § 78m(b)(7) (2012)).
25. *World-Wide Coin Invs.*, 567 F. Supp at 751.

services get to market; the nature of its work force; the degree of regulation; the extent of its government interaction; and the degree to which it has operations in countries with a high risk of corruption.[26]

A company whose operations expose it to a high risk of corruption will have different internal controls than a company operating in a low corruption environment, just as a bank will be expected to devise and employ different internal controls than a manufacturer.[27]

> Good internal controls can prevent not only FCPA violations, but also other illegal or unethical conduct by the company, its subsidiaries, and its employees. DOJ and SEC have repeatedly brought FCPA cases that also involved other types of misconduct, such as financial fraud, commercial bribery, export controls violations, and embezzlement or self-dealing by company employees.
>
> —*FCPA Guide*[28]

Notes and Questions

Although § 13(b) of the Exchange Act does not require proof of scienter to establish civil liability, subsection (b)(5)—which imposes criminal liability—requires proof that the defendant "knowingly circumvent[ed] or knowingly fail[ed] to implement a system of internal accounting controls or knowingly falsif[ied] any book, record, or account . . . ."[29] In *United States v. Reyes*,[30] the Ninth Circuit analyzed the prosecution's burden of proof in establishing the intent element:

> As explained to the [Senate] committee, the term "knowingly" connotes a "conscious undertaking." Thus these paragraphs proscribe and make unlawful conduct which is rooted in a conscious undertaking to falsify records or mislead auditors through a statement or conscious omission of material facts.
>
> The committee believes that the inclusion of the "knowingly" standard is appropriate because of the danger, inherent in matters relating to financial recordkeeping, that inadvertent misstatements or minor discrepancies arising from an unwitting error in judgment might be deemed actionable. The committee does not, however, intend that the use of the term "knowingly" will provide a defense for those who shield themselves from the facts. The knowledge required is that the defendant be aware that he is committing the act which is false — not that he knows that his conduct is illegal.

The final report on [§ 13 (b)(5)] that was adopted in 1988 and that provided it was a crime to "knowingly falsify" books or records, explained its meaning as follows:

> The Conferees intend to codify current Securities and Exchange Commission (SEC) enforcement policy that penalties not be imposed for insignificant or

---

26. FCPA Guide, *supra* note 1, at 40.
27. *Id.*
28. *Id.* at 41.
29. 15 U.S.C. § 78m(b)(5) (2012).
30. 577 F.3d 1069 (9th Cir. 1992).

technical infractions or inadvertent conduct. The amendment adopted by the Conferees accomplishes this by providing that criminal penalties shall not be imposed for failing to comply with the FCPA's books and records or accounting control provisions. This provision is meant to ensure that criminal penalties would be imposed where acts of commission or omission in keeping books or records or administering accounting controls have the purpose of falsifying books, records or accounts, or of circumventing the accounting controls set forth in the Act. This would include the deliberate falsification of books and records and other conduct calculated to evade the internal accounting controls requirement.

The district court correctly concluded that the congressional history confirms that Congress intended "knowingly" only to require that the jury find that [the defendant] "was aware of that falsification and did not falsify through ignorance, mistake, or accident."[31]

SEC v. World-Wide Coin Investments, Ltd.

United States District Court, N.D. Georgia 567 F. Supp 724 (1983)

MEMORANDUM OPINION AND ORDER

VINING, District Judge.

This is a securities fraud action in which the Securities and Exchange Commission (SEC) seeks a permanent injunction against World-Wide Coin Investments, Ltd. (World-Wide) and the individual defendants as well as an order for a full accounting and disclosure of wrongfully received benefits. In an order entered March 29, 1983, this court directed the clerk to enter judgment for the SEC on all counts of the complaint and further directed defendants Hale and Seibert to (1) retain an independent auditor to perform a full accounting of World-Wide of all receipts and disbursements of cash and all purchases and sales and other acquisitions and dispositions of inventory and assets since July 1, 1979, and (2) return whatever shares of World-Wide stock they might hold to World-Wide. Finally, the court ordered World-Wide to make a full disclosure to its present shareholders with respect to all material information relating to its operations since July 1, 1979. The following memorandum opinion will constitute this court's findings of fact and conclusions of law as required by Fed.R.Civ.P. 52(a).

FACTUAL BACKGROUND

World-Wide Coin Investments, Ltd., is a Delaware corporation with its principal offices in Atlanta, Georgia, and is engaged primarily in the wholesale and retail sale of rare coins, precious metals, gold and silver coins, bullion, and, until 1979, in the retail sale of camera equipment.

. . . .

---

31. *Id.* at 1080–81 (citations omitted).

. . . Prior to July 1979, the company's assets totaled over $2,000,000, and it had over 40 employees. In August 1981, the time of the filing of this lawsuit, the company's assets amounted to less than $500,000, and it had only three employees.

Defendant Joseph H. Hale took over the management and control of World-Wide on July 24, 1979, as the controlling shareholder, chairman of the board, chief executive officer, and president. He was formerly a national bank examiner with the United States Treasury Department and was employed as an accountant and auditor for General Motors and the Glidden Company, where he obtained an understanding of the importance of internal controls and the concept of "GAAP" (generally accepted accounting principles). Following these experiences, he became a broker-dealer and is registered with the National Association of Securities Dealers (NASD) and the New York Stock Exchange.

Defendant Floyd Seibert is an employee of Health-Care International, Inc., a member of the board of directors of Florafax, Inc., and in September 1979 became a member of World-Wide's board of directors; he also constitutes World-Wide's one-man audit committee.

I. HALE'S TAKEOVER OF WORLD-WIDE

Prior to 1979, World-Wide was managed by John Hamrick, who held the positions of president, chief executive officer, and chairman of the board. During his tenure at World-Wide, Hamrick was involved in the rare coin business and operated two subsidiaries, World-Wide Camera Fair and Chattanooga Coin and Stamp, both of which significantly contributed to World-Wide's profits. Hamrick met Hale in 1979, when Hale made an offer of 25¢ a share to purchase control of World-Wide. This offer was not accepted, but Hale subsequently increased his offer to 75¢ a share, and on July 24, 1979, Hale acquired 51% of the common stock of World-Wide from Hamrick, approximately 290,000 shares. Hamrick then resigned as chairman of the board, president, and chief executive officer, and Hale was elected as his successor at a board meeting of the company on that date. Shortly thereafter, the remaining directors of World-Wide resigned, and on September 1, 1979, Hale appointed Jones and Seibert to comprise, in addition to himself, the three member World-Wide board.

. . . .

II. HALE'S PUBLIC TENDER OFFER

On July 30, 1979, Hale commenced a tender offer to purchase the remaining common shares of World-Wide stock for 75 ¢ per share on or before September 27, 1979. In connection with this tender offer, Hale directed World-Wide's transfer agent, the National Bank of Georgia, to mail an offering circular that he had personally prepared without the assistance of counsel to the remaining 401 shareholders of World-Wide. By way of this tender offer, Hale subsequently acquired approximately 10,000 additional shares from World-Wide public shareholders.

. . . .

III. EVENTS FOLLOWING HALE'S TAKEOVER

Prior to Hale's obtaining control of the company in July 1979, the accounting firm of Kanes, Benator & Co. (Kanes, Benator) was retained as World-Wide's independent auditor . . . . Also prior to the takeover, World-Wide apparently had an adequate system of internal accounting controls, since the company kept books and records which accurately reflected its transactions and dispositions of assets in reasonable detail. Furthermore, all employees followed internal control procedures, and the company had a policy of requiring supporting documents to be prepared for all transactions. It is the deterioration of World-Wide's internal controls and accounting procedures that constitutes the primary thrust of the SEC's complaint. The SEC contends that the combination of late filings, lack of internal controls, transactions unsupported by adequate documentation, and a total disregard for proper accounting procedures resulted in the precarious position of the company at the time the lawsuit was filed. . . .

A. 1979 10K Report[32] and Related Events

. . . .

On November 5, 1979, Kanes, Benator wrote a letter to Hale following a routine, required evaluation of World-Wide's system of internal controls, expressing grave concern over certain accounting procedures and lack of internal controls that Kanes, Benator considered to be detrimental to the company. In this letter, Kanes, Benator noted the following material weaknesses and conditions: (1) An evaluation of the company's internal controls during the period subsequent to the fiscal year ending July 31, 1979, disclosed that an adequate segregation of duties between employees was not properly maintained. One employee was posting the cash receipts journal, the disbursements journal, the general ledger, and the accounts receivable subsidiary ledger, filing all sales invoices, making bank deposits, reconciling bank statements, and issuing disbursement checks. (2) Numerous transactions recorded on the company books by general entries were not properly explained nor accompanied by readily available documentation. (3) The accounting records in general were not properly filed nor available for proper inspection. (4) The accounting and other staff familiar with the company's procedures were not available to assist the auditors at the requested or even at a prearranged time.

This letter from Kanes, Benator officially notified World-Wide of its deficiencies in its internal accounting controls and further stated that these deficiencies would be considered by Kanes, Benator in its examinations of the company's

---

32. The SEC provides the following description of a 10-K report:

> The federal securities laws require public companies to disclose information on an ongoing basis. . . . The annual report on Form 10-K provides a comprehensive overview of the company's business and financial condition and includes audited financial statements.

Securities and Exchange Commission, *Fast Answers, available at,* https://www.sec.gov/fast-answers/answers-form10khtm.html.

financial statements in the future. Even with this official notice that improvements were needed, Hale and Seibert did nothing to remedy the situation, and the criticisms of Kanes, Benator were virtually ignored. Kanes, Benator was dismissed as the company's auditor following this 1979 audit, and May, Zima & Co. was selected as the replacement on May 6, 1980 . . . .

. . . .

B. 1980 10K Report and Related Events

The company's problems increased in 1980, mostly resulting from its chaotic bookkeeping practices and total disregard for an adequate internal control system. World-Wide's problems in this regard will be emphasized in the following subsection of this order; the focus of this subsection will be the misrepresentations and omissions contained in the 1980 10K report. May, Zima & Co., World-Wide's independent auditor for its 1980 10K report, declined to give an opinion with respect to the company's 1980 financial statements stating:

> [T]he company was advised of an uncertainty relating to a possible violation of the provisions of the Foreign Corrupt Practices Act of 1977. The ultimate outcome of the implications of the violations of the federal act cannot be determined and no provision for any liability that may result has been made in the 1980 financial statements.
>
> The company had significant deficiencies in internal controls including the lack of detailed records and certain supporting data which were not available for our examination. Therefore, we were not able to obtain sufficient evidence in order to form an opinion on the accompanying financial statements including whether the inventory at July 31, 1980 ($450,750) was stated at the lower of the cost or market or whether the detailed subscription revenue ($60,878) is an adequate estimate for the applicable liability. . ..
>
> Because of the significance of the matters discussed in the preceding paragraphs, the scope of our work was not sufficient to enable us to express, and we do not express, an opinion on the accompanying financial statements and related schedules.

This 1980 10K report, also prepared by Hale and Seibert without assistance of counsel, indicated that the company was in the process of correcting the deficiencies in its internal accounting controls because of May, Zima's disclaimer opinion. It soon became apparent, however, that no substantive improvements were ever made.

. . . .

C. Problems with Internal Controls and Accounting Procedures

On November 5, 1979, Kanes, Benator, as World-Wide's independent auditor, warned Hale and World-Wide that a good and sound internal accounting control system was necessary to ensure the safeguarding of assets against losses from unauthorized use of dispositions and of financial records for preparing financial statements and maintaining accountability for assets. Although the company was notified of the importance of a good system of internal controls, this warning was ignored, and any control system that had existed at World-Wide ceased to exist. The problems that occurred at the company with respect to internal controls and accounting procedures can be divided into three areas: (1) inventory problems, (2) problems with separation of duties and the lack of documentation of transactions, and (3) problems with the books, records, and accounting procedures of the company.

(1) Inventory Problems

The safeguarding of World-Wide's physical inventory was one of its most severe problems; there was considerable testimony at trial to the effect that the company's vault, where most of the rare coins were kept, was unguarded and left open all day to all employees. Furthermore, no one employee was responsible for the issuance of coins from the vault, according to the accountants from May, Zima, who performed the 1980 audit. Scrap silver and bags of silver coins were left unattended in the hallways and in several cluttered, unlocked rooms at World-Wide's offices. During the trial, Hale admitted that he was worried about thefts due both to faulty record-keeping and the system of safeguarding the assets.

Hale also failed to initiate an adequate system of itemizing World-Wide's physical inventory. Rather than maintaining a perpetual inventory system, the company relied on a manual quarterly system, which, in light of the company's inadequate securities measures, was not effective in safeguarding the assets or in keeping an accurate account of the inventory. World-Wide's system made it relatively simple for an employee to improperly value and/or misappropriate large items of inventory undetected. Furthermore, employees were allowed to take large amounts of inventory off the premises of World-Wide for purposes of effecting a sale without giving a receipt.

. . . .

[Robert] Nofal ["a coin expert hired by May, Zima to determine the value of World-Wide's coin inventory"] testified that he could not determine how much was actually paid for the coins in World-Wide's inventory, since there were no backup documents and only a few coins were cost-coded. Nofal further testified that there was no organization of the inventory and that the vault was open without a guard when he came into the store.

(2) Separation of Duties

The lack of qualified personnel working in World-Wide's offices and the company's policy of allowing one individual to accomplish numerous transactions was another primary reason for May, Zima's disclaimed opinion, and was a major concern of Kanes, Benator in its letter of November 5, 1979. This court has previously noted the lack of supervision over the accounting department, managed by Patricia Allen, and her lack of expertise in the area. World-Wide maintains no separation of duties in the area of purchase and sales transactions, and valuation procedures for ending inventory. For instance, a single salesperson can do all the following tasks without supervision or review by another employer or officer: appraise a particular coin offered for purchase by a customer, purchase that coin with a check that the salesperson alone has drawn, count that same coin into inventory, value the coin for inventory purposes, and sell the coin to another purchaser.

Employees, none of whom was bonded, were also allowed to take large amounts of inventory off the company's premises for purposes of effecting a sale without giving a receipt, as well as being given cash to purchase the precious metals and coins at various locations, also without giving a receipt. Nor were employees required to write source documents relating to the purchase and sale of coins, bullion, and other inventory, making it impossible, as Haygood ["the accountant from May, Zima who performed field work for the 1980 audit'] testified, to ascertain whether a particular inventory item had been sold at a profit or loss, or whether it had even been sold. Although pre-numbered invoices could have been used to help alleviate this problem, they were not; there was a complete lack of control over any retail counter sales, and Haygood testified that he could not match cash coming in or out with the merchandise going out. The company apparently did have a daily report of cash coming in, but there was no record of items purchased or sold. Hale himself admitted that he told his employees to write down the sales of total bullion rather than writing receipts for individual coins.

Additionally, there were no procedures enforced with respect to writing checks; for instance, no system has been implemented to ensure that the purpose for which a check is written can be ascertained. Since employees have been allowed to write checks without noting the purpose of the transaction on the instrument or on any other document, source documents for most checks do not exist. All employees have had access to presigned checks, and there has been no dollar limit over which an employee cannot write a check. Furthermore, employees have not been required to get approval before writing a check. These policies have caused World-Wide to bounce over 100 checks since Hale took over the management of the company. Because of World-Wide's propensity for having their checks returned due to insufficient funds, the National Bank of Georgia, the company's transfer agent, requested World-Wide to close its account and take its business elsewhere.

Evidence introduced at trial further revealed that approximately $1.7 million worth of checks were written to Hale, his affiliates, or to cash, all without supporting documentation or any indication of the purpose of the checks. Hale testified that approximately $250,000 worth of these checks were repayments of loans he had personally made to the company, but he failed to introduce any executed promissory notes or any document to support that claim. The SEC also introduced various checks to and/or bills from local bars and restaurants written by Hale and reimbursed by either World-Wide or East Coast Coin. Numerous checks written to Hale on World-Wide's account were superimposed over purchase orders, supposedly as source documentation for the transactions.

(3) Books and Records

The lack of qualified accounting personnel not only created problems with World-Wide's inventory but also resulted in completely inaccurate and incomplete books and records. World-Wide, Hale, and Seibert have failed to make and keep books, records, and accounts which accurately and clearly reflect the transactions and dispositions of World-Wide's assets. As discussed previously, World-Wide employees have not been required to write purchase orders or any source document relating to the purchase and sale of coins and bullion, rendering it impossible to arrive at an accurate count or valuation of the inventory.

During his inspection of World-Wide's offices, Haygood stated that the records of operations for Hale's subsidiaries, such as World-Wide Camera Fair, were scattered throughout the office and were not in any order. Although Haygood was aware of the existence of World-Wide Camera Fair following a review of Kanes, Benator's work papers from 1979, he stated that he was unsure about the documentation and the sale of other companies such as World-Wide Rare Metals and Chattanooga Coin and Stamp. With respect to this latter subsidiary, Haygood was unable to identify it as a separate and existing corporation since it had been merged into World-Wide's balance sheet, making it impossible to differentiate between the good will of World-Wide and that of Chattanooga Coin and Stamp. Furthermore, this failure to consolidate the subsidiaries into the form and financial statements rendered the 10Q[33] reports incorrect for fiscal year 1980.

Haygood also testified the company's books were chaotic with respect to the deferred revenue received from subscriptions to the company newspaper, *The Coin Wholesaler*. There were no accurate records setting out the dates of subscriptions; therefore, the amount of deferred revenue simply had to be estimated on the company's books.

During May, Zima's inspection at the premises, on July 31, 1980, Haygood and other representatives from May, Zima met with Jones and Seibert to express their concern about the state of World-Wide's control procedures and accounting methods. Each item of concern was discussed in detail including questions from Seibert and Jones relative to the evaluation of the potential effects on the company and the continued trading of the common stock. May, Zima explained the position of Robert Nofal and offered to have a second opinion in order to confirm his initial evaluation that the grading policy and inventory values were significantly higher than was appropriate. Seibert and Jones acknowledged the problems noted and agreed that a totally separate inventory would be prepared by Nofal and later compared to the inventory prepared by the company's employee with appropriate reconciliation of differences in order to establish an acceptable, reasonable valuation of inventory. Robert Johnson, a partner at May, Zima, suggested that the company immediately obtain and consult with a securities attorney relative to the necessary action that should be taken as a result of the information May, Zima provided concerning its evaluation of the

---

33. SEC mandated quarterly reports by public companies are filed on Form 10-Q.

company's internal accounting control system and the effect on May, Zima's opinion. Johnson further indicated that there was a possible violation of the Foreign Corrupt Practices Act and that World-Wide should seek advice concerning that possibility. Johnson explained that May, Zima would be willing to assist World-Wide through further discussions of these matters and/or offer suggestions to remedy the situations noted. Furthermore, Haygood offered to go to the Securities and Exchange Commission with the company to resolve their problems, but Seibert stated that he would rather take his chances and not contact the SEC in the hope that the SEC would not contact him.

World-Wide eventually agreed to retain the law firm of Jones, Bird & Howell and met with Frank Bird of that firm on August 18, 1980. At that meeting, there was a discussion of how World-Wide should communicate to the SEC. Bird agreed that the disclosure should be made immediately and that a Form 8K should be filed on the report received from the company's auditors advising it of a possible problem with the provisions of the Foreign Corrupt Practices Act, a possible disclaimer of opinion on the company's financial statements and the effects on the company's estimated net income resulting from the write-off of investments and subsidiaries. Seibert agreed to draft a Form 8K to disclose these items and to make a press release on the revised estimated income.

Following the initial meeting on July 31, 1980, May, Zima wrote a letter to World-Wide on August 21, 1980, detailing the weaknesses noted in its system of internal accounting controls. In this letter, May, Zima listed the following deficiencies: (1) a lack of supervision in the accounting department, (2) a lack of reliability in the bookkeeping department because of no supervision, (3) a lack of segregation of duties in the accounting department, emphasizing that the segregation of duties would allow for proper checks and balances in the company's accounting system, (4) a lack of control over retail counter sales in that there were no prenumbered invoices and the company could not match cash coming in with merchandise going out, (5) a lack of segregation of duties in the department of purchases and sales of coins, (6) the lack of determined value on some of the items of inventory such as the Coca-Cola memorabilia, (7) problems with "related-party" transactions (transactions between World-Wide and insiders or stockholders).

On October 22, 1980, May, Zima wrote a memorandum to the board of directors of World-Wide, setting forth certain recommendations of procedures which the accounting firm felt would improve and strengthen the company's present system. May, Zima suggested (1) a change in the company's system of cash received and disbursements, suggesting that a listing of mail receipts be prepared by the individual who opens the mail and compared to the bank deposit slip and amounts recorded in the cash receipts journal, (2) petty cash reimbursements should be drawn to the petty cash custodian and not to cash, (3) aging accounts receivable should be reviewed on a periodic basis by an appropriate official separate from the accounting department, (4) an improvement in the safeguarding of the assets of the company, and a provision for regular inspection of the assets, (5) routine procedures to be developed providing for prompt and adequate reporting to the accounting department of sales and/or disposals of property and equipment, (6) utilization of prenumbered inventory tags to facilitate accounting for, and control of, the inventory, (7) obtaining cancelled notes payable from creditors when paid, (8) the maintenance of personnel files for all employees and the rotation of the distribution of payroll checks among appropriate officials, (9) the bonding of employees who receive, disburse, or handle cash or who have access to assets and records, (10) full documentation of travel and entertainment expenses, and (11) a mathematical check for sales and vendor invoices.

Although notified of a possible violation of the Foreign Corrupt Practices Act and of severe problems in the company's internal controls system and accounting procedures, World-Wide did little, if anything, to change its methods of operation. Steve Watson, a staff accountant with the SEC, reviewed World-Wide's accounting records in September 1981 and concluded that there was still inadequate documentation to support purchases made and that the internal controls of the company were inadequate. Watson indicated at trial that the company currently issues receipts for cash sales and has started taking quarterly inventories but that the controls of the company are still inadequate since there are no controls over the inventory itself. He further stated that he was unable to determine the cost of inventory in accordance with generally accepted accounting principles.

. . . .

APPLICATION OF LAW

Foreign Corrupt Practices Act

The Foreign Corrupt Practices Act, 15 U.S.C. § 78m(b)(2) (Amend.1977) ("FCPA") was enacted by Congress as an amendment to the 1934 Securities Exchange Act and was the legislative response to numerous questionable and illegal foreign payments by United States corporations in the 1970s. Although one of the major substantive provisions of the FCPA is to require corporate disclosure of assets as a deterrent to foreign bribes, the more significant addition of the FCPA is the accounting controls or "books and records" provision, which gives the SEC authority over the entire financial management and reporting requirements of publicly held United States corporations.

The FCPA was enacted on the principle that accurate recordkeeping is an essential ingredient in promoting management responsibility and is an affirmative requirement for publicly held American corporations to strengthen the accuracy of corporate books and records, which are "the bedrock elements of our system of corporate disclosure and accountability." A motivating factor in the enactment of the FCPA was a desire to protect the investor, as was the purpose behind the enactment of the Securities Acts. It is apparent that investors are entitled to rely on the implicit representations that corporations will account for their funds properly and will not channel funds out of the corporation or omit to include such funds in the accounting system so that there are no checks possible on how much of the corporation's funds are being expended in the manner management later claims.

Like the anti-fraud provisions of the 1934 Securities Exchange Act, the FCPA's provisions on accounting controls are short and deceptively straightforward. Section 13(b)(2) of the FCPA provides that every issuer having a class of securities registered pursuant to section 12 of the Exchange Act shall:

(a) Make and keep books, records, and accounts which, in reasonable detail, accurately and fairly reflect the transactions and dispositions of the assets of the issuer; and

(b) Devise and maintain a system of internal accounting controls sufficient to provide reasonable assurances that

   (i) transactions are executed in accordance with management's general or specific authorization;

   (ii) transactions are recorded as necessary (I) to permit preparation of financial statements in conformity with generally accepted accounting principles or any other criteria applicable to such statements, and (II) to maintain accountability for assets;

   (iii) access to assets is permitted only in accordance with management's general or specific authorization; and

   (iv) the recorded accountability for assets is compared with the existing assets at reasonable intervals and appropriate action is taken with respect to any differences.

Moreover, SEC Regulation 13b2 was promulgated pursuant to section 13(b)(2) and is entitled "Maintenance of Records and Preparation of Required Reports," contains the following rules:

Rule 13b2–1: No person shall, directly or indirectly, falsify or cause to be falsified, any book, record or account subject to Section 13(b)(2)(A) of the Securities Exchange Act.

Rule 13b2–2: No director or officer of an issuer shall, directly or indirectly,

(a) make or cause to be made a materially false or misleading statement, or

(b) omit to state, or cause another person to omit to state, any material fact necessary in order to make statements made, in light of the circumstances under which such statements were made, not misleading to an accountant in connection with (1) any audit or examination of the financial statements of the issuer required to be made pursuant to this subpart or (2) the preparation or filing of any document or report required to be filed with the Commission pursuant to this subpart or otherwise.

It is clear that section 13(b)(2) and the rules promulgated thereunder are rules of general application which were enacted to (1) assure that an issuer's books and records accurately and fairly reflect its transactions and the disposition of assets, (2) protect the integrity of the independent audit of issuer financial statements that are required under the Exchange Act, and (3) promote the reliability and completeness of financial information that issuers are required to file with the Commission or disseminate to investors pursuant to the Exchange Act.

The accounting provisions of the FCPA will undoubtedly affect the governance and accountability mechanisms of most major and minor corporations, the work of their independent auditors, and the role of the Securities and Exchange Commission. The maintenance of financial records and internal accounting controls are major every-day activities of every registered and/or reporting company. The FCPA also has important implications for the SEC, since the incorporation of the accounting provisions into the federal securities laws confers on the SEC new rulemaking and enforcement authority over the control and record-keeping mechanisms of its registrants. The FCPA reflects a congressional determination that the scope of the federal securities laws and the SEC's authority should be expanded beyond the traditional ambit of disclosure requirements. The consequence of adding these substantive requirements governing accounting control to the federal securities laws will significantly augment the degree of federal involvement in the internal management of public corporations.

Since the FCPA became effective, the SEC has interpreted its authority to enforce the act's requirements quite broadly, taking the position that "it is important that issuers . . . review their accounting procedures, systems of internal accounting controls and business practices in order that they may take any actions necessary to comply with the requirements contained in the Act." The SEC has three basic tools to enforce the requirements of the FCPA: (1) judicial injunctions to prevent violations pursuant to section 21(d) of the 1934 Securities Exchange Act, 15 U.S.C. § 78u(d), (2) the ability to institute administrative proceedings to compel issuer compliance with the provisions of the FCPA or to discipline certain categories of persons who cause violations pursuant to section 15(c)(4) of the 1934 Act, 15 U.S.C. § 78*o* (c)(4), and Rule 2(e) of the SEC's Rules of Practice, 17 C.F.R. § 201.2e, and (3) the opportunity to refer the case to the Department of Justice for criminal proceedings.

From 1977 to 1979, the SEC was primarily preoccupied with the prevention of the foreign bribery provisions of the FCPA; however, the thrust of its enforcement proceedings at present are with the section 13(b)(2) violations. The FCPA actions currently being litigated by the SEC indicate that it apparently intends to rely heavily on the Act to address management misfeasance, misuse of corporate assets and other conduct reflecting adversely on management's integrity. The instant case is the first action to be litigated throughout trial; most of the other cases have been settled prior to trial or have not been brought to trial.

Section 13(b)(2) contains two separate requirements for issuers in complying with the FCPA's accounting provisions: (1) a company must keep accurate books and records reflecting the transactions and dispositions of the assets of the issuer, and (2) a company must maintain a reliable and adequate system of internal accounting controls. In applying these two separate requirements to the instant case, the court will examine the requirements of each provision and the problems inherent in their interpretation.

The "books and records" provision, contained in section 13(b)(2)(A) of the FCPA has three basic objectives: (1) books and records should reflect transactions in conformity with accepted methods of reporting economic events, (2) misrepresentation, concealment, falsification, circumvention, and other deliberate acts resulting in inaccurate financial books and records are unlawful, and (3) transactions should be properly reflected on books and records in such a manner as to permit the preparation of financial statements in conformity with GAAP and other criteria applicable to such statements.

Congress' use of the term "records" suggests that virtually any tangible embodiment of information made or kept by an issuer is within the scope of section 13(b)(2)(A) of the FCPA, such as tape recordings, computer print-outs, and similar representations. As indicated above, the purpose of this provision is to strengthen the accuracy of records and the reliability of audits.

During congressional consideration of the accounting provisions, there were numerous objections to the requirement that records be "accurate," which noted, for example, that inventories are typically valued on either the assumption that costs are recognized on a first-in, first-out basis or a last-in, first-out basis. Both of these theories, if correctly and honestly applied, produce "accurate" records, even though each may yield considerably different results in terms of the monetary value of inventories. Several objecting groups recommended that the accuracy requirement be subject to a materiality test so that inaccuracies involving small dollar amounts would not be actionable. This view is not accepted, but Congress did make it clear that:

> The term "accurately" in the bill does not mean exact precision as measured by some abstract principle. Rather, it means that an issuer's records should reflect transactions in conformity with accepted methods of recording economic events.

The only express congressional requirement for accuracy is the phrase "in reasonable detail." Although section 13(b)(2) expects management to see that the corporation's recordkeeping system is adequate and effectively implemented, how the issuer goes about this task is up to management; the FCPA provides no guidance, and this court cannot issue any kind of advisory opinion.

Just as the degree of error is not relevant to an issuer's responsibility for any inaccuracies, the motivations of those who erred are not relevant. There are no words in section 13(b)(2)(A) indicating that Congress intended to impose a scienter requirement, although there is some support among officials at the Securities and Exchange Commission for the addition of a scienter requirement and a form of a materiality standard to the FCPA. Senate Bill No. 708, a proposal which would impose a scienter requirement on the accounting provisions of the FCPA, has met with substantial opposition in Congress, and it does not appear that it will be enacted as an amendment to the FCPA in the near future. The concept that the books and records provision of the Act embodies a scienter requirement would be inconsistent with the language of section 13(b)(2)(A), which contains no words indicating that Congress intended to impose such a requirement. Furthermore, either inadvertent or intentional errors could cause the misapplication or unauthorized use of corporate assets that Congress seeks to prevent. Also, a scienter requirement is inappropriate because the difficulty of proving intent would render enforcement extremely difficult. As a practical matter, the standard of accuracy in records will vary with the nature of the transaction involved.

The second branch of the accounting provisions—the requirement that issuers maintain a system of internal accounting controls—appears in section 13(b)(2)(B). Like the recordkeeping provisions of the Act, the internal controls provision is not limited to material transactions or to those above a specific dollar amount. While this requirement is supportive of accuracy and reliability in the auditor's review and financial disclosure process, this provision should not be analyzed solely from that point of view. The internal controls requirement is primarily designed to give statutory content to an aspect of management steward-ship responsibility, that of providing shareholders with reasonable assurances that the business is adequately controlled.

Internal accounting control is, generally speaking, only one aspect of a company's total control system; in order to maintain accountability for the disposi-tion of its assets, a business must attempt to make it difficult for its assets to be misappropriated. The internal accounting controls element of a company's control system is that which is specifically designed to provide reasonable, cost-effective safeguards against the unauthorized use or disposition of company assets and reasonable assurances that financial records and accounts are suffi-ciently reliable for purposes of external reporting. "Internal accounting controls" must be distinguished from the accounting system typically found in a com-pany. Accounting systems process transactions and recognize, calculate, classify, post, summarize, and report transactions. Internal controls safeguard assets and assure the reliability of financial records, one of their main jobs being to prevent and detect errors and irregularities that arise in the accounting systems of the company. Internal accounting controls are basic indicators of the reliability of the financial statements and the accounting system and records from which finan-cial statements are prepared.

Among the factors that determine the internal accounting control environ-ment of a company are its organizational structure, including the competence of personnel, the degree and manner of delegation and responsibility, the qual-ity of internal budgets and financial reports, and the checks and balances that separate incompatible activities. The efficiency of the internal control system of a company cannot be evaluated without considering the company's organiza-tional structure, the caliber of its employees, the strength of its audit committee, the effectiveness of its internal audit operation, and a host of other factors which, while not part of the internal control system itself, have an impact on the func-tion of the system.

Although not specifically delineated in the Act itself, the following directives can be inferred from the internal controls provisions: (1) Every company should have reliable personnel, which may require that some be bonded, and all should be supervised. (2) Account functions should be segregated and procedures designed to prevent errors or irregularities. The major functions of recordkeep-ing, custodianship, authorization, and operation should be performed by differ-ent people to avoid the temptation for abuse of these incompatible functions.

(3) Reasonable assurances should be maintained that transactions are executed as authorized. (4) Transactions should be properly recorded in the firm's accounting records to facilitate control, which would also require standardized procedures for making accounting entries. Exceptional entries should be investigated regularly. (5) Access to assets of the company should be limited to authorized personnel. (6) At reasonable intervals, there should be a comparison of the accounting records with the actual inventory of assets, which would usually involve the physical taking of inventory, the counting of cash, and the reconciliation of accounting records with the actual physical assets. Frequency of these comparisons will usually depend on the cost of the process and upon the materiality of the assets involved.

The main problem with the internal accounting controls provision of the FCPA is that there are no specific standards by which to evaluate the sufficiency of controls; any evaluation is inevitably a highly subjective process in which knowledgeable individuals can arrive at totally different conclusions. Any ruling by a court with respect to the applicability of both the accounting provisions and the internal accounting control provisions should be strictly limited to the facts of each case.

The defendants in the instant case contend that the SEC has misconstrued the provisions of the FCPA relating to a knowledge requirement, contending that the SEC must show scienter. The defendants further state that the SEC does not allege a knowing attempt to circumvent for an improper purpose an internal control system required by law and that the complaint ignores all considerations of the costs and benefits of internal accounting controls and seeks to require World-Wide to maintain a system of controls that would destroy the company.

The definition of accounting controls does comprehend reasonable, but not absolute, assurances that the objectives expressed in it will be accomplished by the system. The concept of "reasonable assurances" contained in section 13(b)(2)(B) recognizes that the costs of internal controls should not exceed the benefits expected to be derived. It does not appear that either the SEC or Congress, which adopted the SEC's recommendations, intended that the statute should require that each affected issuer install a fail-safe accounting control system at all costs. It appears that Congress was fully cognizant of the cost-effective considerations which confront companies as they consider the institution of accounting controls and of the subjective elements which may lead reasonable individuals to arrive at different conclusions. Congress has demanded only that judgment be exercised in applying the standard of reasonableness. The size of the business, diversity of operations, degree of centralization of financial and operating management, amount of contact by top management with day-to-day operations, and numerous other circumstances are factors which management must consider in establishing and maintaining an internal accounting controls system. However, an issuer would probably not be successful in arguing a cost-benefit defense in circumstances where the management, despite warnings by its auditors of significant weaknesses of its accounting control system, had decided, after a cost benefit analysis, not to strengthen them, and then the internal accounting controls proved to be so inadequate that the company was virtually destroyed. It is also true that the internal accounting controls provisions contemplate the financial principle of proportionality—what is material to a small company is not necessarily material to a large company.

This court has already declined to adopt the defense offered by the defendants that the accounting controls provisions of the FCPA require a scienter requirement. The remainder of World-Wide's defense appears to be that such a small operation should not be required to maintain an elaborate and sophisticated internal control system, since the costs of implementing and maintaining it would financially destroy the company. It is true that a cost/benefit analysis is particularly relevant here, but it remains undisputed that it was the lack of any control over the inventory and inadequate accounting procedures that primarily contributed to World-Wide's demise. No organization, no matter how small, should ignore the provisions of the FCPA completely, as World-Wide did. Furthermore, common sense dictates the need for such internal controls and procedures in a business with an inventory as liquid as coins, medals, and bullion.

The evidence in this case reveals that World-Wide, aided and abetted by Hale and Seibert, violated the provisions of section 13(b)(2) of the FCPA. As set forth in the factual background portion of this order, the internal recordkeeping and accounting controls of World-Wide has been sheer chaos since Hale took over control of the company. For example, there has been no procedure implemented with respect to writing checks: employees have had access to pre-signed checks; source documents were not required to be prepared when a check was drawn; employees have not been required to obtain approval before writing a check; and, even when a check was drawn to "cash," supporting documentation was usually not prepared to explain the purpose for which the check was drawn. In addition to extremely lax security measures such as leaving the vault unguarded, there has been no separation of duties in the areas of purchase and sales transactions, and valuation procedures for ending inventory. Furthermore, no promissory notes or other supporting documentation has been prepared to evidence purported loans to World-Wide by Hale or by his affiliate companies.

Since Hale obtained control of World-Wide, employees have not been required to write source documents relating to the purchase and sale of coins, bullion, or other inventory. Because of this total lack of an audit trail with respect to these transactions and the disposition of World-Wide's assets, it has been virtually impossible to determine if an item has been sold at a profit or at a loss. Furthermore, there are more than $1,700,000 worth of checks drawn to Hale or to Hale's affiliates, or to cash, for which no adequate source documentation exists. Furthermore, Hale and Seibert knew that the medallions that were sold to World-Wide by Hale in 1979 were overvalued and unmarketable. Even so, they allowed the incorrect value of the medallions to be entered on the books of World-Wide. They also knew that the company's books and records were neither accurate nor complete. Pursuant to their directives, source documents were not prepared with respect to the transfer of funds; additionally, no audit trail was maintained for the acquisition and disposition of inventory. Furthermore, it appears that there were numerous false and misleading statements and omissions in the company's numerous reports to the SEC, many of which were filed late or not at all.

Individually, the acts of these defendants do not appear so egregious as to warrant the full panoply of relief requested by the SEC nor to impose complete liability under the FCPA. However, the court cannot ignore the all-pervasive effect of the combined failure to act, failure to keep accurate records, failure to maintain any type of inventory control, material omissions and misrepresentations, and other activities which caused World-Wide to decrease from a company of 40 employees and assets over $2,000,000 to a company of only three employees and assets of less than $500,000. It is evident that World-Wide, Hale, and Seibert violated all provisions contained in section 13(b)(2)(A) and (B) and the SEC's rules promulgated thereunder.

. . . .

[The Court ordered Hale to forfeit his World-Wide stock pending a full accounting of the fraud].

Notes and Questions

1) The District Court's opinion in *World-Wide Coin* is the only instance where a federal court has analyzed an issuer's obligation under the FCPA's internal control provisions. Why is there such scarcity of judicial opinions on this important issue?
2) What was World-Wide's defense to the charge of violating the FCPA?
3) What burden of proof did the SEC have to meet in establishing intent?
4) How would that burden of proof differ in a criminal case?

SEC v. Oracle Corp.

United States District Court, N.D. California No. CV-12-4310 CRB (2012)

COMPLAINT

. . . .

SUMMARY OF THE ACTION

This matter involves violations of the books and records and internal controls provisions of the Foreign Corrupt Practices Act ("FCPA") by Oracle Corporation ("Oracle" or "the Company"), a Redwood Shores, California-based software company. From 2005 to 2007, certain employees of Oracle's Indian subsidiary Oracle India Private Limited ("Oracle India") secretly "parked" a portion of the proceeds from certain sales to the Indian government and put the money to unauthorized use, creating the potential for bribery or embezzlement. These Oracle India employees structured more than a dozen transactions so that a total of around $2.2 million was held by the Company's distributors and kept off Oracle India's corporate books. The Oracle India employees would then direct its distributor to disburse payments out of the unauthorized side funds to purported local "vendors." Several of the "vendors" were merely storefronts that did not provide any services.

Oracle failed to accurately record these side funds on the Company's books and records, and failed to implement or maintain a system of effective internal accounting controls to prevent improper side funds in violation of the FCPA, which requires public companies to keep books and records that accurately reflect their operations.

The Commission seeks an order permanently enjoining Oracle from violations of the books and records and internal controls provisions of the FCPA, and requiring Oracle to pay a civil monetary penalty.

JURISDICTION AND VENUE

This Court has jurisdiction over this action pursuant to Sections 21(d) and 27 of the Securities Exchange Act of 1934 ("Exchange Act") [15 U.S.C. §§ 78u(d) and 78aa]. Defendant has, directly or indirectly, made use of the means and instrumentalities of interstate commerce and of the mails in connection with the acts, transactions, practices and courses of business alleged in this Complaint.

. . . .

DEFENDANT

Oracle Corporation is a Delaware corporation with headquarters in Redwood Shores, California. Oracle is an enterprise software company and a provider of computer hardware products and services. Shares of Oracle stock are registered with the Commission pursuant to Section12(b) of the Exchange Act and the company files reports pursuant to Section 13 of the Exchange Act. The company's shares are listed on the NASDAQ National Market under the symbol "ORCL." Oracle operates in India through its wholly-owned subsidiary Oracle India Private Limited.

FACTUAL ALLEGATIONS

A. Oracle India Employees Created a Side Fund at Its Distributors and Did Not Properly Account for It

From 2005 to 2007, Oracle India sold products and services to the Indian government and end users through local distributors and then directed excess funds from the sales to be "parked" outside Oracle's books and records.

At the time, Oracle India's typical business model involved selling Oracle software licenses and services through local distributors who had written agreements with Oracle India. In the transactions at issue, Oracle India was heavily involved in identifying and working with the end user customers in selling products and services to them and negotiating the final price. The purchase order, however, was placed by the customer with Oracle India's distributor. The distributor bought the licenses and services directly from Oracle, and then resold them to the customer at the higher price that had been negotiated by Oracle India. The difference between what the government end user paid the distributor and what the distributor paid Oracle typically is referred to as "margin," which the distributor generally retains as payment for its services.

On approximately 14 occasions related to 8 different government contracts between 2005 and 2007, certain Oracle India employees created extra margins between the end user and distributor price and directed the distributors to hold the extra margin in side funds. Oracle India's employees made these margins large enough to ensure a side fund existed to pay third parties. At the direction of the Oracle India employees, the distributor then made payments out of the side funds to third parties, purportedly for marketing and development expenses. Some of the recipients of these payments were not on Oracle's approved local vendor list; indeed, some of the third parties did not exist and were merely storefronts.

Because the Oracle India employees concealed the existence of the side fund, Oracle did not properly account for these side funds. These funds constituted prepaid marketing expenses incurred by Oracle India and should have been recorded as an asset and rolled up to Oracle's corporate books and records. These marketing expenses should then have been reflected in the income statement once they were used. Instead, the parked funds were not reflected on Oracle India's books and were not properly recorded as prepaid marketing expenses. This incorrect accounting in turn affected Oracle's books and records.

Between 2005 and 2007, government customers paid Oracle India's distributors at least $6.7 million on these sales, with Oracle receiving approximately $4.5 million in revenue, resulting in about $2.2 million in funds improperly "parked" with the Company's distributors.

B. Absent Proper Controls, Oracle India Employees Used Side Funds to Pay Unauthorized Third Parties

Oracle India's parked funds created a risk that they potentially could be used for illicit means, such as bribery or embezzlement. Such risk can be highlighted by the following example of the largest government contract that involved parked funds used for unauthorized third party payments.

In May 2006, Oracle India secured a $3.9 million deal with India's Ministry of Information Technology and Communications as payment for the distributor's services. Oracle's distributor accepted payment from the end user for the full $3.9 million. Under the direction of Oracle India's then Sales Director, the distributor sent approximately $2.1 million to Oracle, which Oracle booked as revenue on the transaction.

Oracle India employees then directed the distributor to keep approximately $151,000. The Oracle India employees further instructed the distributor to "park" the remaining approximately $1.7 million to be used for disbursement towards "marketing development purposes." Several Oracle India employees were aware of the parked funds arrangement, which violated Oracle's internal corporate policies.

Two months later, an Oracle India employee provided Oracle India's distributor with eight invoices for payments to third party vendors, in amounts ranging from approximately $110,000 to $396,000. These invoices were later found to be fake. None of these third parties, which were just storefronts and provided no services on the deal, were on Oracle's approved vendor list. As directed by the Oracle India employees, the distributor sent out the third party payments, which created the potential that they could be used for bribery or embezzlement.

Oracle lacked the proper controls to prevent its employees at Oracle India from creating and misusing the parked funds. For example, Oracle knew distributor discounts created a margin of cash from which distributors received payments for their services. Before 2009, however, the Company failed to audit and compare the distributor's margin against the end user price to ensure excess margins were not being built into the pricing structure.

In addition, although Oracle maintained corporate policies requiring approvals for payment of marketing expenses, Oracle failed to seek transparency in or audit third party payments made by distributors on Oracle India's behalf. This control would have enabled Oracle to check that payments were made to appropriate recipients.

C. Oracle Later Implemented Remedial Measures to Improve FCPA Compliance

By November 2007, Oracle India's Senior Channel Sales Manager had resigned and left Oracle India. As a result of an internal investigation that the Oracle Asia division escalated after a local tax inquiry to Oracle India's distributor, Oracle terminated four other Oracle India employees based on their knowledge that Oracle India parked funds at its distributors.

In addition, Oracle took other remedial measures to address the risk and controls related to parked funds, including: conducting additional due diligence in its partner transactions in India so that Oracle had greater transparency into end user pricing in government contracts; terminating its relationship with the distributor involved in the transactions at issue; directing its distributors not to allow the creation of side funds; requiring additional representations and warranties from distributors to include the fact that no side funds exist; and enhancing training for its partners and employees to address anti-corruption policies.

FIRST CLAIM FOR RELIEF

Violations of Section 13(b)(2)(A) of the Exchange Act (Books and Records) [15 U.S.C. § 78m(b)(2)(A)]

....

As described above, Oracle failed to make and keep books, records and accounts which, in reasonable detail, accurately and fairly reflected its transactions and dispositions of its assets.

By reason of the foregoing, Defendant violated, and unless restrained and enjoined will continue to violate, the books-and-records provision of the FCPA, codified as Section 13(b)(2)(A) of the Exchange Act [15 U.S.C. § 78m(b)(2)(A)].

SECOND CLAIM FOR RELIEF

Violations of Section 13(b)(2)(8) of the Exchange Act (Internal Controls) [15 U.S.C. § 78m(b)(2)(8)]

. . . .

With respect to the side funds and payments described above, Oracle failed to devise and maintain a system of internal accounting controls sufficient to provide reasonable assurances that: (i) transactions were executed in accordance with management's general or specific authorization; and (ii) transactions were recorded as necessary to permit the preparation of financial statements in conformity with generally accepted accounting principles or any other criteria applicable to such statements, and to maintain accountability for its assets.

By reason of the foregoing, Defendant violated, and unless restrained and enjoined will continue to violate, the internal-controls provision of the FCPA, codified as Section 13(b)(2)(8) 15 of the Exchange Act [15 U.S.C. § 78m(b)(2)(8)].

. . . .

Notes and Questions

1) Which controls should Oracle have instituted:
   a) at the level of the parent?
   b) at the level of the subsidiary?
2) Did the complaint against Oracle allege misuse of corporate funds?
3) How did Oracle violate its duty to maintain accurate books and records?

A. The COSO Framework

In 1985, five private-sector groups[34] formed the Commission on Fraudulent Financial Reporting, better known as the Treadway Commission, "to identify causal factors that can lead to fraudulent financial reporting and steps to reduce its incidence."[35] The Commission's final report concluded that:

> For the top management of a public company to discharge its obligations to oversee the financial reporting process, it must identify, understand, and assess the factors that may cause the financial statements to be fraudulently misstated.[36]

The report recommended that sponsoring organizations "work together to integrate the various internal control concepts and definitions and

---

34. The American Accounting Association, American Institute of Certified Public Accountants, Financial Executives International, Institute of Management Accountants and the Institute of Internal Auditors.

35. Nat'l Comm'n on Fraudulent Fin. Reporting, Report of the National Comm'n on Fraudulent Fin. Reporting 1 (1987), https://www.coso.org/Documents/NCFFR.pdf.

36. *Id.* at 33.

develop a common reference point."[37] In 1992, the Committee of Sponsoring Organizations of the Treadway Commission ("COSO") published guidance titled "Internal Control—Integrated Framework" ("COSO Framework").[38] The COSO Framework was created to help public companies, auditors, advisors, and regulators better understand the key elements of an effective control framework.[39] It has become the most authoritative guidance on internal controls, and is recognized by the SEC as an acceptable framework for internal control.[40] Virtually all issuers who file financial reports with the SEC follow the COSO Framework to ensure compliance with the FCPA's internal accounting control requirements.

In 2013, COSO released an updated Framework to conform to "higher expectations regarding governance oversight, risk management, and the detection and prevention of fraud."[41] The updated Framework was expanded to address the totality of a company's internal control system. Below is a broad conceptual look at the 2013 COSO Framework.

> An effective system of internal control demands more than rigorous adherence to policies and procedures: it requires the use of judgment. Management and boards of directors use judgment to determine how much control is enough. Management and other personnel use judgment every day to select, develop, and deploy controls across the entity. Management and internal auditors, among other personnel, apply judgment as they monitor and assess the effectiveness of the system of internal control.
>
> —*COSO Executive Summary*[42]

1. Defining Internal Control

COSO defines internal control as:

[A] process, effected by an entity's board of directors, management, and other personnel, designed to provide reasonable assurance regarding the achievement of objectives relating to operations, reporting, and compliance.[43]

Under this definition, the purpose of an internal control system is to assist the board of directors and management in achieving specific objectives. It is a dynamic and iterative process, meaning that it consists of ongoing tasks and activities subject to regular review and improvement that define how a business is run. It is important to note that internal control is "not merely about policy and procedure manuals, systems, and forms, but about people

---

37. *Id.* at 48.

38. Comm. of Sponsoring Orgs. of the Treadway Comm'n, Internal Control — Integrated Framework (2013) [hereinafter COSO Framework].

39. Comm. of Sponsoring Orgs. of the Treadway Comm'n, Internal Control — Integrated Framework: Executive Summary i–ii (2013) [hereinafter COSO Executive Summary].

40. Management's Report on Internal Control Over Financial Reporting and Certification of Disclosure in Exchange Act Periodic Reports, Final Rule, 68 Fed. Reg. 36,635, 36,642 (June 18, 2003) (codified at 17 C.F.R. pt. 210, 228, 229, 240, 249, 270 and 274) ("The COSO Framework satisfies our criteria and may be used as an evaluation framework for purposes of management's annual internal control evaluation and disclosure requirements. However, the final rules do not mandate use of a particular framework, such as the COSO Framework, in recognition of the fact that other evaluation standards exist outside of the United States.").

41. *See* J. Stephen McNally, The 2013 COSO Framework & SOX Compliance, Strategic Finance, June 2013, at 2.

42. COSO Executive Summary, *supra* note 39, at 1.

43. *Id.* at 3.

and the actions they take at every level of an organization to affect internal control."[44]

Given that "[a]bsolute assurance is not possible,"[45] an effective internal control system provides reasonable assurance that specified objectives will be met.[46] "[T]he likelihood of achievement [of objectives] is affected by limitations inherent in all systems of internal control, such as human error, the uncertainty inherent in judgment, and the potential impact of external events outside management's control."[47]

COSO's definition of internal control is intentionally broad so that it can be adapted to different types of businesses, industries, and geographic regions.[48] This breadth also allows the Framework's application to be applied not only to an entire organization, but also to a "subsidiary, division, operating unit, or business process."[49]

2. Objectives

According to the COSO Framework, an internal control system advances three categories of objectives, as follows:

> *Operations Objectives*—These pertain to effectiveness and efficiency of the entity's operations, including operational and financial performance goals, and safeguarding assets against loss.

> *Reporting Objectives*—These pertain to internal and external financial and nonfinancial reporting and may encompass reliability, timeliness, transparency, or other terms as set forth by regulators, recognized standard setters, or the entity's policies.

> *Compliance Objectives*—These pertain to adherence to laws and regulations to which the entity is subject.[50]

"Operations objectives relate to the achievement of an entity's basic mission and vision—the fundamental reason for its existence . . . . [T]hey may relate to improving financial performance, productivity . . . quality, environmental practices, innovation, and customer and employee satisfaction."[51] Protecting the value of the organization's assets (both tangible and intangible) is another operational objective.[52]

Reporting objectives broadly cover financial and nonfinancial reports to both internal and external stakeholders. External financial reporting objectives

---

44. *Id.*
45. COSO Framework, *supra* note 38, at 4.
46. COSO Executive Summary, *supra* note 39, at 3.
47. COSO Framework, *supra* note 38.
48. *Id.*
49. COSO Executive Summary, *supra* note 39, at 3.
50. *Id.* at 3–6.
51. COSO Framework, *supra* note 38, at 7.
52. *See id.*

are directed at satisfying legal requirements as well as the expectations of shareholders and the investing public. "Internal reporting objectives are driven by internal requirements in response to a variety of potential needs such as the entity's strategic directions, operating plans, and performance metrics at various levels."[53] They include, for example, the provision of information necessary for the board of directors to effectively manage the organization.[54]

> The *Framework* requires judgment in designing, implementing, and conducting internal control and assessing its effectiveness. The use of judgment, within the boundaries established by laws, rules, regulations, and standards, enhances management's ability to make better decisions about internal control, but cannot guarantee perfect outcomes.
>
> — *COSO Executive Summary*[57]

Finally, compliance objectives are geared toward conforming an organization's activities to relevant laws and regulations. In setting compliance objectives, an organization must understand not only the laws that apply across the entity, but also those applicable to operations in foreign jurisdictions.[55] Since "[l]aws and regulations [only] establish minimum standards of conduct expected of the entity . . . [s]ome organizations will set objectives to a higher level of performance than established by laws and regulations."[56]

3. Components of Internal Control

The FCPA Guide explains that, in order to comply with the FCPA's internal control requirements, an issuer's internal control system must have the following five components:

> [A] control environment that covers the tone set by the organization regarding integrity and ethics; risk assessments; control activities that cover policies and procedures designed to ensure that management directives are carried out (e.g., approvals, authorizations, reconciliations, and segregation of duties); information and communication; and monitoring.[58]

The COSO Framework elaborates on these same five components. First is the Control Environment, which is the reflection of the "tone at the top" of the organization:

> The control environment is the set of standards, processes, and structures that provide the basis for carrying out internal control across the organization. The board of directors and senior management establish the tone at the top regarding the importance of internal control including expected standards of conduct. Management reinforces expectations at the various levels of the organization. The control environment comprises the integrity and ethical values of the organization; the parameters enabling the board of directors to carry out its governance

---

53. *Id.* at 8.
54. *See id.* at 11.
55. *See id.*
56. *Id.* at 11.
57. COSO Executive Summary, *supra* note 39, at 8.
58. FCPA Guide, *supra* note 1, at 40.

oversight responsibilities; the organizational structure and assignment of authority and responsibility; the process for attracting, developing, and retaining competent individuals; and the rigor around performance measures, incentives, and rewards to drive accountability for performance. The resulting control environment has a pervasive impact on the overall system of internal control.[59]

The board of directors and management lead by example, demonstrating the importance of integrity and ethical values through their "directives, actions, and behavior."[60] They set expectations concerning standards of conduct, communicate them to all levels of the organization and establish processes for evaluating performance against those standards. They also establish appropriate structures within the organization that assign authority and accountability, including lines of reporting.

The second component, Risk Assessment, predicts and measures the threats that the company faces or may face in the future:

> Every entity faces a variety of risks from external and internal sources. Risk is defined as the possibility that an event will occur and adversely affect the achievement of objectives. Risk assessment involves a dynamic and iterative process for identifying and assessing risks to the achievement of objectives. Risks to the achievement of these objectives from across the entity are considered relative to established risk tolerances. Thus, risk assessment forms the basis for determining how risks will be managed.
>
> A precondition to risk assessment is the establishment of objectives, linked at different levels of the entity. Management specifies objectives within categories relating to operations, reporting, and compliance with sufficient clarity to be able to identify and analyze risks to those objectives. Management also considers the suitability of the objectives for the entity. Risk assessment also requires management to consider the impact of possible changes in the external environment and within its own business model that may render internal control ineffective.[61]

The risk assessment process "considers factors that influence the severity, velocity, and persistence of . . . risk, likelihood of the loss of assets, and the related impact on operations, reporting, and compliance activities."[62] It takes into account all internal and external interactions of an organization, including its subunits, subsidiaries and divisions, as well as suppliers, distributors and other third parties with whom the organization collaborates.[63]

The third component of internal control, Control Activities, is directed at mitigating the risks identified in the risk assessment process.

> Control activities are the actions established through policies and procedures that help ensure that management's directives to mitigate risks to the achievement of objectives are carried out. Control activities are performed at all levels

---

59. COSO Executive Summary, *supra* note 39, at 4.
60. COSO Framework, *supra* note 38, at 33.
61. COSO Executive Summary, *supra* note 39, at 4.
62. COSO Framework, *supra* note 38, at 70.
63. *See id.* at 71.

of the entity, at various stages within business processes, and over the technology environment. They may be preventive or detective in nature and may encompass a range of manual and automated activities such as authorizations and approvals, verifications, reconciliations, and business performance reviews. Segregation of duties is typically built into the selection and development of control activities. Where segregation of duties is not practical, management selects and develops alternative control activities.[64]

"Transaction controls are the most fundamental control activities in an entity since they directly address risk responses in the business processes in place to meet management's objectives."[65] Authorizations check the validity of a transaction, usually through approval by a higher level of authority within the organization. Verifications generally confirm the completeness, accuracy or validity of a transaction. Reconciliations compare two or more data elements to verify that they are in agreement (for example, comparing an expense report to a credit card statement to verify the charges). Segregation of duties involves division of responsibility among different employees to "reduce the risk of error or inappropriate or fraudulent actions."[66] For example, if an employee is requesting authorization for an expense, a different employee should be in charge of approving and verifying that expense. Similarly, an employee who receives a commission on a particular transaction should not be in charge of setting the transaction price.[67]

The fourth component of internal control is Information and Communication. This component relates to how an organization establishes information flows, internally and externally, in achieving its objectives:

> Management obtains or generates and uses relevant and quality information from both internal and external sources to support the functioning of other components of internal control. Communication is the continual, iterative process of providing, sharing, and obtaining necessary information.[68]

"Maintaining quality of information is necessary to an effective internal control system, particularly with today's volume of data and dependence on sophisticated, automated information systems."[69] The quality of information used by an organization depends on several factors, including accessibility (those who need it can access it), correctness, currency (it is up-to-date), protectedness (access is restricted where appropriate), sufficiency, timeliness (it is available when needed), validity (it was obtained properly), and verifiability.[70]

There are two types of communication: internal and external. Internal communication disseminates information within the organization, "flowing up, down, and across the entity."[71] "It enables personnel to receive a clear message

---

64. COSO Executive Summary, *supra* note 39, at 4.
65. COSO Framework, *supra* note 38, at 90.
66. *Id.* at 95.
67. *See id.* at 96.
68. COSO Executive Summary, *supra* note 39, at 5.
69. COSO Framework, *supra* note 38, at 111.
70. *See id.*
71. COSO Executive Summary, *supra* note 39, at 5.

from senior management that control responsibilities must be taken seriously."[72] One of the most important kinds of internal communication occurs between management and the board of directors, as it allows the board to properly discharge its oversight responsibilities.[73]

External communication, on the other hand, describes the processes by which the organization communicates with the outside world.[74] External communication has two aspects: first, it directs "inbound communication of relevant external information,"[75] that is, it ensures that information from external sources reaches the right people within the organization and is properly processed. And second, "it provides information to external parties in response to requirements and expectations."[76]

The fifth component of internal control is Monitoring Activities, which covers controls that measure how the system performs in achieving its objectives:

> Ongoing evaluations, separate evaluations, or some combination of the two are used to ascertain whether each of the five components of internal control, including controls to effect the principles within each component, is present and functioning. Ongoing evaluations, built into business processes at different levels of the entity, provide timely information. Separate evaluations, conducted periodically, will vary in scope and frequency depending on assessment of risks, effectiveness of ongoing evaluations, and other management considerations. Findings are evaluated against criteria established by regulators, recognized standard-setting bodies or management and the board of directors, and deficiencies are communicated to management and the board of directors as appropriate.[77]

"[M]onitoring activities identify and examine expectation gaps relating to anomalies and abnormalities, which may indicate one or more deficiencies in an entity's system of internal control."[78] Ongoing evaluations are built into business operations and monitor activities as they occur, such as having a compliance officer embedded in a business unit or automated software that flags suspicious transactions. Separate evaluations are performed periodically and include internal and external audits.

A direct relationship exists between objectives, which are what an entity strives to achieve; components, which represent what is required to achieve the objectives; and the organizational structure of the entity (the operating units, legal entities, and other). The relationship can be depicted in the form of a cube (see Figure 4-1).

- The three categories of objectives—operations, reporting, and compliance—are represented by the columns.
- The five components are represented by the rows.
- An entity's organizational structure is represented by the third dimension.

---

72. *Id.*
73. *See* COSO Framework, *supra* note 38, at 114-15.
74. COSO Executive Summary, *supra* note 39, at 5.
75. *Id.*
76. *Id.*
77. *Id.*
78. COSO Framework, *supra* note 38, at 124.

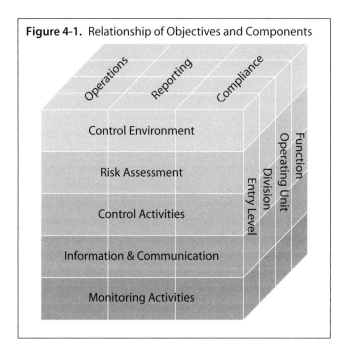

Figure 4-1. Relationship of Objectives and Components

4. The Seventeen Principles

COSO has identified seventeen principles for assessing an internal control system, each of which relates to one of the five components of internal control:[79]

Control Environment

1) Commitment to integrity and ethical values
2) Exercise of oversight responsibility
3) Establishment of structure, authority, and responsibility
4) Demonstration of a commitment to competence
5) Enforcement of accountability

Risk Assessment

6) Specification of objectives
7) Identification and analysis of risk
8) Assessment of fraud risk
9) Identification and analysis of significant change

Control Activities

10) Selection and development of control activities
11) Selection and development of general controls over technology
12) Deployment through policies and procedures

---

79. COSO Executive Summary, *supra* note 39, at 6–7.

Information and Communication

13) Use of relevant information
14) Internal communication
15) External communication

Monitoring

16) Conduct of ongoing and/or separate evaluations
17) Evaluation and reporting of deficiencies.[80]

All five components of internal control and all seventeen principles must be "present and functioning" before management can appropriately conclude its system of internal control.[81] "Present" means that all the appropriate controls are in place, and "functioning" means that they effectively prevent major deficiencies in achieving the company's objectives.[82] Lastly, "[t]he *Framework* requires that all components operate together in an integrated manner."[83]

Hypothetical: Initiatives to Prevent Foreign Corruption

Clyde, Inc. ("Clyde") is a manufacturer of heavy construction equipment, whose shares trade on the NYSE. Following several instances where Clyde employees were found to have secured sales contracts by illegally bribing government officials in emerging markets, Clyde's board of directors and senior management decided to take the following actions:

1) Revise Clyde's policies and code of conduct to place greater emphasis on preventing corruption
2) Hold a series of town hall meetings to discuss the potential consequences of corruption for the company and send a clear message to employees that corruption will not be tolerated
3) Require approval of all payments by sales staff in emerging markets
4) Require that all checks for amounts in excess of $10,000 be co-signed by a supervisor

To which component of internal control does each of the above actions belong?

---

80. *Id.*
81. *See, e.g., id.* at 8.
82. *Id.*
83. *Id.*

Hypothetical: Confidential Hotline

Warren, Inc. ("Warren") is a pharmaceutical company with divisions in thirty countries, whose shares trade on the NYSE. Recently, Warren established a confidential hotline that any employee can call to report a suspected violation of U.S. or foreign law.

To which component of internal control does the hotline belong?

Notes and Questions

Below are examples of internal controls. To which component of internal control does each belong?

- Policies and procedures
- Code of conduct
- Training
- Due diligence
- Authorizations
- Verifications
- Segregation of duties
- Audits

Volkswagen to Spend Up to $14.7 Billion to Settle Allegations of Cheating Emissions Tests and Deceiving Customers on 2.0 Liter Diesel Vehicles[84]

In two related settlements, one with the United States and the State of California, and one with the U.S. Federal Trade Commission (FTC), German automaker Volkswagen AG and related entities have agreed to spend up to $14.7 billion to settle allegations of cheating emissions tests and deceiving customers. Volkswagen will offer consumers a buyback and lease termination for nearly 500,000 model year 2009-2015 2.0-liter diesel vehicles sold or leased in the U.S., and spend up to $10.03 billion to compensate consumers under the program. In addition, the companies will spend $4.7 billion to mitigate the pollution from these cars and invest in green vehicle technology.

The settlements partially resolve allegations by the Environmental Protection Agency (EPA), as well as the California Attorney General's Office and the California Air Resources Board (CARB) under the Clean Air Act, California Health and Safety Code, and California's Unfair Competition Laws, relating to the vehicles' use of

---

84. Press Release, U.S. Dep't of Justice, Volkswagen to Spend Up to $14.7 Billion to Settle Allegations of Cheating Emissions tests and Deceiving Customers on 2.0 Liter Diesel Vehicles (June 28, 2016), https://www.justice.gov/opa/pr/volkswagen-spend-147-billion-settle-allegations-cheating-emissions-tests-and-deceiving.

"defeat devices" to cheat emissions tests. The settlements also resolve claims by the FTC that Volkswagen violated the FTC Act through the deceptive and unfair advertising and sale of its "clean diesel" vehicles. The settlements do not resolve pending claims for civil penalties or any claims concerning 3.0 liter diesel vehicles. Nor do they address any potential criminal liability.

The affected vehicles include 2009 through 2015 Volkswagen TDI diesel models of Jettas, Passats, Golfs and Beetles as well as the TDI Audi A3.

"By duping the regulators, Volkswagen turned nearly half a million American drivers into unwitting accomplices in an unprecedented assault on our environment," said Deputy Attorney General Sally Q. Yates. "This partial settlement marks a significant first step towards holding Volkswagen accountable for what was a breach of its legal duties and a breach of the public's trust. And while this announcement is an important step forward, let me be clear, it is by no means the last. We will continue to follow the facts wherever they go."

"Today's settlement restores clean air protections that Volkswagen so blatantly violated," said EPA Administrator Gina McCarthy. "And it secures billions of dollars in investments to make our air and our auto industry even cleaner for generations of Americans to come. This agreement shows that EPA is committed to upholding standards to protect public health, enforce the law, and to find innovative ways to protect clean air."

"Today's announcement shows the high cost of violating our consumer protection and environmental laws," said FTC Chairwoman Edith Ramirez. "Just as importantly, consumers who were cheated by Volkswagen's deceptive advertising campaign will be able to get full and fair compensation, not only for the lost or diminished value of their car but also for the other harms that VW caused them."

According to the civil complaint against Volkswagen filed by the Justice Department on behalf of EPA on January 4, 2016, Volkswagen allegedly equipped its 2.0 liter diesel vehicles with illegal software that detects when the car is being tested for compliance with EPA or California emissions standards and turns on full emissions controls only during that testing process. During normal driving conditions, the software renders certain emission control systems inoperative, greatly increasing emissions. This is known as a "defeat device." Use of the defeat device results in cars that meet emissions standards in the laboratory, but emit harmful NOx at levels up to 40 times EPA-compliant levels during normal on-road driving conditions. The Clean Air Act requires manufacturers to certify to EPA that vehicles will meet federal emission standards. Vehicles with defeat devices cannot be certified.

The FTC sued Volkswagen in March, charging that the company deceived consumers with the advertising campaign it used to promote its supposedly "clean diesel" VWs and Audis, which falsely claimed that the cars were low-emission, environmentally friendly, met emissions standards and would maintain a high resale value.

The settlements use the authorities of both the EPA and the FTC as part of a coordinated plan that gets the high-polluting VW diesels off the road, makes the environment whole, and compensates consumers.

The settlements require Volkswagen to offer owners of any affected vehicle the option to have the company buy back the car and to offer lessees a lease cancellation at no cost. Volkswagen may also propose an emissions modification plan to EPA and CARB, and if approved, may also offer owners and lessees the option of having their vehicles modified to substantially reduce emissions in lieu of a buyback. Under the U.S./California settlement, Volkswagen must achieve an overall recall rate of at least 85% of affected 2.0 liter vehicles under these programs or pay additional sums into the mitigation trust fund. The FTC order requires Volkswagen to compensate consumers who elect either of these options.

Volkswagen must set aside and could spend up to $10.03 billion to pay consumers in connection with the buy back, lease termination, and emissions modification compensation program. The program has different potential options and provisions for affected Volkswagen diesel owners depending on their circumstances[.]

State of New York v. Volkswagen Aktiengesellschaft

Supreme Court of the State of New York, County of Albany (2016)

COMPLAINT

. . . .

1. Introduction

The State of New York and the New York State Department of Environmental Conservation ("NYSDEC") (collectively, "State") seek civil court redress, including civil penalties and injunctive relief, in New York State Supreme Court for the egregious and pervasive violations of its codified civil environmental laws caused by the defendants (collectively "Volkswagen" or "Defendants") in their efforts to boost sales of their diesel automobiles in the United States and in New York. Defendants' efforts succeeded to the extent of selling nearly 600,000 diesel vehicles to U.S. consumers, including more than 25,000 in New York, from 2008 to 2015. Defendants' violations strike at the heart of New York's civil environmental laws designed to protect public health by strictly limiting motor vehicle pollution. Those civil laws rest on the foundation that prohibiting the sale of vehicles that fail emissions tests reflecting real-world driving conditions will help protect New Yorkers from smog and other pollutants that cause premature deaths and respiratory illness.

Volkswagen defrauded the public and government regulators, including the State, by designing and deploying air pollution control "defeat devices" that detected and then switched on (or ramped up) air pollution control equipment when their diesel vehicles were undergoing emissions tests, and then turned off (or dialed back) the pollution control when the vehicles were driven on the road. Despite being required under law to disclose the existence of any defeat devices,

Volkswagen concealed them for a decade, across multiple Volkswagen, Audi, and Porsche makes and models. The defeat devices concealed that these vehicles: (a) did not comply, or come close to complying, with applicable state emission standards during normal driving; and (b) were not the "clean" "green" vehicles described in Defendants' extensive marketing campaign aimed at American consumers.

Volkswagen has admitted all this. At a September 2015 event to promote the 2016 Passat, Michael Horn, then-President and CEO of Volkswagen Group of America, Inc., was plain-spoken, telling the audience "[l]et's be clear about this. Our company was dishonest with the EPA and the California Air Resources Board and with all of you, and, in my German words, we have totally screwed up."

A few weeks later, in prepared testimony before the House Committee on Energy and Commerce Subcommittee on Oversight and Investigations on October 8, 2015, Horn offered more detail, confirming "that emissions in [Volkswagen's] four cylinder diesel vehicles from model years 2009-2015 contained a 'defeat device' in the form of hidden software that could recognize whether a vehicle was being operated in a test laboratory or on the road. The software made those vehicles emit higher levels of nitrogen oxides when the vehicles were driven in actual road use than during laboratory testing."

The decision to install defeat devices was not, however, made by "a couple of software engineers," as Horn suggested in his testimony. Nor was it confined to the 2.0 liter diesel vehicles that were the focus of the 2014 independent study that led to the exposure of Volkswagen's emissions fraud to the public. Rather, it was the result of a willful and systematic scheme of cheating by dozens of employees at all levels of the company regarding emissions, after Volkswagen was unwilling to manufacture diesel vehicles that would meet federal and state standards in the United States. This scheme, which extended over nearly a decade, was perpetrated by Volkswagen AG and its Audi, Volkswagen and Porsche subsidiaries, through their employees, executives, and officers.

Defendants' unlawful conduct involved different engineering and testing teams—operating across different facilities in both Germany and the United States—and the placement of the illegal defeat devices in over a dozen separate U.S.-market Audi, Volkswagen and Porsche models equipped with 2.0 liter and 3.0 liter diesel engines (the "Subject Vehicles") from the 2009–2016 model years, which were sold between 2008 and 2015.

In addition to defrauding the state and federal agencies responsible for regulating car emissions, Volkswagen carried out a cynical fraud on the American car-buying public. It traded on the reputation for stellar engineering that Audi (whose slogan is "Truth in Engineering"), Porsche and Volkswagen enjoyed, by aggressively marketing the non-compliant diesel engines to U.S. consumers as the product of environmentally-friendly German advanced technology, thereby obtaining premiums for the vehicles on the basis of this fundamentally dishonest marketing.

Volkswagen's illegal and deceptive conduct had the following interrelated objectives: (i) increasing sales and market share in the U.S., part of the company's stated goal of becoming the world's highest-selling car manufacturer, (ii) marketing supposedly "green" diesel vehicles to create an environmental "halo" effect (and thus boost brand equity) across the full spectrum of the company's car offerings, (iii) enabling Volkswagen to bring diesel cars to the U.S. market more rapidly and more cheaply than building truly emissions-compliant engines would have permitted, and (iv) allowing Volkswagen and Audi to compensate for and conceal a number of technological and design deficiencies, including durability problems associated with several of its key drivetrain components, underperforming diesel particulate (soot) filters, and the fact that the urea tanks in Subject Vehicles equipped with selective catalytic reduction emission control systems were significantly undersized.

For years after its initial adoption of defeat devices in the U.S.-market Audi Q7 SUV and the Volkswagen Jetta, and as new diesel car models were introduced or updated, Volkswagen continued to cheat by adapting its defeat device software to the modified engines and emissions systems associated with the newer models.

Even when independent real-world driving test results in 2014 threatened public exposure of Volkswagen's systemic emissions deception, the company continued to actively conceal the existence of the defeat devices by repeatedly denying the validity of testing that exposed the gap between the Subject Vehicles' emissions on the road, as contrasted with emissions in testing conditions, and by conducting sham recalls in 2014–2015 to deflect regulatory scrutiny about the emissions problems. Indeed, even after state and federal regulators began asking tough questions in April 2014, Defendants continued their deceptive marketing campaign in the United States, spending tens of millions of dollars to promote the Subject Vehicles as "clean" and "green," and selling more than 144,000 of the Subject Vehicles from April 2014 (when the Subject Vehicles' high real driving NOx (oxides of nitrogen) emissions first came to light in the U.S.) through September 2015.

As a result of Volkswagen's scheme, the Subject Vehicles were certified for sale throughout the United States, enabling Volkswagen to sell nearly 600,000 Subject Vehicles nationwide and more than 25,000 in New York. Based on initial estimates, the defeat devices were responsible for more than 45,000 additional tons of NOx pollution being emitted into the air from these vehicles driven on highways and streets in New York and in other states.

Because internal combustion engines emit a variety of air pollutants harmful to human health and the environment, and motor vehicles are a significant source of air pollution, the federal Clean Air Act requires the Administrator of the Environmental Protection Agency ("EPA") in Section 202 to establish national emission standards for new motor vehicles. 42 U.S.C. § 7521. Section 177 of the Act, 42 U.S.C. § 7507, authorizes the State of California to adopt emission standards more stringent than the federal standards, and further authorizes other states to adopt those same standards for new motor vehicles sold within their states.

New York has adopted as state law California's strict emission control standards for NOx emissions as part of New York's effort to address pervasive ground-level ozone (smog) pollution, especially in the New York City metropolitan area. Ozone is formed when NOx, emitted by motor vehicles and other sources, combines in the atmosphere with volatile organic compounds ("VOCs") in a complicated reaction in the presence of heat and sunlight. Ozone causes or contributes to many human respiratory health problems, including chest pains, shortness of breath, coughing, nausea, throat irritation and increased susceptibility to respiratory infections, such as asthma, and disproportionately affects vulnerable members of society, particularly children and the elderly.

In New York, the concentration of ground-level ozone exceeds the maximum level allowed under the 2008 national ambient air quality standards in ten counties, with a combined population of approximately 12.4 million people.

Thus, approximately 64 percent of New Yorkers live in communities with ozone pollution above the level established by EPA as necessary to protect human health.

Emissions of NOx also cause eutrophication of and excess nutrient loading in coastal and other waters, reduce the diversity of fish and other life in these waters and, along with sulfur dioxide found in the atmosphere from other sources, contribute to the creation of fine nitrate and sulfate particles. Like ozone, fine particulate matter affects New York's residents by causing human respiratory distress, cardiovascular disease, and even premature mortality. Fine nitrate and sulfate particles are also toxic to aquatic life and vegetation.

With utter disregard for the environment and the health effects of its conduct, Volkswagen implemented the emissions control defeat devices in willful contempt of the environmental laws of the State of New York and other United States jurisdictions.

Volkswagen believed that its deceit would go undetected, and that even if caught, the consequences would be manageable. A February 29, 2016 court filing by Volkswagen in a European shareholder lawsuit provides an illuminating insight into its cost-benefit calculation when it comes to whether to break the law:

> [B]eginning in the 1970s, violations of the prohibition against defeat devices under U.S. environmental law had recurred at irregular intervals in the United States, the theoretical possibility that sanctions might be imposed due to a potential violation of U.S. environmental protection provisions seemed at the time to pose only a moderate cost risk. The fines imposed for such violations in the 1990s against automobile manufacturers that were also well-known (including General Motors, Ford, and Honda) were for relatively low amounts. Even the highest fine to date, which amounted to U.S.-$ 100 million and was imposed in 2014 against the Hyundai/Kia group, was at the lower end of the statutory range of fines. This case involved roughly 1.1 million vehicles, which works out to a fine of barely U.S.-$ 91 per vehicle. It is obvious that fines in this amount are not even remotely capable of influencing the share price of a globally operative company such as VOLKSWAGEN. Even if the fine were U.S.-$100 per vehicle, the total penalty in the present case would amount to U.S. $50 million, which would have no potential effect whatsoever on share prices.

Braunschweig, Case No. 02106-15/BE/Hn, Defendants' Answer (Feb. 29, 2016) at 47.

Worse yet, Volkswagen employees destroyed documents in the wake of the defeat device scandal after being alerted to an impending litigation hold, and Volkswagen AG Supervisory Board awarded Management Board members $70 million in executive compensation for 2015 alone. These actions highlight how stubborn and unrepentant the culture at Volkswagen is that gave rise to the systematic cheating and deception described in this Complaint.

On June 28, 2016, Volkswagen announced that it had reached a partial settlement that, if approved by a federal court, would resolve (a) claims brought by car owners and the Federal Trade Commission for consumer deception in connection with its marketing and sale of the 2.0-liter Subject Vehicles, and (b) claims for injunctive relief to redress environmental harm brought by the U.S. Environmental Protection Agency, California, and the California Air Resources Board. On the same date, many states, including New York, announced that they had settled their claims against Volkswagen for penalties arising under state laws that prohibit consumer deception. None of these settlements address the civil penalty claims of the state governments, including New York, for Volkswagen's systematic, repeated and egregious violations of state environmental laws; indeed, Volkswagen's liability for appropriately stiff environmental penalties, which is the subject of the present Complaint, was expressly left open by New York and other states in their partial settlement with Volkswagen.

The State of New York and the NYSDEC (collectively, "Plaintiffs" or "State"), by and through the Attorney General of the State of New York, Eric T. Schneiderman, bring this action against Defendants to enforce: (a) article 19 of the New York Environmental Conservation Law ("ECL"), which protects the State's air quality from pollution, and its implementing regulations found at 6 NYCRR Parts 200, et seq., including the "Emission Standards for Motor Vehicles and Motor Vehicle Engines" set forth in 6 NYCRR Part 218; and (b) New York Executive Law § 63(12). These statutory and regulatory schemes are described in more detail in paragraphs 248 to 256, infra.

Together with appropriate injunctive and equitable relief and reasonable costs of investigation and litigation, the State seeks imposition against Defendants of civil penalties in amounts sufficient to punish them for their conduct and deter them, as well as other automakers, from engaging in and repeating this form of deliberate misconduct.

Notes and Questions

The settlement and pending civil action against Volkswagen illustrate the potentially devastating consequences of a deficient internal control system.

1) Using the facts from the Volkswagen case study and the COSO Framework, design at least one control for each of the seventeen principles that Volkswagen could have implemented to prevent its illegal conduct.
2) Did Volkswagen's conduct violate the FCPA accounting provisions? If so, how?

In the Matter of BHP Billiton Ltd. and BHP Billiton Plc

Exchange Act Release No. 34-74998 (May 20, 2015)[85]

Order Instituting Cease-and-Desist Proceedings Pursuant to Section 21C of the Securities Exchange Act of 1934, Making Findings, and Imposing a Cease-and-Desist Order

. . . .

III.

. . . .

Background

[BHP Billiton ("BHPB")] is a global resources company that is among the world's leading producers of major commodities, including iron ore, coal, oil and gas, copper, aluminum, manganese, uranium, nickel, and silver. As of June 30, 2014, the end of its most recently completed fiscal year, BHPB had a market capitalization of approximately $190 billion, with over 140 locations, operations in 25 countries, and a workforce of more than 128,000 employees and contractors.

During the relevant period, BHPB operated through different business divisions, called Customer Sector Groups ("CSGs"). These CSGs included Iron Ore, Aluminum, Petroleum, Base Metals, Diamonds and Specialty Products, Stainless Steel Materials, Manganese, Metallurgical Coal, and Energy Coal. Each CSG had its own president, which reported to a member of BHPB's Group Management Committee. BHPB also had a Minerals Exploration Group ("MinEx") that assisted the CSGs with exploration activities.

Under BHPB's operating model during the relevant period, each CSG President was responsible for ensuring their businesses' compliance with the company's Guide to Business Conduct. Every CSG President also was required to certify annually that they had read and understood the Guide, confirmed that their direct reports had done the same, and discussed it with their direct reports. BHPB had a centralized legal department. In addition, it had an advisory body with internal and external membership called the Global Ethics Panel ("Ethics Panel"), which advised business leaders on compliance with the Guide to Business Conduct and other business ethics issues. BHPB did not have an independent, centralized compliance group within its legal department, or otherwise.

BHPB's Hospitality Program for the 2008 Beijing Summer Olympic Games

A. The Scope and Goals of BHPB's Olympic Hospitality Program

In December 2005, BHPB and the Beijing Organizing Committee announced their agreement for BHPB to become an official sponsor of the 2008 Beijing Olympic Games. Under this agreement, BHPB paid a sponsorship fee and supplied the raw materials used to make the Olympic medals. In exchange, BHPB

---

85. BHP Billiton Ltd., Exchange Act Release No. 74998, 2015 WL 2393657 (May 20, 2015).

received the rights to use the Olympic trademark and other intellectual property in public announcements and advertisements, as well as priority access to tickets, hospitality suites, and accommodations in Beijing during the August 2008 Games.

BHPB established an Olympic Sponsorship Steering Committee ("OSSC") to plan, oversee, and implement its sponsorship program, which involved multiple different branding, promotion, and relationship-building initiatives. The chair of the OSSC, who also was the chair of the Ethics Panel, reported directly to BHPB's CEO.

One of BHPB's objectives for the sponsorship was "to reinforce and develop relationships with key stakeholders" in China and in "product and investor markets, and regions where we have or would like to have operations." BHPB's strategy for accomplishing its objectives included "[u]tiliz[ing] Olympic hospitality to motivate China-based stakeholders, including customers, suppliers, government and media, to enhance business opportunities for BHP Billiton in China" and "[u]tiliz[ing] Olympic hospitality to build relationships with stakeholders from product and investor markets, and regions where we have or would like to have operations."

One of the company's sponsorship-related initiatives was a global hospitality program under which BHPB invited guests from around the world, including foreign government officials and representatives of state-owned enterprises, to attend the Beijing Olympics on three to four day hospitality packages. The hospitality packages included luxury hotel accommodations, meals, event tickets, and sightseeing excursions, at a cost of approximately $12,000 to $16,000 per package. In addition, BHPB executives approved the offer of round trip business class airfare to approximately 51 foreign government officials, as well as the airfares for 35 of these government officials' spouses or guests. Apart from BHPB's desire to enhance business opportunities by strengthening relationships with its guests, these trips had no other business purpose.

An internal e-mail to CSG presidents and other senior BHPB business managers emphasized the importance of the hospitality program to the success of BHPB's sponsorship, stating, "[a]s you know, we have made a commitment to support the Beijing Olympic Games in 2008. One of the core objectives is to maximise the commercial investment made in the Games through assisting [BHPB] to strengthen relationships with key local and global stakeholders, e.g.: Government Ministers, Suppliers, and Customers. The BHP Billiton Hospitality Program is a primary vehicle to ensure this goal is achieved."

In early 2007, BHPB employees prepared country-specific Olympic Leverage Plans, which summarized BHPB's business and Olympic-related objectives. In a number of instances, these plans discussed inviting key stakeholders, including government officials, to help BHPB develop relationships with a view to increasing or maintaining its business opportunities. For example, the Olympic Leverage Plan prepared for one country stated that BHPB's business objectives in that country included "gaining access to regions that will provide growth for [BHPB's] business" and "gaining port access." The plan further stated that the hospitality program would "provide useful relationship building opportunity for . . . stakeholders" and that the invitees would include the country's Minister of Mines and Minister of Transport. The Olympic Leverage Plan for another country, while not specifically addressing the hospitality program, stated that one of the goals for the sponsorship was "us[ing] Olympics program to strengthen and build the govt's confidence and relationship with [BHPB], to help facilitate approvals for future projects."

After Olympic Leverage Plans were prepared for each country, BHPB business managers submitted lists of potential invitees and were instructed to rank them in order of importance, with "Category A" being those "most critical to the business." Internal BHPB presentations discussed the need to establish "the business benefit" of an Olympic invitation.

Eventually, BHPB invited approximately 650 people to attend the Beijing Olympics, including 176 government officials, 98 of whom were representatives of state-owned enterprises that were BHPB customers or suppliers. BHPB also invited the spouses of 102 of these government officials. Most of the invited government officials were from countries in Africa and Asia where there was a known risk of corruption. Sixty of these government officials ultimately attended, 24 of them with their spouses or guests. A number of other invited government officials accepted their invitations, but then cancelled before the Olympics began.

B. BHPB's Insufficient Internal Controls Over the Olympic Hospitality Program

Early in its planning for the Olympics, BHPB identified the risk that inviting government officials to the Olympics could potentially violate anti-corruption laws and the company's own Guide to Business Conduct. The company relied on its existing operating model and an Olympic-specific internal approval process to address this risk. However, these internal controls, and BHPB's implementation of them, were insufficient.

BHPB developed a hospitality application which business managers were required to complete for any individuals, including government officials, whom they wished to invite. These applications included the following questions [question numbers revised]:

[1]. What business obligation exists or is expected to develop between the proposed invitee and BHP Billiton?

[2]. Is BHP Billiton negotiating or considering any contract, license agreement or seeking access rights with a third party where the proposed invitee is in a position to influence the outcome of that negotiation?

[3]. Do you believe that the offer of the proposed hospitality would be likely to create an impression that there is an improper connection between the provision of the hospitality and the business that is being negotiated, considered or conducted, or in any way might be perceived as breaching the Company's Guide to Business Conduct?

If yes, please provide details.

[4]. Are there other matters relating to the relationship between BHP Billiton and the proposed invitee that you believe should be considered in relation to the provision of hospitality having regard to BHP Billiton's Guide to Business Conduct?

BHPB required each such application to be filled out and signed by an employee with knowledge of the invitee's relationship with the company, and approved in writing by the president of the relevant CSG or the BHPB country president. A cover sheet that accompanied the blank forms included a short description of anti-bribery provisions in the Guide to Business Conduct and urged employees to re-read the section of the Guide concerning travel, entertainment, and gifts before completing the form. However, the controls did not adequately address the anti-bribery risks associated with offering expensive travel and entertainment packages to government officials.

First, BHPB did not require independent legal or compliance review of hospitality applications by someone outside the CSG that was submitting the application, and did not clearly communicate to its employees the fact that the Ethics Panel was not reviewing and approving each invitation to a government official. On the one hand, BHPB's internal website stated that the hospitality applications were subject to "scrutiny by the Ethics Panel [steering committee]," and the hospitality applications themselves stated that, "[r]equests for travel and accompanying spouses will be approved by the Olympic Sponsorship Steering Committee and the Global Ethics Panel Sub-Committee." E-mails sent to some BHPB business managers by a member of the OSSC staff stated that the Ethics Panel had "approved" their applications.

However, other than reviewing approximately 10 hospitality applications for government officials in mid-2007 in order to assess the invitation process, the OSSC and the Ethics Panel subcommittee did not review the appropriateness of individual hospitality applications or airfare requests. The Ethics Panel's charter stated that its role simply was to provide advice on ethical and compliance matters, and that "accountability rest[ed] with business leaders." Members of the Ethics Panel understood that, consistent with their charter, their role with respect to implementation of the hospitality program was purely advisory. As a result, business managers had sole responsibility for reconciling the competing goals of inviting guests—including government officials—who would "maximize [BHPB's] commercial investment made in the Olympic Games" without violating anti-bribery laws.

Second, some hospitality applications were not accurate or complete. Many applications identified an employee of a state-owned enterprise as a "Customer," but failed to identify the invitee as a "Representative of Government." In addition, a number of applications contained "No" responses to Question [2], even when BHPB had pending negotiations, efforts to obtain access rights, regulatory actions, or other business dealings in which the government official was directly involved or in a position to influence. Furthermore, in a number of instances, BHPB business people were provided with examples of language that had been used by other employees when responding to Questions [2] and [3] in order to explain why an invitation was appropriate, even when there was a "Yes" response to Questions [2-4]. As a result, many hospitality applications contained the exact same statements in response to Questions [2] and [3] rather than a description of the specific facts and circumstances relating to that government official.

Third, while BHPB had an annual Guide to Business Conduct review and certification process, and generalized training, it did not provide its employees and executives with any specific training on how to fill out the hospitality forms or how to evaluate whether an invitation to a government official complied with the Guide. During the relevant period, this portion of the Guide included a case example concerning a negotiation between BHPB and a Ministry for Planning in a particular country, in which the Minister indicated that it would help his consideration of the company's application if the Minister and his wife could visit BHPB's operations in Australia. The example stated that "this kind of situation requires the utmost caution and you must consult senior management. You must not offer to provide anything that could be reasonably regarded as an attempt to unduly influence the Minister's decision. This means that you must not pay for travel by the Minister's wife." However, BHPB did not provide any guidance to its senior managers on how they should apply this portion of the Guide when determining whether to approve invitations and airfares for government officials' spouses.

Fourth, although the form asked whether any business was "expected to develop" with the invitee, BHPB did not institute a process for updating hospitality applications or reassessing the appropriateness of invitations to government officials if conditions changed. Almost all of the hospitality applications relating to government officials were approved and submitted in mid-2007. However, BHPB did not require hospitality forms to be updated, or invitations to be reconsidered, in those situations when government officials subsequently became involved in negotiations, attempts by BHPB to obtain access rights, or other pending matters.

Fifth, hospitality applications were submitted by individual CSGs, and generally only reflected negotiations between the government official and that CSG. While lists of invitees were circulated among senior BHPB business managers, BHPB had no process in place to determine whether the invited government official also was involved in other CSGs' negotiations, efforts to obtain access rights, or other business dealings.

C. As a Result of Its Insufficient Internal Controls, BHPB Invited Government Officials Who Were Directly Involved in, or in a Position to Influence, Pending Negotiations, Regulatory Actions, or Business Dealings with BHPB

As a result of its failure to design and maintain sufficient internal controls over the Olympic global hospitality program, BHPB invited a number of government officials who were directly involved with, or in a position to influence, pending negotiations, efforts by BHPB to obtain access rights, or other pending matters.

Republic of Burundi

In mid-2007, BHPB's MinEx group submitted a hospitality application form to invite the as-yet-unidentified Burundi Minister of Mines and spouse to the Olympics, with airfare included. Because BHPB was not currently in negotiations with the Minister of Mines at the time, the hospitality application form contained a "No" response to Question [2]. However, BHPB had a joint venture ("JV") in Burundi with an entity that was in danger of losing a nickel exploration permit unless it made a substantial near-term financial investment in the project or negotiated a renewal or amendment of the permit. Under Burundi law, the Minister of Mines was responsible for reviewing an application to renew or amend a mining permit and presenting the application to the country's Council of Ministers for final approval.

In late 2007 and early 2008, BHPB began to negotiate directly with the newly-appointed Minister of Mines to extend and modify the JV's nickel exploration permit. However, BHPB employees did not update the hospitality application or take steps to re-review the appropriateness of the invitation after these negotiations began. As noted above, no such re-review was required by the internal controls that BHPB relied upon for the Olympic hospitality program. The Minister of Mines and his wife attended the Olympics as BHPB's guests for four days.

Republic of the Philippines

In July 2007, BHPB became embroiled in a dispute with a local JV partner concerning a prospective nickel mining operation in the Philippines. The JV partner sued BHPB in local court and filed requests with the country's Secretary of Department of Environment and Resources ("DENR"), requesting reversion of the mining rights that the JV partner had assigned to the JV.

In October 2007, a BHPB employee from the Stainless Steel Materials CSG submitted a hospitality application to invite the Secretary and his spouse to attend the Olympics, with airfare included. The completed application contained a "Yes" response to Question [2], but only described a technical services agreement that BHPB was considering submitting to the DENR for the Secretary's approval. Question [2] of the hospitality form did not explicitly require, and the employee's response did not provide, any information about the Secretary's role in reviewing the JV partner's reversion request or the fact that the President of the Philippines had designated the Secretary to mediate the dispute between BHPB and its JV partner. The form included a "No" response to Question [3].

The Secretary accepted BHPB's invitation in December 2007. In March 2008, he issued a decision denying the JV partner's reversion request and continued during the ensuing months to mediate the parties' dispute. In late July, BHPB became concerned that the company's JV partner had learned about the Olympics invitation. As a result, BHPB withdrew the invitation shortly before the Olympics began.

Democratic Republic of the Congo

In mid-2007, MinEx submitted a hospitality application form to invite the Governor of the Katanga Province in the Democratic Republic of the Congo (the "DRC") and his spouse, with airfare included. Following its June 2007 review of 10 invitations to government officials, the Ethics Panel subcommittee advised MinEx to provide more detail about whether the invitation involved Gecamines, a state-owned entity with which BHPB was attempting to negotiate a copper exploration deal. In response, MinEx submitted a revised application that contained a "No" response to Question [2], stating, "[t]he issuing and management of mineral titles and negotiations with third parties in DRC have nothing to do with the Governor's roles and responsibilities. Although [BHPB] are currently engaged in negotiations with State copper company, Gecamines, the Governor of Katanga will have no influence in these dealings."

Later in 2007, however, BHPB employees held several meetings with the Governor. Internal summaries of these meetings noted that the Governor was "a close ally of [the DRC] President" and that having the Governor as BHPB's ally "could be the key to unlock a successful entry in a deal with Gecamines." In spite of obtaining this information after making the initial decision to invite the Governor of Katanga and his wife to the Olympics, BHPB employees did not update the hospitality application form or take steps to re-review the appropriateness of the invitation. No such re-review was required under the internal controls that BHPB relied upon for the Olympic hospitality program. The Governor accepted the invitation, but then cancelled before the Olympics.

Republic of Guinea

In May 2007, MinEx submitted a hospitality application to invite the Guinea Minister of Mines and his spouse to the Olympics, with airfare included. The application contained a "No" response to Question [2], and in response to Question [3] it stated, "No. A sound professional relationship with the Guinea Ministry of Mines is key for the success of the [BHPB] exploration and mining business in this country." Following its June 2007 review of 10 invitations to government officials, the Ethics Panel subcommittee advised MinEx to provide additional information concerning this invitation. The MinEx employee who had prepared the original form asked BHPB's Guinea country president to respond to the request for information concerning any pending negotiations with the Minister. The country president replied that "of course" there would be "further negotiations" regarding the upcoming renewal of a bauxite mining concession held by BHPB and the government's intention to review all existing mining concessions, but that the response to Question [3] was "key in that regard."

This information was not passed along to the Ethics Panel subcommittee, however, and the form was not updated to accurately reflect the pending negotiations across all of the CSGs operating in Guinea. Because they received no response to the Guinea country president's email, MinEx officials mistakenly understood that the Ethics Panel had approved the invitation. The Minister accepted the invitation on behalf of himself and his wife in January 2008, but cancelled shortly before the Olympics began.

Legal Standards and FCPA Violations

Under Section 21C(a) of the Exchange Act, the Commission may impose a cease-and-desist order upon any person who is violating, has violated, or is about to violate any provision of the Exchange Act or any rule or regulation thereunder, and upon any other person that is, was, or would be a cause of the violation, due to an act or omission the person knew or should have known would contribute to such violation.

Under Section 13(b)(2)(A) of the Exchange Act, issuers are required to make and keep books, records, and accounts, which, in reasonable detail, accurately and fairly reflect the transactions and disposition of the assets of the issuer.

Under Section 13(b)(2)(B) of the Exchange Act, issuers are required to devise and maintain a system of internal accounting controls sufficient to provide reasonable assurances that (i) transactions are executed in accordance with management's general or specific authorization; (ii) transactions are recorded as necessary (I) to permit preparation of financial statements in conformity with generally accepted accounting principles or any other criteria applicable to such statements, and (II) to maintain accountability for assets; (iii) access to assets is permitted only in accordance with management's general or specific authorization; and (iv) the recorded accountability for assets is compared with the existing assets at reasonable intervals and appropriate action is taken with respect to any differences.

As a result of the conduct described above, BHPB violated Section 13(b)(2)(A) because its books and records, namely certain Olympic hospitality applications, did not, in reasonable detail, accurately and fairly reflect pending negotiations or business dealings between BHPB and government officials invited to the Olympics. BHPB violated Section 13(b)(2)(B) because it did not devise and maintain internal accounting controls over the Olympic hospitality program that were sufficient to provide reasonable assurances that access to assets and transactions were in executed in accordance with management's authorization.

BHPB's Cooperation and Remedial Efforts

In response to the Commission's investigation, BHPB retained outside counsel to assist it with conducting an extensive internal investigation into potential improper conduct in the jurisdictions that were the subject of the staff's inquiry. BHPB provided significant cooperation with the Commission's investigation by voluntarily producing large volumes of business, financial, and accounting documents from around the world in response to the staff's requests, and by voluntarily producing translations of key documents. BHPB's counsel conducted scores of interviews and provided the staff with regular reports on the findings of its internal investigation.

BHPB also has undertaken significant remedial actions. BHPB has created a compliance group within its legal department that is independent from the business units. This compliance group is responsible for FCPA compliance, among other things, and reports directly to BHPB's general counsel and Audit Committee. In addition, it has reviewed its existing anti-corruption compliance program and implemented other changes. These include embedding independent anti-corruption managers into its businesses and further enhancing its policies and procedures concerning hospitality, gift giving, use of third party agents, business partners, and other high-risk compliance areas. BHPB also has enhanced its financial and auditing controls, including policies to specifically address conducting business in high-risk markets. BHPB has conducted extensive employee training on anti-corruption issues and overhauled its processes for conducting internal investigations of potential violations of anti-corruption laws.

IV.

In view of the foregoing, the Commission deems it appropriate to impose the sanctions agreed to in Respondents BHP Billiton Ltd.'s and BHP Billiton Plc's Offers.

Accordingly, it is hereby ORDERED that:

A. Pursuant to Section 21C of the Exchange Act, Respondents cease and desist from committing or causing any violations and any future violations of Sections 13(b)(2)(A) and 13(b)(2)(B) of the Exchange Act.

B. Respondents shall, within 10 days of the entry of this Order, pay a civil money penalty totaling $25,000,000 to the Securities and Exchange Commission for remission to the United States Treasury, subject to Exchange Act Section 21F(g)(3). If timely payment is not made, additional interest shall accrue pursuant to 31 U.S.C. § 3717....

. . . .

C. During a one-year term as set forth below, Respondents shall report to the Commission staff on the operation of BHPB's FCPA and anti-corruption compliance program. If Respondents discover credible evidence, not already reported to the Commission staff, that: (1) questionable or corrupt payments or questionable or corrupt transfers of property or interests may have been offered, promised, paid, or authorized by Respondents, or any entity or person while working directly for Respondents, to any government official; (2) that related false books and records have been maintained; or (3) that Respondents' internal controls failed to detect and prevent such conduct, Respondents shall promptly report such conduct to the Commission staff. During this one-year period:

 (1) Respondents shall submit to the Commission staff a written report within 180 calendar days of the entry of this Order on the operation of BHPB's FCPA and anti-corruption compliance program (the "Initial Report")....

 (2) Respondents shall undertake one follow-up review, incorporating any comments provided by the Commission staff on the Initial Report, to further monitor and assess the operation of its FCPA and

anti-corruption compliance program and whether Respondents' policies and procedures are reasonably designed to detect and prevent violations of the FCPA and other applicable anti-corruption laws (the "Final Report").

. . . .

By the Commission.

Notes and Questions

1) What internal controls could BHPB have put in place to prevent the violations?
2) What, if any, existing internal controls did BHPB employees circumvent, and how?
3) Would the existing facts have been sufficient for a criminal prosecution of BHPB?

Hypothetical: Automated Data Check

Lee, Inc. ("Lee") is a clothing manufacturer whose shares trade on the NYSE. Lee uses an automated system to assure the accuracy of sales figures entered into the company's accounting records. The system checks the data in the accounting records and matches them against original invoices. If there is a discrepancy, or data is not properly formatted, the system provides immediate feedback indicating the error and produces a report.

To which component of internal control does the automated system belong?

United States v. Daimler AG

United States District Court, District of Columbia No. 1:10-CR-063-RJL (March 24, 2010)

United States Sentencing Memorandum

The United States of America, by and through its counsel, the United States Department of Justice, Criminal Division, Fraud Section (the "Department"), hereby submits in the above captioned matters this United States' Sentencing Memorandum. For the reasons outlined below, the Department respectfully requests that the Court approve the disposition of this matter and accept the guilty pleas of DaimlerChrysler Automotive Russia SAO and Daimler Export and Trade Finance GmbH pursuant to Fed. R. Crim. P. 11(c)(l)(C), and sentence them in accordance with the parties' plea agreements, which are being filed simultaneously herewith.

1. BACKGROUND

During the period relevant here, Daimler AG, formerly DaimlerChrysler AG and Daimler Benz AG (collectively "Daimler"), was a German vehicle manufacturing company with business operations throughout the world. Among other things, Daimler sold all manner of cars, trucks, vans, and buses, including Unimogs, heavy duty all terrain trucks primarily used for hauling, and Actros, large commercial tractor/trailer-style vehicles. Daimler was a major global producer of premium passenger cars, as well as the largest manufacturer of commercial vehicles in the world. As a result of its luxury car and commercial vehicles lines, Daimler had among its customers government and state-owned entities from many countries in which it did business. Daimler sold its products worldwide, had production facilities on five continents, did business in many foreign countries, and employed more than 270,000 people.

Daimler is owned by individual and institutional investors in the U.S., Europe, and elsewhere. More than one billion shares of Daimler were in circulation as of December 31, 2007. For purposes of the United States securities laws, Daimler became an "issuer" in 1993, and Daimler's common stock has been traded on the New York Stock Exchange, the Pacific Exchange, the Chicago Stock Exchange, and the Philadelphia Stock Exchange. As a result of Daimler's filing of periodic reports with the Securities and Exchange Commission ("SEC") pursuant to Title 15, United States Code, Section 18m, and Daimler's use of U.S. bank accounts and U.S. companies in transacting certain business with foreign governments and officials, the company is subject to the Foreign Corrupt Practices Act ("FCPA").

In March 2004, a former Daimler employee filed a whistleblower complaint with the U.S. Department of Labor's Occupational Safety & Health Administration pursuant to Section 806 of the Sarbanes-Oxley Act of 2002. In the complaint, the former employee alleged that he was terminated for voicing concerns about Daimler's practice of maintaining secret accounts, including accounts in its own books and records, for the purpose of bribing foreign government officials. In August 2004, the Securities and Exchange Commission granted its staff a formal order to investigate whether Daimler violated the FCPA. Thereafter, the Department opened its own investigation as to whether any such violations were criminal in nature.

Daimler engaged the law firm of Skadden Arps Slate Meagher & Flom ("Skadden") to represent the company in connection with both the SEC and the Department investigations. Skadden was also engaged to conduct a global internal investigation, the results of which were reported to the SEC and the Department. In response to the results of the company's internal investigation, and the SEC and Department investigations, Daimler and the Department have entered into a proposed global disposition for the Court's consideration that would resolve the criminal investigation into Daimler and its subsidiaries.

As in response to the results of these investigations, Daimler has instituted numerous compliance reforms, including linking a portion of board members' compensation to success in compliance-related matters. The company has terminated numerous individuals involved in the criminal wrongdoing described in these matters, and has overhauled its internal compliance organization and its compliance program. Significantly, Daimler did not wait to make these reforms until a final disposition was reached with the Department or the SEC. Instead, Daimler began reforming its worldwide compliance program as its investigation was ongoing, and regularly reported such reforms to the Department.

2. SUMMARY OF FACTS—DAIMLER'S KNOWING FALSIFICATION OF BOOKS AND RECORDS

Daimler's internal investigation, along with the SEC and the Department investigations, revealed that Daimler engaged in a long-standing practice of paying bribes to "foreign officials" as that term is defined in the FCPA (hereinafter "governmental officials") through a variety of mechanisms, including the use of corporate ledger accounts known internally as "third-party accounts" or "TPAs," corporate "cash desks," offshore bank accounts, deceptive pricing arrangements, and third-party intermediaries.

Within Daimler, bribe payments were often identified and recorded as "commissions," "special discounts," and/or "niitzliche AufWendungen" or "N.A." payments, which translates to "useful payment" or "necessary payment," and was understood by certain employees to mean "official bribe."

Between 1998 and January 2008, Daimler made hundreds of improper payments worth tens of millions of dollars to foreign officials in at least 22 countries—including China, Croatia, Egypt, Greece, Hungary, Indonesia, Iraq, Ivory Coast, Latvia, Nigeria, Russia, Serbia and Montenegro, Thailand, Turkey, Turkmenistan, Uzbekistan, Vietnam, and others—to assist in securing contracts with government customers for the purchase of Daimler vehicles valued at hundreds of millions of dollars. In some cases, Daimler wired these improper payments to U.S. bank accounts or to the foreign bank accounts of U.S. shell companies in order to transmit the bribe. In at least one instance, a U.S. shell company was incorporated for the specific purpose of entering into a sham consulting agreement with Daimler in order to conceal improper payments routed through the shell company to foreign government officials. Certain improper payments even continued as late as January 2008. In all cases, Daimler improperly recorded these payments in its corporate books and records.

Daimler's longstanding violations of the FCPA resulted from a variety of factors, including: (1) an inadequate compliance structure; (2) a highly decentralized system of selling vehicles through a myriad of foreign sales forces, subsidiaries, and affiliates, with no central oversight; (3) a corporate culture that tolerated and/or encouraged bribery; and (4) the involvement of certain key executives, such as the then head of its overseas sales division ("DCOS"), the then head of internal audit, and the then CEOs of several subsidiaries and affiliates.

In total, the corrupt transactions with a territorial connection to the United States resulted in over $50,000,000 in pre-tax profits for Daimler.

a. Use of Third Party Accounts to Make Improper Payments

At the time of the merger between Chrysler Corporation and Daimler-Benz in 1998, Daimler maintained over 200 internal "third-party accounts" ("TPAs"), known in German as "interne Fremdkonten." TPAs were maintained as receivable ledger accounts on Daimler's books and were controlled by third parties outside the company or by Daimler's own subsidiaries and affiliates. Daimler used these accounts, among other things, to facilitate the making of improper payments and the provision of gifts to foreign government officials. Funds were credited to these accounts through price inclusions, discounts, rebates, and other mechanisms. Although these accounts appeared in Daimler's books and records, they were accounted for improperly and were not subject to normal auditing or other financial controls. Moreover, certain accounts remained "off the books" of those Daimler affiliates on whose behalf Daimler maintained the accounts.

Daimler had maintained certain written policies governing the operation of TPAs since 1977, although until recently none of those policies addressed improper payments to government officials, or the inaccurate recording of payments to government officials in the company's books and records, or required internal controls to prevent and detect such improper payments and related false accounting. Daimler's written policies provided that TPAs were managed internally by the company at the request of the TPA account holder, and the funds on account were managed according to the instructions of the account holder. In one case, an account was managed by Daimler for the benefit of a foreign government official. Other TPA holders included Daimler's foreign subsidiaries, outside distributors, dealers, or consultants that Daimler used as intermediaries to make payments to foreign government officials. As reflected in a 1986 audit report, the TPAs were maintained with "absolute confidentiality" to protect account holders from having to reveal funds distributed to them from their respective third-party accounts, or to any other ultimate beneficiary. At that time, Daimler was aware that the existence of the accounts may violate the laws of other countries and that disclosure of the accounts to other governments could pose "significant difficulties for the account holder," as well as for Daimler.

Prior to 2002, Daimler's TPA policies permitted Daimler employees to make cash disbursements which were deducted from ledger balances on the TPAs. The cash was disbursed from a corporate "cash desk" located at a Daimler manufacturing facility in Stuttgart, Germany. In some instances, Daimler employees then took the cash and transported it to other countries, where the funds were used to pay bribes to governmental officials.

b. Daimler's Oil for Food Contracts

Daimler, or its intermediaries, agreed to pay a 10% commission to the government of Iraq in connection with sales of its vehicles under the Oil for Food ("OFF") program. In cases where Daimler entered into contracts to sell vehicles to the Iraqi government under the OFF program but the contracts were never executed (either because they failed to receive U.N. approval or the Iraqi government decided not to make the purchase), Daimler offered to make payments worth 10% of the contract value to the government of Iraq. Daimler entered into side agreements or side letters with its Iraqi government customers in which Daimler expressly promised to kick back 10% of the anticipated contract value to the Iraqi government.

c. DaimlerChrysler Automotive Russia SAO

DaimlerChrysler Automotive Russia SAO ("DCAR"), now known as Mercedes-Benz Russia SAO, was a Moscow-based, wholly owned subsidiary of Daimler AG. DCAR sold Daimler spare parts, assisted with the sale of vehicles from various Daimler divisions in Germany, including in particular DCOS, to government customers in the Russian Federation ("Russia"), and also imported Daimler passenger and commercial vehicles into Russia for sale to customers and distributors. Daimler sold passenger cars and commercial vehicles directly from its headquarters in Stuttgart, Germany, to its Russian government clients with the assistance of DCAR and Daimler's representative office in Moscow. Daimler carried out such sales from DCOS with DCAR acting as an agent to assist with such direct sales. DCAR and Daimler sold passenger cars, commercial vehicles, and Unimogs in Russia.

Daimler's business in Russia was substantial. DCAR and Daimler's government customers in Russia included the Russian Ministry of Internal Affairs, the Russian military, the City of Moscow, the City of Ufa, and the City of Novi Urengoi, among others. Daimler, through DCAR, made improper payments at the request of Russian government officials or their designees in order to secure business from Russian government customers. Payments of this nature were made with the knowledge and participation of the former senior management of DCAR and DCOS.

Daimler and DCAR sometimes made improper payments to government officials in Russia to secure business by over-invoicing the customer and paying the excess amount back to the government officials, or to other designated third parties that provided no legitimate services to Daimler or DCAR with the understanding that such payments would be passed on, in whole or in part, to Russian government officials. When payments were made to third parties, the payments were recorded on one of at least nine Daimler debtor accounts.

These overpayments were maintained as reserves on Daimler's books and records in certain internal debtor accounts, including debtor accounts that were identified by the name of the government customer with which Daimler and DCAR did business. When requested, Daimler employees wired and authorized the wiring of payments from Daimler's bank accounts in Germany to, among other destinations, U.S. and Latvian bank accounts beneficially owned by shell companies with the understanding that the money, in whole or in part, was for the benefit of Russian government officials.

Daimler and DCAR employees also made and authorized the making of cash payments to Russian government officials employed at Russian government customers, or their designees, in order to induce sales of Unimogs to several Russian government municipalities.

Daimler and DCAR recorded improper payments to Russian government officials or their designees, in their books and records as "commissions," "special discounts," and "N.A."

Overall, between 2000 and 2005, Daimler's vehicle sales in Russia, consisting of sales of passenger vehicles, commercial vehicles, and Unimogs, totaled approximately €1.4 billion, of which approximately 5% or €64,660,000 was derived from the sale of vehicles to Russian government customers. In connection with these vehicle sales, DCAR and Daimler made over €3 million in improper payments to Russian government officials employed at their Russian governmental customers, their designees, or to third-party shell companies that provided no legitimate services to Daimler or DCAR with the understanding that the funds would be passed on, in whole or in part, to Russian government officials.

d. Daimler Export and Trade Finance GmbH

Daimler Export and Trade finance GmbH ("ETF"), a German corporation, was a wholly owned, German-based subsidiary of Daimler Financial Services AG ("DFS"), which was itself a wholly owned subsidiary of Daimler. ETF formerly was known as "debis International Trading GmbH" ("dIT" or "debis"). ETF specialized in the structuring and arranging of customized financing solutions for exports by Daimler and external customers to countries without a local DFS company. In addition to these financing services, ETF participated in business ventures outside of Daimler's core businesses of the manufacture and sale of passenger cars and commercial vehicles.

ETF made improper payments directly to Croatian government officials and to third parties with the understanding that the payments would be passed on, in whole or in part, to Croatian government officials, to assist in securing the sale of 210 fire trucks (the "Fire Trucks Contracts") to the government of Croatia. In total, between 2002 and January 2008, ETF made approximately €4.69 million in such payments.

e. DaimlerChrysler China Ltd.

DaimlerChrysler China Ltd. ("DCCL"), now known as Daimler North East Asia Ltd., was a Beijing-based wholly owned Daimler subsidiary and cost center that managed Daimler's business relationships in China, assisted Daimler in selecting and managing its joint ventures in China, and helped manage Daimler's expatriate employees in China.

Although DCCL did not itself sell any vehicles directly into China, certain DCCL employees assisted with the sale of vehicles by various Daimler divisions in Germany to government customers in China, including principally the Bureau of Geophysical Prospecting ("BGP"), a division of the China National Petroleum Corporation, a Chinese state-owned oil company, and Sinopec Corp. ("Sinopec"), a Chinese state-owned energy company. Both BGP and Sinopec were involved in, among other things, exploration for oil and gas.

Between 2000 and 2005, DCCL employees and/or Daimler employees through DCCL made at least €4, 173,944 in improper payments in the form of "commissions," delegation travel, and gifts for the benefit of Chinese government officials or their designees, in connection with over €112,357,719 in sales of commercial vehicles and Unimogs to Chinese government customers. These sales were made directly from Daimler's commercial vehicles and Unimog divisions in Germany through various intermediaries to Chinese government customers with the assistance of DCCL employees in the commercial vehicles division.

To make improper payments to Chinese government officials, Daimler and DCCL typically inflated the sales price of vehicles sold to Chinese government customers and maintained the overpayments in debtor accounts on Daimler's books and records, including one debtor account called the "special commissions" account. The "special commissions" account; also known as the "819" account for the last three digits of the account number, was used by Daimler to make improper payments to Chinese government officials.

DCCL and Daimler also employed agents to assist in securing commercial vehicles and Unimog business from Chinese government customers. Neither DCCL nor Daimler performed due diligence on these agents, and there were inadequate controls in place to ensure that payments made to agents were not passed on to Chinese government officials and their designees. The agency agreements were often not in writing. In addition, DCCL and Daimler lacked adequate oversight into the appropriateness or purpose of payments from debtor accounts that ultimately went to government officials in China and their designees.

3. DISPOSITIONS WITH DAIMLER, DCAR, ETF, AND DCCL

a. Overall Summary

The Department and Daimler agree that the appropriate resolution of this matter consists of (1) a deferred prosecution agreement ("DPA") with Daimler AG, the parent company; (2) a DPA with DCCL, the Chinese subsidiary; (3) guilty pleas pursuant to plea agreements with DCAR, the Russian subsidiary, and ETF, the Daimler Finance subsidiary; (4) overall payment of a $93.6 million criminal penalty, which is apportioned, based on a Guidelines analysis, among the subsidiaries and the parent company; (5) continued obligation to provide full, complete, and truthful cooperation to the Department and any other law enforcement agency, domestic or foreign; (6) implementation of rigorous compliance enhancements, including periodic testing of same, with a recognition that the Company has already implemented substantial compliance changes due to the investigation; and (7) the imposition of a corporate compliance monitor who will, over a three-year term, conduct a review of the compliance code, the Company's internal controls and related issues, and will prepare periodic reports on his reviews.

In accordance with the Department's Principles of Federal Prosecution of Business Organizations, the Department considered a number of factors in its decisions regarding the overall disposition. Those factors included, but were not limited to, Daimler's cooperation and remediation efforts, as well as any collateral consequences, including whether there would be disproportionate harm to the shareholders, pension holders, employees, and other persons not proven personally culpable, and the impact on the public, arising from the prosecution. The Department's analysis of collateral consequences included the consideration of the risk of debarment and exclusion from government contracts, and in particular included European Union Directive 2004/181EC, which provides that companies convicted of corruption offenses shall be mandatorily excluded from government contracts in all EU countries.

b. Charges

The information filed against Daimler AG contains two counts, including conspiracy to commit an offense against the United States in violation of 18 U.S.C. § 371, that is, to violate the books and records provisions of the FCPA, as amended, 15 U.S.C. §§ 78m(b)(2)(A), 78m(b)(5), and 78ff(a) (Count One); and violating the books and records provisions of the FCPA, 15 U.S.C. §§ 78m(b)(2)(A), 78m(b)(5), and 78ff(a), and 18 U.S.C. § 2 (Count Two).

The information filed against the three subsidiaries—DCAR, ETF, and DCCL—also each contain two counts, including conspiracy to commit an offense against the United States, in violation of 18 U.S.C. § 371, that is, to violate the anti-bribery provisions of the FCPA, as amended, 15 U.S.C. § 78dd-3 (Count One), and violating of the anti-bribery provisions of the FCPA, 15 U.S.C. § 78dd-3 (Count Two).

c. Sentencing Guidelines Calculation and Criminal Penalties

. . . .

The overall criminal penalty of $93,600,000 is approximately 20% below the bottom of the Sentencing Guidelines fine range of $116,000,000. The parties believe that such a reduction is appropriate given the nature and extent of Daimler's cooperation in this matter, including sharing information with the Department regarding evidence obtained as a result of Daimler's extensive investigation of corrupt payments made by Daimler in various countries around the world. Indeed, because Daimler did not voluntarily disclose its conduct prior to the filing of the whistleblower lawsuit, it only receives a two-point reduction in its culpability score. The Department respectfully submits that such reduction is incongruent with the level of cooperation and assistance provided by the company in the Department's investigation. The three subsidiary agreements—guilty pleas for DCAR and ETF and a DPA for DCCL—contain separate Guidelines analyses for the transactions applicable to those entities. Those analyses yield criminal penalties attributable to the subsidiaries in the following amounts: (1) $5,040,000 (DCCL); (ii) $27,360,000 (DCAR); and (iii) $29,120,000 (ETF).

DCAR and ETF are pleading guilty pursuant to Fed. R. Crim. P. 11(c)(1)(C). Under Fed. R. Crim. P. 11(c)(1)(C), the Department respectfully submits that the appropriate criminal penalties in this case are as reflected in these Guidelines calculations, in light of Daimler's (a) assistance in the investigation, (b) its payments of fines or disgorgement in other related proceedings, and (c) its compliance and remediation efforts. The Department also respectfully submits that such a disposition adequately takes into account the nature and circumstances of the offense, reflects the seriousness of the offense, promotes respect for the law, provides just punishment, and affords adequate deterrence to criminal conduct for Daimler and the marketplace generally. *See* 18 U.S.C. § 3553(a). On this point, the Department notes that, when combined with Daimler's payment to the SEC, the instant disposition represents one of the largest payments in the history of the FCPA.

d. Daimler's Cooperation and Remediation Efforts

The Department considers Daimler's cooperation in this investigation to have been excellent. Specifically, Daimler conducted a worldwide internal investigation, involving dozens of countries and every major market in which the company does business. The company regularly presented its findings to the Department. In addition, Daimler made certain witnesses available to the Department, and voluntarily complied with requests for the production of documents from overseas.

Often, when Daimler would present its findings to the Department, it would also inform the Department about disciplinary actions that had already been taken by the company against culpable employees. These disciplinary actions resulted in sanctions against over 60 company employees, with approximately 45 employees being terminated or separated under termination agreements.

Finally, and perhaps most significantly, Daimler began to reform its anti-bribery compliance program while the investigation was still ongoing, without waiting until the finalization of a disposition with the Department. Daimler regularly updated the Department on the changes being made to its compliance program, including the following:

- Centralization of Corporate Compliance Operations ("CCO")—this initiative has resulted in the increase in CCO to approximately 60 full-time staff, plus 85 Local Compliance Managers in 41 countries who cover a total of 95 entities and business units." The company also retained external compliance experts, including a former German prosecutor. The CCO is integrated into Daimler's organization. This represents a significantly more robust compliance organization than existed previously.
- Centralization of Corporate Audit ("CA")—key CA initiatives include standardizing the methodology used by CA staff to conduct its audits, the express inclusion of control objectives from CCO in its work plans, and the performance of ad hoc audits. The CA staff consists of a total of 150 employees. Again, this is a more robust CA department than existed previously.
- Inclusion of compliance component in board-level compensation— the company began including compliance as a component of Board of Management compensation. Specifically, failure to reach compliance targets can reduce a Board of Management member's personal bonus by up to 25%. The company also now includes compliance, including FCPA and anti-corruption compliance, as part of its regular performance evaluation process.

- The company has established a whistleblower hotline, managed by the Business Practice Office ("BPO"), which falls under the CCO. The BPO's quarterly reports are provided to the Audit Committee. This reform is significant, given that the allegations of foreign bribery in this case first surfaced as the result of a Sarbanes Oxley whistleblower complaint filed against the company.
- The company has established a sales practices hotline known as the Compliance Consultation Desk, which also falls under the CCO. There are nine CCO employees dedicated to fielding and responding to hotline inquiries. Among other things, these employees counsel others in the prevention of bribery in connection with benefits such as discounts and donations, as well as in the prevention of bribery in business transactions with government bodies, consultants and intermediaries, and due diligence of third parties.
- The company now requires anti-bribery contract terms and audit rights for its intermediaries, including provisions that allow for unilateral termination by Daimler. This requirement has resulted in over 15,000 company contracts being amended.
- The company has instituted numerous other policies and training initiatives regarding FCPA compliance, including the implementation of company-wide rules regarding the use of bank accounts, gifts and entertainment, signature authorities, and approvals.
- Finally, the company has instituted a zero-tolerance policy for violations of the company's Integrity Code as well as other laws and regulations.

CONCLUSION

For the foregoing reasons, the Department respectfully recommends that the Court approve the disposition of this matter as described in this memorandum and accept the guilty pleas of DCAR and ETF pursuant to Fed. R. Crim. P. 11(c)(1)(C).

Notes and Questions

1) What methods did Daimler and its subsidiaries use to circumvent internal controls?
2) What internal controls could Daimler have employed to prevent the violations?
3) Notice that there are no charges against Daimler for violating the anti-bribery provisions of the FCPA, and instead, all of the charges relate to violations of the accounting provisions. Why do you think the DOJ chose this strategy?
4) How effectively did Daimler mitigate the potential losses resulting from its criminal conduct?

IV. Who Is Covered Under the FCPA Accounting Provisions?

A. Issuers and Their Subsidiaries

The FCPA Accounting Provisions apply to "issuers," defined as any foreign or domestic companies whose securities trade on a U.S. securities exchange or on the over-the-counter market[86] and who file periodic reports with the SEC.[87] Because an issuer's books include those of its consolidated subsidiaries, those entities are also subject to the FCPA Accounting Provisions.[88]

With respect to subsidiaries in which an issuer owns less than a majority interest, § 13(b)(6) of the Exchange Act provides:

> Where an issuer . . . holds 50 per centum or less of the voting power with respect to a domestic or foreign firm . . . the issuer [is required to] proceed in good faith to use its influence, to the extent reasonable under the issuer's circumstances, to cause such domestic or foreign firm to devise and maintain a system of internal accounting controls consistent with [the FCPA Accounting Provisions]. Such circumstances include the relative degree of the issuer's ownership of the domestic or foreign firm and the laws and practices governing the business operations of the country in which such firm is located. An issuer which demonstrates good faith efforts to use such influence shall be conclusively presumed to have complied with the requirements of [the FCPA Accounting Provisions].[89]

Thus, any ownership interest in another entity triggers an obligation to attempt to persuade that entity to adopt FCPA-compliant internal controls.

Hypothetical: Minority-Held Subsidiaries and the FCPA

Peach, Inc. ("Peach") is a U.S.-based technology company with a net worth of $1 billion, whose shares trade on the NYSE. In the last six months, Peach's management has made several strategic investments in small technology start-ups in emerging markets. Most of these start-ups are not in compliance with the FCPA Accounting Provisions.

---

86. Many stocks, corporate bonds, government bonds, and certain derivative products are traded in the over-the-counter (OTC) market, which is decentralized and less transparent than a securities exchange. *See Over-the-Counter Market*, SEC. & EXCH. COMM'N (May 9, 2013), https://www.sec.gov/divisions/marketreg/mrotc.shtml.

87. 15 U.S.C. § 78m(b)(2) (2012) (stating that Section 13(b) applies to "every issuer which has a class of securities registered pursuant to section 78*l* of this title [or] which is required to file reports pursuant to section 78o(d) of this title . . . .").

88. FCPA GUIDE, *supra* note 1, at 42–43.

89. 15 U.S.C. § 78m(b)(6) (2012).

1) What, if any, good faith efforts should Peach make to convince the start-ups to comply with the FCPA Accounting Provisions?
2) Does Peach have any other options to ensure that its investments do not violate the FCPA Accounting Provisions?

In the Matter of BellSouth Corp.

Exchange Act Release No. 45279 (January 15, 2002)[90]

Order Instituting Proceedings Pursuant to Section 21C of the Securities Exchange Act of 1934, Making Findings and Imposing a Cease-and-Desist Order

. . . .

III.

Findings

The Commission makes the following findings:

A. Respondent

BellSouth is a Georgia corporation with its headquarters in Atlanta, Georgia. The common stock of BellSouth has been registered with the Commission since 1983 pursuant to Section 12(b) of the Exchange Act and its common stock is listed on the New York Stock Exchange.

B. Other Relevant Entities

BellSouth International, Inc. ("BSI"), also headquartered in Atlanta, Georgia, is an indirectly wholly-owned subsidiary of BellSouth.

Telcel, C.A. ("Telcel"), a Venezuelan corporation headquartered in Caracas, Venezuela, is an indirectly majority-owned subsidiary of BellSouth. Since August 1997, BellSouth has indirectly held a majority interest in Telcel.

Telefonia Celular de Nicaragua, S.A. ("Telefonia"), a Nicaraguan corporation headquartered in Managua, Nicaragua, is an indirectly majority-owned subsidiary of BellSouth. Telefonia is Nicaragua's only provider of wireless telephone services. From March 1997 through June 2000, BellSouth held a 49 percent ownership interest in Telefonia and an option for an additional 40 percent. During that same period, BSI controlled Telefonia's operations by contractual agreement between BSI and Telefonia, and controlled Telefonia's management through a majority presence on Telefonia's board of directors. BellSouth increased its ownership interest in Telefonia to 89 percent in June 2000.

---

90. SEC v. BellSouth Corp., Civil Action No. 1:02-CV-0113 (N. D. Ga.) (filed Jan. 15, 2002).

C. Facts

1. Introduction

Over the last decade, BellSouth expanded its operations into Latin America by acquiring telephone companies in 11 Latin American countries: Venezuela, Brazil, Argentina, Colombia, Peru, Chile, Panama, Ecuador, Uruguay, Nicaragua and Guatemala. In the early years of BellSouth's expansion into Latin America, BellSouth acquired minority ownership positions in the local companies and allowed its local in-country partners to manage the companies' daily operations. In a gradual shift of strategy, BellSouth began acquiring majority ownership of the local companies and exercising greater management control over their operations. The violations of law that underlie this Order stem from actions and omissions relating to BellSouth's Latin American subsidiaries in Venezuela and Nicaragua.

2. Telcel

In 1991, BellSouth acquired a minority interest in Telcel. BellSouth eventually increased its ownership percentage in Telcel, acquiring a majority interest in August 1997. Telcel has become Venezuela's leading wireless provider, and contributes more revenue to BellSouth's Latin American Group segment than any other Latin American BellSouth operation.

Between September 1997 and August 2000, former Telcel senior management authorized payments totaling approximately $10.8 million to six offshore companies (the "Companies"). Telcel recorded the disbursements in Telcel's books and records based on fictitious invoices. The invoices indicated, without detail, that Telcel had received from the Companies professional, computer and contracting services. However, there were no service or vendor agreements supporting the alleged services, and, in fact, no services were rendered. BellSouth has been unable to reconstruct the circumstances or purpose of the payments, or the identity of their ultimate recipients.

3. Telefonia

In 1997, BellSouth acquired a 49 percent ownership interest in Telefonia, and an option granted by members of a Nicaraguan family (the "Nicaraguan co-owners") to acquire an additional 40 percent. At the time of BellSouth's acquisition of its minority interest in Telefonia, a Nicaraguan law, Article 29 of the General Law of Telecommunications and Postal Services (the "foreign ownership restriction"), prohibited foreign companies such as BellSouth from acquiring a majority interest in Nicaraguan telecommunications companies. BellSouth intended to exercise its 40 percent option, but could do so only in the event that the Nicaraguan legislature repealed the Article 29 foreign ownership restriction.

In connection with BellSouth's acquisition of Telefonia, BSI and the Nicaraguan co-owners executed an agreement ceding to BSI operational control of Telefonia ("the Operating Agreement"). Under the Operating Agreement, BSI became responsible for Telefonia's daily operations and for its long-term business planning. Additionally, after BellSouth's investment in Telefonia, there was a restructuring of Telefonia's board of directors, including the filling of four of the six Telefonia board seats by BSI personnel.

In October 1998, Telefonia retained the wife of the chairman of the Nicaraguan legislative committee ("Committee") with oversight of Nicaraguan telecommunications. Pursuant to their agreement, the wife was to be responsible for providing various regulatory and legislative services, including lobbying for repeal of the foreign ownership restriction. Although the wife ("lobbyist") had prior financial and operations experience in the telecommunications area, she had no prior legislative experience. Telefonia and the lobbyist agreed that she would provide services to Telefonia over a three-month trial period for a monthly fee of $6,500, making her the second most highly paid individual compensated by Telefonia.

Ultimately, the lobbyist worked predominantly on the repeal of the foreign ownership restriction. Because the lobbyist's husband chaired the legislative committee with jurisdiction over the foreign ownership restriction, BSI knew that its payments to the lobbyist could implicate the Foreign Corrupt Practices Act ("FCPA"). Although a former in-house BSI attorney approved the wife's retention, BSI officials knew, or should have known, that the counsel lacked sufficient experience or training to enable him properly to opine on the matter.

During the lobbyist's retention, the legislator/husband drafted the text of the proposed repeal of the foreign ownership restriction and enlisted support for the proposed repeal from other Committee members. The husband scheduled and presided at a hearing in April 1999, during which his Committee heard arguments from BSI and others advocating repeal of the foreign ownership restriction.

In May 1999, Telefonia terminated the lobbyist. In June 1999, Telefonia made a severance payment to her. Telefonia recorded the total sum of $60,000 paid to the lobbyist as consulting services and as a severance payment. In September 1999, the Committee referred the proposed amendment for approval by the Nicaraguan National Assembly. In December 1999, the National Assembly voted to repeal the foreign ownership restriction. BellSouth exercised its 40 percent option and increased its ownership interest in Telefonia to 89 percent in June 2000.

IV.

Discussion

Sections 13(b)(2)(A) and 13(b)(2)(B) of the Exchange Act, commonly referred to as the "books and records" and "internal controls" provisions, respectively, of the FCPA, require generally that issuers with a class of securities registered pursuant to Section 12 of the Exchange Act ("Section 12 issuers") make and keep books, records and accounts, which, in reasonable detail, accurately and fairly reflect their transaction and disposition of assets, and devise and maintain a system of internal accounting controls sufficient to provide reasonable assurances that: transactions are executed in accordance with management's general or specific authorization; transactions are recorded as necessary to permit preparation of financial statements in conformity with generally accepted accounting principles or any other criteria applicable to such statements and to maintain accountability for assets; access to assets is permitted only in accordance with management's general or specific authorization; and the recorded accountability for assets is compared with the existing assets at reasonable intervals and appropriate action is taken with respect to any differences.

Telcel created false books and records by improperly recording the falsely documented, unsubstantiated payments to the offshore companies as bona fide services. In addition, Telcel's internal controls failed to detect the unsubstantiated payments for a period of at least two years. This control deficiency has further prevented BellSouth from being able to reconstruct the circumstances of the payments, or the identity of the ultimate recipients of the payments.

Pursuant to Section 13(b)(6) of the Exchange Act, Section 12 issuers are required, with respect to entities of which they hold 50 percent or less of the voting power, to proceed in good faith to use their influence, to the extent reasonable under the circumstances, to cause the entity to comply with the FCPA's "books and records" and "internal controls" provisions. BellSouth, during the relevant period, held less than 50 percent of the voting power of Telefonia, but through its operational control, had the ability to cause Telefonia to comply with the FCPA's books and records and internal controls provisions. Despite BellSouth's ability to cause Telefonia's compliance, Telefonia created false books and records by improperly recording payments to the wife of the Nicaraguan legislator as "consulting services." BellSouth failed to devise and maintain a system of internal accounting controls at Telefonia sufficient to detect and prevent FCPA violations.

V.

As a result of the conduct described above, the Commission finds that BellSouth violated Sections 13(b)(2)(A) and 13(b)(2)(B) of the Exchange Act.

VI.

In determining to accept BellSouth's Offer, the Commission considered BellSouth's cooperation with the Commission staff after BellSouth was advised of the staff's investigation. The Commission also considered remedial actions BellSouth has undertaken, including the disciplining and termination of various employees. Finally, the Commission considered the steps BellSouth has taken to enhance its FCPA compliance program, which currently consists of a number of components, including corporate governance, policies and procedures, training, internal auditing, and corrective action and discipline.

VII.

Accordingly, IT IS HEREBY ORDERED, pursuant to Section 21C of the Exchange Act, that BellSouth cease and desist from committing or causing any violation, and any future violation, of Sections 13(b)(2)(A) and 13(b)(2)(B) of the Exchange Act.

By the Commission.

Notes and Questions

1) What operational control did BellSouth have over Telefonia?
2) What should BellSouth have done to ensure that Telefonia complied with the FCPA Accounting Provisions?

B. Affiliates

Although on its face § 13(b) of the Exchange Act only applies to issuers and their subsidiaries, the DOJ and SEC interpret it more broadly to cover affiliates of issuers:

> An issuer's responsibility thus extends to ensuring that subsidiaries or affiliates under its control, including foreign subsidiaries and joint ventures, comply with the accounting provisions.[91]

The SEC defines an "affiliate" as "a person that directly, or indirectly . . . controls, or is controlled by, or is under common control with, the person specified."[92] Control is defined as:

> [T]he possession, direct or indirect, of the power to direct or cause the direction of the management and policies of a person, whether through the ownership of voting securities, by contract, *or otherwise*.[93]

Thus, the DOJ and SEC extend the reach of § 13(b) beyond subsidiaries to include any entity over which the issuer has power or influence.[94]

Multinational enterprises typically wield considerable leverage over their collaborators around the world—joint venture partners, distributors, licensees, franchisees, and many others—who depend on them for business. Unlike ownership of shares, such leverage is not amenable to measurement, making it difficult for issuers to determine whether a foreign collaborator might qualify as an affiliate under the SEC definition.

Even where an issuer's collaborator does not qualify as an affiliate, the DOJ and SEC's interpretation of § 13(b) arguably requires "good faith efforts" to convince that collaborator to comply with the FCPA Accounting Provisions. It falls on multinational enterprises to decide where to draw the line; that is, to decide: (1) which foreign collaborators could qualify as affiliates; and (2) what steps they should take to convince those collaborators to comply with the FCPA Accounting Provisions.

---

91. FCPA Guide, *supra* note 1, at 42–43.
92. 17 C.F.R. § 240.12b-2 (2017).
93. *Id.* (emphasis added).
94. *See* FCPA Guide, *supra* note 1, at 42–43.

Hypothetical: Books and Records of Third Parties

Delisco, Inc. ("Delisco"), a U.S.-based producer of packaged food products, has appointed Vietnamese Co. as its exclusive distributor in Vietnam. Delisco's products account for 90 percent of Vietnamese Co.'s sales.

Unbeknownst to Delisco, Vietnamese Co. maintains doctored books and records in order to avoid paying local taxes. Delisco respects Vietnamese Co.'s privacy and independence, and has never demanded information about Vietnamese Co.'s accounts and operations.

Vietnamese Co. was raided by the local tax authority, which uncovered evidence of corrupt payments to local customs officials to obtain import permits. Subsequently, the DOJ brought charges against Delisco for violating the FCPA Accounting Provisions in connection with Vietnamese Co.'s corrupt payments.

What is the DOJ's strongest theory of liability against Delisco?

V. Interplay Between the FCPA Accounting Provisions and the Sarbanes-Oxley Act of 2002 ("SOX")

Although the FCPA Accounting Provisions constituted a step forward in corporate governance, they are toothless absent a mechanism for verifying issuers' compliance. The FCPA does not obligate issuers to periodically evaluate the accuracy of their books and records or the effectiveness of their internal control system, and it does not explicitly hold senior management accountable for noncompliance. This means that, unless some extrinsic event brings violations to the attention of shareholders or regulators, those violations can continue indefinitely.

The SEC tried to address this problem in 1988 after the Treadway Commission exposed the poor state of governance in public companies, proposing rules that imposed an affirmative duty on the principal officers of public companies to certify compliance with the FCPA.[95] An aggressive counter-lobby put a quick end to those SEC proposals, however.[96] It took fourteen years and the corporate fraud scandals of the early 2000s to provide the needed impetus for the passage of SOX, which was largely modeled on the SEC's 1988 proposals.

SOX was passed "[t]o protect investors by improving the accuracy and reliability of corporate disclosures made pursuant to the securities laws[.]"[97] SOX

---

95. Tim J. Leech, Sarbanes-Oxley Sections 302 & 404: A White Paper Proposing Practical, Cost Effective Compliance Strategies 4 (2003), https://www.sec.gov/rules/proposed/s74002/card941503.pdf.

96. *Id.*

97. This is the introductory sentence at the top of the Sarbanes-Oxley Act. Sarbanes-Oxley Act of 2002, Pub. L. No. 107-204, § 805(a), 116 Stat. 802, 802 (2002).

includes two key sections—302 and 404—which reinforce the FCPA Accounting Provisions. Section 302 requires senior management to personally certify the accuracy of the issuer's financial reports.[98] Section 404 requires senior management and an outside auditor to separately evaluate an issuer's internal control system annually, and report any deficiencies discovered in the process.[99]

> Widely deemed the most important piece of security legislation since formation of the [SEC] in 1934, [SOX] was born into a climate still reeling from . . . [the] fraud scandals at Enron and WorldCom. . . . Despite high initial costs of the internal control mandate, evidence shows that it has proved beneficial.
>
> —Julia Hanna, Associate Editor,
> HBS Alumni Bulletin[100]

Report of Investigation by the Special Investigative Committee of the Board of Directors of WorldCom, Inc.[101]

March 31, 2003

. . . .

I. SUMMARY AND CONCLUSIONS

The Special Investigative Committee ("Committee") of the Board of Directors of WorldCom, Inc. ("WorldCom" or the "Company") submits this Report of Investigation. This Summary and Conclusions section highlights important parts of the Report and sets out our conclusions.

From 1999 until 2002, WorldCom suffered one of the largest public company accounting frauds in history. As enormous as the fraud was, it was accomplished in a relatively mundane way: more than $9 billion in false or unsupported accounting entries were made in WorldCom's financial systems in order to achieve desired reported financial results. The fraud did not involve WorldCom's network, its technology, or its engineering. Most of WorldCom's people did not know it was occurring. Rather, the fraud occurred as a result of knowing misconduct directed by a few senior executives centered in its Clinton, Mississippi headquarters, and implemented by personnel in its financial and accounting departments in several locations. The fraud was the consequence of the way WorldCom's Chief Executive Officer, Bernard J. Ebbers, ran the Company. Though much of this Report details the implementation of the fraud by others, he was the source of the culture, as well as much of the pressure, that gave birth to this fraud. That the fraud continued as long as it did was due to a lack of courage to blow the whistle on the part of others in WorldCom's financial and accounting departments; inadequate audits by Arthur Andersen; and a financial system whose controls were

---

98. *Id.* at § 302 (codified at 15 U.S.C. § 7241).

99. *Id.* at § 404 (codified at 15 U.S.C. § 7262).

100. Julia Hanna, *The Costs and Benefits of Sarbanes-Oxley*, FORBES (Mar. 10, 2014), https://www.forbes.com/sites/hbsworkingknowledge/2014/03/10/the-costs-and-benefits-of-sarbanes-oxley/#40336b7e478c.

101. DENNIS R. BERESFORD ET AL., REPORT OF INVESTIGATION BY THE SPECIAL INVESTIGATIVE COMMITTEE OF THE BOARD OF DIRECTORS OF WORLDCOM, INC. (2003), https://www.sec.gov/Archives/edgar/data/723527/000093176303001862/dex991.htm.

sorely deficient. The setting in which it occurred was marked by a serious corporate governance failure.

Background

On June 25, 2002, WorldCom announced that it intended to restate its financial statements for 2001 and the first quarter of 2002. It stated that it had determined that certain transfers totaling $3.852 billion during that period from "line cost" expenses (costs of transmitting calls) to asset accounts were not made in accordance with generally accepted accounting principles ("GAAP"). Less than one month later, WorldCom and substantially all of its active U.S. subsidiaries filed voluntary petitions for reorganization under Chapter 11 of the Bankruptcy Code. WorldCom subsequently announced that it had discovered an additional $3.831 billion in improperly reported earnings before taxes for 1999, 2000, 2001 and first quarter 2002. It has also written off approximately $80 billion of the stated book value of the assets on the Company's balance sheet at the time the fraud was announced.

On June 26, 2002, the United States Securities and Exchange Commission ("SEC") filed a lawsuit captioned Securities and Exchange Commission v. WorldCom, Inc., No. 02-CV-4963 (JSR). On July 3, the Honorable Jed S. Rakoff, of the United States District Court for the Southern District of New York, appointed Richard C. Breeden, former Chairman of the SEC, as Corporate Monitor, with the consent of WorldCom.

. . . .

The accounting records that should have documented the transactions under review were, in many cases, either non-existent or in such disarray—for example, in a storage room that was disorganized and had piles of paper on the floor and spilling from boxes—that enormous effort was required to locate and identify them. Through time-consuming review, along with examination of millions of pages of other documents and electronic files, we believe we have been able to understand the events in question.

. . . .

While our investigation has proceeded, WorldCom has taken action to remake itself. Under the supervision of Judge Rakoff and Mr. Breeden, WorldCom has adopted new practices designed to address both the conduct described in this Report and the culture that permitted that conduct to occur. WorldCom now has an entirely new Board of Directors and a new Chief Executive Officer, none of whom was at the Company when these events occurred. The Company no longer employs the people whose culpable conduct was principally responsible for the events described below.

Summary of Findings

In the 1990s, the principal business strategy of WorldCom's Chief Executive Officer, Bernard J. Ebbers, was growth through acquisitions. The currency for much of that strategy was WorldCom stock, and the success of the strategy depended on a consistently increasing stock price. WorldCom pursued scores of increasingly large acquisitions. The strategy reached its apex with WorldCom's acquisition in

1998 of MCI Communications Corporation ("MCI"), a company more than two-and-a-half times WorldCom's size (by revenues). Ebbers' acquisition strategy largely came to an end by early 2000 when WorldCom was forced to abandon a proposed merger with Sprint Corporation because of antitrust objections.

At that point, WorldCom's continued success became dependent on Ebbers' ability to manage the internal operations of what was then an immense company, and to do so in an industry-wide downturn. He was spectacularly unsuccessful in this endeavor. He continued to feed Wall Street's expectations of double-digit growth, and he demanded that his subordinates meet those expectations. But he did not provide the leadership or managerial attention that would enable WorldCom to meet those expectations legitimately.

Ebbers presented a substantially false picture to the market, to the Board of Directors, and to most of the Company's own employees. At the same time he was projecting, and then reporting, continued vigorous growth, he was receiving internal information that was increasingly inconsistent with those projections and reports. Moreover, he did not disclose the persistent use of non-recurring items to boost reported revenues. Ebbers was aware, at a minimum, that WorldCom was meeting revenue expectations through financial gimmickry. Yet he kept making unrealistic promises, and failed to disclose the existence of these devices or their magnitude.

Ebbers directed significant energy to building and protecting his own personal financial empire, with little attention to the risks these distractions and financial obligations placed on the Company that was making him one of the highest paid executives in the country. It was when his personal financial empire was under the greatest pressure—when he had the greatest need to keep WorldCom's stock price up in order to avoid margin calls that he could not meet—that the largest part of the fraud occurred. And it was shortly after he left that it was discovered and disclosed.

The fraud was implemented by and under the direction of WorldCom's Chief Financial Officer, Scott Sullivan. As business operations fell further and further short of financial targets announced by Ebbers, Sullivan directed the making of accounting entries that had no basis in generally accepted accounting principles in order to create the false appearance that WorldCom had achieved those targets. In doing so he was assisted by WorldCom's Controller, David Myers, who in turn directed the making of entries he knew were not supported. This was easily accomplished, because it was apparently considered acceptable for the General Accounting group to make entries of hundreds of millions of dollars with little or no documentation beyond a verbal or an e-mail directive from senior personnel.

There is clear evidence that Ebbers was aware of certain practices Sullivan and Myers used to inflate reported revenues. Moreover, after the capitalization of line costs had been discovered, Sullivan said that Ebbers had known of it; however, we do not have direct evidence concerning Ebbers' knowledge. Since we were unable to interview these three individuals, we have not heard their side of this story.

Awareness of this financial fraud was not confined to just two or three people. Others at WorldCom either knew or suspected that senior financial management was engaged in improper accounting. These included not only people in the General Accounting group (generally located at the Clinton, Mississippi corporate headquarters) who ordered or implemented the entries, but people in other financial reporting and accounting groups whose responsibilities were affected by them. Employees in several such groups suggested, made or knew of entries that were not supportable, or prepared reports that were false or misleading as a consequence. Remarkably, these employees frequently did not raise any objections despite their awareness or suspicions that the accounting was wrong, and simply followed directions or even enlisted the assistance of others. Some of them complained to their supervisors or, in a handful of cases, refused to take actions they considered inappropriate. However, none took effective action to try to halt or expose these practices until the Spring of 2002. Employees in the financial and accounting groups believed that forcefully objecting to conduct that they knew was being directed by Sullivan would cost them their jobs; few of them were prepared to take that risk.

The Board of Directors does not appear to have known of the fraud, nor did it receive information we believe should have put it on notice. However, the Board was so passive and reliant on Ebbers and Sullivan that it had little opportunity to learn of the fraud. Moreover, by authorizing WorldCom to lend Ebbers hundreds of millions of dollars so he could meet margin calls without selling his stock, and by creating a bonus plan that rewarded short-term revenue growth, the Board—and more specifically the Compensation and Stock Option Committee (the "Compensation Committee")—created incentives that may have played a role in motivating the misconduct that occurred at WorldCom.

. . . .

The subsections of this Summary that follow briefly describe our understanding of: the nature of the accounting fraud; how the systems at WorldCom facilitated this fraud and permitted it to continue as long as it did; why the fraud was not discovered by WorldCom's outside auditors; and the role of the Board of Directors with respect to the accounting issues and, more generally, in the governance of WorldCom.

A. The Nature of the Accounting Fraud

WorldCom's improper accounting took two principal forms: reduction of reported line costs, WorldCom's largest category of expenses; and exaggeration of reported revenues. The overall objective of these efforts was to hold reported line costs to approximately 42% of revenues (when in fact they typically reached levels in excess of 50%), and to continue reporting double-digit revenue growth when actual growth rates were generally substantially lower.

. . . .

B. WorldCom's Culture

Numerous individuals—most of them in financial and accounting departments, at many levels of the Company and in different locations around the world—became aware in varying degrees of senior management's misconduct.

Had one or more of these individuals come forward earlier and raised their complaints with Human Resources, Internal Audit, the Law and Public Policy Department, Andersen, the Audit Committee, individual Directors and/or federal or state government regulators, perhaps the fraud would not have gone on for so long. Why didn't they? The answer seems to lie partly in a culture emanating from corporate headquarters that emphasized making the numbers above all else; kept financial information hidden from those who needed to know; blindly trusted senior officers even in the face of evidence that they were acting improperly; discouraged dissent; and left few, if any, outlets through which employees believed they could safely raise their objections.

This culture began at the top. Ebbers created the pressure that led to the fraud. He demanded the results he had promised, and he appeared to scorn the procedures (and people) that should have been a check on misreporting. When efforts were made to establish a corporate Code of Conduct, Ebbers reportedly described it as a "colossal waste of time." He showed little respect for the role lawyers played with respect to corporate governance matters within the Company. While we have heard numerous accounts of Ebbers' demand for results—on occasion emotional, insulting, and with express reference to the personal financial harm he faced if the stock price declined—we have heard none in which he demanded or rewarded ethical business practices.

Through a variety of mechanisms, senior management tightly controlled financial information so that only a few learned about the size and nature of the accounting irregularities. The key financial information was shared only within a closed, inner circle of senior executives, although as time went on more and more employees were exposed to elements they considered improper. While confidentiality is a legitimate concern, at WorldCom it extended to concealing information from those with a need to know, in order to hide the fraud. There was obvious concern at the top level about sharing corporate accounting adjustments with others; for example, Director of General Accounting Yates told Controller Myers in May 2001 that "we 'Took' $327 [m[illion] of the [MCI Balance Sheet] reserves in the 2nd Q[uarter] of last year. They [MCI personnel] DO NOT know this." When an employee in Wireless Accounting started asking questions about a $150 million corporate reduction in line costs, Yates asked Walter Nagel, the General Tax Counsel, to stop the inquiry because "the entry he asks about is one of the 'I'll need to kill him if I tell him'"—even though the employee was trying to determine whether the adjustment affected one of the Company's state tax returns. We came across e-mails and a voicemail in which senior management directed employees not to discuss in e-mail or writing certain items that had raised concerns. Access to the Company's computerized accounting system, particularly the accounts where senior officials made corporate adjustments, was restricted to a handful of people and kept from others who needed access. In July 2001, for example, after Myers learned that Internal Audit had started a line cost review, Myers instructed the employee in charge of security for the accounting system not to give Internal Audit access to the area showing corporate adjustments; the employee complied.

Consolidated financial information was available only at the most senior levels and not shared with officers who normally would have access to such information in most companies. In 1999, when Cynthia Cooper, the Vice President of Internal Audit, requested a copy of the MonRev report for an Internal Audit project that she was working on for Ebbers, Sullivan wrote to Lomenzo: "Do not give her the total picture—i.e. she does not need international, other revenues, etc." Senior management particularly restricted the distribution of internal reports that could have revealed the accounting fraud. In September 2000, Myers wrote to Sullivan about limiting the distribution of a line cost report that showed corporate reductions: "You did ask/demand and we did nip it in the bud immediately. We stopped producing the report completely." Other examples of similar instructions are discussed throughout our Report. More than one employee described WorldCom as a series of isolated "silos" where each group knew and understood its own costs and revenues but had no knowledge about other groups and never shared information with the others. When employees raised concerns about reductions of their accruals or other apparent misconduct, senior management could always—and frequently did— say that the issue was resolved and acceptable at the consolidated, total company level.

The geographic isolation of various business units contributed to this closed atmosphere. While the Company's headquarters were in Clinton, Mississippi, its Property Accounting group was in Richardson, Texas; its Law and Public Policy Department and head of sales were in Washington, D.C.; its Human Resources group was in Boca Raton, Florida and New York, N.Y.; its Business Operations group was in Alpharetta, Georgia; and its UUNET business and its Network Financial Management group were in Ashburn, Virginia.

There was also a systemic attitude conveyed from the top down that employees should not question their superiors, but simply do what they were told. Employees told us that personnel were discouraged from challenging anyone above them in the corporate hierarchy, and senior officers and managers made it clear that their actions should not be questioned. Staff accountants in the General Accounting group frequently and without question entered large, round-dollar journal entries—in the tens, and often hundreds, of millions of dollars—after the close of a quarter, without being provided *any* supporting documentation whatsoever. Many, even those with accounting degrees and CPA designations, told us that they viewed their job as simply entering numbers. Several employees told us that, upon identifying something unusual or an apparent discrepancy between internally and externally reported numbers, they relied on the fact that Sullivan was trusted and well-respected in the industry. In 1998, CFO Magazine called Sullivan a "whiz kid" and awarded him a CFO Excellence Award. To many, Sullivan had a reputation of impeccable integrity. Some who learned about the capitalization of line costs said they simply rationalized that Sullivan must have found an accounting loophole or legitimate way to justify these entries.

Employees who learned about improper corporate adjustments appear to have feared senior management's criticism or even the loss of their jobs. It was common for employees to be denigrated in public about their work. We were told that many who had concerns about what they observed probably did not report their concerns because they were worried about losing their jobs, particularly in Mississippi where WorldCom was one of the largest, most prestigious and highest paying employers in its area.

When financial personnel did raise questions about accounting discrepancies, senior management often stymied those inquiries through intimidation and belittling e-mails. For example, when a financial analyst in the Budget Department prepared a budget that incorporated estimates of actual costs and corporate adjustments, Sullivan wrote to this employee and her supervisor: "This is complete, complete garbage . . . . What am I supposed to do with this? What have we been doing for the last six months. This is a real work of trash." After a senior UUNET employee refused to reduce line costs without support, Myers threatened to fly from Mississippi to Washington, D.C. and book the entry himself if the employee did not comply. When another employee went to Yates for an explanation of a large discrepancy, Yates reportedly berated him and said, "show those numbers to the damn auditors and I'll throw you out the f*****g window."

At other times, senior management responded to questions about corporate adjustments with evasive or confusing explanations. One such example occurred in July 2000 after an employee asked about corporate adjustments that she observed in the computerized reporting system. Yates wrote Myers that he was "always concerned" when employees asked about adjustments to general and administrative expenses and "the big item that concerns all of us is the reserve release," and stated that "[it's] just the packaging of the response to skirt the issue that we need to ensure works." Finally, at times senior management simply refused to answer employee questions, and often referred those asking to Sullivan, whom it seems the lower level employee would never contact directly.

We asked many of the employees who said they had concerns about senior management's conduct at the time why they failed to bring their complaints to the attention of others. Often, these employees said that they did not feel there was an independent outlet for voicing their concerns. WorldCom's written policy directed employees who felt that they had "been instructed or requested by anyone acting on behalf of the Company to engage or participate in any unlawful or unethical activity" to immediately contact their manager, Human Resources, or the Law and Public Policy Department. However, we learned of only two complaints alleging unethical behavior relating to accounting that were raised with Human Resources. Neither resulted in the Company taking any action, and both employees left the Company shortly after lodging their complaints. The Law and Public Policy Department consisted largely of legacy MCI employees and was located in Washington, D.C., hundreds of miles away from the Company's headquarters in Mississippi. Perhaps for those reasons, legacy WorldCom employees would not normally come to the Department with questions or concerns. In addition, there was a near-universal failure on the part of WorldCom employees to understand the role of the Department.

Moreover, prior to April 2002, it appears that no employee raised any concerns about accounting irregularities with Internal Audit. Indeed, one senior manager told us that he had never even heard of Internal Audit. Internal Audit was engaged principally in operational audits, and management had a strong influence over the types of audits that the department conducted. Others thought—or learned from the Company's internal website—that Internal Audit reported directly to Sullivan and, therefore, felt that it was not a productive avenue for pursuing claims of wrongdoing by Sullivan. One employee told us that he did not present his concerns to Internal Audit because he believed it would have put his job in jeopardy.

C. Compromising Financial Arrangements

Ebbers and Sullivan engaged in financial dealings that, while not necessarily improper in themselves, created conflicting loyalties and disincentives to insist on proper conduct. In 2000 and 2002, Ebbers personally loaned Ron Beaumont, the Chief Operating Officer, a total of $650,000 over a sixteen month period: a $250,000 loan in October 2000 and a $400,000 loan in February 2002. Both loans were still outstanding as of October 2002. Although Beaumont told us that Ebbers' loans to him were arm's-length, financial arrangements such as these create an inherent conflict between the duty of loyalty of an officer to the corporation and financial dependence on the Chief Executive Officer personally. At a minimum, they would create a financial incentive for Beaumont to avoid any conflict with Ebbers.

In late 2000, Sullivan gave personal gifts totaling at least $140,000 to certain managers at the Company. Sullivan gave $20,000 to each of the following people, writing one personal check in the amount of $10,000 to each officer and a second in the same amount to the officer's spouse: Myers; Yates; Lomenzo; Vice President of Financial Reporting Stephanie Scott; Director of Financial Reporting Mark Willson; Vice President of Investor Relations Scott Hamilton; and Director of Investor Relations Blair Bingham. Sullivan told them that he had received a large bonus ($10 million), that he felt the bonus was partially due to the hard work of others, and that he wanted them to view the money as coming from the Company. These individuals have told us that Sullivan did not ask for anything in return for the money.

Although we found no Company rule prohibiting Sullivan's gifts or requiring that they be reported within the Company, in our view large personal gifts from a senior officer to subordinates are inappropriate. As with Ebbers' loans to Beaumont, gifts of this sort inherently compromise the employees' loyalty to the institution. They create the appearance, or even a reality, of an effort to buy loyalty to the individual donor that may be inconsistent with the Company's best interest.

D. Why WorldCom's Auditors Did Not Discover the Fraud

We have found no evidence that WorldCom's independent, external auditors, Arthur Andersen, were aware of the capitalization of line costs or determined that WorldCom's revenues were improperly reported. We had access to only a portion of Andersen's documents, and Andersen personnel refused to speak with us. Therefore, we cannot answer with certainty the question why Andersen failed to detect such a large fraud.

Based on the materials available to us, the blame for Andersen's failure to detect the fraud appears to lie with personnel both at Andersen and at WorldCom. There were apparent flaws in Andersen's audit approach, which limited the likelihood it would detect the accounting irregularities. Moreover, Andersen appears to have missed several opportunities that might have led to the discovery of management's misuse of accruals, the capitalization of line costs, and the improper recognition of revenue items. For their part, certain WorldCom personnel maintained inappropriately tight control over information that Andersen needed, altered documents with the apparent purpose of concealing from Andersen items that might have raised questions, and were not forthcoming in other respects. Andersen, knowing in some instances that it was receiving less than full cooperation on critical aspects of its work, failed to bring this to the attention of WorldCom's Audit Committee.

Andersen employed an approach to its audit that it itself characterized as different from the "traditional audit approach." It focused heavily on identifying risks and assessing whether the Company had adequate controls in place to mitigate those risks, rather than emphasizing the traditional substantive testing of information maintained in accounting records and financial statements. This approach is not unique to Andersen, and it was disclosed to the Audit Committee. But a consequence of this approach was that if Andersen failed to identify a significant risk, or relied on Company controls without adequately determining that they were worthy of reliance, there would be insufficient testing to make detection of fraud likely.

Andersen does not appear to have performed adequate testing to justify reliance on WorldCom's controls. We found hundreds of huge, round-dollar journal entries made by the staff of the General Accounting group without proper support; examples include unsupported journal entries of $334,000,000 and $560,000,000 on July 21, 2000, and July 17, 2001, respectively. We also found accrual reversals were made with little or no support. And where we did find documentary support it was frequently disorganized and maintained haphazardly. These deficiencies made reliance on controls impossible. We do not understand how they escaped Andersen's notice.

Andersen concluded year after year that the risk of fraud was no greater than a moderate risk, and thus it never devised sufficient auditing procedures to address this risk. It did so despite rating WorldCom a "maximum risk" client—an assessment Andersen never disclosed to the Audit Committee—and having given management less than favorable ratings in a few areas (such as accounting and disclosure practices, behavior toward Andersen's work, and policies to prevent or detect fraud) in Andersen internal documents. Andersen relied heavily on senior management and did not conduct tests to corroborate the information it received in many areas. It assumed incorrectly that the absence of variances in the financial statements and schedules—in a highly volatile business environment—indicated there was no cause for heightened scrutiny. As a result,

Andersen conducted only very limited audit procedures in many areas where we found accounting irregularities.

. . . .

WorldCom, for its part, exerted excessive control over Andersen's access to information, and was not candid in at least some of its dealings with Andersen. The WorldCom personnel who dealt most often with Andersen controlled Andersen's access to information in several respects. They denied Andersen's requests to speak with some employees. They "struck" Andersen's requests for detailed information, supporting documentation, or material that they felt was overly burdensome. WorldCom personnel also repeatedly rejected Andersen's requests for access to the computerized General Ledger through which Internal Audit and others discovered the capitalization of line costs. And they fostered an attitude in which questions from Andersen were to be parried, rather than answered openly. Of course, it was Andersen's responsibility to overcome those obstacles to perform an appropriate audit, and to inform the Audit Committee of the difficulties it faced, but it did not do so.

Moreover, certain members of WorldCom's management altered significant documents before providing them to Andersen, with the apparent purpose of hampering Andersen's ability to identify problems at the Company. In the Sections that follow we discuss in detail two examples where documents were changed because of concerns about disclosing questionable revenue items. The first involves the preparation of "Special MonRevs" for Andersen after the third and fourth quarters of 2001. The altered documents removed revenue items from the Corporate Unallocated schedule and shifted them elsewhere in the document where they would be less obvious. The second involves the preparation of an analysis of certain balance sheet reserve accounts for Andersen after the fourth quarter of 2000. This altered document downplayed the significance of problematic entries by combining certain accounts so as to make the entries less obvious. Our Report points out other examples where documents were altered or actions taken for the apparent purpose of deceiving Andersen.

E. WorldCom's Governance

WorldCom's collapse reflected not only a financial fraud but also a major failure of corporate governance. The Board of Directors, though apparently unaware of the fraud, played far too small a role in the life, direction and culture of the Company. Although the Board, at least in form, appeared to satisfy many checklists of the time, it did not exhibit the energy, judgment, leadership or courage that WorldCom needed.

1. Board's Lack of Awareness of Accounting Fraud

We found no evidence that members of the Board of Directors, other than Ebbers and Sullivan, were aware of the improper accounting practices at the time they occurred. We have reviewed materials (including slide presentations) the Board received and have not found information that should reasonably have led it to detect the practices or to believe that further specific inquiry into the accounting practices at issue was necessary.

. . . .

2. Adequacy of Board's Oversight of Company

The Board and its Committees did not function in a way that made it likely that they would notice red flags. The outside Directors had little or no involvement in the Company's business other than through attendance at Board meetings. Nearly all of the Directors were legacies of companies that WorldCom, under Ebbers' leadership, had acquired. They had ceded leadership to Ebbers when their companies were acquired, and in some cases viewed their role as diminished. Ebbers controlled the Board's agenda, its discussions, and its decisions. He created, and the Board permitted, a corporate environment in which the pressure to meet the numbers was high, the departments that served as controls were weak, and the word of senior management was final and not to be challenged.

The Audit Committee in particular needed an understanding of the Company it oversaw in order to be effective. However, the Audit Committee members do not appear to have had a sufficient understanding of the Company's internal financial workings or its culture, and they devoted strikingly little time to their role, meeting as little as three to five hours per year. WorldCom was a complicated Company in a fast-evolving industry. It had expanded quickly, through a series of large acquisitions, and there had been virtually no integration of the acquisitions. WorldCom had accounting-related operations scattered in a variety of locations around the country. These facts raised significant accounting, internal control and systems concerns that required Audit Committee knowledge and attention, and that should also have elicited direct warnings from Andersen. However, the Audit Committee members apparently did not even understand—though the evidence indicates that Andersen disclosed—the non-traditional audit approach Andersen employed. To gain the knowledge necessary to function effectively as an Audit Committee would have required a very substantial amount of energy, expertise by at least some of its members, and a greater commitment of time.

Neither WorldCom's legal department nor Internal Audit was structured to maximize its effectiveness as a control structure upon which the Board could depend. At Ebbers' direction, the Company's lawyers were in fragmented groups, several of which had General Counsels who did not report to WorldCom's General Counsel for portions of the relevant period; they were not located geographically near senior management or involved in its inner workings; and they had inadequate support from senior management. Internal Audit—though eventually successful in revealing the fraud—had been structured in ways that made this accomplishment more difficult: it reported in most respects to Sullivan, and until 2002 its duties generally did not include financial reporting matters.

The outside Directors had virtually no interaction with Company operational or financial employees other than during the presentations they heard at meetings. While in this respect the Directors were far from unique among directors of large corporations, this lack of contact meant that they had little sense of the culture within the Company, or awareness of issues other than those brought to them by a few senior managers. They were not themselves visible to employees, and there were no systems in place that could have encouraged employees to contact them with concerns about either the accounting entries or operational matters. In short, the Board was removed and detached from the operations of WorldCom to the extent that its members had little sense of what was really going on within the Company.

Ebbers was autocratic in his dealings with the Board, and the Board permitted it. With limited exceptions, the members of the Board were reluctant to challenge Ebbers even when they disagreed with him. They, like most observers, were impressed with the Company's growth and Ebbers' reputation, although they were in some cases mystified or perplexed by his style. This was Ebbers' company. Several members of the Board were sophisticated, yet the members of the Board were deferential to Ebbers and passive in their oversight until April 2002.

The deference of the Compensation Committee and the Board to Ebbers is illustrated by their decisions beginning in September 2000 to authorize corporate loans and guaranties that grew to over $400 million, so that Ebbers could avoid selling WorldCom stock to meet his personal financial obligations. This was not the first occasion on which Ebbers had overextended himself financially and borrowed from the Company: he had done so in 1994 as well. On neither occasion did anyone on the Board challenge Ebbers with respect to his use of WorldCom stock to extend his personal financial empire to the point that it threatened to cause involuntary liquidation of his stock. The approach of the Board, as one member characterized his own view, was to say nothing to Ebbers because they thought Ebbers was a grownup and could manage his own affairs—even though Ebbers' management of his own affairs involved the use of Company funds, eventually to the tune of hundreds of millions of dollars.

We believe that the extension of these loans and guaranties was a 19-month sequence of terrible decisions—badly conceived, and antithetical to shareholder interests—and a major failure of corporate governance. Indeed, we do not understand how the Compensation Committee or the Board could have concluded that these loans were an acceptable use of more than $400 million of the shareholders' money. These decisions reflected an uncritical solicitude for Ebbers' financial interests, a disregard of the incentives the situation created for Ebbers' management of the Company, and a willingness to subordinate shareholders' interests to Ebbers' financial wellbeing.

A second example of the Board's deference is its failure to challenge Ebbers on the extent of his substantial outside business interests (and the resulting claim on his time and energies). Those interests included a Louisiana rice farm, a luxury yacht building company, a lumber mill, a country club, a trucking company, a minor league hockey team, an operating marina, and a building in downtown Chicago. We do not believe most properly-run Boards of Directors would permit a Chief Executive Officer to pursue an array of interests such as these, certainly not without careful examination of the time and energy commitments they would require. Yet we have seen no evidence of any such challenge.

3. Stock Sales

A number of WorldCom Directors, officers, and employees sold WorldCom stock in or after 2000. WorldCom had a policy with regard to trading in its securities that was insufficient and that was applied haphazardly and inconsistently. It was disregarded in connection with a transaction in which Ebbers agreed to sell three million shares of WorldCom stock on September 28, 2000. The sale occurred less than 30 days before an earnings announcement, in violation of a policy Ebbers himself had circulated just a few months earlier. Moreover, there is compelling evidence that this sale took place while Ebbers was in possession of significant nonpublic information about a downturn in revenue growth and about proposed actions that could have a negative impact on WorldCom's stock price.

In addition, two Directors were given clearance by the Company to sell stock without adequate attention to whether they possessed information about the then-undisclosed Company loans to Ebbers and whether that information was important enough to preclude the trades. In one case, the Chairman of the Compensation Committee, Stiles Kellett, Jr., having approved loans to Ebbers to keep him from selling stock and thereby depressing the stock price, sold WorldCom stock before those loans were disclosed to the public.

4. Lease of Airplane to Chairman of Compensation Committee

During the period under investigation, WorldCom did not have a comprehensive written policy governing the use of the three to seven airplanes that comprised the WorldCom airplane fleet. The lack of written policies or effective procedures regarding the use of a fleet of corporate airplanes created an environment in which the use of airplanes was largely a perquisite to be dispensed at the discretion of Ebbers, and individuals had varying, inconsistent, and on occasion impermissible arrangements with the Company for personal use of the WorldCom airplanes.

In the Spring of 2001, Kellett, the Chairman of the Compensation Committee, entered into a lease arrangement with WorldCom for a Falcon 20 airplane. The arrangement was made between Kellett and Ebbers and was not disclosed to the Board or the public. The details of this arrangement and its impropriety were described in a report to the Board by Mr. Breeden, the Corporate Monitor, in August 2002. The lease arrangement was, in our judgment, at below-market rates, and it should not have occurred. First, it is an unacceptable governance practice for the Chairman of a Compensation Committee to receive anything of value in a deal with the Chief Executive Officer of a company; its nondisclosure to other members of the Committee and the Board made it even worse, because it might have affected their level of deference to the Chairman in the conduct of the Committee's business. This was all the more objectionable in light of the public controversy at the time surrounding the Company's loans to Ebbers. Second, if the jet was actually an unneeded asset, the Company at least should have considered selling it, or sought the best lease terms available from third parties, instead of entering into a lease arrangement with a member of the Board. Third, under governing regulations the lease arrangement with Kellett was required to be disclosed to the public, which it was not.

We also found arrangements for the personal use of airplanes by senior executives that were not in compliance with applicable regulations, although they did not raise the same governance issues.

Following the Corporate Monitor's report to the Board and a response by Kellett, Kellett resigned from the Board, and Kellett and WorldCom entered into an agreement resolving potential claims arising from the airplane lease.

* * *

In sum, WorldCom was a company driven overwhelmingly by a perceived need to meet unrealistic securities market expectations that its own executives had fostered, without an institutional culture in which integrity was valued, without the benefit of policies and procedures covering important matters of governance, and without the effective oversight of an active and engaged Board of Directors. It was headed by a Chief Executive Officer with a dominant personality, who was able to act largely unchecked. The Chief Financial Officer—himself a strong figure—could direct employees to take action they knew or believed was improper, and the employees would comply.

This Committee believes that the most important remedial action for WorldCom includes the installation of new management and a new Board, with a clear commitment to integrity and sound governance, and removal of all personnel who participated in the accounting manipulations or who failed to take necessary action to stop it (every individual identified as having a meaningful role in these events has left the Company or been terminated). Both new management and a new Board with this commitment are now in place, along with the Corporate Monitor whose actions have expedited dramatic change at WorldCom. At the end of this Report, we identify a number of general concepts to be considered in effecting further healthy change. These steps, along with an open acknowledgment of the misconduct that occurred in the past, are part of the effort at reform.

Notes and Questions

1) Using the seventeen principles of the COSO Framework, evaluate WorldCom's internal control system.
2) How could SOX have led to earlier discovery of the fraud?
3) What did WorldCom's board of directors do wrong?

THE FALL OF ENRON: HOW COULD IT HAVE HAPPENED?

S. Hrg. 107-376 (January 24, 2004) [102]

Hearing Before the Committee on Governmental Affairs
United States Senate, One Hundred Seventh Congress,
Second Session

ENRON CORPORATION

In July, 1985 Kenneth Lay ("Lay") was appointed chairman and chief executive officer after Enron was formed from the merger of Houston Natural Gas and InterNorth, a natural gas pipeline company. In December of 1996 Jeffrey K. Skilling ("Skilling") became Enron's president and chief operating officer. Kenneth Lay remained as Chairman of the Board.

Enron conducted business as a pipeline company and grew to be a dominant force controlling major pipelines throughout the United States. During the 1990's Enron ventured into the trading of oil, gas and electricity. It was instrumental in the development of an energy trading system utilizing a relative new breed of financial instruments that allowed them to manage their risk such that they became the dominant energy trader in the United States. This quick success let Enron to move away from the traditional energy business into other emerging markets involving telecommunications, broadband and other Internet related businesses.

Enron maintained its headquarters in Houston, Texas. Its securities were listed on the New York Stock Exchange and it was required to file reports with the United States Securities and Exchange Commission ("SEC") pursuant to the federal securities laws. In August, 2000 Enron was ranked by *Fortune* magazine as the seventh largest company in the United States based on market capitalization. At that time its common stock was trading in the $90 range, having increased 1,700% since its first shares were issued in the 1980's.

On October 16, 2001 Enron reports its first quarterly loss in over 4 years after taking charges of $1 billion on poorly performing businesses and a $1.2 billion charge against shareholder' equity relating to dealings with "off-balance" sheet entities. This disclosure resulted in the announcement of an SEC inquiry.

THE BANKRUPTCY FILING

In June 2001, after questions arose about the validity of Enron's stock valuation, the company's top executives were apparently engaged in a systematic effort to sell off many of their shares resulting in an estimated $1.1 billion return to these executives. CEO Skilling announced his resignation in August and Kenneth Lay resumed the position of chief executive officer.

---

102. *The Fall of Enron: How Could It Have Happened?: Hearing Before the S. Comm. On Governmental Affairs*, 107th Cong. 43–46 (2002).

On October 22, 2001 Enron reported a third quarter loss of $618 million and the SEC announced an inquiry into its operations. On November 8, the company amended and restated its financial reports back to 1997 showing that profits had been overstated by $586 million. As a result of its financial practices, credit reporting agencies, financial analysts and the investing public lost confidence in the company resulting in a total collapse of its business operations and its share value.

Sophisticated financial engineering, risky corporate ventures, overstatements of asset value and understatement of liabilities forced Enron into bankruptcy on December 2, 2001 in a New York bankruptcy court. This represents the largest bankruptcy filing in U.S. history. At the time of the petition, the assets of the company were estimated to be about $50 billion and its liabilities approximately $40 billion.

ENERGY TRADING

Enron engaged in a successful and sophisticated financial trading system involving the trading of energy contracts including oil, gas and electricity. By the development of a state of the art trading environment, Enron was able to engage in massive bilateral trading contracts that were outside the overview of the SEC or the United States Commodities Futures Trading Commission ("CFTC"). The CFTC overview of such contracts was excluded or exempted as the result of a recent amendment to the federal commodities futures trading law, even though these contracts are similar to other futures contracts regulated by the CFTC.

This type trading is risky but apparently necessary in order to provide an open market in these commodities. For example, by engaging in appropriate risk management techniques a supplier can assure a future market for its products and a user can assure the availability of the product at an established price. In order to track supply and demand it is necessary to have state of the art hardware and software and the personnel resources trained in such trading environments.

Even though energy futures contract trading is a risky business, the meltdown of Enron was accelerated as a result of action by credit reporting agencies that downgraded them from investment grade to junk status. An energy trading entity will not be able to remain in the market once they have lost financial integrity and confidence by their trading partners. The disclosure of their serious financial problems, the lost value in their shares, the off-balance sheet financial engineering and the decline in the broadband telecommunications business, all came to light much in the manner of the weather systems in the movie "The Perfect Storm."

ENRON'S QUESTIONABLE CORPORATE, AUDITING,
AND FINANCIAL PRACTICES

- The use of off-balance sheet transactions involving entities that were formed by, and controlled by, Enron or its executives, that were created without complying with Rule 140 of Financial Accounting Standards Board.

It has been reported that certain of these entities were created by Enron executives borrowing funds from Enron's bankers using Enron compensating balances and its shares as guarantees.

- Enron failed to disclose the formation of these entities resulting in the failure to disclose material financial transaction and the understatement of corporate liabilities. This resulted in continued positive ratings by credit rating agencies and financial analysts.

- The use of mark to market evaluation reports of certain Enron assets by these entities resulted in false and significant valuations of Enron's assets.

- On October 17, 2001 Enron apparently decides to change plan administrators for its employee's 401(k) plan resulting in significant restrictions being placed on Enron's employees ability to dispose of their Enron shares. Enron later issued press releases stating that the lock-down period was from October 29 through November 12, 2001. This lock-down was eventually lifted on or about November 19, 2001 after Enron shares declined approximately 71% to $9.06 per share.

- The downgrading by major credit agencies of Enron's bonds to "junk" status on November 28, 2001.

- Enron's filing and disclosure of materially false financial statements that were relied on by the markets, credit reporting agencies and financial analysts.

- The financial practices engaged in by Enron may have resulted in its executive employing a device, scheme, or artifice to defraud market investors and engaging in acts, practices, or a course of business that operates or would operate as a fraud or deceit upon a purchaser or holder of Enron securities.

- The financial practices engaged in by Enron resulted in omissions to state material facts necessary in order to make the statements made, in the light of the circumstances under which they are made, not misleading.

- Enron executives sold approximately $1.1 billion of their shares on the market. As an example, on August 14, 2001, Skilling, Enron's president and chief executive officer, resigns citing a decline of share price and personal reasons after selling shares for an aggregate value of approximately $17.5 million. The sale and distribution of Enron shares by its executive officers may constitute the offer or sale of securities by means of insider information not available to the investing public. The questions that must be answered regarding these transactions include what information the executive knew, or should have known regarding the questionable financial transactions engaged in by Enron and when did such information become known to each of them.

- The compensation and profits paid to Enron employees engaged in the off-balance sheet entities.

- The use of market appraisals from affiliated, off-balance sheet entities that resulted in inflated mark to market asset values.

- The use of over-valued and misleading broadband and telecommunications assets to maintain its bond rating status.
- The failure of the Arthur Andersen auditing team to explore and report on the questionable financial transactions and accounting practices.
- The destruction of audit records and documents by employees of Arthur Andersen.
- The payment of significant compensation, reported to be $55 million to 500 executives, on the eve of the bankruptcy filing.
- Possible conflicts of interest charges involving Enron, its accountants and consultants and an investment advisor's employee being a member of the Enron board.
- The untimely and questionable selection of a new plan administrator that resulted in Enron employees being unable to dispose of their Enron shares for an extended period of time when the Enron shares were declining in value as a result of newly reported material changes to Enron's financial condition.
- The use of plan restrictions limiting the ability of employees to dispose of their company match shares prior to age 50.
- The SEC oversight and reviews of the filings of public companies.

  . . . .

- The Enron campaign contributions further reveal the flaws in our system of financing the campaigns of candidates for the Congress, the President, and other federal officeholders.

THE RISING TIDE OF SECURITIES FRAUD

Top securities watchdogs in the United States have constantly warned investors that the explosion in the stock market has brought with it a sharp rise in securities sales fraud and stock price manipulation. The past year or so have proved them to be correct. At a town meeting in Los Angeles, Former SEC Chairman Levitt cautioned that investors are "more vulnerable than ever to fraud." This concern continues to be echoed by others who point to a disturbing rise in the level of securities fraud and allegations.

What is unusual about the increasing evidence of wrongdoing in the stock market is that shady practices usually go unnoticed in the heady days of a strong bull market. As in the Enron matter, the misconduct is normally uncovered only after a sharp market drop. This has many in the regulatory community wary about what they will be facing if we continue to see other Enron type market collapses.

The challenge to government and industry self-regulators in keeping up with the job of policing a marketplace that is undergoing explosive growth was graphically illustrated several years ago in *Forbes Magazine* ("Swindlers' Paradise"). *Forbes* writer Gretchen Morgenson cautioned that "greed makes people careless" but that investors "shouldn't count on the cops to protect them." In this regard you must also include the financial market regulators.

Make no mistake about who it is that suffers at the hand of securities fraud. It is retirees living on fixed incomes, families struggling to make ends meet and save a little for their children's education, teachers, factory workers, bankers, and others; it is, in short, the everyday man and woman who works so hard for every dime they earn.

. . . .

Each day, equally devastating cases are brought to the attention of securities regulators, law enforcement officers, and attorneys representing the interests of defrauded investors. Financial fraud is a serious and growing problem that must be addressed by the United States Congress.

. . . .

CONCLUSIONS

It is my firm belief that the United States Senate must fully explore the Enron financial collapse in order to present for debate and consideration changes in our financial and market regulatory programs that will deter the use of illegal and improper financial engineering practices to conceal losses and overstate assets resulting in a market confidence that is bound to collapse.

Question

What were the main control deficiencies that caused WorldCom and Enron's downfall?

A. Section 302: Officer Certification

SOX § 302 squarely places responsibility for the accuracy of an issuer's financial reports with its CEO and CFO. It requires each to certify the integrity of their company's financial reports by signing and affirming that:

1) the signing officer has reviewed the report;
2) based on the officer's knowledge, the report does not contain any untrue statement of a material fact or omit to state a material fact necessary in order to make the statements made, in light of the circumstances under which such statements were made, not misleading;
3) based on such officer's knowledge, the financial statements, and other financial information included in the report, fairly present in all material respects the financial condition and results of operations of the issuer as of, and for, the periods presented in the report;
4) the signing officers—
   (A) are responsible for establishing and maintaining internal controls;
   (B) have designed such internal controls to ensure that material information relating to the issuer and its consolidated subsidiaries is made known to such officers by others within those entities, particularly during the period in which the periodic reports are being prepared;

     (C)   have evaluated the effectiveness of the issuer's internal controls as of a date within 90 days prior to the report; and

     (D)   have presented in the report their conclusions about the effectiveness of their internal controls based on their evaluation as of that date[.][103]

Officers who knowingly certify fraudulent financial statements can face severe criminal penalties.[104]

> [Senator Paul] Sarbanes told a story of a man who approached him and lauded the bill. Sarbanes was skeptical because he was used to hearing criticism, so he asked the man what he did for a living. The man was an internal auditor. "Before your bill came along, if I wanted to see the CEO or CFO, I could never get in to see them," Sarbanes recalls the man saying " . . . Now, since your bill, any time I want to see them, I walk right into their office."
>
> —*Interview with Former Senator Paul Sarbanes*[106]

It is important to note that § 302 does not directly repeat the requirements of the FCPA Accounting Provisions; that is, it does not require that all of the issuer's books and records be accurate, but rather that the financial reports produced on the basis of those books and records contain no *material* misstatements. A material misstatement is not defined by the statute, but it is generally considered to be a deviation of more than 5 percent in the company's reported financial figures.[105]

B. Section 404: Reporting on the Adequacy of Internal Controls

SOX § 404 reinforces the FCPA internal controls provisions by holding principal officers responsible for testing those controls annually and reporting any deficiencies. It requires that:

     (a) [E]ach annual report . . . contain an internal control report, which shall—

     . . . .

         (2) [C]ontain an assessment . . . of the effectiveness of the internal control structure and procedures of the issuer for financial reporting.

     (b) [E]ach registered public accounting firm that prepares or issues the audit report for the [company] shall attest to, and report on, the assessment made by the management of the [company].[107]

Section 404 does not cover the entire internal control system, but only those controls directed at ensuring the accuracy of a company's financial reports.[108] Still, § 404 requires a massive investment of time and resources, especially

---

103. Sarbanes-Oxley Act of 2002, Pub. L. No. 107-204, § 302, 116 Stat. 745 (codified at 15 U.S.C. § 7241).

104. *Id.* at § 906 (codified at 18 U.S.C. § 1350).

105. *See generally* SEC Staff Accounting Bulletin: No. 99, Exchange Act Release No. SAB 99, 64 Fed. Reg. 45150 (Aug. 19, 1999).

106. Neil Amato, *Lawmakers Reflect on Sarbanes-Oxley's Effect on Corporate Culture*, J. Acct. (July 30, 2012), http://journalofaccountancy.com/news/2012/jul/20126140.html.

107. 18 U.S.C. § 1350 (a)–(b).

108. *Id.*; *see supra* note 1, Chapter 4, Section II.

because subsection (2)(b) requires a redundant second assessment by the company's outside auditor.[109]

Internal Controls Over Financial Reporting ("ICFR"),[110] the SEC rule implementing § 404, defines the assessment process as:

> A process designed by . . . the [company's] principal executive and principal financial officers . . . to provide reasonable assurance regarding the reliability of financial reporting and the preparation of financial statements for external purposes in accordance with generally accepted accounting principles and includ[ing] those policies and procedures that:
>
> (1) pertain to the maintenance of records that in reasonable detail accurately and fairly reflect the transactions and dispositions of the assets of the registrant;
>
> (2) provide reasonable assurance that transactions are recorded as necessary to permit preparation of financial statements in accordance with generally accepted accounting principles . . . ; and
>
> (3) provide reasonable assurance regarding prevention or timely detection of unauthorized acquisition, use or disposition of the registrant's assets that could have a material effect on the financial statements.[111]

Pursuant to the ICFR, the company's assessment need only provide a "reasonable assurance" of reliability and accuracy—the same standard as the FCPA's accounting provisions. That standard requires "such level of detail and degree of assurance as would satisfy prudent officials in the conduct of their own affairs," but not absolute exactitude.[112]

Commission Guidance Regarding Management's Report on Internal Control over Financial Reporting under Section 13(a) of 15(d) of the Securities Exchange Act of 1934

Release Nos. 33-8810; 34-55929, 17 CFR Part 241 (June 20, 2007)

I. INTRODUCTION

Management is responsible for maintaining a system of internal control over financial reporting ("ICFR") that provides reasonable assurance regarding the reliability of financial reporting and the preparation of financial statements for external purposes in accordance with generally accepted accounting principles. The rules we adopted in June 2003 to implement Section 404 of the Sarbanes-Oxley Act of 2002 ("Sarbanes-Oxley") require management to annually evaluate

---

109. *See* Deloitte & Touche LLP, Taking Control: A Guide to Compliance with Section 404 of the Sarbanes-Oxley Act of 2002, 3-4 (2004), http://www.iasplus.com/en/binary/dttpubs/0407takingcontrol.pdf.

110. Final Rule: Management's Report on Internal Control Over Financial Reporting and Certification of Disclosure in Exchange Act Periodic Reports, Exchange Act Release Nos. 33-8238 & 34-47986, 2003 WL 21294970 (June 5, 2003) [hereinafter ICFR].

111. *Id.*

112. FCPA Guide, *supra* note 1, at 40 (quoting 15 U.S.C. § 78m(b)(7) (2012)).

whether ICFR is effective at providing reasonable assurance and to disclose its assessment to investors. Management is responsible for maintaining evidential matter, including documentation, to provide reasonable support for its assessment. This evidence will also allow a third party, such as the company's external auditor, to consider the work performed by management.

ICFR cannot provide absolute assurance due to its inherent limitations; it is a process that involves human diligence and compliance and is subject to lapses in judgment and breakdowns resulting from human failures. ICFR also can be circumvented by collusion or improper management override. Because of such limitations, ICFR cannot prevent or detect all misstatements, whether unintentional errors or fraud. However, these inherent limitations are known features of the financial reporting process, therefore, it is possible to design into the process safeguards to reduce, though not eliminate, this risk.

. . . .

. . . The Commission has long held that "reasonableness" is not an "absolute standard of exactitude for corporate records." In addition, the Commission recognizes that while "reasonableness" is an objective standard, there is a range of judgments that an issuer might make as to what is "reasonable" in implementing Section 404 and the Commission's rules. Thus, the terms "reasonable," "reasonably," and "reasonableness" in the context of Section 404 implementation do not imply a single conclusion or methodology, but encompass the full range of appropriate potential conduct, conclusions or methodologies upon which an issuer may reasonably base its decisions.

Since companies first began complying in 2004, the Commission has received significant feedback on our rules implementing Section 404. This feedback included requests for further guidance to assist company management in complying with our ICFR evaluation and disclosure requirements. This guidance is in response to those requests and reflects the significant feedback we have received, including comments on the interpretive guidance we proposed on December 20, 2006. In addressing a number of the commonly identified areas of concerns, the interpretive guidance:

- Explains how to vary evaluation approaches for gathering evidence based on risk assessments;
- Explains the use of "daily interaction," self-assessment, and other on-going monitoring activities as evidence in the evaluation;
- Explains the purpose of documentation and how management has flexibility in approaches to documenting support for its assessment;
- Provides management significant flexibility in making judgments regarding what constitutes adequate evidence in low-risk areas; and
- Allows for management and the auditor to have different testing approaches.

The Interpretive Guidance is organized around two broad principles. The first principle is that management should evaluate whether it has implemented controls that adequately address the risk that a material misstatement of the financial statements would not be prevented or detected in a timely manner. The guidance describes a top-down, risk-based approach to this principle, including the role of entity-level controls in assessing financial reporting risks and the adequacy of controls. The guidance promotes efficiency by allowing management to focus on those controls that are needed to adequately address the risk of a material misstatement of its financial statements. The guidance does not require management to identify every control in a process or document the business processes impacting ICFR. Rather, management can focus its evaluation process and the documentation supporting the assessment on those controls that it determines adequately address the risk of a material misstatement of the financial statements. For example, if management determines that a risk of a material misstatement is adequately addressed by an entity-level control, no further evaluation of other controls is required.

The second principle is that management's evaluation of evidence about the operation of its controls should be based on its assessment of risk. The guidance provides an approach for making risk-based judgments about the evidence needed for the evaluation. This allows management to align the nature and extent of its evaluation procedures with those areas of financial reporting that pose the highest risks to reliable financial reporting (that is, whether the financial statements are materially accurate). As a result, management may be able to use more efficient approaches to gathering evidence, such as self-assessments, in low-risk areas and perform more extensive testing in high- risk areas. By following these two principles, we believe companies of all sizes and complexities will be able to implement our rules effectively and efficiently.

The Interpretive Guidance reiterates the Commission's position that management should bring its own experience and informed judgment to bear in order to design an evaluation process that meets the needs of its company and that provides a reasonable basis for its annual assessment of whether ICFR is effective. This allows management sufficient and appropriate flexibility to design such an evaluation process. Smaller public companies, which generally have less complex internal control systems than larger public companies, can use this guidance to scale and tailor their evaluation methods and procedures to fit their own facts and circumstances. We encourage smaller public companies to take advantage of the flexibility and scalability to conduct an evaluation of ICFR that is both efficient and effective at identifying material weaknesses.

The effort necessary to conduct an initial evaluation of ICFR will vary among companies, partly because this effort will depend on management's existing financial reporting risk assessment and control monitoring activities. After the first year of compliance, management's effort to identify financial reporting risks and controls should ordinarily be less, because subsequent evaluations should be more focused on changes in risks and controls rather than identification of all financial reporting risks and the related controls. Further, in each subsequent year, the documentation of risks and controls will only need to be updated from the prior year(s), not recreated anew. Through the risk and control identification process, management will have identified for testing only those controls that are needed to meet the objective of ICFR (that is, to provide reasonable assurance regarding the reliability of financial reporting) and for which evidence about their operation can be obtained most efficiently. The nature and extent of procedures implemented to evaluate whether those controls continue to operate effectively can be tailored to the company's unique circumstances, thereby avoiding unnecessary compliance costs.

The guidance assumes management has established and maintains a system of internal accounting controls as required by the FCPA. Further, it is not intended to explain how management should design its ICFR to comply with the control framework management has chosen. To allow appropriate flexibility, the guidance does not provide a checklist of steps management should perform in completing its evaluation.

The guidance in this release shall be effective immediately upon its publication in the Federal Register.

. . . .

II. INTERPRETIVE GUIDANCE—EVALUATION AND ASSESSMENT OF INTERNAL CONTROLS OVER FINANCIAL CONTROLS

. . . .

A. The Evaluation Process

The objective of internal control over financial reporting ("ICFR") is to provide reasonable assurance regarding the reliability of financial reporting and the preparation of financial statements for external purposes in accordance with generally accepted accounting principles ("GAAP"). The purpose of the evaluation of ICFR is to provide management with a reasonable basis for its annual assessment as to whether any material weaknesses in ICFR exist as of the end of the fiscal year. To accomplish this, management identifies the risks to reliable financial reporting, evaluates whether controls exist to address those risks, and evaluates evidence about the operation of the controls included in the evaluation based on its assessment of risk. The evaluation process will vary from company to company; however, the top-down, risk-based approach which is described in this guidance will typically be the most efficient and effective way to conduct the evaluation.

The evaluation process guidance is described in two sections. The first section explains the identification of financial reporting risks and the evaluation of whether the controls management has implemented adequately address those risks. The second section explains an approach for making judgments about the methods and procedures for evaluating whether the operation of ICFR is effective. Both sections explain how entity-level controls impact the evaluation process, as well as how management should focus its evaluation efforts on the highest risks to reliable financial reporting.

Under the Commission's rules, management's annual assessment of the effectiveness of ICFR must be made in accordance with a suitable control framework's definition of effective internal control. These control frameworks define elements of internal control that are expected to be present and functioning in an effective internal control system. In assessing effectiveness, management evaluates whether its ICFR includes policies, procedures and activities that address the elements of internal control that the applicable control framework describes as necessary for an internal control system to be effective. The framework elements describe the characteristics of an internal control system that may be relevant to individual areas of the company's ICFR, pervasive to many areas, or entity-wide. Therefore, management's evaluation process includes not only controls involving particular areas of financial reporting, but also the entity-wide and other pervasive elements of internal control defined by its selected control framework. This guidance is not intended to replace the elements of an effective system of internal control as defined within a control framework.

1. Identifying Financial Reporting Risks and Controls

Management should evaluate whether it has implemented controls that will achieve the objective of ICFR (that is, to provide reasonable assurance regarding the reliability of financial reporting). The evaluation begins with the identification and assessment of the risks to reliable financial reporting (that is, materially accurate financial statements), including changes in those risks. Management then evaluates whether it has controls placed in operation (that is, in use) that are designed to adequately address those risks. Management ordinarily would consider the company's entity-level controls in both its assessment of risks and in identifying which controls adequately address the risks.

The evaluation approach described herein allows management to identify controls and maintain supporting evidential matter for its controls in a manner that is tailored to the company's financial reporting risks (as defined below). Thus, the controls that management identifies and documents are those that are important to achieving the objective of ICFR. These controls are then subject to procedures to evaluate evidence of their operating effectiveness, as determined pursuant to Section II.A.2.

a. Identifying Financial Reporting Risks

Management should identify those risks of misstatement that could, individually or in combination with others, result in a material misstatement of the financial statements ("financial reporting risks"). Ordinarily, the identification of financial reporting risks begins with evaluating how the requirements of GAAP apply to the company's business, operations and transactions. Management must provide investors with financial statements that fairly present the company's financial position, results of operations and cash flows in accordance with GAAP. A lack of fair presentation arises when one or more financial statement amounts or disclosures ("financial reporting elements") contain misstatements (including omissions) that are material.

Management uses its knowledge and understanding of the business, and its organization, operations, and processes, to consider the sources and potential likelihood of misstatements in financial reporting elements. Internal and external risk factors that impact the business, including the nature and extent of any changes in those risks, may give rise to a risk of misstatement. Risks of misstatement may also arise from sources such as the initiation, authorization, processing and recording of transactions and other adjustments that are reflected in financial reporting elements. Management may find it useful to consider "what could go wrong" within a financial reporting element in order to identify the sources and the potential likelihood of misstatements and identify those that could result in a material misstatement of the financial statements.

The methods and procedures for identifying financial reporting risks will vary based on the characteristics of the company. These characteristics include, among others, the size, complexity, and organizational structure of the company and its processes and financial reporting environment, as well as the control framework used by management. For example, to identify financial reporting risks in a larger business or a complex business process, management's methods and procedures may involve a variety of company personnel, including those with specialized knowledge. These individuals, collectively, may be necessary to have a sufficient understanding of GAAP, the underlying business transactions and the process activities, including the role of computer technology, that are required to initiate, authorize, record and process transactions. In contrast, in a small company that operates on a centralized basis with less complex business processes and with little change in the risks or processes, management's daily involvement with the business may provide it with adequate knowledge to appropriately identify financial reporting risks.

Management's evaluation of the risk of misstatement should include consideration of the vulnerability of the entity to fraudulent activity (for example, fraudulent financial reporting, misappropriation of assets and corruption), and whether any such exposure could result in a material misstatement of the financial statements. The extent of activities required for the evaluation of fraud risks is commensurate with the size and complexity of the company's operations and financial reporting environment.

Management should recognize that the risk of material misstatement due to fraud ordinarily exists in any organization, regardless of size or type, and it may vary by specific location or segment and by individual financial reporting element. For example, one type of fraud risk that has resulted in fraudulent financial reporting in companies of all sizes and types is the risk of improper override of internal controls in the financial reporting process. While the identification of a fraud risk is not necessarily an indication that a fraud has occurred, the absence of an identified fraud is not an indication that no fraud risks exist. Rather, these risk assessments are used in evaluating whether adequate controls have been implemented.

b. Identifying Controls That Adequately Address Financial Reporting Risks

Management should evaluate whether it has controls placed in operation (that is, in use) that adequately address the company's financial reporting risks. The determination of whether an individual control, or a combination of controls, adequately addresses a financial reporting risk involves judgments about whether the controls, if operating properly, can effectively prevent or detect misstatements that could result in material misstatements in the financial statements. If management determines that a deficiency in ICFR exists, it must be evaluated to determine whether a material weakness exists. The guidance in Section II.B.1. is designed to assist management with that evaluation.

Management may identify preventive controls, detective controls, or a combination of both, as adequately addressing financial reporting risks. There might be more than one control that addresses the financial reporting risks for a financial reporting element; conversely, one control might address the risks of more than one financial reporting element. It is not necessary to identify all controls that may exist or identify redundant controls, unless redundancy itself is required to address the financial reporting risks. To illustrate, management may determine that the risk of a misstatement in interest expense, which could result in a material misstatement of the financial statements, is adequately addressed by a control within the company's period-end financial reporting process (that is, an entity-level control). In such a case, management may not need to identify, for purposes of the ICFR evaluation, any additional controls related to the risk of misstatement in interest expense.

Management may also consider the efficiency with which evidence of the operation of a control can be evaluated when identifying the controls that adequately address the financial reporting risks. When more than one control exists and each adequately addresses a financial reporting risk, management may decide to select the control for which evidence of operating effectiveness can be obtained more efficiently. Moreover, when adequate information technology ("IT") general controls exist and management has determined that the operation of such controls is effective, management may determine that automated controls are more efficient to evaluate than manual controls. Considering the efficiency with which the operation of a control can be evaluated will often enhance the overall efficiency of the evaluation process.

In addition to identifying controls that address the financial reporting risks of individual financial reporting elements, management also evaluates whether it has controls in place to address the entity-level and other pervasive elements of ICFR that its chosen control framework prescribes as necessary for an effective system of internal control. This would ordinarily include, for example, considering how and whether controls related to the control environment, controls over management override, the entity-level risk assessment process and monitoring activities, controls over the period-end financial reporting process, and the policies that address significant business control and risk management practices are adequate for purposes of an effective system of internal control. The control frameworks and related guidance may be useful tools for evaluating the adequacy of these elements of ICFR.

When identifying the controls that address financial reporting risks, management learns information about the characteristics of the controls that should inform its judgments about the risk that a control will fail to operate as designed.

This includes, for example, information about the judgment required in its operation and information about the complexity of the controls. Section II.A.2. discusses how these characteristics are considered in determining the nature and extent of evidence of the operation of the controls that management evaluates.

At the end of this identification process, management has identified for evaluation those controls that are needed to meet the objective of ICFR (that is, to provide reasonable assurance regarding the reliability of financial reporting) and for which evidence about their operation can be obtained most efficiently.

c. Consideration of Entity-Level Controls

Management considers entity-level controls when identifying financial reporting risks and related controls for a financial reporting element. In doing so, it is important for management to consider the nature of the entity-level controls and how those controls relate to the financial reporting element. The more indirect the relationship to a financial reporting element, the less effective a control may be in preventing or detecting a misstatement.

Some entity-level controls, such as certain control environment controls, have an important, but indirect, effect on the likelihood that a misstatement will be prevented or detected on a timely basis. These controls might affect the other controls management determines are necessary to adequately address financial reporting risks for a financial reporting element. However, it is unlikely that management will identify only this type of entity-level control as adequately addressing a financial reporting risk identified for a financial reporting element.

Other entity-level controls may be designed to identify possible breakdowns in lower-level controls, but not in a manner that would, by themselves, adequately address financial reporting risks. For example, an entity-level control that monitors the results of operations may be designed to detect potential misstatements and investigate whether a breakdown in lower-level controls occurred. However, if the amount of potential misstatement that could exist before being detected by the monitoring control is too high, then the control may not adequately address the financial reporting risks of a financial reporting element.

Entity-level controls may be designed to operate at the process, application, transaction or account-level and at a level of precision that would adequately prevent or detect on a timely basis misstatements in one or more financial reporting elements that could result in a material misstatement of the financial statements. In these cases, management may not need to identify or evaluate additional controls relating to that financial reporting risk.

d. Role of Information Technology General Controls

Controls that management identifies as addressing financial reporting risks may be automated, dependent upon IT functionality, or a combination of both manual and automated procedures. In these situations, management's evaluation process generally considers the design and operation of the automated or IT dependent application controls and the relevant IT general controls over the applications providing the IT functionality. While IT general controls alone ordinarily do not adequately address financial reporting risks, the proper and consistent operation of automated controls or IT functionality often depends upon effective IT general controls. The identification of risks and controls within IT should not be a separate evaluation. Instead, it should be an integral part of management's top-down, risk-based approach to identifying risks and controls and in determining evidential matter necessary to support the assessment.

Aspects of IT general controls that may be relevant to the evaluation of ICFR will vary depending upon a company's facts and circumstances. For purposes of the evaluation of ICFR, management only needs to evaluate those IT general controls that are necessary for the proper and consistent operation of other controls designed to adequately address financial reporting risks. For example, management might consider whether certain aspects of IT general control areas, such as program development, program changes, computer operations, and access to programs and data, apply to its facts and circumstances. Specifically, it is unnecessary to evaluate IT general controls that primarily pertain to efficiency or effectiveness of a company's operations, but which are not relevant to addressing financial reporting risks.

e. Evidential Matter to Support the Assessment

As part of its evaluation of ICFR, management must maintain reasonable support for its assessment. Documentation of the design of the controls management has placed in operation to adequately address the financial reporting risks, including the entity-level and other pervasive elements necessary for effective ICFR, is an integral part of the reasonable support. The form and extent of the documentation will vary depending on the size, nature, and complexity of the company. It can take many forms (for example, paper documents, electronic, or other media). Also, the documentation can be presented in a number of ways (for example, policy manuals, process models, flowcharts, job descriptions, documents, internal memorandums, forms, etc). The documentation does not need to include all controls that exist within a process that impacts financial reporting. Rather, the documentation should be focused on those controls that management concludes are adequate to address the financial reporting risks.

In addition to providing support for the assessment of ICFR, documentation of the design of controls also supports other objectives of an effective system of internal control. For example, it serves as evidence that controls within ICFR, including changes to those controls, have been identified, are capable of being communicated to those responsible for their performance, and are capable of being monitored by the company.

2. Evaluating Evidence of the Operating Effectiveness of ICFR

Management should evaluate evidence of the operating effectiveness of ICFR. The evaluation of the operating effectiveness of a control considers whether the control is operating as designed and whether the person performing the control possesses the necessary authority and competence to perform the control effectively. The evaluation procedures that management uses to gather evidence about the operation of the controls it identifies as adequately addressing the financial reporting risks for financial reporting elements (pursuant to Section II.A.1.b) should be tailored to management's assessment of the risk characteristics of both the individual financial reporting elements and the related controls (collectively, ICFR risk). Management should ordinarily focus its evaluation of the operation of controls on areas posing the highest ICFR risk. Management's assessment of ICFR risk also considers the impact of entity-level controls, such as the relative strengths and weaknesses of the control environment, which may influence management's judgments about the risks of failure for particular controls.

> Management should ordinarily focus its evaluation of the operation of controls on areas posing the highest ICFR risk.

Evidence about the effective operation of controls may be obtained from direct testing of controls and on-going monitoring activities. The nature, timing and extent of evaluation procedures necessary for management to obtain sufficient evidence of the effective operation of a control depend on the assessed ICFR risk. In determining whether the evidence obtained is sufficient to provide a reasonable basis for its evaluation of the operation of ICFR, management should consider not only the quantity of evidence (for example, sample size), but also the qualitative characteristics of the evidence. The qualitative characteristics of the evidence include the nature of the evaluation procedures performed, the period of time to which the evidence relates, the objectivity of those evaluating the controls, and, in the case of on-going monitoring activities, the extent of validation through direct testing of underlying controls. For any individual control, different combinations of the nature, timing, and extent of evaluation procedures may provide sufficient evidence. The sufficiency of evidence is not necessarily determined by any of these attributes individually.

a. Determining the Evidence Needed to Support the Assessment

Management should evaluate the ICFR risk of the controls identified in Section II.A.1.b as adequately addressing the financial reporting risks for financial reporting elements to determine the evidence needed to support the assessment. This evaluation should consider the characteristics of the financial reporting elements to which the controls relate and the characteristics of the controls themselves. This concept is illustrated in Figure 4-2.

. . . .

B. Reporting Considerations

1. Evaluation of Control Deficiencies

In order to determine whether a control deficiency, or combination of control deficiencies, is a material weakness, management evaluates the severity of each control deficiency that comes to its attention. Control deficiencies that are determined to be a material weakness must be disclosed in management's annual report on its assessment of the effectiveness of ICFR. Control deficiencies that

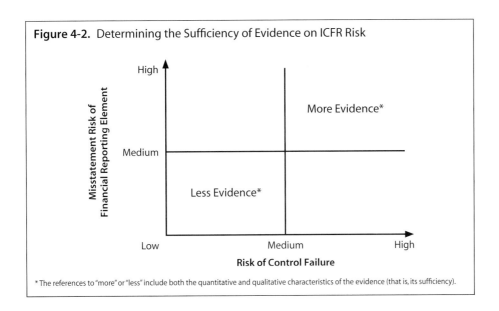

Figure 4-2. Determining the Sufficiency of Evidence on ICFR Risk

* The references to "more" or "less" include both the quantitative and qualitative characteristics of the evidence (that is, its sufficiency).

are considered to be significant deficiencies are reported to the company's audit committee and the external auditor pursuant to management's compliance with the certification requirements in Exchange Act Rule 13a-14.

Management may not disclose that it has assessed ICFR as effective if one or more deficiencies in ICFR are determined to be a material weakness. As part of the evaluation of ICFR, management considers whether each deficiency, individually or in combination, is a material weakness as of the end of the fiscal year. Multiple control deficiencies that affect the same financial statement amount or disclosure increase the likelihood of misstatement and may, in combination, constitute a material weakness if there is a reasonable possibility that a material misstatement of the financial statements would not be prevented or detected in a timely manner, even though such deficiencies may be individually less severe than a material weakness. Therefore, management should evaluate individual control deficiencies that affect the same financial statement amount or disclosure, or component of internal control, to determine whether they collectively result in a material weakness.

The evaluation of the severity of a control deficiency should include both quantitative and qualitative factors. Management evaluates the severity of a deficiency in ICFR by considering whether there is a reasonable possibility that the company's ICFR will fail to prevent or detect a misstatement of a financial statement amount or disclosure; and the magnitude of the potential misstatement resulting from the deficiency or deficiencies. The severity of a deficiency in ICFR does not depend on whether a misstatement actually has occurred but rather on whether there is a reasonable possibility that the company's ICFR will fail to prevent or detect a misstatement on a timely basis.

Risk factors affect whether there is a reasonable possibility that a deficiency, or a combination of deficiencies, will result in a misstatement of a financial statement amount or disclosure. These factors include, but are not limited to, the following:

- The nature of the financial reporting elements involved (for example, suspense accounts and related party transactions involve greater risk);
- The susceptibility of the related asset or liability to loss or fraud (that is, greater susceptibility increases risk);
- The subjectivity, complexity, or extent of judgment required to determine the amount involved (that is, greater subjectivity, complexity, or judgment, like that related to an accounting estimate, increases risk);
- The interaction or relationship of the control with other controls, including whether they are interdependent or redundant;
- The interaction of the deficiencies (that is, when evaluating a combination of two or more deficiencies, whether the deficiencies could affect the same financial statement amounts or disclosures); and
- The possible future consequences of the deficiency.

Factors that affect the magnitude of the misstatement that might result from a deficiency or deficiencies in ICFR include, but are not limited to, the following:

- The financial statement amounts or total of transactions exposed to the deficiency; and
- The volume of activity in the account balance or class of transactions exposed to the deficiency that has occurred in the current period or that is expected in future periods.

. . . [I]n many cases, the probability of a small misstatement will be greater than the probability of a large misstatement.

Management should evaluate the effect of compensating controls when determining whether a control deficiency or combination of deficiencies is a material weakness. To have a mitigating effect, the compensating control should operate at a level of precision that would prevent or detect a misstatement that could be material.

> To have a mitigating effect, the compensating control should operate at a level of precision that would prevent or detect a misstatement that could be material.

In determining whether a deficiency or a combination of deficiencies represents a material weakness, management considers all relevant information. Management should evaluate whether the following situations indicate a deficiency in ICFR exists and, if so, whether it represents a material weakness:

- Identification of fraud, whether or not material, on the part of senior management;
- Restatement of previously issued financial statements to reflect the correction of a material misstatement;
- Identification of a material misstatement of the financial statements in the current period in circumstances that indicate the misstatement would not have been detected by the company's ICFR; and

- Ineffective oversight of the company's external financial reporting and internal control over financial reporting by the company's audit committee.

When evaluating the severity of a deficiency, or combination of deficiencies, in ICFR, management also should determine the level of detail and degree of assurance that would satisfy prudent officials in the conduct of their own affairs that they have reasonable assurance that transactions are recorded as necessary to permit the preparation of financial statements in conformity with GAAP. If management determines that the deficiency, or combination of deficiencies, might prevent prudent officials in the conduct of their own affairs from concluding that they have reasonable assurance that transactions are recorded as necessary to permit the preparation of financial statements in conformity with GAAP, then management should treat the deficiency, or combination of deficiencies, as an indicator of a material weakness.

Notes and Questions

1) The FCPA Accounting Provisions and SOX §§ 302 and 404 only apply to "issuers." Should nonissuers voluntarily establish accurate books and records and adequate internal controls?
2) What is the difference between a control deficiency and a material weakness?
3) How must issuers document their compliance with SOX § 404? What purpose does such documentation serve?

In the Matter of Marc Sherman

Exchange Act Release No. 72723 (July 30, 2014)

Order Instituting Cease-and-Desist Proceedings Pursuant to Section 21C of the Securities Exchange Act of 1934

I.

The Securities and Exchange Commission ("Commission") deems it appropriate that cease-and-desist proceedings be, and hereby are, instituted pursuant to Section 21C of the Securities Exchange Act of 1934 ("Exchange Act") against Marc Sherman ("Respondent" or "Sherman").

II.

After an investigation, the Division of Enforcement alleges that:

A. Summary

During its 2008 fiscal year and continuing up to its filing for Chapter 11 bankruptcy on July 2, 2009 (the "relevant period"), QSGI Inc. ("QSGI" or the "Company") was a reseller of and maintenance services provider for used computer equipment. Sherman, who during the relevant period served as QSGI's Chief Executive Officer and Chairman, was aware of deficiencies in and the circumvention of internal controls for inventory and the resulting falsification of the Company's books and records. On occasion in 2008 and increasing in frequency in 2009, Sherman improperly accelerated the recognition on QSGI's books and records of accounts receivable and receipt of inventory in order to increase the borrowing base available under a revolving credit facility with the Company's chief creditor. Sherman withheld this information from the Company's external auditors in connection with their audit of the financial statements for the fiscal year ended December 31, 2008 and review of the financial statements for the quarter ended March 31, 2009, and made affirmative material misrepresentations and statements that were materially misleading as a result of his omission of information in management representation letters to the auditors about the design, maintenance, and operation of internal controls. Further, Sherman signed a Form 10-K and a Form 10-K/A for the 2008 fiscal year, each containing a management's report on internal control over financial reporting ("ICFR"), as required by Section 404 of the Sarbanes-Oxley Act of 2002 ("Sarbanes-Oxley Act") and Exchange Act Rule 13a-15(c), which falsely represented that he, in his capacity as CEO, had participated in assessing the effectiveness of the Company's ICFR. Sherman also signed certifications required under Section 302 of the Sarbanes-Oxley Act and Rule 13a-14 of the Exchange Act included in filings with the Commission falsely representing that he had evaluated ICFR and, based on this evaluation, disclosed all significant deficiencies to the auditors. The certifications were attached to the 2008 Forms 10-K and 10-K/A, and to the first quarter 2009 Form 10-Q filed with the Commission, which Sherman also signed.

B. Respondent

Sherman, age 50 and a resident of West Palm Beach, Florida, founded QSGI in 2001. He has since served as QSGI's CEO and Chairman of its Board of Directors. After the Company filed for bankruptcy and until at least July 2010, he served as Chief Financial Officer and Chief Accounting Officer.

C. Relevant Entity

QSGI, Inc., incorporated in 1967 in Delaware under a different name and headquartered during the relevant period in West Palm Beach, Florida, is engaged in the business of purchasing, refurbishing, selling, and servicing used computer equipment, parts and mainframes. On May 4, 2011, the U.S. Bankruptcy Court for the Southern District of Florida, West Palm Beach Division, confirmed QSGI's plan of reorganization pursuant to which, effective June 17, 2011, the corporate shell merged with a private company which had been founded by Sherman and others. The Company's common stock is registered with the Commission pursuant to Section 12(g) of the Exchange Act and quoted on the OTC Link (formerly "Pink Sheets") operated by OTC Markets Group Inc.

D. Sherman's Awareness of Deficiencies in and Circumvention of Inventory Controls

During the relevant period, QSGI maintained inventory principally at facilities in New Jersey and Minnesota. The New Jersey inventory, which comprised 50% of the company's reported gross inventory and 55% of its reported net inventory, after reduction for reserves, as of the close of its fiscal year ended December 31, 2008, was comprised of laptops, monitors, and other consumer electronics and components. The Minnesota inventory, which comprised 40% of QSGI's reported gross inventory and 35% of its reported net inventory, after reduction for reserves, as of the close of QSGI's 2008 fiscal year, was comprised chiefly of servers, mainframes, and component parts.

For a period of years prior to the Company filing for bankruptcy in 2009, QSGI experienced recurring inventory control problems. Throughout the relevant period, Company personnel: (1) shipped certain inventory received into its facilities out to customers without making the appropriate entries into the Company's books and records; and (2) removed items from physical inventory without relieving the inventory from the Company's books and records. Company personnel removed component parts from the physical inventory for such parts without recording the parts removed and occasionally stripped component parts from operating systems without recording the parts removed. As a result, the Company's books and records incorrectly reflected certain components in inventory and operating systems as intact systems. These component parts were then sold by the Company or used for the Company's maintenance services.

These internal control problems resulted in the falsification of QSGI's books and records relating to QSGI's inventory.

These inventory control problems escalated at the Minnesota facility beginning in 2007 for several reasons. First, a manufacturer's policy of curtailing resellers' ability to modify machines to customers' specifications hastened QSGI's shift from selling machines to selling parts and providing repair and maintenance services. This, in turn, exacerbated the problem in Minnesota of personnel removing component parts from operating systems without any corresponding adjustment to the Company's books and records. The units continued to be recorded on the books and records as intact systems. Second, key personnel, including accounting personnel, left the Minnesota operations in late 2007. Personnel designated to replace the departed accounting staff lacked an accounting background and failed to fully carry out their responsibilities. Third, while QSGI management had undertaken to design, document, and implement internal controls to come into compliance with federal securities law requirements, such efforts were not begun in earnest in Minnesota until late 2007, after the departure of key personnel. Prior to that point, QSGI senior management had accorded Minnesota personnel a fair amount of autonomy, including using an accounting system that differed from the one used in New Jersey.

The Company's efforts to introduce new controls to the Minnesota operations during the 2008 fiscal year largely failed. More particularly, the Company failed to design procedures taking into account the existing control environment, including the qualifications and experience level of persons employed to handle accounting. Training of accounting, sales, and warehouse personnel either did not take place or was inadequate. As a result, controls the Company attempted to implement in February 2008 were widely ignored during the ensuing ten months of the 2008 fiscal year and well into the 2009 fiscal year. For example, sales and warehouse personnel often failed to document their removal of items from inventory or, to the extent they did prepare the paperwork, accounting personnel often failed to process the paperwork and to adjust inventory in the company's financial reporting system. The Company's attempts to monitor compliance on an ongoing basis were also inadequate. Company personnel regularly circumvented controls.

In periodic filings with the Commission relating to the relevant period and certifications included therein pursuant to Rule 13a-14 of the Exchange Act, Sherman acknowledged his responsibility for the design and operation of internal controls.

During the relevant period, Sherman knew of ongoing deficiencies in and the circumvention of internal controls relating to inventory. For example, in the final days of the 2008 fiscal year, QSGI senior management, including Sherman, communicated openly amongst themselves about the failed implementation, including training in, and circumvention of controls introduced to the Minnesota operations earlier in the year. Management agreed that corrective action was needed which, given the timing, could not be undertaken until 2009. Based on further communications, management, including Sherman, was aware that the problems continued through the Company filing for bankruptcy in July 2009.

E. Sherman's Improper Acceleration of Recognition of Inventory and Accounts Receivable

QSGI reported net losses in each fiscal year from 2005 through 2008. Under these circumstances, QSGI's ability to procure operating funds was critical to the Company's survival.

In mid-2008, QSGI entered into a revolving credit facility with its chief creditor. QSGI's inventory and accounts receivable factored into the weekly calculation of the borrowing base under the revolving credit facility. A QSGI employee calculated the borrowing base and reported it to Sherman and to QSGI's Chief Financial Officer, subsequently redesignated QSGI's Vice President of Finance and Controller, ("PFO") for their review prior to sending it to the chief creditor.

On occasion in 2008 and continuing on a more frequent basis up until the company filed for bankruptcy in July 2009, the weekly calculations would show that QSGI had exceeded its borrowing limit or would not be able to borrow enough to continue operations through the upcoming week. When this occurred, Sherman, either directly or indirectly through the PFO, directed the QSGI employee to not report the calculations to the creditor pending other items being posted to the books and records so that the employee could redo the weekly calculation.

In order to increase the borrowing base, Sherman directed the accelerated recognition of accounts receivable and/or the receipt of product into inventory on QSGI's books and records. Under generally accepted accounting principles, recognition of the accounts receivables and receipt of product into inventory should not have occurred until days or up to approximately a week later, when all conditions for recognition had been satisfied.

Once the accounts receivable and/or receipt of inventory were improperly recorded on QSGI's books and records, the QSGI employee would recalculate the borrowing base using the new figures.

F. Sherman Misled Qsgi's External Auditors

At no time during the relevant period did Sherman disclose, or direct anyone else to disclose, to QSGI's external auditors the foregoing inventory and accounts receivable issues and the resulting falsification of QSGI's books and records.

To the contrary, in management representations letters to the auditors, Sherman made affirmative misrepresentations and made statements that were misleading as a result of his omitting material facts which were necessary in order to make the statements made not misleading. Sherman affirmatively represented in management representation letters he provided to the auditors in connection with their review of quarterly financial statements in 2008 that either there were no significant deficiencies or that he had disclosed to the auditors all such deficiencies. At the conclusion of the fiscal year, he provided yet another management representation letter in connection with the external auditors' audit of the 2008 fiscal year financial statements in which he acknowledged his responsibility for establishing and maintaining ICFR. Omitted from the letter was any reference to the existence, or his disclosure to the auditors, of significant deficiencies. Following on his management representation letters for the first three quarters of 2008, however, and in the context of his having acknowledged in the year-end management representation letter his responsibility for establishing and maintaining ICFR, the omission of any reference to significant deficiencies implied falsely that none existed. In the management representation letter relating to the external auditors' review of the first quarter 2009 financial statements, Sherman affirmatively misrepresented that he had disclosed to the auditors all significant deficiencies.

Had Sherman disclosed to the external auditors the deficiencies in and the circumvention of inventory controls and the improper acceleration of accounts receivable and inventory recognition described above, the auditors would have changed the nature, timing, and extent of their procedures in conducting the audit of the financial statements for the fiscal year ended December 31, 2008 and review of the financial statements for the quarter ended March 31, 2009.

G. Sherman's False Representations in Management's Report on ICFR and Concerning Qsgi's Critical Accounting Policies

QSGI's Form 10-K for the fiscal year ended December 31, 2008 included a Company management's report on ICFR, as required by Section 404 of the

Sarbanes-Oxley Act and Exchange Act Rule 13a-15(c). A management's report on ICFR was also included in a Form 10-K/A for the 2008 fiscal year.

The management report included in both filings falsely represented that QSGI's management, with the participation of QSGI's CEO, Sherman, had evaluated QSGI's ICFR as of December 31, 2008 using the criteria set forth by the Committee of Sponsoring Organizations of the Treadway Commission in Internal Control – Integrated Framework. In fact, Sherman, in his capacity as CEO, did not participate in any evaluation and was unfamiliar with the referenced framework.

The discussion on critical accounting policies in QSGI's Form 10-K for the fiscal year ended December 31, 2008 falsely stated that: (1) QSGI "recognize[d] revenue when it is realized or realizable and earned"; and (2) "[m]anagement continually monitors its inventory valuation . . . ."

The discussion on critical accounting policies included in QSGI's Form 10-K/A for the fiscal year ended December 31, 2008 falsely stated that, "[m]anagement closely monitors and analyzes inventory for potential obsolescence and slow-moving items on an item-by-item basis . . . ."

Sherman knew, or was reckless in not knowing, that these statements were materially false and misleading. During the relevant period, he had directed the improper accelerated recognition of accounts receivable, which would have had the effect of improperly increasing revenue by a commensurate amount. He also knew that the Company did not closely monitor inventory in the manner described because the Company lacked the necessary resources.

Sherman signed the 2008 Form 10-K in his capacity as Chief Executive Officer and Chairman of QSGI's Board of Directors. Sherman signed the 2008 Form 10-K/A in his capacity as Chairman, CEO, CFO and CAO. He was the sole signing officer of the Form 10-K/A. The 2008 Form 10-K and Form 10-K/A were filed with the Commission on March 31, 2009 and July 23, 2010, respectively.

H. Sherman's False Sarbanes-Oxley Certifications

Pursuant to Sarbanes-Oxley Act Section 302 and Exchange Act Rule 13a-14, Sherman signed certifications which were attached to QSGI's 2008 Forms 10-K and 10-K/A and Form 10-Q for the periods ended December 31, 2008 and March 31, 2009, respectively.

Sherman individually certified in each filing that, based on his and the other certifying officer's "most recent evaluation of [ICFR]," they had disclosed to QSGI's external auditors all significant deficiencies, "in the design or operation of [ICFR] which are reasonably likely to adversely affect [QSGI's] ability to record, process, summarize and report financial information." Omitted from the certification attached to the Form 10-K, but included in the certification attached to the Form 10-Q, were Sherman's certifications to the effect that the other certifying officer and he: (1) had been responsible for establishing and maintaining ICFR and designing, or supervising others in the design of, ICFR; and (2) had designed, or caused to be designed, such ICFR.

Sherman's certifications were false because: (1) he had not participated in designing, establishing, or maintaining ICFR, and had not evaluated ICFR; (2) he and others had on occasion circumvented QSGI's internal controls in accelerating improperly the recognition of accounts receivable and inventory; and (3) the other certifying officer and Sherman had not made the referenced disclosures to the external auditors.

Sherman knew, or was reckless in not knowing, that his certifications were materially false and misleading.

As mentioned, Sherman signed the 2008 Form 10-K and Form 10-K/A, which were filed with the Commission. Sherman also signed the Form 10-Q for the first quarter of 2009 in his capacity as CEO and Chairman of the Board of Directors, which was filed with the Commission on May 14, 2009.

I. Violations

As a result of the conduct described above, Sherman violated Section 10(b) of the Exchange Act and Rule 10b-5 thereunder, which prohibits fraudulent conduct in connection with the purchase or sale of any security involving: a) the use of any device, scheme, or artifice to defraud; b) the making of material misrepresentations or omissions; and c) any act, practice, or course of business which operates or would operate as a fraud or deceit upon any person.

As a result of the conduct described above, Sherman caused QSGI's violations of Exchange Act Sections 13(b)(2)(A) and 13(b)(2)(B), which require reporting issuers to make and keep accurate books and records and devise and maintain effective internal accounting controls, respectively.

As a result of the conduct described above, Sherman violated Exchange Act Section 13(b)(5), which prohibits any person from knowingly circumventing or knowingly failing to implement a system of internal accounting controls or knowingly falsifying any book, record or account subject to Exchange Act Section 13(b)(2). Sherman also violated Exchange Act Rule 13b2-1, which prohibits any person from, directly or indirectly, falsifying or causing to be falsified, any book, record or account subject to Exchange Act Section 13(b)(2).

As a result of the conduct described above, Sherman violated Exchange Act Rule 13b2-2, which prohibits any director or officer of an issuer from, directly or indirectly: (a) making or causing to be made a materially false or misleading statement; or (b) omitting or causing another person to omit to state a material fact necessary in order to make statements made, in light of the circumstances under which such statements were made, not misleading, to an accountant in connection with financial statement audits, reviews, or examinations or the preparation or filing of any document or report required to be filed with the Commission.

As a result of the conduct described above, Sherman violated Exchange Act Rule 13a-14(a), which requires that an issuer's principal executive officer, or person's performing similar functions, certify each periodic report containing financial statements filed by an issuer pursuant to Section 13(a) of the Exchange Act.

III.

In view of the allegations made by the Division of Enforcement, the Commission deems it necessary and appropriate that cease-and-desist proceedings be instituted to determine:

A. Whether the allegations set forth in Section II hereof are true and, in connection therewith, to afford Respondent an opportunity to establish any defenses to such allegations;

B. Whether, pursuant to Section 21C of the Exchange Act, Respondent should be ordered to cease and desist from committing or causing violations of and any future violations of Sections 10(b), 13(b)(2)(A), 13(b)(2)(B) and 13(b)(5) of the Exchange Act and Rules 10b-5, 13a-14, 13b2-1 and 13b2-2 thereunder;

C. What, if any, remedial action is appropriate against Respondent, including, but not limited to, civil penalties pursuant to Section 21B(a) of the Exchange Act;

D. Whether, pursuant to Section 21C(f) of the Exchange Act, Respondent should be prohibited, conditionally or unconditionally, and permanently or for such period of time as it shall determine, from acting as an officer or director of any issuer that has a class of securities registered pursuant to Section 12 of the Exchange Act, or that is required to file reports pursuant to Section 15(d) of the Exchange Act; and

IV.

IT IS ORDERED that a public hearing for the purpose of taking evidence on the questions set forth in Section III hereof shall be convened not earlier than 30 days and not later than 60 days from service of this Order at a time and place to be fixed, and before an Administrative Law Judge to be designated by further order as provided by Rule 110 of the Commission's Rules of Practice, 17 C.F.R. § 201.110.

IT IS FURTHER ORDERED that Respondent shall file an Answer to the allegations contained in this Order within twenty (20) days after service of this Order, as provided by Rule 220 of the Commission's Rules of Practice, 17 C.F.R. § 201.220.

If Respondent fails to file the directed answer, or fails to appear at a hearing after being duly notified, the Respondent may be deemed in default and the proceedings may be determined against him upon consideration of this Order, the allegations of which may be deemed to be true as provided by Rules 155(a), 220(f), 221(f) and 310 of the Commission's Rules of Practice, 17 C.F.R. §§ 201.155(a), 201.220(f), 201.221(f) and 201.31

This Order shall be served forthwith upon Respondent personally or by certified mail.

IT IS FURTHER ORDERED that the Administrative Law Judge shall issue an initial decision no later than 300 days from the date of service of this Order, pursuant to Rule 360(a)(2) of the Commission's Rules of Practice.

In the absence of an appropriate waiver, no officer or employee of the Commission engaged in the performance of investigative or prosecuting functions in this or any factually related proceeding will be permitted to participate or advise in the decision of this matter, except as witness or counsel in proceedings held pursuant to notice. Since this proceeding is not "rule making" within the meaning of Section 551 of the Administrative Procedure Act, it is not deemed subject to the provisions of Section 553 delaying the effective date of any final Commission action.

By the Commission.

Notes and Questions

1) The order instituting cease-and-desist proceedings states:

   > On occasion in 2008 and increasing in frequency in 2009, Sherman improperly accelerated the recognition on QSGI's books and records of accounts receivable and receipt of inventory in order to increase the borrowing base available under a revolving credit facility with the Company's chief creditor.

   What does this mean, and how did this conduct violate SOX § 302?

2) What were the inventory control problems at QSGI, and what control deficiencies did they reflect?

3) What controls could have been implemented by QSGI to address those control deficiencies?

4) Could Sherman have been criminally prosecuted for the violations enumerated in the order instituting cease-and-desist proceedings? If so, under what provision?

CHAPTER 5

The FCPA Anti-Bribery Provisions

I. Introduction
II. What Is Covered Under the FCPA Anti-Bribery Provisions?
   A. The Business Purpose Test
   B. "Anything of Value"
      1. Charitable Donations
      2. Gifts, Travel, and Entertainment
      3. Exceptions and Affirmative Defenses to "Anything of Value"
   C. Meaning of "Foreign Official"
   D. Prohibited Intent (Corruptly, Willfully, Knowingly)
   E. Successor Liability
III. Who Is Covered Under the FCPA Anti-Bribery Provisions?
   A. Scope of the Extraterritorial Application of the FCPA
   B. The Presumption Against Extraterritoriality
   C. Jurisdictional Scope of the FCPA Anti-Bribery Provisions in Light of the Presumption Against Extraterritoriality
      1. Issuers (15 U.S.C. § 78dd-1)
      2. Domestic Concerns (15 U.S.C. § 78dd-2)
      3. Territorial Jurisdiction (15 U.S.C. § 78dd-3)
   D. Responsibility for the Conduct of Others
      1. Agency
      2. Concert of Action

I. Introduction

Does the FCPA's prohibition of foreign corrupt payments impose American values on other countries? After all, conduct that may be considered customary in one part of the world could be offensive or wrong in another. And so, the argument goes, the United States should not impose its own moralistic anticorruption laws on countries where bribery is a part of local culture.[1]

---

1. *See, e.g.*, John N. Hooker, *Corruption from a Cross-Cultural Perspective*, 16 CROSS CULTURAL MGMT. 251, 267 (2009), http://repository.cmu.edu/cgi/viewcontent.cgi?article=1144&context=tepper ("Rather than fight corruption by trying to standardize behavior worldwide, it seems best to allow each cultural system to evolve organically in its own direction and work out its own problems, with enough interaction to exchange goods and ideas, but not so much as to create interference and dysfunction. Cultural diversity, no less than ecological diversity, is good for the planet.").

Another objection to the FCPA anti-bribery provisions is that they disadvantage U.S. businesses in favor of competitors from countries that do not subscribe to the United States' anticorruption agenda.[2] Some argue that the FCPA and similar anticorruption laws act as *de facto* sanctions against countries where corruption is rampant by elevating the legal risk of investment, thereby depriving some of the poorest nations of needed foreign capital.[3]

Regardless of the merits of these objections to the FCPA, corporate leaders can only express them at their peril. Senior management is responsible for setting the right "tone at the top"—one that advances the company's compliance objectives, including compliance with the FCPA anti-bribery provisions. Corporate leaders are therefore limited in their freedom to express personal opinions that might set a permissive or tolerant tone with respect to corrupt dealings with foreign officials and government-controlled entities.[4]

What is the correct tone? The preamble to the U.N. Convention Against Corruption is instructive. It states:

> Corruption is an insidious plague that has a wide range of corrosive effects on societies. It undermines democracy and the rule of law, leads to violations of human rights, distorts markets, erodes the quality of life and allows organized crime, terrorism and other threats to human security to flourish.
>
> This evil phenomenon is found in all countries—big and small, rich and poor—but it is in the developing world that its effects are most destructive. Corruption hurts the poor disproportionately by diverting funds intended for development, undermining a Government's ability to provide basic services, feeding inequality and injustice and discouraging foreign aid and investment. Corruption is a key element in economic underperformance and a major obstacle to poverty alleviation and development.[5]

All members of the Organisation for Economic Co-operation and Development ("OECD") are signatories to the OECD Anti-Bribery Convention,[6] and more than 100 nations are signatories to the U.N. Convention Against

---

2. *See, e.g.*, Andrew Brady Spalding, *Unwitting Sanctions: Understanding Anti-Bribery Legislation as Economic Sanctions Against Emerging Markets*, 62 FLA. L. REV. 351, 397 (2010) ("'[B]lack knights' will move in to fill the void created by the economic withdrawal of countries that are enforcing the OECD convention. Companies from countries that either have not ratified the OECD convention or do not enforce it, such as China or Russia, may not hesitate to invest in these countries.").

3. *See, e.g., id.*

4. U.S. DEP'T. OF JUST. & U.S. SEC. AND EXCH. COMM'N, FCPA: A RESOURCE GUIDE TO THE U.S. FOREIGN CORRUPT PRACTICES ACT 4 (2012) [hereinafter FCPA GUIDE], at 3.

5. United Nations Convention Against Corruption, Oct. 31, 2003, S. TREATY DOC. 109-6, 2349 U.N.T.S. 41., at iii.

6. *See generally* Convention on Combating Bribery of Foreign Public Officials in International Business Transactions, Dec. 17, 1997, S. TREATY DOC. 105-43, 2802 U.N.T.S. 225 [hereinafter OECD Anti-Bribery Convention].

Corruption.[7] There is no wiggle room for cultural relativism when it comes to corruption, especially not for leaders of global business enterprises.

Notes and Questions

In his 1996 article in the *Harvard Business Review*, Thomas Donaldson posits that cultural absolutism—the notion that there is a universal right and wrong—can lead to disastrous mistakes when conducting business overseas.[9] He calls absolutism "ethical imperialism" and gives the example of gift giving in Japan:

> The United States has a strong national security interest in opposing corruption and bribery worldwide. For example, we want to prevent foreign officials from accepting bribes that might lead to a dangerous container being allowed onto a ship bound for our shores. We want to prevent bribes that might help a criminal or terrorist gain access to our country. And we want to prevent bribes that might provide terrorists with access to nuclear material, chemical and biological weapons, MANPADS [MAN-Portable Air-Defense Systems], or other dangerous items.
>
> —*Richard G. Lugar, Chairman, Senate Committee on Foreign Relations*[8]

> [M]any Western business-people thought that the [Japanese] practice of gift giving might be wrong rather than simply different . . . . As Western companies have become more familiar with Japanese traditions, [they have] come to tolerate the practice and to set different limits on gift giving in Japan . . . .[10]

The issue was raised during the Senate hearings preceding the 1998 amendments to the FCPA:

> **Senator Robb:** Very briefly, Secretary Eizenstat, let me ask you a general question first.
>
> The difficulty, it seems to me, that we have—and we allude to it, but I am not sure that we have discussed it sufficiently—is the culture of bribery which we clearly see as bribery and has frustrated U.S. companies and officials and others who view the transparency and the rule of law that we do, and yet there are a number of countries that, from the very beginning of their business practices, have simply viewed it differently. We do not agree with it all but we do [] understand it. But some view what we see clearly as bribery as a cost of doing business, a middleman, blackmail, hush money. There are a lot of different ways to characterize it, but it has been so fully ingrained in the culture that it is very difficult not to contend with that practice no matter how many laws, treaties, or whatever we come up with.
>
> Is it your belief that this particular treaty will make major inroads into changing the culture so that the international community does not have to continue to deal

---

7. *See generally* United Nations Convention Against Corruption, *supra* note 5.

8. S. EXEC. REP. NO. 109-18, at 12 (2006) (Report of the Senate Committee on Foreign Relations Regarding the United Nations Convention Against Corruption).

9. Thomas Donaldson, *Values in Tension: Ethics Away from Home*, HARV. BUS. REV., Sept.–Oct. 1998, at 49, 52.

10. *Id.* at 54.

with something that is culturally ingrained and viewed differently than we see in very black and white terms here but is seen differently in some other nations?

Mr. Eizenstat: Your question is an important one. I think that there has been a culture which has accepted and even encouraged this as long as the bottom line was getting a contract.

I think one of the prime reasons we have seen the Europeans come around on this is not only the bipartisan urging that we have had for a decade, but it is the fact that their own corporations realize that this is self-defeating. So, I think that there is a change in culture and that there will be, as a result, effective enforcement because the major corporations there recognize that they need an external constraint so they can say to the corrupt foreign official, look, our laws now prevent this, do not ask us. It allows them to put a shield up. So, I think that in many ways we are going to see a change in culture. We are already beginning to see it and this will give them an excuse in effect to avoid doing what they would prefer not to do now.

A TREATY AGAINST BRIBES

Printed in the WASHINGTON POST, May 10, 1998[11]

How's this for a level playing field? U.S. law bans the bribery of foreign officials to win business contracts; French law makes such bribes tax-deductible. For years, the United States has been urging other industrialized countries to erase this discrepancy—to outlaw foreign bribery, as has U.S. law for more than two decades. Now Congress has a chance to help make that happen.

The instrument at hand is the Organization for Economic Cooperation and Development's Convention on Combating Bribery of Foreign Public Officials, which 33 leading developed nations signed last December. Once the treaty goes into effect, every participating country will criminalize bribery of foreign officials. In some ways, the treaty doesn't go as far as the U.S. negotiators would have liked. It doesn't ban payments to political parties or candidates, for example. But it's a huge first step, and other nations have agreed to discuss extending its reach once this treaty goes into effect.

The United States has nothing to lose by ratifying the covenant; it essentially confirms U.S. law. Exactly 10 years ago Congress instructed the executive branch to seek just such a treaty. The only question is whether the Senate will find time to vote on it, and whether both houses of Congress will find time to pass the necessary implementing legislation before everyone goes home to campaign. But timing is urgent. The signatories promised maximum effort to ratify by the end of this year. Any delay here would only give other countries an excuse to deviate from that schedule.

---

11. S. EXEC. REP. NO. 105-19, at 2 (1998) (quoting *A Treaty Against Bribes*, WASH. POST, May 10, 1998) (report of the Senate Committee on Foreign Relations Regarding the OECD Anti-Bribery Convention).

Corruption exists in all countries, and no doubt always will. But in developing nations, and those making a transition from communism to free market, corruption can have an especially debilitating effect. Such countries often lack established courts and law enforcement institutions to keep bribery in check. When ruling elites skim huge portions of incoming investment, they impoverish everyone else while fostering cynicism and a sense that anyone who is honest is also a sap. It's important that all developed countries recognize, as the United States has since 1997, that they have a responsibility to help fight such destructive dishonesty. And once the treaty comes into force, European bribes will not only no longer be legal—they won't be tax deductible, either. That's one more reason for Congress to act fast.

U.S. Targets Overseas Bribery; KBR Exec's Plea Widens Probe

T. Christian Miller, ProPublica (Sept. 9, 2008)[12]

HOUSTON — In the world of Big Oil, Albert "Jack" Stanley was legendary for winning billion-dollar contracts in third world countries, the Halliburton executive who knew all the secrets of deals in places like Malaysia, Egypt and Yemen.

In the wake of his admission in a guilty plea last week that he resorted to bribes, kickbacks and high-level corruption to secure deals in Nigeria, however, Stanley now lies at the center of a widening scandal in the oil industry that has implications for corporations and governments across the globe.

Stanley's case is the first in what federal officials believe will be a string of indictments in coming months against U.S. corporate executives who have participated in bribing foreign officials in recent years.

By agreeing to cooperate with prosecutors, Stanley, who ran KBR when it was a subsidiary to Halliburton, promises to become a hammer for federal investigators seeking to crack open additional cases under a 30-year-old statute designed to halt overseas corporate corruption. Around 80 cases involving major corporations accused of overseas bribery were under investigation as of last year, a high-level Justice Department official said.

In addition, Stanley's cooperation may provide a new tool for encouraging industrial countries in Europe and Asia to get more serious about enforcing anti-bribery laws against corporations based there. The $182 million in bribes were allegedly paid not just by Halliburton, but by its partners, an international consortium of engineering companies from France, Italy and Japan. The U.K. has jurisdiction as well because much of the bribery scheme was, according to court documents, hatched in London where Stanley maintained a sumptuous home.

"We are very pleased to see that there has been an uptick in enforcement not only in the U.S. but in other countries as well," said Patrick McCormick, a spokesman for Transparency International USA, an anti-corruption group funded by donations from government development agencies and private businesses and foundations. "We are hoping that it [this case] is a sign of things to come."

---

12. T. Christian Miller, *U.S. Targets Overseas Bribery; KBR Exec's Plea Widens Probe*, PROPUBLICA (Sept. 9, 2008, 1:12 PM), https://www.propublica.org/article/kbr-exec-plea-widens-probe-909.

The intensifying level of this government effort, pushed by a Republican administration normally friendly to business, cuts two ways for American business executives.

For those who may have been involved in bribery to secure construction contracts or equipment sales in developing countries around the world, it represents a nightmare.

The active involvement of the FBI is particularly worrisome to such people. In contrast to white-collar investigations handled by Justice and the Securities and Exchange Commission, the FBI is believed to be prepared to use techniques more familiar to investigations of organized crime, including wiretapping and undercover agents.

Stanley's high profile and punishment—he faces a potential seven-year sentence, the longest in the history of the federal statute outlawing bribing foreign officials—also signal the federal government's willingness to seek long jail terms rather than fines and court injunctions.

For those who fret they have been losing out to foreign competitors in jurisdictions less likely to prosecute bribery, it offers hope that the playing field will soon be leveled.

Stanley has already acknowledged paying bribes to unnamed senior Nigerian officials, although reports have identified the primary recipient as the late president of Nigeria, Sani Abacha. He also admitted to receiving kickbacks of $10.8 million from contracts that Halliburton and predecessor companies signed with governments in Nigeria, Malaysia, Egypt, [and] Yemen. Government officials in those countries, with the exception of President Abacha, have not yet been implicated, according to a person familiar with the investigation.

Stanley's testimony may also pose concerns for Vice President Dick Cheney, who ran Halliburton between 1995 and 2000, when Stanley was appointed as KBR's chief executive officer. Cheney has consistently denied wrongdoing.

Law enforcement officials familiar with the investigation said that in previous interviews, Stanley repeatedly said that then-CEO Cheney had no knowledge of the bribes. At the time, however, Stanley was not a cooperating witness, a stance which changed in June when he was confronted with evidence of his involvement in the bribery scheme. The officials said they had not ruled out pursuing Cheney and other executives as the investigation continues.

The Vice President's office declined comment, citing the ongoing litigation.

Larry Veselka, Stanley's lawyer, said that his client would cooperate fully in any investigation. A judge will determine Stanley's final sentence depending on his compliance with the plea agreement.

"He's going to cooperate with wherever they want to go and whatever they want him to do," Veselka said on Thursday.

Stanley's rise and fall, detailed in U.S. and leaked French court documents, show what can happen when corporate greed mixes with the autocratic governments that control valuable natural resources like oil and copper in lawless corners of the globe.

Now 65, Stanley spent nearly his entire career in the oil business, a globetrotting high-level roustabout who made a specialty of dealing with governments in resource rich, accountability poor countries. He owned a million-dollar home in Texas and a property in one of London's swankest neighborhoods—a residence that he will now have to sell under his plea agreement.

A fearsome competitor, Stanley had a reputation as a hard drinker. At his hearing in Texas, Stanley held himself up by gripping the podium, and appeared frail. He appeared to wince at references to alcoholism as a mitigating factor for his actions, and to statements by the government prosecutor William Stuckwisch who characterized Stanley's behavior as "egregious."

"Jack was an extremely capable, smart and totally dedicated to the company," said one former colleague, who declined to be named because of the ongoing investigation. "I was shocked like everyone else when we heard about the bribes."

Others expressed less surprise that Halliburton was involved. Walter Carrington was the U.S. Ambassador to Nigeria in 1994, when Stanley acknowledged making the first bribe payments to the Nigerian government.

"I used to brag that because of our Foreign Corrupt Practices Act Americans weren't involved as other countries were. American businessmen would complain that it wasn't fair, other countries really ought to be doing more to keep people from doing this. It was a competitive disadvantage," said Carrington, who did not recall meeting Stanley. "Halliburton was a different kettle of fish. There were always stories going on about the way in which their people operated."

Stanley began his rise up the corporate ladder with M.W. Kellogg, an oil infrastructure company then owned by Dresser Industries. Dresser would later merge with Halliburton and Kellogg would become KBR.

Stanley was working as a senior executive at Kellogg in the 1990s when the firm formed a joint venture called TSKJ to pursue contracts to construct a liquefied natural gas plant on Bonny Island off Nigeria's oil-rich coast. Besides Kellogg, the TSKJ companies were France's Technip SA, Snamprogetti Netherlands B.V., an affiliate of Italy's ENI SpA, and Japan's JGC Corporation.

As Nigerian officials weighed the consortium's bid against a competing group led by San Francisco–based Bechtel Engineering, Stanley decided to improve the chances of winning by offering bribes, according to court documents filed by the Justice Department and the Securities and Exchange Commission.

He hatched a plan to hire consultants who could direct the money to Nigerian officials, the court documents said. One consultant, from England, would pay off higher-level Nigerian officials while a second, from Japan, would be responsible for bribing lower-ranking officials.

In November 1994, the U.K. consultant, who was not identified, allegedly told an associate that it would take $60 million to secure the contract, the court documents said. Of that money, $40 million to $45 million would go to the "first top-level executive branch" of Nigerian officials, while another $15 million to $20 million would go to other Nigerian officials.

Later that month, Stanley himself traveled to the Nigerian capital to meet with senior officials and confirm that the U.K. consultant would serve as a go-between, according to court documents and officials familiar with the investigation.

Over the next year, TSKJ, operating through subsidiary companies in the Portuguese offshore tax haven of Madeira Island, signed agreements to transfer millions of dollars to the U.K. consultant, according to court documents and people familiar with the investigation.

In December 1995, the Nigerian government awarded the first of the gas plant contracts to TSKJ. Over the next decade, the government awarded TSKJ four contracts worth a total of $6 billion to build and expand the plant.

Throughout that time, Stanley continued traveling to Nigeria to meet with senior officials and continued arranging payments through the U.K. and Japanese consultant firms, according to the court documents.

Abacha died suddenly in 1998. His death, according to Nigerian press accounts, was either the result of a marathon orgy with four prostitutes fueled by Viagra, or a conspiracy among his closest confidantes to poison him. No autopsy was ever performed. In the decade since Abacha's death, Switzerland alone has returned at least $500 million in his bank accounts to the government of Nigeria.

All told, Stanley traveled to Nigeria to meet with top officials on four occasions between 1994 and 2001 as part of the bribery scheme. TSKJ paid out $130 million in bribes through the U.K. consultant and $50 million through the Japanese firm, according to the court documents.

Although he was not identified or charged in U.S. court documents, French and Nigerian investigators have identified the primary consultant to the consortium as Jeffrey Tesler, a London attorney who worked with Nigerian immigrants, according to a transcript of testimony from the French case.

Tesler, who has been investigated by British and French authorities, has never been charged with wrongdoing. Last year, British authorities conducted a search of his London office at the urging of U.S. officials. A woman who answered the phone at Tesler's law office on Thursday said the attorney could not be reached and would have no comment.

In the middle of the bribery and plant construction, Kellogg changed hands. In 1998, Kellogg's parent company, Dresser Industries, merged with Halliburton, the oil services giant.

Cheney, then-CEO of Halliburton, arranged the merger during a quail hunting trip. Afterwards, Cheney appointed Stanley to head KBR, a newly formed construction and logistics subsidiary that grew out of the merger.

In a 1999 article in *Middle East Economic Digest*, Cheney praised Stanley: "We took Jack Stanley [and a colleague] . . . to head up the organization and that has helped tremendously."

As allegations of corruption mounted, however, Halliburton conducted its own internal investigation into the charges. In June 2004, the company publicly fired Stanley, then working as a consultant, for improper personal enrichment. The company also severed all relations with Tesler's firm, Tri-Star Investments.

The bribery scandal is one of many involving Halliburton's KBR subsidiary in the past several years. KBR has repeatedly been criticized for overbilling the U.S. government for providing food, fuel and other services to U.S. soldiers in Iraq. Last year, Halliburton spun off KBR into a separate corporation.

KBR spokeswoman Heather Browne said the company had not yet reviewed the plea agreement. "KBR does not in any way condone or tolerate illegal or unethical behavior. The company stands firm in its unwavering commitment to conduct business with the utmost integrity," she said in a prepared statement.

Halliburton spokeswoman Cathy Mann declined comment, saying the company had not yet reviewed the plea agreement. Earlier this year, Halliburton reported that the Securities and Exchange Commission was dramatically widening the scope of the investigation to cover projects in multiple countries built during the last 20 years.

Those investigation may focus on Stanley's activities in other countries. Court documents show that Stanley worked with another consultant, identified as a dual national Lebanese and American citizen, in an elaborate kickback scheme.

Under the scheme, Stanley hired the consultant to help Halliburton and its predecessor firms arrange deals to build liquid natural gas projects not only in Nigeria, but also in Egypt, Yemen and Malaysia. From 1991 to 2004, the consultant directed a total of $10.8 million of the proceeds back to Stanley through a Swiss bank account. These deals involved Mr. Stanley's original employer, M.W. Kellogg, as well as KBR.

Reporting: This story is part of a joint reporting project between PBS's Frontline and ProPublica on international bribery, the subject of a coming documentary production. Marlena Telvick and Oriana Zill de Granados reported from Houston, Texas. Additional reporting contributed by Lowell Bergman, Jake Bernstein and T. Christian Miller. The story was written by T. Christian Miller.

II. What Is Covered Under the FCPA Anti-Bribery Provisions?

The FCPA anti-bribery provisions, codified in § 30A of the Exchange Act, prohibit:

> [A]n offer, payment, promise to pay, or authorization of the payment of any money, or offer, gift, promise to give, or authorization of the giving of anything of value to—
> (1) any foreign official for purposes of—
>   (A)
>   (i) influencing any act or decision of such foreign official in his official capacity,

(ii) inducing such foreign official to do or omit to do any act in violation of the lawful duty of such official, or

(iii) securing any improper advantage; or

(B) inducing such foreign official to use his influence with a foreign government or instrumentality thereof to affect or influence any act or decision of such government or instrumentality, in order to assist such issuer in obtaining or retaining business for or with, or directing business to, any person;

(2) any foreign political party or official thereof or any candidate for foreign political office for purposes of—

(A)

(i) influencing any act or decision of such foreign official in his official capacity,

(ii) inducing such foreign official to do or omit to do any act in violation of the lawful duty of such official, or

(iii) securing any improper advantage; or

(B) inducing such party, official, or candidate to use its or his influence with a foreign government or instrumentality thereof to affect or influence any act or decision of such government or instrumentality, in order to assist such issuer in obtaining or retaining business for or with, or directing business to, any person; or

(3) any person, while knowing that all or a portion of such money or thing of value will be offered, given, or promised, directly or indirectly, to any foreign official, to any foreign political party or official thereof, or to any candidate for foreign political office, for purposes of—

(A)

(i) influencing any act or decision of such foreign official, political party, party official, or candidate in his or its official capacity,

(ii) inducing such foreign official, political party, party official, or candidate to do or omit to do any act in violation of the lawful duty of such foreign official, political party, party official, or candidate, or

(iii) securing any improper advantage; or

(B) inducing such foreign official, political party, party official, or candidate to use his or its influence with a foreign government or instrumentality thereof to affect or influence any act or decision of such government or instrumentality, in order to assist such issuer in obtaining or retaining business for or with, or directing business to, any person.[13]

In any case involving a potential violation of the FCPA anti-bribery provisions, the prosecution has the burden of proving the following four elements beyond a reasonable doubt: that the defendant (1) sought to obtain a business advantage, (2) by offering, promising, or giving something of value (3) to a foreign official (4) with corrupt intent to induce that official to abuse his office. We examine each of these elements in the sections below.

---

13. 15 U.S.C. § 77dd-1 (2012).

Notes and Questions

Given the scarcity of FCPA case law, the DOJ remains the primary authority for interpreting the provisions of the statute. Issuers, U.S. companies, and individuals, under 28 C.F.R. § 80.1 *et seq.,* may request and receive guidance from the DOJ in the form of an opinion release. As will become clear in the following chapters, many aspects of the FCPA anti-bribery provisions remain ambiguous. In cases where a company is considering entering into a transaction, but is unsure about the legality of that transaction under the FCPA, obtaining an opinion release can provide clarity and help the company in deciding how to proceed. As § 80.1 explains,

> These procedures enable issuers and domestic concerns to obtain an opinion of the Attorney General as to whether certain specified, prospective—not hypothetical—conduct conforms with the Department's present enforcement policy regarding the antibribery provisions of the Foreign Corrupt Practices Act of 1977, as amended, 15 U.S.C. 78dd-1 and 78dd-2.

Opinion releases are based on the facts represented by the requestor, and can provide the requestor with assurance that it will not be prosecuted if it proceeds with the transaction as described in the request. Requesting an opinion release involves a tradeoff:

> [An opinion release] necessarily impose[s] demanding standards and prescriptive timeframes in return for specific assurances from DOJ, which SEC, as a matter of discretion, also honors. . . . [B]ecause of the nature of such an opinion, it will likely contain more stringent requirements than may be necessary in all circumstances.[14]

Section 80.6 sets forth the general requirements for an opinion release request:

> Each request shall be specific and must be accompanied by all relevant and material information bearing on the conduct for which an FCPA Opinion is requested and on the circumstances of the prospective conduct, including background information, complete copies of all operative documents, and detailed statements of all collateral or oral understandings, if any. The requesting issuer or domestic concern is under an affirmative obligation to make full and true disclosure with respect to the conduct for which an opinion is requested. Each request on behalf of a requesting issuer or corporate domestic concern must be signed by an appropriate senior officer with operational responsibility for the conduct that is the subject of the request and who has been designated by the requestor's chief executive officer to sign the opinion request. In appropriate cases, the Department of Justice may require the chief executive officer of each requesting issuer or corporate domestic concern to sign the request. All requests of other domestic concerns must also be signed. The person signing the request

---

14. FCPA Guide, *supra* note 4, at 29.

must certify that it contains a true, correct and complete disclosure with respect to the proposed conduct and the circumstances of the conduct.[15]

A. The Business Purpose Test

The FCPA does not apply to all corrupt payments to foreign officials, but only to those intended to obtain or retain business on behalf of the payor or a third party. This requirement is known as the "business purpose test." The Fifth Circuit found that the business purpose test broadly "target[s] bribery paid to engender assistance in improving the business opportunities of the payor or his beneficiary, irrespective of whether that assistance be direct or indirect, and irrespective of whether it be related to administering the law, awarding, extending, or renewing a contract, or executing or preserving an agreement.[16]

The FCPA Guide lists the following circumstances as satisfying the business purpose test:

- Winning a contract
- Influencing the procurement process
- Circumventing the rules for importation of products
- Gaining access to nonpublic bid tender information
- Evading taxes or penalties
- Influencing the adjudication of lawsuits or enforcement actions
- Obtaining exceptions to regulations
- Avoiding contract termination[17]

A Resource Guide to the U.S. Foreign Corrupt Practices Act

Criminal Division of the U.S. Department of Justice and the Enforcement Division of the U.S. Securities and Exchange Commission[18]

THE BUSINESS PURPOSE TEST

Not surprisingly, many enforcement actions involve bribes to obtain or retain government contracts. The FCPA also prohibits bribes in the conduct of business or to gain a business advantage. For example, bribe payments made to secure favorable tax treatment, to reduce or eliminate customs duties, to

---

15. 28 C.F.R. § 80.6 (2017).
16. United States v. Kay, 359 F.3d 738, 750-51 (5th Cir. 2004).
17. FCPA GUIDE, *supra* note 4, at 13.
18. FCPA GUIDE, *supra* note 4, at 13-14.

obtain government action to prevent competitors from entering a market, or to circumvent a licensing or permit requirement, all satisfy the business purpose test.

In 2004, the U.S. Court of Appeals for the Fifth Circuit addressed the business purpose test in *United States v. Kay* and held that bribes paid to obtain favorable tax treatment—which reduced a company's customs duties and sales taxes on imports—could constitute payments made to "obtain or retain" business within the meaning of the FCPA. The court explained that in enacting the FCPA, "Congress meant to prohibit a range of payments wider than only those that directly influence the acquisition or retention of government contracts or similar commercial or industrial arrangements." The *Kay* court found that: "[t]he congressional target was bribery paid to engender assistance in improving the business opportunities of the payor or his beneficiary, irrespective of whether that assistance be direct or indirect, and irrespective of whether it be related to administering the law, awarding, extending, or renewing a contract, or executing or preserving an agreement."

Accordingly, *Kay* held that payments to obtain favorable tax treatment can, under appropriate circumstances, violate the FCPA:

> Avoiding or lowering taxes reduces operating costs and thus increases profit margins, thereby freeing up funds that the business is otherwise legally obligated to expend. And this, in turn, enables it to take any number of actions to the disadvantage of competitors. Bribing foreign officials to lower taxes and customs duties certainly can provide an unfair advantage over competitors and thereby be of assistance to the payor in obtaining or retaining business.
>
> * * *
>
> [W]e hold that Congress intended for the FCPA to apply broadly to payments intended to assist the payor, either directly or indirectly, in obtaining or retaining business for some person, and that bribes paid to foreign tax officials to secure illegally reduced customs and tax liability constitute a type of payment that can fall within this broad coverage.

In short, while the FCPA does not cover every type of bribe paid around the world for every purpose, it does apply broadly to bribes paid to help obtain or retain business, which can include payments made to secure a wide variety of unfair business advantages.

Hypothetical: Business Purpose Test

Glenville, Inc. ("Glenville") is a U.S.-based multinational company engaged in the provision of engineering consulting services. Glenville was recently awarded a contract to provide consulting services to the government of Albania. In order to perform the contract, Glenville established an office in Tirana, where 20 of its employees will be stationed during the one-year term of the contract. Because of the high incidence of violent crime in Tirana,

> Glenville paid bribes to the Tirana police chief to ensure an increased police presence around its facility.
>
> Do the bribes paid by Glenville meet the business purpose test?

B. "Anything of Value"

The FCPA prohibits an "offer, payment, promise to pay, or authorization of the payment of any money, or offer, gift, promise to give, or authorization of the giving of anything of value to" a foreign official.[19] Similarly to the domestic bribery statute, there is no minimum threshold amount for a corrupt gift or payment under the FCPA.[20] It prohibits even an offer or promise to give something of value to a government official.[21] While cash is the most obvious form of corrupt payment, "[c]ompanies and individuals have faced liability for providing travel and entertainment, offering employment to family members, funneling money to the election campaign of a political candidate, paying for shopping excursions and medical expenses, and for arranging the services of prostitutes."[22]

Courts have broadly defined the term "anything of value" in the context of the domestic bribery statute,[23] holding that "the focus of the . . . term is to be placed on the value which the [recipient] subjectively attaches to the items received."[24] In *U.S. v. Williams*, the Second Circuit held:

> The phrase "anything of value" in bribery and related statutes has consistently been given a broad meaning . . . to carry out the congressional purpose of punishing misuse of public office. Corruption of office occurs when the officeholder agrees to misuse his office in the expectation of gain, whether or not he has correctly assessed the worth of the bribe.[25]

The breadth of the term "anything of value" is constrained by the statute's intent requirement. The FCPA Guide states:

> Regardless of size, for a gift or other payment to violate the statute, the payor must have corrupt intent—that is, the intent to improperly influence the government official. The corrupt intent requirement protects companies that engage in the ordinary and legitimate promotion of their businesses while targeting conduct that seeks to improperly induce officials into misusing their positions.

---

19. 15 U.S.C. § 77dd-1 (2012).

20. *See* FCPA GUIDE, *supra* note 4, at 15. The SEC brought an enforcement action against Delta & Pine Land Co. for improper payments to Turkish officials totaling $43,000 "to obtain governmental reports and certifications that were necessary . . . to operate its business in Turkey." Delta & Pine Land Co. et al., Exchange Act Release No. 56138, 2007 WL 2140170 (July 26, 2007). Similarly, in the enforcement action against Veraz Networks, Inc., a payment of merely $4,500 was deemed to violate the statute. Complaint, SEC v. Veraz Networks, Inc., 10-cv-2849 (N.D. Cal. June 29, 2010), https://www.sec.gov/litigation/complaints/2010/comp21581.pdf.

21. FCPA GUIDE, *supra* note 4, at 23.

22. O'MELVENY & MYERS LLP, FOREIGN CORRUPT PRACTICES ACT: AN O'MELVENY HANDBOOK 19 (7th ed. 2013).

23. *Id.*

24. United States v. Gorman, 807 F.2d 1299, 1305 (6th Cir. 1986).

25. United States v. Williams, 705 F.2d 603, 623 (2d Cir. 1983) (citations omitted).

Thus, it is difficult to envision any scenario in which the provision of cups of coffee, taxi fare, or company promotional items of nominal value would ever evidence corrupt intent, and neither DOJ nor SEC has ever pursued an investigation on the basis of such conduct. Moreover, as in all areas of federal law enforcement, DOJ and SEC exercise discretion in deciding which cases promote law enforcement priorities and justify investigation. Certain patterns, however, have emerged: DOJ and SEC anti-bribery enforcement actions have focused on small payments and gifts only when they comprise part of a systemic or long-standing course of conduct that evidences a scheme to corruptly pay foreign officials to obtain or retain business. These assessments are necessarily fact specific.[26]

> Anti-bribery enforcement actions have focused on small payments and gifts only when they comprise part of a systemic or long-standing course of conduct that evidences a scheme to corruptly pay foreign officials to obtain or retain business.
>
> —FCPA Guide[27]

Hypothetical: Payment of Medical Expenses

The following is an excerpt from DOJ Opinion Release 13-01:[28]

> The Department of Justice (the "Department") has reviewed the Foreign Corrupt Practices Act ("FCPA") Opinion Procedure Request of a U.S. national ("Requestor") that was submitted on October 15, 2013 . . . regarding whether certain specified, prospective—not hypothetical—conduct conforms with the Department's present enforcement policy regarding the anti-bribery provisions of the FCPA.
>
> Relevant Facts and Circumstances
>
> Requestor is a partner with a U.S. law firm (the "Law Firm"). Requestor and other attorneys with the Law Firm have represented Foreign Country A in various international arbitrations. Requestor presently represents Foreign Country A in two international arbitrations for which the Law Firm receives payment. In the past 18 months, the Law Firm has billed fees to Foreign Country A of over $2 million, and Requestor anticipates that in 2014, the fees on matters for Foreign Country A will exceed $2 million.
>
> Over the past several years of these representations, Requestor has become a personal friend of Foreign Official, who works in Foreign Country A's Office of the Attorney General (the "OAG"). The OAG is responsible for selecting and contracting with international counsel on behalf of Foreign Country A. According to Requestor, however, Foreign Official has not had and will not have in the future any role in the selection of Requestor or the Law Firm as counsel for Foreign Country A. Requestor is not the Law Firm's "primary relationship attorney," "originating attorney," or "lead

26. FCPA Guide, *supra* note 4, at 15.
27. *Id.*
28. Foreign Corrupt Practices Act Review, U.S. Dep't of Just., Crim. Div. Opinion 13-01, https://www.justice.gov/sites/default/files/criminal-fraud/legacy/2014/01/02/13-01.pdf.

attorney" for the OAG or the government of Foreign Country A, but has participated in the selection or pitch processes for new business with OAG and/or the government of Foreign Country A, and would expect to do so with regard to future business from these clients.

Requestor proposes to pay the medical expenses of Foreign Official's daughter, who suffers from a severe medical condition that cannot effectively be treated in Foreign Country A or anywhere in the region. The physicians treating Foreign Official's daughter have recommended that she receive inpatient care at a specialized facility located in Foreign Country B. Requestor reports that the treatment will cost between approximately $13,500 and $20,500 and that Foreign Official lacks financial means to pay for this treatment for his daughter.

In addition to the above representations, Requestor has further represented that among other things:

- Requestor's intention in paying for the medical treatment of Foreign Official's daughter is purely humanitarian, with no intent to influence the decision of any foreign official in Foreign Country A with regard to engaging the services of the Law Firm, Requestor, or any third person.
- The funds used to pay for the medical treatment will be Requestor's own personal funds. Requestor will neither seek nor receive reimbursement from the Law Firm for such payments.
- Requestor will make all payments directly to the facility where Foreign Official's daughter will receive treatment in Foreign Country B. Foreign Official will pay for the costs of his daughter's related travel.
- Foreign Country A is expected to retain the Law Firm to work on one new matter in the near future. Requestor is presently unaware of any additional, potential matters as to which Foreign Country A might retain the Law Firm. However, if such a matter develops, Requestor anticipates that Foreign Country A would likely retain the Law Firm given its successful track record and their strong relationship.
- Under the law for Foreign Country A, any government agency such as OAG that hires an outside law firm must publicly publish a reasoned decision justifying the engagement. It is a crime punishable by imprisonment under the penal code of Foreign Country A for any civil servant or public employee to engage in corrupt behavior in connection with public contracting.

In addition, Foreign Official and Requestor have discussed this matter transparently with their respective employers. The government of Foreign Country A and the leadership of the Law Firm have expressly indicated that they have no objection to the proposed payment of medical expenses. Indeed, Requestor has provided a certified letter from the Attorney General of Foreign Country A that represents the following:

- The decision by Requestor to pay for or not to pay for this medical treatment will have no impact on any current or future decisions of the OAG in deciding on the hiring of international legal counsel.

> • In the opinion of the Attorney General, the payment of medical expenses for Foreign Official's daughter under these circumstances would not violate any provision of the laws of Foreign Country A.
>
> The Attorney General further confirms that while Foreign Official handles aspects of the cases on which the Law Firm and Requestor work, Foreign Official has not taken part in any decisions regarding the Firm's retention for any matter, nor would Foreign Official have such a role in any possible future decision regarding contracting outside counsel, as such decisions are outside of Foreign Official's responsibilities.
>
> Finally, Foreign Official has represented and warranted in writing that he has not had, does not have, and will not have any influence in the contracting of international lawyers to represent Foreign Country A; he will not attempt to assist Requestor or the Law Firm in the award of future work; and he would not get involved in any decision that the OAG might make in the future in this regard.
>
> How should the DOJ respond to this request?

In the Matter of JP Morgan Chase & Co.

Release No. 79335 (Nov. 17, 2016)[29]

Order Instituting Cease-and-Desist Proceedings Pursuant to Section 21C of the Securities Exchange Act of 1934, Making Findings, and Imposing a Cease-and-Desist Order

. . . .

II.

In anticipation of the institution of these proceedings, JPMorgan has submitted an Offer of Settlement (the "Offer") which the Commission has determined to accept.

. . . .

III.

On the basis of this Order and JPMorgan's Offer, the Commission finds that:

SUMMARY

This matter concerns violations of the anti-bribery, books and records, and internal controls provisions of the Foreign Corrupt Practices Act ("FCPA") by JPMorgan. Between 2006 and 2013, the firm provided valuable jobs and internships to the relatives and friends of certain key executives of its clients, prospective clients, and foreign government officials in the Asia-Pacific region ("APAC")

---

29. J.P. Morgan Chase & Co., Exchange Act Release No. 79335, 2016 WL 6804113 (Nov. 17, 2016).

as a personal benefit to the requesting officials in order to obtain or retain investment banking business or other benefits for the firm. Many of JPMorgan's clients were state-owned entities ("SOEs"), and therefore the client executives requesting employment for their relatives and friends were foreign government officials under the FCPA. The firm provided these jobs and internships with the intent to corruptly influence the foreign government officials making the requests.

Investment bankers at JPMorgan's subsidiary in Asia, JPMorgan Securities (Asia Pacific) Limited ("JPMorgan APAC"), created a client referral hiring program to leverage the promise of well-paying, career building JPMorgan employment for the relatives and friends of senior officials with its clients in order to assist JPMorgan APAC in obtaining or retaining business. A special hiring program ("Client Referral Program") was created at JPMorgan APAC for referred candidates that bypassed the firm's normal hiring process and was made available exclusively to candidates referred by clients, prospective clients, or foreign government officials ("Referral Hires"). Non-referral JPMorgan APAC hires were subjected to a rigorous screening process and competed against other candidates for a limited number of positions. Referral Hires did not compete against other candidates based on merit and, in most instances, were less qualified than those employees hired through the firm's non-referral hiring programs. Instead, Referral Hires were hired based on direct or potential links to investment banking revenue that could be generated from the referring client in exchange for the hire. Referral Hires whose relationships generated sufficient revenue for JPMorgan APAC were offered longer-term jobs, while others were given shorter terms of employment unless the referring client offered additional business to the firm. In 2010 and 2011, JPMorgan APAC employees created spreadsheets to track the revenue to the firm from clients whose candidates were hired through the Client Referral Program.

Over this seven-year period, JPMorgan hired approximately 200 interns and full-time employees at the request of its APAC clients, prospective clients, and foreign government officials. This included nearly 100 candidates referred by foreign government officials at more than twenty different Chinese SOEs. A number of the referral hires resulted in business for JPMorgan APAC. The referring SOEs entered into transactions totaling more than $100,000,000 in revenue for JPMorgan APAC or its affiliates during this period. JPMorgan also hired referrals from more than 10 different government agencies. JPMorgan APAC bankers leveraged connections with these government agencies to assist other JPMorgan APAC clients and the firm itself in navigating complicated regulatory landscapes.

JPMorgan APAC employees understood that hiring relatives and friends of foreign government officials for the purpose of obtaining or retaining business posed the risk of violating the FCPA. Nonetheless, JPMorgan APAC investment bankers and supporting personnel often provided inaccurate or incomplete information as part of the legal and compliance review designed to prevent these violations or withheld key information so that the Referral Hires would pass compliance review. The legal and compliance review of Referral Hires became a formality in which JPMorgan APAC investment bankers and supporting personnel provided inaccurate or incomplete answers to secure approval for hires without revealing the links to business as a result of certain Referral Hires. Of all the candidates that passed through JPMorgan APAC's Client Referral Program, none were rejected by the legal and compliance review.

JPMorgan failed to devise and maintain a system of internal accounting controls around its hiring practices sufficient to provide reasonable assurances that its employees were not bribing foreign officials in contravention of company policy. Likewise, JPMorgan APAC employees failed to follow the firm's internal accounting controls, and JPMorgan failed to implement other appropriate accounting controls to detect or prevent the Client Referral Program from being used to improperly benefit government officials. JPMorgan APAC employees took steps to hide the magnitude and purpose of the Client Referral Program from others within the firm, and devised a way to avoid having certain Referral Hires in APAC counted within JPMorgan APAC's internal year-end headcount calculations. For Referral Hires that originated in APAC but were employed outside of APAC, JPMorgan APAC employees failed to undertake a compliance review or impose conflict of interest restrictions despite knowledge of the FCPA and other risks.

JPMorgan also violated the books and records provisions of the FCPA. JPMorgan APAC personnel created and implemented a system by which inaccurate or incomplete questionnaires were submitted, reviewed, and approved by compliance in contravention of the internal policy created to prevent improper hiring of Referral Hires. The records reflected that they were hired for legitimate business purposes rather than as hires made to improperly benefit JPMorgan APAC investment banking business. JPMorgan APAC's internal records also inaccurately reflected the true number of client Referral Hires in the APAC region by taking steps to disguise the headcount relating to Referral Hires from others within the firm.

RESPONDENT

JPMorgan Chase & Co. is a Delaware corporation with its headquarters in New York, New York. The company's common stock is registered under Section 12(b) of the Exchange Act and listed on the New York Stock Exchange . . . .

OTHER RELEVANT ENTITIES AND INDIVIDUALS

JPMorgan Securities (Asia Pacific) Ltd. ("JPMorgan APAC") is a Hong Kong registered company and wholly owned and controlled subsidiary of JPMorgan. JPMorgan APAC operated as JPMorgan's investment banking office in Hong Kong and coordinated JPMorgan's investment banking operations in the Asia-Pacific region. JPMorgan APAC is responsible for JPMorgan's investment banking and certain other business in The People's Republic of China, Hong Kong, and other countries in the Asia-Pacific region.

FACTS

JPMorgan's Policies Prohibited the Hiring of Client Referrals in Exchange for Business

As early as 2001, JPMorgan recognized the FCPA risks in hiring the relatives of foreign government officials. JPMorgan therefore took steps to educate its employees on the potential dangers in hiring Referral Hires and the potential FCPA violations that could occur if Referral Hires were tied to business for the firm. JPMorgan's 2001 FCPA Compliance Policy noted that the "[h]iring of family members of foreign officials as employees, agents or consultants" was a "red flag . . . that could result in [an] FCPA violation." JPMorgan's 2005 anti-bribery training included an example where "[a]s an understood part of the deal, the company will hire . . . the daughter of a government official from that country, for an unpaid summer internship." This training noted that the hiring of the daughter could be a bribe because the "internship has some value and is a requirement for the deal to happen."

In or about September 2007, JPMorgan instituted a new Anti-Corruption Policy which provided that "the offer of internships or training for relatives of a public official" required legal and compliance pre-clearance. It also indicated that hiring individuals in order to win business was prohibited. Specifically, the Policy stated that "it is improper for a person to offer or give anything to a public official, either directly or through an intermediary, in an effort to secure an advantage that would not have been granted if the offer or gift had not been made," noting that "'value' can include such things as the offer of internships or training for relatives of a public official." This policy applied to JPMorgan APAC. In addition, in 2007 JPMorgan APAC instituted training for employees in the region specifying that pre-clearance from compliance was required before JPMorgan APAC could hire Referral Hires because "[a]n offer of internship to a relative of a non-U.S. public official suggests an advantage by causing the official to misuse his or her position."

In approximately June 2011, JPMorgan implemented an updated Anti-Corruption Policy which also applied to JPMorgan APAC. Training provided regarding this Policy noted that "almost anything can meet the definition of a 'bribe,' including . . . internships [and] employment." The Policy further stated that "[n]o employee may directly or indirectly offer, promise, grant or authorize the giving of money or anything else of value to a government official to influence official action or obtain an improper advantage."

During this period, JPMorgan APAC also had an established, highly-selective hiring program for undergraduates and graduates to enter JPMorgan APAC's summer internship and analyst/associate employment programs, primarily in Hong Kong. Hiring was done mainly through campus recruiting at prestigious, highly-selective schools in the United States and elsewhere, as well as through an on-line application process. Admission to the JPMorgan APAC hiring program was highly competitive, with candidates competing based on educational background, prior experience, language, and other skills. Successful applicants usually had a minimum grade point average, a demonstrated affinity for and interest in financial services work, language skills, and advanced through multiple rounds of interviews. Throughout this period JPMorgan APAC had more applicants than it had available positions with the firm.

JPMorgan APAC Created a Client Referral Hiring Program in 2006

In or around 2006, JPMorgan APAC's investment banking group created and implemented a referral hiring program (referred to colloquially during the relevant time period as the "Sons & Daughters Program") whereby certain internships and short-term, entry-level employment opportunities were made available only to Referral Hires in order to accommodate frequent requests to hire the relatives and friends of senior executives or officials with its clients, prospective clients, and contacts within foreign government ministries. JPMorgan APAC created the "Sons & Daughters" program based on these requests from senior executives or officials and a perception of similar actions being taken by its competitors. From the outset, the primary goal of client referral hiring was to generate revenue for JPMorgan APAC by extending personal favors to client executives and government officials through hiring their relatives and friends.

By contrast with the established JPMorgan APAC non-referral hiring program, most JPMorgan APAC Referral Hires would not have secured positions with the firm but for the client relationship and request. Referral Hires generally did not meet the minimum educational, grade-point average, or background qualifications that JPMorgan APAC looked for in its non-referral hiring programs. Referral Hires were not subjected to the rigorous, multi-round interviews that non-Referral Hires had to go through before hiring. Likewise, Referral Hires were not evaluated based on merit, but instead were evaluated based on JPMorgan APAC's relationship with and prospects for future revenue from the referring clients.

During this time it was widely recognized within JPMorgan APAC that Referral Hires generally were not subject to the same requirements, workload, and expectations as non-referral APAC employees. Nonetheless, these Referral Hires were given the same titles as non-referral employees as well as significant salaries and other benefits. JPMorgan APAC employees commented on the lack of capabilities of many Referral Hires, with some employees referring to them as "photocopiers." Referral Hires were sometimes given special consideration regarding work assignments and promotions and protected from rigorous work schedules. For example, in 2008, one senior JPMorgan APAC investment banker referred to a Referral Hire as a "protected species requiring [senior management] input. His reporting line to you is accountable but like national service."

JPMorgan APAC investment bankers were made aware of the risks inherent in referral hiring under the FCPA and other laws. In 2006, the head of Junior Resources Management ("JRM") for JPMorgan APAC, a business support team which oversaw the hiring and staffing of all interns and junior investment bankers on transactions in the region, sent an email to JPMorgan APAC investment bankers regarding "Sons & Daughters" which noted that:

> "As you know, the firm does not condone the hiring of the children or other relatives of clients or potential clients of the Firm or other people who might be helpful to the Firm for the purpose of securing or potentially securing business for the Firm. In fact, the firm's policies expressly forbid this. There are no exceptions."

This was further reinforced in 2007 when JPMorgan APAC legal and compliance staff noted in a message to employees that for Referral Hires "[t]he firm should not be currently actively pitching for any transaction of such client" and "[t]he firm should not be subject to any direct regulation of such government authority" making the referral. In analyzing Referral Hires, legal and compliance looked to see that "[t]he candidate should have been through usual interview process and feedback from interviewers should be positive." However, the Client Referral Program frequently did not follow these stated limitations.

Based on the recognition of potential FCPA issues in hiring Referral Hires, in or about 2006, JPMorgan APAC's legal and compliance personnel developed a process to screen prospective Referral Hires for potential FCPA and other risks including conflicts of interest. As part of this screening process, JPMorgan APAC legal and compliance created a "Sons & Daughters" questionnaire to elicit information regarding the potential Referral Hire. Under the process as it was intended to work, each requesting banker was required to fill out the questionnaire for each specific hire, and then submit that questionnaire to JPMorgan APAC legal and compliance staff for review and approval.

The "Sons & Daughters" questionnaire sought information in order to screen for potential FCPA and other risks from hiring a specific Referral Hire. The questionnaire sought confirmation that the Referral Hire: (1) went "through the usual application/interview process," (2) had the "necessary qualifications for the position," and (3) was rated "against other applicants for the position." The questionnaire also sought information regarding the referring client or entity, including whether JPMorgan was "currently working on, or pitching for any deal or transaction" with the referring client or potential client, and whether "JPMorgan [was] seeking future opportunity to work or develop a relationship with such client." Finally, the questionnaire sought information from the referring banker on the "expected benefit to JPMorgan in employing the candidate."

JPMorgan APAC legal and compliance also imposed restrictions on what confidential information Referral Hires were able to access. As part of the "Sons & Daughters" questionnaire review process, JPMorgan APAC legal and compliance made the hiring of most Referral Hires conditional on the bankers "walling off" the Referral Hire from business directly involving or related to the referring client or entity. This was designed to prevent conflicts of interest and the sharing of sensitive, confidential information regarding JPMorgan's clients, or the competitors of those clients, with the relatives and friends of senior officials with those same clients. In cases in which the referring person was employed by a government ministry, Referral Hires were supposed to be walled off from transactions involving that ministry.

Due to the misconduct of JPMorgan APAC investment bankers and the failures of APAC legal and compliance staff, the "Sons & Daughters" questionnaire process was an ineffective review that failed to operate as an effective check on potential violations. JPMorgan APAC legal and compliance staff did not understand the actual nature and operation of the Client Referral Program, and did not take adequate steps to fully investigate the extent and purpose of the Program during the relevant time period. This was due in part to JPMorgan APAC investment bankers failing to share complete information on the Client Referral Program with legal and compliance personnel. It was also due to a fundamental misunderstanding of the Client Referral Program by JPMorgan APAC legal and compliance, and a failure to investigate potential issues when they arose. For example, in 2007 as part of the review of Referral Hires, an attorney with JPMorgan's global legal team conveyed to his colleague in JPMorgan APAC that "I thought the Sons & Daughters Program was ended . . . . [JPMorgan Global Compliance officers] are telling . . . [personnel] that this program doesn't work from an FCPA standpoint. What are your thoughts?" In response, a JPMorgan APAC compliance attorney noted that "'Sons & Daughters' is not an active programme to solicit connected persons to work for us in the hope of obtaining business." Rather, it was described as a "filter process" involving a questionnaire and review by the legal staff. The attorney went on to note: "If we take a Son or Daughter, it is because they have applied for an internship like thousands of others, meet objective academic requirements, there are no FCPA concerns. No favours are done. They get treated like everyone else." This JPMorgan APAC compliance professional's understanding was not an accurate description of the Client Referral Program at the time.

JPMorgan APAC Control Failures

Beginning no later than 2007, JPMorgan APAC investment bankers began using the hiring of Referral Hires to assist in obtaining banking business and other advantages from senior officials at SOEs, private sector clients, and government agencies. In order to achieve the business objectives of the Client Referral Program, JPMorgan APAC investment bankers provided incorrect, misleading, incomplete, or untruthful responses to the "Sons & Daughters" questionnaires. Certain JPMorgan APAC investment bankers used the questionnaire to hide the true purpose of the Referral Hire. Investment banking and legal and compliance support personnel frequently assisted the investment bankers with drafting and modifying questionnaires that failed to state the true purpose for some Referral Hires. Draft questionnaires that suggested a potential improper benefit from hiring a Referral Hire were sometimes edited by bankers and support staff to include responses that would pass scrutiny. In addition, JPMorgan APAC support personnel supplied questionnaires with pre-populated answers to questions, including for example a standard answer that there was "[N]o expected benefit" from hiring a Referral Hire. The questionnaires were also answered as a matter of practice to give the appearance that the Referral Hires went through the non-referral hiring process rather than the special Client Referral Program, which was inaccurate. For these reasons, the "Sons & Daughters" questionnaire that was designed to prevent FCPA violations was wholly ineffective. In fact, JPMorgan's APAC legal and compliance staff did not reject a single Referral Hire candidate from 2007 through 2012.

JPMorgan APAC legal and compliance personnel did not take adequate steps to identify or mitigate the risks of bribery and corruption in approving Referral Hires. For example, in 2006, a JPMorgan APAC paralegal tasked with organizing and submitting Referral Hire questionnaires for review informed a JPMorgan

APAC attorney that she was told by an investment banker that JPMorgan APAC was "now pitching for a . . . project" from a referring client, and that the project "may potentially result from the hiring of [candidate] as a summer analyst. I don't feel quite comfortable about this and would like to have your views." The paralegal drafted a memorandum to members of the APAC legal and compliance staff, noting that "[w]e will be exposed to a risk of being alleged of bribing [the client] for the . . . project or any other . . . projects," especially considering that the candidate would not otherwise be hired on her own merits. The hire was nonetheless approved after another JPMorgan APAC investment banker stated that the hire was not in exchange "for return of any business from [the client]."

JPMorgan APAC support personnel also assisted APAC investment bankers in drafting and modifying "Sons & Daughters" questionnaires in order to avoid scrutiny and receive compliance approval for specific Referral Hires. This led to multiple cases of "Sons & Daughters" questionnaires being revised to remove references to a specific or implied benefit from a client Referral Hire before submitting those questionnaires for final approval. For example, in 2010, a JPMorgan APAC investment banker noted in a questionnaire for a prospective Referral Hire that JPMorgan was pitching for a role in the client's forthcoming IPO. Regarding the "expected benefit" from the Referral Hire, he wrote:

> "It will strengthen our relationship with [client executive] and solidifying [sic] our position as an advisor to him and the IPOs of his companies (expected to be >$500mm in offering size)."

In response, the JPMorgan APAC paralegal tasked with reviewing and commenting on Referral Hire questionnaires noted:

> "The firm does not condone the hiring of client's referred person who might be helpful to the firm for the purpose of securing or potentially securing business for the firm. The above comment is not acceptable from [legal and compliance's] perspective.
>   Please clarify to what extent the proposed hire will affect our position in our participation of the IPO [sic]?

Is hiring of the intern part of any agreement to secure business of the firm?"

In response to these questions, the investment banker contradicted his prior responses, and now replied: (1) "Hiring of this candidate will not benefit the firm," (2) "It will not affect our position," and (3) "No." The JPMorgan APAC attorney reviewing the proposed Referral Hire was then told by the paralegal that the investment banker "has confirmed that the proposed hire will not affect our position in our participation of the IPO and hiring of the candidate is not part of any agreement to secure business of the firm [sic]." The initial answers from the investment bankers were not shared with the JPMorgan APAC attorney, and the Referral Hire request was approved.

None of the hires made through the Client Referral Program were reviewed or assessed alongside normal JPMorgan APAC hires, yet the "Sons & Daughters" questionnaires reviewed by legal and compliance noted that the candidates had the "necessary qualifications" and were rated well against "other applicants" for the position. These responses were inaccurate, as the Client Referral Program operated separate from JPMorgan APAC's normal hiring program and candidates were hired based on the referring client relationship.

For Referral Hires that originated in APAC but were employed outside of the region, such as New York, JPMorgan APAC bankers typically would not submit questionnaires or seek compliance review of the potential hires despite knowledge that such questionnaires were part of the controls for hiring Referral Hires. In such cases, JPMorgan APAC's human resources and legal departments were usually not made aware of the hire. Likewise, their counterparts in the jurisdiction in which the Referral Hire was going to work (such as New York) were usually unaware of any client referral aspect to the hire. Further, JPMorgan did not always restrict such Referral Hires from working on deals involving the referring client because no such instruction came from JPMorgan APAC's compliance department.

Beginning in 2009, JPMorgan APAC personnel structured the contracts for full-time Referral Hires to withhold the total number of Referral Hires in APAC from other parts of the firm and give the appearance of conformity with JPMorgan's internal, year-end global headcount restrictions. The revised Client Referral Program was designed to give offers to Referral Hires from "Jan 15 to Dec 15, thereby avoiding year end count." Referral Hires were given contracts that would end in mid-December and then a new contract would re-start the following January, thus avoiding counting the Referral Hire on JPMorgan APAC's internal, year-end headcount numbers which were reported as of December 31st. This allowed JPMorgan APAC to continue to make Referral Hires but not limit the number of non-referral junior investment bankers hired by JPMorgan APAC who were capable of functioning as junior investment bankers. In 2010, the JPMorgan APAC employee tasked with managing headcount noted he had reached "agreement with [coordinator for Client Referral Program] at start of year was [Referral Hires] would NOT cross year end. We should push [coordinator] on that because we specifically agreed to track them this way to create additional slots for full time staff [sic]." The same JPMorgan APAC employee noted that for Referral Hires, "[f]rom a budget perspective we keep these [Referral Hires] off balance sheet and are supposed to have a maximum of 10 [Client Referral Program] interns at one time on contracts that do not cross a year end." Another JPMorgan APAC employee discussed structuring contracts for Referral Hires so that the contracts would end in December "[i]n order to have them NOT counted toward our year end headcount next year. . . ."

JPMorgan APAC, including legal and compliance, investment banking, and human resources personnel, failed to properly review or stop the Client Referral Program until 2013. At that time, a JPMorgan APAC compliance officer in a newly-created position was tasked with reviewing and approving client Referral Hire questionnaires. In denying a request to hire a Referral Hire, he stated that hiring Referral Hires at the request of clients and outside of the normal hiring system was impermissible under JPMorgan's compliance and anti-corruption policies. He further stated that "I'm afraid from an anti bribery [sic] and corruption standpoint, we cannot create positions to accommodate client requests. . . . Employment within JPMorgan is seen as a significant benefit (in terms of training, experience, and improving the resume)." This effectively ended the Client Referral Program, although new Referral Hires continued to work at JPMorgan APAC in the summer of 2013.

JPMorgan APAC Investment Bankers Knew That Referral Hires Were Hired to Obtain or Retain Business

JPMorgan APAC investment bankers sought to use the Client Referral Program to exchange valuable employment for assistance with obtaining or retaining banking business from senior executives with its clients, potential clients, and foreign government officials. This assistance included the awarding of deals to JPMorgan APAC based in part on hiring Referral Hires, non-public information on clients and future deals, influence with foreign government officials, introductions and meetings, and other benefits.

Over time, senior JPMorgan APAC investment bankers designed a system to provide employment to referrals from "decision-makers" or those with the ability to influence upcoming investment banking transactions at their clients. For example, a senior banker responsible for overseeing JPMorgan APAC junior banking hiring and staffing, including the Referral Hires ("APAC Banker A"), encouraged other bankers to prioritize referral requests received from "decision-makers" or those who had the ability to influence an upcoming banking deal over less influential individuals. APAC Banker A acknowledged in communications with his colleagues that they should consider whether the hire would bring near-term revenue to the firm. In a 2008 email regarding a Referral Hire request from a senior executive with a private sector JPMorgan APAC client in China, APAC Banker A told another investment banker seeking his approval for the hire, copying the head of JPMorgan APAC investment banking, that: "I am supportive of bringing [the referral candidate] on board given what's at stake . . . . A couple of points to discuss and agree prior to any offer being made to [referral candidate]: how do you get the best quid pro quo from the relationship upon confirmation of the offer." The banker seeking to make the hire responded "[t]he client has communicated clearly the quid pro quo on this hire and the team should start working on the [upcoming] IPO asap." Although the questionnaire reviewed by compliance relating to this hire disclosed that JPMorgan APAC was working on one deal for a company affiliated with the referring executive and pitching for another, the questionnaire did not disclose any discussion of the "quid pro quo" from this Referral Hire. Instead, the questionnaire reviewed by compliance indicated that there would be "no expected benefit" to the firm from the hire.

These senior JPMorgan APAC personnel also understood that client Referral Hires were for the most part not qualified on their own merit for the positions they were given when compared with non-referral employees, yet special considerations were taken to benefit the business relationship. For example, in 2010, APAC Banker A wrote to the banker who assisted him with hiring and staffing of junior JPMorgan APAC bankers that "we picked up a new mandate in Taiwan today — all we have to do is get [referral candidate] a full time analyst job at JPM in NY. Mission impossible?" In response, the other banker wrote "Can try . . . his napping habit will be an eye-opening experience for our NY colleagues if he gets a job." APAC Banker A later sent an email titled "client referral" to other investment bankers in the United States in September 2010 in which he wrote: "[w]e have a very good [private sector] client in Taiwan who has asked that we find an IB analyst role for his son in NY. . . . We are being offered now a [mandate] and the quid pro quo, is an analyst IB job for his son. . . . Can we in [an investment banking group in New York] adopt him, or can you recommend a safe place for him where he won't get too scarred." After the candidate was hired by JPMorgan in New York in October 2010, a JPMorgan APAC banker wrote to his colleagues that the Referral Hire was a "happy young man! And his dad will also be very pleased." In response, another JPMorgan APAC banker noted: "I am sure this will go a long way for us in terms of [referring client entity] and [the candidate's father, a senior executive of the entity]."

Other JPMorgan APAC investment bankers understood the true purpose of the program and the potential benefits to JPMorgan APAC's business from hiring Referral Hires. The purpose and benefit of Referral Hires was discussed amongst JPMorgan APAC investment bankers. For example:

- In 2008, one junior banker wrote to a JPMorgan APAC investment banker that she had "reconfirmed that [the requested Referral Hire] is very important to our relationship with [SOE]. [SOE] has a pending placement subject to market condition, and [referring client] made it clear that [referral candidate] is our ticket to this mandate."

- In discussing a potential Referral Hire in 2010 from a private sector client, a senior JPMorgan APAC investment banker wrote to another asking him to interview a referral candidate, writing: "The last thing I want is we go slow and they ask another bank and I am sure someone will give him a full time offer given the mandate up for grabs here. We can give him an offer under the new 'sons and daughters' one-year program . . . They are interested." The second banker noted "Happy to speak with son asap. Seen this movie a lot before, we should consider it part of the pursuit immediately." He went on to note "We do way, way, way too little of this type of hiring and I have been pounding on it with China team for a year. Let me know if you need me to weigh in at all asap. Confidential, just added son of #2 at [Chinese SOE] to my team. I got room for a lot more hires like this ([competitor investment bank] has 25)."

- In 2010, a senior JPMorgan APAC investment banker wrote to a colleague regarding a Referral Hire from a private sector client: "They are close to mandating banks for their IPO. We are a strong contender. Blink blink nod nod, can we find a place for his son (they have only approached us in this regard)?"

The expected financial benefit to JPMorgan APAC from hiring certain Referral Hires was also communicated by JPMorgan APAC investment bankers in certain cases to the referring clients and the Referral Hires themselves. For example, in 2011, a Referral Hire wrote to a senior JPMorgan APAC banker regarding his decision to leave JPMorgan before the expiration of his employment term because despite his hard work "all of my efforts seemed meaningless to you and you tend to judge me solely on the relation part of me. . . . I remember when i [*sic*] first started working here you told me that [other relationship hires] all paid the price for their seats on the floor. Now I had a better understanding of your words after getting to know some of the relationship hires on the floor. I do not think my family is in a position to help you to the extent as others did: bring their family business to the firm. Therefore i [*sic*] decided to leave my head count to those who are more valuable to the company." This Referral Hire went on to write "regarding [two Chinese SOEs], my father would try his best to coordinate the meeting."

JPMorgan APAC Revamped the Client Referral Program in 2009 to Directly Link Referral Hires to New Investment Banking Deal Business

Beginning in or about 2009, JPMorgan APAC investment bankers began a review of all previously hired Referral Hires to determine the success of the program in terms of the "business rationale" for hiring and retaining Referral Hires. Referring bankers were asked to list each client referred hire and to provide the "client affiliation" and "the importance of retaining them from a client/revenue standpoint."

In September 2009, a senior JPMorgan APAC investment banker wrote to the chief executive officer of JPMorgan APAC that:

> "One specific item that we may need your help is how to run a better sons and daughters program, which has *an almost linear relationship* with mandates in China. People believe [other investment banks] are doing a much better job. On the other hand, we J.P. Morgan have had a few disas[t]rous cases which I can share with you later. We have more [lines of business] in China therefore in theory we can accomodate [*sic*] more 'powerful' sons and daughters that could benefit the entire platform." (Emphasis added.)

Following this email, senior JPMorgan APAC investment bankers on multiple occasions discussed reforming the Client Referral Program to improve the ability to obtain specific client business using Referral Hires. Among other things, it was agreed that the Client Referral Program would prioritize referral requests from "decision-makers" or those with the ability to influence upcoming investment banking transactions. It was also agreed to focus on Referral Hires in situations involving near-term transactions.

To that end, in or about September 2009, APAC Banker A wrote to the APAC banker assigned to assist him in running the JRM functions ("APAC Banker B") that he "spoke to [a senior JPMorgan APAC investment banker] about referrals. [W]e want to revisit the programme at two levels." He wrote that for the one-year Referral Hires, they wanted to "plan better" in the areas of "accountability" and "deal conversion or revenue attribution and relationship." JPMorgan Banker A also noted that for one-year Referral Hires, the hire should be made "Jan 15 to Dec 15, thereby avoiding year end count." APAC Banker A noted that doing this "[w]ould be a clever way to manage all 1 yr [sic] program hires if we could align the hiring cycle. Maybe able to even get more people."

Per these instructions, APAC Banker B created a presentation titled "Emerging Asia Client Referral Program (CRP)" in November 2009. The presentation reviewed the "Current state of play" regarding the "full-time referrals program," and noted: "The firm benefits from a CRP to facilitate its business development in China." It further noted that the current program was "designed to hire employees referred by our key clients who may not meet our regular hiring standard. . . . The current program is functional but could be further improved to optimize control/management and enhance contribution to business generation." The presentation noted that "[a]reas for [i]mprovement" for the current program included "[m]onitoring referral deal conversion." The revised program also sought to prioritize requests from "decision-makers" or those with the ability to influence future, near-term deals to benefit JPMorgan APAC.

This presentation first sought to summarize the success of the then-current Client Referral Program. The presentation tracked certain then-current Referral Hires made through the Client Referral Program, and the "Historical deal conversion track record" relating to those hires. The presentation noted deal "[c]onversion" with respect to multiple Referral Hires including (1) conversion of a deal with an SOE after referral of a candidate from a senior member of a foreign political party; and (2) conversion of a deal with an SOE after hiring the daughter of a "Deputy Minister." The presentation also noted "Work in progress" on potential deals involving the "family friend" of the chairman of a Hong Kong company and the daughter of a senior foreign government minister.

A new aspect to JPMorgan APAC's Client Referral Program was also proposed in this presentation. Under the heading "Full-time referrals: Proposed new program," the presentation listed new "Selection [C]riteria" for full-time Referral Hires that would include:

- "Directly attributable linkage to business opportunity," and
- "Clear accountability for deal conversion and accountability for abuse of program."

In 2009, after approval by the head of investment banking for APAC, JPMorgan APAC implemented the revised Client Referral Program. The revised program was managed by the JRM business support team with input from senior JPMorgan APAC investment bankers. Certain senior bankers were given a "quota" of Referral Hires that could be made each year. Subsequent JRM reports from 2009 through 2012 contained the same language regarding the "revised" referral hiring program with the selection criteria of a "[d]irectly attributable linkage to business opportunity." These presentations were discussed with the head of investment banking for JPMorgan APAC and other JPMorgan APAC senior executives.

The JPMorgan APAC investment bankers who created and ran the revised Client Referral Program did not seek a review of the program by the legal and compliance staff, or otherwise inform the legal and compliance staff of the nature and purpose of the revised Client Referral Program. JPMorgan APAC personnel continued to provide inaccurate or incomplete information to JPMorgan APAC legal and compliance staff in order to secure approval for hiring Referral Hires.

Under the revised referral hiring program, Referral Hires were given the same titles as non-Referral Hires, although they typically were paid less than employees hired through JPMorgan APAC's non-referral hiring programs. Referral Hires were generally hired for a one-year term with limited ability to continue with JPMorgan APAC after the conclusion of their contracts. However, exceptions were made based on business needs. In 2011, APAC Banker B wrote to several APAC investment bankers that "[t]he client referral program is strictly one year for everyone else unless [the Referral Hires] bring in a new profitable deal to justify an extension, otherwise they must move on."

Beginning by at least 2009, JPMorgan APAC employees tracked investment banking deals attributable to entities whose officials had requested Referral Hires. In or about December 2010, JPMorgan APAC investment bankers created "Referral Hires vs Revenue" spreadsheets to track revenue from clients whose referrals had been hired by the firm. The spreadsheet included columns listing: (1) type of hire (fixed term versus intern); (2) date of hire; (3) a description of the relationship between the Referral Hire and the referring client or government official ("daughter of Chairman," "family friend of . . . Chairman," "Son of Executive Vice President . . . of [SOE]."); and (4) "[r]evenue" to the firm from those clients.

In March 2011, as part of this review process, JPMorgan APAC personnel estimated that clients who had referred individuals into the Client Referral Program had generated more than $14 million in revenue in 2009 and $19 million in 2010, with $21 million anticipated in the "pipeline" for 2011.

JPMorgan APAC's Client Referral Summer Internship Programs

In addition to providing analyst and associate employment opportunities, in 2009 and 2010 JPMorgan APAC also created summer internship programs to accommodate Referral Hires. Referral Hires were generally not qualified for the regular JPMorgan APAC summer internship program; nonetheless, summer internships in the regular program were sometimes provided by JPMorgan APAC to Referral Hires. In order to accommodate more client referrals, in 2010 JPMorgan APAC also created an unpaid training program in Hong Kong (colloquially referred to as "summer camp") for Referral Hires seeking summer employment or internships with JPMorgan APAC. The "summer camp" consisted mainly of social events, lectures, and classroom speakers. Although the participants were not employed by JPMorgan APAC and were not paid, participants could list the program on their resumes. APAC Banker B noted that one senior APAC investment banker said that he could "sleep better at night knowing that we now have a structured program to entertain the little darlings."

JPMorgan APAC undertook no compliance review of participants in the "summer camp." However, candidates for the "summer camp" were selected based on investment bank client relationships rather than merit. Further, certain client referrals with links to potential revenue were given paid summer internships with JPMorgan APAC rather than the opportunity to participate in the "summer camp."

JPMorgan APAC bankers, including APAC Banker B, managed summer training Referral Hires to generate potential near-term revenue for the firm. APAC Banker B noted in 2010 that sponsoring bankers "need to make a strong case for their referrals — minimum $3m tangible fees sounds like a sensible benchmark." A JPMorgan APAC senior investment banker also suggested making additional accommodations (such as paying for flights) for the children of "SOE clients who are not well paid even at senior levels." This practice continued, and in 2011 APAC Banker B again noted that the summer training program "will most probably follow last year's convention of only considering clients with >$US3 million new revenue contribution for referring candidates into the training program."

JPMorgan APAC Hired SOE Referral Hires to Assist in Winning or Retaining Business

Between 2006 and 2013, JPMorgan APAC hired numerous relatives and friends of officials with foreign government entities and senior officials at foreign SOEs to obtain or retain business for JPMorgan. These hires include:

- Beginning in 2005, JPMorgan APAC hired the son of a key executive with a Chinese manufacturing SOE. The son worked at JPMorgan APAC in various roles from 2005–2008 and then again from 2010 until 2015. Another Referral Hire was given a training opportunity in 2009 based on a request from a senior executive of the same SOE. JPMorgan APAC was awarded an IPO from this SOE in 2006 and further advisory business in 2008. JPMorgan APAC received net profits for its work for this SOE of more than $32 million.
- In 2007, JPMorgan APAC hired the relative of a senior official at a Chinese SOE and the relative of a senior official at the government agency which oversaw that SOE. JPMorgan APAC was working on the IPO for that SOE when it agreed to the hires. The firm hired one of the Referral Hires while negotiating for a better fee from the SOE for its role in that IPO. In part as a result of this Referral Hire, JPMorgan APAC received additional net profits of more than $3.3 million.
- Between 2007 and 2010, JPMorgan APAC made multiple Referral Hires from officials with a Chinese financial SOE. Referral Hires were hired at the request of senior officials with this SOE, including the chairman and chief financial officer. JPMorgan APAC won multiple investment banking deals from this SOE from 2007–2010 resulting in net profits of more than $6.5 million.
- JPMorgan APAC hired at least five Referral Hires from 2007 to 2011 from senior officials with another Chinese financial SOE. This included the hiring of the son of a Chinese government official from the province in which this

institution was located at the request of the Chairman of the SOE. JPMorgan APAC was awarded investment banking business from this SOE in 2008 and 2009, with total net profits to the firm of more than $5.8 million.

- Between 2010 and 2012, JPMorgan APAC hired two Referral Hires at the request of officials with a large Chinese energy-related SOE. In 2012 and 2013, the firm was awarded business from this SOE, including bond issuances, with total net profits of more than $10 million.
- Between 2007 and 2010, JPMorgan APAC hired two employees and a trainee at the request of officials with a large Chinese transportation SOE. The referrals were made by the chief executive officer and other key employees with the SOE. JPMorgan APAC was awarded business from this SOE in 2010 totaling more than $10 million in net profits.
- JPMorgan APAC hired two employees and a trainee referred by officials at a Chinese financial SOE between 2008 and 2012. The requests were made by the chairman of the SOE and another senior official. For one of the Referral Hires, his parents were both Chinese government officials at different ministries. JPMorgan APAC was awarded a role in this SOE's 2012 IPO and received net profits of more than $2.6 million.

Referral Hire Employed in New York in Order to Obtain IPO Roles for JPMorgan APAC

In 2007, JPMorgan APAC hired the son ("Referral Hire A") of an executive ("Official A") of an energy related Chinese SOE ("SOE A") for a summer internship position in China based on the request of Official A. Subsequently, in 2009, the firm hired Referral Hire A for a position in its Hong Kong internship program, again upon the request of Official A.

Before Referral Hire A started his Hong Kong internship, the referring JPMorgan APAC banker noted that Official A "was recently promoted to the current position and is said to be very close to the president [of SOE A]. Maybe we should use [Official A's] ask to take over the relationship" from a former APAC banker. The JPMorgan APAC banker ("APAC Banker C") who had taken over responsibility for JPMorgan's relationship with SOE A noted as part of discussions regarding what information to put in the "Sons & Daughters" questionnaire that "[w]e are pitching for a couple of M+A deals . . . and we have been in constant dialogue for a potential block trade. Also, we need to establish broad relationship with this client as we could provide a broad spectrum of products (corporate, commodities) to them." APAC Banker C then submitted the "Sons & Daughters" questionnaire for Referral Hire A, after being advised by the referring APAC banker that for the question regarding potential deals with SOE A, he should "limit[] this to real pitches only to avoid challenges by legal and compliance."

After the hire was approved, APAC Banker C then asked "shall we coordinate so I can hook up with his father? I will be in [Beijing] next week and we actually have some meetings with [SOE A] so would be good to do this in time." The meeting was arranged with Official A.

During Referral Hire A's summer internship in Hong Kong, APAC Banker C asked Referral Hire A to get non-public information about potential JPMorgan SOE clients from SOE A through his father in order to assist JPMorgan APAC in pitching for new business. Referral Hire A did not provide non-public information to APAC Banker C. Later that summer, Referral Hire A was told by APAC Banker C that in order to receive a full-time offer from JPMorgan APAC, he would need to "bring in a deal" for JPMorgan APAC.

Referral Hire A specifically wanted an analyst position with JPMorgan in New York. Therefore, in the fall of 2009, Official A sought assistance from his friend, another senior executive at a Chinese SOE ("Official B"), to help get Referral Hire A a job with the firm in New York. Official B was a senior executive with a large Chinese state-owned financial institution ("SOE B"). In 2009, SOE B was in the process of preparing for an initial public offering ("IPO") in Hong Kong that was expected to be lucrative for investment banks working on the transaction. Official B had significant influence over the decision-making as to which firms would be designated to participate in the forthcoming IPO of SOE B ("IPO Mandate").

In fall 2009, Officials A and B each sent multiple messages and made multiple calls to JPMorgan APAC investment bankers seeking a job with JPMorgan in New York for Referral Hire A. In late 2009 and early 2010, JPMorgan APAC bankers noted that Official B kept "pushing" for the hire. Official B requested that the Referral Hire request be kept from JPMorgan APAC bankers involved in the deal. One senior APAC banker wrote in January 2010 that "to avoid any 'complication,' [Official B] has asked to keep this confidential and particularly away from the '[SOE B] pitch team.' But I have kept [a senior banker on the pitch team] in the loop. . . . Would be great if you could give this a push in NY. . . . Many thanks."

Based upon the requests from Officials A and B and the forthcoming IPO Mandate, senior JPMorgan APAC investment bankers undertook steps to secure a position for Referral Hire A with the firm in New York. These bankers believed that JPMorgan APAC could receive a more significant and lucrative role in the IPO Mandate if the firm hired Referral Hire A, and would risk JPMorgan APAC's position or its entire role in the IPO Mandate if they did not.

In December 2009, JPMorgan APAC investment bankers sought the assistance of a JPMorgan banker in New York who reported to the then-head of JPMorgan APAC ("JPMorgan Banker D") with finding a job for Referral Hire A. JPMorgan Banker D reported back that Referral Hire A was not qualified for a position with the firm in New York, causing one of the JPMorgan APAC bankers seeking the hire to note that "Jpm in NY won't give [Referral Hire A] a preference. Spoke with a few people who know [him]. Unlikely to pass thorugh [sic] regular process." A JPMorgan recruiter in New York noted that "[r]elative to other candidates, his technological and quantitative skills were light (this is an extremely quantitative position). We plan on notifying him this week that he will not be moving forward in the process." Referral Hire A interviewed with multiple groups at JPMorgan in New York, and each rejected hiring him despite the client relationship. JPMorgan

Banker D noted that, according to two JPMorgan groups in New York, "while [Referral Hire A] has solid technical skills, his communication and marketing skills as well as his overall credentials on other metrics fell short of JPM standards. Both groups cite these deficiencies as reason not to pursue his case further, making the point that is hard to argue, that lowering the highly competitive recruitment bar at JPM is not a desirable option."

Despite this negative feedback, in February 2010 the JPMorgan APAC investment bankers emailed the then-chief executive officer of JPMorgan APAC and the head of human resources for JPMorgan Hong Kong to state they had "reached consensus among us to offer [Referral Hire A] a one-year fixed-term position at [JPMorgan Banker D's] team in our New York office. We understand that you have been always supportive of this hire. [I]t is time to ask your approval to proceed on that basis. [Official B] called and sent sms to [two JPMorgan APAC bankers] several times to ask the status. If we can get this hire done soon, that will be very helpful." The next day, the head of the JPMorgan APAC group handling the IPO Mandate noted that he had a meeting with the chairman of another Chinese entity at which he learned "[v]ery interesting info re [SOE B]: will launch [IPO Mandate] process just before or just after chinese new year. Very definitive. So we should act reg [sic] this young guy and place him in [JPMorgan Banker D]'s group. One-year analyst." The hire was thereafter approved by the chief executive officer of JPMorgan APAC, and Referral Hire A began working in New York in 2010 as part of JPMorgan Banker D's group.

In April 2010, JPMorgan APAC was selected for a significant role in the IPO Mandate. In June 2010, a JPMorgan APAC banker sent an email to JPMorgan Banker D stating that "I understand from his father, [Official A], that [Referral Hire A] will start today in office. His uncle [Official B] did deliver [SOE B] IPO and his father is helping us on [an energy-related] ipo." Later in July 2010, an APAC banker noted that "we are on track to make [SOE B] the largest IPO ever."

In 2010, JPMorgan APAC investment bankers learned that Referral Hire A's father, Official A, had assisted JPMorgan APAC in securing a mandate from a Chinese energy company that was preparing for its own IPO. In August 2010, Referral Hire A was added to JPMorgan APAC's team working on that IPO. In November 2010, JPMorgan APAC bankers consulted with Official A regarding this IPO pitch. Later discussions regarding the "game plan" included that "[Official A] will help us from the side." In December 2010, an APAC banker told other senior APAC bankers that Referral Hire A, described as the referral from Official B and "the analyst we placed under [JPMorgan Banker D]'s team in NY, has played a critical role in helping secure this mandate. [Referral Hire A']s father is a senior executive at [SOE A]. FYI." JPMorgan Banker D responded "He is a quietly efficient worker. . ."

In January 2011, a JPMorgan APAC banker emailed the then-CEO of JPMorgan APAC regarding Referral Hire A's application to be transferred to a different department at JPMorgan in New York, noting that "[Referral Hire A] (and his family) has been instrumental in helping us on both the [SOE B] IPO and [another] IPO." He further noted that Referral Hire A's "father is helping us on [other companies] at the moment as well." The then-CEO of JPMorgan APAC then wrote to another senior banker at the firm to ask him to help Referral Hire A find another job within JPMorgan, stating "[h]is Dad is pretty important in China and I am happy to keep him on my headcount if you can use him." In March 2011, the firm then hired Referral Hire A into another position when his initial fixed-term Referral Hire contract expired.

JPMorgan APAC did not inform JPMorgan APAC legal and compliance about the 2010 hire of Referral Hire A in New York. Therefore, a "Sons & Daughters" questionnaire was not completed or reviewed. In July 2010, JPMorgan's compliance group became aware that Referral Hire A had been hired without compliance review or a "Sons & Daughters" questionnaire for his 2010 hire. A JPMorgan compliance officer noted "[c]learly, in a perfect world, it would be best if this had gone through another formal review prior to the position being offered. However, since [Referral Hire A] had already been reviewed in the past for at least his 2009 internship, I am not sure what value there would be in reviewing again at this point in time." No additional inquiry was undertaken, and instead JPMorgan APAC reviewed the questionnaire that was submitted in 2009 prior to Referral Hire A's Hong Kong internship. That questionnaire had no reference to SOE B, the IPO Mandate, or the other IPO which Official A helped JPMorgan APAC secure. Although JPMorgan APAC legal and compliance had required Referral Hire A to be walled off from pitches involving SOE A (where his father worked) at the time of his summer internship, this was not communicated to JPMorgan legal and compliance in New York and nothing was done to enforce this restriction even after JPMorgan APAC legal and compliance learned of Referral Hire A's position in New York. At no point after he was hired in 2010 was Referral Hire A walled off from transactions involving either his father, Official A, entities related to SOE A, or his father's friend, Official B, and entities relating to him.

JPMorgan APAC participated in the IPO for SOE B in 2010. For its efforts, the firm received net profits of more than $23 million. In 2010, JPMorgan APAC also worked on the IPO for another Chinese SOE which was connected to SOE A, where Referral Hire A's father was an official. For its efforts on the latter IPO, JPMorgan APAC received more than $3.7 million in net profits.

Referral Hire from Government Ministry in Order to Obtain Favorable Treatment for JPMorgan

In 2006, a JPMorgan APAC investment banker sought to find a job with the firm in New York for the son ("Referral Hire X") of a deputy minister ("Official X") at a Chinese government agency. In seeking the hire, a JPMorgan APAC investment banker wrote of Official X that "[a]lthough he is now promoted to be a government official, his influence remains strong both personally as well as in an official capacity [at the Ministry] . . . [and] a good indepth [sic] relationship with the Ministry will pave the ground for us in many large and important industries in China as well as large cap companies, despite the fact some of them are 'independent' commercial entities, a unique feature of the Chinese/government business alliance."

Referral Hire X interviewed for the position in New York but was not selected for hire. He nonetheless received an offer for an analyst position in November 2006 based on the referral request. Referral Hire X then sought to start his employment one month earlier than planned. To do so, Referral Hire X contacted an executive at a Chinese company who then contacted a different JPMorgan APAC investment banker about the request. In December 2006, an employee with the firm in New York emailed the JPMorgan APAC banker seeking the early start for Referral Hire X that Referral Hire X "did very very poorly in interviews — some [managing directors] said he was the worst [business analyst] candidate they had ever see [sic] — and we obviously had to extend him an offer . . . [o]bviously, we will need to accommodate due to client pressure, but we're going to have to handle this very carefully." In or about mid-2007, Referral Hire X began working as an analyst in Corporate Finance in New York on a one-year contract.

In May 2008, during Referral Hire X's first year of work with the firm in New York, Official X requested that a JPMorgan APAC investment banker provide his son with another job after the expiration of his one-year term. In June 2008, a JPMorgan APAC senior banker sent his supervisor an email in which he stated: "The father indicated to me repeatedly that he is willing to go extra mile to help JPM in whatever way we think he can. And I do have a few cases where I think we can leverage the father's connection. . . . [G]iven the above, I'd like to discuss with you and seek your advice/support on how to handle the son in NY and leverage the father in China."

In July 2008, JPMorgan Banker D offered a position in his group to Referral Hire X. After he was hired, JPMorgan Banker D wrote to the JPMorgan APAC banker in Hong Kong that "I don't have the details of the incident but apparently last Friday when I was out of the office, [Referral Hire X] sent out an email (which he inadvertently copied to an HR Person), where he made inappropriate . . . remarks." In August 2008, JPMorgan Banker D wrote that there was a "general consensus among seniors in our group" that Referral Hire X was "immature, irresponsible, and unreliable" and that one banker was "no longer will[ing] to have [Referral Hire X] as part of the pool [of junior analysts on his deals] . . . there is also concern about his reliability on confidentiality of client records/documents which means that we may not be able to let him have access to sensitive transactional records/documents." Referral Hire X remained in his position until it was eliminated 10 months later.

Hiring of Referral Hire to Initiate Client Relationship with SOE

In 2010, JPMorgan APAC began taking steps to hire the son ("Referral Hire Z") of the chairman ("Official Z") of another large Chinese financial SOE, at his father's request. Official Z had asked a senior JPMorgan APAC banker to hire his son at the firm during an in-person meeting. In an email to other senior bankers, this APAC banker noted "[g]iven the size of the group and the existing and potential business opportunities from this group to both FIG [Financial Institutions Group] and GI [group within investment banking], I responded to this request positively. Let's gather our thought on how we can leverage more on this account going forward."

JPMorgan APAC bankers discussed that hiring Referral Hire Z could help the firm win future business from Official Z's SOE entity. A senior banker wrote in 2010 in response to the request to hire the son "[a]gree with [other banker]. [Official Z's entity] is an important client. We need to help his son that definately [sic] will give us leverage of business opportunities for both fig and non fig for jpm." The head of FIG within JPMorgan APAC's investment bank later checked to make sure that JPMorgan had in fact followed through and "onboarded" Official Z's son.

Steps were taken to hire Referral Hire Z for a fixed-term position with JPMorgan APAC. The compliance questionnaire for Referral Hire Z noted that his father was the CEO of a Chinese SOE and that JPMorgan APAC was in discussions with a subsidiary of the SOE for a "potential financing transaction at the moment." It also noted that JPMorgan APAC intended "to maintain a close relationship with the client." The questionnaire falsely stated that there was "No expected benefit" from hiring Referral Hire Z.

A few weeks after JPMorgan APAC offered Referral Hire Z a one-year position, the same banker who proposed the hire noted to a senior JPMorgan APAC banker that the firm had won "a mandate to be sole bookrunner for a USD300mm+ placement of [Official Z's SOE]'s listed subsidiary in HK. This will be our first transaction for this group." One year later, JPMorgan APAC was mandated for the IPO for Official Z's SOE, but the firm withdrew from that deal in 2013. In 2010, JPMorgan APAC also worked on a private placement for Official Z's SOE for which the firm received net profits of more than $1.4 million.

LEGAL STANDARDS AND VIOLATIONS

Under Section 21C(a) of the Exchange Act, the Commission may impose a cease-and-desist order upon any person who is violating, has violated, or is about to violate any provision of the Exchange Act or any regulation thereunder, and upon any other person that is, was, or would be a cause of the violation, due to an act or omission the person knew or should have known would contribute to such violation.

FCPA Violations

Anti-Bribery Violations

JPMorgan violated the anti-bribery provisions of the federal securities laws by corruptly providing valuable internships and employment to relatives and friends of foreign government officials in order to assist JPMorgan in retaining and obtaining business.

As a result of the conduct described above, JPMorgan violated Section 30A of the Exchange Act which prohibits any issuer with a class of securities registered pursuant to Section 12 of the Exchange Act, or any officer, director, employee, or agent acting on behalf of such issuer, in order to obtain or retain business, from corruptly giving or authorizing the giving of, anything of value to any foreign official for the purposes of influencing the official or inducing the official to act in violation of his or her lawful duties, or to secure any improper advantage, or to induce a foreign official to use his influence with a foreign governmental instrumentality to influence any act or decision of such government or instrumentality. [15 U.S.C. § 78dd-1.]

Books and Records Violations

JPMorgan violated the books and records provisions of the FCPA in conjunction with certain Referral Hires. Under Section 13(b)(2)(A) of the Exchange Act, JPMorgan was required to make and keep books, records, and accounts, which, in reasonable detail, accurately and fairly reflect the transactions and dispositions of the assets of the issuer. JPMorgan APAC's controls required that investment bankers submit accurate questionnaires to compliance for review before client referrals from SOEs and foreign government officials could be hired. Contrary to that requirement, JPMorgan APAC personnel submitted, reviewed, and approved inaccurate compliance questionnaires containing false and incomplete information which failed to disclose the intended, improper purpose of making certain client Referral Hires. JPMorgan's internal records also inaccurately reflected the true number of client Referral Hires in the APAC region by taking steps to withhold certain headcount information relating to Referral Hires. [15 U.S.C § 78m(b)(2)(A).]

Internal Controls Violations

JPMorgan violated the internal accounting controls provisions of the FCPA in conjunction with certain Referral Hires. JPMorgan failed to devise and maintain an effective system of internal accounting controls. JPMorgan's internal accounting controls were insufficiently designed to prevent the corruption risks inherent in the hiring of Referral Hires, and therefore inadequate to enforce or effectuate JPMorgan's referral hiring policy. JPMorgan recognized the inherent risks in hiring Referral Hires, yet proceeded with a system that failed adequately to address those risks. The safeguards put in place by JPMorgan APAC to minimize compliance and FCPA risks were not effective to curb the true purpose of the Client Referral Program. JPMorgan APAC's referral hiring questionnaire was designed to ensure that Referral Hires were hired based on merit and not for improper purposes. However, in practice the Client Referral Program operated as a separate tier of employment within JPMorgan APAC where hiring and retention decisions were based on client relationships and potential revenue and not employee merit.

Referral Hires were subject to a completely separate hiring process, and once hired their jobs and terms of employment were likewise different than non-Referral Hires. The interview and screening process for Referral Hires was perfunctory, with candidates receiving an offer based on the perceived strength of the client relationship and prospect for future business. Referral Hires were also generally less qualified than employees hired through the non-referral, entry-level hiring program, and once hired the Referral Hires were generally not expected to do the same work as non-referral employees in similar positions.

JPMorgan APAC attempted to put in place protections to mitigate the inherent conflicts and FCPA risks in hiring Referral Hires. However, these protections were insufficient to prevent the violations. While legal and compliance staff were required to approve Referral Candidates before they could be hired, in practice they never failed to approve a Referral Candidate. In certain cases, the protections were ignored. JPMorgan APAC bankers sought to have certain Referral Hires work outside of APAC at the request of the APAC-based client or prospective client seeking the employment. These Referral Hires did not go through the normal hiring process for that region, and instead were hired based on the perceived benefit to JPMorgan APAC from the hire. In such cases, a compliance questionnaire was not completed and therefore no review was made to analyze the potential conflicts of interest and FCPA violations inherent in referral hiring. In cases in which the Referral Hire was hired outside of APAC, the conflict of interest prohibitions were not imposed or enforced. This led to Referral Hires being staffed on the deal teams for the referring person's entity, often at the request of the referring person, in direct contravention of the conflict of interest rules imposed on the referral hiring program.

Under Section 13(b)(2)(B) of the Exchange Act issuers are required to devise and maintain a system of internal accounting controls sufficient to provide reasonable assurances that (i) transactions are executed in accordance with management's general or specific authorization; (ii) transactions are recorded as necessary (I) to permit preparation of financial statements in conformity with generally accepted accounting principles or any other criteria applicable to such statements, and (II) to maintain accountability for assets; (iii) access to assets is permitted only in accordance with management's general or specific authorization; and (iv) the recorded accountability for assets is compared with the existing assets at reasonable intervals and appropriate action is taken with respect to any differences. [15 U.S.C § 78m(b)(2)(B).]

. . . .

NON-PROSECUTION AGREEMENT

JPMorgan APAC has entered into a non-prosecution agreement with the Department of Justice that acknowledges responsibility for criminal conduct relating to certain findings in the Order.

By the Commission

Notes and Questions

In April 2015, the *Wall Street Journal* reported a wide-ranging U.S. government probe of several major financial institutions for their hiring of relatives of influential foreign government officials, most notably Chinese "princelings."[30]

---

30. Jean Eaglesham et al., *Wall Street Pushes Back on Foreign Bribery Probe*, WALL ST. J. (Apr. 29, 2015, 7:24 PM) https://www.wsj.com/articles/wall-street-pushes-back-on-foreign-bribery-probe-1430349863.

In addition to JPMorgan, the probe covered Goldman Sachs Group, Inc., Citigroup, Inc., BNY Mellon, Credit Suisse Group AG, Deutsche Bank AG, Morgan Stanley, and UBS AG.[31]

The banks vociferously opposed the government's position, arguing that the FCPA only prohibits hiring "done solely to win specific deals."[32] They contended that the government's position "would redefine bribery law by punishing firms for hiring qualified but well-connected people who are later linked to certain deals," and that hiring relatives of influential statesmen was "only one part of large, complex relationships with clients, who didn't award deals purely as a result of any such hires."[33]

The question of indirect payments to family members of foreign officials was addressed in the Senate hearings preceding the 1998 amendments to the FCPA. As noted by the Committee's report:

> [T]he Committee is concerned by a potential loophole in the definition of foreign public officials that would allow individuals or corporations to bribe family members of foreign public officials without penalty. In a response to a question for the record, the State Department described the reach of the Convention to family members:
>
>> The Convention, like the U.S. Foreign Corrupt Practices Act, covers bribes offered or paid to a foreign public official so that the official will take certain action, or refrain from acting, in the performance of official duties. Bribes to a family member of a foreign public official are covered in circumstances where (1) a bribe is paid to a family member as a conduit or intermediary, who in turn passes it to the foreign public official, the intended recipient; or (2) a foreign public official directs that a bribe, intended to induce that official to take certain action or refrain from acting, be paid to a family member.
>
> The Committee is concerned that in many instances the connection between the payment to immediate family members and the influence on a foreign public official will not be evident. Payments to a family member who does not pass it on to a family member who is a public official, yet enriches the family, would not be covered under the proposed Convention. The Committee directs the President to describe efforts by the United States to amend the Convention to expand the definition of "foreign public official," so as to make illegal the bribery of immediate family members of foreign public officials.[34]

BNY Mellon, which had hired three student interns related to foreign government officials affiliated with a Middle Eastern sovereign wealth fund, settled with the SEC in August 2015, and agreed to a cease-and-desist order and payment of $14.8 million in penalties. The order noted that the three interns, hired as a special favor to their relatives, were:

---

31. *Id.*
32. *Id.*
33. *Id.*
34. S. Exec. Rep. No. 105-19, at 2 (1998).

[L]ess than exemplary employees. On at least one occasion, Interns A and B were confronted by a BNY Mellon human resources employee concerning their repeated absences from work. A Boutique portfolio manager who worked with Intern C observed that his performance was "okay" and that "he wasn't actually as hardworking as I would have hoped." Despite these issues, BNY Mellon accommodated the Interns in order to favorably influence Officials X and Y.

1) Does the government's position force businesses to forgo hiring of qualified individuals because they are related to a government official?
2) Under what circumstances, if any, does the FCPA allow a business to hire a government official's relative without fearing an FCPA prosecution?

1. Charitable Donations

Charitable donations may be required as a condition to enter some markets or be a "part of legitimate local outreach. The FCPA does not prohibit charitable contributions or prevent corporations from acting as good corporate citizens."[35] However, if such donations are made as a way to "funnel bribes to government officials,"[36] they violate the FCPA. If a donation to a specific charity is made at the request of a government official, or if the donor fails to conduct proper due diligence to ensure that the donation is in fact used for a charitable purpose, the DOJ and SEC will deem it a corrupt payment.

> For example, a pharmaceutical company used charitable donations to a small local castle restoration charity headed by a foreign government official to induce the official to direct business to the company. Although the charity was a bona fide charitable organization, internal documents at the pharmaceutical company's subsidiary established that the payments were not viewed as charitable contributions but rather as "dues" the subsidiary was required to pay for assistance from the government official. . . .
>
> Proper due diligence and controls are critical for charitable giving. In general, the adequacy of measures taken to prevent misuse of charitable donations will depend on a risk-based analysis and the specific facts at hand. In Opinion Procedure Release No. 10-02, DOJ described the due diligence and controls that can minimize the likelihood of an FCPA violation. In that matter, a Eurasian-based subsidiary of a U.S. non-governmental organization was asked by an agency of a foreign government to make a grant to a local micro finance institution (MFI) as a prerequisite to the subsidiary's transformation to bank status. The subsidiary proposed contributing $1.42 million to a local MFI to satisfy the request. The subsidiary undertook an extensive, three-stage due diligence process to select the proposed grantee and imposed significant controls on the proposed grant, including ongoing monitoring and auditing, ear-marking funds for capacity building, prohibiting compensation of board members, and implementing anti-corruption compliance provisions. DOJ explained that it would not take

---

35. FCPA GUIDE, *supra* note 4, at 16.
36. *Id.*

any enforcement action because the company's due diligence and the controls it planned to put in place sufficed to prevent an FCPA violation.

Other opinion releases also address charitable-type grants or donations. Under the facts presented in those releases, DOJ approved the proposed grant or donation, based on due diligence measures and controls such as:

- certifications by the recipient regarding compliance with the FCPA;
- due diligence to confirm that none of the recipient's officers were affiliated with the foreign government at issue;
- a requirement that the recipient provide audited financial statements;
- a written agreement with the recipient restricting the use of funds;
- steps to ensure that the funds were transferred to a valid bank account;
- confirmation that the charity's commitments were met before funds were disbursed; and
- on-going monitoring of the efficacy of the program.

Legitimate charitable giving does not violate the FCPA. Compliance with the FCPA merely requires that charitable giving not be used as a vehicle to conceal payments made to corruptly influence foreign officials.[37]

Five Questions to Consider When Making Charitable Payments in a Foreign Country

1. What is the purpose of the payment?
2. Is the payment consistent with the company's internal guidelines on charitable giving?
3. Is the payment at the request of a foreign official?
4. Is a foreign official associated with the charity and, if so, can the foreign official make decisions regarding your business in that country?
5. Is the payment conditioned upon receiving business or other benefits?

— FCPA Guide[38]

Hypothetical: Charitable Donation

Commonwealth, Inc. ("Commonwealth") is a corporation based in Boston, Massachusetts, which engages in mineral exploration and extraction in different countries around the world. Commonwealth is interested in exploring new mineral deposits in a Latin American country and has engaged in preliminary negotiations with the country's authorities regarding the project. The authorities have offered to pass special legislation allowing Commonwealth to purchase the public land containing the deposits,

---

37. *Id.* at 17–19.
38. *Id.* at 19.

> provided that the corporation makes a substantial charitable contribution to a hospital recently inaugurated by the president.
>
> 1) Do the FCPA anti-bribery provisions prohibit Commonwealth from entering into the proposed deal?
> 2) Would your analysis be different if the proposed deal allowed Commonwealth to make a contribution to a charity of its choice? If so, what conditions should Commonwealth attach to its contribution?

2. Gifts, Travel, and Entertainment

Companies often provide gifts, travel, and entertainment to their customers as a way of expressing gratitude and building relationships. When the customer is a foreign government, however, this can violate the FCPA. From the DOJ and SEC's perspective, two key distinctions between a legal gift and a bribe are: (1) the intent behind the gift and (2) its relative value.

> Some hallmarks of appropriate gift-giving are when the gift is given openly and transparently, properly recorded in the giver's books and records, provided only to reflect esteem or gratitude, and permitted under local law.
>
> Items of nominal value, such as cab fare, reasonable meals and entertainment expenses, or company promotional items, are unlikely to improperly influence an official, and, as a result, are not, without more, items that have resulted in enforcement action by DOJ or SEC. The larger or more extravagant the gift, however, the more likely it was given with an improper purpose. DOJ and SEC enforcement cases thus have involved single instances of large, extravagant gift-giving (such as sports cars, fur coats, and other luxury items) as well as widespread gifts of smaller items as part of a pattern of bribes. For example, in one case brought by DOJ and SEC, a defendant gave a government official a country club membership fee and a generator, as well as household maintenance expenses, payment of cell phone bills, an automobile worth $20,000, and limousine services. The same official also received $250,000 through a third-party agent.
>
> In addition, a number of FCPA enforcement actions have involved the corrupt payment of travel and entertainment expenses. Both DOJ and SEC have brought cases where these types of expenditures occurred in conjunction with other conduct reflecting systemic bribery or other clear indicia of corrupt intent.
>
> A case involving a California-based telecommunications company illustrates the types of improper travel and entertainment expenses that may violate the FCPA. Between 2002 and 2007, the company spent nearly $7 million on approximately 225 trips for its customers in order to obtain systems contracts in China, including for employees of Chinese state-owned companies to travel to popular tourist destinations in the United States. Although the trips were purportedly for the individuals to conduct training at the company's facilities, in reality, no training occurred on many of these trips and the company had no facilities at those locations. Approximately $670,000 of the $7 million was falsely recorded as "training" expenses.
>
> . . . .

Companies also may violate the FCPA if they give payments or gifts to third parties, like an official's family members, as an indirect way of corruptly influencing a foreign official. For example, one defendant paid personal bills and provided airline tickets to a cousin and close friend of the foreign official whose influence the defendant sought in obtaining contracts. The defendant was convicted at trial and received a prison sentence.

As part of an effective compliance program, a company should have clear and easily accessible guidelines and processes in place for gift-giving by the company's directors, officers, employees, and agents. Though not necessarily appropriate for every business, many larger companies have automated gift-giving clearance processes and have set clear monetary thresholds for gifts along with annual limitations, with limited exceptions for gifts approved by appropriate management. Clear guidelines and processes can be an effective and efficient means for controlling gift-giving, deterring improper gifts, and protecting corporate assets.

The FCPA does not prohibit gift-giving. Rather, just like its domestic bribery counterparts, the FCPA prohibits the payments of bribes, including those disguised as gifts.[39]

Gifts, Meals, and Entertainment

Alexandra Wrage, TRACE[40]

Rules prohibiting bribes to Government officials are straightforward. Most companies have little trouble recognizing the risk inherent in wiring money to a foreign official's numbered bank account in order to secure a large Government contract. Written policies, employee training, internal hotlines and remedial action all contribute to greater transparency and less risk to reputation and shareholder value. Guidelines on gifts and entertainment for Government officials, however, are far less clear.

Are fruit baskets and other perishables appropriate and defensible gestures of goodwill? Is it appropriate to give a gift of higher value if the item carries the company's logo? Cash isn't ever an acceptable gift for a foreign official, of course. Or is it? If local custom is a reliable guide, China's New Year tradition of hong bao—giving little red envelopes containing small amounts of cash—remains widespread. Extravagant gifts to a foreign official should be easy to spot, but "extravagant" may be interpreted differently by a highly compensated executive of a major multinational travelling on an expense account and a foreign official living locally on a modest salary.

Meals provide another area of risk with even less guidance. Few would find any impropriety in a working lunch provided at company facilities, but what about a lavish dinner with spouses at a top London restaurant? If you lose control of the wine list, the bill can quickly exceed the monthly salary of some

---

39. *See* FCPA Guide, *supra* note 4, at 16.

40. Alexandra Wrage, *Gifts Meals and Entertainment*, *in* John Bray et al., Business Against Corruption: Case Stories and Examples 80 (2006).

Government officials. Enforcement authorities usually stop short of declaring that all hospitality is suspect, but their admonition that it be "reasonable" under the circumstances is of little help.

Companies addressing the issue must consider not only the laws of their home country, but also the local laws of the foreign official's country, where the law may be unclear and the risk of reputational damage is often greatest. Many countries have enacted laws forbidding their Government officials to accept anything of value from any supplier or potential supplier; some of these laws expressly include gifts, meals, entertainment and travel. It is corrosive of good governance to permit employees to ignore these laws, but it's simply not feasible to expect a Government official to pay for his own coffee. Risk analysis may dictate that no company will be prosecuted for a modest meal, but recent prosecutions have highlighted patterns of hospitality as evidence of weak internal controls.

Earlier this year, TRACE undertook a review of more than 80 corporate policies addressing the question of whether or under what circumstances business people should provide gifts, meals, and entertainment to foreign Government officials. Almost all companies surveyed during this research agreed with the nine principles that have been adopted as TRACE guidelines on this issue.

TRACE GIFTS AND HOSPITALITY GUIDELINES

All benefits provided to a foreign official should:
- Be reasonable and customary under the circumstances;
- Not be motivated by a desire to influence the foreign official inappropriately;
- Be tasteful and commensurate with generally accepted standards for professional courtesy in the country where the company has its headquarters;
- Be provided openly and transparently;
- Be given in good faith and without expectation of reciprocity;
- Be provided in connection with a recognized gift-giving holiday or event in the case of gifts;
- Be provided in connection with a bona fide and legitimate business purpose in the case of hospitality and travel;
- Not be provided to any foreign official or group of foreign officials with such regularity or frequency as to create an appearance of impropriety or undermine the purpose of this policy;
- Comply with the local laws and regulations that apply to the foreign official.

COMPANY POLICIES ON GIFTS, MEALS, AND ENTERTAINMENT

Companies may choose to take a generally rules-based approach, providing strict dollar thresholds for gifts and meals. This approach is particularly popular with companies based in the United States. Or, companies may take a values-based approach, counselling employees that no gift, meal, or entertainment may be provided with corrupt intent, but that reasonable and customary gifts and meals may be provided at the employee's discretion. Regardless of the approach taken, internal conflicts can arise as companies balance the interests of their business development groups, tasked with customer relations and the development of goodwill, against the concerns of their legal and compliance organizations.

When capturing either approach in their compliance programmes, TRACE research indicates that companies tend to approach the question of gifts, meals, and entertainment in one of three ways. Companies fall fairly evenly into two of these categories, regardless of industry or region; the exception is the third category, which includes US companies almost exclusively.

1. **Employee discretion:** Gifts, meals, and entertainment may be provided at the employees' discretion, subject typically to budget restraints and an overriding code of ethics.
2. **Fixed monetary threshold:** All gifts, meals, and entertainment under a financial threshold, which varies from US$20 to US$250, are permitted. All expenditures over the threshold are either prohibited or permitted only with additional internal approvals. These thresholds may vary:
   a. By country or region;
   b. By seniority of employee; or
   c. By seniority of recipient.
3. **Management approval:** All gifts and hospitality over a low minimum threshold require approval of a compliance officer or the legal department.

Of the companies that TRACE interviewed, those that use monetary thresholds typically use a similar model for receipt by employees of gifts, meals, and entertainment from suppliers. This was widely described as an intuitive and consistent approach that was easily understood by employees. Of the companies relying on employee discretion, there was generally a high level of confidence that the company's broad code of conduct would minimize abuses.

ADDRESSING FOREIGN LAW

In addition to the laws of the country in which a company has its headquarters, it is possible that local laws of foreign countries in which the company operates may regulate or prohibit nationals from receiving this sort of benefit. TRACE research shows that the codes of conduct of most companies operating internationally state that the companies will comply with all local laws. Most companies, however, are not familiar with the local laws governing gifts and hospitality. Those that are spend enormous sums keeping their information on numerous countries up to date. The written laws of some Gulf States, for example, prohibit all gifts and hospitality to Government officials. This is problematic in part because the practice of dining out is widespread and expected and in part because it isn't always clear who fits the definition of a Government official in countries where members of the royal family may hold honorary or paid positions within quasi-Governmental enterprises. To address the question of local law, TRACE has worked with more than 50 law firms worldwide to develop an on-line matrix of local regulations, addressing the black letter law as well as providing comments on local custom.

Simply dismissing the issue of local law as low risk is no longer advisable. Recent cases and investigations in Europe and the United States demonstrate that the media and enforcement agencies are paying attention to corporate practices in this area and that both liability and reputational damage can result.

CASE STORIES: DILEMMA SITUATIONS

Due to the uncertainty of the law in this area and an increasingly aggressive enforcement climate, we have provided a series of case studies without attribution to specific companies. Despite the difficulty of the decisions facing these companies, it was encouraging to see the level of interest in this issue and the commitment to provide resources to work toward solutions that balanced the need to support internal marketing efforts with the company's need to proceed in a transparent and ethical manner.

Surprise Spouse

Company A complained of an event that was planned far in advance for two employees and four Government officials. Local law provided only vague guidance that Government officials should not accept anything that might influence them unduly. The Company in question had a policy with strict monetary limits and the restaurant had been chosen with care in order to ensure that those limits were observed. On the evening of the dinner, the four Government officials arrived with their four spouses and the sister of one of the spouses, for a total of five guests. They ordered expansively, including several bottles of expensive wine.

Many company policies prohibit gifts, meals, and entertainment for the spouses of Government officials on the premise that there is no business purpose for them to attend. Others require that the value of anything provided to the spouse of a Government official be added to the value of what is provided to the official himself, for purposes of monetary thresholds.

In this case, the employees had taken the appropriate steps to ensure compliance with the company's policy, but nevertheless ended up with a violation. The short-term response was to inform management that the policy violation was inadvertent and to account for the expense accurately in their books and records. The long-term response was the creation of an informal policy to favour business lunches over dinners, except in exceptional circumstances. Lunches are often less expensive than dinners, and spouses are far less likely to arrive unexpectedly.

Signing Ceremonies

Company B described a signing ceremony for an important and long-term contract. It was to be the third major contract signed with the same senior Government official. For each ceremony, the Company executive was expected to present his pen to the Government official after the signing and to accept the Government official's pen in return. This was a long-standing tradition and it launched the project with goodwill and positive publicity. The Company expressed concern, however, that the Government official had made clear the brand of pen he expected, going so far as to encourage the executive to buy it at the tax-free shop at the airport; it was determined that the cost of each pen was over US$300. The pen provided by the Government official in return was of little or no value, but that probably wasn't relevant to a bribery risk assessment, as it was the Government official who held decision-making authority over the contract. What may have been relevant was that US$300 was only slightly less than a mid-level Government official's monthly salary in the country in question and that this was the third pen presented in two years.

In this case, the Company determined that: (1) there was no tactful way to provide a less prestigious pen than the brand that had been requested; (2) no local laws prohibited a gift of this kind; (3) the nature of the event was sufficiently transparent to mitigate the high relative value of the item given; and (4) the contract had been awarded already and no immediate procurement decisions were before the Government official in question. Based on this analysis, the expenditure was approved.

Involuntary Entertainment

Company C described repeated requests by Government officials that fell outside permitted corporate entertainment policy thresholds. In one case, the Government officials were travelling to corporate headquarters for three days of meetings at the Company's expense. The trip was approved in accordance with the Company's policy, which required review and approval by the legal department. Shortly before their arrival, the Government officials indicated that they wanted to stay over for the weekend and visit local attractions. They asked to be escorted and made it clear that they expected the Company to pay for the weekend excursion.

The Company concluded that the weekend activities were outside the scope of the trip's legitimate business purpose and therefore could not be approved. Their compromise was to offer to book—but not pay for—a rental car for the Government officials for the weekend. When the Government officials realized that they would have to pay for the excursion themselves, they departed after the meetings as originally planned. The Company's response illustrates careful and diplomatic application of the Company's policy, although some within the Company believe that this response soured business relations with these important customers. Addressing gifts or hospitality requested by Government officials is among the greatest challenges to a robust anti-bribery compliance programme. Training employees to decline inappropriate requests is more difficult than training them not to offer inappropriate gifts or hospitality.

Meetings Prolonged for Legitimate Reasons

Unlike the previous example, Company D planned a business trip for foreign Government officials that was prolonged for legitimate reasons, raising the question of entertaining the Government officials over the weekend. This is largely uncharted water under anti-bribery laws, and companies must apply a standard of reasonableness. The Company in this case made arrangements for the weekend, but largely at the customer's expense. There was a major attraction nearby. The Company chose to provide transportation to and from the site, but it required the Government officials to bear their own costs once inside.

Just Between Friends

Company E's policy on gifts for Government officials includes monetary thresholds of US$50 which cannot be exceeded without the prior approval of the legal department. An employee who had lived in-country for many years was invited to his primary customer's house for dinner to celebrate a local holiday. The employee decided to bring a more lavish gift than Company policy permitted, worth approximately US$120. He submitted the expense falsely, recording it as two gifts given on two separate occasions; he then paid the remaining US$20 himself. The Company had several reasons for concern, including deliberate circumvention of Company policy and a books and record violation. When the Company met with the employee to discuss the situation, he indicated that the Government official was a personal friend and that he would have been happy to pay the additional amount himself.

This situation arises quite frequently when employees live overseas for long periods and develop friendships within the business community. Nevertheless, there was a breakdown in the policy that the Company needed to address. They revised their internal guidelines by: (1) limiting the frequency with which gifts can be given to Government officials to one major gift-giving holiday per year; (2) prohibiting employees from paying their own money for gifts for Government officials that are not permitted under Company policy (unless prior approval has been obtained); and (3) requiring more rigorous audits of expenditures on gifts, meals, and entertainment.

Some may find this level of compliance needlessly restrictive, and for some industries and regions it may be. However, most companies that TRACE interviewed preferred a comprehensive global approach to this issue over a regional approach or fact-specific analysis.

Per Diem

Payment of a per diem for travel expenses has long been thought a reasonable approach to managing legitimate expenses. Company F used an international table to determine an appropriate rate of per diem for a Government official's multi-city tour of the Company's facilities and then paid it in advance to ensure the official had sufficient funds upon arrival. The Government official then permitted the Company to pay for almost all meals and even some hotel rooms as these expenses arose. As a result, the Government official received double payment of his expenses. This was a violation of the Company's policy and probably of US law, which applied in this case.

The Company has since revised its policy. Now, in all cases where per diem payments will be made, the policy dictates that the per diem amount must be disclosed to the superiors of the Government official (as a part of the initial invitation) and that the amount should be paid in part upon arrival in the country and at appropriate intervals thereafter. In addition, rather than trying to monitor who would pay for each meal, the per diem was set at such a level as to anticipate that it would cover only lodging and those meals that the Government official ate alone. There are frequent stories of customers sharing hotel rooms in order to save a portion of their per diem, but there is little that companies can reasonably be expected to do to police this sort of behaviour.

Widely Attended Events

Company G sponsors frequent seminars, conferences, and trade shows to promote its products internationally. Elaborate refreshments and gifts bearing the Company's logo are typically provided at these events. The Company has been concerned in the past that they cannot monitor attendance, restrict participation by spouses, or assess the value of hospitality and gifts flowing to any one Government official.

Many companies struggle with different approaches to hospitality provided to Government officials at widely attended events. Accurately tracking attendance is not possible for companies hosting events of this kind. One event may flow into another, and Government officials may attend multiple events but stay only briefly at each one. To address this problem, TRACE researched how its member companies deal with this situation and provided a proposed model policy with criteria that, if met, would exempt an event from the Company's usual policy on gifts, meals, and entertainment. Company G adopted this policy with the criteria set forth below:

- No corrupt intent;
- More than 25 participants;
- Nationals of more than two countries, such that a country-by-country legal analysis would be impracticable;
- Reasonable and customary for the country in which the event is held;
- Per person cost of event not to exceed (monetary threshold to be determined by Company, in this case US $125).

CONCLUSION

Regardless of which approach a company takes when establishing and enforcing its gifts, meals, and entertainment policy, the issue should be addressed clearly and consistently. A consistent approach will make oversight easier and will reduce both employee confusion and the compliance or legal resources otherwise required to address this issue on an ad hoc basis.

While approving expensive gifts and lavish hospitality is less likely to undermine a company's culture of compliance than the payment of a traditional bribe, it can be symptomatic of weak internal controls. In addition, details of lavish gift-giving are often featured in media accounts of anti-bribery enforcement actions. One recent US enforcement action involved large cash transactions, but the enforcement agency nevertheless decided to include in its summary details of pedicures provided to the spouses of Government officials. The relative value of these items is often very small, but the reputational damage they can cause is extraordinary.

---

3. Exceptions and Affirmative Defenses to "Anything of Value"

a. Local Law Affirmative Defense

The 1988 amendments to the FCPA created an affirmative defense for situations where "the payment, gift, offer, or promise of anything of value that was made, was lawful under the written laws and regulations of the foreign official's . . . country."[41] However, this defense is virtually never available because no country's laws authorize bribery of its government officials. As the FCPA Guide notes:

> Congress sought "to make clear that the absence of written laws in a foreign official's country would not by itself be sufficient to satisfy this defense." Thus, the fact that bribes may not be prosecuted under local law is insufficient to establish the defense. . . . Nevertheless, if a defendant can establish that conduct that otherwise falls within the scope of the FCPA's anti-bribery provisions was lawful under written, local law, he or she would have defense to prosecution.[42]

The scope of the local law affirmative defense was discussed in *U.S. v. Kozeny*,[43] where the defendant argued that "the alleged payments were legal under Azeri law and thus under the FCPA . . . because . . . pursuant to Azeri law, any criminality associated with the payments was excused when he reported them to the President of Azerbaijan."[44] The court rejected this argument, holding:

> [T]here is no immunity from prosecution under the FCPA if a person could not have been prosecuted in the foreign country due to a technicality (e.g., time-barred) or because a provision in the foreign law "relieves" a person of criminal responsibility. An individual may be prosecuted under the FCPA for a payment that violates foreign law even if the individual is relieved of criminal responsibility for his actions by a provision of the foreign law.[45]

b. Reasonable and Bona Fide Expenditures Affirmative Defense

The FCPA provides a second affirmative defense for reasonable and bona fide expenditures:

> (2) the payment, gift, offer, or promise of anything of value that was made, was a reasonable and bona fide expenditure, such as travel and lodging expenses, incurred by or on behalf of a foreign official, party, party official, or candidate and was directly related to—
>
> (A) the promotion, demonstration, or explanation of products or services; or

---

41. 15 U.S.C. § 78dd-1(c)(1) (2012); 15 U.S.C. § 78dd-2(c)(1) (2012); 15 U.S.C. § 78dd-3(c)(1) (2012).
42. FCPA Guide, supra note 4, at 23 (citation omitted).
43. United States v. Kozeny, 582 F. Supp. 2d 535 (S.D.N.Y. 2008).
44. *Id.* at 537.
45. *Id.* at 539.

(B) the execution or performance of a contract with a foreign government or agency thereof.[46]

The DOJ and SEC interpret this affirmative defense to cover three types of expenditures: (1) "travel and expenses to visit company facilities or operations"; (2) "travel and expenses for training"; and (3) "product demonstration or promotional activities, including travel and expenses for meetings."[47] The FCPA Guide provides the following guidance to businesses seeking to take advantage of this affirmative defense:

- Do not select the particular officials who will participate in the party's proposed trip or program or else select them based on pre-determined, merit-based criteria.
- Pay all costs directly to travel and lodging vendors and/or reimburse costs only upon presentation of a receipt.
- Do not advance funds or pay for reimbursements in cash.
- Ensure that any stipends are reasonable approximations of costs likely to be incurred and/or that expenses are limited to those that are necessary and reasonable.
- Ensure the expenditures are transparent, both within the company and to the foreign government.
- Do not condition payment of expenses on any action by the foreign official.
- Obtain written confirmation that payment of the expenses is not contrary to local law.
- Provide no additional compensation, stipends, or spending money beyond what is necessary to pay or actual expenses incurred.
- Ensure that costs and expenses on behalf of the foreign officials will be accurately recorded in the company's books and records.[48]

Hypothetical: Gifts, Travel, and Entertainment[49]

Company A is a large U.S. engineering company with global operations in more than 50 countries, including a number that have a high risk of corruption, such as Foreign Country. Company A's stock is listed on a national U.S. stock exchange. In conducting its business internationally, Company A's officers and employees come into regular contact with foreign officials, including officials in various ministries and state-owned entities. At a trade show, Company A has a booth at which it offers free pens, hats, t-shirts, and other similar promotional items with Company A's logo. Company A also serves free coffee, other beverages, and snacks at the booth. Some of the visitors to the booth are foreign officials.

---

46. 15 U.S.C. § 78dd-1 (2012).
47. FCPA GUIDE, *supra* note 4, at 24.
48. *Id.*
49. FCPA GUIDE, *supra* note 4, at 17–18 (hypothetical reproduced verbatim, with answers excluded) (emphasis added).

Is Company A in violation of the FCPA?

At the trade show, Company A invites a dozen current and prospective customers out for drinks, and pays the moderate bar tab. Some of the current and prospective customers are foreign officials under the FCPA.

Is Company A in violation of the FCPA?

Two years ago, Company A won a long-term contract to supply goods and services to the state-owned Electricity Commission in Foreign Country. The Electricity Commission is 100 percent owned, controlled, and operated by the government of Foreign Country, and employees of the Electricity Commission are subject to Foreign Country's domestic bribery laws. Some Company A executives are in Foreign Country for meetings with officials of the Electricity Commission. The General Manager of the Electricity Commission was recently married, and during the trip Company A executives present a moderately priced crystal vase to the General Manager as a wedding gift and token of esteem.

Is Company A in violation of the FCPA?

During the course of the contract described above, Company A periodically provides training to Electricity Commission employees at its facilities in Michigan. The training is paid for by the Electricity Commission as part of the contract. Senior officials of the Electricity Commission inform Company A that they want to inspect the facilities and ensure that the training is working well. Company A pays for the airfare, hotel, and transportation for the Electricity Commission senior officials to travel to Michigan to inspect Company A's facilities. Because it is a lengthy international flight, Company A agrees to pay for business class airfare, to which its own employees are entitled for lengthy flights. The foreign officials visit Michigan for several days, during which the senior officials perform an appropriate inspection. Company A executives take the officials to a moderately priced dinner, a baseball game, and a play.

Do any of these actions violate the FCPA? Would this analysis be different if Company A instead paid for the senior officials to travel first class with their spouses for an all-expenses-paid, week-long trip to Las Vegas, where Company A has no facilities?

Company A's contract with the Electricity Commission is going to expire, and the Electricity Commission is offering the next contract through its tender process. An employee of the Electricity Commission contacts Company A and offers to provide Company A with confidential, nonpublic bid information from Company A's competitors if Company A will pay for a vacation to Paris for him and his girlfriend. Employees of Company A accede to the official's request, pay for the vacation, receive the confidential bid information, and yet still do not win the contract.

Has Company A violated the FCPA?

c. Exception for Facilitating or Expediting Payments

In some countries, securing routine nondiscretionary government services—like visa processing or mail delivery—requires payment of a petty bribe. The FCPA excepts such payments, referred to as "facilitating" or "grease" payments:

(b) Exception for routine governmental action

> [The FCPA anti-bribery provisions] shall not apply to any facilitating or expediting payment to a foreign official, political party, or party official the purpose of which is to expedite or to secure the performance of a routine governmental action by a foreign official, political party, or party official.[50]

"In exempting facilitating payments, Congress sought to distinguish them as payments which merely move a particular matter toward an eventual act or decision or which do not involve any discretionary action." In *United States v. Kay*,[51] the Fifth Circuit underscored the limited nature of this exception:

> A brief review of the types of routine governmental actions enumerated by Congress shows how limited Congress wanted to make the grease exceptions. Routine governmental action, for instance, includes "obtaining permits, licenses, or other official documents to qualify a person to do business in a foreign country," and "scheduling inspections associated with contract performance or inspections related to transit of goods across country." Therefore, routine governmental action does not include the issuance of *every* official document or *every* inspection, but only (1) documentation that qualifies a party to do business and (2) scheduling an inspection—very narrow categories of largely non-discretionary, ministerial activities performed by mid- or low-level foreign functionaries.[52]

The FCPA Guide lists several circumstances under which a payment to a government official qualifies under this exception:

- Obtaining permits, licenses, or other official documents to qualify a person to do business in a foreign country;
- Processing governmental papers, such as visas and work orders;
- Providing police protection, mail pickup, and delivery, or scheduling inspections associated with contract performance or inspections related to transit of goods across country;
- Providing phone service, power, and water supply, loading and unloading cargo, or protecting perishable products or commodities from deterioration; or
- Actions of a similar nature.[53]

---

50. 15 U.S.C. § 78dd-1(b) (2012).
51. United States v. Kay, 359 F.3d 738, 750–51 (5th Cir. 2004) (internal footnote omitted) (emphasis in original).
52. FCPA Guide, *supra* note 4, at n.161 (quoting *id.*).
53. *See* FCPA Guide, *supra* note 4, at 25.

Nonetheless, the DOJ and SEC strongly discourage companies from making "grease" payments in reliance on this exception:

> Although true facilitating payments are not illegal under the FCPA, they may still violate local law in the countries where the company is operating, and the OECD's Working Group on Bribery recommends that all countries encourage companies to prohibit or discourage facilitating payments, which the United States has done regularly. In addition, other countries' foreign bribery laws, such as the United Kingdom's, may not contain an exception for facilitating payments. Individuals and companies should therefore be aware that although true facilitating payments are permissible under the FCPA, they may still subject a company or individual to sanctions. As with any expenditure, facilitating payments may still violate the FCPA if they are not properly recorded in an issuer's books and records.[54]

Facilitation Payments

Alexandra Wrage & Kerry Mandernach, TRACE (2006)[55]

Most multinational companies have made progress toward eliminating traditional bribes from their business practices. They have done this by implementing comprehensive compliance programmes, by training local and foreign employees and business intermediaries, and by rigorous internal enforcement. Some of these companies are now taking steps to eliminate "facilitation payments" from their business practices as well. These small bribes, permitted under an exception in the US Foreign Corrupt Practices Act and under the laws of some countries, are made to Government officials to encourage them to perform or expedite routine, non-discretionary Governmental tasks.

. . . .

THE PROBLEM

In many companies, a distinction has long been drawn between major bribes and mere "facilitation payments." The distinction has been confusing. Bribes and "facilitation payments" are both payments or gifts to, or favours for, Government officials in exchange for preferential treatment. If companies pay these small bribes willingly, they are nevertheless bribes. If companies pay these bribes because they believe they have no choice, they are extortionate.

54. *Id.* at 25–26.
55. Alexandra Wrage & Kerry Mandernach, *Facilitation Payments, in* BRAY ET AL., *supra* note 40, at 69–71.

Double Standard

Of the countries that permit these small bribes overseas, none permits them at home. A Canadian or American who makes a "grease payment" to a foreign customs official would face criminal penalties for making the same payment to an official at home. Permitting the citizens of one country to violate the laws of another on the grounds that it is "how they do business there," corrodes international legal standards that otherwise benefit multinational corporations.

A Slippery Slope

The mixed message of permissible small bribes versus impermissible large bribes creates a risky arena for business activities. Many companies interviewed complained that small bribes involving routine Governmental tasks are both difficult to define and impossible to control. They found that some employees, responding to pressure to ensure timely contract performance, paid bribes for distinctly non-routine services. Furthermore, it is difficult to convey to employees why the payment of large bribes to foreign Government officials is likely to cost the employee his job and possibly his freedom, but that the payment of small bribes is acceptable.

Loss of Local Community's Confidence

It is difficult to maintain a good reputation within a local business community when your company is believed to buy its way past the administrative obstacles that local citizens and companies must endure. When a bureaucratic delay is legitimate—rather than created by the bribe-taker—purchasing preferential treatment for your company bumps others further down the waiting list.

Inherent Illegality

Every bribe of a Government official—regardless of size—breaks the law of at least one country. There is no country anywhere with a written law permitting the bribery of its officials. A lack of resources, political will or interest has meant violations are rarely prosecuted, but that is changing. Some countries, eager to be seen combating corruption, are prosecuting the payment of small bribes with increasing frequency. As a result, there is widespread concern amongst the companies that TRACE interviewed that small bribes could lead to costly legal complications.

Accounting Dilemma

The laws of countries that permit the payment of these bribes abroad also require companies to maintain detailed and accurate records of each transaction. Many businesspeople interviewed expressed reluctance to record on company books a "payment to Government official for routine task"—creating a record of a violation of local law. Yet, failure to keep accurate records of the expense constitutes a violation of law even in countries where the underlying payment does not. Consequently, companies making these payments must choose between falsifying their records in violation of their own laws or recording the payment accurately and documenting a violation of local law.

Foreign Subsidiaries

With the implementation in many countries of new laws criminalizing the payment of small bribes to foreign Governments, there is also an increasing risk that a multinational company with foreign subsidiaries will violate the laws of the country where the subsidiary is based. Companies with offices in more than one country expressed concern that if they do not abolish the use of small bribes altogether, they must undertake different compliance programmes based not only upon the location of each office, but the citizenship of the people working there.

International Security

In addition to the legal issues, there is a growing concern regarding national security. One US company reported that the terrorist attacks of September 2001 put a new face on the practice of paying small bribes. That company had routinely paid foreign officials for processing work permits and visas, but is now very uncomfortable promoting corruption in this area. If visas can be bought, borders won't be safe. The practice of bribing immigration officials can lead to serious entanglements with the enhanced security laws of the company's home country.

Bad for Business

Paying small bribes is poor legal practice, but more to the point, it is bad business practice. Widespread small bribes set a permissive tone, which invites more and greater demands. Every company that TRACE interviewed expressed dissatisfaction with these small bribes. They told us that they amount to a hidden tax on business, they tend to proliferate, they buy an uncertain, unenforceable advantage and—the most common complaint—they are simply irritating. Well-run businesses seek clear, dependable terms and enforceable contracts. Small bribes introduce uncertainty, risk and delay.

Reputation as a "Soft Touch"

The standard argument in defence of bribery is that it is impossible to conduct business successfully overseas without paying bribes to ease the bureaucratic and regulatory burden. If true, business should be more efficient for companies paying bribes, yet this argument is not supported by research or anecdote. Two World Bank researchers studied the premise that small bribes reduce red tape and found that "contrary to the efficient grease theory . . . firms that pay more bribes are also likely to spend more, not less, management time with bureaucrats negotiating regulations and face higher, not lower, cost of capital."

. . . .

MEDICAL AND SAFETY EMERGENCY EXCEPTION

Employees of multinational companies are occasionally asked to travel and live abroad in countries where the standard of living is lower than their own country and the risks to health and safety are higher. Many companies currently rely on the good judgement of their employees in these situations, but some have created a formal medical and safety emergency exception. The situation should be a true emergency and the payment should be accounted for appropriately and reported through management channels both to conform to books and records requirements and to ensure that management is apprised of and can track the risks to personnel in that country.

Questions

1) Other than illegality under local law, why else should companies prohibit facilitating payments?
2) Under what circumstances, if any, should a company tolerate the use of grease payments?

Hypothetical: Facilitating Payments

SwissCo. is an issuer headquartered in Geneva, Switzerland, that produces seeds for agricultural wholesale. In July, SwissCo. makes a large shipment of highly perishable seeds to its subsidiary in Tanzania ("SwissCo. TZ"). Just as SwissCo. TZ's employees in Dar es Salaam take delivery of the seeds, their warehouse loses power—a frequent occurrence.

Without refrigeration, the seeds will quickly perish. An employee of the public utility company offers to turn the power back on immediately in exchange for $10,000.

SwissCo.'s code of conduct strictly prohibits facilitation payments. The manager of SwissCo. TZ makes an appeal to SwissCo.'s chief compliance officer ("CCO") to allow the payment to save the seeds.

How should SwissCo.'s CCO respond?

Hypothetical: Facilitating Payments[56]

Company A is a large multinational mining company with operations in Foreign Country, where it recently identified a significant new ore deposit. It has ready buyers for the new ore but has limited capacity to get it to market. To increase the size and speed of its ore export, Company A will need to build a new road from its facility to the port that can accommodate larger trucks. Company A retains an agent in Foreign Country to assist it in obtaining the required permits, including an environmental permit, to build the road. The agent informs Company A's vice president for international operations that he plans to make a one-time small cash payment to a clerk

---

56. FCPA GUIDE, *supra* note 4, at 26 (hypothetical reproduced verbatim, with answers excluded) (emphasis added).

in the relevant government office to ensure that the clerk files and stamps the permit applications expeditiously, as the agent has experienced delays of three months when he has not made this "grease" payment. The clerk has no discretion about whether to file and stamp the permit applications once the requisite filing fee has been paid. The vice president authorizes the payment.

A few months later, the agent tells the vice president that he has run into a problem obtaining a necessary environmental permit. It turns out that the planned road construction would adversely impact an environmentally sensitive and protected local wetland. While the problem could be overcome by rerouting the road, such rerouting would cost Company A $1 million more and would slow down construction by six months. It would also increase the transit time for the ore and reduce the number of monthly shipments. The agent tells the vice president that he is good friends with the director of Foreign Country's Department of Natural Resources and that it would only take a modest cash payment to the director and the "problem would go away." The vice president authorizes the payment, and the agent makes it. After receiving the payment, the director issues the permit, and Company A constructs its new road through the wetlands.

Was the payment to the clerk a violation of the FCPA? Was the payment to the director a violation of the FCPA?

C. Meaning of "Foreign Official"

Section 30A of the Exchange Act defines the term "foreign official" as:

> [A]ny officer or employee of a foreign government or any department, agency, or instrumentality thereof, or of a public international organization, or any person acting in an official capacity for or on behalf of any such government or department, agency, or instrumentality, or for or on behalf of any such public international organization.[57]

The DOJ and SEC interpret this provision to mean that any employee of a foreign government qualifies as a foreign official, regardless of rank or function.

Construing the term government "instrumentality" has been problematic because the distinction between government and private enterprise is often blurred in countries transitioning from planned to market economies.[58] For example, as one practitioner observed:

> We have found that our clients are frequently and particularly challenged in China, where there may be a governmental hand in many aspects of private life.

---

57. 15 U.S.C. § 78dd-1(f)(1)(A) (2012); 15 U.S.C. § 78dd-2(h)(2)(A) (2012); 15 U.S.C. § 78dd-3(f)(2)(A) (2012).

58. *See* U.S. Dep't of Commerce, Business Ethics: A Manual for Managing A Responsible Business Enterprise in Emerging Market Economies 274 (2004) [hereinafter BEM].

That involvement may not be completely obvious to an outsider. For example, because China has socialized medicine, doctors in most Chinese hospitals would be considered government officials for purposes of the [FCPA].[59]

The legal distinction between a state "instrumentality" and a private entity carries enormous consequences: If an entity qualifies as a government instrumentality, each of its employees will be considered a government official.[60]

A Resource Guide to the U.S. Foreign Corrupt Practices Act

Criminal Division of the U.S. Department of Justice and the Enforcement Division of the U.S. Securities and Exchange Commission[61]

WHO IS A FOREIGN OFFICIAL?

The FCPA's anti-bribery provisions apply to corrupt payments made to (1) "any foreign official"; (2) "any foreign political party or official thereof"; (3) "any candidate for foreign political office"; or (4) any person, while knowing that all or a portion of the payment will be offered, given, or promised to an individual falling within one of these three categories. Although the statute distinguishes between a "foreign official," "foreign political party or official thereof," and "candidate for foreign political office," the term "foreign official" in this guide generally refers to an individual falling within any of these three categories.

. . . .

[T]he FCPA broadly applies to corrupt payments to "any" officer or employee of a foreign government and to those acting on the foreign government's behalf. The FCPA thus covers corrupt payments to low-ranking employees and high-level officials alike.

The FCPA prohibits payments to foreign officials, not to foreign governments. That said, companies contemplating contributions or donations to foreign governments should take steps to ensure that no monies are used for corrupt purposes, such as the personal benefit of individual foreign officials.

DEPARTMENT, AGENCY, OR INSTRUMENTALITY OF A FOREIGN GOVERNMENT

Foreign officials under the FCPA include officers or employees of a department, agency, or instrumentality of a foreign government. When a foreign government is organized in a fashion similar to the U.S. system, what constitutes a government department or agency is typically clear (e.g., a ministry of energy, national security agency, or transportation authority). However, governments can be organized in very different ways. Many operate through state-owned

---

59. Amy Westbrook, *Enthusiastic Enforcement, Informal Legislation: The Unruly Expansion of the Foreign Corrupt Practices Act*, 45 GA. L. REV. 489, 534 (2011) (citations omitted).

60. FCPA GUIDE, *supra* note 4, at 19-21.

61. *Id.*

and state-controlled entities, particularly in such areas as aerospace and defense manufacturing, banking and finance, healthcare and life sciences, energy and extractive industries, telecommunications, and transportation. By including officers or employees of agencies and instrumentalities within the definition of "foreign official," the FCPA accounts for this variability.

The term "instrumentality" is broad and can include state-owned or state-controlled entities. Whether a particular entity constitutes an "instrumentality" under the FCPA requires a fact-specific analysis of an entity's ownership, control, status, and function. A number of courts have approved final jury instructions providing a non-exclusive list of factors to be considered:

- the foreign state's extent of ownership of the entity;
- the foreign state's degree of control over the entity (including whether key officers and directors of the entity are, or are appointed by, government officials);
- the foreign state's characterization of the entity and its employees;
- the circumstances surrounding the entity's creation;
- the purpose of the entity's activities;
- the entity's obligations and privileges under the foreign state's law;
- the exclusive or controlling power vested in the entity to administer its designated functions;
- the level of financial support by the foreign state (including subsidies, special tax treatment, government-mandated fees, and loans);
- the entity's provision of services to the jurisdiction's residents;
- whether the governmental end or purpose sought to be achieved is expressed in the policies of the foreign government; and
- the general perception that the entity is performing official or governmental functions.

Companies should consider these factors when evaluating the risk of FCPA violations and designing compliance programs.

DOJ and SEC have pursued cases involving instrumentalities since the time of the FCPA's enactment and have long used an analysis of ownership, control, status, and function to determine whether a particular entity is an agency or instrumentality of a foreign government. For example, the second-ever FCPA case charged by DOJ involved a California company that paid bribes through a Mexican corporation to two executives of a state-owned Mexican national oil company. And in the early 1980s, DOJ and SEC brought cases involving a $1 million bribe to the chairman of Trinidad and Tobago's racing authority.

DOJ and SEC continue to regularly bring FCPA cases involving bribes paid to employees of agencies and instrumentalities of foreign governments. In one such case, the subsidiary of a Swiss engineering company paid bribes to officials of a state-owned and controlled electricity commission. The commission was created by, owned by, and controlled by the Mexican government, and it had a monopoly on the transmission and distribution of electricity in Mexico. Many of the commission's board members were cabinet-level government officials, and the director was appointed by Mexico's president. Similarly, in another recent case, Miami telecommunications executives were charged with paying bribes to employees of Haiti's state-owned and controlled telecommunications company. The telecommunications company was 97% owned and 100% controlled by the Haitian government, and its director was appointed by Haiti's president.

While no one factor is dispositive or necessarily more important than another, as a practical matter, an entity is unlikely to qualify as an instrumentality if a government does not own or control a majority of its shares. However, there are circumstances in which an entity would qualify as an instrumentality absent 50% or greater foreign government ownership, which is reflected in the limited number of DOJ or SEC enforcement actions brought in such situations. For example, in addition to being convicted of funneling millions of dollars in bribes to two sitting presidents in two different countries, a French issuer's three subsidiaries were convicted of paying bribes to employees of a Malaysian telecommunications company that was 43% owned by Malaysia's Ministry of Finance. There, notwithstanding its minority ownership stake in the company, the Ministry held the status of a "special shareholder" had veto power over all major expenditures and controlled important operational decisions. In addition, most senior company officers were political appointees, including the Chairman and Director, the Chairman of the Board of the Tender Committee, and the Executive Director. Thus, despite the Malaysian government having a minority shareholder position, the company was an instrumentality of the Malaysian government as the government nevertheless had substantial control over the company.

Companies and individuals should also remember that, whether an entity is an instrumentality of a foreign government or a private entity, commercial (i.e., private-to-private) bribery may still violate the FCPA's accounting provisions, the Travel Act, anti-money laundering laws, and other federal or foreign laws. Any type of corrupt payment thus carries a risk of prosecution.

PUBLIC INTERNATIONAL ORGANIZATIONS

In 1998, the FCPA was amended to expand the definition of "foreign official" to include employees and representatives of public international organizations. A "public international organization" is any organization designated as such by Executive Order under the International Organizations Immunities Act, 22 U.S.C. § 288, or any other organization that the President so designates. Currently, public international organizations include entities such as the World Bank, the International Monetary Fund, the World Intellectual Property Organization, the World Trade Organization, the OECD, the Organization of American States, and numerous others.

Notes and Questions

The original FCPA enacted in 1977 did not explicitly cover "employees" of foreign governments, but only their "officials." By adding the term "employees" in the 1988 amendments, Congress significantly broadened the definition of the term "foreign official." However, at the same time, Congress added the exception for facilitating payments.

> Prior to 1988, the "facilitating payments" exception was incorporated into the definition of "foreign official," which excluded from the statute's purview officials whose duties were primarily ministerial or clerical. See Foreign Corrupt Practices Act of 1977 (providing that the term foreign official "does not include any employee of a foreign government or any department, agency, or instrumentality thereof whose duties are essentially ministerial or clerical"). The original exception thus focused on the duties of the recipient, rather than the purpose of the payment. In practice, however, it proved difficult to determine whether a foreign official's duties were "ministerial or clerical." Responding to criticism that the statutory language "does not clearly reflect Congressional intent and the boundaries of the prohibited conduct," Congress revised the FCPA to define the exception in terms of the purpose of the payment. In doing so, Congress reiterated that while its policy to exclude facilitating payments reflected practical considerations of enforcement, "such payments should not be condoned."[62]

1) Why did Congress originally exclude government employees whose duties were ministerial or clerical?

2) Does the exception for facilitating payments in the 1988 amendment effectively serve the same purpose?

A foreign official is defined by the OECD Anti-Bribery Convention as:

> [A]ny person holding a legislative, administrative or judicial office of a foreign country, whether appointed or elected; any person exercising a public function for a foreign country, including for a public agency or public enterprise; and any official or agent of a public international organization[.][63]

3) Is the FCPA's definition of "foreign official" broader than that of the OECD Anti-Bribery Convention? If so, what are the implications?

Hypothetical: Hiring Royal Family Member as Consultant

The following is an excerpt from FCPA Opinion Release 12-01:[64]

The Department of Justice (the "Department") has reviewed the Foreign Corrupt Practices Act ("FCPA") Opinion Procedure Request of a U.S. lobbying firm (the "Requestor") that was submitted on February 15, 2012 (the "Request") . . . regarding whether certain specified, prospective—not hypothetical—conduct conforms with the Department's present enforcement

---

62. FCPA Guide, *supra* note 4, at 111 n.159.
63. OECD Anti-Bribery Convention, *supra* note 6, at 229.
64. U.S. Dep't. of Justice, Criminal Division, Opinion Release on Foreign Corrupt Practices Act, No. 12-01 (Sept. 18, 2012), https://www.justice.gov/sites/default/files/criminal-fraud/legacy/2012/09/27/1201.pdf.

policy regarding the anti-bribery provisions of the FCPA. The Requestor represents that the facts and circumstances are as set forth below.

The Requestor wishes to represent the Embassy of a foreign country (the "Foreign Country") to the United States and the Foreign Country's Foreign Ministry (collectively, the "Foreign Country Embassy") in its lobbying activities in the United States. To facilitate that lobbying representation, the Requestor further wishes to contract with a third party (the "Consulting Company") to introduce the Requestor to the Foreign Country Embassy, to advise the Requestor on cultural awareness issues in dealing with the Foreign Country's officials and businesses, to act as the Requestor's sponsor in the Foreign Country, to help the Requestor establish an office in the Foreign Country, and to identify additional business opportunities for the Requestor in the Foreign Country. One of the partners in the Consulting Company is a member of the royal family of the Foreign Country (the "Royal Family Member"), although he holds no position in the government. The Requestor requests an FCPA Opinion Release regarding: (1) whether the Royal Family Member is a "foreign official" under the FCPA; and (2) whether the Requestor's proposed engagement with the Consulting Company would result in any enforcement action by the Department.

Based on the Department's review of the Request, as well as the additional information received from the Requestor, it is the Department's opinion that the Royal Family Member does not qualify as a foreign official under 15 U.S.C. § 78dd-2(h)(2)(A), so long as the Royal Family Member does not directly or indirectly represent that he is acting on behalf of the royal family or in his capacity as a member of the royal family. Accordingly, based on the facts as represented by the Requestor, the Requestor's proposed engagement of the Consulting Company to assist in its potential representation of the Foreign Country Embassy in its U.S. lobbying efforts may go forward without enforcement action. The Department does not opine about any other aspect of the proposed engagement.

BACKGROUND

I. The Requestor

The Requestor, which is a partnership engaged in lobbying activities, is organized under U.S. law and headquartered in the United States. As such, it is a domestic concern under 15 U.S.C. § 78dd-2(h)(1)(B).

II. The Consulting Company

The Consulting Company is a limited liability company located in both the United States and the Foreign Country. The Consulting Company has three partners, one of which is the Royal Family Member.

The Royal Family Member holds no title or position in the government, has no governmental duties or responsibilities, is a member of the royal family through custom and tradition rather than blood relation, and has no benefits or privileges because of his status. The Royal Family Member has held only one governmental position in the Foreign Country: in the late 1990s, he served for less than twelve months in a position overseeing a governmental construction project.

Other than this one previous governmental position, the Royal Family Member does not act—and has never acted—in any capacity for, or on behalf of, the Foreign Country, or any department, agency, or instrumentality of the Foreign Country. The Royal Family Member has also never had any role in any public organization. The Royal Family Member's position in the royal family does not put him in line to ascend to any governmental post.

Any private sector company planning to open an office or operate a business in the Foreign Country is required by law to have local sponsorship. The Royal Family Member has sponsored numerous foreign companies wishing to do business in the Foreign Country. In his work on behalf of these foreign companies, the Royal Family Member interacts in his personal capacity (i.e., not on behalf of the royal family) with government officials of the Foreign Country who are not themselves members of the royal family.

III. The Requestor's Engagement of the Consulting Company

The Requestor wishes to provide the Foreign Country Embassy with lobbying, business development, and policy services in the United States.

At present, neither the Requestor nor anyone from the Consulting Company, including the Royal Family Member, has had any contact with any member of the Foreign Country Embassy or any other governmental agency regarding the proposed engagement. The Foreign Country's Ambassador to the United States will personally make the decision whether to retain the Requestor. Once the Ambassador makes a decision, he will then forward his recommendation to the Foreign Country's Foreign Minister for his formal approval. If approved, the subsequent agreement will then be signed by the Ambassador on behalf of the Foreign Country's government. The Royal Family Member does not have any relationship—familial, professional, or personal—with the Ambassador and does not personally know the Ambassador. The Royal Family Member also does not have any relationship—familial, professional, or personal—with the Foreign Minister but is an acquaintance.

In this engagement, the Requestor would monitor actions taken by the U.S. Congress and the U.S. Administration that could impact the Foreign Country, present analyses of those activities, and recommend appropriate courses of action. As necessary, the Requestor would then engage in lobbying services for the Foreign Country related to U.S. governmental activity. The Requestor would also introduce Foreign Country officials to Members of Congress and Administration officials who may be able to take appropriate actions that may help improve the Foreign Country's economic and business relationship with the United States. Those contacted would also be asked to raise awareness within the United States about the Foreign Country and improve the Foreign Country's image with the people of the United States. The Requestor would create a strategic plan to raise the Foreign Country's visibility in the United States. The Requestor and the Consulting Company would create culturally appropriate promotional materials to complement this strategic plan.

A. The Consulting Company's Services

The Requestor wishes to retain the Consulting Company to introduce the Requestor to the Foreign Country Embassy and assist the Requestor in providing services to the Foreign Country Embassy. Under the terms of the proposed agreement between the Requestor and the Consulting Company,[65] the Consulting Company would provide "strategic advice and counsel on public policy and business development issues of interest to the [Foreign Country Embassy], as well as make selected liaisons with U.S. and [Foreign Country] interlocutors on behalf of the [Foreign Country Embassy]." The Requestor believes that the Royal Family Member's experience and expertise in matters relating to the Foreign Country are essential to its successful lobbying efforts on behalf of the Foreign Country Embassy.

In addition to these services, the Consulting Company may also work to identify additional business opportunities in the Foreign Country for the Requestor. Any such additional work would be the subject of a separate engagement letter between the Requestor and the Consulting Company.

B. The Structure and Payment Terms of the Agreement

The proposed agreement between the Requestor and the Consulting Company includes the Consulting Company's representation that "none of its members, or principals are 'foreign officials' as that term is defined in the FCPA." The Consulting Company "further represents that its principals and members are familiar with, and agree to abide by, the FCPA and all U.S. and [Foreign Country] anti-bribery and anticorruption laws."[66] In addition, the Consulting Company's principals have adopted the Good Practice Guidance on Internal Controls, Ethics and Compliance issued by the Organization for Economic Cooperation and Development (OECD) and have pledged that all partners and employees would be bound by the procedures covered in the Good Practices Guide.

---

65. The proposed agreement also provides that "[b]oth [the Requestor] and [the Consulting Company] agree that [the Requestor] will submit this proposed contract to the United States Department of Justice for review under its Foreign Corrupt Practices Act Opinion Procedure and that this agreement will not become effective until such approval is received."

66. The Foreign Country has signed and ratified the United Nations Convention Against Corruption, which prohibits bribery of both domestic and foreign public officials.

Further, the Requestor has committed that "to ensure this arrangement is transparent to the [Foreign Country] and the general public, full disclosure of [the Royal Family Member]'s relationship to the royal family will be made to all relevant parties in both the United States and the [Foreign Country]." The Requestor has also committed that, "[i]n the spirit of full disclosure, [the Consulting Company]'s name, and the names of its partners, will be included in [the Requestor]'s contract with the [Foreign Country], and [the Consulting Company] also will sign the contract."

The Foreign Country Embassy in the United States would pay the Requestor for its lobbying services through a retainer agreement. The Requestor and the Foreign Country Embassy would negotiate the monthly fee for the services to be provided. The Requestor has represented that it anticipates being paid within a typical range at the going fair market rate.

Pursuant to the terms of the proposed engagement contract between the Requestor and the Consulting Company, the Foreign Country Embassy would pay fees to the Requestor and, in turn, the Requestor would compensate the Consulting Company for the services it performs. The Requestor anticipates paying to the Consulting Company twenty percent of what it receives from the Foreign Country Embassy, so long as that percentage accurately reflects the amount of work provided. For each set of services the Consulting Company provides, the Requestor and the Consulting Company would agree in advance on the scope of the Consulting Company's work. For additional contracts, the percentage may be higher depending on the Consulting Company's role.

The Consulting Company would split its portion of the payment equally among its three partners, one of whom is the Royal Family Member. The amount paid to the Consulting Company by the Requestor would be on a pro-rata basis. The Requestor anticipates that the monthly payment to each of the three principals would likely be approximately $2,000.

The Requestor represents that the fee it anticipates paying to the Consulting Company is at or below that charged by other entities, including the Requestor itself, for similar services.

Although the Requestor anticipates contracting with the Foreign Country Embassy and the Consulting Company separately, it has represented that there is no provision of the Foreign Country's law that would prohibit the Foreign Country Embassy from directly contracting with or paying the Consulting Company or the Royal Family Member. The Requestor has represented that it prefers the current arrangement, under which the Foreign Country Embassy would retain the Requestor and the Requestor would in turn retain the Consulting Company.

How should the DOJ respond to this request?

United States v. Esquenazi

U.S. Court of Appeals for the Eleventh Circuit, 752 F.3d 912 (11th Cir. 2014)

OPINION

MARTIN, Circuit Judge:

Joel Esquenazi and Carlos Rodriguez appeal their convictions and sentences imposed after a jury convicted them of conspiracy, violating the Foreign Corrupt Practices Act, and money-laundering. After careful review, and with the benefit of oral argument, we affirm.

I.

In December 2009, a grand jury indicted Messrs. Esquenazi and Rodriguez on 21 counts. Two of these were conspiracy charges that spanned November 2001 through March 2005: conspiracy to violate the Foreign Corrupt Practices Act (FCPA) and commit wire fraud, all in violation of 18 U.S.C. § 371 (Count 1); and conspiracy to launder money, in violation of 18 U.S.C. § 1956 (Count 9). Counts 2 through 8 charged substantive violations of the FCPA, 15 U.S.C. § 78dd–2. And Counts 10 through 21 charged acts of concealment money laundering, in violation of 18 U.S.C. § 1956(a)(1)(B)(i).

A. Trial

Messrs. Esquenazi and Rodriguez co-owned Terra Telecommunications Corp. (Terra), a Florida company that purchased phone time from foreign vendors and resold the minutes to customers in the United States. Mr. Esquenazi, Terra's majority owner, served as President and Chief Executive Officer. Mr. Rodriguez, the company's minority owner, served as Executive Vice President of Operations. James Dickey served as Terra's general counsel and Antonio Perez as the company's comptroller.

One of Terra's main vendors was Telecommunications D'Haiti, S.A.M. (Teleco). Because the relationship of Teleco to the Haitian government was, and remains, at issue in this case, the government presented evidence of Teleco's ties to Haiti. Former Teleco Director of International Relations Robert Antoine testified that Teleco was owned by Haiti. An insurance broker, John Marsha, testified that, when Messrs. Rodriguez and Esquenazi were involved in previous contract negotiations with Teleco, they sought political-risk insurance, a type of coverage that applies only when a foreign government is party to an agreement. In emails with Mr. Marsha copied to Messrs. Esquenazi and Rodríguez, Mr. Dickey called Teleco an "instrumentality" of the Haitian government.

An expert witness, Luis Gary Lissade, testified regarding Teleco's history. At Teleco's formation in 1968, the Haitian government gave the company a monopoly on telecommunication services. Teleco had significant tax advantages and, at its inception, the government appointed two members of Teleco's board of directors. Haiti's President appointed Teleco's Director General, its top position, by an executive order that was also signed by the Haitian Prime Minister, the minister of public works, and the minister of economy and finance. In the early 1970s, the National Bank of Haiti gained 97 percent ownership of Teleco. From that time forward, the Haitian President appointed all of Teleco's board members. Sometime later, the National Bank of Haiti split into two separate entities, one of which was the Banque de la Republique d'Haiti (BRH). BRH, the central bank of Haiti, is roughly equivalent to the United States Federal Reserve. BRH retained ownership of Teleco. In Mr. Lissade's expert opinion, for the years relevant to this case, Teleco belonged "totally to the state" and "was considered . . . a public entity."

Mr. Lissade also testified that Teleco's business entity suffix, S.A.M., indicates "associate anonymous mixed," which means the "Government put money in the corporation." Teleco's suffix was attached not by statute, but "de facto" because "the government consider[ed] Teleco as its . . . entity." In 1996, Haiti passed a "modernization" law, seeking to privatize many public institutions. As a result, Haiti privatized Teleco sometime between 2009 and 2010. Ultimately, Mr. Lissade opined that, during the years relevant to this case, "Teleco was part of the public administration." He explained: "There was no specific law that . . . decided that at the beginning that Teleco is a public entity but government, officials, every-one consider[ed] Teleco as a public administration." And, he said, "if there was a doubt whatsoever, the [anti-corruption] law [that] came in 2008 vanish[ed] com-pletely this doubt . . . by citing Teleco as a public administration" and by requiring its agents—whom Mr. Lissade said were public agents—to declare all assets to avoid secret bribes.

In 2001 Terra contracted to buy minutes from Teleco directly. At that time, Teleco's Director General was Patrick Joseph (appointed by then-President Jean-Bertrand Aristide), and the Director of International Relations was Robert Antoine. Mr. Antoine had two friends and business associates who played a role in this case: Jean Fourcand, a grocery-store owner, and Juan Diaz.

By October 2001, Terra owed Teleco over $400,000. So Mr. Perez testified, Mr. Esquenazi asked him to contact Mr. Antoine and negotiate an amortization deal or, alternatively, to offer a side payment. Mr. Perez met with Mr. Antoine, who rejected the idea of amortization but agreed to a side payment to ease Terra's debt. The deal, according to Mr. Perez, was that Mr. Antoine would shave min-utes from Terra's bills to Teleco in exchange for receiving from Terra fifty percent of what the company saved. Mr. Antoine suggested that Terra disguise the pay-ments by making them to sham companies, which Terra ultimately did. Mr. Perez returned to Mr. Esquenazi and told him the news and later shared details of the deal in a meeting with Messrs. Esquenazi, Rodriguez, and Dickey. The four dis-cussed "the fact that Robert Antoine had accepted an arrangement to accept . . . payments to him in exchange for reducing [Terra's] bills." Mr. Perez testified: "[Mr. Esquenazi] was happy, and both James Dickey and Carlos Rodriguez also congratulated me on a job well done."

The following month, in November 2001, Terra began funneling personal payments to Mr. Antoine using the following subterfuge. Mr. Dickey, on Terra's behalf, drafted a "consulting agreement" between Terra and a company Mr. Antoine had suggested be called J.D. Locator. J.D. Locator, an otherwise insolvent company, was owned by Mr. Antoine's friend Juan Diaz. During the course of the next several months, Messrs. Rodriguez and Esquenazi authorized payments to J.D. Locator via "check requests," forms Terra used to write checks without invoices. Mr. Diaz testified that he knew the payments Terra made were not for legitimate consulting services and that he never intended to provide such services. Instead, Mr. Diaz retained ten percent of the funds Terra paid J.D. Locator and disbursed the remainder, usually either to Mr. Antoine or his business associate Mr. Fourcand. Mr. Fourcand testified that he knew he was receiving money from Terra (through J.D. Locator) that would ultimately go to Mr. Antoine and that Mr. Antoine asked him to be part of that deal. All told, while Mr. Antoine remained at Teleco, Terra paid him and his associates approximately $822,000. And, during that time, Terra's bills were reduced by over $2 million.

In April 2003, President Aristide removed Mr. Antoine and named Alphonse Inevil as his replacement. Mr. Inevil soon replaced Mr. Joseph as Director General, and Jean Rene Duperval replaced Inevil. Later that year, with Terra still behind on its bills, Mr. Esquenazi helped Mr. Duperval form a shell company, Telecom Consulting Services Corporation (TCSC), through which Esquenazi ultimately would make side payments to Mr. Duperval. TCSC's president was Margurite Grandison, Mr. Duperval's sister; its incorporator and registered agent was Mr. Dickey; and the company's principal business address was a post office box that named Mr. Duperval as the person empowered to receive mail through it. Ms. Grandison executed a "commission agreement" with Terra, which Mr. Esquenazi signed. And on November 20, Mr. Rodriguez authorized the first transfer, $15,000, to TCSC. Over the next five months, although Terra received no invoices to reflect money owed TCSC, Terra made six additional transfers to TCSC totaling $60,000. Each of these seven transfers is the subject of the substantive FCPA counts. Ms. Grandison then disbursed money from TCSC's account to Mr. Duperval and his associates. She made a number of transfers, twelve of which constitute the substantive money-laundering counts.

During the Internal Revenue Service's investigation of the case, Mr. Esquenazi admitted he had bribed Mr. Duperval and other Teleco officials. He and Mr. Rodriguez nonetheless pleaded not guilty, proceeded to trial, and were found guilty on all counts.

B. Post-Trial

Five days after the jury convicted Messrs. Esquenazi and Rodriguez, the government received from an attorney involved in Patrick Joseph's defense a declaration by the Haitian Prime Minister, Jean Max Bellerive. The declaration, marked with a date that fell in the middle of the jury trial, stated: "Teleco has never been and until now is not a State enterprise." In a second declaration, made later and provided by the government to defense counsel, Prime Minister Bellerive confirmed that "the facts mentioned in the [first] statement are truthful," but clarified: "The only legal point that should stand out in this statement is that there exists no law specifically designating Teleco as a public institution." In this second declaration, Prime Minister Bellerive also stated, "this does not mean that Haiti's public laws do not apply to Teleco even if no public law designates it as such." The second declaration detailed the public aspects of Teleco, many of which the government's expert had discussed at trial. Messrs. Esquenazi and Rodriguez moved for a judgment of acquittal and a new trial on the basis of the declarations, which the district court denied.

The presentence investigation report prepared in advance of Mr. Esquenazi's sentencing calculated a base offense level of 12, under United States Sentencing Commission, *Guidelines Manual* (USSG) § 2C1.1(a)(2); a 2–level enhancement because the offense involved more than one bribe, under USSG § 2C1.1(b)(1); a 16–level enhancement based on Terra's receipt of $2.2 million from the bribery scheme, under USSG § 2B1.1(b)(1)(I); a 4–level enhancement for Esquenazi's leadership role in the offense, under USSG § 3B1.1(a); and a 2–level obstruction-of-justice enhancement, under USSG § 3C1.1. With a criminal history category I, Mr. Esquenazi's guideline range was 292 to 365 months imprisonment. The district court ultimately imposed a below-guideline sentence of 180 months imprisonment. Mr. Rodriguez, with a guideline range of 151 to 188 months imprisonment, received 84 months. Before sentencing, the district court entered a forfeiture order holding Messrs. Esquenazi and Rodriguez responsible for $3,093,818.50, which was ultimately made a part of the judgment entered against them.

This is the appeal brought by Messrs. Esquenazi and Rodriguez.

II.

The FCPA prohibits "any domestic concern" from "mak[ing] use of the mails or any means . . . of interstate commerce corruptly in furtherance of" a bribe to "any foreign official," or to "any person, while knowing that all or a portion of such money or thing of value will be offered, given, or promised, directly or indirectly, to any foreign official," for the purpose of "influencing any act or decision of such foreign official . . . in order to assist such domestic concern in obtaining or retaining business for or with, or directing business to, any person." 15 U.S.C. §§ 78dd–2(a)(1), (3). A "foreign official" is "any officer or employee of a foreign government or any department, agency, or *instrumentality* thereof." *Id.* § 78dd–2(h)(2)(A) (emphasis added). The central question before us, and the principal source of disagreement between the parties, is what "instrumentality" means (and whether Teleco qualifies as one).

The FCPA does not define the term "instrumentality," and this Court has not either. For that matter, we know of no other court of appeals who has. The definition matters in this case, in light of the challenges to the district court's jury instructions on "instrumentality"; to the sufficiency of the evidence that Teleco qualified as an instrumentality of the Haitian government; and to Mr. Esquenazi's contention that the statute is unconstitutionally vague. Before we address these challenges, however, we must define "instrumentality" for purposes of the FCPA.

We begin, as we always do when construing statutory text, with the plain meaning of the word at issue. According to Black's Law Dictionary, an instrumentality is "[a] means or agency through which a function of another entity is accomplished, such as a branch of a governing body." Webster's Third New

International Dictionary says the word means "something that serves as an intermediary or agent through which one or more functions of a controlling force are
carried out: a part, organ, or subsidiary branch esp. of a governing body." These
dictionary definitions foreclose Mr. Rodriguez's contention that only an actual
part of the government would qualify as an instrumentality—that contention
is too cramped and would impede the "wide net over foreign bribery" Congress
sought to cast in enacting the FCPA. *United States v. Kay,* 359 F.3d 738, 749 (5th
Cir. 2004). Beyond that argument, the parties do not quibble over the phrasing of
these definitions, and they agree an instrumentality must perform a government
function at the government's behest. The parties also agree, however, and we
have noted in other cases interpreting similar provisions, that the dictionary definitions get us only part of the way there. Thus, we turn to other tools to decide
what "instrumentality" means in the FCPA.

To interpret "instrumentality" as used in the Americans with Disabilities Act,
we relied upon what the Supreme Court has called the "commonsense canon
of *noscitur a sociis,*"—that is, "a word is known by the company it keeps." In the
FCPA, the company "instrumentality" keeps is "agency" and "department," entities
through which the government performs its functions and that are controlled
by the government. We therefore glean from that context that an entity must be
under the control or dominion of the government to qualify as an "instrumentality" within the FCPA's meaning. And we can also surmise from the other words in
the series along with "instrumentality" that an instrumentality must be doing the
business of the government. What the defendants and the government disagree
about, however, is what functions count as the government's business.

To answer that question, we examine the broader statutory context in which
the word is used. In this respect, we find one other provision of the FCPA and
Congress's relatively recent amendment of the statute particularly illustrative.
First, the so-called "grease payment" provision establishes an "exception" to FCPA
liability for "any facilitating or expediting payment to a foreign official . . . the
purpose of which is to expedite or to secure the performance of a *routine governmental action* by a foreign official." 15 U.S.C. § 78dd–2(b). "Routine governmental action" is defined as "an action . . . ordinarily and commonly performed by
a foreign official in," among other things, "providing phone service." *Id.* § 78dd–
2(h)(4)(A). If an entity involved in providing phone service could never be a foreign official so as to fall under the FCPA's substantive prohibition, there would
be no need to provide an express exclusion for payments to such an entity. In
other words, if we read "instrumentality," as the defendants urge, to categorically
exclude government-controlled entities that provide telephone service, like
Teleco, then we would render meaningless a portion of the definition of "routine governmental action" in section 78dd–2(b). "It is a cardinal rule of statutory
construction that significance and effect shall, if possible, be accorded to every
word." *Regions Hosp. v. Shalala,* 522 U.S. 448, 467 (1998). Thus, that a government-
controlled entity provides a commercial service does not automatically mean it
is not an instrumentality. In fact, the statute expressly contemplates that in some
instances it would.

Next, we turn to Congress's 1998 amendment of the FCPA, enacted to ensure the United States was in compliance with its treaty obligations. That year, the United States ratified the Organization for Economic Cooperation and Development's Convention on Combating Bribery of Foreign Public Officials in International Business Transactions (OECD Convention). In joining the OECD Convention, the United States agreed to "take such measures as may be necessary to establish that it is a criminal offence under [United States] law for any person intentionally to offer, promise or give . . . directly or through intermediaries, to a *foreign public official* . . . in order that the official act or refrain from acting in relation to the performance of official duties, in order to obtain or retain business or other improper advantage in the conduct of international business." OECD Convention art. 1.1. "Foreign public official" is defined to include "any person exercising a public function for a foreign country, including for a . . . public enterprise." *Id.* art. 1.4(a). The commentaries to the OECD Convention explain that: "A 'public enterprise' is any enterprise, regardless of its legal form, over which a government, or governments, may, directly or indirectly, exercise a dominant influence." *Id.* art. 1.4, cmt. 14. The commentary further explains: "An official of a public enterprise shall be deemed to perform a public function unless the enterprise operates on a normal commercial basis in the relevant market, *i.e.,* on a basis which is substantially equivalent to that of a private enterprise, without preferential subsidies or other privileges." *Id.* art. 1.4, cmt. 15. In addition to this, the OECD Convention also requires signatories make it a crime to pay bribes to agents of any "public international organisation." *Id.* art. 1.4(a).

To implement the Convention's mandates, Congress amended the FCPA in 1998. The only change to the definition of "foreign official" in the FCPA that Congress thought necessary was the addition of "public international organization." 15 U.S.C. 78dd–2(h)(2)(A). This seems to demonstrate that Congress considered its preexisting definition *already to cover* a "foreign public official" of an "enterprise . . . over which a government . . . exercise[s] a dominant influence" that performs a "public function" because it does not "operate[ ] on a normal commercial basis . . . substantially equivalent to that of . . . private enterprise[s]" in the relevant market "without preferential subsidies or other privileges." OECD Convention art. 1.4(a) & cmt. 14, 15. Although we generally are wary of relying too much on later legislative developments to decide a prior Congress's legislative intent, the circumstances in this case cause us less concern in that regard. This is not an instance in which Congress merely discussed previously enacted legislation and possible changes to it. Rather, Congress *did* make a change to the FCPA, and it did so specifically to ensure that the FCPA fulfilled the promise the United States made to other nations when it joined the Convention. The FCPA after those amendments is a different law, and we may consider Congress's intent in passing those amendments as strongly suggestive of the meaning of "instrumentality" as it exists today.

We are not alone in finding instruction from the obligations the United States undertook in the OECD Convention and Congress's resulting amendment of the FCPA made in order to comply with those obligations. The Fifth Circuit, in

United States v. Kay, concluded that, when Congress amended the FCPA to comply with the duties the United States assumed under the OECD Convention and left intact the FCPA's language outlawing bribery for the purpose of "obtaining or retaining business," the preexisting language should be construed to cover the Convention's mandate that signatories prohibit bribery "to obtain or retain business *or other improper advantage* in the conduct of international business." "Indeed, given the United States's ratification and implementation of the Convention without any reservation, understandings or alterations specifically pertaining to its scope," the Fifth Circuit concluded the defendants' narrow construction of the FCPA "would likely create a conflict with our international treaty obligations, with which we presume Congress meant to fully comply."

Indeed, since the beginning of the republic, the Supreme Court has explained that construing federal statutes in such a way to ensure the United States is in compliance with the international obligations it voluntarily has undertaken is of paramount importance. "If the United States is to be able to gain the benefits of international accords and have a role as a trusted partner in multilateral endeavors, its courts should be most cautious before interpreting its domestic legislation in such manner as to violate international agreements." ("An act of Congress ought never to be construed to violate the law of nations if any other possible construction remains.") We are thus constrained to interpret "instrumentality" under the FCPA so as to reach the types of officials the United States agreed to stop domestic interests from bribing when it ratified the OECD Convention.

Based upon this reading, we must also reject the invitation from Messrs. Esquenazi and Rodriguez to limit the term only to entities that perform traditional, core government functions. Nothing in the statute imposes this limitation. And were we to limit "instrumentality" in the FCPA in that way, we would put the United States out of compliance with its international obligations.

The Supreme Court has cautioned that "the concept of a 'usual' or a 'proper' governmental function changes over time and varies from nation to nation." That principle guides our construction of the term "instrumentality." Specifically, to decide in a given case whether a foreign entity to which a domestic concern makes a payment is an instrumentality of that foreign government, we ought to look to whether that foreign government considers the entity to be performing a governmental function. And the most objective way to make that decision is to examine the foreign sovereign's actions, namely, whether it *treats* the function the foreign entity performs as its own. Presumably, governments that mutually agree to quell bribes flowing between nations intend to prevent distortion of the business they conduct on behalf of their people. We ought to respect a foreign sovereign's definition of what that business is. Thus, for the United States government to hold up its end of the bargain under the OECD Convention, we ought to follow the lead of the foreign government itself in terms of which functions it treats as its own.

Although we believe Teleco would qualify as a Haitian instrumentality under almost any definition we could craft, we are mindful of the needs of both corporations and the government for *ex ante* direction about what an instrumentality is. With this guidance, we define instrumentality as follows. An "instrumentality" under section 78dd–2(h)(2)(A) of the FCPA is an entity controlled by the government of a foreign country that performs a function the controlling government treats as its own. Certainly, what constitutes control and what constitutes a function the government treats as its own are fact-bound questions. It would be unwise and likely impossible to exhaustively answer them in the abstract. Because we only have this case before us, we do not purport to list all of the factors that might prove relevant to deciding whether an entity is an instrumentality of a foreign government. For today, we provide a list of some factors that may be relevant to deciding the issue.

To decide if the government "controls" an entity, courts and juries should look to the foreign government's formal designation of that entity; whether the government has a majority interest in the entity; the government's ability to hire and fire the entity's principals; the extent to which the entity's profits, if any, go directly into the governmental fisc, and, by the same token, the extent to which the government funds the entity if it fails to break even; and the length of time these indicia have existed. We do not cut these factors from whole cloth. Rather, they are informed by the commentary to the OECD Convention the United States ratified. They are also consistent with the approach the Supreme Court has taken to decide if an entity is an agent or instrumentality of the government in analogous contexts.

We then turn to the second element relevant to deciding if an entity is an instrumentality of a foreign government under the FCPA—deciding if the entity performs a function the government treats as its own. Courts and juries should examine whether the entity has a monopoly over the function it exists to carry out; whether the government subsidizes the costs associated with the entity providing services; whether the entity provides services to the public at large in the foreign country; and whether the public and the government of that foreign country generally perceive the entity to be performing a governmental function. Just as with the factors indicating control, we draw these in part from the OECD Convention. And we draw them from Supreme Court cases discussing what entities properly can be considered carrying out governmental functions.

III.

A. The Foreign Corrupt Practices Act Convictions

We now turn to Esquenazi's and Rodriguez's specific challenges to their convictions under the FCPA.

1. The District Court's "Instrumentality" Instruction

With the definition of "instrumentality" in mind, we now examine what Messrs. Esquenazi and Rodriguez assert was the district court's chief error with respect to whether Teleco was an instrumentality of the Haitian government—the jury instructions. Notably, the list of factors we identified, although a bit more detailed, is not so different from what the district court laid out in its instructions to the jury here. We review *de novo* the district court's instructions to determine whether they misstated the law or prejudicially misled the jury. *United States v. Felts*, 579 F.3d 1341, 1342 (11th Cir. 2009). The district court instructed the jury:

> An instrumentality of a foreign government is a means or agency through which a function of the foreign government is accomplished. State-owned or state-controlled companies that provide services to the public may meet this definition.
>
> To decide whether Telecommunications D'Haiti or Teleco is an instrumentality of the government of Haiti, you may consider factors including, but not limited to:
>
> One, whether it provides services to the citizens and inhabitants of Haiti.
>
> Two, whether its key officers and directors are government officials or are appointed by government officials.
>
> Three, the extent of Haiti's ownership of Teleco, including whether the Haitian government owns a majority of Teleco's shares or provides financial support such as subsidies, special tax treatment, loans or revenue from government mandated fees.
>
> Four, Teleco's obligations and privileges under Haitian law, including whether Teleco exercises exclusive or controlling power to administer its designated functions.
>
> And five, whether Teleco is widely perceived and understood to be performing official or governmental functions.

Both Mr. Esquenazi and Mr. Rodriguez contend these instructions caused the jury to convict them based only on the fact that Teleco was a government-owned entity that performed a service, without any determination that the service it performed was a governmental function. We cannot agree. Read in context, the district court's instructions make plain that provision of a service by a government-owned or controlled entity is *not* by itself sufficient. The district court explained only that an entity that provides a public service "may" meet the definition of "instrumentality," thus indicating that providing a service is not categorically excluded from "a function of the foreign government." But the sentence just before explained with no equivocation that only "a means or agency [that performs] a *function of the foreign government*" would qualify as an instrumentality. Although, read in isolation, the portions of the instruction addressing the provision of services could sweep too broadly, when constrained by the actual definition of "instrumentality" the district court gave and the other guiding factors the district court outlined, we find no error in these instructions. Indeed, they substantially cover the factors we previously outlined. The instructions, we conclude, neither misstated the law nor prejudicially misled the jury regarding the definition of "instrumentality." *Felts*, 579 F.3d at 1342.

....

Affirmed.

Notes and Questions

The DOJ and SEC published the FCPA Guide in 2012 and the *Esquenazi* opinion followed two years later. Each set forth a slightly different test for determining whether an entity qualifies as a government instrumentality.

1) List the substantive differences between the two tests.
2) Which test should companies use, and why?

The *Esquenazi* opinion heavily relied on the provisions of the OECD Convention in defining the meaning of the term "foreign official" under the FCPA. In so doing, the court stated:

> Although we generally are wary of relying too much on later legislative developments to decide a prior Congress's legislative intent, the circumstances in this case cause us less concern in that regard. This is not an instance in which Congress merely discussed previously enacted legislation and possible changes to it. Rather, Congress *did* make a change to the FCPA, and it did so specifically to ensure that the FCPA fulfilled the promise the United States made to other nations when it joined the Convention. The FCPA after those amendments is a different law, and we may consider Congress's intent in passing those amendments as strongly suggestive of the meaning of "instrumentality" as it exists today.[67]

3) Why are the provisions of the OECD Convention relevant to the interpretation of the FCPA?
4) Which definition of "government instrumentality" is more consistent with the OECD Anti-Bribery Convention: that of the FCPA Guide or the *Esquenazi* opinion?

Hypothetical: Government Instrumentality

Albatel is a telecommunications services provider based in Albania, which transitioned to a market economy in the late 1990s. Albatel had been a state-owned monopoly prior to the transition. Albatel was privatized in 1998 through a lottery process, which was manipulated to allow government insiders to acquire most of Albatel's shares.

Today, Albatel is one of ten telecommunications providers operating in Albania, each covering a specific region. The Ministry of Telecommunications regulates telephone and cable prices and has extended $1 billion in interest-free loans to Albatel—the bulk of which remain outstanding.

UStel, a U.S.-based manufacturer of telecommunications equipment, is in the process of negotiating a $50 million sale to Albatel. During the negotiations, Albatel's CEO, a former telecommunications minister, asks UStel's

---

67. United States v. Esquenazi, 752 F.3d 912, 925 (11th Cir. 2014).

CEO to secure her son admission to a prestigious U.S. law school as a personal favor.

1) Is performance of the favor requested by Albatel's CEO prohibited by the FCPA?
2) What, if any, additional information would you like to know in answering question one?

D. Prohibited Intent (Corruptly, Willfully, Knowingly)

In civil and criminal cases against corporations, the government must prove the defendant acted "corruptly," meaning that the defendant had "an intent or desire to wrongfully influence the recipient."[68] In criminal cases against individuals, the government must also prove "willfulness," that is, the defendant acted with a bad purpose.[69] The defendant must have "knowledge that his conduct was illegal"[70]—an exception "to the maxim that ignorance of the law is no excuse."[71]

The overwhelming majority of enforcement actions do not involve direct payments by corporations or their employees, but rather payments through third parties, such as consultants, distributors, freight forwarders or someone else assisting the corporation.[72] The FCPA explicitly prohibits "payments made to 'any person, *while knowing* that all or a portion of such money or thing of value will be offered, given, or promised, directly or indirectly,' to a foreign official."[73] Therefore, in cases involving payment of bribes through third parties, the government must prove that the corporation acted knowingly.

Although in common parlance knowledge means consciousness of a certain fact, the FCPA defines that term to mean something less:

> [T]he so-called "head-in-the-sand" problem—variously described in the pertinent authorities as "conscious disregard," "willful blindness" or "deliberate ignorance"—should be covered so that management officials could not take refuge from the Act's prohibitions by their unwarranted obliviousness to any action (or inaction), language or other "signaling device" that should reasonably alert them of the "high probability" of an FCPA violation.[74]

---

68. FCPA Guide, *supra* note 4, at 14.
69. *Id.*
70. *Id.*
71. Gregory M. Lipper, *Foreign Corrupt Practices Act and the Elusive Question of Intent*, 47 Am. Crim. L. Rev. 1463, 1484–85 (2010) (internal quotations omitted).
72. O'Melveny & Myers LLP, Foreign Corrupt Practices Act: An O'Melveny Handbook 21 (7th ed. 2013).
73. FCPA Guide, *supra* note 4, at 21 (quoting 15 U.S.C. § 78dd-1(a)(3); 15 U.S.C. §§ 78dd-2(a)(3); 15 U.S.C. §§ 78dd-3(a)(3)) (emphasis added).
74. FCPA Guide, *supra* note 4, at 22 (quoting H.R. Rep. No. 100-576 (1988)).

As Judge Posner put it, this doctrine can be understood by "thinking carefully about just what it is that real ostriches do: They are not merely careless birds . . . [t]hey deliberately avoid acquiring unpleasant knowledge."[75]

What is the practical implication of this standard for multinational enterprises? Lack of actual knowledge about a bribery scheme offers no protection against liability. Rather, businesses must actively look for and act upon "red flags"; that is, circumstances that should alert them to the probability of corruption in a transaction or scheme. The DOJ and SEC identify several such red flags in association with payments to third parties:

1) excessive commissions to third-party agents or consultants;
2) unreasonably large discounts to third-party distributors;
3) third-party "consulting agreements" that include only vaguely described services;
4) the third-party consultant is in a different line of business than that for which it has been engaged;
5) the third party is related to or closely associated with the foreign official;
6) the third party became part of the transaction at the express request or insistence of the foreign official;
7) the third party is merely a shell company incorporated in an offshore jurisdiction; and
8) the third party requests payment to offshore bank accounts.[76]

A Resource Guide to the U.S. Foreign Corrupt Practices Act

Criminal Division of the U.S. Department of Justice and the Enforcement Division of the U.S. Securities and Exchange Commission[77]

WHAT DOES "CORRUPTLY" MEAN?

To violate the FCPA, an offer, promise, or authorization of a payment, or a payment, to a government official must be made "corruptly." As Congress noted when adopting the FCPA, the word "corruptly" means an intent or desire to wrongfully influence the recipient:

The word "corruptly" is used in order to make clear that the offer, payment, promise, or gift, must be intended to induce the recipient to misuse his official position; for example, wrongfully to direct business to the payor or his client, to obtain

---

75. Lipper, *supra* note 71, at 1486-88 (quoting United States v. Giovannetti, 919 F.2d 1223, 1228 (7th Cir. 1990)) (internal quotations omitted); *see also* United States v. Kozeny, 667 F.3d 122, 134 (2d Cir 2011) ("It is not uncommon for a finding of conscious avoidance to be supported primarily by circumstantial evidence. Indeed, the very nature of conscious avoidance makes it unlikely that the record will contain directly incriminating statements. Just as it is rare to find direct record evidence of an employer stating, "I am not going to give you a raise because you are a woman . . .").

76. FCPA GUIDE, *supra* note 4, at 22–23.

77. *Id.* at 14, 21–22.

preferential legislation or regulations, or to induce a foreign official to fail to perform an official function.

Where corrupt intent is present, the FCPA prohibits paying, offering, or promising to pay money or anything of value (or authorizing the payment or offer). By focusing on intent, the FCPA does not require that a corrupt act succeed in its purpose. Nor must the foreign official actually solicit, accept, or receive the corrupt payment for the bribe payor to be liable. For example, in one case, a specialty chemical company promised Iraqi government officials approximately $850,000 in bribes for an upcoming contract. Although the company did not, in the end, make the payment (the scheme was thwarted by the U.S. government's investigation), the company still violated the FCPA and was held accountable.

Also, as long as the offer, promise, authorization, or payment is made corruptly, the actor need not know the identity of the recipient; the attempt is sufficient. Thus, an executive who authorizes others to pay "whoever you need to" in a foreign government to obtain a contract has violated the FCPA—even if no bribe is ultimately offered or paid.

WHAT DOES "WILLFULLY" MEAN AND WHEN DOES IT APPLY?

In order for an individual defendant to be criminally liable under the FCPA, he or she must act "willfully." Proof of willfulness is not required to establish corporate criminal or civil liability, though proof of corrupt intent is.

The term "willfully" is not defined in the FCPA, but it has generally been construed by courts to connote an act committed voluntarily and purposefully, and with a bad purpose, i.e., with "knowledge that [a defendant] was doing a 'bad' act under the general rules of law." As the Supreme Court explained in Bryan v. United States, "[a]s a general matter, when used in the criminal context, a 'willful' act is one undertaken with a 'bad purpose.' In other words, in order to establish a 'willful' violation of a statute, 'the Government must prove that the defendant acted with knowledge that his conduct was unlawful.'"

Notably, as both the Second Circuit and Fifth Circuit Courts of Appeals have found, the FCPA does not require the government to prove that a defendant was specifically aware of the FCPA or knew that his conduct violated the FCPA. To be guilty, a defendant must act with a bad purpose, i.e., know generally that his conduct is unlawful.

. . . .

HOW ARE PAYMENTS TO THIRD PARTIES TREATED?

The FCPA expressly prohibits corrupt payments made through third parties or intermediaries. Specifically, it covers payments made to "any person, while knowing that all or a portion of such money or thing of value will be offered, given, or promised, directly or indirectly," to a foreign official. Many companies doing business in a foreign country retain a local individual or company to help them conduct business. Although these foreign agents may provide entirely legitimate advice regarding local customs and procedures and may help facilitate business transactions, companies should be aware of the risks involved in engaging third-party agents or intermediaries. The fact that a bribe is paid by a third party does not eliminate the potential for criminal or civil FCPA liability.

For instance, a four-company joint venture used two agents—a British lawyer and a Japanese trading company—to bribe Nigerian government officials in order to win a series of liquefied natural gas construction projects. Together, the four multi-national corporations and the Japanese trading company paid a combined $1.7 billion in civil and criminal sanctions for their decade-long bribery scheme. In addition, the subsidiary of one of the companies pleaded guilty and a number of individuals, including the British lawyer and the former CEO of one of the companies' subsidiaries, received significant prison terms.

Similarly, a medical device manufacturer entered into a deferred prosecution agreement as the result of corrupt payments it authorized its local Chinese distributor to pay to Chinese officials. Another company, a manufacturer of specialty chemicals, committed multiple FCPA violations through its agents in Iraq: a Canadian national and the Canadian's companies. Among other acts, the Canadian national paid and promised to pay more than $1.5 million in bribes to officials of the Iraqi Ministry of Oil to secure sales of a fuel additive. Both the company and the Canadian national pleaded guilty to criminal charges and resolved civil enforcement actions by SEC.

In another case, the U.S. subsidiary of a Swiss freight forwarding company was charged with paying bribes on behalf of its customers in several countries. Although the U.S. subsidiary was not an issuer under the FCPA, it was an "agent" of several U.S. issuers and was thus charged directly with violating the FCPA. Charges against the freight forwarding company and seven of its customers resulted in over $236.5 million in sanctions.

Because Congress anticipated the use of third-party agents in bribery schemes—for example, to avoid actual knowledge of a bribe—it defined the term "knowing" in a way that prevents individuals and businesses from avoiding liability by putting "any person" between themselves and the foreign officials. Under the FCPA, a person's state of mind is "knowing" with respect to conduct, a circumstance, or a result if the person:

- is aware that [he] is engaging in such conduct, that such circumstance exists, or that such result is substantially certain to occur; or
- has a firm belief that such circumstance exists or that such result is substantially certain to occur.

Thus, a person has the requisite knowledge when he is aware of a high probability of the existence of such circumstance, unless the person actually believes that such circumstance does not exist.

Notes and Questions

What if a bribe is paid in response to an extortionate threat? Can the payor of such a bribe be said to have the requisite corrupt intent? In passing the FCPA in 1977, the Senate recognized that "true extortion situations would not be covered by [the Act] since a payment to an official to keep an oil rig from being dynamited should not be held to be made with the requisite corrupt purposes."[78]

The DOJ and SEC recognize duress or coercion as a defense to an FCPA violation, but caution:

> Mere economic coercion, however, does not amount to extortion. As Congress noted when it enacted the FCPA: "The defense that the payment was demanded on the part of a government official as a price for gaining entry into a market or to obtain a contract would not suffice since at some point the U.S. company would make a conscious decision whether or not to pay a bribe." The fact that the payment was "first proposed by the recipient . . . does not alter the corrupt purpose on the part of the person paying the bribe."
>
> This distinction between extortion and economic coercion was recognized by the court in *United States v. Kozeny*. There, the court concluded that although an individual who makes a payment under duress (i.e., upon threat of physical harm) will not be criminally liable under the FCPA, a bribe payor who claims payment was demanded as a price for gaining market entry or obtaining a contract "cannot argue that he lacked the intent to bribe the official because he made the 'conscious decision' to pay the official." While the bribe payor in this situation "could have turned his back and walked away," in the oil rig example, "he could not."
>
> Businesses operating in high-risk countries may face real threats of violence or harm to their employees, and payments made in response to imminent threats to health or safety do not violate the FCPA. If such a situation arises, and to ensure the safety of its employees, companies should immediately contact the appropriate U.S. embassy for assistance.[79]

Specifically, proof of duress or coercion requires a defendant to:

> [D]emonstrate that the defendant was under unlawful, present, immediate, and impending threat of death or serious bodily injury; that the defendant did not negligently or recklessly create a situation where he would be forced to engage in criminal conduct (e.g., had been making payments as part of an ongoing bribery scheme); that the defendant had no reasonable legal alternative to violating the law; and that there was a direct causal relationship between the criminal action and the avoidance of the threatened harm.[80]

---

78. S. Rep. No. 95-114, at 11 (1977).

79. FCPA Guide, *supra* note 4, at 27 (footnotes omitted).

80. *Id.* at 111–12 n.169. *See also* Eleventh Circuit Pattern Jury Instr., Special Instr. No. 16 (2003); Fifth Circuit Pattern Jury Instr. No. 1.36 (2001); Sixth Circuit Pattern Jury Instr. No. 6.05 (2010); Seventh Circuit Pattern Jury Instr. No. 6.08 (1998); Ninth Circuit Pattern Jury Instr. No. 6.5 (2010); Kevin F. O'Malley, Jay E. Grenig, & Hon. William C. Lee, Federal Jury Practice and Instructions § 19.02 (6th ed. 2008 & Supp. 2012).

United States v. Kozeny

United States Court of Appeals for the Second Circuit, 667 F.3d 122 (2d Cir. 2011)

OPINION

Pooler, Circuit Judge:

Azerbaijan reclaimed its independence in 1991 following the collapse of the Soviet Union, gaining control over its rich stores of oil and natural gas. In the mid-1990s, Azerbaijan began privatizing various state assets. The candidates for privatization included the state-owned oil company, SOCAR. The government alleged that in an attempt to capitalize on this opportunity, Viktor Kozeny and Frederic Bourke Jr. conspired with others in a scheme to illegally purchase SOCAR by bribing the Azerbaijani president and other officials. After a jury trial, Bourke was convicted of conspiring to violate the Foreign Corrupt Practices Act ("FCPA"), 15 U.S.C. § 78dd—1 et seq., 18 U.S.C. § 371, and the Travel Act, 18 U.S.C. § 1953, and of making false statements in violation of 18 U.S.C. § 1001. The district court denied Bourke's motions for new trial and for judgment of acquittal.

On appeal, Bourke vigorously attacks his conviction on several fronts. Including (1) the correctness of the jury instruction given, (2) the sufficiency of the evidence, and (3) the propriety of certain evidentiary rulings made by the district court. For the reasons given below, we affirm.

BACKGROUND

Bourke co-founded the accessory company Dooney & Bourke, and considers himself an inventor, investor and philanthropist. In the mid 1990s, Bourke met Viktor Kozeny. Dubbed the "Pirate of Prague" by Fortune magazine, Kozeny is an international entrepreneur known for shady dealings. In a December 1996 article, Fortune detailed how Kozeny and his partner engaged in massive fraud during the privatization of the state-owned industries in the Czech Republic, including engaging in insider trading, purchasing state secrets and participating in various other unsavory business practices. Testimony at trial established that Bourke was aware of Kozeny's "Pirate of Prague" moniker.

In the late 1990s, Azerbaijan began converting state-controlled industries to private ownership through a voucher-based initiative, similar to the one used in the Czech Republic. Among the assets being considered for privatization was SOCAR, the state-owned Azerbaijani oil company. However, observers considered it unlikely that SOCAR would ever actually be privatized, given its economic importance to the country. As part of the privatization process, the Azerbaijani government issued each citizen a voucher book with four coupons. The coupons, which could be freely traded, were used to bid at auction for shares of state-owned enterprises being privatized. Foreigners seeking to participate in the auction needed to pair their vouchers with options issued by the State Property Committee ("SPC"), the entity charged with administrating the privatization process. Every coupon needed to be matched with an option, so to bid a complete voucher book a foreigner needed to match the four coupons with four options. Voucher books sold for roughly $12.

In May 1997, Kozeny invited Bourke to travel with him to examine potential investments. Their journey included a stop in Azerbaijan. Kozeny created two entities upon returning from the trip: the Minaret Group, an investment bank; and Oily Rock, an entity formed to purchase and own the privatization vouchers issued by the Azerbaijani government. Kozeny recruited Thomas Farrell to work for the entities, and instructed Farrell and other employees to start purchasing vouchers. The vouchers were purchased using U.S. currency flown in on private jets from Zurich or Moscow. Altogether, about $200 million worth of vouchers were purchased.

Kozeny and Farrell were introduced to Ilham Aliyev, the then-president's son and vice-president of SOCAR. Aliyev introduced the two to Nadir Nasibov, chair of the SPC, and his deputy, Barat Nuriyev. Kozeny discussed acquiring SOCAR at auction with Nuriyev, an auction that would not be conducted absent a presidential decree. . . .

In addition, Nuriyev demanded that two-thirds of Oily Rock's voucher books and options be transferred to Azerbaijani officials. The officials would then be able to receive two-thirds of the profits from SOCAR's eventual privatization without actually investing any money. To make the transfer possible, in September 1997 Kozeny instructed his attorney, Hans Bodmer, to set up a complex corporate structure involving multiple parent and holding companies. In December 1997, Nuriyev told Farrell that Aliyev had doubled the voucher book requirement from one to two million vouchers. At the time Nuriyev had this conversation with Farrell, voucher books had increased in price to approximately $100 each.

This development spurred Kozeny to start seeking out additional investors, an effort he kicked off with a lavish holiday party at his home in Aspen, Colorado. Bourke attended, as did Tom McCloskey, another Aspenite who had previously invested in Oily Rock. In January 1998, Kozeny took a group of potential investors to Azerbaijan, including Bourke and his friend, Robert Evans. The group met with Nuriyev and toured the Minaret Group offices. Carrie Wheeler traveled with the group on behalf of a potential investor. She testified that, "it seemed like the gist of the meeting was to communicate [to] investors that [Kozeny] had a relationship with the government in some way."

Bourke and Evans returned to the Azerbaijani capital, Baku, with Kozeny in February 1998. Bodmer, who traveled separately, testified that Bourke approached him in Baku and questioned him regarding the Azerbaijanis. Bodmer testified that during this so-called "walk-talk," he told Bourke of the nature of the bribery scheme and the corporate structures created to carry it out. Bodmer conveyed the substance of his conversation with Bourke to Rolf Schmid, an associate at Bodmer's law firm. Schmid memorialized Bodmer's description of the conversation years later in a memorandum:

> Ricky Bourke asked Hans Bodmer about the legal structures of Oily Rock and its subsidiaries, the ownership of vouchers and options by the holding companies,

etc. Hans Bodmer remembers that—probably at the beginning of 1998—he left together with Ricky Bourke . . . in Baku and went for a walk together with Ricky Bourke. During this walk he briefed Ricky Bourke in detail about the involvement of the Azeri interests . . . the 2/3:1/3 arrangement. . . .

After traveling to Baku, Bourke set up Blueport, an investment company incorporated in the British Virgin Islands, and invested $7 million in the company. He also recruited other American investors to invest via Blueport, including former Senator George Mitchell. Over time, Blueport would invest roughly $8 million in Oily Rock. In April 1998, Bourke traveled back to Baku for the official opening of the Minaret offices. Mitchell also traveled to Baku for this event, and met with President Aliyev to discuss Oily Rock's investment. Following his conversation, Mitchell told Bourke and Kozeny that the president intended to go forward with SOCAR's privatization. During this same period, Bourke also asked Farrell several times whether "Viktor [was] giving enough" and "[h]as Viktor given them enough money?"

Bourke made another trip to Baku shortly after the Minaret office opening. When he returned home, Bourke contacted his attorneys to discuss ways to limit his potential FCPA liability. During the call, Bourke raised the issue of bribe payments and investor liability. Bourke's attorney advised him that being linked to corrupt practices could expose the investors to FCPA liability. Bourke and fellow Oily Rock investor Richard Friedman agreed to form a separate company affiliated with Oily Rock and Minaret. This separate company would shield U.S. investors from liability for any corrupt payments made by the companies and Kozeny. To that end, Oily Rock U.S. Advisors and Minaret U.S. Advisors were formed, and Bourke joined the boards of both on July 1, 1998. Directors of the advisory companies each received one percent of Oily Rock for their participation.

In mid-1998, Kozeny and Bodmer told Bourke that an additional 300,000,000 shares of Oily Rock would be authorized and transferred to the Azeri officials. Bourke told a Minaret employee, Amir Farman-Farma, that "Kozeny had claimed that the dilution was a necessary cost of doing business and that he had issued or sold shares to new partners who would maximize the chances of the deal going through, the privatization being a success."

Bodmer set up a Swiss bank account for several Azeri officials—including Nuriyev, his son and another relative, as well as President Aliyev's daughter. From May to September 1998, nearly $7 million in intended bribe payments was wired to these accounts. In addition to the evidence of cash bribes, the government adduced evidence that Bourke and other conspirators arranged and paid for medical care, travel and lodging in the United States for both Nuriyev and his son.

By the end of 1998, Kozeny had abandoned all hope of SOCAR's privatization, and began winding down the investment scheme. The Minaret Group fired most of its employees by the end of January 1999, and drastically reduced the pay of the few who remained. Kozeny told the investors that the vouchers were worthless, good only for "wallpaper." Around that same time, Bourke resigned from the advisory company boards. As time went on, the privatization scheme became an issue in civil litigation by investors in the United Kingdom. Kozeny's attorneys contacted the U.S. Attorney's office in late 2000, and Bourke was subsequently advised he was the subject of an investigation. Bourke entered into a proffer agreement on April 26, 2002. Bourke also waived attorney-client privilege and instructed his attorneys to answer questions from investigators. During his proffer sessions, Bourke was asked specifically about whether Kozeny made corrupt payments, transfers and gifts to Azeri officials, and Bourke denied any such knowledge.

On May 12, 2005, Bourke, Kozeny and David Pinkerton, a managing director for American International Group responsible for its investments in Oily Rock and Minaret, were indicted. Kozeny remains a fugitive in the Bahamas and has never faced trial. The indictment charged Bourke with five counts of violating FCPA, 15 U.S.C. § 78dd-1 et seq.; two counts of violating the Travel Act, 18 U.S.C. § 1952; one count of conspiracy to violate FCPA and the Travel Act, 18 U.S.C. § 371; two counts of money laundering, 18 U.S.C. § 1956; one count of conspiracy to commit money laundering, 18 U.S.C. § 371; and one count of making false statements to FBI agents, 18 U.S.C. § 1001. Bourke moved to dismiss all of the counts of the indictment save the false statement charge on statute of limitations grounds. The district court partially granted his motion, *United States v. Kozeny*, 493 F. Supp. 2d 693 (S.D.N.Y. 2007), and this Court affirmed, *United States v. Kozeny*, 541 F.3d 166 (2d Cir. 2008). Bourke ultimately went to trial on three counts: conspiracy to violate FCPA and the Travel Act, conspiracy to launder money, and making false statements to the FBI.

The trial lasted five weeks. At the close of the government's case, Bourke moved pursuant to Federal Rule of Criminal Procedure 29 for a judgment of acquittal, which the district court denied. After three days of deliberations, the jury convicted Bourke on Count One (FCPA conspiracy) and Count Three (false statements) of the indictment, but acquitted on Count Two (conspiracy to commit money laundering). Bourke moved again for a judgment of acquittal or, in the alternative, a new trial. The district court denied the motion. This appeal followed.

DISCUSSION

Bourke raised numerous challenges to his conviction. He primarily argues the district court erred in (1) instructing the jury, (2) allowing his conviction to stand without being supported by sufficient evidence, and (3) certain evidentiary rulings. We address each of his arguments in turn.

I. Jury Instructions

Bourke challenges the jury instructions on four primary grounds. First, he argues the district court erred in refusing to instruct the jury that it needed to agree unanimously on a single overt act committed in furtherance of the conspiracy. Second, he argues the district court improperly charged the jury on conscious avoidance because, (1) there was no factual basis for such a charge; and (2) the government waived its reliance on the conscious avoidance theory. Third, he argues the district court erred by failing to instruct the jury that the government needed to prove Bourke acted "corruptly" and "willfully" to sustain a conviction on FCPA conspiracy. Finally, he argues the district court erred in failing to give the jury Bourke's proposed good-faith instruction.

We review claims of error in jury instructions de novo. *United States v. Wilkerson*, 361 F.3d 717, 732 (2d Cir. 2004). "An erroneous instruction, unless harmless, requires a new trial." *Anderson v. Branen*, 17 F.3d 552, 556 (2d Cir. 1994). An error is harmless if it is "clear beyond a reasonable doubt that a rational jury would have found the defendant guilty absent the error." *Neder v. United States*, 527 U.S. 1, 18, 119 S. Ct 1827, 144 L.Ed.2d. 35 (1999). "[A] defendant who requests an instruction bears the burden of showing that the requested instruction accurately represented the law in every respect and that, viewing as a whole the charge actually given, he was prejudiced." *Wilkerson*, 361 F.3d at 732 (internal quotation marks omitted).

. . . .

B. Conscious Avoidance

The district court instructed the jury on conscious avoidance as part of its charge on the substantive FCPA Violation (Count One):

> The FCPA provides that a person's state of mind is knowing with respect to conduct, a circumstance, or a result if, and I'm quoting from the statute, the FCPA, if such person is aware that such person is engaging in such conduct; that such circumstance exist [*sic*] or that such result substantially is certain to occur, or such person has a firm belief that such circumstances exist or that such result is substantially certain to occur.
>
> When knowledge of existence of a particular fact is an element of the offense, such knowledge may be established when a person is aware of a high probability of its existence, and consciously and intentionally avoided confirming that fact. Knowledge may be proven in this manner if, but only if, the person suspects the fact, realized its high probability, but refrained from obtaining the final confirmation because he wanted to be able to deny knowledge.
>
> On the other hand, knowledge is not established in this manner if the person merely failed to learn the fact through negligence or if the person actually believed that the transaction was legal.

"A conscious avoidance instruction permits a jury to find that a defendant had culpable knowledge of a fact when the evidence shows that the defendant intentionally avoided confirming the fact." *United States v. Ferrarini*, 219 F.3d 145, 154 (2d Cir. 2000). The jury may be instructed on conscious avoidance only where "(1) the defendant asserts the lack of some specific aspect of knowledge required for conviction, and (2) the appropriate factual predicate for the charge exists, i.e., the evidence is such that a rational juror may reach the conclusion beyond a reasonable doubt that the defendant was aware of a high probability of the fact in dispute and consciously avoided confirming that fact." *Id.* (internal quotation marks, alterations and citations omitted). Without either of those factors, as we explained in *Ferrarini*:

> [A] jury could be given a conscious avoidance instruction in a case where there was only equivocal evidence that the defendant had actual knowledge and

where there was no evidence that the defendant deliberately avoided learning the truth. Under those circumstances, a jury might conclude that no actual knowledge existed but might nonetheless convict, if it believed that the defendant had not tried hard enough to learn the truth.

Id. at 157.

Bourke first argues that the conscious avoidance charge lacks a factual predicate. We disagree. While the government's primary theory at trial was that he had actual knowledge of the bribery scheme, there is ample evidence to support a conviction based on the alternate theory of conscious avoidance. The testimony at trial demonstrated that Bourke was aware of how pervasive corruption was in Azerbaijan generally. Bourke knew of Kozeny's reputation as the "Pirate of Prague." Bourke created the American advisory companies to shield himself and other American investors from potential liability from payments made in violation of FCPA, and joined the boards of the American companies instead of joining the Oily Rock board. In so doing, Bourke enabled himself to participate in the investment without acquiring actual knowledge of Oily Rock's undertakings.

The strongest evidence demonstrating that Bourke willfully avoided learning whether corrupt payments were made came from tape recordings of a May 18, 1999, phone conference with Bourke, fellow investor Friedman and their attorneys, during which Bourke voiced concerns about whether Kozeny and company were paying bribes:

I mean, they're talking about doing a deal in Iran. . . . Maybe they . . . bribed them, . . . with . . . ten million bucks. I, I mean, I'm not saying that's what they're going to do, but suppose they do that.

Later in the conversation, Bourke remarks:

I don't know how you conduct business in Kazakhstan or Georgia or Iran, or Azerbaijan, and if they're bribing officials and that comes out . . . Let's say . . . one of the guys at Minaret says to you, Dick, you know, we know we're going to get this deal. We've taken care of this minister of finance, or this minister of this or that. What are you going to do with that information?

He goes on to say:

What happens if they break a law in . . . Kazakhstan, or they bribe somebody in Kazakhstan and we're at dinner and . . . one of the guys says, "Well, you know, we paid some guy ten million bucks to get this now." I don't know, you know, if somebody says that to you, I'm not part of it . . . I didn't endorse it. But let's say [ ] they tell you that. You got knowledge of it. What do you do with that? . . . I'm just saying to you in general . . . do you think business is done at arm's length in this part of the world.

Finally, Bourke's attorney testified that he advised Bourke that if Bourke thought there might be bribes paid, Bourke could not just look the other way. Taken together, a rational juror could conclude that Bourke deliberately avoided confirming his suspicions that Kozeny and his cohorts may be paying bribes.

Of course, this same evidence may also be used to infer that Bourke actually knew about the crimes. See *United States v. Svoboda,* 347 F.3d 471, 480 (2d Cir. 2003). Relying on *Ferrarini* (citation omitted), Bourke argues that the conscious avoidance charge was given in error because the government argued Bourke actually knew of the bribes. We disagree. In *Svoboda* we held that:

> [T]he same evidence that will raise an inference that the defendant had actual knowledge of the illegal conduct ordinarily will also raise the inference that the defendant was subjectively aware of a high probability of the existence of illegal conduct. Moreover, [conscious avoidance] may be established where, a defendant's involvement in the criminal offense may have been so overwhelmingly suspicious that the defendant's failure to question the suspicious circumstances establishes the defendant's purposeful contrivance to avoid guilty knowledge.

347 F.3d at 480 (citation, emphasis and internal quotation marks omitted); *see also United States v. Carlo,* 507 F.3d 799, 802 (2d Cir. 2007) ("The conscious avoidance charge was appropriate because [defendant] asserted that he did not know that his statements were false and the government presented an adequate factual predicate for the charge."); *United States v. Aina-Marshall*, 336 F.3d 167, 171 (2d Cir. 2003) (approving conscious avoidance charges where defendant "admitted possession of contraband but . . . denied knowledge of its nature," because "the defendant herself has directly put in issue whether the circumstances were such as to alert her to a high probability that the goods were contraband and what steps she took to learn the extent of the danger").

It is not uncommon for a finding of conscious avoidance to be supported primarily by circumstantial evidence. Indeed, the very nature of conscious avoidance makes it unlikely that the record will contain directly incriminating statements. Just as it is rare to find direct record evidence of an employer stating, "I am not going to give you a raise because you are a woman," it is highly unlikely a defendant will provide direct record evidence of conscious avoidance by saying, "Stop! I think you are about to discuss a crime and I want to be able to deny I know anything about it!" Here, the evidence adduced by the government at trial suffices to support the giving of a conscious avoidance charge.

Finally, Bourke argues that the conscious avoidance charge improperly allowed the jury to convict him based on negligence, rather than based on evidence that he avoided learning the truth. As detailed above, the record contains ample evidence that Bourke had serious concerns about the legality of Kozeny's business practices and worked to avoid learning exactly what Kozeny was doing. Bourke also argues that the risk of the jury convicting on negligence was heightened here because the district court erroneously admitted the testimony of Wheeler and James Rossman, the attorney also conducting due diligence for Texas Pacific Group ("TPG"). At one time, TPG considered investing with Kozeny, but decided against it. Rossman and Wheeler testified regarding the due diligence they undertook on Oily Rock. Rossman testified that as part of his due diligence, he traveled to Switzerland to meet with Bodmer, and that Bodmer provided Rossman with documents related to the Oily Rock investment. Bodmer also discussed the involvement of the Azeri investors with Rossman. Based on his conversations with Bodmer, and his knowledge of Kozeny's reputation gleaned from news articles, Rossman advised TPG that Oily Rock "was a dumb investment," with "a significant risk because of the lack of information about the other shareholders, [and because] there could be a FCPA issue."

We find no grounds supporting the proposition that Wheeler and Rossman's testimony, coupled with the jury charge, allowed Bourke to be convicted based on negligence. The government offered the testimony to demonstrate that others with access to the same sources of information available to Bourke were able to figure out Kozeny's scheme and avoid participating. It was entirely proper for the government to argue that Bourke refrained from asking his attorneys to undertake the same due diligence done by Rossman and Wheeler because Bourke was consciously avoiding learning about the bribes. This is distinguishable from *United States v. Kaplan,* 490 F.3d 110 (2d. Cir. 2007). Bourke relies on *Kaplan* for the proposition that a court abuses its discretion when it admits testimony about a third party's knowledge of fraud where "the Government failed to offer evidence that would explain how [the] defendant . . . would have obtained the third parties' knowledge of the criminal scheme." *Id.* at 121. Here, Bourke went to Azerbaijan on the same trip as Wheeler, and like Rossman had access to Bodmer. This is the type of explanation *Kaplan* contemplates. *Id.* ("Evidence of others' knowledge would have been highly relevant had it been supplemented by evidence supporting the conclusion that such knowledge was communicated to [the defendant], or that [the defendant] had been exposed to the same sources from with these others derived their knowledge of the fraud.").

Finally, the district court specifically charged the jury not to convict based on negligence. There is no reason to suspect that the jury ignored that instruction.

. . . .

D. Proposed Good Faith Instructions

. . . .

Bourke argues the district court erred in not giving the jury a separate good faith instruction with respect to FCPA and false statement counts. Even assuming *arguendo* that Bourke's proposed instruction was legally correct with an adequate basis in the record, his argument fails because the theory was effectively presented elsewhere in the charge. [This standard set forth in *U.S. v. Doyle,* 130 F.3d 523, 540 (2d Cir. 1997) (discussed in omitted materials).] The district court instructed the jury that the government did not meet its burden if the defendant "merely failed to learn the fact through negligence or if the person actually believed that the transaction was legal." It also charged that "the government must prove beyond a reasonable doubt that the defendant knew that he was a member of an operation or conspiracy that committed or was going to commit a crime, and that his actions of joining such an operation or conspiracy was not due to carelessness, negligence or mistake." The jury was told that it "must first find that [Bourke] knowingly joined in the unlawful agreement or plan." The jurors were instructed that "knowingly" meant "deliberately and voluntarily," and could not be a "mistake or accident or mere negligence or some other innocent reason."

The instructions given here were strikingly similar to the ones given in *Doyle*. There, we found that:

> The indictment charged, and the court instructed, that knowledge and willfulness concerning the ultimate destination of the equipment is an element of the offense that the Government was required to prove beyond a reasonable doubt. It was not error for the court to refuse to charge that the Government had the burden to prove bad faith, when it had already charged that the Government had to prove willfulness and that good faith was a defense to the willfulness element.

130 F.3d at 540-41. Failure to give a specific good faith charge does not require a reversal.

. . . .

CONCLUSION

We have examined the remainder of Bourke's arguments and we find them to be without merit. For the reasons given above, we affirm his conviction.

Hypothetical: Head in the Sand

Briball, Inc. ("Briball") is a U.S.-based pharmaceutical company engaged in the manufacture and sale of drugs throughout the world. Briball's main distributor in China was convicted of bribing state-employed doctors to inflate sales of Briball's prescription drugs. The conviction prompted the DOJ to investigate and eventually indict Briball for violating the FCPA anti-bribery provisions.

The DOJ investigation did not uncover any emails or other communication informing Briball of the bribery scheme. Instead, their case rests on the allegation that "Briball consciously disregarded circumstances indicating a high probability of bribery."

In preparing for trial,

1) What types of evidence should Briball's counsel expect the prosecution to present?
2) What types of evidence should Briball's counsel present in negating her client's knowledge of the bribery?

E. Successor Liability

Successor liability attaches when a purchaser of assets in a merger or acquisition is "treated as a 'successor' to the transferor, [and held] liable for the transferor's debts as though it were the transferor."[81] Thus, even though a merger or acqui-

---

81. Marie T. Reilly, *Making Sense of Successor Liability*, 31 Hofstra L. Rev. 745, 746 (2002).

sition may be a desirable way to establish a presence in a foreign country, the acquirer may face liability for the target's past FCPA violations.

"Successor liability in asset purchase transactions has generated controversy because the asset seller usually remains a separate legal entity capable of paying the costs of its misconduct, unlike in a merger transaction."[82] The DOJ and SEC take the position that, so long as a target was subject to the FCPA prior to the acquisition, the acquirer inherits its FCPA liability regardless of how the transaction is structured.

There is a dearth of federal case law on this subject, particularly in the FCPA context.[83] Given the DOJ and SEC's position, companies intending to merge with or acquire another company commonly undertake extensive due diligence procedures to avoid being held liable for a target's past conduct. "The result is that [mergers and acquisitions] deals quickly [have become] more complex, time-consuming and expensive."[84] Despite this fact, the DOJ and SEC strongly encourage companies to perform pre-acquisition due diligence and consider such efforts when deciding whether to bring enforcement action against an acquirer for a target's past FCPA violations.[85]

A Resource Guide to the U.S. Foreign Corrupt Practices Act

Criminal Division of the U.S. Department of Justice and the Enforcement Division of the U.S. Securities and Exchange Commission[86]

SUCCESSOR LIABILITY

Companies acquire a host of liabilities when they merge with or acquire another company, including those arising out of contracts, torts, regulations, and statutes. As a general legal matter, when a company merges with or acquires

---

82. Daniel J. Grimm, *The Foreign Corrupt Practices Act in Merger and Acquisition Transactions: Successor Liability and Its Consequences*, 7 N.Y.U. J.L. & Bus. 247, 282 (2010).

83. The closest the Supreme Court has come to addressing this issue was in a criminal anti-trust case, *Melrose Distillers, Inc. v. United States*, 359 U.S. 271 (1959). There, several wholly-owned subsidiaries of the same parent corporation had been indicted for violating the Sherman Act. Three of those subsidiaries were dissolved and moved to dismiss the indictments on the ground that they no longer existed. The Court held the successor-in-interest to those subsidiaries liable, reasoning that:

> Petitioners were wholly owned subsidiaries of Schenley Industries, Inc. After dissolution they simply became divisions of a new corporation under the same ultimate ownership. In this situation there is no more reason for allowing them to escape criminal penalties than damages in civil suits. As the Court of Appeals noted, a corporation cannot be sent to jail. The discharge of its liabilities whether criminal or civil can be effected only by the payment of money. *Id.* at 274.

Melrose Distillers was unique in that it did not involve an acquisition, but rather the dissolution of a subsidiary. More on point is the seminal administrative decision in *Sigma-Aldrich Bus. Holdings, Inc.*, 01-BXA-06 (U.S. Dep't of Commerce Bureau of Indus. & Sec. 2002), http://www.bis.doc.gov/enforcement/casesummaries/sigma_aldrich_alj_decision_02.pdf, which involved violations of export control laws. There, the acquirers were held liable for the target's preacquisition violations because they knew of those violations.

84. Grimm, *supra* note 82, at 281.

85. *See* FCPA GUIDE, *supra* note 4, at 28–29.

86. *Id.* at 28–30 (footnotes omitted).

another company, the successor company assumes the predecessor company's liabilities. Successor liability is an integral component of corporate law and, among other things, prevents companies from avoiding liability by reorganizing. Successor liability applies to all kinds of civil and criminal liabilities, and FCPA violations are no exception. Whether successor liability applies to a particular corporate transaction depends on the facts and the applicable state, federal, and foreign law. Successor liability does not, however, create liability where none existed before. For example, if an issuer were to acquire a foreign company that was not previously subject to the FCPA's jurisdiction, the mere acquisition of that foreign company would not retroactively create FCPA liability for the acquiring issuer.

DOJ and SEC encourage companies to conduct pre-acquisition due diligence and improve compliance programs and internal controls after acquisition for a variety of reasons. First, due diligence helps an acquiring company to accurately value the target company. Contracts obtained through bribes may be legally unenforceable, business obtained illegally may be lost when bribe payments are stopped, there may be liability for prior illegal conduct, and the prior corrupt acts may harm the acquiring company's reputation and future business prospects. Identifying these issues before an acquisition allows companies to better evaluate any potential post-acquisition liability and thus properly assess the target's value. Second, due diligence reduces the risk that the acquired company will continue to pay bribes. Proper pre-acquisition due diligence can identify business and regional risks and can also lay the foundation for a swift and successful post-acquisition integration into the acquiring company's corporate control and compliance environment. Third, the consequences of potential violations uncovered through due diligence can be handled by the parties in an orderly and efficient manner through negotiation of the costs and responsibilities for the investigation and remediation. Finally, comprehensive due diligence demonstrates a genuine commitment to uncovering and preventing FCPA violations.

In a significant number of instances, DOJ and SEC have declined to take action against companies that voluntarily disclosed and remediated conduct and cooperated with DOJ and SEC in the merger and acquisition context. And DOJ and SEC have only taken action against successor companies in limited circumstances, generally in cases involving egregious and sustained violations or where the successor company directly participated in the violations or failed to stop the misconduct from continuing after the acquisition. In one case, a U.S.-based issuer was charged with books and records and internal controls violations for continuing a kickback scheme originated by its predecessor. Another recent case involved a merger between two tobacco leaf merchants, where prior to the merger each company committed FCPA violations through its foreign subsidiaries, involving multiple countries over the course of many years. At each company, the bribes were directed by the parent company's senior management. The two issuers then merged to form a new public company. Under these circumstances—the merger of two public companies that had each engaged in bribery—both the new entity and the foreign subsidiaries were liable under the FCPA. The new parent entered into a non-prosecution agreement with DOJ and settled a civil action with SEC, while the company's subsidiaries, which also merged, pleaded guilty.

More often, DOJ and SEC have pursued enforcement actions against the predecessor company (rather than the acquiring company), particularly when the acquiring company uncovered and timely remedied the violations or when the government's investigation of the predecessor company preceded the acquisition. In one such case, an Ohio-based health care company's due diligence of an acquisition target uncovered FCPA violations by the target's subsidiary, and, before the merger was completed, the subsidiary's violations were disclosed to DOJ and SEC. The subsidiary pleaded guilty and paid a $2 million criminal fine, the acquisition target settled with SEC and paid a $500,000 civil penalty, and no successor liability was sought against the acquiring entity. In another case, a Pennsylvania-based issuer that supplied heating and air conditioning products and services was subject to an ongoing investigation by DOJ and SEC at the time that it was acquired; DOJ and SEC resolved enforcement actions only against the predecessor company, which had by that time become a wholly owned subsidiary of the successor company.

DOJ and SEC have also brought actions only against a predecessor company where its FCPA violations are discovered after acquisition. For example, when a Florida-based U.S. company discovered in post-acquisition due diligence that the telecommunications company (a domestic concern) it had acquired had engaged in foreign bribery, the successor company disclosed the FCPA violations to DOJ. It then conducted an internal investigation, cooperated fully with DOJ, and took appropriate remedial action—including terminating senior management at the acquired company. No enforcement action was taken against the successor, but the predecessor company pleaded guilty to one count of violating the FCPA and agreed to pay a $2 million fine. Later, four executives from the predecessor company were convicted of FCPA violations, three of whom received terms of imprisonment.

On occasion, when an enforcement action has been taken against a predecessor company, the successor seeks assurances that it will not be subject to a future enforcement action. In one such case, a Dutch predecessor resolved FCPA charges with DOJ through a deferred prosecution agreement. While both the predecessor and successor signed the agreement, which included a commitment to ongoing cooperation and an improved compliance program, only the predecessor company was charged; in signing the agreement, the successor company gained the certainty of conditional release from criminal liability, even though it was not being pursued for FCPA violations. In another case, after a Connecticut-based company uncovered FCPA violations by a California company it sought to acquire, both companies voluntarily disclosed the conduct to DOJ and SEC. The predecessor company resolved its criminal liability through a non-prosecution agreement with DOJ that included an $800,000 monetary penalty and also settled with SEC, paying a total of $1.1 million in disgorgement, pre-judgment interest, and civil penalties. The successor company proceeded with the acquisition and separately entered into a non-prosecution agreement with DOJ in which it agreed, among other things, to ensure full performance of the predecessor company's non-prosecution agreement. This agreement provided certainty to the successor concerning its FCPA liability.

Importantly, a successor company's voluntary disclosure, appropriate due diligence, and implementation of an effective compliance program may also decrease the likelihood of an enforcement action regarding an acquired company's post-acquisition conduct when pre-acquisition due diligence is not possible.

FCPA Opinion Procedure Release No. 14-02

U.S. Department of Justice, Criminal Division (Nov. 7, 2014)[87]

The Department reviewed the Foreign Corrupt Practices Act ("FCPA") Opinion request of a United States consumer products company (the "Requestor") that was initially submitted on April 30, 2014 (the "Request"). Requestor provided supplemental information on May 12, 2014, July 30, 2014, and October 9, 2014. Requestor is an "issuer" of securities within the meaning of 15 U.S.C. §§ 78c(a)(8) and 78dd-1 and therefore is eligible to submit an opinion procedure request.

Requestor is a multinational company headquartered in the United States. Requestor intends to acquire a foreign consumer products company and its wholly owned subsidiary (collectively, the "Target Company"), both of which are incorporated and operate in a foreign country ("Foreign Country"). In the course of its pre-acquisition due diligence of the Target Company, Requestor identified a number of likely improper payments—none of which had a discernible jurisdictional nexus to the United States—by the Target Company to government officials of Foreign Country, as well as substantial weaknesses in accounting and recordkeeping. In light of the bribery and other concerns identified in the due diligence process, Requestor has set forth a plan that includes remedial pre-acquisition measures and detailed post-acquisition integration steps.

Requestor seeks an Opinion as to whether the Department, based on the facts and representations provided by Requestor that the pre-acquisition due diligence process did not bring to light any potentially improper payments that were subject to the jurisdiction of the United States, would presently intend to bring an FCPA enforcement action against Requestor for the Target Company's pre-acquisition conduct. Requestor does not seek an Opinion from the Department as to Requestor's criminal liability for any post-acquisition conduct by the Target Company.

---

87. U.S. Dep't of Justice, FCPA Opinion Procedure Release No. 14-02 (Nov. 7, 2014), https://www.justice.gov/sites/default/files/criminal-fraud/legacy/2014/11/14/14-02.pdf.

BACKGROUND

Requestor intends to acquire 100% of the Target Company's shares beginning in 2015. The Target Company's shares are currently held almost exclusively by another foreign corporation ("Seller"), which is listed on the stock exchange of Foreign Country. Seller is a prominent consumer products manufacturer and distributor in Foreign Country, with more than 5,000 full-time employees and annual gross sales in excess of $100 million. The Target Company represents part of Seller's consumer products business in Foreign Country and sells its products through several related brands.

Seller and the Target Company largely confine their operations to Foreign Country, have never been issuers of securities in the United States, and have had negligible business contacts, including no direct sale or distribution of their products, in the United States.

In preparing for the acquisition, Requestor undertook due diligence aimed at identifying, among other things, potential legal and compliance concerns at the Target Company. Requestor retained an experienced forensic accounting firm ("the Accounting Firm") to carry out the due diligence review. This review brought to light evidence of apparent improper payments, as well as substantial accounting weaknesses and poor recordkeeping. On the basis of a risk profile analysis of the Target Company, the Accounting Firm reviewed approximately 1,300 transactions with a total value of approximately $12.9 million. The Accounting Firm identified over $100,000 in transactions that raised compliance issues. The vast majority of these transactions involved payments to government officials related to obtaining permits and licenses. Other transactions involved gifts and cash donations to government officials, charitable contributions and sponsorships, and payments to members of the state-controlled media to minimize negative publicity. None of the payments, gifts, donations, contributions, or sponsorships occurred in the United States and none was made by or through a U.S. person or issuer.

The due diligence showed that the Target Company has significant recordkeeping deficiencies. The vast majority of the cash payments and gifts to government officials and the charitable contributions were not supported by documentary records. Expenses were improperly and inaccurately classified in the Target Company's books. In fact, the Target Company's accounting records were so disorganized that the Accounting Firm was unable to physically locate or identify many of the underlying records for the tested transactions. Finally, the Target Company has not developed or implemented a written code of conduct or other compliance policies and procedures, nor have the Target Company's employees, according to the Accounting Firm, shown adequate understanding or awareness of anti-bribery laws and regulations. In light of the Target Company's glaring compliance, accounting, and recordkeeping deficiencies, Requestor has taken several pre-closing steps to begin to remediate the Target Company's weaknesses prior to the planned closing in 2015.

Requestor anticipates completing the full integration of the Target Company into Requestor's compliance and reporting structure within one year of the closing. Requestor has set forth an integration schedule of the Target Company that encompasses risk mitigation, dissemination and training with regard to compliance procedures and policies, standardization of business relationships with third parties, and formalization of the Target Company's accounting and recordkeeping in accordance with Requestor's policies and applicable law.

ANALYSIS

Based upon all of the facts and circumstances, as represented by Requestor, the Department does not presently intend to take any enforcement action with respect to pre-acquisition bribery Seller or the Target Company may have committed.

It is a basic principle of corporate law that a company assumes certain liabilities when merging with or acquiring another company. In a situation such as this, where a purchaser acquires the stock of a seller and integrates the target into its operations, successor liability may be conferred upon the purchaser for the acquired entity's pre-existing criminal and civil liabilities, including, for example, for FCPA violations of the target.

"Successor liability does not, however, create liability where none existed before. For example, if an issuer were to acquire a foreign company that was not previously subject to the FCPA's jurisdiction, the mere acquisition of that foreign company would not retroactively create FCPA liability for the acquiring issuer." *FCPA–A Resource Guide to the U.S. Foreign Corrupt Practices Act*, at 28 ("FCPA Guide"). This principle, illustrated by hypothetical successor liability "Scenario 1" in the FCPA Guide, squarely addresses the situation at hand. *See* FCPA Guide, at 31 ("Although DOJ and SEC have jurisdiction over Company A because it is an issuer, neither could pursue Company A for conduct that occurred prior to the acquisition of Foreign Company. As Foreign Company was neither an issuer nor a domestic concern and was not subject to U.S. territorial jurisdiction, DOJ and SEC have no jurisdiction over its pre-acquisition misconduct.").

Assuming the accuracy of Requestor's representations, none of the potentially improper pre-acquisition payments by Seller or the Target Company was subject to the jurisdiction of the United States. For example, none of the payments occurred in the United States, and Requestor has not identified participation by any U.S. person or issuer in the payments. Requestor also represents that, based on its due diligence, no contracts or other assets were determined to have been acquired through bribery that would remain in operation and from which Requestor would derive financial benefit following the acquisition. The Department would thus lack jurisdiction under the FCPA to prosecute Requestor (or for that matter, Seller or the Target Company) for improper payments made by Seller or the Target Company prior to the acquisition. *See* 15 U.S.C. §§ 78dd-1, *et seq.* (setting forth statutory jurisdictional bases for anti-bribery provisions).

The Department expresses no view as to the adequacy or reasonableness of Requestor's integration of the Target Company. The circumstances of each corporate merger or acquisition are unique and require specifically tailored due diligence and integration processes. Hence, the exact timeline and appropriateness of particular aspects of Requestor's integration of the Target Company are not necessarily suitable to other situations.

To be sure, the Department encourages companies engaging in mergers and acquisitions to (1) conduct thorough risk-based FCPA and anti-corruption due diligence; (2) implement the acquiring company's code of conduct and anti-corruption policies as quickly as practicable; (3) conduct FCPA and other relevant training for the acquired entity's directors and employees, as well as third-party agents and partners; (4) conduct an FCPA-specific audit of the acquired entity as quickly as practicable; and (5) disclose to the Department any corrupt payments discovered during the due diligence process. *See* FCPA Guide at 29. Adherence to these elements by Requestor may, among several other factors, determine whether and how the Department would seek to impose post-acquisition successor liability in case of a putative violation.

This FCPA Opinion Release has no binding application to any party that did not join in the request, and can be relied on by Requestor only to the extent that the disclosure of facts and circumstances in its request and supplements is accurate and complete.

Notes and Questions

In Opinion Release No. 14-02, the DOJ partly based its decision on the following:

> Requestor also represents that, based on its due diligence, no contracts or other assets were determined to have been acquired through bribery that would remain in operation and from which Requestor would derive financial benefit following the acquisition.[88]

Does this mean that, where a target was not subject to the FCPA before the acquisition, but held contracts or assets acquired through bribery, the target and/or the acquirer may be liable? If so, is this inconsistent with the FCPA Guide?

Hypothetical: Successor Liability Where Acquired Company Was Not Previously Subject to the FCPA[89]

Company A is a Delaware corporation with its principal offices in the United States and whose shares are listed on a national U.S. exchange. Company A is considering acquiring Foreign Company, which is not an issuer or a domestic concern. Foreign Company takes no actions within the United States

---

88. *Id.* at 3.
89. FCPA GUIDE, *supra* note 4, at 31–32 (hypothetical reproduced verbatim, with answers excluded) (emphasis added).

that would make it subject to territorial jurisdiction. Company A's proposed acquisition would make Foreign Company a subsidiary of Company A.

Scenario 1

Prior to acquiring Foreign Company, Company A engages in extensive due diligence of Foreign Company, including: (1) having its legal, accounting, and compliance departments review Foreign Company's sales and financial data, its customer contracts, and its third-party and distributor agreements; (2) performing a risk-based analysis of Foreign Company's customer base; (3) performing an audit of selected transactions engaged in by Foreign Company; and (4) engaging in discussions with Foreign Company's general counsel, vice president of sales, and head of internal audit regarding all corruption risks, compliance efforts, and any other corruption-related issues that have surfaced at Foreign Company over the past ten years. This due diligence aims to determine whether Foreign Company has appropriate anti-corruption and compliance policies in place, whether Foreign Company's employees have been adequately trained regarding those policies, how Foreign Company ensures that those policies are followed, and what remedial actions are taken if the policies are violated.

During the course of its due diligence, Company A learns that Foreign Company has made several potentially improper payments in the form of an inflated commission to a third-party agent in connection with a government contract with Foreign Country. Immediately after the acquisition, Company A discloses the conduct to DOJ and SEC, suspends and terminates those employees and the third-party agent responsible for the payments, and makes certain that the illegal payments have stopped. It also quickly integrates Foreign Company into Company A's own robust internal controls, including its anticorruption and compliance policies, which it communicates to its new employees through required online and in-person training in the local language. Company A also requires Foreign Company's third-party distributors and other agents to sign anticorruption certifications, complete training, and sign new contracts that incorporate FCPA and anticorruption representations and warranties and audit rights.

Based on these facts, could DOJ or SEC prosecute Company A?

Scenario 2

Company A performs only minimal and pro forma pre-acquisition due diligence. It does not conduct a risk-based analysis, and its review of Foreign Company's data, contracts, and third-party and distributor agreements is cursory. Company A acquires Foreign Company and makes it a wholly owned subsidiary. Although Company A circulates its compliance policies to all new personnel after the acquisition, it does not translate the compliance policies into the local language or train its new personnel or third-party agents on anticorruption issues.

A few months after the acquisition, an employee in Company A's international sales office (Sales Employee) learns from a legacy Foreign Company employee that for years the government contract that generated most of Foreign Company's revenues depended on inflated commissions to a third-party agent "to make the right person happy at Foreign Government Agency." Sales Employee is told that unless the payments continue the business will likely be lost, which would mean that Company A's new acquisition would quickly become a financial failure. The payments continue for two years after the acquisition. After another employee of Company A reports the long-running bribe scheme to a director at Foreign Government Agency, Company A stops the payments and DOJ and SEC investigate.

Based on these facts, would DOJ or SEC charge Company A?

Scenario 3

Under local law, Company A's ability to conduct pre-acquisition due diligence on Foreign Company is limited. In the due diligence it does conduct, Company A determines that Foreign Company is doing business in high-risk countries and in high-risk industries but finds no red flags specific to Foreign Company's operations. Post-acquisition, Company A conducts extensive due diligence and determines that Foreign Company had paid bribes to officials with Foreign Government Agency. Company A takes prompt action to remediate the problem, including following the measures set forth in Opinion Procedure Release No. 08-02. Among other actions, it voluntarily discloses the misconduct to DOJ and SEC, ensures all bribes are immediately stopped, takes remedial action against all parties involved in the corruption, and quickly incorporates Foreign Company into a robust compliance program and Company A's other internal controls.

Based on these facts, would DOJ or SEC prosecute Company A?

Hypothetical: Successor Liability Where Acquired Company Was Already Subject to the FCPA[90]

Both Company A and Company B are Delaware corporations with their principal offices in the United States. Both companies' shares are listed on a national U.S. exchange.

Scenario 1

Company A is considering acquiring several of Company B's business lines. Prior to the acquisition, Company A engages in extensive due diligence, including: (1) having its legal, accounting, and compliance departments review Company B's sales and financial data, its customer contracts, and its third-party

---

90. *Id.* at 32–33.

and distributor agreements; (2) performing a risk-based analysis of Company B's customer base; (3) performing an audit of selected transactions engaged in by Company B; and (4) engaging in discussions with Company B's general counsel, vice president of sales, and head of internal audit regarding all corruption risks, compliance efforts, and any other major corruption-related issues that have surfaced at Company B over the past ten years. This due diligence aims to determine whether Company B has appropriate anticorruption and compliance policies in place, whether Company B's employees have been adequately trained regarding those policies, how Company B ensures that those policies are followed, and what remedial actions are taken if the policies are violated.

During the course of its due diligence, Company A learns that Company B has made several potentially improper payments in connection with a government contract with Foreign Country. As a condition of the acquisition, Company A requires Company B to disclose the misconduct to the government. Company A makes certain that the illegal payments have stopped and quickly integrates Company B's business lines into Company A's own robust internal controls, including its anticorruption and compliance policies, which it communicates to its new employees through required online and in-person training in the local language. Company A also requires Company B's third-party distributors and other agents to sign anticorruption certifications, complete training, and sign new contracts that incorporate FCPA and anticorruption representations and warranties and audit rights.

Based on these facts, would DOJ or SEC prosecute?

Scenario 2

Company A plans to acquire Company B. Although, as in Scenario 1, Company A conducts extensive due diligence, it does not uncover the bribery until after the acquisition Company A. It then makes certain that the illegal payments stop and voluntarily discloses the misconduct to DOJ and SEC. It quickly integrates Company B into Company A's own robust internal controls, including its anticorruption and compliance policies, which it communicates to its new employees through required online and in-person training in the local language. Company A also requires Company B's third-party distributors and other agents to sign anticorruption certifications, complete training, and sign new contracts that incorporate FCPA and anticorruption representations and warranties and audit rights.

Based on these facts, would DOJ or SEC prosecute?

Scenario 3

Company A merges with Company B, which is in the same line of business and interacts with the same Foreign Government customers, and forms Company C. Due diligence before the merger reveals that both Company A and Company B have been engaging in similar bribery. In both cases, the bribery was extensive and known by high-level management within the companies.

Based on these facts, would DOJ or SEC prosecute?

II. Who Is Covered Under the FCPA Anti-Bribery Provisions?

A. Scope of the Extraterritorial Application of the FCPA

Large multinational enterprises typically operate in many different jurisdictions—either directly or through third parties who act on their behalf. From their perspective, each country's laws should only have effect within its own territory, since overlapping legal obligations imposed by different countries create uncertainty, complicate risk management and drive up the cost of doing business.

Endeavoring to create such certainty and predictability, U.S. courts have traditionally drawn a bright line that limits the reach of most U.S. laws to the border's edge. In *Morrison v. National Australia Bank Ltd.*,[91] the U.S. Supreme Court reinforced this line, stating:

> It is a "longstanding principle of American law 'that legislation of Congress, unless a contrary intent appears, is meant to apply only within the territorial jurisdiction of the United States.'" This principle represents a canon of construction, or a presumption about a statute's meaning . . . . Thus, "unless there is the affirmative intention of the Congress clearly expressed" to give a statute extraterritorial effect, "we must presume it [has none]."[92]

The Court was adamant that the presumption against extraterritoriality applies to every federal statute;[93] and, even "when a statute provides for some extraterritorial application, the presumption . . . operates to limit that provision to its terms."[94]

The FCPA explicitly covers three classes of persons: (1) issuers; (2) so-called "domestic concerns," which are defined as U.S. citizens and permanent residents as well as juridical entities established under U.S. laws; and (3) foreign individuals and juridical entities acting inside U.S. territory. Indisputably, the statute holds U.S. individuals and corporations responsible for their world-wide conduct—meaning that they can be prosecuted for actions that entirely take place overseas.

When it comes to foreign individuals and corporations, however, the jurisdictional analysis becomes more complex. Foreign issuers and foreign employees and agents of U.S. corporations are covered only to the extent that they use

---

91. Morrison v. Nat'l Austl. Bank Ltd., 561 U.S. 247 (2010).

92. *Id.* at 255 (citations omitted). Morrison put an end to a type of class action known as "foreign-cubed" or "f-cubed" lawsuits, so named because they involve foreign investors suing foreign companies to recover losses from trading on foreign exchanges. *See generally id.*

93. *See id.* at 261.

94. *Id.* at 265.

the mails or instruments of interstate commerce. Thus, for example, before a foreign issuer can be prosecuted for conduct outside U.S. territory, the prosecution must prove a nexus between the foreign issuer's conduct and U.S. commerce. The precise scope of that nexus is not defined by statute, leaving it to the courts to settle.

The advent of diversion agreements (DPAs and NPAs) has significantly curtailed the judiciary's role in corporate prosecutions; and as a result, the question of the FCPA's extraterritoriality has thus far been set by the DOJ and SEC. They have interpreted the statute's extraterritorial reach very broadly, extending the FCPA to foreign individuals and corporations with remote, if any, connection to U.S. territory.

This chapter examines the DOJ and SEC's position regarding the extraterritorial application of the FCPA in light of the Supreme Court's recent decisions reinforcing the presumption against extraterritoriality and the statute's legislative history. The second part of the chapter focuses on the DOJ and SEC's use of the principles of agency (*respondeat superior*) and conspiracy to extend the statute's extraterritorial application—a practice that has been rejected by one district court and is currently on appeal before the U.S. Court of Appeals for the Second Circuit.

A Resource Guide to the U.S. Foreign Corrupt Practices Act

Criminal Division of the U.S. Department of Justice and the Enforcement Division of the U.S. Securities and Exchange Commission[95]

WHO IS COVERED BY THE ANTI-BRIBERY PROVISIONS?

The FCPA's anti-bribery provisions apply broadly to three categories of persons and entities: (1) "issuers" and their officers, directors, employees, agents, and shareholders; (2) "domestic concerns" and their officers, directors, employees, agents, and shareholders; and (3) certain persons and entities, other than issuers and domestic concerns, acting while in the territory of the United States.

Issuers—15 U.S.C. § 78dd-1

Section 30A of the Securities Exchange Act of 1934 (the Exchange Act), which can be found at 15 U.S.C. § 78dd-1, contains the anti-bribery provision governing issuers. A company is an "issuer" under the FCPA if it has a class of securities registered under Section 12 of the Exchange Act or is required to file periodic and other reports with SEC under Section 15(d) of the Exchange Act. In practice, this means that any company with a class of securities listed

---

95. FCPA Guide, *supra* note 4, at 12.

on a national securities exchange in the United States, or any company with a class of securities quoted in the over-the-counter market in the United States and required to file periodic reports with SEC, is an issuer. A company thus need not be a U.S. company to be an issuer. Foreign companies with American Depository Receipts that are listed on a U.S. exchange are also issuers. As of December 31, 2011, 965 foreign companies were registered with SEC. Officers, directors, employees, agents, or stockholders acting on behalf of an issuer (whether U.S. or foreign nationals), and any co-conspirators, also can be prosecuted under the FCPA.

Domestic Concerns—15 U.S.C. § 78dd-2

The FCPA also applies to "domestic concerns." A domestic concern is any individual who is a citizen, national, or resident of the United States, or any corporation, partnership, association, joint-stock company, business trust, unincorporated organization, or sole proprietorship that is organized under the laws of the United States or its states, territories, possessions, or commonwealths or that has its principal place of business in the United States. Officers, directors, employees, agents, or stockholders acting on behalf of a domestic concern, including foreign nationals or companies, are also covered.

Territorial Jurisdiction—15 U.S.C. § 78dd-3

The FCPA also applies to certain foreign nationals or entities that are not issuers or domestic concerns. Since 1998, the FCPA's anti-bribery provisions have applied to foreign persons and foreign non-issuer entities that, either directly or through an agent, engage in any act in furtherance of a corrupt payment (or an offer, promise, or authorization to pay) while in the territory of the United States. Also, officers, directors, employees, agents, or stockholders acting on behalf of such persons or entities may be subject to the FCPA's anti-bribery prohibitions.

WHAT JURISDICTIONAL CONDUCT TRIGGERS THE ANTI-BRIBERY PROVISIONS?

The FCPA's anti-bribery provisions can apply to conduct both inside and outside the United States. Issuers and domestic concerns—as well as their officers, directors, employees, agents, or stockholders—may be prosecuted for using the U.S. mails or any means or instrumentality of interstate commerce in furtherance of a corrupt payment to a foreign official. The Act defines "interstate commerce" as "trade, commerce, transportation, or communication among the several States, or between any foreign country and any State or between any State and any place or ship outside thereof . . . ." The term also includes the intrastate use of any interstate means of communication, or any other interstate instrumentality. Thus, placing a telephone call or sending an e-mail, text message, or fax from, to, or through the United States involves interstate commerce—as does sending a wire transfer from or to a U.S. bank or otherwise using the U.S. banking system, or traveling across state borders or internationally to or from the United States.

Those who are not issuers or domestic concerns may be prosecuted under the FCPA if they directly, or through an agent, engage in any act in furtherance of a corrupt payment while in the territory of the United States, regardless of whether they utilize the U.S. mails or a means or instrumentality of interstate commerce. Thus, for example, a foreign national who attends a meeting in the United States that furthers a foreign bribery scheme may be subject to prosecution, as may any co-conspirators, even if they did not themselves attend the meeting. A foreign national or company may also be liable under the FCPA if it aids and abets, conspires with, or acts as an agent of an issuer or domestic concern, regardless of whether the foreign national or company itself takes any action in the United States.

In addition, under the "alternative jurisdiction" provision of the FCPA enacted in 1998, U.S. companies or persons may be subject to the anti-bribery provisions even if they act outside the United States. The 1998 amendments to the FCPA expanded the jurisdictional coverage of the Act by establishing an alternative basis for jurisdiction, that is, jurisdiction based on the nationality principle. In particular, the 1998 amendments removed the requirement that there be a use of interstate commerce (e.g., wire, email, telephone call) for acts in furtherance of a corrupt payment to a foreign official by U.S. companies and persons occurring wholly outside of the United States.

Questions

What is the minimum connection with the U.S. that the DOJ and SEC would consider sufficient to prosecute any of the following under the FCPA?

1) A foreign issuer?
2) A foreign individual?
3) A wholly-owned foreign subsidiary of a U.S. corporation?

B. The Presumption Against Extraterritoriality

Since 2010, the Supreme Court has applied the presumption against extraterritoriality three times to limit the reach of federal statutes to U.S. territory. In *Morrison*, the Court addressed the extraterritorial scope of § 10(b) of the Exchange Act—the same Act that includes the FCPA. Like the FCPA Anti-Bribery Provisions, § 10(b) subjects foreign individuals and corporations to U.S. jurisdiction *only* if they made use of the U.S. mails or instruments of interstate commerce.

Morrison v. National Australia Bank Ltd.

Supreme Court of the United States, 561 U.S. 247 (2010)[96]

OPINION

JUSTICE SCALIA delivered the opinion of the Court.

. . . .

I.

Respondent National Australia Bank Limited (National) was, during the relevant time, the largest bank in Australia. Its Ordinary Shares—what in America would be called "common stock"—are traded on the Australian Stock Exchange Limited and on other foreign securities exchanges, but not on any exchange in the United States. There are listed on the New York Stock Exchange, however, National's American Depositary Receipts (ADRs), which represent the right to receive a specified number of National's Ordinary Shares. *Morrison v. National Australia Bank Ltd.* 547 F.3d 167, 168, and n.1 (2d Cir. 2008).

The complaint alleges the following facts, which we accept as true. In February 1998, National bought respondent HomeSide Lending, Inc., a mortgage servicing company headquartered in Florida. HomeSide's business was to receive fees for servicing mortgages (essentially the administrative tasks associated with collecting mortgage payments, see J. Rosenberg, Dictionary of Banking and Financial Services 600 (2d ed. 1985)). The rights to receive those fees, so-called mortgage-servicing rights, can provide a valuable income stream. See 2 The New Palgrave Dictionary of Money and Finance 817 (P. Newman, M. Milgate, & J. Eatwell eds.1992). How valuable each of the rights is depends, in part, on the likelihood that the mortgage to which it applies will be fully repaid before it is due, terminating the need for servicing. HomeSide calculated the present value of its mortgage-servicing rights by using valuation models designed to take this likelihood into account. It recorded the value of its assets, and the numbers appeared in National's financial statements.

From 1998 until 2001, National's annual reports and other public documents touted the success of HomeSide's business, and respondents Frank Cicutto (National's managing director and chief executive officer), Kevin Race (HomeSide's chief operating officer), and Hugh Harris (HomeSide's chief executive officer) did the same in public statements. But on July 5, 2001, National announced that it was writing down the value of HomeSide's assets by $450 million; and then again on September 3, by another $1.75 billion. The prices of both Ordinary Shares and ADRs slumped. After downplaying the July write-down, National explained the September write-down as the result of a failure to anticipate the lowering of prevailing interest rates (lower interest rates lead to more refinancings, *i.e.,* more early repayments of mortgages), other mistaken

---

assumptions in the financial models, and the loss of goodwill. According to the complaint, however, HomeSide, Race, Harris, and another HomeSide senior executive who is also a respondent here had manipulated HomeSide's financial models to make the rates of early repayment unrealistically low in order to cause the mortgage-servicing rights to appear more valuable than they really were. The complaint also alleges that National and Cicutto were aware of this deception by July 2000, but did nothing about it.

As relevant here, petitioners Russell Leslie Owen and Brian and Geraldine Silverlock, all Australians, purchased National's Ordinary Shares in 2000 and 2001, before the write-downs. They sued National, HomeSide, Cicutto, and the three HomeSide executives in the United States District Court for the Southern District of New York for alleged violations of §§ 10(b) and 20(a) of the Securities and Exchange Act of 1934, 48 Stat. 891, 15 U.S.C. §§ 78j(b) and 78t(a), and SEC Rule 10b–5, 17 CFR § 240.10b–5 (2009), promulgated pursuant to § 10(b). They sought to represent a class of foreign purchasers of National's Ordinary Shares during a specified period up to the September write-down. *Morrison*, 547 F.3d at 169.

Respondents moved to dismiss for lack of subject-matter jurisdiction under Federal Rule of Civil Procedure 12(b)(1) and for failure to state a claim under Rule 12(b)(6). The District Court granted the motion on the former ground, finding no jurisdiction because the acts in this country were, "at most, a link in the chain of an alleged overall securities fraud scheme that culminated abroad." *In re National Australia Bank Securities Litigation,* No. 03 Civ. 6537(BSJ), 2006 WL 3844465, *8 (S.D.N.Y., Oct. 25, 2006). The Court of Appeals for the Second Circuit affirmed on similar grounds. The acts performed in the United States did not "compris[e] the heart of the alleged fraud." *Morrison*, 547 F.3d at 175-76. We granted certiorari, 558 U.S. 1047.

II.

Before addressing the question presented, we must correct a threshold error in the Second Circuit's analysis. It considered the extraterritorial reach of § 10(b) to raise a question of subject-matter jurisdiction, wherefore it affirmed the District Court's dismissal under Rule 12(b)(1). See *Morrison*, 547 F.3d at 177. In this regard it was following Circuit precedent, see *Schoenbaum v. Firstbrook,* 405 F.2d 200, 208, modified on other grounds en banc, 405 F.2d 215 (1968). The Second Circuit is hardly alone in taking this position, see, *e.g., In re CP Ships Ltd. Securities Litigation,* 578 F.3d 1306, 1313 (11th Cir. 2009); *Continental Grain (Australia) Pty. Ltd. v. Pacific Oilseeds, Inc.,* 592 F.2d 409, 421 (8th Cir. 1979).

But to ask what conduct § 10(b) reaches is to ask what conduct § 10(b) prohibits, which is a merits question. Subject-matter jurisdiction, by contrast, "refers to a tribunal's power to hear a case." *Union Pacific R. Co. v. Locomotive Engineers and Trainmen Gen. Comm. of Adjustment, Central Region,* 558 U.S. 67, 81 (2009) (quoting *Arbaugh v. Y & H Corp.,* 546 U.S. 500, 514 (2006) [(internal quotation marks omitted)], in turn quoting *United States v. Cotton,* 535 U.S. 625, 630 (2002)). It presents an issue quite separate from the question whether the allegations the plaintiff makes entitle him to relief. See *Bell v. Hood,* 327 U.S. 678, 682 (1946). The District Court here had jurisdiction under 15 U.S.C. § 78aa to adjudicate the question whether § 10(b) applies to National's conduct.

In view of this error, which the parties do not dispute, petitioners ask us to remand. We think that unnecessary. Since nothing in the analysis of the courts below turned on the mistake, a remand would only require a new Rule 12(b)(6) label for the same Rule 12(b)(1) conclusion. As we have done before in situations like this, we proceed to address whether petitioners' allegations state a claim.

III.

A.

It is a "longstanding principle of American law that legislation of Congress, unless a contrary intent appears, is meant to apply only within the territorial jurisdiction of the United States." *EEOC v. Arabian American Oil Co.,* 499 U.S. 244, 248 (1991) *(Aramco).* This principle represents a canon of construction, or a presumption about a statute's meaning, rather than a limit upon Congress's power to legislate. It rests on the perception that Congress ordinarily legislates with respect to domestic, not foreign matters. Thus, "unless there is the affirmative intention of the Congress clearly expressed" to give a statute extraterritorial effect, "we must presume it is primarily concerned with domestic conditions." *Aramco, supra,* at 248 (internal quotation marks omitted). The canon or presumption applies regardless of whether there is a risk of conflict between the American statute and a foreign law, see *Sale v. Haitian Centers Council, Inc.,* 509 U.S. 155, 173–174 (1993). When a statute gives no clear indication of an extraterritorial application, it has none.

Despite this principle of interpretation, long and often recited in our opinions, the Second Circuit believed that, because the Exchange Act is silent as to the extraterritorial application of § 10(b), it was left to the court to "discern" whether Congress would have wanted the statute to apply. This disregard of the presumption against extraterritoriality did not originate with the Court of Appeals panel in this case. It has been repeated over many decades by various courts of appeals in determining the application of the Exchange Act, and § 10(b) in particular, to fraudulent schemes that involve conduct and effects abroad. That has produced a collection of tests for divining what Congress would have wanted, complex in formulation and unpredictable in application.

As of 1967, district courts at least in the Southern District of New York had consistently concluded that, by reason of the presumption against extraterritoriality, § 10(b) did not apply when the stock transactions underlying the violation occurred abroad. See *Schoenbaum v. Firstbrook,* 268 F. Supp. 385, 392 (1967). *Schoenbaum* involved the sale in Canada of the treasury shares of a Canadian corporation whose publicly traded shares (but not, of course, its treasury shares) were listed on both the American Stock Exchange and the Toronto

Stock Exchange. Invoking the presumption against extraterritoriality, the court held that § 10(b) was inapplicable (though it incorrectly viewed the defect as jurisdictional). The decision in *Schoenbaum* was reversed, however, by a Second Circuit opinion which held that "neither the usual presumption against extra-territorial application of legislation nor the specific language of [§]30(b) show Congressional intent to preclude application of the Exchange Act to transactions regarding stocks traded in the United States which are effected outside the United States . . . ." *Schoenbaum,* 405 F.2d at 206. It sufficed to apply § 10(b) that, although the transactions in treasury shares took place in Canada, they affected the value of the common shares publicly traded in the United States. Application of § 10(b), the Second Circuit found, was "necessary to protect American investors," *id.* at 206.

The Second Circuit took another step with *Leasco Data Processing Equip. Corp. v. Maxwell,* 468 F.2d 1326 (2d Cir. 1972), which involved an American company that had been fraudulently induced to buy securities in England. There, unlike in *Schoenbaum,* some of the deceptive conduct had occurred in the United States but the corporation whose securities were traded (abroad) was not listed on any domestic exchange. *Leasco* said that the presumption against extraterritoriality applies only to matters over which the United States would not have prescriptive jurisdiction. Congress had prescriptive jurisdiction to regulate the deceptive conduct in this country, the language of the Act could be read to cover that conduct, and the court concluded that "if Congress had thought about the point," it would have wanted § 10(b) to apply. *Id.* at 1334–1337.

With *Schoenbaum* and *Leasco* on the books, the Second Circuit had excised the presumption against extraterritoriality from the jurisprudence of § 10(b) and replaced it with the inquiry whether it would be reasonable (and hence what Congress would have wanted) to apply the statute to a given situation. As long as there was prescriptive jurisdiction to regulate, the Second Circuit explained, whether to apply § 10(b) even to "predominantly foreign" transactions became a matter of whether a court thought Congress "wished the precious resources of United States courts and law enforcement agencies to be devoted to them rather than leave the problem to foreign countries." *Bersch v. Drexel Firestone, Inc.,* 519 F.2d 974, 985 (2d Cir. 1975).

The Second Circuit had thus established that application of § 10(b) could be premised upon either some effect on American securities markets or investors (*Schoenbaum*) or significant conduct in the United States (*Leasco*). It later formalized these two applications into (1) an "effects test," "whether the wrongful conduct had a substantial effect in the United States or upon United States citizens," and (2) a "conduct test," "whether the wrongful conduct occurred in the United States." *SEC v. Berger,* 322 F.3d 187, 192–193 (2d Cir. 2003). These became the north star of the Second Circuit's § 10(b) jurisprudence, pointing the way to what Congress would have wished. Indeed, the Second Circuit declined to keep its two tests distinct on the ground that "an admixture or combination of the two often gives a better picture of whether there is sufficient United States involvement to justify the exercise of jurisdiction by an American court." *Itoba Ltd. v. Lep Group PLC,* 54 F.3d 118, 122 (2d Cir. 1995). The Second Circuit never put forward a textual or even extratextual basis for these tests. As early as *Bersch,* it confessed that "if we were asked to point to language in the statutes, or even in the legislative history, that compelled these conclusions, we would be unable to respond," 519 F.2d at 993.

As they developed, these tests were not easy to administer. The conduct test was held to apply differently depending on whether the harmed investors were Americans or foreigners: When the alleged damages consisted of losses to American investors abroad, it was enough that acts "of material importance" performed in the United States "significantly contributed" to that result; whereas those acts must have "directly caused" the result when losses to foreigners abroad were at issue. See *Bersch,* 519 F.2d at 993. And "merely preparatory activities in the United States" did not suffice "to trigger application of the securities laws for injury to foreigners located abroad." *Id.* at 992. This required the court to distinguish between mere preparation and using the United States as a "base" for fraudulent activities in other countries. *Vencap, supra,* at 1017–1018. But merely satisfying the conduct test was sometimes insufficient without "some additional factor tipping the scales" in favor of the application of American law. *Interbrew v. Edperbrascan Corp.,* 23 F. Supp. 2d 425, 432 (S.D.N.Y. 1998). District courts have noted the difficulty of applying such vague formulations. There is no more damning indictment of the "conduct" and "effects" tests than the Second Circuit's own declaration that "the presence or absence of any single factor which was considered significant in other cases . . . is not necessarily dispositive in future cases." *IIT v. Cornfeld,* 619 F.2d 909, 918 (1980).

Other Circuits embraced the Second Circuit's approach, though not its precise application. Like the Second Circuit, they described their decisions regarding the extraterritorial application of § 10(b) as essentially resolving matters of policy. See, *e.g., SEC v. Kasser,* 548 F.2d 109, 116 (3d Cir. 1977); *Continental Grain,* 592 F.2d, at 421–422; *Grunenthal GmbH v. Hotz,* 712 F.2d 421, 424–425 (9th Cir. 1983); *Kauthar SDN BHD v. Sternberg,* 149 F.3d 659, 667 (7th Cir. 1998). While applying the same fundamental methodology of balancing interests and arriving at what seemed the best policy, they produced a proliferation of vaguely related variations on the "conduct" and "effects" tests. As described in a leading Seventh Circuit opinion: "Although the circuits . . . seem to agree that there are some transnational situations to which the antifraud provisions of the securities laws are applicable, agreement appears to end at that point." *Id.* at 665.

At least one Court of Appeals has criticized this line of cases and the interpretive assumption that underlies it. In *Zoelsch v. Arthur Andersen & Co.,* 824 F.2d 27, 32 (D.C. Cir. 1987), the District of Columbia Circuit observed that rather than courts' "divining what Congress would have wished if it had addressed the problem[, a] more natural inquiry might be what jurisdiction Congress in fact thought about and conferred." Although tempted to apply the presumption against extraterritoriality and be done with it, that court deferred to the Second Circuit because of its "preeminence in the field of securities law," *id.* at 32.

Commentators have criticized the unpredictable and inconsistent applica-tion of § 10(b) to transnational cases. Some have challenged the premise under-lying the Courts of Appeals' approach, namely that Congress did not consider the extraterritorial application of § 10(b) (thereby leaving it open to the courts, supposedly, to determine what Congress would have wanted). Others, more fundamentally, have noted that using congressional silence as a justification for judge-made rules violates the traditional principle that silence means no extra-territorial application.

The criticisms seem to us justified. The results of judicial-speculation-made-law—divining what Congress would have wanted if it had thought of the situ-ation before the court—demonstrate the wisdom of the presumption against extrater-ritoriality. Rather than guess anew in each case, we apply the presumption in all cases, preserving a stable background against which Congress can legislate with predictable effects.

> Rather than guess anew in each case, we apply the presumption in all cases, preserving a stable background against which Congress can legislate with predictable effects.

B.

Rule 10b–5, the regulation under which petitioners have brought suit, was promulgated under § 10(b), and "does not extend beyond conduct encom-passed by § 10(b)'s prohibition." *United States v. O'Hagan,* 521 U.S. 642, 651, (1997). Therefore, if § 10(b) is not extraterritorial, neither is Rule 10b–5.

On its face, § 10(b) contains nothing to suggest it applies abroad:

> "It shall be unlawful for any person, directly or indirectly, by the use of any means or instrumentality of interstate commerce or of the mails, or of any facility of any national securities exchange . . . [t]o use or employ, in connection with the pur-chase or sale of any security registered on a national securities exchange or any security not so registered, . . . any manipulative or deceptive device or contrivance in contravention of such rules and regulations as the [Securities and Exchange] Commission may prescribe . . . ." 15 U.S.C. 78j(b).

Petitioners and the Solicitor General contend, however, that three things indi-cate that § 10(b) or the Exchange Act in general has at least some extraterritorial application.

First, they point to the definition of "interstate commerce," a term used in § 10(b), which includes "trade, commerce, transportation, or communication . . . between any foreign country and any State." 15 U.S.C. § 78c(a)(17). But "we have repeatedly held that even statutes that contain broad language in their definitions of 'commerce' that expressly refer to '*foreign* commerce' do not apply abroad." *Aramco,* 499 U.S. at 251; see *id.,* at 251–252. The general reference to foreign commerce in the definition of "interstate commerce" does not defeat the presumption against extraterritoriality.

Petitioners and the Solicitor General next point out that Congress, in describ-ing the purposes of the Exchange Act, observed that the "prices established and offered in such transactions are generally disseminated and quoted throughout the United States and foreign countries." 15 U.S.C. § 78b(2). The antecedent of "such transactions," however, is found in the first sentence of the section, which declares that "transactions in securities as commonly conducted upon securities exchanges and over-the-counter markets are affected with a national public interest." § 78b. Nothing suggests that this *national* public interest pertains to transactions conducted upon *foreign* exchanges and markets. The fleeting reference to the dissemination and quotation abroad of the prices of securities traded in domestic exchanges and markets cannot overcome the presumption against extraterritoriality.

Finally, there is § 30(b) of the Exchange Act, 15 U.S.C. § 78dd(b), which *does* mention the Act's extraterritorial application: "The provisions of [the Exchange Act] or of any rule or regulation thereunder shall not apply to any person insofar as he transacts a business in securities without the jurisdiction of the United States," unless he does so in violation of regulations promulgated by the Securities and Exchange Commission "to prevent . . . evasion of [the Act]." (The parties have pointed us to no regulation promulgated pursuant to § 30(b).) The Solicitor General argues that "[this] exemption would have no function if the Act did not apply in the first instance to securities transactions that occur abroad." Brief for United States as *Amicus Curiae* 14.

We are not convinced. In the first place, it would be odd for Congress to indicate the extraterritorial application of the whole Exchange Act by means of a provision imposing a condition precedent to its application abroad. And if the whole Act applied abroad, why would the Commission's enabling regulations be limited to those preventing "evasion" of the Act, rather than all those preventing "violation"? The provision seems to us directed at actions abroad that might conceal a domestic violation, or might cause what would otherwise be a domestic violation to escape on a technicality. At most, the Solicitor General's proposed inference is possible; but possible interpretations of statutory language do not override the presumption against extraterritoriality. See *Aramco, supra,* at 253.

The Solicitor General also fails to account for § 30(a), which reads in relevant part as follows:

> "It shall be unlawful for any broker or dealer . . . to make use of the mails or of any means or instrumentality of interstate commerce for the purpose of effecting on an exchange not within or subject to the jurisdiction of the United States, any transaction in any security the issuer of which is a resident of, or is organized under the laws of, or has its principal place of business in, a place within or subject to the jurisdiction of the United States, in contravention of such rules and regulations as the Commission may prescribe. . . ." 15 U.S.C. § 78dd(a).

Subsection 30(a) contains what § 10(b) lacks: a clear statement of extraterritorial effect. Its explicit provision for a specific extraterritorial application would be quite superfluous if the rest of the Exchange Act already applied to transactions on foreign exchanges—and its limitation of that application to securities of domestic issuers would be inoperative. Even if that were not true, when a statute provides for some extraterritorial application, the presumption against extraterritoriality operates to limit that provision to its terms. No one claims that § 30(a) applies here.

The concurrence claims we have impermissibly narrowed the inquiry in evaluating whether a statute applies abroad, citing for that point the dissent in *Aramco,* see *post,* at 2891. But we do not say, as the concurrence seems to think, that the presumption against extraterritoriality is a "clear statement rule," *ibid.,* if by that is meant a requirement that a statute say "this law applies abroad." Assuredly context can be consulted as well. But whatever sources of statutory meaning one consults to give "the most faithful reading" of the text, *post,* at 2892, there is no clear indication of extraterritoriality here. The concurrence does not even try to refute that conclusion, but merely puts forward the same (at best) uncertain indications relied upon by petitioners and the Solicitor General. As the opinion *for the Court* in *Aramco* (which we prefer to the dissent) shows, those uncertain indications do not suffice.

In short, there is no affirmative indication in the Exchange Act that § 10(b) applies extraterritorially, and we therefore conclude that it does not.

IV.

A.

Petitioners argue that the conclusion that § 10(b) does not apply extraterritorially does not resolve this case. They contend that they seek no more than domestic application anyway, since Florida is where HomeSide and its senior executives engaged in the deceptive conduct of manipulating HomeSide's financial models; their complaint also alleged that Race and Hughes made misleading public statements there. This is less an answer to the presumption against extraterritorial application than it is an assertion—a quite valid assertion—that that presumption here (as often) is not self-evidently dispositive, but its application requires further analysis. For it is a rare case of prohibited extraterritorial application that lacks *all* contact with the territory of the United States. But the presumption against extraterritorial application would be a craven watchdog indeed if it retreated to its kennel whenever *some* domestic activity is involved in the case. The concurrence seems to imagine just such a timid sentinel, see *post,* at 2892, but our cases are to the contrary. In *Aramco,* for example, the Title VII plaintiff had been hired in Houston, and was an American citizen. The Court concluded, however, that neither that territorial event nor that relationship was the "focus" of congressional concern, but rather domestic employment.

Applying the same mode of analysis here, we think that the focus of the Exchange Act is not upon the place where the deception originated, but upon purchases and sales of securities in the United States. Section 10(b) does not punish deceptive conduct, but only deceptive conduct "in connection with the purchase or sale of any security registered on a national securities exchange or any security not so registered." 15 U.S.C. § 78j(b). Those purchase-and-sale transactions are the objects of the statute's solicitude. It is those transactions that the statute seeks to "regulate," see *Superintendent of Ins. of N.Y. v. Bankers Life &*

Casualty Co., 404 U.S. 6, 12 (1971); it is parties or prospective parties to those transactions that the statute seeks to "protec[t]," *id.* at 10. And it is in our view only transactions in securities listed on domestic exchanges, and domestic transactions in other securities, to which § 10(b) applies.

The primacy of the domestic exchange is suggested by the very prologue of the Exchange Act, which sets forth as its object "[t]o provide for the regulation of securities exchanges . . . operating in interstate and foreign commerce and through the mails, to prevent inequitable and unfair practices on such exchanges . . . ." 48 Stat. 881. We know of no one who thought that the Act was intended to "regulat[e]" *foreign* securities exchanges—or indeed who even believed that under established principles of international law Congress had the power to do so. The Act's registration requirements apply only to securities listed on national securities exchanges. 15 U.S.C. § 78l(a).

With regard to securities *not* registered on domestic exchanges, the exclusive focus on *domestic* purchases and sales is strongly confirmed by § 30(a) and (b), discussed earlier. The former extends the normal scope of the Exchange Act's prohibitions to acts effecting, in violation of rules prescribed by the Commission, a "transaction" in a United States security "on an exchange not within or subject to the jurisdiction of the United States." § 78dd(a). And the latter specifies that the Act does not apply to "any person insofar as he transacts a business in securities without the jurisdiction of the United States," unless he does so in violation of regulations promulgated by the Commission "to prevent evasion [of the Act]." § 78dd(b). Under both provisions it is the foreign location of the *transaction* that establishes (or reflects the presumption of) the Act's inapplicability, absent regulations by the Commission.

The same focus on domestic transactions is evident in the Securities Act of 1933, 48 Stat. 74, enacted by the same Congress as the Exchange Act, and forming part of the same comprehensive regulation of securities trading. That legislation makes it unlawful to sell a security, through a prospectus or otherwise, making use of "any means or instruments of transportation or communication in interstate commerce or of the mails," unless a registration statement is in effect. 15 U.S.C. § 77e(a)(1). The Commission has interpreted that requirement "not to include . . . sales that occur outside the United States." 17 CFR § 230.901 (2009).

Finally, we reject the notion that the Exchange Act reaches conduct in this country affecting exchanges or transactions abroad for the same reason that *Aramco* rejected overseas application of Title VII to all domestically concluded employment contracts or all employment contracts with American employers: The probability of incompatibility with the applicable laws of other countries is so obvious that if Congress intended such foreign application "it would have addressed the subject of conflicts with foreign laws and procedures." 499 U.S. at 256. Like the United States, foreign countries regulate their domestic securities exchanges and securities transactions occurring within their territorial jurisdiction. And the regulation of other countries often differs from ours as to what constitutes fraud, what disclosures must be made, what damages are recoverable, what discovery is available in litigation, what individual actions may be joined in a single suit, what attorney's fees are recoverable, and many other matters. See, *e.g.,* Brief for United Kingdom of Great Britain and Northern Ireland as *Amicus Curiae* 16–21. The Commonwealth of Australia, the United Kingdom of Great Britain and Northern Ireland, and the Republic of France have filed *amicus* briefs in this case. So have (separately or jointly) such international and foreign organizations as the International Chamber of Commerce, the Swiss Bankers Association, the Federation of German Industries, the French Business Confederation, the Institute of International Bankers, the European Banking Federation, the Australian Bankers' Association, and the Association Francaise des Entreprises Privées. They all complain of the interference with foreign securities regulation that application of § 10(b) abroad would produce, and urge the adoption of a clear test that will avoid that consequence. The transactional test we have adopted—whether the purchase or sale is made in the United States, or involves a security listed on a domestic exchange—meets that requirement.

B.

The Solicitor General suggests a different test, which petitioners also endorse: "[A] transnational securities fraud violates [§] 10(b) when the fraud involves significant conduct in the United States that is material to the fraud's success." Brief for United States as *Amicus Curiae* 16; see Brief for Petitioners 26. Neither the Solicitor General nor petitioners provide any textual support for this test. The Solicitor General sets forth a number of purposes such a test would serve: achieving a high standard of business ethics in the securities industry, ensuring honest securities markets and thereby promoting investor confidence, and preventing the United States from becoming a "Barbary Coast" for malefactors perpetrating frauds in foreign markets. Brief for United States as *Amicus Curiae* 16–17. But it provides no textual support for the last of these purposes, or for the first two as applied to the foreign securities industry and securities markets abroad. It is our function to give the statute the effect its language suggests, however modest that may be; not to extend it to admirable purposes it might be used to achieve.

If, moreover, one is to be attracted by the desirable consequences of the "significant and material conduct" test, one should also be repulsed by its adverse consequences. While there is no reason to believe that the United States has become the Barbary Coast for those perpetrating frauds on foreign securities markets, some fear that it has become the Shangri-La of class-action litigation for lawyers representing those allegedly cheated in foreign securities markets.

As case support for the "significant and material conduct" test, the Solicitor General relies primarily on *Pasquantino v. United States,* 544 U.S. 349 (2005). In that case we concluded that the wire-fraud statute, 18 U.S.C. § 1343 (2009 ed., Supp. II), was violated by defendants who ordered liquor over the phone from a store in Maryland with the intent to smuggle it into Canada and deprive the Canadian Government of revenue. 544 U.S. at 353, 371. Section 1343 prohibits "any scheme or artifice to defraud"—fraud *simpliciter,* without any requirement that it be "in connection with" any particular transaction or event. The *Pasquantino* Court said that the petitioners' "offense was complete the moment they executed the scheme inside the United States," and that it was "[t]his domestic element of petitioners' conduct [that] the Government is punishing." 544 U.S. at 371. Section 10(b), by contrast, punishes not all acts of deception, but only such acts "in connection with the purchase or sale of any security registered on a national securities exchange or any security not so registered." Not deception alone, but deception with respect to certain purchases or sales is necessary for a violation of the statute.

The Solicitor General points out that the "significant and material conduct" test is in accord with prevailing notions of international comity. If so, that proves that *if* the United States asserted prescriptive jurisdiction pursuant to the "significant and material conduct" test it would not violate customary international law; but it in no way tends to prove that that is what Congress has done.

Finally, the Solicitor General argues that the Commission has adopted an interpretation similar to the "significant and material conduct" test, and that we should defer to that. In the two adjudications the Solicitor General cites, however, the Commission did not purport to be providing its own interpretation of the statute, but relied on decisions of federal courts—mainly Court of Appeals decisions that in turn relied on the *Schoenbaum* and *Leasco* decisions of the Second Circuit that we discussed earlier. We need "accept only those agency interpretations that are reasonable in light of the principles of construction courts normally employ." *Aramco,* 499 U.S. at 260 (SCALIA, J., concurring in part and concurring in judgment). Since the Commission's interpretations relied on cases we disapprove, which ignored or discarded the presumption against extraterritoriality, we owe them no deference.

Section 10(b) reaches the use of a manipulative or deceptive device or contrivance only in connection with the purchase or sale of a security listed on an American stock exchange, and the purchase or sale of any other security in the United States. This case involves no securities listed on a domestic exchange, and all aspects of the purchases complained of by those petitioners who still have live claims occurred outside the United States. Petitioners have therefore failed to state a claim on which relief can be granted. We affirm the dismissal of petitioners' complaint on this ground.

It is so ordered.

Notes and Questions

The opinion in *Morrison* is especially relevant to the jurisdictional scope of the FCPA, because § 10(b) of the Exchange Act (the antifraud provision) and § 30A of the same Act (the FCPA Anti-Bribery Provisions) contain the same jurisdictional requirement: that the defendant have made use of the U.S. mails or instruments of interstate commerce. Notwithstanding this similarity, however, the two statutes are directed at different types of conduct. While § 10(b) prohibits fraud in connection with sales of securities on U.S. stock exchanges, the FCPA Anti-Bribery Provisions are directed at bribes paid to foreign officials—a kind of transaction that typically takes place abroad. As the *Morrison* opinion notes, the fact that § 10(b) is focused on domestic transactions was relevant to its conclusion that the statute did not evince a clear indication of extraterritoriality.

In *Kiobel v. Royal Dutch Petroleum Co.*,[97] decided three years after *Morrison*, the Court addressed a civil suit for damages by Nigerian nationals residing in the United States under the Alien Tort Statute ("ATS"),[98] "alleging that . . . certain Dutch, British, and Nigerian corporations—aided and abetted the Nigerian Government in committing violations of the law of nations in Nigeria."[99] The ATS provides:

> The district courts shall have original jurisdiction of any civil action by an alien for a tort only, committed in violation of the law of nations or a treaty of the United States.[100]

Rejecting the plaintiffs' claims under the ATS, the Court held:

> [T]o rebut the presumption, the ATS would need to evince a "clear indication of extraterritoriality." It does not.
>
>   To begin, nothing in the text of the statute suggests that Congress intended causes of action recognized under it to have extraterritorial reach. The ATS covers actions by aliens for violations of the law of nations, but that does not imply extraterritorial reach—such violations affecting aliens can occur either within or outside the United States. Nor does the fact that the text reaches "any civil action" suggest application to torts committed abroad; it is well established that generic terms like "any" or "every" do not rebut the presumption against extraterritoriality.[101]

More recently, in *RJR Nabisco*[102]—a case involving alleged violations of the Racketeer Influenced and Corrupt Organizations Act ("RICO")—the Court further clarified how the presumption against extraterritoriality should be applied:

> Twice in the past six years we have considered whether a federal statute applies extraterritorially. In *Morrison*, we addressed the question whether § 10(b) of the Securities Exchange Act of 1934 applies to misrepresentations made in connection with the purchase or sale of securities traded only on foreign exchanges. We first examined whether § 10(b) gives any clear indication of extraterritorial effect, and found that it does not. We then engaged in a separate inquiry to determine whether the complaint before us involved a permissible *domestic* application of § 10(b) because it alleged that some of the relevant misrepresentations were made in the United States. At this second step, we considered the "'focus' of congressional concern," asking whether § 10(b)'s focus is "the place where the deception originated" or rather "purchases and sale of securities in the United States." We concluded that the statute's focus is on domestic securities transactions, and we

---

97. Kiobel v. Royal Dutch Petroleum Co., 133 S. Ct. 1659, 1660 (2013).
98. *Id.* (citing Alien Tort Statute, 28 U.S.C. § 1350 (2012)).
99. *Id.*
100. *Id.* (citing 28 U.S.C. § 1350).
101. Slip op. at 7.
102. RJR Nabisco, Inc. v. European Cmty., 136 S. Ct. 2090 (2016).

therefore held that the statute does not apply to frauds in connection with foreign securities transactions, even if those frauds involve domestic misrepresentations.

In *Kiobel*, we considered whether the Alien Tort Statute (ATS) confers federal-court jurisdiction over causes of action alleging international-law violations committed overseas. We acknowledged that the presumption against extraterritoriality is "typically" applied to statutes "regulating conduct," but we concluded that the principles supporting the presumption should "similarly constrain courts considering causes of action that may be brought under the ATS." We applied the presumption and held that the ATS lacks any clear indication that it extended to the foreign violations alleged in that case. Because "all the relevant conduct" regarding those violations "took place outside the United States," we did not need to determine, as we did in *Morrison*, the statute's "focus."

Morrison and *Kiobel* reflect a two-step framework for analyzing extraterritoriality issues. At the first step, we ask whether the presumption against extraterritoriality has been rebutted—that is, whether the statute gives a clear, affirmative indication that it applies extraterritorially. We must ask this question regardless of whether the statute in question regulates conduct, affords relief, or merely confers jurisdiction. If the statute is not extraterritorial, then at the second step we determine whether the case involves a domestic application of the statute, and we do this by looking to the statute's "focus." If the conduct relevant to the statute's focus occurred in the United States, then the case involves a permissible domestic application even if other conduct occurred abroad; but if the conduct relevant to the focus occurred in a foreign country, then the case involves an impermissible extraterritorial application regardless of any other conduct that occurred in U.S. territory.[103]

The Court also noted that when a statute does not "give[] a clear, affirmative indication that it applies extraterritorially," the inquiry turns on whether "the conduct relevant to the statute's focus occurred in the United States."[104]

1) Assuming that § 78dd-1 does not extend to the extraterritorial conduct of foreign issuers, what is the focus of the FCPA anti-bribery provisions and what domestic conduct would be relevant to that focus?

2) At the outset of the *Morrison* opinion, the Court found error in the district court's dismissal under Federal Rule of Civil Procedure 12(b)(1) instead of Rule 12(b)(6). Why is the distinction relevant, and how does it impact similar cases in the future?

3) In *Morrison*, the defendant's alleged fraudulent conduct largely took place in the U.S. Why was such conduct deemed insufficient to trigger the application of § 10(b)?

4) Why did the Supreme Court reject the "conduct test" and the "effects test" articulated by the Second Circuit?

5) What meaning did *Morrison* attach to the phrase "to make use of the mails or of any means or instrumentality of interstate commerce"?

---

103. *Id.* at 2100-01 (citations omitted).
104. *Id.* 136 S. Ct. at 2101.

C. Jurisdictional Scope of the FCPA Anti-Bribery Provisions in Light of the Presumption Against Extraterritoriality

1. Issuers (15 U.S.C. § 78dd-1)

Section 78dd-1 treats domestic and foreign issuers differently for jurisdictional purposes.[105] U.S.-based issuers, and their employees and agents who are U.S. persons, are addressed in § 78dd-1(g), titled "Alternative jurisdiction," which expressly covers their conduct outside the United States:

> It shall also be unlawful for any issuer organized under the laws of the United States . . . or for any United States person that is an officer, director, employee, or agent of such issuer or a stockholder thereof acting on behalf of such issuer, to corruptly do any act *outside the United States* in furtherance of [a bribe] . . . .[106]

Foreign issuers, as well as foreign employees and foreign agents of all issuers, are only covered to the extent they "make use of the [U.S.] mails or any means or instrumentality of interstate commerce . . . in furtherance" of a bribe.[107]

Morrison made clear when addressing the meaning of the phrase "by the use of any means or instrumentality of interstate commerce or of the mails"[108] in the context of § 10(b) of the Exchange Act, that "[t]he general reference to foreign commerce in the definition of 'interstate commerce' does not defeat the presumption against extraterritoriality."[109] Justice Antonin Scalia, writing for the majority, explained:

> [I]t is a rare case of prohibited extraterritorial application that lacks *all* contact with the territory of the United States. But the presumption against extraterritorial application would be a craven watchdog indeed if it retreated to its kennel whenever *some* domestic activity is involved in the case.[110]

Making no reference to the presumption against extraterritoriality, the DOJ and SEC interpret the phrase "use of the mails or interstate commerce" to require only tenuous connections with the United States: The FCPA's anti-bribery provisions can apply to conduct both inside and out- side the United States. . . . [P]lacing a telephone call or sending an e-mail, text message, or fax from, to, or through the United States involves interstate commerce—as does sending a wire transfer from or to a U.S. bank or otherwise using the U.S. banking system.[111]

---

105. 15 U.S.C. § 78dd-1 (2012).

106. *Id.* § 78dd-1(g) (emphasis added).

107. *Id* § 78dd-1(a).

108. Morrison v. Nat'l Austl. Bank Ltd., 561 U.S. 247, 262 (2010) (citing 15 U.S.C. 78j(b)).

109. *Id.* at 263; *see also* Norex Petroleum Ltd. v. Access Indus., Inc., 631 F.3d 29, 33 (2d Cir. 2010) (holding that RICO statute's reference to "any enterprise which is engaged in, or that activities of which affect, interstate or foreign commerce" does not mean that the statute was intended to apply extraterritorially (citing *Morrison*, 561 U.S. at 262-63)).

110. *Morrison*, 561 U.S. at 266.

111. FCPA Guide, *supra* note 4, at 11.

15 U.S.C. § 78dd-1

(A) PROHIBITION

It shall be unlawful for any issuer . . . or for any officer, director, employee, or agent of such issuer or any stockholder thereof acting on behalf of such issuer, to make use of the mails or any means or instrumentality of interstate commerce corruptly in furtherance of an offer, payment, promise to pay, or authorization of the payment of any money, or offer, gift promise to give, or authorization of the giving of anything of value to . . . any foreign official.

. . . .

(G) ALTERNATIVE JURISDICTION

(1) It shall also be unlawful for any issuer organized under the laws of the United States, or a State, territory, possession, or commonwealth of the United States or a political subdivision thereof . . . or for any United States person that is an officer, director, employee, or agent of such issuer or a stockholder thereof acting on behalf of such issuer, to corruptly do any act outside the United States in furtherance of [a bribe,] irrespective of whether such issuer or such officer, director, employee, agent, or stockholder makes use of the mails or any means or instrumentality of interstate commerce in furtherance of such [bribe].

(2) As used in this subsection, the term "United States person" means a national of the United States . . . or any corporation, partnership, association, joint-stock company, business trust, unincorporated organization, or sole pro-prietorship organized under the laws of the United States or any State, territory, possession, or commonwealth of the United States, or any political subdivision thereof.

House Report: International Anti-Bribery and Fair Competition Act of 1998

H.R. Rep. No. 105-802 (1998)[112]

SECTION 2.—AMENDMENTS TO THE FOREIGN CORRUPT PRACTICES ACT GOVERNING ISSUERS

. . . .

Subsection (c) implements the OECD Convention by creating an additional basis for jurisdiction over foreign bribery by U.S. issuers and U.S. persons that are officers, directors, employees, or agents, or stockholders of such issuers. See OECD Convention, Art. 4, para. 2. This section extends coverage for acts outside the United States to U.S. issuers that are organized under the laws of the United

---

112. COMM. ON COMMERCE, INTERNATIONAL ANTI-BRIBERY AND FAIR COMPETITION ACT OF 1998, H.R. REP. No. 105-802, at 19–20 (1998).

States or of a State, territory, or commonwealth, or a political subdivision thereof and U.S. persons acting on such issuers' behalf. Under the new Sec. 30A(g) of the Securities Exchange Act, U.S. issuers or U.S. persons acting on a U.S. issuer's behalf violate the FCPA if they make any of the payments prohibited under the existing statute outside of the United States, irrespective of whether in doing so they make any use of the mails or means or instrumentality of interstate commerce. Although this section limits liability to U.S. issuers and U.S. persons acting on U.S. issuers' behalf, it is expected that the established principles of liability, including principles of vicarious liability, that apply under the current version of the FCPA shall apply to the liability of U.S. issuers for acts taken on their behalf by their officers, directors, employees, agents, or stockholders outside the territory of the United States, regardless of the nationality of the officer, director, employee, agent, or stockholder. The subsection also inserts references to the new offense in the provisions of the existing statute governing exceptions and affirmative defenses.

Subsection (d) implements the OECD Convention by amending Sec. 32(c) of the Securities Exchange Act (15 U.S.C. 78 ff (c)) to eliminate the current disparity in treatment between U.S. nationals that are employees or agents of issuers and foreign nationals that are employees or agents of issuers. Presently, foreign nationals who are employees or agents (as opposed to officers or directors) are subject only to civil sanctions. Eliminating this preferential treatment implements the OECD Convention's requirement that "[e]ach Party shall take such measures as may be necessary to establish that it is a criminal offense under its law for any person to [make unlawful payments]." OECD Convention, Article 1. In addition, subsection (d) provides that the same penalties shall apply to issuers for violation of the new provisions for acts outside the United States as apply to violations of the existing statute.

Hypothetical: Extraterritorial Application of the FCPA

You are a clerk to one of the Justices of the Supreme Court of the United States. Before the Court is a case involving the following undisputed facts:

> Defendant Albert Camus is being prosecuted for violating the FCPA anti-bribery provisions. Camus is a French citizen employed by FrenchCo., a pharmaceutical company based in Paris, France. FrenchCo.'s shares trade on the NYSE, and it maintains several production facilities in the U.S.
>
> Camus paid a bribe to an Algerian government official in 2015, which resulted in a $1 million sales contract for FrenchCo. A portion of the goods involved in the sales contract, valued at $300,000, was shipped to Algeria from the United States. Camus never set foot in the United States and had no contact with anyone in the United States. No citizens or residents of the United States knew about or were in any way involved in the transaction.

> The district court dismissed the case, holding that the presumption against extraterritoriality precludes the prosecution of Camus. The court of appeals affirmed the dismissal.
>
> 1) Is Camus' conduct covered by the FCPA?
> 2) Articulate a test to guide similar cases in the future.

2. Domestic Concerns (15 U.S.C. § 78dd-2)

Section 78dd-2 covers "domestic concerns" together with their employees and agents to the extent they "make use of the mails or any means or instrumentality of interstate commerce . . . in furtherance of [a bribe.]"[113] A domestic concern is defined as:

> **(A)** any individual who is a citizen, national, or resident of the United States; and
> **(B)** any corporation, partnership, association, joint-stock company, business trust, unincorporated organization, or sole proprietorship which has its principal place of business in the United States, or which is organized under the laws of a State of the United States or a territory, possession, or commonwealth of the United States.[114]

Like § 78dd-1, § 78dd-2 contains an alternative jurisdiction clause which provides:

> **(1)** It shall also be unlawful for any United States person to corruptly do any act outside the United States in furtherance of an offer, payment, promise to pay, or authorization of the payment of any money, or offer, gift, promise to give, or authorization of the giving of anything of value to any of the persons or entities set forth in paragraphs (1), (2), and (3) of subsection (a) of this section, for the purposes set forth therein, irrespective of whether such United States person makes use of the mails or any means or instrumentality of interstate commerce in furtherance of such offer, gift, payment, promise, or authorization.
> **(2)** As used in this subsection, the term "United States person" means a national of the United States . . . or any corporation, partnership, association, joint-stock company, business trust, unincorporated organization, or sole proprietorship organized under the laws of the United States or any State, territory, possession, or commonwealth of the United States, or any political subdivision thereof.[115]

The only class excluded from the alternative jurisdiction clause is foreign employees and foreign agents of domestic concerns. Thus, § 78dd-2 also bifurcates jurisdiction based on nationality, applying extraterritorially to U.S. persons but not to foreign entities and individuals.

---

113. 15 U.S.C. § 78dd-2(a) (2012).
114. *Id.* § 78dd-2(h)(1).
115. *Id.* § 78dd-2(i).

House Report: International Anti-Bribery and Fair Competition Act of 1998

H.R. Rep. No. 105-802 (1998)[116]

SECTION 3.—AMENDMENTS TO THE FOREIGN CORRUPT PRACTICES ACT GOVERNING DOMESTIC CONCERNS

. . . .

Subsection (b) implements the OECD Convention by eliminating the current disparity in treatment between U.S. nationals that are employees or agents of domestic concerns and foreign nationals that are employees or agents of domestic concerns. Presently, foreign nationals who are employees or agents (as opposed to officers or directors) are subject only to civil sanctions. Eliminating this preferential treatment implements the OECD Convention's requirement that "[e]ach Party shall take such measures as may be necessary to establish that it is a criminal offense under its law for any person to [make unlawful payments]." OECD Convention, Article 1. In addition, section 3(b) provides that the same penalties shall apply to U.S. persons for violation of the new Sec. 104(i) for acts outside the United States as apply to violations of the existing FCPA.

. . . .

Subsection (d) implements the OECD Convention by creating an additional basis for jurisdiction over foreign bribery by U.S. persons. See OECD Convention, Art. 4, para. 2. This section limits coverage to businesses organized under the laws of the United States, a State, territory, possession, or commonwealth, or a political subdivision thereof, or U.S. nationals. U.S. nationals are defined by reference to the Immigration and Nationality Act, 8 U.S.C. Sec. 1101(22), which defines a "national of the United States" as "(A) a citizen of the United States, or (B) a person, who though not a citizen, owes permanent allegiance to the United States." Under the new Sec. 104(i), a U.S. person violates the FCPA if it makes any of the payments prohibited under the existing statute outside of the United States, irrespective of whether in doing so it makes any use of the mails or means or instrumentality of interstate commerce. Although this section imposes liability only on U.S. persons, it is expected that the established principles of liability, including principles of vicarious liability, that apply under the current version of the FCPA shall apply to the liability of U.S. businesses for acts taken on their behalf by their officers, directors, employees, agents or stockholders outside the United States, regardless of the nationality of the officer, director, employee, agent, or stockholder. Subsection (d) also inserts references to the new offense in the provisions of the existing statute governing exceptions, affirmative defenses, and injunctive relief.

---

116. Comm. on Commerce, International Anti-Bribery and Fair Competition Act of 1998, H.R. Rep. No. 105-802, at 20–21 (1998).

Notes and Questions

The alternative jurisdiction clauses of §§ 78dd-1 and 78dd-2 were added as part of the 1998 amendments to conform the FCPA to the OECD Anti-Bribery Convention.

Which provision of the OECD Anti-Bribery Convention, if any, mandated their addition?

Hypothetical: Foreign Employee of a Domestic Concern

Hans Schmidt is a citizen and resident of Germany who is employed by Newbury, Inc. ("Newbury"), a privately held investment management company registered in the United States. Schmidt bribed an Indonesian official to obtain business on behalf of Newbury. The DOJ has indicted Schmidt for violating § 78dd-2.

Which of the following statements is true, and why?

1) The DOJ must prove that Schmidt "[made] use of the mails or any means or instrumentality of interstate commerce . . . in furtherance of" the bribe.
2) Schmidt may be held liable under § 78dd-2 "irrespective of whether [he made] use of the mails or any means or instrumentality of interstate commerce in furtherance of" the bribe.

---

3. Territorial Jurisdiction (15 U.S.C. § 78dd-3)

Section 78dd-3, also added as part of the 1988 amendments to the FCPA, provides in part:

> It shall be unlawful for any person other than an issuer that is subject to section 78dd-1 of this title or a domestic concern (as defined in section 78dd-2 of this title), or for any officer, director, employee, or agent of such person or any stockholder thereof acting on behalf of such person, *while in the territory of the United States* . . . to make use of the mails or any means or instrumentality of interstate commerce or to do any other act in furtherance of [a bribe].[117]

"Person" is defined as:

> [A]ny natural person other than a national of the United States . . . or any corporation, partnership, association, joint-stock company, business trust, unincorporated organization, or sole proprietorship organized under the law of a foreign nation or a political subdivision thereof.[118]

---

117. § 78dd-3(a) (emphasis added).
118. § 78dd-3(f)(1).

Inclusion of the term "while in the territory of the United States" is significant because this limitation does not appear anywhere else in the U.S. Code.[119] Section 78dd-3's legislative history confirms what its plain language suggests:

> [T]he offense created under this section requires that an act in furtherance of the bribe be taken within the territory of the United States. The OECD Convention requires each Party to "take such measures as may be necessary to establish its jurisdiction over the bribery of a foreign public official when the offense is committed in whole or in part in its territory." OECD Convention, Art. 4, para. 1. The new offense complies with this section by providing for criminal jurisdiction in this country over bribery by foreign nationals of foreign officials when the foreign national takes some act in furtherance of the bribery within the territory of the United States. . . .
>
> As envisioned by the negotiators, Congress intends that "the territorial basis for jurisdiction should be interpreted broadly so that an extensive physical connection to the bribery act is not required." *See* Commentaries on the Convention on Combating Bribery of Foreign Public Officials in International Business Transactions (OECD Commentary) at para. 24. . . .
>
> Although this section limits jurisdiction over foreign nationals and companies to instances in which the foreign national or company takes some action while physically present within the territory of the United States, Congress does not thereby intend to place a similar limit on the exercise of U.S. criminal jurisdiction over foreign nationals and companies under any other statute or regulation.
>
> The second difference from the existing FCPA provisions is that this section expands the commerce nexus to include not only the use of the mails or any means or instrumentality of interstate commerce but "any other act" within the United States. It is the view of Congress that any act committed by a foreign national within the United States that is in furtherance of a bribe paid to a foreign official falls within the Congress' power to regulate "Commerce with foreign Nations." U.S. Const., Art. 1, sec. 8, cl. 3.[120]

Section 78dd-3 requires some "action while physically present within the territory of the United States."[121] In this sense, § 78dd-3 imposes a stronger territorial limitation than §§ 78dd-1 and 78dd-2.[122]

---

119. *See* Lauren Ann Ross, Note, *Using Foreign Relations Law to Limit Extraterritorial Application of the Foreign Corrupt Practices Act*, 62 DUKE L.J. 445, 466 (2012) (noting that this territorial limitation is not in any other U.S. Code provision).

120. COMM. ON BANKING, HOUS., & URBAN AFFAIRS, THE INTERNATIONAL ANTI-BRIBERY ACT OF 1998, S. REP. NO. 105-277, at 5–6 (1998).

121. *Id.* at 6.

122. *See* United States v. Patel, No. 1:09-CR-00335, Trial Tr. 5:11–14, 7:17–8:2 (D.D.C. June 6, 2011) (holding that attendance at a single meeting in the United States was insufficient to confer jurisdiction under Section 78dd-3).

15 U.S.C. § 78dd-3

(A) PROHIBITION

It shall be unlawful for any person other than an issuer that is subject to section 78dd-1 of this title or a domestic concern (as defined in section 78dd-2 of this title), or for any officer, director, employee, or agent of such person or any stockholder thereof acting on behalf of such person, while in the territory of the United States, corruptly to make use of the mails or any means or instrumentality of interstate commerce or to do any other act in furtherance of [a bribe].

. . . .

(F) DEFINITIONS

For purposes of this section:

(1) The term "person," when referring to an offender, means any natural person other than a national of the United States . . . or any corporation, partnership, association, joint-stock company, business trust, unincorporated organization, or sole proprietorship organized under the law of a foreign nation or a political subdivision thereof.

House Report: International Anti-Bribery and Fair Competition Act of 1998

H.R. Rep. No. 105-802 (1998)[123]

SECTION 4.—AMENDMENTS TO THE FOREIGN CORRUPT PRACTICES ACT GOVERNING OTHER PERSONS

Section 4 creates a new section in the FCPA, Sec. 104A, providing for criminal and civil penalties over persons not covered under the existing FCPA provisions regarding issuers and domestic concerns. This section closes the gap left in the original FCPA and implements the OECD Convention's requirement that Parties criminalize bribery by "any person." OECD Convention, Art. 1, para. 1. The prohibited acts are the same as those covered by Sec. 30A(a) of the Securities Exchange Act, 15 U.S.C. 78dd-1(a), and Sec. 104(a) of the FCPA, 15 U.S.C. 78dd-2(a), with two qualifications.

First, the offense created under this section requires that an act in furtherance of the bribe be taken within the territory of the United States. The OECD Convention requires each Party to "take such measures as may be necessary to establish its jurisdiction over the bribery of a foreign public official when the offense is committed in whole or in party in its territory." OECD Convention, Art. 4, para. 1. The new offense complies with this section by providing for criminal

---

123. COMM. ON COMMERCE, INTERNATIONAL ANTI-BRIBERY AND FAIR COMPETITION ACT OF 1998, H.R. REP. NO. 105-802, at 21–22 (1998).

jurisdiction in this country over bribery by foreign nationals of foreign officials when the foreign national takes some act in furtherance of the bribery within the territory of the United States. It is expected that the established principles of liability, including principles of vicarious liability, that apply under the current version of the FCPA shall apply to the liability of foreign businesses for acts taken on their behalf by their officers, directors, employees, agents or stockholders in the territory of the United States, regardless of the nationality of the officer, director, employee, agent, or stockholder.

As envisioned in the OECD the territorial basis for jurisdiction should be interpreted broadly so that an extensive physical connection to the bribery act is not required. See Commentaries on the Convention on Combating Bribery of Foreign Public Officials in International Business Transactions (OECD Commentary) at para. 24. Further, "territory of the United States" should be understood to encompass all areas over which the United States asserts territorial jurisdiction. See 18 U.S.C. Sec. 5 ("The term 'United States,' as used in this title in a territorial sense, includes all places and waters, continental or insular, subject to the jurisdiction of the United States, except the Canal Zone."); 18 U.S.C. Sec. 7 (special maritime and territorial jurisdiction of the United States, 49 U.S.C. Sec. 46501(2) (special aircraft jurisdiction of the United States)).

Although this section limits jurisdiction over foreign nationals and companies to instances in which the foreign national or company takes some action while physically present within the territory of the United States, Congress does not thereby intend to place a similar limit on the exercise of U.S. criminal jurisdiction over foreign nationals and companies under any other statute or regulation.

The second difference from the existing FCPA provisions is that this section expands the commerce nexus to include not only the use of the mails or any means or instrumentality of interstate commerce but "any other act" within the United States.

Notes and Questions

The FCPA Guide states:

> Those who are not issuers or domestic concerns may be prosecuted under the FCPA if they directly, or through an agent, engage in *any* act in furtherance of a corrupt payment while in the territory of the United States, regardless of whether they utilize the U.S. mails or a means or instrumentality of interstate commerce. Thus, for example, a foreign national who attends a meeting in the United States that furthers a foreign bribery scheme may be subject to prosecution . . . .[124]

Does a plain reading of § 78dd-3 support this position, or does it require that all acts in furtherance of a bribe be committed in the territory of the U.S.?

---

124. FCPA Guide, *supra* note 4, at 11–12 (footnote omitted).

D. Responsibility for the Conduct of Others

The DOJ and SEC take the position that agency and concert of action extend the FCPA's extraterritorial application to foreign nonissuers with remote, if any, ties to the U.S.

The FCPA Guide States:

> A foreign national or company may also be liable under the FCPA if it aids and abets, conspires with, or acts as an agent of an issuer or domestic concern, regardless of whether the foreign national or company itself takes any action in the United States.[125]

Agency,[126] or *respondeat superior*, involves situations where one person acts on behalf of another, as in the case of an employee acting for his employer.[127] By contrast, concert of action involves situations where several people work together to achieve a common illicit goal, and includes conspiracy, aiding and abetting, and causing.[128] The DOJ and SEC commonly use more than one theory in the same case.

1. Agency

Sections 78dd-1 and 78dd-2 explicitly cover agents of issuers and domestic concerns. As previously discussed, an agency relationship arises in situations where a person or entity acts on behalf of another.[129] According to the FCPA Guide:

> The fundamental characteristic of agency is control. Accordingly, DOJ and SEC evaluate the parent's control—including the parent's knowledge and direction of the subsidiary's actions, both generally and in the context of the specific transaction—when evaluating whether a subsidiary is an agent of the parent. Although the formal relationship between the parent and subsidiary is important in this analysis, so are the practical realities of how the parent and subsidiary actually interact.
>
> If an agency relationship exists, a subsidiary's actions and knowledge are imputed to its parent. Moreover, under traditional principles of *respondeat superior*.... [T]he parent is liable for bribery committed by the subsidiary's employees.[130]

Since agency can extend indefinitely, multinational enterprises face indeterminate exposure to civil and criminal liability for the conduct of foreign third

---

125. *Id. supra* note 4, at 12.

126. *See, e.g.,* Information at 7–17, United States v. JGC Corp., No. 4:11-CR-00260 (S.D. Tex. Apr. 6, 2011) (noting that the DOJ predicated jurisdiction over the Japanese defendant not only based remote connections with the United States—like the passage of funds through the United States— but also on allegations of agency and conspiracy between JGC and another co-defendant who was a U.S. corporation); Deferred Prosecution Agreement at 1–14, United States v. Snamprogetti Netherlands B.V., No. 4:10-CR-00460 (S.D. Tex. July 7, 2010) (charging foreign nonissuer for conspiracy based on ties with U.S. corporation).

127. *See* FCPA GUIDE, *supra* note 4, at 10–12, 27.

128. *See, e.g.,* 18 U.S.C. § 371 (2012).

129. *See* FCPA GUIDE, *supra* note 4, at 10–12.

130. *Id. supra* note 4, at 27, 112 n.178 (footnotes omitted) (first citing Pacific Can Co. v. Hewes, 95 F.2d 42, 46 (9th Cir. 1938) ("Where one corporation is controlled by another, the former acts not for itself but as directed by the latter, the same as an agent, and the principal is liable for the acts of its agent within the scope of the agent's authority."); then citing United States v. NYNEX Corp., 788 F. Supp. 16, 18 n.3 (D.D.C. 1992) (holding that "[a] corporation can of course be held criminally liable for the acts of its agents," including "the conduct of its subsidiaries")).

parties with whom they have a substantial relationship. Multinational enterprises must decide which third-party relationships—extending beyond just the subsidiaries they own to also include distributors, vendors, consultants, and others—could fall under the DOJ and SEC's broad definition of "agent." Once they determine that a risk of liability exists, they must take appropriate measures to ensure the third party's compliance with the FCPA.

Department of Justice, Office of Public Affairs, FOR IMMEDIATE RELEASE, Monday, April 22, 2013

Ralph Lauren Corporation Resolves Foreign Corrupt Practices Act Investigation and Agrees to Pay $882,000 Monetary Penalty[131]

Ralph Lauren Corporation (RLC), a New York based apparel company, has agreed to pay an $882,000 penalty to resolve allegations that it violated the Foreign Corrupt Practices Act (FCPA) by bribing government officials in Argentina to obtain improper customs clearance of merchandise, announced Mythili Raman, the Acting Assistant Attorney General for the Criminal Division, and Loretta E. Lynch, the United States Attorney for the Eastern District of New York.

According to the agreement, the manager of RLC's subsidiary in Argentina bribed customs officials in Argentina over the span of five years to improperly obtain paperwork necessary for goods to clear customs; permit clearance of items without the necessary paperwork and/or the clearance of prohibited items; and on occasion, to avoid inspection entirely. RLC's employee disguised the payments by funneling them through a customs clearance agency, which created fake invoices to justify the improper payments. During these five years, RLC did not have an anti-corruption program and did not provide any anti-corruption training or oversight with respect to its subsidiary in Argentina.

In addition to the monetary penalty, RLC agreed to cooperate with the Department of Justice, to report periodically to the department concerning RLC's compliance efforts, and to continue to implement an enhanced compliance program and internal controls designed to prevent and detect FCPA violations. If RLC abides by the terms of the agreement, the Department will not prosecute RLC in connection with the conduct.

The agreement acknowledges RLC's extensive, thorough, and timely cooperation, including self-disclosure of the misconduct, voluntarily making employees available for interviews, making voluntary document disclosures, conducting a worldwide risk assessment, and making multiple presentations to the Department on the status and findings of the internal investigation and the risk assessment. In addition, RLC has engaged in early and extensive remediation, including conducting extensive FCPA training for employees worldwide, enhancing the company's existing FCPA policy, implementing an enhanced gift

---

131. Press Release, U.S. Dep't of Justice, Ralph Lauren Corporation Resolves Foreign Corrupt Practices Act Investigation and Agrees to Pay $882,000 Monetary Penalty (Apr. 22, 2013), https://www.justice.gov/opa/pr/ralph-lauren-corporation-resolves-foreign-corrupt-practices-act-investigation-and-agrees-pay.

policy and other enhanced compliance, control and anti-corruption policies and procedures, enhancing its due diligence protocol for third-party agents, terminating culpable employees and a third-party agent, instituting a whistleblower hotline, and hiring a designated corporate compliance attorney.

In a related matter, the U.S. Securities and Exchange Commission today announced a non-prosecution agreement with RLC, in which RLC agreed to pay $734,846 in disgorgement and prejudgment interest.

Notes and Questions

The DOJ did not allege that RLC participated in, or even knew about, the FCPA violations committed by its Argentine subsidiary's manager ("Manager"), nor that the alleged acts had any connection to the United States. The DOJ's theory imputed liability from the Manager to the subsidiary, and from the subsidiary to RLC.

1) Was the conduct of RLC's Argentine subsidiary covered under §§ 78dd-1, 78dd-2, 78dd-3, or any other provision of the FCPA?
2) Assume that the RLC case was litigated in the federal district court and RLC raised the presumption against extraterritoriality in its defense. What would be RLC's defense theory? What would be the likely result?
3) Can FCPA liability be imputed in reverse—that is, from a parent to its foreign subsidiary?[132]

Hypothetical: Agency

Walden, Inc. ("Walden"), a clothing retailer based in the United States, has contracted Bangladeshi Co. to produce some of its products. The contract requires minimum annual purchases by Walden at a substantially higher price than Bangladeshi Co. receives from its other customers. Bangladeshi Co. has allocated 80 percent of its production capacity to Walden's orders.

Walden's representatives visit Bangladeshi Co.'s production facilities at least once a year for quality-control purposes. Walden pays Bangladeshi Co. six (6) months in advance for all purchases, allowing Bangladeshi Co. to finance costs of labor and materials.

1) Is Bangladeshi Co. an agent of Walden? What additional information, if any, would you like to have in answering that question?
2) What recommendations would you make to Walden to mitigate its FCPA risk?

---

132. *See, e.g.*, Deferred Prosecution Agreement at 1-14, United States v. Snamprogetti Netherlands B.V., No. 4:10-CR-00460 (S.D. Tex. July 7, 2010) (involving a foreign nonissuer who was at relevant times owned by ENI S.p.A., who was an issuer); Information at 1-25, United States v. Alstom S.A., No. 3:14-CR-00246 (D. Conn. Dec. 22, 2014) (indictment of a Swiss company based on agency relationship with foreign issuer).

2. Concert of Action

If agency creates a chain of liability, then the concert of action doctrine—which includes conspiracy, aiding and abetting and causing—creates a web of liability. The federal aiding and abetting and causing statute provides:

> (a) Whoever commits an offense against the United States or aids, abets, counsels, commands, induces or procures its commission, is punishable as a principal.
> (b) Whoever willfully causes an act to be done which if directly performed by him or another would be an offense against the United States, is punishable as a principal.[133]

Similarly, the federal conspiracy statute provides:

> If two or more persons conspire either to commit any offense against the United States, or to defraud the United States, or any agency thereof in any manner or for any purpose, and one or more of such persons do any act to effect the object of the conspiracy, each shall be fined under this title or imprisoned not more than five years, or both.
>
> If, however, the offense, the commission of which is the object of the conspiracy, is a misdemeanor only, the punishment for such conspiracy shall not exceed the maximum punishment provided for such misdemeanor.[134]

Under the doctrine articulated in *Pinkerton v. United States*,[135] the acts of one joint participant in furtherance of a crime are imputed to all other participants—even if they did not know about them—so long as those acts were reasonably foreseeable.[136] Thus, the acts of one co-conspirator may be used to satisfy the elements of the substantive crime with respect to the other co-conspirators.[137]

The DOJ and SEC extend the *Pinkerton* doctrine so that a co-conspirator's territorial ties to the U.S. are also imputed to all other co-conspirators for purposes of conferring territorial jurisdiction over them:[138]

> A foreign company or individual may be held liable for aiding and abetting an FCPA violation or for conspiring to violate the FCPA, even if the foreign company or individual did not take any act in furtherance of the [violation] while in the territory of the United States. In conspiracy cases, the United States generally has jurisdiction over all the conspirators where at least one conspirator is an issuer, domestic concern, or commits a reasonably foreseeable overt act within the United States.[139]

The DOJ and SEC's position flouts the FCPA's specific jurisdictional standards which only cover the extraterritorial acts of U.S. persons.[140] By alleging

---

133. 18 U.S.C. § 2 (2012).

134. *Id.* § 371.

135. Pinkerton v. United States, 328 U.S. 640 (1946).

136. *See id.* at 646–47.

137. *See id.* at 647.

138. *See, e.g.*, *Alstom*, No. 3:14-cr-00246 (indictment of Swiss company based on conspiracy with U.S. concern).

139. FCPA GUIDE, *supra* note 4, at 34 (footnote omitted).

140. *See, e.g.*, United States v. Hoskins, 123 F. Supp. 3d 316, 327 (D. Conn. 2015), *appeal docketed*, No. 16-1010 (2d Cir. Apr. 4, 2016) ("Congress did not intend to impose accomplice liability on non-resident foreign nationals who were not subject to direct liability.").

that different defendants acted as joint participants, the DOJ and SEC extend the FCPA's extraterritorial application to non-U.S. persons regardless of whether they independently meet the statute's jurisdictional requirements.

The so-called "African Sting" case illustrates how far these theories can stretch the limits of the FCPA.[141] The case involved twenty-two co-conspirators who allegedly paid bribes to obtain a government contract in Gabon. Many of the defendants did not know each other and were connected only through an FBI informant.[142] Judge Leon of the Southern District of New York dismissed the case at the end of the second trial, noting:

> Two years ago, at the very outset of this case I expressed more than my fair share of concerns on the record regarding the way this case has been charged and was being prosecuted. Later, during the two trials that I presided over I specifically commented again on the record regarding the government's very, very aggressive conspiracy theory that was pushing its already generous elasticity to its outer limits. Of course, in the second trial that elastic snapped in the absence of the necessary evidence to sustain it.[143]

Judge Leon did not specifically address whether joint participation confers jurisdiction over a defendant who does not otherwise meet the FCPA's jurisdictional requirements. However, the issue came before the Connecticut District Court in *U.S. v. Hoskins*,[144] where the defendant, a non-U.S. person who did not commit any acts in the United States, was prosecuted as a co-conspirator for violating the FCPA. The court dismissed the conspiracy charge, holding that "Congress did not intend to impose accomplice liability on non-resident foreign nationals who were not subject to direct liability."[145]

A Resource Guide to the U.S. Foreign Corrupt Practices Act

Criminal Division of the U.S. Department of Justice and the Enforcement Division of the U.S. Securities and Exchange Commission[146]

ADDITIONAL PRINCIPLES OF CRIMINAL LIABILITY FOR ANTI-BRIBERY VIOLATIONS: AIDING AND ABETTING AND CONSPIRACY

Under federal law, individuals or companies that aid or abet a crime, including an FCPA violation, are as guilty as if they had directly committed the offense

---

141. *See* Superseding Indictment, United States v. Goncalves, No. 09-CR-00335-RJL (D.D.C. Apr. 6, 2010).

142. *See id.*

143. Transcript of Judge Leon's Remarks Dismissing the Indictments with Prejudice for Amaro Goncalves and 15 Co-Defendants at 6–7, United States v. Goncalves, No. 09-CR-00335-RJL (D.D.C. Feb. 21, 2012) (on file with DOJ).

144. *See Hoskins*, 123 F. Supp. at 318.

145. *Id.* at 327.

146. FCPA GUIDE, *supra* note 4, at 34.

themselves. The aiding and abetting statute provides that whoever "commits an offense against the United States or aids, abets, counsels, commands, induces or procures its commission," or "willfully causes an act to be done which if directly performed by him or another would be an offense against the United States," is punishable as a principal. Aiding and abetting is not an independent crime, and the government must prove that an underlying FCPA violation was committed.

Individuals and companies, including foreign nationals and companies, may also be liable for conspiring to violate the FCPA—i.e., for agreeing to commit an FCPA violation—even if they are not, or could not be, independently charged with a substantive FCPA violation. For instance, a foreign, non-issuer company could be convicted of conspiring with a domestic concern to violate the FCPA. Under certain circumstances, it could also be held liable for the domestic concern's substantive FCPA violations under Pinkerton v. United States, which imposes liability on a defendant for reasonably foreseeable crimes committed by a co-conspirator in furtherance of a conspiracy that the defendant joined.

A foreign company or individual may be held liable for aiding and abetting an FCPA violation or for conspiring to violate the FCPA, even if the foreign company or individual did not take any act in furtherance of the corrupt payment while in the territory of the United States. In conspiracy cases, the United States generally has jurisdiction over all the conspirators where at least one conspirator is an issuer, domestic concern, or commits a reasonably foreseeable overt act within the United States. For example, if a foreign company or individual conspires to violate the FCPA with someone who commits an overt act within the United States, the United States can prosecute the foreign company or individual for the conspiracy. The same principle applies to aiding and abetting violations. For instance, even though they took no action in the United States, Japanese and European companies were charged with conspiring with and aiding and abetting a domestic concern's FCPA violations.

ADDITIONAL PRINCIPLES OF CIVIL LIABILITY FOR ANTI-BRIBERY VIOLATIONS: AIDING AND ABETTING AND CAUSING

Both companies and individuals can be held civilly liable for aiding and abetting FCPA anti-bribery violations if they knowingly or recklessly provide substantial assistance to a violator. Similarly, in the administrative proceeding context, companies and individuals may be held liable for causing FCPA violations. This liability extends to the subsidiaries and agents of U.S. issuers.

In one case, the U.S. subsidiary of a Swiss freight forwarding company was held civilly liable for paying bribes on behalf of its customers in several countries. Although the U.S. subsidiary was not an issuer for purposes of the FCPA, it was an "agent" of several U.S. issuers. By paying bribes on behalf of its issuers' customers, the subsidiary both directly violated and aided and abetted the issuers' FCPA violations.

Pinkerton v. United States

Supreme Court of the United States, 328 U.S. 640 (1946)[147]

OPINION

Mr. Justice DOUGLAS delivered the opinion of the Court.

Walter and Daniel Pinkerton are brothers who live a short distance from each other on Daniel's farm. They were indicted for violations of the Internal Revenue Code. The indictment contained ten substantive counts and one conspiracy count. The jury found Walter guilty on nine of the substantive counts and on the conspiracy count. It found Daniel guilty on six of the substantive counts and on the conspiracy count. Walter was fined $500 and sentenced generally on the substantive counts to imprisonment for thirty months. On the conspiracy count he was given a two-year sentence to run concurrently with the other sentence. Daniel was fined $1,000 and sentenced generally on the substantive counts to imprisonment for thirty months. On the conspiracy count he was fined $500 and given a two-year sentence to run concurrently with the other sentence. The judgments of conviction were affirmed by the Circuit Court of Appeals. The case is here on a petition for a writ of certiorari which we granted, because one of the questions presented involved a conflict between the decision below and *United States v. Sall*, 116 F.2d 745, decided by the Circuit Court of Appeals for the Third Circuit.

A single conspiracy was charged and proved. Some of the overt acts charged in the conspiracy count were the same acts charged in the substantive counts. Each of the substantive offenses found was committed pursuant to the conspiracy. Petitioners therefore contend that the substantive counts became merged in the conspiracy count, and that only a single sentence not exceeding the maximum two-year penalty provided by the conspiracy statute [] could be imposed. Or to state the matter differently, they contend that each of the substantive counts became a separate conspiracy count but since only a single conspiracy was charged and proved, only [a] single sentence for conspiracy could be imposed. They rely on *Braverman v. United States*, 317 U.S. 49 (1942).

In the *Braverman* case the indictment charged no substantive offense. Each of the several counts charged a conspiracy to violate a different statute. But only one conspiracy was proved. We held that a single conspiracy, charged under the general conspiracy statute, however diverse its objects may be, violates but a single statute and no penalty greater than the maximum provided for one conspiracy may be imposed. That case is not apposite here. For the offenses charged and proved were not only a conspiracy but substantive offenses as well.

Nor can we accept the proposition that the substantive offenses were merged in the conspiracy. There are, of course, instances where a conspiracy charge may not be added to the substantive charge. One is where the agreement of two

---

147. Pinkerton v. United States, 328 U.S. 640 (1946).

persons is necessary for the completion of the substantive crime and there is no ingredient in the conspiracy which is not present in the completed crime. Another is where the definition of the substantive offense excludes from punishment for conspiracy one who voluntarily participates in another's crime. *Gebardi v. United States, supra.* But those exceptions are of a limited character. The common law rule that the substantive offense, if a felony, was merged in the conspiracy, has little vitality in this country. It has been long and consistently recognized by the Court that the commission of the substantive offense and a conspiracy to commit it are separate and distinct offenses. The power of Congress to separate the two and to affix to each a different penalty is well established. A conviction for the conspiracy may be had though the substantive offense was completed. And the plea of double jeopardy is no defense to a conviction for both offenses. It is only an identity of offenses which is fatal. A conspiracy is a partnership in crime. It has ingredients, as well as implications, distinct from the completion of the unlawful project. As stated in *United States v. Rabinowich*, 238 U.S. 78, 88 (1915):

> For two or more to confederate and combine together to commit or cause to be committed a breach of the criminal laws is an offense of the gravest character, sometimes quite outweighing, in injury to the public, the mere commission of the contemplated crime. It involves deliberate plotting to subvert the laws, educating and preparing the conspirators for further and habitual criminal practices. And it is characterized by secrecy, rendering it difficult of detection, requiring more time for its discovery, and adding to the importance of punishing it when discovered.

Moreover, it is not material that overt acts charged in the conspiracy counts were also charged and proved as substantive offenses. As stated in *Sneed v. United States, supra,* 298 F. at page 913, "If the overt act be the offense which was the object of the conspiracy, and is also punished, there is not a double punishment of it." The agreement to do an unlawful act is even then distinct from the doing of the act.

It is contended that there was insufficient evidence to implicate Daniel in the conspiracy. But we think there was enough evidence for submission of the issue to the jury.

There is, however, no evidence to show that Daniel participated directly in the commission of the substantive offenses on which his conviction has been sustained, although there was evidence to show that these substantive offenses were in fact committed by Walter in furtherance of the unlawful agreement or conspiracy existing between the brothers. The question was submitted to the jury on the theory that each petitioner could be found guilty of the substantive offenses, if it was found at the time those offenses were committed petitioners were parties to an unlawful conspiracy and the substantive offenses charged were in fact committed in furtherance of it.

Daniel relies on *United States v. Sall, supra*. That case held that participation in the conspiracy was not itself enough to sustain a conviction for the substantive offense even though it was committed in furtherance of the conspiracy. The court held that, in addition to evidence that the offense was in fact committed in furtherance of the conspiracy, evidence of direct participation in the commission of the substantive offense or other evidence from which participation might fairly be inferred was necessary.

We take a different view. We have here a continuous conspiracy. There is here no evidence of the affirmative action on the part of Daniel which is necessary to establish his withdrawal from it. As stated in that case, "having joined in an unlawful scheme, having constituted agents for its performance, scheme and agency to be continuous until full fruition be secured, until he does some act to disavow or defeat the purpose he is in no situation to claim the delay of the law. As the offense has not been terminated or accomplished, he is still offending. And we think, consciously offending,—offending as certainly, as we have said, as at the first moment of his confederation, and consciously through every moment of its existence." And so long as the partnership in crime continues, the partners act for each other in carrying it forward. It is settled that "an overt act of one partner may be the act of all without any new agreement specifically directed to that act." Motive or intent may be proved by the acts or declarations of some of the conspirators in furtherance of the common objective. A scheme to use the mails to defraud, which is joined in by more than one person, is a conspiracy. Yet all members are responsible, though only one did the mailing. The governing principle is the same when the substantive offense is committed by one of the conspirators in furtherance of the unlawful project. The criminal intent to do the act is established by the formation of the conspiracy. Each conspirator instigated the commission of the crime. The unlawful agreement contemplated precisely what was done. It was formed for the purpose. The act done was in execution of the enterprise. The rule which holds responsible one who counsels, procures, or commands another to commit a crime is founded on the same principle. That principle is recognized in the law of conspiracy when the overt act of one partner in crime is attributable to all. An overt act is an essential ingredient of the crime of conspiracy under § 37 of the Criminal Code, 18 U.S.C. § 88, 18 U.S.C.A. § 88. If that can be supplied by the act of one conspirator, we fail to see why the same or other acts in furtherance of the conspiracy are likewise not attributable to the others for the purpose of holding them responsible for the substantive offense.

A different case would arise if the substantive offense committed by one of the conspirators was not in fact done in furtherance of the conspiracy, did not fall within the scope of the unlawful project, or was merely a part of the ramifications of the plan which could not be reasonably foreseen as a necessary or natural consequence of the unlawful agreement. But as we read this record, that is not this case.

Affirmed.

Notes and Questions

Pinkerton imputes one co-conspirator's foreseeable actions to another for purposes of liability for the substantive crime. Does it follow that the same actions should be imputed for purposes of jurisdiction? For example, if one co-conspirator commits acts in the territory of the United States, should a foreign co-conspirator, who never set foot on U.S. soil, also become subject to U.S. jurisdiction?

United States v. Hoskins

United States District Court, D. Connecticut 123 F. Supp. 3d 316 (2015)[148]

RULING ON DEFENDANT'S SECOND MOTION TO DISMISS THE INDICTMENT

JANET BOND ARTERTON, District Judge.

Defendant Lawrence Hoskins moves . . . to Dismiss Count One of the Third Superseding Indictment . . . on the basis that it charges a legally invalid theory that he could be criminally liable for conspiracy to violate the Foreign Corrupt Practices Act ("FCPA"), 15 U.S.C. § 78dd–1 *et seq.,* even if the evidence does not establish that he was subject to criminal liability as a principal, by being an "agent" of a "domestic concern." Relatedly, the Government moves *in limine* to preclude Defendant from arguing to the jury that it must prove that he was the agent of a domestic concern because the Government contends that Defendant can also be convicted under theories of accomplice liability. For the reasons that follow, Defendant's Motion to Dismiss Count One of the Third Superseding Indictment will be granted in part to preclude Defendant's FCPA conspiracy prosecution from being de-linked from proof that he was an agent of a domestic concern and the Government's Motion *in Limine* is denied.

I. BACKGROUND

The facts of this case are set forth in detail in the Ruling on Defendant's First Motion to Dismiss the Indictment and will be repeated only as necessary for the legal analysis herein. Briefly, Mr. Hoskins is alleged to have participated in a bribery scheme that spanned from 2002 through 2009 for Alstom Power, Inc. ("Alstom Power U.S."), a company headquartered in Windsor, Connecticut, to secure a $118 million project to build power stations for Indonesia's state-owned and state-controlled electricity company, Perusahaan Listrik Negara, known as the Tarahan Project.

From October 2001 through August 2004, Mr. Hoskins was employed as a Senior Vice President for the Asia Region by Alstom UK and assigned to Alstom Resources Management S.A. in France where he is alleged to have "performed functions and support services for and on behalf of various other Alstom

---

148. United States v. Hoskins, 123 F. Supp. 3d 316 (D. Conn. 2015), *appeal docketed,* No. 16-1010 (2d Cir. Apr. 4, 2016).

subsidiaries, including Alstom Power U.S." It is alleged that Mr. Hoskins's "responsibilities at Alstom included oversight of the hiring of consultants in connection
with Alstom's and Alstom's subsidiaries' efforts to obtain contracts with new
customers and to retain contracts with existing customers in Asia, including the
Tarahan Project" and "[t]hus HOSKINS was an agent of a 'domestic concern,' Alstom
Power U.S., as that term is used in the FCPA." It is in this capacity that Mr. Hoskins
is alleged to have been responsible for approving and authorizing payments to
"consultants" retained for the purpose of "pay[ing] bribes to Indonesian officials
who had the ability to influence the award of the Tarahan Project contract."

On July 31, 2014, Defendant Hoskins moved to dismiss the Second Superseding
Indictment in its entirety, contending, in relevant part, that the indictment failed
to allege that Mr. Hoskins, as an employee of a non-U.S. Alstom subsidiary, could
have been an "agent of a domestic concern" subject to liability under the FCPA.
The Court denied Defendant's motion, holding that the indictment alleged that
Mr. Hoskins worked as an agent of Alstom Power U.S. despite being employed by
an overseas subsidiary and the "existence of an agency relationship is a 'highly
factual' inquiry" and it was "for a jury at trial in the first instance, and not the
Court on a motion to dismiss, to determine whether the Government has proven
Defendant to have been an 'agent'" of Alstom Power U.S. (Ruling on 1st Mot.
Dismiss at 14–16.)

As relevant here, the Third Superseding Indictment altered the charging language of Count One, the FCPA conspiracy count, which originally charged Mr.
Hoskins with "being a domestic concern and an employee and agent of [Alstom
Power U.S.]" and replaced it with the allegation that Mr. Hoskins conspired by
acting "together with" a domestic concern to violate 15 U.S.C. § 78dd–2 (prohibiting domestic concerns from using interstate commerce corruptly to promise,
authorize, or give anything of value to a foreign official) and 15 U.S.C. § 78dd–3
(prohibiting any person from taking acts in furtherance of the corrupt scheme
while in the United States). Defendant now moves to dismiss only Count One of
the Third Superseding Indictment.

II. DISCUSSION

Defendant contends that with the Third Superseding Indictment "the government makes plain . . . its view of the law" that Mr. Hoskins "could be prosecuted for conspiracy to violate the FCPA even when he himself was not subject to
the statute." The Government maintains that the Third Superseding Indictment is
adequately pled under the governing pleading standards and faults Defendant
for attempting "to assign to the Government a particular 'view of the law' based
on [the] change" from the Second to Third Superseding Indictments. But the
Government acknowledges that its theory is that "even were the jury to find
that the defendant was not an 'agent' of a domestic concern, [it] may still convict the defendant on one or more of the remaining accomplice theories," i.e.,
"aiding and abetting, causing, and *Pinkerton*" liability and moves *in limine* to preclude Defendant from arguing to the contrary. (Gov't Mot. to Preclude Def. from
Arguing that Agency is Sole Basis for Conviction.)

Therefore, these two motions put before the Court the question of whether a nonresident foreign national could be subject to criminal liability under the FCPA, even where he is not an agent of a domestic concern and does not commit acts while physically present in the territory of the United States, under a theory of conspiracy or aiding and abetting a violation of the FCPA by a person who is within the statute's reach. The Court concludes that the answer is "no" and that accomplice liability cannot extend to this Defendant under such circumstances and thus Defendant's Motion to Dismiss Count One is granted in part and the Government's Motion *in Limine* is denied.

A. FCPA

As explained in greater detail below, the FCPA in its current form prohibits bribery of foreign governmental officials and has three jurisdictional bases: (1) where a "domestic concern" or U.S. "issuer" of securities, or any officer, director, employee, or agent thereof (regardless of their nationality) makes use of U.S. interstate commerce in furtherance of a corrupt payment, 15 U.S.C. §§ 78dd–1(a), 78dd–2(a); (2) where a U.S. citizen, national, or resident acts outside the United States in furtherance of a corrupt payment, regardless of whether they make use of U.S. interstate commerce, *id*. § 78dd–2(i); and (3) where any other person, while in the territory of the United States, acts in furtherance of a corrupt payment, regardless of nationality and the use of interstate commerce, *id*. § 78dd–3.

Defendant maintains that these provisions demonstrate that "Congress deliberately intended to exclude [non-resident foreign nationals] from the statute's reach so long as they did not act while in the territory of the United States (Section 78dd–3) and did not fall into an enumerated class of persons with threshold ties to a U.S. securities issuer (Section 78dd–1) or U.S. domestic concern (Section 78dd–2)" and "the government cannot nullify that intent by charging such individuals with conspiracy to violate that statute." (Def.'s Mem. Supp. at 5–7.) The Government does not dispute the premise of Defendant's argument—that if Defendant is not proven to be an agent of a domestic concern, he cannot be held liable directly under the FCPA—but it maintains that "[a]s a general rule, the conspiracy and accomplice liability statutes apply to classes of persons who lack the capacity to commit a violation of the underlying substantive crime" and the two narrow exceptions to this rule do not apply in this case. (Gov't's Opp'n at 1.)

B. The *Gebardi* Principle

Theories of accomplice liability under the general conspiracy statute, 18 U.S.C. § 371, and aiding and abetting statute, 18 U.S.C. § 2, generally apply across the United States Code to impose liability upon those who conspire with or aid and abet in the commission of any federal crime. Thus, ever since 18 U.S.C. § 2 was enacted in 1909, "every time Congress has passed a new criminal statute the aider and abettor provision has automatically kicked in and made the aiders and abettors of violations of the new statute punishable as principals." *United States v. Pino–Perez*, 870 F.2d 1230, 1233 (7th Cir. 1989). Likewise, 18 U.S.C. § 371, which has existed in essentially the same form since 1867, generally criminalizes a conspiracy to commit any federal offense. *Gebardi v. United States,* 287 U.S. 112, 121 n.4 (1932); *Iannelli v. United States,* 420 U.S. 770, 777 (1975) ("Conspiracy is an inchoate offense, the essence of which is an agreement to commit an unlawful act.").

In *Gebardi,* the Supreme Court considered whether a woman could be convicted of conspiracy to violate the Mann Act, which outlaws transporting across state lines "any woman or girl for the purpose of prostitution or debauchery, or for any other immoral purpose[]" where she acquiesced to her own transport. 287 U.S. at 118 (quoting 18 U.S.C. § 398(2)). The Supreme Court explained that the conspiracy statute generally prohibits conspiring to commit any crime and the "[i]ncapacity of one to commit the substantive offense does not necessarily imply that he may with impunity conspire with others who are able to commit it," because "it is the collective planning of criminal conduct at which the statute aims." *Id.* at 120–21. Thus, for example, the Supreme Court explained, it is a crime for a bankrupt to conceal property from a trustee, which can necessarily only be committed by a bankrupt, but a non-bankrupt person can be charged with conspiring to conceal such property. *Id.* at 121 n. 5.

However, *Gebardi* reasoned that "Congress set out in the Mann Act to deal with cases which frequently, if not normally, involve consent and agreement on the part of the woman to the forbidden transportation" and "[y]et this acquiescence . . . was not made a crime under the Mann Act itself." *Id.* at 119, 121. Thus, a woman not subject to liability as a principal under the Mann Act could not be charged with conspiracy to violate the Act, because the Supreme Court "perceive[d] in the failure of the Mann Act to condemn the woman's participation in those transportations which are effected with her mere consent, evidence of an affirmative legislative policy to leave her acquiescence unpunished," which would be "contravene[d]" if such "immunity" could be "withdraw[n] by the conspiracy statute." *Id.* at 123.

Thus, the *Gebardi* principle is that where Congress chooses to exclude a class of individuals from liability under a statute, "the Executive [may not] . . . override the Congressional intent not to prosecute" that party by charging it with conspiring to violate a statute that it could not directly violate. *United States v. Castle,* 925 F.2d 831, 833 (5th Cir. 1991); *see also United States v. Bodmer,* 342 F. Supp. 2d 176, 181 n.6 (S.D.N.Y. 2004) ("In *Gebardi,* the Supreme Court held that where Congress passes a substantive criminal statute that excludes a certain class of individuals from liability, the Government cannot evade Congressional intent by charging those individuals with conspiring to violate the same statute."). The *Gebardi* principle also applies to aiding and abetting liability. *United States v. Amen,* 831 F.2d 373, 381 (2d Cir. 1987).

In determining whether the *Gebardi* principle applies, the question is "not whether Congress *could have*" reached a certain class of individuals under the conspiracy or aiding and abetting statutes, "but rather whether Congress *intended to do so,* or more specifically, whether Congress intended the general conspiracy statute" to apply to these individuals. *Castle,* 925 F.2d at 835 (emphasis in original).

The Government maintains that *Gebardi* recognized only a "narrow exception to [the] long-established legal principle" that "the conspiracy and accomplice liability statutes apply to classes of persons who lack the capacity to commit a violation of the underlying substantive crime." (Gov't's Opp'n at 1.) It maintains that this exception only "applies in two limited circumstances: (1) where a class of person is a *necessary party* to the crime and was specifically excluded from prosecution for the substantive violation by Congress (*e.g.,* the foreign official who receives the bribe payment under the FCPA, or the woman who is transported across state lines under the Mann Act); or (2) where the substantive statute was enacted to protect the class of person to which the individual belongs (*e.g.,* victims)." *Id.* at 1–2 (emphasis in original). Defendant maintains that *Gebardi* applies whenever "Congress affirmatively chooses to exclude a certain class of individuals from liability under a criminal statute." (Def.'s Mem. Supp. at 19.)

The Court agrees with Defendant that the Government's interpretation of *Gebardi* is too narrow and that while the two "[f]actual scenarios . . . posited by the government bring Congress's intent into view and, thereby, make it easier to glean the existence of an affirmative legislative policy," Congressional intent can be evident in other circumstances. (Reply at 12.) For example, in *Amen,* the Second Circuit applied *Gebardi* and held that a person who was not the head of a criminal enterprise could not be subject to the drug "kingpin" statute's sentencing enhancement under a theory that he aided and abetted a violation, because "[w]hen Congress assigns guilt to only one type of participant in a transaction, it intends to leave the others unpunished for the offense." 831 F.2d at 381.

The Second Circuit's reasoning was not, as the Government maintains, that a violation of the kingpin statute requires "the participation of two classes of persons—those who lead a criminal enterprise, on the one hand, and those who are led, on the other" and that "Congress chose only to provide for an enhanced punishment of one of those necessary parties." (Gov't's Opp'n at 21–22.) Rather, the Second Circuit reasoned that while the statute's "legislative history makes no mention of aiders and abettors, it makes it clear that the purpose . . . was not to catch in the [kingpin] net those who aided and abetted the supervisors' activities." *Amen,* 831 F.2d at 382.

C. Application

The clearest indication of legislative intent is the text and structure of the FCPA, which carefully delineates the classes of people subject to liability and excludes nonresident foreign nationals where they are not agents of a domestic concern or did not take actions in furtherance of a corrupt payment within the territory of the United States. *See Community for Creative Non–Violence v. Reid,* 490 U.S. 730, 739 (1989) ("The starting point for [the] interpretation of a statute is always its language.").

In *United States v. Castle,* 925 F.2d 831, 832 (5th Cir. 1991), the Fifth Circuit applied *Gebardi* to conclude that another class of individuals not subject to liability as principals under the FCPA—the foreign officials who accept bribes—could not be prosecuted for conspiracy to violate the FCPA. The Fifth Circuit found an intent in the FCPA to exclude the foreign bribe recipients because, in enacting the FCPA in 1977 in the aftermath of the Watergate scandal, Congress was principally "concerned about the domestic effects of such payments," such as "the distortion of, and resulting lack of confidence in, the free market system within the United States." *Id.* at 834–35.

Congress was aware that it "could, consistently with international law, reach foreign officials in certain circumstances," but it was also concerned about "the 'inherent jurisdictional, enforcement, and diplomatic difficulties raised by the application of the bill to non-citizens of the United States'" and decided not to do so. *Id.* at 835 (quoting H.R. Conf. Rep. No. 831, 95th Cong., 1st Sess. 14, *reprinted in* 1977 U.S. Code Cong. & Admin. News 4121, 4126). From the text of the statute and the legislative history expressing concern about reaching non-citizens, the Fifth Circuit found "in the FCPA what the Supreme Court in *Gebardi* found in the Mann Act: an affirmative legislative policy to leave unpunished a well-defined group of persons who were necessary parties to the acts constituting a violation of the substantive law." *Id.* at 836.

D. Legislative History of 1977

Although the text and structure of the FCPA provide strong indication that Congress did not intend for non-resident foreign nationals to be subject to the FCPA unless they were agents of a domestic concern or acted in the territory of the United States, the Court also considers the legislative history of the Act.

While the extensive legislative history of the enactment of the FCPA in 1977 and its amendments in 1998 identified by the parties contain little discussion of accomplice liability, that which does exist is consistent with what the plain text and structure of the final enactment implies regarding the limits of liability for non-resident foreign nationals. The initial version of the Senate bill introduced by the Committee on Banking, Housing and Urban Affairs on June 2, 1976 made it unlawful for any U.S. "issuer" or "domestic concern" to use any means or instrumentality of interstate commerce to authorize or pay a bribe. S. 3664, 94th Cong. (1976) (Ex. 9 to Def's Mem. Supp.). "Domestic concern" was defined to include (1) U.S. citizens and nationals and (2) entities owned or controlled by U.S. citizens and nationals that were either incorporated in or had a principal place of business in the United States. *Id.* at 7.

An amendment to the Senate bill responded to a request by the administration of President Carter "to clearly cover under the bill individuals making payments" that was not "crystal clear" in the original version. Markup Session on S. 305, Senate Comm. on Banking, Housing and Urban Affairs, 95th Cong., 8 (Apr. 6, 1977) (Ex. 11 to Def's Mem. Supp.). The definition of domestic concern was left unchanged, but the proposal added that officers, directors, employees and stockholders acting on behalf of U.S. issuers or domestic concerns, irrespective of nationality, would be liable for making bribes on behalf of the company. S. Rep. No. 95–114, at 11; 123 Cong. Rec. 13817 (1977) (Ex. 13 to Def's Mem. Supp.). Although the Carter Administration requested that liability be extended to foreign subsidiaries of U.S. companies, Markup Session on S. 305 at 9, the Senate declined to do so, S. Rep. No. 95–114.

A competing House bill introduced on February 22, 1977 provided for broader liability for non-resident foreign nationals than the Senate bill, proposing liability not just for non-U.S. officers, directors, and employees of domestic concerns, but also (1) any "agent" of a U.S. issuer or domestic concern who "carried out" a bribe and (2) officers, directors, and employees of foreign affiliates irrespective of nationality. H.R. 3815 §§ 30A(c)(2), 3(c)(2), 3(f)(2)(A), 95th Cong. (1977) (Ex. 14 to Def.'s Mem. Supp.).

The FCPA as enacted included elements from both the Senate and House bills, extending liability to agents of domestic concerns as the House proposed, but limiting criminal liability of agents and employees of domestic concerns to a person who was a "United States citizen, national, or resident or is otherwise subject to the jurisdiction of the United States," and predicated such person's criminal liability on a finding that the domestic concern itself had violated the statute. 15 U.S.C. § 78dd–2(b)(1)(B)(3) (1977).

The final bill excluded foreign affiliates of U.S. companies, as the Senate proposed, which the House Conference Report described as a "recogni[tion] [of] the inherent jurisdictional, enforcement and diplomatic difficulties raised by the inclusion of foreign subsidiaries of U.S. companies in the direct prohibitions of the bill." H.R. Conf. Rep. No. 95–831, at *14, 1977 U.S.C.C.A.N. at 4126. The Report explained, however, that because U.S. citizens, nationals, and residents were defined as domestic concerns, they could be liable for engaging in bribery "indirectly" through another person and that the "jurisdictional, enforcement and diplomatic difficulties" that applied to extending liability to foreign subsidiaries did not apply to "citizens, nations, or residents of the United States." *Id.*

The Government notes that early versions of the Senate and House committee reports discussed accomplice liability:

> The committee fully recognizes that the proposed law will not reach all corrupt payments overseas. For example, Sections 2 and 3 would not permit prosecution of a foreign national who paid a bribe overseas acting entirely on his own initiative. The committee notes, however, that in the majority of bribery cases investigated by the SEC some responsible official or employee of the U.S. parent company had knowledge of the bribery and either explicitly or implicitly approved the practice. Under the bill as reported, such persons could be prosecuted. The concepts of aiding and abetting and joint participation would apply to a violation under this bill in the same manner in which those concepts have always applied in both SEC civil actions and in implied private actions brought under the securities laws generally.

H.R. Rep. No. 95–640, at 8 (1977); S. Rep. No. 94–1031, at 7 (1976).

As discussed above, this legislative history discussing an early version of the bill was later clarified in response to concerns by the Carter Administration that the extent of individual liability (including for U.S. nationals) was not "crystal clear." Rather than resorting to concepts of accomplice liability, the enacted version specifically delineated the extent of individual liability by "mak[ing] it clear that" the delineated individuals were "covered directly." Markup Session on S. 305, Senate Comm. on Banking, Housing and Urban Affairs, 95th Cong., 8, 12 (Apr. 6, 1977). Therefore, the discussion of accomplice liability cited by the Government does not suggest that Congress intended for those who were excluded from direct liability under the Act to be subject to accomplice liability but only shows that Congress considered imposing individual liability based on concepts of accomplice liability but instead chose to do so directly and carefully delineated the class of persons covered to address concerns of overreaching.

Thus, as in *Amen* and *Gebardi,* even absent explicit discussion in the legislative history of accomplice liability, the carefully-crafted final enactment evinces a legislative intent to cabin such liability. *See Amen,* 831 F.2d at 382; *Gebardi,* 287 U.S. at 123. As the Fifth Circuit explained, when Congress "listed all the persons or entities who could be prosecuted" under the FCPA, it "intended that these persons would be covered by the Act itself, without resort to the conspiracy statute" and, as in *Gebardi,* that intent cannot be circumvented by resort to conspiracy and aiding and abetting liability. *Castle,* 925 F.2d at 836.

E. 1998 Amendments

While the Government argues that the original version of the FCPA in 1977 provided for accomplice liability, it maintains that after the 1998 amendments to the FCPA "Congress unequivocally provided that it intended the accomplice liability and conspiracy statutes to apply to foreign nationals not otherwise subject to the FCPA as principals." (Gov't's Opp'n at 27.) The 1998 amendments to the FCPA were "enacted to ensure the United States was in compliance with its treaty obligations," *United States v. Esquenazi,* 752 F.3d 912, 923 (11th Cir. 2014), after the United States ratified the Organization for Economic Cooperation and Development's Convention on Combating Bribery of Foreign Public Officials in International Business Transactions ("OECD Convention"). Dec. 17, 1997, S. Treaty Doc. No. 105–43, 37 I.L.M.; International Anti-Bribery and Fair Competition Act of 1998, Pub. L. No. 105–366, 112 Stat. 3302.

The OECD Convention required each signatory country to "take such measures as may be necessary to establish that it is a criminal offence under its law for any person intentionally" to bribe foreign officials. OECD Convention art. 1.1. In response, the 1998 amendments expanded the scope of liability in three ways. First, Congress added 15 U.S.C. § 78dd–3(a), which prohibited those individuals or entities that did not already fall under other provisions of the statute from taking action "while in the territory" of the United States in furtherance of corrupt payments. 15 U.S.C. § 78dd–3(a). Second, the 1998 amendments eliminated a disparity in penalties between U.S. and foreign nationals acting as agents of domestic concerns whereby previously foreign nationals were subject only to civil penalties. The amendment made clear that foreign nationals acting as agents of domestic concerns could be criminally prosecuted for violating the FCPA if they used some manner or means of interstate commerce. 15 U.S.C. § 78dd–2. Third, Congress provided for nationality jurisdiction, providing that it "shall also be unlawful for any United States person to corruptly do any act outside the United States in furtherance of" a foreign bribe. 15 U.S.C. § 78dd–2(i)(1); *see also* S. Rep. 105–277, at *2–3 (1998) (describing these three changes to the FCPA as being intended "to conform it to the requirements of and to implement the OECD Convention").

The Government maintains that because the OECD Convention required each signatory country to make it a "criminal offense under its law for *any person*" to pay a foreign bribe, OECD Convention, art. 1.1 (emphasis added), the "1998 amendments expanded the jurisdictional reach of the FCPA to cover any person over whom U.S. courts have jurisdiction" and a contrary interpretation "would place the United States in violation of its treaty obligations" (Gov't's Opp'n at 28, 30). While the Supreme Court has admonished that "courts should be most cautious before interpreting . . . domestic legislation in such manner as to violate international agreements," *Vimar Seguros y Reaseguros, S.A. v. M/V Sky Reefer,* 515 U.S. 528, 539 (1995), this Court does not agree with the Government's contention that the OECD Convention required or even contemplated the extent of liability sought by the Government here by using the term "any person."

Rather, the OECD's reference to "any person" is cabined by Article 4 of the Convention, addressing jurisdiction, which provides that each signatory "shall take such measures as may be necessary to establish its jurisdiction over the bribery of a foreign public official when the offense is [1] committed in whole or in part in its territory" (OECD Convention, art. 4.1) or [2] by its own nationals while abroad (*id.,* art. 4.2). Therefore, there is no indication that the OECD Convention requires the United States to prosecute foreign bribery committed abroad by non-resident foreign nationals who conspire with United States citizens.

Based on the text and structure of the FCPA and the legislative history accompanying its enactment and its amendment, the Court concludes that Congress did not intend to impose accomplice liability on non-resident foreign nationals who were not subject to direct liability. Count One will not be dismissed in its entirety, however, because if the Government proceeds under the theory that Mr. Hoskins is an agent of a domestic concern and thus subject to direct liability under the FCPA, *see* Note 1, *supra,* the *Gebardi* principle would not preclude his criminal liability for conspiring to violate the FCPA. The Government may not argue, however, that Defendant could be liable for conspiracy even if he is not proved to be an agent of a domestic concern.

III. CONCLUSION

For the reasons set forth above, Defendant's Motion [Doc. # 254] to Dismiss Count One of the Third Superseding Indictment is GRANTED in PART and the Government's Motion [Doc. # 232] *in Limine* to Preclude Defendant from Arguing that Agency is Sole Basis for Conviction is DENIED.

IT IS SO ORDERED.

Notes and Questions

As the *Hoskins* opinion explains:

> The Third Superseding Indictment altered the charging language of Count One, the FCPA conspiracy count, which originally charged Mr. Hoskins with "being a domestic concern and an employee and agent of [Alstom Power U.S.]" and replaced it with the allegation that Mr. Hoskins conspired by acting "together with" a domestic concern to violate 15 U.S.C. § 78dd–2 (prohibiting domestic concerns from using interstate commerce corruptly to promise, authorize, or give anything of value to a foreign official) and 15 U.S.C. § 78dd–3 (prohibiting any person from taking acts in furtherance of the corrupt scheme while in the United States).[149]

Figure 5-1. Relationship Between Alstom, Its Foreign Subsidiaries, and Hoskins

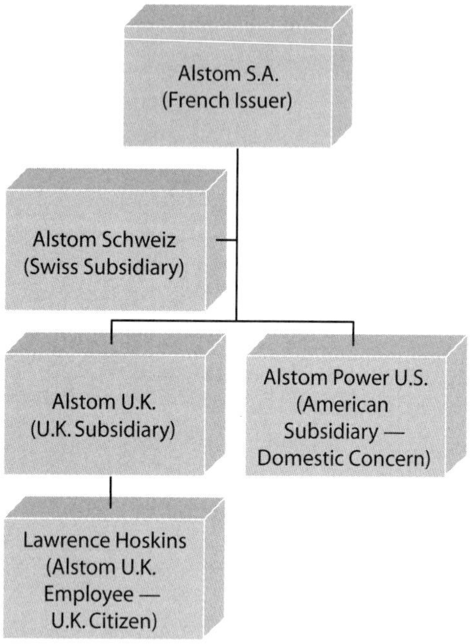

Alstom S.A.
(French Issuer)

Alstom Schweiz
(Swiss Subsidiary)

Alstom U.K.
(U.K. Subsidiary)

Alstom Power U.S.
(American Subsidiary —
Domestic Concern)

Lawrence Hoskins
(Alstom U.K.
Employee —
U.K. Citizen)

1) What do you think was the government's strategy in filing the superseding indictment? As the chart in Figure 5-1 illustrates, Hoskins was an employee of Alstom U.K., who was not a defendant.
2) As of this writing, *Hoskins* is pending before the United States Court of Appeals for the Second Circuit. Should the district court opinion be upheld, what would be the consequences for multinational enterprises?

United States v. JGC Corp.

United States District Court, S.D. Texas Criminal No. 11-CR-260 (April 6, 2011)[150]

INFORMATION

The United States charges:

. . . .

RELEVANT ENTITIES AND INDIVIDUALS

The Defendant

Defendant JGC CORPORATION ("JGC") was a Japanese company headquartered in Yokohama, Japan. JGC was engaged in the business of providing engineering, procurement, and construction ("EPC") services around the world.

---

149. *Id.* at 318.
150. Information, United States v. JGC Corp., No. 11-CR-00260 (S.D. Tex. Apr. 6, 2011), https://www.justice.gov/sites/default/files/criminal-fraud/legacy/2011/04/27/04-6-11jgc-corp-info.pdf.

TSKJ, Its Members, and Related Entities

"TSKJ" was a four-company venture formed in 1990 for the purposes of bidding on and, if successful, performing a series of EPC contracts to design and build a liquefied natural gas ("LNG") plant and several expansions on Bonny Island, Nigeria ("the Bonny Island Project"). TSKJ consisted of Technip S.A., Snamprogetti Netherlands B.V., Kellogg, Brown & Root, Inc., and JGC. The Steering Committee of TSKJ consisted of high-level executives from each of the four joint venture companies. Pursuant to a joint venture agreement, the Steering Committee made major decisions on behalf of TSKJ, including whether to hire agents to assist TSKJ in winning EPC contracts, whom to hire as agents, and how much to pay the agents. Profits, revenues, and expenses generally were shared equally among the four joint venture partners.

Kellogg, Brown & Root, Inc. and, before September 1998, its predecessor company, The M. W. Kellogg Company (collectively, "KBR"), were engaged in the business of providing EPC services around the world. KBR was incorporated in Delaware and headquartered in Houston, Texas. As such, KBR was a "domestic concern" within the meaning of the FCPA, Title 15, United States Code, Section 78dd-2.

Albert Jackson Stanley ("Stanley") was a United States citizen and a resident of Houston, Texas. Stanley served in various capacities as an officer and/or director of KBR, and also served on TSKJ's Steering Committee. Stanley was a "domestic concern" and an officer, employee, and agent of a "domestic concern" within the meaning of the FCPA, Title 15, United States Code, Section 78dd-2.

Technip S.A. ("Technip"), a French corporation headquartered in Paris, France, was engaged in the business of providing EPC services around the world. In August 2001, Technip registered a class of securities with the United States Securities and Exchange Commission ("SEC") and in October 2001 became listed on the New York Stock Exchange. As an issuer of publicly traded securities registered pursuant to Section 12(b) of the Securities Exchange Act of 1934, Title 15, United States Code, Section 78l, Technip was required to file periodic reports with the SEC under Section 13 of the Securities Exchange Act, Title 15, United States Code, Section 78m. Accordingly, beginning in August 2001, Technip was an "issuer" within the meaning of the FCPA, Title 15, United States Code, Section 78dd-l.

Snamprogetti Netherlands B.V. ("Snamprogetti") was a Dutch corporation headquartered in Amsterdam, The Netherlands, and a wholly owned subsidiary of Snamprogetti S.p.A., an Italian EPC company headquartered in Milan, Italy.

M.W. Kellogg Ltd. was a corporation organized under the laws of the United Kingdom. At all relevant times, M.W. Kellogg Ltd. was 55% owned by KBR and 45% owned by JGC.

TSKJ operated through three Portuguese special purpose corporations based in Madeira, Portugal: "Madeira Company 1," "Madeira Company 2," and "Madeira Company 3." Both Madeira Company 1 and Madeira Company 2 were owned equally by the four Joint Venture companies. Madeira Company 3, the entity that

TSKJ used to enter into consulting agreements with TSKJ's agents, was 50% owned by M.W. Kellogg Ltd., 25% owned by Snamprogetti, and 25% owned by Technip.

TSKJ's Agents

Jeffrey Tesler was a citizen of the United Kingdom and a resident of London, England. TSKJ hired Tesler to help it obtain business in Nigeria, including by offering to pay and paying bribes to high-level Nigerian government officials. Tesler was an agent of TSKJ and of each of the joint venture companies.

Tri-Star Investments Ltd. ("Tri-Star") was a Gibraltar corporation that Tesler used as a corporate vehicle to enter into agent contracts with and receive payments from TSKJ. By the time TSKJ had stopped paying Tri-Star in January 2004, TSKJ had paid Tri-Star over $130 million for use in bribing Nigerian government officials. Tri-Star was an agent of TSKJ and of each of the joint venture companies.

Consulting Company B was a global trading company headquartered in Tokyo, Japan. TSKJ hired Consulting Company B to help it obtain business in Nigeria, including by offering to pay and paying bribes to Nigerian government officials. By the time TSKJ had stopped paying Consulting Company B in June 2004, TSKJ had paid Consulting Company B over $50 million for use in bribing Nigerian government officials. Consulting Company B was an agent of TSKJ and of each of the joint venture companies.

The Nigerian Government Entities

The Nigerian National Petroleum Corporation ("NNPC") was a Nigerian government-owned company charged with development of Nigeria's oil and gas wealth and regulation of the country's oil and gas industry. NNPC was a shareholder in certain joint ventures with multinational oil companies. NNPC was an entity and instrumentality of the Government of Nigeria and its officers and employees were "foreign officials," within the meaning of the FCPA, Title 15, United States Code, Sections 78dd-l(t)(1)(A), 78dd-2(h)(2)(A), and 78dd-3(t)(2)(A).

Nigeria LNG Limited ("NLNG") was created by the Nigerian government to develop the Bonny Island Project and was the entity that awarded the related EPC contracts. The largest shareholder of NLNG was NNPC, which owned 49% of NLNG. The other owners of NLNG were multinational oil companies. Through the NLNG board members appointed by NNPC, among other means, the Nigerian government exercised control over NLNG, including but not limited to the ability to block the award of EPC contracts. NLNG was an entity and instrumentality of the Government of Nigeria and its officers and employees were "foreign officials," within the meaning of the FCPA, Title 15, United States Code, Sections 78dd-1(t)(1)(A), 78dd-2(h)(2)(A), and 78dd-3(t)(2)(A).

The Bonny Island Project

Between 1995 and 2004, TSKJ was awarded four EPC contracts to build the Bonny Island Project. Each EPC contract corresponded to one of the four phases in which the Bonny Island Project was constructed. An LNG "train" is the infrastructure necessary to pipe raw natural gas from wellheads, convert the raw gas to purified LNG, and deliver that LNG to a tanker. The first phase of the Bonny

Island Project consisted of two trains (Trains 1 and 2), the second phase consisted of one train (Train 3), the third phase consisted of two trains (Trains 4 and 5), and the fourth phase consisted of one train (Train 6). The first EPC contract, covering Trains 1 and 2, was awarded to TSKJ through an ostensibly competitive international tender. The other three EPC contracts were awarded to TSKJ on a sole-source, negotiated basis. The four EPC contracts awarded to TSKJ collectively were valued at over $6 billion.

COUNT 1

Conspiracy to Violate the Foreign Corrupt Practices Act (18 U.S.C. § 371)

. . . .

From at least in or around August 1994, to on or about June 15, 2004, in the Southern District of Texas, and elsewhere, defendant JGC did unlawfully, willfully, and knowingly combine, conspire, confederate, and agree with TSKJ, KBR, Technip, Snamprogetti, Stanley, Tesler, Tri-Star, Consulting Company B, and others, known and unknown, to commit offenses against the United States, that is, to willfully make use of the mails and means and instrumentalities of interstate commerce corruptly in furtherance of an offer, payment, promise to pay, and authorization of the payment of any money, offer, gift, promise to give, and authorization of the giving of anything of value to any foreign officials, and to any person while knowing that all or a portion of such money or thing of value would be or had been offered, given, or promised, directly or indirectly, to foreign officials, for purposes of: (i) influencing acts and decisions of such foreign officials in their official capacities; (ii) inducing such foreign officials to do and omit to do acts in violation of the lawful duties of such officials; (iii) securing an improper advantage; and (iv) inducing such foreign officials to use their influence with a foreign government and instrumentalities thereof to affect and influence acts and decisions of such government and instrumentalities, in order to assist JGC, KBR, Technip, TSKJ, and others in obtaining and retaining business for and with, and directing business to, JGC, KBR, Technip, TSKJ and others, in violation of Title 15, United States Code, Sections 78dd-l and 78dd-2.

Purpose of the Conspiracy

The purpose and object of the conspiracy was to obtain and retain billions of dollars in contracts related to the Bonny Island Project through the promise and payment of tens of millions of dollars in bribes to officials of the executive branch of the Government of Nigeria, officials of NNPC, officials of NLNG, and others.

Manner and Means of the Conspiracy

JGC and its co-conspirators employed various manner and means to carry out the conspiracy, including but not limited to the following:

a. Employees, and agents of JGC and their co-conspirators, including Consulting Company B, held so-called "cultural meetings" at which they discussed, among other things, the use of particular agents, including Tesler and Consulting Company B, to pay bribes to officials of the Government of Nigeria in order to secure the officials' support for TSKJ in obtaining and retaining contracts to build the Bonny Island Project.

b. Senior Executives, employees, and agents of JGC and their co-conspirators agreed that TSKJ would hire Tri-Star to pay bribes to high-level Nigerian government officials, including top-level executive branch officials, and Consulting Company B to pay bribes to lower-level Nigerian government officials, including employees of NLNG, in exchange for the officials' assistance in obtaining and retaining contracts to build the Bonny Island Project.

c. Senior executives, employees, and agents of JGC and their co-conspirators caused Madeira Company 3 to execute consulting contracts with Tri-Star and Consulting Company B providing for the payment of tens of millions of dollars in consulting fees in exchange for vaguely described marketing and advisory services, when in fact the primary purpose of the contracts was to facilitate the payment of bribes on behalf of TSKJ and its members to Nigerian government officials.

d. Prior to NLNG's award to TSKJ of the various EPC contracts, Stanley and other co-conspirators met with successive holders of a top-level office in the executive branch of the Government of Nigeria and subsequently negotiated with the office holders' representatives regarding the amount of the bribes that TSKJ would pay to the Nigerian government officials.

e. Senior executives, employees, and agents of JGC and their co-conspirators caused wire transfers totaling approximately $132 million to be sent from Madeira Company 3's bank account in Amsterdam, The Netherlands, to bank accounts in New York, New York, to be further credited to bank accounts in Switzerland and Monaco controlled by Tesler for Tesler to use to bribe Nigerian government officials.

f. On behalf of TSKJ and the four joint venture companies, Tesler wire transferred bribe payments to or for the benefit of various Nigerian government officials, including officials of the executive branch of the Government of Nigeria, NNPC, and NLNG, and for the benefit of a political party in Nigeria.

g. Senior executives, employees, and agents of JGC and their co-conspirators caused wire transfers totaling over $50 million to be sent from Madeira Company 3's bank account in Amsterdam, The Netherlands, to Consulting Company B's bank account in Japan for Consulting Company B to use to bribe Nigerian government officials.

Overt Acts

In furtherance of the conspiracy and to achieve its purpose and object, at least one of the co-conspirators committed or caused to be committed, in the Southern District of Texas, and elsewhere, the following overt acts, among others:

a. On or about August 3, 1994, Wojciech Chodan ("Chodan"), an M. W. Kellogg Ltd. salesperson responsible for the Bonny Island Project, sent a facsimile from London, England, to Stanley in Houston, Texas, two executives of JGC, and another co-conspirator stating, among other things, that Stanley, an executive of JGC, and other top executives of the joint venture companies had agreed to send a message "to the top man that we are ready to do business in the customary manner" and to ask Consulting Company B to secure support from the key individuals at the working level of NLNG.

b. On or about November 2, 1994, Tesler told Chodan that he had spoken with a senior official of the Nigerian Ministry of Petroleum, that Tesler's fee would be $60 million, that the first top-level executive branch official of the Government of Nigeria would get $40–45 million of that fee, that other Nigerian government officials would get the remaining $15–20 million of that fee, and that there would be a meeting between Stanley and the first top-level Nigerian executive branch official before the execution of any written agreement between TSKJ and Tesler.

c. On or about November 30, 1994, Stanley and other co-conspirators met in Abuja, Nigeria, with the first top-level executive branch official of the Government of Nigeria to verify that the official was satisfied with TSKJ using Tesler as its agent and to confirm that the first top-level executive branch official wanted TSKJ to negotiate with the senior official of the Ministry of Petroleum the amounts of bribes to various Nigerian government officials.

d. On or about March 20,1995, Madeira Company 3 entered into an agreement with Tri-Star providing, among other things, that Madeira Company 3 would pay $60 million to Tri-Star if TSKJ was awarded a contract to construct Trains 1 and 2 of the Bonny Island Project.

e. On or about December 27, 1995, Madeira Company 3 wire transferred $1,542,000 to Tri-Star, via a correspondent bank account in New York, New York, in payment of Tri-Star's first invoice under the consulting agreement for Trains 1 and 2.

f. On or about April 9, 1996, Madeira Company 3 entered into an agreement with Consulting Company B whereby it agreed to pay Consulting Company B $29 million for assisting TSKJ in winning the contract to build Trains 1 and 2 of the Bonny Island Project.

g. On or about July 26, 1996, Tesler caused $63,000 to be wire transferred to a Swiss bank account controlled by the senior official of the Ministry of Petroleum.

h. On or about May 1, 1997, Stanley and other co-conspirators met in Abuja, Nigeria, with the first top-level executive branch official of the Government of Nigeria and requested that the official designate a representative with whom TSKJ should negotiate the bribes to Nigerian government officials in exchange for the first top-level executive branch official's support of the award of the Train 3 EPC contract to TSKJ.

i. On or about February 28, 1999, Stanley and other co-conspirators met in Abuja, Nigeria, with a second top-level executive branch official of the

Government of Nigeria to request that the official designate a representative with whom TSKJ should negotiate the bribes to Nigerian government officials in exchange for the second top-level executive branch official's support of the award of the Train 3 EPC contract to TSKJ.

j. On or about March 5, 1999, Stanley, two JGC executives, and other co-conspirators met in London, England, with the representative designated by the second top-level executive branch official of the Government of Nigeria to negotiate the bribes to Nigerian government officials in exchange for the award of the Train 3 EPC contract to TSKJ.

k. On or about March 18, 1999, Madeira Company 3 entered into an agreement with Tri-Star providing, among other things, that Madeira Company 3 would pay $32.5 million to Tri-Star if TSKJ was awarded a contract to construct Train 3 of the Bonny Island Project.

l. On or about March 13, 2000, Madeira Company 3 entered into a consulting agreement with Consulting Company B promising to pay it $4 million in connection with Train 3 of the Bonny Island Project.

m. On or about January 16, 2001, Tesler caused $2.5 million to be wire transferred to a Swiss bank account controlled by the representative designated by the second top-level executive branch official of the Government of Nigeria.

n. On or about November 11, 2001, Stanley and a KBR salesperson met in Abuja, Nigeria, with a third top-level executive branch official of the Government of Nigeria and an NNPC official (the "NNPC Official") to request that the third top-level executive branch official designate a representative with whom TSKJ should negotiate the bribes to Nigerian government officials in exchange for the third top-level executive branch official's support of the award of the Trains 4 and 5 EPC contract to TSKJ.

o. On or about December 24, 2001, Madeira Company 3 entered into an agreement with Tri-Star providing, among other things, that Madeira Company 3 would pay $51 million to Tri-Star if TSKJ was awarded a contract to construct Trains 4 and 5 of the Bonny Island Project.

p. On or about May 28, 2002, an executive of JGC and others authorized Madeira Company 3 to sign a consulting agreement with Tri-Star for the Train 6 contract.

q. In or about June 2002, Tesler, the NNPC Official, and an employee of one of TSKJ's subcontractors (the "Subcontractor") met at a hotel in London, England, to discuss the NNPC Official's request that the Subcontractor help funnel payments from Tesler to a political party in Nigeria.

r. On or about June 14, 2002, Madeira Company 3 entered into a consulting agreement with Consulting Company B providing, among other things, that Madeira Company 3 would pay $25 million to Consulting Company B in connection with Trains 4 and 5 of the Bonny Island Project.

s. On or about June 28, 2002, Madeira Company 3 entered into an agreement with Tri-Star providing, among other things, that Madeira Company

3 would pay $23 million to Tri-Star if TSKJ was awarded a contract to con-
struct Train 6 of the Bonny Island Project.

t. On or about August 2002, an employee of the Subcontractor, using funds
that Tesler had caused to be wire transferred to the Subcontractor, delivered a pilot's briefcase containing one million U.S. dollars in one-hundred
dollar bills to the NNPC Official at a hotel in Abuja, Nigeria, for the benefit
of a political party in Nigeria.

u. On or about March 4, 2003, Chodan caused to be e-mailed to two KBR
executives in Houston, Texas, a draft memo for release to French authorities investigating potential crimes in connection with the Bonny Island
Project that included false statements about how Tesler had helped TSKJ
to win the various EPC contracts.

v. On or about April 2003, an employee of the Subcontractor, using funds
that Tri-Star had wire transferred to the Subcontractor, delivered a vehicle
containing Nigerian currency valued at approximately $333,333 to the
hotel of the NNPC Official in Abuja, Nigeria, for the benefit of a political
party in Nigeria.

w. On or about May 30, 2003, Madeira Company 3 wire transferred $123,500
to Tri-Star, via a correspondent bank account in New York, New York, in
payment of one of Tri-Star's invoices under the consulting agreement for
Train 3 of the Bonny Island Project.

x. On or about June 15, 2004, Madeira Company 3 wire transferred $3 million
to Consulting Company B in payment of one of Consulting Company B's
invoices under the consulting agreement for Trains 4 and 5 of the Bonny
Island Project.

All in violation of Title 18, United States Code, Section 371.

COUNT 2

Aiding and Abetting Violations of Foreign Corrupt Practices Act (15 U.S.C. § 78dd-2 & 18 U.S.C. § 2)

. . . .

On or about the dates set forth below, in the Southern District of Texas, and
elsewhere, defendant JGC willfully did aid, abet, counsel, command, induce, procure, and cause the commission of an offense against the United States, that is,
the willful use by KBR, a domestic concern, of instrumentalities of interstate commerce corruptly in furtherance of an offer, payment, promise to pay, and authorization of the payment of money to a person, while knowing that all or a portion
of such money would be or had been offered, given, or promised, directly or
indirectly, to foreign officials, for purposes of: (i) influencing acts and decisions
of such foreign officials in their official capacities; (ii) inducing such foreign officials to do and omit to do acts in violation of the lawful duties of such officials;
(iii) securing an improper advantage; and (iv) inducing such foreign officials to
use their influence with a foreign government and instrumentalities thereof to

affect and influence acts and decisions of such government or instrumentalities, in order to assist defendant JGC, KBR, TSKJ, and others in obtaining and retaining business for and with, and directing business to, defendant JGC, KBR, TSKJ, and others, to wit, defendant JGC aided and abetted KBR in causing the following corrupt U.S. dollar payments to be wire transferred from Madeira Company 3's bank account in Amsterdam, The Netherlands, via correspondent bank accounts in New York, New York, to bank accounts of Tri-Star in Switzerland for use in part to bribe Nigerian government officials:

. . . .

All in violation of Title 15, United States Code, Section 78dd-2, and Title 18, United States Code, Section 2.

Notes and Questions

In 2011, JGC Corporation ("JGC") entered into a DPA with the DOJ, agreeing to pay over $200 million in fines. Rather than immediately capitulate, JGC initially resisted the claims by asserting jurisdictional defenses—a response the DOJ considered a refusal to cooperate.[151]

1) What was the DOJ's basis for asserting jurisdiction over JGC?
2) Applying the rationale of the decision in *Hoskins* to the JGC case, what should be the outcome?

---

151. Deferred Prosecution Agreement at 3–4, United States v. JGC Corp., No. 4:11-CR-00260 (S.D. Tex. Apr. 6, 2011), https://www.justice.gov/criminal/fraud/fcpa/cases/jgc-corp/04-6-11jgc-corp-dpa.pdf.

TEST YOUR KNOWLEDGE
FCPA Violations

Statement of Facts

Zezla S.p.A. ("Zezla") is an Italian corporation that manufactures commercial trucks and whose shares trade on the New York Stock Exchange. Zezla's annual revenues exceed $1 billion, and it employs 20,000 persons around the world.

Zezla's second largest market after Italy is Russia, where it operates through a wholly owned subsidiary, ZezlaR, which was established in August 2014. ZezlaR's largest customer is the Russian Ministry of Transportation ("MOT"), whose purchases generate 30% of Zezla's total revenues.

ZezlaR's relationship with the MOT is handled by ZezlaR's Government Procurement Business Unit ("GPBU"), which employs three persons: Dmitry, Olga, and Natasha. GPBU performs the following tasks:

- Receipt of inquiries from the MOT;
- Preparation and submission of offers to the MOT;
- Handling of all negotiations with the MOT;
- Coordination of after-sales services.

Dmitry has been single-handedly responsible for cultivating ZezlaR's relationship with the MOT. His father is a close advisor to the Russian president and wields considerable influence over the MOT. Because of Dmitry's critical importance to the success of ZezlaR, he has been given a free hand to run the GPBU and is allowed to control virtually all aspects of the ZezlaR's relationship with the Russian government. Dmitry is the only person allowed to communicate with the MOT.

Dmitry was hired by ZezlaR's current CEO during a trip to Russia in December 2014 on the recommendation of the Russian Minister of Transportation. Dmitry graduated from public high school in Moscow in May 2014 and worked for his father's consulting company for three months before being hired by ZezlaR. Dmitry's base salary is $500,000 plus a 0.5% commission on all sales to the MOT. Olga and Natasha were both hired by Dmitry and report exclusively to him. They each receive an annual salary of $80,000.

In January 2016, ZezlaR retained Olig S.A. ("Olig"), a corporation registered in Geneva, Switzerland, as a consultant in connection with ZezlaR's sales to the MOT. ZezlaR has a 1-page contract with Olig signed by Dmitry, which gives Olig the right to a 1% commission on all ZezlaR sales to the MOT in exchange for "Marketing services and assistance in securing sales through Olig's extensive contacts with the Russian government."

At Dmitry's request, ZezlaR waived its third-party due diligence procedures with respect to Olig. Since 2015, ZezlaR has paid more than $3.8 Million from its bank account in Russia to Olig's Swiss bank account "for consulting services."

Zezla has an FCPA compliance program, which includes:

- an anticorruption policy, which strictly prohibits corrupt payments to foreign officials;
- a code of conduct that addresses, gifts, travel expenses, and charitable contributions, among other things;
- annual training of sales personnel; and
- due diligence procedures applicable prior to entering into relationships with third parties, including consultants.

Zezla has a Chief Compliance Officer ("CCO") who manages a dedicated compliance staff. The CCO reports weekly to the CEO and quarterly to the Compliance Committee of Zezla's Board of Directors regarding the performance of the compliance function. ZezlaR currently employs no dedicated compliance staff—though the CCO visits ZezlaR once a year.

After the 2008 financial crisis and subsequent fall in sales, Zezla was forced to significantly reduce its compliance program's budget and cut its compliance staff from 100 to 20. Although Zezla's sales have returned to pre-2008 levels, its compliance program budget has not been increased.

In December 2015, Zezla's CCO attempted to perform an FCPA audit of the GPBU, but Dmitry refused to cooperate and threatened to leave the company. The CCO subsequently withdrew her request and refrained from further attempts to look into GPBU's operations.

In November 2017, Zezla's hotline received a tip from an anonymous caller who stated that all of ZezlaR's sales to the Russian government had been secured through bribes paid to senior Russian government officials, including the Minister of Transportation. The caller, who only identified herself as a ZezlaR employee, offered to provide detailed information about the bribery scheme in exchange for $50,000 and assurances that ZezlaR would not retaliate against her.

Upon learning of the anonymous call, the CCO immediately reported the matter to Zezla's Board of Directors, which retained Law Firm for advice on how Zezla should proceed. You are an associate at Law Firm and have been asked to prepare a memorandum:

a) answering the questions below based on the given facts; and,
b) specifying any additional facts that you would like to know to complete your analysis.

Questions

1) Is Zezla potentially liable under the FCPA and/or SOX? Explain.
2) Assess the likelihood that Zezla may face indictment for violating the FCPA.
3) What steps should Zezla take to mitigate the likelihood of indictment and its costs in connection with any potential violations of the FCPA?

THE EFFECTIVE COMPLIANCE PROGRAM

*E*thos is an Aristotelian concept that describes an orator's character—his integrity, truthfulness, and general disposition.[1] An orator's *ethos* was separate and apart from his spoken words; it was an abstract and intangible expression of his identity.[2]

According to Professor Pamela Bucy, a business organization can be distinguishable by its *ethos* or prevalent culture, which is separate from what the corporation does or the sector in which it operates.[3] This identity, she explains, "results from the dynamic of many individuals working together toward corporate goals."[4] It is a "tone of sentiment" in the group that covers "[s]uperficial things such as the manner of dress and the camaraderie of the employees as well as formal, written goals and policies."[5]

In a landmark 1991 paper, *Corporate Ethos: A Standard for Imposing Corporate Criminal Liability,* Bucy proposed a new conceptual paradigm that would impose criminal liability based on a corporation's *ethos*—where criminal intent would be established by determining if the corporation's prevailing culture encouraged the crime at issue.[6] She argued that if "the criminal conduct is predictable and consistent with corporate goals, policies, and ethos . . . [then] this translates into [criminal intent]."[7]

Our present corporate criminal justice system has in many ways come to resemble the conceptual paradigm proposed by Bucy, but with one significant difference. While Bucy envisioned juries reviewing evidence adduced at trial to decipher a corporation's ethos,[8] the current system has prosecutors—not juries—decide whether a corporation's culture encouraged criminality. In these situations, the first thing that prosecutors will do in order to evaluate a

---

1. *See* Pamela H. Bucy, *Corporate Ethos: A Standard for Imposing Corporate Criminal Liability*, 75 MINN. L. REV. 1095, 1121–23 (1991).
2. *Id.* at 1123.
3. *Id.*
4. *Id.* at 1099.
5. *Id.* at 1123.
6. *Id.* at 1099.
7. *Id.*
8. *Id.* at 1101.

corporation's *ethos* is to examine its compliance program. While organizations face broad corporate liability under the *respondeat superior* doctrine, penalties can be greatly mitigated if a corporation maintains an effective compliance and ethics program.

Surveys have consistently found that an organization's culture significantly impacts the effectiveness of its compliance program in reducing misconduct. The FCPA Guide[9] emphasizes this connection:

> [E]thical culture is the single biggest factor determining the amount of misconduct that will take place in a business. Metrics of ethical culture include ethical leadership (tone at the top), supervisor reinforcement of ethical behavior (middle management reinforcement), and peer commitment (supporting one another in doing the right thing). Strong ethical cultures and strong ethics and compliance programs are related, as data show that a well-implemented program helps lead to a strong ethical culture. . . . To create an ethical culture, attention must be paid to norms at all levels of an organization, including the "tone at the top," "mood in the middle," and "buzz at the bottom."[10]

The FCPA Guide also notes:

> Within a business organization, compliance begins with the board of directors and senior executives setting the proper tone for the rest of the company. . . . Thus, DOJ and SEC consider the commitment of corporate leaders to a culture of compliance and look to see if this high-level commitment is also reinforced and implemented by middle managers and employees at all levels of a business.[11]

Similarly, the Federal Sentencing Guidelines for Organizations requires organizations to maintain "compliance and ethics program[s]" that not only "prevent and detect criminal conduct" but also "promote an organizational culture that encourages ethical conduct and a commitment to compliance with the law."[12]

Additional Reading Materials

Gebler, David. *Is Your Culture a Risk Factor?*, 111 Bus. & Soc'y Rev. 337 (2006).

---

9. Criminal Div. of the U.S. Dep't of Justice & the Enf't Div. of the U.S. Sec. and Exch. Comm'n, A Resource Guide to the U.S. Foreign Corrupt Practices Act (2012), *available at* http://www.justice.gov/sites/default/files/criminal-fraud/legacy/2015/01/16/guide.pdf [hereinafter FCPA Guide].

10. *Id.* at 57 & 117 n.312 (2012) (first quoting Ethics Res. Ctr., 2009 National Business Ethics Survey: Ethics in the Recession 41 (2009); then quoting Ethics Res. Ctr., 2011 National Business Ethics Survey: Workplace Ethics in Transition 19, 34 (2012); and then quoting David Gebler, *The Role of Culture, in* Society of Corporate Compliance and Ethics, The Complete Compliance Ethics Manual 1.9–1.10 (2011)).

11. FCPA Guide at 57 (footnote omitted).

12. U.S. Sentencing Guidelines Manual § 8B2.1(a) (U.S. Sentencing Comm'n 2016).

CHAPTER 6

The Ten Hallmarks of an Effective Compliance Program

I.   Commitment from Senior Management and a Clearly Articulated Policy Against Corruption
II. Code of Conduct and Compliance Policies and Procedures
III. Oversight, Autonomy, and Resources
IV. Risk Assessment
  A. Measuring and Mitigating Risk
  B. Documenting the Results
V.   Training and Continuing Advice
VI. Incentives and Disciplinary Measures
VII. Third-Party Due Diligence and Payments
  A. Defining the Scope of the Process
  B. Assessing Risk
    1. Agency
    2. Accounting and Internal Control Practices
    3. Geography
    4. Industry/Sectoral Risk
    5. Products
    6. History of Prior Misconduct
    7. Identity of the Third Party, Its Owners, and Key Employees
    8. Nature of the Third Party's Involvement and Compensation
    9. Risk Ratings
  C. Conducting Due Diligence
    1. Obtain Relevant Information from the Third Party
    2. Verification of Data and Resolution of Red Flags
  D. Approving and Monitoring the Program
VIII. Confidential Reporting and Internal Investigations
  A. The Confidential Hotline and Whistleblowers
  B. Internal Investigations
    1. Should We Investigate?
    2. Who Should Conduct the Investigation?
    3. What Should Be the Scope of the Investigation?
    4. Should the Investigation Be Referred to Outside Counsel?

C. Self-Disclosure and Cooperation
IX. **Continuous Improvement: Periodic Testing and Review**
   A. Monitoring
   B. Auditing
X. **Pre-Acquisition Due Diligence and Post-Acquisition Integration**

While the Committee of Sponsoring Organizations of the Treadway Commission ("COSO") lays out a broad framework for advancing a company's compliance objectives, the Foreign Corrupt Practices Act Resource Guide ("FCPA Guide") provides a detailed description of the controls necessary to create an effective FCPA compliance program, grouping them into ten categories called "Hallmarks."[2] Notwithstanding their specificity, the Hallmarks do not set forth a universal formula that companies can apply mechanically as a "one-size-fits-all program."[3] The DOJ and SEC ask three basic questions in assessing the effectiveness of an anticorruption compliance program:

> In 2012, the DOJ and the SEC published the Foreign Corrupt Practices Act, or FCPA, Resource Guide, which contains an entire section entitled, "Hallmarks of Effective Compliance Programs." While the Hallmarks in the FCPA Guide are focused on anti-corruption compliance programs, the principles identified apply universally.
>
> —*Deputy Assistant Attorney General Marshall L. Miller*[1]

1) Is it well designed?
2) Is it being applied in good faith?
3) Does it work?[4]

Overview of Corporate Anti-Corruption Programmes

Susan Côté-Freeman, Transparency International[5]

DEVELOPING AN EFFECTIVE PROGRAMME TO COUNTER BRIBERY

[T]he implementation of effective anti-bribery programmes requires a consistent level of effort. This can at first sight seem an onerous burden for small and medium-size companies that have limited financial and human resources, but respecting the law is essential for all companies, regardless of size.

... [T]he first step for a company wishing to develop an effective anti-bribery programme is to articulate a clear policy that promotes zero tolerance of corrupt

---

1. Marshall L. Miller, Principal Deputy Assistant Attorney Gen. ["DAAG"], Criminal Div., Remarks at the Advanced Compliance and Ethics Workshop (Oct. 7, 2014), https://www.justice.gov/opa/speech/remarks-principal-deputy-assistant-attorney-general-criminal-division-marshall-l-miller-0.
2. *Id.*
3. Criminal Div. of the U.S. Dep't of Justice & the Enf't Div. of the U.S. Sec. and Exch. Comm'n, A Resource Guide to the U.S. Foreign Corrupt Practices Act (2012), available at http://www.justice.gov/sites/default/files/criminal-fraud/legacy/2015/01/16/guide.pdf [hereinafter FCPA Guide], at 57.
4. FCPA Guide, *supra* note 3, at 56.
5. Susan Côté-Freeman, *Overview of Corporate Anti-Corruption Programmes*, in Business Against Corruption: Case Stories and Examples 47, 49–50 (Brigit Errath ed., 2006), https://www.unglobalcompact.org/docs/issues_doc/7.7/BACbookFINAL.pdf.

practices. This policy must be accompanied by a detailed implementation programme to ensure that every employee in the company is knowledgeable in all aspects of the policy and trained in coping with ambiguous situations. Too often, good policies are developed and announced by top management, but they remain theoretical because not enough effort is devoted to making sure that they are adhered to throughout the company, especially in locations where business conditions are challenging.

A critical condition to successful implementation is top-level commitment to the anti-bribery policy. The Board and high-level management must demonstrate their full commitment by addressing employees and making public their unequivocal stance on bribery and corruption. It is difficult to resist the temptation to mention the now legendary Enron code of conduct developed by the defunct US energy firm. The Enron code was exemplary in its formulation but proved to be worthless when it was suspended by the company's venal executives.

A programme tailored to address the risks that are specific to a company is required to protect it against instances of bribery and corruption. However, the company must be mindful that beyond the behaviour of its own employees, it must ensure that business partners, including subsidiaries, joint venture partners, agents, contractors and other third parties with whom it has a business relationship, are carefully selected by reference to the company's zero tolerance rules.

... [C]ompanies must exercise great care in choosing business partners, particularly in countries or in business sectors where corruption is known to be widespread. Due diligence must be undertaken in hiring agents, and their compensation must be commensurate with the services they provide.

The company's zero tolerance policy should be clearly communicated to all employees, particularly to those in sales, marketing, purchasing, and project management, as well as to sales representatives and other agents. Employees should be given practical guidance on how to deal with recognized areas of risk, such as payments to and by sales representatives and other agents; gifts, entertainment and travel allowances; political contributions and facilitation payments.

If company efforts to uphold a zero tolerance policy on bribery and corruption are to be successful, all aspects of human resources management, such as recruitment, promotion, and performance reviews, should reflect the commitment to this policy. This may mean reviewing human resource practices to introduce schemes that concretely reward integrity .... Failing the introduction of an integrity incentive scheme, it should be made clear that no employee will be penalized for having lost business that was deemed to be tainted or to have the potential to be so. Appropriate sanction mechanisms must be built into an anticorruption programme, and if employees are to be rewarded for their honesty, those who deviate from company policy must be submitted to appropriate disciplinary action.

Employees should be provided with secure and accessible channels for raising concerns and reporting violations, and whistle-blowers must be protected from reprisals. Anti-bribery communication channels increase the likelihood that the actions of wrongdoers will be exposed. Such channels give honest employees and business partners a means through which they can report bribery and corruption and contribute to creating a culture of prevention.

These communication channels can also play an important role in providing advice to employees who have questions about the company's programme and its implementation and can encourage employee feedback on the programme. This role can be extended to providing advice to business partners and other stakeholders interested in the company's programme.

Very often, bribes have been paid out of "slush funds" or secret reserves that were established in order to pay costs of any kind that cannot be justified. Accurate accounting and record keeping is therefore of the utmost importance in the fight against bribery and corruption. Robust internal systems of accounting controls must be put in place to safeguard assets and ensure the reliability of financial records. Regular audits must be performed to provide assurance that the internal controls are effective in preventing corrupt practices.

Finally, but equally important, a company's anti-bribery programme should be reviewed periodically by senior management for its suitability and effectiveness. The process of improvement should be seen as a continuous one. It is only through regular reviews of the effectiveness of its systems that a company can develop and maintain appropriate protection against corruption.

BUILDING CREDIBILITY

As with any voluntary standard, the credibility of companies that subscribe to anti-bribery principles will depend on their effectiveness in improving company behaviour. Apart from the complexities involved in adapting to the laws and regulations of each country where a company operates, changed behaviour will not be achieved by focusing solely on legal compliance programmes; commitment to ethical principles must be established throughout the company. This approach can be demonstrated by appropriate and fair disclosure in annual reports, social responsibility reports or website postings, and supplemented by independent verification of the systems in place, where credibility is critical.

Companies cannot fully come to grips with the pervasive issue of bribery and corruption on their own. However, the combination of an expanding legal framework and its vigorous enforcement with enhanced company compliance through voluntary codes can contribute to creating a climate where bribery and corruption are increasingly viewed as a risky and costly way of doing business.

Companies that have joined the United Nations Global Compact are now faced with the challenge of implementing the 10th Principle. What does this mean practically for United Nations Global Compact signatories? Companies that already have in place programmes to counter bribery and corruption must assess their effectiveness periodically and take the lead in providing meaningful reporting on their efforts. Companies that are at an earlier stage must devote time and resources to assessing their risk exposure and developing adequate policies and programmes that can be fully integrated into their business. This is a time-consuming and sometimes costly process. But the alternative can be costlier still.

I. Commitment from Senior Management and a Clearly Articulated Policy Against Corruption

The FCPA Guide underscores that "[a]n effective compliance program promotes 'an organizational culture that encourages ethical conduct and a commitment to compliance with the law.'"[6] The board of directors and senior executives are tasked with creating this culture by tempering the organization's drive to maximize profits in order to adapt to legal and ethical norms.

> A well-designed compliance program that is not enforced in good faith, such as when corporate management explicitly or implicitly encourages employees to engage in misconduct to achieve business objectives, will be ineffective.
>
> —FCPA Guide[7]

In global business, the temptation to pay bribes can be overwhelming, as it often means the difference between winning and losing lucrative business opportunities. A sense that "everyone else is doing it" adds to the pressure to succumb to corruption. In those circumstances, a strong culture of compliance and ethics serves as the corporation's conscience to keep temptation in check.

Senior management's position on bribery springs naturally from its commitment to ethics. This commitment is expressed formally through a statement of the company's policy against corruption:[8]

> [The] DOJ and SEC thus evaluate whether senior management has clearly articulated company standards, communicated them in unambiguous terms, adhered to them scrupulously, and disseminated them throughout the organization.[9]

Senior management's role, however, goes well beyond stating a policy against corruption; it involves teaching the values that underlie the global fight against corruption. Corporate leaders must engage their audience as a Greek orator would—by expressing the *ethos* or character that defines the organization's core values. Thus, the policy statement will be a written expression of a message conveyed through everything that corporate leaders say and do.[10]

Vitally, senior management's policy messaging should be designed with the company's particular operations and constituencies in mind. This involves not only the message, but also the information and instructions for each constituency. For example, special focus should

> By adhering to ethical standards, senior managers will inspire middle managers to reinforce those standards. Compliant middle managers, in turn, will encourage employees to strive to attain those standards throughout the organizational structure.
>
> —FCPA Guide[11]

---

6. FCPA Guide, *supra* note 3, at 56 (quoting U.S. Sentencing Guidelines Manual § 8B2.1(b) (U.S. Sentencing Comm'n 2011)).

7. FCPA Guide, *supra* note 3, at 57.

8. *Id.*

9. *Id.*

10. *See id.*

11. *Id.*

be placed on the messaging directed to employees and agents who are exposed to the greatest risk of corruption, such as sales staff and local sales agents in corrupt markets.[12]

Additional Reading Materials

Greenberg, Michael D. PERSPECTIVES OF CHIEF ETHICS AND COMPLIANCE OFFICERS ON THE DETECTION AND PREVENTION OF CORPORATE MISDEEDS: WHAT THE POLICY COMMUNITY SHOULD KNOW (2009), http://www.rand.org/content/dam/rand/pubs/conf_proceedings/2009/RAND_CF258.pdf.

Notes and Questions

In his article, *Is Your Culture a Risk Factor?*, David Gebler notes that Enron exemplified:

> [F]orm over substance with regard to ethics and compliance. Enron had put into place most, if not all, of the basic elements that had been set out by the federal sentencing guidelines. But there is no evidence that the board weighed the impact of Enron's culture on the risks [it] faced.[13]

As Enron demonstrates, a formal policy statement alone is not sufficient to address the risks faced by a company, including the risk of corruption.

1) What are some actions that a company's senior managers can take to build a corporate culture that combats corruption?
2) Which component(s) of internal control does the first Hallmark engage?

Hypothetical: Top-Level Commitment[14]

A small- to medium-sized component manufacturer [(Quince Inc.)] is seeking contracts in markets abroad where there is a risk of bribery. As part of its preparation, a senior manager has devoted some time to participation in the development of a sector-wide anti-bribery initiative.

The top-level management of the manufacturer could consider any or a combination of the following:

- The making of a clear statement disseminated to its staff and key business partners of its commitment to carry out business fairly, honestly

---

12. *See, e.g., id.*

13. David Gebler, *Is Your Culture a Risk Factor?*, 111 BUS. & SOC'Y REV. 337, 339 (2006).

14. The following is reproduced from MINISTRY OF JUSTICE, THE BRIBERY ACT 2010: GUIDANCE 42 (2011) (U.K.), http://www.justice.gov.uk/downloads/legislation/bribery-act-2010-guidance.pdf [hereinafter MOJ Bribery Act Guidance].

and openly, referencing its key bribery prevention procedures and its involvement in the sectoral initiative.

- Establishing a code of conduct that includes suitable anti-bribery provisions and making it accessible to staff and third parties on its website.
- Considering an internal launch of a code of conduct, with a message of commitment to it from senior management.
- Senior management emphasising among the workforce and other associated persons the importance of understanding and applying the code of conduct and the consequences of breaching the policy or contractual provisions relating to bribery prevention for employees and managers and external associated persons.
- Identifying someone of a suitable level of seniority to be a point-person for queries and issues relating to bribery risks.

Assume that you have been brought in by Quince Inc. as a compliance consultant, and they have asked you to pick two of the above strategies for immediate implementation.

1) Which two do you choose and why?
2) Based on your first answer, what risks, if any, do you think Quince remains most exposed to?

Hypothetical: The Anticorruption Policy Statement

Xenon, Inc. ("Xenon") is a corporation registered in the United States with manufacturing facilities in the United States and 20 other countries. Xenon employs 20,000 foreign workers. Because of the nature and location of its operations, Xenon is exposed to a high risk of corruption. Last year, Xenon's operations in China and Vietnam were found to be involved in bribing government workplace safety inspectors, leading to the company's entry into an NPA with the DOJ and payment of a $2 million fine. As part of the NPA, Xenon agreed to significantly improve its compliance program.

Assume you are the CEO preparing Xenon's new anticorruption policy.

1) Make a summary of the points that you plan to discuss in the policy.
2) How should you communicate the policy?

II. Code of Conduct and Compliance Policies and Procedures

A company's code of conduct puts into effect the detailed rules and instructions that implement its anticorruption policy. The code should be "clear, concise, and accessible to all employees and to those conducting business on the company's behalf."[15] It should specifically address the circumstances that employees and agents may face and provide clear instructions on what to do—again, focusing on employees and agents who are exposed to the greatest corruption risks.[16] It should also "outline responsibilities for compliance within the company, detail proper internal controls, auditing practices, and documentation policies, and set forth disciplinary procedures."[17]

The code should be based on "an in-depth understanding of the company's business model, including its products and services, third-party agents, customers, government interactions, and industry and geographic risks."[18] For example, a company whose products are highly regulated or primarily used by governments in emerging markets will require a more elaborate anticorruption code of conduct than a company that sells unregulated products in developed markets. In certain circumstances, such as dealings with high risk countries, it is good practice to implement a supplemental code of conduct for frontline staff addressing the particular risks they are likely to face.

An anticorruption code of conduct typically addresses:

- Dealings with government officials
- Gifts
- Hospitality, entertainment, travel and other expenses
- Customer travel
- Political contributions
- Charitable contributions
- Sponsorships
- Grease/facilitation payments
- Use of third parties
- Dealings with state-owned enterprises
- Dealings with relatives of government officials
- Solicitation and extortion
- Documentation
- Division of responsibilities
- Audit procedures
- Instructions detailing proper internal controls
- Reporting
- Disciplinary procedures.[19]

After taking care to tailor the code of conduct to the particular risks and constituencies of the company, the next step is to ensure that the code is effectively

---

15. FCPA Guide, *supra* note 3, at 57.
16. *See id.* at 56–58.
17. *Id.* at 58.
18. *Id.*
19. *See id.* at 58; *see generally* Jon Jordan, *The Need for a Comprehensive International Foreign Bribery Compliance Program, Covering A to Z, in an Expanding Global Anti-Bribery Environment,* 117 Penn St. L. Rev. 89, 124–32 (2012).

communicated to employees and others acting on the company's behalf. Beyond making the code available in the appropriate languages, companies should ensure communication through proper use of available information and communication technology.[20]

Emphasizing this point about technology, the FCPA Guide provides an example of a web-based approach:

> [S]ome companies with global operations have created web-based approval processes to review and approve routine gifts, travel, and entertainment involving foreign officials and private customers with clear monetary limits and annual limitations. Many of these systems have built-in flexibility so that senior management, or in-house legal counsel, can be apprised of and, in appropriate circumstances, approve unique requests.[21]

The code of conduct is worthless unless its rules, policies and procedures are enforced consistently at all levels of the company.[22] Senior management should set an example of diligent adherence to the code as part of its obligation to set the right tone for the entire organization.[23]

The anticorruption policy and code of conduct should be continually updated to reflect the current corruption risks facing the enterprise: "[a]s companies change over time, so must compliance policies."[24] The code should also be regularly updated to reflect changing laws and regulations as well as lessons learned in the course of operations.[25]

Notes and Questions

Which component(s) of internal control does this Hallmark engage?

Hypothetical: Preparing the Code of Conduct

Holden, Inc. ("Holden") is a U.S.-based publishing company that sells educational content to several countries in South America. Holden operates in Argentina through a wholly owned subsidiary and sells its products directly to the Ministry of Education. Recently, Holden discovered that its sales

---

20. *See* FCPA Guide, *supra* note 3, at 57–58.
21. *Id.* at 58.
22. *See id.*
23. *See* Comm. of Sponsoring Orgs. of the Treadway Comm'n, Internal Control — Integrated Framework: Executive Summary 4 (2013), https://na.theiia.org/standards-guidance/topics/Documents/Executive_Summary.pdf [hereinafter COSO Executive Summary].
24. Miller, *supra* note 1.
25. *See* FCPA Guide, *supra* note 3, at 61–62.

> manager (now replaced) had paid bribes to officials in exchange for inflated sales orders.
>
> Following this discovery, Holden has asked you to prepare a special anti-corruption code of conduct for its Argentinian subsidiary. What information would you like to have in preparing the code?

III. Oversight, Autonomy, and Resources

This Hallmark is patterned after FSGO § 8B2.1(b)(2), which provides:

> (2)
>
> (A) The organization's governing authority shall be knowledgeable about the content and operation of the compliance and ethics program and shall exercise reasonable oversight with respect to the implementation and effectiveness of the compliance and ethics program.
>
> (B) High-level personnel of the organization shall ensure that the organization has an effective compliance and ethics program, as described in this guideline. Specific individual(s) within high-level personnel shall be assigned overall responsibility for the compliance and ethics program.
>
> (C) Specific individual(s) within the organization shall be delegated day-to-day operational responsibility for the compliance and ethics program. Individual(s) with operational responsibility shall report periodically to high-level personnel and, as appropriate, to the governing authority, or an appropriate subgroup of the governing authority, on the effectiveness of the compliance and ethics program. To carry out such operational responsibility, such individual(s) shall be given adequate resources, appropriate authority, and direct access to the governing authority or an appropriate subgroup of the governing authority.[26]

> The quickest way to check on that commitment [to compliance] is to take a look at corporate structure. If you see compliance executives sitting in true positions of authority at a corporation, reporting directly to independent monitoring bodies, like internal audit committees or boards of directors, you likely are looking at a strong compliance program. Compliance programs also need to be resourced; they need to have teeth and respect. By contrast, for years, Wall Street banks housed their compliance programs across the Hudson River, in New Jersey. They were out of sight, out of mind. Compliance programs need to have appropriate stature within corporations.
>
> —*DAAG Marshall L. Miller*[27]

In this Hallmark, the DOJ and SEC set three parameters for the compliance program:

Oversight: A company must assign responsibility for the oversight and implementation of the compliance program to one or more specific senior executives within an organization.

Autonomy: The compliance staff must be given adequate autonomy from management, including direct access to an organization's board of directors.

---

26. U.S. Sentencing Guidelines Manual § 8B2.1(b)(2) (U.S. Sentencing Comm'n 2016).
27. Miller, *supra* note 1.

Resources: Adequate resources should be devoted to compliance based on "the company's size, complexity, industry, geographical reach, and risks associated with the business."[28]

By making compliance program independent from business operations and giving it the right resources, corporate leaders empower the compliance staff to do the work necessary to make sure the company meets its legal and ethical obligations. Also, by furnishing the compliance staff with appropriate authority and resources, management signals its serious commitment to compliance to all employees. As discussed above, the DOJ and SEC take a company's size, complexity, and risk profile into consideration when assessing whether a company has provided adequate resources and staffing to its compliance program.

Additional Reading Materials

Comm. of Sponsoring Orgs. of the Treadway Comm'n. Internal Control Integrated Framework 147–58 (2013).

Felson, Eileen, and Frederic Miller. The Board's Role in Anti-Corruption Compliance: Guardian and Guide, White Collar Crime Committee Newsl. (Am. Bar Ass'n, Criminal Justice Section, D.C.), Winter/Spring 2014, https://www.americanbar.org/content/dam/aba/publications/criminaljustice/wcc2014_FelsonMiller.authcheckdam.pdf.

Reichert, Todd. *The Roles of General Counsel and Chief Compliance Officers*, Corp. Compliance Insights (Jan. 18, 2011), http://corporatecomplianceinsights.com/the-roles-of-general-counsel-and-chief-compliance-officers/.

Snell, Roy. *Compliance Officer Independence*, Compliance & Ethics Blog (May 28, 2014), http://complianceandethics.org/compliance-officer-independence/.

Volkov, Michael, The Volkov Law Grp. *Redefining the Relationship of the General Counsel and Chief Compliance Officer*, in Transforming Compliance: Emerging Paradigms for Boards, Management, Compliance Officers, and Government 56 (2014), http://www.rand.org/content/dam/rand/pubs/conf_proceedings/CF300/CF322/RAND_CF322.pdf.

IV. Risk Assessment

The COSO Framework defines risk as "the possibility that an event will occur and adversely affect the achievement of objectives."[29] In the context of the FCPA anti-bribery provisions, the risks to be managed are those that might adversely impact a company's objective to prevent and detect corrupt payments to foreign officials.

---

28. *See* FCPA Guide, *supra* note 3, at 58.
29. COSO Executive Summary, *supra* note 23, at 4.

A risk-based anticorruption program collects relevant information and uses a consistent methodology for measuring corruption risks across an enterprise so that each risk can be objectively compared to others. In this way, an enterprise can tailor controls and allocate proportionate resources to the mitigation of each risk. It can identify not only areas where controls are insufficient but also where excessive controls burden operations to address a relatively low risk.[30] This systematic approach to the assessment and mitigation of risk is the distinguishing feature of a "well-designed" FCPA compliance program.[31]

The risk assessment process must be conducted with the support of the board of directors and senior management, given sufficient resources, and managed by knowledgeable and accountable staff.[32] Risk assessment involves (a) measuring and mitigating risks and (b) documenting such process. The measuring and mitigating of risks encompasses (1) planning, (2) identifying risks through information gathering and analysis, (3) rating the risks, (4) employing mitigating controls, and (5) measuring the residual risk.[33]

A. Measuring and Mitigating Risk

Various methodologies can be used to assess a company's corruption risks. The OECD has proposed a five-step process, summarized below.

1. Step One

Define the responsible individuals, resources to be invested, information needed, and the framework to be used in the risk assessment process.[34]

2. Step Two

Identify risks by determining which of the risk factors (circumstances that elevate the risk of corruption discussed below) apply.

Geographic Risk

Businesses operating in countries with a high incidence of corruption face enormous pressure to pay bribes to obtain licenses, win government contracts, or even turn on the lights. This elevates the risk that an employee or an intermediary engaged by the company will violate the FCPA. Transparency International's Corruption Perceptions Index (as shown in Figure 6-1) ranks each country according to its perceived level of relative corruption.[35]

---

30. *See* Inst. of Risk Mgmt. & Transparency Int'l U.K., Bribery Risk Guide 8 (2016), https://www.theirm.org/media/2218767/IRM-TI-UK-Bribery-Guide-A5-V6-Low-Res-proof.pdf [hereinafter Bribery Risk Guide].

31. FCPA Guide, *supra* note 3, at 57–59.

32. *See* Bribery Risk Guide, *supra* note 30, at 11.

33. *See id.*

34. *See* Org. for Econ. Cooperation and Dev. [OECD] et al., Anti-Corruption Ethics and Compliance Handbook for Business, at 10 (2013), www.oecd.org/corruption/Anti-CorruptionEthicsCompliance-Handbook.pdf [hereinafter OECD Handbook].

35. *Corruption Perceptions Index* (2016) by Transparency International is licensed under CC-BY-ND 4.0,

Figure 6-1. Transparency International Rankings of Countries According to Their Perceived Levels of Relative Corruption

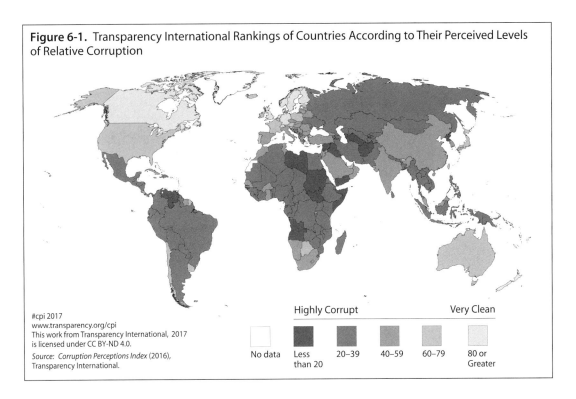

#cpi 2017
www.transparency.org/cpi
This work from Transparency International, 2017 is licensed under CC BY-ND 4.0.

Source: Corruption Perceptions Index (2016), Transparency International.

Highly Corrupt					Very Clean
No data	Less than 20	20–39	40–59	60–79	80 or Greater

Sectoral Risk

Certain industries are inherently more prone to corruption risk. Typically, those sectors are associated with:

- High levels of government interaction
- High levels of regulation
- Large and/or long-term contracts
- Complex projects requiring many business partners.[36]

---

https://www.transparency.org/news/feature/corruption_perceptions_index_2016. Transparency International's website offers the following responses to frequently asked questions:

What Is the Corruption Perceptions Index (CPI)?

The CPI scores and ranks countries/territories based on how corrupt a country's public sector is perceived to be. It is a composite index, a combination of surveys and assessments of corruption, collected by a variety of reputable institutions. The CPI is the most widely used indicator of corruption worldwide.

Why is the CPI based on perceptions?

Corruption generally comprises illegal activities, which are deliberately hidden and only come to light through scandals, investigations, or prosecutions. There is no meaningful way to assess absolute levels of corruption in countries or territories on the basis of hard empirical data. Possible attempts to do so, such as by comparing bribes reported, the number of prosecutions brought, or studying court cases directly linked to corruption, cannot be taken as definitive indicators of corruption levels. Instead, they show how effective prosecutors, the courts, or the media are in investigating and exposing corruption. Capturing perceptions of corruption of those in a position to offer assessments of public sector corruption is the most reliable method of comparing relative corruption levels across countries.

Transparency Int'l, *Corruption Perception Index 2016: Frequently Asked Questions*, at 1 (2016), http://files.transparency.org/content/download/2058/13244/file/CPI_2016_FAQs_EN.pdf.

36. Bribery Risk Guide, *supra* note 30, at 16.

High-risk sectors include the extractive industries (*e.g.,* oil and mineral exploration and extraction), construction and infrastructure, defense, and telecommunications.

Transaction Risk

A transaction may pose an elevated risk of corruption depending on location, subject matter, parties involved, how critical it is to a company, size, and urgency.[37] Examples of high risk transactions include:

- Government procurement
- Provision of gifts, hospitality and/or travel expenses
- Political or charitable donations
- Transactions requiring government permits and/or licenses such as customs clearance
- Hiring of current or former government officials, their relatives, or persons closely associated with them.[38]

Business Opportunity Risk

Business opportunity risks are those that "might arise in high value projects or with projects involving many contractors or intermediaries; or with projects which are not apparently undertaken at market prices, or which do not have a clear legitimate objective."[39]

Business Partnership Risk

"[C]ertain relationships may involve higher risk, for example, the use of intermediaries in transactions with foreign public officials; consortia or joint venture partners; and relationships with politically exposed persons where the proposed business relationship involves, or is linked to, a prominent public official."[40]

The information needed to evaluate the above risk factors may be gathered through various methods, including:

- Employee interviews and surveys
- Questionnaires submitted to business units
- Web or database searches
- Audit reports
- Mining data on government enforcement actions relating to particular industries.[41]

---

37. *See id.* at 17.
38. *See id.*
39. MOJ Bribery Act Guidance, *supra* note 14, at 26.
40. *Id.*
41. *See* Bribery Risk Guide, *supra* note 30, at 13–14; OECD *Handbook, supra* note 34, at 11.

3. Step Three

Rate the risks identified in Step Two by assigning a relative value—called inherent risk—to each. This allows for meaningful differentiation between risks and the allocation of resources commensurate with each specific risk.[42] Inherent risk is composed of two elements: probability and magnitude.[43]

Probability is derived by analyzing the presence of risk factors. "The more significant and/or numerous the risk factors associated with a particular activity, the higher the likelihood that an adverse event might occur in the context of that activity."[44]

Magnitude measures the impact of "financial, legal/regulatory, commercial and reputational fallout" on a company should a risk materialize.[45] Although impact is difficult to predict, a risk manager can use the factors enumerated in the FSGO and the United States Attorneys' Manual (USAM) to gauge the range of penalties that might be imposed on the company. In particular, companies can look to the Federal Sentencing Guidelines for the formula used to impose base penalties for FCPA violations. By the same token, legal expenses and damage to

Table 6-1. Sample Magnitude Scale

Qualitative Rating	Description
High	• Fines and penalties exceeding $100M and/or debarment • Other financial loss exceeding $20M • Significant negative media coverage • Loss of market share exceeding 3% • Termination of one or more senior executives
Medium	• Fines and penalties between $1M and $100M • Other financial loss between $500K and $20M • Negative media coverage • Loss of market share below 3% • Termination of one or more mid-level executives
Low	• Fines and penalties below $1M • Other financial loss below $500K • Limited negative local media coverage • Drop in employee morale • Termination or suspension of one or more employees

---

42. *See* FCPA Guide, *supra* note 3 at 58–59; OECD *Handbook*, *supra* note 34, at 11–12.
43. *See* OECD *Handbook*, *supra* note 34, at 11.
44. Bribery Risk Guide, *supra* note 30, at 20.
45. *Id.* at 22.

reputation may be estimated based on the size of the transaction and nature of the offense.[46]

A quantitative or qualitative value can be assigned to each of the above elements.[47] For example, a company can use a numerical scale of 1 to 5, that is, a quantitative approach, or, it can use descriptions such as "high," "medium," and "low," a qualitative approach.[48] Each approach has advantages and disadvantages. A qualitative assessment is quicker to produce and easy to understand, but it provides limited differentiation between various levels of risk and cannot be numerically aggregated. A quantitative assessment, by contrast, permits numerical aggregation and cost-benefit analysis, but it is more expensive to produce and manage.[49] Regardless of which approach a company chooses, it should be applied consistently throughout the risk assessment process.

4. Step Four

Employ appropriate controls to mitigate the risk (mitigating controls).[50] The COSO Framework recognizes that "[t]here is no practical way to reduce risk to zero."[51] Therefore, "[m]anagement must determine how much risk is to be prudently accepted, [and] strive to maintain risk within these levels."[52] This is known as *risk tolerance,* "the acceptable variation in performance relative to the achievement of objectives."[53]

Mitigating controls are employed to reduce inherent risks to a level within the organization's risk tolerance and defined by their:

1) **Scope:** Are they generally applicable at the level of the company (entity-level controls), or are they are specific to the risk identified (scheme-specific controls)?
2) **Function:** Are they intended to prevent a violation (preventive controls) or designed to uncover a violation after it has occurred (detective controls)?[54]

5. Step Five

Measure the *residual risk,* that is, the level of remaining risk after employing the selected controls.[55] By measuring residual risk, the company can determine if it has employed sufficient controls to mitigate inherent risk to a level within

---

46. *See id.*
47. *See* OECD *Handbook, supra* note 34, at 12.
48. *See id.*
49. *See* Patchin Curtis & Mark Carey, Deloitte & Touche LLP, *Risk Assessment in Practice,* COSO 8, https://www2.deloitte.com/content/dam/Deloitte/global/Documents/Governance-Risk-Compliance/dttl-grc-riskassessmentinpractice.pdf.
50. *See* OECD Handbook, *supra* note 34, at 12.
51. COSO Executive Summary *supra* note 23, at 60.
52. *Id.*
53. *Id.* at 61.
54. *See* OECD Handbook, *supra* note 34, at 12.
55. *See id.*

the company's risk tolerance. If the residual risk exceeds the company's risk tolerance, Steps Three through Five should be repeated until the risk is sufficiently mitigated.

B. Documenting the Results

The entire process of selecting and employing mitigating controls must be documented in detail.[56] This is an important part of the enterprise's systematic effort to prevent and detect crime; should a violation occur, it serves as a means by which the organization can demonstrate its concrete compliance efforts.

A company's anticorruption risk assessment can be documented in different ways. Two options are proposed in the OECD Risk Assessment Handbook: a spreadsheet/database or a heat map.[57]

A risk register is a database template that documents the rating of each risk as well as the mitigating controls. A risk register allows for "[e]ach risk factor, risk, and scheme [to] be documented individually."[58] Table 6-2 illustrates a risk register.[59]

Alternatively, a heat map shows corruption risks according to their likelihood and potential impact. "Simple heat maps typically have sections that are red, yellow, or green, denoting high-risk, medium-risk, and low-risk, respectively."[60] They can be used to illustrate a single risk, an enterprise-wide view, or views by location or function.[61] Figure 6-2 provides an example of a heat map, using increasingly dark shades of grey to indicate the levels of risk.

Table 6-2. Sample Risk Register

Location/ Region: ABC	
Business Unit: XYZ	
Corruption Risk Factor	Local business climate
Corruption Risk	Bribery of a government official
Corruption Scheme	Potential improper payments to government officials in order to obtain permits
Probability	Medium
Potential Impact	High

---

56. *See* OECD Handbook, *supra* note 34, at 13.
57. *Id.* at 13–14.
58. *Id.*
59. *Id.* at 13.
60. *Id.*
61. *Id.*

Table 6-2. Sample Risk Register—*Cont'd*

Location/ Region: ABC	
Business Unit: XYZ	
Anticorruption Controls	• Global anticorruption policy and procedures including specific content on payments to government officials • Anticorruption training for employees that is tailored for select regions and key functions • Global whistleblower hotline
	Annual anticorruption audits on payments to government officials
Control Risk Rating	Effective
Residual Risk Rating	Medium

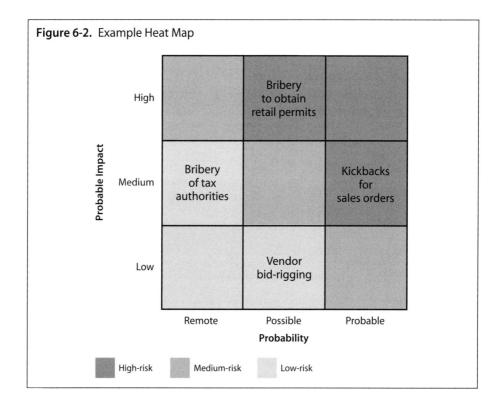

Figure 6-2. Example Heat Map

Notes and Questions

"There is no meaningful way to assess absolute levels of corruption in countries or territories on the basis of hard empirical data,"[62] as bribes by their very nature

---

62. Transparency Int'l, *supra* note 35, at 1.

are concealed. Nonetheless, various indirect methods can be used in measuring corruption, each of which has its own strengths and weaknesses. The two main kinds of corruption indicators are perception- and experience-based indicators and proxy indicators.[63]

Perception-based indicators, such as the CPI, use surveys to gauge public opinion and perception of corruption; experience-based indicators survey peoples' actual experiences with corruption in their daily lives.[64] A disadvantage of this method is that people are generally reluctant to discuss this issue for fear of retribution.[65]

Proxy indicators "assess corruption through indirect measures by aggregating many 'voices' and signals of corruption, or by measuring the opposite: anti-corruption, good governance and public accountability mechanisms."[66] These indicators "range from surveys of where and how money from the public purse gets allocated (and misallocated) to analyzing which companies get public sector contracts and on what terms."[67] Public expenditure tracking surveys, for example, "highlight cases where public money has either not ended up where it should have or can't actually be accounted for at all."[68]

The Millennium Challenge Corporation, a U.S. government aid agency dedicated to fighting global poverty, uses a corruption indicator that "measures the extent to which public power is exercised for private gain . . . as well as 'capture' of the state by elites and private interests."[69] It evaluates countries based on the following factors:

---

63. *See* Raymond June et al., U.N. Dev. Programme [UNDP], *A User's Guide to Measuring Corruption*, at 9–10 (2008), http://www.undp.org/content/dam/aplaws/publication/en/publications/democratic-governance/dg-publications-for-website/a-users-guide-to-measuring-corruption/users_guide_measuring_corruption.pdf [hereinafter UNDP User's Guide].

64. *See id.*

65. *See id.*

66. *Id.* at 9.

67. Dan Hough, *There's More to Measuring Corruption than Transparency International's Annual Index, Just Released*, Wash. Post (Jan. 26, 2017), https://www.washingtonpost.com/news/monkey-cage/wp/2017/01/26/theres-more-to-measuring-corruption-than-transparency-internationals-annual-index-just-released/.

68. *Id.*

69. *Guide to the Indicators, FY 2016*, Millennium Challenge Corp. (Nov. 20, 2015), https://www.mcc.gov/resources/doc/guide-to-the-indicators-fy-2016. The Millennium Challenge Corporation posits that:

> Corruption hinders economic growth by increasing costs, lowering productivity, discouraging investment, reducing confidence in public institutions, limiting the development of small and medium-sized enterprises, weakening systems of public financial management, and undermining investments in health and education. Corruption can also increase poverty by slowing economic growth, skewing government expenditure in favor of the rich and well-connected, concentrating public investment in unproductive projects, promoting a more regressive tax system, siphoning funds away from essential public services, adding a higher level of risk to the investment decisions of low-income individuals, and reinforcing patterns of unequal asset ownership, thereby limiting the ability of the poor to borrow and increase their income.

Id. (footnote omitted).

- The frequency of "irregular payments" associated with import and export permits, public contracts, public utilities, tax assessments, and judicial decisions
- Nepotism, cronyism, and patronage in the civil service
- The estimated cost of bribery as a share of a company's annual sales
- The perceived involvement of elected officials, border officials, tax officials, judges, and magistrates in corruption
- The strength and effectiveness of a government's anticorruption laws, policies, and institutions
- Public trust in the financial honesty of politicians
- The extent to which:
  - processes are put in place for accountability and transparency in decision-making and disclosure of information at the local level;
  - government authorities monitor the prevalence of corruption and implement sanctions transparently;
  - conflict of interest and ethics rules for public servants are observed and enforced;
  - the income and asset declarations of public officials are subject to verification and open to public and media scrutiny;
  - senior government officials are immune from prosecution under the law for malfeasance;
  - the government provides victims of corruption with adequate mechanisms to pursue their rights;
  - the tax administrator implements effective internal audit systems to ensure the accountability of tax collection;
  - the executive budget-making process is comprehensive and transparent and subject to meaningful legislative review and scrutiny;
  - the government ensures transparency, open-bidding, and effective competition in the awarding of government contracts;
  - there are legal and functional protections for whistleblowers, anticorruption activists, and investigators;
  - allegations of corruption at the national and local level are thoroughly investigated and prosecuted without prejudice;
  - government is free from excessive bureaucratic regulations, registration requirements, and/or other controls that increase opportunities for corruption;
  - citizens have a legal right to information about government operations and can obtain government documents at a nominal cost.[70]

The type of indicator used depends on the form of corruption being assessed. Corruption may be classified as petty or grand. Petty corruption involves low- to

---

70. *Id.*

mid-level government officials asking for small bribes to perform routine services such as turning on water or electricity.[71] Perception- and experience-based surveys are useful in measuring petty corruption, because they gauge the impact of corruption on the everyday lives of citizens.[72]

Grand corruption, by contrast, infects the country's political institutions and the legitimacy of its leaders. Large public projects and procurement contracts are typical examples of transactions associated with grand corruption. Proxy indicators are better suited to measuring grand corruption, because they reflect the overall health of the country's public institutions.[73]

OECD Foreign Bribery Report: An Analysis of the Crime of Bribery of Foreign Public Officials[74]

KEY FINDINGS

The following statistics are based on analysis of the information contained in enforcement actions against 263 individuals and 164 entities for the foreign bribery offence (a total of 427 cases) concluded between the entry into force of the OECD Anti-Bribery Convention (15 February 1999) and 1 June 2014. The data was not always available for all categories in all cases; therefore some percentages may be from a reduced data set. Please refer to the relevant section of the report for a detailed description of the data set for each category.

Two-thirds of the foreign bribery cases occurred in four sectors: extractive (19%); construction (15%); transportation and storage (15%); and information and communication (10%).

Almost half of the cases involved bribery of public officials from countries with high (22%) to very high (21%) levels of human development.

In 41% of cases management-level employees paid or authorised the bribe, whereas the company CEO was involved in 12% of cases. In one case, a congressman was convicted of conspiracy to bribe foreign public officials.

Intermediaries were involved in 3 out of 4 foreign bribery cases. These intermediaries were agents, such as local sales and marketing agents, distributors and brokers, in 41% of cases. Another 35% of intermediaries were corporate vehicles, such as subsidiary companies, local consulting firms, companies located in off-shore financial centres or tax havens, or companies established under the beneficial ownership of the public official who received the bribes.

---

71. *See* UNDP *User's Guide, supra* note 63, at 8.

72. *See id.*

73. *See id.* at 8–10.

74. Org. for Econ. Cooperation and Dev. [OECD], *OECD Bribery Report: An Analysis of the Crime of Bribery of Foreign Public Officials*, at 8-36 (2014), http://globalinvestigationsreview.com/digital_assets/64d2bf01-7ad8-43da-950c-d8d643b31260/1360-2-ForeignBribery-Embargo.pdf (footnotes omitted).

Bribes were promised, offered or given most frequently to employees of public enterprises (state-owned or controlled enterprises, SOEs) (27%), followed by customs officials (11%), health officials (7%) and defence officials (6%).

In the majority of cases, bribes were paid to obtain public procurement contracts (57%), followed by clearance of customs procedures (12%). On average, bribes equalled 10.9% of the total transaction value and 34.5% of the profits.

One in three cases came to the attention of authorities through self-reporting by defendant companies or individuals. The next most common sources were investigations initiated directly by law enforcement authorities (13%) and foreign bribery cases that came to light in the context of formal or informal mutual legal assistance between countries (13%). Whistleblower reports and media coverage very rarely instigated a foreign bribery investigation (2% and 5%, respectively).

Companies that self-reported became aware of the foreign bribery in their international operations primarily through internal audits (31%) and merger and acquisition due diligence procedures (28%).

Prison sentences were handed down to 80 individuals who were found guilty of foreign bribery. The longest combined prison sentence imposed to date in a case involving a conviction for conspiracy to commit foreign bribery is 13 years for one individual. Another 38 individuals received suspended prison sentences.

In total, there were 261 fines imposed on individuals and companies with the highest combined fine against a single company totalling EUR 1.8 billion. The highest monetary sanction imposed against an individual in a foreign bribery case was a forfeiture order amounting to USD 149 million.

In 69% of foreign bribery cases, sanctions were imposed by way of settlement, using procedures including corporate probation (Canada); section 153(a) of the Criminal Procedure Code (Germany); *Patteggiamento* (Italy); Penalty Notice (Norway); *Réparation* under article 53 of the Penal Code (Switzerland); Non-Prosecution Agreements (NPAs), Deferred Prosecution Agreements (DPAs) and Plea Agreements (US).

The United States has sanctioned individuals and entities for the foreign bribery offence in connection with 128 separate foreign bribery schemes since the entry into force of the OECD Anti-Bribery Convention. Germany has sanctioned individuals and entities for the foreign bribery offence in connection with 26 separate schemes, Korea in connection with 11 and Italy, Switzerland and the United Kingdom in connection with 6.

. . . .

FOREIGN BRIBERY: THE WHO, WHAT, WHERE, WHY, AND HOW

Thanks to the increase in global enforcement of the crime of foreign bribery, there is more information available now than ever before on how this crime is carried out, including who is bribing and who is receiving the bribes, what is the cost of a bribe, how bribes are being paid, where and for what reason.

WHO IS BRIBING?

The OECD Anti-Bribery Convention requires its Parties to hold their citizens and companies liable for the crime of bribing foreign public officials in international business transactions. On the basis of the data available for this report, 263 individuals and 164 entities were sanctioned for the crime of foreign bribery.

Figure 6-3 illustrates the size of companies that have been involved in foreign bribery, or whose representatives have bribed foreign public officials. Only 4% of sanctioned companies were small and medium-sized enterprises (SMEs). In 60% of cases, the company associated with the corrupt transaction had more than 250 employees. The size of the company involved was unknown in 36% of cases.

Figure 6-4 illustrates the sector of activity of the defendant individuals and companies sanctioned for foreign bribery. Sectors were determined depending on the particular role that the company in question played in the specific case. For example, if an engineering company worked primarily in the extractive industry and was sanctioned for bribery in the construction of an oil rig, then it would be deemed to be in the extractive industry. On the basis of this analysis, companies from the extractive (19%), construction (15%), transportation and storage (15%), information and communication (10%), and manufacturing (8%) industries have been most often sanctioned for foreign bribery. This data can be contrasted with the 2011 Transparency International Bribe Payers' Index (BPI), which ranks the public works contracts and construction (5.3), utilities (6.1), real estate, property, legal and business services (6.1), oil and gas (6.2), and extractive (6.3) sectors as most prone to bribery. These rankings are based on a survey of more than 3,000 business executives worldwide of the likelihood of bribes being paid by companies in 19 different business sectors. Sectors are scored on a scale of 0 to 10, where a maximum score of 10 corresponds with the view that companies in that sector never bribe and 0 corresponds with the view that they always do.

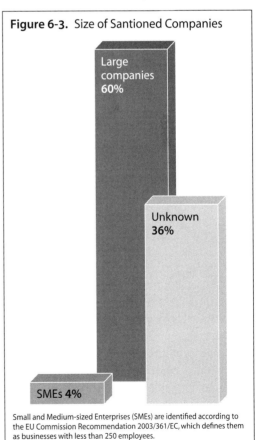

Figure 6-3. Size of Santioned Companies

Large companies 60%

Unknown 36%

SMEs 4%

Small and Medium-sized Enterprises (SMEs) are identified according to the EU Commission Recommendation 2003/361/EC, which defines them as businesses with less than 250 employees.

Source: OECD analysis of foreign bribery cases concluded between 15/02/1999 and 01/06/2014.

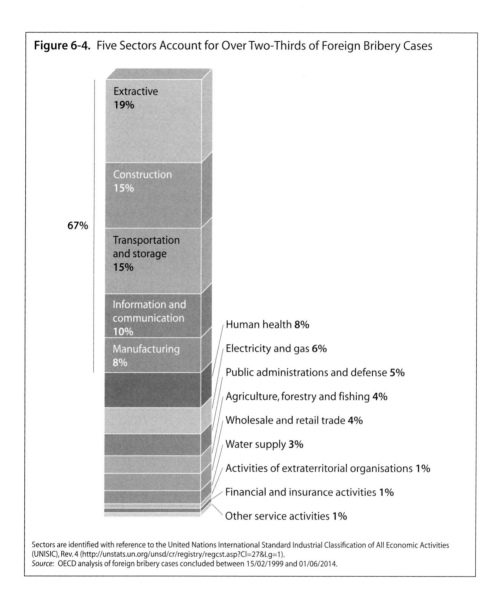

Figure 6-4. Five Sectors Account for Over Two-Thirds of Foreign Bribery Cases

67%

Extractive
19%

Construction
15%

Transportation
and storage
15%

Information and
communication
10%

Manufacturing
8%

Human health **8%**

Electricity and gas **6%**

Public administrations and defense **5%**

Agriculture, forestry and fishing **4%**

Wholesale and retail trade **4%**

Water supply **3%**

Activities of extraterritorial organisations **1%**

Financial and insurance activities **1%**

Other service activities **1%**

Sectors are identified with reference to the United Nations International Standard Industrial Classification of All Economic Activities (UNISIC), Rev. 4 (http://unstats.un.org/unsd/cr/registry/regcst.asp?Cl=27&Lg=1).
Source: OECD analysis of foreign bribery cases concluded between 15/02/1999 and 01/06/2014.

Figure 6-5 indicates the level within the company of the person who paid, was aware of, or authorised the foreign bribery in question. There were often overlaps between the categories in a single case when numerous individuals at various levels of the company were involved and multiple entries were each therefore counted individually. In the majority of cases, corporate management (41%) or even the CEO (12%) was aware of and endorsed the bribery, debunking the "rogue employee" myth and demonstrating the need for a clear "tone from the top" in implementing corporate anti-bribery policies, as referred to in the OECD *Good Practice Guidance on Internal Controls, Ethics and Compliance.*

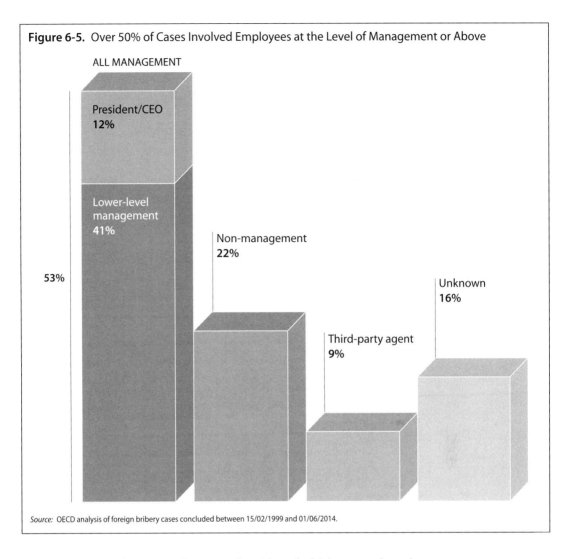

Figure 6-5. Over 50% of Cases Involved Employees at the Level of Management or Above

ALL MANAGEMENT

President/CEO
12%

Lower-level management
41%

53%

Non-management
22%

Third-party agent
9%

Unknown
16%

Source: OECD analysis of foreign bribery cases concluded between 15/02/1999 and 01/06/2014.

Figures 6-4 and 6-5 provide a very clear idea of which sectors have been sanctioned most often, the level within the company of the person who paid, was aware of or authorised the foreign bribery and, based on Figure 6-6, the common use of intermediaries to channel the bribe.

WHO IS RECEIVING THE BRIBE?

While the OECD Anti-Bribery Convention focuses on the supply side of bribes in international business, it is also important to consider who is on the receiving end of a corrupt transaction, bearing in mind the difficult question of bribe solicitation by public officials. This section illustrates the so-called "demand side" of a foreign bribery transaction.

Figure 6-6 shows the role of the foreign public officials who received or solicited the bribes in these cases, and the percentage of total bribes they received.

For further information on each category of public official, please refer to the Glossary of Terms. The largest category of foreign public officials who were bribed is that of employees of SOEs, or public enterprises, who received the bribes in 27% of cases. In terms of the role of the SOE official who received the bribe, this ranged from CEO or President-level, to management (e.g. Environment Director; Finance Director; International Relations Director) and even lower-level employees. In some cases, the SOE official had a dual role, such as transport minister or advisor to a senior government official. In one case the SOE official was the son of a former head of state and president of a subsidiary of the national oil company. This data raises the issue of the integrity of corporate governance practices and, relatedly, the implementation and supervision of decision-making

Figure 6-6. Proportion of Bribes Paid, per Category of Public Official

PERCENTAGE OF OFFICIALS WHO TOOK THE BRIBE		PERCENTAGE OF BRIBES PROMISED, OFFERED OR GIVEN
27%	SOE official	80.11%
11%	Customs official	1.14%
7%	Health official	0.92%
6%	Defense official	2.93%
4%	Resource official	0.08%
4%	IO official	0.22%
4%	Tax official	0.21%
4%	Elected official	0.55%
3%	Minister	4.08%
3%	Transport official	0.06%
3%	Procurement official	0.25%
3%	Family of public official	UNKNOWN AMOUNT
2%	Maritime official	<0.01%
2%	Law enforcement official	0.07%
2%	Head of state	6.97%
2%	Intelligence official	0.01%
1%	Diplomatic official	0.18%
1%	Environment official	<0.01%
1%	Immigration official	<0.01%
1%	Political party	0.05%
<0.1%	Local government official	<0.01%
<0.1%	Vice minister	<0.01%
<0.1%	Education official	<0.01%
11%	Unknown	2.17%

Source: OECD analysis of foreign bribery cases concluded between 15/02/1999 and 01/06/2014.

processes in SOEs. It highlights the importance of effective measures for managing conflicts of interest and transparent and accountable SOE procurement procedures. The next largest category involves customs officials (11%), followed by health (7%) and defence (6%) officials. Heads of State and Ministers were bribed in a total of 5% of cases.

Figure 6-6 also sets out the percentage of the total bribes offered, promised or given relative to each category of public official. This can only be a very rough estimation, given that the case information rarely specified exactly how much was paid and to whom. The data set also did not enable double counting when more than one category of official was involved in a transaction. On the basis of the available data (in 224 cases), SOE officials were bribed in 27% of cases but received 80.11% of total bribes. Heads of State and Ministers were bribed in a total of 5% of cases but received 11% of total bribes. This could confirm a preconceived notion that the more powerful the official, the more s/he receives in bribes. Customs officials were bribed in 11% of cases and received only 1.14% of total bribes, suggesting that bribes in these cases would have been more in the nature of "small facilitation payments."

Figure 6-7 shows that 95.1% of the bribes were paid to public officials in only five categories. In all other categories, the ratio was less than 1%. While not within the scope of this report, future work could analyse whether the public officials on the receiving end of the bribes in these cases were brought to justice.

Figure 6-7. Ninety-Five Percent of Bribes Were Paid to Officials in 5 Categories

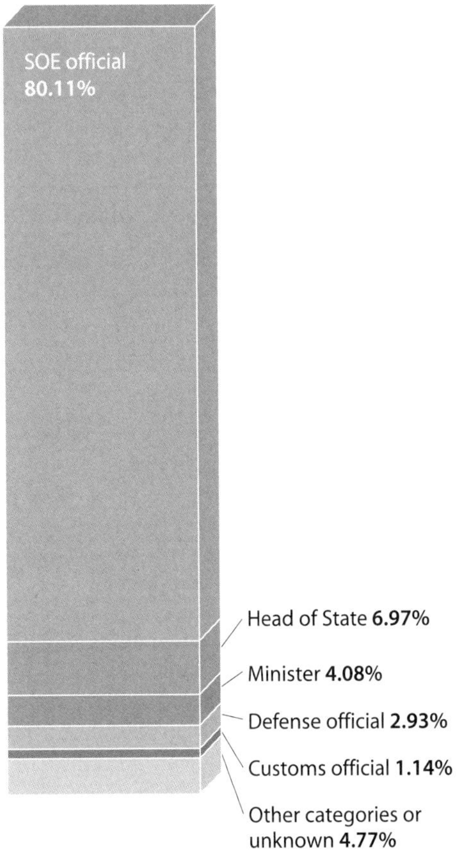

SOE official 80.11%

Head of State **6.97%**
Minister **4.08%**
Defense official **2.93%**
Customs official **1.14%**
Other categories or unknown **4.77%**

Source: OECD analysis of foreign bribery cases concluded between 02/15/1999 and 06/01/2014.

WHAT IS THE COST OF A BRIBE?

A monetary figure for the value of the bribes that were paid was available in 224 cases. It is important to note that the amount of bribes indicates only those values appearing in official judgments or documents finalising settlements; the total amount of bribes promised or paid in any particular case may be consistently higher than reported. The highest total amount offered in bribes in a single foreign bribery scheme was USD 1.4 billion while the smallest was USD 13.17. The total amount of bribes paid in the 224 cases where this information available is USD 3.1 billion. Given the very complex and concealed nature of corrupt transactions, it is without doubt the mere tip of the iceberg.

Information on the value of the bribe and the total value of the transaction resulting from the bribery was available in 55 cases. For example, one decision stated the total value of the particular contract that was obtained (USD 6 million) but noted that the bribes were paid with a view to securing ongoing contracts worth up to USD 100 million. In that instance, both values were counted. However, this information was not available in all cases and it is important to bear in mind that even in cases where the total transaction value is specified, the defendant company or individual may have obtained other, more significant benefits that are difficult to quantify, for example entry into a new market or a dominant position or monopoly in a certain sector. For the purposes of this report, the value of the entire transaction has been called "transaction value," it is different (and greater to) to the profits obtained by individuals and companies from foreign bribery transactions.

Figure 6-8 contemplates the 55 cases which contained information both on the amount paid in bribes and on the transaction value. It shows the distribution

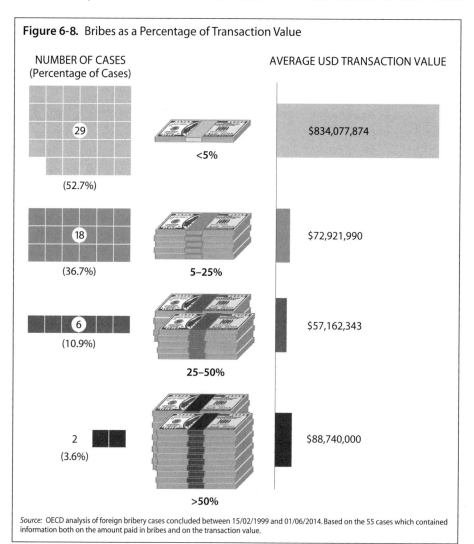

Figure 6-8. Bribes as a Percentage of Transaction Value

NUMBER OF CASES
(Percentage of Cases)

AVERAGE USD TRANSACTION VALUE

29

<5%

$834,077,874

(52.7%)

18

5–25%

$72,921,990

(36.7%)

6

(10.9%)

25–50%

$57,162,343

2

(3.6%)

$88,740,000

>50%

Source: OECD analysis of foreign bribery cases concluded between 15/02/1999 and 01/06/2014. Based on the 55 cases which contained information both on the amount paid in bribes and on the transaction value.

of bribes paid as a percentage of the transaction value, tracked against the average transaction value for each category. For most cases, the amount of bribes promised, offered or given is up to 5% of the transaction value. These cases also involve the highest average transaction value (USD 834 million). In eight out of 57 cases, bribes amounted to more than 25% of the transaction value, although the average transaction value in these cases did not surpass USD 100 million. On average, bribes equaled 10.9% of the transaction value and 34.5% of the profits.

As stated in the OECD Issues Paper on Corruption and Economic Growth, "[T]he true social cost of corruption cannot be measured by the amount of bribes paid or even the amount of state property stolen. Rather, it is the loss of output due to the misallocation of resources, distortions of incentives and other inefficiencies caused by corruption that represent its real cost to society." In this context, the average of 10.9% of the transaction value spent on bribes means that the bribing individual or company would have to somehow recover or offset those costs. Some companies might do this by paying employees less in countries with weaker employment laws. Others might inflate the quote for the goods or services to be provided, therefore requiring more public money to be spent on the project than should otherwise have been allocated. Companies might also recover costs by cutting expenses in the delivery of goods and services. For example, cutting costs in the construction sector could result in faulty roads, bridges or public buildings. Cutting costs in the health sector could mean out-of-date, harmful or ineffective medicines and medical equipment. In the services sector, this could mean that citizens are required to pay more than they otherwise should for a public service. In one case, bribes were paid in the context of a national identity card project to influence officials to issue a decree requiring citizens to purchase the identity cards, ostensibly in order to recover price concessions made in the corrupt procurement process. The project was ultimately abandoned and the decree was never issued.

Figure 6-9 considers this information on the basis of the sectors involved. It displays the percentage of the total amount paid in bribes relative to the transaction value by sector, to show the relative "cost" of bribes per sector in the 57 cases where information from both data sets was available. There was a surprising variation between the sectors, with bribes in the water supply and education sectors each amounting to 2% of the transaction value compared to the extractive and wholesale and retail trade sectors, where bribes amounted to 21% and 19% of the transaction value, respectively.

Another point of interest in the "return on investment" hypothesis for corrupt transactions is the correlation between the amount imposed in monetary sanctions and the amount obtained in profits, or proceeds, as a result of the bribes paid. This comparison also contributes towards an evaluation of whether the monetary sanctions imposed in a particular case are "effective, proportionate and dissuasive," in accordance with Article 3 of the OECD Anti-Bribery Convention. Of course, and as mentioned above, there are other substantial costs involved in foreign bribery enforcement actions that either cannot be quantified in monetary terms or do not constitute official sanctions.

. . . .

Figure 6-9. Bribes as a Percentage of the Transaction Value per Sector

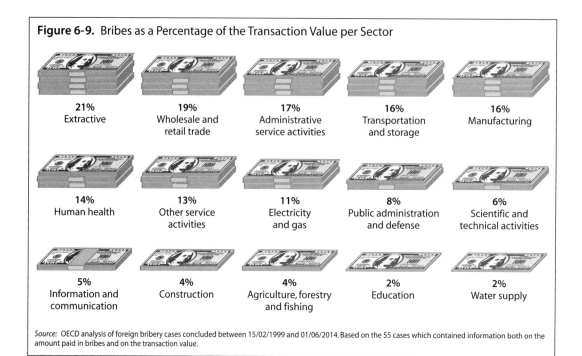

21% Extractive	**19%** Wholesale and retail trade	**17%** Administrative service activities	**16%** Transportation and storage	**16%** Manufacturing
14% Human health	**13%** Other service activities	**11%** Electricity and gas	**8%** Public administration and defense	**6%** Scientific and technical activities
5% Information and communication	**4%** Construction	**4%** Agriculture, forestry and fishing	**2%** Education	**2%** Water supply

Source: OECD analysis of foreign bribery cases concluded between 15/02/1999 and 01/06/2014. Based on the 55 cases which contained information both on the amount paid in bribes and on the transaction value.

HOW ARE BRIBES BEING PAID?

It is clear from the case analysis which forms the basis of this report that in the vast majority of foreign bribery cases, the bribery was carried out via an agent or intermediary. This report uses the definition of intermediary as set out in the OECD Typologies on the Role of Intermediaries in International Business Transactions:

> . . . an intermediary is defined or described as a person who is put in contact with or in between two or more trading parties. In the business context, an intermediary usually is understood to be a conduit for goods or services offered by a supplier to a consumer. Hence, the intermediary can act as a conduit for legitimate economic activities, illegitimate bribery payments, or a combination of both. . . Both natural and legal persons, such as consulting firms and joint ventures are included.

Figure 6-10 shows the percentage of cases where intermediaries were involved in at least one bribe payment. Three out of four foreign bribery cases involved payments through intermediaries. It also shows the role of the intermediary in the 304 cases in which intermediaries were used. An "Agent" was used in 41% of cases; this category includes sales and marketing agents, distributors and brokers based either locally in the country where the bribes were paid, or elsewhere. Future work could consider the range of "fees" charged by such agents, and how much more this adds to the cost of the bribe itself. The second largest category of intermediaries, used in 35% of cases, is that of the "Corporate vehicle." This category includes subsidiary companies, local consulting firms, companies located

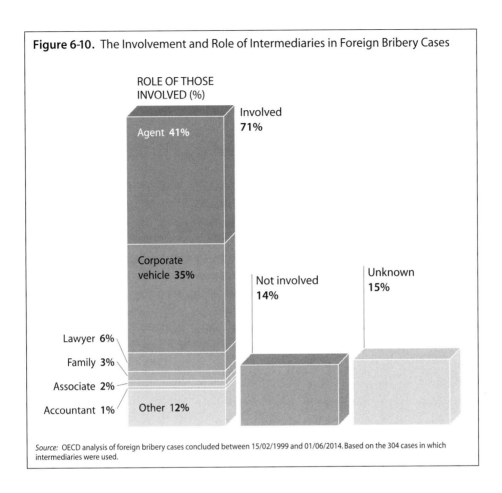

Figure 6-10. The Involvement and Role of Intermediaries in Foreign Bribery Cases

ROLE OF THOSE INVOLVED (%)

Agent **41%**

Involved **71%**

Corporate vehicle **35%**

Not involved **14%**

Unknown **15%**

Lawyer **6%**
Family **3%**
Associate **2%**
Accountant **1%**
Other **12%**

Source: OECD analysis of foreign bribery cases concluded between 15/02/1999 and 01/06/2014. Based on the 304 cases in which intermediaries were used.

in offshore financial centres or tax havens or companies established under the beneficial ownership of either the public official who received the bribes or the individual or entity paying the bribes. Lawyers were used as intermediaries in 6% of cases. Family members of the public official were used as intermediaries in 3% of cases. Accountants and associates (including advisors) of the public official were used in 1% and 2% of cases respectively. The nature of the intermediary was not specified in 12% of cases.

WHERE ARE BRIBES BEING PAID?

A common perception of bribery in international business is that business people and companies from the wealthiest, most developed economies only bribe officials from least developed countries to win lucrative contracts. The analysis in this report suggests that this perception needs to be revisited.

Figure 6-11 illustrates that, among the 427 cases in this report, the majority of bribes paid abroad were not paid to public officials from developing countries. In fact, almost one in two cases involved bribery of foreign public officials from countries with high to very-high levels of human development, based on the UN Human Development Index (HDI) of the country where the bribery took place, at

Figure 6-11. Two-Thirds of Bribes Were Paid to Officials in Countries Medium or Higher on the UN Human Development Index

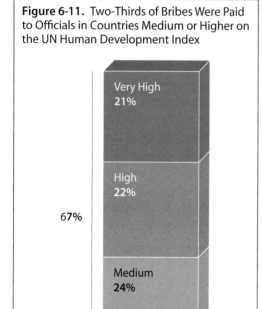

Very High
21%

High
22%

67%

Medium
24%

Low
17%

Unknown
16%

Source: OECD analysis of foreign bribery cases concluded between 15/02/1999 and 01/06/2014.

the time it took place. For cases that took place before 2012, reference was made to the 2011 HDI, whereas cases added post 2012 refer to the 2013 HDI. Where bribes were paid in multiple countries in a single case, the HDI for each country was counted.

One in five bribes was paid in countries with "very high" human development. Figure 6-12 displays the countries whose public officials received or were offered bribes. These include 24 out of the 41 member countries of the OECD WGB and 15 out of the 19 member countries of the G20 (the 20th member of the Group is the European Union). There could be many reasons for this outcome, including that countries with higher levels of human development may have greater capacity to cooperate in foreign bribery investigations, such as detecting, collecting, and providing evidence to foreign law enforcement authorities. They might also be more inclined to share information, since they have less to lose when a major investor pulls out of their markets. In any case, the data certainly shows that bribes are being paid to officials in economies at all stages of development, not just developing economies, as many might have believed.

. . . .

WHY ARE BRIBES BEING PAID?

In order to better understand and thereby combat the crime of foreign bribery, it is important to know the motive of those who pay bribes to win business. The data allowed an analysis of the nature of the advantage sought by paying the bribe.

Figure 6-13 sets out the categories of advantages that were sought by individuals and companies in the context of the bribes they paid in international business. In the majority of cases, bribes were paid to obtain public procurement contracts (57%), followed by clearance of customs procedures (12%), favourable tax treatment (6%), and other preferential treatment (7%). Bribes were paid to obtain a license or other form of authorisation in 6% of cases, whereas in 4% of cases, bribes were in return for access to confidential information. Bribes were paid for travel visas in 1% of cases. The purpose of the bribe was unspecified in 7% of cases.

. . . .

Figure 6-12. Countries Whose Public Officials Received Bribes in the Context of International Business Transactions

Albania, Algeria, Angola, Argentina, Azerbaijan, Bahrain, Bangladesh, Belgium, Benin, Brazil, Bulgaria, Cameroon, Chad, China, Costa Rica, Croatia, Democratic Republic of Congo, Djibouti, Ecuador, Egypt, Former Yugoslav Republic of Macedonia, France, Georgia, Germany, Ghana, Greece, Haiti, Honduras, Hungary, India, Indonesia, Iran, Iraq, Israel, Italy, Ivory Coast, Jamaica, Kazakhstan, Kenya, Korea, Kyrgyzstan, Latvia, Liberia, Libya, Lithuania, Madagascar, Malawi, Malaysia, Mali, Mauritania, Mexico, Mongolia, Montenegro, Mozambique, Myanmar, Netherlands, Niger, Nigeria, Panama, Philippines, Poland, Portugal, Russia, Romania, Rwanda, Saudi Arabia, Senegal, Serbia, Slovak Republic, Slovenia, Spain, Sweden, Syria, Chinese Taipei, Thailand, Tunisia, Turkey, Turkmenistan, Uganda, United Arab Emirates, United Kingdom, United States, Uzbekistan, Venezuela, Vietnam, Yemen.

Source: OECD analysis of foreign bribery cases concluded between 15/02/1999 and 01/06/2014.

PRELIMINARY CONCLUSIONS

The OECD Foreign Bribery Report provides a clearer picture of the crime of foreign bribery and how it has been committed to date. The scope of the report is limited and the conclusions found here will benefit from further, in-depth analysis as more cases evolve. Based on the current analysis, certain preliminary observations can be made regarding the foreign bribery cases that have been concluded since the entry into force of the OECD Anti-Bribery Convention.

Foreign bribery is a complex crime. It is not surprising, therefore, that the majority of foreign bribery cases are carried out via an agent or intermediary. It would be interesting to analyse in future work whether the use of intermediaries is higher in foreign bribery cases than in cases involving bribery of domestic public officials, along with the proportion by which agency "fees" inflate the already significant cost of bribery for business.

One of the most remarkable outcomes is the fact that in foreign bribery cases concluded to date, corruption is not, as some would believe, the scourge solely of developing economies. With almost one in two concluded foreign bribery cases involving officials from countries with high to very-high HDI rankings, it is clear that this is a crime that takes place in countries at all levels of development.

These preliminary findings indicate that the pressure on governments to step up their enforcement of anti-bribery laws and to ensure that penalties for this crime are effective, proportionate, and dissuasive, is well-placed. There has,

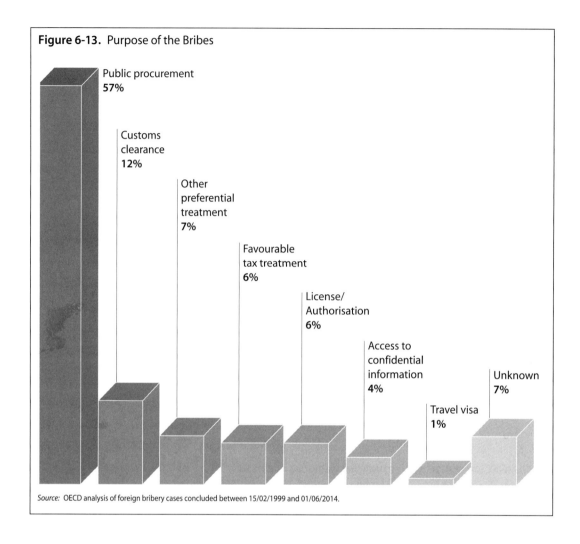

Figure 6-13. Purpose of the Bribes

Public procurement
57%

Customs clearance
12%

Other preferential treatment
7%

Favourable tax treatment
6%

License/ Authorisation
6%

Access to confidential information
4%

Travel visa
1%

Unknown
7%

Source: OECD analysis of foreign bribery cases concluded between 15/02/1999 and 01/06/2014.

indeed, been progress in the fight against foreign bribery, but clearly, much more must be done to be successful in this fight. The following suggestions are designed to help attain that goal:

. . . .

COMPLIANCE PROGRAMMES

In a number of foreign bribery cases concluded to date, the bribes have been paid or authorised by representatives at the highest level of a company, showing the ongoing need for executives to lead by example in implementing their companies' anti-bribery compliance programmes. While SMEs were among the minority of companies sanctioned (4%), companies of all sizes involved in international business should implement measures to combat the risk of foreign bribery.

The overwhelming use of intermediaries in foreign bribery cases demonstrates the need for enhanced and effective due diligence, oversight and application of the company's compliance programme to third parties (whether individuals or companies) in international business transactions. Compliance programmes should focus specifically on due diligence with respect to agents and on verifying the rationale and beneficial ownership of other companies involved in the transaction.

Noting that bribes have been paid to officials from countries at various stages of development, bribery risk assessments should focus instead on the context of the transaction, for example, whether it involves partnering with a public company (in 27% of cases bribes were paid to SOE officials), public procurement processes (the context of the bribery in 57% of cases), or the use of intermediaries (which occurred in 71% of cases).

There is also scope for greater incentivising preventive anti-bribery compliance programmes, including by recognising the existence and effectiveness of such programmes in mitigation of sanctions in foreign bribery cases.

Anti-bribery risk assessments and compliance are equally critical on the demand side of a foreign bribery transaction. Governments should therefore ensure that public officials that have regular contact with business and the private sector are properly trained and informed of the risks and consequences of bribery.

PUBLIC PROCUREMENT

The high number (57%) of cases in which bribes were paid in the context of public procurement reinforces the need for greater integrity in public procurement processes. Raising the overall awareness of procurement officials though tailored trainings and providing them with tools to prevent, to detect and to address corporate crimes such as corruption, collusion and money laundering should be a government priority.

In the same vein, the fact that only 2 out of 427 cases resulted in debarment demonstrates that countries need to do more to ensure that those who are sanctioned for having bribed foreign public officials are suspended from participation in national public procurement contracting.

NEXT STEPS

While this report constitutes a first attempt to measure transnational corruption, there is scope for much more to be done, both in terms of further, in-depth analysis and additional, horizontal studies. The following is a list of ideas for future work to build on the findings of this first OECD Foreign Bribery Report and to reinforce efforts to better understand and combat this crime.

- The OECD Foreign Bribery Report could be a regular publication, updated annually depending on whether there are sufficient numbers of new foreign bribery cases to generate new data or trends.

- The data behind the OECD Foreign Bribery Report could be made public in an online database to be maintained by the OECD.
- Further analysis could focus on differences in sanctions between cases concluded through criminal trials and those that are settled. It could also compare prison sentences imposed on individual defendants to evaluate the standard of "effective, proportionate and dissuasive" sanctions when it comes to deprivation of liberty.
- Future work could focus on the role of SOEs or public companies as both bribe givers and bribe takers. Areas of focus could include how many of the companies sanctioned were wholly or partially state-owned, along with the integrity of corporate governance practices in SOEs, namely the implementation and supervision of decision-making processes and measures for managing conflicts of interest in SOE procurement procedures. This analysis would feed into ongoing OECD work in the field of corporate governance of SOEs.
- While the OECD Foreign Bribery Report has focused on the supply-side of bribery of foreign public officials, future work could analyse the proportion of foreign bribery cases in which the public official actively solicited the bribes and examine whether the public officials who solicited or received the bribes were brought to justice.
- To build on OECD work in the field of bribery and official export credits and bribery and official development assistance, future analysis could focus on cases involving bribery in the context of projects financed by these two categories of public funds. This could be complemented by an analysis of the cases involving projects funded by multilateral development banks.
- Further analysis could contribute to broader OECD work in the field of compliance and government policies aimed at preventing and tackling corporate crimes. Cases in which companies have been sanctioned for various corporate offences, such as bribery, money laundering, anti-trust, tax offences, environmental offences, fraud and UN sanctions violations could be compared and contrasted.

Hypothetical: Assessing and Mitigating a Specific Risk

Ruby, Inc. ("Ruby") is a multinational enterprise engaged in the manufacture and sale of telecommunications equipment, with its principal place of business in the United States and over 100,000 employees around the world. Seventy percent (70%) of Ruby's international sales are to foreign governments.

As part of a recent review of its compliance program, Ruby's compliance staff selected certain high-risk markets for special scrutiny, including Russia, where Ruby operates through a wholly-owned subsidiary, Ruby Russia. The compliance staff has begun its review by conducting a risk assessment of Ruby Russia's business unit in charge of bidding for, and overseeing performance of, government contracts. The business unit has one employee who oversees preparation and submission of bids, and supervises the execution of contracts. He receives a base salary of $35,000 and an annual bonus based on the total value of contracts won.

Figure 6-14 is a flowchart showing the life cycle of a typical contract handled by the business unit. The process begins with the business unit's receipt of information regarding a project. The bidding process usually involves closed bids submitted to the Ministry of Telecommunications and Mass Media. Following submission of a bid, there is a question and answer process during which the business unit and the government discuss details of the bid. Although bid price is a major consideration in the Ministry's evaluation of bids, Ministry officials have discretion to award contracts based on other undefined criteria. After the government awards the contract, the project is executed under the business unit's supervision.

Ruby Russia has performed contracts with the Russian government ranging in value from $100 million to $300 million. It is preparing bids in relation to three contracts, which if won, would make Russia Ruby's biggest area of operations outside the United States.

Prepare a risk register for the corruption risk posed by Ruby Russia's government procurement department, including the controls that Ruby should employ to mitigate the risk.

Figure 6-14. Flowchart of the Life Cycle of a Typical Contract Handled by Ruby Russia's Business Unit

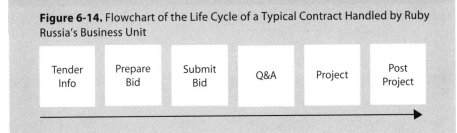

V. Training and Continuing Advice

Training "covers company policies and procedures, instruction on applicable laws, practical advice to address real-life scenarios, and case studies."[75] Training

---

75. FCPA Guide, *supra* note 3, at 59.

should reinforce information and instructions outlined in the code of conduct. Like other aspects of the compliance program, training must be specifically tailored to the corruption risks faced by each area of operations.[76] Thus, employees and agents exposed to the greatest risk of corruption should receive targeted training designed to prepare them to deal with specific scenarios and issues.

> [C]ompanies may want to consider providing different types of training to their sales personnel and accounting personnel with hypotheticals or sample situations that are similar to the situations they might encounter. In addition . . . a company should develop appropriate measures . . . to provide guidance and advice on complying with the company's ethics and compliance program, including when such advice is needed urgently.[77]

It is important to employ the most effective means of delivering the training. For larger companies, the FCPA Guide proposes a "mix of web-based and in-person training conducted at varying intervals."[78] The FCPA Guide also mandates an all-encompassing scope for the training program, covering "all directors, officers, relevant employees, and, where appropriate, [third-party] agents and business partners."[79]

In addition to covering company policies and procedures, training should prepare employees to recognize and report corruption red flags, particularly when dealing with foreign officials, distributors, consultants, and entities owned or controlled by foreign governments. Role-play exercises involving real-life scenarios, including examples drawn from the company's operations and experiences, can be especially helpful in this respect.

Employee attendance at training sessions (both online and in person) should be required, and assessments should be given to verify that the training is effective in accomplishing its objectives. Training should be continuously updated to reflect changes in company policies, controls, and procedures, as well as changes in the code of conduct.

Notes and Questions: Rules-Based vs. Values-Based Approach to Training

Brian Martin, Executive Vice President, General Counsel and Corporate Secretary at KLA-Tencor Corporation, believes that "[e]thical decision-making is not synonymous with compliance with laws—it is bigger,"[80] and, that "[t]oo often, codes of conduct are heavy on formalistic and complex policy and legal

---

76. *See id.*
77. *Id.*
78. *Id.*
79. *Id.*
80. Brian Martin, *Teaching Ethics with Real-Life Scenarios*, Law.com (Mar. 1, 2011), https://www.law.com/almID/4dcafb8e160ba0ad570021a1/?t=department-operations.

compliance statements, [and] light on values and ethics."[81] Martin set out to fill the gap between policy and real life, through the company's values. He conducted an in-person daylong training called "You Make the Call."[82] Attendees were given real-life scenarios that "were designed so that references to company policies would not resolve the issue; instead, corporate and personal ethics were called upon to address the scenarios."[83] Martin noted that this "compelled the trainees to reference corporate and personal values, and it reinforced the supremacy of 'doing the right thing,'" concluding that "[t]he ethics training equipped the business teams with ethical decision-making paradigms that are more durable than any policy could be."[84]

Implicit in Martin's values-based approach is the idea that people, if properly selected and trained, are capable of doing the right thing in different situations without the need for detailed instructions.[85] In contrast, a rules-based approach tries to predict all the different scenarios that an employee may face and set detailed rules for what the employee must do in each situation.

Proponents of a values-based approach argue that it is impossible to formulate enough rules to address every situation and that employees can be trusted to do the right thing. Proponents of a rule-based approach, on the other hand, argue that employees should be taught exactly what is against the rules and when they will be punished.[86] TRACE president, Alexandra Wrage, believes that neither approach will work alone.[87]

According to Wrage, employees fall into four categories: idealists, the ethical majority, box-checkers, and criminals—each requiring a different training approach.[88] Idealist employees are committed to the greater community and good corporate citizenship and are most responsive to values-based training.[89] The most effective method of training them is to discuss the negative impact of corruption on communities.[90] Employees who belong to the ethical majority are not as concerned with social responsibility, but they certainly care about their company's reputation.[91] "[T]hese employees will understand the New York Times test: Would you be content to read about this conduct on the front page of the New York Times tomorrow?"[92] Box-checkers want to understand the rules so that they can get as close to the line as possible without crossing it.[93] They view good corporate citizenship and ethics as a waste of money and hindrance

---

81. *Id.*
82. *Id.*
83. *Id.*
84. *Id.*
85. *See id.*
86. Alexandra Wrage, *Training: What Works?*, TRACE: TRACE TRENDS, A COMPLIANCE CONVERSATION (Apr. 09, 2009), https://www.traceinternational.org/blog/711/Training_What_Works.
87. *See id.*
88. *See id.*
89. *See id.*
90. *See id.*
91. *See id.*
92. *Id.*
93. *See id.*

to operations.[94] This group responds best to a rules-based approach, particularly reminders of how transgressions will be punished.[95] Finally, there are some criminals inside every company—those who violate the law for their personal benefit.[96] Wrage believes that a values-based approach for this group would be "disastrous."[97] "These employees need to leave training asking themselves whether they look good in orange."[98]

Hypothetical: Compliance Training Program

Bentley, Inc. is a U.S.-based corporation that engages in the manufacture and sale of medical devices around the world. It has a wholly owned subsidiary in China whose annual turnover exceeds $100 million. In 2016, Chinese authorities discovered that several Bentley sales agents in its Chinese subsidiary had paid bribes to local doctors, who were employed by the Chinese government. Two doctors who received bribes from Bentley sales agents were subsequently arrested and jailed, leading to extensive negative coverage of the incident in the Chinese and U.S. media.

Following an internal investigation, Bentley learned that as a result of the corrupt payments, doctors in several rural areas had purchased Bentley medical devices in lieu of other equipment and medications necessary for their patients' care. Consequently, numerous patients were unable to receive adequate treatment.

Bentley promptly reported the corrupt payments to the DOJ and entered into a DPA, paying $10 million in penalties and agreeing to strengthen the controls in the Chinese subsidiary.

You have been retained by Bentley to assist in designing a targeted training program for its sales agents in China aimed at mitigating the risk of corrupt payments in the future. You have determined that Bentley's Chinese training program should include a mix of various approaches to ensure its effectiveness in training different types of employees: idealists, ethical majority, box-checkers, and criminals.

Describe the main features of the training program that you will design for Bentley.

---

94. *See id.*
95. *See id.*
96. *See id.*
97. *Id.*
98. *Id.*

VI. Incentives and Disciplinary Measures

People engage in corruption for personal gain. By raising the cost of corrupt behavior and incentivizing ethical conduct, a company can alter a bribe payor's cost-benefit calculus. This can be accomplished through an appropriate system of punishments and rewards. FSGO § 8B2.1(b)(6) requires:

- *Incentives (rewards)* — to perform in accordance with the compliance and ethics program; and,
- *Disciplinary measures (penalties)* — for engaging in misconduct or failing to detect or report it.[99]

The FCPA Guide and the FSGO place incentives before deterrents, stressing the power of rewards in shaping individual and group behavior.[101] That is because the reward system in an organization is an important gauge of a company's priorities and values. Promotions, for example, show "[w]ho are the heroes and who are the goats."[102]

> [M]ake integrity, ethics and compliance part of the promotion, compensation and evaluation processes as well. For at the end of the day, the most effective way to communicate that "doing the right thing" is a priority, is to reward it. Conversely, if employees are led to believe that, when it comes to compensation and career advancement, all that counts is short-term profitability, and that cutting ethical corners is an acceptable way of getting there, they'll perform to that measure.
>
> —*Director Stephen M. Cutler, SEC*[100]

"Culture-shaping managers . . . seek ways to provide frequent and visible praise or other recognition for even modest contributions to the service of important values." Those who are recognized can become the heroes and part of the stories of the company's history.[103]

The FCPA Guide provides several examples of ways companies can promote desired conduct by rewarding employees who embrace compliance goals:

- Incorporate desired conduct into evaluations and promotion criteria
- Recognize efforts to improve and foster the compliance program
- Reward those exhibiting leadership in ethics and compliance
- Include a prominent compliance metric in calculations of managers' bonuses

---

99. U.S. Sentencing Guidelines Manual § 8B2.1(b)(6) (U.S. Sentencing Comm'n 2016).

100. Stephen M. Cutler, Dir., Div. of Enf't, Sec. and Exch. Comm'n, Speech at the Second Annual General Counsel Roundtable: Tone at the Top: Getting It Right (Dec. 3, 2004), https://www.sec.gov/news/speech/spch120304smc.htm.

101. *See* FCPA Guide, *supra* note 3, at 59–60; U.S. Sentencing Guidelines Manual § 8B2.1(b)(6) (U.S. Sentencing Comm'n 2016).

102. Joseph E. Murphy, Soc'y of Corp. Compliance and Ethics, Using Incentives in Your Compliance and Ethics Program 32 (2011), https://www.hcca-info.org/Portals/0/PDFs/Resources/library/814_0_IncentivesCEProgram-Murphy.pdf.

103. *Id.* at 28 (footnote omitted) (quoting Terrence E. Deal & Allan A. Kennedy, Corporate Cultures: The Rites and Rituals of Corporate Life 169 (Addison-Wesley 1982)).

> If compliance and ethics really does matter, then service in that area should be considered a positive factor in selecting people for promotion. A stint in the compliance and ethics program would become a ticket that needs to be punched for those who want to get ahead in the company.
>
> —*Joe Murphy, Society of Corporate Compliance and Ethics*[105]

- Highlight the contributions of compliance professionals and internal audit staff
- Creating advancement opportunities for the compliance team[104]

Nevertheless, the core purpose of a compliance program is to self-police, and that means enforcing the policies, codes, and procedures of the company to deter violations. Hence the second prong of this Hallmark relates to disciplinary measures. The DOJ and SEC will consider three factors in evaluating the adequacy of a company's disciplinary measures:

- Whether . . . a company has appropriate and clear disciplinary procedures,
- Whether those procedures are applied reliably and promptly, and
- Whether they are commensurate with the violation.[106]

A company can underscore its serious commitment to compliance by putting in place strong disciplinary measures and making sure that no one—including senior management—is out of reach. Discipline for a violation of company policy or code of conduct can take different forms, including "counseling training, verbal warnings, written reprimands, job reassignment, suspension with pay, suspension without pay, and termination."[107] Termination is appropriate if the employee commits a criminal violation, subjects the company to significant civil liability, causes injury or risk of harm to others, or repeatedly violates company rules.[108] Lesser punishment can be imposed for lesser infractions, such as failure to complete compliance training or improper documentation of expenses.[109]

Additional Reading Materials

Banks, Theodore, and Gretchen Winter. *Employee Discipline and Compliance*, THE COMPLETE COMPLIANCE AND ETHICS MANUAL, SOCIETY OF CORPORATE COMPLIANCE AND ETHICS, 3.311–317 (2016).

Murphy, Joseph E., Soc'y of Corp. Compliance and Ethics. USING INCENTIVES IN YOUR COMPLIANCE AND ETHICS PROGRAM 33 (2011), http://www.hcca-info.org/Portals/0/PDFs/Resources/library/814_0_IncentivesCEProgram-Murphy.pdf.

---

104. FCPA GUIDE, *supra* note 3, at 59–60. For further guidance on the role of incentives in promoting compliance, *see also* MURPHY, *supra* note 102, at 28–33.

105. MURPHY, *supra* note 102, at 33.

106. FCPA GUIDE, *supra* note 3, at 59.

107. Theodore Banks and Gretchen Winter, *Employee Discipline and Compliance*, THE COMPLETE COMPLIANCE AND ETHICS MANUAL, SOCIETY OF CORPORATE COMPLIANCE AND ETHICS, 3.311–317 (2016), at 3.314.

108. *See id.*

109. *See id.*

Notes and Questions: Game Theory

This Hallmark raises a broader question of why people engage in fraud or corruption. In a 2009 *New Yorker* article titled "Rational Irrationality," John Cassidy discussed "behavior that, on the individual level, is perfectly reasonable but that, when aggregated in the marketplace, produces calamity."[110] Using game theory, Cassidy explained how individual market participants continued to extend credit—even though they were aware of the collective risk—because other market participants were doing so and benefiting from their behavior. "Attempts to act responsibly and achieve a cooperative solution cannot be sustained, because they leave you vulnerable to exploitation by others."[111]

In a market where corruption is pervasive, "rational irrationality" dictates that participants will pay bribes for fear of being left at a competitive disadvantage, despite knowing their behavior is detrimental to the community. While this may make sense for each participant, corruption increases costs and distorts markets.[112] It follows that enhanced punishment, combined with a greater likelihood of getting caught, would reduce the likelihood of misconduct.[113]

What are the lessons of "rational irrationality" for compliance officers?

VII. Third-Party Due Diligence and Payments

The FCPA Guide notes that "third parties, including agents, consultants, and distributors, are commonly used to conceal the payment of bribes to foreign officials in international business transactions."[114] In light of this fact, it is not surprising that over ninety percent of FCPA enforcement actions involve corrupt payments by third parties.[115] The DOJ and SEC pay particular attention to a company's third-party due diligence procedures when evaluating the effectiveness of its compliance program.[116] The FCPA Guide notes:

> Many companies doing business in a foreign country retain a local individual or company to help them conduct business. Although these foreign agents may provide entirely legitimate advice regarding local customs and procedures and

---

110. John Cassidy, *Rational Irrationality*, New Yorker (Oct. 5, 2009), http://www.newyorker.com/magazine/2009/10/05/rational-irrationality; *see also* John MacRae, *Underdevelopment and the Economics of Corruption: A Game Theory Approach*, 10 World Dev. 677 (1982), http://projects.iq.harvard.edu/gov2126/files/macrae_1982.pdf; Fumiko Nagano, *Corruption, Game Theory, and Rational Irrationality*, World Bank: Blogs (Nov. 16, 2009), http://blogs.worldbank.org/publicsphere/corruption-game-theory-and-rational-irrationality.

111. Cassidy, *supra* note 110.

112. *See* MacRae, *supra* note 110, at 684–86; *see generally* Sun Lianju & Peng Luyan, *Game Theory Analysis of the Bribery Behavior*, 2 Int'l J. Bus. & Soc. Sci. 104 (2011), http://ijbssnet.com/journals/Vol._2_No._8;_May_2011/13.pdf.

113. *See* Lianju & Luyan, *supra* note 112, at 107.

114. FCPA Guide, *supra* note 3, at 59.

115. O'Melveny & Myers LLP, Foreign Corrupt Practices Act: An O'Melveny Handbook 65 (7th ed. 2013).

116. *See* FCPA Guide, *supra* note 3, at 60.

may help facilitate business transactions, companies should be aware of the risks involved in engaging third-party agents or intermediaries. The fact that a bribe is paid by a third party does not eliminate the potential for criminal or civil FCPA liability.[117]

The *respondeat superior* doctrine renders an issuer or domestic concern vicariously liable for the conduct of a third party that is owned or controlled by it—regardless of knowledge or participation. FCPA liability can be established, even where a third party does not qualify as an "agent," if an issuer or domestic concern ignores red flags signaling a high risk of corruption.

Third-party due diligence is a four-step process that helps companies to "understand the risks each third party represents and to apply a heightened standard of care or even perhaps terminate relationships with intermediaries that pose the highest risk."[118] A typical program includes successive stages: (1) defining the program's scope, (2) assessing risk, (3) conducting due diligence, and (4) approving and monitoring the program.[119]

A. Defining the Scope of the Process

At the outset, an enterprise faces the critical decision regarding where to set the threshold for including a third party in the due diligence process. Since some third parties pose little or no risk of corruption, their inclusion would divert limited compliance resources. Therefore, setting the scope of the due diligence process requires the use of judgment regarding which third-party relationships pose a sufficiently high risk as to justify the added cost and operational burden of being included in the process.[120]

The first step in determining scope of the process is to understand and categorize the universe of third-party relationships in both sales and supply channels.[121] The following is a nonexhaustive list of relationships that may qualify:

- Joint venture partners
- Agents
- Advisors (legal, financial, tax)
- Consultants
- Contractors and subcontractors
- Suppliers
- Distributors

---

117. *Id.* at 21–22.
118. Protiviti, A Strong Compliance Culture Starts with Managing Third-Party Corruption 1 (2014), https://www.protiviti.com/sites/default/files/united_states/strong-compliance-culture-starts-with-managing-third-party-corruption-protiviti.pdf.
119. *See* World Econ. Forum [WEF], *Good Practice Guidelines on Conducting Third-Party Due Diligence*, at 7-15 (2013), http://www3.weforum.org/docs/WEF_PACI_ConductingThirdPartyDueDiligence_Guidelines_2013.pdf [hereinafter WEF *Guidelines*].
120. *See* Protiviti, *supra* note 118, at 8.
121. *See* WEF *Guidelines*, *supra* note 119, at 8.

- Customers
- Service providers.[122]

A company can narrow the scope by asking the following basic questions designed to quickly eliminate third parties that require no due diligence:

- Is the third party located in a high-risk industry or geographic location?
- Does the third party potentially qualify as an agent of the company?
- Is the third party likely to have contact with foreign government officials?[123]

If the answer to all three questions is negative, the third party can be presumed not to pose a sufficiently high risk of corruption and therefore can be eliminated from the due diligence process.

B. Assessing Risk

For each third party determined to be "in scope," risk assessment should be performed to determine the appropriate level of due diligence; that is, the amount of resources that should be expended to ensure that the third party will not violate the FCPA. This is accomplished by examining the number and seriousness of risk factors that indicate a heightened risk of corruption, such as the following.

> As organizations consider which third parties need to go through due diligence, they may also need to determine how far down the supply chain their due diligence efforts should go. Indeed, an organization's third party may itself use another third party to perform their contract, thereby pushing corruption risks further down the supply chain. Therefore, organizations should consider the potential business and compliance risks which may be found in their third parties' supply chains when deciding whether to extend their due diligence efforts to the suppliers of their suppliers.
>
> —*WEF: Partnering Against Corruption Initiative*[124]

1. Agency

Since the conduct of an agent is directly imputed to the principal, a third party who qualifies as an agent should receive heightened scrutiny. According to the FCPA Guide, "[t]he fundamental characteristic of agency is control," which is defined as the power to direct "the management and policies of a person, whether through the ownership of voting securities, by contract, *or otherwise*."[125] Therefore, the inquiry regarding a third party's status as agent should focus on whether the company has the *power* to direct the management and policies of the third party, regardless of whether that power is exercised.

2. Accounting and Internal Control Practices

If a third party does not maintain accurate books and records, it is impossible to fully understand its activities, including whether it engages in bribery. Moreover,

---

122. *See id.* Many other types of relationships are typically included in the process, including: accounting firms; charitable organizations; channel partners; customs brokers; freight forwarders; contractors; private investigators; and lobbyists, among others. *Id.; see also* Protiviti, *supra* note 118, at 6.

123. *See* WEF *Guidelines, supra* note 119, at 8.

124. *Id.*

125. FCPA Guide, *supra* note 3, at 27; 17 C.F.R. § 230.405 (2017) (emphasis added).

the DOJ and SEC take the position that issuers are obligated to make a good faith effort to ensure that third parties comply with the FCPA accounting provisions, even where an agency relationship does not exist. Hence, a third party's accounting and internal control practices have a significant bearing on the level of risk it poses.

3. Geography

The corruption risk posed by a third party is higher if it is located in a jurisdiction with a high incidence of corruption or a jurisdiction with bank secrecy laws that facilitate flows of illicit funds.[126]

4. Industry/Sectoral Risk

Highly regulated industries and those with a high level of government interaction pose a higher risk of corruption.[127] Beyond looking at an industry in general, companies should examine how that industry is regulated and how it operates in the particular country where the third party is located. Transparency International's *Gateway: Mapping the Corruption Assessment Landscape*,[128] is a tool for in-depth analysis of sectoral risk. Other potential sources for analyzing sectoral risk include competitors and subject matter experts.[129]

5. Products

Certain products are primarily used by governments. If a third party handles such products on behalf of a company, the third party will have greater interaction with government officials and pose a higher risk of corruption.

6. History of Prior Misconduct

If a third party has previously committed violations of anti-bribery laws or appears on a U.S. government watchlist as a result of prior misconduct, it poses a higher corruption risk.[130]

7. Identity of the Third Party, Its Owners, and Key Employees

The DOJ and SEC demand that a company "understand the qualifications and associations of its third-party partners, including its business reputation, and relationship, if any, with foreign officials."[131] Therefore, the risk is elevated if the initial information about a third party indicates that it (1) does not have a good reputation for integrity; (2) is owned or managed by, or closely associated with,

---

126. SEE WEF GUIDELINES, *supra* note 119, at 9.
127. *See, e.g.,* BRIBERY RISK GUIDE, *supra* note 30, at 16.
128. *Anti-Corruption Knowledge Hub*, TRANSPARENCY INT'L (2018), http://gateway.transparency.org/files/uploads/GATEway_report_for_web.pdf.
129. *See, e.g.,* BRIBERY RISK GUIDE, *supra* note 30, at 14.
130. *See, e.g.,* WEF *Guidelines, supra* note 119, at 9.
131. FCPA GUIDE, *supra* note 3, at 60.

a government official; or (3) is unqualified to perform the tasks for which it is being retained.

8. Nature of the Third Party's Involvement and Compensation

As the DOJ and SEC observe:

> [C]ompanies should have an understanding of the business rationale for including the third party in the transaction. Among other things, the company should understand the role of and need for the third party and ensure that the contract terms specifically describe the services to be performed. Additional considerations include payment terms and how those payment terms compare to typical terms in that industry and country, as well as the timing of the third party's introduction to the business. Moreover, companies may want to confirm and document that the third party is actually performing the work for which it is being paid and that its compensation is commensurate with the work being provided.[132]

9. Risk Ratings

For each of the above risk factors, a risk rating of low, medium, or high should be assigned to a third party.[133] The results should then be reviewed together, and, depending on the number and seriousness of risk factors present, the third party's overall risk (high, medium, or low) should be assessed. This classification will dictate the level of due diligence applied to the third party.

C. Conducting Due Diligence

While the DOJ and SEC have provided no guidance specifying the exact process for conducting due diligence, the FCPA Guide and enforcement actions to date suggest the following process:

1) Obtain relevant information from the third party and the person or business unit within the company responsible for the relationship.
2) Verify the information obtained and take action on red flags.[134]

1. Obtain Relevant Information from the Third Party

Questionnaires are typically used to obtain relevant information from a third party. While each company must design its own third-party questionnaire tailored to its particular activities, questionnaires commonly elicit the categories of information shown in Table 6-3.

---

132. *Id.*
133. *See* WEF *Guidelines, supra* note 119, at 9.
134. *See* WEF *Guidelines, supra* note 119, at 11; O'MELVENY & MYERS LLP, *supra* note 115, at 81.

Table 6-3. Categories of Information Typically Included in Third-Party Questionnaires

INFORMATION CATEGORY	COMMON RED FLAGS
Organization and Associations	
Contact information for all owners, executives, members of the board of directors and key managers	
Whether the third party is controlled by, or employs, one or more government officials or their relatives	
Whether "the third party is related to or closely associated with [a] foreign official"[135]	
The financial status of the third party	• Current or previous bankruptcy, or financial distress • Outstanding loans from or to government officials
The location of the third party's banking institution	• Offshore bank account • Bank account in a third country
The structure of the third party, both in terms of ownership and, if possible, reporting responsibilities/chain of command	• "[T]he third party is merely a shell company incorporated in an offshore jurisdiction."[136] • Absence of structure or accountability • Third party is state owned or controlled
"Downstream" relationships of the third party	• Third party's agents and/or collaborators pose a high risk of corruption
Background and Reputation	
Length of time the third party has been in business	• Third party came into existence shortly before its retention by the company
Prior history of violations of the FCPA or other U.S. or local law	
History of unethical or inappropriate conduct	• Third party previously engaged in fraudulent or misleading business practices, maintained an unsafe workplace, committed environmentally unsafe practices or other unethical conduct • Pattern of lawsuits against the third party by employees, customers, consumers and/or NGOs

---

135. FCPA GUIDE, *supra note 3, at* 22.
136. FCPA Guide, *supra note 3, at* 23.

INFORMATION CATEGORY	COMMON RED FLAGS
Detailed history of past dealings between the company and the third party or any of its directors, executives, or key managers	• Third party has a history of delinquent payments or other questionable conduct
Obtain references from the third party's bank, customers, and any multinational companies with whom the third party previously worked	
Accounting and Internal Control Practices	
Whether the third party maintains accurate books and records, and adequate internal controls	• Third party unable to produce an audited financial statement[137]
Whether the third party has an effective anticorruption compliance program	• Third party lacks an anticorruption policy or code of conduct
Whether the third party has a sophisticated ethics program	
Reasons for Involvement	
Whether there is a clear explanation of and justification for the third party's relationship with the company	• "[T]he third party became part of the transaction at the express request or insistence of the foreign official."[138] • "[T]hird-party 'consulting agreements' that include only vaguely described services." • The third party's services are unnecessary[139]
Documentation and explanation of the hiring process for the third party, including details of all parties originally considered and the analysis/reasons used in making the final selection	• The third party was retained without consideration of alternatives
Qualifications	
Does the third party possess the necessary expertise, experience, and qualification (including license or certificate when necessary) to perform the work for which it has been hired?	• "[T]he third-party consultant is in a different line of business than that for which it has been engaged."[140]

---

137. An audited financial statement is prepared according to generally accepted accounting principles ("GAAP") and audited by a certified accountant. It typically includes income statements, balance sheets, earnings statements, and cash flows.

138. FCPA Guide, *supra note 3, at 23.*

139. *Id.*

140. *Id.*

INFORMATION CATEGORY	COMMON RED FLAGS
Payment	
Whether payments being made to the third party are reasonable relative to what is being provided	• "[E]xcessive commissions to third-party agents or consultants." • "[U]nreasonably large discounts to third-party distributors."
Detailed documentation that connects each payment made to an understandable good purchased or service provided	• "[T]hird-party 'consulting agreements' that include only vaguely described services." [141]
Means of payment to the third party	• Payments to an individual or entity other than the third party • Third party insists on cash payment • Payments to an offshore bank account[142]

2. Verification of Data and Resolution of Red Flags

Information collected from the third party and the responsible business unit should next be verified.[143] In addition, information gaps, inconsistencies, and any red flags revealed by the data should be resolved. Verification of data and resolution of red flags can be accomplished through the use of outside sources, follow-up interviews, and follow-up questionnaires. Below are some of the outside sources of information that companies can use for this purpose.

a. Internet and Database Searches

Depending on the level of risk, the names of the third party's owners, key employees, and any close associates should be screened using Internet search engines and various databases, including:

- U.S. government watch lists[144]
- Databases of "politically exposed persons"[145]

---

141. *Id.* at 22.

142. *See id.* at 22–23.

143. *See* WEF *Guidelines, supra* note 119, at 11–12.

144. *See* United States Government Consolidated Screening List, https://www.export.gov/article?id= Consolidated-Screening-List.

145. From the Federal Financial Institutions Examination Council, Bank Secrecy Act/Anti-Money Laundering InfoBase:

The term "politically exposed person" ("PEP") generally includes a current or former senior foreign political figure, their immediate family, and their close associates. Interagency guidance issued in January 2001 offers banks resources that can help them to determine whether an individual is a PEP. More specifically:

- A "senior foreign political figure" is a senior official in the executive, legislative, administrative, military or judicial branches of a foreign government (whether elected or not), a senior official of a major foreign political party, or a senior executive of a foreign government-owned corporation.

- Media searches
- Local company registers
- Litigation records

b. Boots on the Ground

For medium- or high-risk third parties, it may be necessary to perform enhanced due diligence in the form of one or more of the following:

- Manual public records searches to (1) verify the third party's registration and the identities of its owners and key officers; and (2) uncover any lawsuits or criminal proceedings against the third party
- Local media searches to find negative press coverage about the third party
- Site visits to ensure that the third party exists and has the necessary staff and qualifications
- Interviews of the third party's employees
- Interviews of other local persons with knowledge of the third party's activities.[146]

c. Audits

It may be appropriate to conduct an audit of the third party in the same way as if the third party was the target of an acquisition, particularly if it qualifies as an agent of the company.

D. Approving and Monitoring the Program

After all the relevant data has been collected, a decision must be made to either approve or reject the third party. This question turns on whether all of the red flags that surfaced during the due diligence process have been resolved and whether the risk posed by the third party after the employment of mitigating controls falls within the company's risk tolerance. If certain red flags have not been resolved or if the residual risk is higher than the company's risk tolerance,

---

In addition, a senior foreign political figure includes any corporation, business, or other entity that has been formed by, or for the benefit of, a senior foreign political figure.

- The "immediate family" of a senior foreign political figure typically includes the figure's parents, siblings, spouse, children, and in-laws.
- A "close associate" of a senior foreign political figure is a person who is widely and publicly known to maintain an unusually close relationship with the senior foreign political figure, and includes a person who is in a position to conduct substantial domestic and international financial transactions on behalf of the senior foreign political figure.

The definition of senior official or executive must remain sufficiently flexible to capture the range of individuals who, by virtue of their office or position, potentially pose a risk that their funds may be the proceeds of foreign corruption.

Fed. Fin. Insts. Examination Council, Bank Secrecy Act/Anti-Money Laundering Examination Manual 290-91 (2014) (footnotes omitted), https://www.ffiec.gov/bsa_aml_infobase/documents/BSA_AML_Man_2014_v2.pdf.

146. *See, e.g.*, WEF *Guidelines*, *supra* note 119, at 12–13.

the decision whether to approve a third party will be escalated to a person with sufficient authority. The decision should be made by the compliance function so that the decision maker does not have an interest in the relationship.

After a third party has been approved, it is important to memorialize the relationship in a formal contract that includes anticorruption provisions designed to mitigate corruption risk.[147] Below are examples of such provisions:

- Describe the third party's work clearly and in sufficient detail.
- Require adherence to company code of conduct and policies, especially regarding bribery and facilitation payments.
- If applicable, include a "no agency" clause, stating that the third party is not the company's agent and is not authorized to act on behalf of the company.
- Allow for immediate termination without penalty in the event of a violation.
- Require compliance certifications and attendance of compliance training as and when required by the company.
- Require compliance with all laws with specific reference to anti-bribery laws.
- Provide for indemnity in the event of a breach by the third party.
- Prohibit the third party from assigning its obligations to other third parties.
- Set forth detailed procedures for payments to the third party.
- Oblige the third party to maintain accurate and transparent records.
- Provide for a right of audit.[148]

Finally, as the FCPA Guide cautions, it is imperative that companies be subject to continual scrutiny after the initial due diligence process. The FCPA Guide recommends that a company should:

> [U]ndertake some form of ongoing monitoring of third-party relationships. Where appropriate, this may include updating due diligence periodically, exercising audit rights, providing periodic training, and requesting annual compliance certifications by the third party.[149]

A Resource Guide to the U.S. Foreign Corrupt Practices Act

Criminal Division of the U.S. Department of Justice and the Enforcement Division of the U.S. Securities and Exchange Commission[150]

Compliance Program Case Study

Recent DOJ and SEC actions relating to a financial institution's real estate transactions with a government agency in China illustrate the benefits of implementing and enforcing a comprehensive risk-based compliance program. The

---

147. *See* FCPA GUIDE, *supra* note 3, at 60–61.
148. *See, generally,* ANJA MANUEL, COMPREHENSIVE FCPA GUIDE TO DUE DILIGENCE FOR THIRD PARTIES (2011); WEF *Guidelines, supra* note 119, at 14.
149. FCPA GUIDE, *supra* note 3, at 60 (footnote omitted).
150. *Id.* at 61.

case involved a joint venture real estate investment in the Luwan District of Shanghai, China, between a U.S.-based financial institution and a state-owned entity that functioned as the District's real estate arm. The government entity conducted the transactions through two special purpose vehicles ("SPVs"), with the second SPV purchasing a 12% stake in a real estate project.

The financial institution, through a robust compliance program, frequently trained its employees, imposed a comprehensive payment-approval process designed to prevent bribery, and staffed a compliance department with a direct reporting line to the board of directors. As appropriate given the industry, market, and size and structure of the transactions, the financial institution (1) provided extensive FCPA training to the senior executive responsible for the transactions and (2) conducted extensive due diligence on the transactions, the local government entity, and the SPVs. Due diligence on the entity included reviewing Chinese government records; speaking with sources familiar with the Shanghai real estate market; checking the government entity's payment records and credit references; conducting an on-site visit and placing a pretextual telephone call to the entity's offices; searching media sources; and conducting background checks on the entity's principals. The financial institution vetted the SPVs by obtaining a letter with designated bank account information from a Chinese official associated with the government entity (the "Chinese Official"); using an international law firm to request and review 50 documents from the SPVs' Canadian attorney; interviewing the attorney; and interviewing the SPVs' management.

Notwithstanding the financial institution's robust compliance program and good faith enforcement of it, the company failed to learn that the Chinese Official personally owned nearly 50% of the second SPV (and therefore a nearly 6% stake in the joint venture) and that the SPV was used as a vehicle for corrupt payments. This failure was due, in large part, to misrepresentations by the Chinese Official, the financial institution's executive in charge of the project, and the SPV's attorney that the SPV was 100% owned and controlled by the government entity. [The] DOJ and SEC declined to take enforcement action against the financial institution, and its executive pleaded guilty to conspiracy to violate the FCPA's internal control provisions and also settled with SEC.

Case Story: Integrity Due Diligence[151]

Michael Price, Statoil[152]

Integrity Due Diligence is the process of mitigating risk arising from association with a third party who may be or may have been engaged in unethical or illegal practices. The risk may exist as a direct liability incurred by the company through its

---

151. Michael Price, *Case Story: Integrity Due Diligence, in* Business Against Corruption: Case Stories and Examples 119, 119-26 (Brigit Errath ed., 2006), https://www.unglobalcompact.org/docs/issues_doc/7.7/BACbookFINAL.pdf.

152. Vice President Business Integrity, HSE, Statoil ASA.

association, or it may take the form of reputation damage as guilt by association. This type of risk is particularly significant when the company is operating in an unfamiliar environment where local partners are previously unknown to the company and information on local ethical practices is scarce.

The process of Integrity Due Diligence seeks to secure as much information as possible about a prospective third party before any business relationship is entered into. The process covers the third party's interests, reputation, activities, associations, track record and motives, and may be used for assessing any type of business associate, from prospective partners, suppliers, customers, consultants or agents to candidates for prospective mergers.

The Integrity Due Diligence process is progressive and layered. It begins with the acquisition of basic information directly from the third party and open inquiries made to follow up the business and financial references provided. Depending on what this information shows, specific issues may then be examined in more depth. Open sources such as the Internet can be supplemented with the services of external consultants and some confidential field work in order to identify and further investigate specific indicators. The extent and level of detail of this further research will depend on several factors, including the financial value involved, the commercial importance of the third party, and how much is already known about them.

If carried out thoroughly and early enough, the Integrity Due Diligence process will provide valuable "red flag" warnings indicating that further checks and mitigation are needed or even that the business relationship being considered should not be pursued at all. Integrity Due Diligence also provides useful documentation of a company's own risk management. The very fact of having executed an Integrity Due Diligence process may help to meet criticism if a business relationship should later lead to liability or reputation damage in spite of the investigation.

THE RISK ENVIRONMENT

In short-term relationships involving agents or intermediaries, a company may be at risk by association if these third parties pay or take bribes on its behalf. The third parties may also have vested interests that are unknown to the company and in conflict with its own interests. In longer-term partnerships and joint ventures, the company's risk exposure may also stem from hidden differences, concealed information and ulterior motives, or there may be a failure to comply with applicable laws. In the case of a merger or acquisition, the acquiring company should be aware of additional so-called legacy risks if the enterprise being acquired is engaged in unethical or illegal practices or is in possession of assets that have been obtained through such practices.

Generally, the level of risk to which companies are exposed through their relationships with third parties is increasing as business becomes more international. Opportunities now arise more often in unfamiliar environments where the ground rules may be different or unclear. At the same time, international legislation is becoming stricter, and practices that were generally accepted less than a generation ago are now criminal offences with serious legal, commercial and reputation consequences.

The United Nations Convention against Corruption, which came into force at the end of 2005, is the first global legally binding instrument on corruption and includes measures on prevention, criminalization and international cooperation, as well as specifying groundbreaking provisions on asset recovery. The Convention is the latest and most wide-reaching addition to an expanding legal framework to combat corruption, in which the 1997 OECD Convention on Combating Bribery of Foreign Public Officials in International Business Transactions and the pioneering US Foreign Corrupt Practices Act of 1977 are also important elements.

BASIC INFORMATION

The extent of the initial screening in preparing an Integrity Due Diligence will depend on the nature and reputation of the third party under consideration. The scope should be decided in consultation with people who are familiar with the due diligence process and the applicable laws and regulations. The process should then be explained fully to the third party in order to secure their cooperation, possibly extending to the provision of a formal letter of authorization for the Integrity Due Diligence team to use when carrying out their research.

The research team should request basic information about the third party, including ownership information, corporate structure, place of incorporation, composition of boards and higher level committees, and the names, locations, telephone numbers, and C.V.'s of officers and key personnel. Ownership interests in the company should also be given with company registration details for the parent company and any holding companies. A full description of the company, including a brief history, should also be requested.

Ownership and interests held by the third party, key management personnel and their immediate family in other organizations should be stated, in order to identify possible conflicts of interest. The third party's business, Governmental and political affiliations, including those of key management personnel and their immediate families should also be documented and particular attention given to any relationships with Government officials.

Local laws protecting privacy need to be considered in carrying out this research. In countries with unstable political regimes, a confidentiality agreement may be useful in persuading a third party to provide details of political affiliations.

Business and financial references capable of verification should be obtained and the third party asked to notify referees. Obtaining audited financial statements for the previous two years is advisable, but failing this, unaudited accounts certified by senior management may be accepted.

The standard terms of business, if any, of the third party should be requested together with instructions required for invoice payment. Legal disclosures should be requested regarding any involvement by the third party or key management personnel in previous, pending or potential insolvency proceedings, criminal convictions or investigations, or civil litigation.

Finally, it may be a good idea to compare local market rates with rates quoted by the third party for the supply of any goods or services.

VERIFICATION AND FURTHER RESEARCH

The next phase of the Integrity Due Diligence work comprises verification and follow-up of the basic information. It may be that this work can be completed using only open sources such as the Internet, subscription databases, media searches, public records and industry information. However, independent field work may be needed to supplement these results, involving the use of external sources. Here it should be borne in mind that any information obtained will be only as good as the source that provides it and that checking the credentials of external sources may also be a necessary, if time-consuming, feature of this work. In order to ensure impartiality, personnel independent of the business unit concerned should be responsible for any external research.

A growing demand for support services related to Integrity Due Diligence has unfortunately encouraged some unqualified individuals to pass themselves off as specialists. This problem, and the likelihood of unacceptable methods being used to obtain information, can mean a company risks compromising its own standards in the process of trying to document that they are being met.

The following areas should be considered in carrying out the verification and completion of an Integrity Due Diligence process:

Business and Financial References

Independent confirmation of reputation, integrity, and political relationships should be obtained directly from the referees provided by the third party. If personal interviews cannot be obtained, then a telephone conversation or a written statement on a reference form may be acceptable. Audited financial records for at least two years should be examined, but failing that, a financial referee may give an opinion on reliability, probity, and financial capability. A bank reference should always be obtained.

Ownership Interests and Accounts

Official registries of companies and other organizations usually make their records available to the public in some form, by personal application at the office concerned, by written request or even online. Examples of company registries available over the Internet are the UK Companies House on www.companies-house.gov.uk and the United States Securities and Exchange Commission on www.sec.gov.

Key Personnel and Officers

For information on individuals connected with the third party, a variety of sources may be used, including electoral records, local Government business records and commercial business libraries. Local resources may be useful in tracing the appropriate sources. Criminal records should be checked for key personnel, if this is legally permissible in the country concerned and if necessary with the authority of the subject of enquiry. Court judgements, like the official registries of organizations, are normally available for public scrutiny, either by visits to the court involved, through websites, or, if sufficiently serious, in local or international media reports. An example of an on-line service is the site for judgements handed down in the UK High Courts on www.courtservice.gov.uk/judgments/judg_home.htm.

Credit Ratings and Restrictions

Credit ratings are available for many companies from one of the reputable commercial sources offering a rating service on individuals and organizations. Other facilities for checking bankruptcy or insolvency records include registers available to public scrutiny and Internet listings. Such a service covering insolvency notices and databases, creditor meetings, liquidations, receiverships and administrations in the UK can be viewed at www.insolvency.co.uk. A check should also be made to see that the third party does not appear on local or international listings of individuals or organizations restricted by trade regulations imposed by certain countries or debarred from bidding for contracts. The World Bank site at www.worldbank.org/html/opr/procure/debarr.html provides a list of debarred individuals and companies judged to have committed acts of bribery or corruption in bid processes.

Media Search and Local Legal Assistance

Free and subscription databases should be used to research the third party, beginning with a simple Internet search using one of the larger search engines, such as www.google.com. If the third party has a website, this should be examined together with Government sites designed for use in combating cartel activity or fraud. Here too, there are many large international commercial concerns that will carry out media searches for a fee. If advice on the local legal system and practices is not available from internal resources, a reputable local legal firm could explain their significance. Such a firm would also be able to assist with the verification of local corporate registration, or in checking local criminal or civil court records.

Field Work

Some information may be obtained only through discreet and sensitive research in the field. This should be carried out by qualified professionals. Considerable caution needs to be exercised to avoid methods that may compromise the company ethically and legally.

"RED FLAG" WARNING SIGNALS

The following sections give examples of so-called "red flags," the warning signals indicating that further research is needed or that a relationship with the third party may not be advisable:

"Red Flags" in the Basic Information Provided by the Third Party

- A public official holds interests in the third party in a personal capacity rather than in an official one;

- The third party has been recommended by an official who has discretionary authority or influence over the business in question;
- An officer, executive or key employee of the third party has interests in a competitor or is related to someone there;
- The business or financial references are ambiguous or missing information;
- The third party's normal terms of business differ significantly from local business terms and conditions;
- Payment instructions given by the third party include split payments, payments to unrelated entities, or payments to a bank account in an offshore tax regime;
- Company auditors have qualified the accounts produced by the third party;
- The information makes mention of a criminal charge, the conviction of an employee for bribery and corruption, or the unsuccessful defence of a civil action for such an offence;
- The third party discloses previous involvement in insolvency proceedings;
- There is a significant difference between the remuneration rates quoted by the third party and local market rates;
- The third party refuses to sign a statement promising to abide by all local and international laws regarding bribery and corruption or by the company's business ethics policy;
- The third party refuses to disclose the identity of the directors, owners or employees.

"Red Flags" in Verification and Further Research

- Qualifications claimed by the company are denied by the issuing body, or the issuing body is not a bona fide professional entity;
- Written business references differ significantly from what the referees say in interviews;
- Financial referees express reservations regarding the financial probity of the third party;
- The third party is a shell company or has some other unorthodox corporate structure;
- Records from the official registry of companies do not agree with the information given by the third party on ownership, directorships, or any other details in required official documentation;
- The company or its holding company is registered in an offshore tax haven;
- The company representative refuses to reveal the identity of the owners or directors;
- Records show a different location for the company;
- There is a record of a criminal charge, a conviction of an employee for bribery and corruption, or the unsuccessful defence of a civil action for such an offence, which has not been disclosed by the third party;
- A reputable credit agency has provided a poor credit rating on the third party or has drawn attention to previous liquidity problems not disclosed by the applicant;

- The third party appears on a list of organizations debarred from bidding on local, national, or international contracts;
- Media searches reveal potentially damaging information regarding the applicant;
- Research uncovers close associations with local or national politicians, potential competitors, criminals or political activists.

DOCUMENTATION AND CONCLUSIONS

A final Integrity Due Diligence report should be prepared documenting the scope and individual phases of the investigation, summarizing the findings, specifying areas of uncertainty and drawing conclusions on their potential consequences for the company. This will form the basis for management to decide whether or not to proceed with the business relationship.

Case Studies

CASE STUDY A: BETA ENERGY

Business Opportunity

Beta Energy was a Western oil and gas exploration and production company with interests in several developing countries, including B_____. Statoil was considering the acquisition of Beta Energy's B_____ portfolio by purchasing the company's local subsidiary outright.

Reasons for Integrity Due Diligence

Any business relationship between Statoil and Beta Energy would be limited to the purchase of the subsidiary company and would cease as soon as this was completed. However, corruption was known to be endemic in B_____, and as Beta Energy was a company unknown to Statoil, there were questions related to how it had acquired its assets.

Basic Information

A preliminary study showed nothing irregular in the formalities concerning Beta Energy's establishment as a company and its initial domestic trading. However, a look at its more recent history showed that Beta Energy had experienced a rapid expansion into international exploration beginning less than ten years ago. This came after many years of unremarkable performance in its domestic oil and gas business. Beta Energy's international attention was quickly focused on B_____, where it soon acquired the central assets in its current portfolio in negotiations with the national oil company, NOCB. The speed with which these negotiations were concluded and the successful outcome for Beta Energy were said to have surprised many observers, especially as the company's evident optimism was soon vindicated by the discovery of substantial reserves. The suspicion that the main asset may have been secured by unethical or illegal means made further investigation advisable.

Verification and "Red Flags"

- During further investigations, it became clear that Beta Energy had encountered a certain Dr. F_____, working for Gamma Services, a foreign petroleum consulting company, as their business development expert for B_____. Dr. F_____ had also previously worked at NOCB;
- When inviting bids for the license in which Beta Energy later made their hydrocarbon discoveries, NOCB made 30 per cent of their technical information available to interested parties. According to a reliable source, Dr. F_____ had paid a named NOCB technician to gain privileged access to a further 40 per cent of the technical information on the relevant area. This gave Beta Energy prior knowledge that the license had a high potential for a discovery, prompting the company to make a more generous offer than its competitors, and ensuring its success;
- After the license had been awarded, it was alleged that the same NOCB technician had continued to receive payments from Dr. F_____, acting on behalf of Gamma Services, for further information supposedly required by Beta Energy prior to drilling;
- Two years after the license award, Beta Energy granted a 10 per cent net profit interest in the asset to another company, Delta Petroleum, of which Dr. F_____ was believed to be part-owner. No contracts between this company and Beta Energy, apart from the net profit interest agreement, could be traced. Based on subsequent estimates of producible reserves, the agreement was said to be worth over US$80 million at the time it was made.

Assessment

- Although the reported account of Beta Energy's acquisition of its main asset in B_____ was impossible to verify, two independent investigating entities had encountered the same story;
- The payments allegedly made to the NOCB technician implied bribery of an official, which indicated that Beta Energy had acquired its assets in an unethical and illegal manner;
- The net profit interest granted to Delta Petroleum was substantial and raised serious questions as to whether it was appropriate and proportionate to services rendered.

Conclusion

Statoil's evaluation of Beta Energy's assets in B_____ with a view to negotiating their acquisition was terminated.

CASE STUDY B: OMEGA OFFSHORE

Business Opportunity

Statoil was looking for a service company to act for it in marketing a drilling rig it wished to sub-contract. The rig was available for use in an area off the coast of C_____, a developing country with an established oil and gas industry. The most competitive terms had been offered by a local company, Omega Offshore.

Reasons for Integrity Due Diligence

Corruption was endemic in C_____, Omega was a company not well known to Statoil, and there were questions related to its ownership and associations.

Basic Information

Omega Offshore responded to Statoil's request for information by filling in the candidate questionnaire satisfactorily and providing external business references, which included two international oil companies. Among the entities specified in the questionnaire as owners, partners, or shareholders, the name of a holding company, Epsilon Investments, appeared as owning over 90 per cent of Omega Offshore's shares. This entry was followed by a breakdown of the ownership of Epsilon Investments, in which appeared the following:

"14 per cent held by Caicos Trust Company in a blind trust for the benefit of Mr. J_____, serving politician in the Government of C_____."

This information was confirmed further on with affirmative responses to the questions "Have any of the key people mentioned above ever held a Government job or served in the military?", "Do any . . . perform services for any Government-controlled entity?" and "Do any . . . currently hold any position with or have any duties for any political party or political campaign?"

In each case the name of Mr. J_____ appeared. The question "Will Omega Offshore market to a Government or Government agency, including the military?" was also answered in the affirmative, and the agency was identified as the national oil company of C_____.

Verification and "Red Flags"

- In following up the references provided by Omega Offshore, it became evident that several of the referees had not been aware of the interest held by Caicos Trust Company for the benefit of Mr. J_____, although there was no evidence from their response to Statoil that Omega Offshore had ever intended to conceal the fact;
- The concept of an interest being held for someone in a "blind trust" was then discussed in detail with a specialist, who confirmed that this was an acknowledged step that could be taken in order to minimize the risk of a conflict of interest in such a case. The trust had total discretion to invest, buy, or sell assets and to gather the benefit of the assets on behalf of the beneficiary of the trust, who had no insight into the management of the assets and so, in theory, had no motivation to act in a manner that might benefit any of the holdings. This arrangement was mandatory under the laws of C_____.

Assessment

- The Integrity Due Diligence check had been carried out openly with Omega Offshore, and without the need for any investigation other than the questionnaire and reference verification.
- The arrangement of placing Mr. J_____'s interest in a "blind trust" appeared to mitigate the risk of an actual conflict of interest, especially as the trust itself was based outside C_____.

- The senior position of Mr. J_____ in the Government of C_____, and the possibility of their rig being marketed to the national oil company of C_____ made it extremely important for Statoil to err on the side of caution, to avoid not only actual conflict of interest but also any appearance of such a conflict.
- The security given by the "blind trust" arrangement was not considered to be evident enough to outside observers to mitigate sufficiently the risk of reputation damage to Statoil in the event of controversy about Mr. J_____'s interest in Omega Offshore.

Conclusion

Omega Offshore was dropped from the list of bidders for the services required by Statoil.

CASE STUDY C: ALPHA EXPLORATION

Business Opportunity

Statoil was offered the opportunity to participate in an exploration license in A_____, by entering into partnership with a local oil and gas company, Alpha Exploration. The license in question was to be awarded to Alpha Exploration independently of the normal oil and gas bidding rounds in A_____.

Reasons for Integrity Due Diligence

Corruption was endemic in A_____, Alpha Exploration was a company unknown to Statoil, and there were questions related to its associations and to the process by which it expected to acquire the asset it was now offering to share.

Basic Information

A candidate questionnaire submitted to Alpha Exploration was returned completed and accompanied by C.V.'s for officers and references for the company. On examination these were found to contain nothing to raise suspicions. However, the recent date of registration of the company, only a little over a year previously, seemed to limit significantly the value of these findings. It was therefore decided to carry out further research.

Verification and "Red Flags"

- The personal references provided for officers of Alpha Exploration were checked and revealed nothing that contradicted the positive impression given by the initial information. In the course of further investigations, however, the name of a certain Mr. G_____ was mentioned by several independent sources as having recently been an adviser to Alpha Exploration;
- Mr. G_____ had attracted a lot of negative publicity in recent years because of the activities of a company belonging to a group owned by him, which had allegedly been involved in criminal activity. An external investigation of the matter was still ongoing and, in the meantime, several libel

actions brought by Mr. G_____ against those who had made or repeated the accusations against him had been dropped;

- When researchers took up with Alpha Exploration the matter of their use of Mr. G_____, the company claimed they had since severed their connections with him but that, in any case, they had not believed the allegations against him;
- Further investigation showed that other business connections might exist between Mr. G_____ and several key officers of Alpha Exploration, as well as members of the ruling family in A_____. The main representative of Alpha Exploration in A_____ was said to be a personal friend of a member of the President's family, while the registered owner of Alpha Exploration was also reported to be employed as general manager of a company in Mr. G_____'s group. Another of Alpha Exploration's owners was said to have been a technical director for the same group and to have graduated from the same college and at the same time as Mr. G_____.

Assessment

- The possibility that Mr. G_____ was still associated with Alpha Exploration could not be ignored, and it may even have been the case that he was the company's real beneficial owner;
- The reputation damage that Statoil risked by being seen to be associated with Mr. G_____ was considerable;
- The connection to the ruling family in A_____ raised the possibility that the expected license award would be made to Alpha Exploration on a discretionary basis in which personal relationships and privilege would play a part;
- Taking advantage of a business opportunity that existed because of a possible abuse of entrusted power was not consistent with Statoil's values;
- No conclusive evidence was likely to be obtainable to finally confirm or deny continuing connections between Alpha Exploration and Mr. G_____ and Mr. G_____ and the ruling family in A_____.

Conclusion

Statoil decided to refuse the offer of participation with Alpha Exploration in the license it expected to be awarded.

Hypothetical: Third-Party Vetting[153]

Part 1: Consultants

Company A, a U.S. issuer headquartered in Delaware, wants to start doing business in a country that poses high risks of corruption. Company A learns about a potential $50 million contract with the country's Ministry of

---

153. FCPA Guide, *supra* note 3, at 63–65 (hypothetical reproduced verbatim, with answers excluded).

Immigration. This is a very attractive opportunity to Company A, both for its profitability and to open the door to future projects with the government. At the suggestion of the company's senior vice president of international sales (Sales Executive), Company A hires a local businessman who assures them that he has strong ties to political and government leaders in the country and can help them win the contract. Company A enters into a consulting contract with the local businessman (Consultant). The agreement requires Consultant to use his best efforts to help the company win the business and provides for Consultant to receive a significant monthly retainer as well as a success fee of 3% of the value of any contract the company wins.

1) What steps should Company A consider taking before hiring Consultant?

. . . .

Part 2: Distributors and Local Partners

Assume the following alternative facts:

Instead of hiring Consultant, Company A retains an often-used local distributor (Distributor) to sell Company A's products to the Ministry of Immigration. In negotiating the pricing structure, Distributor, which had introduced the project to Company A, claims that the standard discount price to Distributor creates insufficient margin for Distributor to cover warehousing, distribution, installation, marketing, and training costs and requests an additional discount or rebate, or, in the alternative, a contribution to its marketing efforts, either in the form of a lump sum or as a percentage of the total contract. The requested discount/allowance is significantly larger than usual, although there is precedent at Company A for granting this level of discount in unique circumstances. Distributor further advises Company A that the Ministry's procurement officials responsible for awarding the contract have expressed a strong preference for including a particular local company (Local Partner) in the transaction as a subcontractor of Company A to perform installation, training, and other services that would normally have been performed by Distributor or Company A. According to Distributor, the Ministry has a solid working relationship with Local Partner, and it would cause less disruption for Local Partner to perform most of the on-site work at the Ministry. One of the principals (Principal 1) of the Local Partner is an official in another government ministry.

2) What additional compliance considerations do these alternative facts raise?

. . . .

Assume the following additional facts:

Under its company policy for a government transaction of this size, Company A requires both finance and compliance approval. The finance officer is concerned that the discounts to Distributor are significantly larger than what they have approved for similar work and will cut too deeply into Company A's profit margin. The finance officer is also skeptical about including Local Partner to perform some of the same services that Company A is paying Distributor to perform. Unsatisfied with Sales Executive's explanation, she requests a meeting with Distributor and Principal 1. At the meeting, Distributor and Principal 1 offer vague and inconsistent justifications for the payments and fail to provide any supporting analysis, and Principal 1 seems to have no real expertise in the industry. During a coffee break, Distributor comments to Sales Executive that the finance officer is naïve about "how business is done in my country." Following the meeting, Sales Executive dismisses the finance officer's concerns, assuring her that the proposed transaction structure is reasonable and legitimate. Sales Executive also reminds the finance officer that "the deal is key to their growth in the industry."

The compliance officer focuses his due diligence on vetting Distributor and Local Partner and hires a business investigative firm to conduct a background check. Distributor appears reputable, capable, and financially stable and is willing to take on real risk in the project, financial and otherwise. However, the compliance officer learns that Distributor has established an off-shore bank account for the transaction. The compliance officer further learns that Local Partner's business was organized two years ago and appears financially stable but has no expertise in the industry and has established an off-shore shell company and bank account to conduct this transaction. The background check also reveals that Principal 1 is a former college roommate of a senior official of the Ministry of Immigration. The Sales Executive dismisses the compliance officer's concerns, commenting that what Local Partner does with its payments "isn't our problem." Sales Executive also strongly objects to the compliance officer's request to meet with Principal 1 to discuss the off-shore company and account, assuring him that it was done for legitimate tax purposes and complaining that if Company A continues to "harass" Local Partner and Distributor, they would partner with Company A's chief competitor. The compliance officer and the finance officer discuss their concerns with each other but ultimately sign off on the deal even though their questions had not been answered. Their decision is motivated in large part by their conversation with Sales Executive, who told them that this was the region's most important contract and that the detailed FCPA questionnaires and robust anticorruption representations in the contracts placed the burden on Distributor and Local Partner to act ethically.

Company A goes forward with the Distributor and Local Partner agreements and wins the contract after six months. The finance officer approves Company A's payments to Local Partner via the offshore account, even though Local Partner's invoices did not contain supporting detail or documentation of any services provided. Company A recorded the payments as legitimate operational expenses on its books and records. Sales Executive received a large year-end bonus due to the award of the contract.

In fact, Local Partner and Distributor used part of the payments and discount margin, respectively, to funnel bribe payments to several Ministry of Immigration officials, including Principal 1's former college roommate, in exchange for awarding the contract to Company A. Thousands of dollars are also wired to the personal offshore bank account of Sales Executive.

3) How would [the] DOJ and SEC evaluate the potential FCPA liability of Company A and its employees?

. . . .

Hypothetical: Large-Scale Screening of Third Parties

Computerm, Inc. ("Computerm") is a U.S. corporation engaged in the manufacture and sale of computer hardware for private and government use and sells its products through a network of 10,000 distributors worldwide. In general, Computerm's distributors are:

- Responsible for handling all aspects of sales and marketing in their territories
- Responsible for handling all interactions with local government
- Authorized to use Computerm's logo and trademark to market Computerm's products
- Non-exclusive; that is, they are authorized to represent other manufacturers of electronic products
- Required to meet annual purchase targets, which vary according to market
- Handled through Computerm's regional sales teams headed by a relationship manager

Computerm would like to conduct a screening of all of its distributors to ensure compliance with the FCPA. Propose a framework for Computerm to accomplish this task.

For additional guidance, see PROTIVITI, A STRONG COMPLIANCE CULTURE STARTS WITH MANAGING THIRD PARTY CORRUPTION (2014), https://www.protiviti.com/sites/default/files/united_states/strong-compliance-culture-starts-with-managing-third-party-corruption-protiviti.pdf.

VIII. Confidential Reporting and Internal Investigations

This Hallmark deputizes multinational enterprises as law enforcement agents, delegating to them a detective function. It requires companies to (1) implement an internal reporting system that channels information about potential violations; (2) put in place an internal investigative mechanism for probing potential violations; and (3) disclose detected violations to the authorities and fully cooperate with their investigation.[154]

FSGO § 8B2.1(b) requires that:

> (5) The organization shall take reasonable steps—
>
> ....
>
> (C) to have and publicize a system, which may include mechanisms that allow for anonymity or confidentiality, whereby the organization's employees and agents may report or seek guidance regarding potential or actual criminal conduct without fear of retaliation.[155]
>
> ....
>
> (7) After criminal conduct has been detected, the organization shall take reasonable steps to respond appropriately to the criminal conduct and to prevent further similar criminal conduct, including making any neccessary modifications to the organization's compliance and ethics program.[156]

The FCPA Guide states:

> Companies may employ, for example, anonymous hotlines or ombudsmen. Moreover, once an allegation is made, companies should have in place an efficient, reliable, and properly funded process for investigating the allegation and documenting the company's response, including any disciplinary or remediation measures taken. Companies will want to consider taking "lessons learned" from any reported violations and the outcome of any resulting investigation to update their internal controls and compliance program and focus future training on such issues, as appropriate.[157]

A. The Confidential Hotline and Whistleblowers

Discovery and voluntary disclosure of a violation by an organization entitles it to substantial cooperation credit, provided that the authorities do not discover the violation before the company's self-disclosure. SOX and the Dodd-Frank Act of 2010 add another dimension to this process by incentivizing and protecting whistle-blowers who report violations directly to the SEC:

> Sarbanes-Oxley prohibits issuers from retaliating against whistleblowers and provides that employees who are retaliated against for reporting possible securities law violations may file a complaint with the Department of Labor, for which they would be eligible to receive reinstatement, back pay, and other compensation.

---

154. *See* FCPA Guide, *supra* note 3, at 61.
155. U.S. Sentencing Guidelines Manual § 8B2.1(b)(5)(C) (U.S. Sentencing Comm'n 2016).
156. *Id.* at § 8B2.1(b)(7).
157. FCPA Guide, *supra* note 3, at 61.

Sarbanes-Oxley also prohibits retaliation against employee whistleblowers under the obstruction of justice statute.

In 2010, the Dodd-Frank Act added Section 21F to the Exchange Act, addressing whistleblower incentives and protections. Section 21F authorizes SEC to provide monetary awards to eligible individuals who voluntarily come forward with high quality, original information that leads to an SEC enforcement action in which over $1,000,000 in sanctions is ordered. The awards range is between 10% and 30% of the monetary sanctions recovered by the government. The Dodd-Frank Act also prohibits employers from retaliating against whistleblowers and creates a private right of action for employees who are retaliated against.[158]

Thus, anyone who discovers evidence of a potential violation must choose between reporting the violation internally to the company or directly to the authorities in exchange for a monetary reward. It is, therefore, "more crucial than ever that companies have effective whistleblower hotlines as part of their corporate compliance programs so that employees (and other company stakeholders, such as vendors) are motivated to report suspected unethical or unlawful conduct internally and not incentivized to first turn to regulators."[159]

Companies should do everything possible to maximize the likelihood that whistleblowers report internally through the confidential hotline. In their article, *Silence Is Not Necessarily Golden: Elements of an Effective Whistleblower Hotline*, William Libit, Walter Draney and Todd Freier propose the following steps:[160]

1) **Make the hotline an integral part of the compliance program.** Managers should encourage the use of the hotline at every opportunity, emphasizing that all reports will be strictly confidential with no possibility of retaliation. Company procedures for reporting should be well communicated and easy to understand.

2) **Guarantee anonymity and no retaliation.** Employees need to know that using the hotline will not lead to adverse consequences, such as being labeled a "snitch" by their peers or facing retaliation. Complete anonymity, coupled with the knowledge that retaliation is illegal and unacceptable, will provide such assurance.

3) **Provide financial and nonfinancial reporting incentives.** In light of the SEC Whistleblower Program, companies should consider providing monetary rewards for reporting violations.[161] Importantly, there should

---

158. FCPA GUIDE, *supra* note 3, at 82 (footnotes omitted).

159. William M. Libit et al., *Silence Is Not Necessarily Golden: Elements of an Effective Whistleblower Hotline*, INSIGHTS (Oct. 2014), at 1, 2, http://www.chapman.com/media/publication/436_Chapman_Insights_Corporate_Securities_Law_Advisor_Silence_Not_Necessarily_Golden_1014.pdf.

160. *Id.* at 4–6.

161. One company has reportedly paid $55,000 to an employee and another $135,000 to "a group of employees for reporting suspected [FCPA] violations. . . . [W]hile SEC whistleblowers might be awarded much larger awards . . . 'the prospect of a $55,000 bonus . . . without the hassle or retribution attendant to whistle blowing might give them pause.'" RICHARD M. STEINBERG, GOVERNANCE, RISK MANAGEMENT, AND COMPLIANCE: IT CAN'T HAPPEN TO US —AVOIDING CORPORATE DISASTER WHILE DRIVING SUCCESS.

also be nonmonetary rewards to reflect the value the company attaches to internal reporting.[162]

4) **Have a positive "tone at the top."** The board of directors and senior managers should foster a culture that values and protects use of the hotline and makes tipsters "feel less intimidated when they decide whether to report to the internal hotline in the future."[163]

5) **Make the hotline also a helpline.** If the hotline also serves as a resource for obtaining advice regarding compliance or ethical issues, employees will be less inclined to perceive it in a negative light.

6) **Provide alternative means of reporting.** In addition to a dedicated phone line, companies should have a designated website, email address, and mailing address for submitting tips.

7) **Periodically test and audit the hotline.** Like all other aspects of the compliance program, the hotline should be subject to regular evaluation to ensure its effectiveness.

8) **Train third parties and provide them access to the hotline.** "Regularly educating other stakeholders and agents on the who-what-when-where-why-how of reporting suspected wrongdoing by way of the company's hotline may prove beneficial to the company through an increased number of substantiated hotline reports."[164]

Knowing When to Blow the Whistle

Jeremy Simon[165]

If your company wants to be alerted to internal wrongdoing, it takes more than offering your employees an anonymous whistleblower hotline, according to experts at the McCombs School of Business.

In the case of National Security Agency whistleblower Edward Snowden, the government certainly did not want the whistle blown publicly on their surveillance programs. But within companies, corporate executives usually want to hear about internal problems, says McCombs Lecturer Grace Renbarger, who spent four years as the chief ethics and compliance officer at Dell.

"They can't stop it if they don't know about it," she says.

Many large companies offer mechanisms such as ethics hotlines that enable workers to anonymously report misconduct. Under the Sarbanes-Oxley Act, which was passed in 2002, all publicly traded companies must have mechanisms for the reporting of accounting or audit fraud.

But those hotlines don't always get used. According to NPR, research from the University of Michigan shows that as many as one in five workers report

---

162. *See* Murphy, *supra* note 102, at 33–36.
163. Libit, *supra* note 159, at 5.
164. *Id.* at 6.
165. Jeremy Simon, *Knowing When to Blow the Whistle*, Texas Enterprise (University of Texas at Austin; June 10, 2013), http://www.texasenterprise.utexas.edu/2013/06/10/leadership/knowing-when-blow-whistle.

observing violations of their companies' code of conduct, even though only half of the employees spoke up about the violations.

Why don't more employees report wrongdoing? One problem could be a corporate culture that discourages it. To get more employees to speak up, "you have to tackle the culture itself," says Associate Professor of Management Ethan Burris.

WHISTLEBLOWING ISN'T EASY

The consequences of becoming a whistleblower are "generally pretty awful," says Robert Prentice, professor and interim chair of the Business, Government, and Society department.

Prentice explains that whistleblowers are often shunned by coworkers, may be fired, and can have difficulty finding work in their industry ever again.

Some companies require whistleblowers to file an internal report before they can go to outside regulators, such as the Securities and Exchange Commission, at the risk of being discredited by their employer. Unemployment, combined with years spent in court battling former employers, can drag whistleblowers into bankruptcy. In the most extreme cases, whistleblowers may be the victims of physical intimidation or even murder. There is speculation, for example, that the 1974 death of nuclear safety activist Karen Silkwood may have been linked to her public opposition to unsafe practices at her company.

"Being a whistleblower is far from rosy," Prentice says.

Things may not turn out so great for the company, either. Employee whistleblowing can potentially mean fines, lawsuits, or government investigations of the company, Prentice says. If the whistleblowing case isn't handled well internally or high-level executives are involved, expect the press to pick up on it. "You're going to hear a lot of publicity about the really catastrophic ones," Renbarger says.

Just ask the NSA.

INTERNAL MECHANISMS

For companies, it's important to get workers to speak up before problems get too serious.

Companies should consider how they are soliciting employee input. Renbarger says most large U.S. corporations have toll-free hotlines or Web portals managed by third-party vendors that allow employees to blow the whistle while remaining anonymous.

Some experts say more needs to be done. Anonymous hotlines are important "symbolic actions," but they aren't enough, says Burris, who researches how employees share feedback in the workplace. "To me, that is really just sticking a Band-Aid on the underlying issue," Burris says.

A hotline doesn't change the wider corporate culture that not only allowed wrongdoing to occur, but also made the employee feel the need to seek out an independent third party, either inside or outside the organization, to resolve the issue, Burris says.

CHANGING CORPORATE CULTURE

Instead, Burris says employees should be talking about serious workplace problems with their managers. The company can encourage discussion by letting workers know that it's safe and worthwhile to speak up about sensitive issues, and by letting managers know that it's safe and worthwhile to address problems and make changes, rather than continuing with the status quo.

"Unless you have both pieces involved, you're not really going to change the equation all that dramatically for employees," Burris says.

Renbarger agrees that corporations need to set the proper tone.

"If the culture is one of openness and transparency, that values integrity and encourages people to speak up, then I think there will be more reporting," she says. "On the other hand, if the culture is authoritarian, greed-obsessed, and lacking in values, then there will be a lot less reporting because people are either afraid or don't care —they just want to keep their heads down, get their paycheck, and go home."

Burris' research has shown that to get employees talking, managers should be physically present, open and nice about receiving employee feedback, and willing to take action when appropriate. They also should let employees know how their feedback is being used — or not used — and why. Most importantly, managers need to visit employees on their turf and request input, rather than waiting for employees to come to them.

In other words, touting your open-door policy doesn't mean much on its own, Burris says. "Unless you actually do something with [employee feedback], why would I want to waste my time going out of my way and sticking my neck out to tell you how things really are if nothing is going to change?"

For companies that want their employees to speak up, hiring good management isn't enough, though. Employers need to take a holistic approach to the corporate culture, since the company as a whole has a greater influence than the malleable personalities of individual managers.

"If the culture's terrible, they're going to adapt to that terrible culture," Burris says.

Internal Reporting and Whistle-Blowing

Jose A. Tabuena and Chris Mondini, Deloitte Financial Advisory Services LLP[166]

The popularity of helplines is expanding internationally along with the global nature of company business practices. According to a Conference Board survey on the ethics programme of 165 companies worldwide, numerous countries have

---

166. José A. Tabuena & Chris Mondini, *Internal Reporting and Whistle-Blowing, in* Business Against Corruption: Case Stories and Examples 92, 92-95 (Birgit Errath ed., 2006) (footnotes omitted), https://www.unglobalcompact.org/docs/issues_doc/7.7/BACbookFINAL.pdf.

significant percentages of organizations with policies and procedures that encourage employee reporting of violations.

HELPLINES ACROSS THE WORLD

Such global popularity has led to new legal and regulatory concerns regarding the use of helplines. For instance, the European legal system differs from the US one, and privacy laws vary tremendously. This can be especially challenging for businesses when exchanging information between multiple jurisdictions.

Recent legal decisions in France and Germany, ruling that "anonymous employee whistle-blowing hotlines, without certain precautions, are invalid or unlawful in those countries," are now causing concern for many multinational public companies that must comply with the US Sarbanes-Oxley law and related rules. For several European Union Member States (EU), Sarbanes-Oxley requirements may be in direct conflict with these decisions. US companies who have subsidiaries and employees in the EU with reporting mechanisms in place must now consider additional options to minimize risks in those countries.

Another consequence of the globalization of helplines is the potential impact of cultural differences that may govern its use. A World Bank Conference Board study found culture-based resistance to whistle-blowing to be less common in East Asia than in Europe. This study suggests that a lower incidence of whistle-blowing in Western Europe may "reflect a preference for other channels, such as work councils, labour unions, or even direct discussions with appropriate company executives." The study further notes that whistle-blowing may be a risky proposition in France because Article 214 of the French Criminal Code makes denunciation of another person without just cause a criminal offence.

Anecdotal explanations have been generally offered in countries where there may be a culture-based resistance. For instance, respect for the chain of command is said to be embedded in Japanese business culture, thus making it unlikely that someone will feel comfortable reporting an issue outside that chain of command. According to Clarisse Girot, senior legal advisor for the Commission nationale de l'informatique et de libertés (CNIL), for cultural and historical reasons anonymous whistle-blowers are discouraged in France. "It's very much related to World War II. Anonymous reports do not raise good memories in our minds," says Girot referring to the experience under German occupation.

The historical stigma of the whistle-blower as informer has its various cultural explanations, yet the discomfort is apparently universal. At this time there is no universal solution for disparate regulations and cultural norms, thus companies should monitor and perform a country-by-country analysis pending future multinational resolution.

Whistle-blower reporting mechanisms remain, however, one of the most effective means of fighting corruption and detecting fraud in organizations, be they public, private or governmental, or non-governmental. Because the most developed systems and the longest experience with whistle-blower programmes are found within the US private sector, the case story below is drawn from that pool of examples.

WHISTLE-BLOWER CASE STORY

The attached case story is a short and specific account of the use of a whistle-blower helpline in working against corruption within an organization.

Background

This case description involves a large, publicly traded health benefits company in the United States that provides a range of medical and specialty products, including network-based health care services. The company offers various health plans, pharmacy, life and disability benefits in over 10 states.

The Problem

The company had a large Information Technology (IT) department that tended to be viewed as a separate part of the organization. As a result, they were often overlooked when it came time to communicate and promote company-wide initiatives. The IT department was also suffering from poor morale and frequent turnover of programming staff.

A compliance and ethics programme, including a telephone helpline had been in place for approximately two years. A broad range of issues were reported through the helpline, including allegations of regulatory violations and employee misconduct. Feedback from employees regarding the helpline was generally positive with a percentage of callers (approximately 15 per cent) using the mechanism to seek guidance.

The helpline was active and averaged a volume of 1.5 per cent calls per 1,000 employees each year since inception. However, it was observed by the Compliance department that the IT department was the only segment of the organization that did not have a single employee make a report or seek guidance through the helpline. The Compliance department then realized that while all company regions provided basic training on the compliance and ethics programme, regional Compliance officers did not include IT staff as "regional" employees. Similarly, the corporate units did not include IT in their compliance training.

Drivers of Change, Key Players, and Trigger Stakeholder Group

The Compliance officer determined that a compliance liaison needed to be formally designated for the IT function. This liaison would be responsible for ensuring implementation of core compliance and ethics programme activities for the department. A new Chief Information Officer had recently been hired who was supportive of the ethics and compliance programme. As a result, IT employees finally began receiving basic training and communications regarding the company helpline. The stakeholders most responsible for bringing pressure to bear in addressing the problem were the IT department employees.

What Happened

As training to IT employees became implemented across the organization, the usual initial surge of calls started coming to the helpline. The Compliance and

Ethics department observed that calls coming from IT employees concerned the following major issues:

- Questions regarding conflict of interests and hiring of family members;
- Allegations that certain managers (director-level and above) were manipulating certain metrics to maximize their annual bonus.

The Issues

Conflicts of Interest

Upon evaluating questions regarding conflicts of interest and the hiring of family members, the compliance and ethics staff learned there was a widespread perception of favouritism and inappropriate reporting relations in the IT department. A review was conducted with the support of Human Resources (HR) that included questioning all IT managers about their direct reports and employees of their unit. It was determined that there was one instance of a family member (brother-in-law) of a manager who had been hired, but that person did not report to the manager and was in a different section of the IT organization. Still, managers occasionally would refer a friend or family member to another manager, and employees believed the referring managers exerted influence in the hiring process.

Because of the misperceptions, which were believed to be impacting morale, all the IT managers received training on appropriate employment practices (hiring, performance reviews, discipline, and retention). Communications were also delivered to all IT employees explaining policies and practices regarding the hiring of family members.

Follow-up with callers to the helpline was conducted. Most of the callers were not anonymous, but confidentiality of their identity was maintained. The callers stated that the work environment in the IT department had noticeably improved. They also expressed gratitude that their questions had been answered and that the issue had been addressed. The callers felt their concerns were taken seriously when they saw the communications on hiring practices and when they were able to discuss issues with managers during staff meetings. Staff retention started improving in the department.

Manipulation of Data Impacting Incentive Compensation

Efforts were made to get more detail on these allegations from an anonymous caller. The HR leader responsible for incentive compensation noted that the same allegation was made by an anonymous letter the prior year, but it was difficult to investigate the matter due to limited information. For instance, there were over 10 managers with varying compensation factors who could potentially fall under the allegations. Further, the data sources on which some of the metrics were based were not centrally maintained, and controls were loose. A comprehensive investigation would have been difficult and time-intensive.

Through the telephone mechanism, ethics and compliance staff were able to obtain more information from the callers, thus isolating the metrics and impacted individuals. It was determined that the bonuses of a select few IT managers were indeed influenced by the data source in question, which was controlled by a non-manager with minimal oversight and controls.

Following interviews with the key individual and review of the data file (including forensic analysis), it was determined that one IT manager had misrepresented information provided to the staff person maintaining the data. Notably, this staff person also reported to this manager. As a result, the IT manager's bonus compensation was inflated.

The IT manager was subsequently terminated. The compliance and ethics department also worked with HR to review all bonus compensation arrangements to assess appropriateness and potential for data manipulation. Performance incentives were adjusted, and stricter controls on pertinent data files were implemented. The board and senior leadership began considering linking ethics and compliance-oriented conduct and measures to bonus compensation and other company incentives.

CONCLUSION: SUCCESS IN THE CORRECTION OF FAILURES

This case story provides support for several basic tenets of an effective ethics and compliance helpline in uncovering, investigating and mitigating corruption.

First, a helpline is of no value if the workforce is not aware of it. Although a helpline was in place, it became apparent that a segment of the company had not been informed. It was helpline data that revealed this gap. Through a review and comparison of the data segmented by region, department and incident classification, it became obvious that the IT department had not used the helpline.

Once the IT department became part of the helpline communication plan, they began to call the helpline. Fortunately, promotion of the helpline to IT staff was not done in isolation. The Ethics and Compliance office obtained support from the CIO for designating an accountable liaison within the IT function. The support of department leadership likely influenced the success of the training and communications delivered by the Ethics and Compliance staff.

Awareness of a helpline is not sufficient to ensure success. The company made sure that issues and allegations were addressed and investigated, as needed. During assessment work we've done for Fortune 500 companies, employees who choose not to report wrongdoing indicate a belief that nothing will be done anyway, so why should they take the risk? Employees also cite fear of retaliation as a reason for not reporting.

Here, the Ethics and Compliance office established the credibility of the helpline as a resource to raise issues and report misconduct. The concern regarding nepotism and conflicts of interest was taken seriously, and although the situation did not exist as thought, the review went a long way to clearing the air.

Similarly, the investigation and dismissal of the manager who manipulated data to increase bonus compensation sent a message to the department that such conduct would not be tolerated. Without the report by an anonymous caller, it is highly unlikely this scheme would have been uncovered. And the telephone mechanism enabled a degree of interactivity that supported a detailed investigation, which had not been possible by submission of an anonymous letter.

Finally, it should be apparent that the helpline, in addition to addressing the problem of corruption, proved to be a successful management tool. Before the helpline was utilized, the IT function was a hotbed of discontent and high turnover. Once underlying concerns were safely raised and addressed, employee satisfaction and retention improved. Clearly, the helpline supported a culture of compliance and ethical behaviour, which in turn fostered satisfaction in the workplace.

2015 Annual Report to Congress on the Dodd-Frank Whistleblower Program[167]

. . . .

HISTORY AND PURPOSE

The Dodd-Frank Act amended the Securities Exchange Act of 1934 (the "Exchange Act") by, among other things, adding Section 21F, entitled "Securities Whistleblower Incentives and Protection." Section 21F directs the Commission to make monetary awards to eligible individuals who voluntarily provide original information that leads to successful Commission enforcement actions resulting in monetary sanctions over $1 million, and successful related actions.

Awards are required to be made in an amount equal to 10 to 30% of the monetary sanctions collected. To ensure that whistleblower payments would not diminish the amount of recovery for victims of securities law violations, Congress established a separate fund, called the Investor Protection Fund ("Fund"), out of which eligible whistleblowers would be paid.

The Commission established [the Office of the Whistleblower ("OWB")], a separate office within the SEC's Division of Enforcement, to administer and effectuate the whistleblower program. It is OWB's mission to administer a vigorous whistleblower program that will help the Commission identify and halt frauds early and quickly to minimize investor losses.

In addition to establishing an awards program to encourage the submission of high-quality information, the Dodd-Frank Act and the Commission's implementing regulations (the "Whistleblower Rules") prohibit retaliation against whistleblowers who report possible wrongdoing based on a reasonable belief that a possible securities violation has occurred, is in progress, or is about to occur.

The whistleblower program was designed to complement, rather than replace, existing corporate compliance programs. While it provides incentives for insiders and others with information about unlawful conduct to come forward, it

---

167. U.S. Sec. & Exch. Comm'n, 2015 Annual Report to Congress on the Dodd-Frank Whistleblower Program 4-8 (2015) (footnotes omitted), https://www.sec.gov/files/owb-annual-report-2015.pdf.

also encourages them to work within their company's own compliance structure, if appropriate.

. . . .

ACTIVITIES OF THE OFFICE OF THE WHISTLEBLOWER

Section 924(d) of the Dodd-Frank Act directed the Commission to establish a separate office within the Commission to administer and to enforce the provisions of Section 21F of the Exchange Act. . . . Below is an overview of OWB's primary responsibilities and activities over the past fiscal year.

Assessment of Award Applications

The whistleblower program was designed, in part, to provide a monetary incentive to corporate insiders and others with relevant information concerning potential securities violations to report their information to the Commission. As such, much of what OWB does relates to the assessment of claims for whistleblower awards.

OWB posts a Notice of Covered Action ("NoCA") on its website for every Commission enforcement action that results in monetary sanctions of over $1 million. Anyone who believes that they are entitled to a whistleblower award may submit an application in response to a posted NoCA. Before submitting an application, however, a whistleblower should check to make sure that there is a nexus between the tip he or she provided to the Commission and what was ultimately charged in the enforcement matter.

OWB staff attempts to track investigations where a whistleblower has provided information or assistance to Enforcement staff. This case-tracking initiative is intended to help OWB know which cases may involve a potential award payout. Although it is ultimately a whistleblower's responsibility to make a timely application for an award, OWB often contacts whistleblowers who have been actively working with Enforcement staff to confirm they are aware of the NoCA posting and applicable deadline for submitting a claim for award.

After receiving an application for an award, OWB attorneys assess the application and confer with relevant Enforcement or Exam staff to understand in more detail the contribution of the claimant, if any. OWB then makes recommendations to the Claims Review Staff, comprised of five senior members of Enforcement, as to award eligibility. . . .

. . . .

Advancing Anti-Retaliation Protections

OWB identifies and monitors whistleblower complaints alleging retaliation by employers or former employers in response to the employee's reporting of possible securities law violations internally or to the Commission. The Commission has authority to enforce all the provisions of the Exchange Act, including the whistleblower anti-retaliation protections under the Dodd-Frank Act. As discussed in last year's report, the Commission brought its first anti-retaliation case against an employer in June 2014. OWB continues to work with Enforcement staff on identifying potential anti-retaliation enforcement actions. OWB also monitors federal court cases involving the anti-retaliation provisions of the Dodd-Frank Act and the Sarbanes-Oxley Act of 2002. Finally, OWB works with the SEC's Office of the General Counsel, which has appeared in federal courts around the country in support of the Commission's position that the anti-retaliation provisions of the Dodd-Frank Act protect individuals who report internally to their companies, as well as those who report directly to the Commission. . . .

Intake of Whistleblower Tips

The Commission developed its Tips, Complaints, and Referrals Intake and Resolution System ("TCR System"), an internal database, to serve as a central repository for all tips and complaints, as well as referrals from other government agencies or self-regulatory organizations, that are received by the Commission. Exchange Act Rule 21F-9 provides whistleblowers the option of either submitting their tips directly into the TCR System through the Commission's online portal, or by mailing or faxing a hard-copy Form TCR to OWB. This procedure assists whistleblowers who may not have ready access to a computer or who, for other reasons, may prefer to submit their information in hard copy. In those cases where whistleblowers elect to send in a Form TCR, OWB manually enters it into the TCR System so that it can be appropriately reviewed, assigned and tracked in the same manner as tips received through the online portal. . . .

Communications with Whistleblowers

The Office serves as the primary liaison between the Commission and individuals who have submitted information or are considering whether to submit information to the agency concerning a possible securities violation. OWB created a whistleblower hotline that has been in operation since May 2011 to respond to questions from the public about the whistleblower program. Individuals leave messages on the hotline, which are returned by OWB attorneys within 24 business hours. To protect the identity of whistleblowers, OWB will not leave return messages unless the caller's name is clearly and fully identified on the caller's voicemail box. If we are not able to leave a message because the individual's name is not identified or if it appears to be a shared voicemail box, OWB attorneys make two additional attempts to contact the individual.

During Fiscal Year 2015, the Office returned over 2,801 phone calls from members of the public. Many of the calls the Office receives relate to how the caller should submit a tip in order to be eligible for an award; concerns about how the Commission will maintain the confidentiality of a whistleblower's identity; requests for information on the investigative process or tracking an individual's complaint status; or focus on whether the SEC is the appropriate agency to handle the caller's tip.

In addition to communicating with whistleblowers through the hotline, the Office regularly communicates with whistleblowers who have submitted tips, additional information, claims for awards, and other correspondence to OWB.

. . . .

Notes and Questions

What if a company takes steps to stop a whistleblower from cooperating with the government, for example, by entering into a confidentiality agreement and paying the whistleblower? The SEC answered that question in its cease and desist order against Anheuser-Busch InBev ("AB InBev"). AB InBev's wholly owned subsidiary in India, Crown Beers India Private Limited ("Crown"), was involved in making "improper payments to Indian government officials to obtain beer orders and to increase brewery hours for Crown in 2011."[168] After a Crown employee informed the SEC about the payments, Crown successfully stopped the employee from further cooperating. As explained in the Order:

> In 2010 and 2011, a Crown employee (the "Crown Employee") informed AB InBev personnel that, among other things, IIIPL may have been using Promoter Company A to make improper payments to government officials. The Crown Employee also raised concerns to AB InBev about Promoter Company B, questioning its lack of sales experience, staff, and infrastructure. The Crown Employee reported to AB InBev personnel that the Principal had a local reputation for "taking care of" government officials and suggested that AB InBev perform due diligence on him.
>
> During the relevant period, the Crown Employee was employed by an AB InBev subsidiary.
>
> In early 2012, AB InBev's subsidiary terminated the Crown Employee's employment. The Crown Employee and AB InBev's subsidiary subsequently engaged in mediation regarding potential employment law claims related to this termination. In late 2012, the Crown Employee and AB InBev's subsidiary entered into a Confidential Agreement and General Release (the "Separation Agreement") that resolved the Crown Employee's claims.
>
> Paragraph 7.A of the Separation Agreement includes the following language:
>
> [The Crown Employee] agrees to keep in strict secrecy and confidence any and all unique, confidential and/or proprietary information and material belonging or relating to [the AB InBev subsidiary] that is not a matter of common knowledge or otherwise generally available to the public including, but not limited to, business, government affairs, communications, financial, trade, technical or technological information. [The Crown Employee] acknowledges and agrees that [the Crown Employee] remains subject to the "Employment Agreement as to Intellectual Property and Confidentiality," which [the Crown Employee] previously signed and is incorporated into the Agreement by reference.
>
> Paragraph 7.C of the Separation Agreement includes the following language:
>
> [The Crown Employee] agrees not to disclose, directly or indirectly, any information regarding the substance of this Agreement to any person other than [the Crown Employee's] spouse, attorney, or financial or tax advisor, except to the extent such disclosure may be required for accounting or tax purposes or as otherwise required by law.
>
> Paragraph 7.D of the Separation Agreement includes the following language:

---

168. Anheuser-Busch InBev SA/NV, Exchange Act Release No. 78957, 115 SEC 2 (Sept. 28, 2016) (citation omitted), https://www.sec.gov/litigation/admin/2016/34-78957.pdf.

[The Crown Employee] agrees that, if [the Crown Employee] violates in any way any of the terms and conditions of paragraph 7, [the Crown Employee] shall be liable to [the AB InBev subsidiary], and shall immediately pay to [the AB InBev subsidiary] as liquidated damages and not as a penalty, the total sum of $250,000.00 which represents reasonable compensation for the loss incurred by [the AB InBev subsidiary] as a result of such breach . . . .

After signing the Separation Agreement, the Crown Employee, who was previously voluntarily communicating directly with the Commission staff, stopped doing so. The Crown Employee stopped doing so because he believed that he was prohibited by the recently executed Separation Agreement and any violation of the Separation Agreement would risk triggering the Separation Agreement's liquidated damages provision. Only after the Commission issued an administrative subpoena for testimony and documents did the Crown Employee resume communicating directly with the Commission staff.

AB InBev has used the same or similar language in other agreements in the past.

. . . .

The Dodd-Frank Wall Street Reform and Consumer Protection Act, enacted on July 21, 2010, amended the Exchange Act by adding Section 21F, "Whistleblower Incentives and Protection." The Commission adopted Rule 21F-17(a), which provides that, "No person may take any action to impede an individual from communicating directly with the Commission staff about a possible securities law violation, including enforcing, or threatening to enforce, a confidentiality agreement . . . with respect to such communications." Rule 21F-17(a) became effective on August 12, 2011

. . . .

In addition, AB InBev violated Rule 21F-17(a) because the Separation Agreement contained language that impeded the Crown Employee from communicating directly with the Commission staff. Such restrictions on providing information regarding possible securities law violations to the Commission undermine the purpose of Section 21F, which is to "encourage[e] individuals to report to the Commission," and violate Rule 21F-17(a) by impeding individuals from communicating directly with the Commission staff about possible securities law violations.

AB InBev paid $6 million to settle the charges.

Could AB InBev have structured the separation agreement differently to avoid violating Rule 21F-17(a)?

Hypothetical: Evaluating a Whistleblower Tip

Zebra, Inc. ("Zebra") is a domestic concern engaged in the manufacturing and sales of military equipment. A few days ago, Zebra received a tip through its hotline reporting that Allen, Zebra's star sales agent in the United States, regularly bribed foreign military officials. The tip came from JJ, one of Allen's subordinates who has received several negative performance reviews from Allen. JJ has repeatedly expressed dissatisfaction with his job and is rumored to be looking for other employment.

After being informed about the tip, Zebra's CCO contacted the CEO to discuss the possibility of conducting an internal investigation. The CEO strongly opposed an investigation, expressing doubt about the veracity of JJ's tip and stating that an investigation would negatively impact the company's performance.

1) What should be the CCO's next steps?
2) Has the CCO acted appropriately in response to JJ's tip?

B. Internal Investigations

When a company discovers a potential violation—either through the confidential hotline, an internal audit, or other means—it must conduct an internal investigation. FCPA internal investigations are similar to other internal investigations, using many of the same tools and skills.[169] They are unique, however, in that they are often "transnational, extraterritorial, and focused on foreign government official action, implicating foreign laws, cultures and business practices."[170] In *Effective FCPA Corporate Investigations: Discovering the Whole Truth*, Lucinda Low provides a list of threshold questions involved in determining whether and how to conduct an FCPA internal investigation.[171]

1. Should We Investigate?

Internal investigations are costly, likely to impede operations, and, if made public, can generate negative publicity. Therefore, before an internal investigation is launched, the company should consider the source and whether the allegations are sufficiently credible.[172]

2. Who Should Conduct the Investigation?

When the alleged violation involves a foreign subsidiary or division, the question becomes whether the parent or the foreign entity should conduct the investigation. In most circumstances, the parent bears potential responsibility either for its participation or lack of oversight. "This gives the parent a significant stake in the investigation, and often means that the parent rather than the subsidiary should drive the investigation . . . ."[173]

---

169. *See* Lucinda A. Low, Steptoe & Johnson LLP, Effective FCPA Investigations: Discovering the Whole Truth 2 (Feb. 23, 2015), http://www.americanbar.org/content/dam/aba/administrative/litigation/materials/2015_corporate_counselcleseminar/Materials/3b_12_fcpa_investigations.authcheckdam.pdf.
170. *Id.*
171. *See id.* at 3–12.
172. *See id.* at 3.
173. *Id.* at 3–4.

3. What Should Be the Scope of the Investigation?

At the outset of an FCPA investigation, the true scope of the wrongdoing may not be apparent. Often, an investigation that starts with a single violation will lead to the discovery of a wide-ranging scheme involving multiple business units spanning many countries. At the same time, a violation involving bribery of foreign officials usually implicates the company's books and records and internal controls. "Avoiding a 'runaway' investigation, while at the same time investigating sufficiently to assess root causes of misconduct and properly remediate, requires judgment and experience."[174]

4. Should the Investigation Be Referred to Outside Counsel?

Referral to outside counsel offers several advantages. First, it is costly and inefficient to maintain a dedicated internal investigative staff. Second, in the event it becomes necessary to self-disclose, an outside investigator will be perceived by regulators to be more independent. Third, an investigation by outside counsel will mean that a wider range of documents and information will be protected by the attorney-client and work-product privileges.[175]

In a 2015 speech, Assistant Attorney General Leslie Caldwell explained how the DOJ evaluates a company's internal investigation when considering what, if any, charges to bring:

> While we in the Criminal Division will not tell a company how it should conduct an investigation, we evaluate the quality of a company's internal investigation, both through our own investigation and in considering what if any charges to bring against a company. In that regard, we have seen some "best practices" with regard to internal investigations.
>
> Good internal investigations uncover the facts. They don't promote corporate talking points or whitewash the truth. The investigation should be focused on rooting out the relevant facts, identifying and interviewing the knowledgeable actors and capturing and preserving relevant documents and other evidence. The investigation should seek to identify responsible individuals, even if those individuals hold senior positions at the company.
>
> It is reasonable to take resources—time and money—into account. If an internal investigation unearths criminal conduct, the inquiry should be thorough enough to identify the relevant facts, players, documents and other evidence, and to get a sense of the pervasiveness of the misconduct.
>
> But, we do not believe that it is necessary or productive for a company to employ its internal investigators to look under every rock and pebble—particularly when a company has offices or personnel around the globe that do not appear to be involved in the misconduct at issue.

---

174. *Id.* at 5.
175. *See id.* at 13–14.

In fact, doing so will cost companies much more in the end, both in fees but also because it ultimately will delay our investigation and delay resolution and closure for the company.

For example, if a multinational corporation discovers an FCPA violation in one country, and has no basis to suspect that the misconduct is occurring elsewhere, the Criminal Division would not expect that the internal investigation would extend beyond the country in which the violation was discovered. By contrast, if the known offenders operated in multiple countries, we would expect that the internal investigation would extend into those locations as well.[176]

Notes and Questions

Forensic accounting is a useful competency for conducting FCPA (and other) internal investigations. "Forensic accountants combine their accounting knowledge with investigative skills, using this unique combination in . . . investigative accounting settings. [Unlike] SOX internal auditors [who] are primarily tasked with testing the adequacy of financial controls . . . ."[177]

Forensic accountants go beyond the documentation typically examined by an internal auditor's transaction testing to look at the underlying substance. For example, when examining a transaction involving a company purchase, an invoice that matches the company's purchase order would typically satisfy an internal auditor's documentation requirements.[178] By contrast, a forensic accountant would ask for additional details, such as proof of the service provided, whether the company performed due diligence on the service provider, and whether the invoice reflects the market value of the service.[179] Forensic accountants also perform data mining to look for anomalous patterns and may "[t]est a broader sample of high-risk activities (e.g., payments to agents and high-risk vendors), analysis of cash activities (including petty cash), analysis of travel and entertainment reports, analysis of gift giving and entertainment involving government officials . . . ."[180]

1) Apart from internal investigations, in what FCPA context(s) would forensic accounting be useful?

---

176. Leslie R. Caldwell, Assistant Attorney Gen., U.S. Dep't of Justice, Remarks at the Compliance Week Conference (May 19, 2015), https://www.justice.gov/opa/speech/assistant-attorney-general-leslie-r-caldwell-delivers-remarks-compliance-week-conference.

177. Kristin Rivera & Sulaksh Shah, *FCPA: The Role of Forensic Accountants*, WHITE COLLAR CRIME COMMITTEE NEWSL. (Am. Bar Ass'n, Criminal Justice Section, D.C.), Summer/Fall 2013, https://www.americanbar.org/content/dam/aba/publications/criminaljustice/wcc_shah_rivera.authcheckdam.pdf.

178. *See id.*

179. *See id.*

180. GREG WOLSKI & VIRGINIA ADAMS, ERNST & YOUNG LLP, TYPICAL FORENSIC ACCOUNTANT ROLES IN ANTI-CORRUPTION DUE DILIGENCE 4 (2013), http://www.ey.com/Publication/vwLUAssets/EY-Typical-forensic-accountant-roles-in-anti–corruption-due-diligence/$FILE/EY-Typical-forensic-accountant-roles-in-anti–corruption-due-diligence.pdf.

2) If outside counsel retained for the purpose of conducting an FCPA internal investigation employs a forensic accountant, would privilege protect:
   a) The forensic accountant's work product?
   b) Communications between outside counsel and the forensic accountant?

C. Self-Disclosure and Cooperation

When an internal investigation yields evidence of a violation, the company must decide whether and when to self-disclose. In a 2015 speech, Assistant Attorney General Caldwell provided guidance on the timing and nature of self-disclosure and its impact on the company's receipt of cooperation credit:

> Once your company learns of potential criminal conduct and confirms it through a reasonable internal investigation, the company then must choose whether to disclose the conduct to the government, and whether to cooperate in the government's investigation.
>
> These are the company's choices, and very few companies have a legal obligation to disclose criminal misconduct to the department. Likewise, there is no obligation to cooperate beyond compliance with lawful process.
>
> But if a company chooses to cooperate with the government in its investigation—particularly at an early stage—the company likely will receive significant credit for such efforts when the government is contemplating what prosecutorial action to take.
>
> In conducting an investigation, determining whether to bring charges and negotiating plea or other agreements, federal prosecutors take into account, among other factors, the corporation's timely and voluntary disclosure of wrongdoing and its willingness to cooperate in the investigation of its agents. Prosecutors also consider the availability of alternative or supplemental remedies such as civil or regulatory enforcement action.
>
> To receive cooperation credit, a company must do more than comply with subpoenas or other compulsory process. Companies must provide a full accounting of the known facts about the conduct or events under review, and affirmatively must identify responsible individuals (and provide evidence supporting their culpability), including corporate executives and officers—and they must do so in a timely way.
>
> A company's cooperation may be particularly helpful where the criminal conduct continued over an extended period of time, and the knowledgeable or culpable individuals and/or the relevant documents are dispersed or located abroad.
>
> Under these circumstances, cooperation includes helping to circumvent barriers to the investigation by making knowledgeable personnel available for interviews or testimony, and by producing documents and other evidence that otherwise may not be readily accessible to the government.
>
> . . . .
>
> The consequences of refusing to cooperate in an ongoing investigation are evident in department's recent, landmark criminal resolution with BNP Paribas (BNPP) —the fourth largest bank in the world.
>
> Between 2004 and 2012, BNPP knowingly violated the IEEPA and the Trading with the Enemy Act (TWEA) by moving more than $8.8 billion through

the U.S. financial system on behalf of Sudanese, Iranian and Cuban entities subject to U.S. economic sanctions. The majority of the transactions facilitated by BNPP were on behalf of entities in Sudan, which is subject to a U.S. embargo due to the Sudanese government's role in facilitating terrorism and committing human rights abuses.

BNPP's criminal conduct took place despite repeated warnings expressed by the bank's own compliance officers and its outside counsel. In response to the concerns identified by compliance personnel, high-ranking BNPP officials explained that the questioned transactions had the "full support" of BNPP management in Paris. In short, BNPP expressly elected to favor profits over compliance.

BNPP refused to cooperate with our investigation. In fact, the bank hindered the investigation by dragging its feet and making exaggerated assertions that certain information was precluded from disclosure by foreign data privacy laws. BNPP's intransigence thwarted the government's ability to prosecute responsible individuals or satellite banks.

Ultimately, BNPP pleaded guilty to conspiracy to violate the IEEPA and the TWEA, and agreed to pay record-setting penalties of over $8.9 billion. And the company admitted its misconduct—including its disregard of compliance advice—in a detailed statement of facts that was made public. BNPP's refusal to cooperate was a key factor in the department's decision to seek a parent-level guilty plea.

Corporate accountability through a strong, tailored compliance program and thorough internal investigations should be the standard for your companies.[181]

In a 2016 press release announcing NPAs with two U.S.-based companies whose foreign subsidiaries paid bribes to Chinese officials, the SEC emphasized the importance of early disclosure and explained the essential features of effective cooperation:

> Both companies self-reported the misconduct promptly, and they cooperated extensively with the ensuing SEC investigations. The non-prosecution agreements stipulate that the companies are not charged with violations of the Foreign Corrupt Practices Act (FCPA) and do not pay additional monetary penalties.
>
> . . . .
>
> Among the companies' actions outlined in the NPAs:
>
> - Reported the situation to the SEC on their own initiative in the early stages of internal investigations.
> - Shared detailed findings of the internal investigations and provided timely updates to enforcement staff when new information was uncovered.
> - Provided summaries of witness interviews and voluntarily made witnesses available for interviews, including those in China.
> - Voluntarily translated documents from Chinese into English.
> - Terminated employees responsible for the misconduct.
> - Strengthened their anticorruption policies and conducted extensive mandatory training with employees around the world with a focus on bolstering internal audit procedures and testing protocols.[182]

---

181. Caldwell, *supra* note 176.
182. Press Release, U.S. Sec. & Exch. Comm'n, SEC Announces Two Non-Prosecution Agreements in

In 2016, the DOJ's FCPA Unit launched a pilot program to guide companies on how to (1) conduct an internal FCPA investigation, and (2) disclose a violation to the DOJ. As Assistant Attorney General Caldwell remarked at the time:

> [The] pilot program . . . provides guidance to our prosecutors for corporate resolutions in FCPA cases, and . . . is designed to motivate companies to voluntarily self-disclose FCPA-related misconduct, fully cooperate with the Fraud Section, and, where appropriate, remediate flaws in their controls and compliance programs.
>
> . . . .
>
> The pilot program describes what we mean by "voluntary self-disclosure," "full cooperation," and "remediation." It also explains the credit available to companies that in fact voluntarily self-disclose FCPA misconduct, fully cooperate with investigations, and remediate. . . .
>
> In short, the guidance provides that if a company chooses not to voluntarily disclose its FCPA misconduct, it may receive limited credit if it later fully cooperates and timely and appropriately remediates–but any such credit will be markedly less than that afforded to companies that do self-disclose wrongdoing. By contrast, when a company not only cooperates and remediates, but also voluntarily self-discloses misconduct, it is eligible for the full range of potential mitigation credit. That means that if a criminal resolution is warranted, the Fraud Section may grant a reduction of up to 50 percent below the low end of the applicable U.S. Sentencing Guidelines fine range, and generally will not require appointment of a monitor. In addition, where those same conditions are met, the Fraud Section's FCPA Unit will consider a declination of prosecution.[183]

Caldwell's remarks reflect the great importance the DOJ and SEC place on early self-disclosure. Therefore, companies should report violations as soon as the evidence gathered through an internal investigation confirms that a violation occurred—even if the investigation is in its early stages and the full scope of the wrongdoing is not yet known.

The Fraud Section's Foreign Corrupt Practices Act Enforcement Plan and Guidance

U.S. Department of Justice, Criminal Division, Fraud Section[184]

April 5, 2016

Bribery of foreign officials to gain or retain a business advantage poses a serious systemic criminal problem across the globe. It harms those who play by the rules, siphons money away from communities, and undermines the rule of law.

FCPA Cases (June 7, 2016), https://www.sec.gov/news/pressrelease/2016-109.html.

183. Press Release, Leslie R. Caldwell, Assistant Attorney Gen., U.S. Dep't of Justice, Criminal Division Launches New FCPA Pilot Program (Apr. 5, 2016), https://www.justice.gov/archives/opa/blog/criminal-division-launches-new-fcpa-pilot-program.

184. Memorandum from Andrew Weissmann, Chief, Fraud Section, Criminal Div., U.S. Dep't of Justice, The Fraud Section's Foreign Corrupt Practices Act Enforcement Plan and Guidance 1-9 (Apr. 5, 2016) (footnotes omitted) (citations omitted), https://www.justice.gov/archives/opa/blog-entry/file/838386/download.

Accordingly, the Department of Justice (Department) is committed to enhancing its efforts to detect and prosecute both individuals and companies for violations of the Foreign Corrupt Practices Act (FCPA), which criminalizes various acts of bribery and related accounting fraud. This memorandum sets forth three steps in our enhanced FCPA enforcement strategy.

As the first and most important step in combatting FCPA violations, the Department is intensifying its investigative and prosecutorial efforts by substantially increasing its FCPA law enforcement resources. These new resources will significantly augment the ability of the Criminal Division's Fraud Section and the Federal Bureau of Investigation (FBI) to detect and prosecute individuals and companies that violate the FCPA. Specifically, the Fraud Section is increasing its FCPA unit by more than 50% by adding 10 more prosecutors to its ranks. At the same time, the FBI has established three new squads of special agents devoted to FCPA investigations and prosecutions. The Department's demonstrated commitment to devoting additional resources to FCPA investigations and prosecutions should send a message to wrongdoers that FCPA violations that might have gone uncovered in the past are now more likely to come to light.

Second, the United States is not going at this alone. The Department is strengthening its coordination with foreign counterparts in the effort to hold corrupt individuals and companies accountable. Law enforcement around the globe has increasingly been working collaboratively to combat bribery schemes that cross national borders. In short, an international approach is being taken to combat an international criminal problem. We are sharing leads with our international law enforcement counterparts, and they are sharing them with us. We are also coordinating to more effectively share documents and witnesses. The fruits of this increased international cooperation can be seen in the prosecutions of both individuals and corporations, in cases involving Archer Daniels Midland, Alcoa, Alstom, Dallas Airmotive, Hewlett-Packard, IAP, Marubeni, Vadim Mikerin, Parker Drilling, PetroTiger, Total, and VimpelCom, among many others.

Third, as set forth below, the Fraud Section is conducting an FCPA enforcement pilot program. The principal goal of this program is to promote greater accountability for individuals and companies that engage in corporate crime by motivating companies to voluntarily self-disclose FCPA-related misconduct, fully cooperate with the Fraud Section, and, where appropriate, remediate flaws in their controls and compliance programs. If successful, the pilot program will serve to further deter individuals and companies from engaging in FCPA violations in the first place, encourage companies to implement strong anti-corruption compliance programs to prevent and detect FCPA violations, and, consistent with the memorandum of the Deputy Attorney General dated September 9, 2015 ("DAG Memo on Individual Accountability"), increase the Fraud Section's ability to prosecute individual wrongdoers whose conduct might otherwise have gone undiscovered or been impossible to prove.

We aim to accomplish this goal of greater accountability in part through the increased enforcement measures discussed above— adding additional agents and prosecutors to investigate criminal activity, and enhancing our cooperation with foreign law enforcement authorities where possible. And we also aim to accomplish the same goal by providing greater transparency about what we require from companies seeking mitigation credit for voluntarily self-disclosing misconduct, fully cooperating with an investigation, and remediating, and what sort of credit those companies can receive if they do so consistent with these requirements. Mitigation credit will be available only if a company meets the mandates set out below, including the disclosure of all relevant facts about the individuals involved in the wrongdoing. Moreover, to be eligible for such credit, even a company that voluntarily self-discloses, fully cooperates, and remediates will be required to disgorge all profits resulting from the FCPA violation.

The balance of this memorandum sets forth the Fraud Section's guidance ("Guidance") to our FCPA attorneys about how the Fraud Section will pursue the pilot program. The Guidance first sets forth the standards for what constitutes (1) voluntary self-disclosure of criminality, (2) full cooperation, and (3) remediation by business organizations, for purposes of qualifying for mitigation credit from the Fraud Section in an FCPA matter. Next, the Guidance explains the credit that the Fraud Section will accord under this pilot to business organizations that voluntarily self-disclose, fully cooperate, and remediate. As set forth below, that credit may affect the type of disposition, the reduction in fine, or the determination of the need for a monitor.

By way of background, the Principles of Federal Prosecution of Business Organizations (the "USAM Principles") have long provided guidance on whether a criminal disposition against a company is appropriate and what form that disposition should take. In addition, the United States Sentencing Guidelines ("Sentencing Guidelines") provide for reduced fines for business organizations that voluntarily disclose criminal conduct, fully cooperate, and accept responsibility for the criminal conduct. To provide incentives for organizations to self-disclose misconduct, fully cooperate with a criminal investigation, and timely and appropriately remediate, the Fraud Section has historically provided business organizations that do such things with a reduction below the low end of the Sentencing Guidelines fine range. These fine reductions and other incentives have not previously been articulated in a written framework. By setting forth this Guidance, we intend to provide a clear and consistent understanding of the circumstances in which the Fraud Section may accord additional credit in FCPA matters to organizations that voluntarily disclose misconduct, fully cooperate, and timely and appropriately remediate.

The Guidance does not supplant the USAM Principles. Prosecutors must consider the ten factors set forth in the USAM when determining how to resolve criminal investigations of organizations. Prosecutors must also calculate the appropriate fine range under Chapter 8 of the Sentencing Guidelines. This Guidance, by contrast, sets forth the circumstances in which an organization can receive additional credit in FCPA matters, above and beyond any fine reduction provided for under the Sentencing Guidelines, and the manner in which that additional credit should be determined, whether it be in the type of disposition, the extent of reduction in fine, or the determination of the need for a monitor.

Organizations that voluntarily self-disclose, fully cooperate, and remediate will be eligible for significant credit in all three categories. But, as noted above, to receive this additional credit under the pilot program, organizations must meet the standards described below, which are more exacting than those required under the Sentencing Guidelines.

The pilot program will be effective April 5, 2016 as part of a one-year program applicable to all FCPA matters handled by the Fraud Section. The Guidance is being applied by the Fraud Section to organizations that voluntarily self-disclose or cooperate in FCPA matters during the pilot period, even if the pilot thereafter expires. By the end of this pilot period, the Fraud Section will determine whether the Guidance will be extended in duration and whether it should be modified in light of the pilot experience. The Guidance applies only to the Fraud Section's FCPA Unit and not to any other part of the Fraud Section, the Criminal Division, the United States Attorneys' Offices, any other part of the Department of Justice, or any other agency.

Nothing in the Guidance is intended to suggest that the government can require business organizations to voluntarily self-disclose, cooperate, or remediate. Companies remain free to reject these options and forego the credit available under the pilot program.

This Guidance first sets forth the requirements for a company to qualify for credit for voluntary self-disclosure, cooperation, and timely and appropriate remediation under this pilot program, including exceptions to the general rules. It then sets forth the credit that should be accorded if a company meets these criteria.

A. REQUIREMENTS

1. Voluntary Self-Disclosure in FCPA Matters

Voluntary self-disclosure of an FCPA violation is encouraged. Indeed, in implementing the DAG Memo on Individual Accountability, the Department recently revised the USAM Principles to underscore the importance of voluntary self-reporting of corporate wrongdoing. Under the current USAM Principles, prosecutors are to consider a corporation's timely and voluntary self-disclosure, both as an independent factor and in evaluating the company's overall cooperation and the adequacy of the company's compliance program.

In evaluating self-disclosure during this pilot, the Fraud Section will make a careful assessment of the circumstances of the disclosure. A disclosure that a company is required to make, by law, agreement, or contract, does not constitute voluntary self-disclosure for purposes of this pilot. Thus, the Fraud Section will determine whether the disclosure was already required to be made. In addition, the Fraud Section will require the following items for a company to receive credit for voluntary self-disclosure of wrongdoing under this pilot:

- The voluntary disclosure qualifies under U.S.S.G. § 8C2.5(g)(1) as occurring "prior to an imminent threat of disclosure or government investigation";

- The company discloses the conduct to the Department "within a reasonably prompt time after becoming aware of the offense," with the burden being on the company to demonstrate timeliness; and
- The company discloses all relevant facts known to it, including all relevant facts about the individuals involved in any FCPA violation.

2. Full Cooperation in FCPA Matters

In addition to the USAM Principles, the following items will be required for a company to receive credit for full cooperation under this pilot (beyond the credit available under the Sentencing Guidelines):

- As set forth in the DAG Memo on Individual Accountability, disclosure on a timely basis of all facts relevant to the wrongdoing at issue, including all facts related to involvement in the criminal activity by the corporation's officers, employees, or agents;
- Proactive cooperation, rather than reactive; that is, the company must disclose facts that are relevant to the investigation, even when not specifically asked to do so, and must identify opportunities for the government to obtain relevant evidence not in the company's possession and not otherwise known to the government;
- Preservation, collection, and disclosure of relevant documents and information relating to their provenance;
- Provision of timely updates on a company's internal investigation, including but not limited to rolling disclosures of information;
- Where requested, de-confliction of an internal investigation with the government investigation;
- Provision of all facts relevant to potential criminal conduct by all third-party companies (including their officers or employees) and third-party individuals;
- Upon request, making available for Department interviews those company officers and employees who possess relevant information; this includes, where appropriate and possible, officers and employees located overseas as well as former officers and employees (subject to the individuals' Fifth Amendment rights);
- Disclosure of all relevant facts gathered during a company's independent investigation, including attribution of facts to specific sources where such attribution does not violate the attorney-client privilege, rather than a general narrative of the facts;
- Disclosure of overseas documents, the location in which such documents were found, and who found the documents (except where such disclosure is impossible due to foreign law, including but not limited to foreign data privacy laws);
  - Note: Where a company claims that disclosure is prohibited, the burden is on the company to establish the prohibition. Moreover, a company should work diligently to identify all available legal bases to provide such documents.

- Unless legally prohibited, facilitation of the third-party production of documents and witnesses from foreign jurisdictions; and
- Where requested and appropriate, provision of translations of relevant documents in foreign languages.

Cooperation comes in many forms. Once the threshold requirements of the DAG Memo on Individual Accountability have been met, the Fraud Section should assess the scope, quantity, quality, and timing of cooperation based on the circumstances of each case when assessing how to evaluate a company's cooperation under this pilot. For example, the Fraud Section does not expect a small company to conduct as expansive an investigation in as short a period of time as a Fortune 100 company. Nor do we generally expect a company to investigate matters unrelated in time or subject to the matter under investigation in order to qualify for full cooperation credit. An appropriately tailored investigation is what typically should be required to receive full cooperation credit; the company may, of course, for its own business reasons seek to conduct a broader investigation.

As set forth in USAM 9-28.720, eligibility for full cooperation credit is not predicated upon waiver of the attorney-client privilege or work product protection and none of the requirements above require such waiver. Nothing in the Guidance or the DAG Memo on Individual Accountability alters that policy, which remains in full force and effect. Furthermore, not all companies will satisfy all the components of full cooperation, either because they decide to cooperate only later in an investigation or they timely decide to cooperate but fail to meet all of the criteria listed above. In general, such companies should be eligible for some cooperation credit under this pilot if they meet the DAG Memo on Individual Accountability criteria, but the credit generally will be markedly less than for full cooperation, depending on the extent to which the cooperation was lacking.

3. Timely and Appropriate Remediation in FCPA Matters

Remediation can be difficult to ascertain and highly case specific. In spite of these difficulties, encouraging appropriate and timely remediation is important to reducing corporate recidivism and detecting and deterring individual wrongdoing. The Fraud Section's Compliance Counsel is assisting us in refining our benchmarks for assessing compliance programs and for thoroughly evaluating an organization's remediation efforts.

In evaluating remediation efforts under this pilot program, the Fraud Section will first determine whether a company is eligible for cooperation credit; in other words, a company cannot fail to cooperate and then expect to receive credit for remediation despite that lack of cooperation. The following items generally will be required for a company to receive credit for timely and appropriate remediation under this pilot (beyond the credit available under the Sentencing Guidelines):

- Implementation of an effective compliance and ethics program, the criteria for which will be periodically updated and which may vary based on the size and resources of the organization, but will include:

- Whether the company has established a culture of compliance, including an awareness among employees that any criminal conduct, including the conduct underlying the investigation, will not be tolerated;
- Whether the company dedicates sufficient resources to the compliance function;
- The quality and experience of the compliance personnel such that they can understand and identify the transactions identified as posing a potential risk;
- The independence of the compliance function;
- Whether the company's compliance program has performed an effective risk assessment and tailored the compliance program based on that assessment;
- How a company's compliance personnel are compensated and promoted compared to other employees;
- The auditing of the compliance program to assure its effectiveness; and
- The reporting structure of compliance personnel within the company.
- Appropriate discipline of employees, including those identified by the corporation as responsible for the misconduct, and a system that provides for the possibility of disciplining others with oversight of the responsible individuals, and considers how compensation is affected by both disciplinary infractions and failure to supervise adequately; and
- Any additional steps that demonstrate recognition of the seriousness of the corporation's misconduct, acceptance of responsibility for it, and the implementation of measures to reduce the risk of repetition of such misconduct, including measures to identify future risks.

B. CREDIT FOR BUSINESS ORGANIZATIONS UNDER THE PILOT PROGRAM

1. Limited Credit for Full Cooperation and Timely and Appropriate Remediation in FCPA Matters Without Voluntary Self-Disclosure

If a company has not voluntarily disclosed its FCPA misconduct in accordance with the standards set forth above, it may receive limited credit under this pilot program if it later fully cooperates and timely and appropriately remediates. Such credit will be markedly less than that afforded to companies that do self-disclose wrongdoing, as described immediately below in category B.2. Specifically, in circumstances where no voluntary self-disclosure has been made, the Fraud Section's FCPA Unit will accord at most a 25% reduction off the bottom of the Sentencing Guidelines fine range.

2. Credit for Voluntary Self-Disclosure, Full Cooperation, and Timely and Appropriate Remediation in FCPA Matters

When a company has voluntarily self-disclosed misconduct in an FCPA matter in accordance with the standards set forth above; has fully cooperated in a manner consistent with the DAG Memo on Individual Accountability and the USAM Principles; has met the additional stringent requirements of the pilot program;

and has timely and appropriately remediated, the company qualifies for the full range of potential mitigation credit.

In such cases, if a criminal resolution is warranted, the Fraud Section's FCPA Unit:

- may accord up to a 50% reduction off the bottom end of the Sentencing Guidelines fine range, if a fine is sought; and
- generally should not require appointment of a monitor if a company has, at the time of resolution, implemented an effective compliance program.

Where those same conditions are met, the Fraud Section's FCPA Unit will consider a declination of prosecution. As noted above, this pilot program is intended to encourage companies to disclose FCPA misconduct to permit the prosecution of individuals whose criminal wrongdoing might otherwise never be uncovered by or disclosed to law enforcement. Such voluntary self-disclosures thus promote aggressive enforcement of the FCPA and the investigation and prosecution of culpable individuals. Of course, in considering whether declination may be warranted, Fraud Section prosecutors must also take into account countervailing interests, including the seriousness of the offense: in cases where, for example, there has been involvement by executive management of the company in the FCPA misconduct, a significant profit to the company from the misconduct in relation to the company's size and wealth, a history of non-compliance by the company, or a prior resolution by the company with the Department within the past five years, a criminal resolution likely would be warranted.[185]

Hypothetical: First Response After Discovery of a Potential Violation

Brazilia Co. ("Brazilia") is a manufacturer of pharmaceutical products based in Brazil whose shares trade on the New York Stock Exchange. Brazilia has twenty subsidiaries and divisions outside Brazil, including BraziliaMexico, a wholly owned subsidiary in Mexico. Brazilia's annual revenue exceeds $100 million.

An annual audit of BraziliaMexico's books has revealed a $50,000 payment described as "consulting fees" made to a Panamanian shell company. When confronted, the sales agent who made the payment admitted that it was a bribe paid to a local official to increase sales. The sales agent claimed that he had done it only to compete with other bribe-paying sales agents and that "everybody in the company is doing it." When terminated, the sales agent threatened to "go to the authorities" unless he was reinstated.

---

185. *Id.*

1) Is the sales agent's conduct covered by the FCPA? Why?
2) Assuming that the sales agent's conduct is covered by the FCPA, what should be Brazilia's next steps in conducting an investigation?
3) At what point in the investigation should Brazilia report the violation to the DOJ and/or the SEC?

Which of the following documents should Brazilia consider turning over to the prosecutors, and why?

- A memorandum from a Mexican lawyer to the sales representative, explaining how to set up a shell corporation in Panama.
- A memorandum obtained by Brazilia following discovery of the potential violation containing an opinion by outside counsel regarding Brazilia's potential liability under the FCPA.
- Emails and memoranda generated by Brazilia's legal department discussing the significance of the evidence uncovered by the investigation and how an enforcement action would impact the company.

Following self-disclosure to the DOJ, Brazilia referred the investigation to Edwards & Smith, LLP ("E&S"), a reputable New York law firm with experience in conducting FCPA investigations. E&S immediately retained the services of a forensic accountant to assist in the investigation.

4) What documents should the forensic accountant review in connection with the payment to the shell corporation?
5) What other documents, if any, should the forensic accountant review?
6) Which employee(s) should E&S and/or the forensic accountant interview in the course of the investigation?
7) Should the investigation at any point be expanded to any other subsidiaries and/or divisions of Brazilia outside Mexico? If so, when?

During the investigation, E&S and the forensic accountant discover several corrupt payments to government officials by BraziliaMexico's sales agents via shell corporations.

8) What controls should Brazilia put into place to remediate?

IX. Continuous Improvement: Periodic Testing and Review

The FCPA Guide cautions that "[a]n organization should take the time to review and test its controls, and it should think critically about its potential weaknesses and risk areas."[186] Similarly, FSGO § 8B2.1 provides:

---

186. FCPA GUIDE, *supra* note 3, at 62.

(5) The organization shall take reasonable steps—

(A) to ensure that the organization's compliance and ethics program is followed, including monitoring and auditing to detect criminal conduct;

(B) to evaluate periodically the effectiveness of the organization's compliance and ethics program. . . .[187]

This Hallmark requires ongoing evaluations, which can be divided into monitoring and auditing.[188] Monitoring and auditing are essential because they (1) ensure that the compliance program is functioning properly; and (2) detect violations not otherwise reported through the hotline. In many ways, monitoring and auditing perform a similar function to the testing of internal reporting controls encountered under SOX § 404, with one significant difference. Under SOX § 404, internal controls are tested for *material* weaknesses—that is, weaknesses that may have a material effect on the company's financial reports. By contrast, compliance auditing is not subject to a materiality threshold, since any violation can have a significant negative impact on the company. Compliance auditing ensures that the company operates within the requirements of the law at all times.

A. Monitoring

Monitoring is the observation of the compliance processes in real time with the aim of responding to weaknesses or red flags.[189] Monitoring may involve training personnel, as well as the use of automated technology to identify and respond to suspicious transactions or other red flags. In the context of third parties, monitoring includes continual updating of due diligence information, policies, codes, and training.[190]

Monitoring activities, such as approvals, reconciliations, verifications, and supervision are incorporated into the company's normal operations. They are tailored to the company's specific risks and designed to detect violations in real time. For example, a company engaged in sales to foreign governments will have sophisticated monitoring in place to supervise employee interactions with government officials and prevent improper payments. Similarly, a company with a large number of third-party agents in high-risk countries will have elaborate systems for gathering real-time information regarding distributors' activities.

Monitoring systems may be manual (as in the case of an officer verifying that necessary approvals have been obtained) or automated. Today's complex business operations, which often span many countries, require monitoring systems that can quickly analyze large volumes of data and discern anomalous patterns and suspicious activities. They can also be "designed to incorporate the knowledge and experience of business unit experts, thus greatly surpassing the

---

187. U.S. Sentencing Guidelines Manual § 8B2.1(b)(5) (U.S. Sentencing Comm'n 2016).

188. *See* FCPA Guide, *supra* note 3, at 61–62.

189. *See id.* at 62.

190. *See id.* at 60.

capabilities of individuals. . . ."[191] Automation can assist companies in meeting this challenge. Examples include:

- Identification and analysis of predetermined FCPA red flags
- Timely detection of high-risk transactions, such as "[d]uplicate payments, round-dollar payments, sequential payments, and cash distributions"[192]
- Monitoring of training programs to verify employee completion and certification of training[193]

As part of the design of automated monitoring systems, suspicious transaction rules should be developed in consultation with personnel who work in and have a detailed understanding of the relevant business units. Given that all technologies have inherent limitations, it is important that data generated by such systems be manually reviewed for further action. "[S]till on the horizon is what's considered the 'Holy Grail' of FCPA compliance—continuous monitoring of accounts and transactions using crawling software to identify and stop improper payments before they occur."[194]

B. Auditing

Auditing is the periodic review of internal controls to ensure that weaknesses are uncovered.[195] The FCPA Guide requires that all areas of compliance undergo audits, including internal departments, divisions, and subsidiaries.[196] In contrast to monitoring systems, which continuously observe operations, compliance audits periodically test compliance controls, verify compliance with company policies and detect violations. Audits typically include three stages:

1) Planning, which includes assessing risk and developing a testing plan;
2) Performance of tests; and
3) Reporting of findings and recommendations.[197]

In the planning stage, the auditor sets the scope of the audit by developing a full understanding of the relevant areas of operations and compliance objectives. This allows the auditor to perform a risk assessment that will dictate selection of business units and locations to be included in the scope of the audit. In making this assessment, the auditor conducts interviews of appropriate personnel; and, where necessary, individuals outside of the company such as a regulator or subject matter

---

191. § 13:42. Surveillance process—Surveillance, information systems and statistical analysis, Compliance Programs & Corp Sent Gdlns § 13:42 (2016).

192. DELOITTE, *Using Advanced Management Controls to Strengthen FCPA Compliance*, WALL ST. J. (Mar. 16, 2017, 12:01 AM), http://deloitte.wsj.com/cfo/2017/03/16/using-advanced-management-controls-to-strengthen-fcpa-compliance/.

193. *See id.*

194. *Id.*

195. *See* FCPA GUIDE, *supra* note 3, at 62.

196. *See id.* at 61–62.

197. § 13:17. Auditing process—Scope of auditing, Compliance Programs & Corp Sent Gdlns § 13:17 (2016).

expert. The auditor should also understand the controls that are already in place to achieve the relevant compliance objectives. In the context of an FCPA audit, the controls that typically fall within the scope of the audit are those specified in the FCPA Guide's Hallmarks. Those include, among other things, company policies and the code of conduct, the risk assessment process, due diligence procedures for onboarding third parties, and the functioning of the confidential hotline.

In the testing stage, the auditor evaluates those controls determined to be within the scope of the audit in order to (1) ensure that sufficient controls are present to achieve compliance objectives; and (2) verify that those controls are functioning as intended.[198] The nature and extent of testing of a control, or group of controls, will depend on the probability and potential impact of a control failure on the company. For example, due diligence processes for vetting third parties will be subjected to varying levels of scrutiny depending on the corruption risk posed by the markets in which they operate. Similarly, controls related to business units with high levels of government interaction will be tested more extensively than those applied to units with little or no government interaction.[199]

Tools for performing control testing include interviews with employees, and selection and review of high-risk transactions, such as:

- Payments to consultants
- Payments in connection with licenses and permits
- Payments related to government contracts
- Gift, travel, and entertainment expenses
- Charitable contributions
- Cash transactions and advances[200]

In light of the high volumes of data generated by the audit process, auditors should take advantage of information technology for data analysis and classification.

In addition to control testing, FCPA audits typically include transaction reviews to ensure proper documentation and identify violations. In performing this task, the audit team can be assisted by forensic accountants experienced in corruption investigations who can "appl[y] technical knowledge, experience and seasoned judgment in selecting testing samples and reviewing transactions."[201]

In the final stage, auditors must document, evaluate, and report the results of the audit process to senior management and audit committee of the board of directors. The audit report will contain findings regarding any control deficiencies and/or violations encountered and recommend remediation measures. A key purpose of documenting the audit findings is to provide a baseline so that future audits can ensure that deficiencies have been corrected.[202]

---

198. *See, e.g.,* COSO Executive Summary, *supra* note 23, at 7.

199. *See* Ernst & Young LLP, Anti-Corruption Internal Audits: A Crucial Element of Anti-Corruption Compliance 2, 4 (2013), http://www.ey.com/Publication/vwLUAssets/EY-FIDS-Anti-corruption-internal-audits/$FILE/EY-FIDS-Anti-corruption-internal-audits.pdf.

200. *See id.* at 4.

201. *Id.* at 1.

202. *See* FCPA Guide, *supra* note 3, at 61–62.

Additional Reading Materials

Institute of Internal Auditors [IIA], *Practice Guide: Auditing Anti-Bribery and Anti-Corruption Programs* (2014), http://www.iia.nl/SiteFiles/Nieuws/PG-Auditing-Anti-bribery-and-Anti-corruption-Programs.pdf.

Hypothetical: Defining the Scope of an Audit

Pishie, Inc. ("Pishie") is a U.S.-based issuer engaged in the production and distribution of pharmaceutical products around the world. Forty percent of Pishie's worldwide sales are to foreign governments, including those of China, France, and Nigeria. Pishie is about to conduct an annual audit of its FCPA compliance program. As part of their planning, Pishie's internal auditors would like to identify areas of operation that pose a significant risk of corruption and, therefore should be included within the scope of the audit. Which of the following areas should be included, and why?

- Sales (to the private sector)
- Government procurement
- Human resources
- Shipping
- Real estate (planning, zoning, construction)
- Accounting
- Customer complaints
- Distributors
- Vendors
- Outside consultants
- Insurance
- Legal
- Transportation

X. Pre-Acquisition Due Diligence and Post-Acquisition Integration

In the context of mergers and acquisitions, the DOJ and SEC follow two general principles for deciding when to impose FCPA liability on the acquiring company, the target, or both.[203]

First, if a target company was subject to the FCPA before the closing, the acquiring company generally inherits the target's liabilities for past FCPA

---

203. *See* FCPA Guide, *supra* note 3, at 28.

violations.[204] The acquiring company can substantially mitigate its liability by taking several pre- and post-acquisition steps:

1) Conduct proper risk-based anticorruption due diligence on potential new business acquisitions.
2) Ensure that the acquiring company's code of conduct and compliance policies and procedures apply as quickly as is practicable to newly acquired businesses or merged entities.
3) Train the directors, officers, and employees of newly acquired businesses or merged entities, as well as their agents and business partners, on the FCPA and other relevant anticorruption laws and the company's code of conduct and compliance policies and procedures.
4) Conduct an FCPA-specific audit of all newly acquired or merged businesses as quickly as practicable.
5) Report any corrupt payments discovered as part of due diligence of newly acquired entities or merged entities.[205]

Keep in mind that the target itself remains liable for past violations.[206] The due diligence process is not only essential in mitigating risk of liability, but also in accurately calculating the target's value.

As a second general rule, if a target company was not subject to the FCPA prior to the acquisition, the DOJ and SEC will not retroactively prosecute its past misconduct.[207] Note that both the target and the acquiring company can be prosecuted for any violations that occur after closing.[208] This is because two things happen as soon as the acquisition is completed:

1) The target becomes immediately subject to FCPA jurisdiction by virtue of being owned by the acquiring company.
2) The acquiring company becomes immediately responsible for the target's conduct.[209]

Thus, regardless of whether a target was subject to the FCPA before the acquisition, companies should undertake risk-based pre-acquisition due diligence in order to discover and stop any ongoing violations.[210]

M&A due diligence is similar to third-party due diligence discussed earlier. The objective of pre-acquisition due diligence is to:

- Quantify the risk of past or future FCPA violations by the target.
- Employ investigative tools to detect and report past violations and to stop ongoing violations before the acquisition is completed.

---

204. *See id.*
205. *See id.* at 29.
206. *See id.* at 29–30.
207. *See id.* at 28.
208. *See id.* at 30–32, 62.
209. *See id.* at 28.
210. *See id.* at 62.

- Identify deficiencies in the target's compliance and ethics program and remedy them.[211]

The process begins with an initial assessment of risk by evaluating several risk factors, including:

- Geography
- Industry
- State of the target's books, records, and internal controls
- The target's interactions with government entities
- The target's connections with governments or government officials

These risk factors provide a starting point for setting the appropriate level of scrutiny for the target, after which the level of scrutiny should increase as red flags surface. Keep in mind that the target's relationships with third parties will become the acquiring company's relationships after closing. Therefore, as part of the pre-acquisition due diligence process, those relationships should be subject to the same level of scrutiny as the acquirer's own third-party relationships.

The DOJ and SEC also give substantial weight to the acquiring company's prompt incorporation of the target into its compliance program, specifically:

- "[T]raining new employees,
- [R]eevaluating third parties under company standards, and where appropriate,
- [C]onducting audits on new business units."[212]

FCPA Opinion Procedure Release No. 03-01

No. 2003-01[213]

January 15, 2003

The Requestor is a U.S. issuer. Requestor intends to purchase the stock of Company A, another U.S. company which has both U.S. and foreign subsidiaries, and thereafter operate it as a subsidiary. During its due diligence efforts, Requestor learned that officers of a foreign subsidiary, including officers located within the United States, authorized and made payments to individuals employed by foreign state-owned entities to obtain or retain business. Requestor notified Company A of its findings, and both companies commenced parallel investigations of Company A's operations throughout the world. The companies then disclosed the results of their investigations to

---

211. *See id.* at 28–30, 62.
212. *See* FCPA GUIDE, *supra* note 3, at 62.
213. U.S. Dep't of Justice, FCPA Opinion Procedure Release 2003-01 (Jan. 15, 2003), https://www.justice.gov/sites/default/files/criminal-fraud/legacy/2010/04/11/0301.pdf.

the Department of Justice and the staff of the U.S. Securities and Exchange Commission (the "SEC").

With Requestor's encouragement and approval, Company A has taken certain remedial actions, including making appropriate disclosures to the investing public, issuing instructions to each of its foreign subsidiaries to cease all payments to foreign officials, and suspending the most senior officers and employees implicated in the payments pending the conclusion of its investigation.

Both Requestor and Company A wish to proceed with the acquisition. Requestor, however, is concerned that by acquiring Company A it is also acquiring potential criminal and civil liability under the FCPA for the past acts of Company A's employees.

Requestor undertakes to do the following once the transaction closes and it becomes the owner of Company A:

1. Requestor will continue to cooperate with the Department and the SEC in their respective investigations of the past payments and will similarly cooperate with foreign law enforcement authorities;
2. Requestor will ensure that any employees or officers of Company A found to have made or authorized unlawful payments to foreign officials are appropriately disciplined;
3. Requestor will disclose to the Department any additional pre-acquisition payments to foreign officials made by Company A or its subsidiaries that it discovers after the acquisition;
4. Requestor will extend to Company A its existing compliance program. Such compliance program will, if necessary, be modified to insure that it is reasonably designed to detect and deter, through training and reporting, violations of the FCPA and foreign bribery laws; and
5. Requestor will ensure that Company A implements a system of internal controls and makes and keeps accurate books and records.

Based on all the facts and circumstances, as represented by the Requestor, the Department does not presently intend to take any enforcement action against the Requestor for the pre-acquisition conduct of described in its request of companies that will be wholly owned subsidiaries following the acquisition. This statement of intent does not, of course, apply to any payments made after the date of acquisition, nor does it apply to individuals involved in making or authorizing the payments.

This FCPA Opinion Release has no application to any party which did not join in the request, and can be relied upon by the Requestor only to the extent that the disclosure of facts and circumstances in the request is accurate and complete and continues to accurately and completely reflect such facts and circumstances.

FCPA Opinion Procedure Release No. 08-02

No. 08-02[214]

June 13, 2008

Foreign Corrupt Practices Act Review

Opinion Procedure Release

The Department has reviewed the Foreign Corrupt Practices Act ("FCPA") Opinion Procedure request of Halliburton Company and its controlled subsidiaries ("Halliburton"), a U.S. issuer, which is currently considering making an additional bid to acquire the entire share capital of a company based in the United Kingdom ("Target"). Target is traded on the London Stock Exchange, has approximately 4,000 employees, and operates in over fifty countries, including throughout Africa, the Middle East, Asia, the former Soviet Union, South America, Europe, and North America. Target is involved in well flow management and provides specialized products and services in the upstream oil and gas industry. Target has a number of national oil companies as customers. A company formed by a consortium of primarily foreign investors ("Competitor") is also bidding to acquire Target. Competitor submitted the first, and more recently the highest, bid, which is unconditional.

Halliburton has submitted a request for an opinion regarding the Department's present intention to take enforcement action under the circumstances here, specifically posing the following three questions: (1) whether the proposed acquisition transaction itself would violate the FCPA; (2) whether through the proposed acquisition of Target, Halliburton would "inherit" any FCPA liabilities of Target for pre-acquisition unlawful conduct; and (3) whether Halliburton would be held criminally liable for any post-acquisition unlawful conduct by Target prior to Halliburton's completion of its FCPA and anti-corruption due diligence, where such conduct is identified and disclosed to the Department within 180 days of closing.

CIRCUMSTANCES OF THE REQUEST

The circumstances of the request are as follows: Halliburton represents that, as a result of U.K. legal restrictions inherent in the bidding process for a public U.K. company, it has had insufficient time and inadequate access to information to complete appropriate FCPA and anti-corruption due diligence and that it can only complete such due diligence post-closing. Pursuant to the U.K. bidding process, given that Target's board has already recommended to its shareholders the acceptance of Competitor's bid, Target is legally obliged to provide to Halliburton the same information given to Competitor, but it is not required either to (1) provide any additional information to Halliburton, or (2) agree to entertain an offer

---

214. U.S. Dep't of Justice, FCPA Opinion Procedure Release No. 08-02 (June 13, 2008) (footnote omitted), https://www.justice.gov/sites/default/files/criminal-fraud/legacy/2010/04/11/0802.pdf.

by Halliburton that is subject to any condition that has not already been imposed upon Competitor.

Thus, if Halliburton wanted to condition the making of its bid on the satisfactory completion of FCPA and anti-corruption diligence or on the pre-closing completion of remediation to its satisfaction, Target would be under no legal obligation to agree to any such terms, and might well reject a conditional, higher bid by Halliburton in favor of the lower, but unconditional bid of Competitor.

While in connection with the bidding process Halliburton has had access to a data room with certain information concerning Target, under the terms of a confidentiality agreement entered into between Halliburton and Target, Halliburton is not permitted to discuss with the Department whether any specific FCPA, corruption, or related internal controls or accounting issues have arisen, and if so, the nature and extent of such issues, except as required by applicable law.

Halliburton represents that, in light of the above restrictions, if it makes an additional bid which is successful and thus acquires Target, it intends to implement the following post-closing plan:

Immediately following the closing, Halliburton will meet with the Department to disclose whether the information made available to Halliburton or otherwise learned by Halliburton pre-closing suggests that any FCPA, corruption, or related internal controls or accounting issues exist or existed at Target and, if so, will disclose such information to the Department.

Within ten business days of the closing, Halliburton will present to the Department a comprehensive, risk-based FCPA and anti-corruption due diligence work plan which will address, among other things, the use of agents and other third parties; commercial dealings with state-owned customers; any joint venture, teaming, or consortium arrangements; customs and immigration matters; tax matters; and any government licenses and permits. Such work plan will organize the due diligence effort into high risk, medium risk, and lowest risk elements. Halliburton shall consult with the Department regarding the work plan. Over time, the work plan shall be reviewed and, if necessary, revised as the plan is implemented and more information is learned.

Within 90 days of the closing, Halliburton will report to the Department the results to date of its high risk due diligence. Halliburton will provide the Department periodic progress reports over the course of the 90 days, and thereafter as appropriate.

Within 120 days of the closing, Halliburton will report to the Department the results to date of its medium risk due diligence. Halliburton will provide the Department periodic progress reports over the course of the 120 days, and thereafter as appropriate.

Within 180 days of the closing, Halliburton will report to the Department the results to date of its lowest risk due diligence. Halliburton will provide the Department periodic progress reports over the course of the 180 days, and thereafter as appropriate.

To the extent that issues identified during Halliburton's due diligence require further examination beyond the 180-day period, Halliburton will complete such remaining due diligence expeditiously and provide periodic reports thereof to the Department until concluded.

In any event, Halliburton will complete its due diligence and remediation related to Target, including completing its investigation of any issues that are identified within the 180-day period, by no later than one year from the date of closing.

Halliburton will retain external counsel and third-party consultants, including forensic accountants, as well as utilize internal resources, as appropriate, to conduct the FCPA and anti-corruption due diligence. The due diligence process shall include, under all appropriate circumstances and in all appropriate locations, examination of relevant Target records, including e-mail review and review of company financial and accounting records, as well as interviews of relevant Target personnel and other individuals.

All agents and other third parties associated with Target who are expected to continue to work for Target post-closing, and as to whom there are no compliance issues to be resolved, will as soon as commercially reasonable be required to sign new contracts (rather than contract modifications or extensions) with Halliburton that incorporate appropriate FCPA and anti-corruption representations and warranties, anti-corruption provisions, and audit rights, as provided for under Halliburton's Code of Business Conduct and related policies and procedures. Agents and other third parties who will not continue to work for Target post-closing will be terminated as expeditiously as possible. Based on the results of its due diligence efforts, Halliburton will take appropriate remedial action in the event it discovers any FCPA or corruption-related problems, including suspending or terminating any agents and other third parties and taking appropriate remedial action regarding relevant employees.

Upon closing, Halliburton will immediately impose its own Code of Business Conduct and specific FCPA and anti-corruption policies and procedures on Target, including effectively communicating the same to all Target employees. Within 60 days of the closing, Halliburton will provide FCPA and anti-corruption training to all Target officers and all Target employees whose positions or job responsibilities warrant such training on an expedited basis, including all employees in management, sales, accounting, and financial control positions. Halliburton shall provide all other appropriate Target employees with such training within 90 days of closing.

Halliburton will disclose to the Department all FCPA, corruption, and related internal controls and accounting issues that it uncovers during the course of its 180-day due diligence. Halliburton will complete any additional steps the Department deems necessary to complete the due diligence and remediation plan.

Halliburton further represents that post-closing, it will maintain Target as a wholly owned subsidiary for so long as the Department is investigating any conduct by Target or any of its officers, directors, employees, agents, subsidiaries, and affiliates. Halliburton expressly acknowledges and agrees that Target, and all Target subsidiaries and affiliates, retain their liability for past and future violations of the FCPA, if any.

ANALYSIS AND CONCLUSION

Based upon all the facts and circumstances as represented, and assuming Halliburton satisfactorily completes each of the steps detailed herein, the Department does not presently intend to take any enforcement action against Halliburton for: (1) the acquisition of Target in and of itself; (2) any pre-acquisition unlawful conduct by Target disclosed to the Department within 180 days of the closing; and (3) any post-acquisition conduct by Target disclosed to the Department within 180 days of the closing, and which does not continue beyond the 180-day period or, if in the judgment of the Department the alleged conduct cannot be fully investigated within the 180-day period, which does not continue beyond such time as the conduct can reasonably be stopped. In issuing this Opinion Release, the Department specifically notes the particular circumstances of this transaction, including the foreign legal impediments to robust pre-acquisition due diligence. In the view of the Department, for the reasons set forth below, the issuance of this Opinion Release advances the interests of the Department in enforcing the FCPA and promoting FCPA due diligence in connection with corporate transactions, and permits the Requestor to proceed with an additional bid for Target with the benefit of the protections afforded by the Opinion Release procedure.

First, consistent with precedent, the Department believes that the execution of the transaction here would not, in and of itself, create FCPA liability for Halliburton. In FCPA Opinion Procedure Release 2001-01 (May 24, 2001), the Department addressed whether funds a corporation contributes as part of a corporate combination transaction may be considered a "payment" that is "in furtherance of" a bribe within the meaning of 15 U.S.C. § 78dd-1. The Department discussed the risk that funds contributed to a joint venture by Corporation A might be used to make payments to an agent under pre-existing unlawful contracts that Corporation B contributed to the joint venture. Those issues, however, do not appear to be present here. Target is a public company listed on a major exchange, and at least 65% of its shares are held by large, institutional investors. Any amounts Halliburton pays to acquire Target will go to shareholders and not to Target itself. It is unlikely that any Target shareholders were corruptly given their shares such that the purchase of Target by Halliburton would improperly enrich such shareholders. Moreover, as a practical matter, it is impossible for any acquirer of a substantial public company to determine the identity of all shareholders and investigate how such shares were acquired.

Second, in light of the facts presented here and the particular restrictions in U.K. law regarding the bidding process, the Department does not presently intend to take any enforcement action with respect to any pre-acquisition conduct by Target disclosed to the Department during the 180-day period following the closing, provided Halliburton satisfactorily proceeds in accordance with the post-closing plan and remediation detailed above.

Third, the Department notes that an acquiring company may be held liable as a matter of law for any unlawful payments made by an acquired company or its

520 • Part III. The Effective Compliance Program

personnel after the date of acquisition. In that regard, in a prior Opinion Release, which related to an acquiring corporation's potential FCPA liability based on the target's pre-acquisition conduct, the Department did not provide assurances with respect to unlawful "payments made after the date of acquisition." Release No. 2003-01 (January 15, 2003). Under the circumstances here, however, there is insufficient time and inadequate access to complete appropriate pre-acquisition FCPA due diligence and remediation. As represented by Halliburton, under the application of the U.K. Takeover Code, it has no legal ability to require a specified level of due diligence or to insist upon remedial measures until after the acquisition is completed. As a result, Halliburton's ability to take action to prevent unlawful payments by Target or its personnel during the period immediately after the closing has been severely compromised. Assuming that Halliburton, in the judgment of the Department, satisfactorily implements the post-closing plan and remediation detailed above, and assuming that no Halliburton employee or agent knowingly plays a role in approving or making any improper payment by Target, the Department does not presently intend to take any enforcement action against Halliburton for any post-acquisition violations of the antibribery provisions of the FCPA committed by Target during the 180-day period after closing provided that Halliburton: (a) discloses such conduct to the Department within 180 days of closing; (b) stops and remediates such conduct within 180 days of closing, or, if the alleged conduct, in the judgment of the Department, cannot be fully investigated within the 180-day period, stops and remediates such conduct as soon as it can reasonably be stopped; and (c) completes its due diligence and remediation, including completing its investigation of any issues that are identified within the 180-day period, by no later than one year from the date of closing.

The Department reserves the right, however, to take enforcement action against Halliburton with respect to: (a) any FCPA violations committed by Target during the 180-day period that are not disclosed to the Department during this same time period; (b) any FCPA violations committed by Target at any time where any Halliburton employee or agent knowingly participates in the unlawful conduct; and (c) any issues identified within the 180-day period which are not investigated to conclusion within one year of closing. In no event does this Opinion Release provide any protection for any conduct which occurs after the 180-day period. The Department further reserves the right to prosecute or take enforcement action against Target and any of its subsidiaries and affiliates for any and all violations of the FCPA or any other federal criminal statute either pre- or post-acquisition, whether disclosed to the Department or not. The Department notes, however, that any unlawful conduct by Target disclosed to the Department by Halliburton pursuant to the post-closing plan and this Opinion Request would qualify as a "voluntary disclosure" under the Department's Principles of Federal Prosecution of Business Organizations, Section VII, and such disclosure may be considered by the Department as a factor in any determination whether to charge Target.

This FCPA Opinion Release applies to the Requestor, Halliburton, only, has no binding application to any party which did not join in the request, and can be relied upon by Halliburton only to the extent that the disclosure of facts and circumstances in this request is accurate and complete and continues to accurately and completely reflect such facts and circumstances.

Notes and Question

In opinion release No. 14-02, the DOJ "enourag[ed] companies engaging in mergers and acquisitions to . . . conduct thorough risk-based FCPA and anti-corruption due diligence . . . as quickly as practicable."[215] By contrast, the Halliburton opinion release (No. 08-02) imposed stringent time limits.

What accounts for this apparent inconsistency?

FCPA Opinion Procedure Release No. 08-01

No. 08-01[216]

January 15, 2008

Foreign Corrupt Practices Act Review

Opinion Procedure Release

The Department has reviewed the FCPA Opinion Procedure request and supporting materials, dated January 2, 2008 (the "Request"), submitted by a United States issuer (the "Requestor") under the Foreign Corrupt Practices Act ("FCPA") Opinion Procedure, 28 C.F.R. Part 80. The facts and circumstances are as follows:

OVERVIEW OF THE REQUEST

The Requestor is a Delaware corporation with its principal place of business in the United States, and an issuer within the meaning of the FCPA, 15 U.S.C. §§ 78dd-1, et seq. The Requestor has requested that the Department of Justice issue an Opinion under the FCPA Opinion Procedure, 28 C.F.R. Part 80, stating its enforcement policy with respect to the prospective majority investment by a wholly owned foreign subsidiary of the Requestor in a foreign company that is responsible for managing certain public services for a major foreign municipality. This anticipated investment (the "Proposed Transaction") is described more fully below.

---

215. *See* U.S. Dep't of Justice, FCPA Opinion Procedure Release No. 14-02, at 3 (Nov. 7, 2014), https://www.justice.gov/sites/default/files/criminal-fraud/legacy/2014/11/14/14-02.pdf.

216. U.S. Dep't of Justice, FCPA Opinion Procedure Release No. 08-01 (Jan. 15, 2008) (footnotes omitted), https://www.justice.gov/sites/default/files/criminal-fraud/legacy/2010/04/11/0801.pdf.

The Requestor notes that the Proposed Transaction is a matter of significant importance and urgency to the Requestor, this opportunity is highly valued, and delay by the Requestor in committing to the Proposed Transaction will likely forever preclude its consummation. Accordingly, the Requestor has asked that the Department of Justice consider this opinion request on an expedited basis. The Department of Justice has agreed to and conducted expedited review.

The Requestor: Background

The Requestor is a Fortune 500 company headquartered in the United States, located in over 35 countries, including the country at issue in this Request, and with worldwide annual revenues of several billion dollars. The Requestor's relevant business unit is one of the largest providers of the relevant public services to governments worldwide.

The Investment Target and Other Relevant Parties

The Requestor has made the following representations regarding the operation and ownership of the investment target company in the foreign country (the "Investment Target") and certain relevant parties:

Currently, the relevant public services for the foreign municipality are provided by the Investment Target. The Investment Target currently is jointly owned by a government-owned entity of the foreign country (the "Foreign Government Owner") and a foreign private company (the "Foreign Private Company 1"). A citizen of the foreign country (the "Investment Target Chairman") is the Chairman and formal legal representative of the Investment Target.

The Foreign Government Owner, historically, is the majority owner of the Investment Target and currently holds a 56% ownership share in that company. The Foreign Government Owner's indirect majority parent is the foreign country's governmental entity generally responsible for the management, reform and restructuring of state-owned enterprises (the "State Enterprises Management Entity"). In particular, the State Enterprises Management Entity is responsible for determining from which state-owned companies the government should divest, and for effectuating public offerings or sales of state-owned assets through another governmental entity (the "State Enterprises Divestiture Entity"). In addition to his role at the Investment Target, the Investment Target Chairman is also the General Manager and formal legal representative of the Foreign Government Owner.

Foreign Private Company 1, established under the laws of the foreign country, is the 44% minority owner of the Investment Target. The controlling and ultimate beneficial owner, and the formal legal representative, of Foreign Private Company 1 is a citizen of the foreign country (the "Foreign Private Company Owner"). The Foreign Private Company Owner has substantial business experience in the foreign municipality, and in particular, with the relevant public services provided by the Investment Target. Foreign Private Company 1 has appointed the Foreign Private Company Owner as its representative in the Investment Target. In this role, the Foreign Private Company Owner holds the title of General Manager of the Investment Target. However, the Foreign Private Company Owner is not an employee of the Investment Target and receives no salary or other direct compensation from the Investment Target. Further, the Foreign Private Company Owner has no other formal affiliation with the host country government other than through his involvement in the Investment Target as its General Manager.

The Investment Target Divestiture and the Requestor's Business Opportunity

In its Request, the Requestor has described the origin of the investment opportunity as follows:

Some time prior to November 2007, the Foreign Government Owner and the State Enterprises Management Entity determined to divest the host country government's interest in the Investment Target and, thus, fully privatize the business. Around November 2007, the Foreign Government Owner received formal approval of the State Enterprises Management Entity for such divestiture and, as required under foreign law, the public bid process managed by the State Enterprises Divestiture Entity was initiated for the purpose of selling the entirety of the Foreign Government Owner's 56% share in the Investment Target. Pursuant to the host country government's regulations, the bids themselves were subject to review by the State Enterprises Divestiture Entity, the Foreign Government Owner, and the Foreign Government Owner's direct parent corporations. The Foreign Government Owner and its direct corporate parents have final authority to select and approve a final bid.

After the announcement of the planned divestiture of the Investment Target shares, the Requestor engaged in substantial discussions with the Foreign Private Company Owner regarding the potential entrée of the Requestor into the market for the relevant public services in the foreign country. The Requestor determined that a potential controlling investment in the Investment Target presented an opportunity for a long-term, high-yield return of revenue and profit, and, perhaps more importantly, could provide an unparalleled competitive advantage by securing a foothold for the Requestor in the regional markets generally.

Prior Negotiations

The Requestor has made the following representations regarding the Requestor's prior negotiations with the Foreign Private Company Owner regarding the Investment Target, and the Requestor's identification of, and responses to, FCPA concerns identified in connection with the Proposed Transaction:

In late 2005, the Requestor was first contacted by the Investment Target's representatives who were searching for a foreign investor with relevant expertise. In approximately June 2006, the Requestor began direct discussions with the Foreign Private Company Owner in connection with a possible joint venture through which the Requestor would purchase a controlling interest in the Investment Target following the government's anticipated sale of its portion of the entity. The parties considered a scenario whereby: (1) the Foreign Private Company Owner (through a new company controlled and beneficially owned by him, the "Foreign Private Company 2") would obtain 100%

ownership of the Investment Target by bidding on and hopefully obtaining the Foreign Government Owner's shares of the Investment Target through the State-sponsored sale, and by transferring Foreign Private Company 1's 44% interest to Foreign Private Company 2; and (2) the Requestor would then purchase a controlling interest in the Investment Target from Foreign Private Company 2. Thus, this transaction would result in the Requestor acquiring a controlling interest in the Investment Target, while Foreign Private Company 2 and the Foreign Private Company Owner would retain a minority ownership interest.

THE REQUESTOR'S INITIAL FCPA CONCERNS AND DUE DILIGENCE EFFORTS

The Requestor has represented the following with respect to the due diligence efforts undertaken by it in connection with its potential purchase of a controlling interest in the Investment Target from Foreign Private Company 2, and the Requestor's assessment of the attendant FCPA risks:

Prior to executing a joint venture agreement with the Foreign Private Company Owner, the Requestor conducted due diligence of the potential joint venture to assess, among other things, potential FCPA-related risk. In conducting its due diligence, the Requestor understood that, as General Manager of the Investment Target, a joint venture whose majority owner is a state-owned company, the Foreign Private Company Owner would be considered a "foreign official" for purposes of the FCPA, 15 U.S.C. § 78dd-1(f)(1)(A). Accordingly, the Requestor sought to assure itself that any payment to the Foreign Private Company Owner for the Foreign Private Company 2 shares of the Investment Target would not be in violation of the FCPA, and that the Foreign Private Company Owner did not obtain those shares improperly under foreign law.

The due diligence conducted, none of which identified any negative information regarding the Foreign Private Company Owner, Foreign Private Company 1, or the Investment Target, including the following:

1. The Requestor commissioned a report on the Foreign Private Company Owner by a reputable international investigative firm.
2. The Requestor retained a business consultant in the foreign municipality who provided advice on possible due diligence procedures in the foreign country.
3. The Requestor commissioned International Company Profiles on the Investment Target and Foreign Private Company 1 from the U.S. Commercial Service of the Commerce Department.
4. The Requestor searched the names of all relevant persons and entities, including the Foreign Private Company Owner, the Investment Target, and Foreign Private Company 1, through the various services and databases accessible to the Requestor's International Trade Department—including a private due diligence service—to determine that no relevant parties are included on lists of designated or denied persons, terrorist watches, or similar designations.

5. The Requestor met with representatives of the U.S. Embassy in the foreign municipality and learned that there were no negative records at the
   Embassy regarding any party to the Proposed Transaction.
6. Outside counsel conducted due diligence and issued a preliminary report.
   An updated report is being prepared, and will be completed before closing the Proposed Transaction.
7. An outside forensic accounting firm has prepared a preliminary due diligence report and a final report is being prepared, and will be completed
   before closing the Proposed Transaction.
8. A second law firm has reviewed the due diligence.

The Requestor identified two principal FCPA-related risks to be addressed prior
to its consummation of the Proposed Transaction. First, the Requestor originally
believed that, as General Manager of the Investment Target, the Foreign Private
Company Owner was subject to certain foreign privatization regulations (the
"privatization regulations"), and as such he could only legally participate in the
purchase of the Foreign Government Owner's sale of its shares in the Investment
Target if his ownership interests in Foreign Private Company 1 and Foreign Private
Company 2 were adequately disclosed to the Foreign Government Owner and
its State-owned parent organizations. Second, the Requestor believed that, as
General Manager of the Investment Target, the Foreign Private Company Owner
was legally prohibited from acting on corporate opportunities—for example,
realizing the purchase price premium from the Requestor for the Investment
Target shares—that arguably belonged to a government-owned entity (*i.e.*, the
Foreign Government Owner), without first seeking approval from the Foreign
Government Owner.

When presented with these issues by the Requestor in September 2007, the
Foreign Private Company Owner, through counsel, declined to make or accede
to disclosures to the Foreign Government Owner and its corporate parents
regarding his various roles and beneficial interests for the stated reasons that
in the foreign country it was neither necessary nor customary to do so. In addition, the Foreign Private Company Owner declined to disclose to the Foreign
Government Owner and its corporate parents information concerning the premium the Requestor would agree to pay for the proposed controlling stake in the
Investment Target. At the time, the Foreign Private Company Owner informed
the Requestor that its disclosure requests were inconsistent with business practices in the foreign country and that competitive concerns prevented him from
agreeing to disclose to the Foreign Government Owner and its corporate parents
his bid price on the Investment Target or the spread between his bid and the
price for which the Requestor would agree to purchase the controlling interest
in the Investment Target.

Also at that time, the Requestor believed that the Foreign Private Company
Owner's bid for the government-owned shares in the Investment Target had
been accepted and that the State Enterprises Divestiture Entity–run sale of those
shares would be finalized in the immediate future. In light of the Foreign Private

Company Owner's reluctance to make what the Requestor believed were necessary disclosures, and because it did not appear to the Requestor that post-sale disclosures would be sufficient to bring the Foreign Private Company Owner's acquisition within the strictures of the foreign country's laws, the Requestor decided to abandon the proposed joint venture and so informed the Foreign Private Company Owner.

RESUMPTION OF NEGOTIATIONS AND RENEWED FCPA DUE DILIGENCE

The Requestor has stated the following with respect to the facts and circumstances of the Requestor's resumption of negotiations with the Foreign Private Company Owner and additional due diligence efforts undertaken by the Requestor:

After a period of approximately three weeks, on or about November 1, 2007, the Foreign Private Company Owner requested that the Requestor renew negotiations of the Proposed Transaction. Without engaging the Foreign Private Company Owner in substantive negotiations, the Requestor first reiterated its concern over disclosure and the Foreign Private Company Owner's compliance with the privatization regulations. The Foreign Private Company Owner still resisted such disclosure, but also indicated his belief that, based on a conversation he had with an attorney at the State Enterprises Divestiture Entity (the "Divestiture Entity Lawyer"), the privatization regulations did not apply to him because he was not a paid manager of the Investment Target, but rather a voluntary minority-owner representative at the Investment Target with no real control over that entity. In response, prior to agreeing to renew negotiations of the Proposed Transaction, the Requestor sought to conduct additional due diligence to determine whether, or to what extent, its initial analysis of the application of the privatization regulations had been incorrect as to the Foreign Private Company Owner, and to verify his claims as to both the facts of his involvement at the Investment Target and the foreign law ramifications of the same. The Foreign Private Company Owner did not object to the Requestor's pursuit of these additional due diligence steps.

As part of that additional due diligence, the Requestor learned from the State Enterprises Divestiture Entity officials that although the Foreign Private Company Owner's bid for the Investment Target shares had been accepted by the Foreign Government Owner, the State Enterprises Divestiture Entity, and the State Enterprises Management Entity, the Foreign Private Company Owner was providing the purchase money in installments and that, therefore, his purchase of the Investment Target had not yet been consummated. The Requestor viewed this fact as an opportunity to take affirmative steps as part of its additional due diligence to disclose, prior to finalization of the sale, the Foreign Private Company Owner's beneficial ownership interest in Foreign Private Company 1 and Foreign Private Company 2 to legal representatives and high-ranking officials of relevant government-owned entities. The Foreign Private Company Owner did not object to the Requestor's disclosures to government-owned entities regarding his role and the Proposed Transaction.

Thereafter, the Requestor met with various high-ranking relevant government officials, confirmed certain information, and made certain disclosures (both orally and in writing). First, the Requestor's representatives met with a senior official in the State Enterprises Divestiture Entity (the "Divestiture Entity Senior Official"), who explained that the State Enterprises Divestiture Entity is responsible for managing the sales of government-owned assets, and that it reports to the State Enterprises Management Entity. As part of a State-owned asset sale, the State Enterprises Divestiture Entity is responsible for reviewing the forms required to be filed by the seller, including reviewing paperwork for purposes of determining compliance with the privatization regulations. The Requestor's representatives disclosed to the Divestiture Entity Senior Official that: (1) the Requestor had been negotiating with the Foreign Private Company Owner for over a year to purchase a majority interest in the Investment Target; (2) the Foreign Private Company Owner was in the process of buying the Foreign Government Owner shares in the Investment Target through the State Enterprises Divestiture Entity-run State asset sale; (3) the Foreign Private Company Owner is the current minority beneficial shareholder of the Investment Target and is the General Manager of the Investment Target; and (4) the Requestor is offering the Foreign Private Company Owner a very substantial price premium over the price the Foreign Private Company Owner has agreed to pay for the Foreign Government Owner's shares of the Investment Target. During the meeting, the Divestiture Entity Senior Official expressed no reservations about the appropriateness of the Proposed Transaction and commented specifically that the premium described would not be unusual or unexpected. Subsequent to this meeting, the Requestor reiterated these disclosures by letter to the Divestiture Entity Senior Official.

Soon thereafter, the Requestor's representatives met with a lawyer for the State Enterprises Divestiture Entity (the "Divestiture Entity Lawyer") and disclosed the same details of the Proposed Transaction as had been relayed to the Divestiture Entity Senior Official. The Divestiture Entity Lawyer explained that the Foreign Private Company Owner had been selected as the winning bidder in the Investment Target tender, but that the Foreign Private Company Owner was making payments for the tendered shares in installments and that, as such, the sale and transfer of shares was not complete. Further, the Divestiture Entity Lawyer explained that the State Enterprises Divestiture Entity reviewed the Foreign Private Company Owner's bid in light of potential restrictions under the privatization regulations when the bid process formally began in September 2007, and that the State Enterprises Divestiture Entity had determined that the Foreign Private Company Owner was not a government official for purposes of those regulations because the Foreign Private Company Owner served as General Manager of the Investment Target only in his capacity as the representative of the minority, private owners of the Investment Target shares. The Divestiture Entity Lawyer represented that he personally had confirmed this interpretation of the privatization regulations with a senior official with the State Enterprises Divestiture Entity department responsible for ensuring that the public tender process is run consistent with the State Enterprises Divestiture Entity's procedures. Subsequent to this meeting, via letter to the Divestiture Entity Lawyer, the Requestor reiterated the disclosures noted above.

That same date, representatives of the Requestor met with the Investment Target Chairman. The Foreign Private Company Owner also attended this meeting. The Requestor disclosed to the Investment Target Chairman the same details of the Proposed Transaction as had been relayed to the Divestiture Entity Senior Official and the Divestiture Entity Lawyer. Specifically, the Requestor inquired whether the Investment Target Chairman was aware of the Foreign Private Company Owner's various roles in the Investment Target and Foreign Private Companies 1 and 2, whether the Investment Target Chairman believed the privatization regulations applied to and precluded the Foreign Private Company Owner's participation, and whether the Investment Target Chairman was aware of the substantial premium the Requestor was prepared to offer the Foreign Private Company Owner. The Investment Target Chairman indicated that: (1) he was previously aware of the Foreign Private Company Owner's role as General Manager and minority shareholder of the existing joint venture; (2) he was previously aware of the Foreign Private Company Owner's role as the shareholder of the acquiring entity (Foreign Private Company 2); (3) he did not believe that the privatization regulations applied to the Foreign Private Company Owner in this context because he, the Investment Target Chairman, was the Senior Manager at the Investment Target, and not the Foreign Private Company Owner; and (4) he understood that the Requestor would pay a substantial premium for the Investment Target shares, and he had no objections. Subsequent to this meeting, by letter to the Investment Target Chairman, the Requestor reiterated the oral disclosures and confirmed the substance of the parties' discussions.

Finally, representatives of the Requestor met with staff members of the State Enterprises Divestiture Entity and a supervisor in the State-Owned Asset Department of the State Enterprises Divestiture Entity. The Requestor's representatives disclosed to these officials the same details of the Proposed Transaction as had been relayed in each of the prior meetings described above. One staff member explained that her department at the State Enterprises Divestiture Entity was responsible for determining whether restrictions under the privatization regulations were implicated in the context of proposed sales of State-owned assets. She further explained that pursuant to the State Enterprises Management Entity definitions under privatization regulations, those regulations only apply to "Senior Managers," who are defined as an employee of a State-owned enterprise or an individual assigned by the government to work on behalf of a joint venture owned in part by the government. Based on the Requestor's representation that the Foreign Private Company Owner was the General Manager of the Investment Target, appointed as the minority-owner's representative, one staff member indicated that the Foreign Private Company Owner would not be considered a manager of sufficient authority to come within the privatization regulations because the Foreign Private Company Owner's position at the Investment Target did not convey any state or government status to him. After reviewing the official State Enterprises Divestiture Entity files relating to the Investment Target tender, the staff member confirmed that the State Enterprises Divestiture Entity had explicitly determined that the privatization regulations do not apply to the Foreign Private Company Owner because he is not a government official within the meaning of those regulations, despite his status as the General Manager of The Investment Target. The supervisor in the State-Owned Asset Department of the State Enterprises Divestiture Entity, who was the contact person and coordinator of the Foreign Government Owner share sale, concurred with this interpretation of the privatization regulations. Subsequent to this meeting, the Requester sent a letter to one of the staff members reiterating the same basic disclosures noted above, and specifically confirming the State Enterprises Divestiture Entity's determination that the privatization regulations do not apply to the Foreign Private Company Owner.

REVISED FCPA CONSIDERATIONS

Despite the initial FCPA risks identified by the Requestor, and the Foreign Private Company Owner's initial reluctance to make disclosures believed at that time necessary to alleviate those risks, based on the Requestor's original FCPA due diligence efforts together with its additional due diligence efforts described above, the Requestor has stated that it is prepared to proceed with the Proposed Transaction.

While the Requestor believes that the Foreign Private Company Owner is likely considered a "foreign official" under the FCPA, at least during the period when the Investment Target remains a government-owned entity and he is the General Manager of that entity, the Requestor notes and represents the following:

The Foreign Private Company Owner is purchasing the Investment Target shares without financial assistance from the Requestor. As represented by high-ranking officials at the State Enterprises Divestiture Entity, the Foreign Private Company Owner must provide the entirety of the funds required to purchase the Investment Target shares prior to finalization of the purchase. The Foreign Private Company Owner is in the process of doing so, through installment payments, without the assistance of the Requestor. A necessary and explicit predicate to the Requestor's participation in the Proposed Transaction is Foreign Private Company 2's full and legal ownership of 100% of the Investment Target. Thus, the Requestor will not close the Proposed Transaction until the Foreign Private Company Owner's purchase of the Foreign Government Owner's shares of the Investment Target shares is complete. Further, the Requestor has not made, and warrants that it will not make, any direct or indirect payment to the Foreign Private Company Owner to make possible his intended purchase of those shares.

The Requestor will make no extra or unjustified payments to the Foreign Private Company Owner. The Requestor confirms that it has not made any payments to the Foreign Private Company Owner to date. The Requestor further warrants that, in connection with the Proposed Transaction, it will not pay the Foreign Private Company Owner anything other than the agreed-upon purchase price for the Investment Target shares, and reasonable fees in connection with the Foreign Private Company Owner's actual involvement in the management of the Investment Target joint venture as set out in the final joint venture agreement. The Foreign Private Company Owner has also assured the Requestor that he will not use any payments from the Requestor to pay government officials, and the Foreign Private Company Owner will be required to guarantee as much within the documentation of the Proposed Transaction.

The Requestor will make no payments to any other foreign officials. The Requestor believes, after reasonable inquiry, that no investor of Foreign Private Company 2 from whom the Requestor would purchase shares in the Investment Target, with the exception of the Foreign Private Company Owner, is a foreign official. Moreover, after reasonable inquiry, no owner, officer, director, consultant, representative or agent of Foreign Private Company 2, or close relative of the Foreign Private Company Owner, is known to be a foreign official. Further, under the joint venture agreement, the Foreign Private Company Owner will be required to inform the Requestor of any instances where the government status of those individuals changes.

The premium between the Foreign Private Company Owner's purchase price of the Investment Target shares and the Requestor's purchase price is justified based on legitimate business considerations. The Requestor has confirmed through various due diligence efforts, including conversations with high-ranking State Enterprises Divestiture Entity officials, that: (1) the Foreign Private Company Owner's bid price for the Investment Target shares was appropriate; (2) valuation methodologies in the foreign country differ, sometimes dramatically, from American valuation methodologies in that the foreign country valuations often do not include future value calculations for assets such as the Investment Target shares; and thus, (3) the Requestor's valuation and purchase of the Investment Target shares at a substantial premium over the Foreign Private Company Owner's purchase price is justified based on legitimate business considerations. Lastly, in connection with and as an essential condition of the Proposed Transaction, the Requestor is receiving valuable concessions in the revised joint venture agreement which include, but are not limited to, services and hardware supply contracts between the joint venture and the Requestor's foreign subsidiary, a preferred return, and effective control of the joint venture board and appointment of all senior management.

The Foreign Private Company Owner's status as a "foreign official" will soon cease. The Requestor believes that, upon finalization of the Foreign Private Company Owner's purchase of the Foreign Government Owner's shares of the Investment Target, the Foreign Private Company Owner could no longer be considered a "foreign official" under the FCPA. At that point, the Requestor understands that the Foreign Private Company Owner will have no formal or actual role with any government-owned entity, further decreasing any FCPA risk.

The Foreign Private Company Owner's purchase of the Foreign Government Owner's shares is lawful under the foreign country's laws. The Requestor has learned that the State Enterprises Divestiture Entity does not consider the Foreign Private Company Owner subject to the privatization regulations.

This interpretation was stated orally (and confirmed by the Requestor in writing) by informed government officials specifically responsible for interpreting the privatization regulations, and appears to reflect the official State Enterprises Divestiture Entity determination on that issue. The conclusion apparently reflects the government's conclusion that the Foreign Private Company Owner is not a member of senior management for purposes of the privatization regulations and he does not otherwise have government official status by virtue of any other position he holds. The Requestor is not aware, after making reasonable inquiry, of any other formal connection between the Foreign Private Company Owner and the government aside from his current nominal role at the Investment Target. In light of these facts, the Foreign Private Company Owner's lack of practical control over any government entity, and the government's assertion that the Foreign Private Company Owner does not represent its interests, the Requestor is prepared to proceed with the Proposed Transaction.

In pursuing the Proposed Transaction, the Foreign Private Company Owner is not illegally or inappropriately acting on a corporate opportunity belonging to the joint venture. The State Enterprises Management Entity and the Foreign Government Owner made the decision to divest their shares in the Investment Target. As is required by law, the sale of State assets, in this case the shares in the Investment Target owned by the Foreign Government Owner, was conducted through the public tender process managed by the State Enterprises Divestiture Entity. Prior to concluding that transaction, the existence of the discussions between the Requestor and the Foreign Private Company Owner, his various roles and interests, and the details relating to the Proposed Transaction—including the fact that the Requestor was offering the Foreign Private Company Owner a substantial premium for a controlling interest in the Investment Target—were disclosed to high level officials at the State Enterprises Divestiture Entity and the Foreign Government Owner and its parent shareholders.

The State Enterprises Divestiture Entity officials also have been advised of the Proposed Transaction, including the fact that the Foreign Private Company Owner will receive from the Requestor a significant premium over the price at which he acquired the Investment Target, and such officials have expressed no reservations about the Foreign Private Company Owner's participation, the premium he is to receive from the Requestor on his shares, or otherwise. Even if the Foreign Private Company Owner was subject to the privatization regulations, disclosure has now been made to the relevant government entities. In particular, the Requestor explicitly informed high-ranking officials at the Investment Target, the Foreign Government Owner, and the State Enterprises Divestiture Entity that: (1) the Foreign Private Company Owner was the General Manager of the Investment Target; (2) the Foreign Private Company Owner was the ultimate beneficial owner of Foreign Private Company 1 and Foreign Private Company 2; and (3) the Foreign Private Company Owner, through Foreign Private Company 2, stood to receive a substantial price premium from the Requestor for a portion of his shares in the Investment Target. The government officials with whom the Requestor spoke expressed no reservations about the propriety of the

Foreign Private Company Owner's participation in and profit from the Proposed Transaction.

DUE DILIGENCE DOCUMENTATION AND CONTRACTUAL PROVISIONS

The Requestor has represented in its request that it has fully documented all of the due diligence it conducted with regard to the Proposed Transaction, and will maintain such documentation in the Requestor's offices in the United States.

The Requestor has further represented that the Foreign Private Company Owner, as Chairman, will provide a representation and warranty on behalf of Foreign Private Company 2 that: (1) neither Foreign Private Company 2 nor its owners, directors, officers, employees, agents, or close family members thereof, have made any payment directly or indirectly in violation of relevant anti-corruption laws, including the FCPA; (2) no payment will be made in the future in violation of relevant anti-corruption laws, including the FCPA; and (3) it has an ongoing obligation to comply with relevant anti-corruption laws. The Requestor has further represented that under its joint venture agreement with Foreign Private Company 2, the Requestor will have the right to withhold payments to Foreign Private Company 2 and/or terminate the joint venture agreement and dissolve the joint venture entity in the event of a breach of the agreement, including violations of relevant anti-corruption laws. In addition, the agreement will contain provisions providing for one party to buy out the other in the event of breach of the agreement.

CONCLUSION

Based upon all the facts and circumstances as represented by the Requestor, the Department does not presently intend to take any enforcement action with respect to the Proposed Transaction, a prospective majority investment by the Requestor in the Investment Target, an entity that would be responsible for providing certain public services to a municipality in the host country.

This determination is based on several important factors. First, the Requestor conducted and documented reasonable due diligence of the anticipated seller of privatized shares of the Investment Target, with attention to both FCPA risks and compliance with local laws and regulations, and will maintain such documentation in the United States. Second, the Requestor required and obtained transparency through adequate disclosures to the relevant government entities of the anticipated purchase at a significant premium from the Foreign Private Company Owner of the majority of shares in the Investment Target, following the Foreign Private Company Owner's completion of his purchase of the Foreign Government Owner's shares through the public tender process. Third, the Requestor will obtain from the Foreign Private Company Owner representations and warranties regarding past and future anti-corruption compliance. And fourth, the Requestor will retain the contractual rights to discontinue its business relationship with Foreign Private Company 2 in the event of breach of their joint venture agreement, including violations of anti-corruption laws.

This Opinion, however, is subject to the following important caveats: the FCPA Opinion Letter and Release can be relied upon by you only to the extent that the disclosure of facts and circumstances in your Request is accurate and complete and remains accurate and complete. Additionally, this Opinion Letter and Release have no binding application on any party that did not join in the Request.

Hypothetical: Failure to Conduct Pre-acquisition Due Diligence

ABC S.A. ("ABC") is an Italian corporation engaged in producing food products, whose shares are publicly traded on the New York Stock Exchange ("NYSE"). ABC's annual sales exceed $1 billion. ABC has 60,000 employees and twenty subsidiaries around the world.

In July 2015, ABC entered into a DPA with the DOJ for a violation of the FCPA involving bribes paid by ABC's subsidiary in Vietnam. Pursuant to the terms of the DPA, ABC agreed to:

1) Pay $10 million in penalties; and
2) Upgrade its FCPA compliance program, including its internal controls over foreign subsidiaries and third parties, within one year.

In October 2016, ABC acquired 40 percent of the shares of Indo Co., an Indonesian corporation that produces military Meals-Ready-to-Eat ("MREs"). Prior to the acquisition, Indo. Co. produced 100 percent of its products in Indonesia and sold them exclusively to the country's armed forces. Indo. Co.'s annual sales are approximately $20 million.

ABC's bid to purchase Indo. Co.'s shares was one of several received by Indo. Co.'s board of directors. The other bidders had not conditioned their bids on any pre-acquisition due diligence of Indo. Co. To avoid being placed at a competitive disadvantage vis-à-vis the other bidders, ABC decided to also forgo any pre-acquisition due diligence of Indo. Co.

ABC's bid to purchase Indo. Co.'s shares included a commitment to equip Indo. Co. with ABC's proprietary technology, which would increase the shelf life of MREs from one year to ten years, substantially increasing the marketability of Indo. Co.'s products. In addition, ABC committed to invest $100 million in Indo. Co.'s production facilities and begin marketing Indo. Co.'s products globally, doubling Indo. Co.'s sales within two years.

In November 2016, about one month after the acquisition, ABC's anonymous hotline received a call from an Indo. Co. employee, claiming that Indo. Co. had been paying bribes to senior Indonesian military and political leaders for years to secure its sales contracts with the armed forces.

Answer the following questions and include any additional facts that you would like to know to complete your analysis:

1) Assuming that the anonymous caller is telling the truth, is ABC potentially liable under the FCPA for the bribes paid by Indo. Co.:
   a) Before the acquisition?
   b) After the acquisition?
2) Assess the potential costs, if any, to ABC in connection with Indo. Co.'s alleged bribery of Indonesian government officials.
3) What specific steps would you, as ABC's outside counsel, recommend to mitigate the potential costs?
4) Does ABC face any potential liability under SOX in connection with Indo. Co.? If so, what would be the prosecution's likely theory of liability?

TEST YOUR KNOWLEDGE
Evaluating a Compliance Program

After being caught violating the FCPA, Siemens has scheduled meetings with the DOJ to negotiate its penalty. As part of the negotiations, the parties will discuss the state of Siemens' existing compliance program and steps that Siemens should take to remediate it. You have been retained as Siemens' counsel in the negotiations. Read the following *New York Times* article to get a sense of the corporate culture that led to Siemens' offenses, and then using the facts set forth in the Sentencing Memorandum in *U.S. v. Siemens* and the questions in the DOJ release "Evaluation of Corporate Compliance Programs," perform the following:

1) Where the stated facts permit, answer the questions, identify deficiencies in Siemens' existing FCPA compliance program, and propose remediation steps.
2) If the facts are insufficient to answer a question, assume Siemens cannot answer satisfactorily, and use your knowledge of the Hallmarks to propose remediation steps.

At Siemens, Bribery Was Just a Line Item

By T. Christian Miller, Dec. 20, 2008, 6:59 p.m. EST[1]

In this *Frontline* interview, Reinhard Siekaczek, a former Siemens executive, describes how bribery was "customary" at the company.

This article is a joint report by ProPublica, PBS's FRONTLINE, the The New York Times, and the Investigative Reporting Program at UC Berkeley. A related documentary will be broadcast on Frontline on April 7.

MUNICH—Reinhard Siekaczek was half asleep in bed when his doorbell rang here early one morning two years ago.

---

1. T. Christian Miller, *At Siemens, Bribery Was Just a Line Item*, PROPUBLICA (Dec. 20, 2008), https://www.propublica.org/article/siemens-bribery-1220.

Still in his pajamas, he peeked out his bedroom window, hurried downstairs and flung open the front door. Standing before him in the cool, crisp dark were six German police officers and a prosecutor. They held a warrant for his arrest.

At that moment, Mr. Siekaczek, a stout, graying former accountant for Siemens A.G., the German engineering giant, knew that his secret life had ended.

"I know what this is about," Mr. Siekaczek told the officers crowded around his door. "I have been expecting you."

To understand how Siemens, one of the world's biggest companies, last week ended up paying $1.6 billion in the largest fine for bribery in modern corporate history, it's worth delving into Mr. Siekaczek's unusual journey.

A former midlevel executive at Siemens, he was one of several people who arranged a torrent of payments that eventually streamed to well-placed officials around the globe, from Vietnam to Venezuela and from Italy to Israel, according to interviews with Mr. Siekaczek and court records in Germany and the United States.

What is striking about Mr. Siekaczek's and prosecutors' accounts of those dealings, which flowed through a web of secret bank accounts and shadowy consultants, is how entrenched corruption had become at a sprawling, sophisticated corporation that externally embraced the nostrums of a transparent global marketplace built on legitimate transactions.

Mr. Siekaczek (pronounced SEE-kah-chek) says that from 2002 to 2006 he oversaw an annual bribery budget of about $40 million to $50 million at Siemens. Company managers and sales staff used the slush fund to cozy up to corrupt government officials worldwide.

The payments, he says, were vital to maintaining the competitiveness of Siemens overseas, particularly in his subsidiary, which sold telecommunications equipment. "It was about keeping the business unit alive and not jeopardizing thousands of jobs overnight," he said in an interview.

Siemens is hardly the only corporate giant caught in prosecutors' cross hairs.

Three decades after Congress passed a law barring American companies from paying bribes to secure foreign business, law enforcement authorities around the world are bearing down on major enterprises like Daimler and Johnson & Johnson, with scores of cases now under investigation. Both companies declined comment, citing continuing investigations.

Albert J. Stanley, a legendary figure in the oil patch and the former chief executive of the KBR subsidiary of Halliburton, recently pleaded guilty to charges of paying bribes and skimming millions for himself. More charges are coming in that case, officials say.

But the Siemens case is notable for its breadth, the sums of money involved, and the raw organizational zeal with which the company deployed bribes to secure contracts. It is also a model of something that was once extremely rare: cross-border cooperation among law enforcement officials.

German prosecutors initially opened the Siemens case in 2005. American authorities became involved in 2006 because the company's shares are traded on the New York Stock Exchange.

In its settlement last week with the Justice Department and the Securities and Exchange Commission, Siemens pleaded guilty to violating accounting provisions of the Foreign Corrupt Practices Act, which outlaws bribery abroad.

Although court documents are salted throughout with the word "bribes," the Justice Department allowed Siemens to plead to accounting violations because it cooperated with the investigation and because pleading to bribery violations would have barred Siemens from bidding on government contracts in the United States. Siemens doesn't dispute the government's account of its actions.

Matthew W. Friedrich, the acting chief of the Justice Department's criminal division, called corruption at Siemens "systematic and widespread." Linda C. Thomsen, the S.E.C.'s enforcement director, said it was "egregious and brazen." Joseph Persichini Jr., the director of the F.B.I.'s Washington field office, which led the investigation, called it "massive, willful and carefully orchestrated."

MR. SIEKACZEK'S telecommunications unit was awash in easy money. It paid $5 million in bribes to win a mobile phone contract in Bangladesh, to the son of the prime minister at the time and other senior officials, according to court documents. Mr. Siekaczek's group also made $12.7 million in payments to senior officials in Nigeria for government contracts.

In Argentina, a different Siemens subsidiary paid at least $40 million in bribes to win a $1 billion contract to produce national identity cards. In Israel, the company provided $20 million to senior government officials to build power plants. In Venezuela, it was $16 million for urban rail lines. In China, $14 million for medical equipment. And in Iraq, $1.7 million to Saddam Hussein and his cronies.

The bribes left behind angry competitors who were shut out of contracts and local residents in poor countries who, because of rigged deals, paid too much for necessities like roads, power plants and hospitals, prosecutors said.

Because government contracting is an opaque process and losers don't typically file formal protests, it's difficult to know the identity of competitors who lost out to Siemens. Companies in the United States have long complained, however, that they face an uneven playing field competing overseas.

Ben W. Heineman Jr., a former general counsel at General Electric and a member of the American chapter of Transparency International, a nonprofit group that tracks corruption, says the enforcement of some antibribery conventions still remains scattershot. "Until you have energetic enforcement by the developed-world nations, you won't get strong antibribery programs or high-integrity corporate culture," he said.

Afghanistan, Haiti, Iraq, Myanmar and Somalia are the five countries where corporate bribery is most common, according to Transparency International. The S.E.C. complaint said Siemens paid its heftiest bribes in China, Russia, Argentina, Israel and Venezuela.

"Crimes of official corruption threaten the integrity of the global marketplace and undermine the rule of law in the host countries," said Lori Weinstein, the Justice Department prosecutor who oversaw the Siemens case.

All told, Siemens will pay more than $2.6 billion to clear its name: $1.6 billion in fines and fees in Germany and the United States and more than $1 billion for internal investigations and reforms.

Siemens's general counsel, Peter Y. Solmssen, in an interview outside a marble-lined courtroom in Washington, said the company acknowledged that bribes were at the heart of the case. "This is the end of a difficult chapter in the company's history," he said. "We're glad to get it behind us."

Mr. Siekaczek, who cooperated with German authorities after his arrest in 2006, has already been sentenced in Germany to two years' probation and a $150,000 fine. During a lengthy interview in Munich, a few blocks from the Siemens world headquarters, he provided an insider's account of corruption at the company. The interview was his first with English-language news outlets.

"I would never have thought I'd go to jail for my company," Mr. Siekaczek said. "Sure, we joked about it, but we thought if our actions ever came to light, we'd all go together and there would be enough people to play a game of cards."

Mr. Siekaczek isn't a stereotype of a white-collar villain. There are no Ferraris in his driveway, or villas in Monaco. He dresses in jeans, loafers and leather jackets. With white hair and gold-rimmed glasses, he passes for a kindly grandfather—albeit one who can discuss the advantages of offshore bank accounts as easily as last night's soccer match.

Siemens began bribing long before Mr. Siekaczek applied his accounting skills to the task of organizing the payments.

World War II left the company shattered, its factories bombed and its trademark patents confiscated, according to American prosecutors. The company turned to markets in less developed countries to compete, and bribery became a reliable and ubiquitous sales technique.

"Bribery was Siemens's business model," said Uwe Dolata, the spokesman for the association of federal criminal investigators in Germany. "Siemens had institutionalized corruption."

Before 1999, bribes were deductible as business expenses under the German tax code, and paying off a foreign official was not a criminal offense. In such an environment, Siemens officials subscribed to a straightforward rule in pursuing business abroad, according to one former executive. They played by local rules.

Inside Siemens, bribes were referred to as "NA"—a German abbreviation for the phrase "nützliche Aufwendungen" which means "useful money." Siemens bribed wherever executives felt the money was needed, paying off officials not only in countries known for government corruption, like Nigeria, but also in countries with reputations for transparency, like Norway, according to court records.

In February 1999, Germany joined the international convention banning foreign bribery, a pact signed by most of the world's industrial nations. By 2000, authorities in Austria and Switzerland were suspicious of millions of dollars of Siemens payments flowing to offshore bank accounts, according to court records.

Rather than comply with the law, Siemens managers created a "paper program," a toothless internal system that did little to punish wrongdoers, according to court documents.

Mr. Siekaczek's business unit was one of the most egregious offenders. Court documents show that the telecommunications unit paid more than $800 million of the $1.4 billion in illegal payments that Siemens made from 2001 to 2007. Managers in the telecommunications group decided to deal with the possibility of a crackdown by making its bribery procedures more difficult to detect.

So, on one winter evening in late 2002, five executives from the telecommunications group met for dinner at a traditional Bavarian restaurant in a Munich suburb. Surrounded by dark wood panels and posters celebrating German engineering, the group discussed how to better disguise its payments, while making sure that employees didn't pocket the money, Mr. Siekaczek said.

To handle the business side of bribery, the executives turned to Mr. Siekaczek, a man renowned within the company for his personal honesty, his deep company loyalty—and his experiences in the shadowy world of illegal bribery.

"It had nothing to do with being law-abiding, because we all knew what we did was unlawful." Mr. Siekaczek said. "What mattered here was that the person put in charge was stable and wouldn't go astray."

Although Mr. Siekaczek was reluctant to take the job offered that night, he justified it as economic necessity. If Siemens didn't pay bribes, it would lose contracts and its employees might lose their jobs.

"We thought we had to do it," Mr. Siekaczek said. "Otherwise, we'd ruin the company."

Indeed, he considers his personal probity a point of honor. He describes himself as "the man in the middle," "the banker" or, with tongue in cheek, "the master of disaster." But, he said, he never set up a bribe. Nor did he directly hand over money to a corrupt official.

German prosecutors say they have no evidence that he personally enriched himself, though German documents show that Mr. Siekaczek oversaw the transfer of some $65 million through hard-to-trace offshore bank accounts.

"I was not the man responsible for bribery," he said. "I organized the cash."

Mr. Siekaczek set things in motion by moving money out of accounts in Austria to Liechtenstein and Switzerland, where bank secrecy laws provided greater cover and anonymity. He said he also reached out to a trustee in Switzerland who set up front companies to conceal money trails from Siemens to offshore bank accounts in Dubai and the British Virgin Islands.

Each year, Mr. Siekaczek said, managers in his unit set aside a budget of about $40 million to $50 million for the payment of bribes. For Greece alone, Siemens budgeted $10 million to $15 million a year. Bribes were as high as 40 percent of the contract cost in especially corrupt countries. Typically, amounts ranged from 5 percent to 6 percent of a contract's value.

The most common method of bribery involved hiring an outside consultant to help "win" a contract. This was typically a local resident with ties to ruling leaders. Siemens paid a fee to the consultant, who in turn delivered the cash to the ultimate recipient.

Siemens has acknowledged having more than 2,700 business consultant agreements, so-called B.C.A.'s, worldwide. Those consultants were at the heart of the bribery scheme, sending millions to government officials.

Mr. Siekaczek was painfully aware that he was acting illegally. To protect evidence that he didn't act alone, he and a colleague began copying documents stored in a basement at Siemens's headquarters in Munich that detailed the payments. He eventually stashed about three dozen folders in a secret hiding spot.

In 2004, Siemens executives told him that he had to sign a document stating he had followed the company's compliance rules. Reluctantly, he signed, but he quit soon after. He continued to work for Siemens as a consultant before finally resigning in 2006. As legal pressure mounted, he heard rumors that Siemens was setting him up for a fall.

"On the inside, I was deeply disappointed. But I told myself that people were going to be surprised when their plan failed," Mr. Siekaczek recalled. "It wasn't going to be possible to make me the only one guilty because dozens of people in the business unit were involved. Nobody was going to believe that one person did this on his own."

The Siemens scheme began to collapse when investigators in several countries began examining suspicious transactions. Prosecutors in Italy, Liechtenstein and Switzerland sent requests for help to counterparts in Germany, providing lists of suspect Siemens employees. German officials then decided to act in one simultaneous raid.

The police knocked on Mr. Siekaczek's door on the morning of Nov. 15, 2006. Some 200 other officers were also sweeping across Germany, into Siemens's headquarters in Munich and the homes of several executives.

In addition to Mr. Siekaczek's detailed payment records, investigators secured five terabytes of data from Siemens's offices—a mother lode of information equivalent to five million books. Mr. Siekaczek turned out to be one of the biggest prizes. After calling his lawyer, he immediately announced that he would cooperate.

Officials in the United States began investigating the case shortly after the raids became public. Knowing that it faced steep fines unless it cooperated, Siemens hired an American law firm, Debevoise & Plimpton, to conduct an internal investigation and to work with federal investigators.

As German and American investigators worked together to develop leads, Debevoise and its partners dedicated more than 300 lawyers, forensic analysts and staff members to untangle thousands of payments across the globe, according to the court records. American investigators and the Debevoise lawyers conducted more than 1,700 interviews in 34 countries. They collected more than 100 million documents, creating special facilities in China and Germany to house records from that single investigation. Debevoise and an outside auditor racked up 1.5 million billable hours, according to court documents. Siemens has said that the internal inquiry and related restructurings have cost it more than $1 billion.

Siemens officials "made it crystal clear that they wanted us to get to the bottom of this and follow it wherever the evidence led," said Bruce E. Yannett, a Debevoise partner.

At the same time, Siemens worked hard to purge the company of some senior managers and to reform company policies. Several senior managers have been arrested. Klaus Kleinfeld, the company's C.E.O., resigned in April 2007. He has denied wrongdoing and is now head of Alcoa, the aluminum giant. Alcoa said that the company fully supports Mr. Kleinfeld and declined to comment further.

Last year, Siemens said in S.E.C. filings that it had discovered evidence that former officials had misappropriated funds and abused their authority. In August, Siemens said it seeks to recover monetary damages from 11 former board members for activities related to the bribery scheme. Negotiations on that matter are continuing.

Earlier this year, Siemens's current chief executive, Peter Löscher, vowed to make Siemens "state of the art" in anticorruption measures.

"Operational excellence and ethical behavior are not a contradiction of terms," the company said in a statement. "We must get the best business—and the clean business."

Siemens still faces legal uncertainties. The Justice Department and German officials said that investigations were continuing and that current and former company officials might face prosecution.

Legal experts say Siemens is the latest in a string of high-profile cases that are changing attitudes about corruption. Still, they said, much work remains.

"I am not saying the fight against bribing foreign public officials is a fight full of roses and victories," said Nicola Bonucci, the director of legal affairs for the Organization for Economic Cooperation and Development, which is based in Paris and monitors the global economy. "But I am convinced that it is something more and more people are taking seriously."

For his part, Mr. Siekaczek is uncertain about the impact of the Siemens case. After all, he said, bribery and corruption are still widespread.

"People will only say about Siemens that they were unlucky and that they broke the 11th Commandment," he said. "The 11th Commandment is: 'Don't get caught.'"[2]

---

2. *Id.*

U.S. v. Siemens Aktiengesellschaft

United States District Court, The District of Columbia,
Case 1:08-cr-00367-RJL (2008)[3]

DEPARTMENT'S SENTENCING MEMORANDUM

The United States of America, by and through its counsel, the United States Department of Justice, Criminal Division, Fraud Section, and the United States Attorney for the District of Columbia (collectively, the "Department"), hereby submits in the above-captioned matters the Department's Sentencing Memorandum. For the reasons outlined below, the Department respectfully submits that the Court should accept the guilty pleas of Siemens [et al.] . . . , and sentence them in accordance with the parties' agreement.

1. Background

Siemens is a German engineering company with over 400,000 employees and operations in 191 countries. Siemens, through its operating groups, subsidiaries, officers, directors, employees, and agents, is engaged in, among other things, developing, consulting, selling, and servicing telecommunications equipment and systems; power generation, transmission, and distribution equipment and systems; transportation equipment and systems; medical equipment and systems; and industrial and traffic equipment and systems, for, among others, national, state, and municipal governments. On March 12, 2001, Siemens became listed on the New York Stock Exchange, subjecting itself as an "issuer" [to the] United States' securities laws, including the Foreign Corrupt Practices Act ("FCPA").

In November 2006, the Munich Public Prosecutor's Office conducted raids on multiple Siemens offices and the homes of Siemens employees in and around Munich, Germany, as part of an investigation of possible bribery of foreign public officials and falsification of corporate books and records. Shortly after these raids, Siemens disclosed to the Department and to the Securities and Exchange Commission ("SEC"), which under the FCPA has civil enforcement authority over issuers, potential violations of the FCPA in multiple countries and initiated a sweeping global internal investigation. Siemens engaged Davis Polk & Wardwell to represent the Company, and engaged Debevoise & Plimpton LLP ("Debevoise") to conduct an independent investigation for the Audit Committee. Debevoise, in turn, hired Deloitte & Touche GmbH ("Deloitte"), translators, computer experts, litigation support firms, and other third parties to assist in the investigation.

The scope of Siemens' internal investigation was unprecedented and included virtually all aspects of its worldwide operations, including headquarters components, subsidiaries, and regional operating companies. Compliance, legal, internal

---

3. Sentencing Memorandum for U.S. Dep't of Justice, United States v. Siemens Aktiengesellschaft, No. 1:08-cr-00367-RJL (D.D.C. Dec. 12, 2008) (footnote omitted), https://www.justice.gov/sites/default/files/criminal-fraud/legacy/2013/05/02/12-12-08siemensvenez-sent.pdf.

audit, and corporate finance departments were a significant focus of the investigation and were discovered to be areas of the company that played a significant role in the violations. Finally, the role and awareness of Siemens' Managing Board and Supervisory Board in serious compliance failures were the subject of particular scrutiny of the Audit Committee and the Department. Debevoise and Deloitte, at the direction of Siemens, provided frequent and extensive reports to the Department and the SEC in face-to-face presentations and conference calls that assisted the Department's investigation enormously.

As described below, Siemens has provided extraordinary cooperation in connection with the investigation of its past corporate conduct, and has undertaken uncommonly sweeping remedial actions in response to the discovery of its prior misconduct. In addition, Siemens has provided substantial and timely assistance in the investigation of other persons and entities.

2. Summary of Facts

The Debevoise internal investigation uncovered evidence of corruption by Siemens spanning several decades in many operating groups and regions. Equally if not more important, the internal investigation revealed knowing failures to implement, and circumvention of, internal controls up to the most senior echelons of management. Wilmer Cutler Pickering Hale & Dorr LLP, which was engaged to conduct a related investigation into Siemens' United Nations Oil for Food Program contracts, discovered evidence confirming the Volcker Commission's findings that several Siemens AG subsidiaries made significant kickback payments to the Iraqi government in connection with the Oil for Food Program. The Debevoise internal investigation and the Department's investigation also revealed evidence of corrupt and improperly recorded payments with a strong nexus to the U.S. by two Siemens subsidiaries, Siemens Venezuela and Siemens Bangladesh, as well as evidence of improperly recorded payments with respect to an additional subsidiary, Siemens Argentina.

a. Siemens' Knowing Falsification of Books and Records and Knowing Failures in and Circumvention of Internal Controls

From in or about the mid-1990s to in or about 2007, Siemens engaged in systematic efforts to knowingly falsify its corporate books and records and to knowingly fail to implement and to circumvent existing internal controls. These systematic efforts included, but were not limited to: (a) using off-books accounts for corrupt payments even after compliance risks associated with such accounts were raised at the highest levels of management; (b) entering into purported business consulting agreements with no legitimate business purpose, sometimes after Siemens had won the relevant project; (c) engaging former Siemens employees as purported business consultants to act as conduits for corrupt payments to government officials; (d) justifying payments to purported business consultants based on false invoices; (e) mischaracterizing corrupt payments in the corporate books and records as consulting fees and other seemingly legitimate expenses; (f) limiting the quantity and scope of audits of payments to purported business consultants; (g) accumulating profit reserves as liabilities in internal balance sheet accounts and then using them to make corrupt payments through business consultants as needed; (h) using removable Post-it notes to affix signatures on approval forms authorizing payments to conceal the identity of the signors and obscure the audit trail; (I) allowing third party payments to be made based on a single signature in contravention of Siemens' "four eyes principle" which required authorization of payments by two Siemens managers; (j) drafting and backdating sham business consulting agreements to justify third party payments; and (k) changing the name of purported business consulting agreements to "agency agreements" or similar titles to avoid detection.

1) Siemens' Use of Payment Mechanisms

From on or about March 12, 2001 to in or about 2007, Siemens made payments totaling approximately $1,360,000,000 through various mechanisms. Of this amount, $805,500,000 was intended in whole or in part as corrupt payments to foreign officials through various payment mechanisms, as explained in more detail in the Siemens criminal information.

2) Siemens' United Nations Oil for Food Program Contracts

In addition, from in or about 2000 to in or about 2002, four Siemens AG subsidiaries—Siemens S.A.S. of France ("Siemens France"), Siemens Sanayi ve Ticaret A.S. of Turkey ("Siemens Turkey"), Osram Middle East FZE ("Osram Middle East"), and Gas Turbine Technologies S.p.A. ("GTT")—each wholly owned by Siemens or one of its subsidiaries, were awarded 42 contracts with a combined value of more than $80,000,000 with the Ministries of Electricity and Oil of the Government of the Republic of Iraq under the United Nations Oil for Food Program. To obtain these contracts, Siemens France, Siemens Turkey, Osram Middle East, and GTT paid a total of at least $1,736,076 in kickbacks to the Iraqi government, and they collectively earned over $38,000,000 in profits on those 42 contracts.

In order to generate the funds to pay the kickbacks to the Iraqi government and to conceal those payments, Siemens France, Siemens Turkey, Osram Middle East, and GTT inflated the price of these contracts by approximately 10% before submitting them to the United Nations for approval. In order to conceal on their corporate books and records the kickback payment made to the Iraqi government, Siemens France, Siemens Turkey, Osram Middle East, and GTT improperly characterized payments to purported business consultants, part of which were paid as kickbacks to the Iraqi government, as "commissions" to the business consultants. For the relevant years, the books and records of Siemens France, Siemens Turkey, Osram Middle East, and GTT, including those containing false characterizations of the kickbacks paid to the Iraqi government, were part of the books and records of Siemens.

b. Siemens Argentina's Improperly Recorded Payments

Siemens Argentina was a wholly owned subsidiary of Siemens AG. Beginning around September 1998 and continuing until 2007, Siemens Argentina made and caused to be made significant payments to various Argentine officials, both directly and indirectly, in an effort to retain current business or secure future business.

In or about 1994, the Argentine government issued a tender for bids to replace the then existing manually-created national identity booklets with state of the art national identity cards (the "national identity card project"). The total estimated value of the national identity card project was $1 billion. In February 1998, Siemens Argentina and its affiliates were awarded the national identity card project contract by the Argentine Ministry of the Interior. In approximately September 1998, Siemens Argentina began making and causing to be made multiple payments to a group of purported business consultants (the "Argentine Consulting Group") in connection with the national identity card project, despite the fact that the Argentine Consulting Group provided no legitimate services on the project. Siemens Argentina employees understood these payments to be, at least in part, bribes for the high-level Argentine government officials responsible for awarding Siemens Argentina and its affiliates the identity card project.

From in or about 1997 to in or about January 2007, Siemens Argentina paid or caused to be paid at least $15,725,000 directly to entities controlled by members of the Argentine government, at least $35,150,000 directly to the Argentine Consulting Group, and at least $54,908,000 to other entities. Some of the corrupt payments were approved by Siemens Argentina personnel or agents from within the United States or paid into United States bank accounts. From the date Siemens became an issuer on March 12, 2001 through in or about January 2007, Siemens Argentina made approximately $31,263,000 in corrupt payments through the Argentine Consulting Group and other entities, and improperly characterized those corrupt payments in its books and records as legitimate payments for "consulting fees" or "legal fees." Siemens Argentina's books and records, including those containing the false characterizations of the corrupt payments, were part of the books and records of Siemens.

c. Siemens Bangladesh's Corrupt and Improperly Recorded Payments

From 2000 to 2002, the Bangladesh Telegraph Telephone Board (the "BTTB"), a government-owned telecommunications regulatory entity in Bangladesh, conducted a series of three open tenders for a mobile telephone project (the "BTTB Project") that was ultimately awarded to Siemens. In 2000, the BTTB conducted the first tender for the BTTB Project contract. Siemens was excluded from the first tender for technical non-compliance, but the tender was subsequently cancelled. The second tender in 2001 was cancelled and reissued because of a change in government. Siemens was initially disqualified from the third tender, but in partnership with Siemens Bangladesh and Siemens Mobile Communications S.p.A. (then a Siemens subsidiary located in Milan, Italy), ultimately was awarded part of that tender in June 2004. Siemens' and its subsidiaries' portion of the contract value was $40,887,000.

From May 2001 to August 2006, Siemens Bangladesh, which was responsible for the local operations on the project, engaged or caused to be engaged purported business consultants to pay bribes to various Bangladeshi officials in exchange for favorable treatment during the bidding process. Siemens Bangladesh caused to be paid at least $5,319,839.83 to the purported business consultants. Siemens Bangladesh caused at least one payment to be made to each of these purported consultants from a United States bank account, and the remaining payments to be made through payment intermediaries.

Siemens Bangladesh knew that the purported business consultants were passing along some or all of the money they received from Siemens Bangladesh to senior Bangladeshi government officials in exchange for favorable treatment of Siemens AG in the BTTB Project bid process. In September 2004, Siemens Bangladesh learned that one of the purported business consultants had moved to the United States, after which Siemens Bangladesh continued to cause him to be paid purported consulting fees to an account in Hong Kong. In 2003, Siemens Bangladesh also made payments of at least $16,000 directly to Bangladeshi government officials, or relatives of Bangladeshi officials, with responsibility for awarding the BTTB Project. Siemens Bangladesh caused these payments to be improperly recorded on Siemens' books and records as "consulting fees" and other seemingly legitimate payments.

d. Siemens Venezuela's Corrupt and Improperly Recorded Payments

Beginning around November 2001 and continuing until around May 2007, Siemens Venezuela made and caused to be made significant payments to various Venezuelan officials, indirectly through purported business consultants, in exchange for favorable business treatment. The payments were related to two major transportation infrastructure projects.

1) Metro Valencia Project

In or about 1996, Siemens was awarded a contract to design and build a rail mass transit system in the City of Valencia, Venezuela (the "Metro Valencia project"). Due to the size, cost, and complexity of the project, work was performed in several phases, each of which was governed by a contract between a Siemens entity and the city of Valencia. The total estimated value of all contracts was $240,000,000. Siemens Venezuela was responsible for overseeing certain administrative aspects of the contracts, including the hiring and payment of business consultants.

2) Metro Maracaibo Project

In 2000, the city of Maracaibo, Venezuela, and the State of Zulia, Venezuela, solicited bids for a contract to design and build a rail mass transit system in the city of Maracaibo (the "Metro Maracaibo project"). Siemens Venezuela and its affiliates submitted a bid. Prior to opening the bids, a dispute arose between the Mayor of Maracaibo, who favored the project, and the Governor of the State of Zulia, who opposed the project. In or about 2000, Siemens Venezuela hired a purported business consultant in connection with the dispute. Following that, the project was unanimously approved at a Metro Maracaibo board meeting, which the representatives from the Governor's Office failed to attend. The total value for the contract and project was over $100,000,000. Siemens Venezuela was responsible for overseeing certain administrative aspects of the contracts, including the hiring and payment of business consultants.

3) Total Corrupt Payments by Siemens Venezuela

From in or about November 2001 through in or about May 2007, Siemens Venezuela paid and caused to be paid at least $18,782,965 to various purported business consultants with the understanding that some or all of those funds would be passed along to Venezuelan government officials for the corrupt purpose of obtaining and retaining government contracts in Venezuela relating to the Metro Valencia and Metro Maracaibo projects. Some of those payments were made using United States bank accounts controlled by the purported business consultants. Siemens Venezuela caused these payments to be improperly recorded on Siemens' books and records as "consulting fees," payments for "studies," and other seemingly legitimate payments.

3. Dispositions With Siemens, Siemens Argentina, Siemens Bangladesh, and Siemens Venezuela

a. Summary of Criminal Charges

The Department and Siemens agree that the appropriate resolution of this matter consists of guilty pleas pursuant to plea agreements with Siemens, Siemens Argentina, Siemens Bangladesh, and Siemens Venezuela. The Siemens information charges (a) a violation of the FCPA's internal controls provisions under 15 U.S.C. §§ 78m(b)(2)(B), 78m(b)(5), and 78ff(a) (Count One); and (b) a violation of the FCPA's books and records provisions under 15 U.S.C. §§ 78m(b)(2)(B), 78m(b)(5), and 78ff(a) (Count Two). The Siemens Argentina information charges a single count of conspiracy to commit an offense against the United States, in violation of 18 U.S.C. § 371, with a single object—to violate the books and records provisions of the FCPA. The proposed informations against Siemens Bangladesh and Siemens Venezuela each charge a single count of conspiracy to commit offenses against the United States, in violation of 18 U.S.C. § 371, with two objects—to violate the FCPA's antibribery provisions and to violate the FCPA's books and records provisions.

b. Summary of Plea Agreements

The Proposed plea agreements contain the following core terms: (a) agreement to plead guilty to the charges in the informations in the District of Columbia, the factual allegations of which Siemens, Siemens Venezuela,

Siemens Bangladesh, and Siemens Argentina agree not to contest; (b) a total criminal penalty of $450,000,000, apportioned as follows: a $448,500,000 fine for Siemens; and a $500,000 fine (the statutory maximum for conspiracy) for each of Siemens Argentina, Siemens Bangladesh, and Siemens Venezuela; (c) a continuing obligation to provide full, complete, and truthful cooperation to the Department and any other law enforcement agency, domestic or foreign, with which the Department directs Siemens to cooperate, in particular the Munich Public Prosecutor's Office; (d) implementation of rigorous compliance enhancements, including periodic testing of same, with a recognition that Siemens has already implemented substantial compliance changes over the course of the investigation; and (e) retention of an independent monitor, who will, over a four-year term, conduct a review of the compliance code, Siemens' internal controls and related issues, and will prepare periodic reports on his reviews.

In accordance with the Department's Principles of Federal Prosecution of Business Organizations, the Department considered a number of factors in its decisions regarding the overall disposition. Those factors included, but were not limited to, Siemens' cooperation and remediation efforts, as well as any collateral consequences, including whether there would be disproportionate harm to the shareholders, pension holders, employees, and other persons not proven personally culpable, and the impact on the public, arising from the prosecution. The Department's analysis of collateral consequences included the consideration of the risk of debarment and exclusion from government contracts. In considering the overall disposition, the Department also considered related cases of other governmental authorities.

. . . .

5. Siemens' Substantial Assistance, Cooperation, and Remediation Efforts

The Department believes the above-proposed penalties are appropriate based on Siemens' substantial assistance to the Department in the investigation of other persons and entities, its extraordinary efforts to uncover evidence of prior corrupt activities, and in its extensive commitment to restructure and remediate its operations to make it a worldwide leader in transparent and responsible corporate practices going forward, all of which are described in more detail below.

If the plea agreement were being filed pursuant to Fed. R. Crim. P. 11(c)(1)(B) instead of pursuant to Fed. R. Crim. P. 11(c)(1)(c), the Department believes that the facts contained in the Department's Sentencing Memorandum would merit a motion for downward departure with respect to Siemens. U.S.S.G. § 8C4.1, the corporate analogue to U.S.S.G. §5K1.1, provides for downward departures from the advisory sentencing guideline range based on the defendant's "substantial assistance in the investigation or prosecution of another organization that has committed an offense, or in the investigation or prosecution of an individual not directly affiliated with the defendant who has committed an offense."

If the plea agreement were being filed pursuant to Fed. R. Crim. P. 11(c)(1)(B) and the Department were filing a motion for downward departure with respect to Siemens, it would also argue that under 18 U.S.C. § 3553(b)(1) and the introductory commentary to U.S.S.G. § 8C4, departure is warranted if the court finds "that there exists an aggravating or mitigating circumstance of a kind, *or to a degree*, not adequately taken into consideration by the Sentencing Commission in formulating the guidelines that should result in a sentence different from that described." (Emphasis added). Because Siemens did not voluntarily disclose the conduct before the Munich Public Prosecutor raided its offices, it only receives a two-point reduction in its culpability score, which is incongruent with the level of cooperation and assistance provided by the company in the Department's investigation.

The Department's and Siemens' proposed criminal penalty of $448,500,000 would be the same in the event of a plea under Fed. R. Crim. P. 11(c)(1)(B) accompanied by a motion for downward departure. Nevertheless, the Department and Siemens AG agreed that filing the plea agreement pursuant to Fed. R. Crim. P. 11(c)(1)(c) was more appropriate in this case.

a. Substantial Assistance in the Investigation of Others

As part of its overall cooperation efforts, Siemens (primarily through Debevoise and Deloitte) has developed and timely provided detailed and significant information regarding third parties, including individuals and entities that were used as conduits to conceal corrupt payments made to foreign government officials. Several of these individuals and entities were located in the United States and utilized United States banks to facilitate the payments. Siemens has assisted in the investigation of these individuals and entities by initially disclosing the existence of the activities, and then providing detailed and useful information obtained from interviews of Siemens employees, corporate records, and bank and other financial records. Frequently, this detailed information has been presented during debriefing sessions that included PowerPoint presentations together with binders of pertinent documents. Because many Siemens documents are in German or other foreign languages, Siemens has routinely provided English language translations of documents produced, thereby saving the Department very significant time and expense.

In certain instances, Siemens has provided forensic analyses of bank records and payments that have greatly assisted in the tracing of multi-layered financial transactions. Many of these transactions involved the movement of funds through several countries. It was only through the extensive, worldwide investigative efforts of the internal investigators that these complex criminal activities were uncovered. As a practical matter, it would have been exceedingly difficult for the Department to identify and obtain the necessary foreign financial records, review them, trace proceeds, and identify and interview potential witnesses, all between late 2006 and the present. Furthermore, the documentation and analysis undertaken by Siemens has been possible only because it took aggressive steps starting immediately after the Munich raids to preserve evidence in both electronic and hard copy form. A summary of the specific substantial assistance efforts, identifying the persons and entities involved, appears in a separate pleading being filed under seal.

In addition to the many timely and useful presentations to the Department and the SEC, Siemens has undertaken significant similar efforts to cooperate with foreign law enforcement authorities who have been conducting investigations of alleged improper payments abroad. In addition to the Munich Public Prosecutor's Office, the Department understands that Siemens has cooperated extensively with law enforcement authorities in numerous countries, including but not limited to, Bangladesh, Greece, and Nigeria. Siemens has also fully cooperated with several international development banks, including the World Bank and Inter-American Development Bank, in connection with Siemens projects that received funding from those banks. Siemens interacted with the relevant government and inter-governmental entities in a transparent fashion, such that it facilitated communication between and among the Department and the SEC and these bodies. These efforts have set a standard going forward for the type of multi-national cooperation that can greatly enhance worldwide law enforcement efforts involving corruption of foreign officials.

b. Siemens' Exceptional Cooperation

The Department views as exceptional Siemens' wide-ranging cooperation efforts throughout this investigation, which included a sweeping internal investigation, the creation of innovative and effective amnesty and leniency programs, and exemplary efforts with respect to preservation, collection, testing, and analysis of evidence.

1) Extensive Internal Investigation

Within a short time after the Munich Public Prosecutor's Office conducted raids of Siemens' offices in November 2006, Siemens retained Debevoise "to conduct an independent and comprehensive investigation to determine whether anti-corruption regulations [had] been violated and to conduct an independent and comprehensive assessment of the compliance and control systems at Siemens." Siemens has since then provided its unwavering support and commitment to this investigation. By all indications, Debevoise has been permitted to conduct its investigation in a completely independent fashion, without limitations as to scope or duration. According to Siemens' latest estimates, over 1.5 million hours of billable time by Debevoise and Deloitte professionals have been devoted to the investigation. This includes the extensive and sustained participation of approximately 100 lawyers and 100 support staff from Debevoise and 130 forensic accountants and support staff from Deloitte. The investigative work has taken place in 34 countries and has involved over 1,750 interviews and over 800 informational meetings. Over 100 million documents have been collected and preserved, many of which have been searched or reviewed for evidence relevant to the investigation. Siemens, either directly or through Debevoise, has produced to the Department over 24,000 documents, amounting to over 100,000 pages.

To ensure that Debevoise and Deloitte had the support needed within Siemens to effectively conduct their investigation, Siemens stressed to all employees that they must fully cooperate in the investigation. In addition, Siemens established a Project Office at headquarters staffed by 16 full-time employees that facilitated interviews and document collection. To facilitate visits to regional companies by the investigation team, the Project Office communicated with regional management to explain and prepare them for the interviews and other investigative work.

2) Amnesty and Leniency Programs

In consultation with the Department, Siemens designed and implemented a company-wide amnesty program to facilitate the internal investigation. This amnesty program was implemented on October 31, 2007 and continued until approximately February 29, 2008. The program provided that all but the most senior employees who voluntarily disclosed to Debevoise truthful and complete information about possible violations of relevant anti-corruption laws would be protected from unilateral employment termination and company claims for damages. The policy that implemented the amnesty program made clear that it was in no way binding on any prosecutors or regulators, including the Department and the SEC, but that Siemens would bring an employee's cooperation to the attention of such authorities if he or she were the subject of a government investigation.

For employees too senior to qualify for the amnesty program, as well as those employees who did not come forward during the amnesty program period, Siemens established a similar leniency program on April 4, 2008. The leniency program provided for individualized leniency determinations for cooperating employees. The creation of these two programs was a unique and effective way to further the investigation and it yielded impressive results. Over 100 employees provided information in connection with the programs, including numerous employees who previously provided incomplete or less than truthful information and employees who had not come forward previously.

Shortly after the amnesty program began, the Department and the SEC identified various individuals and projects for more extensive debriefings by Siemens, referred to by the parties as "deep dives." The amnesty and leniency programs were vital to obtaining the types of detailed information needed for the deep dives. These deep dive sessions greatly enhanced the Department's ability to evaluate the overall case, properly target its limited resources, and develop the evidence necessary to bring the charges here.

3) Preservation, Collection, Testing, and Analysis of Evidence

At the outset of the internal investigation, Siemens instituted a worldwide data preservation policy directing that employees secure and preserve, among other things, all documents relating to financial transactions; all corporate books and records; records of any payments to government officials; and records concerning consultants, agents, or other third parties that assisted Siemens in obtaining business. Siemens took extensive steps using technological and human resources to ensure successful preservation of these documents. One of the primary functions of the Project Office has been to ensure that employees have complied with the data preservation policy.

Due to the enormous volume of records and the data protection laws in various countries, document preservation and production have been complex and expensive. Siemens established special offices in Germany and China to collect, review, process, and store documents in connection with the investigation. To date, Siemens has spent more than $100 million on document collection, review, processing and storage, including those facilities in Germany and China. Although data protection laws, including those in Germany, have at times limited or delayed Siemens' production of certain documents, Siemens has worked hard to take necessary steps and, where necessary, obtain approvals from foreign authorities, to make the documents available to the Department and the SEC as promptly as possible and in compliance with relevant data privacy laws and other legal restrictions.

Siemens' extensive efforts in preserving and making available documents from foreign countries have been exemplary and serve as a model to other multinational companies seeking to cooperate with law enforcement authorities.

c. Remediation Efforts

Since the beginning of the internal investigation, Siemens' remediation efforts have been exceptional. Siemens has replaced nearly all of its top leadership, including the Chairman of the Supervisory Board, the Chief Executive Officer, the General Counsel, the Head of Internal Audit, and the Chief Compliance Officer. The Company has terminated members of senior management implicated in the misconduct uncovered by the investigation and has reorganized the Company to be more centralized from both a business and compliance perspective. This includes the creation of a new position on the Managing Board with specific responsibility for legal and compliance matters.

Siemens also overhauled and greatly expanded its compliance organization, which now totals more than 500 full time compliance personnel worldwide. Control and accountability for all compliance matters is vested in a Chief Compliance Officer, who, in turn, reports directly to the General Counsel and the Chief Executive Officer. Siemens has also reorganized its Audit Department, which is headed by a newly appointed Chief Audit Officer who reports directly to Siemens' Audit Committee. To ensure that auditing personnel throughout the company are competent, the Chief Audit Officer required that every member of his 450 person staff reapply for their jobs.

Siemens also has enacted a series of new anti-corruption compliance policies, including a new anti-corruption handbook, sophisticated web-based tools for due diligence and compliance matters, a confidential communications channel for employees to report irregular business practices, and a corporate disciplinary committee to impose appropriate disciplinary measures for substantiated misconduct.

Siemens has organized a working group devoted to fully implementing the new compliance initiatives, which consists of employees from Siemens' Corporate Finance and Corporate Compliance departments, and professionals from PricewaterhouseCoopers ("PwC"). This working group developed a step-by-step guide on the new compliance program and improved financial controls known as the "Anti-Corruption Toolkit." The Anti-Corruption Toolkit and its accompanying guide contain clear steps and [timelines] required of local management in the various Siemens entities to ensure full implementation of the global anti-corruption program and enhanced controls. Over 150 people, including 75 PwC professionals, provided support in implementing the Anti-Corruption Toolkit at 162 Siemens entities, and dedicated support teams spent six weeks on the ground at 56 of those entities deemed to be "higher risk," assisting management in those locations with all aspects of the implementation. The total external cost to Siemens for the PwC remediation efforts has exceeded $150 million.

In addition to these efforts, during the investigation, Siemens imposed a moratorium on entering into new business consulting agreements or making payments under existing business consulting agreements until a complete collection and review was undertaken of all such agreements. Siemens also initiated, and has nearly completed, a review of all third party agents with whom it has agreements. This has resulted in a significant reduction in the number of business consultants used by Siemens.

Siemens also significantly enhanced its review and approval procedures for business consultants, in light of the past problems. The new state-of-the-art system requires any employee who wishes to engage a business consultant to enter detailed information into an interactive computer system, which assesses the risk of the engagement and directs the request to the appropriate supervisors for review and approval. Siemens has also increased corporate-level control over company funds and has centralized and reduced the number of company bank accounts and outgoing payments to third parties.

The reorganization and remediation efforts of Siemens have been extraordinary and have set a high standard for multi-national companies to follow. These measures, in conjunction with Siemens' agreement to retain a Monitor (with support from a U.S. law firm with FCPA and compliance expertise) for a term of four years, highlight the serious commitment of Siemens to ensure that it operates in a transparent, honest, and responsible manner going forward.

CONCLUSION

For the foregoing reasons, the Department respectfully recommends that the Court sentence Siemens to a fine in the amount of $448,500,000 and a special assessment of $800; and that the Court sentence Siemens Venezuela, Siemens Bangladesh, and Siemens Argentina each to a fine in the amount of $500,000 and a special assessment of $400.

U.S. Department of Justice Criminal Division Fraud Section Evaluation of Corporate Compliance Programs[4]

INTRODUCTION

The Principles of Federal Prosecution of Business Organizations in the United States Attorney's Manual describe specific factors that prosecutors should consider in conducting an investigation of a corporate entity, determining whether to bring charges, and negotiating plea or other agreements. These factors, commonly known as the "Filip Factors," include "the existence and effectiveness of the corporation's pre-existing compliance program" and the corporation's remedial efforts "to implement an effective corporate compliance program or to improve an existing one."

Because a corporate compliance program must be evaluated in the specific context of a criminal investigation that triggers the application of the Filip Factors, the Fraud Section does not use any rigid formula to assess the effectiveness of corporate compliance programs. We recognize that each company's risk profile and solutions to reduce its risks warrant particularized evaluation. Accordingly, we make an individualized determination in each case.

There are, however, common questions that we may ask in making an individualized determination. This document provides some important topics and sample questions that the Fraud Section has frequently found relevant in evaluating a corporate compliance program. The topics and questions below form neither a checklist nor a formula. In any particular case, the topics and questions set forth below may not all be relevant, and others may be more salient given the particular facts at issue.

Many of the topics below also appear in the United States Attorney's Manual ("USAM"), in the United States Sentencing Guidelines ("USSG"), in Fraud Section corporate resolution agreements, in A Resource Guide to the U.S. Foreign Corrupt Practices Act ("FCPA Guide") published in November 2012 by the Department of Justice (DOJ) and the Securities and Exchange Commission (SEC), in the Good Practice Guidance on Internal Controls, Ethics, and Compliance adopted by the Organization for Economic Cooperation and Development ("OECD") Council on February 18, 2010, and in the Anti-Corruption Ethics and Compliance Handbook for Business ("OECD Handbook") published in 2013 by OECD, United Nations Office on Drugs and Crime, and the World Bank.

Sample Topics and Questions

1. Analysis and Remediation of Underlying Misconduct
- **Root Cause Analysis**—What is the company's root cause analysis of the misconduct at issue? What systemic issues were identified? Who in the company was involved in making the analysis?

---

4. Fraud Section, U.S. Dep't of Justice, Evaluation of Corporate Compliance Programs (footnotes omitted), https://www.justice.gov/criminal-fraud/page/file/937501/download.

- **Prior Indications**—Were there prior opportunities to detect the misconduct in question, such as audit reports identifying relevant control failures or allegations, complaints, or investigations involving similar issues? What is the company's analysis of why such opportunities were missed?
- **Remediation**—What specific changes has the company made to reduce the risk that the same or similar issues will not occur in the future? What specific remediation has addressed the issues identified in the root cause and missed opportunity analysis?

2. **Senior and Middle Management**
   - **Conduct at the Top**—How have senior leaders, through their words and actions, encouraged or discouraged the type of misconduct in question? What concrete actions have they taken to demonstrate leadership in the company's compliance and remediation efforts? How does the company monitor its senior leadership's behavior? How has senior leadership modelled proper behavior to subordinates?
   - **Shared Commitment**—What specific actions have senior leaders and other stakeholders (*e.g.*, business and operational managers, Finance, Procurement, Legal, Human Resources) taken to demonstrate their commitment to compliance, including their remediation efforts? How is information shared among different components of the company?
   - **Oversight**—What compliance expertise has been available on the board of directors? Have the board of directors and/or external auditors held executive or private sessions with the compliance and control functions? What types of information have the board of directors and senior management examined in their exercise of oversight in the area in which the misconduct occurred?

3. **Autonomy and Resources**
   - **Compliance Role**—Was compliance involved in training and decisions relevant to the misconduct? Did the compliance or relevant control functions (*e.g.*, Legal, Finance, or Audit) ever raise a concern in the area where the misconduct occurred?
   - **Stature**—How has the compliance function compared with other strategic functions in the company in terms of stature, compensation levels, rank/title, reporting line, resources, and access to key decision-makers? What has been the turnover rate for compliance and relevant control function personnel? What role has compliance played in the company's strategic and operational decisions?
   - **Experience and Qualifications**—Have the compliance and control personnel had the appropriate experience and qualifications for their roles and responsibilities?
   - **Autonomy**—Have the compliance and relevant control functions had direct reporting lines to anyone on the board of directors? How often do they meet with the board of directors? Are members of the senior

management present for these meetings? Who reviewed the performance of the compliance function and what was the review process? Who has determined compensation/bonuses/raises/hiring/termination of compliance officers? Do the compliance and relevant control personnel in the field have reporting lines to headquarters? If not, how has the company ensured their independence?

- **Empowerment**—Have there been specific instances where compliance raised concerns or objections in the area in which the wrongdoing occurred? How has the company responded to such compliance concerns? Have there been specific transactions or deals that were stopped, modified, or more closely examined as a result of compliance concerns?

- **Funding and Resources**—How have decisions been made about the allocation of personnel and resources for the compliance and relevant control functions in light of the company's risk profile? Have there been times when requests for resources by the compliance and relevant control functions have been denied? If so, how have those decisions been made?

- **Outsourced Compliance Functions**—Has the company outsourced all or parts of its compliance functions to an external firm or consultant? What has been the rationale for doing so? Who has been involved in the decision to outsource? How has that process been managed (including who oversaw and/or liaised with the external firm/consultant)? What access level does the external firm or consultant have to company information? How has the effectiveness of the outsourced process been assessed?

4. **Policies and Procedures**
   a. **Design and Accessibility**
      - **Designing Compliance Policies and Procedures**—What has been the company's process for designing and implementing new policies and procedures? Who has been involved in the design of policies and procedures? Have business units/divisions been consulted prior to rolling them out?
      - **Applicable Policies and Procedures**—Has the company had policies and procedures that prohibited the misconduct? How has the company assessed whether these policies and procedures have been effectively implemented? How have the functions that had ownership of these policies and procedures been held accountable for supervisory oversight?
      - **Gatekeepers**—Has there been clear guidance and/or training for the key gatekeepers (*e.g.*, the persons who issue payments or review approvals) in the control processes relevant to the misconduct? What has been the process for them to raise concerns?
      - **Accessibility**—How has the company communicated the policies and procedures relevant to the misconduct to relevant employees and third parties? How has the company evaluated the usefulness of these policies and procedures?

b. Operational Integration

- **Responsibility for Integration**—Who has been responsible for integrating policies and procedures? With whom have they consulted (*e.g.*, officers, business segments)? How have they been rolled out (*e.g.*, do compliance personnel assess whether employees understand the policies)?
- **Controls**—What controls failed or were absent that would have detected or prevented the misconduct? Are they there now?
- **Payment Systems**—How was the misconduct in question funded (*e.g.*, purchase orders, employee reimbursements, discounts, petty cash)? What processes could have prevented or detected improper access to these funds? Have those processes been improved?
- **Approval/Certification Process**—How have those with approval authority or certification responsibilities in the processes relevant to the misconduct known what to look for, and when and how to escalate concerns? What steps have been taken to remedy any failures identified in this process?
- **Vendor Management**—If vendors had been involved in the misconduct, what was the process for vendor selection and did the vendor in question go through that process? See further questions below under Item 10, "Third Party Management."

5. Risk Assessment

- **Risk Management Process**—What methodology has the company used to identify, analyze, and address the particular risks it faced?
- **Information Gathering and Analysis**—What information or metrics has the company collected and used to help detect the type of misconduct in question? How has the information or metrics informed the company's compliance program?
- **Manifested Risks**—How has the company's risk assessment process accounted for manifested risks?

6. Training and Communications

- **Risk-Based Training**—What training have employees in relevant control functions received? Has the company provided tailored training for high-risk and control employees that addressed the risks in the area where the misconduct occurred? What analysis has the company undertaken to determine who should be trained and on what subjects?
- **Form/Content/Effectiveness of Training**—Has the training been offered in the form and language appropriate for the intended audience? How has the company measured the effectiveness of the training?
- **Communications about Misconduct**—What has senior management done to let employees know the company's position on the misconduct that occurred? What communications have there been generally when an employee is terminated for failure to comply with the company's policies, procedures, and controls (*e.g.*, anonymized descriptions of the type of misconduct that leads to discipline)?

- **Availability of Guidance**—What resources have been available to employees to provide guidance relating to compliance policies? How has the company assessed whether its employees know when to seek advice and whether they would be willing to do so?

7. **Confidential Reporting and Investigation**
   - **Effectiveness of the Reporting Mechanism**—How has the company collected, analyzed, and used information from its reporting mechanisms? How has the company assessed the seriousness of the allegations it received? Has the compliance function had full access to reporting and investigative information?
   - **Properly Scoped Investigation by Qualified Personnel**—How has the company ensured that the investigations have been properly scoped, and were independent, objective, appropriately conducted, and properly documented?
   - **Response to Investigations**—Has the company's investigation been used to identify root causes, system vulnerabilities, and accountability lapses, including among supervisory manager and senior executives? What has been the process for responding to investigative findings? How high up in the company do investigative findings go?

8. **Incentives and Disciplinary Measures**
   - **Accountability**—What disciplinary actions did the company take in response to the misconduct and when did they occur? Were managers held accountable for misconduct that occurred under their supervision? Did the company's response consider disciplinary actions for supervisors' failure in oversight? What is the company's record (*e.g.*, number and types of disciplinary actions) on employee discipline relating to the type(s) of conduct at issue? Has the company ever terminated or otherwise disciplined anyone (reduced or eliminated bonuses, issued a warning letter, etc.) for the type of misconduct at issue?
   - **Human Resources Process**—Who participated in making disciplinary decisions for the type of misconduct at issue?
   - **Consistent Application**—Have the disciplinary actions and incentives been fairly and consistently applied across the organization?
   - **Incentive System**—How has the company incentivized compliance and ethical behavior? How has the company considered the potential negative compliance implications of its incentives and rewards? Have there been specific examples of actions taken (*e.g.*, promotions or awards denied) as a result of compliance and ethics considerations?

9. **Continuous Improvement, Periodic Testing and Review**
   - **Internal Audit**—What types of audits would have identified issues relevant to the misconduct? Did those audits occur and what were the findings? What types of relevant audit findings and remediation progress have been reported to management and the board on a regular basis? How have management and the board followed up? How often has internal audit generally conducted assessments in high-risk areas?

- **Control Testing**—Has the company reviewed and audited its compliance program in the area relating to the misconduct, including testing of relevant controls, collection and analysis of compliance data, and interviews of employees and third-parties? How are the results reported and action items tracked? What control testing has the company generally undertaken?
- **Evolving Updates**—How often has the company updated its risk assessments and reviewed its compliance policies, procedures, and practices? What steps has the company taken to determine whether policies/procedures/practices make sense for particular business segments/subsidiaries?

10. **Third Party Management**
- **Risk-Based and Integrated Processes**—How has the company's third-party management process corresponded to the nature and level of the enterprise risk identified by the company? How has this process been integrated into the relevant procurement and vendor management processes?
- **Appropriate Controls**—What was the business rationale for the use of the third parties in question? What mechanisms have existed to ensure that the contract terms specifically described the services to be performed, that the payment terms are appropriate, that the described contractual work is performed, and that compensation is commensurate with the services rendered?
- **Management of Relationships**—How has the company considered and analyzed the third party's incentive model against compliance risks? How has the company monitored the third parties in question? How has the company trained the relationship managers about what the compliance risks are and how to manage them? How has the company incentivized compliance and ethical behavior by third parties?
- **Real Actions and Consequences**—Were red flags identified from the due diligence of the third parties involved in the misconduct and how were they resolved? Has a similar third party been suspended, terminated, or audited as a result of compliance issues? How has the company monitored these actions (*e.g.*, ensuring that the vendor is not used again in case of termination)?

11. **Mergers and Acquisitions (M&A)**
- **Due Diligence Process**—Was the misconduct or the risk of misconduct identified during due diligence? Who conducted the risk review for the acquired/merged entities and how was it done? What has been the M&A due diligence process generally?
- **Integration in the M&A Process**—How has the compliance function been integrated into the merger, acquisition, and integration process?

- **Process Connecting Due Diligence to Implementation**—What has been the company's process for tracking and remediating misconduct or misconduct risks identified during the due diligence process? What has been the company's process for implementing compliance policies and procedures at new entities?

THE BUSINESS ETHICS PROGRAM

In 1970, economist Milton Friedman argued that "in a free society, there is one and only one social responsibility of business—to use its resources and engage in activities designed to increase its profits so long as it stays within the rules of the game." Friedman, whose views would largely define conventional wisdom for the next generation, rejected the idea of corporate social responsibility ("CSR") as fundamentally subversive:

> When I hear businessmen speak eloquently about the "social responsibilities of business in a free-enterprise system," I am reminded of the wonderful line about the Frenchman who discovered at the age of 70 that he had been speaking prose all his life. The businessmen believe that they are defending free enterprise when they claim that business is not concerned "merely" with profit but also with promoting desirable "social" ends; that business has a "social conscience" and takes seriously its responsibilities for providing employment, eliminating discrimination, avoiding pollution and whatever else may be the catchwords of the contemporary crop of reformers. In fact they are—or would be if they or anyone else took them seriously—preaching pure and unadulterated socialism. Businessmen who talk this way are unwitting puppets of the intellectual forces that have been undermining the basis of a free society these past decades.[1]

Friedman worried that were CSR to become widely accepted, "the external forces that curb the market [would] not be the social consciences, however highly developed, of the pontificating executives [, but] the iron fist of Government bureaucrats."[2]

Some 50 years later, that prediction has at least partially come to pass. Although no U.S. law imposes a code of CSR, the criminal justice system compels its observance through the same carrot-and-stick regime that forces corporations to self-police. The 2004 amendments to the Federal Sentencing Guidelines for Organizations ("FSGO") introduced CSR by requiring that corporations go

---

1. Milton Friedman, *The Social Responsibility of Business Is to Increase Its Profits*, N.Y. TIMES MAG., Sept. 13, 1970, at 12.
2. *Id.*

beyond mere compliance with the law and make sure that they actively promote a culture of ethics. Thus, in addition to spurring a movement toward corporate self-policing, the FSGO ushered in a new era in corporate ethics:

> The Federal Sentencing Guidelines . . . transformed the way businesses respond to ethics. Formerly, corporations relied on compliance measures which became activated only after wrongdoing occurred. Violations occurred and compliance responses consisted of identifying and punishing those responsible. But the Federal Sentencing Guidelines push corporations toward a much more proactive stance . . . . It is in this new corporate context that corporations have begun to adopt values-based decision making. Instead of setting forth rules that outline minimum levels of forced compliance, they now ask employees to work beyond the moral minimum and seek occasions to actually realize or enhance moral value.[3]

In 2004, the U.S. government moved closer to formally imposing CSR when it issued detailed guidance on what constitutes responsible business conduct in the global economy. Titled *Business Ethics: A Manual for Managing a Responsible Business Enterprise in Emerging Market Economies* ("BEM"),[4] it opens with the following admonition:

> [O]wners and managers must temper the competitive aspects of capitalism with concerned citizenship. They must take individual responsibility for the decisions and activities of their enterprises and their impact on the culture of their enterprise and its stakeholders. A business needs . . . to take the long view and to respect the physical environment and the prospects of future generations.[5]

The BEM is based on the central tenet of CSR: that a business enterprise is responsible not only to its shareholders, but also to its stakeholders—a much larger class that includes any party whose interests may be impacted by the enterprise, including employees, consumers, regulators, environmental interest groups, and the community. Fulfilling that responsibility, the BEM states, involves nothing less than satisfying the reasonable expectations of all those groups, wherever they may be located.[6]

Like the FCPA Guide, which articulates the U.S. government's expectations of corporate compliance programs, the BEM serves the same function with respect to ethics programs. It sketches out components of an effective ethics program that, similarly to the FCPA Guide's "Hallmarks" of an effective compliance program, specify program objectives and the means by which to achieve them. In fact, the FCPA Guide refers to the BEM as additional guidance for creating a compliance and ethics program.[7] Thus, maintaining an

---

3. Jose A. Cruz-Cruz & William Frey, Business Ethics 41 (William Frey ed., 2009).

4. U.S. Dep't of Commerce, Business Ethics: A Manual for Managing A Responsible Business Enterprise in Emerging Market Economies (2004) [hereinafter BEM].

5. *Id.*

6. *See* BEM, *supra* note 4, at 29.

7. *See* Criminal Div. of the U.S. Dep't of Justice & the Enf't Div. of the U.S. Sec. and Exch. Comm'n, A Resource Guide to the U.S. Foreign Corrupt Practices Act 63 (2012), *available at* http://www.justice.gov/sites/default/files/criminal-fraud/legacy/2015/01/16/guide.pdf [hereinafter FCPA Guide].

ethics program patterned after the BEM potentially allows a corporation to avoid prosecution entirely, reduce the penalty when negotiating a deferred prosecution agreement ("DPA"), or, in the event of prosecution, mitigate the sentence.

CSR proponents argue that, far from curbing market forces, the government is simply responding to changed market expectations. As one commentator notes:

> The traditional view of business, summarized by economists such as Milton Friedman in the 1970s . . . is no longer valid, as today's business is about much more than simply providing goods and services to the consumers and paying a fair share of taxes. . . .
>
> Surveys reveal that consumers care about the ethical behavior of companies. The traditional response—that companies are only responsible to their owners—may no longer be valid in today's complex world, where consumers are presented with a variety of options, investors look for stability and security of their investment, and firms face significant legal fines and a myriad of social fears, concerns, and false beliefs. For firms, addressing the role of business in society is vital, because failure to do so can damage their reputation and corporate image, impose additional costs of doing business, and reduce competitiveness. In fact, numerous studies show that responsible business practices—attention to factors other than just maximizing short-term profits—help companies' bottom line[s] and that responsible firms often outperform their competitors.[8]

From this perspective, the government is not levying a cost on corporations, but rather guiding them to generate value in the form of higher productivity, enhanced reputation and social capital, and lower legal risk.

Regardless of the merits of this argument, the shift from Friedman's shareholder theory of corporate governance to the BEM's stakeholder theory confronts multinational enterprises with a new reality, defined by significantly enhanced responsibilities and unclear boundaries. Part IV examines this new reality and its impact on corporate governance structures. Chapter 7 focuses on the changing roles and priorities of corporate leaders and how they can reconcile their traditional obligations to shareholders with their ethical obligations to other stakeholders. Chapter 8 examines the impact of CSR on the compliance function—specifically, how the compliance program interacts with an ethics program that helps satisfy the enterprise's social responsibilities.

Ethics programs are not directed at preventing violations of specific statutes but at addressing the more general international norms of business conduct. Accordingly, Chapter 9 examines the most authoritative source of those norms, the Organisation for Economic Co-operation and Development Guidelines for Multinational Enterprises ("OECD Guidelines").[9] The OECD Guidelines

---

8. Aleksandr Shkolnikov et al., Ctr. For Int'l Private Enter., Issue Paper No. 0410, The Business Case for Corporate Citizenship 1–2 (2004).

9. OECD (2011), *OECD Guidelines for Multinational Enterprises*, OECD Publishing., http://www.oecd.org/daf/inv/mne/48004323.pdf [hereinafter OECD Guidelines].

"have received broad support internationally, and are the only multilaterally agreed and comprehensive code of [CSR] that governments have committed to promoting"[10] and "cover a broad range of corporate practices and issues, such as human rights, environment, labor, anti-bribery, corporate governance, disclosure, supply chain management, and taxation."[11]

---

10. U.S. Dep't of State, A Guide to the U.S. National Contact Point for the OECD Guidelines for the Multinational Enterprises: Your Resource for Responsible Business Conduct, at 4 (2017), [hereinafter Guide to the U.S. NCP OECD Guidelines].

11. *Id.*

CHAPTER 7

The Responsible Business Enterprise ("RBE")

I.   Responsible Conduct
II. Responsible Governance
III. Responsible Management

I. Responsible Conduct

The traditional responsibilities of corporate leaders are defined by the concept of corporate governance, which asks:

- Who can rightfully claim the power to govern an enterprise?
- How can the board of directors and management best protect the rights of shareholders, especially minority shareholders?
- How can the board of directors best guide management to meet the reasonable expectations of shareholders?[2]

> Business enterprises today are expected to meet standards of responsible business conduct that go beyond what had been expected traditionally . . . . [I]t is understood and accepted across the globe that a business enterprise remains a member of its community. The pursuit of profits and economic progress is not a license to ignore community norms, values, and standards of respect, integrity, and quality.
>
> —*Business Ethics: A Manual for Managing a Responsible Business Enterprise in Emerging Market Economies ("BEM")* [1]

Business ethics, as articulated by the BEM, encompasses corporate governance as well as three additional categories of responsibility, which are defined by several questions that corporate executives must ask themselves:

Business and Professional Ethics

- What does a business enterprise owe its customers and consumers?
- What standards of conduct and performance should an enterprise set for its employees and agents?

---

1. U.S. Dep't of Commerce, Business Ethics: A Manual for Managing A Responsible Business Enterprise in Emerging Market Economies (2004) [hereinafter BEM], at 4.

2. *See id.*, at xiii.

- What is the role of industry and government in setting business and professional standards?

Organizational Ethics

- What is the optimal mix of values and rules to guide decision making and action?
- What structures, systems, practices, and procedures will best implement the values and rules of the enterprise?
- What outcomes should one reasonably expect from an enterprise's decisions and activities, and how can an enterprise track, measure, and report them?

Corporate Social Responsibility

- Who are the legitimate stakeholders of an enterprise, and what can they reasonably expect?
- Who speaks for the environment and future generations as stakeholders?
- What is the role of business in sustainable development?[3]

Most of these ethical obligations relate to the treatment of the enterprise's stakeholders. The first two categories aim to protect the enterprise's owners and the consumers of its products, while the third requires that the enterprise meet the reasonable expectations of *all* stakeholders.

BUSINESS ETHICS: A MANUAL FOR MANAGING A RESPONSIBLE BUSINESS ENTERPRISE IN EMERGING MARKET ECONOMIES[4]

The Individual Business in an Emerging Market Economy

. . . .

In an emerging market economy, an RBE must confront and rise above the legacies of a command economy. As a part of the solution to its economy's problems, it can participate in three essential ways: improving its business performance; helping build social capital in its economy; and working with leaders in business, government, and civil society to develop the essential market-oriented legal framework and reliable judicial institutions.

IMPROVING BUSINESS PERFORMANCE

An essential contribution of any business enterprise in the evolution to a market economy is to improve its own business performance. For all business enterprises, this is the first step toward making profits and contributing to economic

---

3. *See* BEM, *supra* note 1, at xii–xiii.
4. BEM, *supra* note 1.

progress. Performance can be improved by expanding and better engaging stakeholders as follows:

- Establishing clear standards and procedures to guide employees and agents
- Focusing on anticipating and meeting the needs and desires of customers and consumers more effectively and efficiently
- Attracting, hiring, and bringing out the best in employees, suppliers, and service providers
- Establishing internal control mechanisms to build confidence among dispersed owners and investors
- Developing and maintaining strategic alliances with enterprises sharing the same values

These best practices are at the heart of a business ethics program. They can significantly improve an enterprise's prospects for success, as described in more detail in Chapter 2 [of the BEM]. They can help an enterprise improve its reputation, manage its risk, protect itself from its own employees and agents, strengthen its competitive position, expand its access to capital and credit, increase profits, sustain long-term growth, and gain international respect.

HELPING BUILD SOCIAL CAPITAL

Respect, shared values, and mutual trust among individuals, businesses, NGOs, and government officials are the foundation of a market economy. To compete effectively and sustain economic growth, enterprises need social capital as well as financial capital. To contribute to this social capital, an RBE can[:]

- Make the case in its community for a market economy and the role of responsible business.
- Develop a reputation for meeting the reasonable expectations of its stakeholders.
- Agree to voluntary forms of alternative dispute resolution, such as mediation and arbitration, while domestic courts are formed.
- Take responsibility for its mistakes and misconduct.
- Be willing to be held accountable for its mistakes and misconduct.
- Correct misunderstandings about its decisions and activities.
- Compete fairly with competition, both foreign and domestic.

How effectively, efficiently, and responsibly an enterprise is able to add value to its community depends, in large part, on how much its stakeholders trust one another. . . . [W]here market participants and community members cannot trust one another, transaction costs soar. It may be that in markets and communities, especially in emerging market economies, the value an RBE most profitably adds is to be worthy of trust—and to encourage other market participants and community members to be trustworthy as well.

WORKING WITH LEADERS IN BUSINESS, GOVERNMENT, AND CIVIL SOCIETY

An RBE helps government create the conditions for a market economy by promoting responsible business conduct—through self-regulation or by conducting a public dialogue with government officials and NGOs. Even where the legal framework of decrees, laws, and regulations is unfair, supporting the rule of law is an important practice for an RBE. Faced with an unfair legal framework, for example, businesses can work with other businesses and NGOs to point out the ethical dimensions of the decree, law, or regulation and to work for change.

Responsible businesses can serve as a voice for the community. They can work with leaders in government, business, and NGOs to do the following:

- Help develop the necessary institutional and legal frameworks for a market economy.
- Support initiatives to develop good public governance on the part of government itself.
- Strengthen NGOs to provide community-building services that business and government are unable to provide.

In economies where the government is unable to provide the social services a community requires, an RBE can work with other businesses and NGOs to identify community needs and can work with community-based organizations to provide such services. For example, the RBE can contribute supplies or services as a part of community-driven development, or it can contribute funds to community foundations. Some enterprises create their own charity programs or foundations or support volunteer work by employees.

. . . .

Notes and Questions

The BEM urges businesses to assume a leadership position in emerging markets to help facilitate the transition to a market economy. Do business executives possess the necessary skills to perform such a task?

Hypothetical: Absence of a Sophisticated Legal System

Netherlands-based Dutch Co. is the largest producer of vegetable seeds in the world. Its shares trade on the AEX (Holland's main stock exchange) as well as the NYSE. Dutch Co.'s onion seed is particularly popular in Asia. In Vietnam, 80 percent of farmers use Dutch Co.'s onion seeds. In northern regions of Vietnam, farmers use a variety called "Long Day," and, in the south, farmers plant a variety called "Short Day." Climatic conditions dictate that each variety be planted in the appropriate region.

Because of an error at Dutch Co.'s packaging facilities in Holland, a batch of onion seeds sold in Vietnam was labeled "Short Day" instead of "Long Day." As a result, virtually all the farmers in the south—whose harvest supplies the entire country during the winter months—planted the wrong seed.

Dutch Co. caught the mistake one week into the planting season in Vietnam and promptly informed senior management. Senior management immediately understood the implications: No onions would grow in Vietnam that winter.

Dutch Co.'s general counsel has conducted a preliminary assessment of the potential legal consequences and concluded that they will be minimal. The farmers' only recourse is a slow and inefficient judicial system that is unlikely, even after many years, to award damages to the farmers beyond the price they paid for the seeds. Dutch Co.'s local distributor strongly urges senior management not to publicly disclose the error and instead wait to see what happens. At most, the local distributor believes, Dutch Co. should only reimburse the farmers for the cost of the seeds.

What should Dutch Co. do next?

Case Study: The Bhopal Disaster

This case study is comprised of two documents: (1) A 2005 report on the 1984 Bhopal disaster published by the National Institutes of Health ("NIH"); and (2) the Order of the District Court for the Southern District of New York granting Union Carbide's Motion to Dismiss claims by survivors for *forum non conveniens*.

The Bhopal Disaster and its Aftermath: A Review[5]

ABSTRACT

On December 3, 1984, more than 40 tons of methyl isocyanate [("MIC")] gas leaked from a pesticide plant in Bhopal, India, immediately killing at least 3,800 people and causing significant morbidity and premature death for many thousands more. The company involved in what became the worst industrial accident in history immediately tried to dissociate itself from legal responsibility. Eventually it reached a settlement with the Indian Government through mediation of that country's Supreme Court and accepted moral responsibility. It paid $470 million in compensation, a relatively small amount of based on significant underestimations of the long-term health consequences of exposure and the number of people exposed. The disaster indicated a need for enforceable

---

5. Edward Broughton, *The Bhopal Disaster and Its Aftermath: A Review*, 4 ENVT'L HEALTH 6 (May 10, 2005), https://www.ncbi.nlm.nih.gov/pmc/articles/PMC1142333/.

international standards for environmental safety, preventative strategies to avoid similar accidents and industrial disaster preparedness.

Since the disaster, India has experienced rapid industrialization. While some positive changes in government policy and behavior of a few industries have taken place, major threats to the environment from rapid and poorly regulated industrial growth remain. Widespread environmental degradation with significant adverse human health consequences continues to occur throughout India.

December 2004 marked the twentieth anniversary of the massive toxic gas leak from Union Carbide Corporation's chemical plant in Bhopal in the state of Madhya Pradesh, India that killed more than 3,800 people. This review examines the health effects of exposure to the disaster, the legal response, the lessons learned and whether or not these are put into practice in India in terms of industrial development, environmental management and public health.

. . . .

HISTORY

In the 1970s, the Indian government initiated policies to encourage foreign companies to invest in local industry. Union Carbide Corporation (UCC) was asked to build a plant for the manufacture of Sevin, a pesticide commonly used throughout Asia. As part of the deal, India's government insisted that a significant percentage of the investment come from local shareholders. The government itself had a 22% stake in the company's subsidiary, Union Carbide India Limited (UCIL). The company built the plant in Bhopal because of its central location and access to transport infrastructure. The specific site within the city was zoned for light industrial and commercial use, not for hazardous industry. The plant was initially approved only for formulation of pesticides from component chemicals, such as MIC imported from the parent company, in relatively small quantities. However, pressure from competition in the chemical industry led UCIL to implement "backward integration"—the manufacture of raw materials and intermediate products for formulation of the final product within one facility. This was inherently a more sophisticated and hazardous process.

In 1984, the plant was manufacturing Sevin at one quarter of its production capacity due to decreased demand for pesticides. Widespread crop failures and famine on the subcontinent in the 1980s led to increased indebtedness and decreased capital for farmers to invest in pesticides. Local managers were directed to close the plant and prepare it for sale in July 1984 due to decreased profitability. When no ready buyer was found, UCIL made plans to dismantle key production units of the facility for shipment to another developing country. In the meantime, the facility continued to operate with safety equipment and procedures far below the standards found in its sister plant in Institute, West Virginia. The local government was aware of safety problems but was reticent to place heavy industrial safety and pollution control burdens on the struggling industry because it feared the economic effects of the loss of such a large employer.

At 11:00 PM on December 2, 1984, while most of the one million residents of Bhopal slept, an operator at the plant noticed a small leak of [MIC] gas and increasing pressure inside a storage tank. The vent-gas scrubber, a safety device designer to neutralize toxic discharge from the MIC system, had been turned off three weeks prior. Apparently a faulty valve had allowed one ton of water for cleaning internal pipes to mix with forty tons of MIC. A 30-ton refrigeration unit that normally served as a safety component to cool the MIC storage tank had been drained of its coolant for use in another part of the plant. Pressure and heat from the vigorous exothermic reaction in the tank continued to build. The gas flare safety system was out of action and had been for three months. At around 1:00 AM, December 3, loud rumbling reverberated around the plant as a safety valve gave way sending a plume of MIC gas into the early morning air. Within hours, the streets of Bhopal were littered with human corpses and the carcasses of buffaloes, cows, dogs, and birds. An estimated 3,800 people died immediately, mostly in the poor slum colony adjacent to the UCC plant. Local hospitals were soon overwhelmed with the injured, a crisis further compounded by a lack of knowledge of exactly what gas was involved and what its effects were. It became one of the worst chemical disasters in history and the name Bhopal became synonymous with industrial catastrophe.

Estimates of the number of people killed in the first few days by the plume from the UCC plant run as high as 10,000, with 15,000 to 20,000 premature deaths reportedly occurring in the subsequent two decades. The Indian government reported that more than half a million people were exposed to the gas. Several epidemiological studies conducted soon after the accident showed significant morbidity and increased mortality in the exposed population. . . .

AFTERMATH

Immediately after the disaster, UCC began attempts to dissociate itself from responsibility for the gas leak. Its principal tactic was to shift culpability to UCIL, stating the plant was wholly built and operated by the Indian subsidiary. It also fabricated scenarios involving sabotage by previously unknown Sikh extremist groups and disgruntled employees but this theory was impugned by numerous independent sources.

The toxic plume had barely cleared when, on December 7, the first multi-billion-dollar lawsuit was filed by an American attorney in a U.S. court. This was the beginning of years of legal machinations in which the ethical implications of the tragedy and its affect on Bhopal's people were largely ignored. In March 1985, the Indian government enacted the Bhopal Gas Leak Disaster Act as a way of ensuring that claims arising from the accident would be dealt with speedily and equitably. The Act made the government the sole representative of the victims in legal proceedings both within and outside India. Eventually all cases were taken out of the U.S. legal system under the ruling of the presiding American judge and placed entirely under Indian jurisdiction much to the detriment of the injured parties.

In a settlement mediated by the Indian Supreme Court, UCC accepted moral responsibility and agreed to pay $470 million to the Indian government to be distributed to claimants as a full and final settlement. The figure was partly based on the disputed claim that only 3000 people died and 102,000 suffered permanent disabilities. Upon announcing this settlement, shares of UCC rose $2 per share or 7% in value. Had compensation in Bhopal been paid at the same rate that asbestosis victims were being awarded in US courts by defendants including UCC—which mined asbestos from 1963 to 1985—the liability would have been greater than the $10 billion the company was worth and insured for in 1984. By the end of October 2003, according to the Bhopal Gas Tragedy Relief and Rehabilitation Department, compensation had been awarded to 554,895 people for injuries received and 15,310 survivors of those killed. The average amount to families of the dead was $2,200.

At every turn, UCC has attempted to manipulate, obfuscate and withhold scientific data to the detriment of victims. Even to this date, the company has not stated exactly what was in the toxic cloud that enveloped the city on that December night. When MIC is exposed to 200° heat, it forms degraded MIC that contains the more deadly hydrogen cyanide (HCN). There was clear evidence that the storage tank temperature did reach this level in the disaster. The cherry-red color of blood and viscera of some victims were characteristic of acute cyanide poisoning. Moreover, many responded well to administration of sodium thiosulfate, an effective therapy for cyanide poisoning but not MIC exposure. UCC initially recommended use of sodium thiosulfate but withdrew the statement later prompting suggestions that it attempted to cover up evidence of HCN in the gas leak. The presence of HCN was vigorously denied by UCC and was a point of conjecture among researchers.

As further insult, UCC discontinued operation at its Bhopal plant following the disaster but failed to clean up the industrial site completely. The plant continues to leak several toxic chemicals and heavy metals that have found their way into local aquifers. Dangerously contaminated water has now been added to the legacy left by the company for the people of Bhopal.

LESSONS LEARNED

The events in Bhopal revealed that expanding industrialization in developing countries without concurrent evolution in safety regulations could have catastrophic consequences. The disaster demonstrated that seemingly local problems of industrial hazards and toxic contamination are often tied to global market dynamics. UCC's Sevin production plant was built in Madhya Pradesh not to avoid environmental regulations in the U.S. but to exploit the large and growing Indian pesticide market. However the manner in which the project was executed suggests the existence of a double standard for multinational corporations operating in developing countries. Enforceable uniform international operating regulations for hazardous industries would have provided a mechanism for significantly improved safety in Bhopal. Even without enforcement, international standards could provide norms for measuring performance of individual companies engaged in hazardous activities such as the manufacture of pesticides and other toxic chemicals in India. National governments and international agencies should focus on widely applicable techniques for corporate responsibility and accident prevention as much in the developing world context as in advanced industrial nations. Specifically, prevention should include risk reduction in plant location and design and safety legislation.

Local governments clearly cannot allow industrial facilities to be situated within urban areas, regardless of the evolution of land use over time. Industry and government need to bring proper financial support to local communities so they can provide medical and other necessary services to reduce morbidity, mortality, and material loss in the case of industrial accidents.

Public health infrastructure was very weak in Bhopal in 1984. Tap water was available for only a few hours a day and was of very poor quality. With no functioning sewage system, untreated human waste was dumped into two nearby lakes, one a source of drinking water. The city had four major hospitals but there was a shortage of physicians and hospital beds. There was also no mass casualty emergency response system in place in the city. Existing public health infrastructure needs to be taken into account when hazardous industries choose sites for manufacturing plants. Future management of industrial development requires that appropriate resources be devoted to advance planning before any disaster occurs. Communities that do not possess infrastructure and technical expertise to respond adequately to such industrial accidents should not be chosen as sites for hazardous industry.

SINCE 1984

Following the events of December 3, 1984 environmental awareness and activism in India increased significantly. The Environment Protection Act was passed in 1986, creating the Ministry of Environment and Forests (MoEF) and strengthening India's commitment to the environment. Under the new act, the MoEF was given overall responsibility for administering and enforcing environmental laws and policies. It established the importance of integrating environmental strategies into all industrial development plans for the country. However, despite greater government commitment to protect public health, forests, and wildlife, policies geared to developing the country's economy have taken precedence in the last 20 years.

India has undergone tremendous economic growth in the two decades since the Bhopal disaster. Gross domestic product (GDP) per capita has increased from $1,000 in 1984 to $2,900 in 2004 and it continues to grow at a rate of over 8% per year. Rapid industrial development has contributed greatly to economic growth but there has been significant cost in environmental degradation and increased public health risks. Since abatement efforts consume a large portion of India's GDP, MoEF faces an uphill battle as it tries to fulfill its mandate of reducing industrial pollution. Heavy reliance on coal-fired power plants and poor enforcement of vehicle emission laws have result from economic concerns taking precedence over environmental protection.

With the industrial growth since 1984, there has been an increase in small-scale industries (SSIs) that are clustered about major urban areas in India. There are generally less stringent rules for the treatment of waste produced by SSIs due to less waste generation within each individual industry. This has allowed SSIs to dispose of untreated wastewater into drainage systems that flow directly into rivers. New Delhi's Yamuna River is illustrative. Dangerously high levels of heavy metals such as lead, cobalt, cadmium, chrome, nickel and zinc have been detected in this river which is a major supply of potable water to India's capital thus posing a potential health risk to the people living there and areas downstream.

Land pollution due to uncontrolled disposal of industrial solid and hazardous waste is also a problem throughout India. With rapid industrialization, the generation of industrial solid and hazardous waste has increased appreciably and the environmental impact is significant.

India relaxed its controls on foreign investment in order to accede to WTO rules and thereby attract an increasing flow of capital. In the process, a number of environmental regulations are being rolled back as growing foreign investments continue to roll in. The Indian experience is comparable to that of a number of developing countries that are experiencing the environmental impacts of structural adjustment. Exploitation and export of natural resources has accelerated on the subcontinent. Prohibitions against locating industrial facilities in ecologically sensitive zones have been eliminated while conservation zones are being stripped of their status so that pesticide, cement and bauxite mines can be built. Heavy reliance on coal-fired power plants and poor enforcement of vehicle emission laws are other consequences of economic concerns taking precedence over environmental protection.

In March 2001, residents of Kodaikanal in southern India caught the Anglo-Dutch company, Unilever, red-handed when they discovered a dumpsite with toxic mercury laced waste from a thermometer factory run by the company's Indian subsidiary, Hindustan Lever. The 7.4-ton stockpile of mercury-laden glass was found in torn stacks spilling onto the ground in a scrap metal yard located near a school. In the fall of 2001, steel from the ruins of the World Trade Center was exported to India apparently without first being tested for contamination from asbestos and heavy metals present in the twin tower debris. Other examples of poor environmental stewardship and economic considerations taking precedence over public health concerns abound.

The Bhopal disaster could have changed the nature of the chemical industry and caused a reexamination of the necessity to produce such potentially harmful products in the first place. However the lessons of the acute and chronic effects of exposure to pesticides and their precursors in Bhopal has not changed agricultural practice patterns. An estimated 3 million people per year suffer the consequences of pesticide poisoning with most exposure occurring in the agricultural developing world. It is reported to be the cause of at least 22,000 deaths in India each year. In the state of Kerala, significant mortality and morbidity have been reported following exposure to Endosulfan, a toxic pesticide whose use continued for 15 years after the events of Bhopal.

Aggressive marketing of asbestos continues in developing countries as a result of restrictions being placed on its use in developed nations due to the well-established link between asbestos products and respiratory diseases. India has become a major consumer, using around 100,000 tons of asbestos per year, 80% of which is imported with Canada being the largest overseas supplier. Mining, production and use of asbestos in India is very loosely regulated despite the health hazards. Reports have shown morbidity and mortality from asbestos related disease will continue in India without enforcement of a ban or significantly tighter controls.

UCC has shrunk to one sixth of its size since the Bhopal disaster in an effort to restructure and divest itself. By doing so, the company avoided a hostile takeover, placed a significant portion of UCC's assets out of legal reach of the victims and gave its shareholder and top executives bountiful profits. The company still operates under the ownership of Dow Chemicals and still states on its website that the Bhopal disaster was "cause by deliberate sabotage."

Some positive changes were seen following the Bhopal disaster. The British chemical company, ICI, whose Indian subsidiary manufactured pesticides, increased attention to health, safety and environmental issues following the events of December 1984. The subsidiary now spends 30–40% of their capital expenditures on environmental-related projects. However, they still do not adhere to standards as strict as their parent company in the UK.

The US chemical giant DuPont learned the lesson of Bhopal in a different way. The company attempted for a decade to export a nylon plant from Richmond, VA to Goa, India. In its early negotiations with the Indian government, DuPont had sought and won a remarkable clause in its investment agreement that absolved it from all liabilities in case of an accident. But the people of Goa were not willing to acquiesce while an important ecological site was cleared for a heavy polluting industry. After nearly a decade of protesting by Goa's residents, DuPont was forced to scuttle plans there. Chennai was the next proposed site for the plastics plant. The state government there made significantly greater demand on DuPont for concessions on public health and environmental protection. Eventually, these plans were also aborted due to what the company called "financial concerns."

CONCLUSION

The tragedy of Bhopal continues to be a warning sign at once ignored and heeded. Bhopal and its aftermath were a warning that the path to industrialization, for developing countries in general and India in particular, is fraught with human, environmental and economic perils. Some moves by the Indian government, including the formation of the MoEF, have served to offer some protection of the public's health from the harmful practices of local and multinational heavy industry and grassroots organizations that have also played a part in opposing rampant development. The Indian economy is growing at a tremendous rate but at significant cost in environmental health and public safety as large and small companies throughout the subcontinent continue to pollute. Far more remains to be done for public health in the context of industrialization to show that the lessons of the countless thousands dead in Bhopal have truly been heeded.[6]

---

6. *Id.*

In re Union Carbide Corp. Gas Plant Disaster at Bhopal, India, 634 F. Supp. 842 (S.D.N.Y. 1986)

United States District Court, S.D. New York.

May 12, 1986.

As Amended June 10, 1986.

[Order Granting Defendant Union Carbide's Motion to Dismiss for *Forum Non Conveniens*]

FACTUAL BACKGROUND

On the night of December 2–3, 1984 the most tragic industrial disaster in history occurred in the city of Bhopal, state of Madhya Pradesh, Union of India. Located there was a chemical plant owned and operated by Union Carbide India Limited ("UCIL"). The plant, situated in the northern sector of the city, had numerous hutments adjacent to it on its southern side which were occupied by impoverished squatters. UCIL manufactured the pesticides Sevin and Temik at the Bhopal plant at the request of, and with the approval of, the Government of India. UCIL was incorporated under Indian law in 1934. 50.9% of its stock is owned by the defendant, Union Carbide Corporation, a New York corporation. Methyl isocyanate (MIC), a highly toxic gas, is an ingredient in the production of both Sevin and Temik. On the night of the tragedy MIC leaked from the plant in substantial quantities for reasons not yet determined.

The prevailing winds on the early morning of December 3, 1984 were from Northwest to Southeast. They blew the deadly gas into the overpopulated hutments adjacent to the plant and into the most densely occupied parts of the city. The results were horrendous. Estimates of deaths directly attributable to the leak range as high as 2,100. No one is sure exactly how many perished. Over 200,000 people suffered injuries—some serious and permanent—some mild and temporary. Livestock were killed and crops damaged. Businesses were interrupted.

On December 7, 1984 the first lawsuit was filed by American lawyers in the United States on behalf of thousands of Indians. *Dawani et al. v. Union Carbide Corp.*, S.D.W.Va. (84-2479). Since then 144 additional actions have been commenced in federal courts in the United States. The actions have all been joined and assigned by the Judicial Panel on Multidistrict Litigation to the Southern District of New York by order of February 6, 1985, 601 F. Supp. 1035.

The individual federal court complaints have been superseded by a consolidated complaint filed on June 28, 1985.

The Indian Government on March 29, 1985 enacted legislation, the Bhopal Gas Leak Disaster (Processing of Claims) Act (21 of 1985) ("Bhopal Act"), providing that the Government of India has the exclusive right to represent Indian plaintiffs in India and elsewhere in connection with the tragedy. Pursuant to the Bhopal Act, the Union of India, on April 8, 1985, filed a complaint with this Court setting forth claims for relief similar to those in the consolidated complaint of June 28, 1985.

By order of April 25, 1985 this Court established a Plaintiffs' Executive Committee, comprised of F. Lee Bailey and Stanley M. Chesley, Esqs., who represented individual plaintiffs and Michael V. Ciresi, Esq., whose firm represents the Union of India. Jack S. Hoffinger, Esq., who represents individual plaintiffs, was appointed liaison counsel for the Plaintiffs' Executive Committee.

On September 24, 1985, pursuant to the Bhopal Act, the Central Government of India framed a "scheme" for the Registration and Processing of Claims arising out of the disaster. According to the Union of India's counsel, over 487,000 claims have been filed in India pursuant to the "scheme."

There presently are 145 actions filed in the United States District Court for the Southern District of New York under the Judicial Panel for Multidistrict Litigation's order of February 6, 1985, involving approximately 200,000 plaintiffs.

Before this Court is a motion by the defendant Union Carbide Corporation ("Union Carbide") to dismiss the consolidated action on the grounds of *forum non conveniens*.

. . . .

C. PROCEDURAL AND PRACTICAL CAPACITY OF INDIAN COURTS.

Plaintiffs contend that the Indian legal system lacks the wherewithal to allow it "to deal effectively and expeditiously" with the issues raised in this lawsuit.

Plaintiffs urge that Indian practitioners emphasize oral skills rather than written briefs. They allegedly lack specialization, practical investigative techniques and coordination into partnerships. These factors, it is argued, limit the Indian bar's ability to handle the Bhopal litigation. As Mr. Dadachanji indicates, Indian lawyers have competently dealt with complex technology transfers, suggesting capability within the technological and scientific areas of legal practice, if not "specialization." Moreover, Indian attorneys use experts, when necessary. As to investigative ability, Mr. Dadachanji persuasively points out that the Central Bureau of Investigation ("CBI") of the Union of India is well equipped to handle factual inquiry, as is the Commission of Enquiry constituted by the state of Madhya Pradesh. While Indian attorneys may not customarily join into large law firms, and as Mr. Palkhivala states, are limited by present Indian law to partnerships of no more than twenty, this alone or even in concert with other factors does not establish the inadequacy of the Indian legal system. There is no reason the Indian legislature could not provide for the expansion of law firms, if such a choice is required. In any event, this Court is not convinced that the size of a law firm has that much to do with the quality of legal service provided. Many small firms in this country perform work at least on a par with the largest firms. Bigger is not necessarily better.

Moreover, since the Union of India purports to represent all the claimants, it is likely that if the case were transferred to India, the Attorney General or Solicitor General of India and the Advocate General of Madhya Pradesh, with attendant staffs, would represent the claimants. The Indian bar appears more than capable of shouldering the litigation if it should be transferred to India.

Next, plaintiffs and Professor Galanter argue that the substantive tort law of India is not sufficiently developed to accommodate the Bhopal claims. Plaintiffs trace the lack of sophistication in Indian tort law to the presence of court fees for litigants as inhibiting the filing of civil suits. Though the filing fees may have had historical significance, they are irrelevant here. Professor Galanter acknowledges that court fees may be waived for "poor parties or for specific classes of litigants." In fact, filing fees have been waived for claimants in India in the Bhopal litigation already begun there.

Professor Galanter asserts that India lacks codified tort law, has little reported case law in the tort field to serve as precedent, and has no tort law relating to disputes arising out of complex product or design liability. As an illustration of the paucity of Indian tort law, Professor Galanter states that a search through the *All-India Reports* for the span from 1914 to 1965 revealed only 613 tort cases reported. Mr. Dadachanji responds that tort law is sparsely reported in India due to frequent settlement of such cases, lack of appeal to higher courts, and the publication of tort cases in specialized journals other than the *All-India Reports*. In addition, tort law has been codified in numerous Indian statutes.

As Professor Galanter himself states, "the major categories of tort, their elements, the [theories] of liability, defenses, *respondeat superior,* the theories of damages—are all familiar." What is different, Galanter asserts, is the complete absence of tort law relating to high technology or complex manufacturing processes. This is of no moment with respect to the adequacy of the Indian courts. With the groundwork of tort doctrine adopted from the common law and the precedential weight awarded British cases, as well as Indian ones, it is obvious that a well-developed base of tort doctrine exists to provide a guide to Indian courts presiding over the Bhopal litigation. In any event, much tort law applied in American cases involving complex technology has its source in legal principles first enunciated in Victorian England. As Mr. Palkhivala stated in his affidavit:

> The plant itself was the product of highly complex technology, but complexity of the technology cannot be equated with complexity of legal issues. The principles of liability and damages involved in the Bhopal cases are all well established in India. The complexity is not in the nature or determination of legal issues but in the application of the law to the events which took place in Bhopal. Well settled law is to be applied to an unusual occurrence.

Plaintiffs next assert that India lacks certain procedural devices which are essential to the adjudication of complex cases, the absence of which prevent India from providing an adequate alternative forum. They urge that Indian pretrial discovery is inadequate and that therefore India is an inadequate alternative forum. Professor Galanter states that the only forms of discovery available in India are written interrogatories, inspection of documents, and requests for admissions. Parties alone are subject to discovery. Third-party witnesses need not submit to discovery. Discovery may be directed to admissible evidence only, not material likely to lead to relevant or admissible material, as in the courts of the United States. Parties are not compelled to provide what will be actual proof at trial as part of discovery.

These limits on discovery are adopted from the British system. Similar discovery tools are used in Great Britain today. This Court finds that their application would perhaps, however, limit the victims' access to sources of proof. Therefore, pursuant to its equitable powers, the Court directs that the defendant consent to submit to the broad discovery afforded by the United States Federal Rules of Civil Procedure if or when an Indian court sits in judgment or presides over pretrial proceedings in the Bhopal litigation. Any dismissal of the action now before this Court is thus conditioned on defendant›s consent to submit to discovery on the American model, even after transfer to another jurisdiction.

The ostensible lack of devices for third-party impleader or for organizing complex cases under the law of the state of Madhya Pradesh are two other procedural deficiencies which plaintiffs assert preclude a finding that India offers an adequate alternative forum. Assuming for the moment that, upon appropriate transfer, the Bhopal litigation would be adjudicated by the local district court in Bhopal, and that the law of Madhya Pradesh would be applied, this Court is still not moved by plaintiffs' argument regarding impleader or complex litigation.

Although no specific provision in the Indian Code of Civil Procedure permits the impleading of third-parties from whom contribution is sought, other provisions in the Code do provide for impleader. As both parties to this motion state, Order 1, Rule 10(2) of the Indian Code of Civil Procedure "allows the court to add additional parties if the presence of those parties is 'necessary in order to enable the Court effectively and completely to adjudicate upon and settle all questions involved in the suit.'" Professor Galanter posits that a joint tortfeasor would not be considered a necessary party, and would not be joined. Defendant›s expert, conversely, asserts that a party can be added to prevent multiplicity of suits and conflicts of decisions. Thus, Mr. Dadachanji argues, defendants would be able to seek contribution from third parties if joinder would prevent repetitive litigation or inconsistency. Moreover, the broad provision of inherent powers to aid the ends of justice, as codified at Section 151 of the Indian Code of Civil Procedure would prevent an ultimate miscarriage of justice in the area of impleader.

The absence of procedures or mechanisms within the Indian judiciary to handle complex litigation is presented as support for plaintiffs' position regarding the nonexistence of an adequate alternative forum. Professor Galanter asserts, for example, that Indian judges do not promote settlements. The point is wholly irrelevant to the question of whether an adequate alternative forum exists. In any event, this Court has labored hard and long to promote settlement between the parties for over a year, to no avail. It would appear that settlement, although desirable for many reasons, including conservation of attorneys' fees and costs of litigation, preservation of judicial resources, and speed of resolution, is unlikely regardless of the level of activism of the presiding judge.

Plaintiffs' next contention is that since no class action procedure exists in India expeditious litigation of the Bhopal suits would be impossible. As with all of plaintiffs' other arguments, this purported deficiency does not constitute "no remedy" at all. Professor Galanter himself acknowledges that Order 1, Rule 8 of the Indian Code of Civil Procedure provides a mechanism for "representative" suits, "where there are numerous persons having the same interest in one suit." Even if the current state of Indian law regarding "representative" suits involves application of the mechanism to pre-existing groups such as religious sects or associations, there is no reason to conclude that the Indian legislature, capable of enacting the Bhopal Act, would not see its way to enacting a specific law for class actions. In addition, it does not appear on the face of Order 1, Rule 8 that the "representative" suit is expressly limited to preexisting groups. The Indian district court could adopt the rule for use in a newly created class of injured, whose members all have "the same interest" in establishing the liability of the defendant. An Indian court has law available to create a representative class, or perhaps a few different representative classes. The "scheme" for registration and processing of claims could perform the task of evaluating the specific amounts of claims. Moreover, Mr. Dadachanji gives at least three examples where Indian courts have consolidated suits pursuant to their inherent power under Section 151 of the Indian Code of Civil Procedure. In at least one case, such consolidation allegedly occurred without consent of the parties. The absence of a rule for class actions which is identical to the American rule does not lead to the conclusion that India is not an adequate alternative forum.

Final points regarding the asserted inadequacies of Indian procedure involve unavailability of juries or contingent fee arrangements in India. Plaintiffs do not press these arguments, but Mr. Palkhivala touches upon them. They are easily disposed of. The absence of juries in civil cases is a feature of many civil law jurisdictions, and of the United Kingdom. Furthermore, contingency fees are not found in most foreign jurisdictions. In any event, the lack of contingency fees is not an insurmountable barrier to filing claims in India, as demonstrated by the fact that more than 4,000 suits have been filed by victims of the Bhopal gas leak in India, already. According to Mr. Palkhivala, moreover, well-known lawyers have been known to serve clients without charging any fees.

Plaintiffs' final contention as to the inadequacy of the Indian forum is that a judgment rendered by an Indian court cannot be enforced in the United States without resort to further extensive litigation. Conversely, plaintiffs assert, Indian law provides *res judicata* effect to foreign judgments, and precludes plaintiffs from bringing a suit on the same cause of action in India. Mr. Dadachanji disputes this description of the Indian law of *res judicata*. He asserts that the pendency, or even final disposition, of an action in a foreign court does not prevent plaintiffs from suing in India upon the original cause of action. Plaintiffs would not be limited, Mr. Dadachanji argues, to an Indian action to enforce the foreign judgment. In addition, he states that an Indian court, before ordering that a foreign judgment be given effect, would seek to establish whether the foreign court had failed to apply Indian law, or misapplied Indian law.

The possibility of non-enforcement of a foreign judgment by courts of either country leads this Court to conclude that the issue must be addressed at this time. Since it is defendant Union Carbide which, perhaps ironically, argues for the sophistication of the Indian legal system in seeking a dismissal on grounds of *forum non conveniens,* and plaintiffs, including the Indian Government, which state a strong preference for the American legal system, it would appear that both parties have indicated a willingness to abide by a judgment of the foreign nation whose forum each seeks to visit. Thus, this Court conditions the grant of a dismissal on *forum non conveniens* grounds on Union Carbide's agreement to be bound by the judgment of its preferred tribunal, located in India, and to satisfy any judgment rendered by the Indian court, and affirmed on appeal in India. Absent such consent to abide by and to "make good" on a foreign judgment, without challenge except for concerns relating to minimal due process, the motion to dismiss now under consideration will not be granted. The preference of both parties to play ball on a distant field will be taken to its limit, with each party being ordered to be bound by the decision of the respective foreign referees.

To sum up the discussion to this point, the Court determines that the Indian legal system provides an adequate alternative forum for the Bhopal litigation. Far from exhibiting a tendency to be so "inadequate or unsatisfactory" as to provide "no remedy at all," the courts of India appear to be well up to the task of handling this case. Any unfavorable change in law for plaintiffs which might be suffered upon transfer to the Indian courts, will . . . not be given "substantial weight." Differences between the two legal systems, even if they inure to plaintiffs' detriment, do not suggest that India is not an adequate alternative forum. As Mr. Palkhivala asserts with some dignity, "while it is true to say that the Indian system today is different in some respects from the American system, it is wholly untrue to say that it is deficient or inadequate. Difference is not to be equated with deficiency."

. . . .

CONCLUSION

It is difficult to imagine how a greater tragedy could occur to a peacetime population than the deadly gas leak in Bhopal on the night of December 2–3, 1984. The survivors of the dead victims, the injured and others who suffered, or may in the future suffer due to the disaster, are entitled to compensation. This Court is firmly convinced that the Indian legal system is in a far better position than the American courts to determine the cause of the tragic event and thereby fix liability. Further, the Indian courts have greater access to all the information needed to arrive at the amount of the compensation to be awarded the victims.

The presence in India of the overwhelming majority of the witnesses and evidence, both documentary and real, would by itself suggest that India is the most convenient forum for this consolidated case. The additional presence in India of all but the less than handful of claimants underscores the convenience of holding trial in India. All of the private interest factors . . . weigh heavily toward dismissal of this case on the grounds of *forum non conveniens*.

The public interest factors . . . also favor dismissal. The administrative burden of this immense litigation would unfairly tax this or any American tribunal. The cost to American taxpayers of supporting the litigation in the United States would be excessive. When another, adequate, and more convenient forum so clearly exists, there is no reason to press the United States judiciary to the limits of its capacity. No American interest in the outcome of this litigation outweighs the interest of India in applying Indian law and Indian values to the task of resolving this case.

The Bhopal plant was regulated by Indian agencies. The Union of India has a very strong interest in the aftermath of the accident which affected its citizens on its own soil. Perhaps Indian regulations were ignored or contravened. India may wish to determine whether the regulations imposed on the chemical industry within its boundaries were sufficiently stringent. The Indian interests far outweigh the interests of citizens of the United States in the litigation.

Plaintiffs, including the Union of India, have argued that the courts of India are not up to the task of conducting the Bhopal litigation. They assert that the Indian judiciary has yet to reach full maturity due to the restraints placed upon it by British colonial rulers who shaped the Indian legal system to meet their own ends. Plaintiffs allege that the Indian justice system has not yet cast off the burden of colonialism to meet the emerging needs of a democratic people.

The Court thus finds itself faced with a paradox. In the Court's view, to retain the litigation in this forum, as plaintiffs request, would be yet another example of imperialism, another situation in which an established sovereign inflicted its rules, its standards and values on a developing nation. This Court declines to play such a role. The Union of India is a world power in 1986, and its courts have the proven capacity to mete out fair and equal justice. To deprive the Indian judiciary of this opportunity to stand tall before the world and to pass judgment on behalf of its own people would be to revive a history of subservience and subjugation from which India has emerged. India and its people can and must vindicate their claims before the independent and legitimate judiciary created there since the Independence of 1947.

This Court defers to the adequacy and ability of the courts of India. Their interest in the sad events of December 2–3, 1984 at the UCIL plant in the City of Bhopal, State of Madhya Pradesh, Union of India, is not subject to question or challenge. The availability of the probative, relevant, material and necessary evidence to Indian courts is obvious and has been demonstrated in this opinion.

Therefore, the consolidated case is dismissed on the grounds of *forum non conveniens* under the following conditions:

1. Union Carbide shall consent to submit to the jurisdiction of the courts of India, and shall continue to waive defenses based upon the statute of limitations;
2. Union Carbide shall agree to satisfy any judgment rendered against it by an Indian court, and if applicable, upheld by an appellate court in that country, where such judgment and affirmance comport with the minimal requirements of due process;
3. Union Carbide shall be subject to discovery under the model of the United States Federal Rules of Civil Procedure after appropriate demand by plaintiffs.

SO ORDERED.

Notes and Questions

The Bhopal disaster is an example of a multinational enterprise operating in an emerging market whose laws and regulations did not adequately protect the health and safety of its citizens.

1) In your opinion, would Union Carbide have observed a higher safety standard had the plant been located in a developed country like the United States?
2) Regardless of whether Union Carbide violated any laws, did it act ethically in operating its Bhopal plant?
3) Had the Bhopal plant been in operation after the FSGO and BEM went into effect, would Union Carbide have acted differently?

Union Carbide strongly resisted the claims arising from the disaster, raising several unsubstantiated theories to deflect responsibility:

> [C]ompany lawyers submitted a clipping of a newspaper story [saying] that a group of Sikh extremists . . . had claimed responsibility for the Bhopal disaster. . . . [T]he company had earlier tried to lay the responsibility on a Sikh employee . . . dismissed along with several dozen other company officials after the leak.[7]

In the legal proceedings in the United States, the claims were consolidated before a single district judge who ultimately dismissed them. This decision led to the transfer of the claims to India, where the legal system provided the plaintiffs with a much more limited opportunity to collect a large damages award.

4) How should Union Carbide have responded to the plaintiffs' claims?
5) Should Union Carbide have refrained from seeking dismissal of the claims in the United States?

Case Study: The BP Deepwater Horizon Oil Spill

This case study is comprised of two documents: (1) the report of the National Commission on the BP Deepwater Horizon Oil Spill; and (2) the DOJ press release announcing the settlement between BP and five Gulf states.

Deepwater: The Gulf Oil Disaster and the Future of Offshore Drilling[8]

The explosion that tore through the Deepwater Horizon drilling rig last April 20, as the rig's crew completed drilling the exploratory Macondo well deep under

---

7. Rajiv Desai, *An Ill Wind, for the People of Once-Prosperous Bhopal, The Horror of History's Worst Industrial Disaster May Never End,* CHI. TRIB. (Nov. 30, 1986), http://articles.chicagotribune.com/1986-11-30/features/8603300912_1_bhopal-plant-mic-unit-disgruntled.

8. NAT'L COMM'N ON THE BP DEEPWATER HORIZON OIL SPILL AND OFFSHORE DRILLING, DEEP WATER: THE GULF OIL DISASTER AND THE FUTURE OF OFFSHORE DRILLING vi–viii, 217–47 (2011) [hereinafter BP DEEPWATER REPORT] (reporting findings of the Commission to the President).

the waters of the Gulf of Mexico, began a human, economic, and environmental disaster.

Eleven crew members died, and others were seriously injured, as fire engulfed and ultimately destroyed the rig. And, although the nation would not know the full scope of the disaster for weeks, the first of more than four million barrels of oil began gushing uncontrolled into the Gulf—threatening livelihoods, precious habitats, and even a unique way of life. A treasured American landscape, already battered and degraded from years of mismanagement, faced yet another blow as the oil spread and washed ashore. Five years after Hurricane Katrina, the nation was again transfixed, seemingly helpless, as this new tragedy unfolded in the Gulf. The costs from this one industrial accident are not yet fully counted, but it is already clear that the impacts on the region's natural systems and people were enormous, and that economic losses total tens of billions of dollars.

On May 22, 2010, President Barack Obama announced the creation of the National Commission on the BP Deepwater Horizon Oil Spill and Offshore Drilling: an independent, nonpartisan entity, directed to provide a thorough analysis and impartial judgment. The President charged the Commission to determine the causes of the disaster, and to improve the country's ability to respond to spills, and to recommend reforms to make offshore energy production safer. And the President said we were to follow the facts wherever they led.

. . . .

As a result of our investigation, we conclude:

- The explosive loss of the Macondo well could have been prevented.
- The immediate causes of the Macondo well blowout can be traced to a series of identifiable mistakes made by BP, Halliburton, and Transocean that reveal such systematic failures in risk management that they place in doubt the safety culture of the entire industry.
- Deepwater energy exploration and production, particularly at the frontiers of experience, involve risks for which neither industry nor government has been adequately prepared, but for which they can and must be prepared in the future.
- To assure human safety and environmental protection, regulatory oversight of leasing, energy exploration, and production require reforms even beyond those significant reforms already initiated since the *Deepwater Horizon* disaster. Fundamental reform will be needed in both the structure of those in charge of regulatory oversight and their internal decisionmaking process to ensure their political autonomy, technical expertise, and their full consideration of environmental protection concerns.

  . . . .

- The technology, laws and regulations, and practices for containing, responding to, and cleaning up spills lag behind the real risks associated with deepwater drilling into large, high-pressure reservoirs of oil and gas located far offshore and thousands of feet below the ocean's surface. Government must close the existing gap and industry must support rather than resist that effort.

- Scientific understanding of environmental conditions in sensitive environments in deep Gulf waters, along the region's coastal habitats, and in areas proposed for more drilling, such as the Arctic, is inadequate. The same is true of the human and natural impacts of oil spills.

. . . .

Offshore oil and gas exploration and production are risky. But even the most inherently risky industry can be made much safer, given the right incentives and disciplined systems, sustained by committed leadership and effective training. The critical common element is an unwavering commitment to safety at the top of an organization: the CEO and board of directors must create the culture and establish the conditions under which everyone in a company shares responsibility for maintaining a relentless focus on preventing accidents. Likewise, for the entire industry, leadership needs to come from the CEOs collectively, who can apply pressure on their peers to enhance performance.

Properly managed, the presence of risk does not mean that accidents have to happen. As Magne Ognedal, Director General of Norway's Petroleum Safety Authority, put it: "risk must be managed at every level and in every company involved in this business. . . . In this way, risk in the petroleum sector can be kept at a level society is willing to accept. And we can reduce the probability that major accidents will hit us again."

BP'S SAFETY CULTURE

BP has proclaimed the importance of safety for its vast worldwide operations. "Our goal of 'no accidents, no harm to people and no damage to the environment' is fundamental to BP's activities," stated the company's Sustainability Review 2009. "We work to achieve this through consistent management processes, ongoing training programmes, rigorous risk management and a culture of continuous improvement." It added that "creating a safe and healthy working environment is essential for our success. Since 1999, injury rates and spills have reduced by approximately 75%."

Yet despite the improvement in injury and spill rates during that decade, BP has caused a number of disastrous or potentially disastrous workplace incidents that suggest its approach to managing safety has been on individual worker occupational safety but not on process safety. These incidents and subsequent analyses indicate that the company does not have consistent and reliable risk-management processes—and thus has been unable to meet its professed commitment to safety. BP's safety lapses have been chronic.

. . . .

DEEPWATER HORIZON

BP's safety culture failed on the night of April 20, 2010, as reflected in the actions of BP personnel on- and offshore and in the actions of BP's contractors. . . . BP, Halliburton, and Transocean did not adequately identify or address risks of an accident—not in the well design, cementing, or temporary abandonment procedures. Their management systems were marked by poor communications among BP, Transocean, and Halliburton employees regarding the risks associated with decisions being made. The decision-making process on the rig was excessively compartmentalized, so individuals on the rig frequently made critical decisions without fully appreciating just how essential the decisions were to well safety—singly and in combination. As a result, officials made a series of decisions that saved BP, Halliburton, and Transocean time and money—but without full appreciation of the associated risks.

BP conducted its own accident investigation of *Deepwater Horizon*, but once again kept its scope extremely narrow. Professor Najmedin Meshkati of the University of Southern California, Los Angeles—a member of the separate National Academy of Engineering committee investigating the oil spill—criticized BP's accident report for neglecting to "address human performance issues and organizational factors which, in any major accident investigation, constitute major contributing factors." He added that BP's investigation also ignored factors such as fatigue, long shifts, and the company's poor safety culture.

Upon reading the BP report, this Commission's Chief Scientific and Engineering Advisor, Richard Sears, commented that "it appeared that for BP, the accident happened at 9:49 p.m. on April 20; whereas in some ways, the blowout began in early 2009 when they initially designed the well."

THE CULTURE ON THE RIG

BP was operator of the Macondo well and in that capacity had both the overall responsibility for everything that went on and was in the best position to promote a culture of safety on the rig, including in the actions of its two significant contractors, Halliburton and Transocean. But the extensive involvement of those contractors in the mistakes that caused the Macondo well blowout underscores the compelling need for a fundamental shift in industry culture that extends beyond BP. . . .

. . . .

A survey of the Transocean crew regarding "safety management and safety culture" on the *Deepwater Horizon* conducted just a few weeks before the accident hints at the organizational roots of the problem. The research, conducted at Transocean's request, involved surveys and interviews with hundreds of employees onshore and on four rigs, including *Deepwater Horizon*, which was surveyed from March 12 to March 16. The reviewers found *Deepwater Horizon* "relatively strong in many of the core aspects of safety management." But there were also weaknesses. Some 46 percent of crew members surveyed felt that some of the workforce feared reprisals for reporting unsafe situations, and 15 percent felt that there were not always enough people available to carry out work safely. Some Transocean crews complained that the safety manual was "unstructured," "hard to navigate," and "not written with the end user in mind"; and that there is "poor distinction between what is required and how this should be achieved." According to the final survey report, Transocean's crews "don't always know what they don't know. [F]ront line crews are potentially working with a mindset that they believe they are fully aware of all the hazards when it's highly likely that they are not."

Halliburton, BP's other major contractor for the Macondo well, is one of the world's largest providers of products and services to the energy industry. It has offices in 70 countries, and Halliburton-affiliated companies have participated in the majority of producing deepwater wells and contributed to most of the world's deepwater well completions. Yet notwithstanding its clear experience and expertise in cementing—a $1.7 billion business for the company in 2009—Halliburton prepared cement for the Macondo well that had repeatedly failed Halliburton's own laboratory tests . . . . And then, despite those test results, Halliburton managers onshore let its crew and those of Transocean and BP on the Deepwater Horizon continue with the cement job apparently without first ensuring good stability results.

Halliburton also was the cementer on a well that suffered a blowout in August 2009, in the Timor Sea off Australia. The *Montara* rig caught fire and a well leaked tens of thousands of barrels of oil over two and a half months before it was shut down. The leak occurred because the cement seal failed, the government report into the accident found. However, the report said it would not be appropriate to criticize Halliburton, because the operator "exercised overall control over and responsibility for cementing operations." The inquiry concluded that "Halliburton was not required or expected to 'value add' by doing more than complying with [the operator's] instructions." In this, *Montara* offers yet another example of a lack of communication between operators and service providers and of the gaps between the silos of expertise that exist in the deepwater oil and gas industry.

. . . .

INDUSTRY SELF-POLICING AS A SUPPLEMENT TO GOVERNMENT REGULATION

One of the key responsibilities of government is to regulate—to direct the behavior of individuals and institutions according to rules. Many businesses and business groups are involved in internal standard-setting, evaluation, and other activities that constitute self-policing or self-regulation. Such oversight can be conducted by a private entity established and supported by an industry to ensure safe operations by individual members (among other purposes), often because industry leaders recognize that a misstep by any one member necessarily has significant repercussions for them all. But even in industries with strong self-policing, government also needs to be strongly present, providing oversight and/or additional regulatory control—responsibilities that cannot be abdicated if public safety, health, and welfare are to be protected.

The Logic of Self-Policing

Industry-standard setting and self-policing organizations are widespread in the United States and in most industrialized nations—typically for operations marked by technical complexity, such as the chemical, nuclear power, civil aviation, and oil and gas industries, where government oversight is also present. These processes coexist where there are, as a practical matter, relatively limited numbers of people with the requisite expertise and experience, making it hard for government to be able to rely solely on its own personnel (especially when government cannot compete with private-sector salaries for those experts). . . .

The Limits of Unregulated Self-Policing

Industry self-policing is not a substitute for government but serves as an important supplement to government oversight. And the cost of forgetting that essential premise can be calamitous. In the financial sector, for example, the Securities and Exchange Commission's Consolidated Supervised Entities Program had, in 2004, delegated regulatory risk assessment of global investment bank conglomerates to the banks themselves. The program was designed to cover a regulatory gap left by Congress amid changes in global finance, but it was entirely voluntary. Four years later, Securities and Exchange Commission Chairman Christopher Cox ended the program, declaring it a failure—indeed "fundamentally flawed"—after companies like Bear Sterns failed to adequately assess the risk of a sharp downturn in housing prices on their large, leveraged investments in mortgage-backed securities.

A second cautionary tale involves an environmental disaster. When political opposition stymied federal and state regulation of toxic coal ash and other residues from power generation, the electric utilities that had opposed regulations deferred to the Utilities Solid Wastes Activities Group's voluntary "Action Plan" to manage such wastes. The U.S. Environmental Protection Agency stepped back from regulating such hazards. And, in 2008, an earthen dam containing coal ash gave way in eastern Tennessee, releasing more than a billion gallons of coal ash across a large portion of Roane County and polluting rivers that carried the hazardous wastes farther afield.

. . . .

THE CHALLENGE OF CHANGE

. . . .

The oil and gas industry needs now to regain [the nation's] trust, but doing so will require it to take bold action to make clear that business will no longer be conducted as usual in the Gulf. Industry must seize the opportunity to demonstrate that it is fully committed to subjecting its own internal operations to fundamental change and not merely because it is being forced to do so. Underscoring the sincerity and depth of their commitment to embracing a new safety culture, company leaders will need to lead the effort to guarantee that risk management improves throughout the industry to ensure that the mistakes made at the Macondo well are not repeated. And those leaders must also demonstrate an equal commitment to ensuring adequate containment and response technology and resources in case another spill happens. Only then will the oil and gas industry truly demonstrate that it is ready, willing, and able to engage in the kind of responsible offshore drilling practices upon which the nation's basic energy supplies depend.

U.S. and Five Gulf States Reach Historic Settlement with BP to Resolve Civil Lawsuit Over Deepwater Horizon Oil Spill (Press Release)

U.S. Department of Justice (October 5, 2015)[9]

Total Value of Global Settlement Will Top $20 Billion Largest with a Single Entity in Justice Department History Assures Continued Restoration of the Gulf Coast

The United States today joins the five Gulf states in announcing a settlement to resolve civil claims against BP arising from the April 20, 2010 Macondo well blowout and the massive oil spill that followed in the Gulf of Mexico.

This global settlement resolves the governments' civil claims under the Clean Water Act and natural resources damage claims under the Oil Pollution Act, as well as economic damage claims of the five Gulf states and local governments. Taken together this global resolution of civil claims is worth $20.8 billion, and is the largest settlement with a single entity in the department's history.

. . . .

"Building on prior actions against BP and its subsidiaries by the Department of Justice, this historic resolution is a strong and fitting response to the worst environmental disaster in American history," said Attorney General Loretta Lynch. "BP is receiving the punishment it deserves, while also providing critical compensation for the injuries it caused to the environment and the economy of the Gulf region. I am proud that the Department of Justice has helped lead the way from tragedy to opportunity, and I am confident that our actions today will help to ensure that Gulf communities emerge from this disaster stronger and more resilient than ever before."

. . . .

On Dec. 15, 2010, Attorney General Eric Holder announced a civil lawsuit against BP and several co-defendants, seeking to hold them accountable for the Deepwater Horizon disaster. The federal lawsuit culminated in a three-phase civil trial in which the United States proved, among other things, that the spill was caused by BP's gross negligence.

Each of the Gulf states—Alabama, Florida, Louisiana, Mississippi, and Texas—also filed civil claims against BP relating to the spill, including claims for economic losses and natural resource damages.

. . . .

---

9. U.S. Dep't of Justice, Office of Pub. Affairs, Press Release No. 15-1231, U.S. and Five Gulf States Reach Historic Settlement with BP to Resolve Civil Lawsuit Over Deepwater Horizon Oil Spill (2015).

Notes and Questions

BP's Deepwater Horizon oil spill and Union Carbide's Bhopal disaster are two of the most devastating industrial accidents of the last 50 years.

1) What conclusions can be drawn from their respective legal outcomes?
2) Has the increased attention paid to CSR made a difference in corporate behavior?
3) What is the right balance between self-regulation and government regulation?
4) Why do these tragedies continue to occur, and how might they be prevented in the future?

II. Responsible Governance

As discussed in Part I, the FSGO holds an organization's board of directors responsible for overseeing the implementation and operation of the compliance program. This responsibility also extends to the ethics program:

> Corporate governance is concerned with holding the balance between economic and social goals and between individual and communal goals. . . . The aim is to align as nearly as possible the interests of individuals, corporations, and society.
>
> —*Sir Adrian Cadbury*[10]

(b) Due diligence and the promotion of an organizational culture that encourages ethical conduct and a commitment to compliance with the law within the meaning of subsection (a) minimally require the following:

. . . .

(2)(A) The organization's governing authority shall be knowledgeable about the content and operation of the compliance and ethics program and shall exercise reasonable oversight with respect to the implementation and effectiveness of the compliance and ethics program.[11]

The BEM recognizes that "while the board owes faithful attention to the interests of shareholders, it also must pay attention to social order and must see that the enterprise is a good member of a community."[12] This does not mean the board should divide its loyalty between the owners of the company and its other stakeholders; rather, the board's primary responsibility is always to pursue the ends specified by the company's shareholders. The interests of stakeholders are taken into account only when defining the means by which the organization pursues those ends. As the BEM explains, compliance with the law and due consideration for the interests of stakeholders:

---

10. Adrian Cadbury, *Foreword* to Magdi R. Iskander & Nadereh Chamlou, World Bank Group [WBG], *Corporate Governance: A Framework for Implementation—Overview*, at vi (2000), http://documents.worldbank.org/curated/en/831651468781818619/pdf/30446.pdf.

11. U.S. Sentencing Guidelines Manual § 8B2.1(b)(U.S. Sentencing Comm'n 2016).

12. BEM, *supra* note 1, at 97.

[A]re means issues. They are not the reason for the enterprise's existence, but they suggest how it may obtain its objectives. For example, the enterprise's legal obligations and its relationships with stakeholders, while critical, are not the reason the enterprise exists. To preserve management flexibility, therefore, the board should establish policies that define the boundaries of management authority, rather than offer prescriptions for action.[13]

In this manner, the BEM resolves the tension between Friedman's shareholder theory and the increasingly accepted notion that a corporation owes ethical obligations to all of its stakeholders.

Business Ethics: A Manual for Managing a Responsible Business Enterprise in Emerging Market Economies[14]

Responsible Governance

There is a flow of authority, responsibility, and accountability throughout all enterprises. At the top of this flow are the owners or their representatives. The owners or representatives of an RBE follow a three-step process to establish policy guidelines for responsible governance. First, they delegate some measure of authority to managers. Next, they establish the purpose of the enterprise, including the value it brings to its community. Third, they establish clear limitations or constraints on the exercise of the authority they granted. These policy categories are comprehensive: they embrace all choices and actions of the enterprise's employees and agents—managers, supervisors, and workers.

Following the responsible governance policies and procedures of the owners or their representatives, managers define methods, activities, conduct, and tasks for employees at all levels and for agents. They define the core beliefs of the enterprise and establish the guidance that employees and agents need to meet reasonable stakeholder expectations.

Where there are owner representatives, such as a board of directors, these representatives also define the purpose, functions, and character of their own governance. These policies define how they will work together and their commitment to doing so.

RESPONSIBLE GOVERNANCE PROCESS

. . . Three specific provisions are particularly important: accountability, social responsibility, and directors' conduct. An accountability philosophy statement affirms the board's understanding that its primary responsibility is to the shareholders it represents, not management. A social responsibility statement affirms the board's understanding that, while the board owes faithful attention to the interests of shareholders, it also must pay attention to social order and must see

---

13. *Id.* at 99.
14. *Id.* at 96–99.

that the enterprise is a good member of a community. Finally, a director's conduct statement commits individual board members to ethical, businesslike, and lawful conduct.

BOARD–MANAGEMENT DELEGATION

In situations when owners are not actively engaged in an enterprise, they or their representatives will delegate a substantial amount of their authority to management. Responsible governance calls for such authority to be delegated to one person. That person, whether called the chief executive officer (CEO), president, or general director, is given the authority to manage everyone else in the enterprise. . . .

Under this arrangement, the lines of authority are clear. The owner representatives have one employee for operational purposes: the CEO. The CEO, in turn, is accountable to the board itself. The CEO will delegate some of his or her authority to other employees through standards, procedures, and expectations, but the CEO remains accountable to the board for all decisions made and actions taken.

OWNER EXPECTATIONS OF MANAGEMENT PERFORMANCE

Owner policies regarding management performance relate to the ends sought for the enterprise. The CEO is not entitled to make any choices or to take any actions that are not reasonably calculated to achieve the designated ends of the enterprise.

Policies Defining Ends

Responsible governance calls for precise definition of the ends of the enterprise. There are three components to an effective ends statement: "first, the *results* for which the [enterprise] exists; second, the *recipients* of those results; and third, the *relative worth* of those results."

At first glance, the *results* component relates to financial performance. Certainly for enterprises whose shares are actively traded results must be related to financial performance. As one scholar, John Carver, notes, however, this is not always the case:

> In some small start-up companies, for example, desired results may include working independently with trusted partners in an exciting field—plus satisfactory financial return. In some family-owned companies, the value owners want is satisfaction of having family members working together in the same business—plus satisfactory financial return.

A range of performance results is possible: market share, long-term capital growth, profits, reliable income, and successful research and development. Owner representatives must take the desires of all owners into account to determine what the desired results of the enterprise are and how to communicate them to employees and other stakeholders.

The *recipients* component seems clear enough, since the owners are the recipients. However, as Carver notes, "owners do not all have the same interests, and the board represents all owners." The board must take into account the diverse interests of the owners. The relative strength of blocs of shareholders must also be considered. Although majority shareholders are entitled to a proportionate share of enterprise results, the board must not disproportionately benefit majority shareholders.

Finally, the *relative worth* component requires that the owner representatives prioritize among the results and recipients it has identified. Rarely will all owners have the same desired performance results. Some, for example, may be willing to forgo current income in favor of capital investment in research and development. Others may be certain that their majority interest entitles them to disproportionate returns or influence over the board. Whatever a given ends statement might contain, management deserves a clear statement from the owners or their representatives as to what successful enterprise performance looks like.

Policies Defining Means

When the board is setting management limitations, Carver suggests they set "basic executive constraints." It is up to management to decide how to achieve the ends of the enterprise within the authority granted to it by the board. Given that the ends of an RBE are ultimately to produce value for the owners, what about the many other considerations of the RBE, such as other stakeholders, the rule of law, and ethical conduct?

These are means issues. They are not the reason for the enterprise's existence, but they suggest how it may obtain its objectives. For example, the enterprise's legal obligations and its relationships with stakeholders, while critical, are not the reason the enterprise exists. To preserve management flexibility, therefore, the board should establish policies that define the boundaries of management authority, rather than offer prescriptions for action.

Carver recommends that the board ask itself, "What management situations, activities, or decisions would be unacceptable to us even if they worked? Even if the ends are being achieved, what risks, ethical violations, and proprieties does the board want to put off limits?" When the board has answered these questions, responsible governance requires that it specify all the limitations it intends to place on management authority. . . . The power of this approach is that management authority not expressly limited is, in effect, authorized. Management authority exercised within those boundaries—and reasonably intended in good faith to achieve the ends of the enterprise—has bounded freedom to be agile and creative.

. . . .

Hypothetical: Eduardo's Legacy

Camarillo, Inc. ("Camarillo") is a family-owned business incorporated in Arizona that operates a chain of supermarkets in the United States and

Mexico. Camarillo was founded by Eduardo Gonzalez in 1960 and has grown from a single storefront into a chain of 100 supermarkets with 5,000 employees and annual revenues exceeding $500 million. Gonzalez owns 70 percent of the shares of Camarillo and his three children, Eduardo Jr., Alejandro, and Maria, each own 10 percent. Eduardo is seventy years old and intends to retire this year. The board, which is composed of seven representatives appointed by Eduardo and three representatives appointed by his children, has hired a new CEO and would like to instruct her regarding the ends to be pursued by Camarillo.

- Having grown up in an impoverished neighborhood in Mexico City, Eduardo feels a strong sense of responsibility towards his employees in Mexico and has always paid them the same wage that Camarillo pays its U.S. employees ($10 per hour). Eduardo believes that this enhances Camarillo's reputation and social capital, leading to better long-term performance. Eduardo also places much importance on his legacy and would like to be admired by his employees.
- Eduardo's children are interested in maximizing short-term revenue and profits by paying the minimum wage legally allowable in Mexico ($4 per day).

Camarillo's board of directors has retained the services of a consulting firm, which has advised as follows:

- The minimum wage in Mexico is insufficient to support a small family.
- The minimum wage required to support a family is $3 per hour.
- Paying employees in Mexico at least $3 per hour will generate substantial goodwill among the employees and customers and lead to better growth prospects for Camarillo in the long run.
- Paying in excess of $5 per hour yields negligible benefits with respect to goodwill and Camarillo's long-term growth prospects in Mexico.
- If Camarillo were to pay its employees in Mexico the minimum allowable wage, its profits would increase by 50 percent.

1) How should the board of directors define the ends to be pursued by the new CEO?
2) What limitations, if any, should the board of directors place on the means by which the new CEO pursues those ends?

Looking Toward the Future: The Business Case for Corporate Governance[15]

John D. Sullivan and Anna Nadgrodkiewicz

January 31, 2013

PREFACE

Historically, in the developed economies, key drivers for the adoption of good corporate governance have been the following: the search for investment capital, the desire to list on major global stock exchanges, the need to gain access to technology, and the desire to build solid supply chains. In today's global economy, corporate governance is becoming increasingly recognized as a key factor affecting businesses' success in emerging markets as well.

Opportunities and competitive threats created by the global economy make instituting good corporate governance practices key to developing a strategy for the company to prosper. Improving corporate governance allows companies to attract greater investment at lower cost, strengthens corporate strategy and its implementation, clarifies accountability, enhances shareholder protection, and helps to attract and retain quality employees. This is true not only for large publicly listed multinationals but for other types of companies as well. For controlling shareholders, corporate governance clarifies roles and improves accountability, enhances senior executives' professionalization, and increases company value. Crucially, for society as a whole, corporate governance minimizes the occurrence of corruption, reduces the risk of devastating systemic crises, and improves productivity.

UNDERSTANDING CORPORATE GOVERNANCE

Corporate governance is at the core of a modern company's strategy and operations because it addresses issues vital to that company's performance and to its very survival. From board selection and strategic decision-making to day-to-day operations and legal compliance, corporate governance is a way for companies to create a framework for sound business practices, sustained growth, and risk management.

The basic concept of corporate governance is a principal-agent model used to ensure the profitable performance of corporations and the efficient use of resources, and to solve problems related to the separation of ownership and control. The principals are owners of company assets; the agents are managers responsible for company operations. The idea behind corporate governance is to ensure that the agent—the manager—acts in the best interest of the principal. Therefore, at its core corporate governance entails an internal control system

---

15. John D. Sullivan & Anna Nadgrodkiewicz, *Looking Toward the Future: The Business Case for Corporate Governance*, CIPE Economic Reform Feature Service (January 31, 2013).

for transparent decision making to which company executives should be held accountable.

In this basic model, directors represent the shareholders; vote on key matters and appoint and monitor the management, while the management carries out core company functions and reports to the board of directors. Many people think of corporate governance as limited to this internal company dynamic between the shareholders, board of directors, and management. The revised Principles of Corporate Governance published by the Organisation for Economic Co-operation and Development (OECD) in 2004 capture the essence of that dynamic:

> Corporate governance involves a set of relationships between a company's management, its board, its shareholders and other stakeholders. Corporate governance also provides the structure through which the objectives of the company are set and the means of attaining those objectives and monitoring performance are determined.

However, the OECD Principles also make it clear that corporate governance involves more than just internal company structures and requires external supporting institutions that promote transparent and efficient markets.

Many people also think of corporate governance as something applicable only to large corporations in developed economies with little relevance to the broader private sector or to issues affecting the development of countries around the world. In the global economy, however, it has become increasingly obvious that the external factors that guide the behavior of companies, such as regulatory frameworks and market institutions, are equally important to making the system of corporate governance work. Moreover, in many countries publicly listed corporations are not the most important economic actors in terms of employment and growth. Instead, other types of business—from family-owned companies to small enterprises—play a dominant role in the economy. Those companies also need good corporate governance for better sustainability and in order to become integrated into the global supply chains.

As a result, the understanding and application of corporate governance has evolved in the last few decades, as people recognize that corporate governance does not exist in a vacuum. Its successful implementation depends on a country's overall institutional environment, not just on a company's internal practices. Therefore, to strengthen private sector governance, countries and companies alike should also focus on broader reforms of the judicial systems, property rights, freedom of information, and other institutions key to market economies and democratic governance. These institutional dimensions of corporate governance must be understood in order to appreciate corporate governance's importance for business growth, especially in emerging markets.

INSTITUTIONAL DIMENSIONS OF CORPORATE GOVERNANCE

The external factors that affect corporate behavior include various stakeholders who need to be considered in decision making, such as employees, customers, suppliers, lenders, and communities in which the company operates.

Reputational agents, such as accountants and independent auditors, lawyers, credit rating agencies, investment bankers and advisors, financial media, and corporate governance analysts, are also crucial in shaping company decisions. So are shareholder rights organizations, corporate governance institutes, and directors' associations, given their role in corporate governance-related advocacy, professional standards, and self-regulation.

Another key external factor is the regulatory environment. It involves various standards (accounting and auditing, for instance); laws and regulations applied to companies; stock exchange and securities market regulations; debt and equity requirements of the financial sector; rules governing market competition; investment; and corporate control.

The growing recognition that corporate governance requires the functioning of both internal controls and external supporting institutions is illustrated by the evolution of the OECD Principles of Corporate Governance. The OECD Principles were created in 1999 and initially focused on five core areas of corporate governance: the rights of shareholders and key ownership structures; equitable treatment of shareholders; the role of stakeholders; disclosure and transparency; and the responsibilities of the board. However, it soon became apparent that this scope did not sufficiently reflect the external, institutional factors that drive corporate governance.

When the authors drafted the original Principles, they primarily looked at the OECD countries with developed capital markets and well-established corporate structures. The Principles assumed that all the other institutions of a market economy were in place. Furthermore, they did not touch upon forms of business common in many countries such as family firms or state-owned enterprises (SOEs), nor did they address the differences between dispersed and concentrated ownership structures. Those shortcomings highlighted a discrepancy between the traditional definition of corporate governance and its actual practice.

That is why, in 2004, a revision of the OECD Principles added another key tenet to the existing five: ensuring the basis for an effective corporate governance framework. It states that "the corporate governance framework should promote transparent and efficient markets, be consistent with the rule of law and clearly articulate the division of responsibilities among different supervisory, regulatory and enforcement authorities." This principle now makes it explicit that the existence of good public governance and market institutions cannot be assumed and should be enhanced through reforms where needed.

The revision process, in which the Center for International Private Enterprise (CIPE) and its partners from around the world participated, also captured the fact that the value of corporate governance goes beyond the performance of individual companies. The private sector, as a whole, plays a vital role in market economies and development prospects of countries. Therefore, institutions of good corporate governance—in order to operate effectively—must exist in the context of broader institutions that guarantee transparent governance and competitive markets.

BUSINESS CASE FOR CORPORATE GOVERNANCE

Given that corporate governance is relevant to individual companies and countries alike, building a business case for implementing good corporate governance practices has two equally crucial aspects: it needs to demonstrate benefits both at a company level and at a systemic country level.

BUSINESS CASE FOR COMPANIES

As mentioned earlier, corporate governance traditionally has been associated with large companies in developed markets for which the key benefit of good governance is being listed on a stock exchange and able to raise outside capital. However, corporate governance can deliver benefits to other types of companies because it provides a framework for efficient, transparent, and accountable decision making. That framework is needed in every enterprise regardless of the size or form of ownership. All companies must have a way of reconciling divergent interests, planning for strategy and succession, accessing capital, cultivating company image in the community, and ensuring legal compliance. Corporate governance is a key tool for achieving those business goals.

Family firms are one such example. Given that their owners and managers are the same, the conventional model of corporate governance has generally not been deemed applicable to them. Yet, those firms—prevalent in many developing countries—face serious governance challenges that require clear rules and decision-making frameworks. Common problems in family-owned firms include nepotism, personal conflicts between different family members, lack of clear separation of interests and assets between the company and family, and succession issues that threaten the company's survival beyond the founder.

In those companies, good corporate governance can, among other qualities, help ensure sustainability in the second and third generations, improve professionalism of management, enhance access to capital, and increase the price and volume of traded shares. Better corporate governance practices also help family firms achieve clearer distinction between representatives of the ownership (directors) and of management (CEO and other executives) and improve the quality of decision making by recruiting independent board members. Those findings have been borne out by a study of corporate governance practices of 15 largest family-owned companies in Brazil.

Improving corporate governance in the state-owned enterprise (SOE) sector is another example of benefits at a company level. By adopting good corporate governance rules, SOEs can make the state an effective and more responsible owner, improve board quality, tie management incentives to company performance, and establish clear lines of accountability that ultimately go back to the taxpayers.

Small- and medium-sized enterprises (SMEs), although not associated with the classic corporate governance model, can also greatly benefit from improved internal governance. Most leaders of SMEs cite access to credit as one of the biggest challenges they face, especially in economies where capital markets are underdeveloped and small companies primarily rely on banks for financing. Without proper accounting procedures and disclosure of financial information, bank loans are not forthcoming.

Many SME leaders are recognizing the need to improve their companies' accounting procedures and internal control systems to enhance their credit worthiness. They also see the economic value of crafting internal codes of corporate governance for greater sustainability and competitiveness. By adopting such codes, SME leaders can improve the decision-making process between partners or shareholders, the transparency and accuracy of financial information, the role of executive staff, and the relationships with stakeholders.

By requiring better financial information from companies to which they lend, banks can encourage the adoption of improved accounting systems and regular reporting in various types of companies. In doing so, the banking sector can promote good governance in countries where most companies rely on banks rather than stock exchanges to meet their capital needs. To do it effectively, however, leaders of banks themselves must appreciate the benefits of good corporate governance practices.

Financial crises plaguing countries around the world have frequently been linked to insider lending or improper risk management in financial institutions. Those risks are particularly compounded in state-owned banks in which, without proper safeguards, political considerations often trump sound economic decision-making and risk assessment in lending. That is where corporate governance—through more transparency and accountability in the boardroom and through better disclosure— can make a big difference, not just for responsible bank lending but also for macroeconomic stability.

In fact, systemic failure of risk management tied to poor corporate governance practices has been at the core of the recent global financial crisis. As the OECD report on the causes of the crisis observed, "In many cases risk was not managed on an enterprise basis and not adjusted to corporate strategy. (. . .) Most important of all, boards were in a number of cases ignorant of the risk facing the company." The lesson is that risk management was typically not covered, or insufficiently covered, by corporate governance practices. Many companies, including banks, have since improved board performance in this regard by developing policies for identification of the best skill composition of the board or establishing remuneration committees to better monitor the relation between executive compensation and company performance and anticipate potential conflicts of interest.

BUSINESS CASE FOR ECONOMICS

The institutional underpinnings of corporate governance, especially the private sector institutions and regulatory framework that shape business behavior, make it an essential component of public governance and economic development of countries. Many efforts toward strengthening corporate governance in emerging markets have been focused on improving internal company practices. However, improving the broader institutional environment in which those practices are implemented is of equal importance because of the intertwined nature of the internal and external factors that influence business conduct.

Addressing institutional deficiencies that hamper effective corporate governance is one of the core benefits of corporate governance reforms, particularly for developing economies. At the most basic level, a sound corporate governance system helps to ensure that companies operate on a level playing field and that the rights of shareholders and stakeholders are well defined and protected. More broadly, corporate governance requires institutions, such as healthy justice system, to enforce the rules and a vibrant civil society and independent media to monitor company conduct and expose abuses. Building these supporting institutions of corporate governance facilitates the creation of value systems based on transparency, accountability, responsibility, and fairness. Those values are not only important for ethical and sustainable business growth but are also indispensable for democratic governance.

One key area in which countries can greatly benefit from improved corporate governance is in privatization of state-owned enterprises. Introducing good corporate governance in companies scheduled to undergo privatization is particularly crucial in transition economies, in which privatizing state assets is a key part of building a market economy and in which governments depend on income from privatization to deliver services to the public.

The legacy of flawed privatization after the fall of communism in Eastern Europe shows how the lack of proper internal controls, reporting mechanisms, and shareholder protections in privatized firms led to corruption and abuse detrimental not just to those enterprises but to the entire transition process.

The lack of such controls prior to privatization has also contributed to other severe economic crises, such as that of Chile in the 1970s, in which family owned banks unsustainably invested in privatized companies, or the 1994 "tequila crisis" in Mexico, in which government-owned commercial banks were improperly privatized.

Sound corporate governance is also important in state-owned firms with no immediate plans for privatization. In many countries, SOEs account for a large share of employment but are notorious for asset wasting, mismanagement, and entering into political entanglements. Establishing internal controls and clear governance rules can greatly improve the efficiency of their operations and effective use of public resources.

Corporate governance is also crucial for transforming the relationship between businesses and the state away from cronyism and preferential treatment toward transparency and accountability. As financial crises in Asia and Russia in the late 1990s demonstrated, non-transparent relationships between government officials and companies can lead to economic collapse, not just individual company failures.

More recently, the aftermath of the global financial crisis shows the high cost of poor corporate governance . . . is still felt [by societies] around the world. All these examples illustrate that weak corporate governance at a company level has crucial macroeconomic implications and can lead to the inability of countries to attract investment, to public asset stripping, to state capture, and, in extreme cases, to financial disaster.

Corporate governance can also be a key anti-corruption tool with many economic benefits. Certainly, legal reforms, such as better procurement codes or simplification of tax codes, are needed to create stronger anti-corruption environments in countries but robust corporate governance at a company level can greatly supplement such reform efforts. Internal controls limit opportunities for corruption by making bribery harder to conceal, integrating the values of transparency and accountability into a company's operations, and implementing strict policies of zero tolerance for corruption among employees and directors.

In sum, corporate governance clearly delivers palpable economic benefits to countries that put in place better internal and external drivers of company conduct. Studies show that those benefits include higher investment levels, lower costs of capital, and lower costs of doing business, all of which lead to stronger economic growth and more employment opportunities. Improved company performance, through better management and allocation of resources, helps to create wealth and better relationships with stakeholders help improve social and labor relations. Finally, at the systemic level, better corporate governance can help reduce the risk of devastating financial crises.

DRIVERS OF BETTER CORPORATE GOVERNANCE: IN SEARCH OF BENEFITS

Corporate governance reforms can be driven by two distinct factors: crises or searches for benefits. Responses to crises are often rushed, tend to focus on new regulation and stricter penalties, and do not take [into account] many issues affecting corporate behavior. . . . A better approach to corporate governance reforms is the one driven by a search for benefits: for example, the business case for companies and economies to embrace better corporate governance and be proactive about it, rather than simply react to crises. That, in turn, makes them better prepared to deal with a crisis when it does occur.

When considering the significance of corporate governance for business growth, it is therefore important to recognize that drivers of corporate governance are not limited to the rules and competitive pressures that discipline companies into compliance. There are also many positive drivers that incentivize companies to implement good corporate governance in search of benefits, such as attracting investment and lower cost of capital.

A well-governed company, even in a poor investment environment, can do better than its competitors, and that is the premium an investor will pay for. According to the Global Investor Opinion Survey conducted by McKinsey and the Global Corporate Governance Forum (the survey canvassed more than 200 professional investors in 31 countries in Asia, Europe, Latin America, Middle East, Africa, and North America), a significant majority of investors say they are willing to pay a premium for a well-governed company. Corporate governance also helps strengthen competitiveness. Studies show a link between stronger shareholder protection and larger stock markets, stronger corporate governance and lower cost of capital, and greater equity rates equal higher returns on investment relative to the cost of capital.

That said, there is no silver bullet or a single model of good corporate governance that would automatically translate into business growth. Corporate governance systems and their effectiveness in different countries vary depending on the following: if ownership and control of firms is dispersed (as in the United States and United Kingdom) or concentrated (as in continental Europe, Japan, many of the emerging markets); what legal and regulatory frameworks as well as historical and cultural legacies are in place; and which industry sectors are considered. Various models used by companies have their own strengths and weaknesses and the search for best practices and benefits should be considered in that context.

Universally, though, the key benefit that corporate governance can deliver to companies around the world comes down to building a board that performs, since it is the board members who ultimately contribute to generating sustainable business growth. Implementing good corporate governance is, therefore, not a matter of simply ticking a box; rather, it is a process where the core values of transparency, fairness, accountability, and responsibility are integrated both into a company's strategic direction and its day-to-day operations.

Those values can become institutionalized only if a company adopts a robust code of corporate governance, and the board members fulfill their fundamental duties of care and loyalty to place the company's interest always above board members' personal interests. As demonstrated by the failures of corporate governance that contributed to the recent global financial crisis, it is also crucial for the board members to properly understand the business judgment rule and make informed decisions that responsibly take into account the level of associated risk. Good corporate governance is, therefore, a key tool for ensuring ethical business conduct and managing risks.

Skeptics may say that if a company follows good corporate governance and ethics principles it may, in the short run, lose a business deal to a company that is less scrupulous. In an interconnected modern market economy, however, that works only once. Well-run companies that are consistently profitable have to be able to do business repeatedly with the same customers. Thus, ethical business practices translate into the ability to retain existing customers and gain new ones. They also have a positive impact on attracting and retaining top talent, and improve relationships between employees and management. Finally, ethical business practices matter for a company's reputation and long-term prospects. Managing today's global supply chains and serving increasingly value-conscious consumers requires being able to demonstrate proper and fair conduct all the way down that supply chain, including to sub-contractors and vendors.

People should also keep in mind that business ethics comprise a set of evolving guidelines—and the standards in most societies keep going up. Conduct that was acceptable 50 or even 20 years ago in the area of equal employment opportunities or environmental protection, for instance, is no longer acceptable today. Similarly, the current standards keep evolving, especially through the rising pressure on board members to become more sophisticated in risk management, in light of the global financial meltdown. As standards change, companies need to revisit their corporate governance guidelines and ethics codes to update and refresh them as needed.

CONCLUSION

The essence of inclusive market economies is the institutional framework where private entrepreneurs have the opportunities to create and build wealth, to maximize their value to society, and to grow the economy of their countries. Corporate governance is a key element of that framework because it helps create a fair level playing field among companies. Corporate governance can also become a focal point for reform of broader institutions needed for a well-functioning market economy: property rights, judicial system and enforcement mechanisms, securities markets, free press, rating agencies, and other checks and balances.

The importance of corporate governance in today's global economy is magnified by the fact that the principles of good corporate governance are applicable to a wide variety of firms, not just large companies listed on major stock exchanges. From SOEs to family-owned firms and SMEs, corporate governance offers a valuable toolkit for introducing transparency, accountability, responsibility, and fairness into the decision making, helping to ensure greater competitiveness and sustainability.

By improving company procedures and by building responsible boards, corporate governance contributes to business growth. Yet, its significance goes beyond improving company performance and maximizing shareholder value. The external drivers of corporate behavior, from the regulatory framework to independent media, are equally important as internal controls, and reforming them helps to transform the institutional framework in which companies operate. That transformation is of great significance for businesses conducting business in emerging markets and for the overall development prospects of those countries.

Efforts to reform corporate governance around the world must therefore focus on both the internal and external factors that drive corporate behavior. Attempting to transfer international best practices in corporate governance into a country where market and public governance institutions are weak will not succeed unless people pay attention to reforming those broader institutions too. Moreover, reformers should seek to integrate the local business community in the process of developing corporate governance codes in their countries in order to create a sense of ownership and opportunities for feedback.

The ultimate goal of corporate governance reforms is to create value systems that guide ethical company behavior and strengthen the institutions and rights that allow businesses to compete fairly and generate economic growth. There are two paths toward improving corporate governance in companies and countries. One is reactive, associated with failures and collapses; the other is proactive and has to do with the search for benefits. Both have been responsible for bringing attention to corporate governance issues in recent years. Yet, it is the latter that shows the business case for corporate governance and provides positive incentives. By helping companies and countries attract investment, reduce corruption, and facilitate institutional reform, an effective corporate governance framework supports a foundation for sustained growth and a stable and vibrant global economy in the future.

III. Responsible Management

The premise of Friedman's argument is that, as a business enterprise becomes more socially responsible, its costs increase and its resources are diverted from its main mission of generating profits. It follows that CSR forces business executives to divide their loyalty between their shareholders and other stakeholders—serving the latter at the expense of the corporation's owners. The BEM disputes this notion, proposing a way to ensure the opposite result.

According to the BEM, the enterprise can align its own objectives with those of its stakeholders by articulating a "purpose beyond profit," a set of core values and a "vision of a desired future" that is shared by the enterprise and its stakeholders. Assume, for example, that a large multinational enterprise sells packaged food for children in developing countries. Assume further that this enterprise articulates the higher purpose beyond maximizing profits of improving the health of the children who consume its products; sets "compassion" as the core value driving its actions; and proposes a desired vision for itself and its employees of helping end child hunger in underprivileged countries. In this way, the BEM states, the enterprise aligns the objectives of its operations, compliance and ethics function, and its stakeholders, since they share the same objective; as a result, performance is improved through:

> In a free enterprise, private-property system, a corporate executive is an employee of the owners of the business. He has direct responsibility to his employers. That responsibility is to conduct the business in accordance with their desires, which generally will be to make as much money as possible. . . .
>
> . . . .
>
> What does it mean to say that the corporate executive has a "social responsibility" in his capacity as businessman? If this statement is not pure rhetoric, it must mean that he is to act in some way that is not in the interest of his employers. For example, that he is to . . . make expenditures on reducing pollution beyond the amount that is . . . required by law in order to contribute to the social objective of improving the environment. . . .
>
> In [that case], the corporate executive would be spending someone else's money for a general social interest.
>
> —*Milton Friedman*[16]

- Enhanced reputation and goodwill
- Reduced risks
- Reduced costs
- Protection from unethical employees and agents
- Enhanced performance, productivity, and competitive position

---

16. Milton Friedman, *The Social Responsibility of Business Is to Increase Its Profits*, N.Y. Times Mag., Sept. 13, 1970, at 12.

- Expanded access to capital, credit, and foreign investment
- Increased profits and sustained long-term growth
- Increased international respect[17]

Business Ethics: A Manual for Managing a Responsible Business Enterprise in Emerging Market Economies[18]

Management Vision for the Enterprise

Responsible management defines the enterprise's core beliefs: its purpose beyond profit, its core values, and its envisioned future. In addition, as developed at length in Chapter 4 [of the BEM], owners and managers establish expectations for the business ethics program itself by describing supportive cultural characteristics of the organization and expected program outcomes.

Two researchers, James Collins and Jerry Porras, found that what separates good companies from great ones, in large part, is the vision framework they provide their employees and aligning their choices and actions to that framework. The vision framework that they recommend has three components: a core purpose, core values, and an envisioned future.

CORE PURPOSE

Without losing sight of returning value to the owners, responsible management establishes the fundamental reason for the existence of the enterprise in the form of a purpose statement that inspires its employees and agents. An enterprise purpose beyond profit helps define the enterprise. Unlike goals and objectives, the purpose is never actually achieved. As Collins and Porras describe it, enterprise purpose "like a star on the horizon can never be reached; it guides and inspires forever."

Purpose should be a succinct statement of how the enterprise intends to meet some important need of its community. A purpose statement captures the reasons that employees and agents are eager to go to work. It takes as given that owners want profits and that employees want livelihoods. But one can be certain that most employees do not go to work eager to make more money for the owners or even to earn their next paycheck. They go to work eager to contribute because there is something in the purpose of the enterprise that excites them.

Defining an enterprise's purpose is not an easy process. Collins and Porras suggest describing what the enterprise does in business—its mission, for example—and then asking five times: "Why is that important?" Though deceptively simple, asking "Why is that important?" will help establish the value the enterprise brings to the community. This sense of value added becomes the ordering principle of all subsequent decisions and activities.

---

17. BEM, *supra* note 1, at 21–31.
18. *Id.* at 21–31, 102–04.

CORE VALUES

Responsible management defines four or five values to guide the choices and actions for all employees and agents. These core values should be so fundamental to what the enterprise sees itself to be—and the way that it does business—that they will not be sacrificed for short-term gain.

There is no right set of values for an enterprise. Royal Dutch/Shell, for example, has three core values: *honesty*, *integrity*, and *respect for people*. Chiquita Brands, International, which has plantations around the globe, has four core values: *integrity*, *respect*, *opportunity*, and *responsibility*. Alcatel, a multicultural company with employees in 130 countries, has four values as well: *customer focus*, *innovation*, *teamwork*, and *accountability*.

Core values should reflect the fundamental qualities that the enterprise wants to use to guide employee and agent decisions and activities, but they should not be so far removed from the reality of the enterprise that they are impossible to follow or that they breed cynicism. Moreover, the process of defining core values will influence how they are understood, accepted, and followed. The more stakeholders participate in developing the core values, the more likely these core values are to reflect the enterprise and to be accepted by its members and other stakeholders.

Some enterprises arrive at their core values through a carefully crafted survey of their employees, including interviews and focus groups. Others establish advisory groups at various levels of the enterprise to work with a small working group to draft a set of values for further dialogue. A few enterprises survey all or most of their members plus many other stakeholders.

To bring to the surface enterprise values among employees, ask a simple question such as, "What would you tell a new employee who asks 'What does someone have to do to succeed around here?'" Following through on employee and other stakeholder answers to these questions will lead eventually to four or five values that should guide members of the enterprise.

VISION OF A DESIRED FUTURE

Responsible owners and managers visualize enterprise goals and objectives and the enterprise's role in the community over the long term. Goals should include responsibility to the community and to external stakeholders. They should incorporate relevant political, economic, and socio-cultural considerations. From this vision flow the goals, objectives, and expected outcomes of the enterprise's strategies and action plans.

Research suggests that there are two components to an effective envisioned future: (a) a specific goal that gives direction and meaning to enterprise decisions and activities and (b) a vivid description of the desired future. . . .

. . . .

IMPROVING BUSINESS PERFORMANCE

There is much support for the notion that the discipline of responsible business conduct outlined here contributes to improving business performance and expanding opportunities for growth. Principal benefits coming to an enterprise that implements a business ethics program are[:]

. . . .

Enhanced Reputation and Goodwill

. . . .

A business ethics program contributes to the enterprise's reputation for integrity. By giving adequate guidance to employees and agents, it ensures that they know what is responsible business conduct. By helping form reasonable expectations among its stakeholders, it minimizes disputes with customers and other stakeholders and increases stakeholder satisfaction.

Reduced Risks

Every business, even if it strives to comply strictly with the law, is subject to risks such as these:

- Being exposed to criminal prosecution for bribing a government contracting officer
- Being debarred from government contracting or a strategic partnership for an inappropriate gift or gratuity
- Having to recall products for failure to follow quality standards and procedures
- Having to clean up spills of toxic waste
- Dealing with employee claims of sexual harassment
- Dealing with lost employee time for health and safety problems
- Being placed on a blacklist of international, national, or local organizations

An RBE develops processes with which it identifies, assesses, and manages the full range of factors that might pose a risk to social and financial performance. The processes include assessing risks, establishing adequate standards and procedures, training, and monitoring and auditing systems. These processes help owners and managers plan, organize, and control the day-to-day operations of an enterprise to minimize risks to its capital, earnings, and reputation. They include management of risks associated with accidental losses, as well as operational risks such as those arising from financial mismanagement, fraud and embezzlement, corruption, and loss of reputation.

Reduced Costs

By providing employees clear guidelines on how to conduct day-to-day business in compliance with laws and ethics through a business ethics program, the RBE can reduce transaction costs. A business ethics program institutes procedures to detect and to prevent violations of the law and ethics. It provides employees with clear guidelines on a host of day-to-day transactions: how to conduct bids and tenders; how to conclude contracts; how to use confidential information; how to avoid conflicts of interest; and how to work with customers, suppliers, service providers, and competitors.

The cost of bribery, kickbacks, and other forms of illegal or corrupt conduct is not only the amount paid. The full cost includes management effort to allocate time to work with officials, to maintain a second set of books, and to deal with the threat of extortion and blackmail. The real cost is the risk to reputation and pride in the enterprise and the reduced prospects for participating in a market economy.

Protection From Unethical Employees and Agents

It is not pleasant to contemplate, but the enterprise itself is often abused by its employees and agents. Embezzlement of enterprise funds is a major example. Cheating on time cards or carrying off supplies and tools, while relatively minor, add up to significant losses sustained every year by businesses—both large and small. It has been estimated that enterprises in the United States lose some 6 percent of their revenues annually to employee misconduct.

A business ethics program is designed to establish standards and procedures to prevent and detect violations of the trust put in employees. Among these standards and procedures are processes to protect enterprise assets. These specific processes may include establishing standards and procedures, monitoring and auditing systems, and reporting mechanisms.

However, at the heart of a business ethics program is the desire of owners and managers to foster the commitment of their employees to the welfare of the enterprise as a whole. Fostering this sense of loyalty and commitment among employees and agents may be the most effective way in which a business ethics program protects the enterprise from disloyal employees.

Enhanced Performance, Productivity, and Competitive Position

An RBE increases effectiveness and efficiency by enabling all stakeholders to work together closely on the basis of respect, shared values, and mutual trust. Such efforts lead to what one author calls "invisible savings" by reducing employee conduct that is harmful to the enterprise but difficult to detect. After a business ethics program becomes a part of operations, many of the costs of monitoring and supervision can be reduced.

Product quality may improve and transaction costs, such as contracting, may decline. For example, many large, complex enterprises (LCEs), most of which have business ethics programs, are developing preferred supplier lists to reduce the number of suppliers that they deal with. To ensure that there is no interruption in supplies and services, these LCEs require that their supply chains adopt the same good management practices that they follow, including a business ethics program. . . .

Since, in the minds of most employees, ethics are essentially a matter of fairness, a business ethics program often increases employee morale. Better morale leads to increased productivity and innovation. It strengthens the enterprise's competitive position in its industry.

Expanded Access to Capital, Credit, and Foreign Investment

A business ethics program, including aggressive risk management processes, may increase an RBE's attractiveness to investors. Before making loans, international lending institutions and domestic banks perform due diligence on whether an enterprise is managed well. They look to see whether an enterprise has strong financial supervision and internal controls. A business ethics program is designed to prevent and detect illegal and unethical practices. Financial institutions may view management as a worthy credit risk and allow access to capital at lower rates.

When entering new markets, foreign investors seek reliable partners who demonstrate integrity and operate on a transparent basis. A business ethics program reflecting global norms and values provides a common language between an enterprise and foreign investors. It creates opportunity to build partnerships that are based on respect, shared values, and mutual trust.

Increased Profits and Sustained Long-Term Growth

The discipline of responsible business conduct does not deliver instant results. However, a business ethics program—including infrastructure and processes for continuous monitoring of compliance with law and ethics—should help an enterprise be more reliable and stable over time.

Once an RBE has demonstrated its ability to detect and to prevent violations of the law and ethics, it tends to earn stakeholder confidence. This confidence leads to an increase in the value of shares; to wider access to capital and credit; to new clients, customers, and partners; and to further opportunities for expansion.

Increased International Respect

Adhering to the discipline of responsible business conduct can help enterprises gain access to international markets. It encourages compliance with laws and regulations that require a high level of transparency. When the generally accepted business practices of a community are based on sound standards and reasonable expectations, fair competition is the norm and the RBE can operate on a level playing field. Fair competition may encourage trading partners to reduce trade barriers such as tariffs and quotas.

Recent research suggests that a business ethics program is particularly valuable in times of merger, acquisition, and restructuring. It is thought that the essential elements of a business ethics program may help members of often distinct organizational cultures manage their differences until they find common ground. These elements include core beliefs, standards, and procedures; high-level personnel responsible for the program; and dedicated resources to help employees seek advice. Enterprises undergoing privatization should also consider the advantages of a business ethics program as a means to reduce the risks associated with this transition process.

. . . .

Trust and Social Capital

. . . .

Social capital is "performance-based trust." It is "the ability of people to work together for common purposes in groups and organizations." Each participant in a market or society is responsible for contributing to the pattern of reasonable expectations. In such a community, trust will be rewarded. The RBE strives to be a trustworthy member of its community in order to contribute to its social capital.

Social capital is the foundation of a successful market economy. The benefits of operating in a high-trust environment are many. As one scholar observes, "A high-trust society can organize its workplace on a more flexible and group-oriented basis, with more responsibility delegated to lower levels of the organization. Low-trust societies, by contrast, must fence in and isolate their workers with a series of bureaucratic rules."

Another scholar lists eight studies that demonstrate the link between values in general, trust in particular, and profitability. The link is based on an increase in creativity, support of management decisions, knowledge sharing, and pride, among other factors.

. . . .

Social capital also accrues through the efforts of civil society: organizations, such as trade groups, business associations, service clubs, charities, university faculty, and other nongovernmental organizations (NGOs) that aim to hold business and government officials accountable. Business enterprises, in general, have the potential to be powerful and influential members of their communities.

The RBE helps create the conditions for good public governance by promoting responsible business conduct—through self-regulation or through public dialogue with government officials. These forms of voluntary action help build social capital—the trust and shared values among individuals, government officials, civil society, the local community, and business that make it possible to work together on a cooperative basis.

. . . .

Hypothetical: #Purpose #Values #Vision

Assume that Twitter, Inc. ("Twitter") has recently implemented a new ethics program patterned after the guidance provided by the BEM. You are Twitter's CEO. Articulate a core purpose, a set of core values, and a "vision of a desired future" for the company.

CHAPTER **8**

Building the Ethics Program

I. The Program's Objective
II. Program Components
   A. The Ethics Code of Conduct
   B. Ethics Program Infrastructure (Autonomy, Oversight, Resources)
   C. Ethics Training
   D. Incentives and Disciplinary Measures
   E. Reporting and Investigations
   F. Continuous Assessment and Monitoring

I. The Program's Objective

The Federal Sentencing Guidelines for Organizations ("FSGO") and the Resource Guide to the United States Foreign Corrupt Practices Act ("FCPA Guide") evaluate compliance programs in a somewhat binary fashion—as either effective or ineffective. Business Ethics: A Manual for Managing a Responsible Business Enterprise in Emerging Market Economies ("BEM"), by contrast, measures the effectiveness of the ethics program by reference to a spectrum corresponding to degrees of responsible conduct, starting with a program that meets the bare minimum legal requirements and culminating in a program that positively impacts all of the enterprise's stakeholders. As shown in Figure 8-1, there are four levels of enterprise identity along this spectrum: compliance, risk management, reputation enhancement, and added value. As an enterprise continues to improve its compliance and ethics program, it moves along this spectrum from compliance to the value-added level—progressively reducing risk and enhancing performance. By so classifying the different levels of enterprise identity, the BEM allows program designers to set more specific objectives for the program and to measure the program's effectiveness in achieving those objectives.

Take an imaginary multinational enterprise that has built an effective compliance program—one that is reasonably designed to prevent and detect violations of law as minimally required by the FSGO and hallmarks. This enterprise incurs a certain cost in maintaining its program, but that cost is justified because it goes toward mitigating the risk of a much more costly and disruptive enforcement action by the government.

According to the BEM, this state of existence corresponds to the "compliance" level of enterprise identity in which the principal objective of the program is to

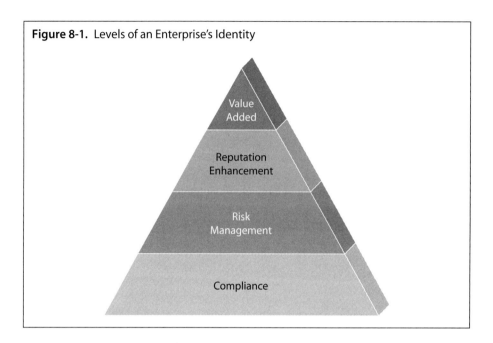

Figure 8-1. Levels of an Enterprise's Identity

protect the enterprise by mitigating legal risk. Although this enterprise might satisfy the government's expectations, it controls employee conduct through strict rules and disciplinary measures instead of by instilling a culture that orients employees toward ethical conduct.

At the next level of enterprise identity—risk management—the enterprise has developed a more sophisticated system for measuring and mitigating risks across the enterprise, and it more efficiently allocates resources to mitigate those risks. At the same time, the corporation's leadership has begun to create a culture of compliance that induces law abidance by inspiring employees to do the right thing. Still, at this level, the compliance program remains a cost center; that is, a net spender of resources—albeit more efficiently—to prevent an enforcement action.

At the next "reputation enhancement" level, the enterprise begins to pay attention to and meet the reasonable expectations of its primary stakeholders; that is, the stakeholders who are most directly impacted by its actions. Other than shareholders, primary stakeholders include employees, consumers, and government regulators. At this level, the corporation begins to generate value through its improved relationships with those stakeholders. It will have happier and more productive employees, more satisfied and loyal customers, and regulators that trust and facilitate its operations. Still, the enterprise remains self-interested, and its efforts to improve its relations with stakeholders are motivated by a desire to enhance its reputation and thereby improve its financial performance.

At the highest "value-added level," the enterprise generates even more value by meeting the reasonable expectations of its more distant stakeholders: communities in which it operates, vulnerable natural resources, competitors who could be harmed by the its monopolistic behavior, and even future generations.

An enterprise at this level carefully modulates its conduct to ensure that its activities positively impact all stakeholders, even though the benefits might not be immediately detectable in terms of improved performance. Since the enterprise's actions are motivated by a genuine desire to benefit its stakeholders, they generate a higher level of trust between the enterprise and its stakeholders. The BEM refers to this enhanced level of trust as social capital—a valuable asset that in the long run results in optimal efficiency and performance.[1]

According to the BEM, to achieve the value-added level of identity, an enterprise must fully embrace all of the three other levels, and it must add value to its community in at least the following ways:

- Serving the most important needs of its customers and consumers,
- Providing gainful employment for its employees and agents, so that they can provide for their families and be responsible citizens,
- Providing an adequate return to investors,
- Purchasing goods and services from suppliers and service providers,
- Competing intensely but fairly,
- Forming strategic partnerships and alliances to create new business opportunities,
- Supporting community infrastructure through taxes and fees,
- Participating in the political process to improve market conditions, and
- Respecting the environment.[2]

Notes and Questions

In September 2015, within days of public disclosures about VW's emissions scandal, the company's publicly traded shares lost around 20 percent of their value—dramatically illustrating the value of social capital.[3] Why did the capital markets dump VW's shares? Was it because of an expectation of a large legal liability, or was it because the markets believed that consumers would no longer place trust in VW's cars?

Case Study: Coca-Cola in Myanmar

The Coca-Cola Company was one of the first American businesses to reenter Myanmar following the country's first democratic elections in 2010. As Coca-Cola noted:

Guided by the UN Guiding Principles on Business and Human Rights, our due diligence included commercial, legal, and environmental aspects and a thorough

---

1. *See* U.S. Dep't of Commerce, Business Ethics: A Manual for Managing A Responsible Business Enterprise in Emerging Market Economies (2004) [hereinafter BEM], at 47.

2. *Id.*, at 17.

3. William Boston, *Volkswagen Shares Tumble, as Emissions Test Scandal Spreads to Europe*, Wall St. J. (Sept. 21, 2015), https://www.wsj.com/articles/volkswagen-shares-tumble-as-emissions-test-scandal-spreads-to-europe-1442844206.

review of human and workplace rights to assess the nature of actual and potential adverse human rights impacts related to future business operations. . . .[4]

Below is Coca-Cola's Responsible Investment Report submitted pursuant to the U.S. State Department Responsible Investment Reporting Requirements.[5]

The Coca-Cola Company: Myanmar Investment Due Diligence 2015 Annual Update Report[6]

EXECUTIVE SUMMARY

In June 2012, The Coca-Cola Company ("TCCC") announced plans to re-enter Myanmar after more than 60 years. As part of the re-entry, the Company completed a rigorous and in-depth due diligence process which is described in detail in the 2013 Responsible Investment Report. The first plant was inaugurated in June 2013 and the business in Myanmar has just completed its second year of operations. This is the third report (second annual update) and continues to focus on mitigation, as well as new challenges and engagement efforts, since the June 30th, 2014 report submission.

Progress made since the June 2014 report submission includes:

- Extensive training to build a culture of safety within the Company. Trainings are designed for roles within the facility as well as for delivery drivers and, along with a focus on workplace safety, include modules on personal health and hygiene.
- Skills and leadership training opportunities to enhance the role of women within the operations.
- A childcare facility at one plant has been established and is expected to be fully operational in Q3 of 2015.
- The construction of one wastewater treatment system is completed and the wastewater treatment at the second plant is in the final stages of construction.

---

4. Brent Wilton, *Growing and Learning in Myanmar* COCA-COLA: UNBOTTLED (Aug. 21, 2015), http://www.coca-colacompany.com/coca-cola-unbottled/growing-and-learning-in-myanmar.

5. 60-Day Notice of Proposed Information Collection: Reporting Requirements for Responsible Investment in Burma, 80 Fed. Reg. 73867 (Nov. 25, 2015). In order to support the Department of State's efforts to assess the extent to which new U.S. investment authorized by GL 17 furthers U.S. foreign policy goals of, inter alia, improving human rights protections and facilitating political reform in Burma, GL 17 requires U.S. persons engaging in new investment in Burma to report to the Department of State information related to such investment, as laid out in the "Reporting Requirements on Responsible Investment in Burma," (hereafter referred to as the "collection"). This collection is authorized by section 203(a)(2) of IEEPA, which grants the President authority to keep a full record of, and to furnish under oath, in the form of reports or otherwise, complete information relative to any act or transaction referred to in section 203(a)(1) of IEEPA. *Id.*

6. THE COCA-COLA COMPANY, RESPONSIBLE INVESTMENT IN MYANMAR 2015 UPDATE (2015), http://photos.state.gov/libraries/burma/895/pdf/20150630TCCCMyanmarDueDiligenceReport.pdf.

- Ongoing efforts to limit overtime, including the creation of more than 200 new positions in the last 12 months and a system to flag when employees are close to reaching overtime limits.
- Wages were reassessed and increased across the board in line with an independent assessment of market pay rates amongst peer companies across sectors.
- The second plant, Hmawbi, unionized so both plants now have unions which meet regularly with management. Issues discussed include compensation and benefits, overtime and safety.
- Operational level grievance mechanisms are functional with grievances raised and addressed via [an ethics hotline]. Worker Committees continue to meet bimonthly with management to discuss workplace issues.
- Comprehensive anti-corruption training workshops held in partnership with a not-for-profit organization, Emerging Markets, for more than 40 local suppliers.

. . . .

- Air quality testing and SWPPs (source water protection plans) completed and being implemented.
- The Swan Yi project, which is funded by The Coca-Cola Company Foundation and implemented by PACT, is on track to meet targets for 2015. The program, which aims to empower women and older girls to increase household income through livelihoods development and community based banking, has reached 25,409 women and has led to $1,865,797 USD in total savings by participating women and $6,945,154 USD in loans.

One key challenge continues to be attracting, training, and retaining talent in the competitive labor market. Another challenge has been the slow construction progress in completing renovations at one plant and the implications this has had on completing the wastewater treatment plant at that plant.

Many of the key human rights risks identified in our initial report remain relevant and, as such, require ongoing due diligence and engagement. In particular these include: environment, excessive hours of work, lack of awareness about health and safety, child labor in downstream and upstream entities, bribery and corruption, land rights, and gender inequality. This update addresses our efforts in these and other areas since the June 2014 report. As Myanmar continues to open up and our business develops, our due diligence will remain ongoing and we will continue to report publically on our findings and mitigation actions.

. . . .

POLICY COMMITMENT AND EMBEDDING RESPECT FOR HUMAN RIGHTS

The foundation of our corporate commitment to respect human rights is grounded in two overarching policies that apply to our operations in Myanmar: our Human Rights Policy and our Supplier Guiding Principles. These policies provide a consistent approach to human and workplace rights across our system and embed the expectation as an integral part of our culture, strategy and day-to-day operations. The Human Rights Policy and Supplier Guiding Principles are translated and shared on our public website as well as with company-owned operations and supplier partners. Additionally the Code of Business Conduct is translated and shared online and with all employees; training is conducted to communicate the expectation of ethical behavior globally.

To help our Company, our bottling partners, and our direct suppliers meet these standards, third party auditors conduct regular human and workplace rights assessments. Where there are gaps in compliance, corrective actions plans are put in place with follow-up assessments to check on whether our standards are being met. Each year, over 2,000 independent assessments are conducted and over 18,000 assessments have been conducted since the program began. The results of these assessments are included in quarterly and annual scorecards. In Myanmar we have completed three audits . . . .

ANTI-BRIBERY AND ANTI-CORRUPTION UPDATE

The Company's Code of Business Conduct, Trade Sanctions Compliance Policy, and Anti-Bribery Policy continue to serve as primary pillars of our strong commitment to doing business in an ethical and transparent manner. Our Myanmar employees are held to the same high integrity standards as the rest of our global associates. As noted previously, we implemented these important policies as a part of integrating the Myanmar bottling operations into our Company.

Progress made since the June 2014 report submission includes:

- Implemented a certification process for our Code of Business Conduct for employees enrolled in online training.
- Conducted a confidential anti-bribery survey to understand local interactions with government for employees who have such interactions as a part of their role.
- Translated online anti-corruption and bribery training course into local language.
- Comprehensive anti-bribery and corruption training workshops held in partnership with non-governmental organisation, Emerging Markets, for more than 40 local Coca-Cola Pinya Beverages Myanmar suppliers. The training covered Coca-Cola's Supplier Guiding Principles, its Anti-Bribery Policy and Code of Business Conduct for Suppliers, local and international laws as well as case studies, role play, and group discussion.
- Upgraded fleet thereby reducing the risk of drivers being stopped for routine violations and facing potential bribery requests or excessive fees.
- Refresher anti-bribery and corruption training course with specific and applicable examples including facilitating payments, was implemented for all Company drivers.

As outlined previously, our continued efforts in this area include:

- Ongoing training on the Code of Business Conduct and Anti-Bribery Policy and a module on the topics has been included in the onboarding for new employees.

- Consistent communication of our hotline . . . in all Company facilities via posters translated in Myanmar language.
- Continued screening of potential third-party business partners regarding their possible status as sanctioned parties.

HUMAN AND WORKPLACE RIGHTS UPDATE

In October 2012, a human and workplace rights audit was conducted at the bottling plants in Myanmar. During the assessment, the third-party auditors completed a document review, a facility walk-through, confidential employee interviews, and an opening and closing meeting with the management to discuss the process and findings. The initial audit in 2012 identified a variety of issues, including gender- and age-based discrimination and poor wastewater treatment. The majority of findings from that audit have been resolved and the corrective actions were reported in the June 2014 report. The most recent human and workplace rights audit in May 2015 identified some continued gaps as well as a few new findings.

Progress made to close non-compliances identified in the human and workplace rights audit since the June 2014 report submission include:

- *Wages and Benefits:* The initial audit indicated that overtime payments were either not provided or improperly calculated. To address this issue, the facility moved piece rate workers into prescribed shifts to eliminate excessive overtime. The follow-up audits in 2013 and 2014 confirmed the process was ongoing. The 2015 audit validated that the overtime compensation and mandated leave for piece rate workers has been corrected.
- *Childcare Facilities:* The initial audit in 2012 revealed that there were no onsite childcare facilities as required by local regulation. The 2015 audit indicated that the childcare facility has been established at one plant and is part of the renovations of other plant.
- *Hours of Work:* During the initial audit, overtime above legal limits was observed and rest days were not properly provided. The 2015 audit indicated improvements with regards to the rest day violation, but determined that hours of work remain an ongoing concern. The plant has identified some key causes for the overtime including staff turnover, shortage of required labor force skills, maintenance issues, and production increases since 2012. Ongoing efforts to limit overtime have included the creation of more than 200 new positions and a system to flag when employees are close to reaching overtime limits. A focus has been on improving the tracking and reporting of work hours and monitoring overtime on a weekly basis to reschedule shifts if needed. We are looking to implement new software to track work hours in real time in Q4 2015. Better organization and more efficient use of resources have enabled us to achieve a 14% reduction in excessive overtime during peak season and nearly full compliance during off-peak season. Every Function Head gets a monthly report to review with leadership teams on work hours, and they now have to sign off in advance

on any overtime above normal monthly limits. The enhanced reporting and oversight requirements increase accountability and keeps a focus on the issue. Hiring also remains a priority to further reduce work hours.

Despite the progress there remains additional work to close all gaps identified in the human and workplace rights audit. Construction interruptions have led to a delay in the completion of the wastewater treatment and childcare facility at the one plant. Additionally, new health and safety issues were uncovered in the recent audit including some areas' emergency lighting was not functioning and boilers were lacking a required certificate. As previously reported, follow-up assessments will continue to be conducted every six months until the sites demonstrate sustained compliance over time.

Additional steps taken with regards to human and workplace rights since the June 2014 report submission include:

- *New and Updated Training:* To support a culture of compliance, we have made significant investments in developing and implementing training over the past year and expect to deliver more than 120,000 hours of training in 2015. Each new hire participates in a 2-day onboarding process which covers the mission and values of the Company including modules on the Human Rights Policy and Supplier Guiding Principles, the Code of Business Conduct, [ethics hotline], and safety procedures. In addition to the classroom onboarding, we have a "buddy program" such that new employees are partnered with existing employees for their first 3 months on the job. The buddies offer advice, resources, and guidance regarding the day-to-day aspects of work. Operators participate in the Supply Chain Frontline Excellence training which goes more in-depth on workplace safety and also covers personal hygiene. Our frontline supervisor and manager leadership program, STEP, is a three-part training focused on fostering a positive workplace through ensuring supervisors communicate effectively, provide positive feedback, motivate, coach, and inspire workers around them. The latest STEP program occurred in late May 2015. An estimated 50% of our people leaders will have completed STEP by September 2015. At the leadership level our SUMMIT program is a two-week program to support leaders in building trust and engagement in their organization and also includes a module on diversity and inclusion. Investing in people is an essential component to building a positive and safe workplace.

- *Health and Safety:* Extensive work was done in 2015 to support a safe workplace and increase awareness of safety as a priority. An executive plan with regards to workplace environment, health and safety was developed to highlight risks and develop mitigation and/or proactive strategies with an associated timeline. This plan is overseen by the EOSH committee which includes the General Manager and other members of the senior leadership team. A monthly report articulates statistics, activities and progress according to the executive plan. Reporting revealed that the plant renovation project involved more than 1 million hours of work with one minor safety incident and no serious incidents.

Given the size of the Company truck fleet and the amount of time spent on the road by sales and delivery representatives, vehicular safety is a constant focus. In addition to updating the fleet, three trainings were held in the first half of 2015 to educate drivers and promote fleet safety and seven more are scheduled for the Q3 and Q4. Other training included forklift safety and competency training and fire-fighting equipment training. As part of the executive plan, an Incident Reporting Procedure was developed and implemented, the OHSAS18001 manual completed and a pedestrian walkway throughout the facility was constructed. In addition the Company has implemented a monthly "Safety Heroes" reward program, which identifies and rewards employees demonstrating good safety practices.

- *Grievance Mechanisms:* The Coca-Cola Company believes that workplace issues are best resolved through open communication, and that early resolution of disagreements is the best way to maintain a positive, productive work environment. Company-wide grievance mechanisms were described in detail in the initial report and updates provided in the June 2014 report. Grievances are received via [the ethics hotline], all of which are investigated, tracked, and addressed as appropriate. In addition to [the ethics hotline], the Company provides a number of means for the public and community to air and resolve grievances, including through consumer contact numbers and www.facebook.com/CocaColaMyanmar. We also have a paper form to receive complaints/feedback at the plant reception. The submitter receives a copy and a copy is lodged with management for resolution.

- *Gender Balance:* [Coca-Cola] has developed a three-year gender diversity plan that covers recruitment, development, and workplace equity. As part of this, basic gender metrics are monitored every month including the overall population, recruitment pipeline, hiring, and turnover. In Q1 2015, 32% of new hires were female as opposed to 23% in 2014; the metrics demonstrate improvement, but also highlight the need for additional work. In order to further develop female employees, select workers are invited to join a 3-day training called "Achieve Your Best Self" which focuses on strengthening the pipeline of female leaders. Two sessions are planned for 2015 to reach ~50 workers. Additionally, the "Leveraging and Inspiring Female Talent" (LIFT) training targets mid-level leaders. Three women have participated in the LIFT program so far this year and 4–6 more are scheduled to attend in the second half of 2015. At the workplace level, the plan includes a proposed policy review, ongoing pay review analysis for gender equity and a series of communications to educate managers and supervisors on the case for gender balance. The Women's Leadership Council remains active and submits suggestions to senior leaders on an ongoing basis.

ENVIRONMENTAL UPDATE

The Coca-Cola Company has a set of policies governing plant operating requirements, known as KORE. As described in the previous report, these policies are applicable across the Coca-Cola System, including Myanmar, and guide quality, safety and environmental performance.

Progress made since the June 2014 report submission includes:

- Hired Environment, Health, and Safety managers.
- Hired external organization to conduct a baseline assessment of social or environmental impacts resulting from the brownfield renovation project at one plant. Developed and implemented an environment and social management plan for the renovation project term.
- Source water protection plans completed for both plants. The source water protection plans were completed at the end of 2014 and helped identify vulnerabilities and associated mitigation strategies.
- Air quality testing completed.

As identified in the previous report, local community complaints related to construction works at one plant led to an immediate remediation plan. In addition, an environmental and social management plan was developed, to ensure a robust management system and monitoring plan that met or exceeded the requirements of the national environmental acts, laws, regulations and relevant international guidelines. The plan covered topics such as energy use, water use and waste management and included testing on air quality, groundwater, soil quality, noise levels as well as survey of the ecological setting. Whilst most testing levels were within normal parameters, the study flagged excessive noise from the facility operations as a risk, and this was addressed with louvres and silencers for the generators as well as through limiting generator use by connecting to city power supply. The plant renovation project has been completed and the wastewater treatment facility commissioned. The plant is now operating subject to Coca-Cola's KORE operating requirements and from June 2015 onwards will be subject to regular audits.

The external organization also surveyed the surrounding communities to assess potential community impacts associated with the plant renovation. A baseline socio-economic survey was conducted based on interviews with villagers, consultations with the village leaders and site observations. A public consultation process was undertaken to inform the neighboring community/stakeholders of the details of the renovation and to collect views on the perceived positive and negative impacts. Overwhelmingly the community saw job creation as a positive benefit of the construction project. The potential negative impacts perceived were more varied and included concerns about traffic, noise, waste treatment and water usage. All of these fed into the overall environment and social management plan and informed the establishment of regular quarterly meetings between the Company and leaders from villages surrounding the plant. A mutually beneficial outcome from the first of these meetings in 2014 is that villagers identified a need for soil for rebuilding works related to seasonal monsoon flooding. As a result CCPBM was able to supply more than 60 truckloads of soil from the plant construction works and deliver these to areas where it was needed. Quarterly meetings with the village leaders are ongoing and minutes and any agreed actions are shared after each meeting.

Water source vulnerability assessments (SVA) and protection plans (SWPP) were completed for both plants. These assessments inventory the social, environmental and political risks to the water sources supplying our facilities and the surrounding communities. A full description of what is included in the assessments can be found here.

Because many issues identified in an SVA are concerns shared among many if not all water users in a given watershed, we use our findings to engage governments, local communities, businesses and civil society, and plan for collaborative action.

The assessments help us to identify and implement locally relevant projects that support the sustainability of local watersheds and communities while reducing risks to our business. One salient risk identified in the assessment was poor sanitation conditions in the rural areas surrounding one plant, which present a public health risk from run off into surface water supplies as well as present a potential long-term threat to groundwater quality. As a result of this finding and the community consultation described above, in 2015 the Company, with funding from The Coca-Cola Foundation will implement a WASH (water and sanitation for health) program in three local villages. The program aims include improving access to water and sanitation in the local community and educating the community on water management and sanitation for health. The program will be managed by PACT, an NGO that is currently working with us in these communities on the Swan Yi project. The WASH program is intended to be implemented in collaboration with the Township Authority, Yangon City Development Corporation, with solutions and implementation led by village steering committees including women volunteers from the existing Swan Yi groups. This program is in keeping with The Coca-Cola Company's replenish goal, by 2020.

The SVAs further identified that meteorological data was either difficult to obtain or insufficient to evaluate long-term weather patterns which are linked with water availability in the watershed. As a result of this finding, piezometers and automatic weather stations will be installed at both plants in 2015.

Air quality testing was also completed since the last report. Testing on Stack emission (boilers/generators), ambient air, hazardous air and vehicle emission was completed in Q2 2015 and demonstrated compliance with KORE limits. A plan was agreed to for annual testing on lighting, audiometrics (hearing), boundary noise, and also workplace noise level every two years. The next tests are due in Q4 2015.

In addition, CCPBM is placing energy efficient and 100% HFC free coolers in retailer outlets. CCPBM is also actively lightweighting and reducing packaging and will introduce new lighter weight bottles and smaller closures for Max 2.0 water brand in 2015.

COMMUNITY AND STAKEHOLDER ENGAGEMENT

Stakeholder engagement continues to be an integral part of our work in Myanmar and the Company has continued to participate in multi-stakeholder forums and discussions in Myanmar on topics including responsible investment, transparency, child labor, and workplace rights.

Additional work since the June 2014 report includes:

Tea Shop Study: In addition to our human and workplace audits, we initiated an evaluation of tea shops—venues serving tea and food as well as packaged beverages and snacks—to better understand potential human rights impacts across the value chain, including among customers. These establishments are governed by Myanmar's local law, which cites 13 as the minimum working age. The study indicated the common practice of such young workers relocating from rural areas to the city to work at tea shops. We are actively pursuing opportunities to engage with peers and civil society to reduce this practice including collaborating with the ILO, US government and other governments on the Initiative to Promote Fundamental Labor Rights and Practices in Myanmar. Furthermore, we aim to address root causes through our support of the Swan Yi project (described below), and we are also exploring opportunities for vocational training support for affected young workers. We realise that any holistic solution requires strong government action and a multi-stakeholder approach.

Swan Yi Community Engagement: The Coca-Cola Foundation has partnered with PACT, a respected international non-governmental organization, to empower over 25,000 Myanmar women through village-based banking and microenterprise development. The project, called Swan Yi, operates by gathering 20–25 women in small groups, across hundreds of villages, to undertake financial literacy training, and develop community banks that lend money to fund business start-ups and entrepreneurial efforts. Now in its third year of implementation, 25,409 women have participated in 1,098 groups in eight townships . . . . Nearly all of the women have started saving, with an average of $35 USD per woman and an average loan amount of $137 USD. The total amount of savings by the women is $1,865,797 USD and the total loan value is $6,945,154 USD. Due to the success of the program, we are looking to extend the partnership beyond the original three-year plan and to include an advocacy curriculum based in empowerment principles, to increase participants' confidence on issues such as labor laws, child labor, domestic violence, divorce, and inheritance laws and land ownership as they learn to navigate the changing Myanmar environment.

Although purely philanthropic, the Swan Yi project is consistent with The Coca-Cola Company's existing global commitment to enable the economic empowerment of five million women across its global value chain by 2020 through the 5by20 initiative. Furthermore, by enhancing economic strength of women in villages, we see a potential benefit for the entire family. This, in turn, may reduce the likelihood that their children enter the workforce to augment family income.

Shareholder Due Diligence: Between 2009 and 2012, before entering the market in Myanmar, The Coca-Cola Company conducted comprehensive due diligence based on the information available at that time. In addition to the due diligence that The Coca-Cola Company does as part of its normal acquisition process, including disclosure from the target, the Company conducted a search through independent firms on the reputation, background, and trade sanction risks of the target business and its shareholders and officers. There were no findings that Pinya or its shareholders were deemed Specially Designated Nationals

(SDNs), as identified by the Office of Foreign Assets Control (OFAC). This due diligence was repeated prior to closing in June 2013, as an extra precaution.

In 2015, we completed another level of due diligence after engaging with the NGO Global Witness, which brought to our attention information regarding a Director of Coca-Cola Pinya Beverages Myanmar (CCPBM), Daw Shwe Cynn who is also a shareholder of Pinya Manufacturing. The information from Global Witness showed that the CCPBM Director is also a Director and minority shareholder in Xie Family Company which reportedly operates jade mines in Myanmar.

Our original due diligence was based on the best information available at that time. A number of Directorate of Investment and Company Administration (DICA) records, including the records on Xie Family Company, were only made public in late 2014.

While the jade mining industry is unrelated to our business, we encouraged and facilitated engagement between Daw Shwe Cynn and Global Witness.

Our findings from the additional due diligence conducted in 2015 are in line with our earlier assessment, and we remain confident that our investment is in compliance with applicable laws, and that our local business partners fully understand our expectations regarding human rights, workplace rights, and ethical business conduct.

Part of our long-term investment in and commitment to Myanmar is to continue working with all stakeholders—including government, business and civil society—to encourage transparency and foster greater respect for human rights in Myanmar.

SECURITY PROVIDERS

As outlined in the previous reports, the only security utilized in Company operations in Myanmar is at the plant sites and all security guards are full-time employees. No third-party security firm is currently or will be utilized in the near future. The role of security personnel is to safeguard the facility as well as the workers. Currently TCCC is not operating in known zones of conflict in Myanmar and, as such, the role of security employees is limited.

As part of our human and workplace rights assessments, third-party auditors verify that security personnel employed by the Company do not infringe on the privacy and dignity of employees or conduct themselves in a way that is intimidating, threatening, or which oversteps their authority. The assessment reviews whether policies and procedures are in place to ensure security guards undergo criminal background checks, receive training on the use of force, and that their duties are limited to protecting workers, the facility, and equipment only. The human and workplace rights assessments also review whether security workers are provided the same treatment and benefits as other Company employees. No non-compliances related to security guards were identified.

PROPERTY ACQUISITION

In 2013, The Coca-Cola Company announced a new set of commitments to protect the land rights of farmers and communities . . . As part of these commitments, The Coca-Cola Company conducted a number of country level assessments which focused, in part, on land rights. Although focused on the top sugar- producing regions, the principles are upheld throughout the system.

No land acquisition has been made since the June 30th, 2014 report submission. The Company continues identifying potential areas for a new plant. Once these areas have been identified, a list of possible plant sites will be developed and land rights will be an important component of the plant siting due diligence process. One of the tools used in the process will be the Plant Siting Checklist, one of seven such checklists published on our website, which is used internally as an early issue identification tool.

In addition, suppliers in Myanmar undergoing a Supplier Guiding Principles audit will be assessed against the land rights provisions, including Free, Prior, and Informed Consent of any land acquisition as outlined in our issue guidance on land rights.

. . . .

MILITARY CONTACT

There have been no meetings or communications by any representative of TCCC with the armed forces of Myanmar or other armed groups related to our investment in Myanmar. Furthermore, no third parties have been contracted to contact [the] military. This has and will continue to be our consistent practice.

. . . .

Notes and Questions

Coca-Cola's Myanmar investment report lists various initiatives aimed at protecting human rights, combatting corruption, protecting the environment, and improving work conditions. What is Coca-Cola Myanmar's level of enterprise identity?

II. Program Components

As discussed previously, the ethics program proposed by the BEM is built around several components that closely resemble the hallmarks of an effective FCPA compliance program described in the FCPA Guide. This does not mean that the ethics program operates separately from the compliance program. Rather, there is a single compliance and ethics program whose components meet the criteria set forth in both the FCPA Guide and the BEM.

A. The Ethics Code of Conduct

The ethics code of conduct encapsulates the RBE's core purpose and values and guides their actualization. The BEM stresses that "[t]he process for developing a code of conduct is as important as the code itself."[8] The code must be "comprehensive enough to give guidance on all important matters to employees and agents . . . [and] have had enough participative feedback from internal stakeholders [so] that they will recognize it as their own, support it, and be willing to live by it."[9] It must also "describe external stakeholder expectations well enough that they will recognize the enterprise as a contributing member of the community."[10]

> Organizational culture is shaped by the organization's origin and history as well as the values, norms, and attitudes of its owners, managers, and other stakeholders. It is a bundle of assumptions about the way the world works and the beliefs, values, symbols, languages, rituals, principles, rules, and practices that consciously or unconsciously drive the thoughts, feelings, and actions of the enterprise and its stakeholders.
>
> —*BEM*[7]

Business Ethics: A Manual for Managing a Responsible Business Enterprise in Emerging Market Economies[11]

CODE OF CONDUCT

A code of conduct is often the primary means by which management gives guidance to its employees and agents as to what is expected of them by way of business conduct. Indeed, among large enterprises globally, most now have some form of code of conduct.

A code demonstrates management's commitment to meeting all applicable industry practices and government regulations. Its target audience is the enterprise as a whole. Other, more specific policies and procedures will be directed at specific functions, such as procurement or contracting.

A code of conduct addresses minimum standards of conduct and procedures to reduce the enterprise's risk of liability and damage to its reputation. A code of conduct also goes beyond these minimums to guide employees and agents toward enhancing the enterprise's reputation and adding genuine value to its community.

. . . .

As part of a business ethics program . . . a code is a central component of a process by which the enterprise engages its stakeholders, both internal and external. In recent years, the process of formulating codes of conduct has

---

7. BEM, *supra* note 1, at 66.
8. *Id.* at 114.
9. *Id.*
10. *Id.*
11. *Id.* at 109–16.

become more interactive and inclusive. Increasingly, codes are an essential part of an ongoing dialogue designed to shape programs. Indeed, a senior official at Royal Dutch/Shell has declared:

> Shell is increasingly focusing on dialogue, and we have found many NGOs who are willing to enter into debate with us. Discussion based on a broad framework of principles offers a constructive atmosphere for cooperation—and for the compromise that is sometimes necessary in the face of real-life ambiguities.

An enterprise should carefully examine its relevant context when deciding on the scope of its code of conduct. It should consider the priorities of its community and external stakeholders; the state of decrees, laws, and regulations; and industry standards. It should also show respect for national and organizational culture.

Compliance with the Law

When designing a business ethics program, an enterprise must ensure that it complies with all laws and regulations that govern its area of commerce: local, foreign, and international. The codes themselves tend not to set forth the details of the law. However, they will set the general policy of complying with all laws, and they may refer to laws that have specific application to the enterprise's business conduct such as corporate governance, workplace practices, and relationships with government officials. Where more detail is required, these matters will typically be treated in policies and procedures documents. Working closely with legal counsel, an RBE will incorporate changes and amendments to the law and regulations into its business ethics program on a regular basis.

. . . .

Compliance with Industry Standards

An RBE is often a member of an industry as well as a community. Owners and managers take into account industry-specific issues and standards and procedures. In doing so, they should strive to achieve the highest standards of compliance in their industry. Improved industry standards increase transparency and trust in the marketplace, and they enhance the reputation of the industry as a whole. . . .

Protection of the Environment

A code of conduct should address the enterprise's standards, procedures, and expectations regarding the environment. Governments, local communities, NGOs, and international institutions are increasingly using their influence to promote sound environmental practices by business.

A code should include a statement that the enterprise will abide by both local and international laws and regulations designed to protect the environment. It should address how the business balances production objectives with environmental protection in general. In more detailed standards, procedures, and expectations, the enterprise might discuss how to reduce waste products, how to avoid polluting air and water, and how to manage and report chemical use and disposal.

. . . .

Respect for Cultural Norms

A code of conduct should demonstrate respect for the cultural norms of the society in which the enterprise operates—especially if it is a transnational enterprise. Employees and agents bring their beliefs, values, and cultural norms to the job. Each society has cultural practices that are unique, including practice of religion, gender relations, and power relationships in the workplace. An RBE is sensitive to these practices and ensures that its business ethics program takes them into consideration without sacrificing its core beliefs. Implementing and enforcing a code of conduct that does not take these factors into consideration may be seen as unfair and may lead to confusion and frustration.

A number of responsible business conduct issues are unusually culturally sensitive: dealing with conflicts of interest, accepting and giving gifts and gratuities, making facilitation payments, hiring relatives and friends, seeking advice, and reporting misconduct. Reporting misconduct, in particular, touches on deeply held cultural values and even relatively recent histories . . . .

A best practice for dealing with these cultural nuances is to require regional divisions of an enterprise to formulate local policies and to submit them for approval. Provided that the local policy reflects the spirit of the general policy and is applied consistently, regional policies can be effective ways to address cultural differences. Note, however, that the general rule should apply unless a specific local policy has been proposed and approved. An employee or agent should not be able to claim a regional difference without an approved local policy in place.

Guidelines for Developing a Code

The process for developing a code of conduct is as important as the code itself. Engaging stakeholders, demonstrating management commitment, and honoring core beliefs will lead to a clear statement of what the enterprise values. Moreover, the process is an important step toward reinforcing the desired aspects of organizational culture.

At the end of the process, the code must be comprehensive enough to give guidance on all important matters to employees and agents. It must have had enough participative feedback from internal stakeholders—especially the owners, managers, and workers—that they will recognize it as their own, support it, and be willing to live by it. It must describe external stakeholder expectations well enough that they will recognize the enterprise as a contributing member of the community.

. . . .

A code of conduct should be a practical, easily accessible document. It should be written in plain language, avoiding technical or legal terms. It should be available in the languages key stakeholders understand.

Aspirational versus Obligatory Provisions

Some authors distinguish between code provisions that are aspirational and those that are obligatory. Aspirational provisions are said to be ones that employees and agents are to strive for but for which they will not be held accountable. Obligatory provisions are said to be ones for which employees and agents can be held accountable and ones that will result in punishment if violated.

. . . .

For the most specific standards—rules—good judgment seldom leads one to violate a rule. When rules are violated, punishment is appropriate since a clear intention to violate rules exists. For more general provisions such as values or principles, good judgment is still required, and it makes little sense to describe such provisions as unenforceable. . . .

Adaptations, Updates, and Improvements to the Code

Though a code of conduct is a fundamental document, it is not static. To be effective, it must anticipate the guidance that employees and agents will need to deal appropriately with the challenges they face. Laws and regulations change. Stakeholder expectations change as well. Through commerce with enterprises from different markets, businesses become exposed to new values and beliefs that can affect the way employees view the enterprise and markets. All these tend to create new gray areas for employees.

An RBE should plan in the code itself to monitor closely changes in its relevant context, organizational culture, and stakeholder expectations and to adapt, update, and improve the code accordingly. The RBE must be able to react quickly to changes that affect the enterprise, its markets, and its communities. It must adapt its code to reflect its relationships with new suppliers, service providers, partners, competitors, and markets.

Code Formats

An author who has tracked the trends in drafting codes of conduct has found that most codes apply one or more of three basic formats: (a) compliance codes—specific statements giving guidance and prohibiting certain kinds of conduct; (b) corporate credos—broad general statements of corporate commitments to constituencies, values, and objectives; and (c) management philosophy statements—formal enunciations of the company or CEO's way of doing business.

. . . .

Typical Code of Conduct Provisions[12]

The best way to think about what standards, procedures, and expectations to put in a code of conduct is to try to anticipate, from the points of view of stakeholders, the tough decisions that employees and agents might face. With this

---

12. *Id.* at 117–23.

approach in mind, consider including the items described below. Examples of how some enterprises addressed certain issues are also included. . . .

INTRODUCTORY MATERIALS

What materials should be included? And why? Introductory materials are highly dependent on the situation, needs, and culture of the enterprise. They should begin with a declaration of the enterprise's core beliefs, examples of which were described earlier. An advisable provision to include is a disclaimer. . . . Disclaimers are recommended because some courts have treated similar documents as promises on which stakeholders may justifiably rely.

OWNERS

What relationships and responsibilities to its owners should the enterprise assume? And why? Consider the following:

- Maximizing shareholder value
- Minimizing business risk
- Using business resources prudently
- Engaging in legal and ethical behavior
- Preventing insider trading
- Being responsible to community and environment

CUSTOMERS OR CONSUMERS

What relationship and responsibilities to its customers should the enterprise assume? And why? Here are some examples:

- Providing quality, safe goods, and services
- Representing products or services
- Communicating clearly so that there is no misunderstanding
- Protecting confidential information
- Preventing bribes and kickbacks
- Regulating gifts and entertainment
- Including government customer provisions
- Including foreign government customer provisions
- Ensuring accurate billing procedures
- Safeguarding property of others
- Preventing the disparagement of competitors
- Ensuring fair competition
- Acquiring marketing data properly and legally

EMPLOYEES AND THE ENTERPRISE

What relationships and responsibilities to its employees should an enterprise assume? What do the employees owe the enterprise? And why? Issues include these:

- Promoting respect for one another
- Promoting equal opportunity and anti-harassment

- Creating a hassle-free environment
- Respecting right to privacy
- Promoting workplace health and safety
- Maintaining skills and qualifications
- Preventing substance abuse
- Preventing workplace violence
- Regulating use of company funds
- Regulating company e-mail and computer use
- Preventing conflicts of interest
- Regulating outside business activities
- Regulating gifts and entertainment
- Regulating collective bargaining
- Promoting human rights
- Excluding child labor
- Promoting business with the company
- Regulating employment outside the company
- Encouraging self-development and lifelong learning
- Regulating the hire of closely related people
- Ensuring accurate books and records
- Retaining records

PARTNERS, SUPPLIERS, AND SERVICE PROVIDERS

What relationship and responsibilities to its partners, suppliers, and service providers should the enterprise assume? And why? Consider these issues:

- Treating all suppliers fairly
- Regulating the acceptance or offer of gifts and gratuities
- Respecting intellectual property of others
- Protecting proprietary data of others
- Using software for its intended purposes
- Requiring consultants and suppliers to act legally and ethically

COMPETITORS

What do we owe our competitors? And why? Issues include:

- Dealing fairly with competitors
- Winning on product and service merits
- Discouraging comparisons with and disparagement of competitors
- Prohibiting inducement of others to break binding contracts with competitors
- Discouraging the discussion of pricing, costing, marketing, or product plans with competition
- Prohibiting illegal or unethical methods to gather competitive information
- Preventing unfair competition (antitrust)
- Promoting adherence to principles of free competition

COMMUNITY, GOVERNMENT, AND THE ENVIRONMENT

What relationship and responsibilities to its communities, governments, and the environment should the enterprise assume? And why?

- Obeying both the letter and the spirit of law
- Promoting good competitor relations
- Complying with local laws and customs
- Promoting anticorruption practices
- Excluding foreign corrupt practices
- Regulating political contributions
- Regulating political activity
- Including indigenous peoples
- Promoting sustainable development
- Complying with anti-money-laundering measures
- Complying with anti-boycott laws
- Complying with import-export laws
- Voluntarily disclosing violations
- Cooperating with authorities
- Promoting charitable contributions
- Encouraging employee volunteer work
- Protecting the environment

BUSINESS ETHICS PROGRAM

A business ethic program should cover these issues:

- Ethics and compliance structure and systems
- Responsibility of managers and supervisors
- Need to avoid even the appearance of impropriety
- Monitoring and auditing practices
- Employees' duty to report violations
- Failure to comply
- Failure to detect misconduct
- Methods to seek advice and report misconduct
- Policy concerning false reports
- Enterprise response to reports
- Policy for customer, supplier, and contact agents
- Confidentiality and anonymity policy
- Non-retaliation policy
- Policy for employee misconduct
- Policy for rewarding ethical behavior
- Records retention
- Media contact
- Individual accountability
- Obligation to sign acknowledgment

BUSINESS ETHICS PROGRAM RESOURCES

Resources may include these:
- Ethical decision-making model
- Case studies and examples
- Telephone contact numbers

B. Ethics Program Infrastructure (Autonomy, Oversight, Resources)

Like the third Hallmark of the FCPA Guide—"oversight, autonomy and resources"—the BEM requires that the ethics program be autonomous from operations, overseen by a member or committee of the board of directors and given adequate resources.[13]

Business Ethics: A Manual for Managing a Responsible Business Enterprise in Emerging Market Economies[14]

Determining Systems of Authority, Responsibility, and Accountability

Support for a business ethics program must start at the top of an enterprise. The following general elements of leadership are typically found in successful programs:
- The owners or owner representatives ensure that the program provides them with adequate information regarding enterprise performance.
- The owners and managers set a tone of support for responsible business conduct.
- A high-level person is responsible for the business ethics program.

. . . .

INFRASTRUCTURE FOR OWNER REPRESENTATIVES

A business ethics program provides an information and reporting system for both the owners and the managers. An emerging corporate governance standard is that owner representatives are responsible for ensuring that they receive the information they need to prevent and detect wrongdoing. They may be held individually liable for losses caused by noncompliance with applicable legal standards. While delegating authority to the chief executive officer (CEO) to conduct day-to-day operations, an RBE's board of directors must provide for systematic and rigorous monitoring of enterprise performance through an information and reporting system. Boards often delegate the authority to monitor enterprise performance to a committee, sometimes called an audit committee,

---

13. *See id.* at 43–45.
14. *Id.* at 132–44.

less often a responsible business conduct committee. Delegation of authority, however, does not relieve the board as a whole of its responsibility. It is important that the audit committee have unrestricted access to necessary records and personnel. . . .

An audit committee is usually responsible for arranging for competent independent auditing. In this regard, it should be alert to any conflicts of interest that potential auditors might have, including conflicts stemming from their role as consultants.

Where managers sit on a board, an emerging best practice is for the audit committee to be composed wholly or predominantly of independent directors. If committee members are managers, or are closely allied with managers, the board may be unable to represent the owners without bias in favor of management. This situation is an inherent conflict of interest. Moreover, the confidence of employees and agents to seek advice and report concerns may be compromised for fear of retribution.

HIGH-LEVEL RESPONSIBILITY

A first step toward an effective business ethics program is to assign responsibility for its operation to a specific individual or group of people [called] a responsible officer. A responsible officer may be an individual, a committee, or an individual supported by a committee. An RBE should avoid creating a situation in which no one is responsible because everyone is responsible. In the pressures of day-to-day operations, it is easy for employees and agents to focus on immediate tasks and goals. A single person needs to be tasked with ensuring that responsible business conduct becomes the norm at the enterprise.

For the business ethics program to be effective, the responsible officer, whether an individual or a group, should have a number of basic characteristics:

- Be at a high level of responsibility in the organization
- Have unrestricted access to the CEO and the board, or a designated board committee
- Have a high degree of trust and respect from senior management
- Have access to the resources necessary to ensure that the organization has an effective program
- Be given incentives and rewarded for proactively carrying out the roles and responsibilities of the office
- Have the skills to operate effectively with the media, public forums, government agencies, and the legal process

It is important that the person or group assigned responsibility for the business ethics program be at a high enough level to demonstrate the owners' and managers' commitment to the program. . . . This requires that the person or group have substantial control over the enterprise or a substantial role in making policy.

The responsible officer has three major objectives:

1. Ensuring that the enterprise establishes adequate standards and procedures to guide employees and agents and to create reasonable stakeholder expectations
2. Ensuring that these standards and expectations are institutionalized and enforced within the enterprise
3. Evaluating and reporting on the enterprise's performance against these standards, procedures, and expectations

The reporting relationships of the responsible officer are critical. One key way in which owners and managers demonstrate support for a business ethics program is to demand regular reports on performance. Access of the responsible officer to the board and CEO serves a number of functions: it provides greater opportunity for responsible business conduct to be given due attention; it reinforces the authority and credibility of the responsible officer; and it provides resources to high-level decision-makers for guidance and support in dealing with difficult issues.

The responsible officer function may be served from any number of positions: an executive, a committee, an individual in charge of a business unit or major function, or someone with a substantial ownership interest. The position may be full-time or part-time, depending on the enterprise.

High-level responsibility may also be assigned for specific areas of ethics, compliance, and social responsibility. For example, in enterprises such as hospitals, one person may be responsible for the organizational ethics program and a medical professional may be assigned responsibility for the biomedical ethics program. In an enterprise that does a lot of government contracting, a high-level person may be assigned to monitor that specific function.

In a highly regulated enterprise, legal demands may be such that a compliance officer should be appointed to deal only with compliance issues, in coordination with the ethics and social responsibility functions. This may be the case, for example, in an economy where the enterprise must be especially diligent against corruption. In another enterprise, issues of responsibility to external stakeholders may be so demanding that a social responsibility officer should be appointed to deal with those issues, in close coordination with the responsible business conduct functions. This may be the case, for example, in an economy where environmental issues or relations with indigenous tribes are common.

BUSINESS ETHICS OFFICER

Independent of high-level responsibility for the business ethics program, a number of specific business ethics staff functions must be accomplished for the program to be effective. It is critical that a specific individual or individuals be assigned responsibility for these functions. Responsibilities for reporting to the owners (or their representatives) are typically retained by the responsible officer. However, a best practice is for both the responsible officer and the business ethics officer to have access to the CEO and board.

Roles and Responsibility of the Business Ethics Officer

The business ethics officer is the staff officer responsible for the day-to-day operations of the business ethics program. Two practitioners have identified the following 12 functions of a business ethics officer:

1. Coordinate development and implementation of the business ethics program.
2. Establish and chair a business ethics council representing all levels of the enterprise.
3. Develop and maintain standards of conduct and procedures, as well as related policies, which will guide employees and agents and will foster reasonable stakeholder expectations.
4. Establish internal reporting channels, including, but not limited to, a help line that employees and agents may use to seek advice and report concerns without fear of retribution.
5. Establish or coordinate monitoring controls and measures to ensure that correct processes are established and followed.
6. Implement or coordinate enterprise-wide communication and training programs to ensure that all employees, agents, and other stakeholders are educated on the standards, procedures, and reasonable stakeholder expectations.
7. Coordinate or conduct inquiries and investigations to ensure proper follow-up on reports and resolution.
8. Delegate authority to conduct appropriate inquiries and investigations . . . when necessary.
9. Monitor and evaluate the business ethics program for periodic modifications when needed.
10. Maintain a working knowledge of relevant issues, laws, regulations, and emerging standards of ethics, compliance, and responsibility through periodicals, seminars, training programs, and peer contact, including membership in professional associations.
11. Respond appropriately when a violation of these standards is uncovered, including making a direct report to the board or external agency if a violation of law or regulation is involved.
12. Report quarterly to the appropriate board committees on the status of the business ethics program, report to the CEO or appropriate board committees whenever necessary, and report to stakeholders annually.

Location and Centralization of Business Ethics Offices

The functions of the business ethics officer may be performed by one ethics officer out of a central location or may be decentralized. For example, the business ethics officer may be located at headquarters, or each plant may have a business ethics officer. The significant differences relate to responsibility and reporting. In a decentralized program, the local business ethics officer will be personally responsible for the conduct of the program at the local level and be required—and entitled—to report to the CEO and board on issues of responsible business conduct. He or she may also have more responsibility for training and investigations.

The advantages of centralization include a more consistent message, economies of scale in production and distribution, more effective monitoring of the program, and more uniform and efficient enforcement. Advantages of a more decentralized approach include messages that are more tailored to local circumstances, more employee involvement, and more nuanced and inclusive decision-making.

Business Ethics Officer Qualifications

. . . .

In terms of their operational experience, staff members from departments such as general business, finance, internal audit, and human resources tend to be tapped to be business ethics officers. Appointing a lawyer as business ethics officer, especially where legal compliance is a significant program element, often leads to responsible business conduct being treated as simply an extension of the legal function. However, as two lawyers write, "Compliance is not just another legal matter. It is a management responsibility demanding a full range of management resources and skills, and the exercise of those in the day-to-day management of the business."

BUSINESS ETHICS COUNCIL

The business ethics council serves principally as an adviser on setting policy, resolving issues, and monitoring the business ethics program. In larger enterprises, it often consists of representatives of executive management, including finance, general counsel, human resources, internal audit, quality, and public affairs. It is typically chaired by either the responsible officer or the business ethics officer. It is advisable that all levels of the enterprise be represented so that the council's advice fully reflects the enterprise as a whole. Wider participation may also contribute to greater employee acceptance of the program and its message.

A business ethics council should meet on a regular basis, perhaps monthly or quarterly. It raises issues of concern in the enterprise, reviews disposition of help-line requests for advice or reports of concerns, previews training materials, and recommends policy changes or program modifications. It meets on call when there are urgent matters to address, such as unforeseen conduct issues or a compliance violation that may require disclosure to government agencies.

If the business ethics officer is highly respected and has an extensive network of managers and specialists that he or she can turn to for advice, a business ethics council may not be especially valuable. The risk of not having such a council, however, is that the business ethics program lacks the formal acknowledgment that input from all levels of the enterprise is important to management. Also, the lack of a council tends to identify the business ethics program with one person, which may require restructuring the business ethics program when he or she leaves the post.

PROFESSIONAL ETHICS COUNCIL

The business ethics council is concerned with standards of conduct that affect the RBE as a whole. In many enterprises, well-developed bodies of professional ethics standards guide day-to-day operations. For example, biomedical ethics guide health care providers, especially physicians and nurses. Other examples include legal, engineering, accounting, and environmental ethics, but there are many others, including specific social responsibility issues.

In each of these areas, significant issues will arise that require the same sort of consultation and advice process that the business ethics council provides on more general issues. To address these more specific issues, an RBE might establish a professional ethics council. For example, biomedical ethics is such a significant part of hospital operations that hospitals often have a separate biomedical ethics council, which reports directly to senior management on biomedical issues.

If an enterprise wants to contribute to the welfare of its community as a whole, beyond its essential function as a business, it might appoint a community relations committee. Such a committee might identify specific community needs not met by government or civil society, coordinate with NGOs, and organize voluntary employee work projects. It would usually coordinate closely with the public affairs function to further enhance the reputation of the enterprise.

BUSINESS CONDUCT REPRESENTATIVES

An RBE must also determine how best to engage its employees and agents in its business ethics program. If the enterprise is large or complex, local personnel can be appointed to serve as advisers to local managers, employees, and agents and as channels for communication back to a central business ethics office. An SME will generally not make formal appointments of business conduct representatives at individual units since the responsible officer and business ethics officer will generally be able to give each unit adequate attention.

Business conduct representatives generally report directly to both the senior manager at the location and the business ethics officer. They advise managers and other employees on standards, policies, procedures, and the business ethics program as a whole. They facilitate the functions of responsible business conduct at the local unit, such as training; monitoring, auditing, and investigating; providing employee incentives and discipline; and evaluating the program. They are responsible for coordinating with other functions at the local level such as legal; environment, health, and safety; quality management; and human resources.

Business conduct representatives must be familiar with enterprise standards, procedures, and expectations and all communications channels. They must be able to give unbiased advice that will not interfere with the conduct of their primary duties. For this reason, they should not be appointed from the human resources, procurement, or legal units of the enterprise, which are often either the source of the issue or the unit responsible for resolving the issue.

RELATED EXECUTIVE AND DEPARTMENT FUNCTIONS

The business ethics officer is responsible for coordinating the enterprise's ethics, compliance, and social responsibility programs. This task requires that the business ethics program be integrated well with other enterprise functions.

The chief financial officer, for example, is responsible for maintaining the enterprise's financial integrity, including all of its financial practices, books, and records. He or she will also have significant influence in the allocation of resources for business ethics infrastructure, including training.

An enterprise's internal auditor is closely involved in the enterprise's internal controls and processes. (LCEs will often have an audit department.) The internal auditor will be able to provide significant support to the business ethics officer by providing advice on internal controls and processes and by conducting inquiries and investigations.

The business ethics officer will often turn to the chief legal officer for advice on legal requirements of a compliance program, due process requirements of inquiries and investigations, legal risk analysis, and possible program outcomes.

In the minds of many employees, when one speaks of ethics one speaks of "fairness." Many ethics issues, therefore, involve human resources issues: assignments, compensation and benefits, discipline, employee assistance, and promotions. The business ethics officer will need to recognize human resources issues and work with human resources personnel to resolve them.

Other enterprise functions that the business ethics officer will work with closely are training, education, and development; environment, health, and safety; security; quality management; and operations and administration in general.

INDIVIDUAL RESPONSIBILITY

To be a truly responsible business, the enterprise must articulate the responsibilities of all of its employees and agents in a positive, constructive manner. For owners, managers, and supervisors, this effort may involve complete awareness of the business ethics program itself. Owners, managers, and supervisors must demonstrate commitment to the program in all that they say and do. They are responsible for maintaining an organizational climate in which pressures to violate standards are minimized and incentives to achieve enterprise goals and objectives, pursue the enterprise purpose, and meet reasonable stakeholder expectations are high. Managers and supervisors may be required to certify regularly that they have no conflicts of interest and that they—and those they manage—are following the business ethics program.

For all employees and agents, their specific responsibilities under the business ethics program may require familiarizing themselves with the standards, certifying receipt of the code and compliance with code requirements, attending scheduled training, participating in feedback sessions and investigations, and seeking advice and reporting concerns. They may also be charged with contributing to an organizational climate in which all employees can work together to achieve the enterprise's purposes.

Hypothetical: Fusing the Compliance and Ethics Programs

Bendigo, Inc. ("Bendigo") is a U.S.-based multinational enterprise engaged in the manufacture and sale of automotive parts. Bendigo has 100,000 employees and operates through thirty subsidiaries around the world. It has a robust compliance program, overseen by the audit committee of the board of directors, with three thousand dedicated compliance employees led by the CCO. Bendigo's compliance program has a budget of $75 million.

Bendigo faces the following ethical issues in its global operations:

- Its patented process produces a toxic byproduct, which is only regulated in OECD member states.
- Three of its plants in South America are attempting to unionize the workforce, with a demand for equal wages worldwide.

Bendigo intends to create an ethics program pursuant to guidance provided by the FSGO and the BEM.

1) Should the ethics program be overseen by the audit committee of the board of directors?
2) Should the CCO also act as the business ethics officer?
3) Explain the views of at least two sides for each of Bendigo's ethical dilemmas, and offer some potential solutions. Could your suggestions be integrated into an existing compliance program, or would they require a new, standalone ethics infrastructure?

C. Ethics Training

Business Ethics: A Manual for Managing a Responsible Business Enterprise in Emerging Market Economies[15]

. . . Designing a training program requires the same attention to objectives and outcomes as does the design of the business ethics program as a whole. It requires attention to the situation, resources available, activities and participants, target audiences, outputs, and expected outcomes. Without this attention to detail, neither the business ethics program nor the communications program or training program has any criteria for evaluation. In short, it is not clear to all what success looks like.

Demonstrating Management Commitment

Few decisions symbolize management's commitment to its business ethics program more than devoting time, on a regular basis, to training in responsible

---

15. *Id.* at 155–65.

business conduct. Beyond the skills, knowledge, and understanding developed through such training, the mere fact that management dedicates valuable employee time to such training goes a long way toward demonstrating that it is serious about its standards, procedures, and expectations becoming part of the organizational culture—instead of just a collection of policies sitting on a shelf.

Rescheduling busy day-to-day operations to accommodate regular employee training also conveys an important message from managers and supervisors to their workers. Where training is treated as an integral part of the enterprise, employees tend to value it more than where training is treated as an irritant or necessary evil.

Reinforcing Core Beliefs and Organizational Culture

Training should be designed as an essential link between the enterprise's core beliefs, the business ethics program, and the expected program outcomes. . . .

The training program should reflect the organizational culture of the enterprise. The enterprise needs to project the expected behavior through the training program. Training should also contribute to the expected outcomes of the business ethics program. If an expected program outcome, for example, is that employees come to recognize issues of responsible business conduct more readily and talk about them in terms of enterprise core beliefs, standards, and procedures, then training composed primarily of lectures will not succeed. Where employees are not used to being asked how they would address important issues, let alone raise them, training will need to demonstrate how it is done—and engage the employees as their comfort level increases.

Designing the Program

Training program objectives depend on relevant context, organizational culture, goals and objectives, and expected outcomes for the business ethics program as a whole. . . . The training program should be based on enterprise core beliefs. It must reflect the pressures of the enterprise's context and its organizational culture. Its primary objective is to make a positive contribution toward achieving expected program outcomes.

At a minimum, training sessions should require employees to become familiar with applicable laws and regulations, as well as with the enterprise's procedures for reporting and investigating concerns about responsible business conduct. The training should enhance the ethical awareness of employees and should uncover ethical issues and concerns that relate to their needs as well as those of the enterprise. It should include an examination of the criteria for ethical decision-making. . . .

. . . .

All participants should leave the training program confident that they know what the enterprise expects of them and what they can expect from the enterprise in turn. They should be able to recognize issues of responsible business conduct and have the confidence—and courage—to make the right decision, explain that decision to the appropriate people, and act accordingly. They should understand how the business ethics program relates to strategic issues for the RBE as a whole.

For a training program to contribute to expected outcomes, it requires a heavy emphasis on dialogue and decision-making about issues of responsible business conduct. Beyond developing listening and feedback skills and good judgment in enterprise members, the training program must convey management's sincere desire to know whether its standards and procedures are being followed and whether its stakeholder expectations are being met. The program must also convey management's commitment to support employees and other stakeholders who seek advice and report concerns. This task requires not only encouraging individuals who are inclined to come forward but also explaining to those who do not why their silence is detrimental to enterprise performance.

A typical expected outcome is that employees and agents will use good judgment in addressing issues of responsible business conduct. For the RBE, ethical decision-making is a form of action learning. It is a tool that employees and agents use to learn how to pursue the purpose of the enterprise and meet the reasonable expectations of stakeholders. At a minimum, management might provide a decision-making process that, in a specific incident, enables its employees and agents:

- To define the issues of ethics, compliance, and responsibility
- To demonstrate a grasp of all relevant and material facts, including the stakeholders involved and their interests
- To point to the applicable standards, procedures, and expectations, including decrees, laws, and regulations
- To describe the range of options available
- To explain why, based on these considerations, they made a particular choice or acted in a particular manner

Many ethics and policy decision-making models are available on the Internet. They range from simple, five-step models to multiphase frameworks that include decision criteria. The better models are based on well-developed skills in critical thinking. . . .

A long-term expected program outcome should be an organizational culture in which owners and managers have the information they need to make intelligent decisions for the enterprise. To achieve this, employees must leave training believing that they will not be punished for bringing bad news to management.

Participants must also leave training firmly convinced that, should they make a mistake, they will not be punished if they can demonstrate that they followed the enterprise decision-making process. Employees or agents should not be punished for making a mistake if they can demonstrate that they:

- Recognized the issue
- Had a reasonable grasp of the relevant facts
- Considered enterprise standards, procedures, and expectations
- Explored the range of options available
- Could justify the choice they made or action they took

DELIVERING THE TRAINING PROGRAM

A number of principles characterize effective training programs on responsible business conduct. First, a program should project the core beliefs of the enterprise—not just teach them. Second, owners and managers should be involved in the training in significant, visible ways. Third, the program should recognize the personal values of individual stakeholders but not rely on them. Fourth, the program should be comprehensive, not limited to specific training in responsible business conduct. Finally, it should include action planning and follow-up to reinforce the lessons learned.

Reflecting Core Beliefs

Where expected program objectives include issue recognition, dialogue, and ethical decision-making, the training program should develop those skills and provide the knowledge necessary to apply them. For adults, who tend to learn best while doing, the best training method is often a balance of lectures—to introduce or review standards, procedures, and expectations—and facilitated case studies.

In developing those skills and passing on this knowledge, the program needs to project the core beliefs of the enterprise and the expected program outcomes. Abstract standards, procedures, and expectations take on meaning for employees when relayed in terms of the enterprise's core beliefs. It is one thing to discuss rules governing bribery and corruption because they are in the code of conduct. It is another thing to tell stories about how those rules are applied in practice.

Involving Owners and Managers

Because all training must reflect the relevant context and organizational culture of the enterprise, the precise way to involve owners and managers cannot be specified. A key requirement is that stakeholders, especially employees, believe that management fully supports the training.

Management involvement takes many forms. Some enterprises use cascade training, in which the CEO trains his or her direct subordinates. They, in turn, train those who report to them and so on down the chain of management until supervisors train their workers. This method has the advantage of actively involving managers, which tends to demonstrate commitment. A disadvantage may be that the presence of managers may stifle active involvement of the employees when candid discussion of issues is in order or when the culture of the enterprise is to remain silent on important issues.

Another option is a video of the CEO introducing the training by declaring his or her personal commitment to the training program. Owners and managers may also visit the training, observe it, or be available to answer questions as they arise during the course of the program. In any event, employees are unlikely to value training that management does not appear to support.

Recognizing Personal Values

One of the controversies surrounding training in responsible business conduct is whether one can—or should—teach ethics to adults. It is unlikely that ethics training will change the outlook of most employees. Personal values are usually set in youth—families, schools, churches, and peers subtly guide children as they grow to adulthood. But the purpose of business ethics training is not so much to change adults as it is to support them, admonish them, or reinforce their understanding of management's commitment to enforcing its standards, procedures, and expectations.

Trainers can be confident that what adults bring with them to the enterprise does not include knowledge of enterprise standards, procedures, and expectations. Moreover, it is unlikely that most employees—including owners and managers—are skilled at making the best choice among options where the problem involves complex pressures arising from the relevant context. For some employees and agents, no amount of training is going to change them. Such cases are less a matter of training than of having the right people performing the right tasks . . . .

For the training to be effective, it must appeal to what motivates the participants. The ideal situation permits an appeal to a participant's sense of community. Where participants feel that they share a purpose, values, and a vision of a desired future, trainers may stress responsibilities to stakeholders. But more often, participants respond to a sense of urgency. This sense can be created by recounting stories about what happened when employees and agents violated standards—and the impact on both the enterprise and the individuals involved.

One cost-effective way of creating a sense of urgency is to develop a "parade of horribles" by collecting headlines of powerful enterprises and individuals who have been prosecuted or held liable for misconduct. "The Bigger They Are, the Harder They Fall," said the headline of one recent working paper, which estimated that "the loss of confidence following the collapse of Enron and WorldCom will cost the U.S. economy $37 billion to $42 billion" in reduced gross domestic product. Since these two enterprises, Enron and WorldCom, were accused of major accounting fraud, their stock values have dropped to a fraction of their former values, and senior executives have been indicted. Few responsible business conduct trainers now miss an opportunity to refer to Enron to demonstrate what can happen if managers act irresponsibly—what has come to be known as the "Enron Effect."

Making Training Comprehensive

Training should take place at all levels of the enterprise. From senior managers and owners to workers on the shop floor, every employee and agent should receive training in responsible business conduct specific to his or her level of responsibility. All employees and agents should review enterprise core beliefs, standards, procedures, and expectations, including policies relating to their individual responsibilities.

Managers and supervisors need additional training to reflect their roles and responsibilities as integral parts of the business ethics program. They may need to gain understanding of the issues that affect their performance such as conflicts of interest, anticorruption measures, or emerging global standards. In particular, they must understand that enterprise standards, procedures, and expectations are never to be violated to meet individual and enterprise performance objectives. They must fully appreciate their roles and responsibilities in nurturing an organizational culture in which employees and agents can seek advice and report concerns so that management has the information it needs to guide the enterprise. Finally, they must learn not to fear evaluation of their units' performance, if the enterprise is to learn from experience.

Agents, including consultants, sales agents, brokers, partners, franchisees, and closely allied suppliers and service providers, should be exposed to the enterprise core beliefs; applicable standards, procedures, and expectations; and specific policies relating to their roles and responsibilities.

Training should address pursuing the enterprise's purpose and meeting stakeholder expectations. A training program begins with basic employee recruiting materials and procedures, and never truly ends. Though the emphasis of a business ethics program is on issues of ethics, compliance, and social responsibility, this focus is primarily on reinforcing an enterprise-wide sense of responsibility to the enterprise and its stakeholders in pursuit of the enterprise's purpose.

For example, concerns such as customer service, quality management, fair dealing with suppliers and service providers, environmental protection, proper relationships with government officials, and individual responsibility for developing a healthy workplace require attention to issues far beyond business ethics. Nevertheless, such issues have substantial elements of responsible business conduct. Although basic training in workplace skills is not specifically training in responsible business conduct, ensuring that employees and agents have the requisite skills, knowledge, understanding, and attitudes to pursue the enterprise's purpose and meet reasonable stakeholder expectations is responsible business conduct. Preaching a core value of customer service when employees know they do not have the ability to provide it will build, at best, frustration and cynicism.

In short, the training program should ensure that training in responsible business conduct begins with the earliest opportunity to orient the newly hired or retained and continues to transfer to the workplace as long as the employee remains a stakeholder.

Incorporating Action Planning and Action Learning

One way to make training meaningful is to have participants, individually or as members of a team, develop an action plan for the next three to six months based on what they learned. For senior employees, this action plan may reflect an assessment that some aspects of an enterprise's business ethics program require more support in practice. An example might be recognition that more training is required during the ensuing months on the issue of gifts and gratuities. Another might be a need to develop a division policy on wastewater disposal.

Copies of these action plans should be retained by the business ethics offi-cer or another appropriate officer. Follow-up questionnaires requesting progress reports should be sent regularly. Tracking progress on action plans can give indi-rect feedback or function as a performance evaluation item. It also has the effect of reinforcing perceptions of management's commitment. An important way to demonstrate management commitment is to include participation in the train-ing and action planning as express elements of performance evaluation.

USING THE MODES OF TRAINING

The training program should use all modes appropriate to the organizational culture and stakeholder needs. In general, training should be as interactive, real-istic, and relevant to day-to-day jobs as possible. In a recent study, one researcher found that European "training objectives typically include illumination of the company's and individual's values while in the United States the emphasis is on increasing knowledge of company standards and/or the law." The level of dif-ficulty should challenge but not overwhelm participants.

Some modes of training that enterprises may consider include:

- *Lectures and presentations*. The classic method that adults are familiar with from their school days, lectures are the most effective way to reach a num-ber of people with fairly straightforward information. In the initial rollout of a code, for example, lectures may be the most effective mode of explaining where the code fits into business performance. This mode is also an effec-tive way to describe other resources and ways to access them. If an objec-tive of the training program is to develop dialogue and decision-making skills, it is doubtful that lectures will be effective. Indeed, this mode may be counterproductive if it reinforces an organizational culture in which employees do what they are told and avoid the risks of making decisions.
- *Case studies and scenarios*. After participants understand the purpose of the training and the resources available, issues of responsible business con-duct can be effectively introduced through the study and analysis of cases that have actually occurred to the enterprise or to other similarly situated enterprises. Trainers might also develop their own scenarios to raise a num-ber of issues. Case studies and scenarios help develop dialogue and deci-sion-making skills. Case studies take more time to pass on information than do lectures. But analyzing a situation to isolate an issue, to develop the realistic options available, and to justify a decision to others in a relatively risk-free environment is invaluable. This mode also develops the important skills and attitudes of listening and of giving and receiving feedback.
- *Ethics games*. Many larger enterprises, including Citigroup, Lockheed Martin, and Boeing, have developed games to raise awareness of issues of ethics, compliance, and social responsibility; to develop good reason-ing skills and judgment; to stimulate dialogue; and to demonstrate man-agement commitment. In general, the games involve dividing employees into small teams and placing before them a situation that raises a discrete

issue of ethics, compliance, or social responsibility. The teams are given a few minutes to reach a consensus choice among the four or five alternative responses available to them. Teams are then asked to justify their choice. These games usually stimulate heated discussion. Each answer has a predetermined value in points. A particularly valuable element is that members of senior management sit as an "appeals board" in the event a team disputes the correctness of the answers or their predetermined point values. Participants are then able to observe how senior managers make and justify their decisions.

• *Other modes.* Many companies are now offering quite sophisticated web-based training. This mode may be relatively cost-effective. Videos and self-paced studies may be purchased off the shelf and may expose participants to the basics. These products, while useful, lack the familiarity that customized materials would offer. Yet, such materials do tend to reinforce the notion that the enterprise is engaging in an emerging global effort, and thus they might add some sense of importance to the training.

UPDATING AND MODIFYING THE TRAINING PROGRAM

The training program should be modified over time to ensure that its content contributes to the pursuit of the enterprise's purpose and helps meet reasonable stakeholder expectations. Also, it should be reviewed to ensure that the delivery methods are the most effective available. As the relevant context of an enterprise, its organizational culture, and its stakeholders' expectations change over time, the training program must adapt as well. This effort requires considering feedback from the training program.

Training provides useful feedback to managers on the ways in which the business ethics program is being received. It helps uncover sensitive areas such as insufficient guidance for employees or unreasonable stakeholder expectations, legal issues, unfair treatment of employees, and difficult working conditions. Feedback might reveal that trainers focus on issues that do not reflect the real-life concerns of the participants. It might also show that the sessions need more trainer-trainee interaction or that the materials are dull and do not encourage interaction. If feedback shows that participants need a better understanding of complicated issues, such as conflicts of interest, there may be specific real examples or case studies from the enterprise's experience that could address these concerns.

There are several methods for collecting feedback from training programs. Traditionally, training administrators ask trainees to fill out an evaluation form asking whether they found the training useful and what, if anything, they learned. At the end of the training, administrators should ask participants questions such as:

• How would you rate the overall effectiveness of the training?
• Were the materials helpful and relevant?
• Were the right issues discussed?
• What other topics would you like to discuss in the next training session?

Training administrators might also ask participants to take quizzes before, during, and after the training to determine what they learned.

The action-planning process described earlier is probably the most valuable, though time-consuming, process of collecting feedback because it tracks whether training actually transferred to the workplace.

. . . .

Hypothetical: Ethics Training Program

OceanDrill, Inc. is a U.S.-based multinational corporation that provides services for offshore oil and gas exploration, development, and drilling. OceanDrill has recently expanded its operations to Sri Lanka, which lacks a robust regulatory framework. While OceanDrill believes that Sri Lanka's lack of environmental regulations and protections make it a desirable prospect for future growth, its board of directors is committed to responsible business practices that minimize the risk of harm to the environment and the local population. OceanDrill's mission statement articulates its commitment to "transparency, accountability, safety, and teamwork."

In recent years, other drilling companies operating off the shores of Sri Lanka have had oil spills causing significant damage to wildlife, the fishing industry, and tourism. Wishing to avoid the negative publicity and loss of community goodwill that followed its competitors' accidents, OceanDrill intends to implement a comprehensive ethics training program for its employees and managers who work on the drilling platform to reinforce its commitment to CSR, raise awareness of the negative consequences of unethical behavior and make known the benefits of acting responsibly.

Develop an ethics training program for OceanDrill's managers, engineers, and rig hands stationed on the oil platforms in Sri Lanka.

D. Incentives and Disciplinary Measures

As with the compliance program, a key component of the ethics program is a system of rewards and disciplinary measures. The FSGO provides:

> The organization's . . . ethics program shall be promoted and enforced consistently throughout the organization through (A) appropriate incentives[;] . . . and (B) appropriate disciplinary measures . . . .[16]

Like the FSGO, the BEM prioritizes incentives over deterrents:

---

16. *See* U.S. SENTENCING GUIDELINES MANUAL § 8B2.1(b)(6)(U.S. SENTENCING COMM'N 2016).

The single most important thing that responsible owners and managers can do to encourage responsible business behavior is to recognize the contributions their employees and agents make in pursuit of the purpose of the enterprise.[17]

Nevertheless, unethical conduct should be punished:

Misconduct is intentional, negligent, or reckless disregard for the core beliefs, established standards and procedures, and reasonable expectations of the stakeholders of the enterprise. It also involves violating standards or procedures, including the admonition to obey the letter and spirit of the law.[18]

Misconduct should be distinguished from mistakes.[19] While misconduct should be punished, employees should be encouraged to disclose mistakes without fear of retribution, and managers should make "a sincere effort to learn from what went wrong."[20]

Business Ethics: A Manual for Managing a Responsible Business Enterprise in Emerging Market Economies[21]

REWARD SYSTEMS

An important principle of management is that employees tend to do what is rewarded. If managers want responsible employee and agent behavior that meets standards and procedures and that contributes to meeting reasonable stakeholder expectations, they should pay close attention to what they reward. Few managers plan to reward unethical behavior, but many do. Few managers plan to discourage ethical behavior, but many often do.

Commission schemes are the classic way that managers reward unethical behavior and discourage ethical behavior. If a value of the enterprise is customer service or excellence, the enterprise should aspire to customer satisfaction. However, sales agents and their managers are often compensated not by how well their customers are satisfied, but by how much product is sold. For example, there are numerous instances of sales agents receiving large bonuses based on the volume of their sales, without regard for the number of product returns or customer complaints. In one case, a sales agent, knowing that he was being transferred to another region, colluded with customers to order more products than were needed so that he would receive a bonus that the agent following him would otherwise have received. It is obvious that this "reward system" discourages ethical behavior and encourages unethical behavior.

Employees are quite skilled at finding out what is required for success in an enterprise. Although a code of conduct may say that customer service is a value,

---

17. BEM, *supra* note 1, at 194.
18. *Id.* at 199.
19. *Id.* at 199–200.
20. *Id.* at 200.
21. *Id.* at 195–99.

even one manager saying, "Do whatever it takes," dilutes the message. Sometimes the signal may be more subtle. For example, when an employee's success results from unethical behavior, recognizing his or her efforts can lead to cynicism at best, and other employees joining in at worst.

There is much opposition to rewarding ethical behavior explicitly. First, there is a widespread sense that one should not reward people for doing what they should be doing anyway. Second, in organizational cultures that have a strong group orientation, rewards to an individual may be resented and may even make the individual uncomfortable. In such cultures, a reward to an individual may disrupt the harmony of the group.

The first point merits some further thought. As the sales bonus scheme above reflects, managers often reward people for doing what they should have done all along—in this case, selling products. What is the justification for such incentives? Perhaps to spur employees beyond what would otherwise be the minimum acceptable standard of performance. Here is where rewards for ethical behavior make a lot of sense.

If employees honestly fill out expense reports, as some authors suggest, the behavior is so much the norm, that it makes no sense to reward it. However, consider the employee who reports an apparent violation of standards and procedures for the welfare of the enterprise when other employees do not. Without reports from employees who know what is actually going on in the enterprise, owners and managers might learn of problems too late to prevent serious misconduct or lessen the harm done. Although reporting concerns may be expected of all employees, it is not the norm in most enterprises. Substantial minorities of employees say they would never report misconduct they observed to managers. Many others are as concerned about retaliation from their peers as they are about retaliation from managers.

Whatever the specific circumstances may be—and with due regard to the organizational culture—ethical behavior that goes beyond the norms of conduct in the enterprise should be rewarded. Rewarding employees for reporting concerns makes a lot of sense if it is not the norm, and owners and managers should plan for it. The reward may be as simple as recognition. The reward may also need to be made in private. The behavior should certainly be reflected in performance evaluations.

DISCIPLINE SYSTEMS

Recognition and reward are two means of encouraging employees and agents to follow standards and procedures. But what should owners and managers do when standards and procedures are violated? They need to take all necessary steps to get the violator's attention and to prevent further violations, up to and including dismissal and reporting to law enforcement. They need to do this to protect the enterprise and its stakeholders from further harm.

Take the example of a sales agent who earns bonuses through collusion or by offering improper discounts. Fairness requires that the violator knew or should have known that the choice or action was inconsistent with enterprise core beliefs, standards and procedures, or reasonable stakeholder expectations. It is not fair to discipline an employee or agent for violating norms he or she had no reason to know existed. Fairness also requires that the employee or agent be given the opportunity to explain his or her actions. The discipline, if any, must be proportionate to the offense and legally administered.

But fairness is a concept that has a broader application. It is not fair to the enterprise or its stakeholders, including fellow employees, to fail to enforce standards and procedures. First, irresponsible behavior does not help other employees meet the reasonable expectations of stakeholders. Second, a single act of misconduct may result in prosecution of the enterprise, civil claims, loss of reputation, and removal from preferred provider lists and strategic partnerships. Finally, if environment, health, and safety standards and procedures are violated, the welfare of other employees and the community is put at risk.

Allowing standards and procedures to be violated with impunity sends a powerful message. When managers fail to enforce their own standards, they signal that they do not believe in those standards. Moreover, there is no reason why stakeholders should believe that the one violated standard is the only one in which managers do not believe. The whole set of values may come into question because of one failure to act.

Such questions arise particularly where employees perceive a double standard. Recent research suggests that employee perception of a business ethics program as primarily protecting owners and managers is the single most harmful factor to the prospects of the program's success. If ordinary employees are punished for violating a standard but senior managers are not, the entire business ethics program may be regarded as simply one more way to protect owners and managers.

One final consideration is to avoid the temptation to punish all employees for the violations of some of them by setting new standards or procedures. Often, if managers are uncomfortable with confronting an employee or agent about his or her behavior, they instead admonish the group as a whole or establish another standard or procedure designed to encourage the desired behavior.

. . . .

DEALING WITH MISTAKES AND FAILURES

In many offices, one will find a sign that reads "To err is human, to forgive divine—neither of which is the policy of this company." However, an RBE recognizes that the employee who never fails is probably not contributing his or her fullest in pursuit of the enterprise's purpose. Much can be learned from failure, provided that the effort was intended to achieve enterprise ends and that the means were well chosen and within enterprise boundaries.

An RBE fosters an environment in which the creativity and enthusiasm of its employees and agents are encouraged even in the face of mistakes and failure. There is no surer way of preventing creativity than to punish employees for mistakes made in good faith.

[An ideal] policy statement . . . affirms management's commitment to expect the best from employees and agents while providing responsible criteria for evaluating their choices and actions. It reinforces the responsibility that employees and agents assume: to make responsible choices and to take responsible actions to achieve the ends of the enterprise. It is also a liberating policy, which tends to free employees and agents from the fear of unfair criticism or punishment if they make mistakes or fail.

A responsible response to mistakes of employees includes an evaluation of what happened, and why. It includes a sincere effort to learn from mistakes or failure. Managers may need to modify the standards and procedures that failed to prevent the misconduct. They may choose to retrain or educate the employee or other agent, or they may reassign the person, especially if that person is in a position that has substantial discretionary authority.

. . . .

Hypothetical: Incentives and Deterrents

SuSu Melon, Inc. is a U.S.-based corporation specializing in the manufacture and sale of high-end athletic apparel. SuSu Melon prides itself on designing, manufacturing, and distributing its clothing in an environmentally sustainable and socially responsible manner. SuSu Melon manufactures most of its apparel in its plant in Malaysia, a country where labor and occupational safety regulations are rarely enforced. SuSu Melon's U.S. executives are concerned that managers in its Malaysian factory may not be observing company policies relating to safety standards.

SuSu Melon's business model and culture are based on a strong commitment to providing ethically sourced products manufactured according to the highest international labor standards. The board of directors wants to ensure that labor practices in its Malaysian plant are aligned with the company's values and policies.

The board has retained you to design a system of incentives and disciplinary measures to encourage ethical conduct on the part of the Malaysian supplier. Describe the main features of that system.

E. Reporting and Investigations

Any channel or hotline set up for confidential reporting of legal violations should be expanded to receive reports of ethics violations. Likewise, the internal investigatory mechanisms set up under the compliance program should also be used to address potential ethics violations. The BEM suggests an organizational ombudsman:

> In a number of large, complex enterprises (LCEs), a specific office, called the *ombudsman*, has been established to advise employees and agents of their rights

and duties regarding responsible conduct. In the business enterprise context, the ombudsman is a separate means by which employees and agents can seek advice and report their concerns.

. . . [T]he position of an organizational ombudsman in a business ethics program has evolved to be an independent, neutral, and alternative office where employees and agents can go to seek advice and report concerns. Independent means the ombudsman is not a part of day-to-day staff or operations management. Neutral means it does not function as an advocate for the enterprise or individual. Alternative means the ombudsman does not duplicate any other enterprise function, such as investigations. With few exceptions, the ombudsman is authorized to refer reports of misconduct for investigation only with the express consent of the reporting source.

In some jurisdictions, enterprises can claim that the ombudsman can make an enforceable promise of confidentiality. The enterprise will not be deemed to have notice of the concern until the source registers his or her concerns with the enterprise or authorizes the ombudsman to do so. However, as managers review standards, procedures, and expectations, an ombudsman may contribute what he or she has learned about employee concerns, provided that he or she does not compromise the anonymity and confidentiality of the sources.[22]

Business Ethics: A Manual for Managing a Responsible Business Enterprise in Emerging Market Economies[23]

EMPLOYEES SEEKING ADVICE AND REPORTING CONCERNS

Among the surest sources of information about what is going on in an enterprise—especially behavior that violates enterprise core beliefs, standards, procedures, and expectations—are employees and agents. Most employees and agents recognize management's legitimate need for such information, if the enterprise is to meet the reasonable expectations of its stakeholders.

. . . .

Reporting concerns about the business conduct of co-workers is hard for most employees. Indeed, research suggests that substantial numbers of employees, even in developed economies, are extremely reluctant to report their concerns. Many put loyalty to friends and colleagues above loyalty to the enterprise. Many do not trust that managers—or their peers—will not retaliate against them if they report their concerns.

As two authors have observed:

Both the law and popular opinion have always been ambivalent about whistle-blowers, whether in the elementary school yard, universities, the military or other government agency, or in private life. Are they malcontents, troublemakers, and

---

22. *Id.* at 173.
23. *Id.* at 168–174.

snitches? Or are they brave, ethical individuals who, unlike their fellow beings, coworkers, or superiors, want their company to act legally and ethically as well?

A business ethics program helps employees and agents understand why it is important that they communicate their concerns to management, how they should report their concerns, and why it is safe to do so.

Under a business ethics program, employees and agents are more sensitive to the types of behavior that constitute misconduct or illegality. They are more likely to view reporting misconduct as one of their obligations to the enterprise, their fellow employees, and enterprise stakeholders.

. . . .

In an organizational culture that encourages dialogue, questions, and delivery of bad news, employees find it easier to confront issues of responsible business conduct, to seek advice and report concerns, and to make ethical decisions. In many enterprises, however, employees are uncomfortable with coming forward, especially to report their concerns involving other employees. Owners and managers need to make the case for coming forward in terms that resonate with their employees. . . .

Reporting Violations

Ideally, owners, managers, and supervisors maintain an open-door policy for employees and agents who have concerns that involve responsible business conduct. Often, however, employees and agents are reluctant to bring "bad news" to managers and supervisors. To encourage them to come forward, an enterprise should establish discreet procedures for employees to seek advice and report concerns.

Suggestion boxes, helplines, and whistleblow[er] protection all facilitate reporting of questionable conduct. Reports may also be received from individuals who come to the business ethics office and register a concern. The identity of reporters should be kept confidential (to the extent that the law provides), and sources should not be held liable, discriminated against, or harassed for reporting their concerns.

Once the business ethics officer receives a report, it is important that the enterprise follow through. The officer should:

- Record the reported concern
- Evaluate the concern and develop an action plan for dealing with it
- Initiate or coordinate an investigation or inquiry, if appropriate
- Take appropriate action on findings and conclusions
- Track reported concerns for patterns and trends
- Make recommendations based on lessons learned

Critical to the success of the business ethics program is feedback to the reporting source of the steps taken to investigate the matter, what was found, and what corrective steps—if any—were or will be taken. In many surveys of employee attitudes, when reasons are given for why an employee observing misconduct did not report it, second only to fear of retaliation is the sense that management would not do anything with the information anyway.

Protecting Employees and Agents from Retribution

All reporting procedures should be designed to leave reporters free from fear of retribution. Managers, supervisors, and other employees should understand that direct or indirect retribution for voicing a concern or complaint is not to be tolerated. Retribution by either managers or peers discourages others from reporting their concerns. An RBE, therefore, should have a strict policy that discipline will be imposed for any instance of retribution.

Occasionally, an employee or other agent reporting concerns may make a mistake or abuse the reporting process and cause an investigation that does not lead to further action. Behavior that abuses the reporting process will often violate enterprise core beliefs; however, managers should counsel, but not punish, such a reporter. Maintaining absolute certainty among employees and agents that they can report concerns without fear of retribution is so important that managers should not risk losing that confidence by punishing anyone who used a reporting process. If the enterprise reserves the right to punish those who abuse the process, the published standards, procedures, and expectations will have to leave that possibility open. Where trust in management is not the norm, reporting sources may be uncertain about just how safely they can make reports.

Moreover, it is difficult, at best, to prove that a reported concern was an abuse of the process. Even if a case can be made, it may raise significant questions in the minds of potential sources about just how safe the process is. . . . In short, for all the satisfaction owners and managers may retain in being able to punish someone who abuses the process, the cost in terms of employee confidence in the reporting process is too high to pay.

Although the individual should not be punished to preserve confidence in the business ethics program, other steps can be taken to limit harm to other individuals or to the enterprise. The abusing person or the victim may be reassigned, for example.

. . . .

POLICIES AND PROCEDURES FOR INVESTIGATIONS

It is critical to the success of a business ethics program that reported concerns be investigated. Managers may learn of concerns suggesting that a violation of standards, procedures, and expectations has occurred from a variety of sources, including the help-line. Once on notice, an RBE must take all reasonable steps to determine what happened and how the problem might be avoided in the future.

In developing an investigative plan, managers need to consider the laws of the jurisdiction in which they operate. These laws will affect who conducts the investigation and what rights are afforded to the subjects of the investigation. Investigations should always be conducted with a view to possible government prosecution or civil litigation.

Investigations will typically involve document review and witness interviews. Employees should be instructed to cooperate fully with the investigation, including preserving all relevant documents and materials. The investigator must be alert to avoiding the appearance of influencing witnesses or appearing to speak for the enterprise or another witness.

. . . .

F. Continuous Assessment and Monitoring

In the case of the ethics program, the yardstick for measuring effectiveness is somewhat different from that used for the compliance program. Because the ethics program is mainly directed at meeting the reasonable expectations of stakeholders, appropriate channels of communication are required to gauge stakeholder sentiment:

> Typically, the most important stakeholders to reach will be customers, employees, and agents. Next in priority may be financial stakeholders, such as owners and investors, and then, specific stakeholder advocacy groups. Management needs to conduct this analysis carefully to ensure that its message about standards, procedures, and expectations is communicated as effectively and efficiently as possible. Perhaps most important for long-term program success is consideration of the criteria that will be used to determine whether the program is successful.[24]

The monitoring and auditing processes established for the compliance program should also apply to the ethics program. Since the FSGO explicitly requires the enterprise to promote a culture of ethics,[25] enterprises must find a way to measure and track their culture. Stakeholder surveys may be used for this purpose.

Business Ethics: A Manual for Managing a Responsible Business Enterprise in Emerging Market Economies[26]

. . . Although it is difficult to measure directly the extent to which values such as trust and integrity are shared, there are a number of specific outcomes affecting the organization's culture that can be expected from such a program and that are valuable to monitor, track, and report.

ESSENTIAL CHARACTERISTICS OF ENTERPRISES

A number of elements of organizational culture will give owners and managers a profile of the enterprise to help them design and implement an effective business ethics program. These include five characteristics of a highly effective

---

24. *Id.* at 152.
25. *See* U.S. Sentencing Guidelines Manual § 8B2.1(a)(U.S. Sentencing Comm'n 2016).
26. BEM, *supra* note 1, at 66–69, 234–38.

organization and eight influential cultural factors. When tracked and measured over time, these elements will be extremely valuable in evaluating program success.

Importance of Organizational Culture

The principal predictor of an effective business ethics program is the culture of the organization itself. Responsible owners and managers will shape their management, ethics, compliance, and social responsibility practices to address nuances of the enterprise's organizational culture.

Organizational culture is shaped by the organization's origin and history as well as the values, norms, and attitudes of its owners, managers, and other stakeholders. It is a bundle of assumptions about the way the world works and the beliefs, values, symbols, languages, rituals, principles, rules, and practices that consciously or unconsciously drive the thoughts, feelings, and actions of the enterprise and its stakeholders.

Organizational culture influences what the organization senses, cares about, and is capable of dealing with. It will influence how comfortable employees and agents are with engaging the stakeholders. Culture also is a source of conflict. . . .

Characteristics of Organizational Culture

The first step in developing measures of an enterprise's organizational culture is to develop a profile of the enterprise as a whole. This profile can be captured in the following five characteristics:

1. Extent to which leaders and members alike embrace the organization's core purpose and values . . .
2. Extent to which leaders and members hold themselves responsible—and others accountable—for high standards
3. Extent to which leaders encourage members—and members welcome and accept the opportunity—to participate in organizational affairs
4. Extent to which leaders and members have [access to information] when they need it
5. Extent to which conflict and mistakes made in good faith are seen as opportunities for learning and growth

Indicators of Organizational Culture

More specific than the profile described above are a number of measurable indicators of organizational culture, which tend to be closely associated with expected business ethics program outcomes. Eight such influential factors are set forth below:

1. Perceiving that leadership cares about ethics and values as much as the bottom line
2. Feeling safe to deliver bad news
3. Feeling treated fairly
4. Feeling valued as an employee
5. Not feeling pressured to compromise values

6. Believing ethical behavior is rewarded
7. Believing unethical behavior is punished
8. Recognizing whether the enterprise has an employee, community, or self-interest focus

These factors reflect the styles of leadership and sense of fair play that characterize the enterprise. They are visible aspects of organizational culture.

EXPECTED PROGRAM OUTCOMES

The primary purpose of a business ethics program is to help an enterprise address all four levels of its identity as an RBE. . . . An effective business ethics program will include a performance measurement system that captures program outcomes that reflect the goals and objectives of the enterprise. . . .

Tracking the following nine outcomes will help determine whether a business ethics program is effective for all four levels of [enterprise] identity:

1. How often violations of standards, including legal requirements, can be observed (compliance and risk management levels)
2. How often responsible business conduct issues are raised at the workplace (all four levels)
3. How often employees and agents speak in terms of core beliefs and standards (all four levels)
4. How often employees and agents make decisions based on core beliefs and standards (all four levels)
5. How willing employees and agents are to seek advice on standards (all four levels)
6. How willing employees and agents are to report observed or suspected violations (compliance and risk management levels)
7. How satisfied those who reported observed or suspected violations are with management's response (compliance and risk management levels)
8. How committed employees are to the enterprise (value-added level)
9. How satisfied stakeholders are that the enterprise meets their expectations (reputation enhancement and value-added levels)

BENCHMARKS AND BASELINES

When the data are collected and analyzed, they may be used in a number of ways. They can give owners a picture of the culture, program processes, and business conduct of the enterprise. They can be used as baseline data for comparison with subsequent data. They can also be used to compare the findings with those of other similarly situated enterprises (known as benchmarking).

The first usage is helpful for owners and managers because it gives them a sense of how their employees and agents view the fundamental workings of the enterprise. Particularly valuable is comparing how managers, supervisors, and workers answer the same questions. Often, the answers are so different that one might wonder if the respondents work for different enterprises. These data also permit comparison between different plants and locations. For large, complex enterprises (LCEs), regional differences can be explored.

Where program evaluation is done on a regular basis—every one to three years, for example—the data serve as baseline data. Once a baseline of organizational culture, processes, and expected program outcomes is established, owners and managers can compare later data with the baseline to detect patterns and identify trends over time.

A final use is to compare the organizational culture, program processes, or expected program outcomes with other enterprises that establish benchmarks of practices or conduct. Benchmarking can be an effective practice if it compares program processes, such as code of conduct formats, business ethics office organization, or helpline procedures. For analyzing organizational culture or expected program outcomes, however, benchmarking is very difficult to do well, for a number of reasons.

Very little data are available publicly beyond large national surveys for program outcomes. Enterprises that do evaluate their programs for organizational culture and outcomes seldom share the data with the public. Moreover, business ethics programs are so fundamental to the very identity of an enterprise that it would be difficult to make meaningful comparisons that take into account differing organizational culture, program process, and expected program outcomes.

. . . .

EVALUATING THE PROCESS

Process evaluation looks at how the program works: whether resources are being used well, whether assigned activities are being performed, and whether specific outputs are produced.

Many general management evaluation models, especially in the arena of continuous quality improvement, are process models, including the International Organization for Standardization (ISO) management systems models. The ISO 9000 series for quality certification does not define quality; instead, it examines whether the processes that have been shown to lead to quality goods and services have been followed. The same is true for the ISO 14000 series for environmental management. It does not define what protecting the environment is; instead, it determines whether management systems are in place to protect the environment.

. . . .

Developing a Data Collection Plan

There are a number of classic data collection methods for evaluators to consider in collecting data for the relevant context scan, organizational culture tracking, and process and outcome valuation. . . . [T]hese methods include interviews (including focus groups), surveys, document review, and direct observation. Each has its strengths, weaknesses, and resource demands.

The primary concern is to develop a cost-effective collection plan that encourages employees and agents to be forthcoming and give evaluators, owners and managers, and stakeholders a clear picture of what is going on in the enterprise.

Surveys and document review are valuable for collecting standardized data very cost-effectively . . . . However, they offer no opportunity to follow through on the information gathered. Where the evaluators need the opportunity to follow leads gained from initial impressions or responses, interviews, focus groups, and direct observation are better methods, though generally more expensive. Unless people outside the enterprise are involved in collecting the data, it is difficult to ensure the anonymity or confidentiality often required to secure candid responses.

. . . .

Reporting Program Performance

As they develop a plan to evaluate business ethics program performance, owners and managers need to determine whether the evaluation is intended only for internal consumption or for wider distribution. Since the enterprise cannot report on performance that it has not evaluated, owners and managers must determine the outcomes of legitimate interest to stakeholders and the methods of evaluation and reporting that stakeholders will trust.

REPORTING TO EXTERNAL STAKEHOLDERS

Coupled with the increased activism of civil society, there is an emerging trend among enterprises to report more about their impact on society to more people. One term for this is triple bottom-line reporting. *Triple bottom-line reporting* requires enterprises to evaluate their social and environmental performance to the same degree that they evaluate and report economic performance.

Reporting on an enterprise's performance and impact on society is becoming more common—and expected. Beyond publicizing the enterprise's role in the economic, social, and environmental evolution of its community, expanded reporting requires the enterprise to integrate social and environmental considerations into its strategic and operational decision-making. Considering what outcomes to measure and report, what indicators to measure, how to analyze the data, and how to report data can produce synergies that can be quite energizing—in the long run—for the enterprise.

. . . .

Notes and Questions

1) Should acquiring companies conduct ethics due diligence on their targets in M&A transactions? If so, why?

2) Outline the steps in the process. For guidance, see the excerpt in Chapter 6 from *Case Story: Integrity Due Diligence,* by Michael Price.[27]

---

27. Michael Price, *Case Story: Integrity Due Diligence, in* Business Against Corruption: Case Stories and Examples 119, 119-26 (Birgit Errath ed., 2006), https://www.unglobalcompact.org/docs/issues_doc/7.7/BACbookFINAL.pdf.

OECD Guidelines for Multinational Enterprises

I. Introduction
   A. RBC Due Diligence
   B. Meaningful Stakeholder Engagement
II. Disclosure
III. Human Rights
IV. Employment and Industrial Relations
V. Environment
VI. Consumer Interests
   A. Health and Safety
   B. Consumer Awareness and Education
   C. Dispute Resolution
   D. Consumer Data Protection and Privacy
VII. Science and Technology
VIII. Competition
IX. Taxation

I. Introduction

According to Business Ethics: A Manual for Managing a Responsible Business Enterprise in Emerging Market Economies ("BEM"), each enterprise must ask a fundamental question as it designs its ethics program: "What norms, values, and standards should we set to guide our members and foster reasonable expectations among our stakeholders?"[1] The BEM answers that question by referring to the OECD Guidelines, which, as discussed previously, set forth the international norms of responsible business conduct ("RBC") under nine broad

> **The OECD Guidelines**
>
> I. Disclosure
> II. Human Rights
> III. Employment and Industrial Relations
> IV. Environment
> V. Combating Bribery, Bribe Solicitation, and Extortion
> VI. Consumer Interests
> VII. Science and Technology
> VIII. Competition
> IX. Taxation

---

1. U.S. Dep't of Commerce, Business Ethics: A Manual for Managing a Responsible Business Enterprise in Emerging Market Economies (2004) [hereinafter BEM], at 38.

categories: disclosure, human rights, employment and industrial relations, environment, combating bribery, consumer interests, science and technology, competition and taxation.[2] The OECD Guidelines incorporate two foundational concepts: (1) RBC due diligence and (2) meaningful stakeholder engagement.

A. RBC Due Diligence

RBC due diligence can be differentiated from normal due diligence processes in that the latter are "typically geared towards identifying risks *to* the enterprise, rather than risks *created by* it."[3] In the context of the OECD Guidelines, multinational companies must:

> [U]se due diligence to *identify, prevent and mitigate actual and potential adverse impacts* [on stakeholders.] Due diligence is a flexible, risk-based process and not a specific formula for companies to follow. It requires companies to know and describe the potential effects their operations could have on local communities and on that basis take steps to address the risk. The fundamentals of the concept are familiar to companies working on a daily basis with risk management and management systems. The Guidelines acknowledge that due diligence can be included within broader enterprise risk management systems, provided that it goes beyond simply identifying and managing material risks to the enterprise itself to include the risks of adverse impacts related to matters covered by the Guidelines.[4]

The OECD proposes a five-step framework for conducting RBC due diligence:[5]

> *Step One—Establish strong management systems for due diligence*: Adopt a responsible business conduct policy, build internal capacity & functional alignment, supplier & business partner engagement (outreach, incorporating into contracts, etc.), set-up internal controls & data collection on supply chain[s], establish grievance mechanism[s].
> *Step Two—Identify and assess risks of adverse impacts in the supply chain*: Map operations, business partners & supply chains; prioritize further assessment

---

2. *See generally* OECD (2011), *OECD Guidelines for Multinational Enterprises*, OECD Publishing., http://www.oecd.org/daf/inv/mne/48004323.pdf [hereinafter OECD Guidelines].

3. Org. for Econ. Cooperation and Dev. [OECD], *OECD Due Diligence Guidance for Responsible Business Conduct (Draft 2.1)*, at 8–9 (2016) [hereinafter *OECD Due Diligence Guidance*].

4. U.S. Dep't of State, A Guide to the U.S. National Contact Point for the OECD Guidelines for the Multinational Enterprises: Your Resource for Responsible Business Conduct (2017) [hereinafter U.S. National Contact Point Guide], at 5.

5. In 2009, the OECD initiated a project aimed at producing sector-specific guidance on how to perform due diligence. The project has thus far produced five sector-specific sets of guidance: (1) *OECD Due Diligence Guidance for Responsible Supply Chains in the Garment and Footwear Sector* (2017); (2) *OECD Due Diligence Guidance for Meaningful Stakeholder Engagement in the Extractive Sector* (Feb. 2, 2017); (3) *OECD Due Diligence Guidance for Responsible Supply Chains of Minerals from Conflict-Affected and High-Risk Areas* (3d ed., 2016); (4) *OECD-FAO Guidance for Responsible Agricultural Supply Chains* (2016); and (5) *Responsible Business Conduct for Institutional Investors* (Mar. 28, 2017).

based on severity of harm (sector, counterparty, and site for high-risk issues); identify risks of circumstances inconsistent with standards in the Guidelines.

Step Three—Manage risks in the supply chain: Inform senior management, fix internal systems, build leverage individually or collaboratively, use existing networks to manage risk (e.g. industry, workers' rep[resentatives], non-traditional partnerships), build internal and business partner capacity, provide remedies when [the company has] "caused" or "contributed" to adverse impacts.

Step Four—Verify the effectiveness of the enterprise's due diligence: Where relevant, monitor medium-high-risk operations, products, or services, after a change of circumstance; undertake audits . . . .

Step Five—Report publicly and communicate: With due regard for commercial confidentiality and competitive concerns.[6]

B. Meaningful Stakeholder Engagement

Meaningful stakeholder engagement "refers to ongoing engagement with stakeholders that is two-way, conducted in good faith and responsive."[7]

- Two-way engagement is a process of "sharing of decision-making power through moving away from the enterprise as a primary decision-maker to a more mutual process . . . ."[8]
- Good faith engagement refers to an honest participation in dialogue with a view towards addressing adverse impacts.[9]
- Responsive engagement involves follow-through actions to ensure that adverse impacts are effectively addressed.[10]
- Ongoing engagement "continue[s] throughout the lifecycle of an operation. . . ."[11]

The OECD recommends that enterprises "integrate RBC risk management within broader enterprise risk management systems."[12] This can be accomplished by "[e]mbedding internal controls in management systems to track progress in meeting the Guidelines' recommendations throughout the full lifecycle of the enterprise's operations, products and services."[13]

Members of the OECD have made a "binding commitment" to encourage enterprises operating or based in their territories to voluntarily adhere to the Guidelines.[14]

---

6. Org. for Econ. Cooperation and Dev., *Quantifying the Costs, Benefits and Risks of Due Diligence for Responsible Business Conduct: Framework and Assessment Tool for Companies* (June 2016), at 18.

7. Org. for Econ. Cooperation and Dev., *OECD Due Diligence Guidance for Meaningful Stakeholder Engagement in the Extractive Sector* (Feb. 2, 2017), at 18.

8. *Id.*

9. *See id.*

10. *See id.*

11. *Id.*

12. Org. for Econ. Cooperation and Dev. [OECD], *Due Diligence Companion (Draft)* (2016), at 6 (alteration in original).

13. *Id.* at 6 (alteration in original).

14. *OECD Guidelines, supra* note 2, at 13.

Governments wish to encourage the widest possible observance of the *Guidelines*. While it is acknowledged that small- and medium-sized enterprises may not have the same capacities as larger enterprises, governments adhering to the *Guidelines* nevertheless encourage them to observe the *Guidelines'* recommendations to the fullest extent possible.[15]

OECD General Policies[16]

Enterprises should take fully into account established policies in the countries in which they operate, and consider the views of other stakeholders. In this regard:

A. ENTERPRISES SHOULD:

1. Contribute to economic, environmental and social progress with a view to achieving sustainable development.
2. Respect the internationally recognised human rights of those affected by their activities.
3. Encourage local capacity building through close co-operation with the local community, including business interests, as well as developing the enterprise's activities in domestic and foreign markets, consistent with the need for sound commercial practice.
4. Encourage human capital formation, in particular by creating employment opportunities and facilitating training opportunities for employees.
5. Refrain from seeking or accepting exemptions not contemplated in the statutory or regulatory framework related to human rights, environmental, health, safety, labour, taxation, financial incentives, or other issues.
6. Support and uphold good corporate governance principles and develop and apply good corporate governance practices, including throughout enterprise groups.
7. Develop and apply effective self-regulatory practices and management systems that foster a relationship of confidence and mutual trust between enterprises and the societies in which they operate.
8. Promote awareness of and compliance by workers employed by multinational enterprises with respect to company policies through appropriate dissemination of these policies, including through training programmes.
9. Refrain from discriminatory or disciplinary action against workers who make bona fide reports to management or, as appropriate, to the competent public authorities, on practices that contravene the law, the *Guidelines* or the enterprise's policies.
10. Carry out risk-based due diligence, for example by incorporating it into their enterprise risk management systems, to identify, prevent and mitigate

---

15. *Id.* at 18.
16. *Id.* at 19–26.

actual and potential adverse impacts as described in paragraphs 11 and 12, and account for how these impacts are addressed. The nature and extent of due diligence depend on the circumstances of a particular situation.

11. Avoid causing or contributing to adverse impacts on matters covered by the *Guidelines*, through their own activities, and address such impacts when they occur.

12. Seek to prevent or mitigate an adverse impact where they have not contributed to that impact, when the impact is nevertheless directly linked to their operations, products or services by a business relationship. This is not intended to shift responsibility from the entity causing an adverse impact to the enterprise with which it has a business relationship.

13. In addition to addressing adverse impacts in relation to matters covered by the *Guidelines*, encourage, where practicable, business partners, including suppliers and sub-contractors, to apply principles of responsible business conduct compatible with the *Guidelines*.

14. Engage with relevant stakeholders in order to provide meaningful opportunities for their views to be taken into account in relation to planning and decision making for projects or other activities that may significantly impact local communities.

15. Abstain from any improper involvement in local political activities.

B. ENTERPRISES ARE ENCOURAGED TO:

1. Support, as appropriate to their circumstances, cooperative efforts in the appropriate fora to promote Internet Freedom through respect of freedom of expression, assembly and association online.

2. Engage in or support, where appropriate, private or multi-stakeholder initiatives and social dialogue on responsible supply chain management while ensuring that these initiatives take due account of their social and economic effects on developing countries and of existing internationally recognised standards.

COMMENTARY ON GENERAL POLICIES

1. The General Policies chapter of the *Guidelines* is the first to contain specific recommendations to enterprises. As such it is important for setting the tone and establishing common fundamental principles for the specific recommendations in subsequent chapters.

2. Enterprises are encouraged to co-operate with governments in the development and implementation of policies and laws. Considering the views of other stakeholders in society, which includes the local community as well as business interests, can enrich this process. It is also recognised that governments should be transparent in their dealings with enterprises, and consult with business on these same issues. Enterprises should be viewed as partners with government in the development and use of both voluntary and regulatory approaches (of which the *Guidelines* are one element) to policies affecting them.

3. There should not be any contradiction between the activity of multinational enterprises (MNEs) and sustainable development, and the *Guidelines* are meant to foster complementarities in this regard. Indeed, links among economic, social, and environmental progress are a key means for furthering the goal of sustainable development.

. . . .

5. The *Guidelines* also acknowledge and encourage the contribution that MNEs can make to local capacity building as a result of their activities in local communities. Similarly, the recommendation on human capital formation is an explicit and forward-looking recognition of the contribution to individual human development that MNEs can offer their employees, and encompasses not only hiring practices, but training and other employee development as well. Human capital formation also incorporates the notion of non-discrimination in hiring practices as well as promotion practices, life-long learning and other on-the-job training.

6. The *Guidelines* recommend that, in general, enterprises avoid making efforts to secure exemptions not contemplated in the statutory or regulatory framework related to human rights, environmental, health, safety, labour, taxation, and financial incentives among other issues, without infringing on an enterprise's right to seek changes in the statutory or regulatory framework. The words "or accepting" also draw attention to the role of the State in offering these exemptions. While this sort of provision has been traditionally directed at governments, it is also of direct relevance to MNEs. Importantly, however, there are instances where specific exemptions from laws or other policies can be consistent with these laws for legitimate public policy reasons. . . .

7. The *Guidelines* recommend that enterprises apply good corporate governance practices drawn from the OECD Principles of Corporate Governance. The Principles call for the protection and facilitation of the exercise of shareholder rights, including the equitable treatment of shareholders. Enterprises should recognise the rights of stakeholders established by law or through mutual agreements and encourage active co-operation with stakeholders in creating wealth, jobs, and the sustainability of financially sound enterprises.

8. The Principles call on the board of the parent entity to ensure the strategic guidance of the enterprise, the effective monitoring of management and to be accountable to the enterprise and to the shareholders, while taking into account the interests of stakeholders. In undertaking these responsibilities, the board needs to ensure the integrity of the enterprise's accounting and financial reporting systems, including independent audit, appropriate control systems, in particular, risk management, and financial and operational control, and compliance with the law and relevant standards.

9. The Principles extend to enterprise groups, although boards of subsidiary enterprises might have obligations under the law of their jurisdiction of

incorporation. Compliance and control systems should extend where possible to these subsidiaries. Furthermore, the board's monitoring of governance includes continuous review of internal structures to ensure clear lines of management accountability throughout the group.

10. State-owned multinational enterprises are subject to the same recommendations as privately-owned enterprises, but public scrutiny is often magnified when a State is the final owner. The OECD *Guidelines on Corporate Governance of State-Owned Enterprises* are a useful and specifically tailored guide for these enterprises and the recommendations they offer could significantly improve governance.

11. Although primary responsibility for improving the legal and institutional regulatory framework lies with governments, there is a strong business case for enterprises to implement good corporate governance.

12. An increasing network of non-governmental self-regulatory instruments and actions address aspects of corporate behaviour and the relationships between business and society. Interesting developments in this regard are being undertaken in the financial sector. Enterprises recognise that their activities often have social and environmental implications. The institution of self-regulatory practices and management systems by enterprises sensitive to reaching these goals—thereby contributing to sustainable development—is an illustration of this. In turn, developing such practices can further constructive relationships between enterprises and the societies in which they operate.

13. Following from effective self-regulatory practices, as a matter of course, enterprises are expected to promote employee awareness of company policies. Safeguards to protect bona fide "whistle-blowing" activities are also recommended, including protection of employees who, in the absence of timely remedial action or in the face of reasonable risk of negative employment action, report practices that contravene the law to the competent public authorities. While of particular relevance to anti-bribery and environmental initiatives, such protection is also relevant to other recommendations in the *Guidelines*.

14. For the purposes of the *Guidelines*, due diligence is understood as the process through which enterprises can identify, prevent, mitigate and account for how they address their actual and potential adverse impacts as an integral part of business decision-making and risk management systems. Due diligence can be included within broader enterprise risk management systems, provided that it goes beyond simply identifying and managing material risks to the enterprise itself, to include the risks of adverse impacts related to matters covered by the *Guidelines*. Potential impacts are to be addressed through prevention or mitigation, while actual impacts are to be addressed through remediation. The *Guidelines* concern those adverse impacts that are either caused or contributed to by the enterprise, or are directly linked to their operations, products or services by a business relationship. . . . Due diligence can help enterprises avoid the risk of such

adverse impacts. For the purposes of this recommendation, "contributing to" an adverse impact should be interpreted as a substantial contribution, meaning an activity that causes, facilitates or incentivizes another entity to cause an adverse impact and does not include minor or trivial contributions. The term "business relationship" includes relationships with business partners, entities in the supply chain and any other non-State or State entities directly linked to its business operations, products or services. The recommendation in paragraph A.10 [risk-based due diligence] applies to those matters covered by the *Guidelines* that are related to adverse impacts. It does not apply to the chapters on Science and Technology, Competition and Taxation.

15. The nature and extent of due diligence, such as the specific steps to be taken, appropriate to a particular situation will be affected by factors such as the size of the enterprise, context of its operations, the specific recommendations in the *Guidelines*, and the severity of its adverse impacts. . . .

16. Where enterprises have large numbers of suppliers, they are encouraged to identify general areas where the risk of adverse impacts is most significant and, based on this risk assessment, prioritise suppliers for due diligence.

17. To avoid causing or contributing to adverse impacts on matters covered by the *Guidelines* through their own activities includes their activities in the supply chain. Relationships in the supply chain take a variety of forms including, for example, franchising, licensing or subcontracting. Entities in the supply chain are often multinational enterprises themselves and, by virtue of this fact, those operating in or from the countries adhering to the Declaration are covered by the *Guidelines*.

18. In the context of its supply chain, if the enterprise identifies a risk of causing an adverse impact, then it should take the necessary steps to cease or prevent that impact.

19. If the enterprise identifies a risk of contributing to an adverse impact, then it should take the necessary steps to cease or prevent its contribution and use its leverage to mitigate any remaining impacts to the greatest extent possible. Leverage is considered to exist where the enterprise has the ability to effect change in the wrongful practices of the entity that causes the harm.

20. Meeting the expectation in paragraph A.12 [prevention and mitigation of adverse impacts] would entail an enterprise, acting alone or in co-operation with other entities, as appropriate, to use its leverage to influence the entity causing the adverse impact to prevent or mitigate that impact.

21. The *Guidelines* recognise that there are practical limitations on the ability of enterprises to effect change in the behaviour of their suppliers. These are related to product characteristics, the number of suppliers, the structure and complexity of the supply chain, the market position of the enterprise vis-à-vis its suppliers or other entities in the supply chain. However, enterprises can also influence suppliers through contractual arrangements such as management contracts, pre-qualification requirements for potential

suppliers, voting trusts, and licence or franchise agreements. Other factors relevant to determining the appropriate response to the identified risks include the severity and probability of adverse impacts and how crucial that supplier is to the enterprise.

22. Appropriate responses with regard to the business relationship may include continuation of the relationship with a supplier throughout the course of risk mitigation efforts; temporary suspension of the relationship while pursuing ongoing risk mitigation; or, as a last resort, disengagement with the supplier either after failed attempts at mitigation, or where the enterprise deems mitigation not feasible, or because of the severity of the adverse impact. The enterprise should also take into account potential social and economic adverse impacts related to the decision to disengage.

23. Enterprises may also engage with suppliers and other entities in the supply chain to improve their performance, in co-operation with other stakeholders, including through personnel training and other forms of capacity building, and to support the integration of principles of responsible business conduct compatible with the *Guidelines* into their business practices. Where suppliers have multiple customers and are potentially exposed to conflicting requirements imposed by different buyers, enterprises are encouraged, with due regard to anti-competitive concerns, to participate in industry-wide collaborative efforts with other enterprises with which they share common suppliers to coordinate supply chain policies and risk management strategies, including through information-sharing.

24. Enterprises are also encouraged to participate in private or multi-stakeholder initiatives and social dialogue on responsible supply chain management, such as those undertaken as part of the proactive agenda pursuant to the Decision of the OECD Council on the OECD *Guidelines for Multinational Enterprises* and the attached Procedural Guidance.

25. Stakeholder engagement involves interactive processes of engagement with relevant stakeholders, through, for example, meetings, hearings or consultation proceedings. Effective stakeholder engagement is characterised by two-way communication and depends on the good faith of the participants on both sides. This engagement can be particularly helpful in the planning and decision-making concerning projects or other activities involving, for example, the intensive use of land or water, which could significantly affect local communities.

26. Paragraph B.1 [support for Internet Freedom] acknowledges an important emerging issue. It does not create new standards, nor does it presume the development of new standards. It recognises that enterprises have interests which will be affected and that their participation along with other stakeholders in discussion of the issues involved can contribute to their ability and that of others to understand the issues and make a positive contribution. It recognises that the issues may have a number of dimensions and emphasises that co-operation should be pursued through appropriate fora. . . .

27. Finally, it is important to note that self-regulation and other initiatives in a similar vein, including the *Guidelines*, should not unlawfully restrict competition, nor should they be considered a substitute for effective law and regulation by governments. It is understood that MNEs should avoid potential trade or investment distorting effects of codes and self-regulatory practices when they are being developed.

Notes

Adhering governments are expected to fulfill their obligation to promote the OECD Guidelines through a unique implementation mechanism called a National Contact Point ("NCP"). NCPs are "agencies established by adhering governments to promote and implement the Guidelines."[17] NCPs have three distinct functions:

- *Promote awareness and encourage implementation of the Guidelines* to business, labor, NGOs and other members of civil society, the general public, and the international community.
- *Facilitate practical application of the Guidelines* by bringing business and civil society together to identify potential and emerging RBC-related risks for MNEs and discuss appropriate actions and responses regarding the Guidelines.
- *Offer a "specific instance" mediation process* to be used when a party raises allegations against an MNE's operations, focusing on finding a resolution between the parties through mediated dialogue.[18]

Specific instance mediation is a grievance mechanism that allows a complaint to be filed when alleging violation of the Guidelines by an enterprise. A specific instance "may be brought by a community affected by a company's activities, a company's employees, members of a trade union, an NGO, or an individual."[19] When an NCP accepts a specific instance, it does not acknowledge or determine its merits, but rather makes "an offer to facilitate neutral, third-party mediation or conciliation to assist the parties in voluntary, confidential, and good faith efforts to reach a cooperative resolution of their concerns."[20] As the OECD explains:

> Specific instances are not legal cases and NCPs are not judicial bodies. NCPs focus on problem solving—they offer good offices and facilitate access to consensual and non-adversarial procedures (ex. conciliation or mediation).

---

17. *OECD Guidelines, supra* note 2, at 3; *see also* U.S. National Contact Point Guide, *supra* note 4, at 5.

18. U.S. National Contact Point Guide, *supra* note 4, at 6.

19. *Id.* at 5.

20. *Id.* at 6.

Any party can submit a specific instance to an NCP regarding the alleged non-observance of the Guidelines. Once the specific instance has been submitted, its consideration is composed of three phases:

1) Initial assessment: to determine if the issues raised merit further examination
2) Offer of good offices: to seek advice and facilitate access to consensual and non-adversarial means to resolve the issues
3) Conclusion: to issue statements or reports.[21]

Final Report, Kinross Gold Corporation/Association of Neighborhoods of Paracatu, Allegation of Non-Compliance NCP No. 01/2014[22]

1. SUMMARY OF THE CLAIM.

On 18 June 2013, Brazil National Contact Point (NCP) received a claim of non-observance of the OECD Guidelines for Multinational Enterprises from Paracatu neighboring associations against Kinross Brasil Mineração, which is part of the Kinross Gold Corporation group based in Toronto, Canada.

The complainant associations are composed of residents of the districts of Machadinho, rural community near Paracatu, and three urban districts, Bela Vista II, Alto da Colina, Amoreiras II. According to the allegation, the following conducts of the enterprise are in disagreement with the OECD Guidelines:

a) *The use of explosives in the company's production process would have caused cracks in houses near the mine in Paracatu;*
b) *Rural properties acquired by Kinross were transformed into dams or preservation areas, isolating the rural area of Machadinho, damaging residents' access to the city.*

According to the claimants, the aforementioned conduct would violate the caput and items 1, 2, 7, 11, 12 and 15 of Chapter II, General Policies; Items 1, 2, 3, 4, 5 and 6 of Chapter IV, Human Rights; and items 3, 4, 5, 6 (d) of Chapter VI, Environment, of the Guidelines:

II. General Policies

Enterprises should take fully into account established policies in the countries in which they operate, and consider the views of other stakeholders. In this regard:

---

21. *Specific Instances Mechanism of the OECD Guidelines for Multinational Enterprises*, ORG. FOR ECON. COOPERATION AND DEV. [OECD], http://mneguidelines.oecd.org/specificinstances.htm (last visited Feb. 10, 2018).

22. Brazilian National Contact Point, *Final Rep. KINROSS Gold Corporation/Association of Neighborhoods of Paracatu Allegation of Non-compliance*, NCP No. 01/2014 (Dec. 21, 2016).

A. *Enterprises should:*

1. *Contribute to economic, environmental and social progress with a view to achieving sustainable development.*
2. *Respect the internationally recognised human rights of those affected by their activities. . . .*
7. *Develop and apply effective self-regulatory practices and management systems that foster a relationship of confidence and mutual trust between enterprises and the societies in which they operate. . . .*
11. *Avoid causing or contributing to adverse impacts on matters covered by the Guidelines, through their own activities, and address such impacts when they occur.*
12. *Seek to prevent or mitigate an adverse impact where they have not contributed to that impact, when the impact is nevertheless directly linked to their operations, products or services by a business relationship. This is not intended to shift responsibility from the entity causing an adverse impact to the enterprise with which it has a business relationship. . . .*
15. *Abstain from any improper involvement in local political activities. . . .*

IV. Human Rights

States have the duty to protect human rights. Enterprises should, within the framework of internationally recognised human rights, the international human rights obligations of the countries in which they operate as well as relevant domestic laws and regulations:

1. *Respect human rights, which means they should avoid infringing on the human rights of others and should address adverse human rights impacts with which they are involved.*
2. *Within the context of their own activities, avoid causing or contributing to adverse human rights impacts and address such impacts when they occur.*
3. *Seek ways to prevent or mitigate adverse human rights impacts that are directly linked to their business operations, products or services by a business relationship, even if they do not contribute to those impacts.*
4. *Have a policy commitment to respect human rights.*
5. *Carry out human rights due diligence as appropriate to their size, the nature and context of operations and the severity of the risks of adverse human rights impacts.*
6. *Provide for or co-operate through legitimate processes in the remediation of adverse human rights impacts where they identify that they have caused or contributed to these impacts.*

VI. Environment

. . .

3. *Assess, and address in decision-making, the foreseeable environmental, health, and safety-related impacts associated with the processes, goods, and services of the enterprise over their full lifecycle with a view to avoiding or,*

when unavoidable, mitigating them. Where these proposed activities may have significant environmental, health, or safety impacts, and where they are subject to a decision of a competent authority, prepare an appropriate environmental impact assessment.

4. *Consistent with the scientific and technical understanding of the risks, where there are threats of serious damage to the environment, taking also into account human health and safety, not use the lack of full scientific certainty as a reason for postponing cost-effective measures to prevent or minimise such damage.*

5. *Maintain contingency plans for preventing, mitigating, and controlling serious environmental and health damage from their operations, including accidents and emergencies; and mechanisms for immediate reporting to the competent authorities.*

6. *Continually seek to improve corporate environmental performance, at the level of the enterprise and, where appropriate, of its supply chain, by encouraging such activities as:*

   . . .

d) *exploring and assessing ways of improving the environmental performance of the enterprise over the longer term, for instance by developing strategies for emission reduction, efficient resource utilisation and recycling, substitution or reduction of use of toxic substances, or strategies on biodiversity.*

In a preliminary analysis, this NCP, in accordance with the Brazil NCP Resolution No. 01/2012, concluded that the Allegation of Non-compliance was subject to the themes of the Guidelines. It contained a sufficiently defined focus and presented information that could be analyzed by objective criteria. Thus, this NCP decided to accept the claim and communicated this fact to Kinross, the OECD and Canada NCP.

On a first meeting with the representative of the Rural Community of Machadinho, he reported that Kinross had bought land properties surrounding the Community, modifying the access route of the remaining populations to the city of Paracatu. Because of this, the venal value of these lands would have been diminished.

In relation to the urban communities, the expansion of Kinross's mining activities took place in areas bordering the claimants' neighborhoods. In these regions, mining activities took place in the open and very close to residences. The detonation of explosives caused noise and vibration in the residences. The explosions usually lasted from four to six seconds. The expansion and approximation of mining activities in relation to the urban districts occurred concurrently with the appearance of cracks in the neighborhoods' houses.

Regarding the cracks, Kinross and the National Institute of Colonization and Agrarian Reform of Brazil (INCRA) carried out tests that verified that there was no causal link between the cracks and the activities of the mines. According to the report of the Kinross expertise, the houses had not been built according to rules of the Brazilian Association of Technical Standards (ABNT); that is, the houses should have had more solid structures.

In 2015, the company built acoustic and visual barriers to mitigate the effects of the explosions, but there was no further information on the effectiveness of these activities. According to Kinross, there is a daily relationship between the company and the members of these communities, who participate in monthly relationship forums to carry out different activities.

2. MEETINGS OF MEDIATION.

A. First mediation meeting—September 2015.

The claimants reported that, although the company had expanded its social action activities, concomitantly with the expansion and increase of the intensity of its activities, the residents of both urban and rural areas had not previously been informed about the company's expansion plans, nor on the necessity to have homes with more robust structures. These were the reasons that led them to seek advice from this NCP.

The claimants also reported on a Kinross land regularization project in the region. The project had been conducted in partnership with the Paracatu City Hall. Kinross's Director of Licensing and Sustainability explained that the company seeks to provide a level of comfort to the affected community, and that was done when the use of explosives was introduced. He reaffirmed that, technically, detonations are not responsible for causing cracks in homes. That the company operates below the levels of vibration allowed by Brazilian law, and that these such levels do not cause crackings.

The director concluded that the company would be willing to engage with City Hall and Civil Defense to carry out the risk assessments of the houses but would refuse to admit causal link between the occurrence of cracks and the mining activities.

Kinross had asked the City Hall to carry out a survey of the houses at risk, but the representative of the Associations said he believed that this would not be done, since that was not that body's obligation. He also disputed the explanations given, stating that life is very difficult for those living near the areas of explosion, where there are large amounts of dust, which cause many limitations to domestic life in the region.

The claimants [argued] that they were not dealing here with residences, but above all with the lives of those living in these areas. If there happened to be any collapse, [they] feared for the loss of their lives. The representative of the neighborhood associations also expected to receive compensation for the demolished structures in Machadinho . . . . He would like the company to acknowledge its responsibility for the cracks in Paracatu, and that it would be important to resettle the families whose houses are damaged.

The first meeting was concluded with an agreement that the Neighborhood Associations would draft [proposed compensation], to be funded by Kinross, which proposed a new round of talks for the presentation of the proposals. Proposals would not need to be drawn up by a professional, but it was essential that they be clear and well-structured.

B. Second mediation meeting—March 24, 2016.

According to the first mediation meeting records, Kinross had proposed to pay for a technical survey on the cracks of the urban houses and to receive a compensation proposal for the Machadinho Community.

The Associations presented a budget proposal for the payment of the costs of preparing a study on cracks and another budget for the purchase of rural equipment for the Community of Machadinho. Both were delivered to Kinross earlier in Paracatu, to be discussed later during a second mediation meeting in Brasilia.

The proposal[s] should address the needs of the neighborhood associations of Paracatu. One house [would serve] as a [model], which should be applied to the rest of the houses.

However, in the second mediation in Brasilia, Kinross was against the proposals presented, arguing that each house had its own damage, so each house should be evaluated individually.

The company reiterated that this had been emphasized in the first mediation, and that the most important thing was that the study did not aim to establish responsibilities. The proposal presented also dealt with the houses of a single neighborhood, Alto da Colina, and Kinross needed studies for all three neighborhoods, and required that they be delivered together. The company was looking for a study that assessed the risk of each household, the number of people at risk, and what could be done to help these people.

The company requested that the other stakeholders, including the public sector, participate in this process. Kinross requested the inclusion of a body from the public sector because of the houses at risk and because they were dealing with human lives, and suggested the participation of the City Hall. Under the rules of the company, contracting would have to be done via bidding, with the presentation of at least three executors. However, that was not explained in the first meeting.

Kinross reported on other projects carried out in partnership with the City Hall and stated that it would like to fit the proposals presented in this claim into the existing programs underway with that body. The Generation of Work and Income Program is one these such programs, which is offered through an annual public notice. Thus, the public entity, City Hall, would be the intermediary manager of the proposals, and the rural community and urban associations could execute some of their projects through these programs.

The representative of the Associations reacted by saying that the pilot proposal in the Alto da Colina neighborhood had been treated in the first mediation. He believed that the City Hall would not be the ideal partner for this project because the City Hall was currently short in servants. He believed that they should work with the associations, an executing company and a representative of the public power. In addition, there would have been a major change of focus in this meeting in relation to what had been agreed in the first meeting. At the first mediation, the associations had been asked to provide an estimate of spending for the reform of one hundred houses, as well as the definition of which would be reformed. According to the Associations representative, the discussion under way at this meeting had changed the conditions agreed upon in the first mediation meeting. That was the reason why the representatives of the other neighborhoods were not present at this meeting.

The NCP representative intervened, questioning whether the company would be ready to discuss the proposals presented objectively at this meeting, to which the company replied that it would only discuss a proposal for the three neighborhoods jointly, not just one of them. The company was there to settle the [parameters] and then go on to a specific discussion. They proposed that this detailed meeting could take place in Paracatu in the future.

Regarding the rural areas, the representative of the community of Machadinho [wanted] to involve the community and the City in these surveys. He [wanted] the community to be the protagonist, the manager of this process, not the City Hall.

Kinross requested that the rural areas present proof of ownership of land. Their representative reported that they did not have the lands' registry certificates, and stated that the Community's lands were only listed in the Community's foundation document. He estimated that there were about forty families, prior to the expropriation and land acquisition by Kinross. Some land had been purchased by Kinross from these families.

The representative of the Neighborhood Associations of Paracatu reiterated that all compensation proposals were suggested by Kinross in the first mediation. However, [now] the company was saying that it did not recognize the demands of Machadinho. Kinross disagreed, saying that the points raised [at the meeting] had been dealt with at the meeting in Paracatu. He further stated that the premises presented at this meeting were so because of the proposal delivered in Paracatu. They said they understood that these would be the [parameters] for the proposal to be examined in a later meeting.

At the end of the meeting, Kinross did not agree with the proposed compensation for the area of Machadinho, in the form presented. They would offer compensation within the . . . already existing company's programs. The next program publication would be in December 2016. If Machadinho's proposal met the program's requirements, it would be evaluated and possibly approved. The NCP recommended that Kinross should help by giving guidance in drawing up a viable proposal for the Community to apply for the company's programs. Kinross accepted the recommendation.

The NCP concluded the meeting and proposed a third mediation meeting, which would have the purpose of dealing with the demands of Machadinho and the study on the houses of the three districts of Paracatu.

C. Third mediation meeting—September 23, 2016.

In June 2016, two months after the second mediation meeting, Kinross informed the NCP that the Paracatu City Hall had accepted their partnership proposal. Also in June, they formalized a partnership agreement with the Civil

Defense. However, due to the municipal elections of 2016, the City Hall would not be able to execute new projects until after the elections. The activities of this partnership were said to begin in 2017.

Kinross contacted the Neighborhood Associations' leaders directly in Paracatu, when the partnership project with the City Hall was presented to them. They proposed the project as a viable response to the lawsuits filed with the NCP. The Neighborhood Associations agreed to the partnership with the City Hall and a document was signed by them and sent to this NCP on 29 June 2016. The Associations informed Kinross that they were willing to attend the third NCP mediation meeting in Brasilia to formally register this agreement. Mr. Rosival was not invited to sign or participate in that meeting.

Kinross then requested the third mediation meeting, and the NCP proposed and contacted the parties in June to schedule the third mediation meeting. Only in September did the parties find a common date, 23 September 2016. Surprisingly, on September 22, the Neighborhood Associations representative wrote to the NCP canceling the meeting, claiming that some neighborhood representatives were candidates for the coming election and that they were therefore barred from attending the NCP meeting. This NCP was surprised by the cancellation and Kinross did not accept it. Kinross said that the tickets of its directors had been bought and the daily rates paid, and that they would show up to take part in meeting. The NCP agreed to hold the meeting. Among the representatives of the neighborhood, only Mr. Rosival attended.

On 23 September, to the surprise of those present, the representative of the Associations, Rosival, stated that he had been informed of the legal impediment of representatives of some urban and rural districts only the day before. However, he should have known of the candidacies of his associates if he had been in contact with those representatives since June.

Three Kinross directors, Alderman Rosival, and the NCP coordinator were [in attendance.] The meeting's agenda . . . was divided between [issues] related to the region of Machadinho and the rebuilding of urban houses.

Kinross met in Paracatu with Machadinho's region representative to explain the operation of the Program Integrate and how the urban neighborhoods and Machadinho Community could participate in the Program, as well as how support would be provided in formulating the proposal. The Program Integrate is directed to non-governmental organizations, with the objective of generating work and income, for the period of two years, and the possibility of contribution of up to 80,000 Brazilian Real.

The demand for proof of ownership of the rural lands requested by the NCP at the second mediation meeting was never met. Thus Kinross stated that it did not recognize . . . the rural Community of Machadinho, as the company could not assure who was entitled to compensation. . . . Kinross said the supposed owners were impetuous. They do not live in the region; they live in the city and have productive farms in the region.

The mediator concluded that, without proof of ownership of the land, Kinross would not be able to repair damages or provide compensation, as the allegation process could not appoint who had been harmed. Kinross held the meeting on the Program Integrate in Paracatu with the rural communities and confirmed its commitment to assist them in the preparation of social action projects by the end of 2016.

Mr. Rosival, as representative of the Machadinho residents' Associations, despite the representatives not being present, said that they . . . acknowledged their demand . . . [pertaining to] this part of the allegation of non-compliance would not be able to be resolved as demanded.

As for the urban neighborhoods residents' demand on the consequences of the explosions, the company mentioned a study made by the research company Avalicon, which concluded that cracks were not the result of Kinross activities. Damage to houses occurred because they had not been built according to ABNT technical specifications (Brazilian Association for Technical Norms). Avalicon's report showed that there was no correlation between the explosions and the consequences in the houses. That is, the study found no causality link between the two actions. The analysis showed that the vibration would not have damaged the houses if they had been properly built.

Despite Avalicon's report on causality, Kinross confirmed its intent to repair the homes through a partnership project with the City Hall, with the active participation of affected communities. The company reported that the City Hall has done this action with other neighborhoods of the city, through the "Urbanization Plan for Precarious Settlements."

However, because 2016 was an election year, works in the three neighborhoods cited in this allegation had not yet begun, as the City Hall was prevented from starting new projects . . . . For other districts of Paracatu, which had [previously initiated processes], the City Hall would [continue to] carry[] out the works.

Kinross clarified that the work of the City Hall [would be] done in three strands. The selection of houses that are well, those that need renovation and those that can no longer receive improvements. Those houses in risk areas will have their residents transferred to other locations for resettlement. In case of a need for resettlement, the City Hall will seek for the demanding neighborhoods' similar localities for the construction of new houses.

According to the proposal accepted by the Associations, Kinross [would] transfer resources to the City Hall[] . . . to reform the houses through the "Urbanization Plan for Precarious Settlements." The City Hall civil servants [would] prepare the survey and a company will be hired to do the technical evaluations of the homes that have been considered sensitive. Based on this survey, a reform or resettlement plan will be draw[n].

The NCP questioned whether there would be a guarantee that this project will be executed, due to the dependency of the City Hall. Kinross said yes, that the guarantee is the agreement with the City Hall and the Letter of Intent that establishes the commitment to start in 2017 the "Plan of Urbanization and Precarious Settlements."

Mr. Rosival considered that the City Hall should be a partner, but not the executor of the project, because Kinross would be transferring its obligation to third parties. He complained that the initial proposal was that associations would indicate a company to survey housing needs. He also questioned whether the City Hall projects already underway would be working, as he did not know the program.

An important fact to note is that Mr. Rosival, the petitioner, had no knowledge of the signing of the Letter of Acceptance by the Associations on 28 June 2016. In this third mediation, three months later, Mr. Rosival still did not know about the Associations' agreement or about the signing of this document by the ones whom he represented.

The meeting mediator questioned the company [about] whether the City Hall would make such urban recoveries with or without Kinross's financial backing, as the City Hall would be undertaking city-wide reforms. Kinross replied that this would be the second module of the City Hall program, and that the associations had accepted compensation in this way, although this was not the form of reparation[s] requested in the initial claim.

The copy of the letter of intent was signed by the Associations and sent by Kinross to the NCP on 29 June. The letter contained the signatures of all the members of the Associations . . . . The document is proof that the Associations accepted the partnership between Kinross and the City Hall.

At the end of the meeting, Kinross requested the closing of the claim, saying that they have signed this project with the City Hall, [and that] activities will start in 2017. They will transfer . . . resources the same way the company does with their other partnership projects. Kinross understood that the offer was the viable form the company found to carry out compensation, addressing all the points demanded in the allegation. It may not have done so in the way requested, but due to several events, including political events, the best way the company could address these demands was through the partnership with the City Hall. The company did not wish to play the role of manager in this process, so they decided to finance the project and monitor its execution.

The mediator concluded the meeting, saying that the NCP's guidance in this process is to seek agreement between the parties. Although the associations were not present, they had signed an agreement with Kinross, fulfilling the allegation requirements. On the other hand, the Associations did not inform [the NCP] that they would not attend the meeting, and their absence would prevent them from modifying what had already been agreed. The NCP concluded by saying that this case was successful in finding an agreed solution through the mediation offered.

3. PROPOSALS AND RECOMMENDATIONS.

According to Kinross, the City Hall will make a diagnosis and [meet] with each association of the three urban districts. The City Hall is committed to informing Kinross about this meeting, and about the details of what will be agreed upon.

The NCP asked Kinross to send information about the City Hall program . . . which they will join. The company responded that they will continue to feed the NCP with information about the implementation process of what has been agreed upon.

The NCP requested that Kinross forward a copy of the project document to be established for each area of Paracatu in 2017, for monitoring purposes.

The NCP recommended that Kinross should host the Machadinho community and give guidance in drawing up a viable proposal to apply for the company's programs.

This NCP recommends that Kinross inform[] residents of neighborhoods adjacent to their mines about their work and future plans that may interfere with residents' lives. That shall foster a relationship of trust between the company and the residents of Paracatu.

The NCP also recommends that Kinross conduct due diligence processes that assess the adverse effects of its mining activities, establishing a maximum distance between its mining operations and the home dwellings in the outlying districts of Paracatu.

4. CONCLUSION.

This Brazil NCP concluded that the document of agreement signed by the associations in June with Kinross and the City Hall responds to the demands presented in this allegation. The demands of the rural communities are not going to be addressed as they were not able to provide the requested property documents, which would confirm to whom compensation should be addressed.

[The parties agree] that Kinross will repair the urban neighborhoods' residences, despite not having admitted causality between their mining activities and the cracks presented at the houses.

For all of the above, Brazil NCP provided its good offices and successfully found a negotiated solution for the case.

This allegation [of] non-compliance with the OECD guidelines is now concluded. This NCP expects that the recommendations presented will be considered, and follow-up information and monitoring will take place.

BRAZIL NATIONAL CONTACT POINT
OECD Guidelines for Multinational Enterprises
Brasília, 21 December 2016

II. Disclosure

This guideline relates to the disclosure of core information about the financial state and operations of multinational enterprises. Transparency is necessary for a business to meet the reasonable expectations of its stakeholders. By disclosing its activities and future plans, a company empowers stakeholders to effectively advocate for their interests and creates an opportunity for dialogue before taking action.

OECD Disclosure[23]

1. Enterprises should ensure that timely and accurate information is disclosed on all material matters regarding their activities, structure, financial situation, performance, ownership and governance. This information should be disclosed for the enterprise as a whole, and, where appropriate, along business lines or geographic areas. Disclosure policies of enterprises should be tailored to the nature, size and location of the enterprise, with due regard taken of costs, business confidentiality and other competitive concerns.

2. Disclosure policies of enterprises should include, but not be limited to, material information on:
   a) the financial and operating results of the enterprise;
   b) enterprise objectives;
   c) major share ownership and voting rights, including the structure of a group of enterprises and intra-group relations, as well as control enhancing mechanisms;
   d) remuneration policy for members of the board and key executives, and information about board members, including qualifications, the selection process, other enterprise directorships and whether each board member is regarded as independent by the board;
   e) related party transactions;
   f) foreseeable risk factors;
   g) issues regarding workers and other stakeholders;
   h) governance structures and policies, in particular, the content of any corporate governance code or policy and its implementation process.

3. Enterprises are encouraged to communicate additional information that could include:
   a) value statements or statements of business conduct intended for public disclosure including, depending on its relevance for the enterprise's activities, information on the enterprise's policies relating to matters covered by the Guidelines;
   b) policies and other codes of conduct to which the enterprise subscribes, their date of adoption and the countries and entities to which such statements apply;
   c) its performance in relation to these statements and codes;
   d) information on internal audit, risk management and legal compliance systems;
   e) information on relationships with workers and other stakeholders.

4. Enterprises should apply high quality standards for accounting, and financial as well as non-financial disclosure, including environmental and social reporting where they exist. The standards or policies under which information is compiled and published should be reported. An annual audit

---

23. *OECD Guidelines, supra* note 2, at 27–30.

should be conducted by an independent, competent and qualified auditor in order to provide an external and objective assurance to the board and shareholders that the financial statements fairly represent the financial position and performance of the enterprise in all material respects.

COMMENTARY ON DISCLOSURE

28. The purpose of this chapter is to encourage improved understanding of the operations of multinational enterprises. Clear and complete information on enterprises is important to a variety of users ranging from shareholders and the financial community to other constituencies such as workers, local communities, special interest groups, governments and society at large. To improve public understanding of enterprises and their interaction with society and the environment, enterprises should be transparent in their operations and responsive to the public's increasingly sophisticated demands for information.

29. The information highlighted in this chapter addresses disclosure in two areas. The first set of disclosure recommendations is identical to disclosure items outlined in the OECD Principles of Corporate Governance. Their related annotations provide further guidance and the recommendations in the *Guidelines* should be construed in relation to them. The first set of disclosure recommendations may be supplemented by a second set of disclosure recommendations which enterprises are encouraged to follow. The disclosure recommendations focus mainly on publicly traded enterprises. To the extent that they are deemed applicable in light of the nature, size and location of enterprises, they should also be a useful tool to improve corporate governance in non-traded enterprises; for example, privately held or State-owned enterprises.

30. Disclosure recommendations are not expected to place unreasonable administrative or cost burdens on enterprises. Nor are enterprises expected to disclose information that may endanger their competitive position unless disclosure is necessary to fully inform the investment decision and to avoid misleading the investor. In order to determine what information should be disclosed at a minimum, the *Guidelines* use the concept of materiality. Material information can be defined as information whose omission or misstatement could influence the economic decisions taken by users of information.

31. The *Guidelines* also generally note that information should be prepared and disclosed in accordance with high quality standards of accounting and financial and non-financial disclosure. This significantly improves the ability of investors to monitor the enterprise by providing increased reliability and comparability of reporting, and improved insight into its performance. The annual independent audit recommended by the *Guidelines* should contribute to an improved control and compliance by the enterprise.

32. Disclosure is addressed in two areas. The first set of disclosure recommendations calls for timely and accurate disclosure on all material matters regarding the corporation, including the financial situation, performance, ownership and governance of the company. Companies are also expected to disclose sufficient information on the remuneration of board members and key executives (either

individually or in the aggregate) for investors to properly assess the costs and benefits of remuneration plans and the contribution of incentive schemes, such as stock option schemes, to performance. Related party transactions and material foreseeable risk factors are additional relevant information that should be disclosed, as well as material issues regarding workers and other stakeholders.

33. The *Guidelines* also encourage a second set of disclosure or communication practices in areas where reporting standards are still evolving such as, for example, social, environmental and risk reporting. This is particularly the case with greenhouse gas emissions, as the scope of their monitoring is expanding to cover direct and indirect, current and future, corporate and product emissions; biodiversity is another example. Many enterprises provide information on a broader set of topics than financial performance and consider disclosure of such information a method by which they can demonstrate a commitment to socially acceptable practices. In some cases, this second type of disclosure —or communication with the public and with other parties directly affected by the enterprise's activities—may pertain to entities that extend beyond those covered in the enterprise's financial accounts. For example, it may also cover information on the activities of subcontractors and suppliers or of joint venture partners. This is particularly appropriate to monitor the transfer of environmentally harmful activities to partners.

34. Many enterprises have adopted measures designed to help them comply with the law and standards of business conduct, and to enhance the transparency of their operations. A growing number of firms have issued voluntary codes of corporate conduct, which are expressions of commitments to ethical values in such areas as environment, human rights, labour standards, consumer protection, or taxation. Specialised management systems have been or are being developed and continue to evolve with the aim of helping them respect these commitments—these involve information systems, operating procedures and training requirements. Enterprises are cooperating with NGOs and intergovernmental organisations in developing reporting standards that enhance enterprises' ability to communicate how their activities influence sustainable development outcomes (for example, the Global Reporting Initiative).

35. Enterprises are encouraged to provide easy and economical access to published information and to consider making use of information technologies to meet this goal. Information that is made available to users in home markets should also be available to all interested users. Enterprises may take special steps to make information available to communities that do not have access to printed media (for example, poorer communities that are directly affected by the enterprise's activities).

Hypothetical: Disclosure of Payments to Government

U.S. Mining Co. ("U.S. Mining") is incorporated in Florida and engages in the extraction of mineral deposits around the world. In 2010, U.S. Mining entered into a joint venture with the government of Malaysia for the extraction of copper deposits. Under the terms of the joint venture, U.S. Mining was required to make regular royalty payments to the Malaysian government. Malaysian law requires that a portion of royalties received in connection with any extraction project be reinvested in the local communities surrounding the mine. However, in practice, the Malaysian government significantly delays or never makes such investments.

What, if anything, should U.S. Mining do about this situation?

U.S. National Contact Point for the OECD Guidelines for Multinational Enterprises, Final Statement, Specific Instance between Greenpeace and Herakles Farms and Herakles Capital[24]

Office of the U.S. National Contact Point
May 19, 2014

I. INTRODUCTION

This Final Statement concludes consideration by the United States National Contact Point (U.S. NCP) for the OECD Guidelines for Multinational Enterprises (Guidelines) of the Specific Instance submitted by Greenpeace regarding the actions of Herakles Farms and Herakles Capital. The NCP's review of this Specific Instance is concluded as conditions are not satisfactory to proceed to mediation.

II. CONTEXT AND BACKGROUND ON THE U.S. NCP

The OECD Guidelines for Multinational Enterprises (MNEs) are voluntary, non-binding recommendations for responsible business conduct in a global context. The Guidelines are addressed to MNEs operating in or from the territories of governments adhering to the OECD's Declaration on International Investment and Multinational Enterprises, of which the Guidelines form one part. Adhering governments have committed to a) encouraging their MNEs to follow the Guidelines in their global operations and b) appointing a National Contact Point (NCP) to assist parties in seeking a consensual resolution to issues that may arise under the Guidelines.

As a part of its function, the U.S. NCP receives concerns raised, in the form of a Specific Instance, about the business conduct of an MNE operating in or from the United States. . . . In such circumstances, the NCP's primary function is to assist affected parties, when appropriate, in their efforts to reach a satisfactory and consensual resolution to matters raised under the Guidelines. The NCP's role is to take up issues that are amenable to a consensual resolution under the Guidelines

---

24. U.S. Nat'l Contact Point for the OECD Guidelines for Multinational Enterprises, U.S. Dep't of State, Final Statement: Specific Instance Between Greenpeace and Herakles Farms and Herakles Capital (May 19, 2014).

and, where appropriate, make recommendations as to how the enterprise might make its business practices more consistent with the Guidelines. Consistent with the voluntary nature of the Guidelines, the NCP does not make a determination whether a "violation" of the Guidelines has occurred, nor does the NCP have legal authority to adjudicate disputes submitted under this process.

III. INITIAL ASSESSMENT

The process leading up to completing the Specific Instance includes the Initial Assessment, which determines whether the issues raised merit further examination. The Initial Assessment does not determine whether the company has acted consistently with the Guidelines. Per the OECD Guideline procedures, the Initial Assessment is made based on:

- Identity of the party and its interest in the matter
- Whether the issue is material and substantiated
- Likely link between the enterprise's activities and the issue raised
- Relevance of applicable law and procedures, including court rulings
- Treatment of similar issues in other domestic or international proceedings
- Contribution of the specific issue to the purposes and effectiveness of the Guidelines

IV. THE SPECIFIC INSTANCE

On March 11, 2014, Greenpeace, a nongovernmental organization, submitted a specific instance regarding Herakles Farms and Herakles Capital (Herakles), the former of which is a New York-based entity. In February 2014, Greenpeace wrote a letter to both Herakles Capital and Herakles Farms requesting the following information:

> D. The financial and operating results of the group of enterprises known as Herakles Farms and Herakles Capital, including but not limited to, all affiliates and subsidiaries of said companies, for each of the fiscal years 2008-2013; and the companies' financial contributions to All for Africa and receipts from All for Africa;
>
> E. The major share ownership and voting rights, including the structure of the group of enterprises known as Herakles Farms and Herakles Capital, including, but not limited to, intra-group relations, as well as control enhancing mechanisms and all beneficial ownership.

Greenpeace further requested that this information be provided on a project-by-project basis. Greenpeace cited Chapter III, paragraph 4 of the OECD Guidelines as the basis for its complaint. Herakles did not respond to the Greenpeace letter.

V. DECISION AND CONCLUSION

The NCP determines that the issues raised in the Specific Instance do not merit further examination and declines to offer good offices to seek a mediated resolution between Greenpeace and Herakles.

Greenpeace provided insufficient information to support its allegation that Herakles was not in compliance with the Guidelines. We note that Herakles is a private company, not in fact a multinational corporation, although we do not decline to offer our good offices for the Greenpeace submission based on that fact, nor does its legal status in the United States remove it from the scope of the Guidelines. Rather, the NCP believes that the public documentation that Herakles provides on its website in large measure duplicates the relevant information that shareholders would expect from the annual report of a multinational corporation. Because Herakles' alleged violation of chapter III paragraph four cannot be substantiated based on the specific instance filed, the NCP declines to offer its good offices for mediation.

David M. Birdsey
U.S. National Contact Point for the OECD Guidelines
for Multinational Enterprises

III. Human Rights

"The concept of human rights is as simple as it is powerful: that people have a right to be treated with dignity."[25] The U.N.'s 1948 Universal Declaration of Human Rights (UDHR), signed by all 171 participating countries, encapsulates the definition of human rights.[26] These rights are "inherent to all human beings, regardless of race, sex, nationality, ethnicity, language, religion, or any other status."[27] The UDHR is one of the foundational documents in the body of human rights law—together with the International Covenant on Civil and Political Rights (ICCPR) and the International Covenant on Economic, Social and Cultural Rights (ICESCR), these instruments form the basis of the International Bill of Human Rights.[28]

Numerous other international human rights treaties have been adopted since the passage of the UDHR, including the International Convention on the Elimination of All Forms of Racial Discrimination (ICERD) and the Convention on the Rights of the Child (CRC).[29] As of 2018, each of these Covenants and Conventions has been ratified by over 160 states.[30]

The OECD Guideline on Human Rights requires that business enterprises "[r]espect human rights . . . [and] avoid causing or contributing to adverse

---

25. Monash University Castan Centre for Human Rights Law in collaboration with Office of the United Nations High Commissioner for Human Rights, Human Rights Translated 2.0: A Business Reference Guide ix (2016).

    26. *Id.*

    27. United Nations, Human Rights, http://www.un.org/en/sections/issues-depth/human-rights/.

    28. *Id.*

    29. *Id.*

    30. *Id.*

human rights impacts and address such impacts when they occur."[31] An adverse, or negative human rights impact, is defined as occurring:

> [W]hen an action removes or reduces the ability of an individual to enjoy his or her human rights. Several elements are important in this definition:
>
> - *Negative:* removing or reducing the ability to enjoy human rights;
> - *Action:* the activity (or inactivity) of the company itself or one of its business relationships that leads to or contributes to an impact;
> - *An individual:* somebody affected or harmed (which the Guiding Principles refer to as "potentially affected stakeholders");
> - *Human rights:* the impact is on an internationally recognized human right or rights.[32]

The table below lists the rights included in the International Bill of Human Rights and includes examples of how businesses might impact those rights.[33]

Table 9-1. Rights Included in the International Bill of Human Rights

Relevant Human Right	Brief Explanation of the Right	Examples of How Business Might Be Involved with an Impact on the Right
Right of self-determination [included in ICCPR art. 1 and ICESCR art. 1[34]]	• A right of peoples, rather than individuals. • Peoples are entitled to determine their political status and place in the international community. • It includes the rights to pursue economic, social, and cultural development; to dispose of a land's natural resources; and not to be deprived of the means of subsistence. • A particular right of indigenous peoples to self-determination has been specifically recognized by the international community.	• Engaging in business activities on land that has traditional significance to the peoples that inhabit an area when that land was acquired by a government without due consultation with the local population. • Any activity that might have impacts on indigenous peoples' lands, whether through acquisition, construction, or operation, may give rise to impacts on their right to self-determination.

---

31. *OECD Guidelines, supra* note 2, at 31.

32. Shift, Oxfam, & Global Compact Network Netherlands, Doing Business With Respect for Human Rights: A Guidance Tool for Companies 23 (2d ed. 2016).

33. Shift in association with Mazars, *How Can Businesses Impact Human Rights?*, UN Guiding Principles Reporting Framework, https://www.ungpreporting.org/resources/how-businesses-impact-human-rights/ (last visited Feb. 10, 2018).

34. The United States has not ratified the ICESCR. United Nations Office of Legal Affairs, Status of Treaties: International Covenant on Economic, Social and Cultural Rights (Mar. 13, 2018), https://treaties.un.org/Pages/ViewDetails.aspx?src=TREATY&mtdsg_no=IV-3&chapter=4&clang=_en [hereinafter U.N. OLA, Status of Treaties: ICESCR].

Relevant Human Right	Brief Explanation of the Right	Examples of How Business Might Be Involved with an Impact on the Right
Right to life [included in UDHR art. 3 and ICCPR art. 6]	• Right not to be deprived of life arbitrarily or unlawfully. • Right to have one's life protected, for example, from physical attacks or health and safety risks.	• The lethal use of force by security forces (state or private) to protect company resources, facilities, or personnel. • Operations that pose life-threatening safety risks to workers or neighbouring communities through, for example, exposure to toxic chemicals. • The manufacture and sale of products with lethal flaws.
Rights to liberty and security of the person [included in UDHR art. 3 and ICCPR art. 9]	• These rights involve the prohibition of unlawful or arbitrary detention. • "Lawful" detention is understood to mean that it must be authorized by an appropriate government body, such as the courts, and be capable of being challenged by the detainee. • "Arbitrary" detention is always prohibited. • Security of the person includes protection from physical attacks, threats of such attacks, or other severe forms of harassment, whether or not a person is detained.	• Threatening staff with physical punishment or tolerating severe harassment of some employees, for example, of trade union members or members of a minority ethnic group. • A company whose supplier routinely allows sexual abuse of female workers to go unaddressed in their workplace.
Right not to be subjected to slavery, servitude, or forced labor [included in UDHR art. 4 and ICCPR art. 8]	• Slavery exists when one human effectively owns another. • Freedom from servitude covers other forms of severe economic exploitation or degradation, such as in the trafficking of workers or debt bondage. • Rights to freedom from slavery and servitude are absolute rights. • Forced or compulsory labor is defined by the [International Labour Organization] as all work or service that is extracted under menace of any penalty and for which the person has not voluntarily offered themselves. • Providing payment does not mean that work is not forced labor if the other aspects of the definition are met.	• Businesses may unknowingly benefit through their supply chains from the labor of workers who have been trafficked and are forced to work as slaves, for example, on agricultural plantations. Women and children may be subject to particularly severe impacts in such situations. • A company may be involved in the transportation of people or goods that facilitates the trafficking of individuals. • Forced labor can arise in any sector where an employer puts workers in a position of debt bondage through company loans or the payment of fees to secure a job and/or where the company withholds workers' identity documents. This is a particular risk in the case of migrant workers, a recognized vulnerable group.

continued

Relevant Human Right	Brief Explanation of the Right	Examples of How Business Might Be Involved with an Impact on the Right
Right not to be subjected to torture; cruel, inhuman, and/or degrading treatment; or punishment [included in UDHR art. 5 and ICCPR art. 7[35]]	• An absolute right, which applies in all circumstances. • Torture has been held to involve a very high degree of pain or suffering that is intentionally inflicted for a specific purpose. • Cruel and/or inhuman treatment also entails severe suffering. • Degrading treatment has been held to involve extreme humiliation of the victim.	• Conducting business in countries where State security or police forces protecting company assets do not respect this right. • Failure to foster a workplace that is free from severe forms of harassment that cause serious mental distress. • Manufacture and sale of equipment misused by third parties for torture or cruel treatment or for medical or scientific experimentation without subjects' consent.
Right to recognition as a person before the law [included in UDHR art. 6 and ICCPR art. 16]	• All individuals are entitled to "legal personality," or independent legal recognition.	• Companies may be linked to such an impact, for example, where they benefit from a State-led land acquisition process that pays compensation only to male heads of households because the property of married women is treated as belonging to their husbands under domestic law.
Right to equality before the law, equal protection of the law, and rights of non-discrimination [included in UDHR art. 7 and ICCPR art. 26][36]	• Individuals have a right not to be discriminated against, directly or indirectly, on various grounds, including race, ethnicity, sex, language, religion, political or other opinion, national or social origin, property, and birth or other status (such as sexual orientation or health status, for example, having HIV/AIDS). • This right applies to the enjoyment of all other rights. • The State is allowed to make distinctions where they are in line with international human rights standards. • ILO standards provide further guidance on the content of the right.	• Indirectly discriminating in the recruitment, remuneration or promotion of workers, for example, by offering a training programme that enhances an individual's chance of promotion at a time that is reserved for religious observance by a particular group. • A company offers compensation to men and women in a situation where its operations or products have had negative impacts on their health in a way that discriminates against women (such as by failing to recognize the particular harm to their reproductive health).

continued

---

35. The United States submitted a reservation to article 7 of the ICCPR, noting that the United States "considers itself bound by article 7 to the extent that 'cruel, inhuman or degrading treatment or punishment' means the cruel and unusual treatment or punishment prohibited by the Fifth, Eighth, and/or Fourteenth Amendments to Constitution of the United States." United Nations Office of Legal Affairs, Status of Treaties: International Covenant on Civil and Political Rights (Mar. 13, 2018), https://treaties.un.org/Pages/ViewDetails.aspx?src=IND&mtdsg_no=IV-4&chapter=4&clang=_en [hereinafter U.N. OLA, Status of Treaties: ICCPR].

36. The United States submitted an understanding to article 26 of the ICCPR, noting that distinctions based upon race, sex, language, religion, or other terms used therein are permissible "when such distinctions are, at minimum, rationally related to a legitimate governmental objective." *Id.*

Relevant Human Right	Brief Explanation of the Right	Examples of How Business Might Be Involved with an Impact on the Right
Right to a fair trial [included in UDHR art. 10 and ICCPR art. 14]	• Required in both civil and criminal proceedings, this includes the right to a public hearing before an impartial tribunal. • Additional protections are required in criminal proceedings.	• A business tries to corrupt the judicial process by destroying relevant evidence or by seeking to bribe or otherwise influence judges or witnesses to take certain actions or make certain statements.
Right to be free from retroactive criminal law [included in UDHR art. 11 and ICCPR art. 15[37]]	• The State is prohibited from imposing criminal penalties for an act that was not illegal when it was committed, or from imposing higher penalties than those that were in force at the time.	• Companies may be linked to such an impact, for example, where political dissidents protest about some aspect of a company's operations and the State creates new, punitive measures to prosecute them.
Right of detained persons to humane treatment [included in ICCPR art. 10][38]	• This right requires detention authorities to take special measures for the protection of detainees (such as separating juveniles from other detainees).	• Companies involved in the construction, operation or maintenance of detention facilities (such as a prison or immigration detention facility) where detainees are mistreated.
Right not to be subjected to imprisonment for inability to fulfill a contract [included in ICCPR art. 11]	• This right applies where a person is incapable of meeting a private contractual obligation. • It restricts the type of punishment that the State can impose.	• Companies may be linked to such an impact where this right is not protected by the State, for example, where a small local supplier is genuinely unable to meet their contractual obligations and the company takes action against them.

continued

---

37. The United States submitted a reservation to article 15 of the ICCPR, stating that "because U.S. law generally applies to an offender the penalty in force at the time the offence was committed, the U.S. does not adhere to the . . . clause of . . . article 15" that makes particular reference to retroactive criminal punishment. *Id.*

38. The United States submitted a reservation to article 10 of the ICCPR, noting that while "the policy and practice of the United States are generally in compliance with and supportive of the Covenant's provisions regarding treatment of juveniles in the criminal justice system[,] . . . the United States reserves the right, in exceptional circumstances, to treat juveniles as adults[.]" *Id.* The United States also understands the 'exceptional circumstances' referenced in article 10 to "permit the imprisonment of an accused person with convicted persons where appropriate in light of an individual's overall dangerousness, and to permit accused persons to waive their right to segregation from convicted persons. The United States further understands that . . . article 10 does not diminish the goals of punishment, deterrence, and incapacitation as additional legitimate purposes for a penitentiary system." *Id.*

Relevant Human Right	Brief Explanation of the Right	Examples of How Business Might Be Involved with an Impact on the Right
Right of aliens to due process when facing expulsion [included in ICCPR art. 13]	• Aliens (meaning foreigners) who are legally present in a country are entitled to due process (meaning fair legal procedures) before being forced to leave.	• Where companies rely on migrant workers (either directly or through a third-party agency), there may be a risk of their operations being linked to such an impact.
Right to privacy [included in UDHR art. 12 and ICCPR art. 17]	• Individuals have a right to be protected from arbitrary, unreasonable or unlawful interference with their privacy, family, home or correspondence and from attacks on their reputation. • The State is allowed to authorize restrictions on privacy in line with international human rights standards, but "arbitrary" restrictions are always prohibited.	• Failing to protect the confidentiality of personal data held about employees or contract workers, customers or other individuals. • Requiring pregnancy testing as part of job applications. • Providing information about individuals to State authorities, without that individual's permission, in response to requests that are illegal under national law and/or not in line with international human rights standards. • Selling equipment or technology that can be used to track or monitor individuals' communications and movements to a State with a poor human rights record.
Right to freedom of movement [included in UDHR art. 13 and ICCPR art. 12]	• Individuals who are lawfully in a country have the right to move freely throughout it, to choose where to live and to leave. • Individuals also have the right not to be arbitrarily prevented from entering their own country.	• Relocation of communities because of company operations where that is conducted in an arbitrary or unreasonable manner, without adequate notice, consultation (and, at least in the case of indigenous peoples, consent), or compensation. • Employers withholding workers' identification documents.

continued

---

39. The rights of the child, including the right to protection from sexual and economic exploitation, are primarily codified in the CRC. Convention on the Rights of the Child, Sept. 2, 1990, 1577 U.N.T.S. 3 [hereinafter CRC]. While the United States signed the CRC in 1995, it has not yet ratified the treaty. United Nations Office of Legal Affairs, Status of Treaties: Convention on the Rights of the Child (Mar. 13, 2018), https://treaties.un.org/Pages/ViewDetails.aspx?src=IND&mtdsg_no=IV-11&chapter=4&lang=en. Notably, the United States is the only U.N. member state that is not a party to that Convention. *Id.*

Relevant Human Right	Brief Explanation of the Right	Examples of How Business Might Be Involved with an Impact on the Right
Rights of protection of the family and the right to marry [included in UDHR art. 16 and ICCPR art. 23]	• The concept of a family varies. This includes the rights to enter freely into marriage and to start a family.	• Company policy discriminates against women on the basis of their marital or reproductive status. • (See also the examples below under the right to a family life.)
Rights of protection for the child [included in CRC arts. 7, 32, and 34,[39] and ICCPR art. 24]	• A child has the right to be registered, given a name, and to acquire a nationality.	• Business activities that involve hazardous work (such as cutting sugar cane or mining) performed by persons under the age of 18.
	• Children must be protected from sexual and economic exploitation, including child labour. • ILO standards prohibit hazardous work for all persons under 18 years. They also prohibit labour for those under 15, with limited exceptions for developing States.	• Where child labor is discovered, a company can negatively impact other rights (such as the rights to an adequate standard of living, or security of the person) if they fail to take account of the best interests of the child in determining the appropriate response. For example, simply dismissing the child (or cutting the contract with the relevant supplier) may result in the child having to find alternative, more dangerous forms of work (such as prostitution).
Rights to freedom of thought, conscience, and religion [included in UDHR art. 18 and ICCPR art. 18]	• Individuals have a right to choose, practice, and observe their chosen religion or belief, to be an atheist or not to follow any religion or belief. • It includes the right to worship and to observe rituals, such as the wearing of particular clothing.	• A company's policy prevents workers from wearing clothing or other symbols that express their faith, even though these do not interfere with legitimate safety or performance issues. • A company does not allow its workers to seek reasonable time off for their religious holidays.

continued

Relevant Human Right	Brief Explanation of the Right	Examples of How Business Might Be Involved with an Impact on the Right
Rights to freedom of opinion and expression [included in UDHR art. 19 and ICCPR art. 19]	• The right to hold opinions free from outside interference is an absolute right. • The right to hold opinions free from outside interference is an absolute right. • Individuals have a right to seek, receive and impart ideas in whatever media or form. The State is allowed to authorize restrictions in line with international human rights standards.	• Operating in a country where workers are routinely prevented by law from expressing their opinions in the public domain. • Censoring online or other content at the demand of the State where those requests are illegal under national law and/or not in line with international human rights standards. • Engaging in litigation against individual workers, community members or other stakeholders who have spoken critically about the company where there is an extreme imbalance in the parties' means to fund a legal case.
Rights to freedom from war propaganda, and freedom from incitement to racial, religious, or national hatred [included in ICCPR art. 20][40]	• These rights prohibit certain speech that is not protected by the right to freedom of expression. • Individuals are prohibited from advocating racial, religious, or national hatred that amounts to an incitement to discrimination, hostility, or violence.	• Companies that provide the platform or technology for individuals to express hatred against a particular religious group and to incite others to take certain action against them.
Right to freedom of assembly [included in UDHR art. 20 and ICCPR art. 21]	• Individuals have the right to peacefully assemble for a specific purpose or where there is a public discussion, to put forward ideas or to engage in a demonstration, including marches. • The State is allowed to authorize restrictions in line with international human rights standards.	• Situations where public or private security services protecting company assets forcibly prevent or break up peaceful demonstrations by the local community against a company's operations.

continued

---

40. The United States submitted a reservation to article 20, stating that the article "does not authorize or require legislation or other action by the United States that would restrict the right of free speech and association protected by the Constitution and the laws of the United States." *Id.*

Relevant Human Right	Brief Explanation of the Right	Examples of How Business Might Be Involved with an Impact on the Right
Right to freedom of association [included in UDHR art. 20 and ICCPR art. 22]	• Protects the right to form or join all types of association, including political, religious, sporting/recreational, non-governmental and trade union associations. (See also the right to form and join trade unions below.) • The State is allowed to authorize restrictions in line with international human rights standards.	• A company operates in an area where the State seeks to undermine a local political party that opposes the company's activities by bringing false accusations against its leaders. • (See also the examples below under the right to form and join trade unions.)
Right to participate in public life [included in UDHR art. 21 and ICCPR art. 25]	• Citizens have the right to take part in the conduct of public affairs, including the rights to vote and be elected in free and fair elections and the right of equal access to positions within the public service.	• Failing to give time off to workers for the purpose of voting. • Bribery of political figures or other improper uses of company influence may distort the electoral process or otherwise impede free and fair elections.
Right to work [included in UDHR art. 23 and ICESCR arts. 23 and 6][41]	• Individuals are entitled to the opportunity to make a living by work which they freely choose or accept. The work must be "decent work," meaning that it respects their human rights. • The right includes the prohibition of arbitrary dismissal and the rights to just and favorable conditions of work and to form and join trade unions, discussed below.	• Arbitrarily or unfairly dismissing a worker, even if permissible under local law. • Hindering or failing to provide for the reasonable career advancement aspirations of workers. • (See also the examples under the rights to just and favorable conditions of work and to form and join trade unions.)
Right to enjoy just and favorable conditions of work [included in UDHR art. 23 and ICESCR art. 7][42]	• Individuals have the right to fair remuneration and equal remuneration for work of equal value. Remuneration must enable them, and their families, to have a decent living. • The right includes safe and healthy conditions of work, equality of opportunity for promotion, and a right to rest, leisure and holidays. • ILO standards provide further guidance on the content of the right.	• Failing to address a pattern of accidents highlighting inadequate workplace health and safety. • A company's purchasing practices repeatedly allow changes to the terms of product orders without any changes to price or delivery time, creating pressure on its suppliers, who then demand excessive overtime from their workers. • Using cleaning staff that are employed by a third-party company and are paid extremely low wages with no or very limited entitlements to sick pay or leave.

continued

---

41. The United States has not ratified the ICESCR. U.N. OLA, Status of Treaties: ICESCR, *supra* note 34.
42. The United States has not ratified the ICESCR. *Id.*

Relevant Human Right	Brief Explanation of the Right	Examples of How Business Might Be Involved with an Impact on the Right
Right to form and join trade unions and the right to strike [included in UDHR art. 23, ICCPR art. 22 and ICESCR art. 8][43]	• Individuals have the right to form or join trade unions of their choice. • Trade unions must be permitted to function freely, subject only to limitations that are in line with international human rights standards. • Workers have the right to strike, in conformity with reasonable legal requirements. • ILO standards provide guidance on the content of the right, for example, that workers have the right to bargain collectively with their employers and that workers should not be discriminated against because of trade union membership.	• Creating barriers to the formation of trade unions among employees or contract workers. • Refusing or failing to recognize legitimate workers' associations with which the company can enter into dialogue in countries that prohibit trade unions.
Right to an adequate standard of living [included in UDHR art. 25 and ICESCR art. 11][44]	• This right includes access to adequate housing, food, clothing, and water and sanitation. • Individuals have a right to live somewhere in security, dignity, and peace and that fulfills certain criteria (such as availability of utilities and accessibility).[45] • Food should be available and accessible to individuals, in sufficient quality and quantity, to meet their nutritional needs, free from harmful substances and acceptable to their culture. • The right to water and sanitation was recognized as a distinct right in 2010. Individuals are entitled to sufficient, safe, acceptable, physically accessible and affordable water for personal and domestic use and to sanitation services that fulfill certain criteria (such as being safe, physically accessible, and providing privacy and dignity).[46]	• Poor-quality housing or dormitories provided to workers. • Failing to provide adequate sanitation facilities for workers in a company-owned factory. • The expansion of a company's operations significantly reduces the amount of arable land in an area, affecting local community members' access to food. • Business activities pollute or threaten existing water resources in a way that significantly interferes with local communities' ability to access clean drinking water. In such situations, there may be particular negative impacts on women and girls, who are responsible for water collection in many communities.

continued

---

43. Within the International Bill of Rights, the right to strike is specifically listed only in the ICESCR, to which the U.S. is not a party. *Id.* However, the United States has separately provided for this right in its national legislation. National Labor Relations Act § 7, 29 U.S.C. §§ 151-169 (1935).

44. The United States has not ratified the ICESCR. U.N. OLA, Status of Treaties: ICESCR, *supra* note 34.

45. The U.N. Committee for Economic, Social and Cultural Rights (CESCR) has emphasized that the definition of "adequate housing" should not be interpreted narrowly; rather, it is the right to live somewhere in security, peace, and dignity. Comm. on Econ., Soc. and Cultural Rights, Gen. Cmt. No. 4: The Right to Adequate Housing, § 7, E/1992/23 (1991).

46. The CESCR has determined that the right to water is implicitly found in the right to an adequate standard of living. Comm. on Econ., Soc. and Cultural Rights, Gen. Cmt. No. 15: The Right to Water, § 3, E/C.12/2002/11 (2003). The U.S. has not ratified the ICESCR, U.N. OLA, Status of Treaties: ICESCR, *supra* note 34, and the United States abstained in a vote by the General Assembly on whether to recognize the right to water as an independent human right. Press Release, General Assembly, General Assembly Adopts Resolution Recognizing Access to Clean Water, Sanitation as Human Right, by Record Vote of 122 in Favour, None Against, 41 Abstentions, U.N. Press Release GA/10967 (Jul. 28, 2010).

Relevant Human Right	Brief Explanation of the Right	Examples of How Business Might Be Involved with an Impact on the Right
Right to social security, including social insurance [included in UDHR art. 22 and ICESCR art. 9][47]	• This right obliges the State to create and maintain a system of social security that provides adequate benefits for a range of issues (such as injury or unemployment).	• Denying workers their contractually agreed employment injury benefits. • Offering a private social security scheme that has discriminatory eligibility criteria.
Right to a family life [included in UDHR art. 16, and ICESCR art. 10][48]	• Protection should be given to families during their establishment, and while they are responsible for the care and education of dependent children. • The right includes special protections for working mothers. • The right also includes special protections for children.	• Company practices hinder the ability of workers to adopt a healthy work-life balance that enables them to adequately support their families (such as requiring workers to live on-site in dormitories for extended periods of time without providing adequate periods of leave to enable them to spend time with their families). • (See also the examples in relation to the rights of protection for the child above.)
Right to education [included in UDHR art. 26 and ICESCR art. 13][49]	• All children have the right to free and compulsory primary education. • The right also includes equal access to education and equal enjoyment of educational facilities, among other aspects.	• The presence of child labor in a business or in its supply chain, where those children are unable to attend school. • Limiting access to, or damaging, educational facilities through construction, infrastructure, or other projects.
Rights to take part in cultural life, to benefit from scientific progress, and to protection of the material and moral rights of authors and inventors [included in UDHR art. 27 and ICESCR art. 15][50]	• Individuals have a right to take part in the cultural life of society and enjoy the benefits of scientific progress, especially disadvantaged groups. • This includes protection of an individual author's moral and material interests resulting from any scientific, literary, or artistic production. • This protection extends to the rights of indigenous peoples to preserve, protect, and develop indigenous and traditional knowledge systems and cultural expressions.	• Activities involving resource extraction or new construction (such as laying a pipeline or installing infrastructure networks) could impact this right by separating groups from areas of cultural importance and knowledge, or by damaging their cultural heritage.

continued

---

47. While the right to social security is a part of the UDHR, the right to social insurance is specifically found in the ICESCR, which the United States has not ratified. U.N. OLA, Status of Treaties: ICESCR, *supra* note 34.

48. While the general right to a family life is recognized in the UDHR, specifically enumerated protections for children and working mothers are found in the ICESCR, which has not been ratified by the United States. *Id.*

49. The United States has not ratified the ICESCR. *Id.*

50. The United States has not ratified the ICESCR. *Id.*

Relevant Human Right	Brief Explanation of the Right	Examples of How Business Might Be Involved with an Impact on the Right
Rights of minorities [included in ICCPR art. 27]	• Members of ethnic, religious or linguistic minorities are entitled to enjoy their own culture, practice their religion, and speak their language.	• Failing to make reasonable adjustments for workers who wear a traditional form of headgear where that does not pose a legitimate safety or performance issue. • Using land in a manner that undermines the traditional way of life of a minority group, for example, by preventing them from ceremonial activities.
Right to health [included in UDHR art. 25 and ICESCR art. 12][51]	• Individuals have a right to the highest attainable standard of physical and mental health. • This includes the right to have control over one's health and body, and freedom from interference.	• Pollution from business operations can create negative impacts on the health of workers and/or surrounding communities. • The sale of products that are hazardous to the health of end users or customers. • Failure to implement appropriate health and safety standards leads to long-term negative impacts on workers' health.

OECD Human Rights[52]

States have the duty to protect human rights. Enterprises should, within the framework of internationally recognised human rights, the international human rights obligations of the countries in which they operate as well as relevant domestic laws and regulations:

1. Respect human rights, which means they should avoid infringing on the human rights of others and should address adverse human rights impacts with which they are involved.

2. Within the context of their own activities, avoid causing or contributing to adverse human rights impacts and address such impacts when they occur.

---

51. While the concept of the right to health is mentioned in the UDHR in reference to the right to an adequate standard of living, the right to health is largely found in the ICESCR, which the United States has not ratified. *Id.* Furthermore, while the United States is a party to the ICERD—which articulates a commitment to nondiscrimination in guaranteeing the right to everyone, without distinction, of public health—the United States has noted that this provision "does not affirmatively require State Parties to provide or to ensure observance of each of the listed rights themselves, but rather to prohibit discrimination in the enjoyment of those rights to the extent they are provided by domestic law." Observations by the United States of America on "The Right to Health, Fact Sheet No. 31," https://www.state.gov/documents/organization/138850.pdf.

52. *OECD Guidelines, supra* note 2, at 31–34.

3. Seek ways to prevent or mitigate adverse human rights impacts that are directly linked to their business operations, products or services by a business relationship, even if they do not contribute to those impacts.

4. Have a policy commitment to respect human rights.

5. Carry out human rights due diligence as appropriate to their size, the nature and context of operations and the severity of the risks of adverse human rights impacts.

6. Provide for or co-operate through legitimate processes in the remediation of adverse human rights impacts where they identify that they have caused or contributed to these impacts.

COMMENTARY ON HUMAN RIGHTS

36. This chapter opens with a chapeau that sets out the framework for the specific recommendations concerning enterprises' respect for human rights. It draws upon the United Nations Framework for Business and Human Rights "Protect, Respect and Remedy" and is in line with the Guiding Principles for its Implementation.

37. The chapeau and the first paragraph recognise that States have the duty to protect human rights, and that enterprises, regardless of their size, sector, operational context, ownership and structure, should respect human rights wherever they operate. Respect for human rights is the global standard of expected conduct for enterprises independently of States' abilities and/or willingness to fulfil their human rights obligations, and does not diminish those obligations.

38. A State's failure either to enforce relevant domestic laws, or to implement international human rights obligations or the fact that it may act contrary to such laws or international obligations does not diminish the expectation that enterprises respect human rights. In countries where domestic laws and regulations conflict with internationally recognised human rights, enterprises should seek ways to honour them to the fullest extent which does not place them in violation of domestic law, consistent with paragraph 2 of the Chapter on Concepts and Principles.

39. In all cases and irrespective of the country or specific context of enterprises' operations, reference should be made at a minimum to the internationally recognised human rights expressed in the International Bill of Human Rights, consisting of the Universal Declaration of Human Rights and the main instruments through which it has been codified: the International Covenant on Civil and Political Rights and the International Covenant on Economic, Social and Cultural Rights, and to the principles concerning fundamental rights set out in the 1998 International Labour Organisation Declaration on Fundamental Principles and Rights at Work.

40. Enterprises can have an impact on virtually the entire spectrum of internationally recognised human rights. In practice, some human rights may be at greater risk than others in particular industries or contexts, and therefore will be the focus of heightened attention. However, situations may change, so all rights should be the subject of periodic review. Depending on circumstances,

enterprises may need to consider additional standards. For instance, enterprises should respect the human rights of individuals belonging to specific groups or populations that require particular attention, where they may have adverse human rights impacts on them. In this connection, United Nations instruments have elaborated further on the rights of indigenous peoples; persons belonging to national or ethnic, religious and linguistic minorities; women; children; persons with disabilities; and migrant workers and their families. Moreover, in situations of armed conflict, enterprises should respect the standards of international humanitarian law, which can help enterprises avoid the risks of causing or contributing to adverse impacts when operating in such difficult environments.

41. In paragraph 1, addressing actual and potential adverse human rights impacts consists of taking adequate measures for their identification, prevention, where possible, and mitigation of potential human rights impacts, remediation of actual impacts, and accounting for how the adverse human rights impacts are addressed. The term "infringing" refers to adverse impacts that an enterprise may have on the human rights of individuals.

42. Paragraph 2 recommends that enterprises avoid causing or contributing to adverse human rights impacts through their own activities and address such impacts when they occur. "Activities" can include both actions and omissions. Where an enterprise causes or may cause an adverse human rights impact, it should take the necessary steps to cease or prevent the impact. Where an enterprise contributes or may contribute to such an impact, it should take the necessary steps to cease or prevent its contribution and use its leverage to mitigate any remaining impact to the greatest extent possible. Leverage is considered to exist where the enterprise has the ability to effect change in the practices of an entity that cause adverse human rights impacts.

43. Paragraph 3 addresses more complex situations where an enterprise has not contributed to an adverse human rights impact, but that impact is nevertheless directly linked to its operations, products or services by its business relationship with another entity. Paragraph 3 is not intended to shift responsibility from the entity causing an adverse human rights impact to the enterprise with which it has a business relationship. Meeting the expectation in paragraph 3 would entail an enterprise, acting alone or in co-operation with other entities, as appropriate, to use its leverage to influence the entity causing the adverse human rights impact to prevent or mitigate that impact. "Business relationships" include relationships with business partners, entities in its supply chain, and any other non-State or State entity directly linked to its business operations, products or services. Among the factors that will enter into the determination of the appropriate action in such situations are the enterprise's leverage over the entity concerned, how crucial the relationship is to the enterprise, the severity of the impact, and whether terminating the relationship with the entity itself would have adverse human rights impacts.

44. Paragraph 4 recommends that enterprises express their commitment to respect human rights through a statement of policy that: *(i)* is approved at the most senior level of the enterprise; *(ii)* is informed by relevant internal and/or

external expertise; *(iii)* stipulates the enterprise's human rights expectations of personnel, business partners and other parties directly linked to its operations, products or services; *(iv)* is publicly available and communicated internally and externally to all personnel, business partners and other relevant parties; *(v)* is reflected in operational policies and procedures necessary to embed it throughout the enterprise.

45. Paragraph 5 recommends that enterprises carry out human rights due diligence. The process entails assessing actual and potential human rights impacts, integrating and acting upon the findings, tracking responses as well as communicating how impacts are addressed. Human rights due diligence can be included within broader enterprise risk management systems provided that it goes beyond simply identifying and managing material risks to the enterprise itself to include the risks to rights-holders. It is an on-going exercise, recognising that human rights risks may change over time as the enterprise's operations and operating context evolve. Complementary guidance on due diligence, including in relation to supply chains, and appropriate responses to risks arising in supply chains are provided under paragraphs A.10 to A.12 of the Chapter on General Policies and their Commentaries.

46. When enterprises identify through their human rights due diligence process or other means that they have caused or contributed to an adverse impact, the *Guidelines* recommend that enterprises have processes in place to enable remediation. Some situations require co-operation with judicial or State-based non-judicial mechanisms. In others, operational-level grievance mechanisms for those potentially impacted by enterprises' activities can be an effective means of providing for such processes when they meet the core criteria of: legitimacy, accessibility, predictability, equitability, compatibility with the *Guidelines* and transparency, and are based on dialogue and engagement with a view to seeking agreed solutions. Such mechanisms can be administered by an enterprise alone or in collaboration with other stakeholders and can be a source of continuous learning. Operational-level grievance mechanisms should not be used to undermine the role of trade unions in addressing labour-related disputes, nor should such mechanisms preclude access to judicial or non-judicial grievance mechanisms, including the National Contact Points under the *Guidelines*.

Hypothetical: Suppressing Free Speech in China

Enzyme, Inc. ("Enzyme") is a U.S.-based pharmaceutical company with a wholly owned subsidiary in China that employs 500 workers. Recently, Enzyme's subsidiary was informed by local Chinese intelligence officials that subversive messages posted online had been traced to the subsidiary's IP address. The officials asked Enzyme for time-stamped login data from all computers with internet access. The subsidiary's managing director knows that the person(s) responsible for the anti-government posts might face severe consequences and asks Enzyme's CEO for instructions on how to proceed.

How should Enzyme's CEO respond?

Hypothetical: Sale of Surveillance Software to Bahrain

Disco Systems, Inc. ("Disco") is a U.S. corporation engaged in the manufacture and sale of electronic networking equipment. In 2008, Disco entered into a joint venture agreement with BTE, a South Korean company, whereby BTE was authorized to resell Disco's products in Asia.

Shortly after the joint venture was formed, BTE sold Disco-manufactured surveillance equipment to the government of Bahrain, allowing it to intercept and monitor communications between dissidents.

In 2012, protests broke out across Bahrain by citizens demanding additional political rights. Using Disco's technology, the Bahraini government identified and arrested many protesters, several of whom died in custody.

Disco failed to perform any due diligence with respect to its sale of surveillance technology to BTE, but it had no direct knowledge of the BTE sales to Bahrain.

Did Disco violate the OECD Guideline on human rights?

Hypothetical: Sale of Military Equipment to the Kingdom of Saudi Arabia

USC, Inc. ("USC") is a U.S.-based manufacturer of military equipment whose shares trade on the NYSE. USC has been invited by the Kingdom of Saudi Arabia ("KSA") to participate in a tender involving a multibillion-dollar sale of equipment, including missiles and cluster bombs certain to be used in the KSA's ongoing conflict in Yemen.

On April 20, 2016, the United Nations General Assembly issued a report regarding the KSA's conflict in Yemen, stating:

> The United Nations verified a sixfold increase in the number of children killed and maimed compared with 2014, totalling 1,953 child casualties (785 children killed and 1,168 injured). More than 70 per cent were boys. Of the casualties, 60 per cent . . . were attributed to the Saudi Arabia-led coalition and 20 per cent . . . to the Houthis. . . . Of the child casualties, 60 per cent were caused by air strikes, predominantly in Amanat al-Asimah, Hajjah, and Sa'dah. Significant civilian casualties, including children, as a result of air strikes continued to be documented early in 2016. . . . Child casualties as a result of landmines and explosive remnants of war were documented, with 15 children killed and 67 injured. . . .
>
> . . . .

The United Nations verified 101 incidents of attacks on schools and hospitals, which is double the number of incidents verified in 2014. Of the attacks, 90 per cent caused the partial or complete destruction of schools or health facilities, while the remaining 10 per cent involved attacks on protected personnel, including students. Of the attacks on schools and hospitals, 48 per cent were attributed to the coalition, 29 per cent to the Houthis and 20 per cent to unidentified perpetrators. More than half of the violations occurred in the period from April to June.[53]

Following the report, U.N. Secretary-General Ban Ki-moon "included the Saudi-led military coalition in Yemen on a list of countries, rebel movements, and terrorist organizations that killed, maimed, or otherwise abused children in conflict."[54] However, after the KSA threatened to "break relations with the United Nations and cut hundreds of millions of dollars in assistance,"[55] the U.N. dropped the KSA from the list.

Should USC participate in the tender? Why, or why not?

U.S. National Contact Point for the OECD Guidelines for Multinational Enterprises, Final Statement, Specific Instance between European Centre for Democracy and Human Rights, Defenders for Medical Impartiality, and Arabian Rights Watch Association, and The Boeing Company and Lockheed Martin Corporation[56]

Office of the U.S. National Contact Point
U.S. Department of State
11/18/2016

EXECUTIVE SUMMARY

The U.S. National Contact Point (U.S. NCP) for the OECD Guidelines for Multinational Enterprises (the Guidelines) will not offer mediation in this Specific Instance between the parties—European Centre for Democracy and Human Rights, Defenders for Medical Impartiality, and Arabian Rights Watch Association ("the Submitters") and The Boeing Company and Lockheed Martin Corporation

---

53. U.N. Secretary-General, *Children and Armed Conflict*, ¶ 167-69, U.N. Doc. A/70/836–S/2016/360 (Apr. 20, 2016).

54. Colum Lynch, *Saudi Arabia Threatened to Break Relations with U.N. Over Human Rights Criticism in Yemen*, FOREIGN POLICY (June 7, 2016, 5:55 PM), http://foreignpolicy.com/2016/06/07/saudi-arabia-threatened-to-break-relations-with-un-over-human-rights-criticism-in-yemen/.

55. *Id.*

56. U.S. NAT'L CONTACT POINT FOR THE OECD GUIDELINES FOR MULTINATIONAL ENTERPRISES, U.S. DEP'T OF STATE, FINAL STATEMENT: SPECIFIC INSTANCE BETWEEN EUROPEAN CENTRE FOR DEMOCRACY AND HUMAN RIGHTS, DEFENDERS FOR MEDICAL IMPARTIALITY, AND ARABIAN RIGHTS WATCH ASSOCIATION, AND THE BOEING COMPANY AND LOCKHEED MARTIN CORPORATION (Nov. 18, 2016).

("the Companies")—regarding transactions related to the Government of Saudi Arabia.

The purpose of the Guidelines is to promote responsible business conduct by multinational enterprises. This Specific Instance concerns the conduct of particular States, and would entail an examination of state conduct, which would not serve to advance the Guidelines. Nevertheless, the U.S. NCP offers several recommendations with regards to best practices for implementation of the Guidelines:

RECOMMENDATIONS

- Per the Guidelines, companies in every sector should carry out human rights due diligence and avoid causing or contributing to adverse human rights impacts.
- Companies should consider incorporating the Guidelines into their existing public human rights commitments. The Guidelines recommend that enterprises express their commitment to respect human rights through a statement of policy that is approved at the most senior level of an enterprise and is publicly available.
- The U.S. government regularly engages with civil society and other stakeholders regarding any concerns with U.S. policy, including on the issues raised in the Specific Instance, and is available to discuss the issues further with the submitters.

The U.S. NCP would also note that the U.S. government notifies Congress of proposed Foreign Military Sales (FMS) that meet the monetary thresholds set out in section 36(b) of the Arms Export Control Act, as amended (AECA). In order to provide transparency, this information is made publicly available on the website maintained by the Defense Security Cooperation Agency, at www.dsca.mil/major-arms-sales. Furthermore, the United States continues to participate in and provide relevant arms transfer information to the U.N. Register of Conventional Arms and the U.N. Standardized Instrument for Reporting Military Spending. The U.S. Government also notifies Congress of applications for licenses to export defense articles or defense services satisfying certain dollar-thresholds established in sections 36(c) and 36(d) of the AECA. These notifications are published quarterly in the *Federal Register*.

SUBSTANCE OF THE SPECIFIC INSTANCE

On June 23, 2016, European Centre for Democracy and Human Rights, Defenders for Medical Impartiality, and Arabian Rights Watch Association (collectively "the Submitters"), human rights non-governmental organizations, submitted a Specific Instance with the U.S. NCP alleging conduct inconsistent with Chapter IV (Human Rights), paragraphs 1, 2, 3, 4, and 5 of the Guidelines, involving conduct by the Boeing Company and Lockheed Martin Corporation (collectively "the Companies"). The events addressed in the Specific Instance cover a period from March 2015 to the submission date.

The Submitters alleged that the Companies failed to take appropriate steps to ensure that their products did not cause or contribute to human rights abuses, and that the Companies' products directly contributed to adverse human rights impacts in Yemen through their use by the government of Saudi Arabia. The Submitters also claimed that the Companies did not have a relevant human rights policy and did not carry out appropriate human rights due diligence in the sale of their products.

The Submitters requested that the U.S. NCP facilitate a resolution of the issues raised, specifically: (1) identify whether the Companies have caused or contributed to adverse human rights impacts and provide for or cooperate in legitimate processes in the remediation of any potential impact, (2) make recommendations to uphold the Guidelines, including that the Companies refrain from selling arms to the government of Saudi Arabia, and (3) for the Companies to promulgate a human rights policy and incorporate human rights due diligence in their operations.

Following receipt of the Specific Instance, the U.S. NCP acknowledged receipt to the Submitters and shared the Specific Instance with the Companies. The U.S. NCP offered both the Submitters and Companies the opportunity for a meeting or phone call to discuss the process further. Both the Submitters and Companies accepted this offer, and the U.S. NCP met separately and/or spoke with all parties involved in the Specific Instance to discuss the Initial Assessment process.

While awaiting a response from the Companies, the U.S. NCP undertook an Initial Assessment process by reviewing the issues raised in the Specific Instance, as well as consulting with relevant U.S. government experts, and concluded its Initial Assessment prior [to] a written response from the Companies.

DECISION

After thorough review of information provided, the U.S. NCP has decided not to offer mediation. The purpose of the Guidelines is to promote responsible business conduct by multinational enterprises. This Specific Instance concerns the conduct of particular States, and would entail an examination of state conduct, which would not serve to advance the Guidelines. According to the 2006 Annual Report on the OECD Guidelines, "The Guidelines implementation procedure is not a state-to-state mechanism and is solely concerned with private party dispute resolution."

This Specific Instance is inextricably intertwined with the practices of specific states, including Saudi Arabia and the United States. Arms sales to Saudi Arabia were completed through two processes: transfers completed by the U.S. government through the FMS program and Direct Commercial Sales (DCS) in which the exports were approved by the U.S. government. All arms transfer decisions are reviewed and approved under the criteria outlined in the Conventional Arms Transfer (CAT) Policy. . . . [T]he criteria considered include[] the "likelihood that the recipient would use the arms to commit human rights abuses or serious violations of international humanitarian law, retransfer the arms to those who would commit human rights abuses or serious violations of international humanitarian law." Additionally, for DCS cases, the State Department considers . . . whether the sale would "increase the possibility of outbreak or escalation of conflict" or "support international terrorism." The decision to use arms procured from the United States or these companies is a decision made by Saudi Arabia in its capacity as a sovereign state. However, the use must be consistent with the provisions of the agreement, or license, that was the basis for the sale or approval of the transfer.

Accordingly, this Specific Instance concerns various state practices, which NCPs are not designed to assess. And according to the OECD, "[p]erceptions that the Specific Instance procedure is a channel for intervening inappropriately in the domestic affairs of another country would be highly detrimental to the effectiveness of the Guidelines."

•••

ANNEX: DETAILS OF U.S. NCP SPECIFIC INSTANCE PROCESS

I. Context and Background on the U.S. NCP

The OECD Guidelines for Multinational Enterprises (MNEs) are voluntary recommendations for companies regarding responsible business conduct in a global context. The Guidelines are addressed to MNEs operating in or from the territories of governments adhering to the OECD's Declaration on International Investment and Multinational Enterprises, of which the Guidelines form one part. Adhering governments have committed to encouraging their MNEs to promote and implement the Guidelines in their global operations and appointing a national contact point (NCP) to assist parties in seeking a mutually satisfactory resolution to issues that may arise under the Guidelines.

As a part of its function, the U.S. NCP addresses issues relating to implementation of the Guidelines, raised in the form of a Specific Instance, with regards to the business conduct of an MNE operating or headquartered in the United States. The office of the U.S. NCP handles such instances in accordance with its procedures which are based on Guidelines.

The U.S. NCP's primary function is to assist affected parties, when appropriate, in their efforts to reach a mutually satisfactory resolution and its role is to offer mediation to facilitate the resolution of the matter and, where appropriate, make recommendations as to how the enterprise might make its business practices more consistent with the Guidelines. The U.S. NCP does not make a determination as to whether a party is acting consistently with the Guidelines, and the U.S. NCP does not have legal authority to adjudicate disputes submitted under this process.

Acceptance of the Specific Instance is in no way an acknowledgement of or determination on the merits of the claims presented, but merely an offer to facilitate neutral, third-party mediation or conciliation to assist the parties in voluntarily, confidentially, and in good faith, reaching a cooperative resolution of their concerns. In mediation, the parties are responsible for arriving at their own solution, and the process is designed to create an environment for cooperative problem solving between the parties.

II. Conducting the Initial Assessment

Per the Guidelines procedures, upon receiving a Specific Instance, the U.S. NCP conducts an Initial Assessment. The Initial Assessment does not determine whether the company has acted consistently with the Guidelines, but rather is a process to determine whether the issues raised are bona fide and merit further examination. Per the Guidelines procedures, the Initial Assessment is conducted based on:

- Identity of the party and its interest in the matter
- Whether the issue is material and substantiated
- Likely link between the enterprise's activities and the issue raised
- Relevance of applicable law and procedures, including court rulings
- Treatment of similar issues in other domestic or international proceedings
- Contribution of the specific issue to the purposes and effectiveness of the Guidelines

Under U.S. NCP procedures, acceptance of the Specific Instance would not have indicated that the U.S. NCP considered the Companies to have acted inconsistently with the Guidelines, but rather that the U.S. NCP considers it appropriate to facilitate a discussion between the parties of the issues raised. For the company's part, a decision to participate in this process would not have implied any prima facie admission of conduct inconsistent with the Guidelines. Mediation or conciliation is a voluntary step, providing an opportunity for a neutral third-party to assist parties to reach their own resolution of concerns. In mediation, the parties are responsible for arriving at their own solution, and the process is designed to create an environment for cooperative problem-solving between the parties. The parties are in control of the outcome of an agreement. Participation is voluntary and no parties would be compelled to violate the law or waive their rights under the law during the NCP process. If the parties can reach an agreement through mediation or other means, the U.S. NCP would consider requests by the parties to follow up on implementation.

The U.S. NCP contributes to the resolution of issues that arise relating to implementation of the Guidelines raised in Specific Instances in a manner that is impartial, predictable, equitable and compatible with the principles and standards of the Guidelines. The U.S. NCP works to facilitate dispute resolution in a confidential, efficient, and timely manner with an aim toward a forward-looking, good-faith resolution and in accordance with applicable law.

III. Outcome of the Initial Assessment

Per the Guidelines, the U.S. NCP took the following points into account when considering whether this Specific Instance merited further consideration.

a. Identity of the Party and Its Interest in the Matter

The U.S. NCP is satisfied that Submitters are able to provide information about the Specific Instance and have an interest in the issues raised.

The European Centre for Democracy & Human Rights (ECDHR) is a Brussels-based NGO working to raise awareness of human rights issues in the Middle East and North Africa region and the Gulf Cooperation Council countries. ECDHR promotes policies and actions with European Institutions, key stakeholders, and the media to strengthen advocacy efforts.

The Defenders for Medical Impartiality (DMI) is an initiative of ECDHR that engages with key actors in the international policy and medical community to build a network of support for the international protection of the right to medical impartiality. DMI brings together human rights advocates and healthcare professionals from the Middle East and across the glob[e] to advocate on behalf of codifying and protecting the concept of medical impartiality and to document regional violations.

The Arabian Rights Watch Association (ARWA) is a Washington D.C.-based human rights NGO working to defend human rights worldwide, and particularly the human rights of persons situated in the Arabian Peninsula. ARWA investigates human rights abuses on the ground to ensure accountability and to promote and protect human dignity.

The Boeing Company is the world's largest aerospace company and leading manufacturer of commercial jetliners and defense, space and security systems. A top U.S. exporter, the company supports airlines and U.S. and allied government customers in 150 countries. Boeing products and tailored services include commercial and military aircraft, satellites, weapons, electronic and defense systems, launch systems, advanced information and communication systems, and performance-based logistics and training.

Headquartered in Bethesda, Maryland, Lockheed Martin is a global security and aerospace company that employs approximately 98,000 people worldwide and is principally engaged in the research, design, development, manufacture, integration and sustainment of advanced technology systems, products and services.

b. Whether the Issue Is Material and Substantiated

Submitter(s) have provided information in writing alleging the Companies failed to take appropriate steps to ensure that their products do not cause or contribute to human rights abuses, and that the Companies' products have directly contributed to adverse human rights impacts in Yemen through use by the government of Saudi Arabia. The Submitters also claim that the Companies do not have a relevant human rights policy commitment, and that the Companies did not carry out appropriate human rights due diligence in the sale of their products. The U.S. NCP per its established procedures makes no determination whether a violation of the Guidelines has taken place.

c. Link Between the Companies' Activities and Issues Raised

The Submitters allege that the Companies' ongoing sale of arms to the Government of the Kingdom of Saudi Arabia constitutes a breach of the Guidelines due to how those products are being used in Yemen.

d. Relevance of Applicable Law and Procedures, Including Court Rulings

While the U.S. NCP has determined that the issues raised fall outside the scope of the Office of the U.S. NCP, there are a number of U.S. laws and policies the U.S. NCP would like to highlight and that were discussed with U.S. government officials during the Initial Assessment phase of the Specific Instance:

- Under section 2 of the AECA, the Secretary of State shall, under the direction of the President, be responsible for the continuous supervision and general direction of sales, leases, financing, cooperative projects and exports under the AECA. Under section 38 of the AECA, and pursuant to delegations of authority, the Secretary of State is authorized to control the export of defense articles and defense services, and, except as specifically provided in regulations, no such export may be done without a license or other authorization. The International Traffic in Arms Regulations (ITAR), promulgated by the Department of State, implements section 38 of the AECA.
- Section 40A of the AECA, as delegated to the Secretary of Defense by Executive Order 13637, requires the Department of Defense (DoD) to perform End-Use Monitoring (EUM) of U.S. defense articles and defense services sold, leased, or exported under the AECA.
- *Foreign Military Sales* (FMS) include the sale and transfer of defense articles, or the provisions of defense services, to a partner country either from Department of Defense stock or through new procurement. FMS cases are implemented through government-to-government agreements between the United States and the partner country.
- *Direct Commercial Sales* (DCS) are between a U.S. private entity and the foreign end-user (either private entity or government). The Department of State, in close partnership with the Department of Defense, regulates the export and temporary import of defense articles and services through the ITAR.
- *Congressional Notification*, in the case of Saudi Arabia, is required prior to the issuance of any letter of offer to sell defense articles or defense services for $50 million or more, design and construction services for $200 million or more, or any major defense equipment for $14 million or more. Additional notifications may be required if, before delivery of any defense equipment or articles, the sensitivity of technology or the capability of the equipment is enhanced or upgraded.
- *Congressional Notification* is required for certain DCS license applications for exports to Saudi Arabia including the export of any major defense equipment sold under a contract in the amount of $14,000,000 or more; of defense articles or defense services sold under a contract in the amount of $50,000,000 or more; firearms controlled under category I of the United States Munitions List (USML) in the amount of $1,000,000 or more; or for any commercial technical assistance or manufacturing licensing agreement which involves the manufacture of any item of significant combat equipment on the USML.

e. How Similar Issues Have Been, or Are Being Treated in Other Domestic or International Proceedings

In 2014 the Australian NCP received a Specific Instance regarding the activities of a UK-headquartered company, G4S, in Papua New Guinea. The Australian NCP (ANCP) did not offer mediation, noting "[t]he ANCP considers that aspects of the complaint could be interpreted as commentary on government policy. However, G4S as service provider is not accountable for government policy and other mechanisms exist for review and scrutiny of policy. The ANCP is not the most appropriate vehicle for resolution of such matters. It is not the role of the ANCP to issue commentary, whether intended or otherwise, on government policies or law."

In 2011 the Norway NCP received a Specific Instance regarding the activities of Statoil ASA in Canada. The Norway NCP did not offer mediation, noting "in this Specific Instance the complaint is directed more towards the policy of Canada to allow the development of oil sands rather than at the manner in which Statoil acts within the framework of this policy. The complaint does not concern whether Statoil, in its activities, is in breach of . . . the OECD Guidelines (hereafter the Guidelines). For the NCP to accept the complaint, it would have to specify the manners in which the company has allegedly violated the Guidelines and to substantiate their claim with facts. The complaint should be directed toward the practices of the enterprise rather than at the nature of the business sector and national authorities. The Norwegian NCP thus rejects the complaint on the basis that is does not meet the criteria specified in the OECD Procedural Guidelines, nor does it clearly fall within the scope of the Guidelines."

f. Whether the Consideration of the Specific Instance Would Contribute to the Purposes and Effectiveness of the Guidelines

The purpose of the Guidelines is to promote responsible business conduct by multinational enterprises. This Specific Instance concerns the conduct of particular States, and would entail an examination of state conduct, which would not serve to advance the Guidelines. According to the 2006 Annual Report on the OECD Guidelines, "The Guidelines implementation procedure is not a state-to-state mechanism and is solely concerned with private party dispute resolution."

This Specific Instance is inextricably intertwined with the practices of specific states, including Saudi Arabia and the United States. The arms sales in question were completed by the United States, in the cases involving FMS, or, for DCS, approved through a U.S. regulatory scheme. Accordingly, this Specific Instance is ultimately about various state practices, which NCPs are not designed to assess.

Per U.S. NCP procedures, all parties were given an advance copy of this Final Statement to allow the opportunity for input.

IV. Role of the Interagency Working Group

Per its standard procedures, the U.S. NCP consulted and received input from its U.S. government experts throughout the process, including informing U.S. government experts of the U.S. NCP's decision to not offer mediation.

IV. Employment and Industrial Relations

The guideline on employment and industrial relations requires adherence to internationally recognized standards for the treatment of employees, particularly in industrial settings.[57] The OECD adopts many of the standards articulated by the International Labor Organization ("ILO"), a U.N. agency that "brings together governments, employers and workers' representatives of 187 member States, to set labour standards, develop policies and devise programmes promoting decent work for all women and men."[58]

The ILO's *Tripartite Declaration of Principles Concerning Multinational Enterprises and Social Policy*[59] sets forth guidelines for management of human resources in emerging markets. For example, ILO *Recommendation No. 195* encourages enterprises to "formulate, apply and review national human resources development, education, training and lifelong learning policies which are consistent with economic, fiscal and social policies."[60]

OECD Employment and Industrial Relations[61]

Enterprises should, within the framework of applicable law, regulations and prevailing labour relations and employment practices and applicable international labour standards:

1.

   a) Respect the right of workers employed by the multinational enterprise to establish or join trade unions and representative organisations of their own choosing.

   b) Respect the right of workers employed by the multinational enterprise to have trade unions and representative organisations of their own choosing recognised for the purpose of collective bargaining, and engage in constructive negotiations, either individually or through employers' associations, with such representatives with a view to reaching agreements on terms and conditions of employment.

   c) Contribute to the effective abolition of child labour, and take immediate and effective measures to secure the prohibition and elimination of the worst forms of child labour as a matter of urgency.

   d) Contribute to the elimination of all forms of forced or compulsory

---

57. *See OECD Guidelines, supra* note 2, at 35–41.

58. *See Mission and Impact of the ILO,* Int'l Labor Org., http://www.ilo.org/global/about-the-ilo/mission-and-objectives/lang--en/index.htm (last visited Feb. 10, 2018).

59. Int'l Labor Org. [ILO], *Tripartite Declaration of Principles Concerning Multinational Enterprises and Social Policy* (5th ed. 2017).

60. Int'l Labor Org. [ILO], Recommendation No. 195, *Human Resources Development Recommendation* (June 17, 2004).

61. *OECD Guidelines, supra* note 2, at 35–41.

labour and take adequate steps to ensure that forced or compulsory labour does not exist in their operations.

e) Be guided throughout their operations by the principle of equality of opportunity and treatment in employment and not discriminate against their workers with respect to employment or occupation on such grounds as race, colour, sex, religion, political opinion, national extraction or social origin, or other status, unless selectivity concerning worker characteristics furthers established governmental policies which specifically promote greater equality of employment opportunity or relates to the inherent requirements of a job.

2.

a) Provide such facilities to workers' representatives as may be necessary to assist in the development of effective collective agreements.

b) Provide information to workers' representatives which is needed for meaningful negotiations on conditions of employment.

c) Provide information to workers and their representatives which enables them to obtain a true and fair view of the performance of the entity or, where appropriate, the enterprise as a whole.

3. Promote consultation and co-operation between employers and workers and their representatives on matters of mutual concern.

4.

a) Observe standards of employment and industrial relations not less favourable than those observed by comparable employers in the host country.

b) When multinational enterprises operate in developing countries, where comparable employers may not exist, provide the best possible wages, benefits and conditions of work, within the framework of government policies. These should be related to the economic position of the enterprise, but should be at least adequate to satisfy the basic needs of the workers and their families.

c) Take adequate steps to ensure occupational health and safety in their operations.

5. In their operations, to the greatest extent practicable, employ local workers and provide training with a view to improving skill levels, in co-operation with worker representatives and, where appropriate, relevant governmental authorities.

6. In considering changes in their operations which would have major employment effects, in particular in the case of the closure of an entity involving collective lay-offs or dismissals, provide reasonable notice of such changes to representatives of the workers in their employment and their organisations, and, where appropriate, to the relevant governmental authorities, and co-operate with the worker representatives and appropriate governmental authorities so as to mitigate to the maximum extent practicable adverse effects. In light of the specific circumstances of each case, it would be appropriate if management were able to give such notice prior to the final decision being taken. Other

means may also be employed to provide meaningful co-operation to mitigate the effects of such decisions.

7. In the context of bona fide negotiations with workers' representatives on conditions of employment, or while workers are exercising a right to organise, not threaten to transfer the whole or part of an operating unit from the country concerned nor transfer workers from the enterprises' component entities in other countries in order to influence unfairly those negotiations or to hinder the exercise of a right to organise.

8. Enable authorised representatives of the workers in their employment to negotiate on collective bargaining or labour-management relations issues and allow the parties to consult on matters of mutual concern with representatives of management who are authorised to take decisions on these matters.

COMMENTARY ON EMPLOYMENT AND INDUSTRIAL RELATIONS

47. This chapter opens with a chapeau that includes a reference to "applicable" law and regulations, which is meant to acknowledge the fact that multinational enterprises, while operating within the jurisdiction of particular countries, may be subject to national and international levels of regulation of employment and industrial relations matters. The terms "prevailing labour relations" and "employment practices" are sufficiently broad to permit a variety of interpretations in light of different national circumstances—for example, different bargaining options provided for workers under national laws and regulations.

48. The [ILO] is the competent body to set and deal with international labour standards, and to promote fundamental rights at work as recognised in its 1998 Declaration on Fundamental Principles and Rights at Work. The *Guidelines*, as a non-binding instrument, have a role to play in promoting observance of these standards and principles among multinational enterprises. The provisions of the *Guidelines* chapter echo relevant provisions of the 1998 Declaration, as well as the 1977 ILO Tripartite Declaration of Principles concerning Multinational Enterprises and Social Policy, last revised in 2006 (the ILO MNE Declaration). The ILO MNE Declaration sets out principles in the fields of employment, training, working conditions, and industrial relations, while the OECD *Guidelines* cover all major aspects of corporate behaviour. The OECD *Guidelines* and the ILO MNE Declaration refer to the behaviour expected from enterprises and are intended to parallel and not conflict with each other. The ILO MNE Declaration can therefore be of use in understanding the *Guidelines* to the extent that it is of a greater degree of elaboration. However, the responsibilities for the follow-up procedures under the ILO MNE Declaration and the *Guidelines* are institutionally separate.

49. The terminology used in Chapter V is consistent with that used in the ILO MNE Declaration. The use of the terms "workers employed by the multinational enterprise" and "workers in their employment" is intended to have the same meaning as in the ILO MNE Declaration. These terms refer to workers who are "in an employment relationship with the multinational enterprise." Enterprises wishing to understand the scope of their responsibility under Chapter V will find useful guidance for determining the existence of an employment relationship

in the context of the *Guidelines* in the non-exhaustive list of indicators set forth in ILO Recommendation 198 of 2006, paragraphs 13 (a) and (b). In addition, it is recognised that working arrangements change and develop over time and that enterprises are expected to structure their relationships with workers so as to avoid supporting, encouraging or participating in disguised employment practices. A disguised employment relationship occurs when an employer treats an individual as other than an employee in a manner that hides his or her true legal status.

50. These recommendations do not interfere with true civil and commercial relationships, but rather seek to ensure that individuals in an employment relationship have the protection that is due to them in the context of the *Guidelines*. It is recognised that in the absence of an employment relationship, enterprises are nevertheless expected to act in accordance with the risk-based due diligence and supply chain recommendations in paragraphs A.10 to A.13 of Chapter II on General Policies.

51. Paragraph 1 of this chapter is designed to echo all four fundamental principles and rights at work which are contained in the ILO's 1998 Declaration, namely the freedom of association and right to collective bargaining, the effective abolition of child labour, the elimination of all forms of forced or compulsory labour, and non-discrimination in employment and occupation. These principles and rights have been developed in the form of specific rights and obligations in ILO Conventions recognised as fundamental.

52. Paragraph 1c) recommends that multinational enterprises contribute to the effective abolition of child labour in the sense of the ILO 1998 Declaration and ILO Convention 182 concerning the worst forms of child labour. Long-standing ILO instruments on child labour are Convention 138 and Recommendation 146 (both adopted in 1973) concerning minimum ages for employment. Through their labour management practices, their creation of high-quality, well-paid jobs and their contribution to economic growth, multinational enterprises can play a positive role in helping to address the root causes of poverty in general and of child labour in particular. It is important to acknowledge and encourage the role of multinational enterprises in contributing to the search for a lasting solution to the problem of child labour. In this regard, raising the standards of education of children living in host countries is especially noteworthy.

53. Paragraph 1(d) recommends that enterprises contribute to the elimination of all forms of forced and compulsory labour, another principle derived from the 1998 ILO Declaration. The reference to this core labour right is based on the ILO Conventions 29 of 1930 and 105 of 1957. Convention 29 requests that governments "suppress the use of forced or compulsory labour in all its forms within the shortest possible period," while Convention 105 requests of them to "suppress and not to make use of any form of forced or compulsory labour" for certain enumerated purposes (for example, as a means of political coercion or labour discipline), and "to take effective measures to secure [its] immediate and complete abolition". At the same time, it is understood that the ILO is the competent body to deal with the difficult issue of prison labour, in particular when it comes

to the hiring-out of prisoners to (or their placing at the disposal of) private individuals, companies or associations.

54. The reference to the principle of non-discrimination with respect to employment and occupation in paragraph 1(e) is considered to apply to such terms and conditions as hiring, job assignment, discharge, pay and benefits, promotion, transfer or relocation, termination, training and retirement. The list of non-permissible grounds for discrimination which is taken from ILO Convention 111 of 1958, the Maternity Protection Convention 183 of 2000, Employment (Disabled Persons) Convention 159 of 1983, the Older Workers Recommendation 162 of 1980 and the HIV and AIDS at Work Recommendation 200 of 2010, considers that any distinction, exclusion or preference on these grounds is in violation of the Conventions, Recommendations and Codes. The term "other status" for the purposes of the *Guidelines* refers to trade union activity and personal characteristics such as age, disability, pregnancy, marital status, sexual orientation, or HIV status. Consistent with the provisions in paragraph 1(e), enterprises are expected to promote equal opportunities for women and men with special emphasis on equal criteria for selection, remuneration, and promotion, and equal application of those criteria, and prevent discrimination or dismissals on the grounds of marriage, pregnancy or parenthood.

55. In paragraph 2(c) of this chapter, information provided by companies to their workers and their representatives is expected to provide a "true and fair view" of performance. It relates to the following: the structure of the enterprise, its economic and financial situation and prospects, employment trends, and expected substantial changes in operations, taking into account legitimate requirements of business confidentiality. Considerations of business confidentiality may mean that information on certain points may not be provided, or may not be provided without safeguards.

56. The reference to consultative forms of worker participation in paragraph 3 of the Chapter is taken from ILO Recommendation 94 of 1952 concerning Consultation and Co-operation between Employers and Workers at the Level of the Undertaking. It also conforms to a provision contained in the ILO MNE Declaration. Such consultative arrangements should not substitute for workers' right to bargain over terms and conditions of employment. A recommendation on consultative arrangements with respect to working arrangements is also part of paragraph 8.

57. In paragraph 4, employment and industrial relations standards are understood to include compensation and working-time arrangements. The reference to occupational health and safety implies that multinational enterprises are expected to follow prevailing regulatory standards and industry norms to minimise the risk of accidents and injury to health arising out of, linked with, or occurring in, the course of employment. This encourages enterprises to work to raise the level of performance with respect to occupational health and safety in all parts of their operation even where this may not be formally required by existing regulations in countries in which they operate. It also encourages enterprises to respect workers' ability to remove themselves from a work situation when there is reasonable justification to believe that it presents an imminent and serious risk to health or safety. Reflecting their importance and complementarities

among related recommendations, health and safety concerns are echoed elsewhere in the *Guidelines*, most notably in chapters on Consumer Interests and the Environment. The ILO Recommendation No. 194 of 2002 provides an indicative list of occupational diseases as well as codes of practice and guides which can be taken into account by enterprises for implementing this recommendation of the *Guidelines*.

58. The recommendation in paragraph 5 of the chapter encourages MNEs to recruit an adequate workforce share locally, including managerial personnel, and to provide training to them. Language in this paragraph on training and skill levels complements the text in paragraph A.4 of the General Policies chapter on encouraging human capital formation. The reference to local workers complements the text encouraging local capacity building in paragraph A.3 of the General Policies chapter. In accordance with the ILO Human Resources Development Recommendation 195 of 2004, enterprises are also encouraged to invest, to the greatest extent practicable, in training and lifelong learning while ensuring equal opportunities to training for women and other vulnerable groups, such as youth, low-skilled people, people with disabilities, migrants, older workers, and indigenous peoples.

59. Paragraph 6 recommends that enterprises provide reasonable notice to the representatives of workers and relevant government authorities, of changes in their operations which would have major effects upon the livelihood of their workers, in particular the closure of an entity involving collective layoffs or dismissals. As stated therein, the purpose of this provision is to afford an opportunity for co-operation to mitigate the effects of such changes. This is an important principle that is widely reflected in the industrial relations laws and practices of adhering countries, although the approaches taken to ensuring an opportunity for meaningful co-operation are not identical in all adhering countries. The paragraph also notes that it would be appropriate if, in light of specific circumstances, management were able to give such notice prior to the final decision. Indeed, notice prior to the final decision is a feature of industrial relations laws and practices in a number of adhering countries. However, it is not the only means to ensure an opportunity for meaningful co-operation to mitigate the effects of such decisions, and the laws and practices of other adhering countries provide for other means such as defined periods during which consultations must be undertaken before decisions may be implemented.

Hypothetical: Doing Business in the Kurdish Region of Turkey

Thea, Inc. ("Thea") is a multinational enterprise based in the United States that builds telecommunication networks and provides telecommunication services in various countries. Thea is formulating a plan to invest in upgrading the telecommunications infrastructure in the Kurdish region of Turkey and providing long-term telecommunications services to the local residents.

Thea's senior management has conducted preliminary studies that reveal substantial prospects for economic growth in the Kurdish regions of Turkey and Iraq and believes that investment in Turkey could later be expanded to cover Iraqi Kurdistan, should the conflict there subside. In addition, Thea's management detects a significant probability that an independent state covering Kurdish regions of Iraq and Syria could form in the next decade. In that event, Thea's current investment could provide an advantage to participate in the new state's economy.

Assume the following facts about the Kurdish region of Turkey:

- The level of local education is much lower than non-Kurdish regions of Turkey.
- Local schools lack resources.
- The poverty level is higher than other regions of Turkey.
- It would be cheaper, faster, and easier for Thea to recruit its employees from non-Kurdish, urban areas of Turkey.
- Local recruits will require extensive training and education.
- The cost of training and educating local recruits is estimated at $5 million.

Should Thea recruit local residents? Perform a cost-benefit analysis.

Hypothetical: Sweatshops

Johnny, Inc. ("Johnny") is a U.S.-based manufacturer of running shoes. Johnny contracts with Banglaco, a Bangladeshi supplier, to produce its cheapest and most popular shoe, called the Johnny-Be-Good. Banglaco employs 500 workers in a dilapidated facility near Dhaka, where temperatures often exceed 100 degrees Fahrenheit and which is in danger of imminent collapse.

Banglaco charges Johnny 30 percent of what it would cost Johnny to produce the same shoes in the United States. If Johnny shifts production of the Johnny-Be-Good line to the United States, it would have to dramatically increase its prices and would no longer be competitive.

How should Johnny proceed with respect to its arrangement with Banglaco? What, if any, additional facts would you like to know in answering this question?

Hypothetical: Collective Bargaining

Exeter, Inc. ("Exeter") is a manufacturer of consumer electronics and plans to establish a manufacturing facility in Tijuana, Mexico. Exeter has begun negotiations with a local trade union to employ 300 workers in its new facility.

During the negotiations, Exeter's chief negotiator informs the union representatives that, unless they agree to the wages offered by Exeter, Exeter will abandon its plans for a Tijuana production facility and instead establish one in Peru.

Has Exeter's chief negotiator acted ethically? Why, or why not?

Hypothetical: Enforcing the Islamic Dress Code

Luzerne, AG ("Luzerne") is a Swiss corporation that markets and sells wastewater management systems. Luzerne recently entered into a contract with the government of Iran to build a new water purification facility near Tehran. In order to perform the contract, Luzerne has established an office in Tehran that employs 100 men and women. Luzerne has a general policy against discrimination on the basis of race, gender, or sexual orientation.

Under Iranian law, all women (including non-Iranians) are required to observe the Islamic dress code outside the home. Women must at all times cover their hair and skin, and avoid tight fitting clothes.

Luzerne's Tehran manager has asked the main office for guidance on whether the office should enforce the Islamic dress code. How should Luzerne respond?

U.S. National Contact Point for the OECD Guidelines for Multinational Enterprises, Final Statement, Specific Instance between the International Union of Food, Agricultural, Hotel, Restaurant, Catering, Tobacco and Allied Workers' Associations and PepsiCo, Inc.[62]

April 15, 2016

Office of the U.S. National Contact Point
4/15/2016

I. SUMMARY OF THE OUTCOME OF THE SPECIFIC INSTANCE

This Final Statement concludes consideration by the United States National Contact Point (USNCP) for the OECD Guidelines for Multinational Enterprises (the Guidelines) of the Specific Instance submitted by the International Union of Food, Agricultural, Hotel, Restaurant, Catering, Tobacco and Allied Workers'

---

62. U.S. Nat'l Contact Point for the OECD Guidelines for Multinational Enterprises, U.S. Dep't of State, Final Statement: Specific Instance between the International Union of Food, Agricultural, Hotel, Restaurant, Catering, Tobacco and Allied Workers' Association (IUF) and PepsiCo, Inc. (Apr. 15, 2016).

Associations (IUF) regarding the actions of PepsiCo, Inc. (PepsiCo), through its subsidiary in India. This Final Statement succeeds a previous Final Statement regarding this Specific Instance issued by the USNCP on May 19, 2014. That Final Statement was issued when PepsiCo declined the offer of mediation the USNCP had made.

Though mediation could not be established through the USNCP mechanism at that time, IUF and PepsiCo continued discussions of the allegations in the Specific Instance. In November 2015, PepsiCo reached out to the USNCP to ask if mediation would still be available. The USNCP agreed to mediate the case and both parties returned to the table. The parties entered into three days of mediation under the USNCP and facilitated by the Federal Mediation and Conciliation Service (FMCS) in February 2016. Although they were not able to reach a mediated agreement, the parties and the USNCP found the dialogue and mediation process to be productive and useful. The USNCP believes that the process did lead to greater understanding of the Guidelines and will result in a quicker recognition of and easier resolution of such issues when they arise in the future.

Note: For more information on the USNCP, its mandate, function, and processes, please reference the NCP Guide.

II. SUBSTANCE OF THE SPECIFIC INSTANCE

IUF's Submission

On November 18, 2013, the Office of the USNCP received a Specific Instance from the IUF citing inconsistencies with Chapters IV (Human Rights) and V (Labor) of the Guidelines alleging that between January 5 and April 30, 2013, 162 of the 170 workers employed at three West Bengal warehouses contracted exclusively by PepsiCo were dismissed or compelled to resign solely as a consequence of exercising their right to join a union. IUF stated that the PepsiCo subsidiary in India contracts for warehouse services with the Radhakrishna Food Land Pvt. Ltd. (RKFL), which, in turn, contracts with Weavings Manpower Solutions, a closely related company, to provide labor for the warehouses. IUF alleges that PepsiCo has facilitated the violation of workers' rights through this subcontracting relationship.

In its submission, the IUF specifically alleged that:

- Between January 5 and April 30, 2013, 162 out of the 170 workers employed at three West Bengal warehouses exclusively contracted by PepsiCo were dismissed or compelled to resign solely as a consequence of exercising their right to join a union.
- By "double outsourcing" its employment relationship, PepsiCo invited abuses of basic rights of the workers.
- PepsiCo's contract with RKFL contained no provisions concerning compliance with national and international labor standards, penalties for noncompliance, monitoring or reporting mechanisms or the responsibilities of labor contractors.

- Union members at the warehouses were the subject of harassment, threats and intimidation at the hands of "thugs" brought in by management.
- Union members were dismissed from work for their union activity, and then invited to return to work only on the condition that they renounce their union membership and activities.

IUF requested that the USNCP offer mediation to facilitate a resolution including the re-employment of 28 workers who had refused to renounce their union activity and thus had not been re-employed. They further asked for compensation for the workers and for the establishment of conditions which would guarantee the exercise of the right to form or join a union without fear of reprisal.

PepsiCo Response

In its written response, submitted on January 23, 2014, PepsiCo did not enter into a detailed discussion of the specific allegations contained in the Specific Instance. Rather, the company made three arguments:

- First, PepsiCo argued that in response to the IUF's allegations, and before the submission of the Specific Instance, the company had gone to great lengths to investigate the allegations. PepsiCo reported that the company had received satisfactory answers to its inquiries of RKFL regarding all of the allegations and that PepsiCo had not been able to substantiate any of the allegations. PepsiCo also reported that audits of RKFL by the India Labor Commissioner in May 2013 and by [PricewaterhouseCoopers] in late 2013 unearthed no evidence to support the allegations.
- Second, PepsiCo emphasized that the Specific Instance focused on the alleged actions of its contractor, and not actions by PepsiCo or its subsidiary. PepsiCo stated that regardless of the merit of IUF's allegations against the contractor, PepsiCo had neither the ability nor the obligation under the Guidelines to require reemployment of the workers dismissed by its contractor. PepsiCo maintained that the workers had been terminated as the result of an illegal strike, as employees had implemented a work stoppage without providing the notice required under Indian law. However, PepsiCo also stated that it had leveraged its relationship with RKFL to secure offers of reemployment for all of the workers referred to in the Specific Instance, including the 28 who have not been reemployed. Given the efforts that PepsiCo had already undertaken, including the leveraging of its relationship with RKFL, to obtain offers of reemployment for the workers, PepsiCo concluded that it had fully complied with its obligations and commitments under the OECD Guidelines, "even if one believes all of the allegations" in the Specific Instance.
- Finally, PepsiCo claimed that the true motivation of the IUF in submitting the Specific Instance was not the redress of violations of the Guidelines, but PepsiCo's refusal to enter into a formal global "relationship" with IUF. PepsiCo asserted that this was an abuse of the Specific Instance process.

PepsiCo also noted that prior to the submission of the Specific Instance, the IUF publicized the complaint through social media and engaged in intentional "spamming" of PepsiCo executives through an auto-email system, thus harassing its employees and exhibiting bad faith with regard to the confidentiality of the USNCP process.

III. INITIAL ASSESSMENT AND OFFER OF MEDIATION

The USNCP does not make judgments as to whether parties have or have not violated the Guidelines. As the issues raised by IUF appeared to merit further consideration, despite information PepsiCo had provided noting its efforts to adhere to and promote the Guidelines, the USNCP made a decision to accept the Specific Instance. On February 12, 2014, the USNCP informed both parties of this decision and offered its good offices for mediation with the view that mediation might further dialogue between RKFL and its employees, supported by IUF and PepsiCo.

On March 14, 2014, PepsiCo declined the USNCP's offer of mediation. In declining the offer, the company argued that the remedy sought by the IUF—reinstatement of the workers with back pay—was not something PepsiCo could effectuate. The company stated that it had no ability or obligation under the Guidelines to require that a contractor re-employ workers with back pay. PepsiCo emphasized that it had been in extensive dialogue with IUF before the submission of the Specific Instance, and stated that the issues had not changed and PepsiCo saw no likelihood that a mediated solution could be reached. PepsiCo reiterated its concern regarding the motivation of IUF in submitting the Specific Instance. Finally, PepsiCo reiterated its concerns regarding the IUF's respect for the confidentiality of the process, providing a copy of a circular letter IUF had sent to its affiliates which informed them of the submission of the Specific Instance.

In a response to the PepsiCo decision submitted on April 2, 2014, the IUF regretted the decision by PepsiCo and expressed hope that PepsiCo might reconsider. The IUF acknowledged its ongoing and widely known policy of seeking relationships with multinational companies operating in the sectors in which IUF is active in order to resolve issues such as those raised in this Specific Instance. However, IUF stated that its intention with this Specific Instance was not to make its solution contingent on a more general relationship with PepsiCo, but rather to "seek just solutions to specific abuses" raised in the Specific Instance. IUF highlighted the fact that PepsiCo had chosen not to respond in detail to the allegations included in the Specific Instance, and argued that the audits which had been undertaken provided little assurance about the operations of RKFL, particularly given that the [PricewaterhouseCoopers] audit was not shared with IUF or the USNCP.

On the basis of the PepsiCo decision to decline the offer of mediation, the USNCP issued a Final Statement on May 19, 2014, closing this Specific Instance. That Final Statement is being supplemented by this Statement.

No other NCPs have been involved in this Specific Instance. In accordance with its procedures, throughout this process the USNCP consulted and received input from the U.S. government Interagency Working Group.

Note: Acceptance of a Specific Instance is in no way a determination on the merits of the claims presented in the Specific Instance, but merely an offer to facilitate neutral, third-party mediation or conciliation to assist the parties in voluntarily, confidentially, and in good faith, reaching a cooperative resolution of their concerns.

IV. ACCEPTANCE OF THE OFFER OF MEDIATION

Notably, in November 2015, PepsiCo contacted the USNCP to express interest in exploring the possibility of USNCP-facilitated mediation with IUF. The company informed the USNCP that the parties had engaged in extensive dialogue in an effort to resolve the dispute since the closing of the 2013 Specific Instance. While they had not been able to reach a settlement on their own, both parties hoped mediation might help them to resolve their differences. Seeing both parties come back in good faith to mediate, the USNCP renewed its offer of mediation. Three days of mediation, under the auspices of the Federal Mediation and Conciliation Service, took place in February 2016. IUF, PepsiCo, and PepsiCo contractor RKFL participated in the mediation. Unfortunately, while the parties showed a desire to reach agreement, they were ultimately unable to bridge their differences.

V. CONCLUSIONS AND RECOMMENDATIONS

While it was not ultimately possible for the parties to reach an agreement in mediation, the USNCP and the parties were pleased with the impact of this Specific Instance and the dialogue that was fostered. The Specific Instance brought the parties into a conversation which has continued (to date) for two years, and while a consensual resolution to the particular issues of this case has eluded the parties, the USNCP believes that the process did lead to greater understanding of the Guidelines and will result in a quicker recognition of and easier solution [to] such issues when they arise in the future.

The USNCP commends both parties for their willingness to continue to work to resolve these issues and for their decision to return to the Specific Instance, even after it had been declared concluded, to make an attempt at a mediated solution. Although disappointed by their initial decision not to enter into mediation, the USNCP would like to commend PepsiCo for coming back to the table and attempting to resolve the issues raised in the Specific Instance after initially turning down mediation.

The USNCP notes PepsiCo's actions to improve its responsible business conduct work over the time since the filing of the Specific Instance. PepsiCo reported that since June 2015, when it launched its Sustainable Supplier Program to assesses PepsiCo suppliers and contractors against international human rights standards, 1,765 PepsiCo supplier/contractor sites have been added to the program and undergone a preliminary risk assessment. Of those, 1,178 sites have completed human rights self-assessments (modeled after the SEDEX SMETA self-assessment), and 163 have been audited against international human rights standards.

PepsiCo has also engaged an internationally recognized human rights non-governmental organization to provide guidance to further strengthen its policies and programs. The company has shared that it [is] in the process of updating its Human Rights policy and its Supplier Code of Conduct to better communicate PepsiCo's expectation of its suppliers and contractors. The USNCP hopes that PepsiCo's efforts will help promote the Guidelines by ensuring workers in PepsiCo supplier and contractor sites are able to fully exercise their human rights without fear of retaliation.

Issues Raised in this Specific Instance

This Specific Instance raised three important issues on which the USNCP wishes to comment. Specifically:

Suppliers and Leverage

The Guidelines have this to say about supply chain responsibility:

> "If the enterprise identifies a risk of contributing to an adverse impact, then it should take the necessary steps to cease or prevent its contribution and use its leverage to mitigate any remaining impacts to the greatest extent possible. Leverage is considered to exist where the enterprise has the ability to effect change in the wrongful practices of the entity that causes the harm." (Commentary on General Principles, p.19)

This supply chain responsibility is further clarified in paragraph 20 of the Commentary on General Principles:

> "Meeting the expectation in paragraph A.12 would entail an enterprise, acting alone or in co-operation with other entities, as appropriate, to use its leverage to influence the entity causing the adverse impact to prevent or mitigate that impact."

From these passages it is clear that enterprises are responsible for their supply chains even while suppliers remain responsible for their own actions. These two separate responsibilities do not contradict each other. The local contractor is responsible for any labor rights violations it commits (Guidelines, General Policies, para 12). However, that does not absolve the company contracting with it from the responsibility to do what it can to keep its supply chain free from such abuses, and ensure such a contracting arrangement does not dilute workers' access to their rights. The need for due diligence flows from this responsibility.

It is also clear that the enterprise is responsible for using its leverage to prevent or mitigate adverse impacts. Leverage is a complex issue. How much leverage a company may have in any given supplier relationship depends upon all the variables in play in that specific situation. In many cases, a company may not even be aware of the full extent of (or the limits to) its leverage until it attempts to wield that leverage in that particular case. However, the Guidelines also imply that a lack of leverage does not justify inaction.

The Guidelines recognize that there can be practical limitations on the ability of enterprises to effect change in the behavior of their suppliers, related to, amongst other issues, product characteristics, the number of suppliers and the structure and complexity of the supply chain. Nonetheless, enterprises are expected to influence their suppliers in any way they can, such as through contractual arrangements, voting trusts, and participation in industry-wide collaborative efforts with other enterprises with which they share common suppliers. . . .

PepsiCo maintains it acted consistent[ly[with the leverage elements of the OECD Guidelines. PepsiCo also shared that it investigated IUF's claims against PepsiCo's contractor RKFL and that its own representatives have spent a significant amount of time interviewing RKFL leaders and reviewing RKFL documentation, both before and after the filing of the Specific Instance. PepsiCo has also stated that it has conducted an additional independent human rights audit— conducted by Intertek—since the original closing of the Specific Instance. PepsiCo used its leverage to secure the participation of RKFL in the mediation process.

Mediation, Flexibility and Openness

Submitters of Specific Instances sometimes make explicit within their initial submission the objectives they have for the Specific Instance and any mediation process which may result. This can be useful, as it helps to define the parameters of the Specific Instance and of any mediation up front. However, such objectives should be seen as a starting point for approaching mediation. Mediation, as a process, looks for mutually agreeable solutions to disputes between the parties. Rarely will mediation result in the starting position of one of the parties being adopted in its totality by the other. It is important for both submitting parties and responding parties to recognize this. A submitter should not start the process by putting a "best and final offer" on the table. Likewise, a responder should not reject the offer of mediation simply because it is unwilling or unable to meet the stated objective of the submitting party. A successful mediation may result in a solution which neither party had imagined before entering the process and which improves the situation of both parties.

Confidentiality

The USNCP does not consider that confidentiality was violated in this case, but wants to take the opportunity to clarify our views on this important requirement. USNCP procedures provide that the parties are expected to strictly respect the confidentiality of all communications during the entire Specific Instance process— from submission of the Specific Instance to the issuance of the Final Statement. The purpose of this confidentiality policy is to facilitate the building of mutual trust, which is an important element for reaching any mediated solution. Similarly, and with the same objective in mind, the USNCP recommends that any "campaigning" be suspended for the duration of the Specific Instance process, especially if mediation is offered.

Most Specific Instances come to the USNCP after the substance of the dispute is already public. That is to be expected, and the USNCP takes no position on communications strategies used by the parties before a Specific Instance is submitted. Likewise, the USNCP has no objection to parties informing the public that a Specific Instance has been submitted, though the USNCP does recommend that parties consider whether such an announcement and the way in which it is made might affect the likelihood of successful mediation, if mediation is offered.

Non-public information learned through the process should not be disseminated publicly, and documents internal to the process should not be made public either during or after the process. After the Specific Instance has concluded, information learned through the Specific Instance process should not be made public.

Recommendations

PepsiCo's Human Rights Workplace Policy, which was reviewed by the USNCP in connection with this Specific Instance, dates back to 2009 and establishes compliance with local laws and regulations as the minimum standard for PepsiCo activities. In 2011, the OECD Guidelines were updated to incorporate a new chapter on human rights and a new general principle on the need to exercise due diligence to avoid or mitigate negative impacts, notably with respect to the management of supply chains and other business relationships. The USNCP recommends that PepsiCo update its Human Rights Workplace Policy, committing itself explicitly to the Guidelines and incorporating the human rights and labor chapters of the Guidelines as the standard for PepsiCo activities. PepsiCo has informed the USNCP that an update is already underway.

With this Final Statement, the USNCP brings this Specific Instance to a close.

Melike Ann Yetken
U.S. National Contact Point for the OECD Guidelines
U.S. Department of State

V. Environment

The OECD guideline on the environment requires multinational enterprises to take eight types of initiatives:

1. Environmental Management Systems

The broad aim of an environmental management system (EMS) is to help an organisation achieve its environmental goals through consistent control of its operations, just as internal accounting controls provide intrinsic assurances that financial management systems are functioning well. Whatever the specific goals, the assumption behind the implementation of an EMS is that better environmental management will improve overall business performance.

An EMS is not based on the adoption of uniform standards or benchmarks. Rather, each organisation tailors the starting point, design and content of its EMS to serve its own aspirations, business goals, capacities and experience. However, there is a growing consensus that an EMS should normally encompass key elements, often referred to as "Plan-Do-Check-Improve." These are: undertake an initial environmental review; define an environmental policy; develop an environmental action plan and define environmental responsibilities; develop internal information and training courses; audit the environmental management system and conduct an environmental management review.[63]

2. Public Information and Shareholder Consultation

Information about the activities of enterprises and associated environmental impacts is an important vehicle for building public confidence. This is most effective when information is provided in a transparent manner and when it encourages active consultation with stakeholders so as to promote a climate of long-term trust and understanding of environmental issues of mutual interest. . . .[64]

3. Life-Cycle Assessment

Environmental life-cycle assessment is a tool for systematic evaluation of the environmental aspects of a product or service through its entire life-cycle. A product's life-cycle starts when raw materials are extracted, followed by manufacturing, transport and use, and ends with waste management including recycling and final disposal. There are emissions and consumption of resources at every stage of the life-cycle. Life-cycle assessment (LCA) starts with life-cycle thinking—an understanding that the environmental impacts of the entire life-cycle of products and services need to be addressed.[65]

4. Exercising Precaution

Governments and enterprises are changing the way in which they look at environmental risk. It is increasingly perceived that repairing environmental damage is not enough, but rather that environmental damage, especially when it is

---

Using LCA to Reduce Environmental Impacts

The company 3M, which manufactures a wide range of products from display and graphics, electronics and telecommunications, health care to industrial products, launched a formal LCA initiative, the Life-Cycle Management System (LCM). 3M chose a qualitative approach to LCA: the tool was designed to identify risks and opportunities, particularly during the use/disposal phase of product life. To implement this tool, 3M created an "LCM Screen" that allows managers to identify the environmental, health, and safety opportunities and risks through the stages of the product's life-cycle.

Recent achievements accomplished through LCA include the development of new film, labels, and adhesive. For example, 3M developed new film that is manufactured with 80% less solvent and with less waste. Trim waste is recycled as a raw material back into the process. Also, working with plastics suppliers and a European-based global manufacturer, 3M Europe created new labels that reduce customers' costs for raw materials, labour, and disposal. Compatible labels make plastic recycling easier and more profitable. Appliance manufacturers can now recycle product cases and meet the EU Directive on waste electrical and electronic equipment.

—*Environment and the OECD Guidelines*[66]

---

63. Org. for Econ. Cooperation and Dev. [OECD], *Environment and the OECD Guidelines for Multinational Enterprises: Corporate Tools and Approaches*, at 9–10 (Sept. 5, 2005).

64. *Id.* at 12.

65. *Id.* at 15.

66. *Id.* at 17.

irreversible, should be prevented. While governments are ultimately responsible for the health and welfare of their citizens and the environment, they have increasingly acted to assign a larger burden of liability for specific acts of harm to the private sector. This is in part an outgrowth of the perception that private gains should not be obtained at the cost of the public interest, and in part a recognition that government cannot compensate for specific acts of harm.

The basic premise of the Guidelines is that enterprises should act as soon as possible, and in a proactive way, to avoid, for example, serious or irreversible environmental damage resulting from their activities. For enterprises, precaution is in part a function of how they operate in an everyday setting, and in part how they implement national regulatory requirements. Enterprises may need to exercise precaution in situations where two factors occur: [1] the existence of a risk, *i.e.*, where potentially hazardous effects deriving from an action, product or process have been identified, and [2] lack of scientific certainty on the effects of such action, product or process on human health and the environment, or on the extent of the potential damage.[67]

5. Emergency prevention, preparedness and response

Preventing, mitigating and controlling environmental and health damage that can be caused by a company's operations is at the heart of sound environmental management. The Guidelines address what are commonly considered to be the three core components of emergency management:

- *Prevention.* The minimisation of the likelihood that an accident will occur.
- *Preparedness and mitigation.* The mitigation of the consequences of accidents through emergency planning, land-use planning, and risk communication.
- *Response.* Limiting adverse consequences to health, environment and property in the event of an accident. The response includes actions needed to learn from the experiences of accidents and other unexpected events (follow-up) in order to reduce future incidents (prevention).

Traditionally, most of the responsibility in the area of emergency response fell to experts in government and industry. However, in recent years, the role of communities has become a more prominent component in the emergency planning and response process. As the case for corporate transparency gains ground, corporate environmental, health and safety reports increasingly include information about community involvement in environmental and emergency management.[68]

6. Continuous Improvements in Environmental Performance

Environmental management systems are one (possibly the main) tool to achieve process-related improvements. The commitment to continual improvement of environmental performance is the main raison d'être of any mainstream EMS (see section 1).

---

67. *Id.* at 18.
68. *Id.* at 21.

Environmental metrics is another important approach increasingly used by companies. Companies are unlikely to achieve environmental improvements if they lack data about their performance in the first place. Companies also face expectations from financial and non-financial stakeholders that they quantify their environmental performance and inform the public. Useful tools for measuring environmental performance are indicators, benchmarking, and environmental management accounting (EMA). EMA expresses environmental information in terms of financial costs to the company. It is a tool to identify, collect and analyse information about environment-related, internally absorbed costs.

Raising Consumer Awareness

Product-information tools. Only a minority of consumers seeks information about the environmental performance of products. If companies provide that information, consumers may take this information into account in their purchasing decisions. One tool used by companies to raise consumer awareness is eco-labelling (see section 2).

Company-information tools. Another way to increase awareness among potential consumers is to provide easy-to-access and comparable information about the company's environmental conduct, e.g. through public databases.[69]

7. Environmental Education and Training

The expectation that enterprises will provide environmentally-related training arises from two general objectives: promoting environmental health and safety and implementing environmental management systems. Under environmental and occupational health and safety (OHS) regulations in most countries, employers must train their staff with the purpose of protecting their health and safety, as well as that of the local community. Training activities that relate to more general environmental management aspects are mostly voluntary and focus on achieving both internal environmental goals and compliance with environmental legislation.

- Training must be designed for a specific audience. In general, the audience should be as homogeneous as possible; hence, it is important to identify the needs for each group. Training should be tailored to match the audience's skills and background (i.e. education, job assignments, position levels, experience).
- Trainers must establish clear objectives prior to the start of the training, which would allow them to have measurable results. Training objectives usually need to be stated in terms of how the trainee's behaviour will be affected, such as "What should the participants be able to accomplish at the end of the training?"
- Training should be tailored according to the corporate culture (which can vary within the same company). Multinational enterprises also need to identify key cultural aspects of the country where the training is conducted.[70]

8. Contributing to the Development of Environmental Policy

Partnerships between various stakeholders have become an integral part of the policy-making process and contribute to developing sound public policy from

---

69. *Id.* at 22–24.
70. *Id.* at 25–27.

both economic and environmental standpoints. The involvement of all stake-holders in policy discussions reduces the risk that some problems go unan-ticipated by regulators. By involving the business sector, policy-makers and regulators are better able to design policies to reflect business realities. This may result in better compliance. Conversely, policy changes without consultations with enterprises may lead to unsatisfactory results, insofar as companies may have little scope and incentive to go beyond minimum requirements. Finally, involving enterprises in policy discussions also allows policy-makers to apprise themselves of new technologies, and the feasibility of the changes that may be needed to achieve compliance. Considering the broad ambit of environmental regulations and policies, business contribution in the latter is likely to impact many other aspects of sound environmental management.[71]

OECD Environment[72]

Enterprises should, within the framework of the laws, regulations and admin-istrative practices of the countries in which they operate, and in consideration of relevant international agreements, principles, objectives, and standards, take due account of the need to protect the environment, public health and safety, and generally to conduct their activities in a manner contributing to the wider goal of sustainable development. In particular, enterprises should:

1. Establish and maintain a system of environmental management appropri-ate to the enterprise, including:
   a) collection and evaluation of adequate and timely information regard-ing the environmental, health, and safety impacts of their activities;
   b) establishment of measurable objectives and, where appropriate, tar-gets for improved environmental performance and resource utilisa-tion, including periodically reviewing the continuing relevance of these objectives; where appropriate, targets should be consistent with relevant national policies and international environmental commitments; and
   c) regular monitoring and verification of progress toward environmental, health, and safety objectives or targets.
2. Taking into account concerns about cost, business confidentiality, and the protection of intellectual property rights:
   a) provide the public and workers with adequate, measureable, veri-fiable (where applicable) and timely information on the potential environment[al], health and safety impacts of the activities of the enter-prise, which could include reporting on progress in improving environ-mental performance; and
   b) engage in adequate and timely communication and consultation with the communities directly affected by the environmental, health and safety policies of the enterprise and by their implementation.

---

71. *Id.* at 28.
72. *OECD Guidelines, supra* note 2, at 42–46.

3. Assess, and address in decision-making, the foreseeable environmental, health, and safety-related impacts associated with the processes, goods and services of the enterprise over their full life cycle with a view to avoiding or, when unavoidable, mitigating them. Where these proposed activities may have significant environmental, health, or safety impacts, and where they are subject to a decision of a competent authority, prepare an appropriate environmental impact assessment.

4. Consistent with the scientific and technical understanding of the risks, where there are threats of serious damage to the environment, taking also into account human health and safety, not use the lack of full scientific certainty as a reason for postponing cost-effective measures to prevent or minimise such damage.

5. Maintain contingency plans for preventing, mitigating, and controlling serious environmental and health damage from their operations, including accidents and emergencies, and mechanisms for immediate reporting to the competent authorities.

6. Continually seek to improve corporate environmental performance at the level of the enterprise and, where appropriate, of its supply chain, by encouraging such activities as:

   a) adoption of technologies and operating procedures in all parts of the enterprise that reflect standards concerning environmental performance in the best performing part of the enterprise;

   b) development and provision of products or services that have no undue environmental impacts; are safe in their intended use; reduce greenhouse gas emissions; are efficient in their consumption of energy and natural resources; and can be reused, recycled, or disposed of safely;

   c) promoting higher levels of awareness among customers of the environmental implications of using the products and services of the enterprise, including by providing accurate information on their products (for example, on greenhouse gas emissions, biodiversity, resource efficiency, or other environmental issues); and

   d) exploring and assessing ways of improving the environmental performance of the enterprise over the longer term, for instance by developing strategies for emission reduction, efficient resource utilisation and recycling, substitution or reduction of use of toxic substances, or strategies on biodiversity.

7. Provide adequate education and training to workers in environmental health and safety matters, including the handling of hazardous materials and the prevention of environmental accidents, as well as more general environmental management areas, such as environmental impact assessment procedures, public relations, and environmental technologies.

8. Contribute to the development of environmentally meaningful and economically efficient public policy, for example by means of partnerships or initiatives that will enhance environmental awareness and protection.

COMMENTARY ON THE ENVIRONMENT

60. The text of the Environment Chapter broadly reflects the principles and objectives contained in the Rio Declaration on Environment and Development, in Agenda 21 (within the Rio Declaration). It also takes into account the (Aarhus) Convention on Access to Information, Public Participation in Decision-making, and Access to Justice in Environmental Matters and reflects standards contained in such instruments as the ISO Standard on Environmental Management Systems.

61. Sound environmental management is an important part of sustainable development, and is increasingly being seen as both a business responsibility and a business opportunity. Multinational enterprises have a role to play in both respects. Managers of these enterprises should therefore give appropriate attention to environmental issues within their business strategies. Improving environmental performance requires a commitment to a systematic approach and to continual improvement of the system. An environmental management system provides the internal framework necessary to control an enterprise's environmental impacts and to integrate environmental considerations into business operations. Having such a system in place should help to assure shareholders, employees and the community that the enterprise is actively working to protect the environment from the impacts of its activities.

62. In addition to improving environmental performance, instituting an environmental management system can provide economic benefits to companies through reduced operating and insurance costs, improved energy and resource conservation, reduced compliance and liability charges, improved access to capital and skills, improved customer satisfaction, and improved community and public relations.

63. In the context of these *Guidelines*, "sound environmental management" should be interpreted in its broadest sense, embodying activities aimed at controlling both direct and indirect environmental impacts of enterprise activities over the long-term, and involving both pollution control and resource management elements.

64. In most enterprises, an internal control system is needed to manage the enterprise's activities. The environmental part of this system may include such elements as targets for improved performance and regular monitoring of progress towards these targets.

65. Information about the activities of enterprises, their relationships with sub-contractors and their suppliers, and their associated environmental impacts is an important vehicle for building confidence with the public. This vehicle is most effective when information is provided in a transparent manner and when it encourages active consultation with stakeholders such as employees, customers, suppliers, contractors, local communities and with the public-at-large so as to promote a climate of long-term trust and understanding on environmental issues of mutual interest. Reporting and communication are particularly appropriate where scarce or at-risk environmental assets are at stake either in

a regional, national or international context; reporting standards such as the Global Reporting Initiative provide useful references.

66. In providing accurate information on their products, enterprises have several options such as voluntary labelling or certification schemes. In using these instruments enterprises should take due account of their social and economic effects on developing countries and of existing internationally recognised standards.

67. Normal business activity can involve the *ex ante* assessment of the potential environmental impacts associated with the enterprise's activities. Enterprises often carry out appropriate environmental impact assessments, even if they are not required by law. Environmental assessments made by the enterprise may contain a broad and forward-looking view of the potential impacts of an enterprise's activities and of activities of sub-contractors and suppliers, addressing relevant impacts and examining alternatives and mitigation measures to avoid or redress adverse impacts. The *Guidelines* also recognise that multinational enterprises have certain responsibilities in other parts of the product life cycle.

68. Several instruments already adopted by countries adhering to the *Guidelines*, including Principle 15 of the Rio Declaration on Environment and Development, enunciate a "precautionary approach." None of these instruments are explicitly addressed to enterprises, although enterprise contributions are implicit in all of them.

69. The basic premise of the *Guidelines* is that enterprises should act as soon as possible in a proactive way to avoid . . . serious or irreversible environmental damages resulting from their activities. However, the fact that the *Guidelines* are addressed to enterprises means that no existing instrument is completely adequate for expressing this recommendation. . . .

70. The *Guidelines* are not intended to reinterpret any existing instruments or to create new commitments or precedents on the part of governments—they are intended only to recommend how the precautionary approach should be implemented at the level of enterprises. Given the early stage of this process, it is recognised that some flexibility is needed in its application, based on the specific context in which it is carried out. It is also recognised that governments determine the basic framework in this field, and have the responsibility to consult periodically with stakeholders on the most appropriate ways forward.

71. The *Guidelines* also encourage enterprises to work to raise the level of environmental performance in all parts of their operations, even where this may not be formally required by existing practice in the countries in which they operate. In this regard, enterprises should take due account of their social and economic effects on developing countries.

72. For example, multinational enterprises often have access to existing and innovative technologies or operating procedures which could, if applied, help raise environmental performance overall. Multinational enterprises are frequently regarded as leaders in their respective fields, so the potential for a "demonstration effect" on other enterprises should not be overlooked. Ensuring that the environment[s] of the countries in which multinational enterprises

operate also benefit from available and innovative technologies and practices is an important way of building support for international investment activities more generally.

73. Enterprises have an important role to play in the training and education of their employees with regard to environmental matters. They are encouraged to discharge this responsibility in as broad a manner as possible, especially in areas directly related to human health and safety.

Hypothetical: GM Seeds

Biofarm, Inc. ("Biofarm"), the largest producer of genetically modified ("GM") seeds in the world, is based in St. Louis, Missouri. Biofarm's GM seeds are resistant to herbicides, allowing farmers to apply herbicides in quantities that would kill conventional crops.

Biofarm has obtained permission to introduce its GM seeds in Tanzania. This is the first time that GM seeds will be used in the country, which has no biosafety code (laws that regulate the introduction and use of genetically modified organisms). Use of GM seeds carries the following risks:

- Cross-contamination with local species grown on nearby farms
- Reduced biodiversity
- Excessive use of pesticides, which can harm the environment and wildlife

What steps should Biofarm take in Tanzania to ensure compliance with the OECD Guidelines?

Irish National Contact Point, OECD Guidelines for Multinational Enterprises[73]

Final Statement of the Irish and Netherlands National Contact Points (NCPs) on the notification dated 21st August, 2008, concerning the Corrib Gas project, pursuant to the OECD Guidelines for Multinational Enterprises

SECTION 1—INTRODUCTION TO THE OECD GUIDELINES

The OECD Guidelines for Multinational Enterprises are a set of recommendations of the governments of the 31 OECD member states plus 11 other countries to enterprises operating in and from their territory. They set out voluntary principles and standards to guide companies in their international operations. While implementation of the Guidelines themselves is voluntary, each OECD Member

---

73. Irish National Contact Point & Dutch National Contact Point for the OECD Guidelines for Multinational Enterprises, *Final Statement of the Irish and Netherlands National Contact Points on the Notification Dated 21st August, 2008 Concerning the Corrib Gas Project* (Jul. 30, 2010).

State is, however, obliged to establish a National Contact Point (NCP) to deal with notifications of groups or individuals of alleged violations of the Guidelines by an enterprise in a specific situation. If an NCP, after conducting an initial assessment, decides that the notification merits further consideration, the NCP provides . . . a platform for discussion on the issues raised, where it can play a mediating role. If parties involved do not reach agreement on the issues raised, the NCP issues a statement and makes, where appropriate, recommendations on the implementation of the Guidelines.

On 21 August 2008, the Irish and Dutch NCPs were asked to consider an issue in relation to the development of a gas find off the west coast of Ireland—the "Corrib Gas project." The complaint related to the environmental, health and safety and human rights aspects of the activities of the developers.

While the Irish NCP has the primary responsibility in relation to this specific instance because of the location of the specific instance, the Dutch NCP was asked to cooperate with the Irish NCP, because Shell's parent company is based in The Netherlands. . . . Since the Consortium also consists of a US and a Norwegian company, the NCPs of those OECD countries were also informed. The Canadian NCP was informed following Vermilion Energy Trust's acquisition of Marathon's interest in the Consortium.

The Irish NCP is located in the Department of Enterprise, Trade and Innovation, although the scope of the Guidelines covers several Government Departments and Agencies. The Dutch NCP is an independent entity.

SECTION 2—THE SPECIFIC INSTANCE

Notifiers: Pobal Chill Chomain et al.

The lead notifier is Pobal Chill Chomain, a community group in North Mayo, Ireland. The notification is supported by Action from Ireland (AFRI), an Irish NGO, and its French counterpart Sherpa, hereafter together referred to as "the Notifiers."

Enterprise: Shell Exploration and Production Ireland Limited (SEPIL) et al.

The notification was directed against the oil companies promoting the venture (Shell Exploration and Production Ireland Limited (SEPIL), Statoil Exploration Ireland Limited, and Marathon International Petroleum Hibernia Limited) hereafter the Consortium. In July 2009, Vermilion Energy Trust of Canada announced that it had acquired Marathon's 18.5% interest in the Corrib gas project.

Date of Notification: 21 August 2008

Content of the Notification

Pobal Chill Chomain *et al.* alleged that the operations of the Consortium:

1. posed a safety risk to residents due to the proximity of high pressure pipelines in an unstable field;
2. posed a risk to the local drinking water supply and would be discharging chemicals [into the] air and water;

3. would negatively affect an intricate and ancient drainage system ("bogland");
4. violated the right to private life of local residents due to the presence and actions of Gardai;
5. would negatively affect local capacity building due to effects on tourism and fishing opportunities;
6. were developed without the possibility of public participation in decision making.

The Notifiers alleged that the Consortium violated the following provisions of the Guidelines:

* *Chapter V—Environment, paragraphs 2 and 3;*
* *Chapter II—General Policies, paragraphs 2 and 3.*

The Notifiers also sought to determine whether or not there had been compliance with domestic, EU and international legal rules and principles.

References in Relation to the Irish Government in the Notification

While the Irish Government was not cited as a party to the NCP procedure, the Notifiers alleged that the Irish authorities violated several EU Directives and International legal instruments. They alluded, in particular, to the referral of Ireland by the Commission to the European Court of Justice (ECJ) in 2007 for failures regarding public participation. In addition, Notifiers alleged that [the] Irish Government failed to transpose Environmental Impact Assessments (EIA) Directives into national legislation, citing Case C215/06 Ireland v. Commission [concerning the construction of wind farms]. The Notifiers drew parallels between the latter case and the Corrib Gas Project in relation to project splitting, alleged failures to carry out Environmental Impact Assessments and other aspects.

Administrative and Parallel Legal Procedures

The notification to the NCPs was preceded by and parallel to administrative procedures for [authorizing] the Consortium to (further) develop the Corrib Gas field and to undertake work. Nevertheless, as the notification was largely about the alleged failure of the Consortium to adequately address the concerns of the Notifiers, the NCPs were of the opinion that the NCP procedure could provide for an informal platform for discussion on these concerns between the parties involved.

SECTION 3—BACKGROUND TO THE 'CORRIB GAS PROJECT' AND RECENT DEVELOPMENTS

The Corrib Gas Field was discovered in 1996. It is about 70% the size of the existing Kinsale Head gas field off the south coast of Ireland and has an estimated production life of about 15 years. Originally, Enterprise Energy Ireland, a subsidiary to Enterprise Oil, was set to develop the field and had, in 2001, obtained permission by local authorities for a gas processing plant. Shell bought Enterprise

Oil in April 2002. Currently, the Corrib Gas Field is being developed by Shell Exploration and Production Ireland Limited (SEPIL), Statoil Exploration (Ireland) Limited and Vermilion Energy Trust. SEPIL, on behalf of the other partners, acts as implementing developer of the Corrib field, while the other two partners—Statoil and Vermilion—are co-investors in the project.

Since 2001, the Consortium, in accordance with relevant Irish legislation, obtained the requisite consents, licences and planning permissions for the various works associated with the development of the Corrib Gas Field. These works included laying a pipeline from the field to the landfall, laying a further pipeline from the landfall to an onshore processing facility some miles inland, and the construction of the processing facility itself.

The Corrib Gas Field Plan of Development was approved by former Minister for Marine and Natural Resources, Mr. Frank Fahey T.D., in 2002. Minister Fahey also granted Compulsory Acquisition Orders [CAOs] permitting the Consortium to have access to and use of private land in order to allow for installation of the pipeline. The Consortium secured planning permission for the processing facility at Ballinaboy in October 2004, after a previous application had been rejected by An Bórd Pleanála in 2003.

According to the Notifiers, members of the local community expressed significant safety concerns as work progressed. The Notifiers also stated that opposition to the development plans among local residents grew from 2000 when local residents felt they were not adequately consulted and that they had been misled about the safety of the gas pipeline.

The relationship between the Consortium and the local community deteriorated sharply in 2005 when five local landowners refused to allow the Corrib developers to proceed with construction work relating to the onshore section of pipeline at Ballinaboy. As this was judged to be in contravention of the CAOs, the five local men were subsequently found to be in contempt of court and were jailed for 94 days. In response to this development, in September 2005 the Irish Government announced the establishment of a formal mediation process, designed to address concerns in relation to the Corrib project. This was chaired by Peter Cassells, former Secretary General of the Irish Congress of Trade Unions.

In addition, the following month, October 2005, the Irish Government appointed Advantica Ltd., a UK engineering consultancy, to carry out an independent safety review of the onshore section of the gas pipeline to address community concerns in relation to pipeline safety. Their report published in January 2006 and contained a number of recommendations, one of which limits the pressure in the onshore pipeline to 144 bar.

In July 2006, Peter Cassells concluded in his report that:

"Following seven months of intensive discussions with the Rossport 5 and Shell and detailed consultations with the local community, I have with regret concluded that, despite their best efforts, the parties are unable to resolve the differences between them. I have also concluded, given the different positions on the project and the different approaches to mediation, that no agreement is likely in the foreseeable future."

Mr. Cassels recommended that the route of the onshore section of the Corrib Gas Pipeline be modified *"in the vicinity of Rossport to address community concerns regarding proximity to housing,"* and also that *"consent to operate the pipeline should not be granted to Shell until the limitation on the pressure in the pipeline to 144 bar has been implemented."*

From his discussions with a wide range of people in the area, Mr Cassells also concluded *"that the majority of people in Rossport, the wider Erris area and County Mayo are in favour of the project."* The Notifiers rejected this finding as based on inadequate consultation and information.

With regard to the recommendation in both the Cassells and Advantica reports on the pressure in the pipeline, the Consortium subsequently confirmed that it would put in place measures to reduce the maximum pressure in the onshore section of the pipeline to 144 bar.

Recent Developments

In November 2008, the Minister for Communications, Energy and Natural Resources, Mr. Eamon Ryan T.D., and the Minister for Community, Rural and Gaeltacht Affairs, Mr. Eamon O'Cuiv T.D., jointly announced the establishment of a new Government-backed initiative on the Corrib gas project entitled the "Community Forum for the Development of North-West Mayo." The Forum is intended to act as a vehicle to facilitate (a) discussion on economic and social issues pertaining to the North Mayo Erris area, and (b) discussion of issues relating to the Corrib project including matters of local concern in relation to its implementation, such as environmental issues, fishing rights, details of consents, policing, etc. The Forum was not constituted as a decision-making body. Its overall objective is to ensure that interested parties are accorded the opportunity to directly engage in dialogue, by bringing together local community and interest groups, the Consortium and representatives of its local workforce, concerned Government Ministers and representatives of Government Departments, County Council, locally elected representatives and the Garda Siochana (police). Mr. Joe Brosnan, a retired senior civil servant with extensive experience in mediation and conciliation, was appointed to chair the Forum.

The administrative situation regarding the route of the pipelines continues to evolve; following the recommendations of the mediation process led by Mr. Peter Cassells, the Consortium modified its plans and subsequently submitted new applications for authorisation for development of the Corrib Gas Field. The Consortium selected a new route for the onshore pipeline, following a 14-month selection process, which involved 11 months of public consultation. In April 2008, applications for approval for the preferred route were submitted to An Bórd Pleanála, under the Planning and Development (Strategic Infrastructure) Act 2006, and the Minister for Communications, Energy and Natural Resources under Section 40 of the Gas Act 1976-2000. These were subsequently withdrawn by the Corrib developers in December 2008, to allow for some minor modifications to be made to the preferred route. In February 2009, the Consortium submitted revised applications for the onshore portion of the pipeline to An Bórd

Pleanála, the Department of Communications, Energy and Natural Resources and the Department of Agriculture Fisheries and Food (DAFF), seeking a wider route corridor as well as minor realignments of the preferred route.

In November 2009, An Bórd Pleanála asked Shell Ireland to make several safety changes, particularly to 5.6km of the 9km pipeline which it considered would be too close to homes for safety. Shell was given until the end of May 2010 to address the concerns. It would then have to submit a modified environmental impact statement; the altered application would then go to another public hearing before a report would be sent back to An Bórd Pleanála. Should the developer decide to comply with the An Bord Pleanála invitation, a new application to the Minister for Communications, Energy and Natural Resources with respect to permission to construct the pipeline pursuant to Section 40 of the Gas Act, 1976, as amended will be necessary. A new application to the Minister for the Environment, Heritage and Local Government for a Foreshore Licence will also be necessary. Both applications would be subject to a statutory public consultation process.

On 4 March 2010, the Irish High Court ruled that two members of the Rossport community were entitled to proceed with their counter-claim against Shell regarding the validity of ministerial consent given eight years ago for the Shell Corrib gas pipeline. As far as the NCPs are aware, this decision has not to date been appealed.

SECTION 4—CONSIDERATION OF THE NOTIFICATION UNDER THE OECD GUIDELINES

As stated in section 2, the notification to the NCPs was preceded by and parallel to administrative procedures for authorisation to further develop the Corrib Gas field and to undertake work. Nonetheless, on 19 February 2008, the Irish and Dutch NCPs decided that the issues raised merited their further consideration within the limitations of the mandate of NCPs. Due to the role of the Irish Government in the situation with regard to considering the Consortium's application for consent to further develop the Corrib Gas project, coordination of the decision on NCP involvement was a lengthier process than originally anticipated.

The NCPs made it clear to the Notifiers that adjudication on whether a private entity or a State has acted in compliance with domestic, EC or international law is beyond the competence of NCPs, and that in relation to parallel legal and administrative proceedings, the NCPs would not to be in a position to comment on those, and therefore would have to act within this limitation.

The NCPs identified the facilitation of the resolution of the dispute as being of utmost importance and accordingly they offered a platform for discussion at which the Notifiers and the Consortium, under the guidance of the NCPs, would have the opportunity to discuss their mutual interests in resolving their differences.

Main Issues for Consideration by the NCPs

Of the six issues brought in the original notification, two emerged as the main items of contention in the NCP procedure that could be discussed, insofar as they fall within the scope of the OECD Guidelines. These two issues relate to:

1. the location of the Corrib Gas terminal in Ballinaboy, Co Mayo due to health and safety concerns of the local community; and
2. the extent to which the Corrib developers sufficiently engaged in consultations on health and safety impacts with the community in planning the development of the Corrib Gas Field.

The NCPs therefore focussed on these two issues in their meetings with the parties. As mentioned already, the NCPs are not competent to investigate compliance with national, EU and other international obligations of either a private or legal entity or the state. The role of the NCPs in this instance was therefore to create a platform for dialogue on issues, which may raise underlying questions of legal interpretation or compliance; the scope of the OECD Guidelines and competence of the NCP would however limit the ability of the NCPs to comment on such issues if the dialogue failed to lead to agreement.

SECTION 5—THE POSITIONS OF THE PARTIES

Following their decision that the notification merited further consideration, the Irish and the Dutch NCP engaged in consultations with the Notifiers and with representatives of Shell Ireland acting on behalf of the Consortium, in order to assess the options for a mediatory attempt. In this light, on 21 April 2009, the Irish and Dutch NCPs met separately in Dublin with representatives of the Notifiers and with Shell Ireland, respectively.

Relocation of the Onshore Processing Facility

In the preparatory meetings for mediation the NCPs found that parties disagreed strongly on the question of the location of the onshore processing facility. As in the prior mediatory attempt by Mr. Peter Cassells in 2005, neither of the parties was willing to abandon its position.

Notifiers continued to strongly disagree with the current location of the onshore processing facility and the pipeline in Ballinaboy. They insisted "that the local community had repeatedly demonstrated its willingness to compromise on its original demand that the processing facility should be established at sea, proposing instead that it should be located in a more remote onshore area, such as Glinsk."

For their part, the Consortium rejected any proposal to relocate the facility given the state of completion of the construction. They stated that "the current location was chosen after careful consideration of several options and that it thus far received all necessary government authorisation and licences."

The Consortium maintained their position that they would not move the project to another location, and stressed that they had already agreed to revise the pipeline route on the basis of the recommendations made by former mediator Mr. Peter Cassells. The modified pipeline route was now to be located at a minimum distance of 140 metres from the houses in the Rossport area, instead of the originally planned 70 metres. The Consortium stated that "they had submitted their revised application for the onshore pipeline route, which had been selected following a 14-month selection process involving 11 months of public consultation. This application was further revised, seeking a wider route corridor as well as realignments of the preferred route, and resubmitted in February 2009."

Also following the recommendations by Mr. Peter Cassells and Advantica, with regard to the pressure of the pipeline itself, the Consortium stated that "a third safety valve would be built in the pipeline which regulates the pressure within the pipes, to address the health and safety concerns of the local community."

Meaningful Dialogue with the Public

On this issue parties were equally divided and unable to bridge their differences. The Notifiers held that "the Consortium never held a meaningful dialogue with the local community in Rossport, as meetings were not sufficiently publicised, took place in inconvenient locations, and were not sufficiently informative. This was particularly the case in the initial uptake of the planning of the development of the Corrib Gas Field."

For their part, the Consortium stated that "these meetings were organized according the regulations of the Government and had been announced in inter alia local newspapers, and that everyone was given the opportunity to vent[] concerns orally and/or in writing." The Consortium also acknowledged that the way in which Shell Ireland presented the project during consultations with the local community in the early stages of its involvement in the project did give the impression that there was little room for modifications to adjust to local concerns, which most likely contributed to a sense of mistrust by parts of the community. The Consortium acknowledged that if these early stages could have been redone, it would have acted differently.

Findings of the NCPs: No Apparent Options for Mediation

The issue of the location of the gas processing plant was the main demand of the Notifiers in this NCP procedure. The NCPs regrettably concluded from their discussions with parties and from studying the documentation in relation to the case that the parties seemed to be irreconcilable in relation to the location of the gas processing plant. Both sides had adopted very fixed positions regarding the relocation of the onshore facility and accordingly the NCPs concluded that a mediatory attempt on the basis of this main demand would not yield any results.

In light of the apparent impasse in relation to both issues, the NCPs wrote to the Notifiers on 24 September 2009, setting out their findings and asking whether the Notifiers saw any merit in continued resort to the good offices of both the Irish and Dutch NCPs, taking account of the limited possibilities under the OECD Guidelines and the fact that the Irish authorities have stated that the Corrib developers obtained all of the necessary statutory permissions. The Notifiers responded on 9 January 2010, regretting that the mediation efforts of the NCPs had not been successful and requesting the NCPs issue a final statement in which their notification would be reviewed in the light of the OECD Guidelines.

SECTION 6—NCPS' CONCLUSIONS

Conclusion with Regard to Relocation

As no options for the resolution of the dispute appeared available, the NCPs are now required to issue a statement. It should be noted that it is beyond the competence of the NCPs to make statements on the validity of the location or the way it was chosen, which are legal issues, given the voluntary nature of the OECD Guidelines, as mentioned in section 4. As noted in Section 3, the Irish High Court has recently ruled that members of the local community can challenge the administrative authorisation for the development and location of the pipelines by the Irish authorities.

The NCPs noted that according to the Consortium the modified pipeline proposed by the Consortium will be located at a distance from the houses in the Rossport area that goes beyond the standards and practice in other operations in Europe, including the Netherlands.

The NCPs also noted that the Notifiers felt they had already compromised by agreeing to an onshore processing facility rather than an offshore facility, but they strongly disagreed with the location currently opted for, i.e. Rossport and Ballinaboy. The NCPs therefore regret that it appeared impossible to explore with the parties involved conditions on the basis of mutual interests that could lead to the resolution of the dispute on the location of the processing plant.

Conclusion with Regard to Meaningful Dialogue with Local Communities

The NCPs investigated whether the Consortium engaged in a meaningful dialogue with the public in the development of the Corrib Gas project, as recommended in Chapter V, paragraph 2, of the OECD Guidelines. The Department of Communications, Energy and Natural Resources provided the NCPs with useful information in this regard.

The availability of information about the activities of enterprises and associated environmental impacts is an important vehicle for building confidence with the public. This vehicle is most effective when information is provided in a transparent manner and when it encourages active consultation with stakeholders such as local communities and with the public-at-large so as to promote a climate of long-term trust and understanding on environmental issues of mutual interest. Furthermore, enterprises should endeavour to exceed the basic requirements with regard to the disclosure of environmental information.

In the case of the Corrib Gas project, the Irish Government authorities as well as Shell itself organised several meetings in the locality while the Consortium set up a local agency where people could go with questions or concerns relating to the Corrib Gas project. Recently, the independent planning authority, An Bórd Pleanála, has requested further adjustment of the Consortium's application for consent for the revised onshore pipeline route on the basis of local concerns over health and safety aspects.

As Shell Ireland itself acknowledged, communication with local stakeholders in the early stages of the project was not sufficient, which has led to a situation of mistrust amongst some members of the local community. However, the

Consortium has voluntarily followed up on all recommendations made by former mediator Mr. Peter Cassells and engineering consultancy firm Advantica Ltd. while it was already granted permission to lay the onshore pipeline at a closer distance than is currently planned. Therefore, it could be stated that in the early stages, dialogue with local stakeholders was not in accordance with the spirit of the OECD Guidelines, but since 2005, the Consortium has improved this and has shown willingness to address health and safety concerns, of which the revised route for the onshore part of the pipeline seems the clearest proof.

SECTION 7—FINAL REMARKS AND RECOMMENDATIONS

In the course of this notification procedure the NCPs came across some issues, which they would like to address in general.

1. The contentious issues were not only subject to legal and administrative procedures, they were also subject to earlier unsuccessful mediation attempts. It seemed that the parties had fixed their positions based on desired outcomes, rather than focussing on exploring other possibilities for resolution of the issues. The NCPs take the view that in such circumstances 'good offices' or mediation may not be suitable fashions of dispute resolution.

2. On the basis of EU and their national legislation, the governments of the EU Member States have an obligation to put in place legislation to ensure adequate consultation. The issue as to whether an EU government has adequately implemented and applied national and EU legislation is a legal one and can be addressed through [the] judicial system, including the European Court of Justice. Nonetheless, enterprises have a responsibility to respect the rights of those (groups of) people on whom their activities have an impact. In order to become aware of potential negative impacts and to appropriately and adequately address such impacts, companies are expected to exercise due diligence in the broad sense of the concept, as set out by UN Special Representative for Business and Human Rights, Professor John Ruggie. Consultation with stakeholders can be part of due diligence, even more so in those situations where government organized consultations are unusual in the development of new projects.

When an enterprise in the EU, e.g. in its exercise of due diligence, is faced with concerns of local stakeholders over their situation and rights, the enterprise has the responsibility to consider, where appropriate, going beyond what is legally required when it comes to holding consultations with the local community. This is precisely what is recommended in chapter V of the OECD Guidelines with regard to health and safety aspects of an enterprise's activities.

Dublin, 30 July 2010.

Dympna Hayes
Irish National Contact Point

Mr F.W.R. Evers
Dutch National Contact Point

VI. Consumer Interests

The notion that government intervention is necessary to correct disparities between the consumer and the supplier was endorsed by President John F. Kennedy in his March 15, 1962, *Special Message to the Congress of the United States on Protecting the Consumer Interest,* where he said:

> Consumers by definition, include us all. They are the largest economic group in the economy, affecting and affected by almost every public and private economic decision. Two-thirds of all spending in the economy is by consumers. But they are the only important group in the economy who is not effectively organized whose views are often not heard.
>
> We cannot afford waste in consumption any more than we can afford inefficiency in business or Government. If consumers are offered inferior products, if prices are exorbitant, if drugs are unsafe or worthless, if the consumer is unable to choose on an informed basis, then his dollar is wasted, his health and safety may be threatened, and the national interest suffers.[75]

> Consumer protection addresses disparities found in the consumer-supplier relationship, which include:
> - Bargaining power;
> - Knowledge; and
> - Resources
>
> —*UNCTD Manual on Consumer Protection*[74]

President Kennedy called for legislation that protected the rights of consumers to safe products, choice, accurate information and redress when those rights are violated. Although many countries, including the United States, have robust legal frameworks to protect consumer rights, this is often not the case with emerging economies, necessitating international frameworks to set minimum standards of conduct for multinational enterprises operating in such jurisdictions.

The U.N., the World Trade Organization ("WTO") and the Group of 20 ("G20") have all adopted directives that seek to protect consumers. Those directives are substantially similar to the OECD Guideline on consumer interests, which addresses four broad categories of concerns.

A. Health and Safety

The Guideline requires that enterprises ensure their products "meet all agreed or legally required standards for consumer health and safety."[76] This means minimizing risks to consumers through the proper "design, manufacture, distribution, information provision, support services and . . . recall procedures."[77]

---

74. U.N. Conf. on Trade & Dev., Manual on Consumer Protection, at 2, U.N. Doc. UNCTAD/WEB/DITC/CLP/2016/1 (2016) [hereinafter UNCTAD Manual on Consumer Protection].

75. President John F. Kennedy, Special Message to the Congress on Protecting the Consumer Interest (Mar. 15, 1962), http://www.presidency.ucsb.edu/ws/?pid=9108.

76. *OECD Guidelines, supra* note 2, at 51.

77. Int'l Org. for Standardization [ISO], *ISO 26000 Guidance on Social Responsibility*, at 51 (Nov. 1, 2010) [hereinafter *ISO 26000*].

Assessing risks to consumers is an important component of this process, as is delivery of safety information and instructions on "the proper use of products."[78]

B. Consumer Awareness and Education

The key objective of consumer education is to allow consumers to evaluate products, make comparisons, and be aware of the impact of their choices on sustainable development.[79] "Education and awareness initiatives enable consumers to be well informed, conscious of their rights and responsibilities, more likely to assume an active role [and] . . . make knowledgeable purchasing decisions and consume responsibly."[80]

There is a distinction between consumer education and information.[81] While consumer education focuses on enhancing consumers' ability to make choices, consumer information "refers to the [delivery] of data relating to particular products."[82] "Consumer information is thus 'situation bound' whilst consumer education is not."[83]

The Distinction Between Consumer Education and Information

Consumer Information: Car A gets 25 MPG, Car B gets 8 MPG

Consumer Education: Vehicles with low fuel efficiency are expensive to maintain and contribute to global warming

Both product-specific information and contextual consumer education are necessary for consumers to make informed purchasing decisions.

The importance of consumer education was highlighted following the 2008 financial crisis, when it became apparent that consumers lacked a proper understanding of the financial products they were purchasing. As the OECD noted:

> Innovations and increasing complexity in the credit markets are transferring additional financial risks to individuals, who have difficulty in evaluating credit options . . . . Moreover, surveys in the OECD and other countries continue to show that consumers have low levels of financial literacy and often overestimate their skills, knowledge and awareness.[84]

In light of these concerns, the OECD Committee on Financial Markets and the Insurance and Private Pensions Committee have published *Good Practices on Financial Education and Awareness Relating to Credit*.[85]

---

78. *See id.* at 56.
79. *See id.*
80. *Id.* at 59.
81. UNCTAD MANUAL ON CONSUMER PROTECTION, *supra* note 74, at 79.
82. *Id.*
83. *Id.*
84. Org. for Econ. Cooperation and Dev. [OECD], *Financial Literacy and Consumer Protection: Overlooked Aspects of the Crisis* (June 2009), at 3.
85. *Id.*

C. Dispute Resolution

On July 12, 2007, the OECD adopted a set of recommendations aimed at providing "access to fair, easy-to-use, timely and effective dispute resolution and redress without unnecessary cost or burden."[86] These recommendations call for domestic frameworks that provide different mechanisms for consumer dispute resolution depending on the nature of the complaint.

With respect to consumers acting individually, the recommendations address such issues as accessibility, the relative cost of dispute resolution, information on procedures, and the needs of disadvantaged or vulnerable consumers.[87]

In cases involving collective action by consumers, including class actions, the recommendations address procedures for opting in or out and ensuring that interested consumers receive timely information regarding the pendency of the action and the mechanisms by which such actions may be initiated. Finally, member countries are encouraged to empower enforcement authorities "to take action and obtain or facilitate redress for consumers."[88]

D. Consumer Data Protection and Privacy

The Guideline limits the kind of information collected from consumers and its use. The commentary to the guideline refers to the OECD *Guidelines Governing the Protection of Privacy and Transborder Flows of Personal Data*, which were revised in 2013 and retitled The OECD *Privacy Framework*.[89] The Privacy Framework explains:

> Over the last three decades, personal data have come to play an increasingly important role in our economies, societies and everyday lives. Innovations, particularly in information and communication technologies, have impacted business operation, government administration, and the personal activities of individuals. New technologies and responsible data uses are yielding great societal and economic benefits. The volume of personal data being collected, used and stored is vast and continues to grow. Modern communications networks support global accessibility and continuous, multipoint data flows. The potential uses of personal data have increased tremendously as a result of the wide range of analytics that can provide comprehensive insights into individuals' movements, interests, and activities.
>
> At the same time, the abundance and persistence of personal data have elevated the risks to individuals' privacy. Personal data is increasingly used in ways not anticipated at the time of collection. Almost every human activity leaves behind some form of digital data trail, rendering it increasingly easy to monitor individuals' behaviour. Personal data security breaches are common. These

---

86. Org. for Econ. Cooperation and Dev. [OECD], *OECD Recommendation on Consumer Dispute Resolution and Redress* (July 12, 2007), at 9.
87. *Id.* at 9–10.
88. *Id.* at 11.
89. Org. for Econ. Cooperation and Dev. [OECD], *The OECD Privacy Framework* (2013).

increased risks signal the need for more effective safeguards in order to protect privacy.[90]

The Privacy Framework articulates the following principles:

- *Collection Limitation Principle*: states that collection of personal data should be limited.
- *Data Quality Principle*: requires that collected data be relevant, accurate and current.
- *Purpose Specification Principle*: mandates that data collectors specify at the time of collection the purpose for which data is collected.
- *Use Limitation Principle:* limits the use of data to the purposes disclosed at the time of collection.
- *Security Safeguards Principle:* mandates that data be safeguarded by reasonable security measures.
- *Openness Principle*: requires transparency regarding developments, practices and policies related to personal data.
- *Individual Participation Principle:* gives individuals the right to obtain data collected about them within a reasonable time and in a reasonable manner.
- *Accountability Principle:* holds a data controller accountable for observing these principles.[91]

OECD Consumer Interests[92]

When dealing with consumers, enterprises should act in accordance with fair business, marketing and advertising practices and should take all reasonable steps to ensure the quality and reliability of the goods and services that they provide. In particular, they should:

1. Ensure that the goods and services they provide meet all agreed or legally required standards for consumer health and safety, including those pertaining to health warnings and safety information.

2. Provide accurate, verifiable and clear information that is sufficient to enable consumers to make informed decisions, including information on the prices and, where appropriate, content, safe use, environmental attributes, maintenance, storage and disposal of goods and services. Where feasible this information should be provided in a manner that facilitates consumers' ability to compare products.

3. Provide consumers with access to fair, easy to use, timely and effective non-judicial dispute resolution and redress mechanisms, without unnecessary cost or burden.

---

90. *Id.* at 19–20.
91. *See id.* at 14–15.
92. *OECD Guidelines, supra* note 2, at 51–54.

4. Not make representations or omissions, nor engage in any other practices, that are deceptive, misleading, fraudulent, or unfair.

5. Support efforts to promote consumer education in areas that relate to their business activities, with the aim of, inter alia, improving the ability of consumers to: (i) make informed decisions involving complex goods, services and markets, (ii) better understand the economic, environmental and social impact of their decisions and iii) support sustainable consumption.

6. Respect consumer privacy and take reasonable measures to ensure the security of personal data that they collect, store, process or disseminate.

7. Co-operate fully with public authorities to prevent and combat deceptive marketing practices (including misleading advertising and commercial fraud) and to diminish or prevent serious threats to public health and safety or to the environment deriving from the consumption, use or disposal of their goods and services.

8. Take into consideration, in applying the above principles, i) the needs of vulnerable and disadvantaged consumers and ii) the specific challenges that e-commerce may pose for consumers.

COMMENTARY ON CONSUMER INTERESTS

81. The chapter on consumer interests of the OECD *Guidelines* for Multinational Enterprises draws on the work of the OECD Committee on Consumer Policy and the Committee on Financial Markets, as well as the work of other international organisations, including the International Chamber of Commerce, the International Organization for Standardization and the United Nations (*i.e.,* the *UN Guidelines on Consumer Policy*, as expanded in 1999).

82. The chapter recognises that consumer satisfaction and related interests constitute a fundamental basis for the successful operation of enterprises. It also recognises that consumer markets for goods and services have undergone major transformation over time. Regulatory reform, more open global markets, the development of new technologies and the growth in consumer services have been key agents of change, providing consumers with greater choice and the other benefits which derive from more open competition. At the same time, the pace of change and increased complexity of many markets have generally made it more difficult for consumers to compare and assess goods and services. Moreover, consumer demographics have also changed over time. Children are becoming increasingly significant forces in the market, as are the growing number of older adults. While consumers are better educated overall, many still lack the arithmetic and literacy skills that are required in today's more complex, information-intensive marketplace. Further, many consumers are increasingly interested in knowing the position and activities of enterprises on a broad range of economic, social and environmental issues, and in taking these into account when choosing goods and services.

83. The chapeau calls on enterprises to apply fair business, marketing and advertising practices and to ensure the quality and reliability of the products that they provide. These principles, it is noted, apply to both goods and services.

84. Paragraph 1 underscores the importance for enterprises to adhere to required health and safety standards and the importance for them to provide consumers with adequate health and safety information on their products.

85. Paragraph 2 concerns information disclosure. It calls for enterprises to provide information that is sufficient for consumers to make informed decisions. This would include information on the financial risks associated with products, where relevant. Furthermore, in some instances enterprises are legally required to provide information in a manner that enables consumers to make direct comparisons of goods and services (for example, unit pricing). In the absence of direct legislation, enterprises are encouraged to present information, when dealing with consumers, in a way that facilitates comparisons of goods and services and enables consumers to easily determine what the total cost of a product will be. It should be noted that what is considered to be "sufficient" can change over time and enterprises should be responsive to these changes. Any product and environmental claims that enterprises make should be based on adequate evidence and, as applicable, proper tests. Given consumers' growing interest in environmental issues and sustainable consumption, information should be provided, as appropriate, on the environmental attributes of products. This could include information on the energy efficiency and the degree of recyclability of products and, in the case of food products, information on agricultural practices.

86. Business conduct is increasingly considered by consumers when making their purchasing decisions. Enterprises are therefore encouraged to make information available on initiatives they have taken to integrate social and environmental concerns into their business operations and to otherwise support sustainable consumption. Chapter III of the *Guidelines* on Disclosure is relevant in this regard. [In that chapter, e]nterprises are . . . encouraged to communicate value statements or statements of business conduct to the public, including information on the social, ethical and environmental policies of the enterprise and other codes of conduct to which the company subscribes. Enterprises are encouraged to make this information available in plain language and in a format that is appealing to consumers. Growth in the number of enterprises reporting in these areas and targeting information to consumers would be welcome.

87. Paragraph 3 reflects language that is used in the 2007 Council *Recommendation on Consumer Dispute Resolution and Redress*. The Recommendation establishes a framework for developing effective approaches to address consumer complaints, including a series of actions that industry can take in this respect. It is noted that the mechanisms that many enterprises have established to resolve consumer disputes have helped increase consumer confidence and consumer satisfaction. These mechanisms can provide more practicable solutions to complaints than legal actions, which can be expensive, difficult and time consuming for all the parties involved. For these non-judicial mechanisms to be effective, however, consumers need to be made aware of their existence and would benefit from guidance on how to file complaints, especially when claims involve cross-border or multi-dimensional transactions.

88. Paragraph 4 concerns deceptive, misleading, fraudulent and other unfair commercial practices. Such practices can distort markets at the expense of both consumers and responsible enterprises, and should be avoided.

89. Paragraph 5 concerns consumer education, which has taken on greater importance with the growing complexity of many markets and products. Governments, consumer organisations and many enterprises have recognised that this is a shared responsibility and that they can play important roles in this regard. The difficulties that consumers have experienced in evaluating complex products in financial and other areas have underscored the importance for stakeholders to work together to promote education aimed at improving consumer decision-making.

90. Paragraph 6 concerns personal data. The increasing collection and use of personal data by enterprises, fuelled in part by the Internet and technological advances, has highlighted the importance of protecting personal data against consumer privacy violations, including security breaches.

91. Paragraph 7 underscores the importance of enterprises to work with public authorities to help prevent and combat deceptive marketing practices more effectively. Co-operation is also called for to diminish or prevent threats to public health and safety and to the environment. This includes threats associated with the disposal of goods, as well as their consumption and use. This reflects recognition of the importance of considering the entire life-cycle of products.

92. Paragraph 8 calls on enterprises to take the situations of vulnerable and disadvantaged consumers into account when they market goods and services. Disadvantaged or vulnerable consumers refers to particular consumers or categories of consumers, who because of personal characteristics or circumstances (like age, mental or physical capacity, education, income, language or remote location) may meet particular difficulties in operating in today's information-intensive, globalised markets. The paragraph also highlights the growing importance of mobile and other forms of e-commerce in global markets. The benefits that such commerce provides are significant and growing. Governments have spent considerable time examining ways to ensure that consumers are afforded transparent and effective protection that is not less in the case of e-commerce than the level of protection afforded in more traditional forms of commerce.

Hypothetical: Defective Handlebars

Velo S.p.A. ("Velo") is an Italian corporation that manufactures and sells bicycles. Velo's most economical bicycle, called the Velino, is popular in China, where Velo sells more than 100,000 units annually. In 2016, Velo received reports of fifty accidents involving the Velino, of which forty-eight occurred in China.

Velo conducted tests after the accident reports, which revealed a defect in the Velino's handlebars, rendering them susceptible to breaking when used by individuals weighing more than 200 pounds. Velo promptly fixed the defect by changing the materials used in the handlebars.

Although Chinese consumers have a right to institute legal action for damages when they are harmed by defective products, such actions commonly take more than ten years and rarely lead to adequate compensation for claimants. In all likelihood, few if any impacted Velino purchasers in China will bring legal action against Velo.

What, if anything, should Velo do in connection with the defective Velinos sold in China?

Statement by the UK National Contact Point on National Grid Transco[93]

INTRODUCTION

1. An African non-governmental organisation, Citizens for a Better Environment (CBE), lodged a complaint under the OECD Guidelines for Multinational Enterprises (the Guidelines) against National Grid Transco in July 2003 in relation to the privatisation of Copperbelt Energy Corporation (CEC), formerly Copperbelt Power Company of Zambia Consolidated Copper Mines, which was acquired by Cinergy, a Zambian local management team and National Grid Transco.

SUMMARY DETAILS OF THE COMPLAINT

2. During the negotiations for acquisition of CEC, National Grid Transco solicited (and, at vesting, obtained) concessions that tend to (a) disadvantage consumer interests on tariffs, (b) inhibit competition, (c) unduly stifle the taxation base and sustainable revenue management and (d) inhibit sound employment and industrial relations.

3. At vesting, National Grid Transco partnered with a Zambian local management team[,] some of whose members [had been a part of] the Zambian government negotiating or technical-advisory team during the privatisation negotiations. These people did not declare their interest during the negotiations.

4. National Grid Transco has failed to take due account of the need to protect the environment, public health and safety.

CO-OPERATION WITH NATIONAL GRID TRANSCO

5. The complaint was lodged by CBE in July 2003. Initially, there was a delay while CBE supplied, at the request of the UK National Contact Point (NCP), the

93. United Kingdom National Contact Point for the OECD Guidelines for Multinational Enterprises, *Statement by the UK National Contact Point on National Grid Transco* (Jul. 5, 2005).

specifics of its claims and supporting documentary evidence. This was provided by CBE in October 2003.

6. A copy of the complaint was provided to National Grid Transco on 21 July 2003 and the additional information by 14 October 2003.

7. National Grid Transco provided the NCP with a detailed response to the complaint on 7 November 2003. This was sent to CBE on 17 November 2003. The NCP invited CBE to indicate, having reviewed the documentation, whether the response satisfied its concerns. If not, in line with the provisions of the Guidelines, the NCP would arrange a dialogue between the parties.

CO-OPERATION WITH CBE

8. CBE noted that the Zambian government had been mentioned on several occasions in National Grid Transco's response. Before requesting the NCP to arrange a dialogue, it indicated that it would prefer to seek clarifications from the Zambian government on a number of issues. Additionally, it wished to consult some other stakeholders. CBE would request a dialogue, if appropriate, in the light of these exchanges.

9. Over the succeeding months, CBE was contacted on a regular basis by the NCP and gave several undertakings to keep the NCP informed on progress. CBE did not adhere to these undertakings, indicating that it was having difficulty in getting a response from the Zambian government.

10. On 7 May 2004, the NCP wrote to CBE in the following terms:

> You last contacted me on 23 February suggesting that it would not be long before you would be in a position to respond to National Grid Transco and stating you would supply monthly updates. Given that I sent you the company's response to your allegations on 17 November 2003 (over five months ago), in fairness to the other party, I must ask you if you intend to progress this case and, if so, when I might expect confirmation from you over any remaining areas of disagreement.

11. CBE replied on 24 June 2004, again detailing difficulties in obtaining a response form the Zambian government. This was communicated by the NCP to National Grid Transco.

12. Having had no further communication, despite CBE's undertaking, the NCP wrote again on 19 April 2005 in the following terms:

> Given that you have not contacted me since June last year, would I be correct in concluding that you will not be pursuing this case?

13. The NCP wrote to CBE again on 21 April 2005 clarifying that, since National Grid Transco's response was provided on 17 November 2003 (17 months previously) and the last contact with CBE was on 24 June 2004 (10 months previously), CBE should give notice of its intent to pursue the case by 28 April 2005, in the absence of which the NCP would make a Statement bringing the matter to a close. No response from CBE has been received by the NCP.

NCP COMMENT

In the circumstances, on the basis of the lack of information provided by CBE and the passage of time since a detailed response was provided by National Grid Transco, the NCP concludes that the complaint is closed for want of prosecution.

05 July 2005
UK NCP for the OECD Guidelines for Multinational Enterprises

VII. Science and Technology

In a knowledge-based and globalized economy, access to science and technology is indispensable to sustainable economic development and growth because it enhances productivity and creates jobs.[94]

> Economic literature identifies technology transfers as perhaps the most important channel through which foreign corporate presence may produce positive externalities in the host developing economy. MNEs . . . generally possess a higher level of technology than is available in developing countries, so they have the potential to generate considerable technological spillovers.[95]

Multinational enterprises contribute to the formation of human capital—the main vehicle for technology transfers—through training and on-the-job learning.[96] Although workers employed by subsidiaries of multinational enterprises are the primary beneficiaries, know-how and technology spill over into society at large as those individuals move to other firms or become entrepreneurs.[97]

To a lesser extent, technology transfers occur when multinational enterprises acquire local firms, particularly where the target is a privatized government-owned entity.[98] Experience in Eastern and Central Europe indicates that such acquisitions significantly increase the efficiency and productivity of targeted privatized firms.[99]

OECD Science and Technology[100]

Enterprises should:

1. Endeavour to ensure that their activities are compatible with the science and technology (S&T) policies and plans of the countries in which they operate

---

94. *OECD Guidelines, supra* note 2, at 55–56.
95. Org. for Econ. Cooperation and Dev. [OECD], *Foreign Direct Investment for Development: Maximising Benefits, Minimising Costs* (2002), at 12.
96. *Id.* at 14.
97. *See id.*
98. *See id.* at 17.
99. *See id.* at 18.
100. *OECD Guidelines, supra* note 2, at 55–56.

and as appropriate contribute to the development of local and national innovative capacity.

2. Adopt, where practicable in the course of their business activities, practices that permit the transfer and rapid diffusion of technologies and know-how, with due regard to the protection of intellectual property rights.

3. When appropriate, perform science and technology development work in host countries to address local market needs, as well as employ host country personnel in an S&T capacity and encourage their training, taking into account commercial needs.

4. When granting licenses for the use of intellectual property rights or when otherwise transferring technology, do so on reasonable terms and conditions and in a manner that contributes to the long term sustainable development prospects of the host country.

5. Where relevant to commercial objectives, develop ties with local universities and public research institutions, and participate in co-operative research projects with local industry or industry associations.

COMMENTARY ON SCIENCE AND TECHNOLOGY

93. In a knowledge-based and globalised economy where national borders matter less, even for small or domestically oriented enterprises, the ability to access and utilise technology and know-how is essential for improving enterprise performance. Such access is also important for the realisation of the economy-wide effects of technological progress, including productivity growth and job creation, within the context of sustainable development. Multinational enterprises are the main conduit of technology transfer across borders. They contribute to the national innovative capacity of their host countries by generating, diffusing, and even enabling the use of new technologies by domestic enterprises and institutions. The R&D activities of MNEs, when well connected to the national innovation system, can help enhance the economic and social progress in their host countries. In turn, the development of a dynamic innovation system in the host country expands commercial opportunities for MNEs.

94. The chapter thus aims to promote, within the limits of economic feasibility, competitiveness concerns and other considerations, the diffusion by multinational enterprises of the fruits of research and development activities among the countries where they operate, contributing thereby to the innovative capacities of host countries. In this regard, fostering technology diffusion can include the commercialisation of products that imbed new technologies, licensing of process innovations, hiring and training of S&T personnel and development of R&D co-operative ventures. When selling or licensing technologies, not only should the terms and conditions negotiated be reasonable, but MNEs may want to consider the long-term developmental, environmental and other impacts of technologies for the home and host country. In their activities, multinational enterprises can establish and improve the innovative capacity of their international subsidiaries and subcontractors. In addition, MNEs can call attention to the importance of local scientific and technological infrastructure, both physical and institutional.

In this regard, MNEs can usefully contribute to the formulation by host country governments of policy frameworks conducive to the development of dynamic innovation systems.

Communiqué of the Argentine National Contact Point (ANCP) for the OECD Guidelines for Multinational Enterprises[101]

Buenos Aires, Argentina
12 December 2016

The functions of the Argentine National Contact Point (ANCP) are to promote the Guidelines for Multinational Enterprises of the Organization for Economic Cooperation and Development (OECD) and to contribute to the resolution of issues related to their implementation. The *OECD Guidelines for Multinational Enterprises* are recommendations issued by governments to multinational companies that operate in adhering countries or with headquarters in said countries. The *Guidelines* set forth voluntary principles and rules for responsible corporate conduct that is compatible with applicable legislation and internationally recognized rules.

The ANCP is the authority in charge of receiving claims involving non-compliance with the OECD Guidelines for Multinational Enterprises. The ANCP acts in compliance with the Procedure Manual and within the framework of the above-mentioned Guidelines.

SPECIFIC INSTANCE: RICARDO MOLINA / LAFARGE HOLCIM LTD.

Claimant

In March 2016, Ricardo José Manuel Molina requested the good offices of the ANCP to consider possible non-compliance with the *Guidelines* by company Lafarge Holcim Ltd., particularly in relation to the preface, the concepts and principles, and the chapters on the environment, science and technology.

Mr. Molina stated that he is an electromechanical engineer and that he [had] worked for almost 19 years in the company until he was laid off on 16 October 2014 due to restructuring. At the time he was Head of Production at the Capdeville plant in the province of Mendoza (Argentina).

He explained that, during the last period of his employment, he developed a machine that helps to improve the combustion of a considerable part of hazardous waste, providing thermal energy and partially replacing noble fuels, with the consequent reduction in the cost of the process.

---

101. Argentine National Contact Point for the OECD Guidelines for Multinational Enterprises, *Communique of the Argentine National Contact Point for the OECD Guidelines for Multinational Enterprises* (Dec. 12, 2016).

As explained by Mr. Molina, the machine he invented was patented by Holcim Technology Ltd (currently Lafarge Holcim Ltd.) while he was employed at the company, recognizing him as the inventor in all the countries that are signatories to the European Patent Convention, as well as in Russia, Brazil, Indonesia, Mexico, the Philippines, and Azerbaijan, among others, but not in Argentina, where the patent process is in progress.

The claimant submitted his claim on the grounds of lack of payment of fair compensation that covers the actual and potential economic benefit of his invention in all the countries where it is already patented and the 20-year period of exclusive use established in section 10 of Law No. 24481 (Argentine Patent Law).

Although the company offered Mr. Molina a certain amount of money as compensation, he considered that such amount only covered the partial benefit obtained with the prototype used in Argentina, while in fact Lafarge Holcim patented the final model with all its improvements (submitted in Switzerland on 21 October 2009). Furthermore, the compensation offered did not cover the benefit obtained in all other plants worldwide (a total of 188) nor the 20-year period of exclusive use.

In view of the above, the claimant requested the ANCP that Lafarge Holcim Ltd.:

- Comply with international treaties and applicable Argentine laws, offering fair economic compensation that covers the actual and potential economic benefits of Ricardo José Manuel Molina's invention in all the countries where it has been patented and the 20-year period of exclusive use.
- Disseminate information on the characteristics and possibilities of use of the equipment at least internally among the plants of the group, highlighting its environmental benefits.
- Commit to formally establishing links with associations of inventors in the countries where it has plants, coordinating activities and enhancing benefits for both parties.

Proceedings

In May 2016, following an analysis of the correspondence between Molina's argument, the documents submitted and the objectives proposed by [the] OECD in the Guidelines, as well as the interest in the case, the ANCP declared the formal admissibility of it, since it considered that, prima facie, the complaint submitted by Molina complied with the formal requirements set forth in the OECD Guidelines for Multinational Enterprises.

In this context, the ANCP offered its good offices to the parties in order to facilitate the dialogue process for them to reach an understanding that is beneficial to all parties involved, maintaining individual contact with them.

Holcim (Argentina) S.A. (the local subsidiary of Lafarge Holcim Ltd.) made a submission to the ANCP through its attorneys requesting the termination of the Specific Instance initiated in May 2016, pursuant to the provisions of Article 14 of the ANCP Procedure Manual.

A representative of Holcim (Argentina) S.A. stated that the parties were summoned to the mandatory mediation process provided for in Argentine Law No. 26589 on 17 February 2016, and the mediation process was initiated on 1 March 2016. In the company's view, this meets the requirements of Article 14 of the ANCP Procedure Manual, which reads as follows: *"The ANCP will declare the instance finished if, during the course of the proceedings, either party and/or a third party resorts to a court in order to obtain a judgment on the same facts that gave rise to the proceedings before the ANCP."*

The representative of Holcim (Argentina) S.A. also stated that "... mediation is a mandatory instance prior to certain court procedures, as well as a requirement for the admission of judicial complaints (see Articles 1 and 2 of Law No. 26589)." It follows that mediation itself should be broadly interpreted as a judicial complaint. This line of reasoning was established by the Argentine Supreme Court of Justice ("ASCJ"), which has decided that *"the beginning of the mandatory mediation process can be broadly understood as a judicial complaint."*

The ANCP clarified the issue relating to Article 14 of the ANCP Procedure Manual by stating that in the case under analysis, the judicial mediation process between the parties began (on 1 March 2016) before the specific instance was initiated (May 2016). Article 14 of the ANCP Procedure Manual only raises the incompatibility of the Specific Instance initiated with the subsequent commencement of judicial proceedings. Therefore, in ANCP's view, the requirements of said article were not met, and so the request for termination of the instance must not be admitted, without thereby prejudging the admissibility of the allegations on the merits made by Mr. Molina in his submission, which led to the initiation of this Specific Instance.

It should be noted that paragraph 26 of the "Commentary on implementation procedures of the OECD Guidelines for Multinational Enterprises," included in the latest edition (2011) of the "OECD Guidelines for Multinational Enterprises," provides as follows: "When assessing the significance for the specific instance procedure of other domestic or international proceedings addressing similar issues in parallel, NCPs should not decide that issues do not merit further consideration solely because parallel proceedings have been conducted, are under way or are available to the parties concerned."

Taking the foregoing into consideration, the ANCP deemed it advisable to request that the company provide information on the acceptance or rejection of the ANCP's good offices to resolve the dispute between the parties and state its position (in the event that it should accept the ANCP's good offices) in relation to the substantive issues raised in Mr. Molina's submission. Additionally, Mr. Molina informed the ANCP that—in the event that Lafarge Holcim Ltd. should accept the ANCP's good offices to resolve the dispute—he would suspend the judicial complaint or any other kind of claim involving the initiation of new instances elsewhere until the dispute was resolved.

On 31 October 2016, the company submitted a new document stating as follows:

- since a judicial instance coexists with these proceedings before the ANCP based on the same facts and involving the same parties, its participation in the Specific Instance as it was initiated affected its right to defence at trial, protected by Article 18 of the Argentine Constitution.
- this is so because participating under these circumstances would require Holcim (Argentina) S.A. to produce technically, legally and economically-complex evidence, positions, arguments and defences which should be discussed in parallel, in greater detail, mandatorily and imperatively in court.

Thus, Holcim Argentina S.A., the local subsidiary of Lafarge Holcim Ltd., stated that it was *"obliged to decline to participate in the specific instance initiated by Mr. Molina, as its right to defence at trial was affected by the existence of a parallel judicial instance initiated by Mr. Molina himself against Holcim to obtain a decision on the same events that led to the instance before the ANCP; and, therefore, requests that the ANCP include these considerations in its final report terminating the proceedings and in any subsequent communiqué relating to these proceedings."*

Following the company's submission, the ANCP proposed that the parties conduct an exercise to reach a solution, based on the following parameters:

- the parties were to discuss a purely transactional solution in relation to the amount of compensation requested by Mr. Molina.
- the parties were not to resubmit any proposals which had already been made before (i.e., in the mediation process that had already ended); instead, they were to explore new means that improved on every other option discussed thus far.

The parties accepted the ANCP's proposal; however, the goal was not achieved, and they failed to reach an agreement.

CONCLUSION

The ANPC has duly considered the arguments of the two parties involved and has acted within the framework of the powers and functions vested upon it by the OECD Guidelines.

In this respect, the ANPC has attempted to bring the parties together in order to foster dialogue between them, with a view to complying with the role assigned to it under the Guidelines—that is, the role to serve as a discussion forum for interested parties; however, no agreement was reached.

Based on the foregoing, the ANCP considers that it can no longer persist in its role of facilitator. Consequently, the ANCP should put an end to the proceedings of this specific instance.

It should be noted that the OECD Guidelines provide for the closing of the procedures of a specific stage when no agreement is reached by the parties or when either party is not willing to take part in the proceedings.

Nevertheless, the ANCP encourages the parties to consider finding a way to generate the conditions required to engage in dialogue and constructively work for the resolution of the issues in which they are involved.

VIII. Competition

Competition enhances market efficiency, improves productivity and innovation, reduces prices, contributes to quality of products and services, and expands consumers' choice. For those reasons, the OECD Guidelines discourage conduct that suppresses competition.

Controlling a large share of a given market is not, by itself, considered anti-competitive behavior unless it is combined with abuse of one's dominant market position. Examples of such abuse include price gouging or charging excessively low prices to create barriers to market entry by rivals.

Anticompetitive behaviors, which also include price fixing, collusive tendering and refusals to deal,[102] can generally be categorized as horizontal or vertical restraints on competition. Horizontal restraints involve collusion among competitors in the same market, such as forming a *cartel*—an arrangement among competitors to act collectively on issues such as pricing and market allocation. Alternatively, vertical restraints refer to anticompetitive practices between suppliers and distributors—for example, an exclusive distribution arrangement in which the supplier agrees not to sell its products to anyone else in the same market.

OECD Competition[103]

Enterprises should:

1. Carry out their activities in a manner consistent with all applicable competition laws and regulations, taking into account the competition laws of all jurisdictions in which the activities may have anti-competitive effects.

2. Refrain from entering into or carrying out anti-competitive agreements among competitors, including agreements to:
   a) fix prices;
   b) make rigged bids (collusive tenders);
   c) establish output restrictions or quotas; or
   d) share or divide markets by allocating customers, suppliers, territories or lines of commerce.

3. Co-operate with investigating competition authorities by, among other things and subject to applicable law and appropriate safeguards, providing responses as promptly and completely as practicable to requests for information, and considering the use of available instruments, such as waivers of confidentiality where appropriate, to promote effective and efficient co-operation among investigating authorities.

---

102. UNCTAD Manual on Consumer Protection, *supra* note 74, at 51.
103. *OECD Guidelines, supra* note 2, at 57–59.

4. Regularly promote employee awareness of the importance of compliance with all applicable competition laws and regulations, and, in particular, train senior management of the enterprise in relation to competition issues.

COMMENTARY ON COMPETITION

95. These recommendations emphasise the importance of competition laws and regulations to the efficient operation of both domestic and international markets and reaffirm the importance of compliance with those laws and regulations by domestic and multinational enterprises. They also seek to ensure that all enterprises are aware of developments concerning the scope, remedies and sanctions of competition laws and the extent of co-operation among competition authorities. The term "competition" law is used to refer to laws, including both "antitrust" and "antimonopoly" laws, that variously prohibit: (a) anti-competitive agreements; (b) the abuse of market power or of dominance; (c) the acquisition of market power or dominance by means other than efficient performance; or (d) the substantial lessening of competition or the significant impeding of effective competition through mergers or acquisitions.

96. In general, competition laws and policies prohibit: (a) hard core cartels; (b) other anti-competitive agreements; (c) anti-competitive conduct that exploits or extends market dominance or market power; and (d) anti-competitive mergers and acquisitions. Under the 1998 Recommendation of the OECD Council Concerning Effective Action Against Hard Core Cartels, C(98)35/FINAL, the anti-competitive agreements referred to in sub (a) constitute hard core cartels, but the Recommendation incorporates differences in member countries' laws, including differences in the laws' exemptions or provisions allowing for an exception or authorisation for activity that might otherwise be prohibited. The recommendations in these *Guidelines* do not suggest that enterprises should forego availing themselves of such legally available exemptions or provisions. The categories sub (b) and (c) are more general because the effects of other kinds of agreements and of unilateral conduct are more ambiguous, and there is less consensus on what should be considered anti-competitive.

97. The goal of competition policy is to contribute to overall welfare and economic growth by promoting market conditions in which the nature, quality, and price of goods and services are determined by competitive market forces. In addition to benefiting consumers and a jurisdiction's economy as a whole, such a competitive environment rewards enterprises that respond efficiently to consumer demand. Enterprises can contribute to this process by providing information and advice when governments are considering laws and policies that might reduce efficiency or otherwise reduce the competitiveness of markets.

98. Enterprises should be aware that competition laws continue to be enacted, and that it is increasingly common for those laws to prohibit anti-competitive activities that occur abroad if they have a harmful impact on domestic consumers. Moreover, cross-border trade and investment makes it more likely that anti-competitive conduct taking place in one jurisdiction will have harmful effects in other jurisdictions. Enterprises should therefore take into account both the law

of the country in which they are operating and the laws of all countries in which the effects of their conduct are likely to be felt.

99. Finally, enterprises should recognise that competition authorities are engaging in more and deeper co-operation in investigating and challenging anti-competitive activity. See generally: Recommendation of the Council Concerning Co-operation between Member Countries on Anticompetitive Practices Affecting International Trade, C(95)130/FINAL; Recommendation of the Council on Merger Review, C(2005)34. When the competition authorities of various jurisdictions are reviewing the same conduct, enterprises' facilitation of co-operation among the authorities promotes consistent and sound decision-making and competitive remedies while also permitting cost savings for governments and enterprises.

Final Statement of the Korean NCP for the OECD Guidelines for Multinational Enterprises, Complaint from Korean Metal Workers' Union et al. against Hydis Technologies Co., Ltd., E Ink Holdings, Inc. and Yuen Foon Yu, Inc.[104]

December 8, 2016

1. INTRODUCTION

The OECD Guidelines for Multinational Enterprises (hereinafter "the Guidelines") are a set of recommendations aimed at minimizing adverse impacts from the activities of multinational enterprises and strengthening their social responsibilities.

To ensure the effectiveness of the Guidelines, the government of [the] Republic of Korea established the Korean National Contact Point (KNCP) in 2001 to promote the Guidelines and deal with issues concerning their implementation in specific instances.

2. SUBSTANCE OF THE SPECIFIC INSTANCE

On July 23, 2015, the Korean Metal Workers' Union et al (hereinafter "the Union" or "Complainants") submitted a complaint to the KNCP against Hydis Technologies Co., Ltd. (hereinafter "Hydis"), E Ink Holdings, Inc. (hereinafter "E Ink"), and Yuen Foon Yu, Inc. (hereinafter "YFY") (collectively referred to as "Respondents"). The complaint specifically argued that Respondents acted inconsistently with the Guidelines.

On October 20, 2015, Complainants presented additional submissions, and Respondents submitted their responses to the KNCP on September 11, 2015, and January 7, 2016.

---

104. Korean National Contact Point for the OECD Guidelines for Multinational Enterprises, *Final Statement of the Korean NCP for the OECD Guidelines for Multinational Enterprises: Complaint from Korean Metal Workers' Union et al against Hydis Technologies Co., Ltd., E Ink Holdings, Inc. and Yuen Foon Yu, Inc.* (Dec. 8, 2016).

Complainants argued as follows:

- Hydis conducted surveillance on the activities of the Union and its members in violation of the Guidelines II(A)(2), IV(1), and IV(2).
- After the acquisition of Hydis, E Ink did not make sincere efforts to create new jobs, and laid off employees, or had them retire in violation of the Guidelines II(A)(4).
- E Ink and YFY provided Hydis' technologies to their affiliated companies at unreasonably low prices, resulting in an increase in profit for E Ink and YFY at the expense of Hydis' profitability and competitiveness in violation of the Guidelines II(A)(5), IX(1), and IX(4).
- Despite the Union's request, Hydis did not provide general information about corporate activities, including management performance and financial status, in a timely manner and made the decision to shut down the factory on short notice in violation of the Guidelines III(1), III(2), V(2)(b), V(2)(c), V(6), and V(8).

Respondents answered as follows:

- Contrary to Complaints' argument, "Daily Activities" is not the company's inspection and surveillance report, but only contains a record of negotiations between management and labor, publicly announced information and news articles. It is highly unlikely that Respondents could conduct surveillance on the Union members' activities considering that Hydis management consists of only 10 members.
- All possible measures were deployed to create employment opportunities: borrowing operating funds from the parent company, attempting a merger & acquisition by means of debt repayment, temporarily shutting down the plant, going through organizational restructuring four times, and introducing a performance management system.
- The act of mutually sharing patent rights is not illegal, and it was the best decision for Hydis' business strategy. The shared technology is not subject to the Act on Prevention of Divulgence and Protection of Industrial Technology.
- Hydis' management provided most of the information requested by the Union, including the company's financial and accounting information as well as the workforce status. They also held 16 meetings with the Job Security Committee before they made the final decision for dismissal in order to minimize its impact.

3. PROCEEDINGS OF THE NCP

The Guidelines state,

"In making an initial assessment of whether the issue merits further examination, the NCP will need to determine whether there is a bona fide issue and is relevant to the implementation of the Guidelines. In this context, the NCP will take into account the following:

- *The identity of the party concerned and its interest in the matter.*
- *Whether the issue is material and substantiated.*
- *Whether there seems to be a link between the enterprise's activities and the issue raised in the specific instance*
- *The relevance of applicable law and procedures, including court rulings*
- *How similar issues have been, or are being treated in other domestic or international proceedings.*
- *Whether the consideration of the specific issue would contribute to the purposes and effectiveness of the Guidelines."*

To consider these factors at the initial assessment, the KNCP held meetings with Hydis on February 3, 2016, and June 23, 2016; with Complainants on February 4, 2016; and with both parties on August 19, 2016.

On August 19, 2016, the KNCP made an initial assessment as stated below and informed both parties on August 31, 2016.

- During the individual meetings that occurred in February 2016, each party requested opportunities to have a meaningful and constructive dialogue. In the initial assessment stage, the KNCP found that this specific instance merited further consideration.
- An initial assessment only determines whether the issues raised merit further examination or whether the KNCP can contribute to the resolution of the issue by offering its good offices. Therefore, the decision for further examination does not necessarily mean that the KNCP considers that Respondents have acted inconsistently with the Guidelines.

The Implementation Procedures of the Guidelines state, *"If the issues raised merit further consideration, the NCP will discuss the issue further with the parties involved and offer its good offices in an effort to contribute informally to the resolution of issues."*

The KNCP organized a Mediation Committee, provided its good offices to the parties in an effort to contribute to the resolution of the issues, and requested the parties' voluntary and active participation in the mediation procedure. The Mediation Committee consisted of three members, one from among the KNCP commissioners and two experts from relevant fields. The chairman of the KNCP appointed Mr. Sang-Young Hong (Director General, Development Cooperation Team of Korea Trade-Investment Promotion Agency) to serve as the chairman of the Mediation Committee. Dr. Prof. Sung-Ryong Kim (Kyungpook National University) and Dr. Yeonjae Bae (Yoon & Yang LLC) were appointed as the other two members of the Mediation Committee.

On September 7, 2016, the Mediation Committee members and both parties participated in a mediation meeting held at the Korean Commercial Arbitration Board (Secretariat of the KNCP). Representing Complainants, three members from a local branch of the Union (Hydis' Union) and one representative from the Union participated in the meeting. Representing Respondents, the CEO and a staff member of Hydis participated in the meeting. At the meeting, Respondents insisted that the mediation procedure should be pursued exclusively between the local branch of the Union and Hydis' management, stating that they would not participate should other parties be involved. In response, Complainants argued that the participation of the Union is justifiable.

On September 19, 2016, Respondents refused to participate in the second meeting because the raised issue is a case between Hydis and the local branch of the Union, adding to the fact that both sides have already met for negotiations more than ten times.

4. CONCLUSION

The grievance mechanism in the Implementation Procedures of the Guidelines is based on the voluntary participation of multinational enterprises and stakeholders. The Implementation Procedures of the Guidelines state, "*As part of making available good offices, and where relevant to the issues at hand, NCPs will offer or facilitate access to consensual and non-adversarial procedures, such as conciliation or mediation, to assist in dealing with the issues at hand. In common with accepted practices on conciliation and mediation procedures, these procedures would be used only upon agreement of the parties concerned and their commitment to participate in good faith during the procedure.*"

In an effort to promote understanding and ensure effective implementation of the Guidelines, the KNCP sought to further move forward with this case. Upon the initiation of the mediation process, however, both parties found out that they had different opinions over the scope of participants. For this reason, Respondents refused to further participate in the mediation process.

Despite continued efforts to convene a mediation meeting, the KNCP found no basis to continue the mediation process as both parties could not narrow their difference with regard to the scope of participants. The case would have set a good example of the Guidelines establishing good practices if the parties had participated in the mediation procedure and shown greater flexibility to reach a consensus.

The KNCP would like to recommend that Respondents keep communication channels open and continue to engage in dialogue concerning the issues raised by Complainants.

Korean National Contact Point
for the OECD Guidelines for Multinational Enterprises

IX. Taxation

The Guideline on taxation requires compliance with both the letter and the spirit of the tax laws in all jurisdictions in which a multinational enterprise operates.[105] It also mandates cooperation with authorities to provide relevant and accurate

---

105. *OECD Guidelines, supra* note 2, at 60–63.

information as required by law.[106] Transactions should not be structured to evade or avoid taxes in a manner contrary to the spirit of the law.[107]

An important issue within the topic of taxation is transfer pricing.[108] Transfer pricing becomes relevant when different divisions and/or subsidiaries of a corporation are located in different tax jurisdictions and subject to different rates of taxation. In those circumstances, a corporation may try to minimize its overall tax liability by accumulating its profits in the lowest tax jurisdiction in which it operates. Transfer pricing rules dictate that sales within the same organization must occur at arm's length—that is, "the transfer price should be the same as if the two companies involved are two independent companies and not part of the same corporate structure."[109]

> Abusive transfer pricing practices are considered to pose major risk to the direct tax base of many countries and developing economies, which are particularly vulnerable because corporate tax tends to account for a larger share of their revenue. There are short-term opportunities for countries to catch up and introduce common anti-abuse provisions tailored to country-specific risks and an ever increasing number of emerging and developing economies are following the example of [OECD] economies, which have introduced legislation specifically aimed at regulating transfer pricing for direct taxation purposes.
>
> *Transfer Pricing and Developing Economies, Handbook*[110]

OECD Taxation[111]

1. It is important that enterprises contribute to the public finances of host countries by making timely payment of their tax liabilities. In particular, enterprises should comply with both the letter and spirit of the tax laws and regulations of the countries in which they operate. Complying with the spirit of the law means discerning and following the intention of the legislature. It does not require an enterprise to make payment in excess of the amount legally required pursuant to such an interpretation. Tax compliance includes such measures as providing to the relevant authorities timely information that is relevant or required by law for purposes of the correct determination of taxes to be assessed in connection with their operations and conforming transfer pricing practices to the arm's length principle.

2. Enterprises should treat tax governance and tax compliance as important elements of their oversight and broader risk management systems. In particular, corporate boards should adopt tax risk management strategies to ensure that

---

106. *See id.*

107. *See id.*

108. *See id.*

109. OECD Watch, *Calling for Corporate Accountability: A Guide to the 2011 OECD Guidelines for Multinational Enterprises,* at 30 (June 2013).

110. Joel Cooper et al., Transfer Pricing and Developing Economies: A Handbook for Policy Makers and Practitioners xix (World Bank, 2016).

111. *OECD Guidelines, supra* note 2, at 60–63.

the financial, regulatory and reputational risks associated with taxation are fully identified and evaluated.

COMMENTARY ON TAXATION

100. Corporate citizenship in the area of taxation implies that enterprises should comply with both the letter and the spirit of the tax laws and regulations in all countries in which they operate, co-operate with authorities and make information that is relevant or required by law available to them. An enterprise complies with the spirit of the tax laws and regulations if it takes reasonable steps to determine the intention of the legislature and interprets those tax rules consistent with that intention in light of the statutory language and relevant, contemporaneous legislative history. Transactions should not be structured in a way that will have tax results that are inconsistent with the underlying economic consequences of the transaction unless there exists specific legislation designed to give that result. In this case, the enterprise should reasonably believe that the transaction is structured in a way that gives a tax result for the enterprise that is not contrary to the intentions of the legislature.

101. Tax compliance also entails co-operation with tax authorities and provision of the information they require to ensure an effective and equitable application of the tax laws. Such co-operation should include responding in a timely and complete manner to requests for information made by a competent authority pursuant to the provisions of a tax treaty or exchange of information agreement. However, this commitment to provide information is not without limitation. In particular, the *Guidelines* make a link between the information that should be provided and its relevance to the enforcement of applicable tax laws. This recognises the need to balance the burden on business in complying with applicable tax laws and the need for tax authorities to have the complete, timely and accurate information to enable them to enforce their tax laws.

102. Enterprises' commitments to co-operation, transparency, and tax compliance should be reflected in risk management systems, structures and policies. In the case of enterprises having a corporate legal form, corporate boards are in a position to oversee tax risk in a number of ways. For example, corporate boards should proactively develop appropriate tax policy principles, as well as establish internal tax control systems so that the actions of management are consistent with the views of the board with regard to tax risk. The board should be informed about all potentially material tax risks and responsibility should be assigned for performing internal tax control functions and reporting to the board. A comprehensive risk management strategy that includes tax will allow the enterprise to not only act as a good corporate citizen but also to effectively manage tax risk, which can serve to avoid major financial, regulatory and reputation risk for an enterprise.

103. A member of a multinational enterprise group in one country may have extensive economic relationships with members of the same multinational enterprise group in other countries. Such relationships may affect the tax liability of each of the parties. Accordingly, tax authorities may need information from

outside their jurisdiction in order to be able to evaluate those relationships and determine the tax liability of the member of the MNE group in their jurisdiction. Again, the information to be provided is limited to that which is relevant to or required by law for the proposed evaluation of those economic relationships for the purpose of determining the correct tax liability of the member of the MNE group. MNEs should co-operate in providing that information.

104. Transfer pricing is a particularly important issue for corporate citizenship and taxation. The dramatic increase in global trade and cross-border direct investment (and the important role played in such trade and investment by multinational enterprises) means that transfer pricing is a significant determinant of the tax liabilities of members of a multinational enterprise group because it materially influences the division of the tax base between countries in which the multinational enterprise operates. The arm's length principle, which is included in both the OECD Model Tax Convention and the UN Model Double Taxation Convention between Developed and Developing Countries, is the internationally accepted standard for adjusting the profits between associated enterprises. Application of the arm's length principle avoids inappropriate shifting of profits or losses and minimises risks of double taxation. Its proper application requires multinational enterprises to co-operate with tax authorities and to furnish all information that is relevant or required by law regarding the selection of the transfer pricing method adopted for the international transactions undertaken by them and their related party. It is recognised that determining whether transfer pricing adequately reflects the arm's length standard (or principle) is often difficult both for multinational enterprises and for tax administrations and that its application is not an exact science.

105. The Committee on Fiscal Affairs of the OECD undertakes ongoing work to develop recommendations for ensuring that transfer pricing reflects the arm's length principle. Its work resulted in the publication in 1995 of the *OECD Transfer Pricing Guidelines for Multinational Enterprises and Tax Administrations* (*OECD Transfer Pricing Guidelines*), which was the subject of the Recommendation of the OECD Council on the Determination of Transfer Pricing between Associated Enterprises (members of an MNE group would normally fall within the definition of Associated Enterprises). The *OECD Transfer Pricing Guidelines* and that Council Recommendation are updated on an ongoing basis to reflect changes in the global economy and experiences of tax administrations and taxpayers dealing with transfer pricing. The arm's length principle as it applies to the attribution of profits of permanent establishments for the purposes of the determination of a host State's taxing rights under a tax treaty was the subject of an OECD Council Recommendation adopted in 2008.

106. The *OECD Transfer Pricing Guidelines* focus on the application of the arm's length principle to evaluate the transfer pricing of associated enterprises. The OECD Transfer Pricing *Guidelines* aim to help tax administrations (of both OECD member countries and non-member countries) and multinational enterprises by indicating mutually satisfactory solutions to transfer pricing cases, thereby minimising conflict among tax administrations and between tax administrations and

multinational enterprises and avoiding costly litigation. Multinational enterprises are encouraged to follow the guidance in the *OECD Transfer Pricing Guidelines*, as amended and supplemented, in order to ensure that their transfer prices reflect the arm's length principle.

Hypothetical: Transfer Pricing

Greycliff, Inc. ("Greycliff") is a U.S. corporation engaged in the manufacture and sale of medical devices, and has three subsidiaries in the Democratic Republic of Congo ("DRC"), Switzerland and Austria. Greycliff is subject to the following corporate income tax rates in the different jurisdictions in which it operates: 26 percent in the United States, 32 percent in the DRC, 8 percent in Switzerland, and 30 percent in Austria. Assume that Greycliff manufactures a stent for $5,000 and sells it to its Swiss subsidiary for $5,500; the Swiss subsidiary in turn sells it to the DRC and Austrian subsidiaries for $10,000. The DRC and Austrian subsidiaries sell the stents for $10,200 to retailers. Is Greycliff's pricing structure ethical?

TEST YOUR KNOWLEDGE
Formulating a Responsible Business Strategy for an Enterprise Operating in a Frontier Market

Panjshir Company ("Panjshir") is a corporation engaged in the production and sale of seeds, and is registered under the laws of Afghanistan. It was established in the 1960s by Ahmad Shah Massoud ("Massoud"), an agronomist who recognized the need for introducing new technologies to improve productivity in Afghanistan's agricultural sector, which accounts for 70 percent of the country's GDP.

Having survived decades of war and intermittent international embargoes, today Panjshir is a family owned business and the largest private enterprise operating in Afghanistan's agricultural sector. Specifically, Panjshir controls 60-70 percent of the market in vegetables, corn, grain, and oilseeds.

Approximately half of Panjshir's sales are comprised of seeds produced by Lorosanto Company ("Lorosanto"), a U.S.-based agricultural conglomerate and the largest producer of advanced conventional and genetically modified ("GM") seeds in the world. The Lorosanto-Panjshir partnership represents a rare and important commercial bridge between the two countries.

Panjshir's shares are owned equally by Massoud, his wife, and their two daughters, Bahar and Parvin. Panjshir's Board of Directors is comprised of Massoud's family and three trusted family friends.

In 2017, as an ageing Massoud prepared to retire, he designated his eldest daughter, Bahar, as his successor. Bahar subsequently sought the advice of Jacob Silverstein, a Stanford Graduate School of Business professor, in formulating the company's future business strategy. When the two met in Palo Alto that summer, Silverstein—an expert in agribusiness who had advised some of the largest conglomerates in the world—had only a few words:

> Take a couple of months alone and think about what you want your company to be in 10 years . . . write a paper explaining the trends that you believe will impact your business in that period and articulate a strategy designed to achieve your objectives.

Silverstein also handed over the following documents to Bahar to read:

- A case study involving how agribusiness giant Cargill had transformed itself in the 2000s to adapt to changing trends in global agriculture
- The BEM, and
- The OECD Guidelines.

Below is the strategy paper prepared by Bahar three months after the Palo Alto meeting. It predicts that within the next decade, Panjshir's landscape will be transformed both by economic liberalization that will leverage the untapped potential of Afghanistan's young and skilled population and by the proliferation of new technologies in agriculture. Bahar's proposed strategy leverages Panjshir's current market position to make the company a critical link between global suppliers of advanced agricultural technology and Afghanistan's farming community.

Read Bahar's paper and answer the questions that follow.

COMPANY PROFILE

Organization

Panjshir currently employs about 100 persons in several Afghan cities: Kabul, Mazar-e-Sharif, Herat, Kandahar, and Balkh.

Most of Panjshir's employees have been with the company for more than ten years; as such, they feel a strong sense of pride for their association with Panjshir and are extremely loyal. Panjshir is also ideally positioned to recruit top candidates from the labor force and academic institutions.

Performance

Panjshir's market share in vegetable seeds exceeds 50 percent, and it leads in all product classes. The company projects its vegetable seed sales to grow at 20 percent annually for the next three years. In 2010, Panjshir purchased about $50 million in vegetable seeds from Lorosanto, a fourfold increase since 2000.

Competitive Environment

Vegetable Seeds

Panjshir's competitors consist of small Afghan importers of vegetable seeds and large Arab pesticide producers who also trade in vegetable seeds. Together, they represent all of the other major vegetable seed producers in the world. In terms of sales turnovers, Panjshir's largest competitor is about half the size of Panjshir.

Grains and Oilseeds

There is no private company importing or selling seeds in this product segment. The government has held a monopoly over grain and oilseeds for more than three decades and has imported minor quantities of seed from producers in

Greece, Turkey, Serbia, and Croatia to complete its portfolio of local varieties. Private imports of seeds are also being gradually permitted.

Core competencies

- **Seed Distribution and Marketing.**
- **Seed Production.** Panjshir produces significant quantities of open-pollinated tomato and onion seeds through contracts with large and mid-sized farmers. It processes and packages the seeds in its own facilities.
- **Seed Testing.** Panjshir has three trialling centers in Tehran and Mashhad and conducts extensive field trials in collaboration with select farmers, academic institutions, and the government.
- **Farming Connections.** Though Panjshir works mainly with vegetable seed farmers, it has significant connections to all farming segments. In addition, Panjshir has partnerships with large and technically proficient farmers with whom it coordinates testing of new products, exchange of technical information, and lobbying on policy issues affecting agriculture.
- **Dealer Connections.** Panjshir has an extensive distribution network comprised of small local dealers and national wholesalers.
- **Institutional Connections.** Panjshir conducts joint research and training programs with several universities and government research institutions and is consulted on important policy initiatives.
- **Public Image.** Panjshir enjoys enormous goodwill that extends beyond the agriculture sector. Its image is that of a pioneer of useful agricultural technology that cares deeply for Afghanistan and its farmers.

STRATEGIC INTENT

In 2028, we will measure success by the following criteria:

1) Did we meet the reasonable expectations of our stakeholders?
2) Did we achieve a position of leadership in seed sales in Afghanistan and the region?

TRENDS

Fixed Trends[1]

- Rising demand for food in Afghanistan and the region will continue as populations grow and standards of living improve.
- Global food prices will be significantly higher. Given Afghanistan's growing reliance on food imports, the country will have to significantly boost production to protect its own economy and population from global price fluctuations.

---

1. Fixed trends have trajectories that can be predicted with relative certainty.

- Climate change will profoundly impact the region's dry land agro-eco-system through increased temperatures and changes in the hydrological cycles of severe droughts and floods.
- Water scarcity will pose a growing threat to agricultural output, as increased exposure to droughts and floods destroys opportunities in the agriculture sector. While heavy investment in infrastructure is planned to improve water management, this will only partly alleviate the problem.
- GM Technology will increasingly offer an effective means for Afghanistan to enhance its agricultural productivity, reduce scarce energy and water inputs, and cope with worsening climatic conditions.
- GM technology will be increasingly regulated through international convention and local legislation as regulators attempt to manage its environmental, commercial, and social impact.
- Public scrutiny of GM will persist globally and become more intense in Afghanistan, making the commercial success of the technology increasingly dependent on careful management of public opinion, use, and environmental impact.
- Consolidation of sales and ownership of seed traits will continue, leaving few large producers in control of the seed traits that will be indispensable to Afghanistan's agricultural economy.
- Consolidation of Afghanistan's farming industry will accelerate as a result of investment inflows aimed at increasing productivity, driven by rising prices, infrastructure improvements, and increased allocation of national resources.

Variable Trends[2]

- Economic growth and development in Afghanistan is projected at an average rate of 7 percent over the next decade, positioning the country to have one of the world's fastest-growing economies despite an unfriendly investment climate and limited capital inflows. At the same time, Afghanistan's particular attributes give it the potential to grow and advance much faster should those same conditions improve. For example, Afghanistan's present leadership appears committed to a program of economic reforms, having phased out fuel and food subsidies at great political cost, lifted the monopoly on some agricultural imports, and strengthened its intellectual property protection regime. In a political best-case scenario, Afghanistan could see an influx in foreign investment, which is presently almost nonexistent. The agriculture sector would disproportionately benefit in light of its importance to the national economy and the fact that it currently enjoys the lowest rate of investment and highest returns of all sectors. This will in turn have a significant bearing on the development of Afghanistan's farming industry and the profile of future Panjshir customers.

---

2. Variable trends cannot be easily predicted and are generally more volatile.

- Regional trade and economic integration will vary significantly depending on political developments in Afghanistan and the region.
- Civil society is extremely weak in Afghanistan and virtually nonexistent elsewhere in the region. Yet, the potential exists for the development of national and regional institutions that reinforce and protect citizenship rights. Should that occur, the center of policy and decision-making would shift from a paternalistic bureaucracy to the public, and priorities would shift from maintaining social stability to promoting public interests.
- Risk management will persist as a serious concern if the present government remains in power. An unreliable legal system and opaque policy making will make it difficult to assess and insure against risk, presenting a major deterrent against business expansion.

SCENARIO

We predict that in 2028, the fixed and variable trends will have developed to produce the following scenario:

- Afghanistan remains politically stable, having instituted substantial economic reforms and improved security in main cities and provinces.
- Afghanistan's government has followed the path of China in increasing wealth through economic reforms while maintaining social stability through political, social, and cultural constraints. Communications media and information remains strictly controlled by the government.
- Although intermittent clashes with fundamentalist militias pose some security risks to the farming industry, those risks will not significantly inhibit the industry's rapid growth and modernization.
- Public policy is still formulated through a nontransparent process involving few individuals and groups, and public debate is limited or nonexistent.
- Corruption remains endemic, increasing legal risk for foreign investors and multinational enterprises operating in the country. Afghanistan is ranked the tenth most corrupt country in the world by Transparency International.
- The legal system remains arbitrary, rendering risk management and protection of intellectual property difficult.
- The strategic imperative of increasing food production and maintaining employment in rural areas has compelled the government to significantly increase investment in agriculture; as a result, productivity has improved. A new generation of farmers is educated, entrepreneurial, and ready to embrace new technology and practices.
- The average farm in Afghanistan remains small and family owned, limiting economies of scale.
- Farmers are not organized, as the formation of independent cooperatives or trade associations is discouraged. However, informal collectives have been formed to negotiate pricing with large buyers.

RECOMMENDED STRATEGY

Lorosanto Partner with Advanced Capability to Manage GM Technology in Afghanistan and Region

We recommend that Panjshir leverage its core competencies and current relationship with Lorosanto to effectively introduce and manage of GM technology in Afghanistan in a manner that ensures its responsible use; that is, its use in a manner that meets the reasonable expectations of farmers, consumers, governmental authorities, environmental protection groups, and the country in general. As a leader in Afghanistan's agriculture sector, Panjshir has the opportunity and responsibility to play a critical role in ensuring that GM technology is employed to advance: (1) Afghanistan's food security, (2) sustainable development of its farming industry, and (3) Afghanistan's long-term capability to meet the challenges posed by climate change and water scarcity.

This strategy is predicated on the development of two key relationships—with Lorosanto and with Afghanistan's farming community. Panjshir would work with Lorosanto to achieve a common vision for making Afghanistan a positive example for the responsible and sustainable introduction of GM technology. To that end, Lorosanto and Panjshir should develop a broad plan—addressing potential public relations ("PR"), regulatory, legal, economic, and environmental issues that could arise in connection with GM—to ensure that problems experienced elsewhere are avoided.

Panjshir would further cultivate its relationship with the farming community by (1) sharpening its focus on its customers through training, technical assistance, and responsive claims processing; and by (2) organizing leaders of industry from different regions in informal associations to discuss and prepare for the future. Through these associations, Panjshir would engage the industry and individual farmers on policy issues that affect their interests, assess their technical needs, address ways to improve productivity (including through GM), and plan for the management of the environmental impact of the technology. These relationships will grow with the industry and give Panjshir, and in turn Lorosanto, the level of control over the supply chain that is necessary to ensure GM's success.

Foreseeable Challenges

Panjshir will have to significantly expand not only the size of its operations but also its competencies. Panjshir will have to grow larger and faster not only to develop those competencies, but also to manage a market that's also expanding at an equal or greater rate. Critical new capabilities will include advanced technical, legal, financial, PR, and environmental impact management and lobbying. Although some capabilities may be acquired through partnerships and joint ventures, many will have to be developed in-house. In this regard, Panjshir will have to be flexible enough to acquire new, as-yet-unknown capabilities, on account of the uncertain future political situation in Afghanistan and the evolution of GM. This strategy would also make Panjshir completely dependent on its relationship with Lorosanto, whose strategies and fortunes may change to Panjshir's detriment.

From a PR perspective, by becoming Lorosanto's representative, Panjshir will immediately render its image susceptible to attack via its association with the conglomerate. Panjshir's margin of error in this venture will be extremely narrow, especially if the political and socioeconomic environment in Afghanistan evolves as predicted. Given the intense public scrutiny and political sensitivity associated with GM, small mistakes could lead to a widespread ban of the technology and destroy Panjshir's reputation. Thus, it's necessary for Panjshir to perform not just competently, but flawlessly, rendering its operations more expensive.

Implementation

An indispensable condition to ensuring the success of this strategy is establishing a long-term partnership with Lorosanto that delegates the handling of all of its products to Panjshir. Therefore, an agreement should be in place with Lorosanto before other aspects of the strategy can be executed. The anticipated risk to Panjshir's image should be minimized through a reservation of rights by Panjshir to (1) conduct its own testing and select those varieties that confer value to its customers without posing an unreasonable risk to the environment; and (2) decline any action that it deems inconsistent with its values or that could damage its reputation.

The proposed strategy should be executed through a phased approach, beginning with the introduction of Lorosanto's conventional seeds for grains and oilseeds, preliminary discussions with farmers about GM, organizing farmer groups, and exploring the promulgation of bio-safety regulations with policy makers. New competencies can be developed gradually as events unfold and, depending on when GM is introduced, tailored as needs develop and to spread capital investment over time.

Implementation of this strategy should be designed around a commitment to customers and their needs, which would be established through intimate familiarity with the customers' business and provision of integrated solutions. This will be especially important in Afghanistan, since provincial customers will need professional advice on a range of issues to navigate a rapidly changing and increasingly unfamiliar environment. In this way, Panjshir can strengthen its connections with its customers without becoming formally involved as their partners or financiers.

These challenges are counterbalanced by the prospect of great success, both in making a significant contribution to Afghanistan and in maintaining Panjshir's leadership position in Afghanistan's agriculture. By 2028, this strategy could make Panjshir the conduit for the sale of most of the seeds planted for grains, oilseeds, and vegetables in Afghanistan, and possibly other countries in the region.

Questions

1) If Panjshir's board of directors adopts Bahar's proposed strategy, how should it articulate the end(s) to be achieved by the future CEO, presumably Bahar?

2) How should Panjshir's board of directors define the means by which the CEO should achieve those end(s)?

3) What, if any, core values has the proposed strategy expressed for Panjshir?

4) What, if any, purpose beyond profit has the proposed strategy defined for Panjshir?

5) What is Bahar's vision of a desired future for Panjshir and its employees? Should that vision be better articulated?

6) Can you think of any global legal trends not mentioned in the paper that will likely impact Panjshir in the next decade?

7) Assuming that Panjshir implements the strategy articulated in Bahar's paper, what level of enterprise identity will it achieve?

8) What specific additional competencies must Panjshir develop to achieve its stated strategic objectives?

9) Can Panjshir further elevate its enterprise identity by modifying its strategy? If so, how?

10) Evaluate Panjshir's strategy in terms of its compliance with the OECD guidelines. What, if any, additional steps must Panjshir take to ensure complete compliance with the OECD guidelines?

11) What specific contractual clauses should Panjshir include in its contract with Lorosanto to ensure that both companies act responsibly and that Panjshir can meet the reasonable expectations of its stakeholders?

12) How can Bahar modify her proposed strategy to better meet the reasonable expectations of each of the following stakeholder classes:
   a) Owners
   b) Employees
   c) Regulators
   d) Customers
   e) Consumers
   f) Competitors
   g) The environment
   h) Future generations

Table of Cases

Principal cases are italicized.

Alstom S.A.; United States v., 384, 385
Anheuser-Busch InBev SA/NV, 493-494
Automated Med. Labs., Inc.; United States v., 6

Bank of New England, N.A.; United States v., 13, 20
Barnes v. Andrews, 49
BellSouth Corp., In re, 207
BHP Billiton Ltd. & BHP Billiton Plc, In re, 187
Booker; United States v., 47
Braswell v. United States, 23, 34
Burwell v. Hobby Lobby Stores, 33, 34

Caremark Int'l Inc. Derivative Litig., In re, 48, 51, 52
Citizens United v. Fed. Election Comm'n, 33, 34

Daimler AG; United States v., 196
Delta & Pine Land Co., 268

Esquenazi; United States v., 322, 331

Fokker Services B.V.; United States v. (818 F.3d 733), 79, 81, 82, 84, *85,* 94
Fokker Servs. B.V.; United States v. (79 F. Supp. 3d 160), 95

Gall v. United States, 47
Giovannetti; United States v., 333
Goncalves; United States v. (No. 09-CR-00335-RJL (D.D.C. Feb. 21, 2012)), 386
Goncalves; United States v. (No. 09-CR-00335-RJL (D.D.C. Apr. 6, 2010)), 386
Gorman; United States v., 268

Hoskins; United States v., 385, 386, *391,* 400, 408
HSBC Bank USA, N.A.; United States v. (No. 12-CR-763, 2013 WL 3306161 (E.D.N.Y. July 1, 2013), 81, 95

HSBC Bank USA, N.A.; United States v. (No. 1:12-cr-00763 (E.D.N.Y. filed Dec. 11, 2012)), 131

JGC Corp.; United States v., 382, *400,* 408
JP Morgan Chase & Co., In re, 271

Kay; United States v., 266, 308
Kimbrough v. United States, 47
Kiobel v. Royal Dutch Petroleum Co., 371, 372
Kozeny; United States v., 305, 333, 336, *337*

McBoyle v. United States, 133
Melrose Distillers, Inc. v. United States, 346
Morrison v. National Australia Bank Ltd., 356, 359, *360,* 370, 371, 372, 373

New York Central & Hudson River Railroad Co. v. United States, 6, *7,* 11, 12
New York, State of, v. Volkswagen Aktiengesellschaft, 182
Norex Petroleum Ltd. v. Access Indus., Inc., 373
NYNEX Corp.; United States v., 382

100Reporters LLC v. U.S. Dep't of Justice, 125
Oracle Corp.; SEC v., 167

Pacific Can Co. v. Hewes, 382
Pacific Gas & Elec. Co.; United States v., 22
Patel; United States v., 379
Pinkerton v. United States, 385, *388,* 391

Reyes; United States v., 151
RJR Nabisco, Inc. v. European Cmty., 371, 372

Science Applications Int'l Corp.; United States v., 19, 21
SEC v. *See name of opposing party*

Sherman, In re, 245

Siemens Aktiengesellschaft; United States v., 535, *542*

Sigma-Aldrich Bus. Holdings, Inc., 346

Snamprogetti Netherlands B.V.; United States v., 382, 384

Standard Oil Co. of Tex. v. United States, 6, 11

Stein; United States v. (541 F.3d 130), 84

Stein; United States v. (440 F. Supp. 2d 315), 84, 113-117

Stein; United States v. (435 F. Supp. 2d 330), 83

Union Carbide Corp. Gas Plant Disaster at Bhopal, India, In re, 576

United States v. *See name of opposing party*

Veraz Networks; SEC v., 268

Vitesse Semiconductor Corp.; SEC v., 134

Williams; United States v., 268

World-Wide Coin Investments, Ltd.; SEC v., 148, 149, 150, *152*, 167

Index

Absolutism, 257
Accounting practices
    corporate self-policing. *See* Accounting provisions
        of FCPA
    forensic accounting. *See* Forensic accounting
    risk assessment, 459-460
Accounting provisions of FCPA, 145-253
    affiliates, 211-212
    books and records. *See* Books and records provision
    collaborators of multinational enterprises, 211
    coverage, 206-212
    Enron's fall, 227-231
    expense reports, 149
    internal controls. *See* Internal controls provisions
        of FCPA
    introduction, 145-147
    issuers and their subsidiaries, 206-211
    manipulation of records, 147-148
    material misstatement, 232
    "reasonable assurances." *See* "Reasonable
        assurances"
    "reasonable detail." *See* "Reasonable detail"
    recordkeeping, 146-147, 148
    Sarbanes-Oxley Act interplay with FCPA, 212-253
    scienter, 149, 151, 163-164, 166
    who is covered, 206-212
    WorldCom, Inc., investigation of, 213-226
Acquisitions. *See* Mergers and acquisitions (M&A)
Action learning, 641, 644
Action planning, 606, 642, 644-645
Ad Hoc Advisory Group. *See* Advisory Group
Adelphia Communications, 42
Advice-of-counsel defense, 111
Advisory Group, 41-46, 48, 54, 56-64, 72. *See*
        also Federal Sentencing Guidelines for
        Organizations (FSGO)
Affiliates
    accounting provisions of FCPA, 211-212
    defined, 211
Affirmative defenses, 305-306, 375, 377
"African Sting" case, 386

Agency
    anti-bribery provisions, 382-384
    risk assessment, 459
Aiding and abetting, 382, 385, 386-387, 407-408
Alien Tort Statute (ATS), 371, 372
Allen, William T., 48
Alstom S.A., 384, 385
Alternative jurisdiction clause, 359, 373, 374, 376, 378
Ambiguity
    in anti-bribery provisions of FCPA, 265
    in anti-competitive agreements, 758
    in business or financial references of third party,
        472
Anheuser-Busch InBev, 493-494
Anti-Bribery Convention, 258-259, 374-375, 377, 378,
        379, 381
    monitoring implementation of, 143
    requirements of, 136-137, 142
    signatories, 143, 256
    testimony on, 138-140
Anti-bribery provisions of FCPA, 255-414
    affirmative defenses, 305-306
    agency, 382-384
    aiding and abetting, 382, 385, 386-387, 407-408
    alternative jurisdiction clause, 359, 373, 374, 376,
        378
    ambiguity, 265
    "anything of value," 264, 269-313
    business purpose test, 264, 266-268
    case stories, 301-304
    charitable donations, 295-297
    civil liability, 149, 387
    coercion, proof of, 336
    concert of action, 382, 385-408
    conduct of others, responsibility for, 382-408
    conspiracy, 382, 385-386, 386-387, 388-399,
        403-407
    coverage, 263-355, 356-408
    domestic concerns, 356, 358, 376-378, 458
    duress, proof of, 336
    entertainment, 297-305, 306-307

Anti-bribery provisions of FCPA (*Cont'd*)
    exceptions to "anything of value," 305, 308-313
    expediting payments exception, 308-313
    extraterritoriality, presumption against, 359-372, 373-381
    facilitating payments exception, 308-313, 317
    foreign individuals and juridical entities acting inside U.S. territory, 356, 358
    foreign official, defined, 264, 313-332
    gifts, 297-305, 306-307
    government "instrumentality," 313-314, 331-332
    "grease" payments, 308, 309
    hiring practices, 271-293, 293-294
    hypotheticals, 306-307, 312-313, 352-355, 477-480
    imputed liability, 383-384, 385
    indirect payments to family members of foreign officials, 294
    intent, 264, 332-345
    internship programs, 271-293, 294-295
    introduction, 255-263
    issuers, 356, 357-358, 373-376, 458
    jurisdictional conduct that triggers provisions, 358-359
    jurisdictional scope, 359-372, 373-381
    knowledge, defined, 332-345
    local law affirmative defense, 305
    meals, 298-305
    medical emergency exception, 311-312
    medical expenses, payment of, 269-271
    opinion release request, 265-266. *See also* FCPA Opinion Procedure Releases
    person, defined, 378
    prohibited intent (corruptly, willfully, knowingly), 264, 332-345
    reasonable and bona fide expenditures affirmative defense, 305-306
    red flags, 333, 458
    responsibility for conduct of others, 382-408
    routine governmental action exception, 308
    safety emergency exception, 311-312
    small payments and gifts, 269
    successor liability, 345-355
    territorial jurisdiction, 378-381
    TRACE guidelines on gifts and hospitality, 299
    travel, 297-305, 306-307
    what is covered, 263-355
    who is covered, 356-408
Anti-bribery update, 616-617
Anticompetitive behaviors, 757. *See also* Competition
    cartel formation, 757
    collusive tendering, 757
    exclusive distribution agreement, 757
    horizontal restraints, 757
    price fixing, 757
    refusals to deal, 757
    vertical restraints, 757
Anticorruption update, 616-617
Anti-retaliation protections, 491-492

"Anything of value," 264, 268-269, 269-313. *See also* Anti-bribery provisions of FCPA
Arabian Rights Watch Association, 702-709
Arbitration, 269, 567
Argentina NCP, 753-756
Arthur Andersen, 2, 41, 79, 80, 81, 83, 213, 220, 230
Ashcroft, John, 80, 124, 125, 133-134
Assessment
    environmental impacts, 725
    ethics program, 655-659
    internal controls, 233
    life-cycle, 725
    risk. *See* Risk assessment; Third-party risk assessment
    training, 452
Association of Neighborhoods of Paracatu (in Brazil), 671-680
Attorney-client privilege, 111, 504
    crime-fraud exception, 111
    protection, 108, 109, 110
    waiver, 80, 106, 108, 109, 340, 505
Auditing
    compliance program, 59-60, 509, 510-512, 655
    ethics program, 655
    FSGO, 509
    third-party due diligence, 465
Authorizations
    expenditures, 148, 176
    internal controls provisions, 176
Autonomy
    compliance program, 424, 555-556, 632
    ethics program, 632-639

Bank of New England, N.A., 13-17, 20
Bank Secrecy Act, 127
Barclays PLC, 94
Beale, Sara Sun, 1, 2, 10
BellSouth Corp., 207-210
BEM (*Business Ethics: A Manual for Managing a Responsible Business Enterprise in Emerging Market Economies*), 562-563, 565, 566-568, 590-591, 591-593
    accountability, 632-639
    assessment of ethics program, 655-659
    authority, 632-639
    autonomous ethics program, 632
    business conduct representatives, 637
    business ethics council, 636
    business ethics officer, 634-636
    code of conduct, 625-632. *See also* Code of conduct
    components of ethics program, 624
    core purpose, 605, 610
    core values, 606, 610
    culture of organization, 625
    deterrents, 647, 648, 649-650, 651
    discipline systems, 649-650
    effectiveness of ethics program, 611
    emerging market economy, 566-568
    enterprise identity, levels of, 611-613

failures, 648, 650-651
high-level responsibility, 633-634
incentives, 647-648, 648-649, 651
individual responsibility, 638
investigations, 651-652, 652-655
management vision for enterprise, 605-610
misconduct, 648
mistakes and failures, 648, 650-651
monitoring of ethics program, 655-659
norms, values, and standards to set. *See* OECD
    Guidelines for Multinational Enterprises
organizational culture, 625
owner representatives, infrastructure for, 632-633
professional ethics council, 637
reporting and investigations, 651-652, 652-655
responsibility, 632-639
responsible business ethics, 566-568
responsible governance, 590-591, 591-593
responsible management, 604, 605-610
reward systems, 648-649
social capital, building of, 567, 610, 613
stakeholder theory, 562-563, 590-591, 604-605
training program, 639-647
vision framework, 605-610
vision of desired future, 606, 610
working with leaders, 568
Bharara, Preet, 2
Bhopal disaster, 1, 569-583, 590
    aftermath, 571-572
    case study, 569-583
    history, 570-571
    lessons learned, 572-573
    National Institute of Health review, 569-575
BHP Billiton, 187-196
Blackmail, 257, 608
BNP Paribas, 94, 498
BNY Mellon, 294-295
Boeing Company, 702-709
Books and records provision, 145-146, 459
    cease-and-desist proceedings, 207-210
    complaint, 167-171
    coverage, 147-149
    memorandum opinion and order, 152-167
    reasonable detail. *See* "Reasonable detail"
    text, 146-147
BP Deepwater Horizon oil spill, 1, 583-590
    National Commission report, 583-588
    settlement press release, 583, 589
Brazil NCP, 671-680
Breuer, Lanny, 82, 96
Breuer Memorandum, 125
Bribery, 2, 134, 135, 137
    compliance program, 448-449
    cost of bribe, 441-444
    countries whose public officials received bribes, 447
    "demand side" of transaction, 439-441
    domestic statute. *See* Anti-bribery provisions of
        FCPA; *see also* FCPA

FCPA anti-bribery provisions. *See* Anti-bribery
        provisions of FCPA
    how bribes are being paid, 444-445
    intermediaries, involvement of, 444-445
    key findings, 435-436
    level within company, 438, 439
    OECD Convention. *See* Anti-Bribery Convention
    OECD report, 435-450
    percentage of bribes paid per category of public
        official, 440, 441
    public procurement, 449
    purpose of bribes, 448
    sectors accounting for two-thirds of cases, 438
    size of sanctioned companies, 437
    transaction value, 442-444
    treaty against bribes. *See* Anti-Bribery Convention
    value of transaction, 442-444
    where bribes are being paid, 445-446
    who is bribing, 437-439
    who is receiving bribes, 439-441
    why bribes are being paid, 446
Buchanan, Mary Beth, 43
Bucy, Pamela H., 11-12, 413
Buente, David T., 43
*Business Ethics: A Manual for Managing a Responsible
        Business Enterprise in Emerging Market
        Economies* (BEM). *See* BEM
Business ethics council, 636, 637
Business ethics officer, 634-636
Business ethics program. *See* Ethics program
Business opportunity risk, 428
Business partnership risk, 428
Business purpose test, 264, 266-268

Cadbury, Adrian, 590
Caldwell, Leslie, 496-497, 498-499, 500
Caremark International Inc., 48, 51, 52
Carrot-and-stick approach, 3-4, 40, 79, 83, 97, 561.
        See also Federal Sentencing Guidelines
        for Organizations (FSGO); Prosecutorial
        guidelines for organizations
Cartel formation, 757
Carter, Jimmy, 136
Case studies
    anti-bribery provisions of FCPA, 301-304
    Bhopal disaster, 569-583
    compliance program, 466-467, 467-477
    ethics program, 613-624
    ethics training program, 645
    third-party due diligence, 467, 473-477
    whistleblowers, 487-489
Cassidy, John, 457
Causing, liability for, 387
CCO. *See* Chief Compliance Officer (CCO)
Certification of financial reports, 213, 231-232
    false certification, 232, 245-253
    responsibility for accuracy of financial reports, 213,
        231-232

CESCR. *See* Committee for Economic, Social and Cultural Rights (CESCR)

Charging decisions, 79-80, 85-93. *See also* Discretion of prosecutor

Charitable donations, 295-297. *See also* Anti-bribery provisions of FCPA
    due diligence measures and controls, 296
    questions to consider, 296

Chief Compliance Officer (CCO), 57

Chief Executive Officer (CEO), 57, 231-232

Chief Financial Officer (CFO), 57, 231-232

Chief Operational Officer (COO), 57

Chief Technical Officer (CTO), 57

Church, Frank, 134

Citigroup, Inc., 94, 294

Civil liability, 456
    for aiding and abetting, 387
    for anti-bribery violations, 149, 387
    for books and records provision violation, 149, 151
    for causing, 387
    for damages tortiously caused by employees, 6.
        See also Respondeat superior

Civil War, 6

Coca-Cola Company, 613-624

Code of conduct, 421-424, 452, 625-632
    adaptations, 628
    aspirational provisions, 628
    communication technology, 423
    compliance program, 421-424
    cultural norms, respect for, 627
    environment, protection of, 626-627
    formats, 628
    FSGO, 55
    guidelines for development of, 627
    improvements, 628
    industry standards, compliance with, 626
    information availability, 423
    law and regulations, compliance with, 626
    obligatory provisions, 628
    typical provisions, 628-632
    updates, 423, 628

Coercion, proof of, 336

Cold War, 135, 139

Collaborators of multinational enterprises, 211

Collateral harm, 80, 81

Collective entity rule, 23-35, 37

Collective knowledge doctrine, 13-22, 34, 37

Collusive tendering, 757

Commission on Fraudulent Financial Reporting (Treadway Commission), 171, 172, 212, 250, 416

Committee for Economic, Social and Cultural Rights (CESCR), 695

Committee of Sponsoring Organizations (COSO), 172, 416
    framework, 171-179
    risk, defined, 425
    risk tolerance, 430

Communication
    compliance program, 423, 557
    external communication, 176, 177
    internal communication, 176-177
    internal controls provisions, 176-177, 179
    monitors, 122-123
    technology, 423

Community engagement, 621-623

Community service, 74

Competition
    anticompetitive behaviors. *See* Anticompetitive behaviors
    OECD Guidelines, 661, 662, 757-759, 759-762
    specific instance, 759-762

Compliance culture. *See* Culture of compliance

Compliance level of enterprise identity, 611-612
    Compliance program, 46, 93, 413-534, 562
    auditing, 59-60, 509, 510-512, 655
    autonomy, 424, 555-556, 632
    bribery, 448-449
    building credibility, 418
    case studies, 466-467, 467-477
    code of conduct, 421-424
    communications, 423, 557
    confidential reporting, 480-495, 558
    continuing advice, 451-454
    continuous improvement, 508-512, 558-559
    cooperation, 498-508
    cooperation credit, 498, 505, 506-507
    credibility, 418
    criteria for effective program, 40-41
    development, 416-418
    disciplinary measures, 455-457, 558
    effectiveness, 611
    evaluation of program, 535-560
    FSGO, 52, 53-69, 424, 590, 611
    game theory, 457
    hallmarks of effective program, 415-534, 562, 623, 624, 632
    hotline, 481-495
    incentives, 455-457, 558
    information availability, 423
    internal investigations. *See* Internal investigations
    internal reporting mechanisms, 60-61
    middle management, 419, 555
    monitoring, 59-60, 509-510, 655
    oversight, 424
    overview, 416-418
    "paper program," 104, 105
    parameters, 424-425
    periodic testing and review, 508-512, 558-559
    policies and procedures, 421-424, 556-557
    policy against corruption, 419-421, 556-557
    post-acquisition integration, 512-534
    pre-acquisition due diligence, 512-534
    remediation, 505-506, 506-507, 554-555
    reporting systems, 60-61
    resources, 424-425, 555-556, 632

risk assessment. *See* Risk assessment
self-disclosure, 498-508
senior management commitment, 419-421, 555
small organizations, 59, 60, 66-67
third-party due diligence. *See* Third-party due diligence
third-party payments, 457
training, 58-59, 451-454, 557
updating policy and code of conduct, 423
USAM, 103-105
whistleblowers. *See* Whistleblowers
Concert of action, 382, 385-408
Conduct of others, responsibility for, 382-408
Confidential reporting, 61, 125, 480-495, 558
Confrontation right, 32
Conspiracy, 382, 385-386, 386-387, 388-399, 403-407
Consumer interests under OECD Guidelines, 661, 662
    awareness and education, 743
    complaint, 749-751
    data protection, 744-751
    dispute resolution, 744
    education vs. information, 743
    health and safety, 742-743
    information, 743
    privacy, 744-751
    text of Guidelines, 745-748
Contract life cycle
    flowchart of typical life cycle, 451
Control, 459
    control activities, 175-176, 178
    control environment, 174-175, 178
    defined, 211
    internal controls under FCPA. *See* Internal controls provisions of FCPA
Convention on Combating Bribery of Foreign Public Officials. *See* Anti-Bribery Convention
Convention on the Rights of the Child (CRC), 686, 691, 692
COO. *See* Chief Operational Officer (COO)
Cooperation, 498-508
    no entitlement to immunity, 112-113
    rewarding, 105-117. *See also* Cooperation credit
    USAM, 106-113
    value, 105, 106-108, 109-111. *See also* Cooperation credit
Cooperation credit, 97, 109-112, 113-117, 481, 498, 505, 506-507
Core purpose, 605, 610
Core values, 606, 610
Corporate criminal liability, 1-4
    collective entity rule, 23-35, 37
    collective knowledge doctrine, 13-22, 34, 37
    constitutional rights of corporations, 23-32, 32-34
    FSGO. *See* Federal Sentencing Guidelines for Organizations (FSGO)
    quick facts, 76-77
    respondeat superior, 5-12, 34, 37
    self-incrimination rule, 23-32

sentencing guidelines. *See* Federal Sentencing Guidelines for Organizations (FSGO)
    theoretical underpinnings, 5-35
Corporate ethics. *See* Ethics program
Corporate ethos, 413-414, 419
Corporate fraud scandals, 212, 213-226, 227-231
Corporate governance, 590-593, 595-604
    BEM, 590-591, 591-593
    business case, 595-604
    drivers of reform, 601-603
    institutional dimensions, 596-597
    shareholder theory, 561, 563, 591
    stakeholder theory, 562-563, 590-591, 604-605
    understanding of, 595-596
Corporate social responsibility (CSR), 561-564, 566, 590, 604, 647
Corrib Gas project, 732-741
Corruption indicators, 433-435
Corruption Perceptions Index (CPI), 426, 427, 433
"Corruptly," meaning of, 333-334
COSO. *See* Committee of Sponsoring Organizations (COSO)
Côté-Freeman, Susan, 416-418
Counsel, right to, 32, 83
CPI. *See* Corruption Perceptions Index (CPI)
CRC. *See* Convention on the Rights of the Child (CRC)
Credibility, building of, 418
Credit ratings and restrictions, 471. *See also* Third-party due diligence
Credit Suisse, 94, 294
Crime or fraud exception, 111
Criminal liability, corporate. *See* Corporate criminal liability
Criminal purpose organizations, 70. *See also* Fine calculation
CSR. *See* Corporate social responsibility (CSR)
CTO. *See* Chief Technical Officer (CTO)
Culpability score, 70, 71, 72. *See also* Fine calculation
Cultural absolutism, 257
Cultural relativism, 257
Culture of compliance, 304, 414, 419, 490, 506, 612, 618
Culture of ethics, 562, 655
Culture of organization, 625, 655-657
Currency Transaction Reporting Act, 13-17
Cutler, Stephen M., 455

DAG Memos, 95, 96
    Individual Accountability, 501, 503, 504, 505, 506
    privileged materials, 84
Daimler AG
    compliance program deficiencies, 196-205
    improper payments to foreign government officials, 196-205
Data protection, OECD Guidelines, 744-751
Database searches, 464-465. *See also* Third-party due diligence

Deepwater Horizon disaster. *See* BP Deepwater
    Horizon oil spill
Defenders for Medical Impartiality, 702-709
Deferred prosecution agreement (DPA), 357, 563.
    See also Non-prosecution agreement (NPA)
  critics, 94
  description, 81-82, 84
  duration of agreement, 123-124
  "eggshell defendants," 94
  FCPA enforcement, 133
  Fokker Services B.V., 85-93
  HSBC, 96
  JGC Corporation, 408
  KPMG, 83
  monitors. *See* Monitors
  probation period, 117
  procedure, 81-82, 84, 85-93
  selection and use of monitors, 118-124. *See also*
    Monitors
  success, 93-94
Definitions
  adverse, or negative, human rights impact, 687
  corruptly, 333-334
  domestic concern, 376
  foreign official, 264, 313, 314-316, 317, 331
  governing authority, 55, 66
  intended loss, 70-71
  internal control, 172-173
  knowledge, 332-345
  organizational leadership, 56-57
  pecuniary gain, 71
  pecuniary loss, 70
  person, 378
  "reasonable assurances," 150
  "reasonable detail," 149
  risk, 425
  violations of law, 54
  willfully, 334
Department of Justice (DOJ), 83
  affiliates of issuers, 211
  agency, 382-383
  books and records, 149
  Caremark investigation, 48
  charitable donations, 295
  co-conspirators, 385
  coercion as defense to FCPA violation, 336
  compliance monitor selection process, 125
  compliance programs, 137, 416, 424, 425
    evaluation of, 535, 554-560
    Fraud Section evaluation of, 554-560
    third-party due diligence procedures, 457
  concert of action, 382
  confidentiality of monitor reports, 125
  corporations, criminal charges against, 94, 95, 97,
    496-497
  DAG Memos. *See* DAG Memos
  Deepwater Horizon settlement press release, 589
  directives, 80, 84

disciplinary measures, adequacy of, 456
diversion agreements, 81, 94
due diligence guidance, 461
duress as defense to FCPA violation, 336
enforcement authority, 12, 79-80, 141-142
Enron investigation, 41
extraterritoriality of FCPA, 357, 373, 382, 385-386
FCPA Guide. *See* FCPA Guide
FCPA interpretation, 265
Filip Factors, 97
"foreign official," 313
  gift vs. bribe, 297-298
"grease payments," 309
HSBC investigation, 127, 130
internal investigation, evaluation of, 496-497
JGC Corporation DPA, 408
mergers and acquisitions, 512-514
opinion releases. *See* FCPA Opinion Procedure
  Releases
reasonable and bona fide expenditures affirmative
  defense, 306
red flags in payments to third parties, 333
self-disclosure by companies, 500
successor liability, 346
third-party accounting practices, 460
third-party due diligence procedures, 457
third-party identity, 460
third-party involvement and compensation, 461
Desio, Paula, 37, 41
Deterrents, 455, 647, 651. *See also* Incentives
Deutsche Bank AG, 294
Disciplinary measures, 61, 62
  adequacy of measures, 456
  compliance program, 455-457, 558
  ethics program, 647-651
  forms of discipline, 456
  FSGO, 455
Disclosure
  OECD Guidelines, 661, 662, 680-686
  rewarding of, 105-117
  self-disclosure, 383, 481, 498-508
  specific instance, 684-686
  USAM, 105, 109-110
Discretion of prosecutor, 88, 127-131. *See also*
  Prosecutorial guidelines for organizations
  charging decisions, 80, 89, 90, 92, 98, 99, 114
  dismissal of pending charges, 90
  mitigation credit, 103
Dispute resolution, 567, 744
  arbitration. *See* Arbitration
  mediation. *See* Mediation
Diversion agreements, 81-82, 357
  DPA. *See* Deferred prosecution agreement (DPA)
  negotiating an agreement, 95
  NPA. *See* Non-prosecution agreement (NPA)
Dodd-Frank Act, 481, 482, 490-492, 494
Dodd-Frank Wall Street Reform and Consumer
  Protection Act. *See* Dodd-Frank Act

DOJ. *See* Department of Justice (DOJ)
Domestic concern
    anti-bribery provision coverage, 356, 358, 376-378,
      458
    defined, 376
    amendments governing, 377
Donaldson, Thomas, 257
Double jeopardy, 32, 389
DPA. *See* Deferred prosecution agreement (DPA)
Draney, Walter, 482-483
Due diligence
    charitable donations, 296
    DOJ guidance, 461
    ethics, 659, 662-663
    Integrity Due Diligence, 467-477, 659
    OECD Guidelines, 662-663
    pre-acquisition, 512-534, 559-560, 659
    RBE, 662-663
    report, 614-624
    SEC guidance, 461
    third party. *See* Third-party due diligence
Due process, 7, 32, 581, 582, 638, 691
Duress, 336

E Ink Holdings, Inc., 759-762
Effective compliance program. *See* Compliance
    program
Eggshell defendants, 3, 94
Eighth Amendment, 32
Elkins Act, 6, 7, 9, 11
EMA. *See* Environmental management accounting
    (EMA)
Employment and industrial relations
    OECD Guidelines, 661, 662, 710-715, 717-724
    specific instance, 717-724
EMS. *See* Environmental management system (EMS)
Enron Corporation, 80
    code of conduct, 417
    collapse, 227-231, 643
    collective knowledge doctrine, 18
    corrupt accounting practices, 18, 41, 136, 213,
      227-231
    culture, 420
Enterprise identity, levels of, 611-613, 624
Entertainment, 297-305, 306-307. *See also* Anti-bribery
    provisions of FCPA
Environment
    consumer awareness, 727
    continuous improvements in environmental
      performance, 726-727
    crimes, 70
    development of policy, 727-728
    education, 727
    emergency prevention, preparedness, and response,
      726
    environmental management accounting, 727
    environmental metrics, 727
    life-cycle assessment, 725

OECD Guidelines, 661, 662, 672-674, 724-728,
    728-732, 732-741
    precaution, exercise of, 725-726
    public information, 725
    shareholder consultation, 725
    specific instance, 732-741
    training, 727
Environmental management accounting (EMA), 727
Environmental management system (EMS), 724-725
Environmental update, 619-621
Ethical imperialism, 257
Ethics program, 46, 93, 561-564, 611-659
    assessment, 655-659
    auditing, 655
    autonomy, 632-639
    baselines, 657-658
    BEM guidance. *See* BEM
    benchmarks, 657-658
    building the program, 611-659
    case study, 613-624
    Coca-Cola Company in Myanmar, 613-624
    code of conduct. *See* Code of conduct
    compliance level of enterprise identity, 611-612
    components, 624-659
    continuous assessment and monitoring, 655-659
    culture of organization, 625, 655-657
    disciplinary measures, 647-651
    due diligence report, 614-624
    effectiveness, 611, 655
    employees seeking advice and reporting concerns,
      652-654
    enterprise identity, levels of, 611-613, 624
    essential characteristics of enterprises, 655-657
    evaluation of process, 658-659
    expected outcomes, 657
    FSGO, 52, 53-69, 424, 590, 647
    hotline, 615, 617, 618, 619, 651
    incentives, 647-648, 648-649, 651
    infrastructure, 632-639
    investigations, 651-655
    monitoring, 655-659
    objective of program, 611-624
    organizational culture, 655-657
    oversight, 424, 632-639
    policies and procedures for investigations, 654-655
    RBE. *See* Responsible business enterprise (RBE)
    reporting, 651-655, 659
    reputation enhancement level of enterprise identity,
      611, 612
    resources, 632-639
    retribution, protection of employees and agents, 654
    risk management level of enterprise identity, 611,
      612
    stakeholder sentiment, 655
    stakeholder surveys, 655
    training program. *See* Ethics training program
    value-added level of enterprise identity, 611,
      612-613

Ethics training program, 639-647
    action learning, 641, 644
    action planning, 606, 642, 644-645
    case studies, 645
    core beliefs, reinforcement of, 640, 642
    delivering the program, 642
    designing the program, 640-641
    feedback, collection of, 646-647
    games, 645-646
    lectures, 645
    management commitment, demonstration of,
        639-640
    modes of training, 645-646
    modifying the program, 646
    organizational culture, reinforcement of, 640
    presentations, 645
    scenarios, 645
    updating the program, 646
Ethos, 413-414, 419
European Centre for Democracy and Human Rights,
    702-709
Excessive fines, 32. See also Fine calculation
Exchange Act, 360-370
    anti-bribery provisions, 263-264, 357-358, 359-372,
        373-376, 376-378, 378-381
    15 U.S.C. § 78dd-1, 357-358, 372, 373-376, 378,
        379, 382, 384
    15 U.S.C. § 78dd-2, 358, 376-378, 379, 382, 384,
        400
    15 U.S.C. § 78dd-3, 358, 378-381, 384, 400
    anti-fraud provision, 370
    books and records provision, 146-147
    cease-and-desist proceedings, 187-196, 207-210,
        245-253, 271-293
    domestic concerns, 358, 376-378, 379, 382, 384,
        400
    extraterritorial scope, 359, 360-370, 373
    Foreign Corrupt Practices Act. See FCPA
    "foreign official," defined, 313
    internal controls provisions, 146-147, 150, 151,
        233-245
    issuers and their subsidiaries, 206, 207-210, 211,
        357-358, 375
    recordkeeping and internal controls provisions,
        146-147, 150, 151, 233-245
    territorial jurisdiction, 358, 371, 373, 378-381,
        384, 400
    whistleblower incentives and protections, 482,
        490-492, 494
Exclusive distribution agreement, 757
Expediting payments exception, 308-313. See also
    Anti-bribery provisions of FCPA
Expense reports, 149
Extortion, 139, 309, 336, 422, 608, 661-662
Extraterritorial application of FCPA
    presumption against extraterritoriality, 356,
        359-372, 373-381
    scope, 356-359

Facilitating payments exception, 308-313, 317. See also
    Anti-bribery provisions of FCPA
False certifications, 245-253
False Claims Act (FCA), 19-21
FCPA (Foreign Corrupt Practices Act), 133-411
    accounting provisions. See Accounting provisions
        of FCPA
    anti-bribery provisions. See Anti-bribery provisions
        of FCPA
    domestic concerns, amendments governing, 377
    enforcement plan and guidance, 500-507
    enforcement trends, 133-134
    extraterritoriality. See Extraterritorial application
        of FCPA
    globalization, 136-137
    history, 134-136
    internal controls provisions. See Internal controls
        provisions of FCPA
    issuers, amendments governing, 374-375
    legislative background, 134-136, 149
    other persons, amendments governing, 380-381
    resource guide. See FCPA Guide
    revival in new century, 136-140
    SOX and, 136
    violations, 409-411
FCPA Guide (A Resource Guide to the U.S. Foreign
        Corrupt Practices Act), 137, 611
    accounting provisions, 145, 150-151
    agency, 382-384, 459
    aiding and abetting, 382, 386-387
    anti-bribery provisions
        hypotheticals, 306-307, 312-313, 352-355,
            477-480
        local law affirmative defense, 305
        reasonable and bona fide expenditures
            affirmative defense, 306
        routine governmental action, exception for, 308
        who is covered, 357-359
    "anything of value," 268-269
    audits, 510, 511
    BEM as additional guidance, 562. See also BEM
    business purpose test, 266-267
    causing, liability for, 387
    civil liability for anti-bribery violations, 387
    communication technology, 423
    compliance, culture of, 414
    compliance program, 419, 562. See also Compliance
        program
        case study, 466-467
        effectiveness, 416, 611, 623
        hallmarks of effective programs, 415-534, 562,
            623, 624, 632
    components of internal control system, 174
    conduct of others, responsibility for, 382
    confidential reporting, 481
    conspiracy, 382, 386-387
    control, 459
    "corruptly," meaning of, 333-334

costs of corruption, 141
criminal liability for anti-bribery violations,
    386-387
culture of compliance, 419
deterrents, 455
DOJ, 141-142
ethical culture, 414
foreign official, defined, 314-316
global anticorruption efforts, 142-144
hypotheticals, 477-480
incentives, 455-456
interagency efforts, 141
international landscape, 142
internal controls, 150-151, 174
internal investigations, 481
introduction, 141-144
monitoring of third-party relationships, 466
national landscape, 141-142
other anticorruption conventions, 144
periodic testing and review, 508
prohibited intent, 333-335
rewards, 455-456
SEC, 141, 142
senior and middle managers, 419
small payments and gifts, 269
successor liability, 346-349
third-party due diligence, 461, 466
third-party payments, 457-458
training program, 451, 452
web-based approach, 423
"willfully," meaning and application, 334
FCPA Opinion Procedure Releases, 296, 352, 515
    Opinion Procedure Release No. 01-01, 518
    Opinion Procedure Release No. 03-01, 514-515
    Opinion Procedure Release No. 08-01, 521-533
    Opinion Procedure Release No. 08-02, 354, 516-521
    Opinion Procedure Release No. 10-02, 295
    Opinion Procedure Release No. 12-01, 317-321
    Opinion Procedure Release No. 13-01, 269-271
    Opinion Procedure Release No. 14-02, 349-352, 521
    requests, 265-266
Federal prosecution of business organizations. *See*
    Prosecution of business organizations
Federal Rules of Civil Procedure
    Rule 12(b)(1), 372
    Rule 12(b)(6), 372
Federal Sentencing Guidelines for Organizations
    (FSGO), 37-75, 93, 97, 611
    auditing, 509
    board of directors, responsibility of, 590
    code of conduct, 55
    compliance program, 52, 53-69, 414, 590
        effectiveness, 611
        oversight, 424
        training, 58-59
    confidential reporting, 481
    corporate ethics, 562
    corporate social responsibility, 561-562

culture of ethics, 655
disciplinary measures, 455, 647
ethics program, 52, 53-69, 414, 590
    disciplinary measures, 647
    incentives, 647
    oversight, 424
failure to prevent or detect offense, 69
fine calculation. *See* Fine calculation
fines, 37-38
"governing authority," defined, 55, 66
history, 37-52
incentives, 455, 647
internal controls, 55
Introductory Commentary, 52-53
mail fraud, 37-38
monitoring, 509
1991 FSGO, 39-41
"organizational leadership," defined, 56-57
Part 8B1, 53
Part 8B2, 53-59, 64-69
Part 8B2(a), 53, 54
Part 8B2(b), 53, 55-62
Part 8B2(c), 53-54, 62-64
Part 8D, 74-75
penalties, 429, 455
periodic testing and review, 508-509
probation, 52, 74-75
responsible governance, 590
restitution, 52, 53
rewards, 455
risk assessments, 46, 53, 62-63
standards of conduct, 55
structure of current FSGO, 52-69
text and commentary
    disciplinary measures, 62
    effective compliance and ethics programs, 54,
        55, 57, 58, 64-69
    governing authority obligations, 55
    pecuniary gain, 71
    probation, 74
    remedial order, 53
    restitution, 53
    standards of conduct, 55
2004 revisions, 41-46
"violations of law," defined, 54
Fifth Amendment, 23-32, 34, 35, 83, 84, 114, 116, 504
Filip Factors, 97, 101-102
Filip, Mark, 84, 97
Filip Memo, 84
Financial crisis of 2008, 95, 410, 743
Fine calculation, 52, 70-73
    actual loss, defined, 70
    base fine, 70, 71, 72
    criminal purpose organizations, 70
    culpability score, 70, 71, 72
    "good citizenship," pre- and post-offense, 71, 72
    intended loss, defined, 70-71
    maximum multiplier, 72

Fine calculation (*Cont'd*)
    minimum multiplier, 72
    Offense Level Fine Table, 70
    pecuniary gain, defined, 71
    pecuniary loss, defined, 70
    prior history of misconduct, 72
    senior leadership involvement in or tolerance of
        offense, 72
Fines, 32, 37-38, 77
First Amendment, 32, 33, 34
Fokker Services B.V., 85-93, 94, 95
Ford Pinto, 17-18, 19
Foreign Bribery Report, 435-450
Foreign Corrupt Practices Act. *See* FCPA
Foreign individuals and juridical entities acting inside
    U.S. territory, 356, 358
Foreign official, defined, 264, 313-332
Forensic accounting, 350, 497-498, 508, 511, 518, 525, 550
Fourteenth Amendment, 32
Fourth Amendment, 25, 32
Frankfurter, Felix, 5
Fraud offenses, 18, 60, 63, 68, 76, 145, 151
    accounting or audit fraud, 483
    advertising and commercial fraud, 746, 748
    corporate scandals, 41, 212, 213-226, 227-231
    defense procurement, 71
    Enron. *See* Enron
    financial reporting, 171-172
    fraud scam, 70
    game theory, 457
    internal control over financial reporting, 233-245
    mail fraud, 37, 38, 48, 390
    risk management, 607
    securities fraud, 152-167, 227-231, 251, 361, 363,
        364, 369
    tax shelters, 83
    Volkswagen. *See* Volkswagen emissions scandal
    wire fraud, 322, 369
    WorldCom. *See* WorldCom
Free speech, 32, 33, 665, 693, 700
Freier, Todd, 482-483
Friedman, Milton, 561, 563, 591, 604
FSGO. *See* Federal Sentencing Guidelines for
    Organizations (FSGO)

Game theory, 457
Garrett, Brandon L., 33, 94
Gebler, David, 420
Geographic risk, 426, 460
Gifts
    anti-bribery provisions, 297-305, 306-307
    charitable donations. *See* Charitable donations
    in Japan, 257
Global anticorruption efforts, 142-144
Globalization, 136-137
Goldman Sachs Group, Inc., 294
Governance of RBE, 590-604. *See also* Responsible
    business enterprise (RBE)

Government "instrumentality," 313-314, 331-332
Grand corruption, 434, 435
"Grease" payments, 308, 309
Great Depression, 95
Greenpeace, 684-686
Grindler Memorandum, 125
Group of 20 (G20), 742
Guidelines Governing the Protection of Privacy and
    Transborder Flows of Personal Data, 744
Gulf oil disaster. *See* BP Deepwater Horizon oil spill

Halabi, Sam, 17, 18-19
Halliburton, 2, 259-263, 516-521, 536, 584-587
Hallmarks of effective compliance programs, 415-
    534, 562, 623, 624, 632. *See also* Compliance
    program
Hanna, Julia, 213
Health and safety, OECD Guidelines, 742-743
HealthSouth, 42
Heat map, 431, 432
Heimann, Fritz F., 138-140
Helms, Jesse, 135
Helplines, 483, 485-490, 653, 658. *See also* Hotlines
Herakles Farms and Herakles Capital, 684-686
High-risk sectors, 428, 438
High-risk transactions, 428
Hiring practices, 271-293, 293-294. *See also* Anti-
    bribery provisions of FCPA
Hobby Lobby Stores, 33, 34
Holder, Eric, 80, 96
Holder Memo, 80, 81, 82
Holmes, Oliver Wendell, Jr., 10-11, 133
Horizontal restraints, 757
Hotlines, 22, 61, 481-495, 509, 511
    compliance program, 482-483
    elements, 482-483
    ethics program, 615, 617, 618, 619, 651
    whistleblowing, 482-483, 483-484, 486, 492
HSBC Group, 81, 95-96, 127-131
Human rights, 615-616, 617-619
    adverse or negative impact, defined, 687
    OECD Guidelines, 661, 662, 672, 686-687, 697-709,
        717-724
    rights included in International Bill of Human
        Rights, 687-697
    specific instance, final statement, 702-709, 717-724
Hydis Technologies Co., Ltd., 759-762

Iacocca, Lee, 18, 19
ICCPR. *See* International Covenant on Civil and
    Political Rights (ICCPR)
ICERD. *See* International Convention on the
    Elimination of All Forms of Racial
    Discrimination (ICERD)
ICESCR. *See* International Covenant on Economic,
    Social and Cultural Rights (ICESCR)
ICFR. *See* Internal Control over Financial Reporting
    (ICFR)

IEEPA. *See* International Emergency Economic Powers Act (IEEPA)
ILO. *See* International Labor Organization (ILO)
Imputed liability, 383-384, 385
Incentives, 61, 62
    compliance program, 455-457, 558
    ethics program, 647-648, 648-649, 651
    FSGO, 455
Indictments, 79-80, 81. *See also* Discretion of prosecutor
Indirect payments to family members of foreign officials, 294
Industrial relations, OECD Guidelines, 661, 662, 710-715
Industry risk, 460
Information, criminal charges filed in, 79. *See also* Discretion of prosecutor; Indictments
Inherent risk, 292, 429, 430
Insider trading, 42, 337, 629
Integrity Due Diligence, 467-477, 659
Internal Control—Integrated Framework (COSO Framework), 171-179
Internal Control over Financial Reporting (ICFR), 233
    evaluation of, 233-245, 245-253
    false certifications, 245-253
    guidance on evaluation procedures, 233-245
    misrepresentations, 245-253
    sufficiency of evidence of ICFR risk, 243*f*
Internal control practices, risk assessment, 459-460
Internal control system
    components, 174-178
    deficiencies, 152-167, 167-171, 186, 189
    objectives, 173-174, 177
Internal controls provisions of FCPA, 146-147, 150-205, 207-210
    adequacy of, reporting on, 213, 232-253
    assessment process, 233
    authorizations, 176
    communication, 176-177, 179
    compliance objectives, 173, 174
    components of internal control, 174-178
    control activities, 175-176, 178
    control environment, 174-175, 178
    COSO Framework, 171-179
    deficiencies in internal control system, 152-167, 167-171, 186, 189
    definition of internal control, 172-173
    examples of internal controls, 180
    external communication, 176, 177
    external reporting objectives, 173-174
    false certifications, 245-253
    FSGO, 55
    information and communication, 176-177, 179
    intent element for criminal liability, 151-152
    internal communication, 176-177
    internal reporting objectives, 174
    monitoring activities, 177, 179
    objectives of internal control system, 173-174, 177

operations objectives, 173
    quality of information, 176
    "reasonable assurances." *See* "Reasonable assurances"
    reconciliations, 176
    relationship of objectives and components, 178
    reporting objectives, 173-174
    risk assessment, 175, 178
    segregation of duties, 176
    seventeen principles, 178-179
    transaction controls, 176
    verifications, 176
Internal investigations, 480, 495-498, 558
    forensic accounting, 497-498
    outside counsel, referral to, 496-498
    questions involved, 495-497
    scope, 496
    USAM, 105, 109-110
    whether to investigate, 495
    who should conduct investigation, 495
Internal reporting
    mechanisms, 60-61
    whistleblowers, 485-490
International Anti-Bribery and Fair Competition Act of 1998, 374-375, 377, 380-381
International Bill of Human Rights, 686, 687-697
International Chamber of Commerce, 369
    Anti-Corruption Commission, 148
    consumer interests, 746
    Rules of Conduct to Combat Extortion and Bribery, 139
International Convention on the Elimination of All Forms of Racial Discrimination (ICERD), 686
International Covenant on Civil and Political Rights (ICCPR), 686, 687-695, 697
International Covenant on Economic, Social and Cultural Rights (ICESCR), 686, 687, 694, 695, 696, 697
International Emergency Economic Powers Act (IEEPA), 87, 127, 498, 499, 614
International Labor Organization (ILO), 688, 698, 710
International Union of Food, Agricultural, Hotel, Restaurant, Catering, Tobacco and Allied Workers' Associations, 717-724
Internet searches, 464-465, 471. *See also* Third-party due diligence
Internship programs, 271-293, 294-295. *See also* Anti-bribery provisions of FCPA
Investigations
    compliance program. *See* Internal investigations
    ethics program, 651-655
    internal. *See* Internal investigations
Investment. *See* Responsible Investment Report
Ireland NCP, 732-741
Issuers
    accounting provisions of FCPA, 206-211
    amendments governing, 374-375
    anti-bribery provisions of FCPA, 356, 357-358, 373-376, 458

JGC Corp., 382, 400-408
JP Morgan Chase & Co., 94
  cease-and-desist proceedings, 271-293
  hiring practices, 271-293, 294
  internship programs, 271-293
Jury trial right, 32, 47

KBR, 259-263
Kennedy, John F., 742
Kinross Gold Corporation, 671-680
Kmart, 42
Knowledge, defined, 332-345. See also Scienter
Korea NCP, 759-762
Korean Metal Workers' Union, 759-762
KPMG, 83, 113-117

Labor, OECD Guidelines. See Employment and
    industrial relations
Lafarge Holcim Ltd., 753-756
LCA. See Life-cycle assessment (LCA)
Legal advice, 108, 110-111, 121
Libit, William, 482-483
Life-cycle assessment (LCA), 725. See also
    Environment
Local law affirmative defense, 305. See also
    Anti-bribery provisions of FCPA
Lockheed Martin Corporation, 702-709
Low, Lucinda, 495-497
Lugar, Richard G., 257
Lynch, Loretta, 96, 589

M&A. See Mergers and acquisitions (M&A)
Mail fraud, 37-38, 48, 390
Management of RBE, 604-610. See also Responsible
    business enterprise (RBE)
Mandernach, Kerry, 309-312
Manipulation of records, 147-148. See also Accounting
    provisions of FCPA
Martin, Brian, 452-453
Material misstatement of financial statements, 232,
    233-245
McCallum Memo, 84
McKesson HBOC, 42
McNulty Memo, 84
McNulty, Paul, 124
Meals, 298-305. See also Anti-bribery provisions of FCPA
Mediation, 493, 569, 674-679, 705, 706
  declining offer of, 718, 720, 721
  non-offering of, 684, 686, 702, 704, 709
  social capital, building of, 567
  "specific instance"
    competition, 761-762
    description, 670-671
    employment and industrial relations, 718-719,
      720-721, 723-724
    environment, 735-741
    human rights, 718-719, 720-721, 723-724
    science and technology, 755-756

Medical emergency exception, anti-bribery provisions,
    311-312
Medical expenses, payment of, 269-271
Merck, 18
Mergers and acquisitions (M&A)
  compliance program, incorporation of target into,
    514
  ethics due diligence, 659
  FCPA liability, 512-534
  post-acquisition integration, 512-513, 514, 516-521,
    559-560
  pre-acquisition due diligence, 512-534, 559-560,
    659
  risk assessment, 514
Middle management, 419
Military contact, 624
Millennium Challenge Corporation, 433
Miller, Marshall L., 416, 424
Miller, T. Christian, 259-263, 535-541
Misrepresentations, 50, 155, 163, 167, 245-253,
    371-372, 467
Mitigating risk, 426-431, 467, 513, 612
Mitigation credit, 46, 103, 105, 109, 500, 502, 507
MNEs. See Multinational enterprises (MNEs)
Mondini, Chris, 485-490
Monetary sentences imposed, 77
Monitors and monitoring
  Breuer Memorandum, 125
  communications, 122-123
  compliance program, 59-60, 509-510, 655
  confidentiality of reports, 125
  costly recommendations, 125
  duration of agreement, 123-124
  efficacy, 124
  FSGO, 509
  future compliance, 118-124
Grindler Memorandum, 125
  independence, 121
  misconduct, reporting of, 123
  Morford Memorandum, 118-124, 125
  recommendations, 122-123, 125
  scope of duties, 121-122
  selection of monitor, 119-121, 125
  termination of monitorship, 120, 124
  third-party due diligence, 465-466
  third-party relationships, 466
  use of, USAM, 117-118, 118-124
Morford, Craig S., 118-124
Morford Memorandum, 118-124, 125
Morgan Stanley, 294
Multinational enterprises (MNEs), 400, 563
  agency, 382-383
  bribery red flags, 333
  extraterritorial application of FCPA, 356
  internal investigations, 480-481
  leverage over collaborators, 211
  OECD Guidelines. See OECD Guidelines for
    Multinational Enterprises

self-policing, 93
size and power, 1, 11
Murphy, Diana, 40
Murphy, Joe, 59, 456

Nadgrodkiewicz, Anna, 595-604
Nagel, Ilene H., 38-39, 74
National Australia Bank Ltd., 356, 360-370
National Contact Point (NCP)
    Argentina, 753-756
    Brazil, 671-680
    functions, 670-671
    Ireland, 732-741
    Korea, Republic of, 759-762
    Netherlands, 732-741
    United Kingdom, 749-751
    United States, 684-686, 702-709, 717-724
National Gas Pipeline Safety Act of 1968, 21
National Grid Transco, 749-751
National security interests, 129, 257
Natural Gas Pipeline Safety Act of 1968, 21
NCP. *See* National Contact Point (NCP)
Netherlands NCP, 732-741
New York Central & Hudson River Railroad Co., 6,
    7-10, 11, 12
Nixon, Richard, 134
Non-prosecution agreement (NPA), 118-124, 357, 384,
    499. *See also* Deferred prosecution agreement
    (DPA)
    description, 81-82, 86
    duration of agreement, 123-124
    monitors. *See* Monitors
    procedure, 81-82
    selection and use of monitors, 118-124. *See also*
        Monitors

OECD Convention. *See* Anti-Bribery Convention
OECD Guidelines for Multinational Enterprises, 564,
    661-766
    bribery and extortion, combating of, 661, 662
    competition. *See* Competition
    consumer interests, 661, 662, 742-744, 749-751
        awareness and education, 743
        consumer information, 743
        data protection and privacy, 744-751
        dispute resolution, 744
        education vs. information, 743
        health and safety, 742-743
        privacy, 744-751
        text of Guidelines, 745-748
    data protection, 744-751
    disclosure, 661, 662, 680-686
    dispute resolution, 744
    due diligence to identify risks of potential adverse
        impacts on stakeholders, 662-663
    employment and industrial relations, 661, 662,
        710-715
    environment. *See* Environment

extortion, combating of, 661, 662
general policies, 664-670, 671-672
health and safety, 742-743
human rights. *See* Human rights
industrial relations, 661, 662, 710-715
meaningful stakeholder engagement, 663-680
mediation. *See* "Specific instance" mediation
NCP. *See* National Contact Point (NCP)
non-compliance with guidelines, report of, 671-680
privacy, 744-751
promotion of, 663-680
RBC due diligence, 662-663
risk management, 663
science and technology, 661, 662, 751-753, 753-756
specific instances. *See* Specific instance
stakeholder engagement, 663-680
steps for conducting due diligence, 662-663
taxation. *See* Taxation
technology, 661, 662, 751-756
transparency, 680
Offense Level Fine Table, 70. *See also* Fine calculation
Office of the United States Attorneys (USAO),
    80, 114
Officer certification, 213, 231-232
Offshore drilling, 583-590
Oil spill. *See* BP Deepwater Horizon oil spill
Omnibus Trade and Competitiveness Act of 1998, 136
Opinion releases (DOJ). *See* FCPA Opinion Procedure
    Releases
Oracle Corp., 167-171
Organisation for Economic Co-operation and
    Development (OECD), 256, 596
    Anti-Bribery Convention. *See* Anti-Bribery
        Convention
    Convention to Combat Bribery of Foreign Public
        Officials. *See* Anti-Bribery Convention
    Foreign Bribery Report, 435-450. *See also* Bribery
    foreign official, defined, 317, 331
    Guidelines for Multinational Enterprises. *See*
        OECD Guidelines for Multinational
        Enterprises
    Guidelines Governing the Protection of Privacy
        and Transborder Flows of Personal Data, 744
    Principles of Corporate Governance, 596
    Privacy Framework, 744, 745
    risk assessment, five-step process, 426-431
    Risk Assessment Handbook, 431
Organizational culture, 625, 655-657. *See also* Ethics
    program
Organizational ethics, 566. *See also* BEM; Ethics
    program
OTC. *See* Over-the-counter market (OTC)
Outside counsel, referral to, 496-498
Over-the-counter market (OTC), 206, 246

Pacific Gas and Electric Company (PG&E), 21-22
Pecuniary gain, defined, 71
Pecuniary loss, defined, 70

Penalties, 9, 44, 69, 252, 346, 455, 601
  anti-bribery laws, enforcement of, 447
  BNPP, 499
  BNY Mellon, 294
  business purpose test, 266
  certification of fraudulent financial statements, 232
  Daimler, 203
  Elkins Act, 7
  FCA, 19
  FCPA
    agents of domestic concerns, 398
    "any person," bribery by, 380
    business purpose test, 266
    evading penalties, 266
    foreign nationals acting as agents of U.S.
        companies, 137, 398
    inadvertent conduct, 152
    insignificant or technical infractions, 151-152
    issuers, 375
    U.S. persons for acts outside United States, 377
  Fokker Services, 87
  FSGO, 50, 55, 429, 455
  "grease payment," 310
  human rights, violation of, 690
  mitigation, 414
  OECD Convention, 140
  Siemens, 548
  stick wielded by government, 3
  successor liability, 349
  USAM, 108, 429
  Volkswagen, 181, 182, 186
PepsiCo., 717-724
Periodic testing and review, 508-509
Person, defined, 378
Petty corruption, 434-435
PG&E. See Pacific Gas and Electric Company (PG&E)
Policy commitment, 615-616
"Politically exposed persons," 464-465
Price fixing, 63, 68, 757
Price, Michael, 467-477, 659
Privacy Framework, 744, 745
Privacy, OECD Guidelines, 744-751
Privileges and Immunities Clause, 32
Probation, FSGO, 52, 74-75
Professional ethics, 565-566
Property acquisition, 623-624
Prosecution of business organizations, 1-4
  characteristics of organizational offender, 76
  criminal liability. See Corporate criminal liability
  discretion of prosecutor. See Discretion of
      prosecutor
  fine, restitution, and combined, 77
  fraud offenses, 76
  guidelines. See Prosecutorial guidelines for
      organizations
  level of authority of individuals convicted, 77
  monetary sentences imposed, 77
  number of cases, 76

  offense characteristics, 76
  organizational offender, defined, 76
  primary offense, cases by, 76
  punishment, 77
  quick facts, 76-77
  restitution, 77
  sentencing guidelines. See Federal Sentencing
      Guidelines for Organizations (FSGO)
Prosecutorial guidelines for organizations, 79-126
  charging decisions, 79-80, 85-93
  collateral harm, 80, 81
  compliance programs, shepherding of, 103-105
  cooperation, rewarding of, 105-117
  DAG Memos, 84, 95, 96
  disclosure, rewarding of, 105-117
  diversion agreements, 81-82
  Filip Memo, 84
  future compliance, monitoring of, 117-126
  Holder Memo, 80, 81, 82
  indictments, 79-80
  McCallum Memo, 84
  McNulty Memo, 84
  stages of formal criminal process, 79, 80
  Thompson Memo, 80-95, 97, 114, 133
  USAM. See United States Attorneys' Manual
      (USAM)
  Yates Memo, 95, 96-97, 105
Proxmire, William, 135
Public expenditure tracking surveys, 433

Qualitative risk assessment, 430
Quantitative risk assessment, 430
Quest, 42
Questionnaires, 461-464. See also Third-party due
    diligence

Racketeer Influenced and Corrupt Organizations Act
    (RICO), 371
Ralph Lauren Corporation, 383-384
"Rational irrationality," 457
RBC. See Responsible business conduct (RBC)
RBE. See Responsible business enterprise (RBE)
Reasonable and bona fide expenditures affirmative
    defense, 305-306. See also Anti-bribery
    provisions of FCPA
"Reasonable assurances," 135, 164, 165, 171, 173, 273
  defined, 147, 150
  Exchange Act text, 146, 147, 150, 161, 194, 209, 293
  ICFR, 233-245
  internal control, defined, 172
"Reasonable detail," 145, 147, 150, 154, 163, 170, 292
  defined, 147, 149
  Exchange Act text, 146, 147, 161, 194, 209
  ICFR, 233-245
Reconciliation
  accounting records, 165
  internal controls provisions, 174, 176
  monitoring activities, 509

Recordkeeping, 151, 164, 166. *See also* Books and records
    provision; Internal controls provisions of FCPA
    accuracy, 160, 163
    Exchange Act provisions, 146-147, 148
    pre-acquisition due diligence, 349-351
Red flags
    accounting provisions, 223
    anti-bribery provisions, 274, 333, 458
    compliance program, 452, 458, 509, 510, 514
    corruption, 452, 458
    Deepwater Horizon disaster, 2
    mergers and acquisitions, 514
    monitoring, 509, 510
    third-party due diligence, 415, 458, 461, 462-464,
        464-465, 471-477, 559
        basic information, 471-472
        examples of warning signals, 471-473
        Integrity Due Diligence, 468
        verification and further research, 472-473, 474,
            475, 476-477
Refusals to deal, 757
Relativism, cultural, 257
Religious Freedom Restoration Act of 1993 (RFRA), 33-34
Religious liberty, 33-34
Remediation efforts, 347, 500, 548, 620, 667
    audit report, 511
    FCPA enforcement plan and guidance, 502, 503,
        505-506, 506-507
    human rights impacts, 672, 698, 699, 700, 704
    pre-acquisition, 517, 518, 519, 520
    response to criminal conduct, 68, 87, 131, 202-205,
        383, 481, 552-555
Reporting systems
    compliance program, 60-61
    ethics program, 651-652, 652-655, 659
    internal controls provisions, 173-174
Reputation enhancement level of enterprise identity,
    611, 612
*A Resource Guide to the U.S. Foreign Corrupt
    Practices Act. See* FCPA Guide
Resources
    compliance program, 424-425, 555-556, 632
    ethics program, 632-639
Respondeat superior, 414
    corporate criminal liability, 5-12, 34, 37
    FCPA extraterritorial application, 357, 382
    scope of employment, 12, 101
    third-party due diligence, 458
Responsible business conduct (RBC), 661, 662-663
    categories of RBC, 661-662
    due diligence, 662-663
    international norms. *See* OECD Guidelines for
        Multinational Enterprises
Responsible business enterprise (RBE), 565-610
    Bhopal disaster, 569-583, 590
    BP Deepwater Horizon oil spill, 583-590
    business ethics, 565-566
    case studies, 569-583, 583-590

    conduct, 565-590
    corporate social responsibility, 566
    due diligence, OECD Guidelines, 662-663
    governance, 590-604
    management, 604-610
    operating in frontier market, 767-774
    organizational ethics, 566
    professional ethics, 565-566
Responsible business ethics, 566-568
Responsible conduct, 565-590
Responsible governance, 590-604
Responsible Investment Report, 614-624
    anti-bribery update, 616-617
    anticorruption update, 616-617
    community engagement, 621-623
    environmental update, 619-621
    executive summary, 614-615
    human rights, 615-616, 617-619
    military contact, 624
    policy commitment, 615-616
    property acquisition, 623-624
    security providers, 623
    stakeholder engagement, 621-623
    workplace rights, 617-619
Responsible Investment Reporting Requirements, 614
Responsible management, 604, 605-610
Restitution, 39, 74
    FSGO, 52, 53, 62, 68, 74
    individual offenders, 40
    quick facts, 77
    USAM, 99, 102, 107
Retaliation
    ethics program, 631, 649, 654
    OECD Guidelines, 722
    whistleblowers, 59, 61, 65, 481, 482, 489-492
Retribution, 433, 482, 633, 635, 648, 654
Reward systems. *See also* Incentives
    compliance program, 455-456
    ethics program, 648-649
RFRA. *See* Religious Freedom Restoration Act of 1993
    (RFRA)
RICO. *See* Racketeer Influenced and Corrupt
    Organizations Act (RICO)
Risk assessment, 425-451, 557
    books and records, 459
    business opportunity risk, 428
    business partnership risk, 428
    corruption indicators, 433-435
    definition of risk, 425
    documenting results, 431-450
    example heat map, 432
    experience-based indicators, 433
    five-step process, OECD Guidelines, 426-431
    FSGO, 46, 53, 62-63
    gathering information, 428
    geographic risk, 426
    grand corruption, 434, 435
    heat map, 431, 432

Risk assessment (*Cont'd*)
  high-risk sectors, 428, 438
  high-risk transactions, 428
  inherent risk, 429, 430
  internal controls provisions, 175, 178
  magnitude, 429-430
  measuring risk, 426-431
  methods of gathering information, 428
  mitigating risk, 426-431
  OECD Foreign Bribery Report, 435-450. *See also*
      Bribery
  perception-based indicators, 433
  petty corruption, 434-435
  probability, 429
  proxy indicators, 433, 435
  public expenditure tracking surveys, 433
  qualitative assessment, 430
  quantitative assessment, 430
  residual risk, 430
  risk, defined, 425
  risk register, 431-432
  risk tolerance, 430, 431
  sample magnitude scale, 429
  sample risk register, 431-432
  sectoral risk, 427-428, 437, 438
  steps, 426-430
  third party. *See* Third-party risk assessment
  transaction risk, 428
Risk Assessment Handbook, 431
Risk management
  level of enterprise identity, 611, 612
  OECD Guidelines, 663
Risk register, 431-432
Risk tolerance, 430, 431
RJR Nabisco, 371
Routine governmental action exception, 308. *See also*
      Anti-bribery provisions of FCPA
Royal Bank of Scotland plc, 94
Royal Dutch Petroleum Co., 371, 372

Safety emergency exception, 311-312. *See also*
      Anti-bribery provisions of FCPA
Safety, OECD Guidelines, 742-743
Sarbanes-Oxley Act of 2002 (SOX), 42, 136
  FCPA accounting provisions, interplay with, 212-253
  internal controls, reporting on adequacy of, 213,
      232-253
  officer certification, 213, 231-232
  passage of, 212-213
  Section 302, 213, 231-232, 245, 253
  Section 404, 213, 232-253, 509
  whistleblowers, 481-482
Sarbanes, Paul, 232
Scalia, Antonin, 373
Schwartz, Bart, 124
Science and technology
  OECD Guidelines, 661, 662, 751-753, 753-756
  specific instance, 753-756

Science Applications International Corp., 19, 21
Scienter, 149, 151, 163-164, 166
Searches and seizures, 32
SEC. *See* Securities and Exchange Commission (SEC)
Sectoral risk, 460
Securities and Exchange Commission (SEC), 135, 137
  affiliates of issuers, 211
  agency, 382-383
  books and records, 149
  charitable donations, 295
  co-conspirators, 385
  coercion as defense to FCPA violation, 336
  compliance programs, 137, 416, 424, 425
  concert of action, 382
  cooperation by companies, 499
  disciplinary measures, adequacy of, 456
  due diligence guidance, 461
  duress as defense to FCPA violation, 336
  enforcement authority, 141, 142
  extraterritoriality of FCPA, 357, 373, 382, 385-386
  FCPA Guide. *See* FCPA Guide
  FCPA interpretation, 265
  "foreign official," 313
      gift vs. bribe, 297-298
  "grease payments," 309
  mergers and acquisitions, 512-514
  reasonable and bona fide expenditures affirmative
      defense, 306
  red flags in payments to third parties, 333
  self-disclosure and cooperation by companies, 499
  successor liability, 346
  third-party accounting practices, 460
  third-party due diligence procedures, 457
  third-party identity, 460
  third-party involvement and compensation, 461
Securities Exchange Act of 1934. *See* Exchange Act
Securities fraud, 152-167, 227-231, 251, 361, 363, 364, 369
Security providers, 623
Self-disclosure, 383, 481, 496, 498-508
Self-incrimination, 23-32, 34, 83
Self-policing, 3-4, 5, 41, 69, 93, 456, 561
  limits, 588
  logic, 587-588
Senior management commitment, 419-421, 555
Sentencing Commission, 79
  organizational guidelines, 40, 41, 42, 46, 47, 77
  responsibilities, 38, 39
Sentencing guidelines. *See* Federal Sentencing
      Guidelines for Organizations (FSGO)
Sentencing Reform Act (SRA), 38, 39, 47
Shareholder theory, 561, 563, 591
Sherman Act, 6, 346
Siemens, 2
  amnesty and leniency programs, 551
  bribery and corrupt payments, 535-541, 542-553
  compliance program, 535-541, 542-553
  cooperation, 548-549, 550
  internal investigation, 550-552

remediation, 548-549, 552-553
   sentencing memorandum, 542-553
   substantial assistance, 548-549, 549-550
Simon, Jeremy, 483-485
Sixth Amendment, 32, 47
Small payments and gifts, 269
Social capital, building of, 567, 610, 613
Solomon, Steven Davidoff, 124
SOX. *See* Sarbanes-Oxley Act of 2002 (SOX)
Specific instance
   competition, 759-762
   description, 670-671
   disclosure, 684-686
   employment and industrial relations, 717-724
   environment, 732-741
   human rights, 702-709, 717-724
   mediation. *See* "Specific instance" mediation
   science and technology, 753-756
"Specific instance" mediation
   competition, 761-762
   description, 670-671
   employment and industrial relations, 718-719,
      720-721, 723-724
   environment, 735-741
   human rights, 718-719, 720-721, 723-724
   science and technology, 755-756
Speedy Trial Act, 85-93, 94
Speedy trial right, 32, 85-93, 94
SRA. *See* Sentencing Reform Act (SRA)
Stakeholder engagement, 621-623, 663-680
Stakeholder surveys, 655
Stakeholder theory, 562-563, 590-591, 604-605
Standards of conduct, 565, 625, 635, 637. *See also* Code
      of conduct
   COSO Framework, 174, 175
   FSGO, 55, 66
   multinational enterprises, 742
Stewart, Martha, 42
Successor liability, 345-355. *See also* Anti-bribery
      provisions of FCPA
Sullivan, John D., 595-604
Surveys, 586, 658, 659, 676, 743
   Corruption Perceptions Index, 427, 433
   employee attitudes, 653
   experienced-based, 433, 435
   ethical culture of companies, 414, 563, 655
   perception-based, 427, 433, 435
   public expenditure tracking, 433
   risk assessment, 428
   stakeholder, 655
Swenson, Winthrop M., 38-39, 74

Tabuena, Jose A., 485-490
Taibbi, Matt, 95
Taxation
   OECD Guidelines, 661, 662, 762-763, 763-766
   transfer pricing, 763, 765-766
Technology, OECD Guidelines, 661, 662, 751-756

Territorial jurisdiction, 378-381. *See also*
      Extraterritorial application of FCPA
Terrorism, 96, 134, 141, 256, 257
Third-party due diligence, 457-480, 511
   approval of third party, 465-466
   audits, 465
   basic information, 469-470, 471-472
   boots on the ground, 465
   business references, 470
   case studies, 467, 473-477
   conclusions drawn, 473
   conducting due diligence, 461-465
   credit ratings and restrictions, 471
   database searches, 464-465
   documentation, 473
   enhanced due diligence, 465
   field work, 471
   financial references, 470
   further research, 470-471, 472-473
   Integrity Due Diligence, 467-477, 659
   Internet searches, 464-465, 471
   key personnel and officers, 470-471
   large-scale screening of third parties, 480
   local legal assistance, 471
   management process, 559
   media search, 471
   monitoring the program, 465-466
   obtaining relevant information, 461-464
   ownership interests and accounts, 470
   "politically exposed persons," 464-465
   questionnaires, 461-464
      red flags, 458, 461, 462-464, 464-465, 471-477
      basic information, 471-472
      examples of warning signals, 471-473
      verification and further research, 472-473, 474,
         475, 476-477
   relationships that may qualify, 458-459
   risk assessment. *See* Third-party risk assessment
   scope of process, defining, 458-459
   verifying data, 461, 464-465, 474, 475, 476-477
   verifying information, 470-471, 472-473
   vetting, 477-480, 511
Third-party payments, 457-458
Third-party questionnaires, 461-464
Third-party risk assessment, 459-461
   accounting practices, 459-460
   agency, 459
   geography, 460
   identity of third party, owners, and key employees,
      460-461
   industry/sectoral risk, 460
   internal control practices, 459-460
   nature of third party's involvement and
      compensation, 461
   prior misconduct, history of, 460
   products, 460
   risk ratings, 461
   sectoral risk, 460

Third-party vetting, 477-480, 511
Thompson, Larry, 91, 133
Thompson Memo, 80-95, 97, 114, 133
    3M, 725
Thurlow, Edward, 1, 3
"Too big to jail" effect, 94, 95
TRACE research
    facilitation payments, 309, 310, 311
    gifts, meals, and entertainment, 298, 299-300, 303,
        304
Trading with the Enemy Act (TWEA), 127, 498,
        499
Training, 451-454
    assessments, 452
    compliance program, 58-59, 451-454, 557
    environment, 727
    ethics program, 639-647. See also Ethics training
        program
    risk-based, 557
    role-play exercises, 452
    rules-based vs. values-based approach, 452-454
    updating, 452
    values-based approach, 452-454
Transaction risk, 428
Transparency, 257
    accounting provisions, 170, 173
    anti-bribery provisions, 297, 298, 299, 301, 302,
        306, 321
    compliance program, 434, 441, 466, 485, 502, 532
    corporate governance, 596-603
    ethics program, 616, 621, 623, 626, 647
    internal control system, 173, 596
    OECD Anti-Bribery Convention, 138-140
    OECD Guidelines
        consumer interests, 748
        disclosure, 680, 682, 683
        environment, 725, 726, 730, 740
        General Policies, 665
        human rights, 700, 703
        privacy, 745
        taxation, 764
    responsible business enterprise, 596-603, 609
    Siemens compliance program, 536, 538, 548, 550,
        553
Transparency International, 138-140, 259, 416, 537,
        771
    Bribe Payers' Index, 437
    Corruption Perceptions Index, 426, 427
    rankings of countries according to perceived levels
        of relative corruption, 426, 427
    sectoral risk, tool for analysis of, 460
    testimony on OECD Anti-Bribery Convention,
        138-140
Travel, 297-305, 306-307. See also Anti-bribery
        provisions of FCPA
Treadway Commission, 171, 172, 212, 250, 416
TWEA. See Trading with the Enemy Act (TWEA)
Tyco, 42

UBS AG, 94, 294
UDHR. See Universal Declaration of Human Rights
    (UDHR)
UNCTD. See United Nations, Conference on Trade
    and Development
Union Carbide Corp. Bhopal disaster, 1, 569-575,
    576-582, 583, 590
United Kingdom NCP, 749-751
United Nations
    Committee for Economic, Social and Cultural
        Rights, 695
    Conference on Trade and Development, Manual on
        Consumer Protection, 742
    consumer protection, 742
    Convention Against Corruption, 137, 143-144,
        256-257
    ILO. See International Labor Organization (ILO)
    UDHR. See Universal Declaration of Human Rights
        (UDHR)
United States Attorneys' Manual. See USAM
United States NCP, 684-686, 702-709, 717-724
United States Sentencing Commission. See Sentencing
    Commission
Universal Declaration of Human Rights (UDHR),
    686, 688-697
Updating
    code of conduct, 423
    ethics training program, 646
    policy, 423
    training, 452, 646
USAM (United States Attorneys' Manual), 97-102
    advice-of-counsel defense, 111
    attorney-client privilege, 108, 111
    compliance programs, 103-105
    cooperation, 106-113
        credit, 113-117
        no entitlement to immunity, 112-113
        value of, 105, 106-108, 109-111
    corporate compliance programs, 103-105
    crime or fraud exception, 111
    disclosure, 105, 109-110
    duties of prosecutors and corporate leaders, 98
    factors to be considered, 97, 101-102
    Filip Factors, 97, 101-102
    foundational principles, 97-98
    future compliance, monitoring of, 118-124
    general considerations of corporate liability, 99
    individual wrongdoers, focus on, 100-101
    internal investigation, 105, 109-110
    legal advice, 110-111
    mitigation credit, 103, 105, 109
    monitors, use of, 117-118, 118-124
    obstruction of investigation, 111-112
    penalties, 429
    voluntary disclosure, 113
    work product protection, 108, 110-111
USAO. See Office of the United States Attorneys
    (USAO)

Value-added level of enterprise identity, 611, 612-613
Verifying data, 461, 464-465, 474, 475, 476-477. *See also* Third-party due diligence
Verifying information, 470-471, 472-473
Vertical restraints, 757
Vetting, 477-480, 511. *See also* Third-party due diligence
Vincke, François, 148
Vision framework, ethics program, 605-610
Volkswagen emissions scandal, 1-2, 180-182, 182-186, 613

Walmart, 18
Warren, Elizabeth, 96
Wells Fargo Bank, 96
Whistleblowers, 481-495
    annual report to Congress, 490-492
    anti-retaliation protections, 491-492
    case story, 487-489
    consequences, 484
    Dodd-Frank Act, 481, 482, 490-492
    hotline, 482-483, 483-484, 486, 492
    internal reporting, 485-490

SOX, 481-482
    tips, 492, 494-495
    when to blow whistle, 483-485
        "Willfully," meaning of, 334
Wire fraud, 322, 369
Work product protection, 108, 110-111
Workplace rights, 617-619
WorldCom, Inc., 42, 136
    accounting fraud, report on investigation into, 213-226
    internal control system, 213-226
    investigation of, 213-226
World Trade Organization (WTO), 742
World-Wide Coin Investments, Ltd., 152-167
Wrage, Alexandra, 298-305, 309-312, 453-454
WTO. *See* World Trade Organization (WTO)

Xerox, 42

Yates Memo, 95, 96-97, 105
Yates, Sally, 96
Yuen Foon Yu, Inc., 759-762